Visit classzone and get connected

Online resources for students and parents

ClassZone resources provide instruction, practice, and learning support.

eEdition Plus ONLINE

This interactive version of the text encourages students to explore science.

Content Review Online

Interactive review reinforces the big idea and key concepts of each chapter.

SciLinks

NSTA-selected links provide relevant Web resources correlated to the text.

Chapter-Based Support

Math tutorials, news, resources, test practice, and a misconceptions database help students succeed.

Now it all clicks!™

CLASSZONE.COM

McDougal Littell

OKLAHOMA EDITION

McDougal Littell
Science

GRADE 8

Life Over Time

Earth's Surface

Chemical Interactions

Motion and Forces

The Changing Earth

Waves, Sound, and Light

GRADE 8 CONTENTS

PASS Science Standards	xxvi
Introducing Science	xxx
Unifying Principles of Science	xxxii
The Nature of Science	xxxviii
The Nature of Technology	xlii
Using *McDougal Littell Science*	xliv

1 Motion and Forces
Motion
Forces
Gravity, Friction, and Pressure
Work and Energy
Machines

2 Waves, Sound, and Light
Waves
Sound
Electromagnetic Waves
Light and Optics

3 Chemical Interactions
Atomic Structure and the Periodic Table
Chemical Bonds and Compounds
Chemical Reactions

4 Earth's Surface
Views of Earth Today
Minerals
Rocks
Weathering and Soil Formation
Erosion and Deposition

5 The Changing Earth
Plate Tectonics
Earthquakes
Mountains and Volcanoes
Views of Earth's Past
Natural Resources

6 Life Over Time
The History of Life on Earth
Classification of Living Things
Population Dynamics

Scientific Thinking Handbook	R2
Lab Handbook	R10
Math Handbook	R36
Note-Taking Handbook	R45
Appendix	R52
Glossary	R68
Index	R94
Acknowledgements	R119

Copyright © 2006 by McDougal Littell, a division of Houghton Mifflin Company.

No part of this work may be reproduced or transmitted in any form or by any means, electronic or mechanical, including photocopy and recording, or by any information storage or retrieval system without the prior written permission of McDougal Littell unless such copying is expressly permitted by federal copyright law. Address inquiries to Supervisor, Rights and Permissions, McDougal Littell, P.O. Box 1667, Evanston, IL 60204.

Printed in the United States of America

ISBN-13: 978-0-618-60657-3   2 3 4 5 6 7 8 VJM 09 08 07 06
ISBN-10: 0-618-60657-2
Internet Web Site: http://www.mcdougallittell.com

Science Consultants

Chief Science Consultant
James Trefil, Ph.D. is the Clarence J. Robinson Professor of Physics at George Mason University. He is the author or co-author of more than 25 books, including *Science Matters* and *The Nature of Science*. Dr. Trefil is a member of the American Association for the Advancement of Science's Committee on the Public Understanding of Science and Technology. He is also a fellow of the World Economic Forum and a frequent contributor to *Smithsonian* magazine.

Rita Ann Calvo, Ph.D. is Senior Lecturer in Molecular Biology and Genetics at Cornell University, where for 12 years she also directed the Cornell Institute for Biology Teachers. Dr. Calvo is the 1999 recipient of the College and University Teaching Award from the National Association of Biology Teachers.

Kenneth Cutler, M.S. is the Education Coordinator for the Julius L. Chambers Biomedical Biotechnology Research Institute at North Carolina Central University. A former middle school and high school science teacher, he received a 1999 Presidential Award for Excellence in Science Teaching.

Instructional Design Consultants

Douglas Carnine, Ph.D. is Professor of Education and Director of the National Center for Improving the Tools of Educators at the University of Oregon. He is the author of seven books and over 100 other scholarly publications, primarily in the areas of instructional design and effective instructional strategies and tools for diverse learners. Dr. Carnine also serves as a member of the National Institute for Literacy Advisory Board.

Linda Carnine, Ph.D. consults with school districts on curriculum development and effective instruction for students struggling academically. A former teacher and school administrator, Dr. Carnine also co-authored a popular remedial reading program.

Donald Steely, Ph.D. serves as principal investigator at the Oregon Center for Applied Science (ORCAS) on federal grants for science and language arts programs. His background also includes teaching and authoring of print and multimedia programs in science, mathematics, history, and spelling.

Sam Miller, Ph.D. is a middle school science teacher and the Teacher Development Liaison for the Eugene, Oregon, Public Schools. He is the author of curricula for teaching science, mathematics, computer skills, and language arts.

Vicky Vachon, Ph.D. consults with school districts throughout the United States and Canada on improving overall academic achievement with a focus on literacy. She is also co-author of a widely used program for remedial readers.

Content Reviewers

John Beaver, Ph.D.
Ecology
Professor, Director of Science Education Center
College of Education and Human Services
Western Illinois University
Macomb, IL

Donald J. DeCoste, Ph.D.
Matter and Energy, Chemical Interactions
Chemistry Instructor
University of Illinois
Urbana-Champaign, IL

Dorothy Ann Fallows, Ph.D., MSc
Diversity of Living Things, Microbiology
Partners in Health
Boston, MA

Michael Foote, Ph.D.
The Changing Earth, Life Over Time
Associate Professor
Department of the Geophysical Sciences
The University of Chicago
Chicago, IL

Lucy Fortson, Ph.D.
Space Science
Director of Astronomy
Adler Planetarium and Astronomy Museum
Chicago, IL

Elizabeth Godrick, Ph.D.
Human Biology
Professor, CAS Biology
Boston University
Boston, MA

Isabelle Sacramento Grilo, M.S.
The Changing Earth
Lecturer, Department of the Geological Sciences
San Diego State University
San Diego, CA

David Harbster, MSc
Diversity of Living Things
Professor of Biology
Paradise Valley Community College
Phoenix, AZ

Richard D. Norris, Ph.D.
Earth's Waters
Professor of Paleobiology
Scripps Institution of Oceanography
University of California, San Diego
La Jolla, CA

Donald B. Peck, M.S.
Motion and Forces; Waves, Sound, and Light; Electricity and Magnetism
Director of the Center for Science Education (retired)
Fairleigh Dickinson University
Madison, NJ

Javier Penalosa, Ph.D.
Diversity of Living Things, Plants
Associate Professor, Biology Department
Buffalo State College
Buffalo, NY

Raymond T. Pierrehumbert, Ph.D.
Earth's Atmosphere
Professor in Geophysical Sciences (Atmospheric Science)
The University of Chicago
Chicago, IL

Brian J. Skinner, Ph.D.
Earth's Surface
Eugene Higgins Professor of Geology and Geophysics
Yale University
New Haven, CT

Nancy E. Spaulding, M.S.
Earth's Surface, The Changing Earth, Earth's Waters
Earth Science Teacher (retired)
Elmira Free Academy
Elmira, NY

Steven S. Zumdahl, Ph.D.
Matter and Energy, Chemical Interactions
Professor Emeritus of Chemistry
University of Illinois
Urbana-Champaign, IL

Susan L. Zumdahl, M.S.
Matter and Energy, Chemical Interactions
Chemistry Education Specialist
University of Illinois
Urbana-Champaign, IL

Safety Consultant

Juliana Texley, Ph.D.
Former K–12 Science Teacher and School Superintendent
Boca Raton, FL

English Language Advisor

Judy Lewis, M.A.
Director, State and Federal Programs for reading proficiency and high risk populations
Rancho Cordova, CA

Oklahoma Teacher Reviewers

Jaime Bowlin
Jenks West Intermediate
Jenks, Oklahoma

Kristen Kuepker
Earlywine Elementary School
Oklahoma City, Oklahoma

Katy Leffel
Mayfield Middle School
Oklahoma City, Oklahoma

Gaye Young
Central Middle School
Edmond, Oklahoma

Teacher Panel Members

Carol Arbour
Tallmadge Middle School,
Tallmadge, OH

Patty Belcher
Goodrich Middle School,
Akron, OH

Gwen Broestl
Luis Munoz Marin Middle School,
Cleveland, OH

Al Brofman
Tehipite Middle School,
Fresno, CA

John Cockrell
Clinton Middle School,
Columbus, OH

Jenifer Cox
Sylvan Middle School,
Citrus Heights, CA

Linda Culpepper
Martin Middle School,
Charlotte, NC

Melvin Figueroa
New River Middle School,
Ft. Lauderdale, FL

Doretha Grier
Kannapolis Middle School,
Kannapolis, NC

Robert Hood
Alexander Hamilton Middle School,
Cleveland, OH

Scott Hudson
Covedale Elementary School,
Cincinnati, OH

Loretta Langdon
Princeton Middle School,
Princeton, NC

Carlyn Little
Glades Middle School,
Miami, FL

Ann Marie Lynn
Amelia Earhart Middle School,
Riverside, CA

James Minogue
Lowe's Grove Middle School,
Durham, NC

Kathleen Montagnino-DeMatteo
Jefferson Davis Middle School,
West Palm Beach, FL

Joann Myers
Buchanan Middle School,
Tampa, FL

Barbara Newell
Charles Evans Hughes Middle School,
Long Beach, CA

Anita Parker
Kannapolis Middle School,
Kannapolis, NC

Greg Pirolo
Golden Valley Middle School,
San Bernardino, CA

Laura Pottmyer
Apex Middle School,
Apex, NC

Lynn Prichard
Williams Middle Magnet School,
Tampa, FL

Jacque Quick
Walter Williams High School,
Burlington, NC

Robert Glenn Reynolds
Hillman Middle School,
Youngstown, OH

Stacy Rinehart
Lufkin Road Middle School,
Apex, NC

Theresa Short
Abbott Middle School,
Fayetteville, NC

Rita Slivka
Alexander Hamilton Middle School,
Cleveland, OH

Marie Sofsak
B F Stanton Middle School,
Alliance, OH

Nancy Stubbs
Sweetwater Union Unified School District,
Chula Vista, CA

Sharon Stull
Quail Hollow Middle School,
Charlotte, NC

Donna Taylor
Bak Middle School of the Arts,
West Palm Beach, FL

Sandi Thompson
Harding Middle School,
Lakewood, OH

Lori Walker
Audubon Middle School & Magnet Center,
Los Angeles, CA

Teacher Lab Evaluators

Andrew Boy
W.E.B. DuBois Academy,
Cincinnati, OH

Jill Brimm-Byrne
Albany Park Academy,
Chicago, IL

Gwen Broestl
Luis Munoz Marin Middle School,
Cleveland, OH

Al Brofman
Tehipite Middle School,
Fresno, CA

Michael A. Burstein
The Rashi School,
Newton, MA

Trudi Coutts
Madison Middle School,
Naperville, IL

Jenifer Cox
Sylvan Middle School,
Citrus Heights, CA

Larry Cwik
Madison Middle School,
Naperville, IL

Jennifer Donatelli
Kennedy Junior High School,
Lisle, IL

Melissa Dupree
Lakeside Middle School,
Evans, GA

Carl Fechko
Luis Munoz Marin Middle School,
Cleveland, OH

Paige Fullhart
Highland Middle School,
Libertyville, IL

Sue Hood
Glen Crest Middle School,
Glen Ellyn, IL

William Luzader
Plymouth Community Intermediate School,
Plymouth, MA

Ann Min
Beardsley Middle School,
Crystal Lake, IL

Aileen Mueller
Kennedy Junior High School,
Lisle, IL

Nancy Nega
Churchville Middle School,
Elmhurst, IL

Oscar Newman
Sumner Math and Science Academy,
Chicago, IL

Lynn Prichard
Williams Middle Magnet School,
Tampa, FL

Jacque Quick
Walter Williams High School,
Burlington, NC

Stacy Rinehart
Lufkin Road Middle School,
Apex, NC

Seth Robey
Gwendolyn Brooks Middle School,
Oak Park, IL

Kevin Steele
Grissom Middle School,
Tinley Park, IL

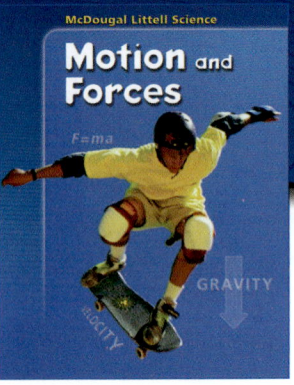

UNIT 1
Motion and Forces

Unit Features

SCIENTIFIC AMERICAN FRONTIERS IN SCIENCE *Robots on Mars* — 2

TIMELINES IN SCIENCE *Understanding Forces* — 108

1 Motion — 6

the BIG idea
The motion of an object can be described and predicted.

1. **An object in motion changes position.** — 9
   SCIENCE ON THE JOB *Physics for Rescuers* — 15
2. **Speed measures how fast position changes.** — 16
   MATH IN SCIENCE *Working with Units* — 24
3. **Acceleration measures how fast velocity changes.** — 25
   CHAPTER INVESTIGATION *Acceleration and Slope* — 32

2 Forces — 38

the BIG idea
Forces change the motion of objects in predictable ways.

1. **Forces change motion.** — 41
   THINK SCIENCE *Why Do These Rocks Slide?* — 48
2. **Force and mass determine acceleration.** — 49
   MATH IN SCIENCE *Using Significant Figures* — 56
3. **Forces act in pairs.** — 57
   CHAPTER INVESTIGATION *Newton's Laws of Motion* — 62
4. **Forces transfer momentum.** — 64

What must happen for a team to win this tug of war? page 38

vi McDougal Littell Science, Grade 8

What forces are acting on this snowboarder? on the snow? page 75

3 Gravity, Friction, and Pressure — 74

the BIG idea
Newton's laws apply to all forces.

1. **Gravity is a force exerted by masses.** — 77
   EXTREME SCIENCE *Bending Light* — 84
2. **Friction is a force that opposes motion.** — 85
   MATH IN SCIENCE *Creating a Line Graph* — 90
3. **Pressure depends on force and area.** — 91
   CHAPTER INVESTIGATION *Pressure in Fluids* — 96
4. **Fluids can exert a force on objects.** — 98

4 Work and Energy — 112

the BIG idea
Energy is transferred when a force moves an object.

1. **Work is the use of force to move an object.** — 115
   MATH IN SCIENCE *Working with Averages* — 120
2. **Energy is transferred when work is done.** — 121
   THINK SCIENCE *How Do They Do It?* — 129
3. **Power is the rate at which work is done.** — 130
   CHAPTER INVESTIGATION *Work and Power* — 136

5 Machines — 142

the BIG idea
Machines help people do work by changing the force applied to an object.

1. **Machines help people do work.** — 145
   MATH IN SCIENCE *Changing Ratios to Percents* — 153
2. **Six simple machines have many uses.** — 154
   CONNECTING SCIENCES *A Running Machine* — 163
3. **Modern technology uses compound machines.** — 164
   CHAPTER INVESTIGATION *Design a Machine* — 170

Visual Highlights

Distance-Time Graph	21
Velocity-Time Graphs	30
Newton's Three Laws of Motion	60
Orbits	81
Conserving Mechanical Energy	127
A Robot at Work	168

Table of Contents vii

UNIT 2
Waves, Sound, and Light

Unit Features

SCIENTIFIC AMERICAN FRONTIERS IN SCIENCE *Sound Medicine* — 178

TIMELINES IN SCIENCE *The Story of Light* — 282

6 Waves — 182

the BIG idea
Waves transfer energy and interact in predictable ways.

1. Waves transfer energy. — 185
   MATH IN SCIENCE *Mean, Median, and Mode* — 191
2. Waves have measurable properties. — 192
   CHAPTER INVESTIGATION *Wavelength* — 198
3. Waves behave in predictable ways. — 200
   CONNECTING SCIENCES *Tsunamis!* — 205

7 Sound — 210

the BIG idea
Sound waves transfer energy through vibrations.

1. Sound is a wave. — 213
   EXTREME SCIENCE *Sonic Booms* — 220
2. Frequency determines pitch. — 221
3. Intensity determines loudness. — 228
   MATH IN SCIENCE *Interpreting Graphs* — 233
4. Sound has many uses. — 234
   CHAPTER INVESTIGATION *Build a Stringed Instrument* — 240

How is this guitar player producing sound? page 210

How does this phone stay connected? page 246

8 Electromagnetic Waves — 246

the BIG idea
Electromagnetic waves transfer energy through radiation.

1. **Electromagnetic waves have unique traits.** — 249
   MATH IN SCIENCE *Using Exponents* — 254
2. **Electromagnetic waves have many uses.** — 255
   THINK SCIENCE *Are Cell Phones Harmful?* — 263
3. **The Sun is the source of most visible light.** — 264
4. **Light waves interact with materials.** — 269
   CHAPTER INVESTIGATION *Wavelength and Color* — 276

9 Light and Optics — 286

the BIG idea
Optical tools depend on the wave behavior of light.

1. **Mirrors form images by reflecting light.** — 289
   MATH IN SCIENCE *Measuring Angles* — 294
2. **Lenses form images by refracting light.** — 295
   CHAPTER INVESTIGATION *Looking at Lenses* — 300
3. **The eye is a natural optical tool.** — 302
4. **Optical technology makes use of light waves.** — 307
   SCIENCE ON THE JOB *Optics in Photography* — 315

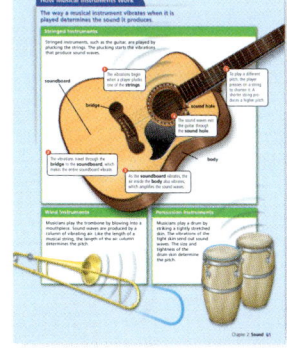

Visual Highlights

Graphing a Wave	195
Sound Frequencies Heard by Animals	223
How Musical Instruments Work	237
The Electromagnetic Spectrum	256
How a Convex Lens Forms an Image	298
Microscopes and Telescopes	309

UNIT 3
Chemical Interactions

Unit Features

FRONTIERS IN SCIENCE *Medicines from Nature* — 322

TIMELINES IN SCIENCE *The Story of Atomic Structure* — 386

10 Atomic Structure and the Periodic Table — 326

the BIG idea
A substance's atomic structure determines its physical and chemical properties.

1. Atoms are the smallest form of elements. — 329
   CONNECTING SCIENCES *Elements of Life* — 336
2. Elements make up the periodic table. — 337
   CHAPTER INVESTIGATION *Modeling Atomic Masses* — 344
3. The periodic table is a map of the elements. — 346
   MATH IN SCIENCE *Using Scientific Notation* — 353

11 Chemical Bonds and Compounds — 358

the BIG idea
The properties of compounds depend on their atoms and chemical bonds.

1. Elements combine to form compounds. — 361
   MATH IN SCIENCE *Calculating Ratios* — 366
2. Chemical bonds hold compounds together. — 367
   THINK SCIENCE *Stick to It* — 375
3. Substances' properties depend on their bonds. — 376
   CHAPTER INVESTIGATION *Chemical Bonds* — 380

How do these skydivers stay together? How is this similar to the way atoms stay together?
page 358

What changes are happening in this chemical reaction?
page 390

12 Chemical Reactions 390

the BIG idea
Chemical reactions form new substances by breaking and making chemical bonds.

1 Chemical reactions alter arrangements of atoms. 393
MATH IN SCIENCE *Analyzing Line Graphs* 401

2 The masses of reactants and products are equal. 402
SCIENCE ON THE JOB *Chemistry in Firefighting* 409

3 Chemical reactions involve energy changes. 410
CHAPTER INVESTIGATION *Exothermic or Endothermic?* 416

4 Life and industry depend on chemical reactions. 418

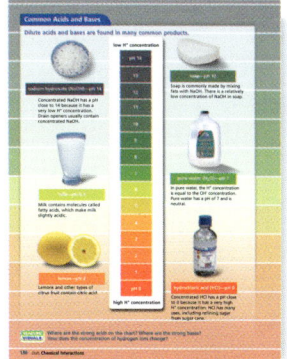

Visual Highlights

The Periodic Table of the Elements	340
Comparing Bonds	372
Balancing Equations with Coefficients	407

Table of Contents **xi**

UNIT 4
Earth's Surface

Unit Features

SCIENTIFIC AMERICAN   **FRONTIERS IN SCIENCE** *Remote Sensing* — 430

TIMELINES IN SCIENCE *History of the Earth System* — 536

13 Views of Earth Today — 434

the BIG idea
Modern technology has changed the way we view and map Earth.

1. Technology is used to explore the Earth system. — 437
2. Maps and globes are models of Earth. — 443
   MATH IN SCIENCE *Using Proportions* — 451
3. Topographic maps show the shape of the land. — 452
   CHAPTER INVESTIGATION *Investigate Topographic Maps* — 456
4. Technology is used to map Earth. — 458
   THINK SCIENCE *Which Site Is Best for an Olympic Stadium?* — 463

14 Minerals — 468

the BIG idea
Minerals are basic building blocks of Earth.

1. Minerals are all around us. — 471
   MATH IN SCIENCE *Writing Fractions as Percents* — 477
2. A mineral is identified by its properties. — 478
   CHAPTER INVESTIGATION *Mineral Identification* — 486
3. Minerals are valuable resources. — 488
   SCIENCE ON THE JOB *Geometry for Gems* — 495

Why can gold be separated from other minerals and rocks in a river? page 468

15 Rocks — 500

the BIG idea
Rocks change into other rocks over time.

1. **The rock cycle shows how rocks change.** — 503
   EXTREME SCIENCE *Rocks from Space* — 509
2. **Igneous rocks form from molten rock.** — 510
   MATH IN SCIENCE *Estimating Area* — 516
3. **Sedimentary rocks form from earlier rocks.** — 517
4. **Metamorphic rocks form as existing rocks change.** — 524
   CHAPTER INVESTIGATION *Rock Classification* — 530

16 Weathering and Soil Formation — 540

the BIG idea
Natural forces break rocks apart and form soil, which supports life.

1. **Mechanical and chemical forces break down rocks.** — 543
   MATH IN SCIENCE *Surface Area of a Prism* — 549
2. **Weathering and organic processes form soil.** — 550
   CHAPTER INVESTIGATION *Testing Soil* — 558
3. **Human activities affect soil.** — 560
   SCIENCE ON THE JOB *Soil, Water, and Architecture* — 565

17 Erosion and Deposition — 570

the BIG idea
Water, wind, and ice shape Earth's surface.

1. **Forces wear down and build up Earth's surface.** — 573
2. **Moving water shapes land.** — 578
   CHAPTER INVESTIGATION *Creating Stream Features* — 584
3. **Waves and wind shape land.** — 586
   CONNECTING SCIENCES *Life on Dunes* — 592
4. **Glaciers carve land and move sediments.** — 593
   MATH IN SCIENCE *Creating a Line Graph* — 599

Visual Highlights

Mineral Formation	491
The Rock Cycle	507
Mechanical Weathering	545
World Soil Types	553
Organisms and Soil Formation	555
Types of Glaciers and Movement	595

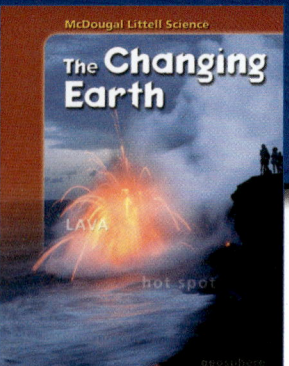

UNIT 5
The Changing Earth

Unit Features

SCIENTIFIC AMERICAN   **FRONTIERS IN SCIENCE** *Studying Volcanoes with Satellites*   606

TIMELINES IN SCIENCE *The Story of Fossils*   744

18 Plate Tectonics   610

the BIG idea
The movement of tectonic plates causes geologic changes on Earth.

1. Earth has several layers.   613
2. Continents change position over time.   618
   CHAPTER INVESTIGATION *Convection Currents and Plate Movement*   624
3. Plates move apart.   626
   MATH IN SCIENCE *Calculating Equivalent Rates*   633
4. Plates converge or scrape past each other.   634
   THINK SCIENCE *What on Earth Is Happening Here?*   641

19 Earthquakes   646

the BIG idea
Earthquakes release stress that has built up in rocks.

1. Earthquakes occur along faults.   649
   EXTREME SCIENCE *When Earth Shakes*   654
2. Earthquakes release energy.   655
   MATH IN SCIENCE *Multiplication*   663
3. Earthquake damage can be reduced.   664
   CHAPTER INVESTIGATION *How Structures React in Earthquakes*   672

What caused these rails to bend, and how long did it take? page 646

How does new land form from molten rock? page 678

20 Mountains and Volcanoes — 678

the BIG idea
Mountains and volcanoes form as tectonic plates move.

1. **Movement of rock builds mountains.** — 681
   MATH IN SCIENCE *Calculating the Mean of a Data Set* — 689
2. **Volcanoes form as molten rock erupts.** — 690
   CHAPTER INVESTIGATION *Make Your Own Volcanoes* — 698
3. **Volcanoes affect Earth's land, air, and water.** — 700
   SCIENCE ON THE JOB *Rangers at Yellowstone* — 707

21 Views of Earth's Past — 712

the BIG idea
Rocks, fossils, and other types of natural evidence tell Earth's story.

1. **Earth's past is revealed in rocks and fossils.** — 715
   CONNECTING SCIENCES *Could T. Rex Win a Race?* — 722
2. **Rocks provide a timeline for Earth.** — 723
   MATH IN SCIENCE *Interpreting Graphs* — 730
3. **The geologic time scale shows Earth's past.** — 731
   CHAPTER INVESTIGATION *Geologic Time* — 738

22 Natural Resources — 748

the BIG idea
Society depends on natural resources for energy and materials.

1. **Natural resources support human activity.** — 751
   CONNECTING SCIENCES *Got Oil Spills?* — 759
2. **Resources can be conserved and recycled.** — 760
   MATH IN SCIENCE *Comparing Decimals* — 764
3. **Energy comes from other natural resources.** — 765
   CHAPTER INVESTIGATION *Wind Power* — 774

Visual Highlights

Tectonic Plate Boundaries	639
Seismic Waves	659
Formation of the Himalayas	685
Fossils in Rocks	719
Radioactive Breakdown	728
Natural Resources	753

eEdition

UNIT 6
Life Over Time

Unit Features

SCIENTIFIC AMERICAN **FRONTIERS IN SCIENCE** *Life by Degrees* — 782

TIMELINES IN SCIENCE *Life Unearthed* — 854

23 The History of Life on Earth — 786

the BIG idea
Living things, like Earth itself, change over time.

1. **Earth has been home to living things for about 3.8 billion years.** — 789
   MATH IN SCIENCE *Using Proportions* — 796
2. **Species change over time.** — 797
   CHAPTER INVESTIGATION *Modeling Natural Selection* — 806
3. **Many types of evidence support evolution.** — 808
   THINK SCIENCE *How Did the Deep-Sea Angler Get Its Glow?* — 815

How do scientists learn about the history of life on Earth? page 786

How many different types of organisms do you see and how would you group them? page 820

24 Classification of Living Things — 820

the BIG idea
Scientists have developed a system for classifying the great diversity of living things.

1. **Scientists develop systems for classifying living things.** — 823
   MATH IN SCIENCE *Writing Percents* — 830
2. **Biologists use seven levels of classification.** — 831
   EXTREME SCIENCE *The Undiscovered* — 839
3. **Classification systems change as scientists learn more.** — 840
   CHAPTER INVESTIGATION *Making a Field Guide* — 848

25 Population Dynamics — 858

the BIG idea
Populations are shaped by interactions between organisms and the environment.

1. **Populations have many characteristics.** — 861
   MATH IN SCIENCE *Finding Averages* — 869
2. **Populations respond to pressures.** — 870
   EXTREME SCIENCE *Seed Survivors* — 877
3. **Human populations have unique responses to change.** — 878
   CHAPTER INVESTIGATION *Sustainable Resource Management* — 886

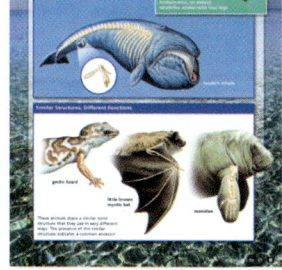

Visual Highlights

Natural Selection	803
Biological Evidence for Evolution	811
Classifying Organisms	835
Dichotomous Key	837
Six Kingdoms	842

Features

Math in Science

MOTION AND FORCES
Working with Units	24
Using Significant Figures	56
Creating a Line Graph	90
Working with Averages	120
Changing Ratios to Percents	153

WAVES, SOUND, AND LIGHT
Mean, Median, and Mode	191
Interpreting Graphs	233
Using Exponents	254
Measuring Angles	294

CHEMICAL INTERACTIONS
Using Scientific Notation	353
Calculating Ratios	366
Analyzing Line Graphs	401

EARTH'S SURFACE
Using Proportions	451
Writing Fractions as Percents	477
Estimating Area	516
Surface Area of a Prism	549
Creating a Line Graph	599

THE CHANGING EARTH
Calculating Equivalent Rates	633
Multiplication	663
Calculating the Mean of a Data Set	689
Interpreting Graphs	730
Comparing Decimals	764

LIFE OVER TIME
Using Proportions	796
Writing Percents	830
Finding Averages	869

Think Science

MOTION AND FORCES
Evaluating Hypotheses	48
Isolating Variables	129

WAVES, SOUND, AND LIGHT
Determining Relevance	263

CHEMICAL INTERACTIONS
Isolating Variables	375

EARTH'S SURFACE
Interpreting Data	463

THE CHANGING EARTH
Evaluating Conclusions	641

LIFE OVER TIME
Evaluating Hypotheses	815

Connecting Sciences

MOTION AND FORCES
Physical Science and Life Science	163

WAVES, SOUND, AND LIGHT
Physical Science and Earth Science	205

CHEMICAL INTERACTIONS
Physical Science and Life Science	336

EARTH'S SURFACE
Earth Science and Life Science	592

THE CHANGING EARTH
Earth Science and Life Science	722
Earth Science and Life Science	759

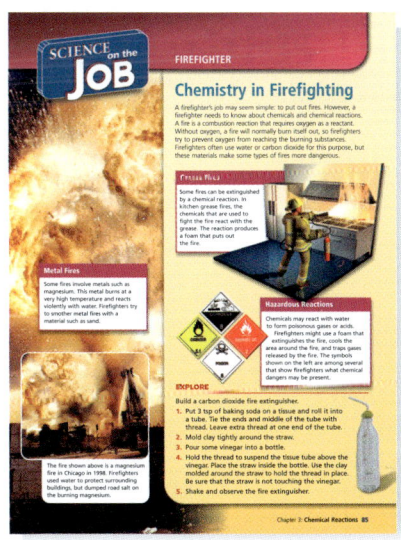

Science on the Job

MOTION AND FORCES
Physics for Rescuers — 15

WAVES, SOUND, AND LIGHT
Optics in Photography — 315

CHEMICAL INTERACTIONS
Chemistry in Firefighting — 409

EARTH'S SURFACE
Geometry for Gems — 495
Soil, Water, and Architecture — 565

THE CHANGING EARTH
Rangers at Yellowstone — 707

Extreme Science

MOTION AND FORCES
Bending Light — 84

WAVES, SOUND, AND LIGHT
Sonic Booms — 220

EARTH'S SURFACE
Rocks from Space — 509

THE CHANGING EARTH
When Earth Shakes — 654

LIFE OVER TIME
The Undiscovered — 839
Seed Survivors — 877

Frontiers in Science

MOTION AND FORCES
Robots on Mars — 2

WAVES, SOUND, AND LIGHT
Sound Medicine — 178

CHEMICAL INTERACTIONS
Medicines from Nature — 322

EARTH'S SURFACE
Remote Sensing — 430

THE CHANGING EARTH
Studying Volcanoes with Satellites — 606

LIFE OVER TIME
Life by Degrees — 782

Timelines in Science

MOTION AND FORCES
Understanding Forces — 108

WAVES, SOUND, AND LIGHT
The Story of Light — 282

CHEMICAL INTERACTIONS
The Story of Atomic Structure — 386

EARTH'S SURFACE
History of the Earth System — 536

THE CHANGING EARTH
The Story of Fossils — 744

LIFE OVER TIME
Life Unearthed — 854

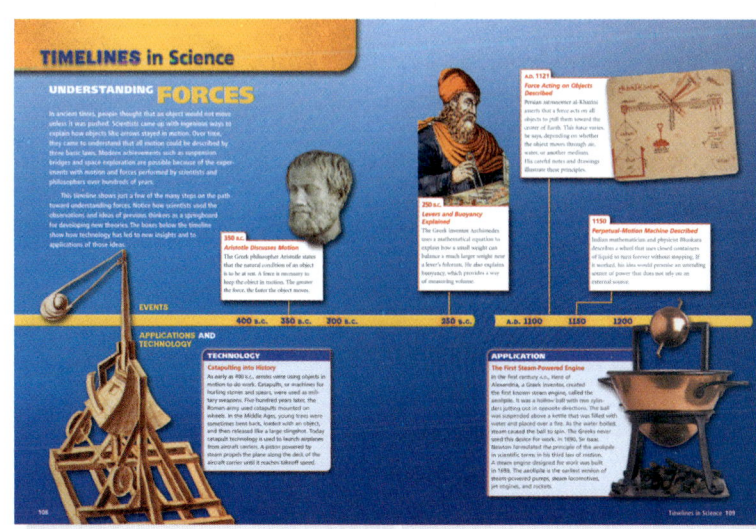

Table of Contents xix

Internet Resources @ ClassZone.com

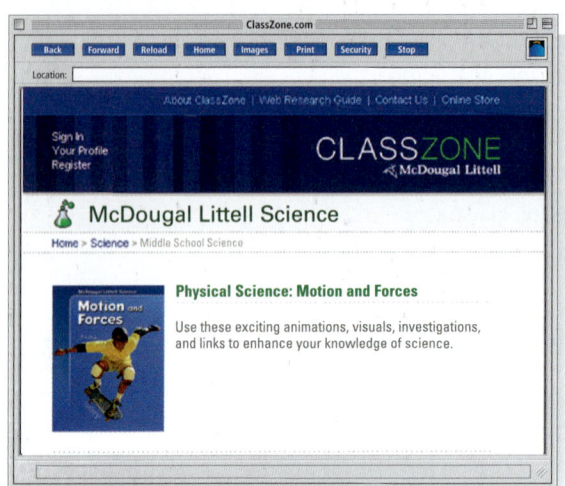

Simulations

MOTION AND FORCES
Changing Acceleration	31
Applying Force	39
Newton's Second Law	50
Fluids and Pressure	93
Work	113
Mechanical Advantage	161

WAVES, SOUND, AND LIGHT
Forces and Waves	183
The Sun at Different Wavelengths	247
Using Lenses to Form Images	299

CHEMICAL INTERACTIONS
Build an Atom	332

EARTH'S SURFACE
Topographic Maps and Surface Features	455
Rock Cycle	501

THE CHANGING EARTH
Create a Volcanic Eruption	679
Nuclear Power Plant	767

LIFE OVER TIME
Matching Finch Beaks to Food	787
Dichotomous Key	836

Visualizations

MOTION AND FORCES
Relative Motion	7
Effect of Gravity in a Vacuum	79
Transfer of Potential and Kinetic Energy	126

WAVES, SOUND, AND LIGHT
Wave Graphing	194
How Sound Travels	211
Doppler Effect	227
Electromagnetic Waves	250
Reflection	291

CHEMICAL INTERACTIONS
Radioactive Decay	352
Ionic and Covalent Bonds	359
Polar Electron Cloud	371
Concentration and Reaction Rate	398
Endothermic and Exothermic Reactions	414

EARTH'S SURFACE
Latitude and Longitude	446
Crystal Growth	474
Igneous Crystal Formation	512
Soil Formation	541
Chemical Weathering	546
Wind Erosion	571
Cave Formation	582

THE CHANGING EARTH
Continental Movement over Time	620
Plate Boundaries	637
Fault Motion	653
Primary-Wave and Secondary-Wave Motion	658
Erupted Volcanic Material	692
Fossil Formation	717
Molten Rock in Sedimentary Layers	725
Hydrogen Fuel Cell	772

LIFE OVER TIME
Fossil Formation	790
Response to Environmental Change	868

Career Centers

Physics and Engineering	5
Audiology	181
Chemistry	325
Mineralogy	433
Volcanology	609
Paleontology	785

Resource Centers

MOTION AND FORCES
Resources for the following topics may be found at ClassZone.com: *Finding Position; Acceleration; Inertia; Moving Rocks; Newton's Laws of Motion; Momentum; Gravity; Gravitational Lenses; Friction, Forces, and Surfaces; Force and Motion Research; Work; Power; Machines in Everyday Objects; Artificial Limbs; Nanomachines; Robots.*

WAVES, SOUND, AND LIGHT
Resources for the following topics may be found at ClassZone.com: *Waves; Wave Speed; Supersonic Aircraft; Sound Safety; Musical Instruments; The Electromagnetic Spectrum; Visible Light; Light Research; Optics; Microscopes and Telescopes; Lasers.*

CHEMICAL INTERACTIONS
Resources for the following topics may be found at ClassZone.com: *Periodic Table; Atom; Elements Important to Life; Chemical Formulas; Properties of Ionic and Covalent Compounds; Balancing Chemical Equations; Catalysts in Living Things.*

EARTH'S SURFACE
Resources for the following topics may be found at ClassZone.com: *Satellite Mapping; Map Projections; GIS; Precious Metals; Minerals; Gemstones; Meteorites and Impacts; Igneous Rocks; Sedimentary Rocks; Metamorphic Rocks; Earth System Research; Weathering; Soil; Mudflows; Rivers and Erosion; Glaciers.*

THE CHANGING EARTH
Resources for the following topics may be found at ClassZone.com: *Earth's Interior; Effects of Plate Movement; Recent Earthquakes; Seismology; Tsunamis; Historic and Current Volcanic Eruptions; Effects of Volcanic Eruptions; Evidence of an Event in Earth's Past; Fossils; Finding the Ages of Rocks; Fossil Research and Excavation; Natural Resources; Pollution-Digesting Microbes; Renewable Energy Resources.*

LIFE OVER TIME
Resources for the following topics may be found at ClassZone.com: *Mass Extinctions; Natural Selection; Evidence Supporting Evolution; Linnaeus; Taxonomy; New Insect Species; Modern Classification; Current Fossil and Living Fossil Finds; Population Dynamics; Human Population Growth; Introduced Species in the United States.*

Math Tutorials

MOTION AND FORCES
Units and Rates	24
Rounding Decimals	56
Creating a Line Graph	90
Finding the Mean	120
Percents and Fractions	153

WAVES, SOUND, AND LIGHT
Finding the Mean, Median, and Mode	191
Interpreting Line Graphs	233
Positive and Negative Exponents	254
Measuring Angles	294

CHEMICAL INTERACTIONS
Scientific Notation	353
Ratios	366
Interpreting Line Graphs	401

EARTH'S SURFACE
Solving Proportions	451
Percents and Fractions	477
Estimating Area	516
Surface Area of Rectangular Prisms	549
Making a Line Graph	599

THE CHANGING EARTH
Rates	633
Multiplication	663
Finding the Mean	689
Reading Line Graphs and Multiplying Whole Numbers	730
Comparing Decimals	764

LIFE OVER TIME
Writing and Solving Proportions	796
Percents and Fractions	830
Finding the Mean	869

NSTA SciLinks

Codes for use with the NSTA SciLinks site may be found on every chapter opener.

Content Reviews

There is a content review for every chapter at ClassZone.com.

Test Practice

There is a standardized test practice for every chapter at ClassZone.com.

Explore the Big Idea

Chapter Opening Inquiry

Each chapter opens with hands-on explorations that introduce the chapter's Big Idea.

Motion and Forces

Off the Wall; Rolling Along	7
Popping Ping-Pong Balls; Take Off!	39
Let It Slide; Under Pressure	75
Bouncing Ball; Power Climbing	113
Changing Direction; Shut the Door!	143

Waves, Sound, and Light

How Can Energy Be Passed Along? How Can You Change a Wave?	183
What Gives a Sound Its Qualities? How Does Size Affect Sound?	211
What Melts the Ice Cubes? What Is White Light Made Of?	247
How Does a Spoon Reflect Your Face? Why Do Things Look Different Through Water?	287

Chemical Interactions

That's Far! Element Safari	327
Mixing It Up; The Shape of Things	359
Changing Steel Wool; A Different Rate	391

Earth's Surface

Earth's Changing Surface; Using Modern Maps	435
How Do You Turn Water into a Mineral? What Makes Up Rocks?	469
How Can Rocks Disappear? What Causes Rocks to Change?	501
Ice Power; Getting the Dirt on Soil	541
Where Has Water Been? How Do Waves Shape Land?	571

The Changing Earth

Watching a Pot Boil; Earth's Moving Surface	611
Can You Bend Energy? How Can Something Move Forward, Yet Sideways?	647
Making Mountains; Under Pressure	679
How Do You Know What Happened? How Long Has That Been There?	713
Sunlight as an Energy Source; Saving Water as You Brush	749

Life Over Time

What Can Rocks Show About Earth's History? Which One of These Things Is Not Like the Others?	787
How Are Fingerprints Different? How Would You Sort Pennies?	821
How Does Population Grow? How Do Populations Differ?	859

Chapter Investigations

Full-Period Labs

The Chapter Investigations are in-depth labs that let you form and test a hypothesis, build a model, or sometimes design your own investigation.

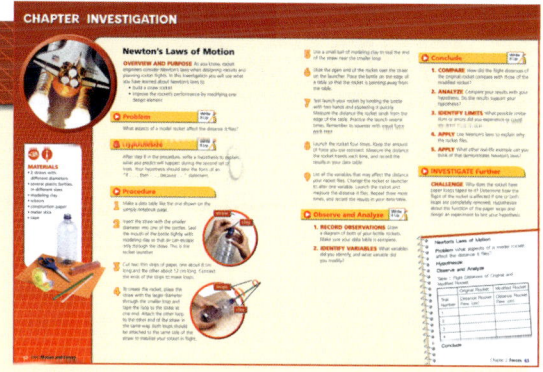

Motion and Forces

Acceleration and Slope	32
Newton's Laws of Motion	62
Pressure in Fluids	96
Work and Power	136
Design a Machine *Design Your Own*	170

Waves, Sound, and Light

Wavelength	198
Build a Stringed Instrument *Design Your Own*	240
Wavelength and Color	276
Looking at Lenses	300

Chemical Interactions

Modeling Atomic Masses	344
Chemical Bonds	380
Exothermic or Endothermic?	416

Earth's Surface

Investigate Topographic Maps	456
Mineral Identification	486
Rock Classification	530
Testing Soil	558
Creating Stream Features	584

The Changing Earth

Convection Currents and Plate Movement	624
How Structures React in Earthquakes *Design Your Own*	672
Make Your Own Volcanoes	698
Geologic Time	738
Wind Power	774

Life Over Time

Modeling Natural Selection	806
Making a Field Guide	848
Sustainable Resource Management	886

Explore

Introductory Inquiry Activities

Most sections begin with a simple activity that lets you explore the Key Concept before you read the section.

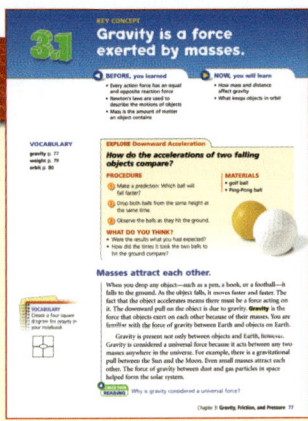

Motion and Forces

Location	9
Speed	16
Changing Motion	41
Acceleration	49
Collisions	64
Downward Acceleration	77
Pressure	91
Forces in Liquid	98
Work	115
Power	130
Machines	145
Changing Forces	154

Waves, Sound, and Light

Waves	185
Reflection	200
Sound	213
Pitch	221
Echoes	234
Electromagnetic Waves	249
Radio Waves	255
Light and Matter	269
Reflection	289
Refraction	295
Focusing Vision	302
Combining Lenses	307

Chemical Interactions

The Size of Atoms	329
Similarities and Differences of Objects	337
Compounds	361
Bonds in Metals	376
Chemical Changes	393
Energy Changes	410

Earth's Surface

Mapping	443
Topographic Maps	452
Minerals	471
Minerals at Your Fingertips	488
Rocks and Minerals	503
Particle Layers	517
Mechanical Weathering	543
Soil Composition	550
Divides	578
Glaciers	593

The Changing Earth

Density	613
Movements of Continents	618
Divergent Boundaries	626
Tectonic Plates	634
Pressure	649
Movement of Energy	655
Shaking	664
Folding	681
Eruptions	690
Rocks	715
Time Scales	731
Energy Use	760
Nuclear Energy	765

Life Over Time

Fossils	789
Evidence	808
Classification	831
Population Density	870
Population Change	878

Investigate

Skill Labs

Each Investigate activity gives you a chance to practice a specific science skill related to the content that you're studying.

Motion and Forces

Changing Positions	Observing	12
Speed and Distance	Design Your Own	19
Acceleration	Measuring	27
Inertia	Design Your Own	46
Motion and Force	Hypothesizing	54
Newton's Third Law	Observing	58
Momentum	Observing	66
Gravity	Predicting	82
Friction in Air	Design Your Own	88
Bernoulli's Principle	Observing	100
Work	Measuring	118
Mechanical Energy	Analyzing Data	125
Power	Measuring	133
Efficiency	Analyzing Data	151
Pulleys	Inferring	157

Waves, Sound, and Light

Wave Types	Comparing	189
Frequency	Collecting Data	196
Diffraction	Predicting	202
Sound Energy	Observing	217
Sound Frequency	Inferring	224
Loudness	Observing	229
Wave Behavior	Design Your Own	252
The Electromagnetic Spectrum	Drawing Conclusions	260
Artificial Lighting	Design Your Own	266
Mixing Colors	Observing	274
The Law of Reflection	Analyzing	291
Vision	Observing	304
Optical Tools	Design Your Own	310

Chemical Interactions

Masses of Atomic Particles	Modeling	333
Radioactivity	Modeling	351
Element Ratios	Modeling	363
Crystals	Observing	373
Chemical Reactions	Inferring	398
Conservation of Mass	Measuring	403
Sugar Combustion	Inferring	419

Earth's Surface

Geosphere's Layers	Modeling	441
Map Projections	Modeling	448
Satellite Imaging	Modeling	460
Crystal Shape	Observing	474
Hardness of Minerals	Classifying	484
Mining	Drawing Conclusions	493
Classification of Rocks	Classifying	505
Crystal Size	Analyzing	513
Rock Layers	Modeling	522
Metamorphic Changes	Modeling	526
Chemical Weathering	Identifying Variables	546
Soil Conservation	Making Models	563
Erosion	Design Your Own	574
Longshore Drift	Observing	588
Kettle Lake Formation	Design Your Own	597

The Changing Earth

Earth's Different Layers	Modeling	616
Magnetic Reversals	Modeling	629
Convergent Boundaries	Design Your Own	637
Faults	Modeling	651
Subduction-Zone Earthquakes	Analyzing	657
Fault-Block Mountains	Modeling	686
Mudflows	Analyzing	703
Learning from Tree Rings	Observing	720
Relative and Absolute Age	Making Models	726
Fossil Fuels	Modeling	757
Conservation	Design Your Own	762

Life Over Time

Fossil Records	Analyzing	791
Genes	Sequencing	813
Classifying Leaves	Classifying	826
Binomial Nomenclature	Classifying	832
Limiting Factors	Design Your Own	874
Population	Graphing data	882

GRADE 8
PASS Science Standards

The chart below shows where Oklahoma's PASS Science Standards for Grade 8 are covered in this book. Process standards are also covered in section Investigates. The six modules that make up *McDougal Littell Science, Oklahoma Edition* for Grade 8 are *Motion and Forces; Waves, Sound, and Light; Chemical Interactions; Earth's Surface; The Changing Earth;* and *Life Over Time.*

SCIENCE PROCESSES AND INQUIRY

Process Standard 1: Observe and Measure—Observing is the first action taken by the learner to acquire new information about an object, organism, or event. Opportunities for observation are developed through the use of a variety of scientific tools. Measurement allows observations to be quantified.

Oklahoma PASS Standard	*McDougal Littell Science,* Grade 8
1. Identify qualitative and/or quantitative changes given conditions (e.g., temperature, mass, volume, time, position, length) before, during, and after an event.	All Chapter Investigations, Investigates, and Explores throughout the book
2. Use appropriate tools (e.g., metric ruler, graduated cylinder, thermometer, balances, spring scales, stopwatches) when measuring objects, organisms, and/or events.	All Chapter Investigations, Investigates, and Explores throughout the book
3. Use appropriate System International (SI) units (i.e., grams, meters, liters, degrees Celsius, and seconds); and SI prefixes (i.e., micro-, milli-, centi-, and kilo-) when measuring objects, organisms, and/or events.	All Chapter Investigations, Investigates, and Explores throughout the book

Process Standard 2: Classify—Classifying establishes order. Objects, organisms, and events are classified based on similarities, differences, and interrelationships.

1. Using observable properties, place an object, organism, and/or event into a classification system (e.g., dichotomous keys).	Chapter 11 Investigation: Chemical Bonds; Chapter 12 Investigation: Exothermic or Endothermic?; Chapter 14 Investigation: Mineral Identification; Chapter 15 Investigation: Rock Classification; Chapter 21 Investigation: Geologic Time; Chapter 24 Investigation: Making a Field Guide
2. Identify properties by which a set of objects, organisms, and/or events could be ordered.	Chapter 10 Investigation: Modeling Atomic Masses; Chapter 11 Investigation: Chemical Bonds; Chapter 14 Investigation: Mineral Identification; Chapter 15 Investigation: Rock Classification; Chapter 16 Investigation: Testing Soil; Chapter 21 Investigation: Geologic Time; Chapter 24 Investigation: Making a Field Guide

Process Standard 3: Experiment—Experimenting is a method of discovering information. It requires making observations and measurements to test ideas.

1. Ask questions about the world and design investigations that lead to scientific inquiry.	Chapter 7 Investigation: Build a Stringed Instrument; Chapter 15 Investigation: Rock Classification; Chapter 19 Investigation: How Structures React to Earthquakes
2. Evaluate the design of a scientific investigation.	Chapter 6 Investigation: Wavelength; Chapter 11 Investigation: Chemical Bonds; Chapter 12 Investigation: Exothermic or Endothermic?; Chapter 16 Investigation: Testing Soil; Chapter 17 Investigation: Creating Stream Features

Process Standard 3: Experiment (continued)

3. Identify variables and/or controls in an experimental setup: independent (tested/experimental) variable and dependent (measured) variable.	Chapter 4 Investigation: Work and Power; Chapter 6 Investigation: Wavelength; Chapter 8 Investigation: Wavelength and Color; Chapter 18 Investigation: Convection Currents; Chapter 19 Investigation: How Structures React to Earthquakes; Chapter 20 Investigation: Make Your Own Volcanoes
4. Identify a testable hypothesis for an experiment.	Chapter 1 Investigation: Acceleration and Slope; Chapter 2 Investigation: Newton's Laws of Motion; Chapter 4 Investigation: Work and Power; Chapter 6 Investigation: Wavelength; Chapter 7 Investigation: Build a Stringed Instrument; Chapter 8 Investigation: Wavelength and Color; Chapter 11 Investigation: Chemical Bonds; Chapter 18 Investigation: Convection Currents; Chapter 19 Investigation: How Structures React to Earthquakes; Chapter 20 Investigation: Make Your Own Volcanoes; Chapter 22 Investigation: Wind Power; Chapter 25 Investigation: Resource Management
5. Design and conduct experiments.	Chapter 1 Investigation: Acceleration and Slope; Chapter 7 Investigation: Build a Stringed Instrument; Chapter 18 Investigation: Convection Currents; Chapter 19 Investigation: How Structures React to Earthquakes
6. Recognize potential hazards and practice safety procedures in all science activities.	All investigations

Process Standard 4: Interpret and Communicate—Interpreting is the process of recognizing patterns in collected data by making inferences, predictions, or conclusions. Communicating is the process of describing, recording, and reporting experimental procedures and results to others. Communication may be oral, written, or mathematical and includes organizing ideas, using appropriate vocabulary, graphs, other visual representations, and mathematical equations.

1. Report data in an appropriate method when given an experimental procedure or data.	Chapter 1 Investigation: Acceleration and Slope; Chapter 2 Investigation: Newton's Laws of Motion; Chapter 4 Investigation: Work and Power; Chapter 6 Investigation: Wavelength; Chapter 9 Investigation: Looking at Lenses; Chapter 10 Investigation: Modeling Atomic Masses; Chapter 16 Investigation: Testing Soil; Chapter 25 Investigation: Resource Management
2. Interpret data tables, line, bar, trend, and/or circle graphs.	Chapter 1 Investigation: Acceleration and Slope; Chapter 14 Investigation: Mineral Identification
3. Evaluate data to develop reasonable explanation, and/or predictions.	Chapter 1 Investigation: Acceleration and Slope; Chapter 3 Investigation: Pressure in Fluids; Chapter 10 Investigation: Modeling Atomic Masses; Chapter 12 Investigation: Exothermic or Endothermic?
4. Accept or reject hypotheses when given results of an investigation.	Chapter 3 Investigation: Pressure in Fluids; Chapter 4 Investigation: Work and Power; Chapter 7 Investigation: Build a Stringed Instrument; Chapter 18 Investigation: Convection Currents; Chapter 22 Investigation: Wind Power; Chapter 25 Investigation: Resource Management
5. Communicate scientific procedures and explanations.	Investigation: Work and Power; Chapter 17 Investigation: Creating Stream Features

Process Standard 5: Inquiry—Inquiry can be defined as the skills necessary to carry out the process of scientific or systemic thinking. In order for inquiry to occur, students must have the opportunity to ask a question, formulate a procedure, and observe phenomena.

1. Use systematic observations, make accurate measurements, and identify and control variables.	Chapter 2 Investigation: Newton's Laws of Motion; Chapter 3 Investigation: Pressure in Fluids; Chapter 4 Investigation: Work and Power; Chapter 10 Investigation: Modeling Atomic Masses; Chapter 12 Investigation: Exothermic or Endothermic?; Chapter 15 Investigation: Rock Classification; Chapter 16 Investigation: Testing Soil; Chapter 22 Investigation: Wind Power; Chapter 24 Investigation: Making a Field Guide; Chapter 25 Investigation: Resource Management
2. Use technology to gather data and analyze results of investigations.	Chapter 11 Investigation: Chemical Bonds; Chapter 16 Investigation: Testing Soil; Chapter 22 Investigation: Wind Power
3. Review data, summarize data, and form logical conclusions.	Chapter 1 Investigation: Acceleration and Slope; Chapter 2 Investigation: Newton's Laws of Motion; Chapter 4 Investigation: Work and Power; Chapter 9 Investigation: Looking at Lenses; Chapter 10 Investigation: Modeling Atomic Masses; Chapter 12 Investigation: Exothermic or Endothermic?
4. Formulate and evaluate explanations proposed by examining and comparing evidence, pointing out statements that go beyond evidence, and suggesting alternative explanations.	Chapter 1 Investigation: Acceleration and Slope; Chapter 3 Investigation: Pressure in Fluids; Chapter 4 Investigation: Work and Power; Chapter 21 Investigation: Geologic Time

PHYSICAL SCIENCE

Standard 1: Properties and Chemical Changes in Matter—Physical characteristics of objects can be described using shape, size, and mass. The materials from which objects are made can be described using color, texture, and hardness. These properties can be used to distinguish and separate one substance from another.

1. Substances react chemically with other substances to form new substances with different characteristics (e.g., rusting, burning, reaction between baking soda and vinegar).	Chapter 10, Atomic Structure and the Periodic Table; Chapter 11, Chemical Bonds and Compounds; Chapter 12, Chemical Reactions
2. Matter has physical properties that can be measured (i.e., mass, volume, temperature, color, texture, density, and hardness). In chemical reactions and physical changes, matter is conserved (e.g., compare and contrast physical and chemical changes).	Chapter 11, Chemical Bonds and Compounds; Chapter 12, Chemical Reactions

Standard 2: Motions and Forces—The motion of an object can be described by its position, direction of motion, and speed.

1. The motion of an object can be measured. The position of an object, its speed and direction can be represented on a graph.	Chapter 1, Motion; Chapter 2 Forces
2. An object that is not being subjected to a net force will continue to move at a constant velocity (in a straight line and a constant speed).	Chapter 2, Forces

LIFE SCIENCE

Standard 3: Diversity and Adaptations of Organisms—Millions of species of animals, plants, and microorganisms are alive today. Although different species might look dissimilar, the unity among organisms becomes apparent from an analysis of internal and external structures. Adaptation involves the selection of naturally occurring variations in populations.

1. By classifying organisms, biologists consider details of internal and external structure.	Chapter 24, Classification of Living Things
2. Organisms have a great variety of internal and external structures that enable them to survive in a specific habitat such as echolocation of bats and seed dispersal methods.	Chapter 25, Population Dynamics

EARTH/SPACE SCIENCE

Standard 4: Structures and Forces of the Earth and Solar System—The earth is mostly rock, three-fourths of its surface is covered by a relatively thin layer of water, and the entire planet is surrounded by a relatively thin blanket of air, and is able to support life.

1. Landforms result from constructive forces such as crystal deformation, volcanic eruption, and deposition of sediment and destructive forces such as weathering and erosion.	Chapter 16, Weathering and Soil Formation
2. The formation, weathering, sedimentation, and reformation of rock constitute a continuing "rock cycle" in which the total amount of material stays the same as its form changes.	Chapter 14, Minerals; Chapter 15, Rocks; Chapter 16, Weathering and Soil Formation; Chapter 17, Erosion and Deposition
3. Gravity is the force that governs the motion of the solar system and holds us to the earth's surface.	Chapter 3, Gravity, Friction, and Pressure

Standard 5: Earth's History—The Earth's history involves periodic changes in the structures of the earth over time.

1. Earth's history has been punctuated by occasional catastrophic events, such as the impact of asteroids or comets, enormous volcanic eruptions, periods of continental glaciation, and the rise and fall of sea level.	Chapter 23, History of Life on Earth
2. Fossils provide important evidence of how life and environmental conditions have changed.	Chapter 23, History of Life on Earth

Introducing Science

Scientists are curious. Since ancient times, they have been asking and answering questions about the world around them. Scientists are also very suspicious of the answers they get. They carefully collect evidence and test their answers many times before accepting an idea as correct.

In this book you will see how scientific knowledge keeps growing and changing as scientists ask new questions and rethink what was known before. The following sections will help get you started.

Unifying Principles of Science   xxxii
What do scientists know? These pages introduce unifying principles that will give you a big picture of science.

The Nature of Science   xxxviii
How do scientists learn? This section provides an overview of scientific thinking and the processes that scientists use to ask questions and to find answers.

The Nature of Technology   xlii
How do we use what scientists learn? These pages introduce you to how people develop and use technologies to design solutions to real-world problems.

Using McDougal Littell Science   xliv
How can you learn more about science? This section provides helpful tips on how to learn and use science from the key parts of this program—the text, the visuals, the activities, and the Internet resources.

What Is Science?

Science is the systematic study of all of nature, from particles too small to see to the human body to the entire universe. However, no individual scientist can study all of nature. Therefore science is divided into many different fields. For example, some scientists are biologists, others are geologists, and still others are chemists or astronomers.

All the different scientific fields can be grouped into three broad categories: life science, earth science, and physical science.

- Life science focuses on the study of living things; it includes the fields of cell biology, botany, ecology, zoology, and human biology.
- Earth science focuses on the study of our planet and its place in the universe; it includes the fields of geology, oceanography, meteorology, and astronomy.
- Physical science focuses on the study of what things are made of and how they change; it includes the fields of chemistry and physics.

McDougal Littell Science, Grade 8

McDougal Littell Science pulls together units from the different categories of science to give you a broad picture of how scientists study nature. For example, physical scientists, earth scientists, and biologists might all study forces and their effects from different points of view. You will learn in Unit 1 how physicists study the strength and the effects of physical forces. In Unit 5 you will read about how earth scientists study the effects of forces generated by volcanoes and earthquakes. In Unit 6 you will see how biologists study the natural forces that have affected entire populations over time.

Even though science has many different fields, all scientists have similar ways of thinking and approaching their work. For example, scientists use instruments as well as their minds to look for patterns in nature. Scientists also try to find explanations for the patterns they discover. As you study each unit, you will in part focus on the patterns that scientists have found within that particular specialized branch. At the same time, as you move from one unit to another, you will be blending knowledge from the different branches of science together to form a more general understanding of our universe.

Unifying Principles

As you learn, it helps to have a big picture of science as a framework for new information. McDougal Littell Science has identified unifying principles from each of the three broad categories of science. These unifying principles are described on the following pages. However, keep in mind that the broad categories of science do not have fixed borders. Earth science shades into life science, which shades into physical science, which shades back into earth science.

> **the BIG idea**
>
> Each chapter begins with a big idea. Keep in mind that each big idea relates to one or more of the unifying principles.

What Is Life Science?

Life science is the study of the great variety of living things that have lived or now live on Earth. Life science includes the study of the characteristics and needs that all living things have in common. It is also a study of changes—both daily changes and those that take place over millions of years. Probably most important, in studying life science you will explore the many ways that all living things—including you—depend on Earth and its resources.

The story of life on Earth is a story of changes. Some changes take place over millions of years. At one time, animals similar to modern fish swam in the area where this lizard now runs.

UNIFYING PRINCIPLES of Life Science

All living things share common characteristics.
Despite the variety of living things on Earth, there are certain characteristics common to all. The basic unit of life is the **cell.** Any living thing, whether it has one cell or many, is described as an **organism.** All organisms are characterized by

- organization—the way that an organism's body is arranged
- growth—the way that an organism grows and develops over its lifetime
- reproduction—the way that an organism produces offspring like itself
- response—the ways an organism interacts with its surroundings

All living things share common needs.
All living things have three basic needs: energy, materials, and living space. Energy enables an organism to carry out all the activities of life. The body of an organism needs water and other materials. Water is important because most of the chemical reactions in a cell take place in water. Organisms also require other materials. Plants, for example, need carbon dioxide to make energy-rich sugars, and most living things need oxygen. Living space is the environment in which an organism gets the energy and materials it needs.

Living things meet their needs through interactions with the environment.
The **environment** is everything that surrounds a living thing. This includes other organisms as well as nonliving factors, such as rainfall, sunlight, and soil. Any exchange of energy or materials between the living and nonliving parts of the environment is an **interaction.** Plants interact with the environment by capturing energy from the Sun and changing that energy into chemical energy that is stored in sugar. Animals can interact with plants by eating the plants and getting energy from the sugars that the plants have made.

The types and numbers of living things change over time.
A **species** is a group of living things so closely related that they can produce offspring together that can also reproduce. Scientists have named about 1.4 million different species. The great variety of species on Earth today is called **biodiversity.** Different species have different characteristics, or **adaptations,** that allow the members of that species to get their needs met in a particular environment. Over the millions of years that life has existed on Earth, new species have come into being and others have disappeared. The disappearance of a species is called **extinction.** Fossils of now extinct organisms is one way that scientists have of seeing how living things have changed over time.

What Is Earth Science?

Earth science is the study of Earth's interior, its rocks and soil, its oceans, its atmosphere, and outer space. For many years, scientists studied each of these topics separately. They learned many important things. More recently, however, scientists have looked more and more at the connections among the different parts of Earth—its oceans, atmosphere, living things, and rocks and soil. Scientists have also been learning more about other planets in our solar system, as well as stars and galaxies far away. Through these studies they have learned much about Earth and its place in the universe.

The lava pouring out of this volcano in Hawaii is liquid rock that was melted by heat energy under Earth's surface.

UNIFYING PRINCIPLES of Earth Science

Heat energy inside Earth and radiation from the Sun provide energy for Earth's processes.

Energy is the ability to cause change. All of Earth's processes need energy to occur. Earth's interior is very hot. This heat energy moves up to Earth's surface, where it provides the energy to build mountains, cause earthquakes, and make volcanoes erupt. Earth also receives energy from the Sun as **radiation**—energy that travels across distances in the form of certain types of waves. Energy from the Sun causes winds to blow, ocean currents to flow, and water to move from the ground to the atmosphere and back again.

Physical forces, such as gravity, affect the movement of all matter on Earth and throughout the universe.

What do the stars in a galaxy, the planet Earth, and your body have in common? For one thing, they are all made of matter. **Matter** is anything that has mass and takes up space. Rocks are matter. You are matter. Even the air around you is matter. Everything in the universe is also affected by the same physical forces. A **force** is a push or a pull. Forces affect how matter moves everywhere in the universe.

Matter and energy move among Earth's rocks and soil, atmosphere, waters, and living things.

Think of Earth as a huge system, or an organized group of parts that work together. Within this system, matter and energy move among the different parts. The four major parts of Earth's system are the

- **atmosphere,** which includes all the air surrounding the solid planet
- **geosphere,** which includes all of Earth's rocks and minerals, as well as Earth's interior
- **hydrosphere,** which includes oceans, rivers, lakes, and every drop of water on or under Earth's surface
- **biosphere,** which includes all the living things on Earth

Earth has changed over time and continues to change.

Events are always changing Earth's surface. Some events, such as the building or wearing away of mountains, occur over millions of years. Others, such as earthquakes, occur within seconds. A change can affect a small area or even the entire planet.

Unifying Principles xxxv

What Is Physical Science?

Physical science is the study of what things are made of and how they change. It combines the study of both physics and chemistry. Physics is the study of matter, energy, and forces, and it includes such topics as motion, light, and electricity and magnetism. Chemistry is the study of the structure and properties of matter. It focuses especially on how substances change into different substances.

You cannot "use up" energy. Even though a camp stove's fuel may be gone and a flashlight's battery is no longer functioning, the energy they provided has not disappeared. It has only changed forms.

UNIFYING PRINCIPLES of Physical Science

Matter is made of particles too small to see.

The tiny particles that make up all matter are called **atoms.** Just how tiny are atoms? They are far too small to see even through a powerful microscope. In fact, an atom is about a million times smaller than the period at the end of this sentence. There are more than 100 basic kinds of matter called **elements.** The atoms of any element are all alike but different from the atoms of any other element. Everything around you is made of atoms and combinations of atoms.

Matter changes form and moves from place to place.

You see objects moving and changing all around you. All changes in matter are the result of atoms moving and combining in different ways. Regardless of how much matter may change, however, under ordinary conditions it is never created or destroyed. Matter that seems to disappear merely changes into another form of matter.

Energy changes from one form to another, but it cannot be created or destroyed.

All the changes you see around you depend on energy. Energy, in fact, means the ability to cause change. Using energy means changing energy. But energy is never created or destroyed, no matter how often it changes form. This fact is known as the **law of conservation of energy.** The energy you may think you've lost when a match has burned out has only been changed into other forms of energy that are less useful to you.

Physical forces affect the movement of all matter on Earth and throughout the universe.

A **force** is a push or a pull. Every time you push or pull an object, you are applying a force to that object, whether or not the object moves. There are several forces—several pushes or pulls—acting on you right now. All these forces are necessary for you to do the things you do, even sitting and reading. **Gravity** keeps you on the ground. Gravity also keeps the Moon moving around Earth, and Earth moving around the Sun. **Friction** is the force that opposes motion. The friction between the bottoms of your shoes and the floor makes it possible for you to walk without slipping. Too much friction between a heavy box and the floor makes it hard to push the box across the floor.

The Nature of Science

You may think of science as a body of knowledge or a collection of facts. More important, however, science is an active process that involves certain ways of looking at the world.

Scientific Habits of Mind

Scientists are curious. They are always asking questions. Scientists have asked questions such as, "What is the smallest form of matter?" and "How do the smallest particles behave?" These and other important questions are being investigated by scientists around the world.

Scientists are observant. They are always looking closely at the world around them. Scientists once thought the smallest parts of atoms were protons, neutrons, and electrons. Later, protons and neutrons were found to be made of even smaller particles called quarks.

Scientists are creative. They draw on what they know to form possible explanations for a pattern, an event, or an interesting phenomenon that they have observed. Then scientists create a plan for testing their ideas.

Scientists are skeptical. Scientists don't accept an explanation or answer unless it is based on evidence and logical reasoning. They continually question their own conclusions and the conclusions suggested by other scientists. Scientists trust only evidence that is confirmed by other people or methods.

Scientists cannot always make observations with their own eyes. They have developed technology, such as this particle detector, to help them gather information about the smallest particles of matter.

Scientists ask questions about the physical world and seek answers through carefully controlled procedures. Here a researcher works with supercooled magnets.

Science Processes at Work

You can think of science as a continuous cycle of asking and seeking answers to questions about the world. Although there are many processes that scientists use, scientists typically do each of the following:

- Observe and ask a question
- Determine what is known
- Investigate
- Interpret results
- Share results

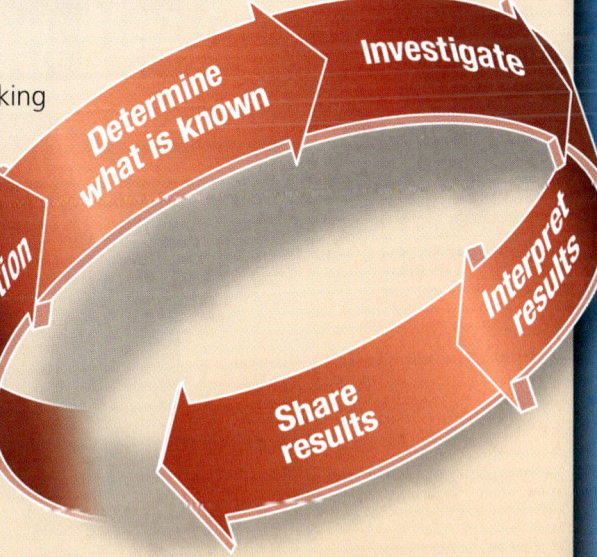

Observe and Ask a Question

It may surprise you that asking questions is an important skill. A scientific process may start when a scientist asks a question. Perhaps scientists observe an event or a process that they don't understand, or perhaps answering one question leads to another.

Determine What Is Known

When beginning an inquiry, scientists find out what is already known about a question. They study results from other scientific investigations, read journals, and talk with other scientists. A scientist working on subatomic particles is most likely a member of a large team using sophisticated equipment. Before beginning original research, the team analyzes results from previous studies.

The Nature of Science xxxix

Investigate

Investigating is the process of collecting evidence. Two important ways of investigating are observing and experimenting.

Observing is the act of noting and recording an event, a characteristic, or anything else detected with an instrument or with the senses. A researcher may study the properties of a substance by handling it, finding its mass, warming or cooling it, stretching it, and so on. For information about the behavior of subatomic particles, however, a researcher may rely on technology such as scanning tunneling microscopes, which produce images of structures that cannot be seen with the eye.

An **experiment** is an organized procedure to study something under controlled conditions. In order to study the effect of wing shape on the motion of a glider, for instance, a researcher would need to conduct controlled studies in which gliders made of the same materials and with the same masses differed only in the shape of their wings.

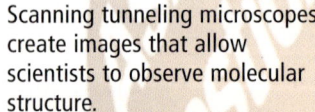

Scanning tunneling microscopes create images that allow scientists to observe molecular structure.

Physical chemists have found a way to observe chemical reactions at the atomic level. Using lasers, they can watch bonds breaking and new bonds forming.

Forming hypotheses and making predictions are two of the skills involved in scientific investigations. A **hypothesis** is a tentative explanation for an observation, a phenomenon, or a scientific problem that can be tested by further investigation. For example, in the mid-1800s astronomers noticed that the planet Uranus departed slightly from its expected orbit. One astronomer hypothesized that the irregularities in the planet's orbit were due to the gravitational effect of another planet—one that had not yet been detected.
A **prediction** is an expectation of what will be observed or what will happen. A prediction can be used to test a hypothesis. The astronomers predicted that they would discover a new planet in the position calculated, and their prediction was confirmed with the discovery of the planet Neptune.

Interpret Results

As scientists investigate, they analyze their evidence, or data, and begin to draw conclusions. **Analyzing data** involves looking at the evidence gathered through observations or experiments and trying to identify any patterns that might exist in the data. Scientists often need to make additional observations or perform more experiments before they are sure of their conclusions. Many times scientists make new predictions or revise their hypotheses.

Often scientists use computers to help them analyze data. Computers reveal patterns that might otherwise be missed.

Scientists use computers to create models of objects or processes they are studying. This model shows carbon atoms forming a sphere.

Share Results

An important part of scientific investigation is sharing results of experiments. Scientists read and publish in journals and attend conferences to communicate with other scientists around the world. Sharing data and procedures gives them a way to test one another's results. They also share results with the public through newspapers, television, and other media.

The Nature of Technology

When you think of technology, you may think of cars, computers, and cell phones, as well as refrigerators, radios, and bicycles. Technology is not only the machines and devices that make modern lives easier, however. It is also a process in which new methods and devices are created. Technology makes use of scientific knowledge to design solutions to real-world problems.

Science and Technology

Science and technology go hand in hand. Each depends upon the other. Even designing a device as simple as a toaster requires knowledge of how heat flows and which materials are the best conductors of heat. Just as technology based on scientific knowledge makes our lives easier, some technology is used to advance scientific inquiry itself. For example, researchers use a number of specialized instruments to help them collect data. Microscopes, telescopes, spectrographs, and computers are just a few of the tools that help scientists learn more about the world. The more information these tools provide, the more devices can be developed to aid scientific research and to improve modern lives.

The Process of Technological Design

The process of technology involves many choices. For example, how does an automobile engineer design a better car? Is a better car faster? safer? cheaper? Before designing any new machine, the engineer must decide exactly what he or she wants the machine to do as well as what may be given up for the machine to do it. A faster car may get people to their destinations more quickly, but it may cost more and be less safe. As you study the technological process, think about all the choices that were made to build the technologies you use.

Identify a Need
Successful technology fills a need; it helps us perform a task we need or want to do. For example, as more cars appear on the road, noise and air pollution become serious threats to the environment and to people's health. Gas consumption also depletes precious petroleum resources. There is a need to find a fuel source for a car that will not pollute the air and that will never run out.

Design and Develop
Hydrogen fuel cells are a potential solution to this need. These cells combine hydrogen and oxygen into water, producing electricity in the process. Engineers have found a way to make fuel cells small enough to fit into a car, yet able to produce enough electricity to power an electric motor. Before arriving at this final design, engineers tried many others.

Test and Improve
Just because a technology works doesn't mean it cannot be improved. A fuel-cell-powered car has been driven from San Francisco to Washington, D.C., but it probably will be a while before it's in dealer showrooms. Engineers won't know how these cars will perform until they're driven in real-world conditions. Engineers also won't know if the average driver will be able to handle the necessary maintenance on the car until the car is made available to ordinary drivers. Improvements in the future may well bring cars powered by fuel cells into garages everywhere.

Using McDougal Littell Science

Reading Text and Visuals

This book is organized to help you learn. Use these boxed pointers as a path to help you learn and remember the **Big Ideas** and **Key Concepts**.

Read the Big Idea.

As you read **Key Concepts** for the chapter, relate them to **the Big Idea**.

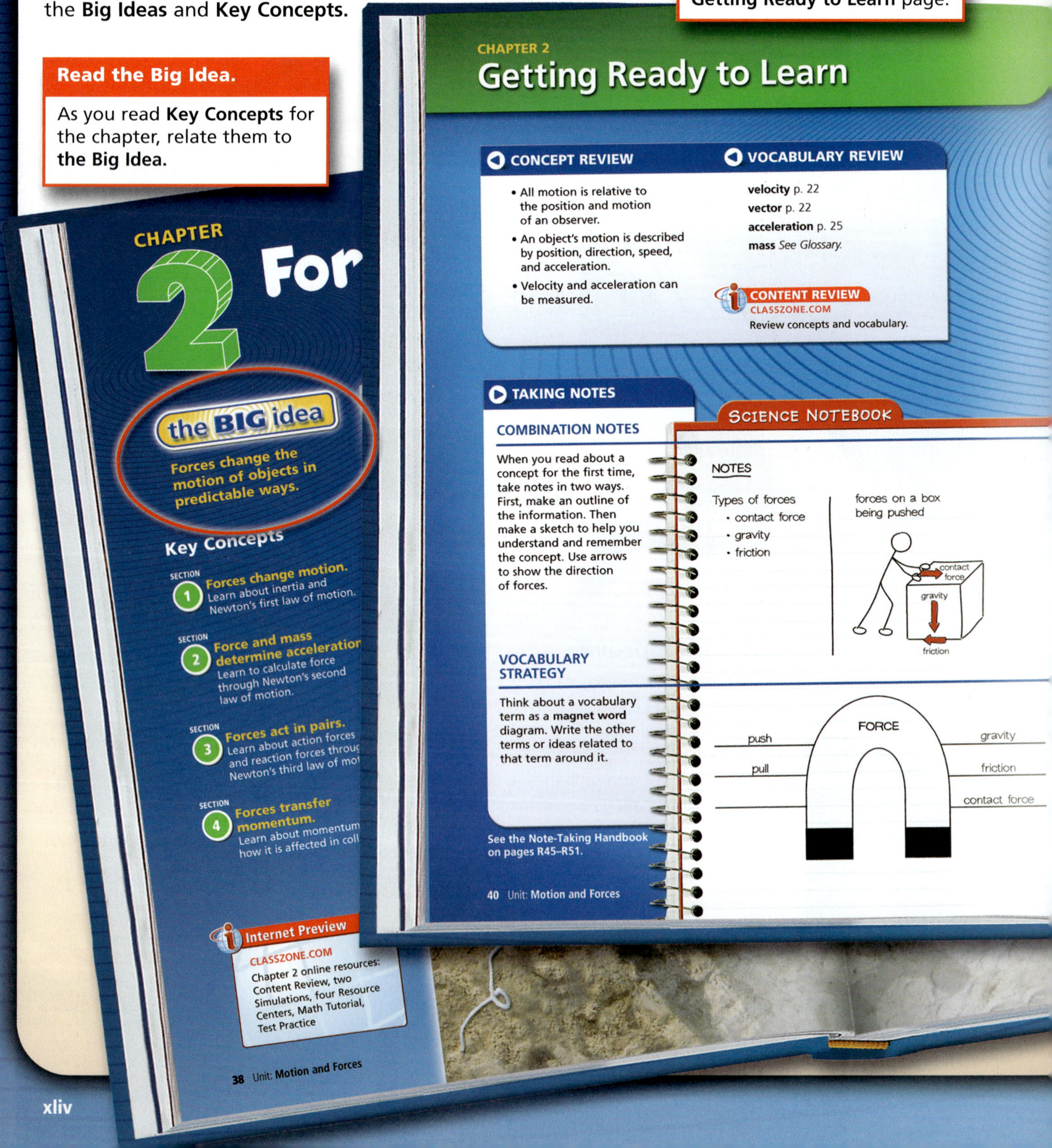

Take notes.

Use the strategies on the **Getting Ready to Learn** page.

> **Read each heading.**
> See how it fits into the outline of the chapter.

KEY CONCEPT

2.1 Forces change motion.

> **Remember what you know.**
> Think about concepts you learned earlier and preview what you'll learn now.

◁ **BEFORE, you learned**
- The velocity of an object is its change in position over time
- The acceleration of an object is its change in velocity over time

▶ **NOW, you will learn**
- What a force is
- How unbalanced forces change an object's motion
- How Newton's first law allows you to predict motion

VOCABULARY
force p. 41
net force p. 43
Newton's first law p. 45
inertia p. 46

EXPLORE Changing Motion

How can you change an object's motion?

PROCEDURE

1. Choose an object from the materials list and change its motion in several ways, from
   - not moving to moving
   - moving to not moving
   - moving to moving faster
   - moving to moving in a different direction

2. Describe the actions used to change the motion.

3. Experiment again with another object. First, decide what you will do; then predict how the motion of the object will change.

MATERIALS
- quarter
- book
- tennis ball
- cup
- feather

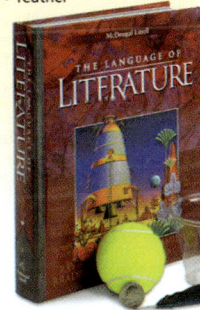

WHAT DO YOU THINK?
In step 3, how were you able to predict the motion of the object?

> **Try the activities.**
> They will introduce you to science concepts.

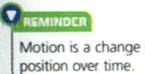
Motion is a change in position over time.

A force is a push or a pull.

Think about what happens during an exciting moment at the ballpark. The pitcher throws the ball across the plate, and the batter hits it high up into the stands. A fan in the stands catches the home-run ball. In this example, the pitcher sets the ball in motion, the batter changes the direction of the ball's motion, and the fan stops the ball's motion. To do so, each must use a **force**, or a push or a pull.

You use forces all day long to change the motion of objects in your world. You use a force to pick up your backpack, to open or close a car door, and even to move a pencil across your desktop. Any time you change the motion of an object, you use a force.

> **Learn the vocabulary.**
> Take notes on each term.

> **Answer the questions.**
> **Check Your Reading** questions will help you remember what you read.

Reading Text and Visuals

> Objects at rest and objects in motion both resist changes in motion. That is, objects at rest tend to stay at rest, and objects that are moving tend to continue moving unless a force acts on them. Galileo reasoned there was no real difference between an object that is moving at a constant velocity and an object that is standing still. An object at rest is simply an object with zero velocity.

CHECK YOUR READING How were Galileo's ideas about objects in motion different from the ideas of the ancient Greeks?

Newton's First Law

Newton restated Galileo's conclusions as his first law of motion. **Newton's first law** states that objects at rest remain at rest, and objects in motion remain in motion with the same velocity, unless acted upon by an unbalanced force. You can easily observe the effects of unbalanced forces, both on the ball at rest and the ball in motion, in the pictures below.

Read one paragraph at a time.

Look for a topic sentence that explains the main idea of the paragraph. Figure out how the details relate to that idea. One paragraph might have several important ideas; you may have to reread to understand.

Answer the questions.

Check Your Reading questions will help you remember what you read.

Study the visuals.

- Read the title.
- Read all labels and captions.
- Figure out what the picture is showing. Notice colors, arrows, and lines.
- Answer the question. **Reading Visuals** questions will help you understand the picture.

Newton's First Law

Objects at rest remain at rest, and objects in motion remain in motion with the same velocity, unless acted upon by an unbalanced force.

An Object at Rest

An object at rest (the ball) remains at rest unless acted upon by an unbalanced force (from the foot).

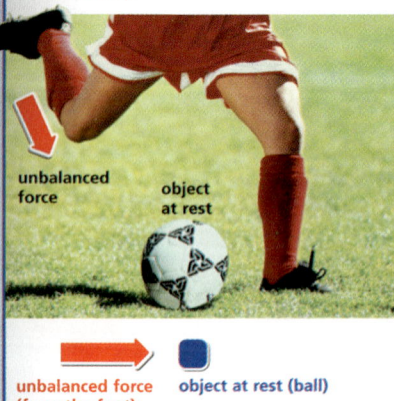

unbalanced force (from the foot) → object at rest (ball)

An Object in Motion

An object in motion (the ball) remains in motion with the same velocity, unless acted upon by an unbalanced force (from the hand).

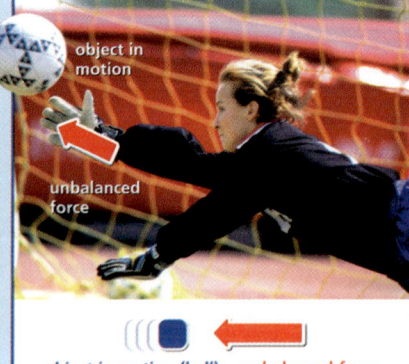

object in motion (ball) ← unbalanced force (from the hand)

READING VISUALS What will happen to the ball's motion in both pictures? Why?

Chapter 2: **Forces** 45

Doing Labs

To understand science, you have to see it in action. Doing labs helps you understand how things really work.

1. Read the entire lab first.
2. Form a hypothesis.
3. Follow the procedure.
4. Record the data.
5. Analyze your results.
6. Write your lab report.

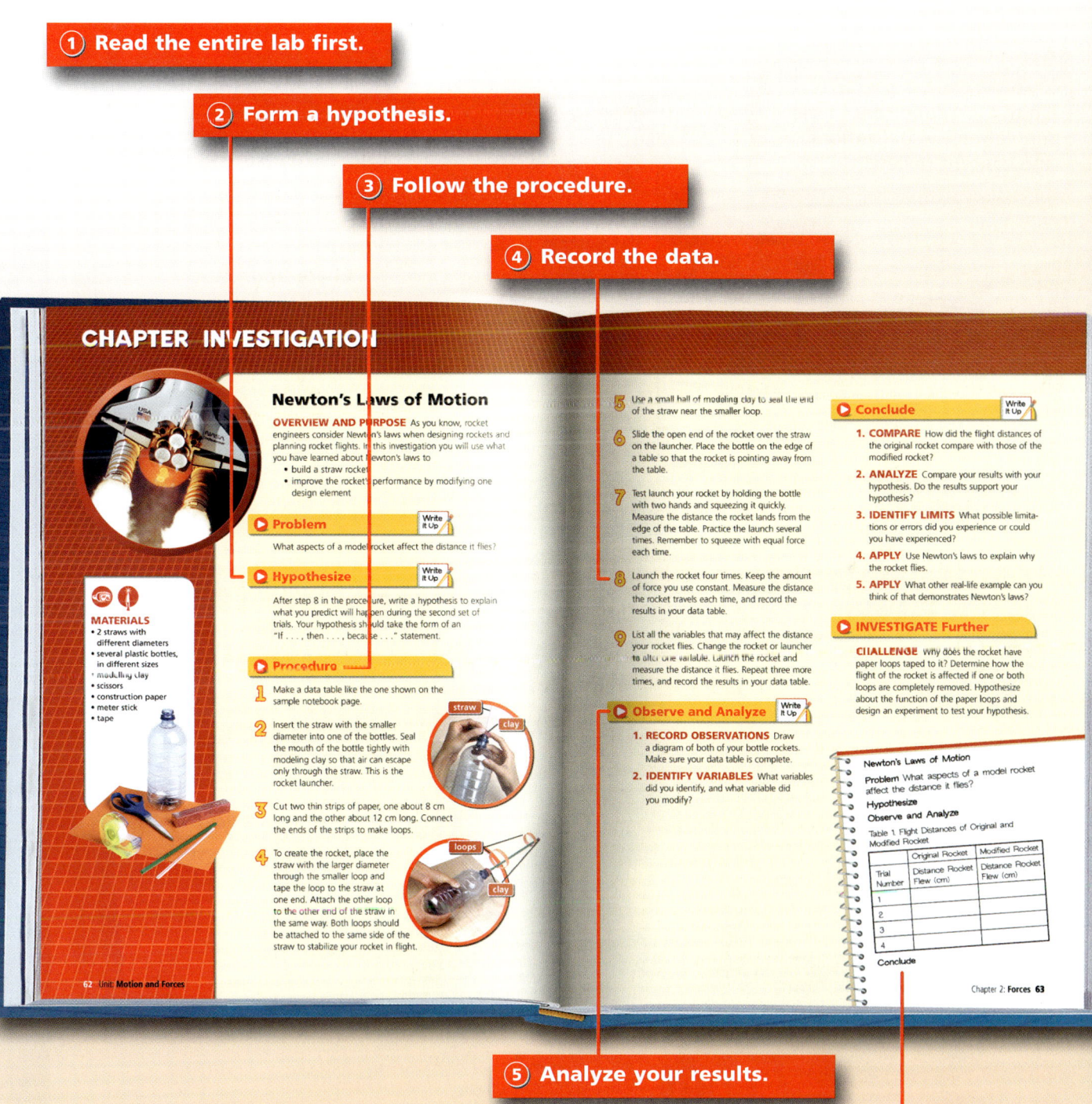

Using Technology

The Internet is a great source of information about up-to-date science. The ClassZone Web site and SciLinks have exciting sites for you to explore. Video clips and simulations can make science come alive.

Look for red banners.

Go to **ClassZone.com** to see simulations, visualizations, and content review.

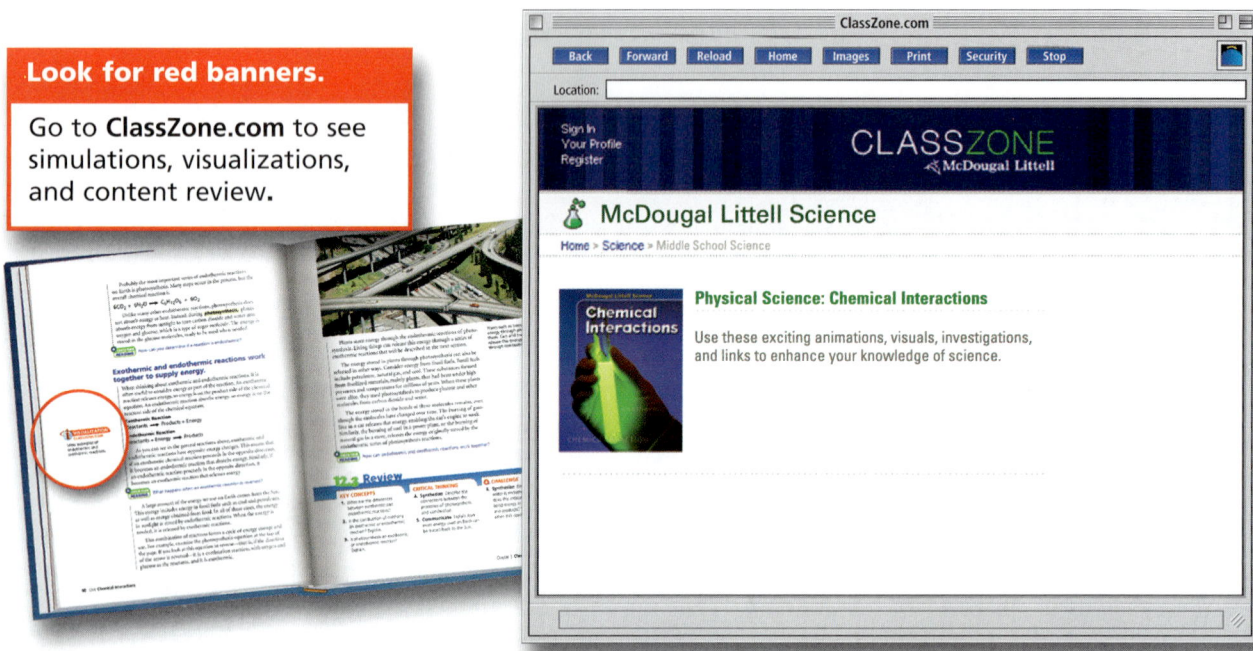

Watch the videos.

See science at work in the **Scientific American Frontiers video.**

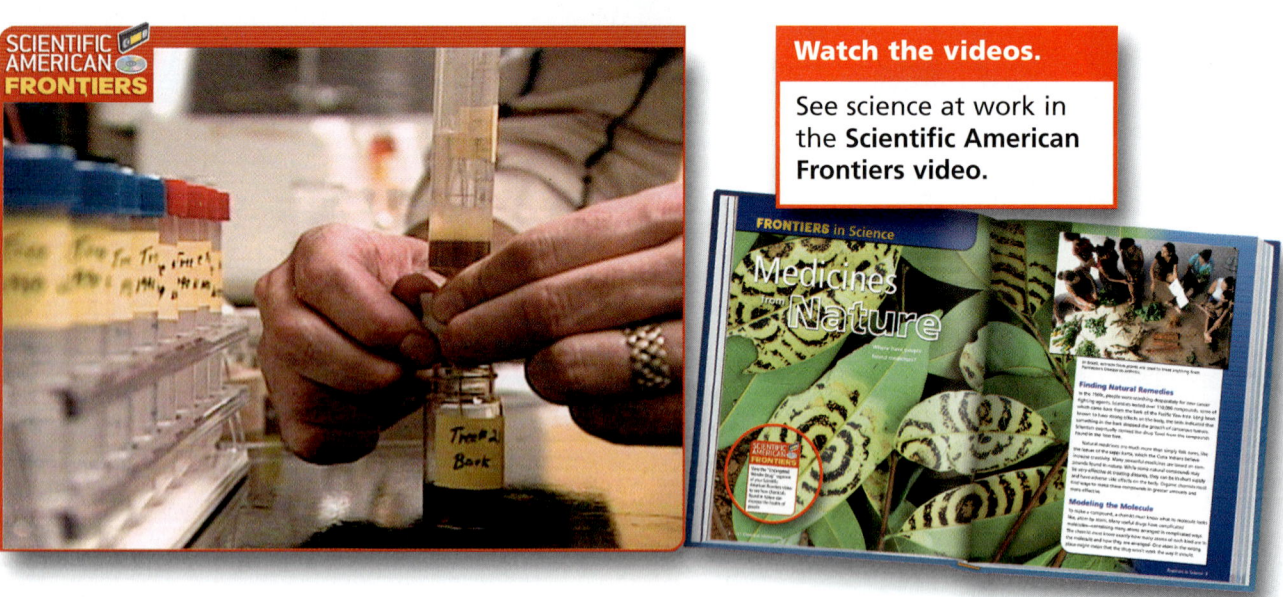

Look up SciLinks.

Go to **scilinks.org** to explore the topic.

Forces **Code: MDL005**

UNIT 1

Motion and Forces

Contents Overview

Frontiers in Science
Robots on Mars — 2

Timelines in Science
Understanding Forces — 108

Chapter 1 Motion — 6
Chapter 2 Forces — 38
Chapter 3 Gravity, Friction, and Pressure — 74
Chapter 4 Work and Energy — 112
Chapter 5 Machines — 142

FRONTIERS in Science

ROBOTS on Mars

If you could design a robot to explore Mars, what would you want it to be able to do?

SCIENTIFIC AMERICAN FRONTIERS

Watch the video segment "Teetering to Victory" to learn about a competition that challenges students to use their knowledge of motion and forces to design a machine.

The surface of Mars looks rocky and barren today, but scientists have long wondered if life might have existed on Mars long ago. That would have been possible only if Mars once had water, which is necessary for all forms of life.

The Design Challenge

It's still not possible to send scientists to Mars to search for signs of water, but in 1999 a team of scientists and engineers began to design two robots for NASA's 2004 mission to Mars. As the team worked, they relied on their scientific understanding of motion, forces, and machines to create and test a successful design.

To identify their goals, the team started by thinking about what scientists would want to do if they could go to Mars. First they would want to look around the landscape to find good areas to study. Then they would need to travel to those areas and analyze rock samples. Finally they would use a variety of tools to analyze the rocks, interpret their data, and communicate their findings back to Earth. Those goals set the basic plan for the Mars Exploration Rovers (MERs).

As you can see in the photograph, the MER team designed a rover with cameras for viewing the surface, wheels for moving around the landscape, and an extendable arm in front equipped with tools for drilling into, observing, and identifying rocks. The rover also has a computer to process information, an antenna for radio communication with Earth, and batteries and solar panels to provide energy for everything.

As in any technology project, the MER team had to work within specific constraints, or limits. The most basic constraints were time and money. They had to design rovers that could be built within NASA's budget and that would be ready in time for launch in 2003. But the team also faced some more challenging

NASA's Mars Exploration Rover (MER) shown in a computer-simulated Martian landscape

Members of the project team stand with a MER and a replica of the much smaller *Sojourner*.

surface of Mars for 12 weeks in 1997. At the left you see one of the MERs next to a replica of *Sojourner*, which was only about 28 centimeters (about 11 in) tall. MER's mast rises up to 1.4 meters (almost 5 ft), giving the cameras, which can be angled up or down, a view similar to what a person would see when standing on the surface of Mars.

Testing the Model

Every part of the MER had to be tested to be sure it would work properly in the harsh conditions on Mars. For example, consider the Rock Abrasion Tool (RAT) at the end of the rover's extendable arm. The RAT is designed to grind off the weathered surface of rock, exposing a fresh surface for examination. Tests with the RAT showed that it worked fine on hard rocks, but its diamond-tipped grinding wheel became clogged with pieces of soft rock. The solution: Add brushes to clean the RAT automatically after each use.

Scientists were also concerned that the RAT's diamond grinding wheel might wear out if it had to grind a lot of hard rocks. An entry from the design team's status report explains why that turned out not to be a problem:

constraints. The rover must survive a rocket launch from Earth as well as a landing on the surface of Mars. This means it must be both lightweight and compact. Engineers designed the MER to fold up into a pyramid-shaped protective compartment, which drops down onto Mars by parachute. Air bags surrounding the compartment absorb the impact, and then the compartment opens and the MER moves down the compartment panels to the planet's surface.

Scientists built on some valuable lessons learned from an earlier robot, *Sojourner*, which explored the

View the "Teetering to Victory" segment of your Scientific American Frontiers video to learn how some students solved a much simpler design challenge.

IN THIS SCENE FROM THE VIDEO
MIT students prepare to test their machines.

BATTLE OF MACHINES Each year more than 100 engineering students at the Massachusetts Institute of Technology (MIT) compete in a contest to see who can design and build the best machine. The challenge this time is to build a machine that starts out sitting on a teeter-totter beam and within 45 seconds manages to tilt its end down against an opponent trying to do the same thing.

Just as the Mars rover designers had to consider the constraints of space travel and Mars' harsh environment, the students had constraints on their designs. They all started with the same kit of materials, and their finished machines had to weigh less than 10 pounds as well as fit inside the box the materials came in. Within these constraints, the student designers came up with an amazing variety of solutions.

The big question, of course, was how things would work under the very cold, dry, low-pressure atmospheric conditions on Mars. We put a RAT into a test chamber recently, took it to real Martian conditions for the first time, and got a very pleasant surprise. The rate at which our diamond studded teeth wear away slowed way down! We're still figuring out why, but it turns out that when you put this Martian RAT into its natural environment, its teeth don't wear down nearly as fast.

Engineers also needed to test the system by which scientists on Earth would communicate with and control the rovers on Mars. For this purpose, they built a smaller version of the real robot, nicknamed FIDO. In tests FIDO successfully traveled to several locations, dug trenches, and observed and measured rock samples.

Goals of the Mission

Technology like the Mars Exploration Rovers extends the power of scientists to gather data and answer questions about our solar system. One main goal of the MER missions is to study different kinds of rock and soils that might indicate whether water was ever present on Mars. From the data gathered by the MERs, scientists hope to find out what factors shaped the Martian landscape. They also hope to check out areas that have been studied only from far away so that the scientists can confirm their hypotheses about Mars.

UNANSWERED Questions

As scientists learn more and more about Mars, new questions always arise.

- What role, if any, did water, wind, or volcanoes play in shaping the landscape of Mars?
- Were the conditions necessary to support life ever present on Mars?
- Could there be bacteria-like life forms surviving below the surface of Mars today?

UNIT PROJECTS

As you study this unit, work alone or with a group on one of these projects.

Build a Mechanical Arm

Design and build a mechanical arm to perform a simple task.

- Plan and sketch an arm that could lift a pencil from the floor at a distance of one meter.
- Collect materials and assemble your arm.
- Conduct trials and improve your design.

Multimedia Presentation

Create an informative program on the forces involved in remote exploration.

- Collect information about the Galileo mission to Jupiter or a similar expedition.
- Learn how engineers use air resistance, gravity, and rocket thrusters to maneuver the orbiter close to the planet and its moons.
- Give a presentation describing what you learned using mixed media, such as a computer slide show and a model.

Design an Experiment

Design an experiment to determine the pressure needed to crush a small object.

- Select a small object, such as a vitamin C tablet, to use in your experiment.
- Collect other materials of your choosing.
- Plan and conduct a procedure to test the pressure required to crush the object. Vary the procedure until you can crush the object using the least amount of force.

CAREER CENTER
CLASSZONE.COM

Learn more about careers in physics and engineering.

CHAPTER 1 Motion

the BIG idea

The motion of an object can be described and predicted.

Where will these people be in a few seconds? How do you know?

Key Concepts

SECTION 1
An object in motion changes position.
Learn about measuring position from reference points, and about relative motion.

SECTION 2
Speed measures how fast position changes.
Learn to calculate speed and how velocity depends on speed and direction.

SECTION 3
Acceleration measures how fast velocity changes.
Learn about acceleration and how to calculate it.

Internet Preview

CLASSZONE.COM
Chapter 1 online resources: Content Review, Visualization, Simulation, two Resource Centers, Math Tutorial, Test Practice

6 Unit 1: Motion and Forces

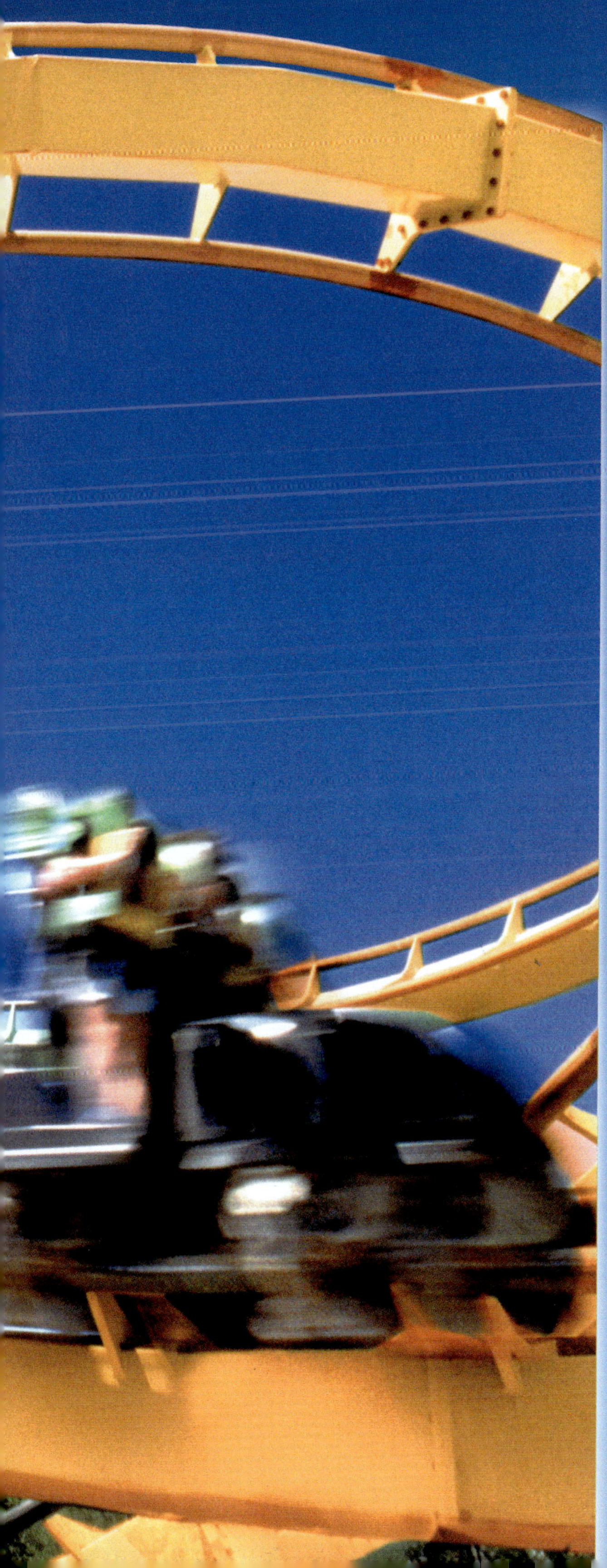

EXPLORE the BIG idea

Off the Wall

Roll a rubber ball toward a wall. Record the time from the starting point to the wall. Change the distance between the wall and the starting point. Adjust the speed at which you roll the ball until it takes the same amount of time to hit the wall as before.

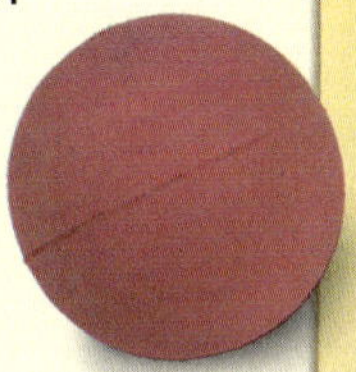

Observe and Think How did the speed of the ball over the longer distance compare with the speed over the shorter distance?

Rolling Along

Make a ramp by leaning the edge of one book on two other books. Roll a marble up the ramp. Repeat several times and notice what happens each time.

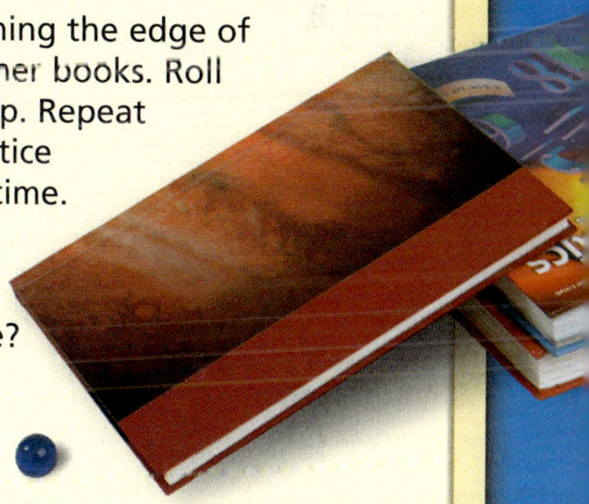

Observe and Think How does the speed of the marble change? At what point does its direction of motion change?

Internet Activity: Relative Motion

Go to **ClassZone.com** to examine motion from different points of view. Learn how your motion makes a difference in what you observe.

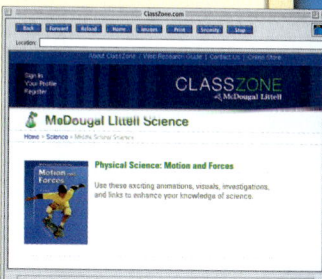

Observe and Think How does the way you see motion depend on your point of view?

Velocity Code: MDL004

CHAPTER 1
Getting Ready to Learn

◁ CONCEPT REVIEW

- Objects can move at different speeds and in different directions.
- Pushing or pulling on an object will change how it moves.

◁ VOCABULARY REVIEW

See Glossary for definitions.

horizontal
meter
second
vertical

Review concepts and vocabulary.

▷ TAKING NOTES

OUTLINE

As you read, copy the headings onto your paper in the form of an outline. Then add notes in your own words that summarize what you read.

VOCABULARY STRATEGY

Place each new vocabulary term at the center of a **description wheel** diagram. As you read about the term, write some words on the spokes describing the term.

See the Note-Taking Handbook on pages R45–R51.

SCIENCE NOTEBOOK

OUTLINE

I. Position describes the location of an object.
   A. Describing a position
      1. A position is compared to a reference point.
      2. Position can be described using distance and direction.

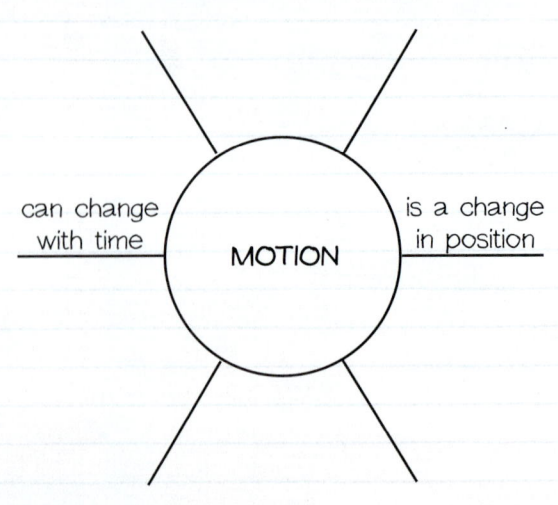

KEY CONCEPT

An object in motion changes position.

 BEFORE, you learned

- Objects can move in different ways
- An object's position can change

 NOW, you will learn

- How to describe an object's position
- How to describe an object's motion

VOCABULARY

position p. 9
reference point p. 10
motion p. 11

EXPLORE Location

How do you describe the location of an object?

PROCEDURE

① Choose an object in the classroom that is easy to see.

② Without pointing to, describing, or naming the object, give directions to a classmate for finding it.

③ Ask your classmate to identify the object using your directions. If your classmate does not correctly identify the object, try giving directions in a different way. Continue until your classmate has located the object.

WHAT DO YOU THINK?
What kinds of information must you give another person when you are trying to describe a location?

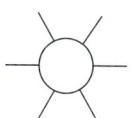

VOCABULARY
Make a description wheel in your notebook for *position*.

Position describes the location of an object.

Have you ever gotten lost while looking for a specific place? If so, you probably know that accurately describing where a place is can be very important. The **position** of a place or an object is the location of that place or object. Often you describe where something is by comparing its position with where you currently are. You might say, for example, that a classmate sitting next to you is about a meter to your right, or that a mailbox is two blocks south of where you live. Each time you identify the position of an object, you are comparing the location of the object with the location of another object or place.

 Why do you need to discuss two locations to describe the position of an object?

Chapter 1: **Motion** 9

Learn more about how people find and describe position.

Describing a Position

You might describe the position of a city based on the location of another city. A location to which you compare other locations is called a **reference point**. You can describe where Santiago, Chile, is from the reference point of the city Brasília, Brazil, by saying that Santiago is about 3000 kilometers (1860 mi) southwest of Brasília.

You can also describe a position using a method that is similar to describing where a point on a graph is located. For example, in the longitude and latitude system, locations are given by two numbers—longitude and latitude. Longitude describes how many degrees east or west a location is from the prime meridian, an imaginary line running north-south through Greenwich, England. Latitude describes how many degrees north or south a location is from the equator, the imaginary circle that divides the northern and southern hemispheres. Having a standard way of describing location, such as longitude and latitude, makes it easier for people to compare locations.

Describing Position

There are several different ways to describe a position. The way you choose may depend on your reference point.

① Reference Point: Brasília

To describe where Santiago is, using Brasília as a reference point, you would need to know how far Santiago is from Brasília and in what direction it is.

② Reference Point: 0° longitude, 0° latitude

In the longitude and latitude system, a location is described by how many degrees north or south it is from the equator and how many degrees east or west it is from the prime meridian.

READING VISUALS Compare and contrast the two ways of describing the location of Santiago as shown here.

10 Unit 1: **Motion and Forces**

Measuring Distance

If you were to travel from Brasília to Santiago, you would end up about 3000 kilometers from where you started. The actual distance you traveled, however, would depend on the exact path you took. If you took a route that had many curves, the distance you traveled would be greater than 3000 kilometers.

The way you measure distance depends on the information you want. Sometimes you want to know the straight-line distance between two positions. Sometimes, however, you might need to know the total length of a certain path between those positions. During a hike, you are probably more interested in how far you have walked than in how far you are from your starting point.

When measuring either the straight-line distance between two points or the length of a path between those points, scientists use a standard unit of measurement. The standard unit of length is the meter (m), which is 3.3 feet. Longer distances can be measured in kilometers (km), and shorter distances in centimeters (cm).

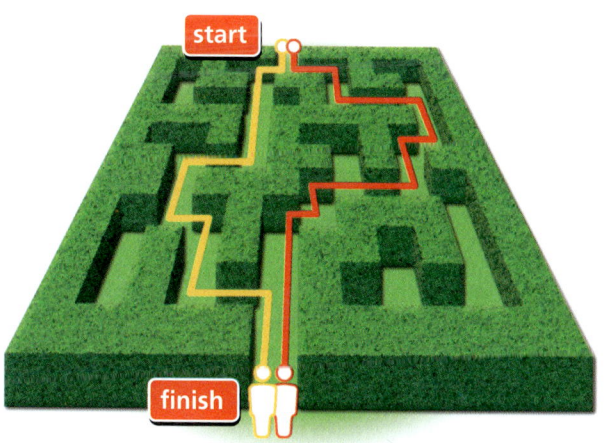

COMPARE How does the distance each person has walked compare with the distance each is from the start of the maze?

Motion is a change in position.

The illustration below shows an athlete at several positions during a long jump. If you were to watch her jump, you would see that she is in motion. **Motion** is the change of position over time. As she jumps, both her horizontal and vertical positions change. If you missed the motion of the jump, you would still know that motion occurred because of the distance between her starting and ending positions. A change in position is evidence that motion happened.

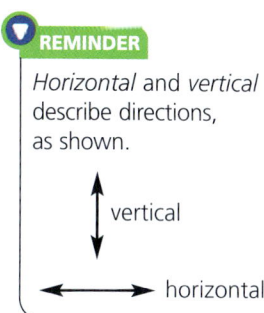

REMINDER

Horizontal and *vertical* describe directions, as shown.

starting position — ending position

INVESTIGATE Changing Position

How are changes in position observed?

PROCEDURE

1. Begin walking while tossing a ball straight up and catching it as it falls back down toward your hand. Observe the changes in the position of the ball as you toss it while walking a distance of about 4 m.

2. Make a sketch showing how the position of the ball changed as you walked. Use your own position as a reference point for the ball's position.

3. Watch while a classmate walks and tosses the ball. Observe the changes in the position of the ball using your own position as a reference point. Make a sketch showing how the ball moved based on your new point of view.

WHAT DO YOU THINK?

- Compare your two sketches. How was the change in position of the ball you tossed different from the change in position of the ball that your partner tossed?
- How did your change in viewpoint affect what you observed? Explain.

CHALLENGE How would the change in position of the ball appear to a person standing 4 m directly in front of you?

SKILL FOCUS
Observing

MATERIALS
- small ball
- paper
- pencil

TIME
20 minutes

Describing Motion

A change in an object's position tells you that motion took place, but it does not tell you how quickly the object changed position. The speed of a moving object is a measure of how quickly or slowly the object changes position. A faster object moves farther than a slower moving object would in the same amount of time.

The way in which an object moves can change. As a raft moves along a river, its speed changes as the speed of the river changes. When the raft reaches a calm area of the river, it slows down. When the raft reaches rapids, it speeds up. The rafters can also change the motion of the raft by using paddles. You will learn more about speed and changing speed in the following sections.

APPLY Describe the different directions in which the raft is moving.

12 Unit 1: **Motion and Forces**

Relative Motion

If you sit still in a chair, you are not moving. Or are you? The answer depends on the position and motion of the person observing you. You do not notice your position changing compared with the room and the objects in it. But if an observer could leave Earth and look at you from outer space, he could see that you are moving along with Earth as it travels around the Sun. How an observer sees your motion depends on how it compares with his own motion. Just as position is described by using a reference point, motion is described by using a frame of reference. You can think of a frame of reference as the location of an observer, who may be in motion.

Consider a student sitting behind the driver of a moving bus. The bus passes another student waiting at a street sign to cross the street.

① To the observer on the bus, the driver is not changing his position compared with the inside of the bus. The street sign, however, moves past the observer's window. From this observer's point of view, the driver is not moving, but the street sign is.

② To the observer on the sidewalk, the driver is changing position along with the bus. The street sign, on the other hand, is not changing position. From this observer's point of view, the street sign is not moving, but the driver is.

OUTLINE
Add relative motion to your outline, along with supporting details.

I. Main idea
   A. Supporting idea
      1. Detail
      2. Detail
   B. Supporting idea

Relative Motion

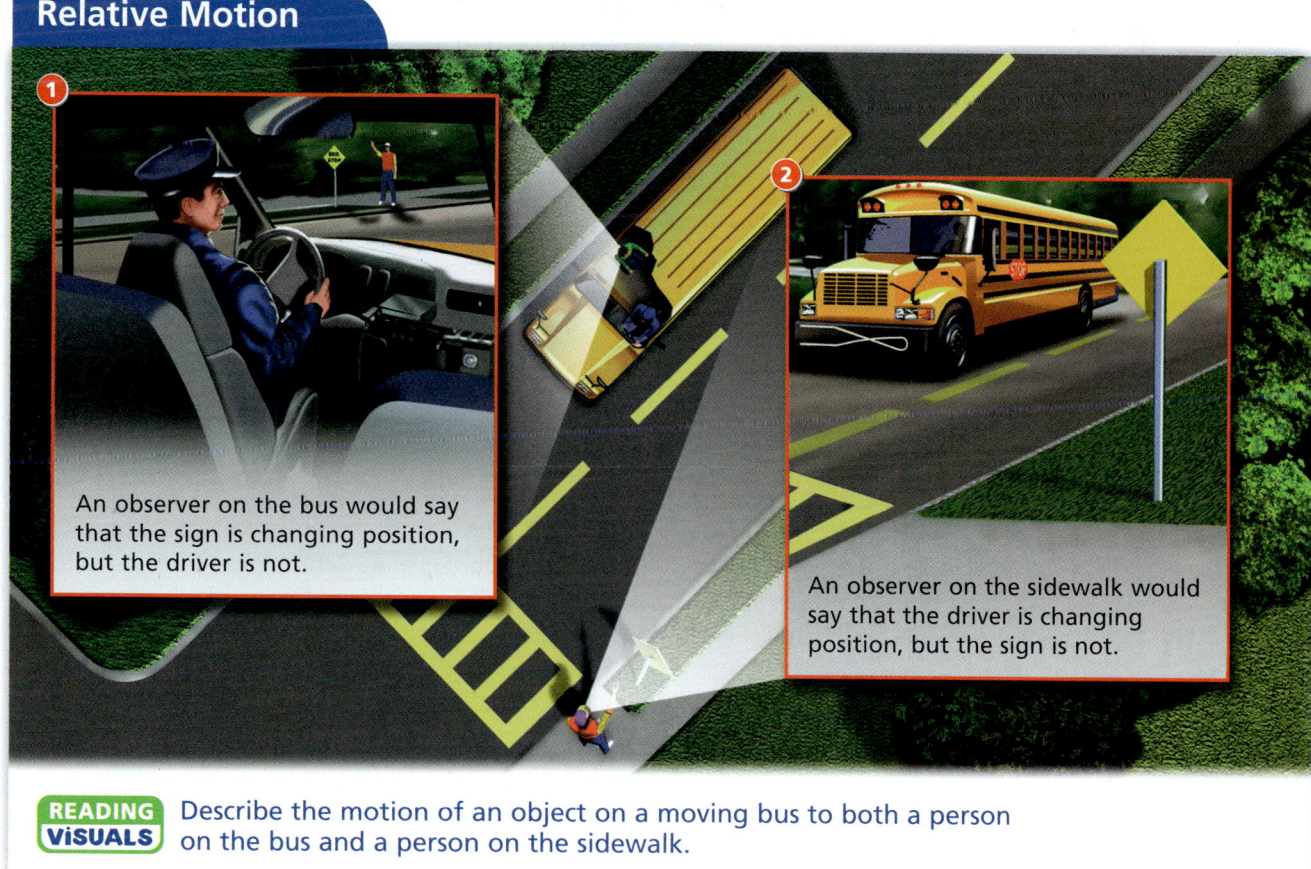

An observer on the bus would say that the sign is changing position, but the driver is not.

An observer on the sidewalk would say that the driver is changing position, but the sign is not.

READING VISUALS Describe the motion of an object on a moving bus to both a person on the bus and a person on the sidewalk.

Chapter 1: **Motion** 13

When you ride in a train, a bus, or an airplane, you think of yourself as moving and the ground as standing still. That is, you usually consider the ground as the frame of reference for your motion. If you traveled between two cities, you would say that you had moved, not that the ground had moved under you in the opposite direction.

If you cannot see the ground or objects on it, it is sometimes difficult to tell if a train you are riding in is moving. If the ride is very smooth and you do not look out the window at the scenery, you might never realize you are moving at all.

Suppose you are in a train, and you cannot tell if you are stopped or moving. Outside the window, another train is slowly moving forward. Could you tell which of the following situations is happening?

- Your train is stopped, and the other train is moving slowly forward.
- The other train is stopped, and your train is moving slowly backward.
- Both trains are moving forward, with the other train moving a little faster.
- Your train is moving very slowly backward, and the other train is moving very slowly forward.

Actually, all four of these possibilities would look exactly the same to you. Unless you compared the motion to the motion of something outside the train, such as the ground, you could not tell the difference between these situations.

APPLY In the top picture, the train is moving compared with the camera and the ground. Describe the relative motion of the train, camera, and ground in the bottom picture.

CHECK YOUR READING How does your observation of motion depend on your own motion?

1.1 Review

KEY CONCEPTS

1. What information do you need to describe an object's location?
2. Describe how your position changes as you jump over an object.
3. Give an example of how the apparent motion of an object depends on the observer's motion.

CRITICAL THINKING

4. **Infer** Kyle walks 3 blocks south from his home to school, and Jana walks 2 blocks north from her home to Kyle's home. How far and in what direction is the school from Jana's home?
5. **Predict** If you sit on a moving bus and toss a coin straight up into the air, where will it land?

CHALLENGE

6. **Infer** Jamal is in a car going north. He looks out his window and thinks that the northbound traffic is moving very slowly. Ellen is in a car going south. She thinks the northbound traffic is moving quickly. Explain why Jamal and Ellen have different ideas about the motion of the traffic.

SCIENCE on the JOB

COAST GUARD RESCUE

Physics for Rescuers

Performing a rescue operation is often difficult and risky because the person in trouble is in a dangerous situation. Coast Guard Search and Rescue Teams have an especially difficult problem to deal with. As a rescue ship or helicopter approaches a stranded boat, the team must get close enough to help but avoid making the problem worse by colliding with the boat. At the same time, wind, waves, and currents cause changes in the motion of both crafts.

Finding the Problem

A stranded boater fires a flare to indicate his location. The observer on the Coast Guard ship tracks the motion of the flare to its source.

Avoiding Collision

As the boats move closer together, the captain assesses their motion relative to each other. The speeds of the boats must match, and the boats must be close enough that a rope can be thrown across the gap. If the sea is rough, both boats will move up and down, making the proper positioning even more difficult.

Rescue from Above

The helicopter pilot determines where to hover so that the rescue basket lands on target. A mistake could be disastrous for the rescuers as well as the people being rescued.

EXPLORE

1. **PREDICT** Tie a washer to a 30 cm piece of string. Using your hand as a helicopter, lower the rescue washer to a mark on the floor. Turn on a fan to create wind. Predict where you will need to hold the string to land the washer on the mark. Place the fan at a different location and try again. How accurate was your prediction? Does your accuracy improve with practice?

2. **CHALLENGE** Have a partner throw a baseball into the air from behind the corner of a wall. Using the motion of the ball, try to determine the position from which it was thrown. When is it easier—when the ball is thrown in a high arc or lower one?

Chapter 1: **Motion** 15

KEY CONCEPT

Speed measures how fast position changes.

BEFORE, you learned
- An object's position is measured from a reference point
- To describe the position of an object, you can use distance and direction
- An object in motion changes position with time

NOW, you will learn
- How to calculate an object's speed
- How to describe an object's velocity

VOCABULARY
speed p. 16
velocity p. 22
vector p. 22

EXPLORE Speed

How can you measure speed?

PROCEDURE

1. Place a piece of tape on the floor. Measure a distance on the floor 2 m away from the tape. Mark this distance with a second piece of tape.

2. Roll a tennis ball from one piece of tape to the other, timing how long it takes to travel the 2 m.

3. Roll the ball again so that it travels the same distance in less time. Then roll the ball so that it takes more time to travel that distance than it did the first time.

MATERIALS
- tape
- meter stick
- tennis ball
- stopwatch

WHAT DO YOU THINK?
- How did you change the time it took the ball to travel 2 m?
- How did changing the time affect the motion of the ball?

Position can change at different rates.

When someone asks you how far it is to the library, you can answer in terms of distance or time. You can say it is several blocks, or you can say it is a five-minute walk. When you give a time instead of a distance, you are basing your time estimate on the distance to the library and the person's speed. **Speed** is a measure of how fast something moves or the distance it moves, in a given amount of time. The greater the speed an object has, the faster it changes position.

VOCABULARY
Make a description wheel in your notebook for *speed*.

CHECK YOUR READING How are speed and position related?

16 Unit 1: **Motion and Forces**

The way in which one quantity changes compared to another quantity is called a rate. Speed is the rate at which the distance an object moves changes compared to time. If you are riding a bike to a movie, and you think you might be late, you increase the rate at which your distance changes by pedaling harder. In other words, you increase your speed.

Calculating Speed

To calculate speed, you need to know both distance and time measurements. Consider the two bike riders below.

1. The two bikes pass the same point at the same time.

2. After one second, the first bike has traveled four meters, while the second has traveled only two meters. Because the first bike has traveled four meters in one second, it has a speed of four meters per second. The second bike has a speed of two meters per second.

3. If each bike continues moving at the same speed as before, then after two seconds the first rider will have traveled eight meters, while the second one will have traveled only four meters.

Comparing Speed

Objects that travel at different speeds move different distances in the same amount of time.

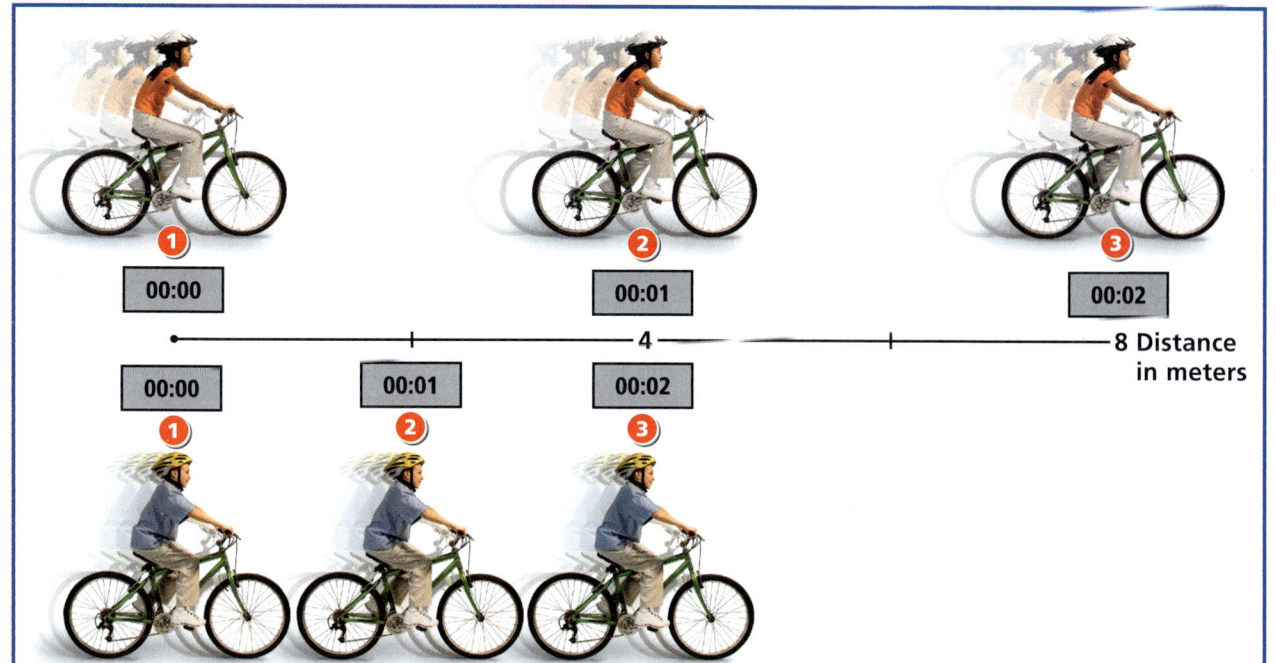

READING VISUALS How far will each rider travel in five seconds?

Racing wheelchairs are specially designed to reach higher speeds than regular wheelchairs.

Speed can be calculated by dividing the distance an object travels by the time it takes to cover the distance. The formula for finding speed is

$$\text{Speed} = \frac{\text{distance}}{\text{time}} \qquad S = \frac{d}{t}$$

Speed is shown in the formula as the letter S, distance as the letter d, and time as the letter t. The formula shows how distance, time, and speed are related. If two objects travel the same distance, the object that took a shorter amount of time will have the greater speed. Similarly, an object with a greater speed will travel a longer distance in the same amount of time than an object with a lower speed will.

The standard unit for speed is meters per second (m/s). Speed is also given in kilometers per hour (km/h). In the United States, where the English system of measurement is still used, speeds are often given in miles per hour (mi/h or mph). One mile per hour is equal to 0.45 m/s.

The man participating in the wheelchair race, at left, will win if his speed is greater than the speed of the other racers. You can use the formula to calculate his speed.

 **CHECK YOUR READING** If two runners cover the same distance in different amounts of time, how do their speeds compare?

Calculating Speed

Sample Problem

A wheelchair racer completes a 100-meter course in 20 seconds. What is his speed?

What do you know?	distance = 100 m, time = 20 s
What do you want to find out?	speed
Write the formula:	$S = \frac{d}{t}$
Substitute into the formula:	$S = \frac{100 \text{ m}}{20 \text{ s}}$
Calculate and simplify:	$S = 5$ m/s
Check that your units agree:	Unit is m/s. Unit of speed is m/s. Units agree.
Answer:	$S = 5$ m/s

Practice the Math

1. A man runs 200 m in 25 s. What is his speed?
2. If you travel 100 m in 50 s, what is your speed?

Average Speed

Speed is not constant. When you run, you might slow down to pace yourself, or speed up to win a race. At each point as you are running, you have a specific speed. This moment-to-moment speed is called your instantaneous speed. Your instantaneous speed can be difficult to measure; however, it is easier to calculate your average speed over a distance.

In a long race, runners often want to know their times for each lap so that they can pace themselves. For example, an excellent middle school runner might have the following times for the four laps of a 1600-meter race: 83 seconds, 81 seconds, 79 seconds, 77 seconds. The lap times show the runner is gradually increasing her speed throughout the race.

The total time for the four laps can be used to calculate the runner's average speed for the entire race. The total time is 320 seconds (5 min 20 s) for the entire distance of 1600 meters. The runner's average speed is 1600 meters divided by 320 seconds, or 5.0 meters per second.

READING TIP
The root of *instantaneous* is *instant*, meaning "moment."

INVESTIGATE Speed and Distance

How does design affect speed?

Cars are built in different shapes. How does the shape of the car affect the way it moves? Design your own car, and see how fast it can go.

DESIGN YOUR OWN EXPERIMENT

PROCEDURE

1. Use the clay, film container lids, and toothpicks to design a car that rolls when it is pushed. The car should have a total mass of 150 g or less.
2. Using any or all of the other materials, design an experiment to measure and compare the speed of your car with the speed of someone else's car. Your experiment should be designed so that the design of the car is the only variable being tested. Write up your procedure.
3. Perform the experiment using your car and another student's car. Record the data you need to calculate the speed of both cars.
4. Calculate the speed of each car, and record which car went faster.

WHAT DO YOU THINK?

- What were the constants in your experiment?
- How would you improve your design if you were to repeat the experiment?

SKILL FOCUS
Designing experiments

MATERIALS
- clay
- film container lids
- toothpicks
- beam balance
- board
- books
- string
- straw
- scissors
- stopwatch

TIME
20 minutes

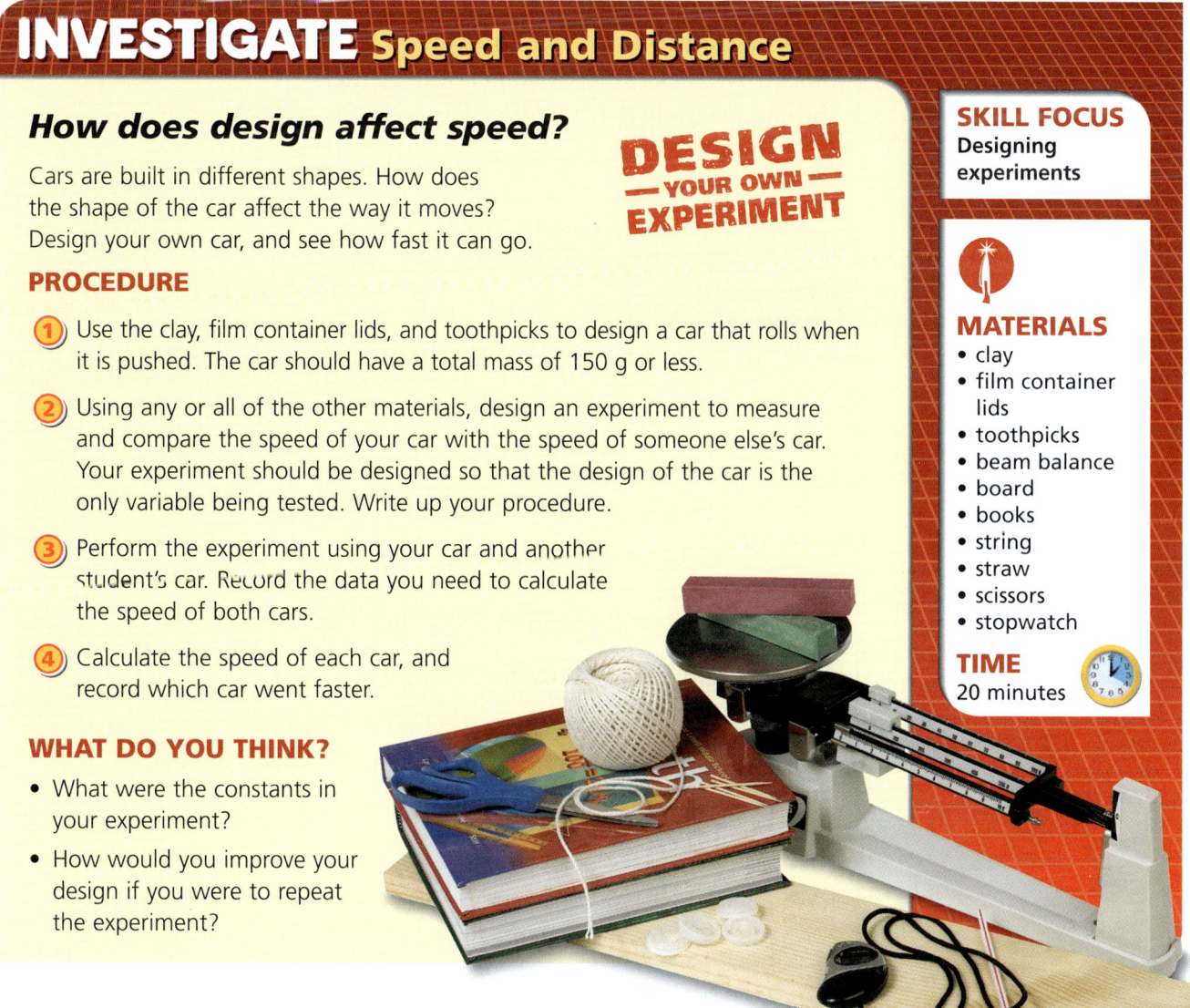

Distance-Time Graphs

A convenient way to show the motion of an object is by using a graph that plots the distance the object has traveled against time. This type of graph, called a distance-time graph, shows how speed relates to distance and time. You can use a distance-time graph to see how both distance and speed change with time.

The distance-time graph on page 21 tracks the changing motion of a zebra. At first the zebra looks for a spot to graze. Its meal is interrupted by a lion, and the zebra starts running to escape.

In a distance-time graph, time is on the horizontal axis, or *x*-axis, and distance is on the vertical axis, or *y*-axis.

❶ As an object moves, the distance it travels increases with time. This can be seen as a climbing, or rising, line on the graph.

❷ A flat, or horizontal, line shows an interval of time where the speed is zero meters per second.

❸ Steeper lines show intervals where the speed is greater than intervals with less steep lines.

You can use a distance-time graph to determine the speed of an object. The steepness, or slope, of the line is calculated by dividing the change in distance by the change in time for that time interval.

> **REMINDER**
> The *x*-axis and *y*-axis are arranged as shown:
>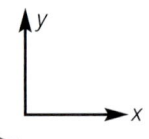

Calculating Speed from a Graph

▶ **Sample Problem**

How fast is the zebra walking during the first 20 seconds?

What do you know? Reading from the graph:
At time = 0 s, distance = 0 m.
At time = 20 s, distance = 40 m.

What do you want to find out? speed

Write the formula: $S = \dfrac{d}{t}$

Substitute into the formula: $S = \dfrac{40 \text{ m} - 0 \text{ m}}{20 \text{ s} - 0 \text{ s}}$

Calculate and simplify: $S = \dfrac{40 \text{ m}}{20 \text{ s}} = 2 \text{ m/s}$

Check that your units agree: Unit is m/s.
Unit of speed is m/s. Units agree.

Answer: $S = 2$ m/s

▶ **Practice the Math**

1. What is the speed of the zebra during the 20 s to 40 s time interval?
2. What is the speed of the zebra during the 40 s to 60 s interval?

20 Unit 1: **Motion and Forces**

Distance-Time Graph

A zebra's speed will change throughout the day, especially if a hungry lion is nearby. You can use a distance-time graph to compare the zebra's speed over different time intervals.

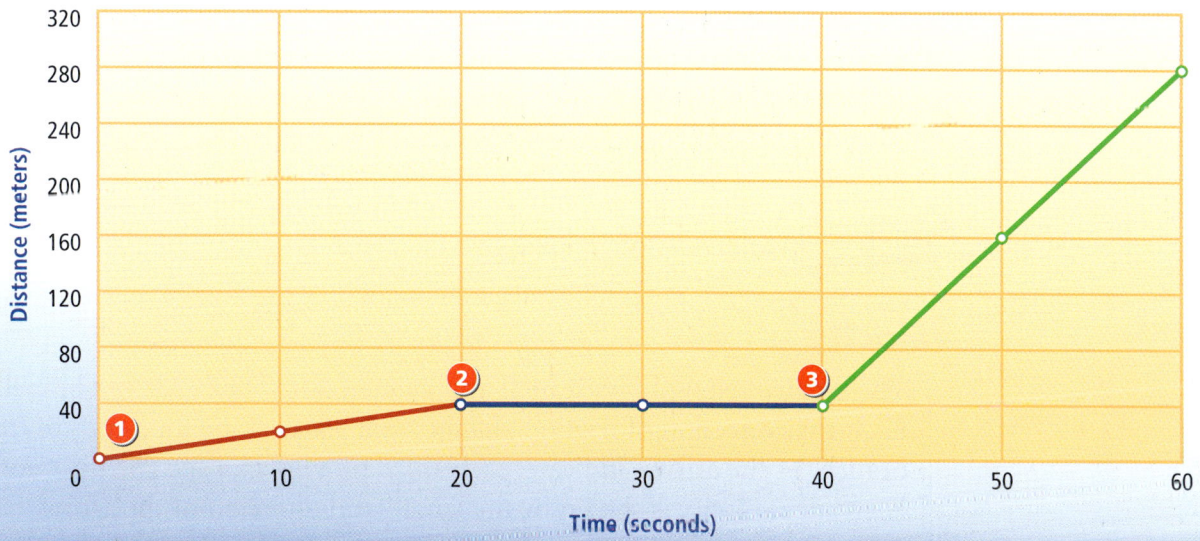

① When the zebra is walking, its distance from its starting point increases. You can see this motion on the graph as a climbing line.

② When the zebra stops to graze, it no longer changes its distance from the starting point. Time, however, continues to pass. Therefore, the graph shows a flat, or horizontal, line.

③ As soon as the zebra notices the lion, it stops grazing and starts to run for its life. The zebra is covering a greater distance in each time interval than it was before the chase started, so the line is steeper.

READING VISUALS How do the distances change over each 10-second time interval?

Chapter 1: **Motion** 21

Velocity includes speed and direction.

Sometimes the direction of motion is as important as its speed. In large crowds, for example, you probably always try to walk in the same direction the crowd is moving and at the same speed. If you walk in even a slightly different direction, you can bump into other people. In a crowd, in other words, you try to walk with the same velocity as the people around you. **Velocity** is a speed in a specific direction. If you say you are walking east at a speed of three meters per second, you are describing your velocity. A person walking north with a speed of three meters per second would have the same speed as you do, but not the same velocity.

 What is velocity? Give an example of a velocity.

Velocity

The picture below shows several ants as they carry leaves along a branch. Each ant's direction of motion changes as it walks along the bends of the branch. As the arrows indicate, each ant is moving in a specific direction. Each ant's velocity is shown by the length and direction of the arrow. A longer arrow means a greater speed in the direction the arrow is pointing. In this picture, for example, the ant moving up the branch is traveling more slowly than the ant moving down the branch.

To determine the velocity of an ant as it carries a leaf, you need to know both its speed and its direction. A change in either speed or direction results in a change in velocity. For example, the velocity of an ant changes if it slows down but continues moving in the same direction. Velocity also changes if the ant continues moving at the same speed but changes direction.

Velocity is an example of a vector. A **vector** is a quantity that has both size and direction. Speed is not a vector because speed is a measure of how fast or slow an object moves, not which direction it moves in. Velocity, however, has a size—the speed—and a direction, so it is a vector quantity.

READING TIP

Green arrows show velocity.
A longer arrow indicates a faster speed than a shorter arrow. The direction of the arrow indicates the direction of motion.

ant moving slowly upward

ant moving quickly downward

INFER How does this ant's velocity compare with those of the other ants?

Velocity Versus Speed

Because velocity includes direction, it is possible for two objects to have the same speed but different velocities. If you traveled by train to visit a friend, you might go 30 kilometers per hour (km/h) north on the way there and 30 km/h south on the way back. Your speed is the same both going and coming back, but your velocity is different because your direction of motion has changed.

Another difference between speed and velocity is the way the average is calculated. Your average speed depends on the total distance you have traveled. The average velocity depends on the total distance you are from where you started. Going north, your average speed would be 30 km/h, and your average velocity would be 30 km/h north. After the round-trip ride, your average traveling speed would still be 30 km/h. Your average velocity, however, would be 0 km/h because you ended up exactly where you started.

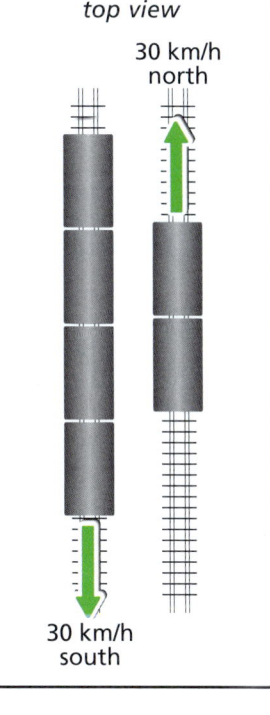

INFER How do the speeds and velocities of these trains compare?

 **CHECK YOUR READING** Use a Venn diagram to compare and contrast speed and velocity.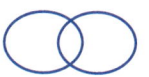

1.2 Review

KEY CONCEPTS

1. How is speed related to distance and time?
2. How would decreasing the time it takes you to run a certain distance affect your speed?
3. What two things do you need to know to describe the velocity of an object?

CRITICAL THINKING

4. **Compare** Amy and Ellie left school at the same time. Amy lives farther away than Ellie, but she and Ellie arrived at their homes at the same time. Compare the girls' speeds.
5. **Calculate** Carlos lives 100 m away from his friend's home. What is his average speed if he reaches his friend's home in 50 s?

CHALLENGE

6. **Synthesize** If you watch a train go by at 20 m/s, at what speed will the people sitting on the train be moving relative to you? Would someone walking toward the back of the train have a greater or lesser speed relative to you? Explain.

Chapter 1: **Motion** 23

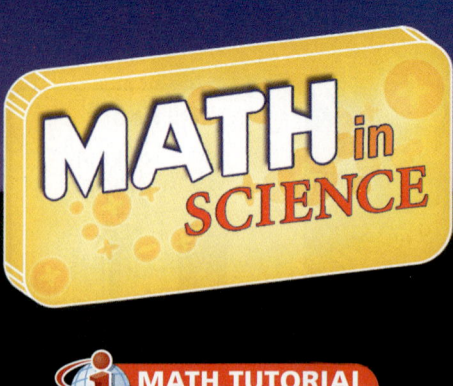

MATH in SCIENCE

MATH TUTORIAL
CLASSZONE.COM
Click on Math Tutorial for more help with units and rates.

SKILL: WORKING WITH UNITS

Time, Distance, and Speed

If someone tells you the store is "five" from the school, you would probably ask, "Five what? Five meters? Five blocks?" You typically describe a distance using standard units of measurement, such as meters, miles, or kilometers. By using units, you help other people understand exactly what your measurement means.

When you work with a formula, the numbers that you substitute into the formula have units. When you calculate with a number, you also calculate with the unit associated with that number.

Example

A cheetah runs at a speed of 30 meters per second. How long does the cheetah take to run 90 meters?

The formula for time in terms of speed and distance is

$$\text{time} = \frac{\text{distance}}{\text{Speed}} \qquad t = \frac{d}{s}$$

(1) Start by substituting the numbers into the formula. Include the units with the numbers.

$$t = \frac{90 \text{ m}}{30 \text{ m/s}}$$

(2) When the units or calculations include fractions, write out the units as fractions as well:

$$t = \frac{90 \text{ m}}{\frac{30 \text{ m}}{s}}$$

(3) Do the calculation and simplify the units by cancellation:

$$t = 90 \text{ m} \cdot \frac{s}{30 \text{ m}} = \frac{90}{30} \cdot \frac{m \cdot s}{m} = 3 \cdot \frac{\cancel{m} \cdot s}{\cancel{m}} = 3 \text{ s}$$

ANSWER 3 seconds

Note that the answer has a unit of time. Use the units to check that your answer is reasonable. An answer that is supposed to have a unit of time, for example, should not have a unit of distance.

Answer the following questions.

1. How long would it take an object traveling 12 m/s to go 60 m? What unit of time is your answer in?

2. If a car travels 60 km/h, how long would it take the car to travel 300 km? What unit of time is your answer in?

3. If a man walks 3 miles in 1 hour, what is his speed? What unit of speed is your answer in? (Use the formula on page 18.)

CHALLENGE Show that the formula *distance = speed • time* has a unit for distance on both sides of the equal sign.

A cheetah can reach a speed of 30 meters per second, but only in short bursts.

KEY CONCEPT

 Acceleration measures how fast velocity changes.

 BEFORE, you learned
- Speed describes how far an object travels in a given time
- Velocity is a measure of the speed and direction of motion

 NOW, you will learn
- How acceleration is related to velocity
- How to calculate acceleration

VOCABULARY

acceleration p. 25

THINK ABOUT

How does velocity change?

The photograph at right shows the path that a bouncing ball takes. The time between each image of the ball is the same during the entire bounce. Is the ball moving the same distance in each time interval? Is the ball moving the same direction in each time interval?

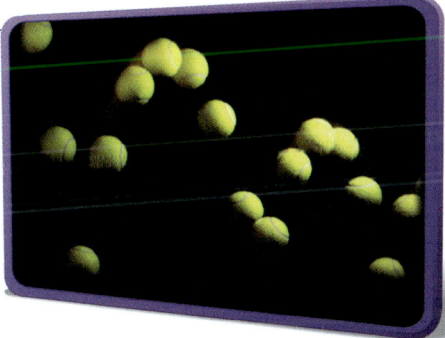

OUTLINE

Remember to use the blue and red headings in this chapter to help you make notes on acceleration.

  I. Main idea
    A. Supporting idea
       1. Detail
       2. Detail
    B. Supporting idea

Speed and direction can change with time.

When you throw a ball into the air, it leaves your hand at a certain speed. As the ball rises, it slows down. Then, as the ball falls back toward the ground, it speeds up again. When the ball hits the ground, its direction of motion changes and it bounces back up into the air. The speed and direction of the ball do not stay the same as the ball moves. The ball's velocity keeps changing.

You can find out how much an object's position changes during a certain amount of time if you know its velocity. In a similar way, you can measure how an object's velocity changes with time. The rate at which velocity changes with time is called **acceleration**. Acceleration is a measure of how quickly the velocity is changing. If velocity does not change, there is no acceleration.

 What is the relationship between velocity and acceleration?

Chapter 1: **Motion** 25

The word *acceleration* is commonly used to mean "speeding up." In physics, however, acceleration refers to any change in velocity. A driver slowing down to stop at a light is accelerating. A runner turning a corner at a constant speed is also accelerating because the direction of her velocity is changing as she turns.

Like velocity, acceleration is a vector, which means it has both size and direction. The direction of the acceleration determines whether an object will slow down, speed up, or turn.

① Acceleration in the Same Direction as Motion When the acceleration is in the same direction as the object is moving, the speed of the object increases. The car speeds up.

② Acceleration in the Opposite Direction of Motion When the acceleration is opposite to the motion, the speed of the object decreases. The car slows down. Slowing down is also called negative acceleration.

③ Acceleration at a Right Angle to Motion When the acceleration is at a right angle to the motion, the direction of motion changes. The car changes the direction in which it is moving by some angle, but its speed does not change.

READING TIP

Orange arrows are used to show acceleration.

Remember that green arrows show velocity.

A longer arrow means greater acceleration or velocity.

CHECK YOUR READING How does acceleration affect velocity? Give examples.

INVESTIGATE Acceleration

When does an object accelerate?

PROCEDURE

1. Use the template and materials to construct an acceleration measuring tool.
2. Hold the tool in your right hand so that the string falls over the 0 m/s² mark. Move the tool in the direction of the arrow. Try to produce both positive and negative acceleration without changing the direction of motion.
3. With the arrow pointing ahead of you, start to walk. Observe the motion of the string while you increase your speed.
4. Repeat step 3, but this time observe the string while slowing down.
5. Repeat step 3 again, but observe the string while walking at a steady speed.

WHAT DO YOU THINK?
- When could you measure an acceleration?
- What was the largest acceleration (positive or negative) that you measured?

CHALLENGE If you moved the acceleration measuring tool backward, how would the measuring scale change?

SKILL FOCUS
Measuring

MATERIALS
- template for tool
- cardboard
- scissors
- glue
- piece of string
- weight

TIME
30 minutes

Acceleration can be calculated from velocity and time.

Suppose you are racing a classmate. In one second, you go from standing still to running at six meters per second. In the same time, your classmate goes from standing still to running at three meters per second. How does your acceleration compare with your classmate's acceleration? To measure acceleration, you need to know how velocity changes with time.

- The change in velocity can be found by comparing the initial velocity and the final velocity of the moving object.
- The time interval over which the velocity changed can be measured.

In one second, you increase your velocity by six meters per second, and your friend increases her velocity by three meters per second. Because your velocity changes more, you have a greater acceleration during that second of time than your friend does. Remember that acceleration measures the change in velocity, not velocity itself. As long as your classmate increases her current velocity by three meters per second, her acceleration will be the same whether she is going from zero to three meters per second or from three to six meters per second.

Chapter 1: **Motion** 27

Calculating Acceleration

If you know the starting velocity of an object, the final velocity, and the time interval during which the object changed velocity, you can calculate the acceleration of the object. The formula for acceleration is shown below.

$$\text{acceleration} = \frac{\text{final velocity} - \text{initial velocity}}{\text{time}}$$

$$a = \frac{v_{final} - v_{initial}}{t}$$

Remember that velocity is expressed in units of meters per second. The standard units for acceleration, therefore, are meters per second over time, or meters per second per second. This is simplified to meters per second squared, which is written as m/s².

As the girl in the photograph at left sleds down the sandy hill, what happens to her velocity? At the bottom of the hill, her velocity will be greater than it was at the top. You can calculate her average acceleration down the hill if you know her starting and ending velocities and how long it took her to get to the bottom. This calculation is shown in the sample problem below.

REMINDER
Remember that velocity is the speed of the object in a particular direction.

Calculating Acceleration

▶ **Sample Problem**

Ama starts sliding with a velocity of 1 m/s. After 3 s, her velocity is 7 m/s. What is Ama's acceleration?

What do you know? initial velocity = 1 m/s, final velocity = 7 m/s, time = 3 s

What do you want to find out? acceleration

Write the formula: $a = \dfrac{v_{final} - v_{initial}}{t}$

Substitute into the formula: $a = \dfrac{7 \text{ m/s} - 1 \text{ m/s}}{3 \text{ s}}$

Calculate and simplify: $a = \dfrac{6 \text{ m/s}}{3 \text{ s}} = 2 \dfrac{\text{m/s}}{\text{s}} = 2 \text{ m/s}^2$

Check that your units agree: $\dfrac{\text{m/s}}{\text{s}} = \dfrac{\text{m}}{\text{s}} \cdot \dfrac{1}{\text{s}} = \dfrac{\text{m}}{\text{s}^2}$

Unit of acceleration is m/s². Units agree.

Answer: $a = 2 \text{ m/s}^2$

▶ **Practice the Math**

1. A man walking at 0.5 m/s accelerates to a velocity of 0.6 m/s in 1 s. What is his acceleration?

2. A train traveling at 10 m/s slows down to a complete stop in 20 s. What is the acceleration of the train?

The sledder's final velocity was greater than her initial velocity. If an object is slowing down, on the other hand, the final velocity is less than the initial velocity. Suppose a car going 10 meters per second takes 2 seconds to stop for a red light. In this case, the initial velocity is 10 m/s and the final velocity is 0 m/s. The formula for acceleration gives a negative answer, -5 m/s^2. The negative sign indicates a negative acceleration—that is, an acceleration that decreases the velocity.

Learn more about acceleration.

 What would be true of the values for initial velocity and final velocity if the acceleration were zero?

Acceleration over Time

Even a very small positive acceleration can lead to great speeds if an object accelerates for a long enough period. In 1998, NASA launched the *Deep Space 1* spacecraft. This spacecraft tested a new type of engine—one that gave the spacecraft an extremely small acceleration. The new engine required less fuel than previous spacecraft engines. However, the spacecraft needed a great deal of time to reach its target velocity.

The acceleration of the *Deep Space 1* spacecraft is less than 2/10,000 of a meter per second per second (0.0002 m/s^2). That may not seem like much, but over 20 months, the spacecraft could increase its speed by 4500 meters per second (10,000 mi/h).

By carefully adjusting both the amount and the direction of the acceleration of *Deep Space 1*, scientists were able to control its flight path. In 2001, the spacecraft successfully flew by a comet, sending back images from about 230 million kilometers (140 million mi) away.

APPLY What makes the new engine technology used by *Deep Space 1* more useful for long-term missions than for short-term ones?

Velocity-Time Graphs

Velocity-time graphs and distance-time graphs are related. This is because the distance an object travels depends on its velocity. Compare the velocity-time graph on the right with the distance-time graph below it.

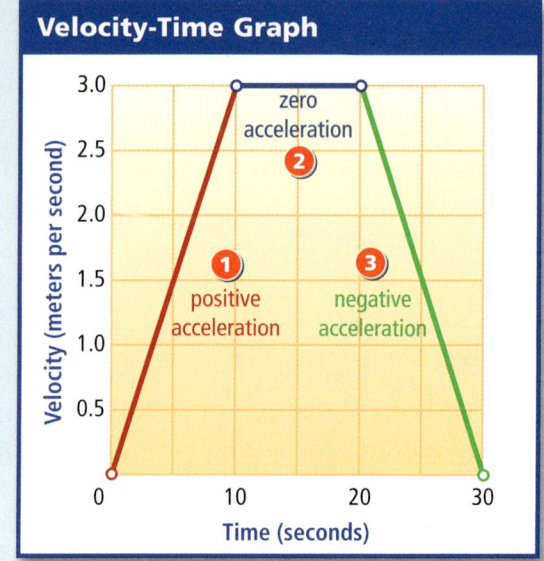

1. As the student starts to push the scooter, his velocity increases. His acceleration is positive, so he moves forward a greater distance with each second that passes.

2. He coasts at a constant velocity. Because his velocity does not change, he has no acceleration, and he continues to move forward the same distance each second.

3. As he slows down, his velocity decreases. His acceleration is negative, and he moves forward a smaller distance with each passing second until he finally stops.

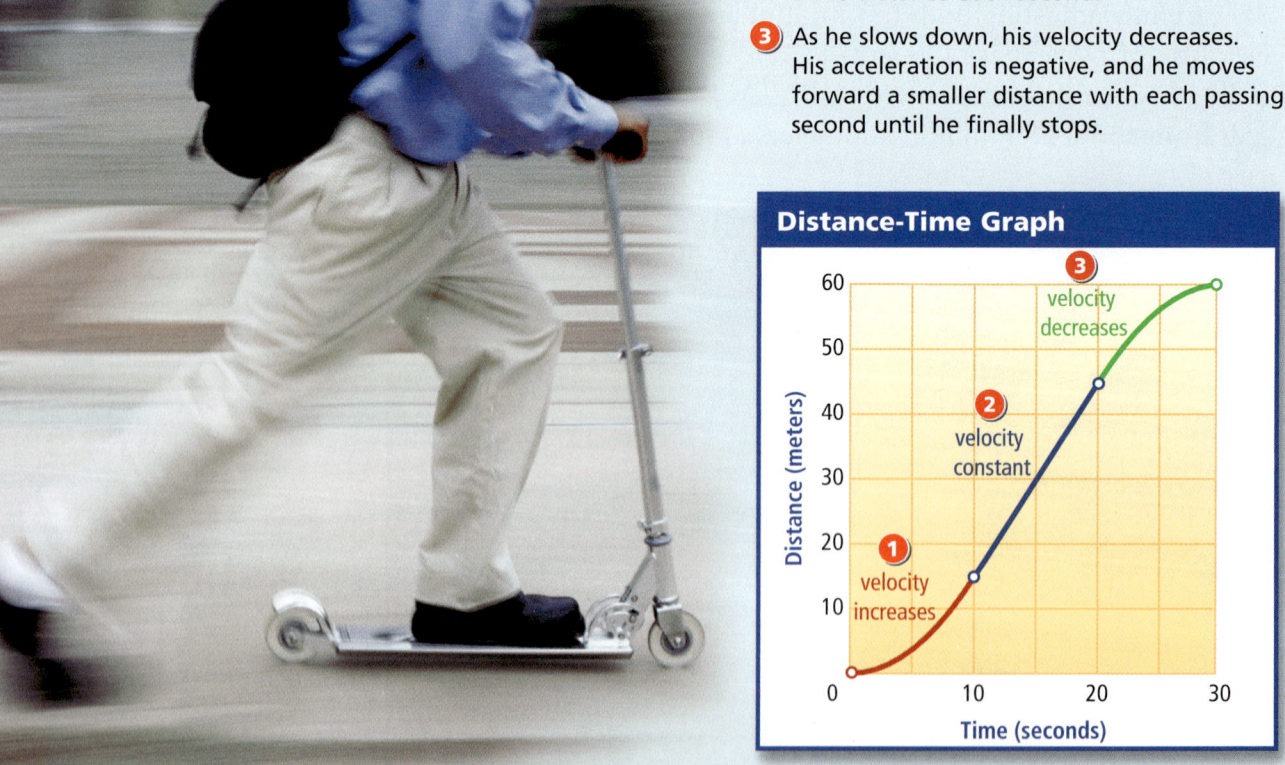

READING VISUALS What velocity does the student have after five seconds? About how far has he moved in that time?

30 Unit 1: **Motion and Forces**

Velocity-Time Graphs

Acceleration, like position and velocity, can change with time. Just as you can use a distance-time graph to understand velocity, you can use a velocity-time graph to understand acceleration. Both graphs tell you how something is changing over time. In a velocity-time graph, time is on the horizontal axis, or *x*-axis, and velocity is on the vertical axis, or *y*-axis.

SIMULATION CLASSZONE.COM
Explore how changing the acceleration of an object changes its motion.

The two graphs on page 30 show a velocity-time graph and a distance-time graph of a student riding on a scooter. He first starts moving and speeds up. He coasts, and then he slows down to a stop.

❶ The rising line on the velocity-time graph shows where the acceleration is positive. The steeper the line, the greater the acceleration. The distance-time graph for the same interval is curving upward more and more steeply as the velocity increases.

❷ The flat line on the velocity-time graph shows an interval of no acceleration. The distance-time graph has a straight line during this time, since the velocity is not changing.

❸ The falling line on the velocity-time graph shows where the acceleration is negative. The same interval on the distance-time graph shows a curve that becomes less and less steep as the velocity decreases. Notice that the overall distance still increases.

Velocity-time graphs and distance-time graphs can provide useful information. For example, scientists who study earthquakes create these graphs in order to study the up-and-down and side-to-side movement of the ground during an earthquake. They produce the graphs from instruments that measure the acceleration of the ground.

What does a flat line on a velocity-time graph represent?

1.3 Review

KEY CONCEPTS

1. What measurements or observations tell you that a car is accelerating?
2. If an object accelerates in the same direction in which it is moving, how is its speed affected?
3. What measurements do you need in order to calculate acceleration?

CRITICAL THINKING

4. **Calculate** A car goes from 20 m/s to 30 m/s in 10 seconds. What is its acceleration?
5. **Infer** Two runners start a race. After 2 seconds, they both have the same velocity. If they both started at the same time, how do their average accelerations compare?

CHALLENGE

6. **Analyze** Is it possible for an object that has a constant negative acceleration to change the direction in which it is moving? Explain why or why not.

CHAPTER INVESTIGATION

Acceleration and Slope

OVERVIEW AND PURPOSE When a downhill skier glides down a mountain without using her ski poles, her velocity increases and she experiences acceleration. How would gliding down a hill with a greater slope affect her acceleration? In this investigation you will

- calculate the acceleration of an object rolling down two ramps of different slopes
- determine how the slope of the ramp affects the acceleration of the object

▶ Problem

How does the slope of a ramp affect the acceleration of an object rolling down the ramp?

▶ Hypothesize

Write a hypothesis to explain how changing the slope of the ramp will affect acceleration. Your hypothesis should take the form of an "If . . . , then . . . , because . . ." statement.

▶ Procedure

MATERIALS
- 2 meter sticks
- masking tape
- marble
- 2 paperback books
- ruler
- stopwatch
- calculator

1. Make a data table like the one shown on the sample notebook page.

2. Make a ramp by laying two meter sticks side by side. Leave a small gap between the meter sticks.

3. Use masking tape as shown in the photograph to join the meter sticks. The marble should be able to roll freely along the groove.

4. Set up your ramp on a smooth, even surface, such as a tabletop. Raise one end of the ramp on top of one of the books. The other end of the ramp should remain on the table.

5. Make a finish line by putting a piece of tape on the tabletop 30 cm from the bottom of the ramp. Place a ruler just beyond the finish line to keep your marble from rolling beyond your work area.

32 Unit 1: Motion and Forces

6. Test your ramp by releasing the marble from the top of the ramp. Make sure that the marble rolls freely. Do not push on the marble.

7. Release the marble and measure the time it takes for it to roll from the release point to the end of the ramp. Record this time under Column A for trial 1.

8. Release the marble again from the same point, and record the time it takes the marble to roll from the end of the ramp to the finish line. Record this time in Column B for trial 1. Repeat and record three more trials.

9. Raise the height of the ramp by propping it up with both paperback books. Repeat steps 7 and 8.

Observe and Analyze

1. **RECORD OBSERVATIONS** Draw the setup of your procedures. Be sure your data table is complete.

2. **IDENTIFY VARIABLES AND CONSTANTS** Identify the variables and constants in the experiment. List them in your notebook.

3. **CALCULATE**

   Average Time For ramps 1 and 2, calculate and record the average time it took for the marble to travel from the end of the ramp to the finish line.

   Final Velocity For ramps 1 and 2, calculate and record v_{final} using the formula below.

   $$v_{final} = \frac{\text{distance from end of ramp to finish line}}{\text{average time from end of ramp to finish line}}$$

   Acceleration For ramps 1 and 2, calculate and record acceleration using the formula below. (**Hint:** Speed at the release of the marble is 0 m/s.)

   $$a = \frac{v_{final} - v_{initial} \text{ (speed at release)}}{\text{average time from release to bottom of ramp}}$$

Conclude

1. **COMPARE** How did the acceleration of the marble on ramp 1 compare with the acceleration of the marble on ramp 2?

2. **INTERPRET** Answer the question posed in the problem.

3. **ANALYZE** Compare your results with your hypothesis. Do your data support your hypothesis?

4. **EVALUATE** Why was it necessary to measure how fast the marble traveled from the end of the ramp to the finish line?

5. **IDENTIFY LIMITS** What possible limitations or sources of error could have affected your results? Why was it important to perform four trials for each measurement of speed?

INVESTIGATE Further

CHALLENGE Design your own experiment to determine how the marble's mass affects its acceleration down a ramp.

Acceleration and Slope

Problem How does the slope of a ramp affect the acceleration of an object rolling down the ramp?

Hypothesize

Observe and Analyze
Table 1. Times for Marble to Travel down Ramp

Height of Ramp (cm)	Trial Number	Column A Time from release to end of ramp	Column B Time from end of ramp to finish line
Ramp 1	1		
	2		
	3		
	4		
	Totals		
		Average	Average

Chapter 1: **Motion** 33

Chapter Review

the BIG idea

The motion of an object can be described and predicted.

CONTENT REVIEW
CLASSZONE.COM

KEY CONCEPTS SUMMARY

1 An object in motion changes position.

Position is measured from a reference point.

Motion is measured relative to an observer.

VOCABULARY
position p. 9
reference point p. 10
motion p. 11

2 Speed measures how fast position changes.
- Speed is how fast positions change with time.
- Velocity is speed in a specific direction.

$$\text{Speed} = \frac{\text{distance}}{\text{time}}$$

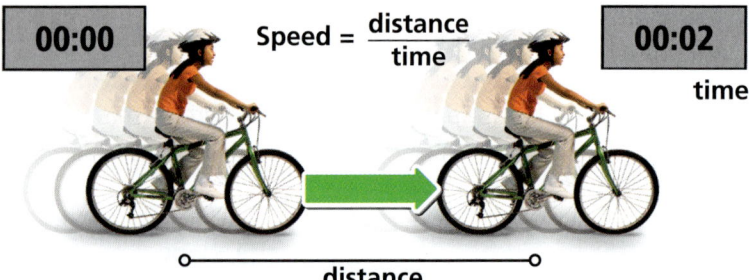

VOCABULARY
speed p. 16
velocity p. 22
vector p. 22

3 Acceleration measures how fast velocity changes.

$$\text{acceleration} = \frac{\text{final velocity} - \text{initial velocity}}{\text{time}}$$

initial velocity   acceleration   final velocity

VOCABULARY
acceleration p. 25

Unit 1: **Motion and Forces**

Reviewing Vocabulary

Copy and complete the chart below. If the left column is blank, give the correct term. If the right column is blank, give a brief description.

Term	Description
1.	speed in a specific direction
2.	a change of position over time
3. speed	
4.	an object's location
5. reference point	
6.	the rate at which velocity changes over time
7.	a quantity that has both size and direction

Reviewing Key Concepts

Multiple Choice *Choose the letter of the best answer.*

8. A position describes an object's location compared to
   a. its motion
   b. a reference point
   c. its speed
   d. a vector

9. Maria walked 2 km in half an hour. What was her average speed during her walk?
   a. 1 km/h
   b. 2 km/h
   c. 4 km/h
   d. 6 km/h

10. A vector is a quantity that has
    a. speed
    b. acceleration
    c. size and direction
    d. position and distance

11. Mary and Keisha run with the same constant speed but in opposite directions. The girls have
    a. the same position
    b. different accelerations
    c. different speeds
    d. different velocities

12. A swimmer increases her speed as she approaches the end of the pool. Her acceleration is
    a. in the same direction as her motion
    b. in the opposite direction of her motion
    c. at right angles to her motion
    d. zero

13. A cheetah can go from 0 m/s to 20 m/s in 2 s. What is the cheetah's acceleration?
    a. 5 m/s^2
    b. 10 m/s^2
    c. 20 m/s^2
    d. 40 m/s^2

14. Jon walks for a few minutes, then runs for a few minutes. During this time, his average speed is
    a. the same as his final speed
    b. greater than his final speed
    c. less than his final speed
    d. zero

15. A car traveling at 40 m/s slows down to 20 m/s. During this time, the car has
    a. no acceleration
    b. positive acceleration
    c. negative acceleration
    d. constant velocity

Short Answer *Write a short answer to each question.*

16. Suppose you are biking with a friend. How would your friend describe your relative motion as he passes you?

17. Describe a situation where an object has a changing velocity but constant speed.

18. Give two examples of an accelerating object.

Chapter 1: **Motion** 35

Thinking Critically

Use the following graph to answer the next three questions.

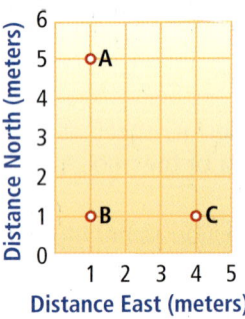

19. OBSERVE Describe the location of point A. Explain what you used as a reference point for your location.

20. COMPARE Copy the graph into your notebook. Draw two different paths an object could take when moving from point B to point C. How do the lengths of these two paths compare?

21. ANALYZE An object moves from point A to point C in the same amount of time that another object moves from point B to point C. If both objects traveled in a straight line, which one had the greater speed?

Read the following paragraph and use the information to answer the next three questions.

In Aesop's fable of the tortoise and the hare, a slow-moving tortoise races a fast-moving hare. The hare, certain it can win, stops to take a long nap. Meanwhile, the tortoise continues to move toward the finish line at a slow but steady speed. When the hare wakes up, it runs as fast as it can. Just as the hare is about to catch up to the tortoise, however, the tortoise wins the race.

22. ANALYZE How does the race between the tortoise and the hare show the difference between average speed and instantaneous speed?

23. MODEL Assume the racetrack was 100 meters long and the race took 40 minutes. Create a possible distance-time graph for both the tortoise and the hare.

24. COMPARE If the racetrack were circular, how would the tortoise's speed be different from its velocity?

25. APPLY How might a person use a floating stick to measure the speed at which a river flows?

26. CONNECT Describe a frame of reference other than the ground that you might use to measure motion. When would you use it?

Using Math Skills in Science

27. José skated 50 m in 10 s. What was his speed?

28. Use the information in the photograph below to calculate the speed of the ant as it moves down the branch.

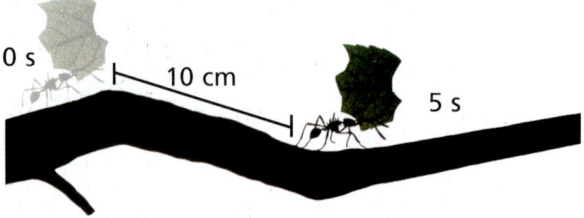

29. While riding her bicycle, Jamie accelerated from 7 m/s to 2 m/s in 5 s. What was her acceleration?

the BIG idea

30. PREDICT Look back at the picture at the beginning of the chapter on pages 6–7. Predict how the velocity of the roller coaster will change in the next moment.

31. WRITE A car is traveling east at 40 km/h. Use this information to predict where the car will be in one hour. Discuss the assumptions you made to reach your conclusion and the factors that might affect it.

UNIT PROJECTS

If you are doing a unit project, make a folder for your project. Include in your folder a list of the resources you will need, the date on which the project is due, and a schedule to keep track of your progress. Begin gathering data.

Standardized Test Practice

Interpreting Graphs

The graph below is a distance-time graph showing a 50-meter race.

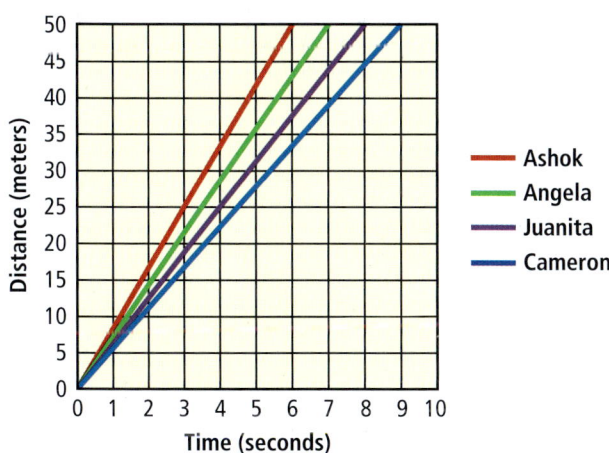

Study the graph and then answer the questions that follow.

1. Which runner reached the finish line first?
   - **a.** Ashok
   - **b.** Angela
   - **c.** Juanita
   - **d.** Cameron

2. How far did Juanita run in the first 4 seconds of the race?
   - **a.** 5 m
   - **b.** 15 m
   - **c.** 25 m
   - **d.** 35 m

3. How much time passed between the time Angela finished the race and Cameron finished the race?
   - **a.** 1 s
   - **b.** 2 s
   - **c.** 3 s
   - **d.** 4 s

4. Which of the following setups would you use to calculate Angela's average speed during the race?
   - **a.** $\dfrac{7\ m}{50\ s}$
   - **b.** $\dfrac{7\ s}{50\ m}$
   - **c.** $\dfrac{50\ m}{6\ s}$
   - **d.** $\dfrac{50\ m}{7\ s}$

5. What can you say about the speed of all of the runners?
   - **a.** They ran at the same speed.
   - **b.** They ran at a steady pace but at different speeds.
   - **c.** They sped up as they reached the finish line.
   - **d.** They slowed down as they reached the finish line.

Extended Response

Answer the two questions below in detail.

6. Suppose you are biking. What is the difference between your speed at any given moment during your bike ride and your average speed for the entire ride? Which is easier to measure? Why?

7. Suppose you are riding your bike along a path that is also used by in-line skaters. You pass a skater, and another biker passes you, both going in the same direction you're going. You pass a family having a picnic on the grass. Describe your motion from the points of view of the skater, the other biker, and the family.

CHAPTER 2 Forces

Forces change the motion of objects in predictable ways.

What must happen for a team to win this tug of war?

Key Concepts

SECTION 1
Forces change motion.
Learn about inertia and Newton's first law of motion.

SECTION 2
Force and mass determine acceleration.
Learn to calculate force through Newton's second law of motion.

SECTION 3
Forces act in pairs.
Learn about action forces and reaction forces through Newton's third law of motion.

SECTION 4
Forces transfer momentum.
Learn about momentum and how it is affected in collisions.

Internet Preview

CLASSZONE.COM

Chapter 2 online resources: Content Review, two Simulations, four Resource Centers, Math Tutorial, Test Practice

EXPLORE the BIG idea

Popping Ping-Pong Balls

Place a Ping-Pong ball in front of a flexible ruler. Carefully bend the ruler back and then release it. Repeat with a golf ball or another heavier ball. Be sure to bend the ruler back to the same spot each time. Predict which ball will go farther.

Observe and Think Which ball went farther? Why?

Take Off!

Blow up a balloon and hold the end closed. Tape the balloon to the top of a small model car. (Put the tape around the car and the balloon.) Predict what will happen to the car when you set it down and let go of the balloon. Will the car move? If so, in what direction? How far?

Observe and Think What happened to the car? If you try it again, will you get the same results? What do you think explains the motion of the car?

Internet Activity: Forces

Go to **ClassZone.com** to change the sizes and directions of forces on an object. Predict how the object will move, and then run the simulation to see if you were right.

Observe and Think What happens if two forces are applied to the object in the same direction? in opposite directions? Why?

Forces Code: MDL005

Chapter 2: **Forces** 39

CHAPTER 2
Getting Ready to Learn

CONCEPT REVIEW

- All motion is relative to the position and motion of an observer.
- An object's motion is described by position, direction, speed, and acceleration.
- Velocity and acceleration can be measured.

VOCABULARY REVIEW

velocity p. 22

vector p. 22

acceleration p. 25

mass *See Glossary.*

CONTENT REVIEW
CLASSZONE.COM
Review concepts and vocabulary.

TAKING NOTES

COMBINATION NOTES

When you read about a concept for the first time, take notes in two ways. First, make an outline of the information. Then make a sketch to help you understand and remember the concept. Use arrows to show the direction of forces.

VOCABULARY STRATEGY

Think about a vocabulary term as a **magnet word** diagram. Write the other terms or ideas related to that term around it.

See the Note-Taking Handbook on pages R45–R51.

SCIENCE NOTEBOOK

NOTES

Types of forces
- contact force
- gravity
- friction

forces on a box being pushed

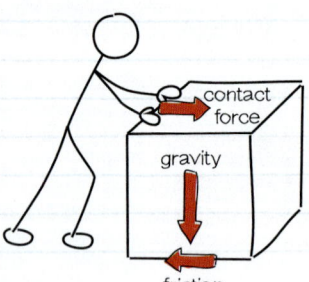

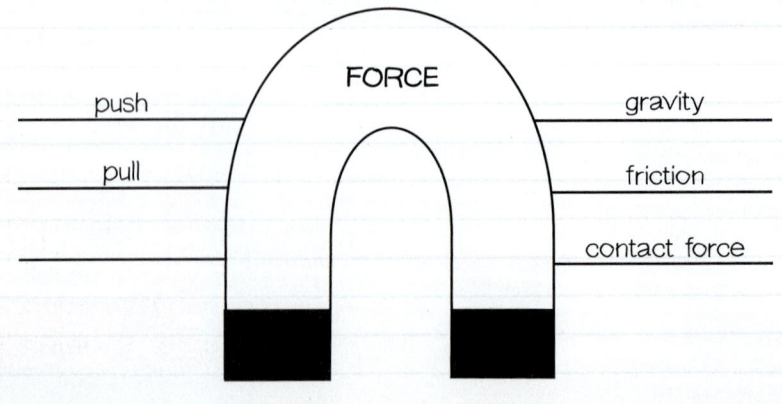

KEY CONCEPT

Forces change motion.

 BEFORE, you learned

- The velocity of an object is its change in position over time
- The acceleration of an object is its change in velocity over time

 NOW, you will learn

- What a force is
- How unbalanced forces change an object's motion
- How Newton's first law allows you to predict motion

VOCABULARY

force p. 41
net force p. 43
Newton's first law p. 45
inertia p. 46

EXPLORE Changing Motion

How can you change an object's motion?

PROCEDURE

1. Choose an object from the materials list and change its motion in several ways, from
   - not moving to moving
   - moving to not moving
   - moving to moving faster
   - moving to moving in a different direction

2. Describe the actions used to change the motion.

3. Experiment again with another object. First, decide what you will do; then predict how the motion of the object will change.

MATERIALS
- quarter
- book
- tennis ball
- cup
- feather

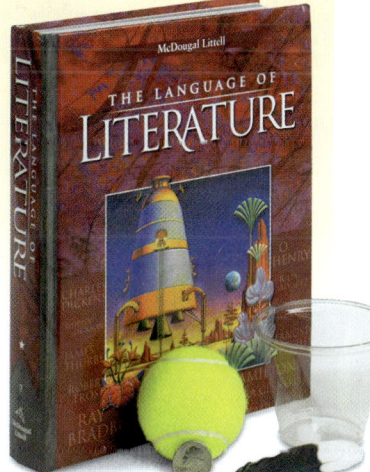

WHAT DO YOU THINK?
In step 3, how were you able to predict the motion of the object?

A force is a push or a pull.

Motion is a change in position over time.

Think about what happens during an exciting moment at the ballpark. The pitcher throws the ball across the plate, and the batter hits it high up into the stands. A fan in the stands catches the home-run ball. In this example, the pitcher sets the ball in motion, the batter changes the direction of the ball's motion, and the fan stops the ball's motion. To do so, each must use a **force,** or a push or a pull.

You use forces all day long to change the motion of objects in your world. You use a force to pick up your backpack, to open or close a car door, and even to move a pencil across your desktop. Any time you change the motion of an object, you use a force.

Chapter 2: **Forces** 41

Types of Forces

A variety of forces are always affecting the motion of objects around you. For example, take a look at how three kinds of forces affect the skater in the photograph on the left.

Gravity pulls the skater toward the ground.

① The ground produces a **contact force** on the skater as she pushes against the ground.

③ There is **friction** between the wheels and the ground.

① **Contact Force** When one object pushes or pulls another object by touching it, the first object is applying a contact force to the second. The skater applies a contact force as she pushes against the ground. The ground applies a contact force that pushes the skater forward.

② **Gravity** Gravity is the force of attraction between two masses. Earth's gravity is pulling on the skater, holding her to the ground. The strength of the gravitational force between two objects depends on their masses. For example, the pull between you and Earth is much greater than the pull between you and a book.

③ **Friction** Friction is a force that resists motion between two surfaces that are pressed together. Friction between the surface of the ground and the wheels of the skates exerts a force that resists the skater's forward motion.

You will learn more about gravity and friction in Chapter 3. In this chapter, most of the examples involve contact forces. You use contact forces constantly. Turning a page, pulling a chair, using a pencil to write, pushing your hair away from your eyes—all involve contact forces.

 What is a contact force? Give an example of a contact force.

Size and Direction of Forces

Like velocity, force is a vector. That means that force has both size and direction. For example, think about what happens when you try to make a shot in basketball. To get the ball through the hoop, you must apply the right amount of force to the ball and aim the force in the right direction. If you use too little force, the ball will not reach the basket. If you use too much force, the ball may bounce off the backboard and into your opponent's hands.

In the illustrations in this book, red arrows represent forces. The direction of an arrow shows the direction of the force, and the length of the arrow indicates the amount, or size, of the force. A blue box represents mass.

Red arrows are used to show force.

Blue boxes show mass.

42 Unit 1: **Motion and Forces**

Balanced and Unbalanced Forces

Considering the size and the direction of all the forces acting on an object allows you to predict changes in the object's motion. The overall force acting on an object when all the forces are combined is called the **net force.**

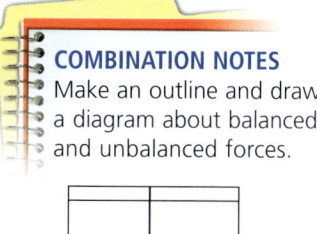

COMBINATION NOTES
Make an outline and draw a diagram about balanced and unbalanced forces.

If the net force on an object is zero, the forces acting on the object are balanced. Balanced forces have the same effect as no force at all. That is, the motion of the object does not change. For example, think about the forces on the basketball when one player attempts a shot and another blocks it. In the photograph below on the left, the players are pushing on the ball with equal force but from opposite directions. The forces on the ball are balanced, and so the ball does not move.

Only an unbalanced force can change the motion of an object. If one of the basketball players pushes with greater force than the other player, the ball will move in the direction that player is pushing. The motion of the ball changes because the forces on the ball become unbalanced.

It does not matter whether the ball started at rest or was already moving. Only an unbalanced force will change the ball's motion.

balanced forces

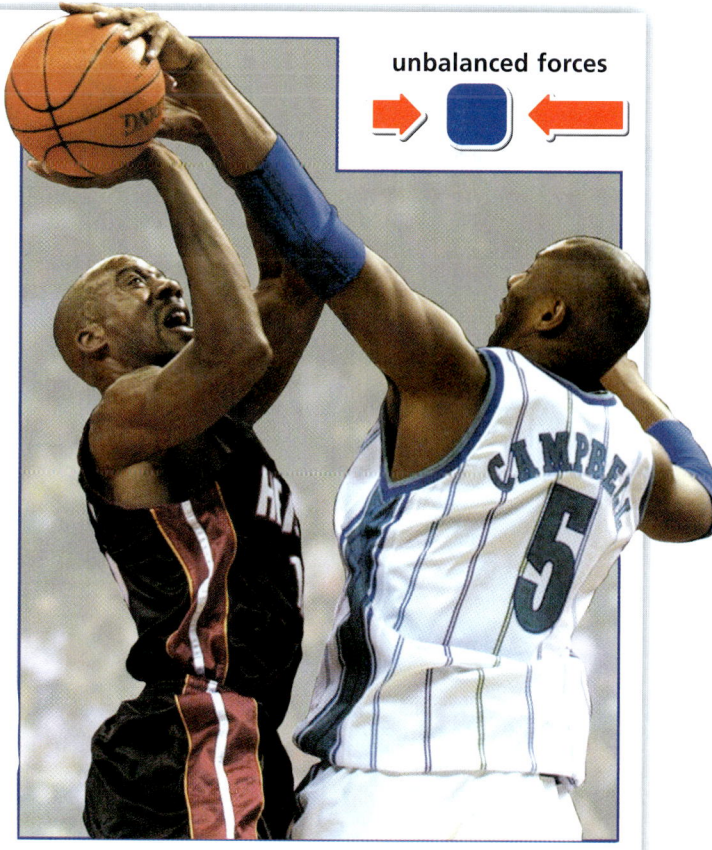

unbalanced forces

READING VISUALS **COMPARE** Compare the net force on the balls in these two photographs. Which photograph shows a net force of zero?

Chapter 2: **Forces** 43

Forces on Moving Objects

An object with forces acting on it can be moving at a constant velocity as long as those forces are balanced. For example, if you ride a bike straight ahead at a constant speed, the force moving the bike forward exactly balances the forces of friction that would slow the bike down. If you stop pedaling, the forces are no longer balanced, and frictional forces slow you down until you eventually stop.

Balanced forces cannot change an object's speed or its direction. An unbalanced force is needed to change an object's motion.

- To increase the speed of your bike, you may exert more forward force by pedaling harder or changing gears. The net force moves the bike ahead faster.
- To turn your bike, you apply an unbalanced force by leaning to one side and turning the handlebars.
- To stop the bike, you use the extra force of friction that your bike brakes provide.

CHECK YOUR READING What happens to a moving object if all the forces on it are balanced? Which sentence above tells you?

Newton's first law relates force and motion.

In the mid-1600s, the English scientist Sir Isaac Newton studied the effects of forces on objects. He formulated three laws of motion that are still helping people describe and predict the motions of objects today. Newton's ideas were built on those of other scientists, in particular the Italian scientist Galileo Galilei (gal-uh-LEE-oh gal-uh-LAY). Both Galileo and Newton overturned thinking that had been accepted since the times of the ancient Greek philosophers.

The ancient Greeks had concluded that it was necessary to apply a continuous force to keep an object in motion. For example, if you set a book on a table and give the book a quick push, the book slides a short way and then stops. To keep the book moving, you need to keep pushing it. The Greeks reasoned that the book stops moving because you stop pushing it.

Galileo's Thought Experiment

READING TIP
Contrast the last sentence of this paragraph with the last sentence of the previous paragraph.

In the early 1600s, Galileo suggested a different way of interpreting such observations. He imagined a world without friction and conducted a thought experiment in this ideal world. He concluded that, in the absence of friction, a moving object will continue moving even if there is no force acting on it. In other words, it does not take a force to keep an object moving; it takes a force—friction—to stop an object that is already moving.

Objects at rest and objects in motion both resist changes in motion. That is, objects at rest tend to stay at rest, and objects that are moving tend to continue moving unless a force acts on them. Galileo reasoned there was no real difference between an object that is moving at a constant velocity and an object that is standing still. An object at rest is simply an object with zero velocity.

CHECK YOUR READING How were Galileo's ideas about objects in motion different from the ideas of the ancient Greeks?

Newton's First Law

Newton restated Galileo's conclusions as his first law of motion. **Newton's first law** states that objects at rest remain at rest, and objects in motion remain in motion with the same velocity, unless acted upon by an unbalanced force. You can easily observe the effects of unbalanced forces, both on the ball at rest and the ball in motion, in the pictures below.

Newton's First Law

Objects at rest remain at rest, and objects in motion remain in motion with the same velocity, unless acted upon by an unbalanced force.

An Object at Rest

An object at rest (the ball) remains at rest unless acted upon by an unbalanced force (from the foot).

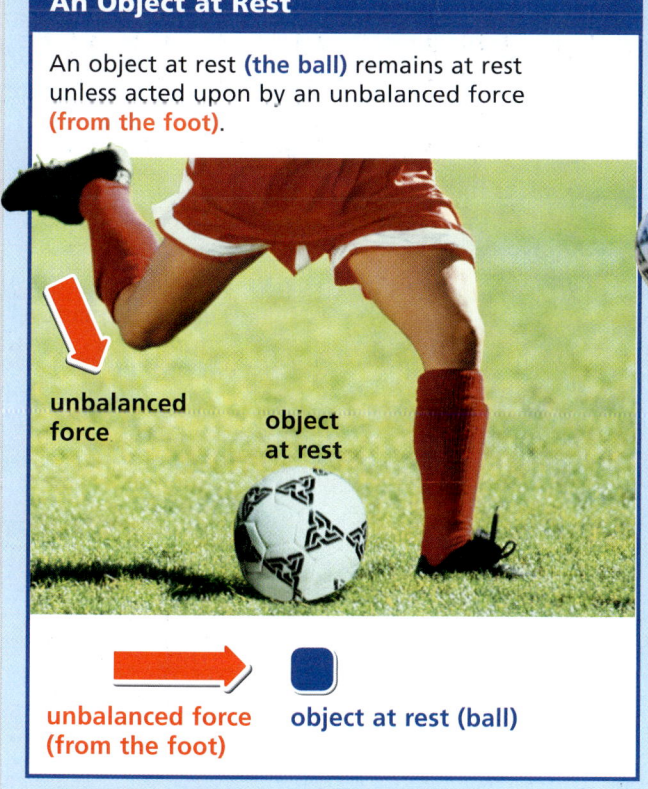

unbalanced force (from the foot) → object at rest (ball)

An Object in Motion

An object in motion (the ball) remains in motion with the same velocity, unless acted upon by an unbalanced force (from the hand).

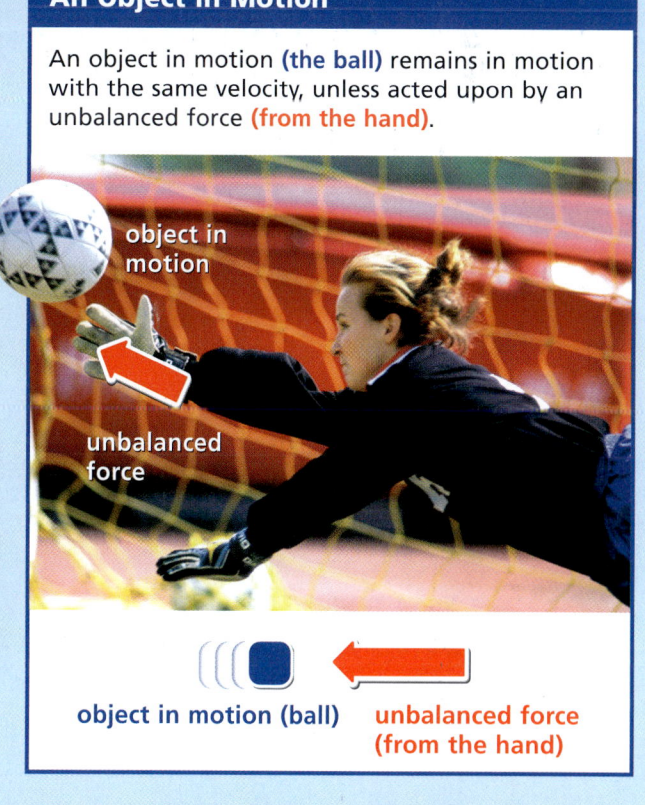

object in motion (ball) ← unbalanced force (from the hand)

READING VISUALS What will happen to the ball's motion in each picture? Why?

You will find many examples of Newton's first law around you. For instance, if you throw a stick for a dog to catch, you are changing the motion of the stick. The dog changes the motion of the stick by catching it and by dropping it at your feet. You change the motion of a volleyball when you spike it, a tennis racket when you swing it, a paintbrush when you make a brush stroke, and an oboe when you pick it up to play or set it down after playing. In each of these examples, you apply a force that changes the motion of the object.

Inertia

VOCABULARY
Make a magnet word diagram for *inertia* in your notebook.

Inertia (ih-NUR-shuh) is the resistance of an object to a change in the speed or the direction of its motion. Newton's first law, which describes the tendency of objects to resist changes in motion, is also called the law of inertia. Inertia is closely related to mass. When you measure the mass of an object, you are also measuring its inertia. You know from experience that it is easier to push or pull an empty box than it is to push or pull the same box when it is full of books. Likewise, it is easier to stop or to turn an empty wagon than to stop or turn a wagon full of sand. In both of these cases, it is harder to change the motion of the object that has more mass.

INVESTIGATE Inertia

Which ball has more inertia?
Two balls have different masses and therefore different amounts of inertia. Use what you know about force and inertia to design an experiment that shows which ball has more inertia. Your procedure cannot include lifting the balls, weighing the balls, or touching the balls with your hands.

DESIGN YOUR OWN EXPERIMENT

PROCEDURE

1. Figure out how to use the meter stick or other materials to compare the inertia of the two balls.
2. Write up your procedure.
3. Test your procedure.

WHAT DO YOU THINK?
- What were the results of your experiment? Did it work? Why or why not?
- What was the variable? What were the constants?
- How does your experiment demonstrate the property of inertia?

SKILL FOCUS
Designing experiments

MATERIALS
- 2 balls of unknown masses
- string
- block
- meter stick

TIME
30 minutes

Inertia is the reason that people in cars need to wear seat belts. A moving car has inertia, and so do the riders inside it. When the driver applies the brakes, an unbalanced force is applied to the car. Normally, the bottom of the seat applies an unbalanced force—friction—which slows the riders down as the car slows. If the driver stops the car suddenly, however, this force is not exerted over enough time to stop the motion of the riders. Instead, the riders continue moving forward with most of their original speed because of their inertia.

RESOURCE CENTER
CLASSZONE.COM
Find out more about inertia.

1 As a car moves forward, the driver—shown here as a crash-test dummy—moves forward with the same velocity as the car.

2 When the driver hits the brakes, the car stops. If the stop is sudden and the driver is not wearing a seat belt, the driver keeps moving forward.

3 Finally, the windshield applies an unbalanced force that stops the driver's forward motion.

If the driver is wearing a seat belt, the seat belt rather than the windshield applies the unbalanced force that stops the driver's forward motion. The force from the seat belt is applied over a longer time, so the force causes less damage. In a collision, seat belts alone are sometimes not enough to stop the motion of drivers or passengers. Air bags further cushion people from the effects of inertia in an accident.

 If a car makes a sudden stop, what happens to a passenger riding in the back seat who is not wearing a seat belt?

2.1 Review

KEY CONCEPTS

1. Explain the difference between balanced and unbalanced forces.
2. What is the relationship between force and motion described by Newton's first law?
3. What is inertia? How is the inertia of an object related to its mass?

CRITICAL THINKING

4. **Infer** Once a baseball has been hit into the air, what forces are acting upon it? How can you tell that any forces are acting upon the ball?
5. **Predict** A ball is at rest on the floor of a car moving at a constant velocity. What will happen to the ball if the car swerves suddenly to the left?

CHALLENGE

6. **Synthesize** What can the changes in an object's position tell you about the forces acting on that object? Describe an example from everyday life that shows how forces affect the position of an object.

Think SCIENCE

SKILL: EVALUATING HYPOTHESES

Why Do These Rocks Slide?

In Death Valley, California, there is a dry lakebed known as Racetrack Playa. Rocks are mysteriously moving across the ground there, leaving tracks in the clay. These rocks can have masses as great as 320 kilograms (corresponding to 700 lb). No one has ever observed the rocks sliding, even though scientists have studied their tracks for more than 50 years. What force moves these rocks? Scientists do not yet know.

▶ Observations

Scientists made these observations.

a. Some rocks left trails that are almost parallel.
b. Some rocks left trails that took abrupt turns.
c. Sometimes a small rock moved while a larger rock did not.
d. Most of the trails are on level surfaces. Some trails run slightly uphill.
e. The temperature in that area sometimes drops below freezing.

A playa was once a shallow lake. The water in it evaporated, leaving a dry lakebed.

This rock made a U-turn.

▶ Hypotheses

Scientists formed these hypotheses about how the rocks move.

- When the lakebed gets wet, it becomes so slippery that gravity causes the rocks to slide.
- When the lakebed gets wet, it becomes so slippery that strong winds can move the rocks.
- When the lakebed gets wet and cold, a sheet of ice forms and traps the rocks. Strong winds move both the ice sheet and the trapped rocks.

▶ Evaluate Each Hypothesis

On Your Own Think about whether all the observations support each hypothesis. Some facts may rule out some hypotheses. Some facts may neither support nor contradict a particular hypothesis.

As a Group Decide which hypotheses are reasonable. Discuss your thinking and conclusions in a small group, and list the reasonable hypotheses.

CHALLENGE What further observations would you make to test any of these hypotheses? What information would each observation add?

 **RESOURCE CENTER** CLASSZONE.COM Learn more about the moving rocks.

48 Unit 1: Motion and Forces

KEY CONCEPT

2.2 Force and mass determine acceleration.

◀ **BEFORE, you learned**
- Mass is a measure of inertia
- The motion of an object will not change unless the object is acted upon by an unbalanced force

▶ **NOW, you will learn**
- How Newton's second law relates force, mass, and acceleration
- How force works in circular motion

VOCABULARY

Newton's second law p. 50
centripetal force p. 54

EXPLORE Acceleration

How are force and acceleration related?

PROCEDURE

1. Tie a paper clip to each end of a long string. Hook two more paper clips to one end.

2. Hold the single paper clip in the middle of a smooth table; hang the other end of the string over the edge. Let go and observe.

3. Add one more paper clip to the hanging end and repeat the experiment. Observe what happens. Repeat.

MATERIALS
- paper clips
- string

WHAT DO YOU THINK?
- What happened each time that you let go of the single paper clip?
- Explain the relationship between the number of hanging paper clips and the motion of the paper clip on the table.

Newton's second law relates force, mass, and acceleration.

Suppose you are eating lunch with a friend and she asks you to pass the milk container. You decide to slide it across the table to her. How much force would you use to get the container moving? You would probably use a different force if the container were full than if the container were empty.

If you want to give two objects with different masses the same acceleration, you have to apply different forces to them. You must push a full milk container harder than an empty one to slide it over to your friend in the same amount of time.

▼ **REMINDER**
Acceleration is a change in velocity over time.

△ **CHECK YOUR READING** What three concepts are involved in Newton's second law?

Chapter 2: **Forces** 49

Newton's Second Law

Explore Newton's second law.

Newton studied how objects move, and he noticed some patterns. He observed that the acceleration of an object depends on the mass of the object and the size of the force applied to it. **Newton's second law** states that the acceleration of an object increases with increased force and decreases with increased mass. The law also states that the direction in which an object accelerates is the same as the direction of the force.

The photographs below show Newton's second law at work in a supermarket. The acceleration of each shopping cart depends upon two things:

- the size of the force applied to the shopping cart
- the mass of the shopping cart

In the left-hand photograph, the force on the cart changes, while the mass of the cart stays the same. In the right-hand photograph, the force on the cart stays the same, while the mass of the cart varies. Notice how mass and force affect acceleration.

Newton's Second Law

The acceleration of an object increases with increased force, decreases with increased mass, and is in the same direction as the force.

Increasing Force Increases Acceleration

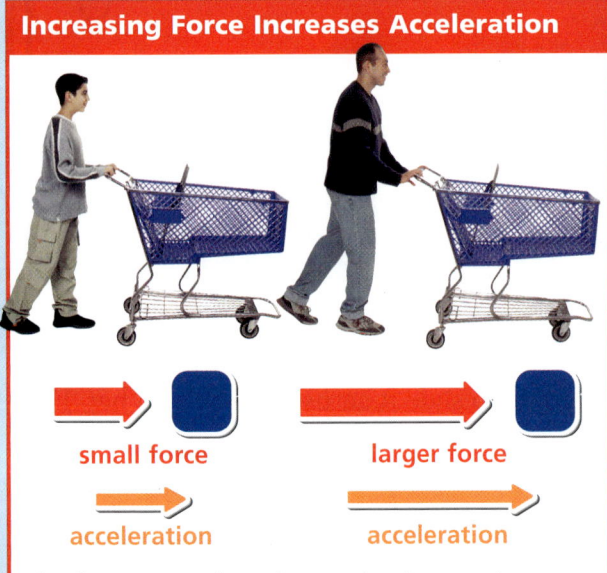

The force exerted on the cart by the man is greater than the force exerted on the same cart by the boy, so the acceleration is greater.

Increasing Mass Decreases Acceleration

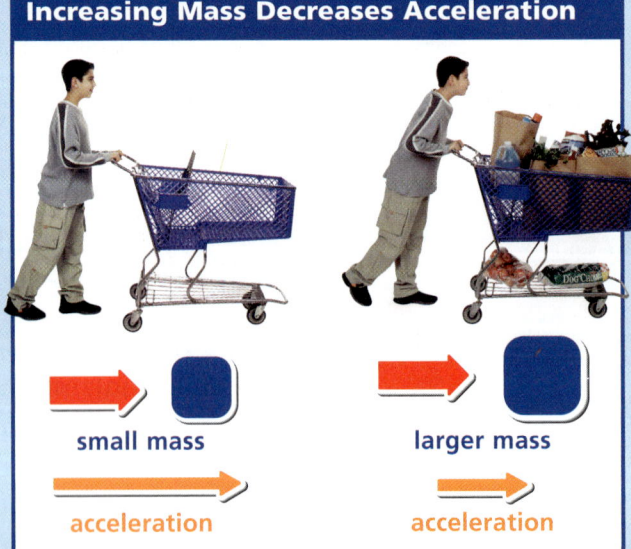

The mass of the full cart is greater than the mass of the empty cart, and the boy is pushing with the same force, so the acceleration is less.

READING VISUALS What do the arrows in these diagrams show?

Force Equals Mass Times Acceleration

Newton was able to describe the relationship of force, mass, and acceleration mathematically. You can calculate the force, the mass, or the acceleration if you know two of the three factors. The mathematical form of Newton's second law, stated as a formula, is

$$\text{Force} = \text{mass} \cdot \text{acceleration}$$
$$F = ma$$

To use this formula, you need to understand the unit used to measure force. In honor of Newton's contribution to our understanding of force and motion, the standard unit of force is called the newton (N). Because force equals mass times acceleration, force is measured in units of mass (kilograms) times units of acceleration (meters per second per second). A newton is defined as the amount of force that it takes to accelerate one kilogram (1 kg) of mass one meter per second per second (1 m/s^2). So 1 N is the same as 1 kg • m/s^2.

REMINDER
Meters per second per second is the same as *m/s^2*, which can be read "meters per second squared."

CHECK YOUR READING If the same force is applied to two objects of different mass, which object will have the greater acceleration?

The mathematical relationship of force, mass, and acceleration allow you to solve problems about how objects move. If you know the mass of an object and the acceleration you want to achieve, you can use the formula to find the force you need to exert to produce that acceleration. Use Newton's second law to find the force that is needed to accelerate the shopping cart in the sample problem.

Calculating Force

Sample Problem

What force is needed to accelerate a 10 kg shopping cart 3 m/s^2?

What do you know?   mass = 10 kg, acceleration = 3 m/s^2

What do you want to find out?   Force

Write the formula: $F = ma$

Substitute into the formula: $F = 10 \text{ kg} \cdot 3 \text{ m/s}^2$

Calculate and simplify: $F = 10 \text{ kg} \cdot \dfrac{3m}{s^2} = 30 \text{ kg} \cdot \text{m/s}^2$

Check that your units agree: Unit is kg • m/s^2.
Unit of force is newton, which is also kg • m/s^2. Units agree.

Answer: $F = 30$ N

Practice the Math

1. If a 5 kg ball is accelerating 1.2 m/s^2, what is the force on it?
2. A person on a scooter is accelerating 2 m/s^2. If the person has a mass of 50 kg, how much force is acting on that person?

This team of 20 people pulled a 72,000-kilogram (159,000 lb) Boeing 727 airplane 3.7 meters (12 ft) in 6.74 seconds.

The photograph above shows people who are combining forces to pull an airplane. Suppose you knew the mass of the plane and how hard the people were pulling. How much would the plane accelerate? The sample problem below shows how Newton's second law helps you calculate the acceleration.

Calculating Acceleration

▶ **Sample Problem**

If a team pulls with a combined force of 9000 N on an airplane with a mass of 30,000 kg, what is the acceleration of the airplane?

What do you know?   mass = 30,000 kg, force = 9000 N

What do you want to find out?   acceleration

Rearrange the formula: $a = \dfrac{F}{m}$

Substitute into the formula: $a = \dfrac{9000 \text{ N}}{30{,}000 \text{ kg}}$

Calculate and simplify: $a = \dfrac{9000 \text{ N}}{30{,}000 \text{ kg}} = \dfrac{9000 \text{ kg} \cdot \text{m/s}^2}{30{,}000 \text{ kg}} = 0.3 \text{ m/s}^2$

Check that your units agree: Unit is m/s². Unit for acceleration is m/s². Units agree.

Answer: $a = 0.3 \text{ m/s}^2$

▶ **Practice the Math**

1. Half the people on the team decide not to pull the airplane. The combined force of those left is 4500 N, while the airplane's mass is still 30,000 kg. What will be the acceleration?
2. A girl pulls a wheeled backpack with a force of 3 N. If the backpack has a mass of 6 kg, what is its acceleration?

Mass and Acceleration

Mass is also a variable in Newton's second law. If the same force acts on two objects, the object with less mass will have the greater acceleration. For instance, if you push a soccer ball and a bowling ball with equal force, the soccer ball will have a greater acceleration.

If objects lose mass, they can gain acceleration if the force remains the same. When a rocket is first launched, most of its mass is the fuel it carries. As the rocket burns fuel, it loses mass. As the mass continually decreases, the acceleration continually increases.

APPLY This NASA launch rocket accelerates with enough force to lift about 45 cars off the ground. As the rocket loses fuel, will it accelerate more or less? Why?

Calculating Mass

▸ **Sample Problem**

A model rocket is accelerating at 2 m/s². The force on it is 1 N. What is the mass of the rocket?

What do you know?   acceleration = 2 m/s², force = 1 N

What do you want to find out?   mass

Rearrange the formula: $m = \dfrac{F}{a}$

Substitute into the formula: $m = \dfrac{1 \text{ N}}{2 \text{ m/s}^2}$

Calculate and simplify: $m = \dfrac{1 \text{ N}}{2 \text{ m/s}^2} = \dfrac{1 \text{ kg} \cdot \text{m/s}^2}{2 \text{ m/s}^2} = 0.5 \text{ kg}$

Check that your units agree: Unit is kg.
Unit of mass is kg. Units agree.

Answer: m = 0.5 kg

▸ **Practice the Math**

1. Another model rocket is accelerating at a rate of 3 m/s² with a force of 1 N. What is the mass of the rocket?
2. A boy pushes a shopping cart with a force of 10 N, and the cart accelerates 1 m/s². What is the mass of the cart?

Forces can change the direction of motion.

Usually, we think of a force as either speeding up or slowing down the motion of an object, but force can also make an object change direction. If an object changes direction, it is accelerating. Newton's second law says that if you apply a force to an object, the direction in which the object accelerates is the same as the direction of the force. You can change the direction of an object without changing its speed. For example, a good soccer player can control the motion of a soccer ball by applying a force that changes the ball's direction but not its speed.

 **CHECK YOUR READING**   How can an object accelerate when it does not change speed?

INVESTIGATE Motion and Force

What affects circular motion?

PROCEDURE

1. Spread newspaper over your work surface. Place the paper plate down on the newspaper.

2. Practice rolling the marble around the edge of the plate until you can roll it around completely at least once.

3. Cut out a one-quarter slice of the paper plate. Put a dab of paint on the edge of the plate where the marble will leave it. Place the plate back down on the newspaper.

4. Hypothesize: How will the marble move once it rolls off the plate? Why?

5. Roll the marble all the way around the paper plate into the cut-away section and observe the resulting motion as shown by the trail of paint.

WHAT DO YOU THINK?

- Did your observations support your hypothesis?
- What forces affected the marble's motion after it left the plate?

CHALLENGE How will changing the speed at which you roll the marble change your results? Repeat the activity to test your prediction.

SKILL FOCUS
Hypothesizing

MATERIALS
- newspaper
- paper plate
- marble
- scissors
- poster paint
- paintbrush

TIME
15 minutes

Centripetal Force

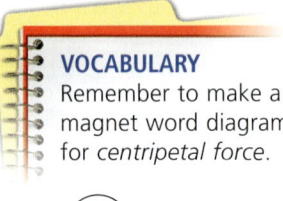

VOCABULARY
Remember to make a magnet word diagram for *centripetal force*.

When you were younger, you may have experimented with using force to change motion. Perhaps you and a friend took turns swinging each other in a circle. If you remember this game, you may also remember that your arms got tired because they were constantly pulling your friend as your friend spun around. It took force to change the direction of your friend's motion. Without that force, your friend could not have kept moving in a circle.

Any force that keeps an object moving in a circle is known as a **centripetal force** (sehn-TRIHP-ih-tuhl). This force points toward the center of the circle. Without the centripetal force, the object would go flying off in a straight line. When you whirl a ball on a string, what keeps the ball moving in a circle? The force of the string turns the ball, changing the ball's direction of motion. When the string turns, so does the ball. As the string changes direction, the force from the string also changes direction. The force is always pointing along the string toward your hand, the center of the circle. The centripetal force on the whirling ball is the pull from the string. If you let go of the string, the ball would fly off in the direction it was headed when you let go.

 How does centripetal force change the motion of an object?

54 Unit 1: **Motion and Forces**

Centripetal force
The force that keeps the female skater moving in a circle is the pull exerted by her partner. The diagram shows the direction of the centripetal force.

Circular Motion and Newton's Second Law

Suppose the male skater shown above spins his partner faster. Her direction changes more quickly than before, so she accelerates more. To get more acceleration, he must apply more force. The same idea holds for a ball you whirl on a string. You have to pull harder on the string when you whirl the ball faster, because it takes more centripetal force to keep the ball moving at the greater speed.

You can apply the formula for Newton's second law even to an object moving in a circle. If you know the size of the centripetal force acting upon the object, you can find its acceleration. A greater acceleration requires a greater centripetal force. A more massive object requires a greater centripetal force to have the same circular speed as a less massive object. But no matter what the mass of an object is, if it moves in a circle, its force and acceleration are directed toward the center of the circle.

CHECK YOUR READING How does increasing the centripetal force on an object affect its acceleration?

2.2 Review

KEY CONCEPTS
1. If the force acting upon an object is increased, what happens to the object's acceleration?
2. How does the mass of an object affect its acceleration?
3. What force keeps an object moving in a circle? In what direction does this force act?

CRITICAL THINKING
4. **Infer** Use Newton's second law to determine how much force is being applied to an object that is traveling at a constant velocity.
5. **Calculate** What force is needed to accelerate an object 5 m/s² if the object has a mass of 10 kg?

CHALLENGE
6. **Synthesize** Carlos pushes a 3 kg box with a force of 9 N. The force of friction on the box is 3 N in the opposite direction. What is the acceleration of the box? **Hint:** Combine forces to find the net force.

Chapter 2: **Forces** 55

MATH in SCIENCE

SKILL: USING SIGNIFICANT FIGURES

Meaningful Numbers

MATH TUTORIAL
CLASSZONE.COM

Click on Math Tutorial for more help with rounding decimals.

A student doing a science report on artificial hearts reads that a certain artificial heart weighs about 2 pounds. The student then writes that the mass of the artificial heart is 0.907185 kilograms. Someone reading this report might think that the student knows the mass to a high precision, when actually he knows it only to one meaningful number.

When you make calculations, the number of digits to include in your answer depends in part on the number of meaningful digits, or significant figures, in the numbers you are working with.

Example

In an experiment to find acceleration, a scientist might record the following data.

Force = 3.1 N   mass = 1.450 kg

In this example, force is given to two significant figures, and mass is given to four significant figures.

(1) Use a calculator and the formula $a = F/m$ to find the acceleration. The display on the calculator shows

2.1379310345

(2) To determine how many of the digits in this answer are really meaningful, look at the measurement with the least number of significant figures. In this example, force is given to two significant figures. Therefore, the answer is meaningful only to two significant figures.

(3) Round the calculated number to two digits.

ANSWER acceleration = 2.1 m/s^2

The AbioCor artificial heart, which has a mass of about 0.9 kg, is designed to fit entirely inside the human body.

Answer the following questions.

For each pair of measurements, calculate the acceleration to the appropriate number of digits.

1. Force = 3.100 N   mass = 3.1 kg
2. Force = 2 N   mass = 4.2 kg
3. Force = 1.21 N   mass = 1.1000 kg

CHALLENGE Suppose a scientist measures a force of 3.25 N and a mass of 3.3 kg. She could round the force to two significant figures and then divide, or she could divide and then round the answer. Compare these two methods. Which method do you think is more accurate?

KEY CONCEPT
2.3 Forces act in pairs.

BEFORE, you learned
- A force is a push or a pull
- Increasing the force on an object increases the acceleration
- The acceleration of an object depends on its mass and the force applied to it

NOW, you will learn
- How Newton's third law relates action/reaction pairs of forces
- How Newton's laws work together

VOCABULARY

Newton's third law p. 57

THINK ABOUT

How do jellyfish move?

Jellyfish do not have much control over their movements. They drift with the current in the ocean. However, jellyfish do have some control over their up-and-down motion. By squeezing water out of its umbrella-like body, the jellyfish shown here applies a force in one direction to move in the opposite direction. If the water is forced downward, the jellyfish moves upward. How can a person or an object move in one direction by exerting a force in the opposite direction?

Newton's third law relates action and reaction forces.

COMBINATION NOTES
In your notebook, make an outline and draw a diagram about Newton's third law.

Newton made an important observation that explains the motion of the jellyfish. He noticed that forces always act in pairs. **Newton's third law** states that every time one object exerts a force on another object, the second object exerts a force that is equal in size and opposite in direction back on the first object. As the jellyfish contracts its body, it applies a downward force on the water. The water applies an equal force back on the jellyfish. It is this equal and opposite force on the jellyfish that pushes it up. This is similar to what happens when a blown-up balloon is released. The balloon pushes air out the end, and the air pushes back on the balloon and moves it forward.

CHECK YOUR READING What moves the jellyfish through the water?

Chapter 2: **Forces** 57

Action and Reaction Pairs

The force that is exerted on an object and the force that the object exerts back are known together as an action/reaction force pair. One force in the pair is called the action force, and the other is called the reaction force. For instance, if the jellyfish pushing on the water is the action force, the water pushing back on the jellyfish is the reaction force. Likewise, if the balloon pushing the air backward is the action force, the air pushing the balloon forward is the reaction force.

You can see many examples of action and reaction forces in the world around you. Here are three:

- You may have watched the liftoffs of the space shuttle on television. When the booster rockets carrying the space shuttle take off, their engines push fuel exhaust downward. The exhaust pushes back on the rockets, sending them upward.
- When you bang your toe into the leg of a table, the same amount of force that you exert on the table is exerted back on your toe.
- Action and reaction forces do not always result in motion. For example, if you press down on a table, the table resists the push with the same amount of force, even though nothing moves.

 Identify the action/reaction forces in each example described above.

INVESTIGATE Newton's Third Law

How do action and reaction forces compare?

PROCEDURE

1. With a partner, hook the two spring scales together.
2. Pull gently on your spring scale while your partner holds but does not pull on the other scale.
3. Observe and record the amount of force that is shown on your scale and on your partner's scale.
4. Both of you pull together. Observe the force shown on each scale.

WHAT DO YOU THINK?

- What happened to your partner's force as your force increased?
- What happened when you both pulled?
- Explain why you think what you observed in each case happened.

CHALLENGE Can you think of a way to use the scales to show Newton's first or second law?

SKILL FOCUS
Observing

MATERIALS
2 spring scales

TIME
15 minutes

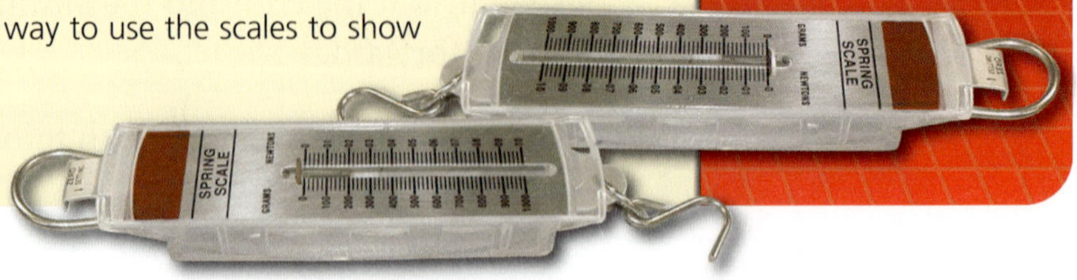

58 Unit 1: Motion and Forces

Action and Reaction Forces Versus Balanced Forces

Because action and reaction forces are equal and opposite, they may be confused with balanced forces. Keep in mind that balanced forces act on a single object, while action and reaction forces act on different objects.

Balanced Forces If you and a friend pull on opposite sides of a backpack with the same amount of force, the backpack doesn't move, because the forces acting on it are balanced. In this case, both forces are exerted on one object—the backpack.

Action and Reaction As you drag a heavy backpack across a floor, you can feel the backpack pulling on you with an equal amount of force. The action force and the reaction force are acting on two different things—one is acting on the backpack, and the other is acting on you.

The illustration below summarizes Newton's third law. The girl exerts an action force on the boy by pushing him. Even though the boy is not trying to push the girl, an equal and opposite reaction force acts upon the girl, causing her to move as well.

Newton's Third Law

When one object exerts a force on another object, the second object exerts an equal and opposite force on the first object.

1 One Skater Pushes

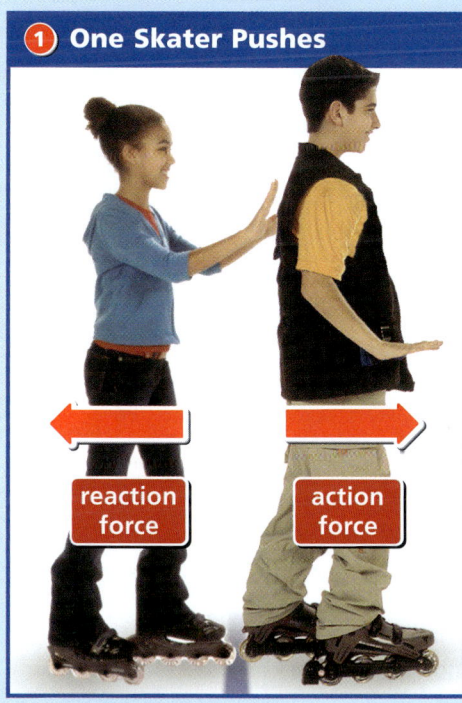

The action force from the girl sets the boy in motion.

2 Both Skaters Move

Even though the boy does not do anything, the reaction force from him sets the girl in motion as well.

READING VISUALS How does the direction of the force on the girl relate to her motion?

Chapter 2: **Forces** 59

Newton's Three Laws of Motion

All three of Newton's laws work together to help describe how an object will move.

Newton's First Law

force of gravity

This kangaroo has jumped, setting itself in motion. If no other forces acted on it, the kangaroo would continue to move through the air with the same motion. Instead, the force of gravity will bring this kangaroo back to the ground.

Newton's Second Law

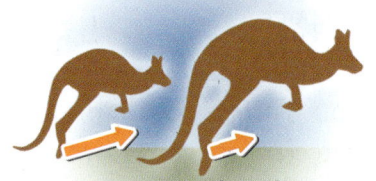

acceleration

The large kangaroo does not have as much acceleration as a less massive kangaroo would if it used the same force to jump. However, the more massive kangaroo can increase its acceleration by increasing the force of its jump.

Newton's Third Law

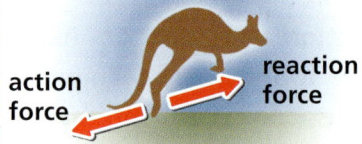

action force   reaction force

A kangaroo applies an action force on the ground with its powerful back legs. The reaction force from the ground can send the kangaroo as far as 8 meters (26 ft) through the air.

READING VISUALS What forces are involved in a kangaroo jump?

Common Name: Red kangaroo
Scientific Name: *Macropus rufus*
Home: Australia
Top Speed: 65 km/h (40 mi/h)
Maximum Leap: 8 m (26 ft)

AUSTRALIA

Newton's three laws describe and predict motion.

Newton's three laws can explain the motion of almost any object, including the motion of animals. The illustrations on page 60 show how all three of Newton's laws can be used to describe how kangaroos move. The three laws are not independent of one another; they are used together to explain the motion of objects.

You can use the laws of motion to explain how other animals move as well. For example, Newton's laws explain why a squid moves forward while squirting water out behind it. These laws also explain that a bird is exerting force when it speeds up to fly away or when it changes its direction in the air.

You can also use Newton's laws to make predictions about motion. If you know the force acting upon an object, then you can predict how that object's motion will change. For example, if you want to send a spacecraft to Mars, you must be able to predict exactly where Mars will be by the time the spacecraft reaches it. You must also be able to control the force on your spacecraft so that it will arrive at the right place at the right time.

Knowing how Newton's three laws work together can also help you win a canoe race. In order to start the canoe moving, you need to apply a force to overcome its inertia. Newton's second law might affect your choice of canoes, because a less massive canoe is easier to accelerate than a more massive one. You can also predict the best position for your paddle in the water. If you want to move straight ahead, you push backward on the paddle so that the canoe moves forward. Together, Newton's laws can help you explain and predict how the canoe, or any object, will move.

Find out more about Newton's laws of motion.

COMBINATION NOTES
Make an outline and draw a diagram showing how all three of Newton's laws apply to the motion of one object.

2.3 Review

KEY CONCEPTS

1. Identify the action/reaction force pair involved when you catch a ball.
2. Explain the difference between balanced forces and action/reaction forces.
3. How do Newton's laws of motion apply to the motion of an animal, such as a cat that is running?

CRITICAL THINKING

4. **Apply** A man pushes on a wall with a force of 50 N. What are the size and the direction of the force that the wall exerts on the man?
5. **Evaluate** Jim will not help push a heavy box. He says, "My force will produce an opposite force and cancel my effort." Evaluate Jim's statement.

CHALLENGE

6. **Calculate** Suppose you are holding a basketball while standing still on a skateboard. You and the skateboard have a mass of 50 kg. You throw the basketball with a force of 10 N. What is your acceleration before and after you throw the ball?

CHAPTER INVESTIGATION

Newton's Laws of Motion

OVERVIEW AND PURPOSE As you know, rocket engineers consider Newton's laws when designing rockets and planning rocket flights. In this investigation you will use what you have learned about Newton's laws to
- build a straw rocket
- improve the rocket's performance by modifying one design element

▶ Problem

What aspects of a model rocket affect the distance it flies?

▶ Hypothesize

After step 8 in the procedure, write a hypothesis to explain what you predict will happen during the second set of trials. Your hypothesis should take the form of an "If . . . , then . . . , because . . ." statement.

▶ Procedure

MATERIALS
- 2 straws with different diameters
- several plastic bottles, in different sizes
- modeling clay
- scissors
- construction paper
- meter stick
- tape

1. Make a data table like the one shown on the sample notebook page.

2. Insert the straw with the smaller diameter into one of the bottles. Seal the mouth of the bottle tightly with modeling clay so that air can escape only through the straw. This is the rocket launcher.

3. Cut two thin strips of paper, one about 8 cm long and the other about 12 cm long. Connect the ends of the strips to make loops.

4. To create the rocket, place the straw with the larger diameter through the smaller loop and tape the loop to the straw at one end. Attach the other loop to the other end of the straw in the same way. Both loops should be attached to the same side of the straw to stabilize your rocket in flight.

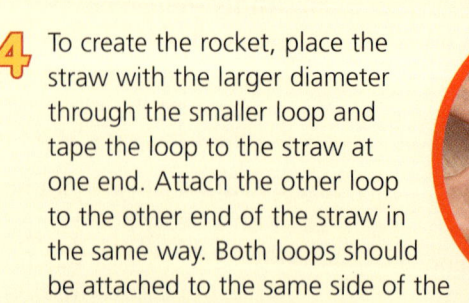

62 Unit 1: Motion and Forces

5. Use a small ball of modeling clay to seal the end of the straw near the smaller loop.

6. Slide the open end of the rocket over the straw on the launcher. Place the bottle on the edge of a table so that the rocket is pointing away from the table.

7. Test launch your rocket by holding the bottle with two hands and squeezing it quickly. Measure the distance the rocket lands from the edge of the table. Practice the launch several times. Remember to squeeze with equal force each time.

8. Launch the rocket four times. Keep the amount of force you use constant. Measure the distance the rocket travels each time, and record the results in your data table.

9. List all the variables that may affect the distance your rocket flies. Change the rocket or launcher to alter one variable. Launch the rocket and measure the distance it flies. Repeat three more times, and record the results in your data table.

Observe and Analyze

1. **RECORD OBSERVATIONS** Draw a diagram of both of your bottle rockets. Make sure your data table is complete.

2. **IDENTIFY VARIABLES** What variables did you identify, and what variable did you modify?

Conclude

1. **COMPARE** How did the flight distances of the original rocket compare with those of the modified rocket?

2. **ANALYZE** Compare your results with your hypothesis. Do the results support your hypothesis?

3. **IDENTIFY LIMITS** What possible limitations or errors did you experience or could you have experienced?

4. **APPLY** Use Newton's laws to explain why the rocket flies.

5. **APPLY** What other real-life example can you think of that demonstrates Newton's laws?

INVESTIGATE Further

CHALLENGE Why does the rocket have paper loops taped to it? Determine how the flight of the rocket is affected if one or both loops are completely removed. Hypothesize about the function of the paper loops and design an experiment to test your hypothesis.

Newton's Laws of Motion

Problem What aspects of a model rocket affect the distance it flies?

Hypothesize

Observe and Analyze

Table 1. Flight Distances of Original and Modified Rocket

Trial Number	Original Rocket Distance Rocket Flew (cm)	Modified Rocket Distance Rocket Flew (cm)
1		
2		
3		
4		

Conclude

Chapter 2: **Forces** 63

KEY CONCEPT

Forces transfer momentum.

 BEFORE, you learned
- A force is a push or a pull
- Newton's laws help to describe and predict motion

 NOW, you will learn
- What momentum is
- How to calculate momentum
- How momentum is affected by collisions

VOCABULARY

momentum p. 64
collision p. 66
conservation of momentum p. 67

EXPLORE Collisions

What happens when objects collide?

PROCEDURE

① Roll the two balls toward each other on a flat surface. Try to roll them at the same speed. Observe what happens. Experiment by changing the speeds of the two balls.

② Leave one ball at rest, and roll the other ball so that it hits the first ball. Observe what happens. Then repeat the experiment with the balls switched.

WHAT DO YOU THINK?
- How did varying the speed of the balls affect the motion of the balls after the collision?
- What happened when one ball was at rest? Why did switching the two balls affect the outcome?

MATERIALS
2 balls of different masses

Objects in motion have momentum.

If you throw a tennis ball at a wall, it will bounce back toward you. What would happen if you could throw a wrecking ball at the wall at the same speed that you threw the tennis ball? The wall would most likely break apart. Why would a wrecking ball have a different effect on the wall than the tennis ball?

A moving object has a property that is called momentum. **Momentum** (moh-MEHN-tuhm) is a measure of mass in motion; the momentum of an object is the product of its mass and its velocity. At the same velocity, the wrecking ball has more momentum than the tennis ball because the wrecking ball has more mass. However, you could increase the momentum of the tennis ball by throwing it faster.

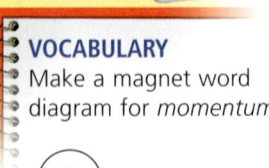

VOCABULARY
Make a magnet word diagram for *momentum*.

64 Unit 1: **Motion and Forces**

Momentum is similar to inertia. Like inertia, the momentum of an object depends on its mass. Unlike inertia, however, momentum takes into account how fast the object is moving. A wrecking ball that is moving very slowly, for example, has less momentum than a fast-moving wrecking ball. With less momentum, the slower-moving wrecking ball would not be able to do as much damage to the wall.

To calculate an object's momentum, you can use the following formula:

$$\text{momentum} = \text{mass} \cdot \text{velocity}$$
$$p = mv$$

In this formula, p stands for momentum, m for mass, and v for velocity. In standard units, the mass of an object is given in kilograms (kg), and velocity is given in meters per second (m/s). Therefore, the unit of momentum is the kilogram-meter per second (kg • m/s). Notice that the unit of momentum combines mass, length, and time.

Like force, velocity, and acceleration, momentum is a vector—it has both a size and a direction. The direction of an object's momentum is the same as the direction of its velocity. You can use speed instead of velocity in the formula as long as you do not need to know the direction of motion. As you will read later, it is important to know the direction of the momentum when you are working with more than one object.

> **REMINDER**
> Inertia is the resistance of an object to changes in its motion.

Explore momentum.

CHECK YOUR READING How do an object's mass and velocity affect its momentum?

Calculating Momentum

Sample Problem

What is the momentum of a 1.5 kg ball moving at 2 m/s?

What do you know?	mass = 1.5 kg, velocity = 2 m/s
What do you want to find out?	momentum
Write the formula:	$p = mv$
Substitute into the formula:	$p = 1.5$ kg • 2 m/s
Calculate and simplify:	$p = 3$ kg • m/s
Check that your units agree:	Unit is kg • m/s.
	Unit of momentum is kg • m/s. Units agree.
Answer:	$p = 3$ kg • m/s

Practice the Math

1. A 3 kg ball is moving with a velocity of 1 m/s. What is the ball's momentum?
2. What is the momentum of a 0.5 kg ball moving 0.5 m/s?

Chapter 2: **Forces** 65

INVESTIGATE Momentum

What happens when objects collide?
PROCEDURE

1. Set up two parallel rulers separated by one centimeter. Place a line of five marbles, each touching the next, in the groove between the rulers.
2. Roll a marble down the groove so that it collides with the line of marbles, and observe the results.
3. Repeat your experiment by rolling two and then three marbles at the line of marbles. Observe the results.

WHAT DO YOU THINK?
- What did you observe when you rolled the marbles?
- Why do you think the marbles moved the way they did?

CHALLENGE Use your answers to write a hypothesis explaining your observations. Design your own marble experiment to test this hypothesis. Do your results support your hypothesis?

SKILL FOCUS
Observing

MATERIALS
- 2 rulers
- 8 marbles

TIME
20 minutes

Momentum can be transferred from one object to another.

If you have ever ridden in a bumper car, you have experienced collisions. A **collision** is a situation in which two objects in close contact exchange energy and momentum. As another car bumps into the back of yours, the force pushes your car forward. Some of the momentum of the car behind you is transferred to your car. At the same time, the car behind you slows because of the reaction force from your car. You gain momentum from the collision, and the other car loses momentum. The action and reaction forces in collisions are one way in which objects transfer momentum.

If two objects involved in a collision have very different masses, the one with less mass has a greater change in velocity. For example, consider what happens if you roll a tennis ball and a bowling ball toward each other so that they collide. Not only will the speed of the tennis ball change, but the direction of its motion will change as it bounces back. The bowling ball, however, will simply slow down. Even though the forces acting on the two balls are the same, the tennis ball will be accelerated more during the collision because it has less mass.

 How can a collision affect the momentum of an object?

Momentum is conserved.

During a collision between two objects, each object exerts a force on the other. The colliding objects make up a system—a collection of objects that affect one another. As the two objects collide, the velocity and the momentum of each object change. However, as no other forces are acting on the objects, the total momentum of both objects is unchanged by the collision. This is due to the conservation of momentum. The principle of **conservation of momentum** states that the total momentum of a system of objects does not change, as long as no outside forces are acting on that system.

> **READING TIP**
>
> A light blue-green arrow shows the momentum of an individual object.
>
>
> A dark blue-green arrow shows the total momentum.
>

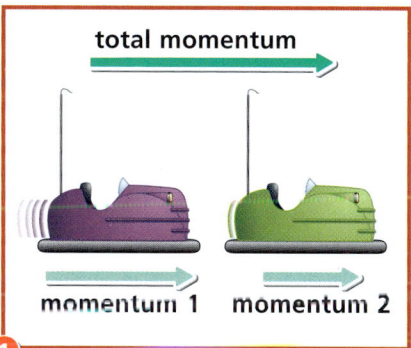
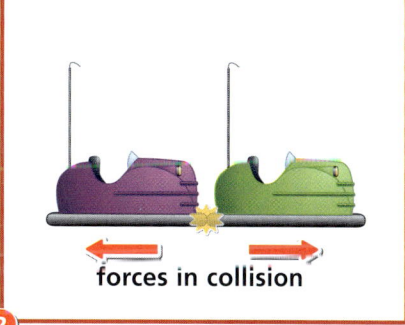
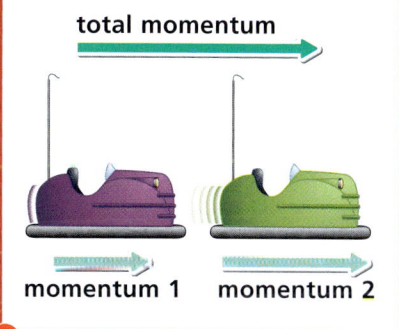

① Before the collision The momentum of the first car is greater than the momentum of the second car. Their combined momentum is the total momentum of the system.

② During the collision The forces on the two cars are equal and opposite, as described by Newton's third law. Momentum is transferred from one car to the other during the collision.

③ After the collision The momentum lost by one car was gained by the other car. The total momentum of the system remains the same as it was before the collision.

How much an object's momentum changes when a force is applied depends on the size of the force and how long that force is applied. Remember Newton's third law—during a collision, two objects are acted upon by equal and opposite forces for the same length of time. This means that the objects receive equal and opposite changes in momentum, and the total momentum does not change.

You can find the total momentum of a system of objects before a collision by combining the momenta of the objects. Because momentum is a vector, like force, the direction of motion is important. To find the total momentum of objects moving in the same direction, add the momenta of the objects. For two objects traveling in opposite directions, subtract one momentum from the other. Then use the principle of conservation of momentum and the formula for momentum to predict how the objects will move after they collide.

> **READING TIP**
>
> The plural of *momentum* is *momenta*.

 What is meant by "conservation of momentum"? What questions do you have about the application of this principle?

Two Types of Collisions

When bumper cars collide, they bounce off each other. Most of the force goes into changing the motion of the cars. The two bumper cars travel separately after the collision, just as they did before the collision. The combined momentum of both cars after the collision is the same as the combined momentum of both cars before the collision.

In this crash test, momentum is conserved, but some of the energy goes into bending the metal in these two cars.

When two cars collide during a crash test, momentum is also conserved during the collision. Unlike the bumper cars, however, which separate, the two cars shown in the photograph above stick and move together after the collision. Even in this case, the total momentum of both cars together is the same as the total momentum of both cars before the collision. Before the crash shown in the photograph, the yellow car had a certain momentum, and the blue car had no momentum. After the crash, the two cars move together with a combined momentum equal to the momentum the yellow car had before the collision.

 **CHECK YOUR READING** Compare collisions in which objects separate with collisions in which objects stick together.

Momentum and Newton's Third Law

Collisions are not the only events in which momentum is conserved. In fact, momentum is conserved whenever the only forces acting on objects are action/reaction force pairs. Conservation of momentum is really just another way of looking at Newton's third law.

When a firefighter turns on a hose, water comes out of the nozzle in one direction, and the hose moves back in the opposite direction. You can explain why by using Newton's third law. The water is forced out of the hose. A reaction force pushes the hose backward. You can also use the principle of conservation of momentum to explain why the hose moves backward:

- Before the firefighter turns on the water, the hose and the water are not in motion, so the hose/water system has no momentum.
- Once the water is turned on, the water has momentum in the forward direction.
- For the total momentum of the hose and the water to stay the same, the hose must have an equal amount of momentum in the opposite direction. The hose moves backward.

If the hose and the water are not acted on by any other forces, momentum is conserved. Water is pushed forward, and the hose is pushed backward. However, the action and reaction force pair acting on the hose and the water are not usually the only forces acting on the hose/water system, as shown in the photograph above. There the firefighters are holding the hose steady.

The force the firefighters apply is called an outside force because it is not being applied by the hose or the water. When there is an outside force on a system, momentum is not conserved. Because the firefighters hold the hose, the hose does not move backward, even though the water has a forward momentum.

Firefighters must apply a force to the water hose to prevent it from flying backward when the water comes out.

CHECK YOUR READING Under what condition is momentum not conserved? What part of the paragraph above tells you?

2.4 Review

KEY CONCEPTS

1. How does increasing the speed of an object change its momentum?
2. A car and a truck are traveling at the same speed. Which has more momentum? Why?
3. Give two examples showing the conservation of momentum. Give one example where momentum is not conserved.

CRITICAL THINKING

4. **Predict** A performing dolphin speeds through the water and hits a rubber ball originally at rest. Describe what happens to the velocities of the dolphin and the ball.
5. **Calculate** A 50 kg person is running at 2 m/s. What is the person's momentum?

CHALLENGE

6. **Apply** A moving train car bumps into another train car with the same mass. After the collision, the two cars are coupled and move off together. How does the final speed of the two train cars compare with the initial speed of the moving train cars before the collision?

Chapter Review

the BIG idea
Forces change the motion of objects in predictable ways.

CONTENT REVIEW
CLASSZONE.COM

KEY CONCEPTS SUMMARY

1 Forces change motion.

Newton's first law
Objects at rest remain at rest, and objects in motion remain in motion with the same velocity, unless acted upon by an unbalanced force.

unbalanced force → object at rest   object in motion ← unbalanced force

VOCABULARY
force p. 41
net force p. 43
Newton's first law p. 45
inertia p. 46

2 Force and mass determine acceleration.

Newton's second law
The acceleration of an object increases with increased force and decreases with increased mass, and is in the same direction as the force.

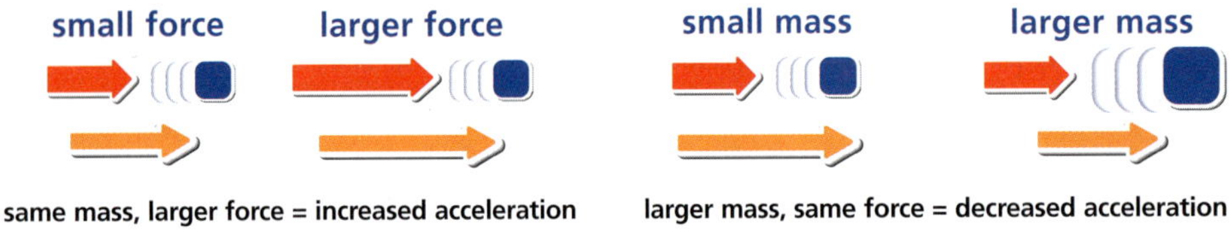

small force   larger force   small mass   larger mass

same mass, larger force = increased acceleration   larger mass, same force = decreased acceleration

VOCABULARY
Newton's second law p. 50
centripetal force p. 54

3 Forces act in pairs.

Newton's third law
When one object exerts a force on another object, the second object exerts an equal and opposite force on the first object.

reaction force   action force

VOCABULARY
Newton's third law p. 57

4 Forces transfer momentum.

- Momentum is a property of a moving object.
- Forces in collisions are equal and opposite.
- Momentum is conserved in collisions.

VOCABULARY
momentum p. 64
collision p. 66
conservation of momentum p. 67

Reviewing Vocabulary

Copy and complete the chart below. If the left column is blank, give the correct term. If the right column is blank, give an example from real life.

Term	Example from Real Life
1. acceleration	
2. centripetal force	
3.	The pull of a handle on a wagon
4. inertia	
5. mass	
6. net force	
7. Newton's first law	
8. Newton's second law	
9.	When you're walking, you push backward on the ground, and the ground pushes you forward with equal force.
10. momentum	

Reviewing Key Concepts

Multiple Choice *Choose the letter of the best answer.*

11. Newton's second law states that to increase acceleration, you
    - a. increase force
    - b. decrease force
    - c. increase mass
    - d. increase inertia

12. What units are used to measure force?
    - a. kilograms
    - b. meters
    - c. newtons
    - d. seconds

13. A wagon is pulled down a hill with a constant velocity. All the forces on the wagon are
    - a. balanced
    - b. unbalanced
    - c. increasing
    - d. decreasing

14. An action force and its reaction force are
    - a. equal in size and direction
    - b. equal in size and opposite in direction
    - c. different in size but in the same direction
    - d. different in size and in direction

15. John pulls a box with a force of 4 N, and Jason pulls the box from the opposite side with a force of 3 N. Ignore friction. Which of the following statements is true?
    - a. The box moves toward John.
    - b. The box moves toward Jason.
    - c. The box does not move.
    - d. There is not enough information to determine if the box moves.

16. A more massive marble collides with a less massive one that is not moving. The total momentum after the collision is equal to
    - a. zero
    - b. the original momentum of the more massive marble
    - c. the original momentum of the less massive marble
    - d. twice the original momentum of the more massive marble

Short Answer *Write a short answer to each question.*

17. List the following objects in order, from the object with the least inertia to the object with the most inertia: feather, large rock, pencil, book. Explain your reasoning.

18. During a race, you double your velocity. How does that change your momentum?

19. Explain how an object can have forces acting on it but not be accelerating.

20. A sea scallop moves by shooting jets of water out of its shell. Explain how this works.

Chapter 2: **Forces** 71

Thinking Critically

Use the information in the photographs below to answer the next four questions.

The photographs above show a toy called Newton's Cradle. In the first picture (1), ball 1 is lifted and is being held in place.

21. Are the forces on ball 1 balanced? How do you know?

22. Draw a diagram showing the forces acting on ball 2. Are these forces balanced?

In the second picture (2), ball 1 has been let go.

23. Ball 1 swung down, hit ball 2, and stopped. Use Newton's laws to explain why ball 1 stopped.

24. Use the principle of conservation of momentum to explain why ball 5 swung into the air.

Copy the chart below. Write what will happen to the object in each case.

Cause	Effect
25. Balanced forces act on an object.	
26. Unbalanced forces act on an object.	
27. No force acts on an object.	

28. **INFER** A baseball is three times more massive than a tennis ball. If the baseball and the tennis ball are accelerating equally, what can you determine about the net force on each?

Using Math Skills in Science

Complete the following calculations.

29. What force should Lori apply to a 5 kg box to give it an acceleration of 2 m/s^2?

30. If a 10 N force accelerates an object 5 m/s^2, how massive is the object?

31. Ravi applies a force of 5 N to a wagon with a mass of 10 kg. What is the wagon's acceleration?

32. Use the information in the photograph on the right to calculate the momentum of the shopping cart.

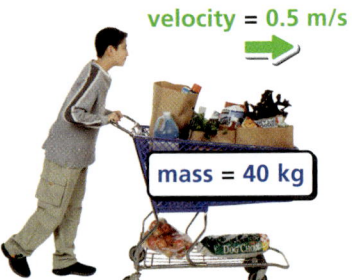

the BIG idea

33. **PREDICT** Look again at the tug of war pictured on pages 38–39. Describe what information you need to know to predict the outcome of the game. How would you use that information and Newton's laws to make your prediction?

34. **WRITE** Pick an activity you enjoy, such as running or riding a scooter, and describe how Newton's laws apply to that activity.

35. **SYNTHESIZE** Think of a question you have about Newton's laws that is still unanswered. What information do you need in order to answer the question? How might you find the information?

UNIT PROJECTS

If you need to do an experiment for your unit project, gather the materials. Be sure to allow enough time to observe results before the project is due.

Standardized Test Practice

For practice on your state test, go to . . .
TEST PRACTICE
CLASSZONE.COM

Analyzing Data

To test Newton's second law, Jodie accelerates blocks of ice across a smooth, flat surface. The table shows her results. (For this experiment, you can ignore the effects of friction.)

Accelerating Blocks of Ice

Mass (kg)	1.0	1.5	2.0	2.5	3.0	3.5	4.0
Acceleration (m/s^2)	4.0	2.7	2.0	1.6	1.3	1.1	1.0

Study the data table and then answer the questions that follow.

1. The data show that as mass becomes greater, acceleration
   a. increases
   b. decreases
   c. stays the same
   d. cannot be predicted

2. From the data, you can tell that Jodie was applying a force of
   a. 1 N
   b. 2 N
   c. 3 N
   d. 4 N

3. If Jodie applied less force to the ice blocks, the accelerations would be
   a. greater
   b. less
   c. the same
   d. inconsistent

4. If Jodie applied a force of 6 N to the 2 kg block of ice, the acceleration would be
   a. 2 m/s^2
   b. 4 m/s^2
   c. 3 m/s^2
   d. 5 m/s^2

5. The average mass of the ice blocks she pushed was
   a. 1.5 kg
   b. 2.5 kg
   c. 3 kg
   d. 4 kg

6. If Jodie used a 3.25 kg block in her experiment, the force would accelerate the block somewhere between
   a. 1.0 and 1.1 m/s^2
   b. 1.1 and 1.3 m/s^2
   c. 1.3 and 1.6 m/s^2
   d. 1.6 and 2.0 m/s^2

Extended Response

Answer the two questions in detail. Include some of the terms shown in the word box. Underline each term you use in your answer.

Newton's second law	velocity
mass	inertia
gravity	balanced forces
centripetal force	unbalanced forces

7. Tracy ties a ball to a string and starts to swing the ball around her head. What forces are acting on the ball? What happens if the string breaks?

8. Luis is trying to pull a wagon loaded with rocks. What can he do to increase the wagon's acceleration?

CHAPTER 3
Gravity, Friction, and Pressure

the BIG idea
Newton's laws apply to all forces.

Key Concepts

SECTION 1
Gravity is a force exerted by masses.
Learn about gravity, weight, and orbits.

SECTION 2
Friction is a force that opposes motion.
Learn about friction and air resistance.

SECTION 3
Pressure depends on force and area.
Learn about pressure and how forces act on objects in fluids.

SECTION 4
Fluids can exert a force on objects.
Learn how fluids apply forces to objects and how forces are transmitted through fluids.

Internet Preview
CLASSZONE.COM
Chapter 3 online resources: Content Review, Simulation, two Visualizations, three Resource Centers, Math Tutorial, Test Practice

EXPLORE the BIG idea

What forces are acting on this snowboarder? What forces are acting on the snow?

Let It Slide

Make a ramp using a board and some books. Slide an object down the ramp. Change the surface of the ramp using various materials such as sandpaper.

Observe and Think What effects did different surfaces have on the motion of the object? What may have caused these effects?

Under Pressure

Take two never-opened plastic soft-drink bottles. Open and reseal one of them. Squeeze each bottle.

Observe and Think How did the fluid inside each bottle react to your force? What may have caused the difference in the way the bottles felt?

Internet Activity: Gravity

Go to **ClassZone.com** to explore gravity. Learn more about the force of gravity and its effect on you, objects on Earth, and orbits of planets and satellites. Explore how gravity determines weight, and find out how your weight would be different on other planets.

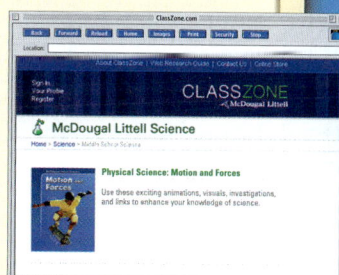

Observe and Think What would you weigh on Mars? What would you weigh on Neptune?

Pressure Code: MDL006

Chapter 3: **Gravity, Friction, and Pressure** 75

CHAPTER 3
Getting Ready to Learn

◀ CONCEPT REVIEW

- The motion of an object will not change unless acted upon by an unbalanced force.
- The acceleration of an object depends on force and mass.
- For every action force there is an equal and opposite reaction.

◀ VOCABULARY REVIEW

force p. 41
Newton's first law p. 45
Newton's second law p. 50
Newton's third law p. 57
density *See Glossary.*

CONTENT REVIEW
CLASSZONE.COM
Review concepts and vocabulary.

▶ TAKING NOTES

SUPPORTING MAIN IDEAS

Make a chart to show main ideas and the information that supports them. Copy the main ideas. Below each main idea, add supporting information, such as reasons, explanations, and examples.

VOCABULARY STRATEGY

Write each new vocabulary term in the center of a **four square** diagram. Write notes in the squares around each term. Include a definition, some characteristics, and some examples of the term. If possible, write some things that are not examples of the term.

See the Note-Taking Handbook on pages R45–R51.

SCIENCE NOTEBOOK

Force of gravity depends on mass and distance.
→ More mass = more gravitational force
→ More distance = less gravitational force

Definition	Characteristics
force of gravity acting on an object	• changes if gravity changes • measured in newtons

WEIGHT

Examples	Nonexamples
A 4 kg bowling ball weighs 39 N.	Mass in kg is not a weight.

KEY CONCEPT

Gravity is a force exerted by masses.

 BEFORE, you learned

- Every action force has an equal and opposite reaction force
- Newton's laws are used to describe the motions of objects
- Mass is the amount of matter an object contains

 NOW, you will learn

- How mass and distance affect gravity
- What keeps objects in orbit

VOCABULARY

gravity p. 77
weight p. 79
orbit p. 80

EXPLORE Downward Acceleration

How do the accelerations of two falling objects compare?

PROCEDURE

1. Make a prediction: Which ball will fall faster?
2. Drop both balls from the same height at the same time.
3. Observe the balls as they hit the ground.

WHAT DO YOU THINK?
- Were the results what you had expected?
- How did the times it took the two balls to hit the ground compare?

MATERIALS
- golf ball
- Ping-Pong ball

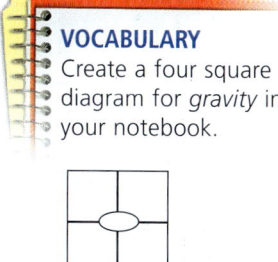

VOCABULARY
Create a four square diagram for *gravity* in your notebook.

Masses attract each other.

When you drop any object—such as a pen, a book, or a football—it falls to the ground. As the object falls, it moves faster and faster. The fact that the object accelerates means there must be a force acting on it. The downward pull on the object is due to gravity. **Gravity** is the force that objects exert on each other because of their masses. You are familiar with the force of gravity between Earth and objects on Earth.

Gravity is present not only between objects and Earth, however. Gravity is considered a universal force because it acts between any two masses anywhere in the universe. For example, there is a gravitational pull between the Sun and the Moon. Even small masses attract each other. The force of gravity between dust and gas particles in space helped form the solar system.

 Why is gravity considered a universal force?

Chapter 3: **Gravity, Friction, and Pressure** 77

SUPPORTING MAIN IDEAS
Support the main ideas about the force of gravity with details and examples.

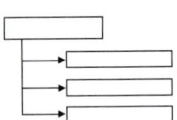

The Force of Gravity

If there is a force between all masses, why are you not pulled toward your desk by the desk's gravity when you walk away from it? Remember that the net force on you determines how your motion changes. The force of gravity between you and the desk is extremely small compared with other forces constantly acting on you, such as friction, the force from your muscles, Earth's gravity, and the gravitational pull from many other objects. The strength of the gravitational force between two objects depends on two factors, mass and distance.

The Mass of the Objects The more mass two objects have, the greater the force of gravity the masses exert on each other. If one of the masses is doubled, the force of gravity between the objects is doubled.

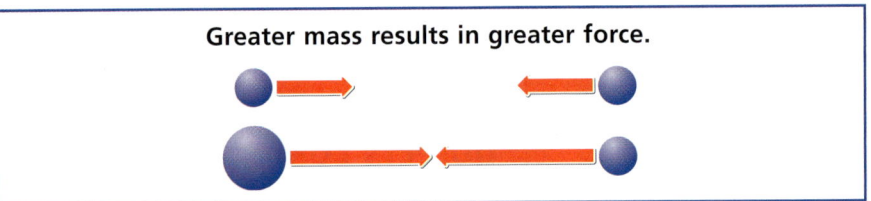

Greater mass results in greater force.

The Distance Between the Objects As distance between the objects increases, the force of gravity decreases. If the distance is doubled, the force of gravity is one-fourth as strong as before.

Greater distance results in smaller force.

 **CHECK YOUR READING** How do mass and distance affect the force of gravity?

Gravity on Earth

The force of gravity acts on both masses equally, even though the effects on both masses may be very different. Earth's gravity exerts a downward pull on a dropped coin. Remember that every action force has an equal and opposite reaction force. The coin exerts an equal upward force on Earth. Because the coin has an extremely small mass compared with Earth, the coin can be easily accelerated. Earth's acceleration due to the force of the coin is far too small to notice because of Earth's large mass.

The acceleration due to Earth's gravity is called g and is equal to 9.8 m/s^2 at Earth's surface. You can calculate the force of gravity on an object using the object's mass and this acceleration. The formula that expresses Newton's second law is $F = ma$. If you use g as the acceleration, the formula for calculating the force due to gravity on a mass close to Earth's surface becomes $F = mg$.

Acceleration Due to Gravity

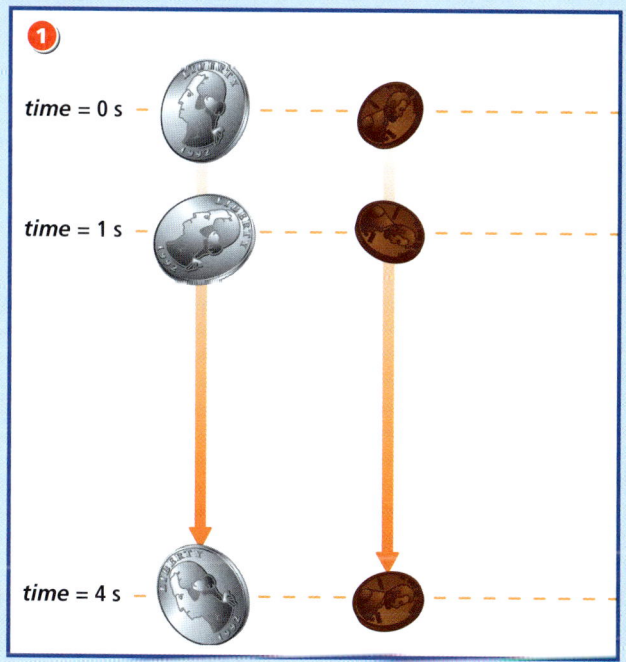
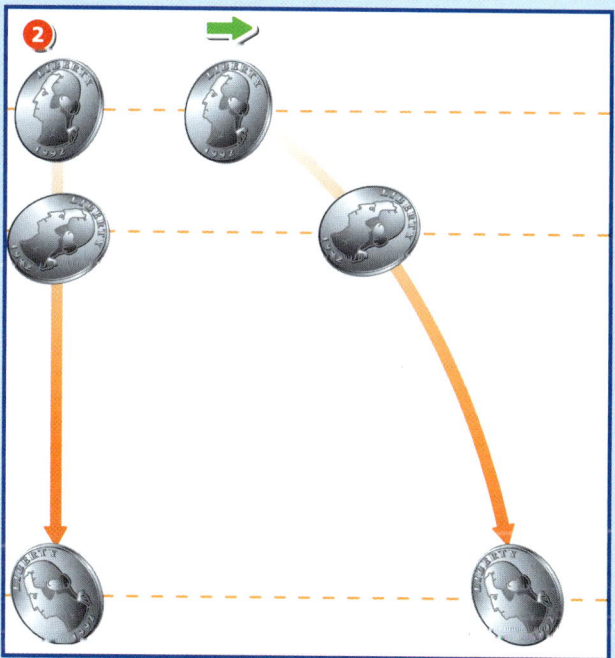

If any two objects are dropped from the same height in a vacuum, they fall at the same rate even if they have different masses.

If an object has a velocity in the horizontal direction when it falls, the horizontal velocity does not change its downward acceleration.

In a vacuum—that is, where there is no air—all falling objects have the same acceleration.

① The quarter falls at the same rate as the penny when they are dropped together. Because the quarter has more mass, gravity exerts more force on it. But greater mass also means more inertia, so the greater force does not produce a larger acceleration. Objects with different masses fall with the same acceleration.

② A coin that is dropped falls at the same rate as one that is thrown forward. Horizontal velocity does not affect acceleration due to gravity. Because gravity is directed downward, it changes only the downward velocity of the coin, not its forward velocity.

Explore how objects fall at the same rate in a vacuum.

CHECK YOUR READING Compare the times it takes two objects with different masses to fall from the same height.

Weight and Mass

While weight and mass are related, they are not the same properties. Mass is a measure of how much matter an object contains. **Weight** is the force of gravity on an object. Mass is a property that an object has no matter where it is located. Weight, on the other hand, depends on the force of gravity acting on that object.

Chapter 3: **Gravity, Friction, and Pressure** 79

On Earth
Mass = 50 kg
Weight = 490 N

On the Moon
Mass = 50 kg
Weight = 82 N

When you use a balance, you are measuring the mass of an object. A person with a mass of 50 kilograms will balance another mass of 50 kilograms whether she is on Earth or on the Moon. Traveling to the Moon would not change how much matter a person is made of. When you use a spring scale, such as a bathroom scale, to measure the weight of an object, however, you are measuring how hard gravity is pulling on an object. The Moon is less massive than Earth, and its gravitational pull is one-sixth that of Earth's. A spring scale would show that a person who has a weight of 490 newtons (110 lb) on Earth would have a weight of 82 newtons (18 lb) on the Moon.

Gravity keeps objects in orbit.

Sir Isaac Newton hypothesized that the force that pulls objects to the ground—gravity—also pulls the Moon in its orbit around Earth. An **orbit** is the elliptical path one body, such as the Moon, follows around another body, such as Earth, due to the influence of gravity. The centripetal force keeping one object in orbit around another object is due to the gravitational pull between the two objects. In the case of the Moon's orbit, the centripetal force is the gravitational pull between the Moon and Earth. Similarly, Earth is pulled around the Sun by the gravitational force between Earth and the Sun.

You can think of an object orbiting Earth as an object that is falling around Earth rather than falling to the ground. Consider what happens to the ball in the illustration on page 81. A dropped ball will fall about five meters during the first second it falls. Throwing the ball straight ahead will not change that falling time. What happens as you throw faster and faster?

Earth is curved. This fact is noticeable only over very long distances. For every 8000 meters you travel, Earth curves downward about 5 meters. If you could throw a ball at 8000 meters per second, it would fall to Earth in such a way that its path would curve the same amount that Earth curves. Since the ball would fall along the curve of Earth, the ball would never actually land on the ground. The ball would be in orbit.

> **READING TIP**
> An ellipse is shaped as shown below. A circle is a special type of ellipse.
>
>

Orbits

An object in orbit, like an object falling to the ground, is pulled toward Earth's center. If the object moves far enough forward as it falls, it orbits around Earth instead of hitting the ground.

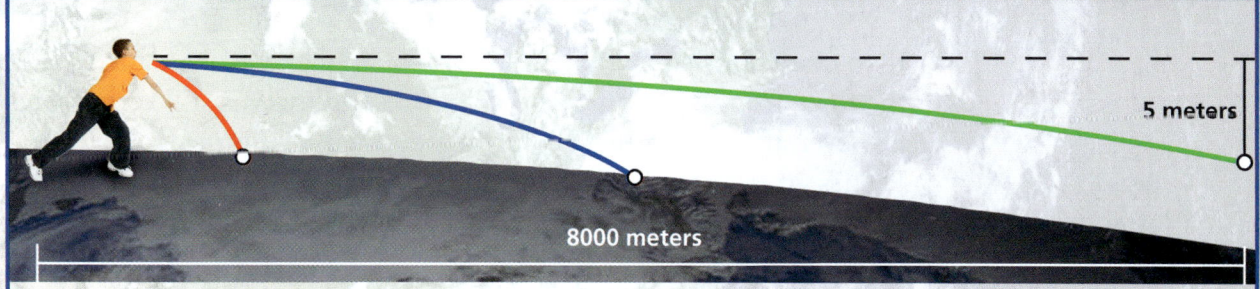

If a ball is thrown straight ahead from a 5-meter height, it will drop 5 meters in the first second it falls. At low speeds, the ball will hit the ground after 1 second.

If the ball is going fast enough, the curvature of Earth becomes important. While the ball still drops 5 meters in the first second, it must fall farther than 5 meters to hit the ground.

If the ball is going fast enough to travel 8000 meters forward as it drops downward 5 meters, it follows the curvature of Earth. The ball will fall around Earth, not into it.

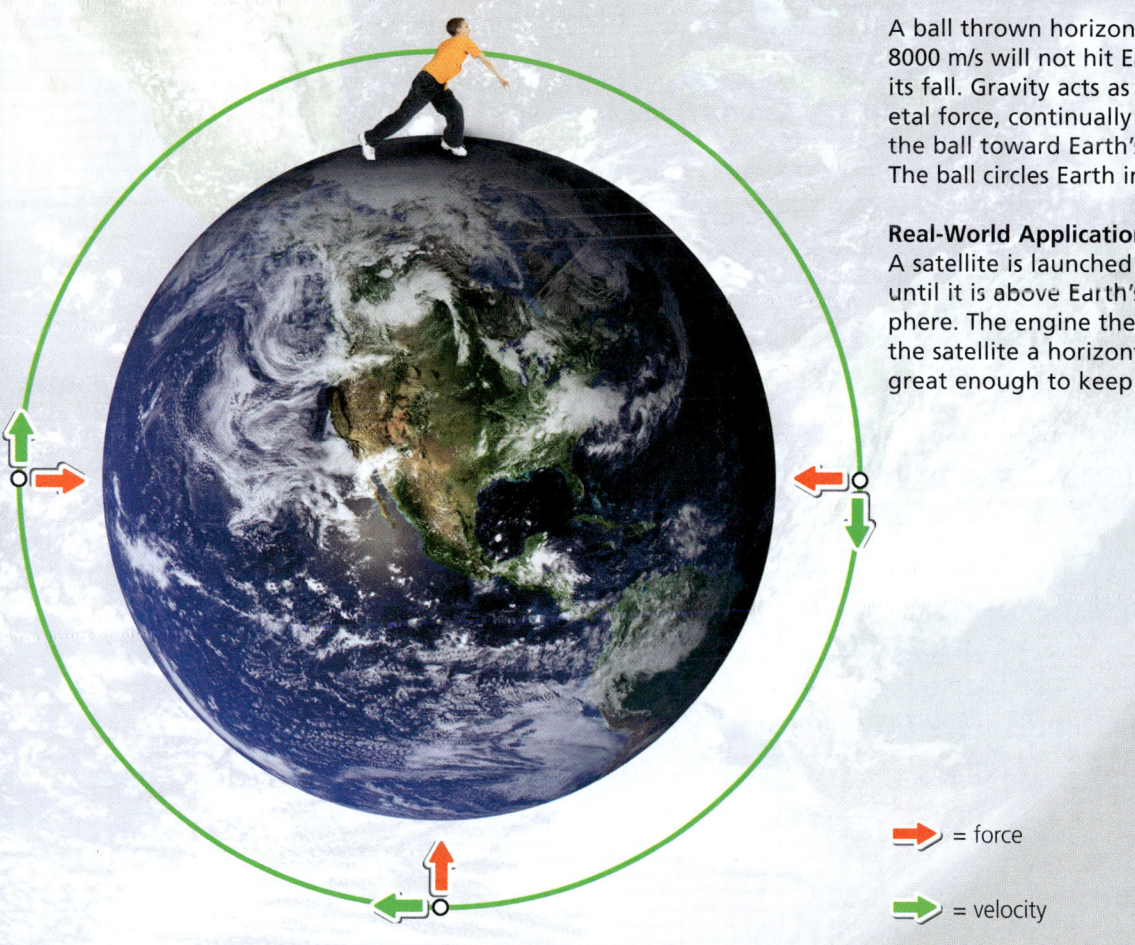

A ball thrown horizontally at 8000 m/s will not hit Earth during its fall. Gravity acts as a centripetal force, continually pulling the ball toward Earth's center. The ball circles Earth in an orbit.

Real-World Application
A satellite is launched upward until it is above Earth's atmosphere. The engine then gives the satellite a horizontal speed great enough to keep it in orbit.

➡ = force

➡ = velocity

READING VISUALS Compare the direction of the velocity with the direction of the force for an object in a circular orbit.

Chapter 3: **Gravity, Friction, and Pressure** 81

Spacecraft in Orbit

The minimum speed needed to send an object into orbit is approximately 8000 meters per second. At this speed, the path of a falling object matches the curve of Earth's surface. If you launch a spacecraft or a satellite at a slower speed, it will eventually fall to the ground.

A spacecraft launched at a greater speed can reach a higher orbit than one launched at a lower speed. The higher the orbit, the weaker the force from Earth's gravity. The force of gravity is still very strong, however. If a craft is in a low orbit—about 300 kilometers (190 mi)—Earth's gravitational pull is about 91 percent of what it is at Earth's surface. The extra distance makes a difference in the force of only about 9 percent.

If a spacecraft is launched with a speed of 11,000 meters per second or more, it is moving too fast to go into an orbit. Instead, the spacecraft will ultimately escape the pull of Earth's gravity altogether. The speed that a spacecraft needs to escape the gravitational pull of an object such as a planet or a star is called the escape velocity. A spacecraft that escapes Earth's gravity will go into orbit around the Sun unless it is also going fast enough to escape the Sun's gravity.

 Did any facts in the text above surprise you? If so, which surprised you and why?

INVESTIGATE Gravity

How does gravity affect falling objects?

PROCEDURE

1. Carefully use the pencil to punch a hole that is the width of the pencil in the side of the cup, about one-third of the way up from the bottom.

2. Holding your finger over the hole, fill the cup three-fourths full of water.

3. Hold the cup above the dishpan. Predict what will happen if you remove your finger from the hole. Remove your finger and observe what happens.

4. With your finger over the hole, refill the cup to the same level as in step 2. Predict how the water will move if you hold the cup 50 cm above the dishpan and drop the cup and its contents straight down into the pan.

5. Drop the cup and observe what happens to the water while the cup is falling.

WHAT DO YOU THINK?
- What happened to the water in step 3? in step 5?
- How did gravity affect the water when you dropped the cup?

CHALLENGE Why did the water behave differently the second time?

SKILL FOCUS
Predicting

MATERIALS
- pencil
- paper cup
- water
- dishpan

TIME
15 minutes

People in Orbit

When an elevator you are riding in accelerates downward, you may feel lighter for a short time. If you were standing on a scale during the downward acceleration, the scale would show that you weighed less than usual. Your mass would not have changed, nor would the pull of gravity. What would cause the apparent weight loss?

When the elevator is still, the entire force of your weight presses against the scale. When the elevator accelerates downward, you are not pressing as hard on the scale, because the scale is also moving downward. Since the scale measures how hard you are pushing on it, you appear to weigh less. If you and the scale were in free fall—a fall due entirely to gravity—the scale would fall as fast as you did. You would not press against the scale at all, so you would appear to be weightless.

Astronaut Mae Jemison is shown here working in a microgravity environment.

A spacecraft in orbit is in free fall. Gravity is acting on the astronauts and on the ship—without gravity, there could be no orbit. However, the ship and the astronauts are falling around Earth at the same rate. While astronauts are in orbit, their weight does not press against the floor of the spacecraft. The result is an environment, called a microgravity environment, in which objects behave as if there were no gravity. People and objects simply float as if they were weightless.

 Why do astronauts float when they are in orbit?

 Review

KEY CONCEPTS
1. What effect would increasing the mass of two objects have on the gravitational attraction between them?
2. What effect would decreasing the distance between objects have on their gravitational attraction to each other?
3. How does gravity keep the Moon in orbit around Earth?

CRITICAL THINKING
4. **Compare** How does the size of the force exerted by Earth's gravity on a car compare with the size of the force the car exerts on Earth?
5. **Apply** What would be the effect on the mass and the weight of an object if the object were taken to a planet with twice the gravity of Earth?

CHALLENGE
6. **Synthesize** Precision measurements of the acceleration due to gravity show that the acceleration is slightly different in different locations on Earth. Explain why the force of gravity is not exactly the same everywhere on Earth's surface. **Hint:** Think about the details of Earth's surface.

Chapter 3: **Gravity, Friction, and Pressure** 83

Extreme Science

GRAVITY IN THE EXTREME

Bending Light

You know that gravity can pull objects toward each other, but did you know that gravity can also affect light? Very extreme sources of gravity cause the normally straight path of a light beam to bend.

Going in Circles
Although Earth is massive, the effects of its gravity on light are not noticeable. However, scientists can model what a familiar scene might look like with an extreme source of gravity nearby. The image to the left shows how the light from the Seattle Space Needle could be bent almost into circles if an extremely small yet extremely massive object, such as a black hole, were in front of it.

Seeing Behind Galaxies
How do we know that gravity can bend light? Astronomers, who study space, have seen the phenomenon in action. If a very bright but distant object is behind a very massive one, such as a large galaxy, the mass of the galaxy bends the light coming from the distant object. This effect, called gravitational lensing, can produce multiple images of the bright object along a ring around the massive galaxy. Astronomers have observed gravitational lensing in their images.

Facts About Bending Light
- Gravitational lensing was predicted by Albert Einstein in the early 1900s, but the first example was not observed until 1979.
- The masses of distant galaxies can be found by observing their effect on light.

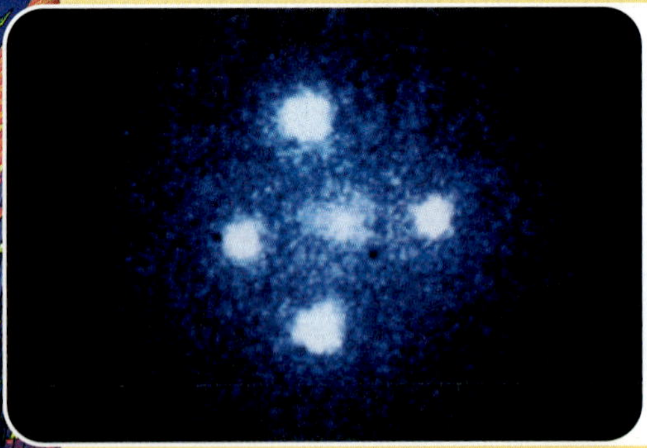

Seeing Quadruple
This gravitational lens is called the Einstein Cross. The four bright objects that ring the central galaxy are all images of the same very bright yet very distant object that is located 20 times farther away than the central galaxy.

EXPLORE

1. **INFER** Why are you unable to notice the gravitational bending of light by an object such as a large rock?
2. **CHALLENGE** Look at the photographs in the Resource Center. Find the multiple images of the distant objects and the more massive object bending the light from them.

RESOURCE CENTER CLASSZONE.COM   Find out more information about gravitational lenses.

KEY CONCEPT

Friction is a force that opposes motion.

 BEFORE, you learned
- Gravity is the attractive force masses exert on each other
- Gravity increases with greater mass and decreases with greater distance
- Gravity is the centripetal force keeping objects in orbit

 NOW, you will learn
- How friction affects motion
- About factors that affect friction
- About air resistance

VOCABULARY

friction p. 85
fluid p. 88
air resistance p. 89

THINK ABOUT

What forces help you to walk?

As a person walks, she exerts a backward force on the ground. A reaction force moves her forward. But some surfaces are harder to walk on than others. Ice, for example, is harder to walk on than a dry surface because ice is slippery. How can different surfaces affect your ability to walk?

Friction occurs when surfaces slide against each other.

Have you ever pushed a heavy box across the floor? You probably noticed that it is easier to push the box over some surfaces than over others. You must apply a certain amount of force to the box to keep it moving. The force that acts against your pushing force is called friction. **Friction** is a force that resists the motion between two surfaces in contact.

When you try to slide two surfaces across each other, the force of friction resists the sliding motion. If there were no friction, the box would move as soon as you applied any force to it. Although friction can make some tasks more difficult, most activities, including walking, would be impossible without it. Friction between your feet and the ground is what provides the action and reaction forces that enable you to walk.

SUPPORTING MAIN IDEAS
Take notes about friction, including details and examples.

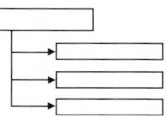

Chapter 3: **Gravity, Friction, and Pressure** 85

Learn more about friction, forces, and surfaces.

Forces and Surfaces

If you look down from a great height, such as from the window of an airplane, a flat field appears to be smooth. If you were to walk in the field, however, you would see that the ground has many bumps and holes. In the same way, a flat surface such as a piece of plastic may look and feel smooth. However, if you look at the plastic through a strong microscope, you see that it has tiny bumps and ridges. Friction depends on how these bumps and ridges on one surface interact with and stick to the bumps and ridges on other surfaces. There are several factors that determine the friction between two surfaces.

Types of Surfaces Friction between two surfaces depends on the materials that make up the surfaces. Different combinations of surfaces produce different frictional forces. A rubber hockey puck sliding across ice has a smaller frictional force on it than the same puck sliding across a wooden floor. The friction between rubber and ice is less than the friction between rubber and wood.

> **REMINDER**
> Remember that balanced forces on an object do not change the object's motion.

Motion of the Surfaces You need a larger force to start something moving than you do to keep something moving. If you have ever tried to push a heavy chair, you may have noticed that you had to push harder and harder until the chair suddenly accelerated forward.

As you apply a force to push a chair or any other object that is not moving, the frictional force keeping it from sliding increases so the forces stay balanced. However, the frictional force has a limit to how

Friction and Motion

Before Object Moves

When an object is standing still, there is a maximum force needed to overcome friction and start it moving. Any force less than this will be exactly balanced by the force of friction, and the object will not move.

While Object Moves

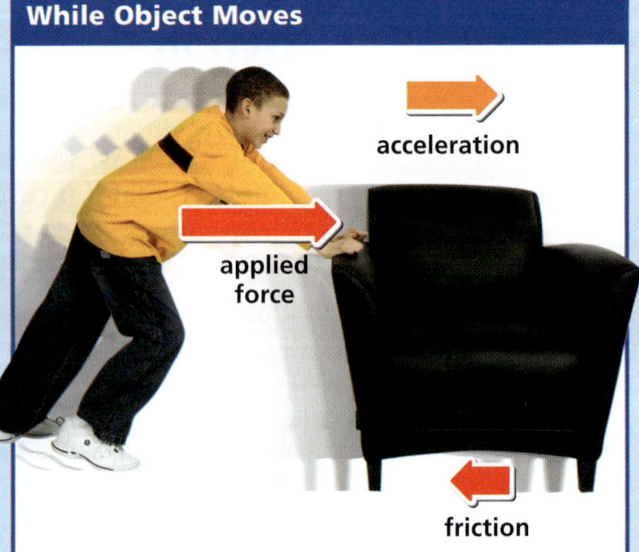

Once the object is moving, the frictional force remains constant. This constant force is less than the maximum force needed to start the object moving.

large it can be. When your force is greater than this limit, the forces on the chair are no longer balanced, and the chair moves. The frictional force remains at a new lower level once the chair is moving.

Force Pressing the Surfaces Together The harder two surfaces are pushed together, the more difficult it is for the surfaces to slide over each other. When an object is placed on a surface, the weight of the object presses on that surface. The surface exerts an equal and opposite reaction force on the object. This reaction force is one of the factors that determines how much friction there is.

If you push a chair across the floor, there will be a certain amount of friction between the chair and the floor. Increasing the weight of the chair increases the force pushing the surfaces together. The force of friction between the chair and the floor is greater when a person is sitting in it than when the chair was empty.

Friction depends on the total force pressing the surfaces together, not on how much area this force acts over. Consider a rectangular cardboard box. It can rest with its smaller or larger side on the floor. The box will have the same force from friction regardless of which side sits on the floor. The larger side has more area in contact with the floor than the smaller side, but the weight of the box is more spread out on the larger side.

 What factors influence frictional force? Give two examples.

Friction and Weight

Less Weight

The force of friction depends on the total force pushing the surfaces together. Here the weight of the chair is the force pressing the surfaces together.

More Weight

The weight of the chair increases when someone sits in it. The force of friction is now greater than when the chair was empty.

Chapter 3: **Gravity, Friction, and Pressure** 87

Friction produces sparks between a match head and a rough surface. The heat from friction eventually lights the match.

Friction and Heat

Friction between surfaces produces heat. You feel heat produced by friction when you rub your hands together. As you rub, friction causes the individual molecules on the surface of your hands to move faster. As the individual molecules in an object move faster, the temperature of the object increases. The increased speed of the molecules on the surface of your hands produces the warmth that you feel.

The heat produced by friction can be intense. The friction that results from striking a match against a rough surface produces enough heat to ignite the flammable substance on the head of the match. In some machines, such as a car engine, too much heat from friction can cause serious damage. Substances such as oil are often used to reduce friction between moving parts in machines. Without motor oil, a car's engine parts would overheat and stop working.

Motion through fluids produces friction.

As you have seen, two objects falling in a vacuum fall with the same acceleration. Objects falling through air, however, have different accelerations. This difference occurs because air is a fluid. A **fluid** is a substance that can flow easily. Gases and liquids are fluids.

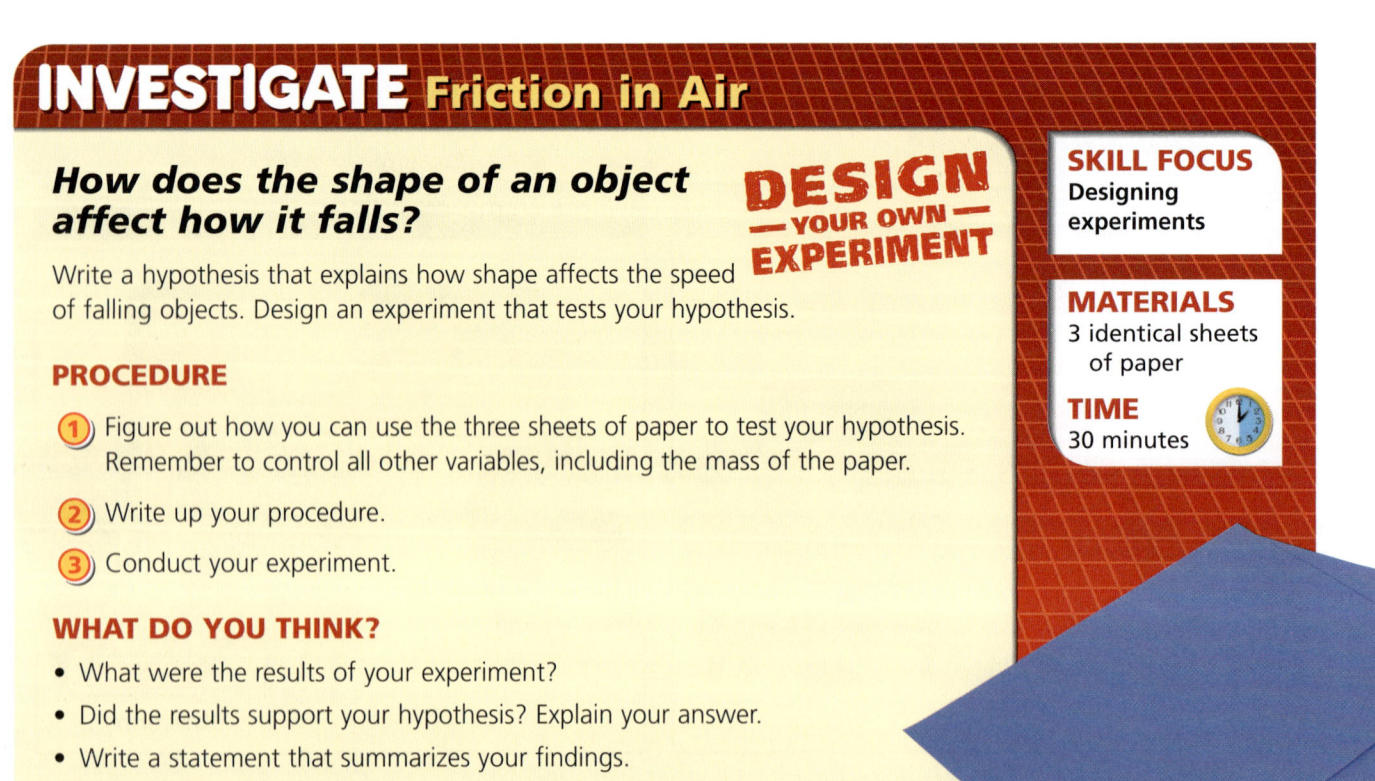

INVESTIGATE Friction in Air

How does the shape of an object affect how it falls?

DESIGN YOUR OWN EXPERIMENT

Write a hypothesis that explains how shape affects the speed of falling objects. Design an experiment that tests your hypothesis.

PROCEDURE

1. Figure out how you can use the three sheets of paper to test your hypothesis. Remember to control all other variables, including the mass of the paper.
2. Write up your procedure.
3. Conduct your experiment.

WHAT DO YOU THINK?
- What were the results of your experiment?
- Did the results support your hypothesis? Explain your answer.
- Write a statement that summarizes your findings.

CHALLENGE What other variable might affect falling time? How could you test it?

SKILL FOCUS
Designing experiments

MATERIALS
3 identical sheets of paper

TIME
30 minutes

When an object moves through a fluid, it pushes the molecules of the fluid out of the way. At the same time, the molecules of the fluid exert an equal and opposite force on the object that slows it down. This force resisting motion through a fluid is a type of friction that is often called drag. Friction in fluids depends on the shape of the moving object. Objects can be designed either to increase or reduce the friction caused by a fluid. Airplane designs, for example, improve as engineers find ways to reduce drag.

The friction due to air is often called **air resistance.** Air resistance differs from the friction between solid surfaces. Air resistance depends on surface area and the speed of an object in the following ways:

- An object with a larger surface area comes into contact with more molecules as it moves than an object with a smaller surface area. This increases the air resistance.
- The faster an object moves through air, the more molecules it comes into contact with in a given amount of time. As the speed of the object increases, air resistance increases.

When a skydiver jumps out of a plane, gravity causes the skydiver to accelerate toward the ground. As the skydiver falls, his body pushes against the air. The air pushes back—with the force of air resistance. As the skydiver's speed increases, his air resistance increases. Eventually, air resistance balances gravity, and the skydiver reaches terminal velocity, which is the final, maximum velocity of a falling object. When the skydiver opens his parachute, air resistance increases still further, and he reaches a new, slower terminal velocity that enables him to land safely.

When the force of air resistance equals the force from gravity, a skydiver falls at a constant speed.

 How do speed and surface area affect air resistance?

3.2 Review

KEY CONCEPTS

1. How does friction affect forward motion? Give an example.
2. Describe two ways to change the frictional force between two solid surfaces.
3. How does air resistance affect the velocity of a falling object?

CRITICAL THINKING

4. **Infer** What two sources of friction do you have to overcome when you are walking?
5. **Synthesize** If you push a chair across the floor at a constant velocity, how does the force of friction compare with the force you exert? Explain.

CHALLENGE

6. **Synthesize** If you push a book against a wall hard enough, it will not slide down even though gravity is pulling it. Use what you know about friction and Newton's laws of motion to explain why the book does not fall.

Chapter 3: **Gravity, Friction, and Pressure** 89

MATH in SCIENCE

SKILL: CREATING A LINE GRAPH

Smoke Jumpers in Action

Scientists often use graphs as a way to present data. Sometimes information is easier to understand when it is presented in graphic form.

Smoke jumpers parachute into burning forests in order to contain the flames.

Example

Smoke jumpers are firefighters who parachute down into a forest that is on fire. Suppose you measured how the velocity of a smoke jumper changed as he was free-falling, and recorded the following data:

Time (s)	0	2	4	6	8	10	12	14	16	18
Velocity (m/s)	0	18	29	33	35	36	36	36	36	36

Follow these steps to make a line graph of the data in the table.

(1) For both variables, decide the scale that each box on your graph will represent and what range you will show for each variable. For the above time data you might choose a range of 0 to 18 s, with each interval representing 2 s. For velocity, a range of 0 to 40 m/s with intervals of 5 m/s each is reasonable.

(2) Determine the dependent and independent variables. In this example, the velocity depends on the falling time, so velocity is the dependent variable.

(3) Plot the independent variable along the horizontal axis, or *x*-axis. Plot the dependent variable along the vertical axis, or *y*-axis. Connect the points with a smooth line.

Use the data below to answer the following questions.

Suppose a smoke jumper varied the mass of his equipment over 5 jumps, and you measured his different terminal velocities as follows:

Extra Mass (kg)	0	5	10	15	20
Terminal Velocity (m/s)	36	37	38	39	40

1. Identify the independent and dependent variables.

2. Choose the scales and intervals you would use to graph the data. **Hint:** Your velocity range does not have to start at 0 m/s.

3. Plot your graph.

CHALLENGE How do different scales give different impressions of the data? Try comparing several different scales for the same data.

KEY CONCEPT

Pressure depends on force and area.

 BEFORE, you learned

- Frictional forces oppose motion when surfaces resist sliding
- Frictional force depends on the surface types and the total force pushing them together
- Air resistance is a type of friction on objects moving through air

 NOW, you will learn

- How pressure is determined
- How forces act on objects in fluids
- How pressure changes in fluids

VOCABULARY

pressure p. 91
pascal p. 92

EXPLORE Pressure

How does surface area affect pressure?

PROCEDURE

1. Place the pencil flat on the Styrofoam board. Balance the book on top of the pencil. After 5 seconds, remove the book and the pencil. Observe the Styrofoam.

2. Balance the book on top of the pencil in an upright position as shown. After 5 seconds, remove the book and the pencil. Observe the Styrofoam.

WHAT DO YOU THINK?

- How did the effect on the Styrofoam change from step 1 to step 2?
- What do you think accounts for any differences you noted?

MATERIALS
- sharpened pencil
- Styrofoam board
- book

Pressure describes how a force is spread over an area.

VOCABULARY
Create a four square diagram for *pressure* in your notebook.

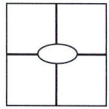

Pressure is a measure of how much force is acting on a certain area. In other words, pressure describes how concentrated a force is. When a cat lies down on your lap, all the force of the cat's weight is spread out over a large area of your lap. If the cat stands up, however, all the force from the cat's weight is concentrated into its paws. The pressure the cat exerts on you increases when the cat stands up in your lap.

While the increased pressure may make you feel as if there is more force on you, the force is actually the same. The cat's weight is simply pressing on a smaller area. How you feel a force when it is pressing on you depends on both the force and the area over which it is applied.

Chapter 3: **Gravity, Friction, and Pressure** 91

One way to increase pressure is to increase force. If you press a wall with your finger, the harder you press, the more pressure you put on the wall. But you can also increase the pressure by decreasing the area. When you push a thumbtack into a wall, you apply a force to the thumbtack. The small area of the sharp point of the thumbtack produces a much larger pressure on the wall than the area of your finger does. The greater pressure from the thumbtack can pierce the wall, while the pressure from your finger alone cannot.

The following formula shows exactly how pressure depends on force and area:

$$\text{Pressure} = \frac{\text{Force}}{\text{Area}} \qquad P = \frac{F}{A}$$

In this formula, P is the pressure, F is the force in newtons, and A is the area over which the force is exerted, measured in square meters (m^2). The unit for pressure is the **pascal** (Pa). One pascal is the pressure exerted by one newton (1 N) of force on an area of one square meter (1 m^2). That is, one pascal is equivalent to one N/m^2.

Sometimes knowing pressure is more useful than knowing force. For example, many surfaces will break or crack if the pressure on them is too great. A person with snowshoes can walk on top of snow, while a person in hiking boots will sink into the snow.

READING TIP
Notice that when a unit, such as pascal or newton, is named for a person, the unit is not capitalized but its abbreviation is.

COMPARE How does the pressure from her snowshoes compare to the pressure from her boots?

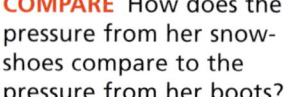

Calculating Pressure

▶ **Sample Problem**

A winter hiker weighing 500 N is wearing snowshoes that cover an area of 0.2 m^2. What pressure does the hiker exert on the snow?

What do you know? Area = 0.2 m^2, Force = 500 N

What do you want to find out? Pressure

Write the formula: $P = \dfrac{F}{A}$

Substitute into the formula: $P = \dfrac{500 \text{ N}}{0.2 \text{ m}^2}$

Calculate and simplify: $P = 2500 \, \dfrac{N}{m^2} = 2500 \text{ N/m}^2$

Check that your units agree: Unit is N/m^2.
Unit of pressure is Pa, which is also N/m^2. Units agree.

Answer: $P = 2500$ Pa

▶ **Practice the Math**

1. If a winter hiker weighing 500 N is wearing boots that have an area of 0.075 m^2, how much pressure is exerted on the snow?
2. A pressure of 2000 Pa is exerted on a surface with an area of 20 m^2. What is the total force exerted on the surface?

Pressure acts in all directions in fluids.

Fluids are made of loosely connected particles that are too small to see. These particles are in constant, rapid motion. The motion is random, which means particles are equally likely to move in any direction. Particles collide with—or crash into—one another and into the walls of a container holding the fluid. The particles also collide with any objects in the fluid.

Explore how a fluid produces pressure.

As particles collide with an object in the fluid, they apply a constant force to the surfaces of the object. This force produces a pressure against the surfaces that the particles come in contact with. A fluid contains many particles, each moving in a different direction, and the force from each particle can be exerted in any direction. Therefore, the pressure exerted by the fluid acts on an object from all directions.

The diver in the picture below experiences a constant pressure from the particles—or molecules—in the water. Water molecules are constantly hitting her body from all directions. The collisions on all parts of her body produce a net force on the surface of her body.

CHECK YOUR READING How does understanding particle motion help you understand fluid pressure?

Pressure in Fluids

Randomly moving water molecules collide with a diver. The net force from the many collisions produces the pressure on the diver.

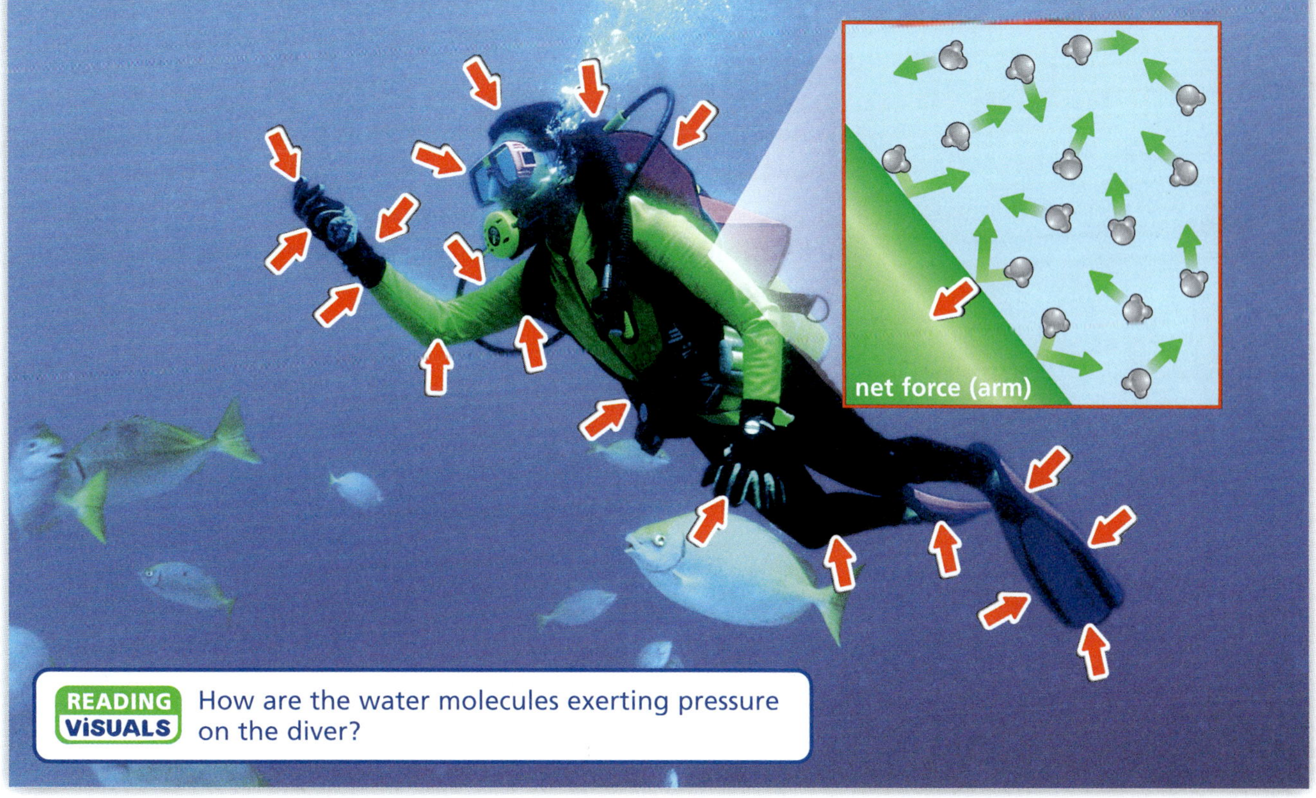

net force (arm)

READING VISUALS How are the water molecules exerting pressure on the diver?

Chapter 3: **Gravity, Friction, and Pressure** 93

Pressure in fluids depends on depth.

The pressure that a fluid exerts depends on the density and the depth of the fluid. Imagine that you have a tall cylinder sitting on the palm of your hand. As you fill the cylinder with water, the force of the water's weight exerts more and more pressure on your hand. The force of the water's weight increases as you put in more water.

Suppose you had two identical cylinders of water sitting on your hand. The cylinders would push with twice the weight of a single cylinder, but the force would be spread over twice the area. Therefore, the pressure would still be the same. The pressure does not depend on the total volume of the fluid, only on the depth and density.

Pressure in Air

Although you do not notice the weight of air, air exerts pressure on you at all times. At sea level, air exerts a pressure on you equal to about 100,000 pascals. This pressure is called atmospheric pressure and is referred to as one atmosphere. At this pressure, every square centimeter of your body experiences a force of ten newtons (2.2 lb). You do not notice it pushing your body inward, however, because the materials in your body provide an equal outward pressure that balances the air pressure.

Changing Elevation Air has weight. The more air there is above you, the greater the weight of that air. As you climb a mountain, the column of air above you is shorter and weighs less, so the pressure of air on you at higher elevations is less than one atmosphere.

Changing Density The air at the top of a column presses down on the air below it. The farther down the column, the more weight there is above to press downward. Air at lower elevations is more compressed, and therefore denser, than air at higher elevations.

Effects on Pressure Pressure is exerted by individual molecules colliding with an object. In denser air, there are more molecules—and therefore more collisions. An increase in the number of collisions results in an increase in the force, and therefore pressure, exerted by the air.

As you travel up a mountain, the air pressure on you decreases. For a short time, the pressure on the inside surface of your eardrum may continue to push out with the same force that balanced the air pressure at a lower elevation. The eardrum is pushed outward, and you may feel pain until your internal pressure adjusts to the new air pressure.

A person at an altitude of 2000 meters experiences approximately 20 percent less atmospheric pressure than a person at sea level.

Pressure in Water

Unlike air molecules, water molecules are already very close together. The density of water does not change very much with depth. However, the deeper you go underwater, the more water there is above you. The weight of that water above you produces the water pressure acting on your body. Just as air pressure increases at lower elevations, water pressure increases with greater water depth.

Water exerts more pressure on you than air does because water has a greater density than air. Therefore, the change in weight of the column of water above you as you dive is greater for each meter that you descend than it is in air. There is a greater difference in pressure if you dive ten meters farther down in the ocean than if you walked ten meters down a mountain. In fact, ten meters of water above you applies about as much pressure on you as the entire atmosphere does.

If you were to dive 1000 meters (3300 ft) below the surface of the ocean, the pressure would be nearly 100 times greater than pressure from the atmosphere. The force of this pressure would collapse your lungs unless you were protected by special deep-sea diving equipment. As scientists explore the ocean to greater depths, new underwater vehicles are designed that can withstand the increase in water pressure. Some whales, however, can dive to a depth of 1000 meters without being injured. As these whales dive to great depths, their lungs are almost completely collapsed by the pressure. However, the whales have adapted to the collapse—they store most of their oxygen intake in their muscles and blood instead of within their lungs.

A deep-diving whale at 1000 meters below the surface experiences about 34 times more pressure than a turtle diving to a depth of 20 meters (65 ft).

 **CHECK YOUR READING** Why is water pressure greater than air pressure?

3.3 Review

KEY CONCEPTS

1. How is pressure related to force and surface area?
2. Describe the way in which a fluid exerts pressure on an object immersed in it.
3. How does changing elevation affect air pressure? How does changing depth affect water pressure?

CRITICAL THINKING

4. **Calculate** If a board with an area of 3 m² has a 12 N force exerted on it, what is the pressure on the board?
5. **Infer** What might cause a balloon blown up at a low altitude to burst if it is taken to a higher altitude?

CHALLENGE

6. **Synthesize** During cold winters, ice can form on small lakes and ponds. Many people enjoy skating on the ice. Occasionally, a person skates on thin ice and breaks through it. Why do rescue workers lie flat on the ice instead of walking upright when reaching out to help rescue a skater?

Chapter 3: **Gravity, Friction, and Pressure** 95

CHAPTER INVESTIGATION

Pressure in Fluids

OVERVIEW AND PURPOSE When you put your hand under a faucet, you experience water pressure. Underwater explorers also experience water pressure. In this investigation you will
- change the depth and volume of a column of water
- determine what factors affect pressure

▶ Problem *Write It Up*

What factors affect water pressure?

▶ Hypothesize *Write It Up*

Write two hypotheses to explain what you expect to happen to the water pressure as you change the depth and volume of the water column. Your hypotheses (one for depth, one for volume) should take the form of "If . . . , then . . . , because . . ." statements.

▶ Procedure

MATERIALS
- nail
- 2 plastic bottles, small and large, with tops cut off
- ruler
- plastic container
- meter stick
- coffee can
- water

1. Create a data table like the one shown on the sample notebook page.

2. Using a nail, poke a hole in the side of each bottle 4 cm from the bottom of the bottle.

3. Set up the materials as shown on the left. Put a ruler in the small bottle so that the lower numbers are at the bottom.

4. Put your finger over the hole so no water will squirt out. Add or remove water (by lifting your finger off the hole) so that the water level is exactly at the 12 cm mark.

step 4

5. Release your finger from the hole, while your partner reads the exact mark where the water hits the meter stick. Cover the hole immediately after your partner reads the distance the water squirted. Record the distance on the line for this depth in your table.

step 3

96

6. Add or remove water so that the water level is now exactly at the 11 cm mark. Repeat step 5.

7. Continue adding, removing, and squirting water at each whole centimeter mark until no more water squirts from the bottle.

8. Repeat steps 4–7 two more times for a total of three trials.

9. Repeat steps 4–8 using the large bottle.

Observe and Analyze *Write It Up*

1. **RECORD OBSERVATIONS** Be sure that your data table is complete.

2. **GRAPH** Construct a graph showing distance versus depth. Draw two curves, one for the small bottle and one for the large bottle. Use different colors for the two curves.

3. **IDENTIFY VARIABLES AND CONSTANTS** List the variables and constants for the experiment using the small bottle and the experiment using the large bottle.

4. **ANALYZE** Is the depth greater when the bottle is more full or more empty? When did the water squirt farther, when the bottle was more full or more empty?

5. **ANALYZE** Did the water squirt farther when you used the small or the large bottle?

Conclude *Write It Up*

1. **INTERPRET** Answer the question posed in the problem.

2. **ANALYZE** Examine your graph and compare your results with your hypotheses. Do your results support your hypotheses?

3. **INFER** How does depth affect pressure? How does volume affect pressure?

4. **IDENTIFY LIMITS** What possible limitations or errors did you experience or could you have experienced with this investigation?

5. **APPLY** Dams store water for irrigation, home use, and hydroelectric power. Explain why dams must be constructed so that they are much thicker at the bottom than at the top.

6. **APPLY** Have you ever dived to the bottom of a swimming pool to pick up a coin? Describe what you felt as you swam toward the bottom.

INVESTIGATE Further

CHALLENGE Repeat the investigation using a liquid with a density that is quite different from water. Measure the distance the liquid travels, and graph the new data in a different color. Is there a difference? Why do you think there is or is not a difference in pressure between liquids of different densities?

Pressure in Fluids

Problem What factors affect water pressure?

Hypothesize

Observe and Analyze

Table 1. Distance Water Squirted with Small Bottle

Depth of water small bottle (cm)	Trial 1	Trial 2	Trial 3	Average
12				
11				
10				

Table 2. Distance Water Squirted with Large Bottle

Depth of water large bottle (cm)	Trial 1	Trial 2	Trial 3	Average
12				
11				
10				

Conclude

KEY CONCEPT

Fluids can exert a force on objects.

◀ **BEFORE, you learned**
- Pressure depends on force and area
- Pressure acts in all directions in fluids
- Density is mass divided by volume

▶ **NOW, you will learn**
- How fluids apply forces to objects
- How the motion of a fluid affects the pressure it exerts
- How forces are transmitted through fluids

VOCABULARY

buoyant force p. 98
Bernoulli's principle p. 100
Pascal's principle p. 102

EXPLORE Forces in Liquid

How does water affect weight?

PROCEDURE

① Tie a piece of string to the middle of the pencil. Tie 4 paper clips to each end of the pencil as shown.

② Move the middle string along the pencil until the paper clips are balanced and the pencil hangs flat.

③ While keeping the pencil balanced, slowly lower the paper clips on one end of the pencil into the water. Observe what happens.

MATERIALS
- 3 pieces of string
- pencil
- 8 paper clips
- cup full of water

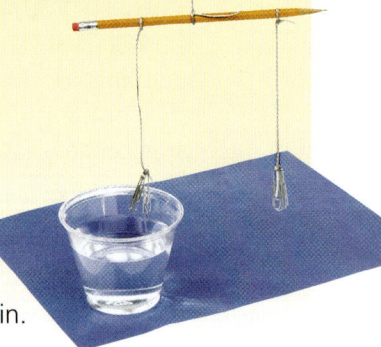

WHAT DO YOU THINK?
- How did the water affect the balance between the two sets of paper clips?
- Did the water exert a force on the paper clips? Explain.

Fluids can exert an upward force on objects.

If you drop an ice cube in air, it falls to the floor. If you drop the ice cube into water, it may sink a little at first, but the cube quickly rises upward until it floats. You know that gravity is pulling downward on the ice, even when it is in the water. If the ice cube is not sinking, there must be some force balancing gravity that is pushing upward on it.

The upward force on objects in a fluid is called **buoyant force**, or buoyancy. Buoyancy is why ice floats in water. Because of buoyant force, objects seem lighter in water. For example, it is easier to lift a heavy rock in water than on land because the buoyant force pushes upward on the rock, reducing the net force you need to lift it.

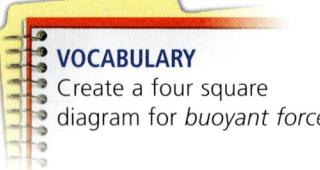

VOCABULARY
Create a four square diagram for *buoyant force*.

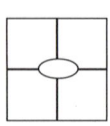

98 Unit 1: Motion and Forces

Buoyancy

The photograph on the right shows a balloon that has been pushed into a beaker of water. Remember that in a fluid, pressure increases with depth. This means that there is greater pressure acting on the bottom of the balloon than on the top of it. The pressure difference between the top and bottom of the balloon produces a net force that is pushing the balloon upward.

When you push a balloon underwater, the water level rises because the water and the balloon cannot be in the same place at the same time. The volume of the water has not changed, but some of the water has been displaced, or moved, by the balloon. The volume of the displaced water is equal to the volume of the balloon. The buoyant force on the balloon is equal to the weight of the displaced water. A deflated balloon would displace less water and would therefore have a smaller buoyant force on it.

net force

CHECK YOUR READING Why does increasing the volume of an object increase the buoyant force on it when it is in a fluid?

Density and Buoyancy

Whether or not an object floats in a fluid depends on the densities of both the object and the fluid. Density is a measure of the amount of matter packed into a unit volume. The density of an object is equal to its mass divided by its volume, and is commonly measured in grams per cubic centimeter (g/cm^3).

If an object is less dense than the fluid it is in, the fluid the object displaces can weigh more than the object. A wooden ball that is pushed underwater, as in the beaker below and on the left, rises to the top and floats. An object rising in a liquid has a buoyant force acting upon it that is greater than its own weight. If an object is floating in a liquid, the buoyant force is balancing the weight.

READING TIP

Remember that both air and water are fluids, and water has a greater density than air. Therefore, water has a greater buoyant force.

If the object is more dense than the fluid it is in, the object weighs more than the fluid it displaces. A glass marble placed in the beaker on the far right sinks to the bottom because glass is denser than water. The weight of the water the marble displaces is less than the weight of the marble. A sinking object has a weight that is greater than the buoyant force on it.

weight — buoyant force — no net force

weight — buoyant force — net force

Chapter 3: **Gravity, Friction, and Pressure** 99

The motion of a fluid affects its pressure.

The motion of a fluid affects the amount of pressure it exerts. A faster-moving fluid exerts less pressure as it flows over the surface of an object than a slower moving fluid. For example, wind blowing over a chimney top decreases the pressure at the top of the chimney. The faster air has less pressure than the slower-moving air in the fireplace. The increased pressure difference more effectively pulls the smoke from a fire out of the fireplace and up the chimney.

Bernoulli's Principle

Bernoulli's principle, named after Daniel Bernoulli (buhr-NOO-lee), a Swiss mathematician who lived in the 1700s, describes the effects of fluid motion on pressure. In general, **Bernoulli's principle** says that an increase in the speed of the motion of a fluid decreases the pressure within the fluid. The faster a fluid moves, the less pressure it exerts on surfaces or openings it flows over.

 **CHECK YOUR READING** What is the relationship between the speed of a fluid and the pressure that the fluid exerts?

INVESTIGATE Bernoulli's Principle

How does the speed of air affect air pressure?

PROCEDURE

1. Use the pen to mark off intervals of 1 cm along the length of one of the straws.
2. Put a drop of food coloring in the cup of water and stir it. Place the marked straw into the cup and hold it upright so that the water level in the straw is at one of the marks. The straw should not touch the bottom of the cup.
3. Position the second straw as shown. Blow across the open end of the marked straw. Observe the level of the water in the marked straw as you blow.
4. Blow harder and then softer. Observe the water level as you change the speed of the air.

WHAT DO YOU THINK?
- What happened to the water in the straw as you blew?
- How did the speed of the air relate to the changes you observed?

CHALLENGE What results would you expect if you blew over the top of a tube with a closed bottom instead of the straw? Explain.

SKILL FOCUS Observing

MATERIALS
- pen
- ruler
- two clear straws
- clear plastic cup filled with water
- food coloring

TIME 15 minutes

100 Unit 1: Motion and Forces

Applying Bernoulli's Principle

Bernoulli's principle has many applications. One important application is used in airplanes. Airplane wings can be shaped to take advantage of Bernoulli's principle. Certain wing shapes cause the air flowing over the top of the wing to move faster than the air flowing under the wing. Such a design improves the lifting force on a flying airplane.

Many racecars, however, have a device on the rear of the car that has the reverse effect. The device is designed like an upside-down airplane wing. This shape increases the pressure on the top of the car. The car is pressed downward on the road, which increases friction between the tires and the road. With more friction, the car is less likely to skid as it goes around curves at high speeds.

A prairie-dog colony also shows Bernoulli's principle in action. The mounds that prairie dogs build over some entrances to their burrows help to keep the burrows well-ventilated.

❶ Air closer to the ground tends to move at slower speeds than air higher up. The air over an entrance at ground level generally moves slower than the air over an entrance in a raised mound.

❷ The increased speed of the air over a raised mound entrance decreases the pressure over that opening.

❸ The greater air pressure over a ground-level entrance produces an unbalanced force that pushes air through the tunnels and out the higher mound entrance.

Bernoulli's Principle in Nature

Bernoulli's principle explains why having two entrances at different heights helps ventilate a prairie-dog burrow.

❶ Air moves more slowly near the ground.

❷ The air over the raised entrance moves faster and has less pressure than the slower-moving air near the ground.

❸ The pressure difference between the two entrances moves air through the tunnel.

Forces can be transmitted through fluids.

Imagine you have a bottle full of water. You place the bottle cap on it, but you do not tighten the cap. You give the bottle a hard squeeze and the cap falls off. How was the force you put on the bottle transferred to the bottle cap?

Pascal's Principle

In the 1600s Blaise Pascal (pa-SKAL), a French scientist for whom the unit of measure called the pascal was named, experimented with fluids in containers. One of his key discoveries is called Pascal's principle. **Pascal's principle** states that when an outside pressure is applied at any point to a fluid in a container, that pressure is transmitted throughout the fluid with equal strength.

You can use Pascal's principle to transmit a force through a fluid. Some car jacks lift cars using Pascal's principle. These jacks contain liquids that transmit and increase the force that you apply.

① The part of the jack that moves down and pushes on the liquid is called a piston. As you push down on the piston, you increase the pressure on the liquid.

② The increase in pressure is equal to your applied force divided by the area of the downward-pushing piston. This increase in pressure is transmitted throughout the liquid.

Pascal's Principle

The pressure from the smaller piston is equal to the pressure pushing up the larger one. The large piston can exert more force because of its greater area.

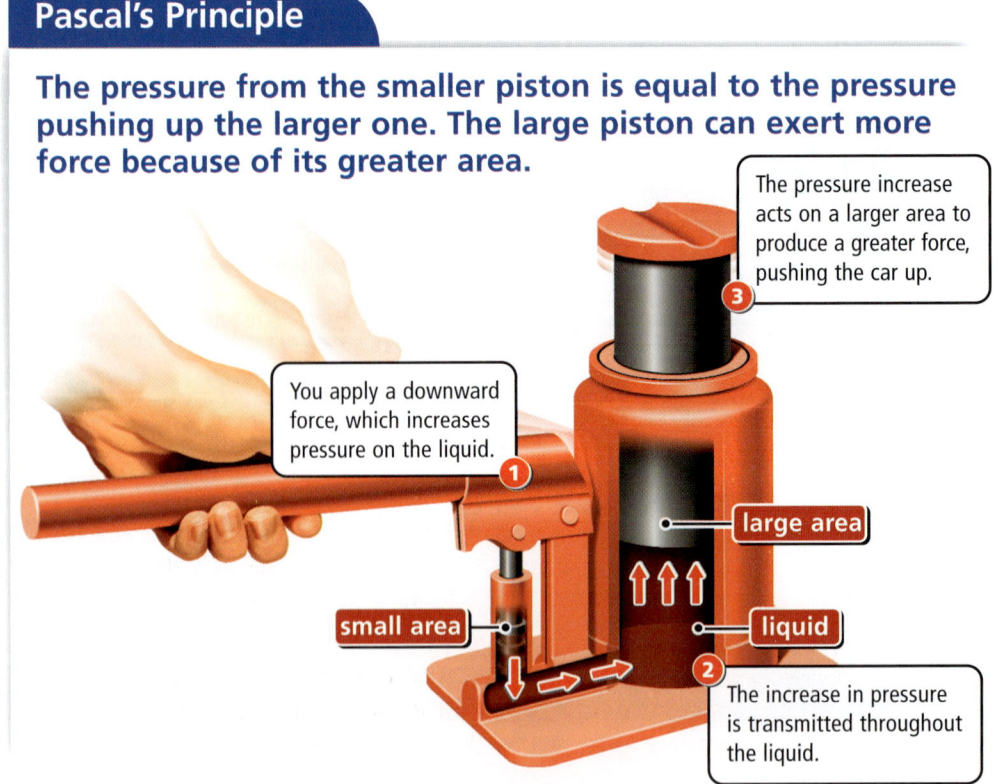

You apply a downward force, which increases pressure on the liquid. ①

The pressure increase acts on a larger area to produce a greater force, pushing the car up. ③

small area

large area

liquid

② The increase in pressure is transmitted throughout the liquid.

❸ The increased pressure pushes upward on another piston, which raises the car. This piston has a large area compared with the first piston, so the upward force is greater than the downward force. A large enough area produces the force needed to lift a car. However, the larger piston does not move upward as far as the smaller one moved downward.

 Describe how pressure is transmitted through a fluid.

Hydraulics

Machines that use liquids to transmit or increase a force are called hydraulic (hy-DRAW-lihk) machines. The advantage to using a liquid instead of a gas is that when you squeeze a liquid, its volume does not change much. The molecules in a liquid are so close together that it is hard to push the molecules any closer. Gas molecules, however, have a lot of space between them. If you apply pressure to a gas, you decrease its volume.

The hydraulic arm on the garbage truck lifts and empties trash cans.

Although hydraulic systems are used in large machines such as garbage trucks, research is being done on using hydraulics on a much smaller scale. Researchers are developing a storage chip similar to a computer chip that uses hydraulics rather than electronics. This chip uses pipes and pumps to move fluid into specific chambers on a rubber chip. Researchers hope that a hydraulic chip system will eventually allow scientists to use a single hand-held device to perform chemical experiments with over a thousand different liquids.

3.4 Review

KEY CONCEPTS

1. Why is there an upward force on objects in water?
2. How does changing the speed of a fluid affect its pressure?
3. If you push a cork into the neck of a bottle filled with air, what happens to the pressure inside the bottle?

CRITICAL THINKING

4. **Infer** Ebony is a dark wood that has a density of 1.2 g/cm^3. Water has a density of 1.0 g/cm^3. Will a block of ebony float in water? Explain.
5. **Analyze** When you use a spray bottle, you force air over a small tube inside the bottle. Explain why the liquid inside the bottle comes out.

CHALLENGE

6. **Synthesize** If you apply a force of 20 N downward on a car jack piston with an area of 2.5 cm^2, what force will be applied to the upward piston if it has an area of 400 cm^2? **Hint:** Remember that pressure equals force divided by area.

Chapter 3: **Gravity, Friction, and Pressure** 103

3 Chapter Review

the BIG idea
Newton's laws apply to all forces.

CONTENT REVIEW
CLASSZONE.COM

KEY CONCEPTS SUMMARY

1 Gravity is a force exerted by masses.

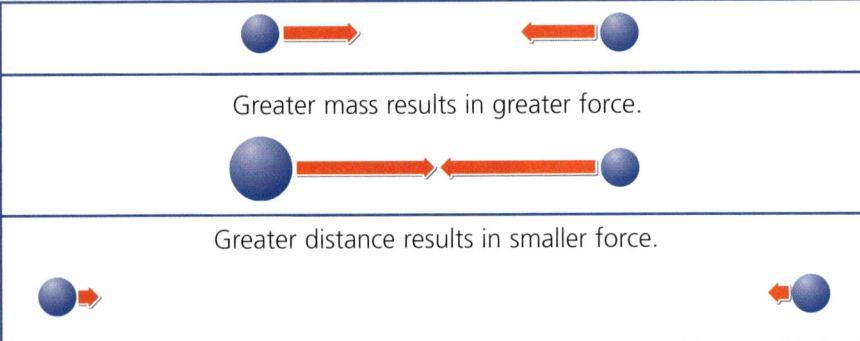

Greater mass results in greater force.

Greater distance results in smaller force.

VOCABULARY
gravity p. 77
weight p. 79
orbit p. 80

2 Friction is a force that opposes motion.

Frictional force depends on—
- types of surfaces
- motion of surfaces
- force pressing surfaces together

Air resistance is a type of friction.

friction

VOCABULARY
friction p. 85
fluid p. 88
air resistance p. 89

3 Pressure depends on force and area.

$$\text{Pressure} = \frac{\text{Force}}{\text{Area}}$$

Pressure in a fluid acts in all directions.

VOCABULARY
pressure p. 91
pascal p. 92

4 Fluids can exert a force on objects.

- Buoyant force is equal to the weight of the displaced fluid.
- A faster-moving fluid produces less pressure than a slower-moving one.
- Pressure is transmitted through fluids.

VOCABULARY
buoyant force p. 98
Bernoulli's principle p. 100
Pascal's principle p. 102

Reviewing Vocabulary

Write a sentence describing the relationship between each pair of terms.

1. gravity, weight
2. gravity, orbit
3. pressure, pascal
4. fluid, friction
5. density, buoyant force
6. fluid, Bernoulli's principle

Reviewing Key Concepts

Multiple Choice *Choose the letter of the best answer.*

7. Which force keeps Venus in orbit around the Sun?
   a. gravity
   b. friction
   c. hydraulic
   d. buoyancy

8. You and a classmate are one meter apart. If you move farther away, how does the gravitational force between you and your classmate change?
   a. It increases.
   b. It decreases.
   c. It stays the same.
   d. It disappears.

9. You kick a ball on a level sidewalk. It rolls to a stop because
   a. there is no force on the ball
   b. gravity slows the ball down
   c. air pressure is pushing down on the ball
   d. friction slows the ball down

10. You push a chair at a constant velocity using a force of 5 N to overcome friction. You stop to rest, then push again. To start the chair moving again, you must use a force that is
    a. greater than 5 N
    b. equal to 5 N
    c. greater than 0 N but less than 5 N
    d. 0 N

11. How could you place an empty bottle on a table so that it produces the greatest amount of pressure on the table?

    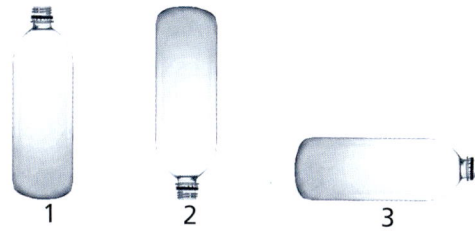

    a. position 1
    b. position 2
    c. position 3
    d. All positions produce the same pressure.

12. As you climb up a mountain, air pressure
    a. increases
    b. decreases
    c. stays the same
    d. changes unpredictably

13. If you squeeze a balloon in the middle, what happens to the air pressure inside the balloon?
    a. It increases only in the middle.
    b. It decreases only in the middle.
    c. It increases throughout.
    d. It decreases throughout.

Short Answer *Write a short answer to each question.*

14. How does the force of attraction between large masses compare with the force of attraction between small masses at the same distance?

15. Explain why a satellite in orbit around Earth does not crash into Earth.

16. You are pushing a dresser with drawers filled with clothing. What could you do to reduce the friction between the dresser and the floor?

17. Why is water pressure greater at a depth of 20 feet than it is at a depth of 10 feet?

18. If you blow over the top of a small strip of paper, the paper bends upward. Why?

Chapter 3: **Gravity, Friction, and Pressure** 105

Thinking Critically

19. **APPLY** Explain why an iron boat can float in water, while an iron cube cannot.

20. **COMPARE** How does the friction between solid surfaces compare with the friction between a moving object and a fluid?

21. **APPLY** Explain why a block of wood gets warm when it is rubbed with sandpaper.

22. **PREDICT** The Moon's orbit is gradually increasing. Each year the Moon is about 3.8 cm farther from Earth than the year before. How does this change affect the force of gravity between Earth and the Moon?

23. **APPLY** The Moon has one-sixth the gravity of Earth. Why would it be easier to launch spacecraft into orbit around the Moon than around Earth?

Use the photograph below to answer the next three questions.

24. **APPLY** A skydiver jumps out of a plane. After he reaches terminal velocity, he opens his parachute. Draw a sketch showing the forces of air resistance and gravity on the skydiver after the parachute opens. Use a longer arrow for a greater force.

25. **SYNTHESIZE** Air is a fluid, which produces a small buoyant force on the skydiver. How does this buoyant force change after he opens his parachute? Why?

26. **INFER** The Moon has no atmosphere. Would it be safe to skydive on the Moon? Why or why not?

27. **INFER** When oil and water are mixed together, the two substances separate and the oil floats to the top. How does the density of oil compare with the density of water?

28. **COMPARE** Three flasks are filled with colored water as shown below. How does the water pressure at the bottom of each flask compare with the water pressure at the bottom of the other two?

1   2   3

Using Math Skills in Science

Complete the following calculations.

29. How much force does a 10 kg marble exert on the ground?

30. A force of 50 N is applied on a piece of wood with an area of 0.5 m². What is the pressure on the wood?

the BIG idea

31. **ANALYZE** Look again at the picture on pages 74–75. What forces are acting on the snowboarder? on the snow? Use Newton's laws to explain how these forces enable the snowboarder to move down the hill.

32. **SYNTHESIZE** Choose two concepts discussed in this chapter, and describe how Newton's laws relate to those concepts.

UNIT PROJECTS

Check your schedule for your unit project. How are you doing? Be sure that you have placed data or notes from your research into your project folder.

Standardized Test Practice

Interpreting Diagrams

Study the diagram and then answer the questions that follow.

Bernoulli's principle states that an increase in the speed of the motion of a fluid decreases the pressure exerted by the fluid. The diagram below relates the movement of a curve ball in baseball to this principle. The ball is shown from above.

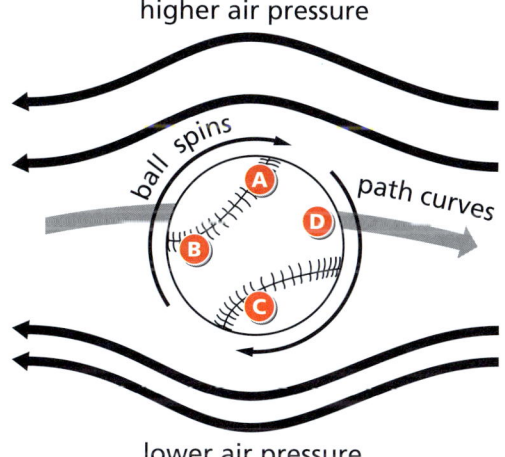

1. To which of these properties does Bernoulli's principle apply?
   a. air pressure
   b. temperature
   c. air resistance
   d. density

2. Where is the air moving fastest in the diagram?
   a. region A
   b. region B
   c. region C
   d. region D

3. Because the ball is spinning, the air on one side is moving faster than on the other side. This causes the ball to curve due to the
   a. air molecules moving slowly and evenly around the ball
   b. forward motion of the ball
   c. difference in air pressure on the ball
   d. changing air temperature around the ball

4. If the baseball were spinning as it moved forward underwater, instead of through the air, how would the pressure of the fluid act on the ball?
   a. The water pressure would be the same on all sides.
   b. The water pressure would vary as air pressure does.
   c. The water pressure would be greatest on the side where air pressure was least.
   d. The water pressure would prevent the ball from spinning.

Extended Response

Answer the two questions below in detail. Include some of the terms from the word box. Underline each term you use in your answer.

acceleration	air resistance	density
fluid	friction	gravity
mass	pressure	velocity

5. If a feather and a bowling ball are dropped from the same height, will they fall at the same rate? Explain.

6. A balloon filled with helium or hot air can float in the atmosphere. A balloon filled with air from your lungs falls to the ground when it is released. Why do these balloons behave differently?

TIMELINES in Science

UNDERSTANDING FORCES

In ancient times, people thought that an object would not move unless it was pushed. Scientists came up with ingenious ways to explain how objects like arrows stayed in motion. Over time, they came to understand that all motion could be described by three basic laws. Modern achievements such as suspension bridges and space exploration are possible because of the experiments with motion and forces performed by scientists and philosophers over hundreds of years.

This timeline shows just a few of the many steps on the path toward understanding forces. Notice how scientists used the observations and ideas of previous thinkers as a springboard for developing new theories. The boxes below the timeline show how technology has led to new insights and to applications of those ideas.

350 B.C.

Aristotle Discusses Motion

The Greek philosopher Aristotle states that the natural condition of an object is to be at rest. A force is necessary to keep the object in motion. The greater the force, the faster the object moves.

EVENTS

400 B.C.   350 B.C.   300 B.C.

APPLICATIONS AND TECHNOLOGY

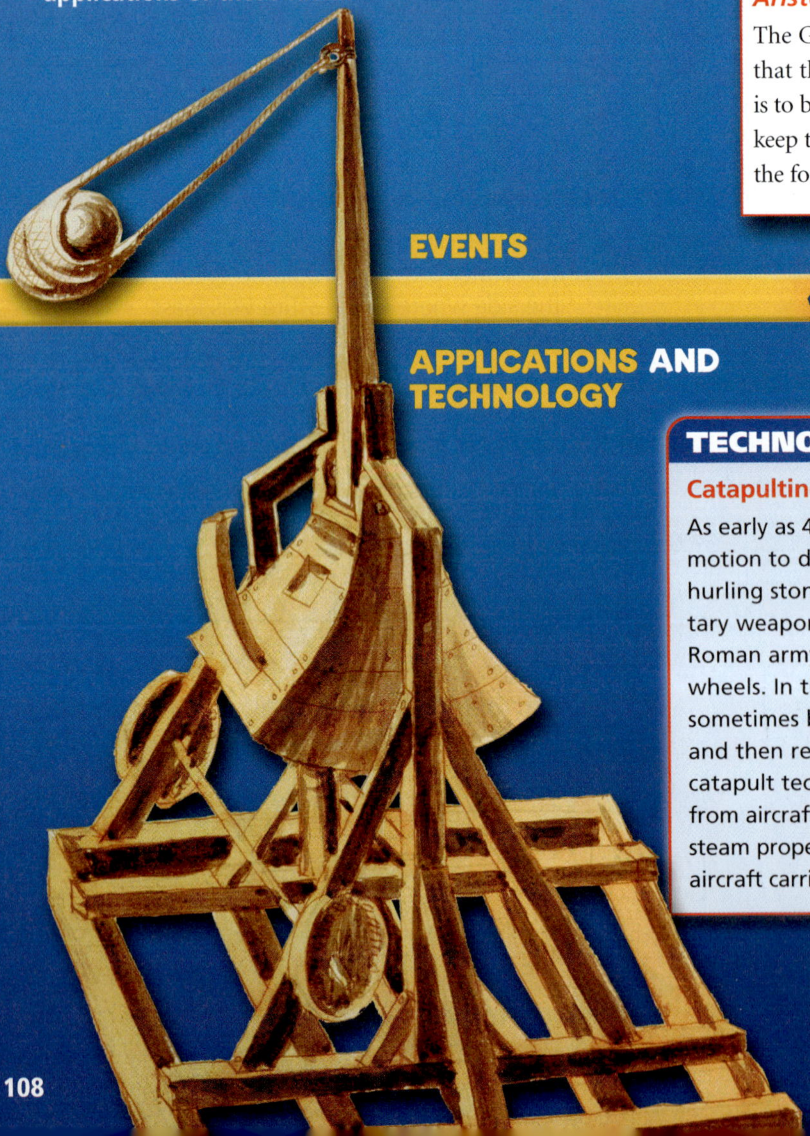

TECHNOLOGY

Catapulting into History

As early as 400 B.C., armies were using objects in motion to do work. Catapults, or machines for hurling stones and spears, were used as military weapons. Five hundred years later, the Roman army used catapults mounted on wheels. In the Middle Ages, young trees were sometimes bent back, loaded with an object, and then released like a large slingshot. Today catapult technology is used to launch airplanes from aircraft carriers. A piston powered by steam propels the plane along the deck of the aircraft carrier until it reaches takeoff speed.

250 B.C.

Levers and Buoyancy Explained

The Greek inventor Archimedes uses a mathematical equation to explain how a small weight can balance a much larger weight near a lever's fulcrum. He also explains buoyancy, which provides a way of measuring volume.

A.D. 1121

Force Acting on Objects Described

Persian astronomer al-Khazini asserts that a force acts on all objects to pull them toward the center of Earth. This force varies, he says, depending on whether the object moves through air, water, or another medium. His careful notes and drawings illustrate these principles.

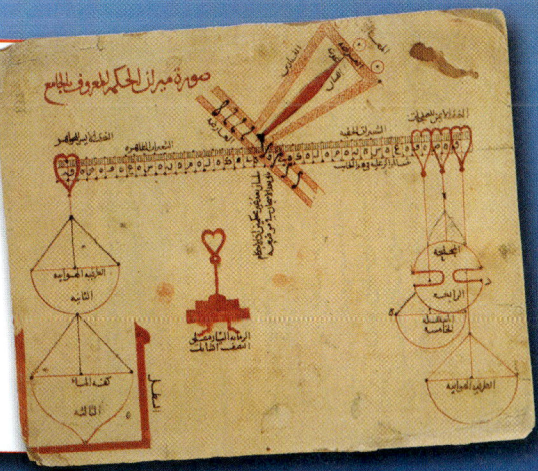

1150

Perpetual-Motion Machine Described

Indian mathematician and physicist Bhaskara describes a wheel that uses closed containers of liquid to turn forever without stopping. If it worked, his idea would promise an unending source of power that does not rely on an external source.

250 B.C.　　A.D. 1100　　1150　　1200

APPLICATION

The First Steam-Powered Engine

In the first century A.D., Hero of Alexandria, a Greek inventor, created the first known steam engine, called the aeolipile. It was a hollow ball with two cylinders jutting out in opposite directions. The ball was suspended above a kettle that was filled with water and placed over a fire. As the water boiled, steam caused the ball to spin. The Greeks never used this device for work. In 1690, Sir Isaac Newton formulated the principle of the aeolipile in scientific terms in his third law of motion. A steam engine designed for work was built in 1698. The aeolipile is the earliest version of steam-powered pumps, steam locomotives, jet engines, and rockets.

1638
Objects Need No Force to Keep Moving
Italian astronomer Galileo Galilei says that an object's natural state is either in constant motion or at rest. Having observed the motion of objects on ramps, he concludes that an object in motion will slow down or speed up only if a force is exerted on it. He also claims that all objects dropped near the surface of Earth fall with the same acceleration due to the force of gravity.

1494
Perpetual-Motion Machine Impossible
Italian painter and engineer Leonardo da Vinci proves that it is impossible to build a perpetual-motion machine that works. He states that the force of friction keeps a wheel from turning forever without more force being applied.

1687
An Object's Motion Can Be Predicted
English scientist Sir Isaac Newton publishes his three laws of motion, which use Galileo's ideas as a foundation. He concludes that Earth exerts a gravitational force on objects on its surface and that Earth's gravity keeps the Moon in orbit.

1500　1550　1600　1650　1700　1750　1800

APPLICATION

A New and Improved Steam Engine
Scottish scientist James Watt designed steam engines that were much more efficient, and much smaller, than older models. About 500 of Watt's engines were in use by 1800. His pump engines drew water out of coal mines, and his rotating engines were used in factories and cotton mills. Watt's steam engines opened the way to the Industrial Revolution. They were used in major industries such as textile manufacturing, railroad transportation, and mining. Watt's steam technology also opened up new areas of research in heat, kinetic energy, and motion.

1919
Gravity Bends Light

A solar eclipse confirms German-American physicist Albert Einstein's modification of Newton's laws. Einstein's theory states that the path of a light beam will be affected by nearby massive objects. During the eclipse, the stars appear to shift slightly away from one another because their light has been bent by the Sun's gravity.

2001
Supercomputers Model Strong Force

Scientists have been using supercomputers to model the force that holds particles in the nucleus of an atom together. This force, called the strong force, cannot be measured directly in the same way that gravity and other forces can. Instead, computer models allow scientists to make predictions that are then compared with experimental results.

RESOURCE CENTER
CLASSZONE.COM
Get current research on force and motion.

1850   1900   1950   2000

INTO THE FUTURE

Since ancient times, scientists and philosophers have tried to explain how forces move objects. We now know that the laws of gravity and motion extend beyond Earth. Engineers have designed powerful spacecraft that can carry robots—and eventually people—to Mars and beyond. Rockets using new technology travel farther on less fuel than liquid-fueled rockets do.

Space travel and related research will continue to unravel the mysteries of forces in the universe. For example, recent observations of outer space provide evidence of an unidentified force causing the universe to expand rapidly. As people venture beyond Earth, we may learn new and unexpected things about the forces we have come to understand so far. The timeline shown here is just the beginning of our knowledge of forces.

TECHNOLOGY
Science Propels Exploration of Outer Space

An increased understanding of forces made space exploration possible. In 1926 American scientist Robert H. Goddard constructed and tested the first liquid-propelled rocket. A replica of Goddard's rocket can be seen at the National Air and Space Museum in Washington, D.C. In 1929 Goddard launched a rocket that carried the first scientific payload, a barometer and a camera.

Many later achievements—including the 1969 walk on the Moon—are a direct result of Goddard's trail-blazing space research.

ACTIVITIES

Reliving History

Bhaskara's design for a perpetual-motion machine involved a wheel with containers of mercury around the rim. As the wheel turned, the mercury would move in such a way that the wheel would always be heavier on one side—and stay in motion. Now we know that this theory goes against the laws of physics. Observe a wheel, a pendulum, or a swing. Think about why it cannot stay in motion forever.

Writing About Science

Suppose you won a trip to outer space. Write a letter accepting or refusing the prize. Give your reasons.

CHAPTER

Work and Energy

the BIG idea

Energy is transferred when a force moves an object.

Key Concepts

SECTION 1
Work is the use of force to move an object.
Learn about the relationship between force and work.

SECTION 2
Energy is transferred when work is done.
Learn how energy is related to work.

SECTION 3
Power is the rate at which work is done.
Learn to calculate power from work and energy.

Which takes more work, lifting a box or holding a box? Why?

Internet Preview

CLASSZONE.COM
Chapter 4 online resources: Content Review, Simulation, Visualization, two Resource Centers, Math Tutorial, Test Practice

EXPLORE the BIG idea

Bouncing Ball

Drop a large ball on a hard, flat floor. Let it bounce several times. Notice the height the ball reaches after each bounce.

Observe and Think
How did the height change? Why do you think this happens? Sketch the path of the ball through several bounces.

Power Climbing

Walk up a flight of stairs wearing a backpack. Run up the same flight of stairs wearing the backpack.

Observe and Think
Compare and contrast both trips up the stairs. Which one took greater effort? Did you apply the same force against gravity each time?

Internet Activity: Work

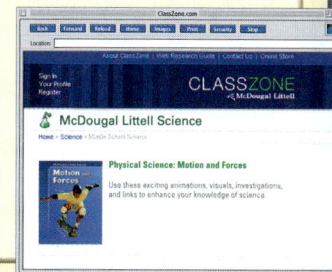

Go to **ClassZone.com** to simulate lifting weights of different masses. Determine how much work is done in lifting each weight by watching your progress on a work meter.

Observe and Think
Do you think more work will be done it the weights are lifted higher?

Potential and Kinetic Energy **Code: MDL007**

Chapter 4: **Work and Energy** 113

CHAPTER 4
Getting Ready to Learn

CONCEPT REVIEW

- Forces change the motion of objects in predictable ways.
- Velocity is a measure of the speed and direction of an object.
- An unbalanced force produces acceleration.

VOCABULARY REVIEW

velocity p. 22
force p. 41

See Glossary for definitions.
energy, mass

CONTENT REVIEW
CLASSZONE.COM
Review concepts and vocabulary.

TAKING NOTES

MAIN IDEA WEB

Write each new blue heading in a box. Then write notes in boxes around it that give important terms and details about that blue heading.

SCIENCE NOTEBOOK

- Work is the use of force to move an object.
- Work = Force • distance
- Force is necessary to do work.
- Joule is the unit for measuring work.
- Work depends on force and distance.

CHOOSE YOUR OWN STRATEGY

Take notes about new vocabulary terms using one or more of the strategies from earlier chapters—**description wheel, magnet words,** or **four square.** Feel free to mix and match the strategies or use a different strategy.

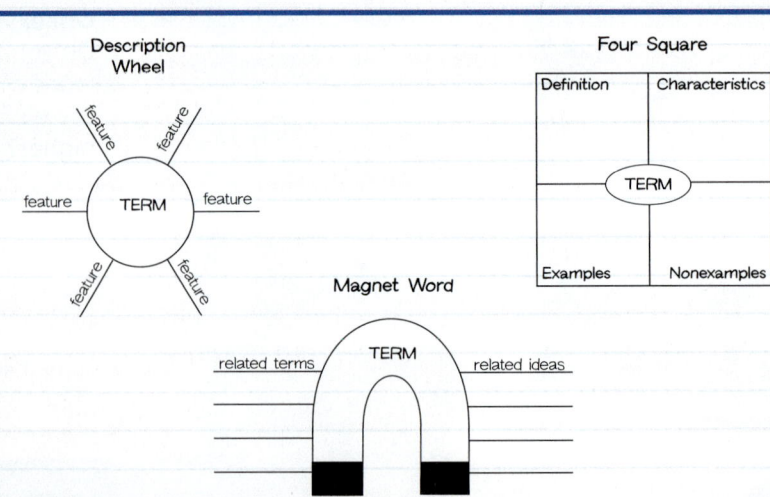

See the Note-Taking Handbook on pages R45–R51.

114 Unit 1: Motion and Forces

KEY CONCEPT

Work is the use of force to move an object.

◁ **BEFORE, you learned**
- An unbalanced force produces acceleration
- Weight is measured in newtons

▷ **NOW, you will learn**
- How force and work are related
- How moving objects do work

VOCABULARY

work p. 115
joule p. 117

EXPLORE Work

How do you work?

PROCEDURE

1. Lift a book from the floor to your desktop. Try to move the book at a constant speed.

2. Now lift the book again, but stop about halfway up and hold the book still for about 30 seconds. Then continue lifting the book to the desktop.

MATERIALS
book

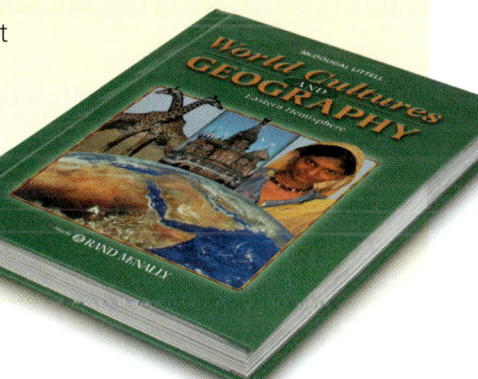

WHAT DO YOU THINK?
- Do you think you did more work the first time you lifted the book or the second time you lifted the book?
- What do you think *work* means?

Force is necessary to do work.

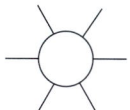

VOCABULARY
You might want to make a description wheel diagram in your notebook for *work*.

What comes to mind when you think of work? Most people say they are working when they do anything that requires a physical or mental effort. But in physical science, **work** is the use of force to move an object some distance. In scientific terms, you do work only when you exert a force on an object and move it. According to this definition of work, reading this page is not doing work. Turning the page, however, would be work because you are lifting the page.

Solving a math problem in your head is not doing work. Writing the answer is work because you are moving the pencil across the paper. If you want to do work, you have to use force to move something.

 How does the scientific definition of work differ from the familiar definition?

Chapter 4: **Work and Energy** 115

RESOURCE CENTER
CLASSZONE.COM
Learn more about work.

Force, Motion, and Work

Work is done only when an object that is being pushed or pulled actually moves. If you lift a book, you exert a force and do work. What if you simply hold the book out in front of you? No matter how tired your muscles may become from holding the book still, you are not doing work unless you move the book.

The work done by a force is related to the size of the force and the distance over which the force is applied. How much work does it take to push a grocery cart down an aisle? The answer depends on how hard you push the cart and the length of the aisle. If you use the same amount of force, you do more work pushing a cart down a long aisle than a short aisle.

Work is done only by the part of the applied force that acts in the same direction as the motion of an object. Suppose you need to pull a heavy suitcase on wheels. You pull the handle up at an angle as you pull the suitcase forward. Only the part of the force pulling the suitcase forward is doing work. The force with which you pull upward on the handle is not doing work because the suitcase is not moving upward—unless you are going uphill.

CHECK YOUR READING Give two examples of when you are applying a force but not doing work.

Work

Work is done by force that acts in the same direction as the motion of an object.

All of the Applied Force Does Work

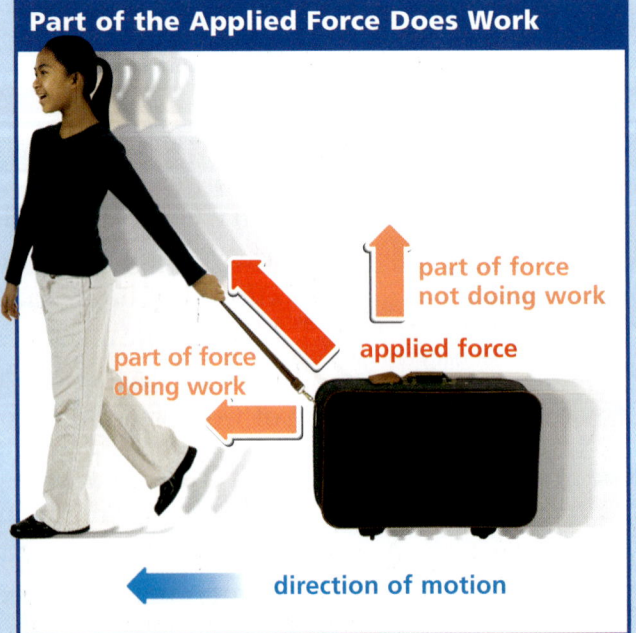

Part of the Applied Force Does Work

READING VISUALS How does changing the direction of the applied force change the amount of the force that is doing work?

116 Unit 1: Motion and Forces

Calculating Work

Work is a measure of how much force is applied over a certain distance. You can calculate the work a force does if you know the size of the force applied to an object and the distance over which the force acts. The distance involved is the distance the object moved in the direction of that force. The calculation for work is shown in the following formula:

$$\text{Work} = \text{Force} \cdot \text{distance}$$
$$W = Fd$$

You read in previous chapters that you can measure force in newtons. You also know that you can measure distance in meters. When you multiply a force in newtons times a distance in meters, the product is a measurement called the newton-meter (N·m), or the **joule** (jool).

The joule (J) is the standard unit used to measure work. One joule of work is done when a force of one newton moves an object one meter. To get an idea of how much a joule of work is, lift an apple (which weighs about one newton) from your foot to your waist (about one meter).

Use the formula for work to solve the problem below.

This man is doing work when he applies force to lift his body.

Calculating Work

▶ Sample Problem

How much work is done if a person lifts a barbell weighing 450 N to a height of 2 m?

What do you know?	force needed to lift = 450 N, distance = 2 m
What do you want to find out?	Work
Write the formula:	$W = Fd$
Substitute into the formula:	$W = 450 \text{ N} \cdot 2 \text{ m}$
Calculate and simplify:	$W = 900 \text{ N·m}$
Check that your units agree:	Unit is newton-meter (N·m). Unit of work is joule, which is N·m. Units agree.
Answer:	$W = 900 \text{ J}$

▶ Practice the Math

1. If you push a cart with a force of 70 N for 2 m, how much work is done?
2. If you did 200 J of work pushing a box with a force of 40 N, how far did you push the box?

▼ REMINDER

You know that $W = Fd$. You can manipulate the formula to find force or distance.
$d = \dfrac{W}{F}$ and $F = \dfrac{W}{d}$

Chapter 4: **Work and Energy**

MAIN IDEA WEB
Remember to organize your notes in a web as you read.

Objects that are moving can do work.

You do work when you pick up your books, hit a baseball, swim a lap, or tap a keyboard. These examples show that you do work on objects, but objects can also do work.

For example, in a bowling alley, the bowling balls do work on the pins they hit. Outdoors, the moving air particles in a gust of wind do work that lifts a leaf off the ground. Moving water, such as the water in a river, also does work. If the windblown leaf lands in the water, it might be carried downstream by the current. As the leaf travels downstream, it might go over the edge of a waterfall. In that case, the gravitational force of Earth would pull the leaf and water down.

You can say that an object or person does work on an object, or that the force the object or person is exerting does work. For example, you could say that Earth (an object) does work on the falling water, or that gravity (a force) does work on the water.

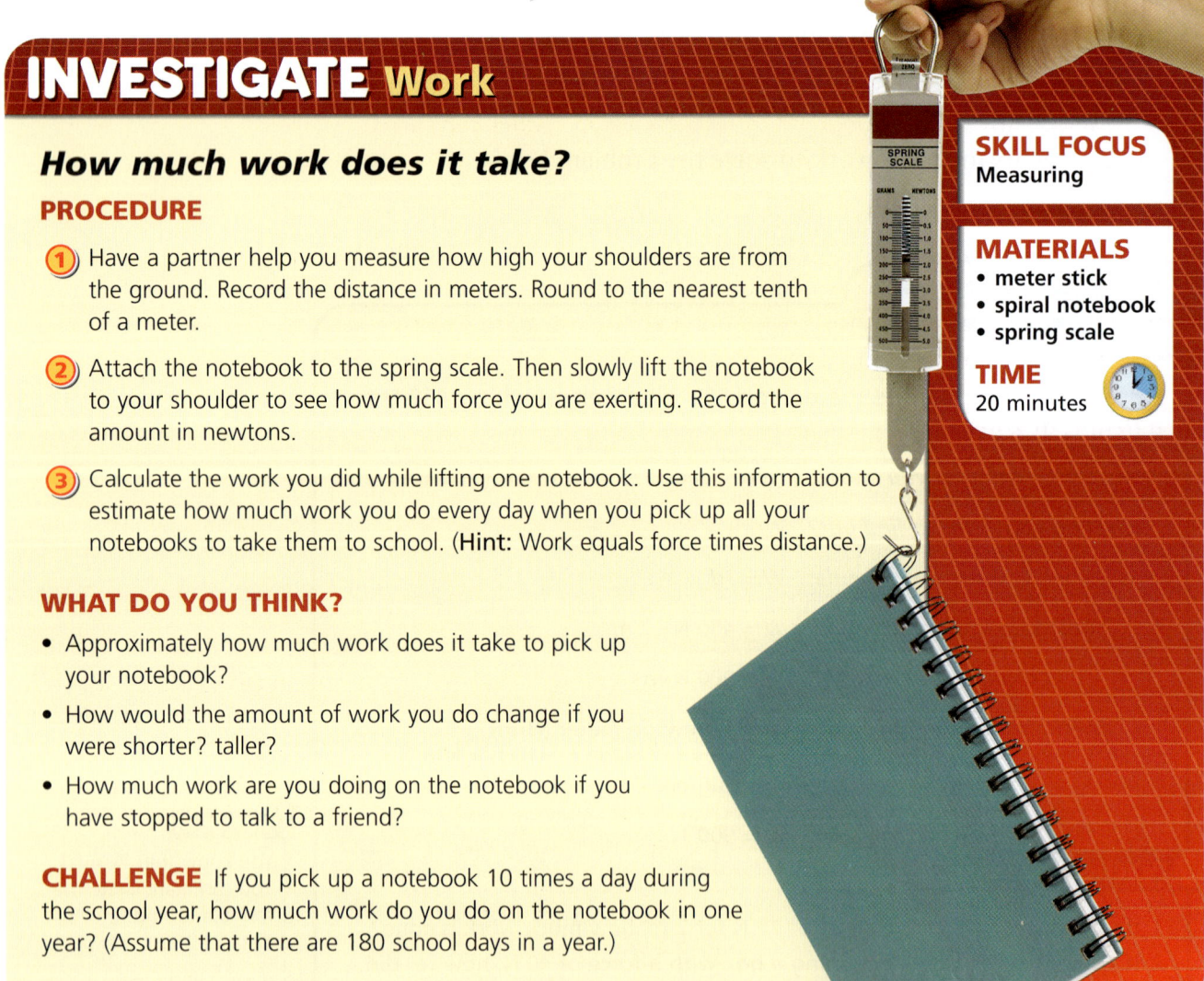

INVESTIGATE Work

How much work does it take?

PROCEDURE

1. Have a partner help you measure how high your shoulders are from the ground. Record the distance in meters. Round to the nearest tenth of a meter.

2. Attach the notebook to the spring scale. Then slowly lift the notebook to your shoulder to see how much force you are exerting. Record the amount in newtons.

3. Calculate the work you did while lifting one notebook. Use this information to estimate how much work you do every day when you pick up all your notebooks to take them to school. (**Hint:** Work equals force times distance.)

SKILL FOCUS
Measuring

MATERIALS
- meter stick
- spiral notebook
- spring scale

TIME
20 minutes

WHAT DO YOU THINK?
- Approximately how much work does it take to pick up your notebook?
- How would the amount of work you do change if you were shorter? taller?
- How much work are you doing on the notebook if you have stopped to talk to a friend?

CHALLENGE If you pick up a notebook 10 times a day during the school year, how much work do you do on the notebook in one year? (Assume that there are 180 school days in a year.)

Unit 1: Motion and Forces

APPLY How could you increase the work done by this water wheel?

Throughout history, people have taken advantage of the capability of objects in motion to do work. Many early cultures built machines such as water wheels to use the force exerted by falling water, and windmills to use the force exerted by moving air. In a water wheel like the one in the photograph, gravity does work on the water. As the water falls, it also can do work on any object that is put in its path. Falling water can turn a water wheel or the turbine of an electric generator.

The water wheel shown above uses the work done by water to turn gears that run a mill and grind grain. In the same way, windmills take advantage of the force of moving air particles. The wind causes the sails of a windmill to turn. The turning sails do work to run machinery or an irrigation system.

 Describe how a water wheel does work.

 Review

KEY CONCEPTS

1. If you push very hard on an object but it does not move, have you done work? Explain.
2. What two factors do you need to know to calculate how much work was done in any situation?
3. Was work done on a book that fell from a desk to the floor? If so, what force was involved?

CRITICAL THINKING

4. **Synthesize** Work is done on a ball when a soccer player kicks it. Is the player still doing work on the ball as it rolls across the ground? Explain.
5. **Calculate** Tina lifted a box 0.5 m. The box weighed 25 N. How much work did Tina do on the box?

CHALLENGE

6. **Analyze** Ben and Andy each pushed an empty grocery cart. Ben used twice the force, but they both did the same amount of work. Explain.

Chapter 4: **Work and Energy** 119

MATH in SCIENCE

SKILL: WORKING WITH AVERAGES

MATH TUTORIAL
CLASSZONE.COM
Click on Math Tutorial for more help with finding the mean.

Eliminating Extreme Values

A value that is far from most others in a set of data is called an outlier. Outliers make it difficult to find a value that might be considered average. Extremely high or extremely low values can throw off the mean. That is why the highest and lowest figures are ignored in some situations.

Example

The data set below shows the work an escalator does to move 8 people of different weights 5 meters. The work was calculated by multiplying the force needed to move each person by a distance of 5 meters.

  4850 J   1600 J   3400 J   2750 J
  2950 J   1750 J   3350 J   3800 J

The mean amount of work done is 3056 J.

(1) To calculate an adjusted mean, begin by identifying a high outlier in the data set.

High outlier: 4850

(2) Discard this value and find the new mean.

1600 J + 3400 J + 2750 J + 2950 J + 1750 J + 3350 J + 3800 J
= 19,600 J

Mean = $\frac{19,600 \text{ J}}{7}$ = 2800 J

ANSWER The mean amount of work done for this new data set is 2800 J.

Answer the following questions.

1. After ignoring the high outlier in the data set, does this new mean show a more typical level of work for the data set? Why or why not?

2. Do you think the lowest value in the data set is an outlier? Remove it and calculate the new average. How did this affect the results?

3. Suppose the heaviest person in the original data set were replaced by a person weighing the same as the lightest person. What would be the new mean for the data set?

CHALLENGE The median of a data set is the middle value when the values are written in numerical order. Find the median of the adjusted data set (without the high outlier). Compare it with the original and adjusted means. Why do you think it is closer to one than the other?

KEY CONCEPT

4.2 Energy is transferred when work is done.

BEFORE, you learned
- Work is the use of force to move an object
- Work can be calculated

NOW, you will learn
- How work and energy are related
- How to calculate mechanical, kinetic, and potential energy
- What the conservation of energy means

VOCABULARY
potential energy p. 122
kinetic energy p. 122
mechanical energy p. 125
conservation of energy p. 126

THINK ABOUT

How is energy transferred?

School carnivals sometimes include dunk tanks. The goal is to hit a target with a ball, causing a person sitting over a tank of water to fall into the water. You do work on the ball as you throw with your arm. If your aim is good, the ball does work on the target. How do you transfer your energy to the ball?

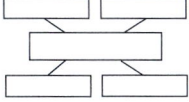

MAIN IDEA WEB
Remember to add boxes to your main idea web as you read.

Work transfers energy.

When you change the position and speed of the ball in the carnival game, you transfer energy to the ball. Energy is the ability of a person or an object to do work or to cause a change. When you do work on an object, some of your energy is transferred to the object. You can think of work as the transfer of energy. In fact, both work and energy are measured in the same unit, the joule.

The man in the photograph above converts one form of energy into another form when he uses his muscles to toss the ball. You can think of the man and the ball as a system, or a group of objects that affect one another. Energy can be transferred from the man to the ball, but the total amount of energy in the system does not change.

 How are work and energy related?

Chapter 4: **Work and Energy** 121

Work changes potential and kinetic energy.

READING TIP
The word *potential* comes from the Latin word *potentia*, which means "power." The word *kinetic* comes from the Greek word *kinetos*, which means "moving."

When you throw a ball, you transfer energy to it and it moves. By doing work on the ball, you can give it **kinetic energy** (kuh-NEHT-ihk), which is the energy of motion. Any moving object has some kinetic energy. The faster an object moves, the more kinetic energy it has.

When you do work to lift a ball from the ground, you give the ball a different type of energy, called potential energy. **Potential energy** is stored energy, or the energy an object has due to its position or its shape. The ball's position in your hand above the ground means that it has the potential to fall to the ground. The higher you lift the ball, the more work you do, and the more potential energy the ball has.

You can also give some objects potential energy by changing their shape. For example, if you are holding a spring, you can do work on the spring by squeezing it. After you do the work, the spring has potential energy because it is compressed. This type of potential energy is called elastic potential energy. Just as position gives the spring the potential to fall, compression gives the spring the potential to expand.

Potential and Kinetic Energy

Potential Energy

The boy has potential energy based on his position because gravity will pull him back down.

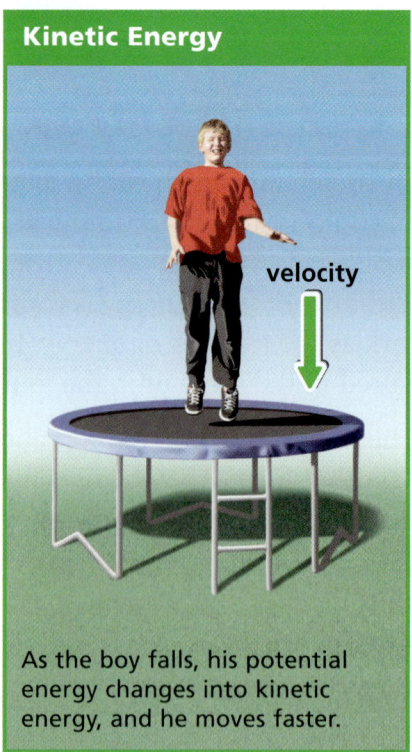

Kinetic Energy

As the boy falls, his potential energy changes into kinetic energy, and he moves faster.

Potential Energy

The trampoline has potential energy because it is stretched.

Calculating Gravitational Potential Energy

Potential energy caused by gravity is called gravitational potential energy. Scientists must take gravitational potential energy into account when launching a spacecraft. Designers of roller coasters must make sure that roller-coaster cars have enough potential energy at the top of a hill to reach the top of the next hill. You can use the following formula to calculate the gravitational potential energy of an object:

Gravitational Potential Energy = mass · gravitational acceleration · height
$$GPE = mgh$$

Recall that g is the acceleration due to Earth's gravity. It is equal to 9.8 m/s² at Earth's surface.

The diver in the photograph below has given herself gravitational potential energy by climbing to the diving board. If you know her mass and the height of the board, you can calculate her potential energy.

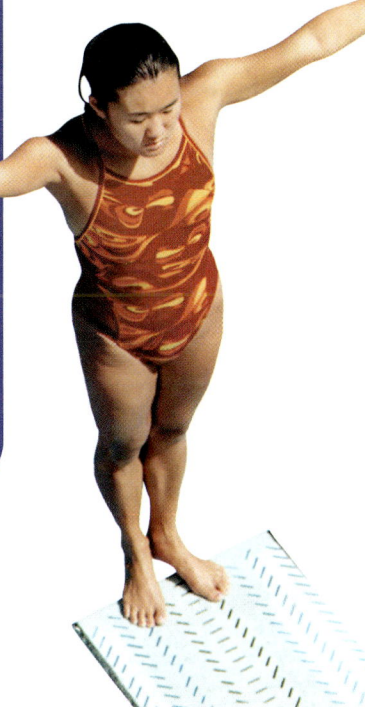

Calculating Potential Energy

Sample Problem

What is the gravitational potential energy of a girl who has a mass of 40 kg and is standing on the edge of a diving board that is 5 m above the water?

What do you know?	mass = 40 kg, gravitational acceleration = 9.8 m/s², height = 5 m
What do you want to find out?	Gravitational Potential Energy
Write the formula:	GPE = mgh
Substitute into the formula:	GPE = 40 kg · 9.8 m/s² · 5 m
Calculate and simplify:	GPE = 1960 kg m²/s²
Check that your units agree:	kg m²/s² = kg · m/s² · m = N·m = J
	Unit of energy is J. Units agree.
Answer:	GPE = 1960 J

> **REMINDER**
> A newton (N) is a kg · m/s², and a joule (J) is a N·m.

Practice the Math

1. An apple with a mass of 0.1 kg is attached to a branch of an apple tree 4 m from the ground. How much gravitational potential energy does the apple have?
2. If you lift a 2 kg box of toys to the top shelf of a closet, which is 3 m high, how much gravitational potential energy will the box of toys have?

The formula for gravitational potential energy is similar to the formula for work $(W = Fd)$. The formula for GPE also has a force (mg) multiplied by a distance (h). To understand why mg is a force, remember two things: force equals mass times acceleration, and g is the acceleration due to Earth's gravity.

Calculating Kinetic Energy

The girl on the swing at left has kinetic energy. To find out how much kinetic energy she has at the bottom of the swing's arc, you must know her mass and her velocity. Kinetic energy can be calculated using the following formula:

$$\text{Kinetic Energy} = \frac{\text{mass} \cdot \text{velocity}^2}{2}$$

$$KE = \frac{1}{2} mv^2$$

Notice that velocity is squared while mass is not. Increasing the velocity of an object has a greater effect on the object's kinetic energy than increasing the mass of the object. If you double the mass of an object, you double its kinetic energy. Because velocity is squared, if you double the object's velocity, its kinetic energy is four times greater.

Calculating Kinetic Energy

▶ Sample Problem

What is the kinetic energy of a girl who has a mass of 40 kg and a velocity of 3 m/s?

What do you know? mass = 40 kg, velocity = 3 m/s

What do you want to find out? Kinetic Energy

Write the formula: $KE = \frac{1}{2} mv^2$

Substitute into the formula: $KE = \frac{1}{2} \cdot 40 \text{ kg} \cdot (3 \text{ m/s})^2$

Calculate and simplify: $KE = \frac{1}{2} \cdot 40 \text{ kg} \cdot \frac{9 \text{ m}^2}{\text{s}^2}$

$$= \frac{360 \text{ kg} \cdot \text{m}^2}{2 \text{ s}^2}$$

$$= 180 \text{ kg} \cdot \text{m}^2/\text{s}^2$$

Check that your units agree: $\frac{\text{kg} \cdot \text{m}^2}{\text{s}^2} = \frac{\text{kg} \cdot \text{m}}{\text{s}^2} \cdot \text{m} = \text{N} \cdot \text{m} = \text{J}$

Unit of energy is J. Units agree.

Answer: $KE = 180 \text{ J}$

▶ Practice the Math

1. A grasshopper with a mass of 0.002 kg jumps up at a speed of 15 m/s. What is the kinetic energy of the grasshopper?
2. A truck with a mass of 6000 kg is traveling north on a highway at a speed of 17 m/s. A car with a mass of 2000 kg is traveling south on the same highway at a speed of 30 m/s. Which vehicle has more kinetic energy?

Calculating Mechanical Energy

Mechanical energy is the energy possessed by an object due to its motion or position—in other words, it is the object's combined potential energy and kinetic energy. A thrown baseball has mechanical energy as a result of both its motion (kinetic energy) and its position above the ground (gravitational potential energy). Any object that has mechanical energy can do work on another object.

Once you calculate an object's kinetic and potential energy, you can add the two values together to find the object's mechanical energy.

Mechanical Energy = Potential Energy + Kinetic Energy

$$ME = PE + KE$$

For example, a skateboarder has a potential energy of 200 joules due to his position at the top of a hill and a kinetic energy of 100 joules due to his motion. His total mechanical energy is 300 joules.

> **VOCABULARY**
> Use a vocabulary strategy to help you remember *mechanical energy*.

CHECK YOUR READING How is mechanical energy related to kinetic and potential energy?

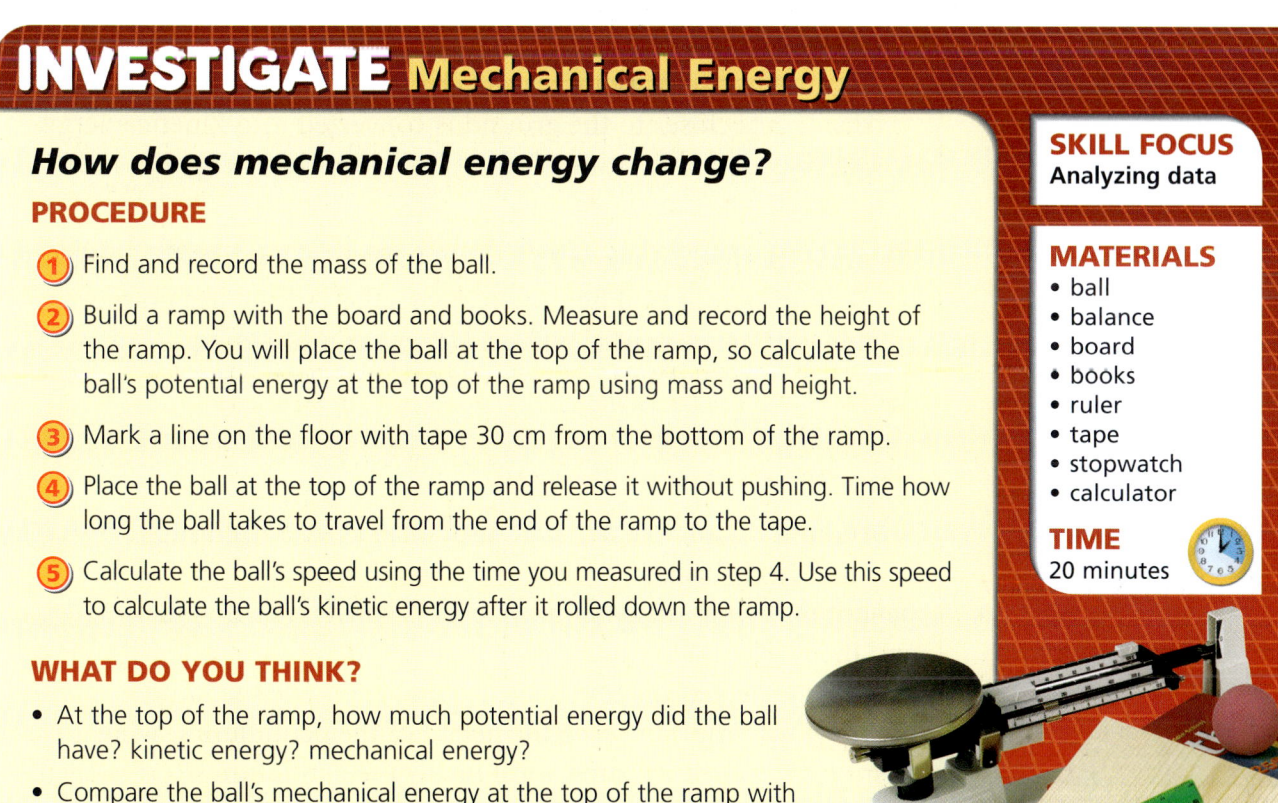

INVESTIGATE Mechanical Energy

How does mechanical energy change?

PROCEDURE

1. Find and record the mass of the ball.
2. Build a ramp with the board and books. Measure and record the height of the ramp. You will place the ball at the top of the ramp, so calculate the ball's potential energy at the top of the ramp using mass and height.
3. Mark a line on the floor with tape 30 cm from the bottom of the ramp.
4. Place the ball at the top of the ramp and release it without pushing. Time how long the ball takes to travel from the end of the ramp to the tape.
5. Calculate the ball's speed using the time you measured in step 4. Use this speed to calculate the ball's kinetic energy after it rolled down the ramp.

WHAT DO YOU THINK?

- At the top of the ramp, how much potential energy did the ball have? kinetic energy? mechanical energy?
- Compare the ball's mechanical energy at the top of the ramp with its mechanical energy at the bottom of the ramp. Are they the same? Why or why not?

CHALLENGE Other than gravity, what forces could have affected the movement of the ball?

SKILL FOCUS
Analyzing data

MATERIALS
- ball
- balance
- board
- books
- ruler
- tape
- stopwatch
- calculator

TIME
20 minutes

Chapter 4: **Work and Energy** 125

The total amount of energy is constant.

Observe how potential and kinetic energy are transferred on an amusement park ride.

You know that energy is transferred when work is done. No matter how energy is transferred or transformed, all of the energy is still present somewhere in one form or another. This is known as the **law of conservation of energy.** As long as you account for all the different forms of energy involved in any process, you will find that the total amount of energy never changes.

Conserving Mechanical Energy

Look at the photograph of the in-line skater on page 127. As she rolls down the ramp, the amounts of kinetic energy and potential energy change. However, the total—or the mechanical energy—stays the same. In this example, energy lost to friction is ignored.

① At the top of the ramp, the skater has potential energy because gravity can pull her downward. She has no velocity; therefore, she has no kinetic energy.

② As the skater rolls down the ramp, her potential energy decreases because the elevation decreases. Her kinetic energy increases because her velocity increases. The potential energy lost as the skater gets closer to the ground is converted into kinetic energy. Halfway down the ramp, half of her potential energy has been converted to kinetic energy.

③ At the bottom of the ramp, all of the skater's energy is kinetic. Gravity cannot pull her down any farther, so she has no more gravitational potential energy. Her mechanical energy—the total of her potential and kinetic energy—stays the same throughout.

Losing Mechanical Energy

A pendulum is an object that is suspended from a fixed support so that it swings freely back and forth under the influence of gravity. As a pendulum swings, its potential energy is converted into kinetic energy and then back to potential energy in a continuous cycle. Ideally, the potential energy at the top of each swing would be the same as it was the previous time. However, the height of the pendulum's swing actually decreases slightly each time, until finally the pendulum stops altogether.

In most energy transformations, some of the energy is transformed into heat. In the case of the pendulum, there is friction between the string and the support, as well as air resistance from the air around the pendulum. The mechanical energy is used to do work against friction and air resistance. This process transforms the mechanical energy into heat. The mechanical energy has not been destroyed; it has simply changed form and been transferred from the pendulum.

APPLY Energy must occasionally be added to a pendulum to keep it swinging. What keeps a grandfather clock's pendulum swinging regularly?

126 Unit 1: **Motion and Forces**

Conserving Mechanical Energy

The potential energy and kinetic energy in a system or process may vary, but the total energy remains unchanged.

1 Top of Ramp

At the top of the ramp, the skater's mechanical energy is equal to her potential energy because she has no velocity.

100% PE

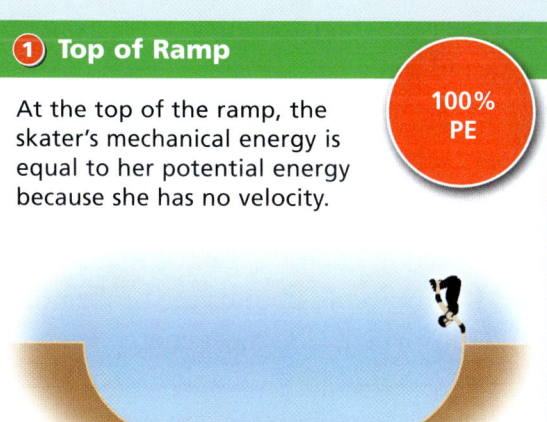

2 Halfway Down Ramp

As the skater goes down the ramp, she loses height but gains speed. The potential energy she loses is equal to the kinetic energy she gains.

50% PE | 50% KE

3 Bottom of Ramp

As the skater speeds along the bottom of the ramp, all of the potential energy has changed to kinetic energy. Her mechanical energy remains unchanged.

100% KE

Fabiola da Silva is a professional in-line skater who was born in Brazil but now lives in California.

READING VISUALS How do the skater's kinetic and potential energy change as she skates up and down the ramp? (Assume she won't lose any energy to friction.)

Chapter 4: **Work and Energy** 127

MAIN IDEA WEB
Include common forms of energy in your web.

Forms of Energy

As you have seen, mechanical energy is a combination of kinetic energy and potential energy. Other common forms of energy are discussed below. Each of these forms of energy is also a combination of kinetic energy and potential energy. Chemical energy, for example, is potential energy when it is stored in bonds.

Thermal energy is the energy an object has due to the motion of its molecules. The faster the molecules in an object move, the more thermal energy the object has.

Chemical energy is the energy stored in chemical bonds that hold chemical compounds together. If a molecule's bonds are broken or rearranged, energy is released or absorbed. Chemical energy is used to light up fireworks displays. It is also stored in food and in matches.

Nuclear energy is the potential energy stored in the nucleus of an atom. In a nuclear reaction, a tiny portion of an atom's mass is turned into energy. The source of the Sun's energy is nuclear energy. Nuclear energy can be used to run power plants that provide electricity.

Electromagnetic energy is the energy associated with electrical and magnetic interactions. Energy that is transferred by electric charges or current is often called electrical energy. Another type of electromagnetic energy is radiant energy, the energy carried by light, infrared waves, and x-rays.

It is possible to transfer, or convert, one energy form into one or more other forms. For example, when you rub your hands together on a cold day, you convert mechanical energy to thermal energy. Your body converts chemical energy stored in food to thermal and mechanical energy (muscle movement).

4.2 Review

KEY CONCEPTS

1. Explain the relationship between work and energy.
2. How are potential energy and kinetic energy related to mechanical energy?
3. When one form of energy changes into one or more other forms of energy, what happens to the total amount of energy?

CRITICAL THINKING

4. **Infer** Debra used 250 J of energy to roll a bowling ball. When the ball arrived at the end of the lane, it had only 200 J of energy. What happened to the other 50 J?
5. **Calculate** A satellite falling to Earth has a kinetic energy of 182.2 billion J and a potential energy of 1.6 billion J. What is its mechanical energy?

CHALLENGE

6. **Apply** At what point in its motion is the kinetic energy of the end of a pendulum greatest? At what point is its potential energy greatest? When its kinetic energy is half its greatest value, how much potential energy did it gain?

Think SCIENCE

SKILL: ISOLATING VARIABLES

How Do They Do It?

Some women in Kenya and other African countries walk many miles every day carrying heavy loads on their heads without an increase in their heart rate. Most have done it since they were children. Scientists have studied African women to learn how they do this.

▶ Variables

In scientific research, variables must be chosen and tested. Variables are usually compared with a control group—that is, a group for whom all potential variables are held constant. Scientists first asked several Kenyan women to walk on a treadmill. The scientists measured the women's heart rate and how much oxygen they used while carrying different weights on their heads. They found that the women could carry as much as 20 percent of their own body weight without using extra oxygen or increasing their heart rate.

The same scientists asked subjects in a control group in the United States to walk on a treadmill. The people in this group wore helmets lined with different amounts of lead. Even the lightest load caused their heart rate and oxygen consumption to increase.

If you were studying the way these African women carry loads, what variables would you choose to isolate? What control group would you use? Here are some variables and controls to consider:

- carrying the load on the head compared with carrying it on the back
- weight of the load
- women compared with men
- African women compared with other women
- method of walking

▶ Isolate the Variables

On Your Own Design an experiment that could test one of the variables without interference from other variables. Can each variable be tested independently?

As a Group Discuss each variable and see if the group agrees that it can be tested independently. Can you eliminate any of the variables based on information on this page?

CHALLENGE How would you measure the amount of energy used for the variable you chose?

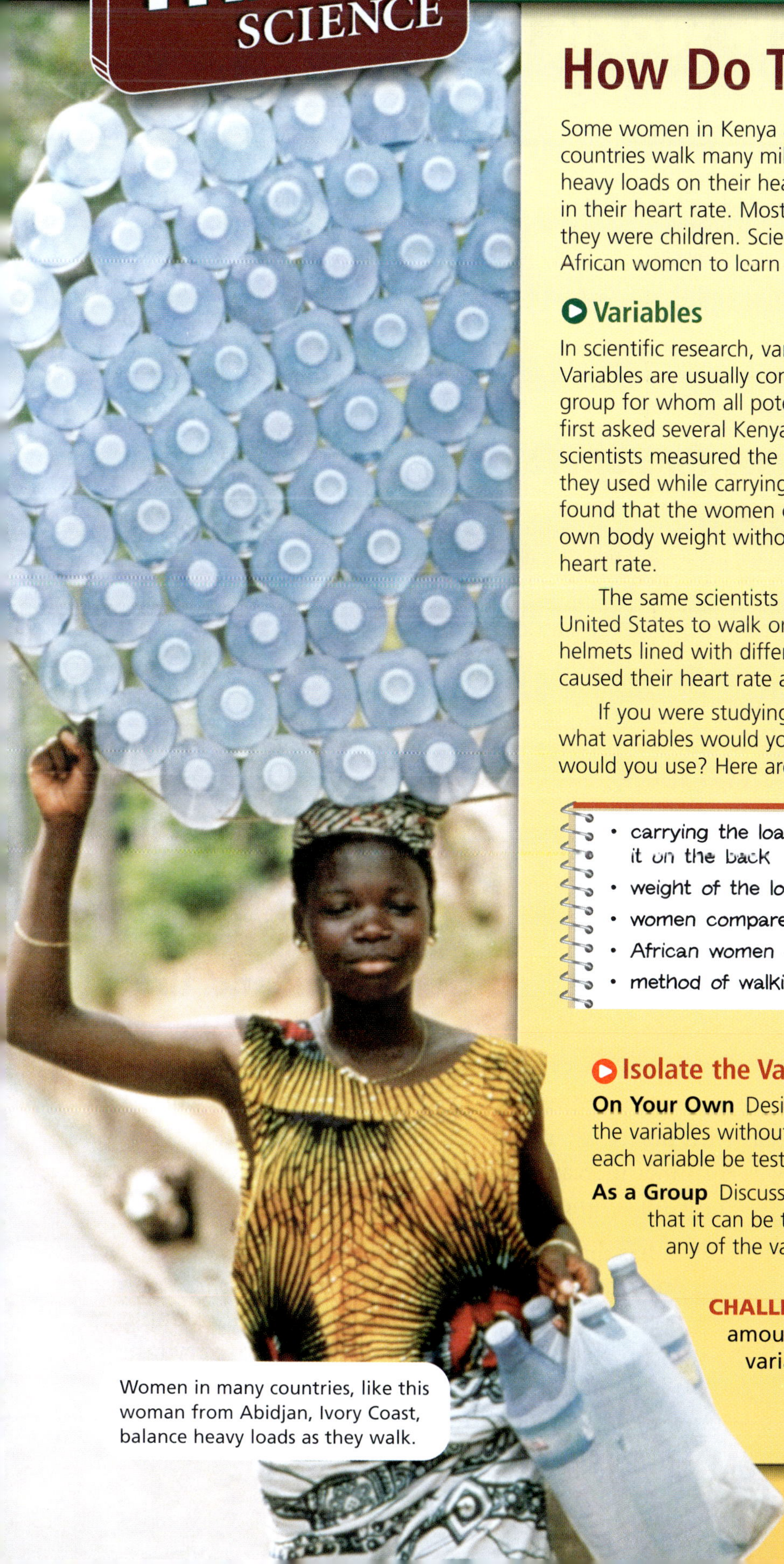

Women in many countries, like this woman from Abidjan, Ivory Coast, balance heavy loads as they walk.

Chapter 4: **Work and Energy** 129

4.3 KEY CONCEPT
Power is the rate at which work is done.

BEFORE, you learned
- Mechanical energy is a combination of kinetic energy and potential energy
- Mechanical energy can be calculated
- Work transfers energy

NOW, you will learn
- How power is related to work and time
- How power is related to energy and time
- About common uses of power

VOCABULARY

power p. 130
watt p. 131
horsepower p. 132

EXPLORE Power

How does time affect work?

PROCEDURE

1. Place the cups side by side. Put all of the marbles in one cup.
2. Place each marble, one by one, into the other cup. Time how long it takes to do this.
3. Set the timer for half that amount of time. Then repeat step 2 in that time.

WHAT DO YOU THINK?
- Did you do more work the first time or the second time? Why?
- What differences did you notice between the two tries?

MATERIALS
- 2 plastic cups
- 10 marbles
- stopwatch

VOCABULARY
Use a vocabulary strategy to help you remember the meaning of *power*.

Power can be calculated from work and time.

If you lift a book one meter, you do the same amount of work whether you lift the book quickly or slowly. However, when you lift the book quickly, you increase your **power**—the rate at which you do work. A cook increases his power when he beats eggs rapidly instead of stirring them slowly. A runner increases her power when she breaks into a sprint to reach the finish line.

The word *power* has different common meanings. It is used to mean a source of energy, as in a power plant, or strength, as in a powerful engine. When you talk about a powerful swimmer, for example, you would probably say that the swimmer is very strong or very fast. If you use the scientific definition of power, you would instead say that a powerful swimmer is one who does the work of moving herself through the water in a short time.

Each of the swimmers shown in the photograph above is doing work—that is, she is using a certain force to move a certain distance. It takes time to cover that distance. The power a swimmer uses depends on the force, the distance, and the time it takes to cover that distance. The more force the swimmer uses, the more power she has. Also, the faster she goes, the more power she has because she is covering the same distance in a shorter time. Swimmers often increase their speed toward the end of a race, which increases their power, making it possible for them to reach the end of the pool in less time.

CHECK YOUR READING Summarize in your own words the difference between work and power.

Calculating Power from Work

You know that a given amount of work can be done by a slow-moving swimmer over a long period of time or by a fast-moving swimmer in a short time. Likewise, a given amount of work can be done by a low-powered motor over a long period of time or by a high-powered motor in a short time.

Because power is a measurement of how much work is done in a given time, power can be calculated based on work and time. To find power, divide the amount of work by the time it takes to do the work.

$$\text{Power} = \frac{\text{Work}}{\text{time}} \qquad P = \frac{W}{t}$$

READING TIP
W (in italicized type) is the letter that represents the variable *Work*. W, not italicized, is the abbreviation for watt.

Remember that work is measured in joules. Power is often measured in joules of work per second. The unit of measurement for power is the **watt** (W). One watt is equal to one joule of work done in one second. If an object does a large amount of work, its power is usually measured in units of 1000 watts, or kilowatts.

Find out more about power.

Calculating Power from Work

Sample Problem

An Antarctic explorer uses 6000 J of work to pull his sled for 60 s. What power does he need?

What do you know? Work = 6000 J, time = 60 s

What do you want to find out? Power

Write the formula: $P = \dfrac{W}{t}$

Substitute into the formula: $P = \dfrac{6000 \text{ J}}{60 \text{ s}}$

Calculate and simplify: $P = 100 \text{ J/s} = 100 \text{ W}$

Check that your units agree: $\dfrac{\text{J}}{\text{s}} = \text{W}$

Unit of power is W. Units agree.

Answer: $P = 100 \text{ W}$

Practice the Math

1. If a conveyor belt uses 10 J to move a piece of candy a distance of 3 m in 20 s, what is the conveyor belt's power?
2. An elevator uses a force of 1710 N to lift 3 people up 1 floor. Each floor is 4 m high. The elevator takes 8 s to lift the 3 people up 2 floors. What is the elevator's power?

Horsepower

James Watt, the Scottish engineer for whom the watt is named, improved the power of the steam engine in the mid-1700s. Watt also developed a unit of measurement for power called the horsepower.

Horsepower is based on what it sounds like—the amount of work a horse can do in a minute. In Watt's time, people used horses to do many different types of work. For example, horses were used on farms to pull plows and wagons.

Watt wanted to explain to people how powerful his steam engine was compared with horses. After observing several horses doing work, Watt concluded that an average horse could move 150 pounds a distance of 220 feet in 1 minute. Watt called this amount of power 1 horsepower. A single horsepower is equal to 745 watts. Therefore, a horsepower is a much larger unit of measurement than a watt.

Today horsepower is used primarily in connection with engines and motors. For example, you may see a car advertised as having a 150-horsepower engine. The power of a motorboat, lawn mower, tractor, or motorcycle engine is also referred to as horsepower.

Both the horse and the tractor use power to pull objects around a farm.

INVESTIGATE Power

How much power do you have?
PROCEDURE

1. Measure a length of 5 meters on the floor. Mark the beginning and the end of the 5 meters with masking tape.
2. Attach the object to the spring scale with a piece of string. Slowly pull the object across the floor using a steady amount of force. Record the force and the time it takes you to pull the object.

WHAT DO YOU THINK?
- How much power did you use to pull the object 5 meters?
- How do you think you could increase the power you used? decrease the power?

CHALLENGE How quickly would you have to drag the object along the floor to produce 40 watts of power?

SKILL FOCUS
Measuring

MATERIALS
- meter stick
- masking tape
- 100 g object
- spring scale
- string
- stopwatch

TIME
15 minutes

Power can be calculated from energy and time.

Sometimes you may know that energy is being transferred, but you cannot directly measure the work done by the forces involved. For example, you know that a television uses power. But there is no way to measure all the work every part of the television does in terms of forces and distance. Because work measures the transfer of energy, you can also think of power as the amount of energy transferred over a period of time.

Calculating Power from Energy

When you turn on a television, it starts using energy. Each second the television is on, a certain amount of electrical energy is transferred from a local power plant to your television. If you measure how much energy your television uses during a given time period, you can find out how much power it needs by using the following formula:

$$\text{Power} = \frac{\text{Energy}}{\text{time}} \qquad P = \frac{E}{t}$$

This formula should look familiar to you because it is very similar to the formula used to calculate power from work.

Chapter 4: **Work and Energy** 133

The photograph shows Hong Kong, China, at night. Every second, the city uses more than 4 billion joules of electrical energy!

You can think about power as any kind of transfer of energy in a certain amount of time. It is useful to think of power in this way if you cannot directly figure out the work used to transfer the energy. Power calculated from transferred energy is also measured in joules per second, or watts.

You have probably heard the term *watt* used in connection with light bulbs. A 60-watt light bulb requires 60 joules of energy every second to shine at its rated brightness.

CHECK YOUR READING In what situations is it useful to think of power as the transfer of energy in a certain amount of time?

REMINDER
Remember that energy and work are both measured in joules.

Calculating Power from Energy

Sample Problem

A light bulb used 600 J of energy in 6 s. What is the power of the light bulb?

What do you know? Energy = 600 J, time = 6 s

What do you want to find out? Power

Write the formula: $P = \dfrac{E}{t}$

Substitute into the formula: $P = \dfrac{600 \text{ J}}{6 \text{ s}}$

Calculate and simplify: $P = 100$ J/s

Check that your units agree: Unit is J/s. Unit for power is W, which is also J/s. Units agree.

Answer: $P = 100$ W

Practice the Math

1. A laptop computer uses 100 J every 2 seconds. How much power is needed to run the computer?
2. The power needed to pump blood through your body is about 1.1 W. How much energy does your body use when pumping blood for 10 seconds?

134 Unit 1: **Motion and Forces**

Everyday Power

Many appliances in your home rely on electricity for energy. Each appliance requires a certain number of joules per second, the power it needs to run properly. An electric hair dryer uses energy. For example, a 600-watt hair dryer needs 600 joules per second. The wattage of the hair dryer indicates how much energy per second it needs to operate.

The dryer works by speeding up the evaporation of water on the surface of hair. It needs only two main parts to do this: a heating coil and a fan turned by a motor.

① When the hair dryer is plugged into an outlet and the switch is turned on, electrical energy moves electrons in the wires, creating a current.

② This current runs an electric motor that turns the fan blades. Air is drawn into the hair dryer through small holes in the casing. The turning fan blades push the air over the coil.

③ The current also makes the heating coil become hot.

④ The fan pushes heated air out of the dryer.

Most hair dryers have high and low settings. At the high power setting, the temperature is increased, more air is pushed through the dryer, and the dryer does its work faster. Some dryers have safety switches that shut off the motor when the temperature rises to a level that could burn your scalp. Insulation keeps the outside of the dryer from becoming hot to the touch.

Many other appliances, from air conditioners to washing machines to blenders, need electrical energy to do their work. Take a look around you at all the appliances that help you during a typical day.

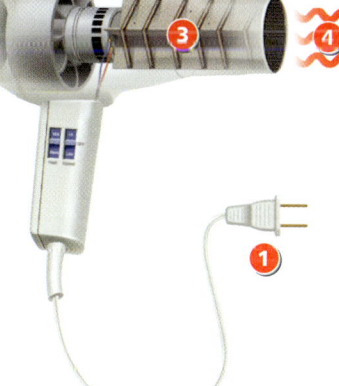

4.3 Review

KEY CONCEPTS

1. How is power related to work?
2. Name two units used for power, and give examples of when each unit might be used.
3. What do you need to know to calculate how much energy a light bulb uses?

CRITICAL THINKING

4. **Apply** Discuss different ways in which a swimmer can increase her power.
5. **Calculate** Which takes more power: using 15 N to lift a ball 2 m in 5 seconds or using 100 N to push a box 2 m in 1 minute?

⚠ CHALLENGE

6. **Analyze** A friend tells you that you can calculate power by using a different formula from the one given in this book. The formula your friend gives you is as follows:

   Power = force • speed

   Do you think this is a valid formula for power? Explain.

CHAPTER INVESTIGATION

Work and Power

OVERVIEW AND PURPOSE People in wheelchairs cannot use steps leading up to a building's entrance. Sometimes there is a machine that can lift a person and wheelchair straight up to the entrance level. At other times, there is a ramp leading to the entrance. Which method takes more power?

▶ Problem

How does a ramp affect the amount of energy, work, and power used to lift an object?

▶ Hypothesize

Write a hypothesis to explain how the potential energy, the amount of work done, and the power required to lift an object straight up compare with the same quantities when the object is moved up a ramp. Your hypothesis should take the form of an "If . . . , then . . . , because . . ." statement.

▶ Procedure

1. Make a data table like the one shown.

2. Lean the board up against the chair seat to create a ramp.

3. Measure and record the vertical distance from the floor to the top of the ramp. Also measure and record the length of the ramp.

4. Tie the string around the wheeled object. Make a loop so that you can hook the string onto the spring scale. Measure and record the weight of the object in newtons.

5. Lift the object straight up to the top of the ramp without using the ramp, as pictured.

MATERIALS
- board
- chair
- meter stick
- string
- small wheeled object
- spring scale
- stopwatch

136 Unit 1: Motion and Forces

6. On the spring scale, read and record the newtons of force needed to lift the object. Time how long it takes to lift the object from the floor to the top of the ramp. Conduct three trials and average your results. Record your measurements in the data table.

7. Drag the object from the bottom of the ramp to the top of the ramp with the spring scale, and record the newtons of force that were needed to move the object and the time it took. Conduct three trials and average your results.

Observe and Analyze *Write It Up*

1. **RECORD OBSERVATIONS** Draw the setup of the procedure. Be sure your data table is complete.

2. **IDENTIFY VARIABLES AND CONSTANTS** List the variables and constants in your notebook.

3. **CALCULATE**
   Potential Energy Convert centimeters to meters. Then calculate the gravitational potential energy (GPE) of the object at the top of the ramp. (Recall that weight equals mass times gravitational acceleration.)

   Gravitational Potential Energy = weight • height

   Work Calculate the work done, first when the object was lifted and then when it was pulled. Use the appropriate distance.

   Work = Force • distance

   Power Calculate the power involved in both situations.

   Power = $\dfrac{\text{Work}}{\text{time}}$

Conclude *Write It Up*

1. **COMPARE** How did the distance through which the object moved when it was pulled up the ramp differ from the distance when it was lifted straight up? How did the amount of force required differ in the two situations?

2. **COMPARE** How does your calculated value for potential energy compare with the values you obtained for work done?

3. **INTERPRET** Answer the question posed in the problem.

4. **ANALYZE** Compare your results with your hypothesis. Did your results support your hypothesis?

5. **IDENTIFY LIMITS** What possible limitations or sources of error could you have experienced?

6. **APPLY** A road going up a hill usually winds back and forth instead of heading straight to the top. How does this affect the work a car does to get to the top? How does it affect the power involved?

INVESTIGATE Further

CHALLENGE Design a way to use potential energy to move the car up the ramp. What materials can you use? Think about the materials in terms of potential energy—that is, how high they are from the ground or how stretched or compressed they are.

Work and Power

Problem How does the amount of energy, work, and power used to lift an object?

Hypothesize

Observe and Analyze

Measured length of ramp = _____ cm

Height object is being lifted = _____ cm

Measured weight of the object = _____ N

Table 1. Measurements for Lifting the Object with and Without the Ramp

	Trial No.	Force (N)	Time (s)
Straight up	1		
	2		
	3		
	Average		
Ramp	1		

Chapter Review

the BIG idea
Energy is transferred when a force moves an object.

KEY CONCEPTS SUMMARY

1. Work is the use of force to move an object.

Work is done by a force that acts in the same direction as the motion of an object.

Work = Force · distance

VOCABULARY
work p. 115
joule p. 117

2. Energy is transferred when work is done.

The amounts of potential energy and kinetic energy in a system or process may vary, but the total amount of energy remains unchanged.

$GPE = mgh$

$KE = \frac{1}{2}mv^2$

$ME = PE + KE$

VOCABULARY
potential energy p. 122
kinetic energy p. 122
mechanical energy p. 125
conservation of energy p. 126

3. Power is the rate at which work is done.

Power can be calculated from work and time.

$$\text{Power} = \frac{\text{Work}}{\text{time}}$$

Power can be calculated from energy and time.

$$\text{Power} = \frac{\text{Energy}}{\text{time}}$$

Power is measured in watts (W) and sometimes horsepower (hp).

VOCABULARY
power p. 130
watt p. 131
horsepower p. 132

Reviewing Vocabulary

Make a four square diagram for each of the terms listed below. Write the term in the center. Define it in one square. Write characteristics, examples, and formulas (if appropriate) in the other squares. A sample is shown below.

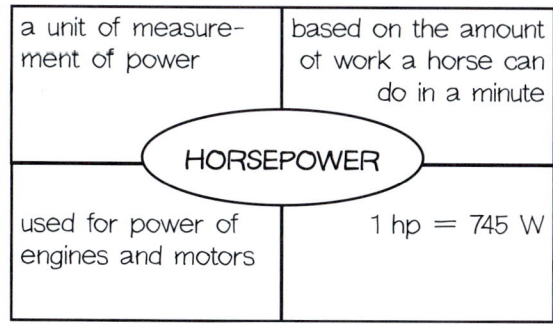

1. work
2. joule
3. potential energy
4. kinetic energy
5. mechanical energy
6. power
7. watt

Reviewing Key Concepts

Multiple Choice *Choose the letter of the best answer.*

8. Work can be calculated from
   a. force and speed
   b. force and distance
   c. energy and time
   d. energy and distance

9. If you balance a book on your head, you are not doing work on the book because
   a. doing work requires moving an object
   b. you are not applying any force to the book
   c. the book is doing work on you
   d. the book has potential energy

10. Energy that an object has because of its position or shape is called
    a. potential energy   c. thermal energy
    b. kinetic energy   d. chemical energy

11. Suppose you are pushing a child on a swing. During what space of time are you doing work on the swing?
    a. while you hold it back before letting go
    b. while your hands are in contact with the swing and pushing forward
    c. after you let go of the swing and it continues to move forward
    d. all the time the swing is in motion

12. A falling ball has a potential energy of 5 J and a kinetic energy of 10 J. What is the ball's mechanical energy?
    a. 5 J   c. 15 J
    b. 10 J   d. 50 J

13. The unit that measures one joule of work done in one second is called a
    a. meter   c. newton-meter
    b. watt   d. newton

14. By increasing the speed at which you do work, you increase your
    a. force   c. energy
    b. work   d. power

15. A ball kicked into the air will have the greatest gravitational potential energy
    a. as it is being kicked
    b. as it starts rising
    c. at its highest point
    d. as it hits the ground

Short Answer *Answer each of the following questions in a sentence or two.*

16. How can you tell if a force you exert is doing work?

17. How does a water wheel do work?

18. State the law of conservation of energy. How does it affect the total amount of energy in any process?

19. Explain why a swing will not stay in motion forever after you have given it a push. What happens to its mechanical energy?

20. What are two ways to calculate power?

21. Why did James Watt invent a unit of measurement based on the work of horses?

Chapter 4: **Work and Energy** 139

Thinking Critically

22. **SYNTHESIZE** A weightlifter holds a barbell above his head. How do the barbell's potential energy, kinetic energy, and mechanical energy change as it is lifted and then lowered to the ground?

23. **SYNTHESIZE** What happens when you wind up a toy car and release it? Describe the events in terms of energy.

Use the photograph below to answer the next three questions.

24. **APPLY** When the boy first pushes on the chair, the chair does not move due to friction. Is the boy doing work? Why or why not?

25. **ANALYZE** For the first two seconds, the boy pushes the chair slowly at a steady speed. After that, he pushes the chair at a faster speed. How does his power change if he is using the same force at both speeds? How does his work change?

26. **SYNTHESIZE** As the boy pushes the chair, he does work. However, when he stops pushing, the chair stops moving and does not have any additional kinetic or potential energy. What happened to the energy he transferred by doing work on the chair?

27. **APPLY** A bouncing ball has mechanical energy. Each bounce, however, reaches a lower height than the last. Describe what happens to the mechanical, potential, and kinetic energy of the ball as it bounces several times.

28. **CONNECT** When you do work, you transfer energy. Where does the energy you transfer come from?

Using Math Skills in Science

Complete the following calculations.

29. Use the information in the photograph below to calculate the work the person does in lifting the box.

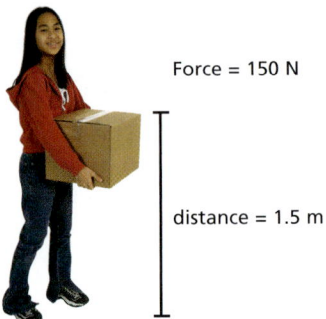

Force = 150 N

distance = 1.5 m

30. If you did 225 J of work to pull a wagon with a force of 25 N, how far did you pull it?

31. A kite with a mass of 0.05 kg is caught on the roof of a house. The house is 10 m high. What is the kite's gravitational potential energy? (Recall that $g = 9.8$ m/s^2.)

32. A baseball with a mass of 0.15 kg leaves a pitcher's hand traveling 40 m/s toward the batter. What is the baseball's kinetic energy?

33. Suppose it takes 150 J of force to push a cart 10 m in 60 s. Calculate the power.

34. If an electric hair dryer uses 1200 W, how much energy does it need to run for 2 s?

the BIG idea

35. **SYNTHESIZE** Look back at the photograph of the person lifting a box on pages 112–113. Describe the picture in terms of work, potential energy, kinetic energy, and power.

36. **WRITE** Think of an activity that involves work. Write a paragraph explaining how the work is transferring energy and where the transferred energy goes.

UNIT PROJECTS

If you need to create graphs or other visuals for your project, be sure you have grid paper, poster board, markers, or other supplies.

Standardized Test Practice

For practice on your state test, go to...
TEST PRACTICE
CLASSZONE.COM

Understanding Experiments

Read the following description of an experiment. Then answer the questions that follow.

James Prescott Joule is well known for a paddle-wheel experiment he conducted in the mid-1800s. He placed a paddle wheel in a bucket of water. Then he set up two weights on either side of the bucket. As the weights fell, they turned the paddle wheel. Joule recorded the temperature of the water before and after the paddle wheel began turning. He found that the water temperature increased as the paddle wheel turned.

Based on this experiment, Joule concluded that the falling weights released mechanical energy, which was converted into heat by the turning wheel. He was convinced that whenever mechanical force is exerted, heat is produced.

1. Which principle did Joule demonstrate with this experiment?
   a. When energy is converted from one form to another, some energy is lost.
   b. The amount of momentum in a system does not change as long as there are no outside forces acting on the system.
   c. One form of energy can be converted into another form of energy.
   d. When one object exerts a force on another object, the second object exerts an equal and opposite force on the first object.

2. Which form of energy was released by the weights in Joule's experiment?
   a. electrical
   b. mechanical
   c. nuclear
   d. heat

3. Which form of energy was produced in the water?
   a. chemical
   b. electrical
   c. nuclear
   d. heat

4. Based on Joule's finding that movement causes temperature changes in water, which of the following would be a logical prediction?
   a. Water held in a container should increase in temperature.
   b. Water at the base of a waterfall should be warmer than water at the top.
   c. Water with strong waves should be colder than calm water.
   d. Water should increase in temperature with depth.

Extended Response

Answer the two questions below in detail. Include some of the terms from the word box. Underline each term you use in your answer.

| potential energy | conservation of energy | force |
| kinetic energy | power | work |

5. A sledder has the greatest potential energy at the top of a hill. She has the least amount of potential energy at the bottom of a hill. She has the greatest kinetic energy when she moves the fastest. Where on the hill does the sledder move the fastest? State the relationship between kinetic energy and potential energy in this situation.

6. Andre and Jon are moving boxes of books from the floor to a shelf in the school library. Each box weighs 15 lb. Andre lifts 5 boxes in one minute. Jon lifts 5 boxes in 30 seconds. Which person does more work? Which person applies more force? Which person has the greater power? Explain your answers.

Chapter 4: **Work and Energy** 141

CHAPTER 5
Machines

the BIG idea

Machines help people do work by changing the force applied to an object.

Key Concepts

SECTION 1
Machines help people do work.
Learn about machines and how they are used to do work.

SECTION 2
Six simple machines have many uses.
Learn about levers and inclined planes and the other simple machines that are related to them.

SECTION 3
Modern technology uses compound machines.
Learn how scientists are using nanotechnology and robots to create new ways for machines to do work.

Internet Preview

CLASSZONE.COM

Chapter 5 online resources: Content Review, Simulation, four Resource Centers, Math Tutorial, Test Practice

Balls move through this sculpture. What do you think keeps the balls in motion?

142 Unit 1: Motion and Forces

EXPLORE the BIG idea

Changing Direction

Observe how a window blind works. Notice how you use a downward force to pull the blind up. Look around you for other examples.

Observe and Think Why does changing the direction of a force make work easier?

Shut the Door!

Find a door that swings freely on its hinges. Stand on the side where you can push the door to close it. Open the door. Push the door closed several times, placing your hand closer to or farther from the hinge each time.

Observe and Think Which hand placement made it easiest to shut the door? Why do you think that is so?

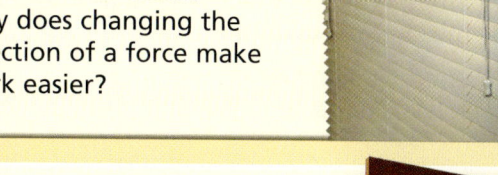

Internet Activity: Machines

Go to **ClassZone.com** to learn more about the simple machines in everyday objects. Select an item and think about how it moves and does its job. Then test your knowledge of simple machines.

Observe and Think What other objects contain simple machines?

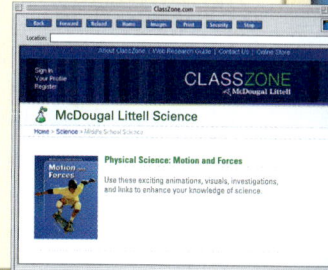

Simple Machines Code: MDL008

Chapter 5: **Machines** 143

CHAPTER 5
Getting Ready to Learn

◁ CONCEPT REVIEW

- Work is done when a force moves an object over a distance.
- Energy can be converted from one form to another.
- Energy is transferred when work is done.

◁ VOCABULARY REVIEW

work p. 115

mechanical energy p. 125

power p. 130

See Glossary for definitions.

energy, technology

CONTENT REVIEW
CLASSZONE.COM

Review concepts and vocabulary.

▷ TAKING NOTES

CHOOSE YOUR OWN STRATEGY

Take notes using one or more of the strategies from earlier chapters—**outline, combination notes, supporting main ideas,** and **main idea web.** Feel free to mix and match the strategies, or use an entirely different note-taking strategy.

VOCABULARY STRATEGY

Draw a **word triangle** diagram for each new vocabulary term. On the bottom line, write and define the term. Above that, write a sentence that uses the term correctly. At the top, draw a small picture to show what the term looks like.

See the Note-Taking Handbook on pages R45–R51.

SCIENCE NOTEBOOK

Outline
I. Main idea
  A. Supporting idea
    1. Detail
    2. Detail
  B. Supporting idea

Combination Notes

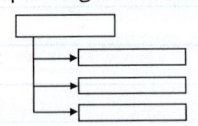

Supporting Main Ideas

Main Idea Web

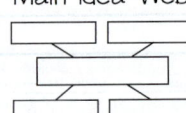

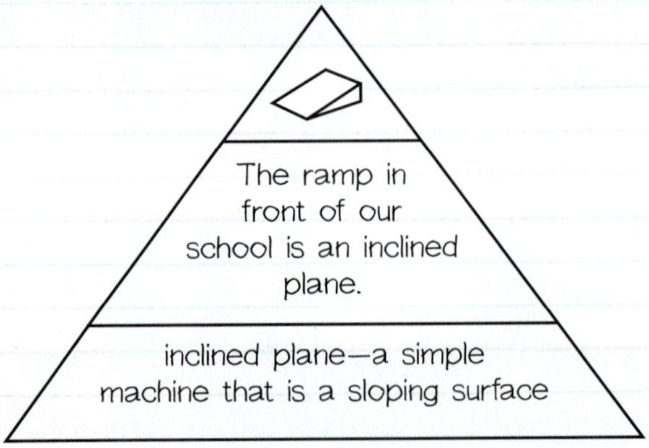

The ramp in front of our school is an inclined plane.

inclined plane—a simple machine that is a sloping surface

144 Unit 1: Motion and Forces

KEY CONCEPT

Machines help people do work.

 BEFORE, you learned
- Work is done when a force is exerted over a distance
- Some work can be converted to heat or sound energy

 NOW, you will learn
- How machines help you do work
- How to calculate a machine's efficiency

VOCABULARY

machine p. 145
mechanical advantage p. 147
efficiency p. 150

EXPLORE Machines

How do machines help you work?

PROCEDURE

1. Look at one of the machines closely. Carefully operate the machine and notice how each part moves.

2. Sketch a diagram of the machine. Try to show all of the working parts. Add arrows and labels to show the direction of motion for each part.

WHAT DO YOU THINK?
- What is the function of the machine?
- How many moving parts does it have?
- How do the parts work together?
- How does this machine make work easier?

MATERIALS
various small machines

Machines change the way force is applied.

For thousands of years, humans have been improving their lives with technology. Technology is the use of knowledge to create products or tools that make life easier. The simplest machine is an example of technology.

A **machine** is any device that helps people do work. A machine does not decrease the amount of work that is done. Instead, a machine changes the way in which work is done. Recall that work is the use of force to move an object. If, for example, you have to lift a heavy box, you can use a ramp to make the work easier. Moving the box up a ramp—which is a machine—helps you do the work by reducing the force you need to lift the box.

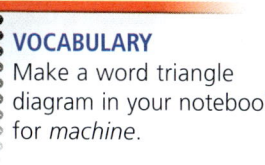

VOCABULARY
Make a word triangle diagram in your notebook for *machine*.

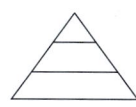

Chapter 5: **Machines** 145

If machines do not reduce the amount of work required, how do they help people do work? Machines make work easier by changing

- the size of the force needed to do the work and the distance over which the force is applied
- the direction in which the force is exerted

Machines can be powered by different types of energy. Electronic machines, such as computers, use electrical energy. Mechanical machines, such as a rake, use mechanical energy. Often this mechanical energy is supplied by the person who is using the machine.

Changing Size and Distance

Some machines help you do work by changing the size of the force needed. Have you ever tried to open a door by turning the doorknob's shaft instead of the handle? This is not easy to do. It takes less force to turn the handle of the doorknob than it does to turn the shaft. Turning the handle makes opening the door easier, even though you must turn it through a greater distance.

If a machine—such as a doorknob attached to a shaft—allows you to exert less force, you must apply that force over a greater distance. The total amount of work remains the same whether it is done with a machine or not. You can think of this in terms of the formula for calculating work—work is force times distance. Because a machine does not decrease the amount of work to be done, less force must mean greater distance.

A doorknob allows you to apply a smaller force over a greater distance. Some machines allow you to apply a greater input force over a shorter distance. Look at the boy using a rake, which is a machine. The boy moves his hands a short distance to move the end of the rake a large distance, allowing him to rake up more leaves.

Input force is the force exerted on a machine. Output force is the force that a machine exerts on an object. The boy in the photograph is exerting an input force on the rake. As a result, the rake exerts an output force on the leaves. The work the boy puts into the rake is the same as the work he gets out of the rake. However, the force he applies is greater than the force the rake can apply to the leaves. The output force is less than the input force, but it acts over a longer distance.

A rake is a machine that changes a large force over a short distance to a smaller force over a larger distance.

CHECK YOUR READING — How can a rake help you do work? Use the word *force* in your answer.

Changing Direction

Machines also can help you work by changing the direction of a force. Think of raising a flag on a flagpole. You pull down on the rope, and the flag moves up. The rope system is a machine that changes the direction in which you exert your force. The rope system does not change the size of the force, however. The force pulling the flag upward is equal to your downward pull.

A shovel is a machine that can help you dig a hole. Once you have the shovel in the ground, you push down on the handle to lift the dirt up. You can use some of the weight of your body as part of your input force. That would not be possible if you were lifting the dirt by using only your hands. A shovel also changes the size of the force you apply, so you need less force to lift the dirt.

Mechanical Advantage of a Machine

When machines help you work, there is an advantage—or benefit—to using them. The number of times a machine multiplies the input force is called the machine's **mechanical advantage** (MA). To find a machine's mechanical advantage, divide the output force by the input force.

$$\text{Mechanical Advantage} = \frac{\text{Output Force}}{\text{Input Force}}$$

For machines that allow you to apply less force over a greater distance—such as a doorknob—the output force is greater than the input force. Therefore, the mechanical advantage of this type of machine is greater than 1. For example, if the input force is 10 newtons and the output force is 40 newtons, the mechanical advantage is 40 N divided by 10 N, or 4.

For machines that allow you to apply greater force over a shorter distance—such as a rake—the output force is less than the input force. In this case, the mechanical advantage is less than 1. If the input force is 10 newtons and the output force is 5 newtons, the mechanical advantage is 0.5. However, such a machine allows you to move an object a greater distance.

Sometimes changing the direction of the force is more useful than decreasing the force or the distance. For machines that change only the direction of a force—such as the rope system on a flagpole—the input force and output force are the same. Therefore, the mechanical advantage of the machine is 1.

APPLY How does the rope system help the man raise the flag?

NOTE-TAKING STRATEGY
Remember to organize your notes in a chart or web as you read.

Work transfers energy.

Machines transfer energy to objects on which they do work. Every time you open a door, the doorknob is transferring mechanical energy to the shaft. A machine that lifts an object gives it potential energy. A machine that causes an object to start moving, such as a baseball bat hitting a ball, gives the object kinetic energy.

Energy

When you lift an object, you transfer energy to it in the form of gravitational potential energy—that is, potential energy caused by gravity. The higher you lift an object, the more work you must do and the more energy you give to the object. This is also true if a machine lifts an object. The gravitational potential energy of an object depends on its height above Earth's surface, and it equals the work required to lift the object to that height.

Recall that gravitational potential energy is the product of an object's mass, gravitational acceleration, and height *(GPE = mgh)*. In the diagram on page 149, the climber wants to reach the top of the hill. The higher she climbs, the greater her potential energy. This energy comes from the work the climber does. The potential energy she gains equals the amount of work she does.

Work

As you have seen, when you use a machine to do work, there is always an exchange, or tradeoff, between the force you use to do the work and the distance over which you apply that force. You apply less force over a longer distance or greater force over a shorter distance.

To reach the top of the hill, the climber must do work. Because she needs to increase her potential energy by a certain amount, she must do the same amount of work to reach the top of the hill whether she climbs a steep slope or a gentle slope.

The sloping surface of the hill acts like a ramp, which is a simple machine called an inclined plane. You know that machines make work easier by changing the size or direction of a force. How does this machine make the climber's work easier?

As the climber goes up the hill, she is doing work against gravity.

❶ One side of the hill is a very steep slope—almost straight up. If the climber takes the steep slope, she climbs a shorter distance, but she must use more force.

❷ Another side of the hill is a long, gentle slope. Here the climber travels a greater distance but uses much less effort.

148 Unit 1: **Motion and Forces**

If the climber uses the steep slope, she must lift almost her entire weight. The inclined plane allows her to exert her input force over a longer distance; therefore, she can use just enough force to overcome the net force pulling her down the inclined plane. This force is less than her weight. In many cases, it is easier for people to use less force over a longer distance than it is for them to use more force over a shorter distance.

Energy and Work

To reach the top of the hill, the climber must do at least as much work as the amount of potential energy she needs to gain.

① The Short Route
By climbing straight up the steep slope, the climber covers a shorter distance but must apply more force against gravity.

② The Long Route
By climbing the gentle slope, the climber covers more distance but uses less force. The work does not decrease even though the force does.

READING VISUALS What combination of forces makes it more difficult to climb a steep slope? How might climbers try to overcome this problem?

Chapter 5: **Machines** 149

VOCABULARY
Write your own definition of *efficiency* in a word triangle.

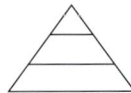

Output work is always less than input work.

The work you do on a machine is called the input work, and the work the machine does in turn is called the output work. A machine's **efficiency** is the ratio of its output work to the input work. An ideal machine would be 100 percent efficient. All of the input work would be converted to output work. Actual machines lose some input work to friction.

You can calculate the efficiency of a machine by dividing the machine's output work by its input work and multiplying that number by 100.

$$\text{Efficiency (\%)} = \frac{\text{Output work}}{\text{Input work}} \cdot 100$$

Recall that work is measured in joules. Suppose you do 600 J of work in using a rope system to lift a box. The work done on the box is 540 J. You would calculate the efficiency of the rope system as follows:

$$\text{Efficiency} = \frac{540 \text{ J}}{600 \text{ J}} \cdot 100 = 90\%$$

CHECK YOUR READING What is a machine's efficiency? How does it affect the amount of work a machine can do?

APPLY The mail carrier is riding a motorized human transport machine. Suppose the machine has an efficiency of 70 percent. How much work is lost in overcoming friction on the sidewalk and in the motor?

Efficiency
The work you put into a machine will always be greater than the work done by the machine. Some input work is always lost in overcoming friction.

Efficiency and Energy

You know that work transfers energy and that machines make work easier. The more mechanical energy is lost in the transfer to other forms of energy, the less efficient the machine. Machines lose some energy in the form of heat due to friction. The more moving parts a machine has, the more energy it loses to friction because the parts rub together. Machines can lose energy to other processes as well.

For example, a car engine has an efficiency of only about 25 percent. It loses much of the energy supplied by its fuel to heat from combustion. By comparison, a typical electric motor has more than an 80 percent efficiency. That means the motor converts more than 80 percent of the input energy into mechanical energy, or motion.

Many appliances come with energy guides that can help a buyer compare the energy efficiency of different models. A washing machine with the highest energy rating may not always save the most energy, however, because users may have to run those machines more often.

INVESTIGATE Efficiency

What is the efficiency of a ramp?
PROCEDURE

1. Build a ramp as shown. Measure the vertical height of the ramp and the length of the ramp in centimeters. Convert these distances to meters and record.

2. Attach the block to the spring scale and measure the force in newtons needed to lift the block straight up. Record this force as the output force. Multiply the output force by the height of the ramp in meters to get the output work. Record the output work.

3. Use the spring scale to pull the block up the ramp with a constant force. Record the force measured on the spring scale as the input force. Multiply the input force by the length of the ramp in meters to get the input work. Record the input work.

4. Use the input work and output work from steps 2 and 3 to calculate the efficiency of the ramp. Record your results.

WHAT DO YOU THINK?
- How did your input work compare with your output work?
- What could you do to increase the efficiency of the ramp?

CHALLENGE Would adding sandpaper on the surface of the ramp increase or decrease the efficiency of the ramp? Why? Test your hypothesis.

SKILL FOCUS
Analyzing data

MATERIALS
- board
- books
- meter stick
- wooden block with eye hook
- spring scale

for Challenge:
- sandpaper

TIME
20 minutes

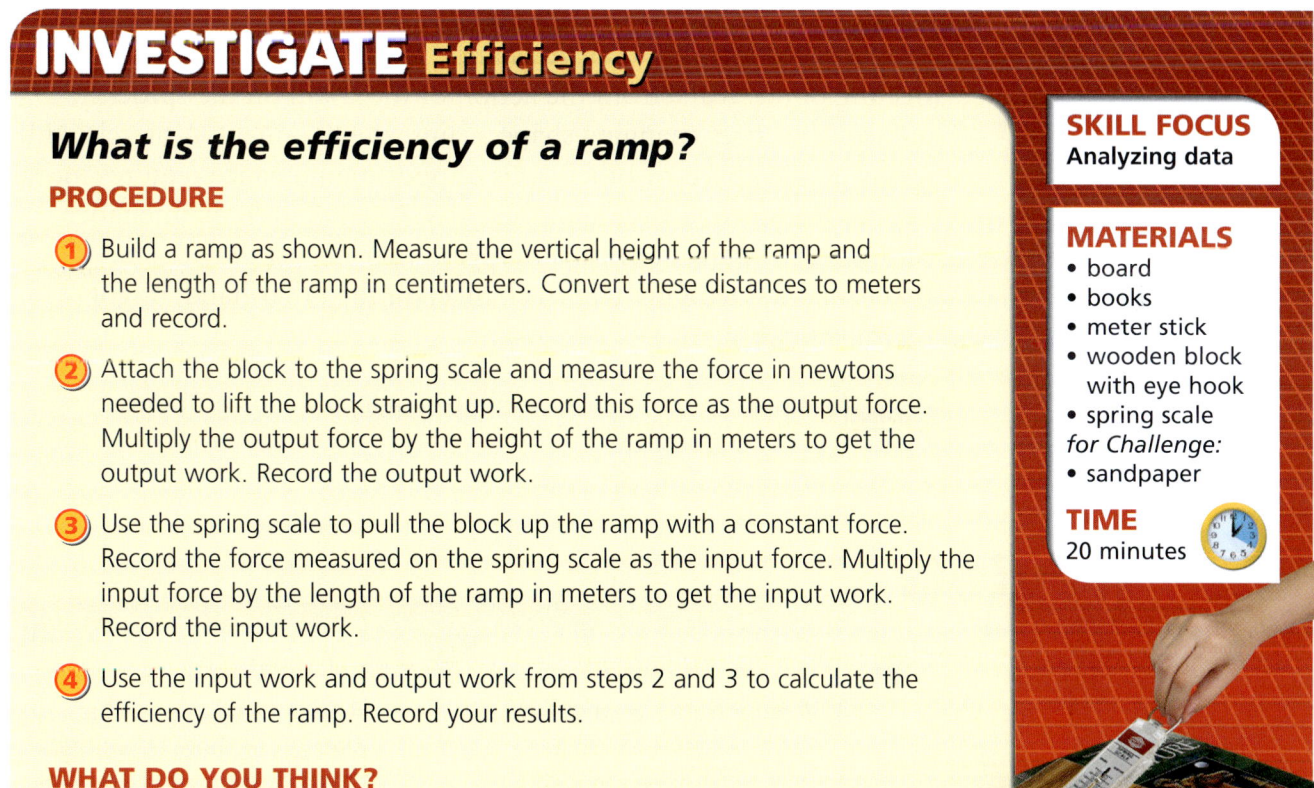

Proper maintenance can help keep a bicycle running as efficiently as possible.

Increasing Efficiency

Because all machines lose input work to friction, one way to improve the efficiency of a machine is by reducing friction. Oil is used to reduce friction between the moving parts of car engines. The use of oil makes engines more efficient.

Another machine that loses input work is a bicycle. Bicycles lose energy to friction and to air resistance. Friction losses result from the meeting of the gears, from the action of the chain on the sprocket, and from the tires changing shape against the pavement. A bicycle with poorly greased parts or other signs of poor maintenance requires more force to move. For a mountain bike that has had little maintenance, as much as 15 percent of the total work may be lost to friction. A well-maintained Olympic track bike, on the other hand, might lose only 0.5 percent.

 What is a common way to increase a machine's efficiency?

5.1 Review

KEY CONCEPTS

1. In what ways can a machine change a force?
2. How is a machine's efficiency calculated?
3. Why is a machine's actual output work always less than its input work?

CRITICAL THINKING

4. **Apply** How would the input force needed to push a wheelchair up a ramp change if you increased the height of the ramp but not its length?
5. **Compare** What is the difference between mechanical advantage and efficiency?

CHALLENGE

6. **Apply** Draw and label a diagram to show how to pull down on a rope to raise a load of construction materials.

152 Unit 1: **Motion and Forces**

MATH in SCIENCE

SKILL: CHANGING RATIOS TO PERCENTS

**MATH TUTORIAL
CLASSZONE.COM**
Click on Math Tutorial for more help with percents and fractions.

How Efficient Are Machines?

A hammer is used to pound in nails. It can also be used to pry nails out of wood. When used to pry nails, a hammer is a machine called a lever. Like all machines, the hammer is not 100 percent efficient.

Efficiency is the amount of work a machine does divided by the amount of work that is done on the machine. To calculate efficiency, you must first find the ratio of the machine's output work to the input work done on the machine. A ratio is the comparison of two numbers by means of division. You convert the ratio to a decimal by dividing. Then convert the decimal to a percent.

Example

A person is doing 1000 joules of work on a hammer to pry up a nail. The hammer does 925 joules of work on the nail to pull it out of the wood.

(1) Find the ratio of output work to input work.

$$\frac{\text{Output work}}{\text{Input work}} = \frac{925 \text{ J}}{1000 \text{ J}} = 0.925$$

(2) To convert the decimal to a percent, multiply 0.925 by 100 and add a percent sign.

$$0.925 \cdot 100 = 92.5\%$$

ANSWER The efficiency of the hammer is 92.5 percent. This means that the hammer loses 7.5 percent of the input work to friction and other products.

No machine, no matter how large or small, is 100 percent efficient. Some of the input energy is lost to sound, heat, or other products.

Answer the following questions.

1. A construction worker does 1000 J of work in pulling down on a rope to lift a weight tied to the other end. If the output work of the rope system is 550 J, what is the ratio of output work to input work? What is the efficiency of the rope system?

2. If a machine takes in 20,000 J and puts out 5000 J, what is its efficiency?

3. You do 6000 J of work to pull a sled up a ramp. After you reach the top, you discover that the sled had 3600 J of work done on it. What is the efficiency of the ramp?

CHALLENGE If you put 7000 J of work into a machine with an efficiency of 50 percent, how much work will you get out?

Chapter 5: **Machines** 153

KEY CONCEPT

5.2 Six simple machines have many uses.

◀ **BEFORE,** you learned
- Machines help you work by changing the size or direction of a force
- The number of times a machine multiplies the input force is the machine's mechanical advantage

▶ **NOW,** you will learn
- How six simple machines change the size or direction of a force
- How to calculate mechanical advantage

VOCABULARY

simple machine p. 154
lever p. 155
fulcrum p. 155
wheel and axle p. 156
pulley p. 156
inclined plane p. 158
wedge p. 158
screw p. 159

EXPLORE Changing Forces

How can you change a force?

PROCEDURE

① Lay one pencil on a flat surface. Place the other pencil on top of the first pencil and perpendicular to it, as shown. Place the book on one end of the top pencil.

② Push down on the free end of the top pencil to raise the book.

③ Change the position of the bottom pencil so that it is closer to the book and repeat step 2. Then move the bottom pencil closer to the end of the pencil you are pushing on and repeat step 2.

MATERIALS
- 2 pencils
- small book

WHAT DO YOU THINK?
- How did changing the position of the bottom pencil affect how much force you needed to lift the book?
- At which position is it easiest to lift the book? most difficult?

NOTE-TAKING STRATEGY
As you read, remember to take notes about the main ideas and supporting details.

There are six simple machines.

You have read about how a ramp and a shovel can help you do work. A ramp is a type of inclined plane, and a shovel is a type of lever. An inclined plane and a lever are both simple machines. **Simple machines** are the six machines on which all other mechanical machines are based. In addition to the inclined plane and the lever, simple machines include the wheel and axle, pulley, wedge, and screw. As you will see, the wheel and axle and pulley are related to the lever, and the wedge and screw are related to the inclined plane. You will read about each of the six simple machines in detail in this section.

154 Unit 1: Motion and Forces

Lever

A **lever** is a solid bar that rotates, or turns, around a fixed point. The bar can be straight or curved. The fixed point is called the **fulcrum.** A lever can multiply the input force. It can also change the direction of the input force. If you apply a force downward on one end of a lever, the other end can lift a load.

The way in which a lever changes an input force depends on the positions of the fulcrum, the input force, and the output force in relation to one another. Levers with different arrangements have different uses. Sometimes a greater output force is needed, such as when you want to pry up a bottle cap. At other times you use a greater input force on one end to get a higher speed at the other end, such as when you swing a baseball bat. The three different arrangements, sometimes called the three classes of levers, are shown in the diagram below.

CHECK YOUR READING What two parts are needed to make a lever?

Levers

Levers can be classified according to where the fulcrum is.

READING TIP
The lengths of the arrows in the diagram represent the size of the force.

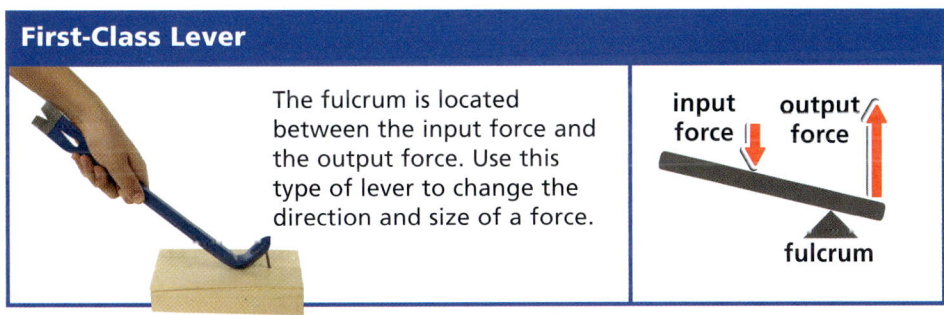

First-Class Lever
The fulcrum is located between the input force and the output force. Use this type of lever to change the direction and size of a force.

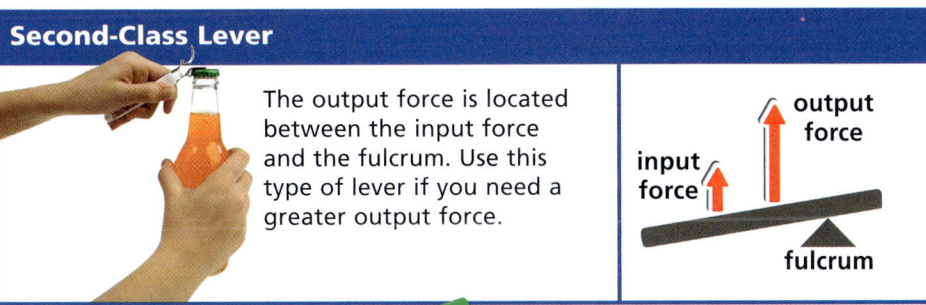

Second-Class Lever
The output force is located between the input force and the fulcrum. Use this type of lever if you need a greater output force.

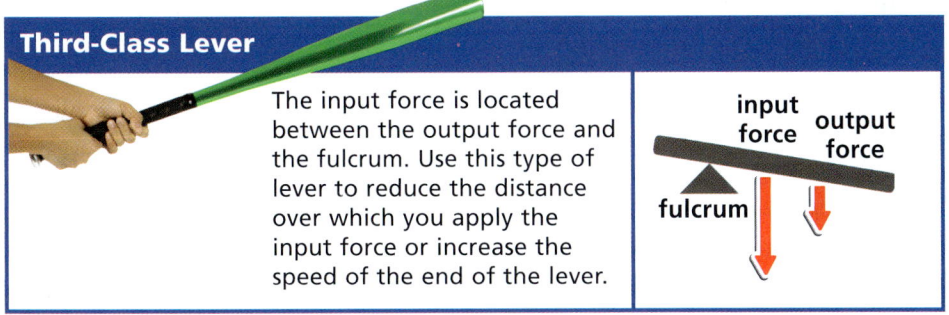

Third-Class Lever
The input force is located between the output force and the fulcrum. Use this type of lever to reduce the distance over which you apply the input force or increase the speed of the end of the lever.

Chapter 5: **Machines** 155

Wheel and Axle

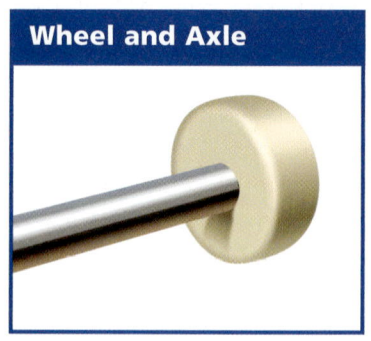

Wheel and Axle

A **wheel and axle** is a simple machine made of a wheel attached to a shaft, or axle. The wheels of most means of transportation—such as a bicycle and a car—are attached to an axle. The wheel and axle act like a rotating collection of levers. The axle at the wheel's center is like a fulcrum. Other examples of wheels and axles are screwdrivers, steering wheels, doorknobs, and electric fans.

Depending on your purpose for using a wheel and axle, you might apply a force to turn the wheel or the axle. If you turn the wheel, your input force is transferred to the axle. Because the axle is smaller than the wheel, the output force acts over a shorter distance than the input force. A driver applies less force to a steering wheel to get a greater turning force from the axle, or steering column. This makes it easier to steer the car.

If, instead, you turn the axle, your force is transferred to the wheel. Because the wheel is larger than the axle, the force acts over a longer distance. A car also contains this use of a wheel and axle. The engine turns the drive axles, which turn the wheels.

 **CHECK YOUR READING** Compare the results of putting force on the axle with putting force on the wheel.

Pulley

A **pulley** is a wheel with a grooved rim and a rope or cable that rides in the groove. As you pull on the rope, the wheel turns.

A pulley that is attached to something that holds it steady is called a fixed pulley. An object attached to the rope on one side of the wheel rises as you pull down on the rope on the other side of the wheel. The fixed pulley makes work easier by changing the direction of the force. You must apply enough force to overcome the weight of the load and any friction in the pulley system.

Fixed Pulley

A fixed pulley allows you to take advantage of the downward pull of your weight to move a load upward. It does not, however, reduce the force you need to lift the load. Also, the distance you pull the rope through is the same distance that the object is lifted. To lift a load two meters using a fixed pulley, you must pull down two meters of rope.

In a movable pulley setup, one end of the rope is fixed, but the wheel can move. The load is attached to the wheel. The person pulling the rope provides the output force that lifts the load. A single movable pulley does not change the direction of the force. Instead, it multiplies the force. Because the load is supported by two sections of rope, you need only half the force you would use with a fixed pulley to lift it. However, you must pull the rope through twice the distance.

Movable Pulley

CHECK YOUR READING How does a single fixed pulley differ from a single movable pulley?

A combination of fixed and movable pulleys is a pulley system called a block and tackle. A block and tackle is used to haul and lift very heavy objects. By combining fixed and movable pulleys, you can use more rope sections to support the weight of an object. This reduces the force you need to lift the object. The mechanical advantage of a single pulley can never be greater than 2. If engineers need a pulley system with a mechanical advantage greater than 2, they often use a block-and-tackle system.

INVESTIGATE Pulleys

What is the mechanical advantage of a pulley system?

PROCEDURE

1. Hang the mass on the spring scale to find its weight in newtons. Record this weight as your output force.

2. Tie the top of one pulley to the ring stand.

3. Attach the mass to the second pulley.

4. Attach one end of the second pulley's rope to the bottom of the first pulley. Then thread the free end of the rope through the second pulley. Loop the rope up and over the first pulley, as shown.

5. Attach the spring scale to the free end of the rope. Pull down to lift the mass. Record the force you used as your input force. Calculate the mechanical advantage of this pulley system.
   Hint: The mechanical advantage can be calculated by dividing the output force by the input force.

WHAT DO YOU THINK?
- How did your input force compare with your output force?
- What caused the results you observed?

CHALLENGE Explain what the mechanical advantage would be for a pulley system that includes another movable pulley.

SKILL FOCUS
Inferring

MATERIALS
- 100 g mass
- spring scale
- 2 pulleys with rope
- ring stand

TIME
20 minutes

Chapter 5: **Machines** 157

Inclined Plane

Recall that it is difficult to lift a heavy object straight up because you must apply a force great enough to overcome the downward pull of the force of gravity. For this reason people often use ramps. A ramp is an **inclined plane,** a simple machine that is a sloping surface. The photograph at the left shows the interior of the Guggenheim Museum in New York City. The levels of the art museum are actually one continuous inclined plane.

Inclined planes make the work of raising an object easier because they support part of the weight of the object while it is being moved from one level to another. The surface of an inclined plane applies a reaction force on the object resting on it. This extra force on the object helps to act against gravity. If you are pushing an object up a ramp, you have to push with only enough force to overcome the smaller net force that pulls the object down parallel to the incline.

The less steep an inclined plane is, the less force you need to push or pull an object on the plane. This is because a less steep plane supports more of an object's weight than a steeper plane. However, the less steep an inclined plane is, the farther you must go to reach a certain height. While you use less force, you must apply that force over a greater distance.

CHECK YOUR READING How do inclined planes help people do work? Your answer should mention force.

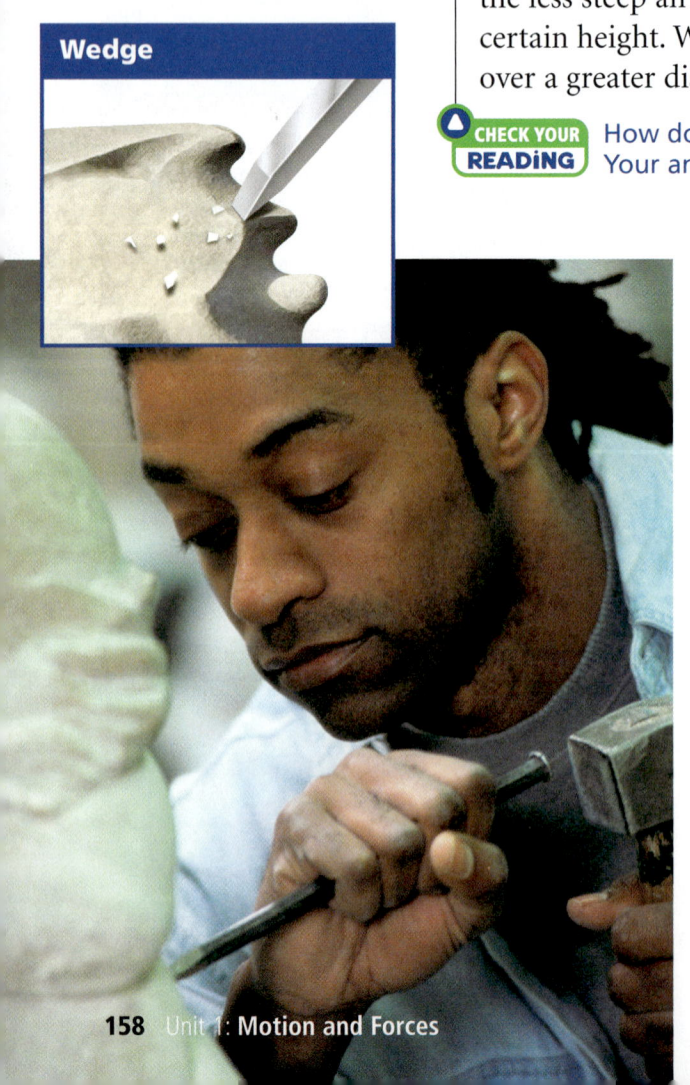

Wedge

A **wedge** is a simple machine that has a thick end and a thin end. Wedges are used to cut, split, or pierce objects—or to hold objects together. A wedge is a type of inclined plane, but inclined planes are stationary, while wedges often move to do work.

Some wedges are single, movable inclined planes, such as a doorstop, a chisel, or an ice scraper. Another kind of wedge is made of two back-to-back inclined planes. Examples include the blade of an axe or a knife. In the photograph at the left, a sculptor is using a chisel to shape stone. The sculptor applies an input force on the chisel by tapping its thicker end with a mallet. That force pushes the thinner end of the chisel into the stone. As a result, the sides of the thinner end exert an output force that separates the stone.

The angle of the cutting edge determines how easily a wedge can cut through an object. Thin wedges have small angles and need less input force to cut than do thick wedges with large angles. That is why a sharp knife blade cuts more easily than a dull one.

You also can think of a wedge that cuts objects in terms of how it changes the pressure on a surface. The thin edges of a wedge provide a smaller surface area for the input force to act on. This greater pressure makes it easier to break through the surface of an object. A sharp knife can cut through an apple skin, and a sharp chisel can apply enough pressure to chip stone.

A doorstop is a wedge that is used to hold objects together. To do its job, a doorstop is pressed tip-first under a door. As the doorstop is moved into position, it lifts the door slightly and applies a force to the bottom of the door. In return, the door applies pressure to the doorstop and causes the doorstop to press against the floor with enough force to keep the doorstop—and the door—from moving.

Screw

A **screw** is an inclined plane wrapped around a cylinder or cone to form a spiral. A screw is a simple machine that can be used to raise and lower weights as well as to fasten objects. Examples of screws include drills, jar lids, screw clamps, and nuts and bolts. The spiraling inclined plane that sticks out from the body of the screw forms the threads of the screw.

In the photograph at right, a person is using a screwdriver, which is a wheel and axle, to drive a screw into a piece of wood. Each turn of the screwdriver pushes the screw farther into the wood. As the screw is turned, the threads act like wedges, exerting an output force on the wood. If the threads are very close together, the force must be applied over a greater distance—that is, the screw must be turned many times—but less force is needed.

The advantage of using a screw instead of a nail to hold things together is the large amount of friction that keeps the screw from turning and becoming loose. Think of pulling a nail out of a piece of wood compared with pulling a screw from the same piece of wood. The nail can be pulled straight out. The screw must be turned through a greater distance to remove it from the wood.

Notice that the interior of the Guggenheim Museum shown on page 158 is not only an inclined plane. It is also an example of a screw. The inclined plane is wrapped around the museum's atrium, which is an open area in the center.

Screw

 Explain how a screw moves deeper into the wood as it is turned.

The mechanical advantage of a machine can be calculated.

Recall that the number of times a machine multiplies the input force is the machine's mechanical advantage. You can calculate a machine's mechanical advantage using this formula:

$$\text{Mechanical Advantage} = \frac{\text{Output Force}}{\text{Input Force}}$$

$$MA = \frac{F_{out}}{F_{in}}$$

This formula works for all machines, regardless of whether they are simple machines or more complicated machines.

If a machine decreases the force you use to do work, the distance over which you have to apply that force increases. It is possible to use this idea to calculate the mechanical advantage of a simple machine without knowing what the input and output forces are. To make this calculation, however, you must assume that your machine is not losing any work to friction. In other words, you must assume that your machine is 100 percent efficient. The mechanical advantage that you calculate when making this assumption is called the ideal mechanical advantage.

Inclined Plane You can calculate the ideal mechanical advantage of an inclined plane by dividing its length by its height.

$$\text{Ideal Mechanical Advantage} = \frac{\text{length of incline}}{\text{height of incline}}$$

$$IMA = \frac{l}{h}$$

READING TIP

Scientists often consider the way in which an object will behave under ideal conditions, such as when there is no friction.

Be sure to use the length of the incline in your calculation, as shown in the diagram, and not the length of the base. If the mover in the photograph on page 160 increased the length of the ramp, he would increase the ramp's mechanical advantage. However, he would also increase the distance over which he had to carry the box.

Wheel and Axle To calculate the ideal mechanical advantage of a wheel and axle, use the following formula:

$$\text{Ideal Mechanical Advantage} = \frac{\text{Radius of input}}{\text{Radius of output}}$$

$$IMA = \frac{R_{in}}{R_{out}}$$

Explore the mechanical advantage of an inclined plane.

REMINDER
The radius is the distance from the center of the wheel or axle to any point on its circumference.

The Ferris wheel below is a giant wheel and axle. A motor applies an input force to the Ferris wheel's axle, which turns the wheel. In this example, the input force is applied to the axle, so the radius of the axle is the input radius in the formula above. The output force is applied by the wheel, so the radius of the wheel is the output radius.

For a Ferris wheel, the input force is greater than the output force. The axle turns through a shorter distance than the wheel does. The ideal mechanical advantage of this type of wheel and axle is less than 1.

Sometimes, as with a steering wheel, the input force is applied to turn the wheel instead of the axle. Then the input radius is the wheel's radius, and the output radius is the axle's radius. In this case, the input force on the wheel is less than the output force applied by the axle. The ideal mechanical advantage of this type of wheel and axle is greater than 1.

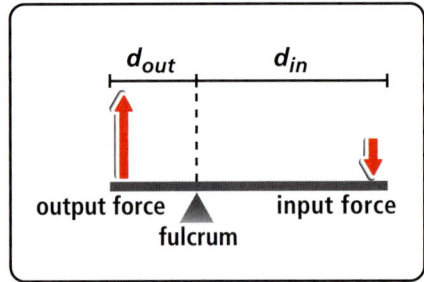

Lever The beam balance above is a lever. The beam is the solid bar that turns on a fixed point, or fulcrum. The fulcrum is the beam's balance point. When you slide the weight across the beam, you are changing the distance between the input force and the fulcrum. The mechanical advantage depends on the distances of the input force and output force from the fulcrum. The output force is applied to balance the beaker.

To calculate the ideal mechanical advantage of a lever, use the following formula:

$$\text{Ideal Mechanical Advantage} = \frac{\text{distance from input force to fulcrum}}{\text{distance from output force to fulcrum}}$$

$$IMA = \frac{d_{in}}{d_{out}}$$

This formula applies to all three arrangements of levers. If the distance from the input force to the fulcrum is greater than the distance from the output force to the fulcrum, the ideal mechanical advantage is greater than 1. The beam balance is an example of this type of lever.

5.2 Review

KEY CONCEPTS

1. Name the six simple machines and give an example of each.
2. Explain how a screw changes the size of the force needed to push it into wood.
3. To calculate mechanical advantage, what two things do you need to know?

CRITICAL THINKING

4. **Synthesize** How is a pulley similar to a wheel and axle?
5. **Calculate** What is the ideal mechanical advantage of a wheel with a diameter of 30 cm fixed to an axle with a diameter of 4 cm if the axle is turned?

CHALLENGE

6. **Infer** How can you increase a wedge's mechanical advantage? Draw a diagram to show your idea.

Connecting Sciences

PHYSICAL SCIENCE AND LIFE SCIENCE

A Running Machine

Marlon Shirley, who lives in Colorado, lost his lower left leg due to an accident at the age of five. He is a champion sprinter who achieved his running records while using a prosthesis (prahs-THEE-sihs), or a device used to replace a body part. Like his right leg, his prosthetic leg is a combination of simple machines that convert the energy from muscles in his body to move him forward. The mechanical system is designed to match the forces of his right leg.

Legs as Levers

Compare Marlon Shirley's artificial leg with his right leg. Both legs have long rods—one made of bone and the other of metal—that provide a strong frame. These rods act as levers. At the knee and ankle, movable joints act as fulcrums for these levers to transfer energy between the runner's body and the ground.

How Does It Work?

1. As the foot—real or artificial—strikes the ground, the leg stops moving forward and downward and absorbs the energy of the change in motion. The joints in the ankle and knee act as fulcrums as the levers transfer the energy to the muscle in the upper leg. This muscle acts like a spring to store the energy.

2. When the runner begins the next step, the energy is transferred back into the leg from the upper leg muscle. The levers in the leg convert the energy into forward motion of the runner's body.

The people who design prosthetic legs study the natural motion of a runner to learn exactly how energy is distributed and converted to motion so that they can build an artificial leg that works well with the real leg.

Other parts of the human body can act like simple machines. For example, teeth work like wedges.

EXPLORE

1. **VISUALIZE** Run across a room, paying close attention to the position of one of your ankles and knees as you move. Determine where the input force, output force, and fulcrum are in the lever formed by your lower leg.

2. **CHALLENGE** Use the library or the Internet to learn more about mechanical legs used in building robots that walk. How do the leg motions of these robots resemble your walking motions? How are they different?

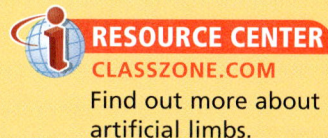
RESOURCE CENTER
CLASSZONE.COM
Find out more about artificial limbs.

Chapter 5: **Machines** 163

KEY CONCEPT
Modern technology uses compound machines.

 BEFORE, you learned
- Simple machines change the size or direction of a force
- All machines have an ideal and an actual mechanical advantage

 NOW, you will learn
- How simple machines can be combined
- How scientists have developed extremely small machines
- How robots are used

VOCABULARY

compound machine p. 164
nanotechnology p. 167
robot p. 169

THINK ABOUT

How does a tow truck do work?

When a car is wrecked or disabled, the owner might call a towing service. The service sends a tow truck to take the car to be repaired. Tow trucks usually are equipped with a mechanism for freeing stuck vehicles and towing, or pulling, them. Look at the tow truck in the photograph at the right. What simple machines do you recognize?

Compound machines are combinations of simple machines.

Like the tow truck pictured above, many of the more complex devices that you see or use every day are combinations of simple machines. For example, a pair of scissors is a combination of two levers. The cutting edges of those levers are wedges. A fishing rod is a lever with the fishing line wound around a wheel and axle, the reel. A machine that is made of two or more simple machines is called a **compound machine.**

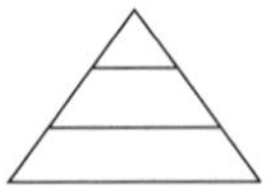

In a very complex compound machine, such as a car, the simple machines may not be obvious at first. However, if you look carefully at a compound machine, you should be able to identify forms of levers, pulleys, and wheels and axles.

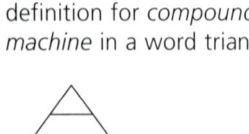

VOCABULARY
Remember to write a definition for *compound machine* in a word triangle.

 How are simple machines related to compound machines?

164 Unit 1: Motion and Forces

The gears in the photograph and diagram are spur gears, the most common type of gear.

Gears

Gears are based on the wheel and axle. Gears have teeth on the edge of the wheel that allow one gear to turn another. A set of gears forms a compound machine in which one wheel and axle is linked to another.

Two linked gears that are the same size and have the same number of teeth will turn at the same speed. They will move in opposite directions. In order to make them move in the same direction, a third gear must be added between them. The gear that turns another gear applies the input force; the gear that is turned exerts the output force. A difference in speed between two gears—caused by a difference in size and the distance each turns through—produces a change in force.

 How do gears form a compound machine?

Mechanical Advantage of Compound Machines

The mechanical advantage of any compound machine is equal to the product of the mechanical advantages of all the simple machines that make up the compound machine. For example, the ideal mechanical advantage of a pair of scissors would be the product of the ideal mechanical advantages of its two levers and two wedges.

The mechanical advantage of a pair of gears with different diameters can be found by counting the teeth on the gears. The mechanical advantage is the ratio of the number of teeth on the output gear to the number of teeth on the input gear. If there are more than two gears, count only the number of teeth on the first and last gears in the system. This ratio is the mechanical advantage of the whole gear system.

Compound machines typically must overcome more friction than simple machines because they tend to have many moving parts. Scissors, for example, have a lower efficiency than one lever because there is friction at the point where the two levers are connected. There is also friction between the blades of the scissors as they close.

Chapter 5: **Machines** 165

APPLY What simple machines do you see in this Jaws of Life cutting tool?

Modern technology creates new uses for machines.

Sophisticated modern machinery is often based on or contains simple machines. Consider Jaws of Life tools, which are used to help rescue people who have been in accidents. These cutters, spreaders, and rams are powered by hydraulics, the use of fluids to transmit force. When every second counts, these powerful machines can be used to pry open metal vehicles or collapsed concrete structures quickly and safely. The cutters are a compound machine made up of two levers—much like a pair of scissors. Their edges are wedges.

Contrast this equipment with a drill-like machine so small that it can be pushed easily through human arteries. Physicians attach the tiny drill to a thin, flexible rod and push the rod through a patient's artery to an area that is blocked. The tip rotates at extremely high speeds to break down the blockage. The tiny drill is a type of wheel and axle.

Microtechnology and Nanotechnology

Manufacturers make machines of all sizes by shaping and arranging pieces of metal, plastic, and other materials. Scientists have used technology to create very small machines through miniaturization—the making of smaller and smaller, or miniature, parts. Micromachines are too small to be seen by the naked eye but are visible under a microscope. There is a limit, however, to how far micromachines can be shrunk.

To develop even tinier machines, scientists needed a new approach. Scientists have used processes within the human body as their model. For example, inside the body a protein molecule carries materials back and forth within a cell on regular paths that are similar to little train tracks. The natural machines in the human body inspired scientists to develop machines that could be 1000 times smaller than the diameter of a human hair.

READING TiP

Micro- means "one-millionth." For example, a microsecond is one-millionth of a second. *Nano-* means "one-billionth." A nanosecond is one-billionth of a second.

These extremely tiny machines are products of **nanotechnology,** the science and technology of building electronic circuits and devices from single atoms and molecules. Scientists say that they create these machines, called nanomachines, from the bottom up. Instead of shaping already formed material—such as metal and plastic—they guide individual atoms of material to arrange themselves into the shapes needed for the machine parts.

Tools enable scientists to see and manipulate single molecules and atoms. The scanning tunneling microscope can create pictures of individual atoms. To manipulate atoms, special tools are needed to guide them into place. Moving and shaping such small units presents problems, however. Atoms tend to attach themselves to other atoms, and the tools themselves are also made of atoms. Thus it is difficult to pick up an atom and place it in another position using a tool because the atom might attach itself to the tool.

RESOURCE CENTER
CLASSZONE.COM
Learn more about nanomachines.

CHECK YOUR READING Compare the way in which nanomachines are constructed with the way in which larger machines are built.

Nanomachines are still mostly in the experimental stage. Scientists have many plans for nanotechnology, including protecting computers from hackers and performing operations inside the body. For example, a nanomachine could be injected into a person's bloodstream, where it could patrol and search out infections before they become serious problems. When the machine had completed its work, it could switch itself off and be passed out of the body. Similar nanomachines could carry anti-cancer drugs to specific cells in the body.

Nanotechnology could also be used to develop materials that repel water and dirt and make cleaning jobs easy. Nanoscale biosensors could be used to detect harmful substances in the environment. Another possible use for nanotechnology is in military uniforms that can change color— the perfect camouflage.

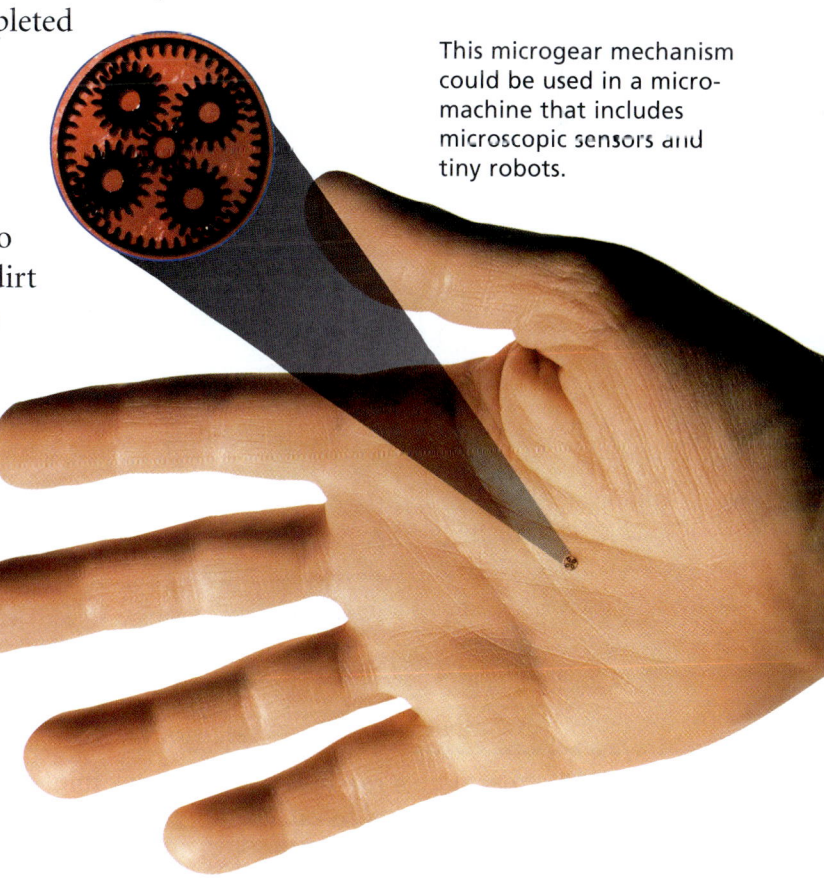

This microgear mechanism could be used in a micro-machine that includes microscopic sensors and tiny robots.

In the future, nanotechnology may change the way almost everything is designed and constructed. As with any new technology, it will be important to weigh both the potential risks and benefits.

Chapter 5: **Machines** 167

A Robot at Work

Scientists are using a robot to unlock the secrets of the Great Pyramid in Egypt.

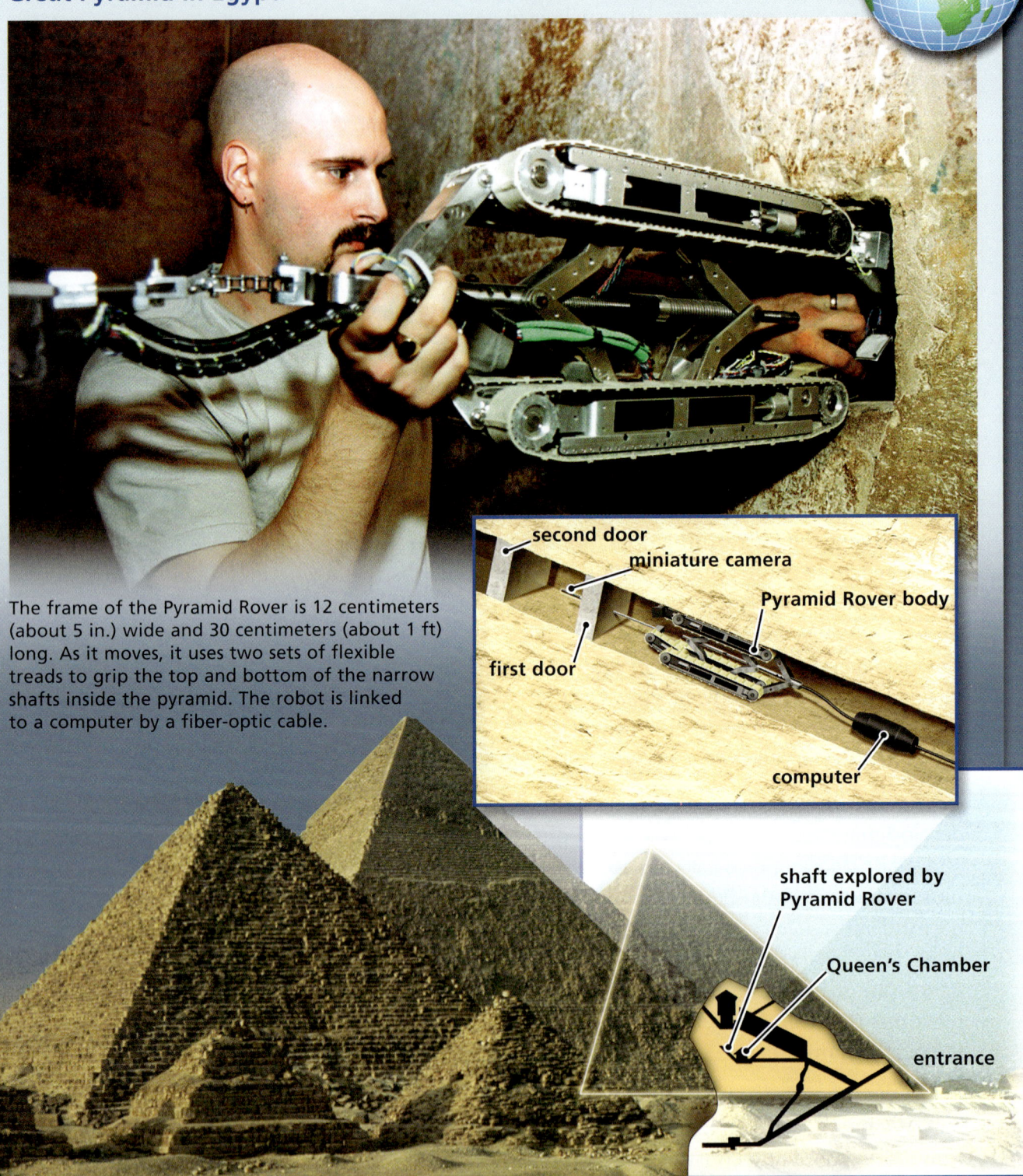

The frame of the Pyramid Rover is 12 centimeters (about 5 in.) wide and 30 centimeters (about 1 ft) long. As it moves, it uses two sets of flexible treads to grip the top and bottom of the narrow shafts inside the pyramid. The robot is linked to a computer by a fiber-optic cable.

READING VISUALS What simple machines do you think might be part of the Pyramid Rover?

Robots

Humans have always taken risks to do jobs in places that are dangerous or difficult to get to. More and more often, robots can be used to do these jobs. A **robot** is a machine that works automatically or by remote control. When many people hear the word *robot*, they think of a machine that looks or moves like a person. However, most robots do not resemble humans at all. That is because they are built to do things humans cannot do or to go places where it is difficult for humans to go.

The Pyramid Rover, shown on page 168, is an example of a robot developed to go where people cannot. After a camera revealed a door at the end of an eight-inch-square shaft inside the Great Pyramid, the Pyramid Rover was sent through the shaft to explore the area. While researchers remained in the Queen's Chamber in the center of the pyramid, the robot climbed the shaft until it came to a door. Using ultrasound equipment mounted on the robot, researchers determined that the door was three inches thick. The robot drilled a hole in the door for a tiny camera and a light to pass through. The camera then revealed another sealed door!

Many companies use robots to manufacture goods quickly and efficiently. Robots are widely used for jobs such as welding, painting, and assembling products. Robots do some repetitive work better than humans, because robots do not get tired or bored. Also, they do the task in exactly the same way each time. Robots are very important to the automobile and computer industries.

Find out more about the Pyramid Rover and other robots.

 How are robots better than humans at some jobs?

5.3 Review

KEY CONCEPTS

1. How do you estimate the mechanical advantage of a compound machine?
2. What are some uses of nanotechnology? Can you think of other possible uses for nanomachines?
3. What are three types of jobs that robots can do?

CRITICAL THINKING

4. **Synthesize** What factors might limit how large or how small a machine can be?
5. **Infer** How do you think the size of a gear compared with other gears in the same system affects the speed of its rotation?

CHALLENGE

6. **Apply** Robots might be put to use replacing humans in firefighting and other dangerous jobs. Describe a job that is dangerous. Tell what a robot must be able to do and what dangers it must be able to withstand to accomplish the required tasks.

CHAPTER INVESTIGATION

Design a Machine

OVERVIEW AND PURPOSE
Although simple machines were developed thousands of years ago, they are still used today for a variety of purposes. Tasks such as cutting food with a knife, using a screwdriver to tighten a screw, and raising a flag on a flagpole all require simple machines. Activities such as riding a bicycle and raising a drawbridge make use of compound machines. In this investigation you will use what you have learned about simple and compound machines to
- choose a machine to design
- build your machine, test it, and calculate its mechanical advantage and efficiency

Procedure

1 Make a data table like the one shown on page 171.

2 From among the three choices listed below, choose which problem you are going to solve.

Carnival Game You work for a company that builds carnival games. Your supervisor has asked you to build a game in which a simple machine moves a 500-gram object from the bottom of the game 1 meter up to the top. This simple machine can be powered only by the person operating the game.

Video Game Contest The marketing department of a video game company is holding a contest. Candidates are asked to submit a working model of a compound machine that will move a 500-gram object a distance of 1 meter. The winning design will be used in a new video game the company hopes to sell. This compound machine must include at least 2 simple machines.

Construction Company You work for a construction company. Your boss has asked you to design a machine for lifting. Your first step is to build a scale model. The model must be a compound machine with a mechanical advantage of 5 that can move a 500-gram object a distance of 1 meter. You also can use a 100-gram object in your design.

MATERIALS
- 500 g object
- 100 g object
- meter stick
- spring scale
- pulleys with rope
- board
- stick or pole

170 Unit 1: Motion and Forces

3. Brainstorm design ideas on paper. Think of different types of machines you might want to build. Choose one machine to build.

4. Build your machine. Use your machine to perform the task of moving a 500-gram object a distance of 1 meter.

   If you chose the third problem, test your compound machine to determine if it has a mechanical advantage of 5. If not, modify your machine and retest it.

5. Record all measurements in your data table.

Observe and Analyze

1. **RECORD OBSERVATIONS** Make a sketch of your machine.

2. **CALCULATE** Use your data to calculate the mechanical advantage and efficiency of your machine. Use the formulas below.

$$\text{Mechanical Advantage} = \frac{\text{Output Force}}{\text{Input Force}}$$

$$\text{Efficiency (\%)} = \frac{\text{Output work}}{\text{Input work}} \cdot 100$$

3. **ANALYZE**

   Carnival Game Add arrows to the drawing of your machine to show the forces involved and the direction of those forces. If your goal was to move the ball from the top of the game to the bottom at a constant speed, how would your machine and diagram have to be changed?

   Video Game Contest Does your machine change the size of the force, the direction of the force, or both? If you used a pulley system (two or more pulleys working together), describe the advantages of using such a system.

   Construction Company Determine whether force or distance is changed by each simple machine in your compound machine. In what ways might you improve your machine to increase its efficiency?

Conclude

1. **INFER** How might changing the arrangement of the parts in your machine affect the machine's mechanical advantage?

2. **IDENTIFY LIMITS** What was the hardest part about designing and constructing your machine?

3. **APPLY** If you needed to lift a large rock from a hole at a construction site, which type of simple machine would you use and why? Which type of compound machine would be useful?

INVESTIGATE Further

CHALLENGE If you made a simple machine, how would you combine it with another simple machine to increase its mechanical advantage?

If you made a compound machine, redesign it to increase its efficiency or mechanical advantage. What made the difference and why?

Draw a plan for the new machine. Circle the parts that were changed. If you have time, build your new machine.

Design a Machine

Observe and Analyze

Table 1. Machine Data

Output force	Input force	Mechanical Advantage
Output work	Input work	Efficiency

Sketch

Chapter Review

the BIG idea

Machines help people do work by changing the force applied to an object.

KEY CONCEPTS SUMMARY

1 Machines help people do work.

When you use a machine to do work, there is always an exchange, or tradeoff, between the force you use and the distance over which you apply that force. You can use less force over a greater distance or a greater force over a shorter distance to do the same amount of work.

VOCABULARY
machine p. 145
mechanical advantage p. 147
efficiency p. 150

2 Six simple machines have many uses.

Simple machines change the size and/or direction of a force.

changes direction

changes size

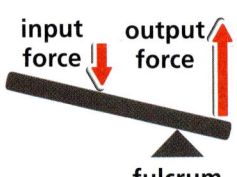
changes both

VOCABULARY
simple machine p. 154
lever p. 155
fulcrum p. 155
wheel and axle p. 156
pulley p. 156
inclined plane p. 158
wedge p. 158
screw p. 159

3 Modern technology uses compound machines.

- Compound machines are combinations of simple machines.

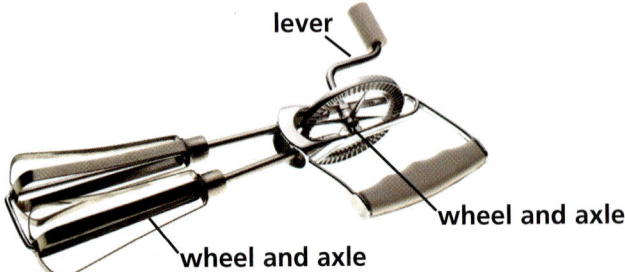

- Modern technology creates new uses for machines.
  —Microtechnology and nanotechnology
  —Robots

VOCABULARY
compound machine p. 164
nanotechnology p. 167
robot p. 169

172 Unit 1: Motion and Forces

Reviewing Vocabulary

Write the name of the simple machine shown in each illustration. Give an example from real life for each one.

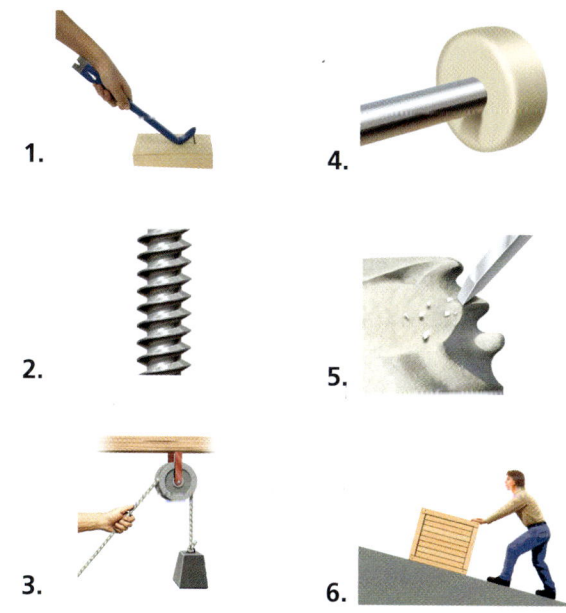

1.
2.
3.
4.
5.
6.

Copy the chart below, and write the definition for each term in your own words. Use the meaning of the term's root to help you.

Term	Root Meaning	Definition
7. machine	having power	
8. nanotechnology	one-billionth	
9. simple machine	basic	
10. efficiency	to accomplish	
11. compound machine	put together	
12. robot	work	
13. fulcrum	to support	

Reviewing Key Concepts

Multiple Choice *Choose the letter of the best answer.*

14. Machines help you work by
    a. decreasing the amount of work that must be done
    b. changing the size and/or direction of a force
    c. decreasing friction
    d. conserving energy

15. To calculate mechanical advantage, you need to know
    a. time and energy
    b. input force and output force
    c. distance and work
    d. size and direction of a force

16. A machine in which the input force is equal to the output force has a mechanical advantage of
    a. 0   c. 1
    b. between 0 and 1   d. more than 1

17. You can increase a machine's efficiency by
    a. increasing force   c. increasing distance
    b. reducing work   d. reducing friction

18. Levers turn around a
    a. fixed point called a fulcrum
    b. solid bar that rotates
    c. wheel attached to an axle
    d. sloping surface called an inclined plane

19. When you bite into an apple, your teeth act as what kind of simple machine?
    a. lever   c. wedge
    b. pulley   d. screw

Short Answer *Answer each of the following questions in a sentence or two.*

20. Describe the simple machines that make up scissors.

21. How do you calculate the mechanical advantage of a compound machine?

22. How did scientists use processes inside the human body as a model for making nanomachines?

Chapter 5: **Machines** 173

Thinking Critically

23. SYNTHESIZE How is a screw related to an inclined plane?

24. INFER Which simple machine would you use to raise a very heavy load to the top of a building? Why?

25. APPLY If you reached the top of a hill by using a path that wound around the hill, would you do more work than someone who climbed a shorter path? Why or why not? Who would use more force?

26. APPLY You are using a board to pry a large rock out of the ground when the board suddenly breaks apart in the middle. You pick up half of the board and use it to continue prying up the rock. The fulcrum stays in the same position. How has the mechanical advantage of the board changed? How does it change your work?

27. SYNTHESIZE What is the difference between a single fixed pulley and a single movable pulley? Draw a diagram to illustrate the difference.

Use the information in the diagram below to answer the next three questions.

28. SYNTHESIZE What is the mechanical advantage of the ramp? By how many times does the ramp multiply the man's input force?

29. SYNTHESIZE If the ramp's length were longer, what effect would this have on its mechanical advantage? Would this require the man to exert more or less input force?

30. INFER If the ramp's length stayed the same but the height was raised, how would this change the input force required?

Using Math Skills in Science

Complete the following calculations.

31. You swing a hockey stick with a force of 10 N. The stick applies 5 N of force on the puck. What is the mechanical advantage of the hockey stick?

32. Your input work on a manual lawn mower is 125,000 J. The output work is 90,000 J. What is the efficiency of the lawn mower?

33. If a car engine has a 20 percent efficiency, what percentage of the input work is lost?

34. A steering wheel has a radius of 21 cm. The steering column on which it turns has a radius of 3 cm. What is the mechanical advantage of this wheel and axle?

35. Two gears with the same diameter form a gear system. Each gear has 24 teeth. What is the mechanical advantage of this gear system?

the BIG idea

36. DRAW CONCLUSIONS Look back at the photograph on pages 142–143. Name the simple machines you see in the photograph. How do you think they work together to move balls through the sculpture? How has your understanding changed as to the way in which machines help people work?

37. SYNTHESIZE Think of a compound machine you have used recently. Explain which simple machines it includes and how they helped you do work.

38. PREDICT How do you think nanotechnology will be useful in the future? Give several examples.

UNIT PROJECTS

Evaluate all of the data, results, and information from your project folder. Prepare to present your project to the class. Be ready to answer questions posed by your classmates about your results.

Standardized Test Practice

Analyzing Graphics

The Archimedean screw is a mechanical device first used more than 2000 years ago. It consists of a screw inside a cylinder. One end of the device is placed in water. As the screw is turned with a handle, its threads carry water upward. The Archimedean screw is still used in some parts of the world to pump water for irrigating fields. It can also be used to move grain in mills.

Study the illustration of an Archimedean screw. Then answer the questions that follow.

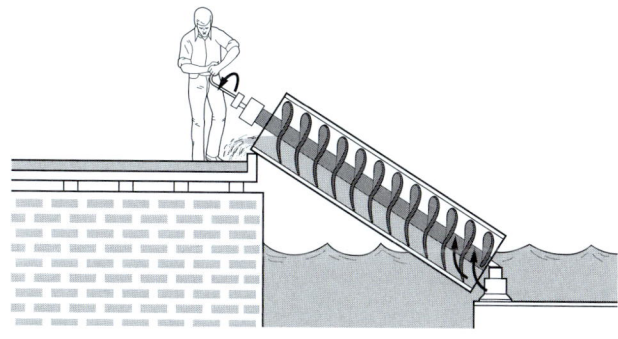

1. Which type of simple machine moves water in the cylinder?
   a. block and tackle
   b. pulley
   c. screw
   d. wedge

2. Which type of simple machine is the handle?
   a. wheel and axle
   b. inclined plane
   c. pulley
   d. wedge

3. What is the energy source for the Archimedean screw?
   a. the water pressure inside the screw
   b. the person who is turning the handle
   c. falling water that is turning the screw
   d. electrical energy

4. How is the Archimedean screw helping the person in the illustration do work?
   a. by decreasing the input force needed to lift the water
   b. by decreasing the work needed to lift the water
   c. by decreasing the distance over which the input force is applied
   d. by keeping the water from overflowing its banks

5. If the threads on the Archimedean screw are closer together, the input force must be applied over a greater distance. This means that the person using it must turn the handle
   a. with more force
   b. fewer times but faster
   c. in the opposite direction
   d. more times with less effort

Extended Response

Answer the two questions below in detail.

6. A playground seesaw is an example of a lever. The fulcrum is located at the center of the board. People seated at either end take turns applying the force needed to move the other person. If one person weighs more than the other, how can they operate the seesaw? Consider several possibilities in your answer.

7. Picture two gears of different sizes turning together. Suppose you can apply a force to turn the larger gear or the smaller gear, and it will turn the other. Discuss what difference it would make whether you turned the larger or smaller gear. Describe the input work you would do on the gear you are turning and the output work that gear would do on the other gear.

Chapter 5: **Machines** 175

UNIT 2
Waves, Sound, and Light

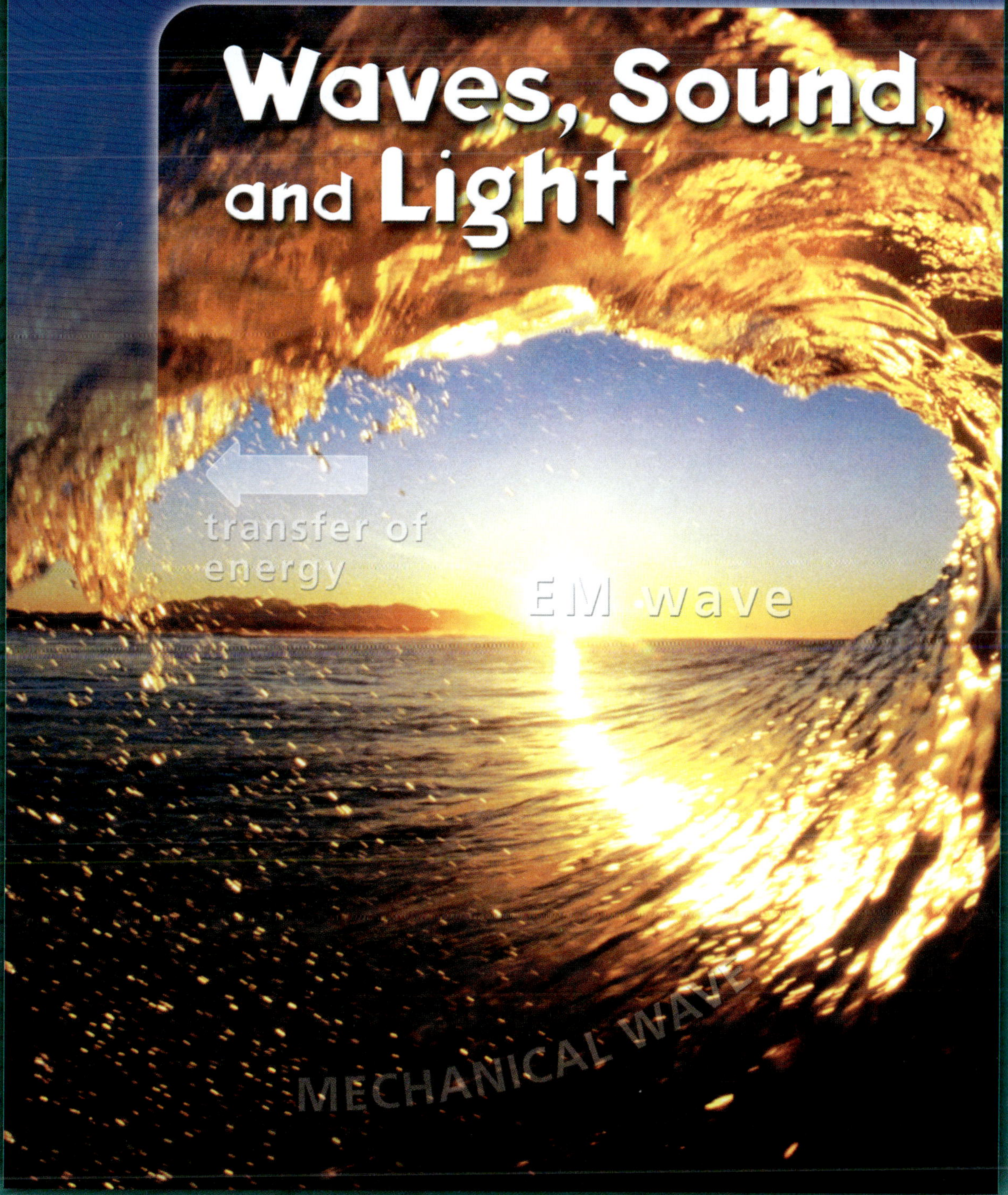

transfer of energy

EM wave

MECHANICAL WAVE

Contents Overview

Frontiers in Science
Sound Medicine   178

Timelines in Science
The Story of Light   282

Chapter 6 Waves   182
Chapter 7 Sound   210
Chapter 8 Electromagnetic Waves   246
Chapter 9 Light and Optics   286

FRONTIERS in Science

SOUND Medicine

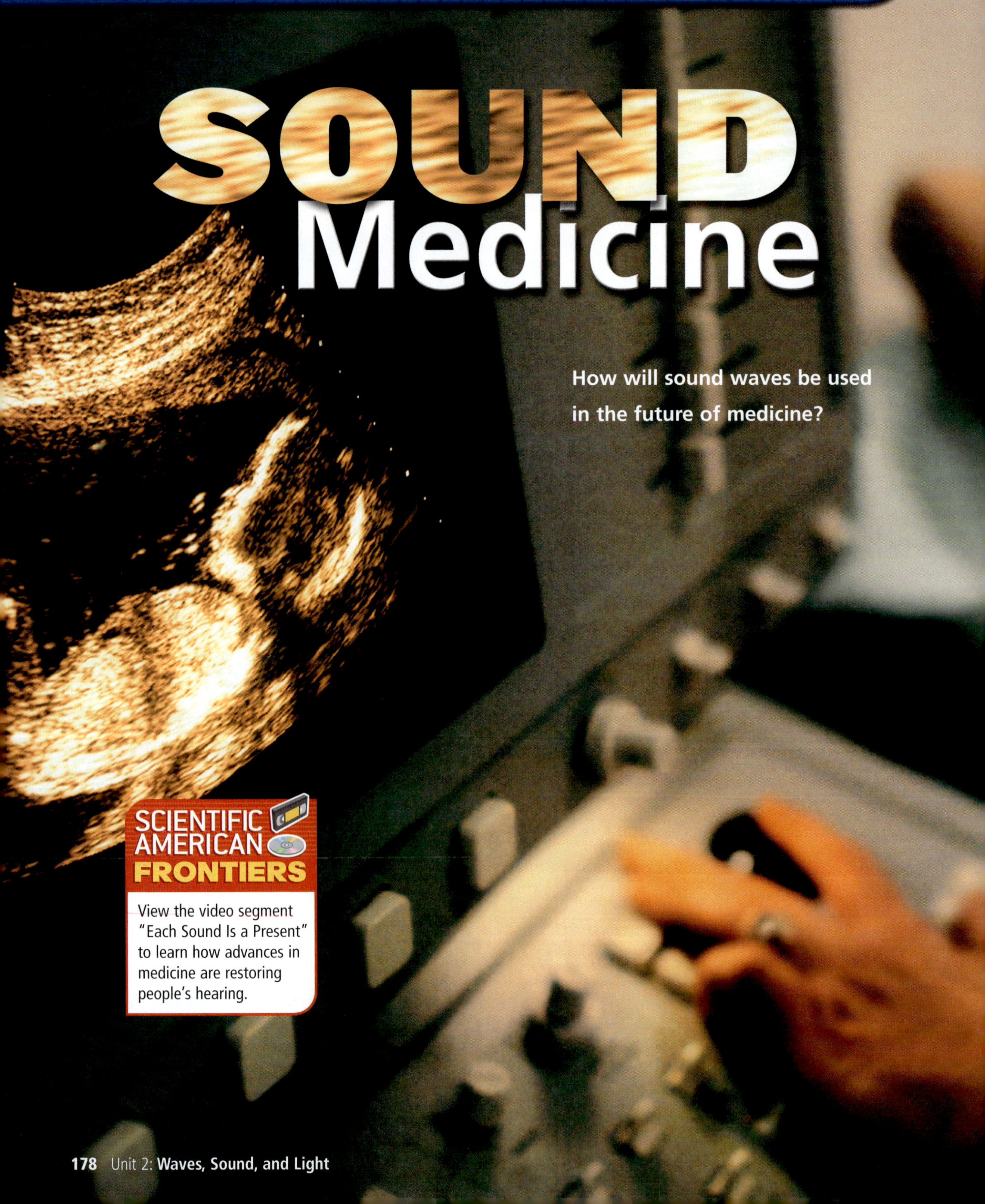

How will sound waves be used in the future of medicine?

SCIENTIFIC AMERICAN FRONTIERS

View the video segment "Each Sound Is a Present" to learn how advances in medicine are restoring people's hearing.

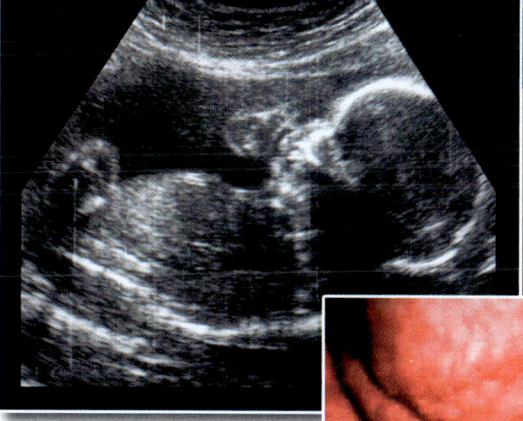

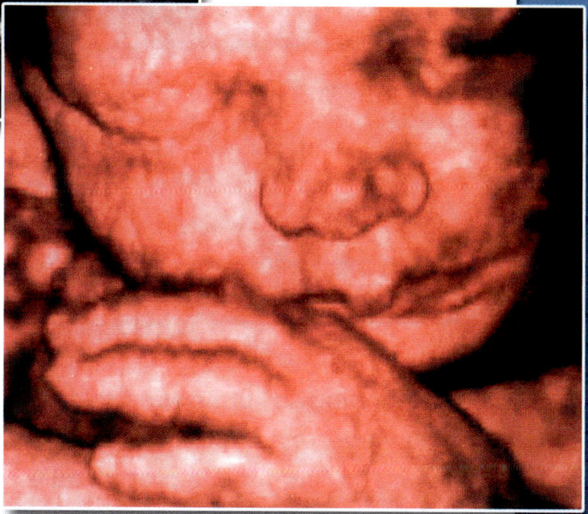

With traditional ultrasound (top), technicians interpret the image of the fetus. With the newer three-dimensional ultrasound (right), the image is much clearer.

Seeing Inside the Body

Have you ever wondered what the inside of your body looks like? Doctors have tried for many years to find ways of seeing what goes on inside a person's body that makes that person sick. Around 100 years ago, scientists found that a kind of wave called x-rays could be used to make images of the bones inside a person. This common method of seeing inside a body, is used mainly to show bones and teeth. However, repeated exposure to x-rays can be damaging to body cells. In the 1960s doctors started using a different kind of wave called ultrasound to make images of the organs inside the body.

Waves are now used in many medical applications. For example, cochlear implants use radio waves to help people hear. Ultrasound now has many new medical applications, from breaking up kidney stones to monitoring the flow of blood in the body.

Sound and Ultrasound

Sound is a type of wave, a vibration in the air. Humans can hear a wide range of different sounds, from very low pitches to very high. Sounds that are higher in pitch than humans can hear are referred to as ultrasound. They are no different from sounds we can hear, except they vibrate much faster than human ears can detect. Many animals can detect ultrasound; for example, dog whistles are in the ultrasound range.

Frontiers in Science 179

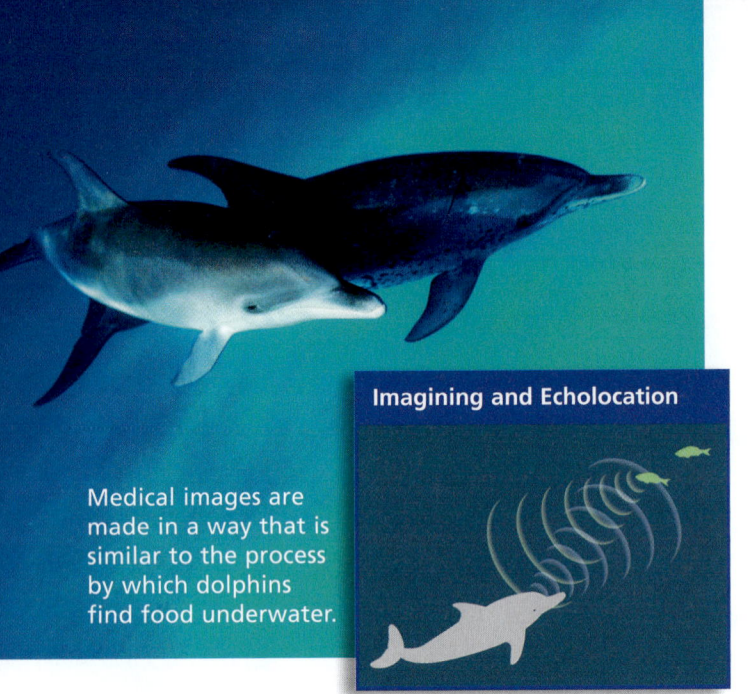

Imagining and Echolocation

Medical images are made in a way that is similar to the process by which dolphins find food underwater.

for the sound to travel to the object and return. Echolocation enables bats to capture flying insects at night and dolphins to catch fish in the ocean depths, where light doesn't penetrate.

Similarly, in ultrasound imaging, a machine sends a beam of ultrasound into a person's body and detects any echoes. The waves reflect whenever they strike a boundary between two objects with different densities. A computer measures the time required for the wave to travel to the boundary and reflect back; this information is used to determine the location and shape of the organ. The computer can then generate a live image of the organ inside the body.

The technology of ultrasound in medicine is based upon a process similar to that used by bats and dolphins to find food, a process called echolocation. The animal emits an ultrasound click or chirp and then listens for an echo. The echo indicates that an object has reflected the sound back to the animal. Over time, these animals have evolved the ability to judge the distance of the object by noting the time required

Ultrasound imaging has been used most often to monitor the development of a fetus inside its mother and to observe the valves of the heart. Blood flow can be color coded with faster flow in one color and slower flow in another color. The colors make it easier to see the location of blockages affecting the rate of flow in the blood vessels. This helps doctors detect blockages and diagnose heart problems.

SCIENTIFIC AMERICAN FRONTIERS

View the "Each Sound Is a Present" segment of your *Scientific American Frontiers* video to learn how a cochlear implant restores hearing to a young girl.

IN THIS SCENE FROM THE VIDEO ▶
A young girl's cochlear implant is turned on for the first time.

HEARING IS A GIFT A recent development in technology is about to give seven-year-old Kelley Flynn something she has always wanted —better hearing. Kelley has been almost completely deaf since she was two years old, and now she is losing the little hearing she does have. The development is a device called a cochlear implant. Cochlear implants work inside the ear, stimulating the brain when a sound is detected.

Normally, sound travels as vibrations from the outer ear, through the middle ear to the inner ear, where thousands of tiny cells—called hair cells— register the quality of the sound and send a signal to the brain. In a cochlear implant, tiny electrical sensors, or electrodes, mimic the hair cells by registering the sound and sending a signal to the brain. The signals get to the electrodes through a system including a computer, microphone, and radio transmitter and receiver. Using this system, people with little or no hearing are able to sense sounds.

180 Unit 2: **Waves, Sound, and Light**

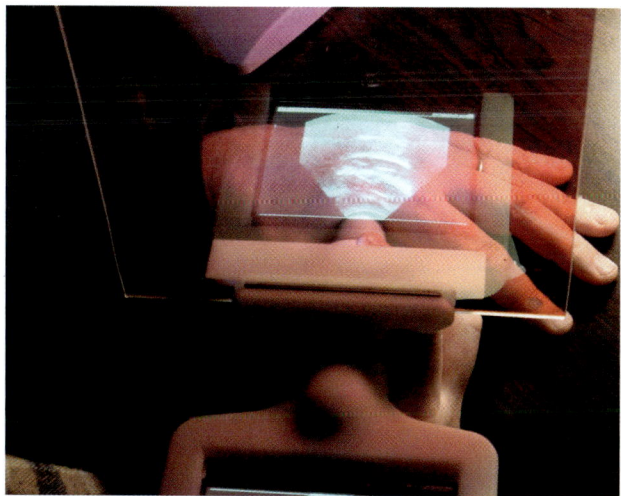

Recent advances in ultrasound technology include the development of portable devices that display images of the body, such as this hand-held device.

Advances in Ultrasound

Waves, including ultrasound, transfer energy. Physical therapists often use this fact when applying ultrasound to sore joints, heating the muscles and ligaments so they can move more freely. If the ultrasound waves are given stronger intensity and sharper focus, they can transfer enough energy to break up kidney stones in the body. The use of focused sound waves is now being tested for its ability to treat other problems, such as foot injuries.

Other recent advances in medical ultrasound include the development of devices that produce clearer images and use equipment that is smaller in size. In the late 1990's portable ultrasound devices were developed that allow the technology to be brought to the patient.

UNANSWERED Questions

As scientists learn more about the use of sound and other types of waves, new questions will arise.

- Will new methods of imaging the body change the way diseases are diagnosed?
- How closely do sounds heard using a cochlear implant resemble sounds heard by the ear?

UNIT PROJECTS

As you study this unit, work alone or with a group on one of these projects.

Magazine Article

Write a magazine article about the medical uses of ultrasound.

- Collect information about medical ultrasound and take notes about applications that interest you.
- If possible, conduct an interview with a medical practitioner who uses ultrasound.
- Read over all your notes and decide what information to include in your article.

Make a Music Video

Make a music video for a song of your choice, and explain how the video uses sound waves and light waves.

- Plan the sound portion of the video, including how the music will be played and amplified.
- For the lighting, use colored cellophane or gels to mix different colors of light. Explain your choices.
- Rehearse the video. Record the video and present it to the class.

Design a Demonstration

Design a hands-on demonstration of echolocation.

- Research the use of echolocation by animals.
- Design a demonstration of echolocation using a tennis ball and an obstacle.
- Present your demonstration to the class.

CAREER CENTER
CLASSZONE.COM

Learn more about careers in audiology.

CHAPTER
6 Waves

the BIG idea
Waves transfer energy and interact in predictable ways.

What is moving these surfers?

Key Concepts

SECTION 1 **Waves transfer energy.**
Learn about forces and energy in wave motion.

SECTION 2 **Waves have measurable properties.**
Learn how the amplitude, wavelength, and frequency of a wave are measured.

SECTION 3 **Waves behave in predictable ways.**
Learn about reflection, refraction, diffraction, and interference.

Internet Preview
CLASSZONE.COM
Chapter 6 online resources: Content Review, Simulation, Visualization, two Resource Centers, Math Tutorial, Test Practice

182 Unit 2: Waves, Sound, and Light

EXPLORE the BIG idea

How Can Energy Be Passed Along?

Stand several videos up in a line. Knock over the first video, and notice the motion of the other videos.

Observe and Think Write down your observations. How far did each video move? What traveled from the beginning to the end of the line? Where did the energy to move the last video come from?

How Can You Change a Wave?

Fill a large bowl half-full of water. Dip a pencil into the water and pull it out quickly. Observe the wave that forms. Now try tapping the bowl with the eraser end of your pencil. What will happen if you use more energy to make the waves? Less energy?

Observe and Think What happened to the size of the waves? The speed? Why do you think that is so?

Internet Activity: Waves

Go to **ClassZone.com** to simulate the effect that different degrees of force have on a wave.

Observe and Think What do you think would happen to the wave if you increased the number of times the flapper moved? What other ways could you affect the wave in the pool?

Seismic Waves **Code: MDL027**

Chapter 6: **Waves** 183

CHAPTER 6
Getting Ready to Learn

◀ CONCEPT REVIEW

- Forces change the motion of objects in predictable ways.
- Energy can be transferred from one place to another.

◀ VOCABULARY REVIEW

See Glossary for definitions.

force
kinetic energy
potential energy

CONTENT REVIEW
CLASSZONE.COM
Review concepts and vocabulary.

▶ TAKING NOTES

COMBINATION NOTES

To take notes about a new concept, write an explanation of the concept in a table. Then make a sketch of the concept and label it so you can study it later.

VOCABULARY STRATEGY

Write each new vocabulary term in the center of a **four square** diagram. Write notes in the squares around each term. Include a definition, some characteristics, and some examples of the term. If possible, write some things that are not examples of the term.

See the Note-Taking Handbook on pages R45–R51.

SCIENCE NOTEBOOK

Concept	Explanation	Sketch
Forces and waves	Forces move a medium up and down or back and forth. A wave moves forward.	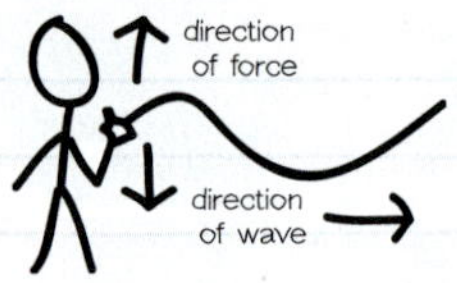 (stick figure with direction of force ↕ and direction of wave →)

Definition	Characteristics
A disturbance that transfers energy from one place to another	Matter moves in place. Energy travels entire distance.

WAVE

Examples	Nonexamples
Water wave	Ball rolling
Sound wave	Water rushing downstream

184 Unit 2: Waves, Sound, and Light

KEY CONCEPT

Waves transfer energy.

 BEFORE, you learned
- Forces can change an object's motion
- Energy can be kinetic or potential

 NOW, you will learn
- How forces cause waves
- How waves transfer energy
- How waves are classified

VOCABULARY

wave p. 185
medium p. 187
mechanical wave p. 187
transverse wave p. 189
longitudinal wave p. 190

EXPLORE Waves

How will the rope move?

PROCEDURE

 Tie a ribbon in the middle of a rope. Then tie one end of the rope to a chair.

② Holding the loose end of the rope in your hand, stand far enough away from the chair that the rope is fairly straight.

③ Flick the rope by moving your hand up and down quickly. Observe what happens.

MATERIALS
- ribbon
- rope
- chair

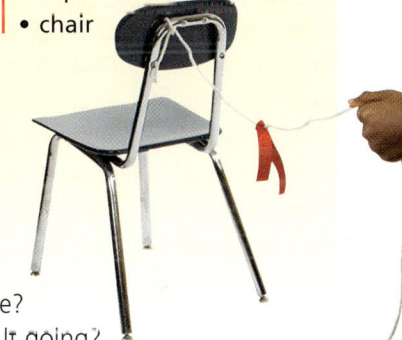

WHAT DO YOU THINK?
- How did the rope move? How did the ribbon move?
- What do you think starts a wave, and what keeps it going?

A wave is a disturbance.

You experience the effects of waves every day. Every sound you hear depends on sound waves. Every sight you see depends on light waves. A tiny wave can travel across the water in a glass, and a huge wave can travel across the ocean. Sound waves, light waves, and water waves seem very different from one another. So what, exactly, is a wave?

A **wave** is a disturbance that transfers energy from one place to another. Waves can transfer energy over distance without moving matter the entire distance. For example, an ocean wave can travel many kilometers without the water itself moving many kilometers. The water moves up and down—a motion known as a disturbance. It is the disturbance that travels in a wave, transferring energy.

READING TIP
To *disturb* means to agitate or unsettle.

 How does an ocean wave transfer energy across the ocean?

Chapter 6: **Waves** 185

Forces and Waves

You know that a force is required to change the motion of an object. Forces can also start a disturbance, sending a wave through a material. The following examples describe how forces cause waves.

Example 1 Rope Wave Think of a rope that is tied to a doorknob. You apply one force to the rope by flicking it upward and an opposite force when you snap it back down. This sends a wave through the rope. Both forces—the one that moves the rope up and the one that moves the rope down—are required to start a wave.

READING TIP
As you read each example, think of how it is similar to and different from the other examples.

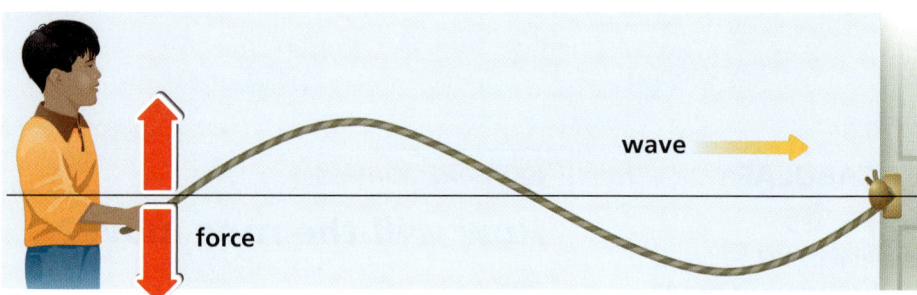

Example 2 Water Wave Forces are also required to start a wave in water. Think of a calm pool of water. What happens if you apply a force to the water by dipping your finger into it? The water rushes back after you remove your finger. The force of your finger and the force of the water rushing back send waves across the pool.

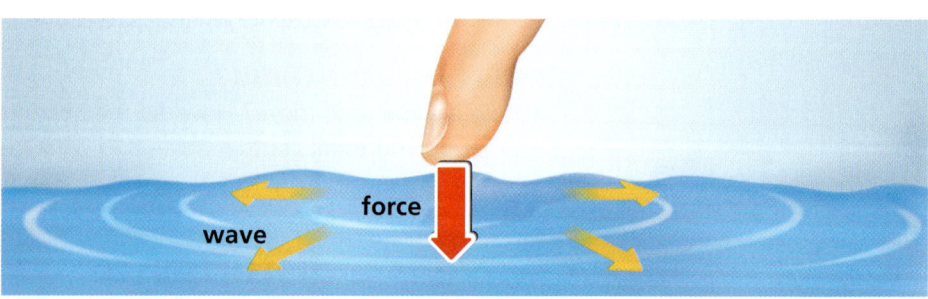

Example 3 Earthquake Wave An earthquake is a sudden release of energy that has built up in rock as a result of the surrounding rock pushing and pulling on it. When these two forces cause the rock to suddenly break away and move, the energy is transferred as a wave through the ground.

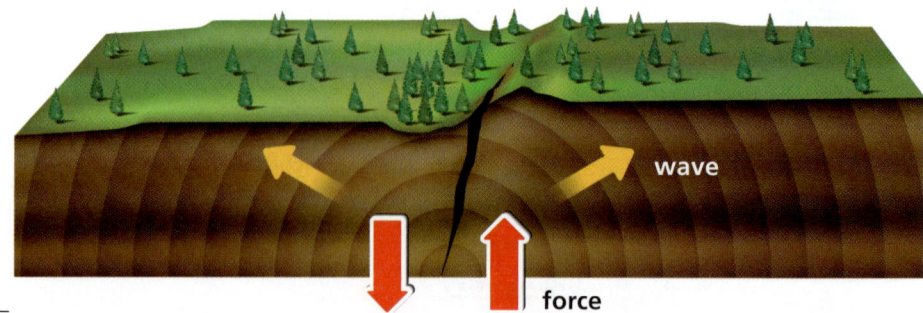

Materials and Waves

A rope tied to a doorknob, water, and the ground all have something in common. They are all materials through which waves move. A **medium** is any substance that a wave moves through. Water is the medium for an ocean wave; the ground is the medium for an earthquake wave; the rope is the medium for the rope wave. In the next chapter, you will learn that sound waves can move through many mediums, including air.

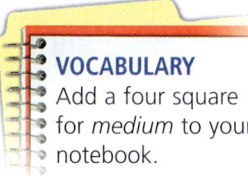
VOCABULARY
Add a four square for *medium* to your notebook.

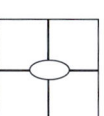

Waves that transfer energy through matter are known as **mechanical waves.** All of the waves you have read about so far, even sound waves, are mechanical waves. Water, the ground, a rope, and the air are all made up of matter. Later, you will learn about waves that can transfer energy through empty space. Light is an example of a wave that transfers energy through empty space.

 How are all mechanical waves similar?

Energy and Waves

The waves caused by an earthquake are good examples of energy transfer. The disturbed ground shakes from side to side and up and down as the waves move through it. Such waves can travel kilometers away from their source. The ground does not travel kilometers away from where it began; it is the energy that travels in a wave. In the case of an earthquake, it is kinetic energy, or the energy of motion, that is transferred.

This photograph was taken after a 1995 earthquake in Japan. A seismic wave transferred enough energy through the ground to bend the railroad tracks, leaving them in the shape of a wave.

Chapter 6: **Waves** 187

A Wave Model

When these fans do "the wave" in a stadium, they are modeling the way a disturbance travels through a medium.

Each person only moves up and down.

The wave can move all the way around the stadium.

READING VISUALS In which direction do people move when doing the stadium wave? In which direction does the wave move?

Look at the illustration of people modeling a wave in a stadium. In this model, the crowd of people represents a wave medium. The people moving up and down represent the disturbance. The transfer of the disturbance around the stadium represents a wave. Each person only moves up and down, while the disturbance can move all the way around the stadium.

Ocean waves are another good example of energy transfer. Ocean waves travel to the shore, one after another. Instead of piling up all the ocean water on the shore, however, the waves transfer energy. A big ocean wave transfers enough kinetic energy to knock someone down.

CHECK YOUR READING How does the stadium wave differ from a real ocean wave?

Waves can be classified by how they move.

As you have seen, one way to classify waves is according to the medium through which they travel. Another way to classify waves is by how they move. You have read that some waves transfer an up-and-down or a side-to-side motion. Other waves transfer a forward-and-backward motion.

Transverse Waves

Think again about snapping the rope with your hand. The action of your hand causes a vertical, or up-and-down, disturbance in the rope. However, the wave it sets off is horizontal, or forward. This type of wave is known as a transverse wave. In a **transverse wave,** the direction in which the wave travels is perpendicular, or at right angles, to the direction of the disturbance. *Transverse* means "across" or "crosswise." The wave itself moves crosswise as compared with the vertical motion of the medium.

READING TIP

Perpendicular means at a 90° angle.

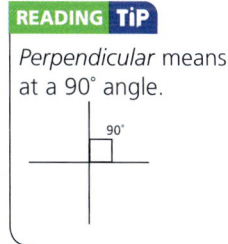

Transverse Wave

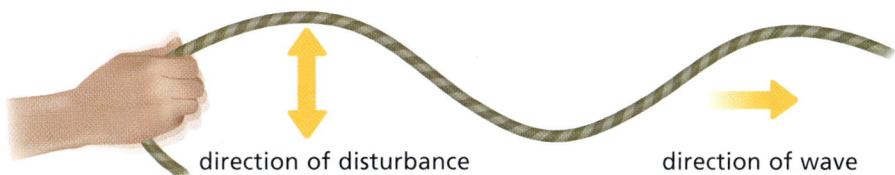

direction of disturbance   direction of wave

Water waves are also transverse. The up-and-down motion of the water is the disturbance. The wave travels in a direction that is perpendicular to the direction of the disturbance. The medium is the water, and energy is transferred outward in all directions from the source.

 What is a transverse wave? Find two examples in the paragraphs above.

INVESTIGATE Wave Types

How do waves compare?

SKILL FOCUS
Comparing

PROCEDURE

1. Place the spring toy on the floor on its side. Stretch out the spring. To start a disturbance in the spring, take one end and move it from side to side. Observe the movement in the spring. Remember that a transverse wave travels at right angles to the disturbance.

2. Put the spring toy on the floor in the same position as before. Think about how you could make a different kind of disturbance to produce a different kind of wave. (**Hint:** Suppose you push the spring in the direction of the wave you expect to make.) Observe the movement in the spring.

WHAT DO YOU THINK?
- Compare the waves you made. How are they alike? How are they different?
- What kind of wave did you produce by moving the spring from side to side?

CHALLENGE Can you think of a third way to make a wave travel through a spring?

MATERIALS
spring toy

TIME
10 minutes

Chapter 6: **Waves** 189

Longitudinal Waves

READING TIP
The word *long* can help you remember longitudinal waves. The disturbance moves along the length of the spring.

Another type of wave is a longitudinal wave. In a **longitudinal wave** (LAHN-jih-TOOD-n-uhl), the wave travels in the same direction as the disturbance. A longitudinal wave can be started in a spring by moving it forward and backward. The coils of the spring move forward and bunch up and then move backward and spread out. This forward and backward motion is the disturbance. Longitudinal waves are sometimes called compressional waves because the bunched-up area is known as a compression. How is a longitudinal wave similar to a transverse wave? How is it different?

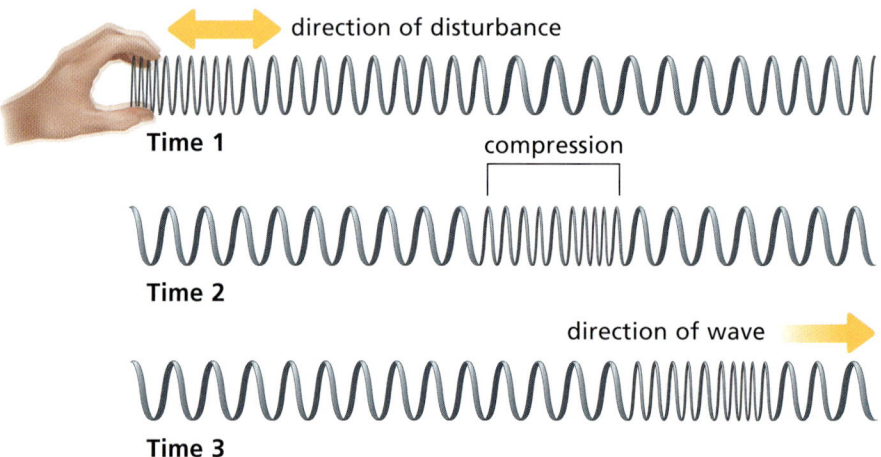

Longitudinal Wave

Learn more about waves.

Sound waves are examples of longitudinal waves. Imagine a bell ringing. The clapper inside the bell strikes the side and makes it vibrate, or move back and forth rapidly. The vibrating bell pushes and pulls on nearby air molecules, causing them to move forward and backward. These air molecules, in turn, set more air molecules into motion. A sound wave pushes forward. In sound waves, the vibrations of the air molecules are in the same direction as the movement of the wave.

6.1 Review

KEY CONCEPTS

1. Describe how forces start waves.
2. Explain how a wave can travel through a medium and yet the medium stays in place. Use the term *energy* in your answer.
3. Describe two ways in which waves travel, and give an example of each.

CRITICAL THINKING

4. **Analyze** Does water moving through a hose qualify as a wave? Explain why or why not.
5. **Classify** Suppose you drop a cookie crumb in your milk. At once, you see ripples spreading across the surface of the milk. What type of waves are these? What is the disturbance?

CHALLENGE

6. **Predict** Suppose you had a rope long enough to extend several blocks down the street. If you were to start a wave in the rope, do you think it would continue all the way to the other end of the street? Explain why or why not.

Math in Science

MATH TUTORIAL
CLASSZONE.COM
Click on Math Tutorial for more help with finding the mean, median, and mode.

Before going out on the water, boaters can check reports on wave conditions in their area.

SKILL: MEAN, MEDIAN, AND MODE

Wave Heights

Tracking stations throughout the world's oceans measure and record the height of water waves that pass beneath them. The data recorded by the stations can be summarized as average wave heights over one hour or one day.

How would you summarize the typical wave heights over one week? There are a few different ways in which data can be summarized. Three common ways are finding the mean, median, and mode.

Example

Wave height data for one week are shown below.

| 1.2 m | 1.5 m | 1.4 m | 1.7 m | 2.0 m | 1.4 m | 1.3 m |

(1) **Mean** To find the mean of the data, divide the sum of the values by the number of values.

$$\text{Mean} = \frac{1.2 + 1.5 + 1.4 + 1.7 + 2.0 + 1.4 + 1.3}{7} = 1.5 \text{ m}$$

ANSWER The mean wave height is 1.5 m.

(2) **Median** To find the median of the data, write the values in order from least to greatest. The value in the middle is the median.

1.2 m   1.3 m   1.4 m   (1.4 m)   1.5 m   1.7 m   2.0 m

ANSWER The median wave height is 1.4 m.

(3) **Mode** The mode is the number that occurs most often.

ANSWER The mode for the data is also 1.4 m.

Use the data to answer the following questions.

The data below show wave heights taken from a station off the coast of Florida over two weeks.

| Wk 1 | 1.2 m | 1.1 m | 1.1 m | 1.5 m | 4.7 m | 1.2 m | 1.1 m |
| Wk 2 | 0.7 m | 0.8 m | 0.9 m | 0.8 m | 1.0 m | 1.1 m | 0.8 m |

1. Find the mean, median, and mode of the data for Week 1.

2. Find the mean, median, and mode of the data for Week 2.

CHALLENGE A storm carrying strong winds caused high waves on the fifth day of the data shown above for Week 1. Which of the following was most affected by the high value—the mean, median, or mode?

Chapter 6: **Waves** 191

KEY CONCEPT

6.2 Waves have measurable properties.

◀ **BEFORE, you learned**

- Forces cause waves
- Waves transfer energy
- Waves can be transverse or longitudinal

▶ **NOW, you will learn**

- How amplitude, wavelength, and frequency are measured
- How to find a wave's speed

VOCABULARY

crest p. 193
trough p. 193
amplitude p. 193
wavelength p. 193
frequency p. 193

THINK ABOUT

How can a wave be measured?

This enormous wave moves the water high above sea level as it comes crashing through. How could you find out how high a water wave actually goes? How could you find out how fast it is traveling? In what other ways do you think a wave can be measured? Read on to find out.

Waves have amplitude, wavelength, and frequency.

COMBINATION NOTES
Use combination notes in your notebook to describe how waves can be measured.

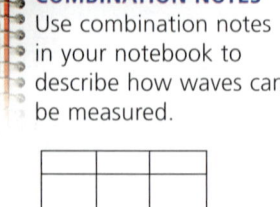

The tallest ocean wave ever recorded was measured from the deck of a ship during a storm. An officer on the ship saw a wave reach a height that was level with a point high on the ship, more than 30 meters (100 ft)! Height is a property of all waves—from ripples in a glass of water to gigantic waves at surfing beaches—and it can be measured.

The speed of a water wave is another property that can be measured—by finding the time it takes for one wave peak to travel a set distance. Other properties of a wave that can be measured include the time between waves and the length of a single wave. Scientists use the terms *amplitude*, *wavelength*, and *frequency* to refer to some commonly measured properties of waves.

CHECK YOUR READING What are three properties of a wave that can be measured?

192 Unit 2: Waves, Sound, and Light

Measuring Wave Properties

A **crest** is the highest point, or peak, of a wave. A **trough** is the lowest point, or valley, of a wave. Suppose you are riding on a boat in rough water. When the boat points upward and rises, it is climbing to the crest of a wave. When it points downward and sinks, the boat is falling to the trough of the wave.

① **Amplitude** for a transverse wave is the distance between a line through the middle of a wave and a crest or trough. In an ocean wave, amplitude measures how far the wave rises above, or dips below, its original position, or rest position.

Amplitude is an important measurement, because it indicates how much energy a wave is carrying. The bigger the amplitude, the more energy the wave has. Find amplitude on the diagram below.

② The distance from one wave crest to the very next crest is called the **wavelength.** Wavelength can also be measured from trough to trough. Find wavelength on the diagram below.

③ The number of waves passing a fixed point in a certain amount of time is called the **frequency.** The word *frequent* means "often," so frequency measures how often a wave occurs. Frequency is often measured by counting the number of crests or troughs that pass by a given point in one second. Find frequency on the diagram below.

VOCABULARY
Remember to add a four square to your notebook for each new term on this page.

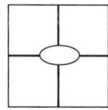

CHECK YOUR READING How is amplitude related to energy?

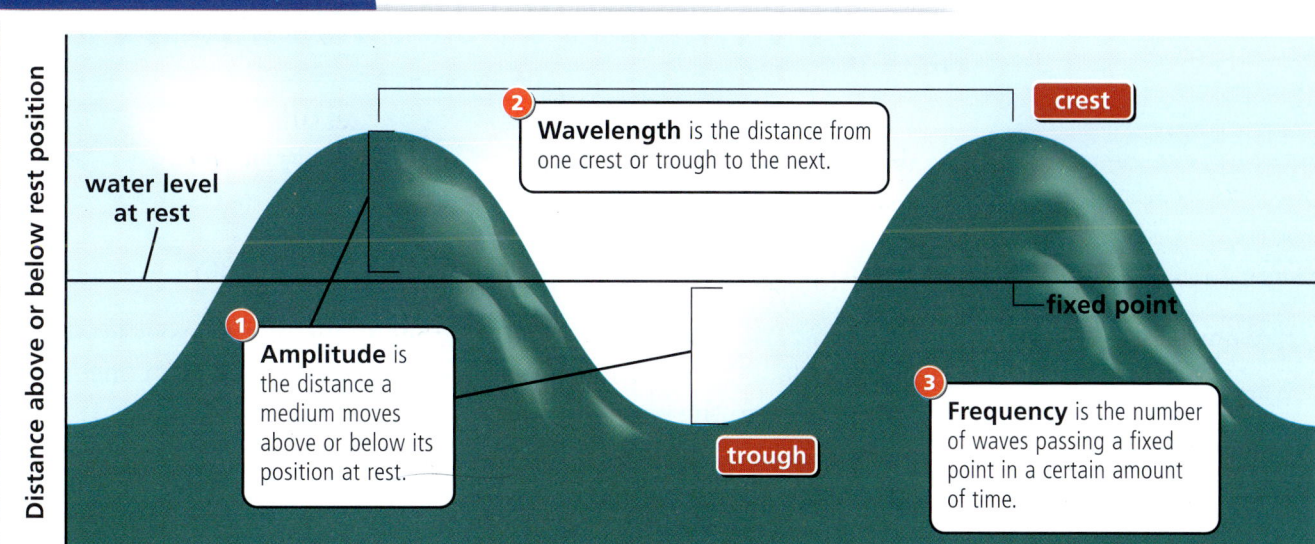

READING VISUALS How many wavelengths are shown in this diagram? How do you know?

Chapter 6: **Waves** 193

How Frequency and Wavelength Are Related

The frequency and wavelength of a wave are related. When frequency increases more wave crests pass a fixed point each second. That means the wavelength shortens. So, as frequency increases, wavelength decreases. The opposite is also true—as frequency decreases, wavelength increases.

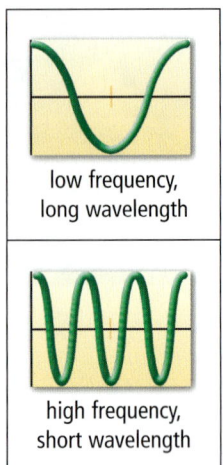

low frequency, long wavelength

high frequency, short wavelength

Suppose you are making waves in a rope. If you make one wave crest every second, the frequency is one wave per second (1/s). Now suppose you want to increase the frequency to more than one wave per second. You flick the rope up and down faster. The wave crests are now closer together. In other words, their wavelengths have decreased.

Graphing Wave Properties

The graph of a transverse wave looks much like a wave itself. The illustration on page 195 shows the graph of an ocean wave. The measurements for the graph come from a float, or buoy (BOO-ee), that keeps track of how high or low the water goes. The graph shows the position of the buoy at three different points in time. These points are numbered. Since the graph shows what happens over time, you can see the frequency of the waves.

> **REMINDER**
> Frequency is the number of waves that pass a given point in a certain amount of time.

Unlike transverse waves, longitudinal waves look different from their graphs. The graph of a longitudinal wave in a spring is drawn below. The coils of the spring get closer and then farther apart as the wave moves through them.

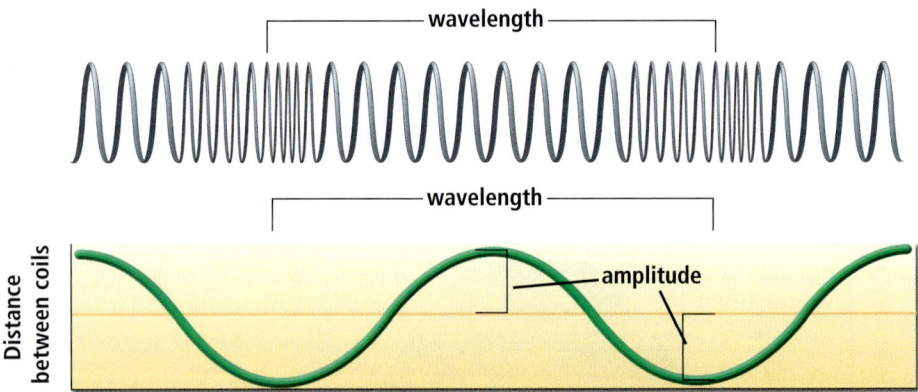

Watch the graph of a wave form.

The shape of the graph resembles the shape of a transverse wave. The wavelength on a longitudinal wave is the distance from one compression to the next. The amplitude of a longitudinal wave measures how compressed the medium gets. Just as in a transverse wave, frequency in a longitudinal wave is the number of waves passing a fixed point in a certain amount of time.

 How are longitudinal waves measured?

194 Unit 2: **Waves, Sound, and Light**

Graphing a Wave

The graph of a transverse wave looks like a wave itself. The graph shows what happens over time.

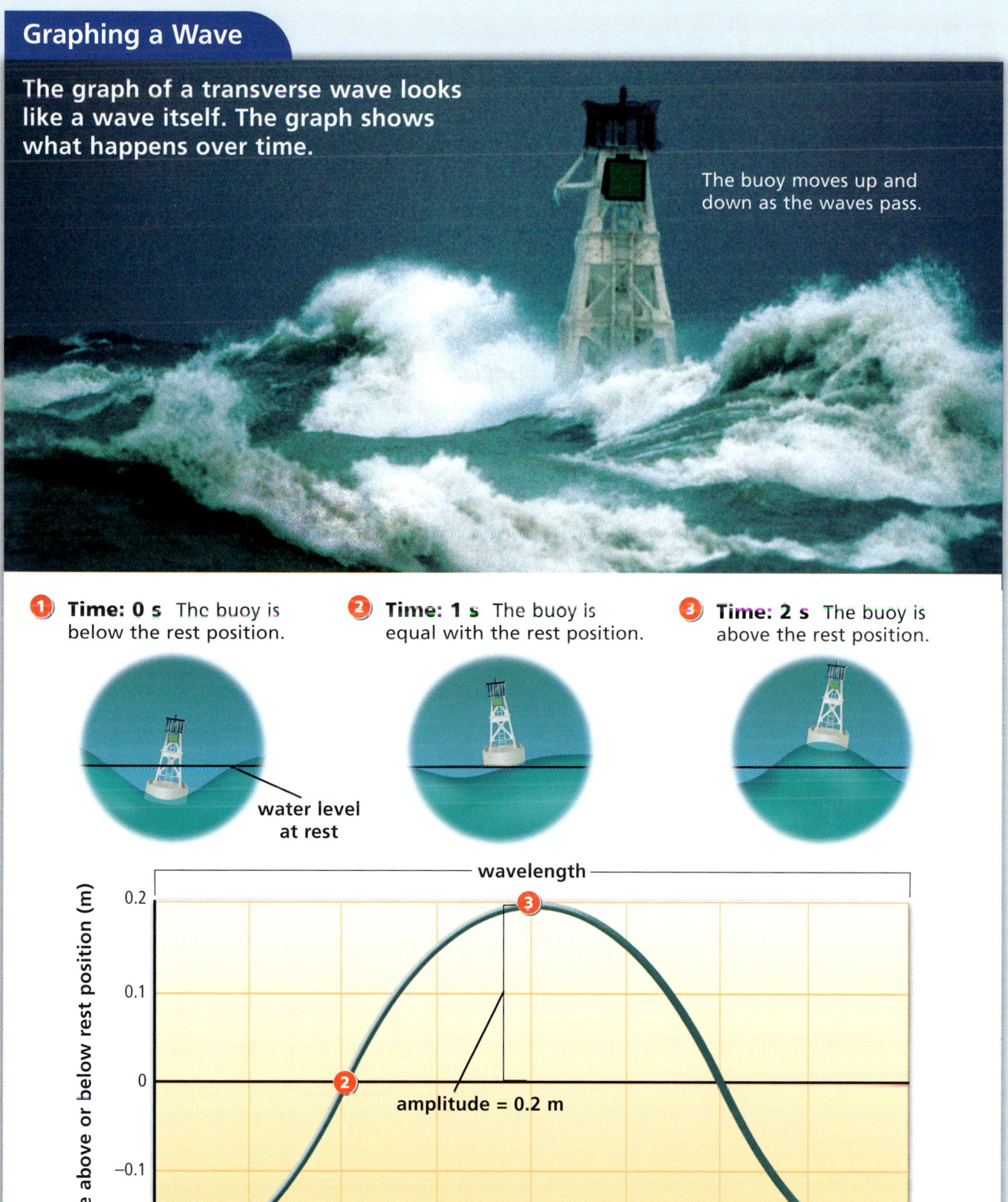

The buoy moves up and down as the waves pass.

① Time: 0 s The buoy is below the rest position.

② Time: 1 s The buoy is equal with the rest position.

③ Time: 2 s The buoy is above the rest position.

water level at rest

wavelength

amplitude = 0.2 m

frequency = 0.25/s

Distance above or below rest position (m)

Time (s)

READING VISUALS How many seconds does it take for one wave to pass? How much of the wave passes in one second?

Chapter 6: **Waves** 195

INVESTIGATE Frequency

How can you change frequency?

SKILL FOCUS
Collecting data

PROCEDURE

1) Tie 3 washers to a string. Tape the string to the side of your desk so that it can swing freely. The swinging washers can model wave action.

2) Pull the washers slightly to the side and let go. Find the frequency by counting the number of complete swings that occur in 1 minute.

3) Make a table in your notebook to record both the length of the string and the frequency.

4) Shorten the string by moving and retaping it. Repeat for 5 different lengths. Keep the distance you pull the washers the same each time.

WHAT DO YOU THINK?

- How did changing the length of the string affect the frequency?
- How does this model represent a wave? How does it differ from a wave?

CHALLENGE How could you vary the amplitude of this model? Predict how changing the amplitude would affect the frequency.

MATERIALS
- 3 metal washers
- piece of string
- tape
- stopwatch
- meter stick

TIME
30 minutes

Wave speed can be measured.

In addition to amplitude, wavelength, and frequency, a wave's speed can be measured. One way to find the speed of a wave is to time how long it takes for a wave to get from one point to another. Another way to find the speed of a wave is to calculate it. The speed of any wave can be determined when both the frequency and the wavelength are known, using the following formula:

$$\text{Speed} = \text{wavelength} \cdot \text{frequency}$$
$$S = \lambda f$$

 **REMINDER**
The symbol λ represents wavelength.

Different types of waves travel at very different speeds. For example, light waves travel through air almost a million times faster than sound waves travel through air. You have experienced the difference in wave speeds if you have ever seen lightning and heard the thunder that comes with it in a thunderstorm. When lightning strikes far away, you see the light seconds before you hear the clap of its thunder. The light waves reach you while the sound waves are still on their way.

How fast do you think water waves can travel? Water waves travel at different speeds. You can calculate the speed using wavelength and frequency.

Suppose you wish to calculate the speed of an ocean wave with a wavelength of 16 meters and a frequency of 0.31 wave per second. When working through the problem in the example below, it is helpful to think of the frequency as

$$f = 0.31 \text{ (wave)/s}$$

even though the units for frequency are just 1/second. You can think of wavelengths as "meters per wave," or

$$\lambda = 16 \text{ m/(wave)}$$

RESOURCE CENTER
CLASSZONE.COM
Find out more about wave speed.

Calculating Wave Speed

Sample Problem

An ocean wave has a wavelength of 16 meters and a frequency of 0.31 wave per second. What is the speed of the wave?

What do you know? wavelength = 16 m, frequency = $0.31 \frac{\text{(wave)}}{\text{s}}$

What do you want to find out? Speed

Write the formula: $S = \lambda f$

Substitute into the formula: $S = 16 \frac{\text{m}}{\text{(wave)}} \cdot 0.31 \frac{\text{(wave)}}{\text{s}}$

Calculate and simplify: $16 \frac{\text{m}}{\text{(wave)}} \cdot 0.31 \frac{\text{(wave)}}{\text{s}} = 5 \frac{\text{m}}{\text{s}}$

Check that your units agree: Unit is m/s. Unit for speed is m/s. Units agree.

Answer: $S = 5$ m/s

Practice the Math

1. In a stormy sea, 2 waves pass a fixed point every second, and the waves are 10 m apart. What is the speed of the waves?
2. In a ripple tank, the wavelength is 0.1 cm, and 10 waves occur each second. What is the speed of the waves (in cm/s)?

6.2 Review

KEY CONCEPTS

1. Make a simple diagram of a wave, labeling amplitude, frequency, and wavelength. For frequency, you will need to indicate a span of time, such as one second.

2. What two measurements of a wave do you need to calculate its speed?

CRITICAL THINKING

3. **Observe** Suppose you are watching water waves pass under the end of a pier. How can you figure out their frequency?

4. **Calculate** A wave has a speed of 3 m/s and a frequency of 6 (waves)/s. What is its wavelength?

CHALLENGE

5. **Apply** Imagine you are on a boat in the middle of the sea. You are in charge of recording the properties of passing ocean waves into the ship's logbook. What types of information could you record? How would this information be useful? Explain your answer.

Chapter 6: **Waves** 197

CHAPTER INVESTIGATION

Wavelength

OVERVIEW AND PURPOSE The pendulum on a grandfather clock keeps time as it swings back and forth at a steady rate. The swings of a pendulum can be recorded as a wave with measurable properties. How do the properties of the pendulum affect the properties of the waves it produces? In this investigation you will use your understanding of wave properties to
- construct a pendulum and measure the waves it produces, and
- determine how the length of the pendulum affects the wavelength of the waves.

▶ Problem

How does changing the length of a pendulum affect the wavelength?

▶ Hypothesize

Write a hypothesis in "If . . . , then . . . , because . . ." form to answer the problem question.

▶ Procedure

MATERIALS
- 1/2 sheet white paper
- tape
- scissors
- string
- meter stick
- fine sand
- graduated cylinder
- 2 sheets colored construction paper

1. Make a data table like the one shown on the sample notebook page.

2. Make a cone with the half-sheet of paper by rolling it and taping it as shown. The hole in the bottom of the cone should be no larger than a pea.

3. Cut a hole in each side of the cone and tie the ends of the string to the cone to make a pendulum.

4. Hold the string on the pendulum so that the distance from your fingers holding the string to the bottom of the cone is 20 cm.

5. Cover the bottom of the cone with your fingertip. While you hold the cone, have your partner pour about 40 mL of sand into the cone.

198 Unit 2: **Waves, Sound, and Light**

6. Hold the pendulum about 5 cm above the construction paper as shown. Pull the pendulum from the bottom to one side of the construction paper. Be careful not to move the pendulum at the top, or to pull the pendulum over the edge of the paper.

7. Let the pendulum go while your partner gently pulls the paper forward so that the sand makes waves on the paper. Be sure to pull the paper at a steady rate. Let the remaining sand pile up on the end of the paper.

8. Measure the wavelength from crest to crest or trough to trough. Record the wavelength in your table.

9. Run two more trials, repeating steps 5–8. Be sure to pull the paper at the same speed for each trial. Calculate the average wavelength over all three trials, and record it in your table.

10. Repeat steps 4–8, changing the length of the pendulum to 30 cm and then to 40 cm.

Observe and Analyze   Write It Up

1. **RECORD OBSERVATIONS** Draw the setup of your procedure. Be sure your data table is complete.

2. **IDENTIFY VARIABLES AND CONSTANTS** Identify the variables and constants that affected the wave produced by the moving pendulum. List them in your notebook.

3. **ANALYZE** What patterns can you find in your data? For example, do the numbers increase or decrease as you read down each column?

Conclude   Write It Up

1. **INFER** Answer your problem question.
2. **INTERPRET** Compare your results with your hypothesis. Do your data support your hypothesis?
3. **IDENTIFY LIMITS** What possible limitations or sources of error could have affected your results?
4. **APPLY** Suppose you were examining the tracing made by a seismograph, a machine that records an earthquake wave. What would happen if you increased the speed at which the paper ran through the machine? What do you think the amplitude of the tracing represents?

INVESTIGATE Further

CHALLENGE Revise your experiment to change one variable other than the length of the pendulum. Run a new trial, changing the variable you choose but keeping everything else constant. How did changing the variable affect the wave produced?

Wavelength

Problem How does changing the length of a pendulum affect the wavelength?

Hypothesize

Observe and Analyze

Table 1. Wavelengths Produced by Pendulums

Pendulum Length (cm)	Trial 1	Trial 2	Trial 3	Average Wavelength (cm)
20				
30				
40				

Conclude

KEY CONCEPT
6.3 Waves behave in predictable ways.

BEFORE, you learned
- Waves transfer energy
- Amplitude, wavelength, and frequency can be measured

NOW, you will learn
- How waves change as they encounter a barrier
- What happens when waves enter a new medium
- How waves interact with other waves

VOCABULARY

reflection p. 201
refraction p. 201
diffraction p. 202
interference p. 203

EXPLORE Reflection
How do ripples reflect?
PROCEDURE

1. Put a few drops of food coloring into the pan of water.
2. Dip the pencil in the water at one end of the pan to make ripples in the water.
3. Observe the ripples as they reflect off the side of the pan. Draw a sketch of the waves reflecting.

MATERIALS
- wide pan, half full of water
- food coloring
- pencil

WHAT DO YOU THINK?
- What happens when the waves reach the side of the pan?
- Why do you think the waves behave as they do?

COMBINATION NOTES
Use combination notes in your notebook to describe how waves interact with materials.

Waves interact with materials.

You have read that mechanical waves travel through a medium like air, water, or the ground. In this section, you will read how the motion of waves changes when they encounter a new medium. For instance, when an ocean wave rolls into a ship or a sound wave strikes a solid wall, the wave encounters a new medium.

When waves interact with materials in these ways, they behave predictably. All waves, from water waves to sound waves and even light waves, show the behaviors that you will learn about next. Scientists call these behaviors reflection, refraction, and diffraction.

CHECK YOUR READING What behaviors do all waves have in common?

200 Unit 2: Waves, Sound, and Light

Reflection

What happens to water waves at the end of a swimming pool? The waves cannot travel through the wall of the pool. Instead, the waves bounce off the pool wall. The bouncing back of a wave after it strikes a barrier is called **reflection.**

Remember what you have learned about forces. A water wave, like all waves, transfers energy. When the water wave meets the wall of the pool, it pushes against the wall. The wall applies an equal and opposite force on the water, sending the wave back in another direction. In the illustration on the right, you can see water waves reflecting off a barrier.

Sound and light waves reflect too. Sound waves reflecting off the walls of a canyon produce an echo. Light waves reflecting off smooth metal behind glass let you see an image of yourself in the mirror. The light waves bounce off the metal just as the water waves bounce off the pool wall. You will learn more about how sound and light waves reflect in the next chapters.

Reflection Water waves move in predictable ways. Here waves are shown from above as they reflect off a barrier.

 How would you define *reflection* in your own words?

Refraction

Sometimes, a wave does not bounce back when it encounters a new medium. Instead, the wave continues moving forward. When a wave enters a new medium at an angle, it bends, or refracts. **Refraction** is the bending of a wave as it enters a new medium at an angle other than 90 degrees. Refraction occurs because waves travel at different speeds in different mediums. Because the wave enters the new medium at an angle, one side of the wave enters the new medium before the rest of the wave. When one side of a wave speeds up or slows down before the other side, it causes the wave to bend.

You have probably noticed the refraction of light waves in water. Objects half-in and half-out of water look broken or split. Look at the photograph of the straw in the glass. What your eyes suggest—that the straw is split—is not real, is it? You are seeing the refraction of light waves caused by the change of medium from air to water. You will learn more about the refraction of light waves in Chapter 9.

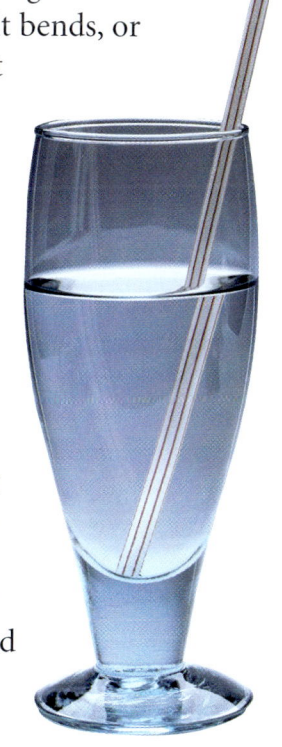

Refraction Light waves refract as they pass from air to water, making this straw look split.

Chapter 6: **Waves** 201

Diffraction

You have seen how waves reflect off a barrier. For example, water waves bounce off the side of a pool. But what if the side of the pool had an opening in it? Sometimes, waves interact with a partial barrier, such as a wall with an opening. As the waves pass through the opening, they spread out, or diffract. **Diffraction** is the spreading out of waves through an opening or around the edge of an obstacle. Diffraction occurs with all types of waves.

Look at the photograph on the right. It shows water waves diffracting as they pass through a small gap in a barrier. In the real world, ocean waves diffract through openings in cliffs or rock formations.

Similarly, sound waves diffract as they pass through an open doorway. Turn on a TV or stereo, and walk into another room. Listen to the sound with the door closed and then open. Then try moving around the room. You can hear the sound wherever you stand because the waves spread out, or diffract, through the doorway and reflect from the walls.

Diffraction through an opening

INVESTIGATE Diffraction

How can you make a wave diffract?

PROCEDURE

1. Put a few drops of food coloring into the container of water.
2. Experiment with quick motions of the ruler to set off waves in the container.
3. Place the block on its side in the center of the container. Set the bag of sand on the block to hold it down. Predict how the waves will interact with the barrier you have added.
4. Make another set of waves, and observe how they interact with the barrier.

WHAT DO YOU THINK?
- How did you make the waves diffract?
- How did your observations compare with your prediction?

CHALLENGE How could you change the experiment to make the effect of the diffraction more obvious?

SKILL FOCUS
Predicting

MATERIALS
- wide pan of water
- food coloring
- ruler
- wooden block
- bag of sand

TIME
20 minutes

202 Unit 2: **Waves, Sound, and Light**

Diffraction also occurs as waves pass the edge of an obstacle. The photograph at the right shows water waves diffracting as they pass an obstacle. Ocean waves also diffract in this way as they pass large rocks in the water.

Light waves diffract around the edge of an obstacle too. The edges of a shadow appear fuzzy because of diffraction. The light waves spread out, or diffract, around the object that is making the shadow.

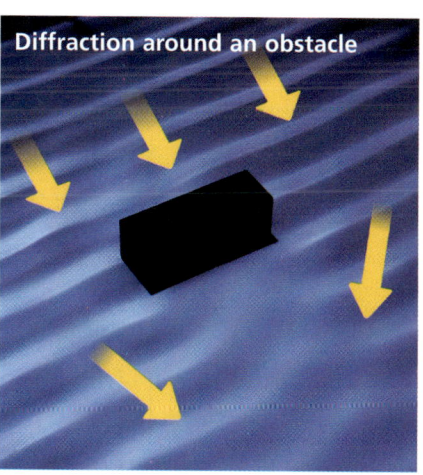
Diffraction around an obstacle

 Describe what happens when waves diffract.

Waves interact with other waves.

Just as waves sometimes interact with new mediums, they can also interact with other waves. Two waves can add energy to or take away energy from each other in the place where they meet. **Interference** is the meeting and combining of waves.

Waves Adding Together

Suppose two identical waves coming from opposite directions come together at one point. The waves' crests and troughs are aligned briefly, which means they join up exactly. When the two waves merge into a temporary, larger wave, their amplitudes are added together. When the waves separate again, they have their original amplitudes and continue in their original directions.

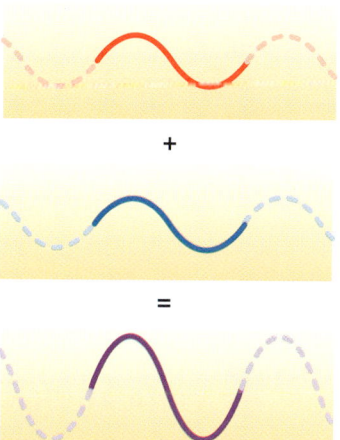

Constructive Interference

The adding of two waves is called constructive interference. It builds up, or constructs, a larger wave out of two smaller ones. Look at the diagram at the right to see what happens in constructive interference.

Because the waves in the example joined together perfectly, the amplitude of the new wave equals the combined amplitudes of the 2 original waves. For example, if the crest of a water wave with an amplitude of 1 meter (3.3 ft) met up with the crest of another wave with an amplitude of 1 meter (3.3 ft), there would be a 2 meter (6.6 ft) crest in the spot where they met.

When two wave crests with amplitudes of 1 m each combine, a wave with an amplitude of 2 m is formed.

Chapter 6: **Waves** 203

Waves Canceling Each Other Out

Imagine again that two very similar waves come together. This time, however, the crest of one wave joins briefly with the trough of the other. The energy of one wave is subtracted from the energy of the other. The new wave is therefore smaller than the original wave. This process is called destructive interference. Look at the diagram below to see what happens in destructive interference.

For example, if a 2-meter (6.6 ft) crest met up with a 1-meter (3.3 ft) trough, there would be a temporary crest of only 1 meter (3.3 ft) where they met. If the amplitudes of the two original waves are identical, the two waves can cancel each other out completely!

When identical waves meet, they are usually not aligned. Instead, the crests meet up with crests in some places and troughs in others. As a result, the waves add in some places and subtract in others. The photograph on the left shows a pattern resulting from waves both adding and subtracting on the surface of a pond. Have you ever listened to music on stereo speakers that were placed at a distance from each other? The music may have sounded loud in some places and soft in others, as the sound waves from the two speakers interfered with each other.

Wave interference produces this pattern on a pond as two sets of waves interact.

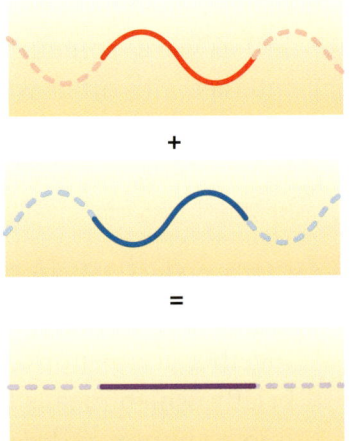

Destructive Interference

When a 1 m wave crest meets a 1 m wave trough, the amplitudes cancel each other out. A wave with an amplitude of 0 m is formed where they meet.

 **CHECK YOUR READING** Summarize in your own words what happens during interference.

 Review

KEY CONCEPTS

1. Explain what happens when waves encounter a medium that they cannot travel through.
2. Describe a situation in which waves would diffract.
3. Describe two ways that waves are affected by interference.

CRITICAL THINKING

4. **Synthesize** Explain how reflection and diffraction can happen at the same time in a wave.
5. **Compare** How is interference similar to net force? How do you think the two concepts might be related? **Hint:** Think about how forces are involved in wave motion.

CHALLENGE

6. **Predict** Imagine that you make gelatin in a long, shallow pan. Then you scoop the gelatin out of one end of the pan and add icy cold water to the exact same depth as the gelatin. Now suppose you set off waves at the water end. What do you think will happen when the waves meet the gelatin?

Connecting Sciences

PHYSICAL SCIENCE AND EARTH SCIENCE

Tsunamis!

Tsunamis (tsu-NAH-mees) are among the most powerful waves on Earth. They can travel fast enough to cross the Pacific Ocean in less than a day! When they reach shore, these powerful waves strike with enough force to destroy whole communities.

What Causes Tsunamis?

Tsunamis are caused by an undersea volcanic eruption, an earthquake, or even a landslide. This deep-sea event sends out a series of waves. Surprisingly, if you were out at sea, you would not even notice these powerful waves. The reason has to do with the physics of waves—their velocity, wavelength, and amplitude.

A tsunami generated by a powerful earthquake struck Japan in 1983. The photograph above shows a scene before the tsunami struck. What changes do you see in the picture below showing the scene after the tsunami struck?

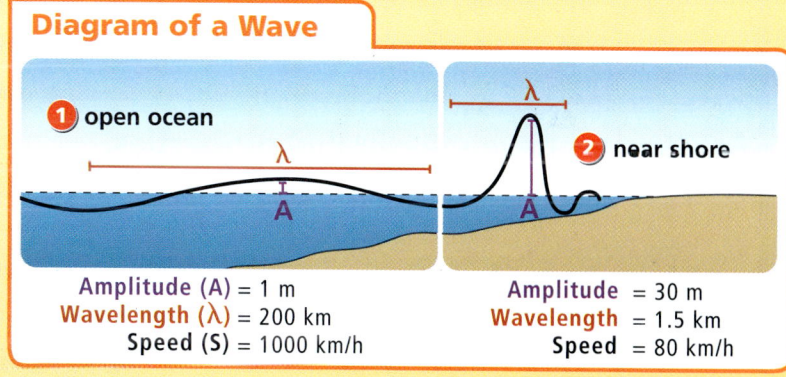

Diagram of a Wave

① open ocean
- Amplitude (A) = 1 m
- Wavelength (λ) = 200 km
- Speed (S) = 1000 km/h

② near shore
- Amplitude = 30 m
- Wavelength = 1.5 km
- Speed = 80 km/h

The Changing Wave

① On the open ocean, the waves of a tsunami are barely visible. The amplitude of the waves is less than a few meters, but the energy of the waves extends to the sea floor. The tsunami's wavelength is extremely long—up to 200 kilometers (120 mi). These long, low waves can travel as fast as a jet—almost 1000 kilometers per hour (600 mi/h).

② Near shore, the waves slow down as they approach shallow water. As their velocity drops, their wavelengths get shorter, but their amplitude gets bigger. All the energy that was spread out over a long wave in deep water is now compressed into a huge wave that can reach a height of more than 30 meters (100 ft).

Individual tsunami waves may arrive more than an hour apart. Many people have lost their lives returning home between waves, making the fatal mistake of thinking the danger was over.

EXPLORE

1. **VISUALIZE** Look at ② on the diagram. How tall is 30 meters (100 ft)? Find a 100-foot building or structure near you to visualize the shore height of a tsunami.
2. **CHALLENGE** Use library or Internet resources to prepare a chart on the causes and effects of a major tsunami event.

Chapter 6: **Waves** 205

Chapter Review

the BIG idea

Waves transfer energy and interact in predictable ways.

CONTENT REVIEW
CLASSZONE.COM

KEY CONCEPTS SUMMARY

1 Waves transfer energy.

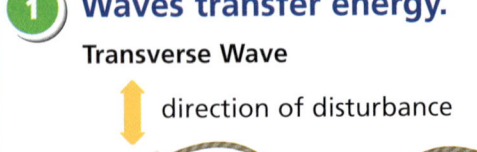

Transverse Wave — direction of disturbance, direction of wave, transfer of energy

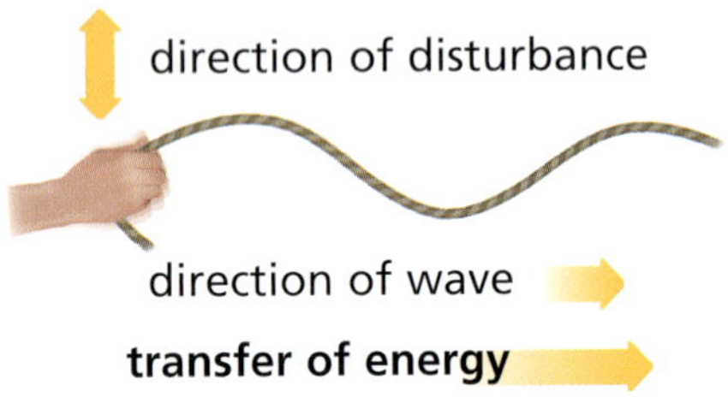

Longitudinal Wave — direction of disturbance, direction of wave, transfer of energy

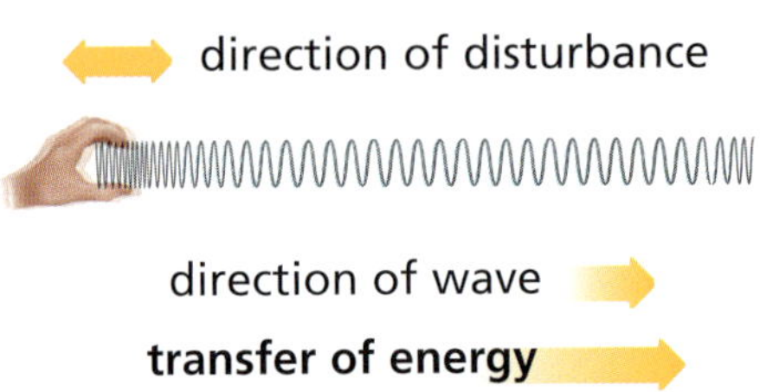

VOCABULARY
wave p. 185
medium p. 187
mechanical wave p. 187
transverse wave p. 189
longitudinal wave p. 190

2 Waves have measurable properties.

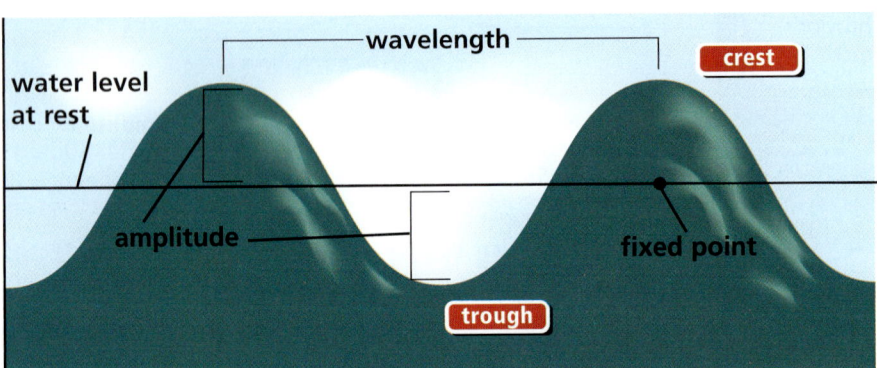

Frequency is the number of waves passing a fixed point in a certain amount of time.

VOCABULARY
crest p. 193
trough p. 193
amplitude p. 193
wavelength p. 193
frequency p. 193

3 Waves behave in predictable ways.

Reflection

Refraction

Diffraction
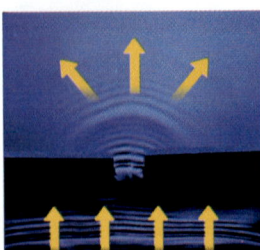

VOCABULARY
reflection p. 201
refraction p. 201
diffraction p. 202
interference p. 203

206 Unit 2: Waves, Sound, and Light

Reviewing Vocabulary

Draw a word triangle for each of the terms below. On the bottom row, write the term and your own definition of it. Above that, write a sentence in which you use the term correctly. At the top, draw a small picture to show what the term looks like. A sample is completed for you.

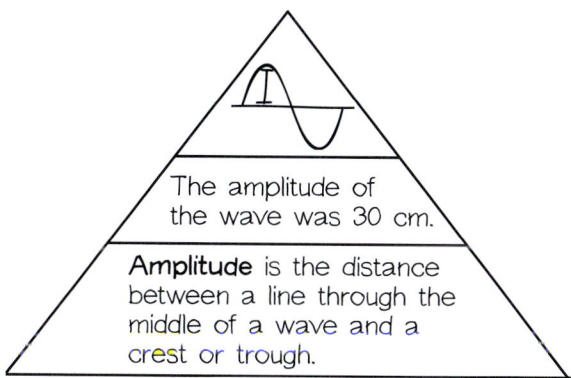

1. transverse wave
2. diffraction
3. frequency
4. medium
5. crest
6. interference
7. reflection
8. trough
9. refraction
10. wavelength

Reviewing Key Concepts

Multiple Choice *Choose the letter of the best answer.*

11. The direction in which a transverse wave travels is
    a. the same direction as the disturbance
    b. toward the disturbance
    c. from the disturbance downward
    d. at right angles to the disturbance

12. An example of a longitudinal wave is a
    a. water wave
    b. stadium wave
    c. sound wave
    d. rope wave

13. Which statement best defines a wave medium?
    a. the material through which a wave travels
    b. a point halfway between the crest and trough of a wave
    c. the distance from one wave crest to the next
    d. the speed at which waves travel in water

14. As you increase the amplitude of a wave, you also increase the
    a. frequency
    b. wavelength
    c. speed
    d. energy

15. To identify the amplitude in a longitudinal wave, you would measure areas of
    a. reflection
    b. compression
    c. crests
    d. refraction

16. Which statement describes the relationship between frequency and wavelength?
    a. When frequency increases, wavelength increases.
    b. When frequency increases, wavelength decreases.
    c. When frequency increases, wavelength remains constant.
    d. When frequency increases, wavelength varies unpredictably.

17. For wave refraction to take place, a wave must
    a. increase in velocity
    b. enter a new medium
    c. increase in frequency
    d. merge with another wave

18. Which setup in a wave tank would best enable you to demonstrate diffraction?
    a. water only
    b. water and sand
    c. water and food coloring
    d. water and a barrier with a small gap

19. Two waves come together and interact to form a new, smaller wave. This process is called
    a. destructive interference
    b. constructive interference
    c. reflective interference
    d. positive interference

Chapter 6: **Waves** 207

Thinking Critically

Use the diagram below to answer the next two questions.

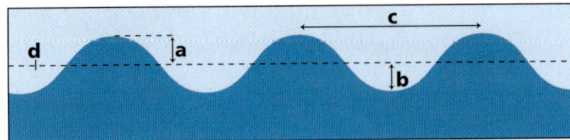

20. What two letters in the diagram measure the same thing? What do they both measure?

21. In the diagram above, what does the letter c measure?

Use the diagram below to answer the next three questions. The diagram shows waves passing a fixed point.

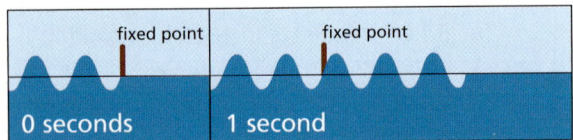

22. At 0 seconds, no waves have passed. How many waves have passed after 1 second?

23. What is being measured in the diagram?

24. How would you write the measurement taken in the diagram?

25. EVALUATE Do you think the following is an accurate definition of medium? Explain your answer.

A **medium** is any solid through which waves travel.

26. APPLY Picture a pendulum. The pendulum is swinging back and forth at a steady rate. How could you make it swing higher? How is swinging a pendulum like making a wave?

27. PREDICT What might happen to an ocean wave that encounters a gap or hole in a cliff along the shore?

28. EVALUATE Do you think *interference* is an appropriate name for the types of wave interaction you read about in Section 6.3? Explain your answer.

Using Math in Science

29. At what speed is the wave below traveling if it has a frequency of 2/s?

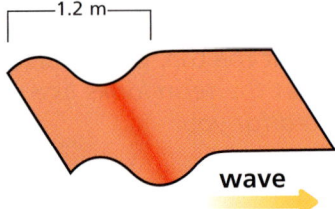

30. An ocean wave has a wavelength of 9 m and a frequency of 0.42/s. What is the wave's speed?

31. Suppose a sound wave has a frequency of 10,000/s. The wave's speed is 340 m/s. Calculate the wavelength of this sound wave.

32. A water wave is traveling at a speed of 2.5 m/s. The wave has a wavelength of 4 m. Calculate the frequency of this water wave.

the BIG idea

33. INTERPRET Look back at the photograph at the start of the chapter on pages 182–183. How does this photograph illustrate a transfer of energy?

34. SYNTHESIZE Describe three situations in which you can predict the behavior of waves.

35. SUMMARIZE Write a paragraph summarizing this chapter. Use the big idea from page 182 as the topic sentence. Then write an example from each of the key concepts listed under the big idea.

UNIT PROJECTS

If you are doing a unit project, make a folder for your project. Include in your folder a list of the resources you will need, the date on which the project is due, and a schedule to track your progress. Begin gathering data.

Standardized Test Practice

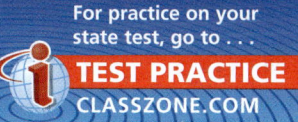

Interpreting Diagrams

Study the illustration below and then answer the questions.

The illustration below shows a wave channel, a way of making and studying water waves. The motor moves the rod, which moves the paddle back and forth. The movement of the paddle makes waves, which move down the length of the channel. The material behind the paddle absorbs the waves generated in that direction.

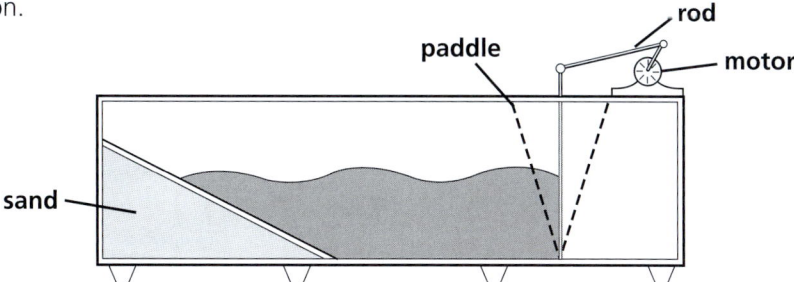

1. An experimenter can adjust the position of the rod on the arm of the motor. Placing it closer to the motor makes shallower waves. Placing it farther from the motor makes deeper waves. What property of waves does this affect?
   a. amplitude
   b. direction
   c. frequency
   d. wavelength

2. By changing motor speeds, an experimenter can make the paddle move faster or slower. What property of waves does this affect?
   a. amplitude
   b. direction
   c. trough depth
   d. wavelength

3. Sand is piled up in the channel at the end of the tank opposite the motor. When waves pass over this sand, their wavelengths shorten. Assuming that the speed of the waves stays the same, their frequency
   a. stays the same
   b. increases
   c. decreases
   d. cannot be predicted

4. Suppose there was no sand at the end of the tank opposite the paddle. In that case, the waves would hit the glass wall. What would they do then?
   a. stop
   b. reflect
   c. refract
   d. diffract

Extended Response

Answer the two questions below in detail.

5. Suppose temperatures in one 10-day period were as follows: 94°, 96°, 95°, 97°, 95°, 98°, 99°, 97°, 99°, and 98°. Make a simple line graph of the data. In what ways is the series of temperatures similar to a wave, and in what ways does it differ?

6. Lydia and Bill each drop a ball of the same size into the same tank of water but at two different spots. Both balls produce waves that spread across the surface of the water. As the two sets of waves cross each other, the water forms high crests in some places. What can you say about both waves? Explain your answer.

Chapter 6: **Waves** 209

CHAPTER 7
Sound

Sound waves transfer energy through vibrations.

Key Concepts

SECTION 1
Sound is a wave.
Learn how sound waves are produced and detected.

SECTION 2
Frequency determines pitch.
Learn about the relationship between the frequency of a sound wave and its pitch.

SECTION 3
Intensity determines loudness.
Learn how the energy of a sound wave relates to its loudness.

SECTION 4
Sound has many uses.
Learn how sound waves are used to detect objects and to make music.

Internet Preview
CLASSZONE.COM
Chapter 7 online resources: Content Review, two Visualizations, three Resource Centers, Math Tutorial, Test Practice

How is this guitar player producing sound?

EXPLORE the BIG idea

What Gives a Sound Its Qualities?

Tap your finger lightly on a table. Then tap it hard. Try scratching the table with your finger. Now, place your head on the table so that your ear is flat against its surface. Tap the table again.

Observe and Think
How did the sounds differ each time? What did you feel?

How Does Size Affect Sound?

Hang three large nails of different sizes from the edge of a table so that they are not touching. Tap each nail with a metal spoon to make it vibrate. Listen to the sounds that are made by tapping each nail.

Observe and Think Which nail produced the highest sound? the lowest? How does the size of a vibrating object affect its sound?

Internet Activity: Sound

Go to **ClassZone.com** to discover how particles move as sound waves move through the air.

Observe and Think
How are the sound waves in the animation similar to the waves you have already learned about?

What Is Sound? Code: MDL028

Chapter 7: **Sound** 211

CHAPTER 7
Getting Ready to Learn

CONCEPT REVIEW

- A wave is a disturbance that transfers energy from one place to another.
- Mechanical waves are waves that travel through matter.

VOCABULARY REVIEW

medium p. 187
longitudinal wave p. 190
amplitude p. 193
wavelength p. 193
frequency p. 193

CONTENT REVIEW
CLASSZONE.COM
Review concepts and vocabulary.

TAKING NOTES

OUTLINE

As you read, copy the headings on your paper in the form of an outline. Then add notes in your own words that summarize what you have read.

VOCABULARY STRATEGY

Place each vocabulary term at the center of a **description wheel** diagram. Write some words on the spokes describing it.

See the Note-Taking Handbook on pages R45–R51.

SCIENCE NOTEBOOK

I. Sound is a type of mechanical wave.
   A. How sound waves are produced
      1.
      2.
      3.
   B. How sound waves are detected
      1.
      2.
      3.

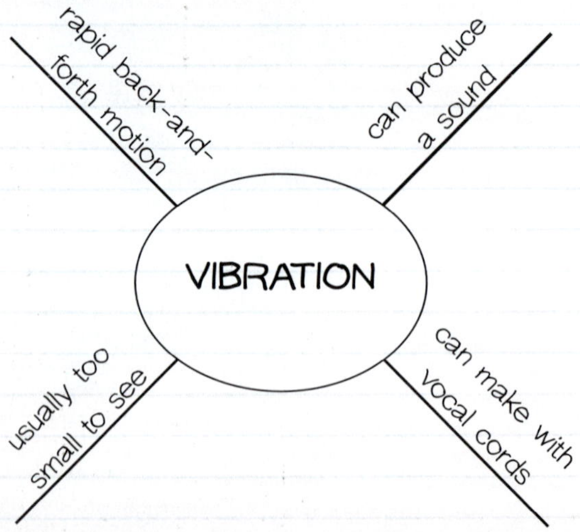

Description wheel for VIBRATION:
- rapid back-and-forth motion
- can produce a sound
- can make with vocal cords
- usually too small to see

7.1 KEY CONCEPT
Sound is a wave.

 BEFORE, you learned
- Waves transfer energy
- Waves have wavelength, amplitude, and frequency

 NOW, you will learn
- How sound waves are produced and detected
- How sound waves transfer energy
- What affects the speed of sound waves

VOCABULARY

sound p. 213
vibration p. 213
vacuum p. 217

EXPLORE Sound

What is sound?

PROCEDURE

1. Tie the middle of the string to the spoon handle.
2. Wrap the string ends around your left and right index fingers. Put the tips of these fingers gently in your ears and hold them there.
3. Stand over your desk so that the spoon dangles without touching your body or the desk. Then move a little to make the spoon tap the desk lightly. Listen to the sound.

MATERIALS
- piece of string
- large metal spoon

WHAT DO YOU THINK?
- What did you hear when the spoon tapped the desk?
- How did sound travel from the spoon to your ears?

OUTLINE
Start an outline for this heading. Remember to leave room for details.

I. Main idea
  A. Supporting idea
    1. Detail
    2. Detail
  B. Supporting idea

Sound is a type of mechanical wave.

In the last chapter, you read that a mechanical wave travels through a material medium. Such mediums include air, water, and solid materials. Sound is an example of a mechanical wave. **Sound** is a wave that is produced by a vibrating object and travels through matter.

The disturbances that travel in a sound wave are vibrations. A **vibration** is a rapid, back-and-forth motion. Because the medium vibrates back and forth in the same direction as the wave travels, sound is a longitudinal wave. Like all mechanical waves, sound waves transfer energy through a medium.

CHECK YOUR READING What do sound waves have in common with other mechanical waves? Your answer should include the word *energy*.

Chapter 7: **Sound** 213

How Sound Waves Are Produced

READING TIP
When you see the word *push* or *pull,* think of force.

The disturbances in a sound wave are vibrations that are usually too small to see. Vibrations are also required to start sound waves. A vibrating object pushes and pulls on the medium around it and sends out waves in all directions.

You have a sound-making instrument within your own body. It is the set of vocal cords within the voice box, or larynx, in your throat. Put several of your fingers against the front of your throat. Now hum. Do you feel the vibrations of your vocal cords?

Your vocal cords relax when you breathe to allow air to pass in and out of your windpipe. Your vocal cords tense up and draw close together when you are about to speak or sing. The illustration below shows how sound waves are produced by the human vocal cords.

❶ Your muscles push air up from your lungs and through the narrow opening between the vocal cords.

❷ The force of the air causes the vocal cords to vibrate.

❸ The vibrating vocal cords produce sound waves.

CHECK YOUR READING  How do human vocal cords produce sound waves?

How Vocal Cords Produce Sound

Sound waves are produced by vibrations.

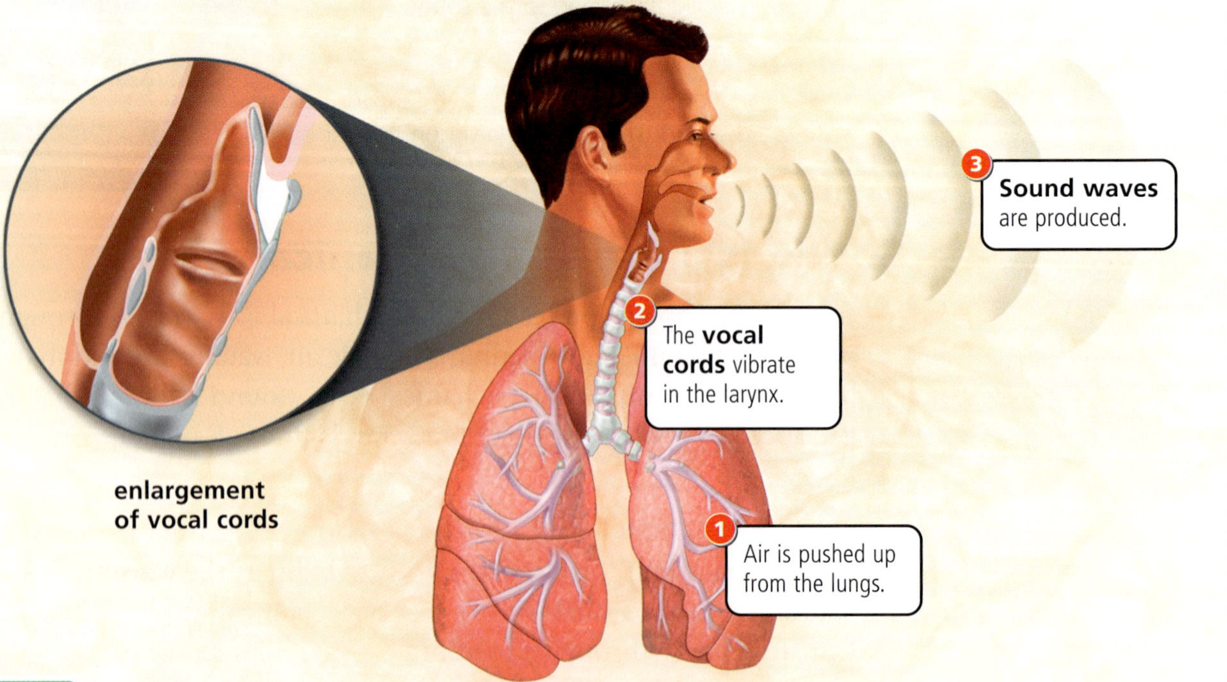

enlargement of vocal cords

❶ Air is pushed up from the lungs.

❷ The **vocal cords** vibrate in the larynx.

❸ Sound waves are produced.

READING VISUALS   What starts the vibrations in the vocal cords?

214 Unit 2: **Waves, Sound, and Light**

How Sound Waves Are Detected

The shape of a human ear helps it collect sound waves. Picture a satellite dish. It collects radio waves from satellites. Your ear works in much the same way. Actually, what we typically call the ear is only the outer section of the ear. The illustration below shows the main parts of the human ear.

❶ Your outer ear collects sound waves and reflects them into a tiny tube called the ear canal. At the end of the ear canal is a thin, skin-like membrane stretched tightly over the opening, called the eardrum. When sound waves strike the eardrum, they make it vibrate.

❷ The middle ear contains three tiny, connected bones called the hammer, anvil, and stirrup. These bones carry vibrations from the eardrum to the inner ear.

❸ One of the main parts of the inner ear, the cochlea (KAWK-lee-uh), contains about 30,000 hair cells. Each of these cells has tiny hairs on its surface. The hairs bend as a result of the vibrations. This movement triggers changes that cause the cell to send electrical signals along nerves to your brain. Only when your brain receives and processes these signals do you actually hear a sound.

READING TIP
As you read each numbered description here, match it to the number on the illustration below.

How the Ear Detects Sound

Sound waves are detected in the human ear, beginning with vibrations of the eardrum.

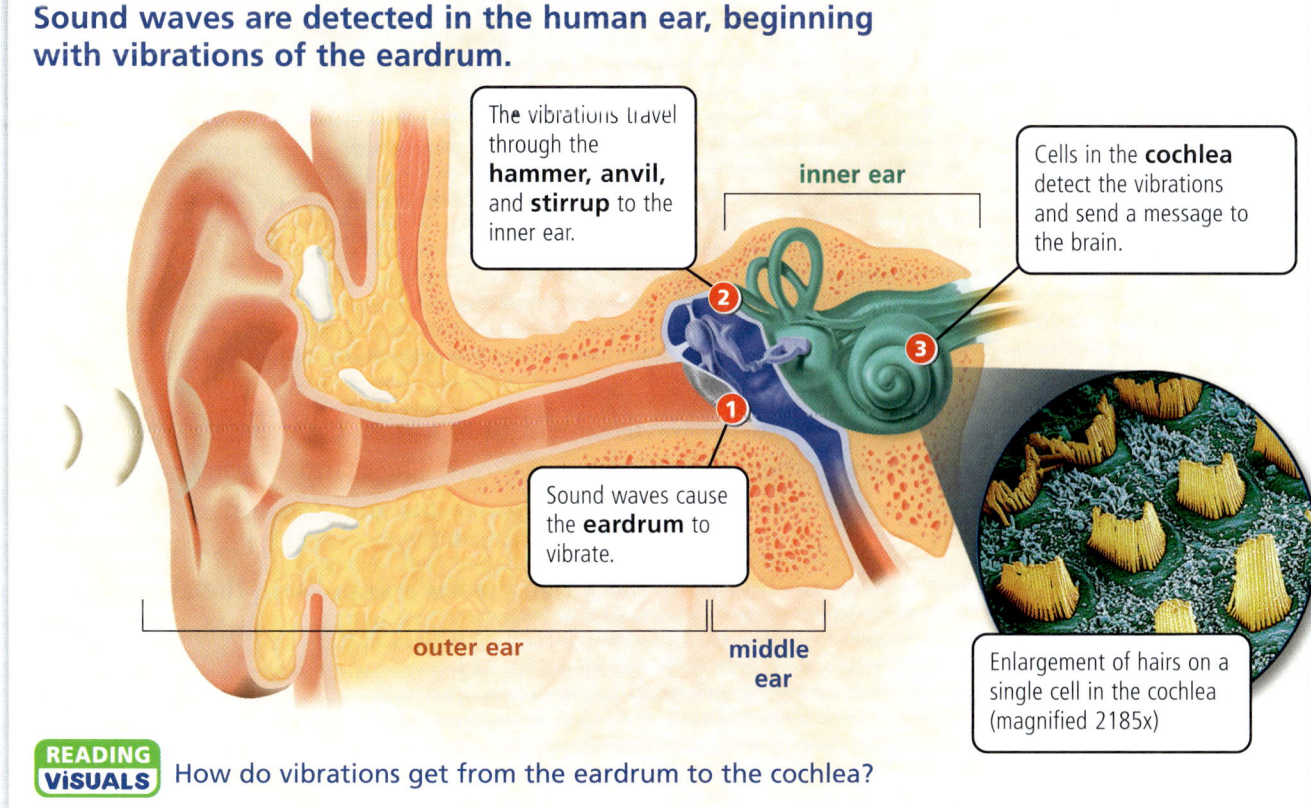

The vibrations travel through the **hammer, anvil, and stirrup** to the inner ear.

Cells in the **cochlea** detect the vibrations and send a message to the brain.

Sound waves cause the **eardrum** to vibrate.

outer ear | middle ear | inner ear

Enlargement of hairs on a single cell in the cochlea (magnified 2185x)

READING VISUALS How do vibrations get from the eardrum to the cochlea?

Sound waves vibrate particles.

You can see the motion of waves in water. You can even ride them with a surfboard. But you cannot see air. How, then, can you picture sound waves moving through air? Sound waves transfer the motion of particles too small to see from one place to another.

For example, think about a drum that has been struck. What happens between the time the drum is struck and the sound is heard?

- The drum skin vibrates rapidly. It pushes out and then in, over and over again. Of course, this happens very, very fast. The vibrating drum skin pushes against nearby particles in the air. The particles in the air become bunched together, or compressed.
- When the drum skin pushes the opposite way, a space opens up between the drum's surface and the particles. The particles rush back in to fill the space.
- The back-and-forth movement, or vibration, of the particles is the disturbance that travels to the listener. Both the bunched up areas, or compressions, and the spaces between the compressions are parts of the wave.

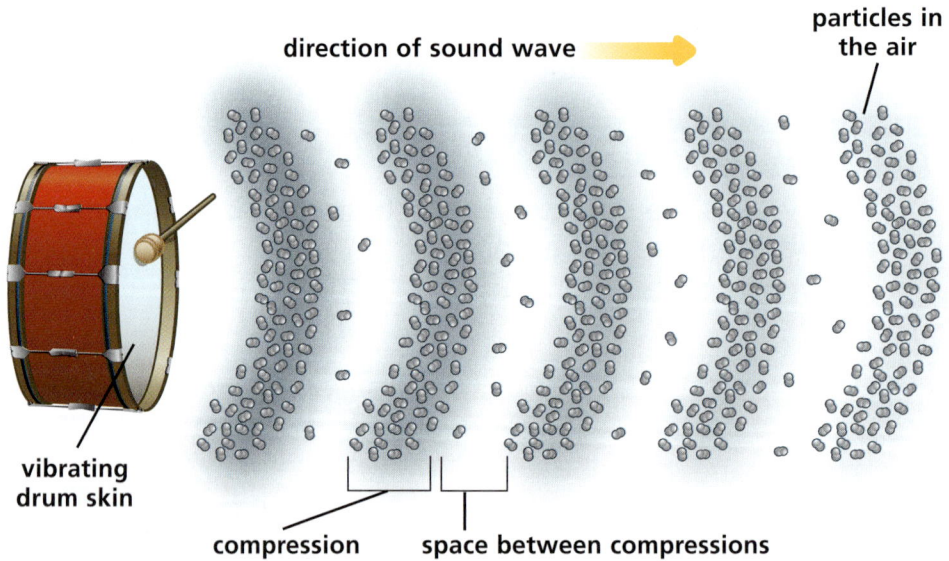

Notice that the waves consist of repeating patterns of compressions and spaces between the compressions. The compressions are areas of high air pressure. The spaces between the compressions are areas of low air pressure. The high- and low-pressure air pushes and pulls on the surrounding air, which then pushes and pulls on the air around that. Soon a sound wave has traveled through the air and has transferred kinetic energy from one place to another.

REMINDER
Kinetic energy is the energy of motion.

CHECK YOUR READING Summarize in your own words how sound travels through air.

In the middle 1600s, scientists began to do experiments to learn more about air. They used pumps to force the air out of enclosed spaces to produce a vacuum. A **vacuum** is empty space. It has no particles—or very, very few of them. Robert Boyle, a British scientist, designed an experiment to find out if sound moves through a vacuum.

Boyle put a ticking clock in a sealed jar. He pumped some air out of the jar and still heard the clock ticking. Then he pumped more air out. The ticking grew quieter. Finally, when Boyle had pumped out almost all the air, he could hear no ticking at all. Boyle's experiment demonstrated that sound does not travel through a vacuum.

The photograph at the right shows equipment that is set up to perform an experiment similar to Boyle's. A bell is placed in a sealed jar and powered through the electrical connections at the top. The sound of the loudly ringing bell becomes quieter as air is pumped out through the vacuum plate.

Sound is a mechanical wave. It can move only through a medium that is made up of matter. Sound waves can travel through air, solid materials, and liquids, such as water, because all of these mediums are made up of particles. Sound waves cannot travel through a vacuum.

Sound Experiment

connections
sealed jar
bell
vacuum plate

INFER As air is pumped out of the jar, the sound of the bell becomes quieter. Why do you think the bell is suspended?

 **CHECK YOUR READING** How did Boyle's experiment show that sound cannot travel through a vacuum?

INVESTIGATE Sound Energy

How does sound transfer energy?
PROCEDURE

1. Sprinkle a few grains of salt into the jar. Put the jar on a flat surface in a well-lit place.
2. Cut off the neck of the balloon with the scissors.
3. Stretch the balloon over the mouth of the jar and pull the sides down past the rim of the jar's mouth. Use a rubber band to make a tight fit.
4. Tap the balloon with the eraser end of the pencil. Observe what happens to the salt on the bottom of the jar.

WHAT DO YOU THINK?
- What happens to the salt?
- How can you explain what you observed?

CHALLENGE Suppose you could pump all the air out of the jar and could leave the salt grains in the jar and the tight rubber cover on top. If you repeated the experiment, do you think the results would be different? Explain your answer.

SKILL FOCUS
Observing

MATERIALS
- clean jar
- table salt
- balloon
- scissors
- rubber band
- pencil with good eraser end

TIME
10 minutes

salt

Chapter 7: **Sound** 217

The speed of sound depends on its medium.

Suppose you are in the baseball stands during an exciting game. A pitch flies from the mound toward home plate, and you see the batter draw back, swing, and hit the ball high. A split second later you hear the crack of the bat meeting the ball. You notice that the sound of the hit comes later than the sight. Just how fast does sound travel?

Sound travels more slowly than light, and it does not always travel at the same speed. Two main factors affect the speed of sound: the material that makes up the medium—such as air or water—and the temperature. If we know the medium and the temperature, however, we can predict the speed of sound.

 Which two factors affect the speed of sound?

The Effect of the Material

You have probably heard sounds in more than one medium. Think about the medium in which you most often hear sound—air. You listen to a radio or a compact disk player. You hear the siren of a fire truck. These sound waves travel through air, a mixture of gases.

Now think about going swimming. You dip below the water's surface briefly. Someone jumps into the water nearby and splashes water against the pool wall. You hear strange underwater sounds. These sound waves travel through water, a liquid.

Sound travels faster through liquids than it does through gases because liquids are denser than gases. That means that the particles are packed closer together. It takes less time for a water particle to push on the water particles around it because the particles are already closer together than are the particles in air. As a result, divers underwater would hear a sound sooner than people above water would.

Sound can also travel through solid materials that are elastic, which means they can vibrate back and forth. In solid materials, the particles are packed even closer together than they are in liquids or gases. Steel is an example of an elastic material that is very dense. Sound travels very rapidly through steel. Look at the chart on the left. Compare the speed of sound in air with the speed of sound in steel.

These divers can hear the motor of a distant boat before their friends above water hear it.

Materials and Sound Speeds

Medium	State	Speed of Sound
Air (20°C)	Gas	344 m/s (769 mi/h)
Water (20°C)	Liquid	1,400 m/s (3,130 mi/h)
Steel (20°C)	Solid	5,000 m/s (11,200 mi/h)

The Effect of Temperature

Sound also travels faster through a medium at higher temperatures than at lower ones. Consider the medium of air, a mixture of gases. Gas particles are not held tightly together as are particles in solids. Instead, the gas particles bounce all around. The higher the temperature, the more the gas particles wiggle and bounce. It takes less time for particles that are already moving quickly to push against the particles around them than it takes particles that are moving slowly. Sound, therefore, travels faster in hot air than in cold air.

Look at the picture of the snowboarders. The sound waves they make by yelling will travel more slowly through air than similar sounds made on a hot day. If you could bear to stand in air at a temperature of 100°C (212°F—the boiling point of water) and listen to the same person yelling, you might notice that the sound of the person's voice reaches you faster.

The chart on the right shows the speed of sound in air at two different temperatures. Compare the speed of sound at the temperature at which water freezes with the speed of sound at the temperature at which water boils. Sound travels about 17 percent faster in air at 100°C than in air at 0°C.

These snowboarders' shouts reach their friends more slowly in this cold air than they would in hot air.

Temperature and Sound Speeds

Medium	Temperature	Speed of Sound
Air	0°C (32°F)	331 m/s (741 mi/h)
Air	100°C (212°F)	386 m/s (864 mi/h)

 **CHECK YOUR READING** What is the difference between the speed of sound in air at 0°C and at 100°C?

 Review

KEY CONCEPTS

1. Describe how sound waves are produced.
2. Describe how particles move as energy is transferred through a sound wave.
3. Explain how temperature affects the speed of sound.

CRITICAL THINKING

4. **Predict** Would the sound from a distant train travel faster through air or through steel train tracks? Explain.
5. **Evaluate** Suppose an audience watching a science fiction movie hears a loud roar as a spaceship explodes in outer space. Why is this scene unrealistic?

CHALLENGE

6. **Evaluate** A famous riddle asks this question: If a tree falls in the forest and there is no one there to hear it, is there any sound? What do you think? Give reasons for your answer.

Chapter 7: **Sound** 219

Extreme Science

SURPASSING THE SPEED OF SOUND

Find out more about supersonic aircraft.

Sonic Booms

Airplanes traveling faster than the speed of sound can produce an incredibly loud sound called a sonic boom. The sonic boom from a low-flying airplane can rattle and even break windows!

How It Works

Breaking the Barrier

The sound waves produced by this airplane begin to pile up and produce a pressure barrier.

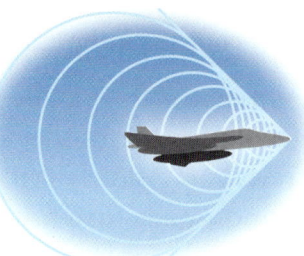

This airplane has broken through the pressure barrier and has produced a loud boom.

This photograph may actually show the wake of a sonic boom. It was taken on a very humid day, and water vapor may have condensed in the low-pressure part of the sound wave.

When an airplane reaches extremely high speeds, it actually catches up to its own sound waves. The waves start to pile up and form a high-pressure area in front of the plane. If the airplane has enough acceleration, it breaks through the barrier, making a sonic boom. The airplane gets ahead of both the pressure barrier and the sound waves and is said to be traveling at supersonic speeds—speeds faster than the speed of sound.

Boom and It's Gone

If an airplane that produces a boom is flying very high, it may be out of sight by the time the sonic boom reaches a hearer on the ground. To make a sonic boom, a plane must be traveling faster than about 1240 kilometers per hour (769 mi/h)! The sound does not last very long—about one-tenth of a second for a small fighter plane to one-half second for a supersonic passenger plane.

Boom Notes

- The pilot of an airplane cannot hear the sonic boom because the sound waves are behind the plane.

- Lightning heats particles in the air so rapidly that they move faster than the speed of sound and cause a shock wave, which is what makes the boom of thunder. If a lightning strike is very close, you will hear a sharp crack.

- Large meteors enter the atmosphere fast enough to make a sonic boom.

EXPLORE

1. **PREDICT** Specially designed cars have traveled faster than the speed of sound. Would you expect them to produce a sonic boom?

2. **CHALLENGE** The space shuttles produce sonic booms when they are taking off and landing, but not while they are orbiting Earth, even though they are moving much faster than 1240 km/h. Can you explain why?

KEY CONCEPT

7.2 Frequency determines pitch.

◀ **BEFORE, you learned**
- Sound waves are produced by vibrations
- Frequency measures the number of waves passing a fixed point per second

▶ **NOW, you will learn**
- How the frequency of a wave affects the way it sounds
- How sound quality differs from pitch
- How the Doppler effect works

VOCABULARY

pitch p. 221
hertz p. 222
ultrasound p. 222
resonance p. 224
Doppler effect p. 226

EXPLORE Pitch

Why does the sound change?

PROCEDURE

1. Hold the ruler flat on the edge of a desk so that it sticks out about 25 centimeters beyond the edge.

2. With your free hand, push the tip of the ruler down and then let it go. As the ruler vibrates, slide it back onto the desk. Listen to the sounds the ruler makes.

WHAT DO YOU THINK?
- What happened to the sound as you slid the ruler back onto the desk?
- Describe the motion of the ruler.

MATERIALS
ruler

VOCABULARY
Remember to add a description wheel in your notebook for each new term.

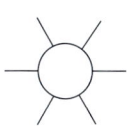

Pitch depends on the frequency of a sound wave.

When you listen to music, you hear both high and low sounds. The characteristic of highness or lowness of a sound is called **pitch.** The frequency of a sound wave determines the pitch of the sound you hear. Remember that frequency is the number of waves passing a fixed point in a given period of time. A high-frequency wave with short wavelengths, such as that produced by a tiny flute, makes a high-pitched sound. A low-frequency wave with long wavelengths, such as the one produced by the deep croak of a tuba, makes a low-pitched sound. An object vibrating very fast produces a high-pitched sound, while an object vibrating slower produces a lower-pitched sound.

 How is frequency related to pitch?

Chapter 7: **Sound** 221

High and Low Frequencies

Frequency is a measure of how often a wave passes a fixed point. One complete wave can also be called a cycle. The unit for measuring frequency, and also pitch, is the hertz. A **hertz** (Hz) is one complete wave, or cycle, per second. For example, a wave with a frequency of 20 hertz has 20 cycles per second. In a wave with a frequency of 100 hertz, 100 waves pass a given point every second. The diagram below shows how frequency and pitch are related.

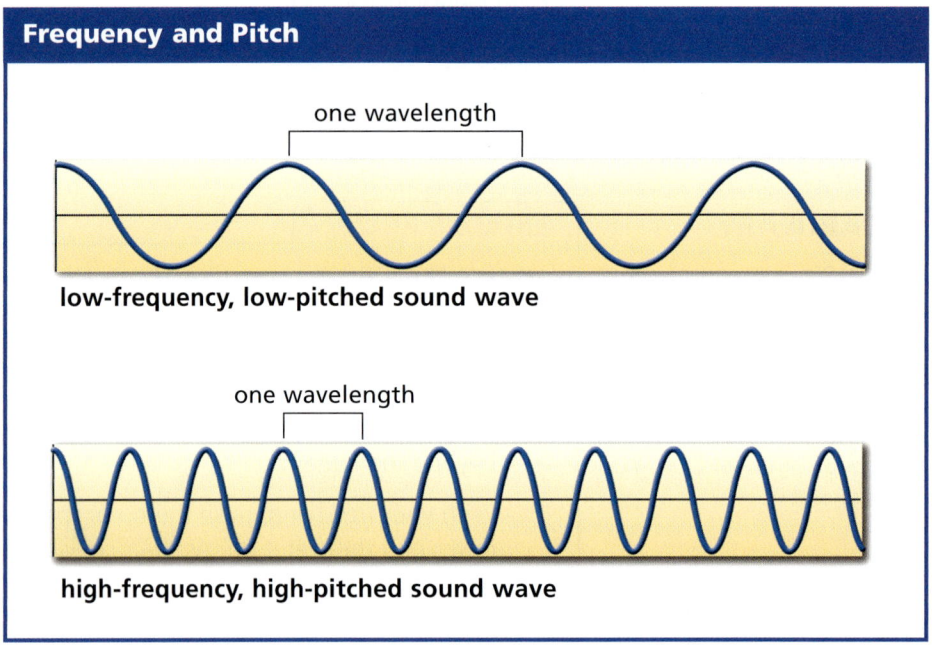

READING TIP

The prefix *infra* means "below," and the prefix *ultra* means "beyond."

Human ears can hear a wide range of pitches. Most people with good hearing can hear sounds in the range of 20 hertz to 20,000 hertz. The note of middle C on a piano, for example, has a frequency of 262 hertz.

Sound waves with wavelengths below 20 hertz are called infrasound. People cannot hear sounds in this range. Infrasound waves have a very long wavelength and can travel great distances without losing much energy. Elephants may use infrasound to communicate over long distances. Some of the waves that elephants use travel through the ground instead of the air, and they may be detected by another elephant up to 32 kilometers (about 20 miles) away.

The highest frequency that humans can hear is 20,000 hertz. Sound waves in the range above 20,000 hertz are called **ultrasound.** Though people cannot hear ultrasound, it is very useful. Later in this chapter, you will learn about some of the uses of ultrasound. Many animals can hear sound waves in the ultrasound range. The chart on page 223 shows the hearing ranges of some animals.

CHECK YOUR READING   What is the range of frequencies that humans can hear?

222 Unit 2: **Waves, Sound, and Light**

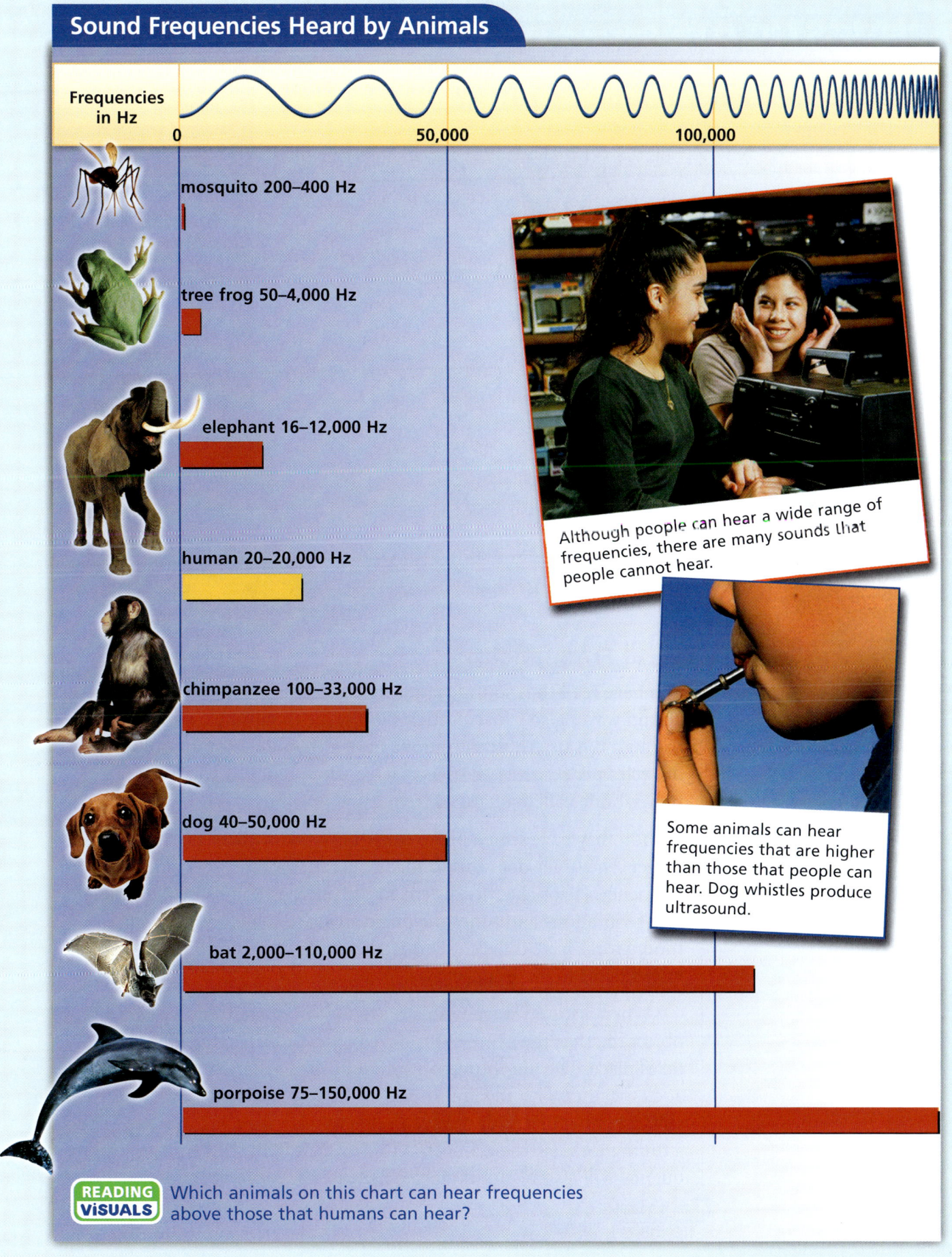

INVESTIGATE Sound Frequency

How is frequency related to pitch?

PROCEDURE

1) Stretch the rubber bands around the open box.
2) Pull one of the rubber bands tightly across the open part of the box so that it vibrates with a higher frequency than the looser rubber band. Tape the rubber band in place.
3) Pluck each rubber band and listen to the sound it makes.

WHAT DO YOU THINK?

- Which rubber band produces a sound wave with a higher pitch?
- How is frequency related to pitch?

CHALLENGE Suppose you are tuning a guitar and want to make one of the strings sound higher in pitch. Do you tighten or loosen the string? Explain your answer.

SKILL FOCUS
Inferring

MATERIALS
- 2 rubber bands of different sizes
- small open box
- tape

TIME
20 minutes

Natural Frequencies

You have read that sound waves are produced by vibrating objects. Sound waves also cause particles in the air to vibrate as they travel through the air. These vibrations have a frequency, or a number of cycles per second. All objects have a frequency at which they vibrate called a natural frequency.

You may have seen a piano tuner tap a tuning fork against another object. The tuner does this to make the fork vibrate at its natural frequency. He or she then listens to the pitch produced by the tuning fork's vibrations and tunes the piano string to match it. Different tuning forks have different frequencies and can be used to tune instruments to different pitches.

When a sound wave with a particular frequency encounters an object that has the same natural frequency, constructive interference takes place. The amplitude of the sound from the vibrating object adds together with the amplitude of the initial sound wave. The strengthening of a sound wave in this way is called **resonance**. When a tuning fork is struck, a nearby tuning fork with the same natural frequency will also begin to vibrate because of resonance.

 How is natural frequency related to resonance?

Sound Quality

Have you ever noticed that two singers can sing exactly the same note, or pitch, and yet sound very different? The singers produce sound waves with their vocal cords. They stretch their vocal cords in just the right way to produce sound waves with a certain frequency. That frequency produces the pitch that the note of music calls for. Why, then, don't the singers sound exactly the same?

Each musical instrument and each human voice has its own particular sound, which is sometimes called the sound quality. Another word for sound quality is timbre (TAM-buhr). Timbre can be explained by the fact that most sounds are not single waves but are actually combinations of waves. The pitch that you hear is called the fundamental tone. Other, higher-frequency pitches are called overtones. The combination of pitches is the main factor affecting the quality of a sound.

Another factor in sound quality is the way in which a sound starts and stops. Think about a musician who is crashing cymbals. The cymbals' sound blasts out suddenly. A sound produced by the human voice, on the other hand, starts much more gently.

CHECK YOUR READING What are two factors that affect sound quality? Which sentences above tell you?

The illustration below shows oscilloscope (uh-SIHL-uh-SKOHP) screens. An oscilloscope is a scientific instrument that tracks an electrical signal. The energy of a sound wave is converted into a signal and displayed on an oscilloscope screen. The screens below show sound wave diagrams made by musicians playing a piano and a clarinet. Both of these musical instruments are producing the same note, or pitch. Notice that the diagrams look slightly different from each other. Each has a different combination of overtones, producing a unique sound quality.

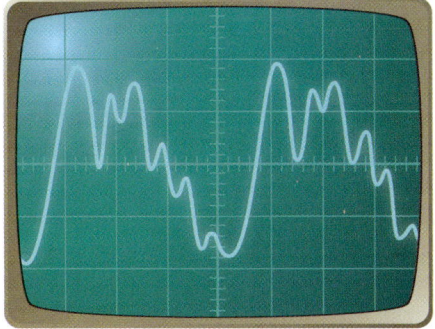

piano   clarinet

Both oscilloscope images at left show diagrams of sound waves of the same pitch produced on two different instruments. The waves, however, have different sound qualities.

Chapter 7: **Sound** 225

The motion of the source of a sound affects its pitch.

Sometimes in traffic, a screeching siren announces that an ambulance must pass through traffic. Drivers slow down and pull over to the side, leaving room for the ambulance to speed by. Suppose you are a passenger in one of these cars. What do you hear?

When the ambulance whizzes past you, the pitch suddenly seems to drop. The siren on the ambulance blasts the same pitches again and again. What has made the difference in what you hear is the rapid motion of the vehicle toward you and then away from you. The motion of the source of a sound affects its pitch.

The Doppler Effect

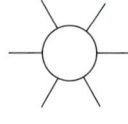

DESCRIPTION WHEEL
Make a description wheel in your notebook for the Doppler effect.

In the 1800s an Austrian scientist named Christian Doppler hypothesized about sound waves. He published a scientific paper about his work. In it, he described how pitch changes when a sound source moves rapidly toward and then away from a listener. Doppler described the scientific principle we notice when a siren speeds by. The **Doppler effect** is the change in perceived pitch that occurs when the source or the receiver of a sound is moving.

Before long, a Dutch scientist learned of Doppler's work. In 1845 he staged an experiment to test the hypothesis that Doppler described. In the experiment, a group of trumpet players were put on a train car. Other musicians were seated beside the railroad track. Those musicians had perfect pitch—that is, the ability to identify a pitch just by listening to it. The train passed by the musicians while the trumpeters on the train played their instruments. The musicians recorded the pitches they heard from one moment to the next. At the end of the demonstration, the musicians reported that they had heard the pitch of the trumpets fall as the train passed. Their experiment showed that the Doppler effect exists.

 CHECK YOUR READING How does the motion of a sound's source affect its pitch?

To listeners outside a train, the sound made by the train seems higher in pitch while it approaches them than while it speeds away.

226 Unit 2: Waves, Sound, and Light

The Doppler Effect

The perceived pitch of a sound changes as the source of the sound moves toward or away from the hearer.

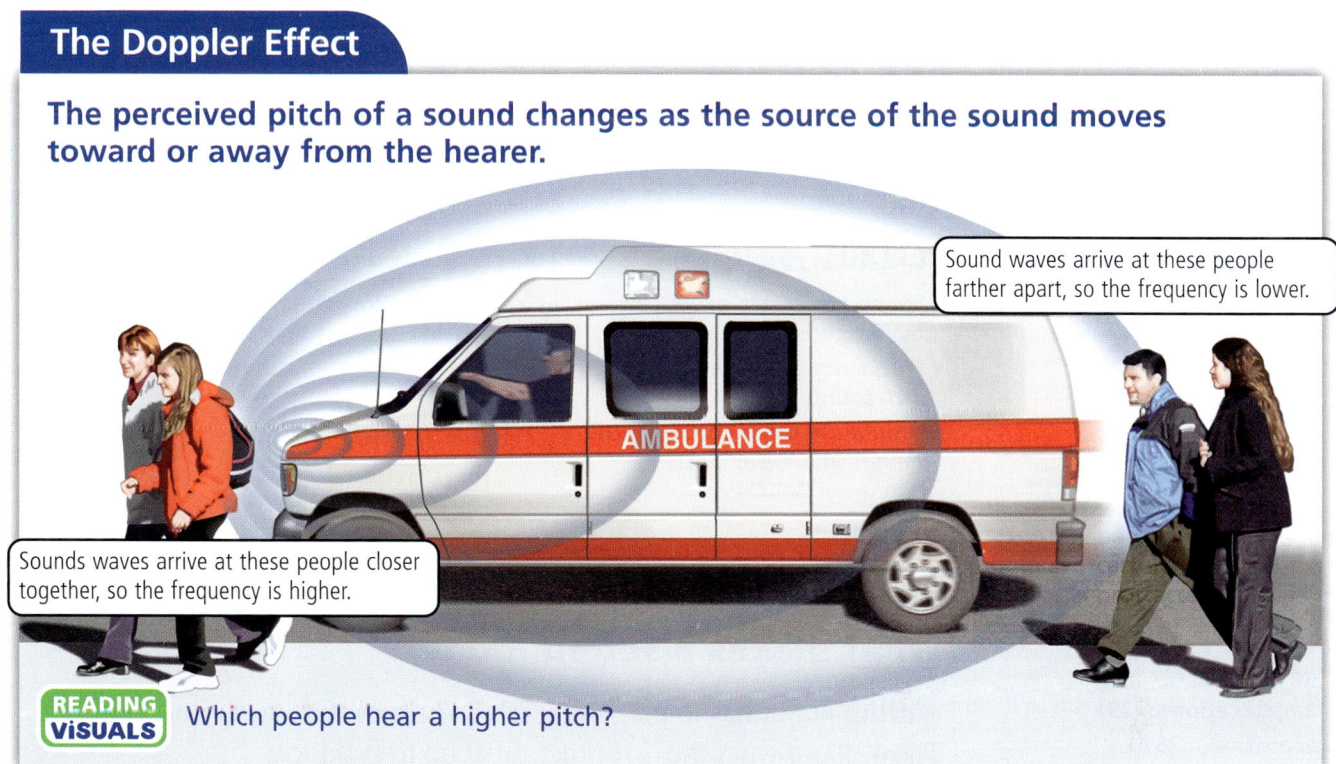

Sound waves arrive at these people farther apart, so the frequency is lower.

Sounds waves arrive at these people closer together, so the frequency is higher.

READING VISUALS Which people hear a higher pitch?

Frequency and Pitch

Again imagine sitting in a car as an ambulance approaches. The siren on the ambulance continually sends out sound waves. As the ambulance pulls closer to you, it catches up with the sound waves it is sending out. As a result, the sound waves that reach your ears are spaced closer together. The frequency, and therefore the pitch, is higher when it reaches you. As the ambulance continues, it gets farther and farther away from you, while the sound waves still move toward you. Now the waves arrive farther and farther apart. As the frequency decreases, you hear a lower pitch.

Explore the Doppler effect.

7.2 Review

KEY CONCEPTS

1. Describe what is different about the sound waves produced by a low note and a high note on a musical instrument.
2. Explain why two people singing the same pitch do not sound exactly the same.
3. How does perceived pitch change as a sound source passes a listener?

CRITICAL THINKING

4. **Apply** How could you produce vibrations in a tuning fork without touching it? Explain your answer.
5. **Predict** Suppose you could view the waves produced by a high-pitched and a low-pitched voice. Which wave would display the greater number of compressions in 1 s? Why?

CHALLENGE

6. **Infer** Offer a possible explanation for why no one noticed the Doppler effect before the 1800s.

7.3 Intensity determines loudness.

BEFORE, you learned
- Sound waves are produced by vibrations
- Frequency determines the pitch of a sound
- Amplitude is a measure of the height of a wave crest

NOW, you will learn
- How the intensity of a wave affects its loudness
- How sound intensity can be controlled
- How loudness can affect hearing

VOCABULARY

intensity p. 228
decibel p. 228
amplification p. 231
acoustics p. 231

THINK ABOUT

What makes a sound louder?

A drum player has to play softly at some times and loudly at others. Think about what the drummer must do to produce each type of sound. If you could watch the drummer in the photograph in action, what would you see? How would the drummer change the way he moves the drumsticks to make a loud, crashing sound? What might he do to make a very soft sound?

Intensity depends on the amplitude of a sound wave.

OUTLINE
Make an outline for this heading. Remember to include main ideas and details.

I. Main idea
　A. Supporting idea
　　1. Detail
　　2. Detail
　B. Supporting idea

Earlier you read that all waves carry energy. The more energy a sound wave carries, the more intense it is and the louder it will sound to listeners. The **intensity** of a sound is the amount of energy its sound wave has. A unit called the **decibel** (dB) is used to measure sound intensity. The faint rustling of tree leaves on a quiet summer day can hardly be heard. Some of the softest sounds measure less than 10 decibels. On the other hand, the noise from a jet taking off or the volume of a TV set turned all the way up can hurt your ears. Very loud sounds measure more than 100 decibels. Remember that amplitude is related to wave energy. The greater the amplitude, the more intensity a sound wave has and the louder the sound will be.

CHECK YOUR READING How is energy related to loudness?

228 Unit 2: Waves, Sound, and Light

INVESTIGATE Loudness

How is amplitude related to loudness?

PROCEDURE

1. Cut a notch in the middle of both ends of the cardboard. Stretch the rubber band around the cardboard so that it fits into the notches as shown.
2. Mark lines on the cardboard at one and four centimeters away from the rubber band.
3. Slide the pencils under the rubber band at each end.
4. Pull the rubber band to the one-centimeter line and let it go so that it vibrates with a low amplitude. Notice the sound it makes. Pull the rubber band to the four-centimeter line and let it go again. This time the amplitude is higher. Notice the sound it makes this time.

WHAT DO YOU THINK?

- How did the loudness of the sounds compare?
- How is amplitude related to loudness?

CHALLENGE Using what you learned from experimenting with the rubber band, explain why swinging a drumstick harder on a drum would make a louder sound than swinging a drumstick lightly.

SKILL FOCUS
Observing

MATERIALS
- piece of cardboard
- scissors
- large rubber band
- 2 pencils
- ruler

TIME
15 minutes

The drummer varies the loudness of a sound by varying the energy with which he hits the drum. Loudness is also affected by the distance between the source and the listener.

Have you ever wondered why sound gradually dies out over distance? Think about someone walking away from you with a radio. When the radio is close, the radio seems loud. As the person walks away, the sound grows fainter and fainter. Sound waves travel in all directions from their source. As the waves travel farther from the radio, their energy is spread out over a greater area. This means that their intensity is decreased. The sound waves with lower intensities are heard as quieter sounds.

Other forces can take energy away from sound waves, too. Forces can act within the medium of a sound wave to decrease the intensity of the waves. This effect on sound is probably a good thing. Imagine what the world would be like if every sound wave continued forever!

Chapter 7: **Sound** 229

Approximate Sound Intensities

dB	Examples
10	leaves rustling
20	light rainfall
30	whisper
50	conversation
60	dog barking
70	traffic
90	lawn mower
100	motorcycle
120	amplified music
140	firecrackers
150	airplane taking off

20 dB light rainfall

150 dB airplane taking off nearby

90 dB lawn mower

60 dB dog barking

10 dB leaves rustling in gentle breeze

READING VISUALS What is the source of the most intense sound in this picture? the least intense?

The intensity of sound can be controlled.

REMINDER
Remember, amplitude is related to wave energy.

Over time and distance, a sound wave gets weaker and weaker until the sound becomes undetectable. The pitch, however, does not typically change as the sound grows weaker. In other words, even as the amplitude decreases, the frequency stays the same.

Sometimes it is desirable to change sound intensity without changing the pitch and quality of a sound. We can do this by adding energy to or taking energy away from a sound wave. As you have already seen, intensity is the amount of energy in a sound wave. Changing the intensity of a sound wave changes its amplitude.

Sound intensity can be controlled in many ways. Mufflers on cars and trucks reduce engine noise. Have you ever heard a car with a broken muffler? You were probably surprised at how loud it was. Burning fuel in an engine produces hot gases that expand and make a very loud noise. A muffler is designed to absorb some of the energy of the sound waves and so decrease their amplitude. As a result, the intensity of the sound you hear is much lower than it would be without the muffler.

CHECK YOUR READING How could you change the intensity of a sound without changing the pitch?

230 Unit 2: Waves, Sound, and Light

Amplification

In addition to being reduced, as they are in a muffler, sound waves can be amplified. The word *amplify* may remind you of *amplitude*, the measure of the height of a wave's crest. These words are related. To amplify something means to make it bigger. **Amplification** is the increasing of the strength of an electrical signal. It is often used to increase the intensity of a sound wave.

When you listen to a stereo, you experience the effects of amplification. Sound input to the stereo is in the form of weak electrical signals from a microphone. Transistors in an electronic circuit amplify the signals. The electrical signals are converted into vibrations in a coil in your stereo's speaker. The coil is attached to a cone, which also vibrates and sends out sound waves. You can control the intensity of the sound waves by adjusting your stereo's volume.

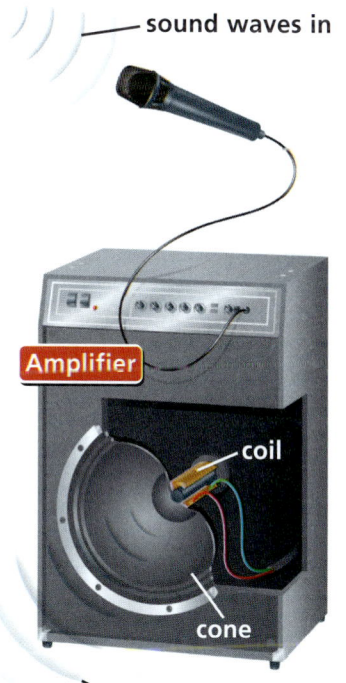

Acoustics

The scientific study of sound is called **acoustics** (uh-KOO-stihks). Acoustics involves both how sound is produced and how it is received and heard by humans and animals.

Acoustics also refers to the way sound waves behave inside a space. Experts called acoustical engineers help design buildings to reduce unwanted echoes. An echo is simply a reflected sound wave. To control sound intensity, engineers design walls and ceilings with acoustical tiles. The shapes and surfaces of acoustical tiles are designed to absorb or redirect some of the energy of sound waves.

The pointed tiles in this sound-testing room are designed to absorb sound waves and prevent any echoes.

The shapes and surfaces in this concert hall direct sound waves to the audience.

READING VISUALS **COMPARE AND CONTRAST** Imagine sound waves reflecting off the surfaces in the two photographs above. How do the reflections differ?

Intense sound can damage hearing.

When a train screeches to a stop in a subway station, the sound of the squealing brakes echoes off the tunnel walls. Without thinking about it, you cover your ears with your hands. This response helps protect your ears from possible damage.

In the first section of this chapter, you read about the main parts of the human ear. The part of the inner ear called the cochlea is lined with special cells called hair cells. As you have seen, these cells are necessary for hearing.

The hair cells are extremely sensitive. This sensitivity makes hearing possible, but it also makes the cells easy to damage. Continual exposure to sounds of 90 dB or louder can damage or destroy the cells. This is one reason why being exposed to very loud noises, especially for more than a short time, is harmful to hearing.

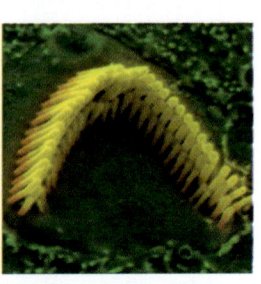
healthy hair cells

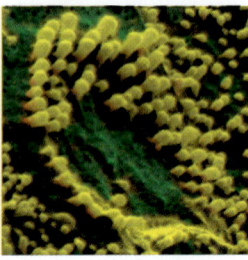
damaged hair cells

CHECK YOUR READING How do high-intensity sounds damage hearing?

Using earplugs can prevent damage from too much exposure to high-intensity sounds such as amplified music. The intensity at a rock concert is between 85 and 120 dB. Ear protection can also protect the hearing of employees in factories and other noisy work sites. In the United States, there are laws that require employers to reduce sounds at work sites to below 90 dB or to provide workers with ear protection.

Even a brief, one-time exposure to an extremely loud noise can destroy hair cells. Noises above 130 dB are especially dangerous. Noises above 140 dB are even painful. It is best to avoid such noises altogether. If you find yourself exposed suddenly to such a noise, covering your ears with your hands may be the best protection.

RESOURCE CENTER
CLASSZONE.COM
Find out more about sound and protecting your hearing.

7.3 Review

KEY CONCEPTS
1. Explain how the terms *intensity, decibel,* and *amplitude* are related.
2. Describe one way in which sound intensity can be controlled.
3. How do loud sounds cause damage to hearing?

CRITICAL THINKING
4. **Synthesize** A wind chime produces both soft and loud sounds. If you could see the waves, how would they differ?
5. **Design an Experiment** How could you demonstrate that sound dies away over distance? Suppose you could use three volunteers, a radio, and a tape recorder.

CHALLENGE
6. **Apply** Which of these acoustical designs would be best for a concert hall? Why?
   a. bare room with hard walls, floor, and ceiling
   b. room padded with sound-absorbing materials such as acoustical tile
   c. room with some hard surfaces and some sound padding

SKILL: INTERPRETING GRAPHS

Click on Math Tutorial for more help with interpreting line graphs.

Measuring Hearing Loss

An audiogram is a graph that can be used to determine if a patient has hearing loss. The vertical axis shows the lowest intensity, in decibels, that the patient can hear for each frequency tested. Notice that intensity is numbered from top to bottom on an audiogram.

To determine the lowest intensity heard at a given frequency, find the frequency on the horizontal axis. Follow the line straight up until you see the data points, shown as ✖ for the right ear and ● for the left ear. Look to the left to find the intensity. For example, the lowest intensity heard in both ears at 250 Hz is 10 dB.

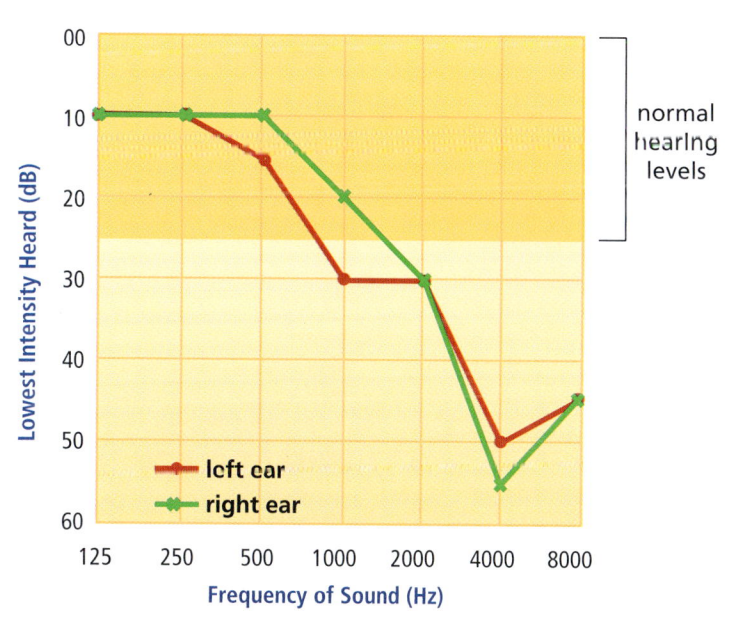

Use the graph to answer the following questions.

1. What is the lowest intensity heard in the patient's left ear at 1000 Hz? the right ear at the same frequency?

2. At which frequencies are the data points for both ears within normal hearing levels?

3. Data points outside the normal hearing levels indicate hearing loss. At which frequencies are the data points for both ears outside the normal levels?

CHALLENGE A dip in the graph at 3000 to 4000 Hz is a sign that the hearing loss was caused by exposure to loud noises. The patient is referred to a specialist for further testing. Should Patient A get further testing? Why or why not?

This air traffic ground controller wears ear protection to prevent hearing loss.

KEY CONCEPT

Sound has many uses.

 BEFORE, you learned
- Sound waves are produced by vibrations
- Sound waves have amplitude, frequency, and wavelength

 NOW, you will learn
- How ultrasound is used
- How musical instruments work
- How sound can be recorded and reproduced

VOCABULARY

echolocation p. 235
sonar p. 235

EXPLORE Echoes

How can you use sound to detect an object?

PROCEDURE

1. Tape the two cardboard tubes onto your desk at a right angle as shown.
2. Put your ear up to the end of one of the tubes. Cover your other ear with your hand.
3. Listen as your partner whispers into the outside end of the other tube.
4. Stand the book upright where the tubes meet. Repeat steps 2 and 3.

MATERIALS
- 2 cardboard tubes
- tape
- book

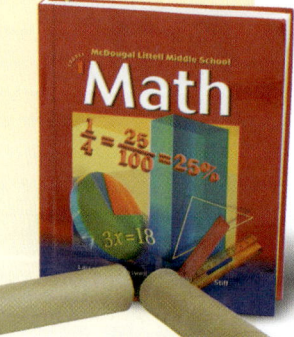

WHAT DO YOU THINK?
- How did the sound change when you added the book?
- How can an echo be used to detect an object?

Ultrasound waves are used to detect objects.

A ringing telephone, a honking horn, and the sound of a friend's voice are all reminders of how important sound is. But sound has uses that go beyond communication. For example, some animals and people use reflected ultrasound waves to detect objects. Some animals, such as bats, use the echoes of ultrasound waves to find food. People use ultrasound echoes to detect objects underwater or even to produce images of the inside of the body.

 Other than communication, what are three uses of sound?

234 Unit 2: **Waves, Sound, and Light**

Echolocation

Sending out ultrasound waves and interpreting the returning sound echoes is called **echolocation** (*echo* + *location*). Bats flying at night find their meals of flying insects by using echolocation. They send out as many as 200 ultrasound squeaks per second. By receiving the returning echoes, they can tell where prey is and how it is moving. They can also veer away from walls, trees, and other big objects.

VOCABULARY
Make description wheels for the terms *echolocation* and *sonar* to help you remember them later.

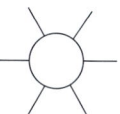

sound waves emitted by bat

sound waves reflected off prey

A number of animals that live in water use echolocation, too. Dolphins, toothed whales, and porpoises produce ultrasound squeaks or clicks. They listen to the returning echo patterns to find fish and other food in the water.

Sonar

People use the principles of echolocation to locate objects underwater. During World War I (1914–1918), scientists developed instruments that used sound waves to locate enemy submarines. Instruments that use echolocation to locate objects are known as **sonar.** Sonar stands for "sound navigation and ranging." The sonar machines could detect sounds coming from submarine propellers. Sonar devices could also send out ultrasound waves and then use the echoes to locate underwater objects. The information from the echoes could then be used to form an image on a screen.

Later, people found many other uses for sonar. Fishing boats use sonar to find schools of fish. Oceanographers—scientists who study the ocean—use it to map the sea floor. People have even used sonar to find ancient sunken ships in deep water.

This woman is using sonar to monitor for submarines.

Sonar is used to locate sunken ships. The image of the sunken ship above was produced on the basis of information from sonar.

Medical Uses of Ultrasound

Ultrasound has many uses in medicine. Because ultrasound waves are not heard by humans, ultrasound can be used at very high intensities. For example, high-intensity vibrations from ultrasound waves are used to safely break up kidney stones in patients. The energy transferred by ultrasound waves is also used to clean medical equipment.

One of the most important medical uses of ultrasound is the ultrasound scanner. This device relies on the same scientific principle as sonar. It sends sound waves into a human body and then records the waves that are reflected from inside the body. Information from these echoes forms a picture on a screen. The ultrasound scanner is used to examine internal organs such as the heart, pancreas, bladder, ovaries, and brain. Doppler ultrasound is a technology that can detect the movement of fluids through the body and is used to examine blood flow.

 How is an ultrasound scanner similar to sonar?

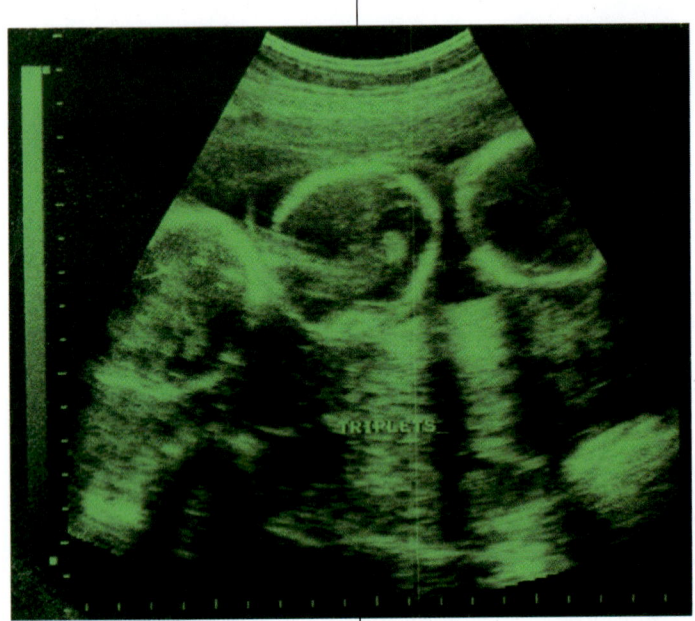

The image of these triplets was produced by reflected ultrasound waves.

One of the most well-known uses of ultrasound is to check on the health of a fetus during pregnancy. Problems that are discovered may possibly be treated early. The scan can also reveal the age and gender of the fetus and let the expecting parents know if they will be having twins or triplets. Ultrasound is safer than other imaging methods, such as the x-ray, which might harm the development of the fetus.

Sound waves can produce music.

Why are some sounds considered noise and other sounds considered music? Music is sound with clear pitches or rhythms. Noise is random sound; that means it has no intended pattern.

Explore musical instruments from around the world.

Musical instruments produce pitches and rhythms when made to vibrate at their natural frequencies. Some musical instruments have parts that vibrate at different frequencies to make different pitches. All of the pitches, together with the resonance of the instrument itself, produce its characteristic sound. The three main types of musical instruments are stringed, wind, and percussion. Some describe electronic instruments as a fourth type of musical instrument. Look at the illustration on the next page to learn more about how each type of musical instrument works.

How Musical Instruments Work

The way a musical instrument vibrates when it is played determines the sound it produces.

Stringed Instruments

Stringed instruments, such as the guitar, are played by plucking the strings. The plucking starts the vibrations that produce sound waves.

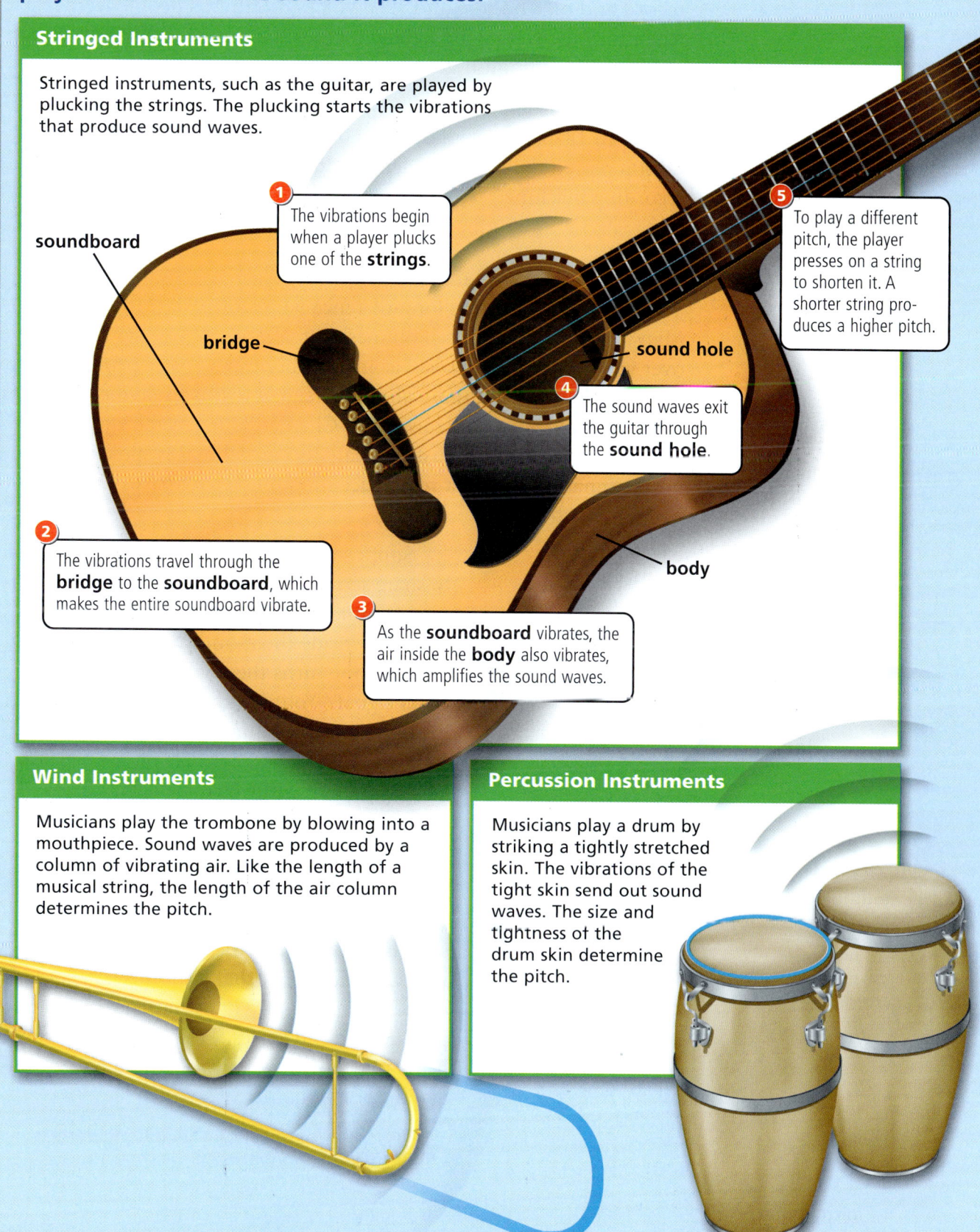

1 The vibrations begin when a player plucks one of the **strings**.

2 The vibrations travel through the **bridge** to the **soundboard**, which makes the entire soundboard vibrate.

3 As the **soundboard** vibrates, the air inside the **body** also vibrates, which amplifies the sound waves.

4 The sound waves exit the guitar through the **sound hole**.

5 To play a different pitch, the player presses on a string to shorten it. A shorter string produces a higher pitch.

Labels: soundboard, bridge, sound hole, body

Wind Instruments

Musicians play the trombone by blowing into a mouthpiece. Sound waves are produced by a column of vibrating air. Like the length of a musical string, the length of the air column determines the pitch.

Percussion Instruments

Musicians play a drum by striking a tightly stretched skin. The vibrations of the tight skin send out sound waves. The size and tightness of the drum skin determine the pitch.

Chapter 7: **Sound** 237

Sound can be recorded and reproduced.

For most of human history, people had no way to send their voices farther than they could shout. Nor could people before the 1800s record and play back sound. The voices of famous people were lost when they died. Imagine having a tape or a compact disk recording of George Washington giving a speech!

Then in the late 1800s, two inventions changed the world of sound. In 1876, the telephone was invented. And in 1877, Thomas Edison played the first recorded sound on a phonograph, or sound-recording machine.

READING TIP
The prefix *phono* means "sound," and the suffix *graph* means "writing."

The Telephone

The telephone has made long-distance voice communication possible. Many people today use cell phones. But whether phone signals travel over wires or by microwaves, as in cell phones, the basic principles are similar. You will learn more about the signal that is used in cell phones when you read about microwaves in Chapter 8. In general, a telephone must do two things. It must translate the sound that is spoken into it into a signal, and it must reproduce the sound that arrives as a signal from somewhere else.

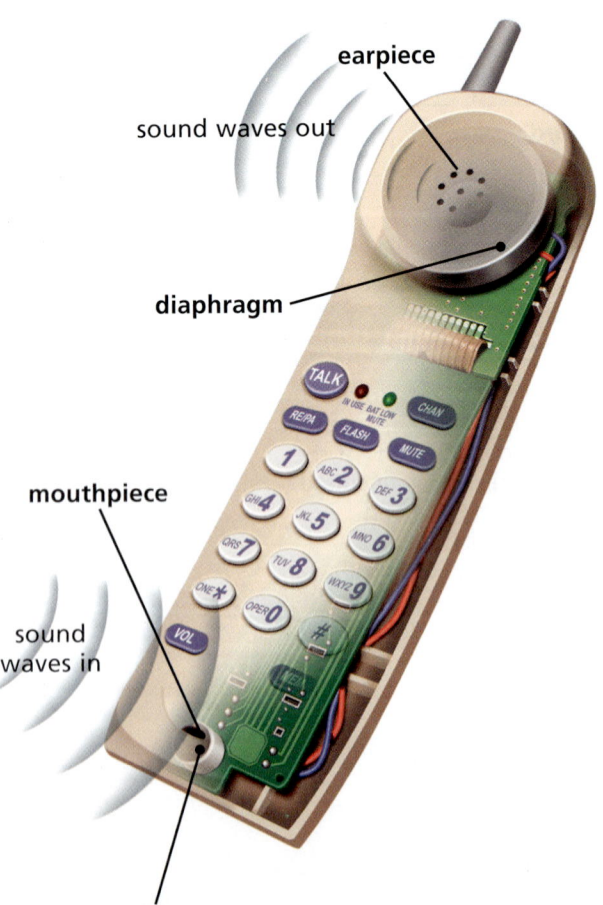

Suppose you are phoning your best friend to share some news. You speak into the mouthpiece. Sound waves from your voice cause a thin disk inside the mouthpiece to vibrate. A microphone turns these vibrations into electrical signals. Your handset sends these signals over wire to a switching station. Computers in the switching station connect phone callers and keep them connected until they finish their conversation.

Your friend receives the news by listening to the earpiece on his handset. There the process is more or less reversed. The electrical signals that arrive in the earpiece are turned into vibrations that shake another thin disk called a diaphragm. The vibrating diaphragm produces sound waves. The sound your friend hears is a copy of your voice, though it sounds like the real you.

CHECK YOUR READING What part of a telephone detects sound waves?

Recorded Sound

Sound occurs in real time, which means it is here for a moment and then gone. That is why Thomas Edison's invention of the phonograph—a way to preserve sound—was so important.

Edison's phonograph had a needle connected to a diaphragm that could pick up sound waves. The vibrations transferred by the sound waves were sent to a needle that cut into a piece of foil. The sound waves were translated into bumps along the grooves cut into the foil. These grooves contained all the information that was needed to reproduce the sound waves. Look at the image on top at the right to view an enlargement of record grooves. To play back the sound, Edison used another needle to track along the grooves etched in the foil. Later, phonographs were developed that changed sound waves into electrical signals that could be amplified.

Most people today listen to music on audio tapes or CDs. Tape consists of thin strips of plastic coated with a material that can be magnetized. Sounds that have been turned into electrical signals are stored on the tape as magnetic information. A CD is a hard plastic disc that has millions of microscopic pits arranged in a spiral. The bottom photograph at the right shows an enlargement of pits on the surface of a CD. These pits contain the information that a CD player can change into electrical signals, which are then turned into sound waves.

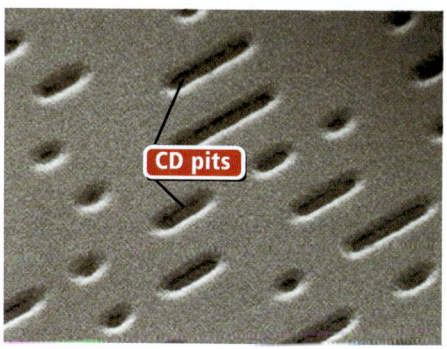

The images above were taken by a scanning electron micrograph (SEM). Both the record grooves (top) and CD pits (bottom) store all of the information needed to reproduce sound.

 Describe three devices on which sound is recorded.

7.4 Review

KEY CONCEPTS

1. Describe one medical use of ultrasound.
2. How are vibrations produced by each of the three main types of musical instruments?
3. How does a telephone record and reproduce sound?

CRITICAL THINKING

4. **Model** Draw a simple diagram to show how telephone communication works. Begin your diagram with the mouthpiece and end with the earpiece.
5. **Classify** The pitch of a musical instrument is changed by shortening the length of a vibrating column of air. What type of instrument is it?

CHALLENGE

6. **Synthesize** How is the earpiece of a telephone similar to the amplifier you read about in Section 3? Look again at the diagram of the amplifier on page 231 to help you find similarities.

CHAPTER INVESTIGATION

Build a Stringed Instrument

OVERVIEW AND PURPOSE

DESIGN YOUR OWN

People make music by plucking strings, blowing through tubes, and striking things. Part of each musical instrument vibrates to produce sounds that form the building blocks of music. In this lab, you will use what you have learned about sound to
- make a simple stringed instrument and see how the vibrating string produces sounds and
- change the design so that your stringed instrument produces more than one pitch.

Problem *Write It Up*

How does the length of a string affect the pitch of the sound it produces when plucked?

Hypothesize *Write It Up*

Write a hypothesis to explain how changing the length of the string affects the pitch of sound that is produced. Your hypothesis should take the form of an "If . . . , then . . . , because . . ." statement. Complete steps 1–3 before writing your hypothesis.

MATERIALS
- book
- 3–5 rubber bands
- 2 pencils
- ruler
- shoebox
- scissors

Procedure

1. Make a data table like the one shown. Try out the following idea for a simple stringed instrument. Stretch a rubber band around a textbook. Put two pencils under the rubber band to serve as bridges.

2. Put the bridges far apart at either end of the book. Find the string length by measuring the distance between the two bridges. Record this measurement in your **Science Notebook.** Pluck the rubber band to make it vibrate. Watch it vibrate and listen to the sound it makes.

3. Move the bridges closer together. What effect does this have on the length of the string? Measure and record the new length. How does this affect the tone that is produced? Record your observations.

240 Unit 2: Waves, Sound, and Light

4. Make a musical instrument based on the principles you just identified. Begin by stretching rubber bands of the same weight or thickness over the box.

5. If necessary, reinforce the box with an extra layer of cardboard or braces so that it can withstand the tension of the rubber bands without collapsing.

6. Place pencils under the rubber bands at each end of the box. Arrange one pencil at an angle so that each string is a different length. Record the length of each string and your observations of the sounds produced. Experiment with the placement of the bridges.

7. You might also try putting one bridge at the center of the box and plucking on either side of it. How does this affect the range of pitches your instrument produces?

8. Experiment with the working model to see how you can vary the sounds. Try this variation: cut a hole in the center of the box lid. Put the lid back on the box. Replace the rubber bands and bridges. How does the hole change the sound quality?

Observe and Analyze

1. **RECORD OBSERVATIONS** Draw a picture of your completed instrument design. Be sure your data table is complete.

2. **ANALYZE** Explain what effect moving the bridges farther apart or closer together has on the vibrating string.

3. **SYNTHESIZE** Using what you have learned from this chapter, write a paragraph that explains how your instrument works. Be sure to describe how sound waves of different frequencies and different intensities can be produced on your instrument.

Conclude

1. **INTERPRET** Answer the question posed in the problem.

2. **ANALYZE** Compare your results with your hypothesis. Did your results support your hypothesis?

3. **EVALUATE** Describe any difficulties with or limitations of the materials that you encountered as you made your instrument.

4. **APPLY** Based on your experiences, how would you explain the difference between music and noise?

INVESTIGATE Further

CHALLENGE Stringed instruments vary the pitch of musical sounds in several other ways. In addition to the length of the string, pitch depends on the tension, weight, and thickness of the string. Design an experiment to test one of these variables. How does it alter the range of sounds produced by your stringed instrument?

Build a Stringed Instrument

Problem How does the length of a string affect the pitch of the sound it produces when plucked?

Hypothesize

Observe and Analyze

Simple instrument: initial string length _____
Simple instrument: new string length _____

Table 1. Stringed Instrument Sound Observations

Stringed Instrument Designs	Length of Strings (cm)	Observations About Pitch and Sound Quality
Bridges at each end		
Bridge in middle		
After adding sound hole		

Conclude

Chapter Review

the BIG idea
Sound waves transfer energy through vibrations.

CONTENT REVIEW
CLASSZONE.COM

KEY CONCEPTS SUMMARY

1. Sound is a wave.

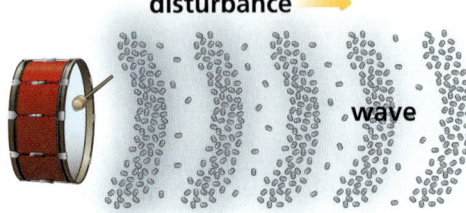

Sound is a longitudinal wave that travels through a material medium, such as air.

VOCABULARY
sound p. 213
vibration p. 213
vacuum p. 217

2. Frequency determines pitch.

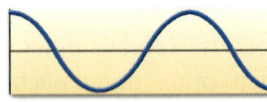

A sound wave with a lower frequency and longer wavelength is perceived to have a lower pitch.

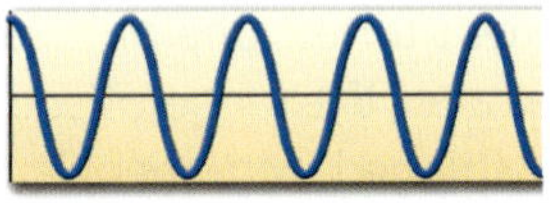

A sound wave with a higher frequency and shorter wavelength is perceived to have a higher pitch.

VOCABULARY
pitch p. 221
hertz p. 222
ultrasound p. 222
resonance p. 224
Doppler effect p. 226

3. Intensity determines loudness.

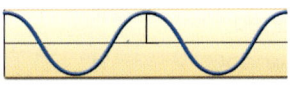

A sound wave with a lower amplitude and energy is perceived as a softer sound.

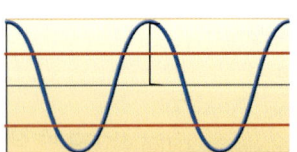

A sound wave with a higher amplitude and energy is perceived as a louder sound.

VOCABULARY
intensity p. 228
decibel p. 228
amplification p. 231
acoustics p. 231

4. Sound has many uses.

Human uses of sound:
sonar
ultrasound
music
telephone
recording

Bats use sound to locate objects.

VOCABULARY
echolocation p. 235
sonar p. 235

242 Unit 2: Waves, Sound, and Light

Reviewing Vocabulary

Copy and complete the chart below by using vocabulary terms from this chapter.

Property of Wave	Unit of Measurement	Characteristic of Sound
Frequency	1.	2.
3.	4.	loudness

Make a frame for each of the vocabulary words listed below. Write the word in the center. Decide what information to frame it with. Use definitions, examples, descriptions, parts, or pictures. An example is shown.

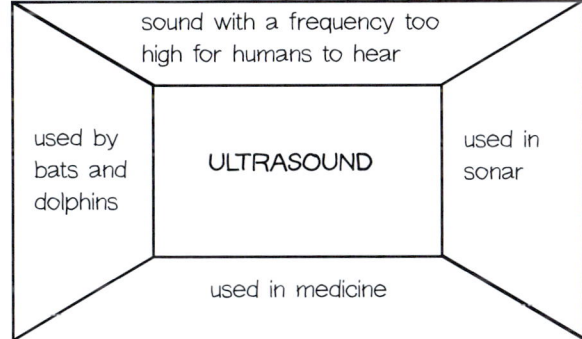

5. resonance
6. Doppler effect
7. amplification
8. acoustics
9. echolocation
10. sonar

Reviewing Key Concepts

Multiple Choice Choose the letter of the best answer.

11. Sound is a mechanical wave, so it always
    a. travels through a vacuum
    b. has the same amplitude
    c. is made by a machine
    d. travels through matter

12. Which unit is a measure of sound frequency?
    a. hertz
    b. decibel
    c. amp
    d. meter

13. In which of the following materials would sound waves move fastest?
    a. water
    b. cool air
    c. hot air
    d. steel

14. Which of the following effects is caused by amplification?
    a. wavelength increases
    b. amplitude increases
    c. frequency decreases
    d. decibel measure decreases

15. The frequency of a sound wave determines its
    a. pitch
    b. loudness
    c. amplitude
    d. intensity

16. As sound waves travel away from their source, their
    a. intensity increases
    b. energy increases
    c. intensity decreases
    d. frequency decreases

17. A telephone mouthpiece changes sound waves into
    a. electric signals
    b. vibrations
    c. CD pits
    d. grooves on a cylinder

Short Answer Look at the diagrams of waves below. For the next two items, choose the wave diagram that best fits the description, and explain your choice.

a.   b.   c.

18. the sound of a basketball coach blowing a whistle during practice

19. the sound of a cow mooing in a pasture

Chapter 7: **Sound** 243

Thinking Critically

Look at the photograph of an instrument above. Write a short answer to the next two questions.

20. HYPOTHESIZE How might sound waves be produced using the instrument in the photograph?

21. APPLY How might a person playing the instrument in the photograph vary the intensity?

22. COMMUNICATE Two people are singing at the same pitch, yet they sound different. Explain why.

23. SEQUENCE Copy the following sequence chart on your paper. Write the events in the correct sequence on the chart.

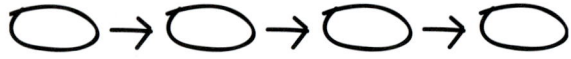

Events
a. Sound waves race out from the wind chime.
b. Forces in air gradually weaken the chime sound.
c. A breeze makes a wind chime vibrate.
d. A person nearby hears the wind chime.

24. COMPARE AND CONTRAST Write a description of the similarities and differences between each of the following pairs of terms: frequency—amplitude; intensity—amplitude; pitch—quality; fundamental tone—overtones.

Using Math in Science

Read the line graph below showing freeway noise levels at a toll collector's booth. Use the data in the graph to answer the next four questions.

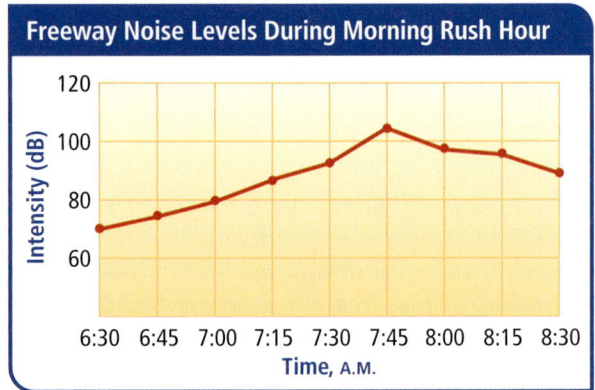

25. Which is the noisiest quarter-hour?

26. Estimate the loudest level of sound that the toll collector is exposed to.

27. If ear protection should be worn for a sound level above 90 dB, should the toll collector wear hearing protection? If so, during which times?

28. Describe how you could turn the line graph into a bar graph. Would the bar graph be as informative? Explain your answer.

the BIG idea

29. ANALYZE Look back at the picture at the start of the chapter on pages 210–211. How are sound waves being produced?

30. SUMMARIZE Write a paragraph summarizing this chapter. Use the Big Idea on page 210 as your topic sentence. Write examples of each key concept listed on page 210.

UNIT PROJECTS

Check your schedule for your unit project. How are you doing? Be sure that you've placed data or notes from your research in your project folder.

Standardized Test Practice

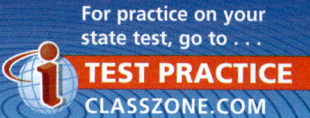

Analyzing Experiments

Read the following description of the way scientists study animals' hearing. Then answer the questions below.

Scientists test the hearing ranges of a human by making a sound and asking the person to say whether it was heard. This cannot be done with animals. Scientists use different methods to find animals' hearing ranges. In some experiments, they train animals—by rewarding them with food or water—to make specific behaviors when they hear a sound. Another method is to study an animal's nervous system for electrical reactions to sounds.

Researchers have found that dogs and cats can hear a wide range of sounds. Both dogs and cats can hear much higher frequencies than humans can. Lizards and frogs can only hear sounds in a much narrower range than humans can. Elephants can hear a wider range than lizards and frogs but not as wide a range as dogs and cats. Elephants can hear the lowest frequency sounds of all these animals.

1. What type of behavior would be best for scientists to train animals to make as a signal that they hear a sound?
   a. a typical motion that the animal makes frequently
   b. a motion that is difficult for the animal to make
   c. a motion the animal makes rarely but does make naturally
   d. a complicated motion of several steps

2. According to the passage, which animals can hear sounds with the highest frequencies?
   a. cats   c. frogs
   b. elephants   d. lizards

3. The high-pitched sounds of car brakes are sometimes more bothersome to pet dogs than they are to their owners. Based on the experimental findings, what is the best explanation for that observation?
   a. The dogs hear high-intensity sounds that their owners cannot hear.
   b. The dogs hear low-intensity sounds that their owners cannot hear.
   c. The dogs hear low-frequency sounds that their owners cannot hear.
   d. The dogs hear high-frequency sounds that their owners cannot hear.

4. Which animal hears sounds with the longest wavelengths?
   a. cat   c. elephant
   b. dog   d. frog

Extended Response

Answer the two questions below in detail. Include some of the terms from the word box in your answer. Underline each term you use in your answer.

| amplitude | distance | Doppler effect |
| frequency | pitch | wavelength |

5. Suppose you are riding in a car down the street and pass a building where a fire alarm is sounding. Will the sound you hear change as you move up to, alongside, and past the building? Why or why not?

6. Marvin had six glass bottles that held different amounts of water. He blew air into each bottle, producing a sound. How would the sounds produced by each of the six bottles compare to the others? Why?

CHAPTER

Electromagnetic Waves

Electromagnetic waves transfer energy through radiation.

Key Concepts

SECTION 1
Electromagnetic waves have unique traits.
Learn how electromagnetic waves differ from mechanical waves.

SECTION 2
Electromagnetic waves have many uses.
Learn about the behaviors and uses of different types of electromagnetic waves.

SECTION 3
The Sun is the source of most visible light.
Learn about the natural and artificial production of light.

SECTION 4
Light waves interact with materials.
Learn how light waves behave in a material medium.

Internet Preview

CLASSZONE.COM

Chapter 8 online resources: Content Review, Simulation, Visualization, two Resource Centers, Math Tutorial, Test Practice.

How does this phone stay connected?

EXPLORE the BIG idea

What Melts the Ice Cubes?

Put an ice cube in each of two sandwich bags, and place the bags in sunlight. Cover one with a sheet of white paper, and cover the other with a sheet of black paper. Lift the sheets of paper every five minutes and observe the cubes. Continue until they are melted.

Observe and Think
What did you notice about the way the ice cubes melted? How can you explain what you observed?

What Is White Light Made Of?

Use the shiny side of a compact disk (CD) to reflect light from the Sun onto a sheet of white paper. If bright sunlight is not available, use a flashlight. Try holding the CD at different angles and at different distances from the paper.

Observe and Think
What did you see on the paper? Where do you think that what you observed came from?

Internet Activity: Electromagnetic Waves

Go to **ClassZone.com** to explore images of the Sun based on different wavelengths.

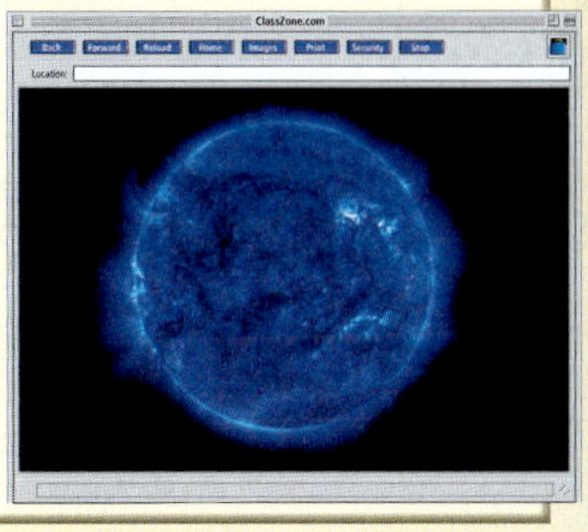

Observe and Think
Why can we see only some of the waves coming from the Sun?

NSTA scilinks.org SciLINKS
Light and Color **Code: MDL029**

CHAPTER 8
Getting Ready to Learn

◄ CONCEPT REVIEW

- A wave is a disturbance that transfers energy.
- Mechanical waves have a medium.
- Waves can be measured.
- Waves react to a change in medium.

◄ VOCABULARY REVIEW

mechanical wave p. 187
wavelength p. 193
frequency p. 193
reflection p. 201
field See Glossary.

CONTENT REVIEW
CLASSZONE.COM
Review concepts and vocabulary.

► TAKING NOTES

SUPPORTING MAIN IDEAS

Make a chart to show main ideas and the information that supports them. Copy each blue heading. Below each heading, add supporting information, such as reasons, explanations, and examples.

VOCABULARY STRATEGY

Write each new vocabulary term in the center of a **frame game** diagram. Decide what information to frame it with. Use examples, descriptions, parts, sentences that use the term in context, or pictures. You can change the frame to fit each term.

See the Note-Taking Handbook on pages R45–R51.

SCIENCE NOTEBOOK

MAIN IDEA
Electromagnetic waves have unique properties.
→ EM waves are disturbances in a field rather than in a medium.
→ EM waves can travel through a vacuum.
→ EM waves travel at the speed of light.

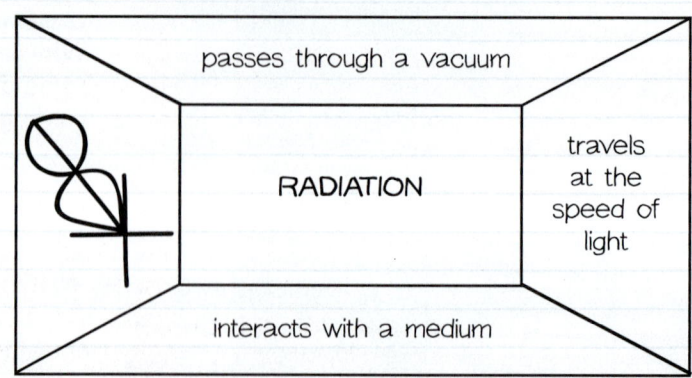

248 Unit 2: Waves, Sound, and Light

KEY CONCEPT
Electromagnetic waves have unique traits.

 BEFORE, you learned
- Waves transfer energy
- Mechanical waves need a medium to travel

 NOW, you will learn
- How electromagnetic waves differ from mechanical waves
- Where electromagnetic waves come from
- How electromagnetic waves transfer energy

VOCABULARY

electromagnetic wave p. 249
radiation p. 251

EXPLORE Electromagnetic Waves

How does the signal from a remote control travel?

PROCEDURE

① Turn the TV on and off using the remote control.

② Work with a partner to try to turn on the TV by aiming the remote control at the mirror.

WHAT DO YOU THINK?
How did you have to position the remote control and the mirror in order to operate the TV? Why do you think this worked?

MATERIALS
- TV with remote control unit
- mirror with stand

An electromagnetic wave is a disturbance in a field.

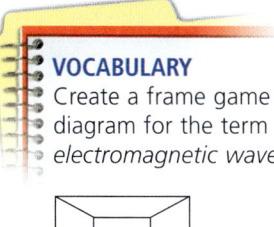

VOCABULARY
Create a frame game diagram for the term *electromagnetic wave.*

Did you know that you are surrounded by thousands of waves at this very moment? Waves fill every cubic centimeter of the space around you. They collide with or pass through your body all the time.

Most of these waves are invisible, but you can perceive many of them. Light is made up of these waves, and heat can result from them. Whenever you use your eyes to see, or feel the warmth of the Sun on your skin, you are detecting their presence. These waves also allow radios, TVs, and cell phones to send or receive information over long distances. These waves have the properties shared by all waves, yet they are different from mechanical waves in important ways. This second type of wave is called an electromagnetic wave. An **electromagnetic wave** (ih-LEHK-troh-mag-NEHT-ihk) is a disturbance that transfers energy through a field. Electromagnetic waves are also called EM (EE-EHM) waves.

Chapter 8: Electromagnetic Waves 249

A field is an area around an object where the object can apply a force—a push or a pull—to another object without touching it. You have seen force applied through a field if you have ever seen a magnet holding a card on the door of a refrigerator. The magnet exerts a pull on the door, even though it does not touch the door. The magnet exerts a force through the magnetic field that surrounds the magnet. When a disturbance occurs in an electric or magnetic field rather than in a medium, the wave that results is an electromagnetic wave.

How EM Waves Form

Learn more about the nature of EM waves.

EM waves occur when electrically charged atomic particles move. Charged particles exert an electric force on each other, so they have electric fields. A moving charged particle creates a magnetic force, so a moving charge also has a magnetic field around it.

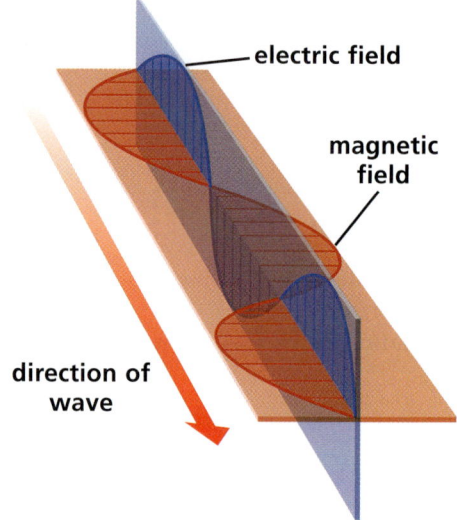

When electrically charged particles move quickly, they can start a disturbance of electric and magnetic fields. The fields vibrate at right angles to each other, as shown in the diagram above. The EM wave travels in the form of these vibrating fields. As you read in Chapter 6, waves have the properties of wavelength and frequency. In an EM wave, both the electric and the magnetic fields have these properties.

 What are the two types of fields that make up an EM wave?

Sources of EM Waves

Many of the EM waves present in Earth's environment come from the Sun. The Sun's high temperature allows it to give off countless EM waves. Other stars give off as many EM waves as the Sun, but because these bodies are so far away, fewer of their EM waves reach Earth. In addition to the Sun, technology is a source of EM waves that humans use for a wide variety of purposes.

EM waves from the Sun provide most of the energy for the environment on Earth. Some of the energy goes into Earth's surface, which then gives off EM waves of different wavelengths.

 What are two sources of EM waves on Earth?

Electromagnetic waves can travel in a vacuum.

Energy that moves in the form of EM waves is called **radiation** (RAY-dee-AY-shuhn). Radiation is different from the transfer of energy through a medium by a mechanical wave. A mechanical wave must vibrate the medium as it moves, and this uses some of the wave's energy. Eventually, every mechanical wave will give up all of its energy to the medium and disappear. An EM wave can travel without a material medium—that is, in a vacuum or space empty of matter—and does not lose energy as it moves. In theory, an EM wave can travel forever.

READING TIP

EM waves are also called rays. The words *radiation* and *radiate* come from the Latin word *radius*, which means "ray" or "spoke of a wheel."

How EM Waves Travel in a Vacuum

Because they do not need a medium, EM waves can pass through outer space, which is a near vacuum. Also, because they do not give up energy in traveling, EM waves can cross the great distances that separate stars and galaxies. For example, rays from the Sun travel about 150 million kilometers (93 million mi) to reach Earth. Rays from the most distant galaxies travel for billions of years before reaching Earth.

Usually, EM waves spread outward in all directions from the source of the disturbance. The waves then travel until something interferes with them. The farther the waves move from their source, the more they spread out. As they spread out, there are fewer waves in a given area and less energy is transferred. Only a very small part of the energy radiated from the Sun is transferred to Earth. But that energy is still a great amount—enough to sustain life on the planet.

The Speed of EM Waves in a Vacuum

In a vacuum, EM waves travel at a constant speed, and they travel very fast—about 300,000 kilometers (186,000 mi) per second. In 1 second, an EM wave can travel a distance greater than 7 times the distance around Earth. Even at this speed, rays from the Sun take about 8 minutes to reach Earth. This constant speed is called the speed of light. The vast distances of space are often measured in units of time traveled at this speed. For example, the Sun is about 8 light-minutes away from Earth. The galaxy shown in the photograph is 60 million light-years from Earth.

The light and other EM waves from this galaxy took approximately 60 million years to reach Earth.

CHECK YOUR READING How are EM waves used to measure distances in space?

Electromagnetic waves can interact with a material medium.

When EM waves encounter a material medium, they can interact with it in much the same way that mechanical waves do. They can transfer energy to the medium itself. Also, EM waves can respond to a change of medium by reflecting, refracting, or diffracting, just as mechanical waves do. When an EM wave responds in one of these ways, its direction changes. When the direction of the wave changes, the direction in which the energy is transferred also changes.

> **REMINDER**
> Potential energy comes from position or form; kinetic energy comes from motion.

Transferring Energy

A mechanical wave transfers energy in two ways. As it travels, the wave moves potential energy from one place to another. It also converts potential energy into kinetic energy by moving the medium back and forth.

In a vacuum, EM waves transfer energy only by moving potential energy from one place to another. But when EM waves encounter matter, their energy can be converted into many different forms.

 In what form do EM waves transfer energy in a vacuum?

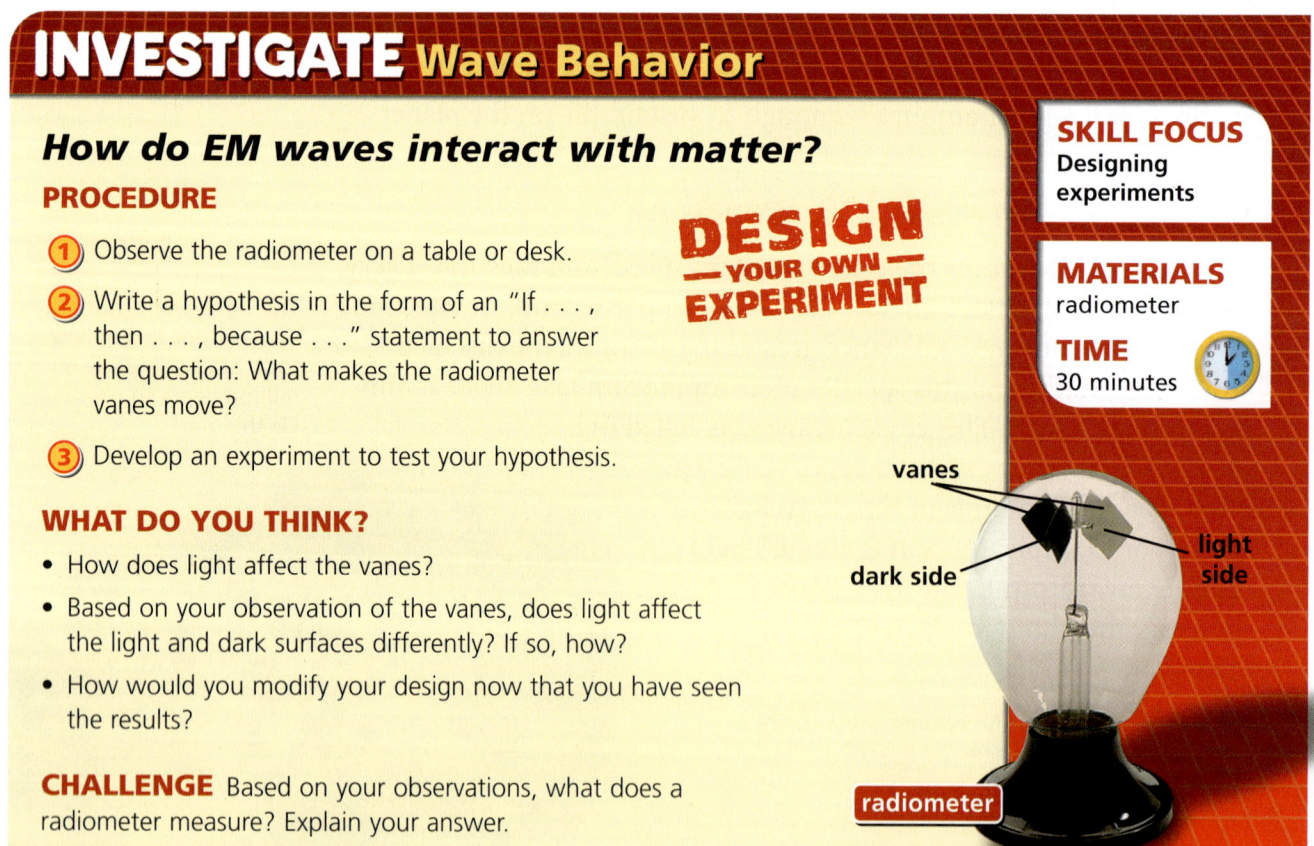

INVESTIGATE Wave Behavior

How do EM waves interact with matter?

PROCEDURE

1. Observe the radiometer on a table or desk.
2. Write a hypothesis in the form of an "If . . . , then . . . , because . . ." statement to answer the question: What makes the radiometer vanes move?
3. Develop an experiment to test your hypothesis.

WHAT DO YOU THINK?
- How does light affect the vanes?
- Based on your observation of the vanes, does light affect the light and dark surfaces differently? If so, how?
- How would you modify your design now that you have seen the results?

CHALLENGE Based on your observations, what does a radiometer measure? Explain your answer.

DESIGN YOUR OWN EXPERIMENT

SKILL FOCUS
Designing experiments

MATERIALS
radiometer

TIME
30 minutes

Converting Energy from One Form to Another

How EM waves interact with a medium depends on the type of the wave and the nature of the material. For example, a microwave oven uses a type of EM wave called microwaves. Microwaves pass through air with very little interaction. However, they reflect off the oven's fan and sides. But when microwaves encounter water, such as that inside a potato, their energy is converted into thermal energy. As a result, the potato gets cooked, but the oven remains cool.

① A device on the oven produces microwaves and sends them toward the reflecting fan.

② Microwaves are reflected in many directions by the blades of the fan and then again by the sides of the oven.

③ Microwaves move through the air without transferring energy to the air.

④ Microwaves transfer energy to the water molecules inside the potato in the form of heat, cooking the potato.

EM waves usually become noticeable and useful when they transfer energy to a medium. You do not observe the microwaves in a microwave oven. All you observe is the potato cooking. In the rest of this chapter, you will learn about different types of EM waves, including microwaves, and about how people use them.

CHECK YOUR READING How does microwave cooking depend on reflection?

8.1 Review

KEY CONCEPTS
1. How are EM waves different from mechanical waves?
2. What are two sources of EM waves in Earth's environment?
3. How can EM waves transfer energy differently in a material medium as compared to a vacuum?

CRITICAL THINKING
4. **Predict** What would happen to an EM wave that never came into contact with matter?
5. **Infer** What might be one cause of uneven heating in a microwave oven?

CHALLENGE
6. **Synthesize** EM waves can interact with a medium. How might this fact be used to make a device for detecting a particular type of EM radiation?

Chapter 8: **Electromagnetic Waves** 253

MATH TUTORIAL
CLASSZONE.COM

Click on Math Tutorial for more help with positive and negative exponents.

SKILL: USING EXPONENTS

EM Frequencies

The Chandra X-Ray Observatory in the photograph is a space telescope that detects high-frequency EM waves called x-rays. A wave's frequency is the number of peaks that pass a given point in 1 second. EM frequencies usually run from about 100 Hz to about 1 trillion trillion Hz. If written in standard form (using zeros), 1 trillion trillion would look like this:

1,000,000,000,000,000,000,000,000

Because this number is hard to read, it would be helpful to write it more simply. Using exponents, 1 trillion trillion can be written as **10^{24}**.

Exponents can also be used to simplify very small numbers. For example, the wavelength of a wave with a frequency of 10^{24} Hz is about one ten-thousandth of one trillionth of a meter. That number can be written in standard form as **0.000,000,000,000,000,1 m**. Using exponents, the number can be written more simply as **10^{-16} m**.

Examples

Large Numbers

To write a multiple of 10 in exponent form, just count the zeros. Then, use the total as the exponent.

(1) 10,000 has 4 zeros.

(2) 4 is the exponent.

ANSWER 10^4 is the way to write 10,000 using exponents.

Decimals

To convert a decimal into exponent form, count the number of places to the right of the decimal point. Then, use the total with a negative sign as the exponent.

(1) 0.000,001 has 6 places to the right of the decimal point.

(2) Add a negative sign to make the exponent –6.

ANSWER 10^{-6} is the way to write 0.000,001 using exponents.

Answer the following questions.

Write each number using an exponent.
   1. 10,000,000   **3.** 100,000   **5.** 10,000,000,000
   2. 0.000,01   **4.** 0.0001   **6.** 0.000,000,001

Write the number in standard form.
   7. 10^8 **9.** 10^{11} **11.** 10^{17}
   8. 10^{-8} **10.** 10^{-12} **12.** 10^{-15}

CHALLENGE Using exponents, multiply 10^2 by 10^3. Explain how you got your result.

The top photograph shows a visible-light image of the Crab Nebula. The bottom photograph shows the same nebula as it appears at higher x-ray frequencies.

KEY CONCEPT

Electromagnetic waves have many uses.

 BEFORE, you learned
- EM waves transfer energy through fields
- EM waves have measurable properties
- EM waves interact with matter

 NOW, you will learn
- How EM waves differ from one another
- How different types of EM waves are used

VOCABULARY

electromagnetic spectrum p. 256
radio waves p. 258
microwaves p. 259
visible light p. 260
infrared light p. 260
ultraviolet light p. 261
x-rays p. 262
gamma rays p. 262

EXPLORE Radio Waves

How can you make radio waves?

PROCEDURE

1. Tape one end of one length of wire to one end of the battery. Tape one end of the second wire to the other end of the battery.
2. Wrap the loose end of one of the wires tightly around the handle of the fork.
3. Turn on the radio to the AM band and move the selector past all stations until you reach static.
4. Hold the fork close to the radio. Gently pull the free end of wire across the fork's prongs.

MATERIALS
- two 25 cm lengths of copper wire
- C or D battery
- electrical tape
- metal fork
- portable radio

WHAT DO YOU THINK?
- What happens when you stroke the prongs with the wire?
- How does changing the position of the dial affect the results?

EM waves have different frequencies.

It might seem hard to believe that the same form of energy browns your toast, brings you broadcast television, and makes the page you are now reading visible. Yet EM waves make each of these events possible. The various types of EM waves differ from each other in their wavelengths and frequencies.

The frequency of an EM wave also determines its characteristics and uses. Higher-frequency EM waves, with more electromagnetic vibrations per second, have more energy. Lower-frequency EM waves, with longer wavelengths, have less energy.

REMINDER

Remember that frequency is the number of waves that pass a given point per second. The shorter the wavelength, the higher the frequency.

Chapter 8: **Electromagnetic Waves** 255

RESOURCE CENTER
CLASSZONE.COM

Learn more about the electromagnetic spectrum.

The Electromagnetic Spectrum

The range of all EM frequencies is known as the **electromagnetic spectrum** (SPEHK-truhm), or EM spectrum. The spectrum can be represented by a diagram like the one below. On the left are the waves with the longest wavelengths and the lowest frequencies and energies. Toward the right, the wavelengths become shorter, and the frequencies and energies become higher. The diagram also shows different parts of the spectrum: radio waves, microwaves, infrared light, visible light, ultraviolet light, x-rays, and gamma rays.

The EM spectrum is a smooth, gradual progression from the lowest frequencies to the highest. Divisions between the different parts of the spectrum are useful, but not exact. As you can see from the diagram below, some of the sections overlap.

The Electromagnetic Spectrum

Frequency in Hertz (1 hertz = 1 wavelength/second)

10^4 10^5 10^6 10^7 10^8 10^9 10^{10} 10^{11} 10^{12} 10^{13}

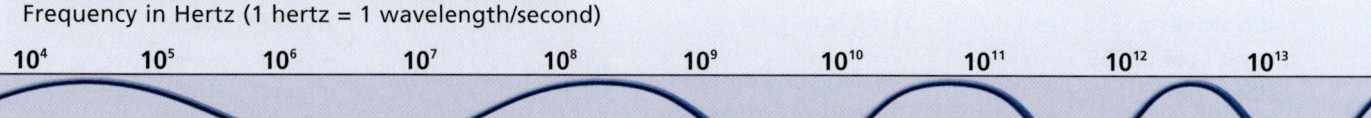

Radio Waves | Infrared Light

Microwaves

This woman is speaking on the radio. **Radio waves** are used for radio and television broadcasts. They are also used for cordless phones, garage door openers, alarm systems, and baby monitors.

Not all astronomy involves visible light. Telescopes like the one above pick up **microwaves** from space. Microwaves are also used for radar, cell phones, ovens, and satellite communications.

The amount of **infrared light** an object gives off depends on its temperature. Above, different colors indicate different amounts of infrared light.

256 Unit 2: **Waves, Sound, and Light**

Measuring EM Waves

Because all EM waves move at the same speed in a vacuum, the frequency of an EM wave can be determined from its wavelength. EM wavelengths run from about 30 kilometers for the lowest-frequency radio waves to trillionths of a centimeter for gamma rays. EM waves travel so quickly that even those with the largest wavelengths have very high frequencies. For example, a low-energy radio wave with a wavelength of 30 kilometers has a frequency of 10,000 cycles per second.

EM wave frequency is measured in hertz (Hz). One hertz equals one cycle per second. The frequency of the 30-kilometer radio wave mentioned above would be 10,000 Hz. Gamma ray frequencies reach trillions of trillions of hertz.

SUPPORTING MAIN IDEAS Write details that support the main idea that EM waves form a spectrum based on frequency.

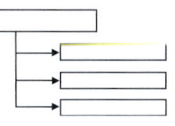

CHECK YOUR READING Why is wavelength all you need to know to calculate EM wave frequency in a vacuum?

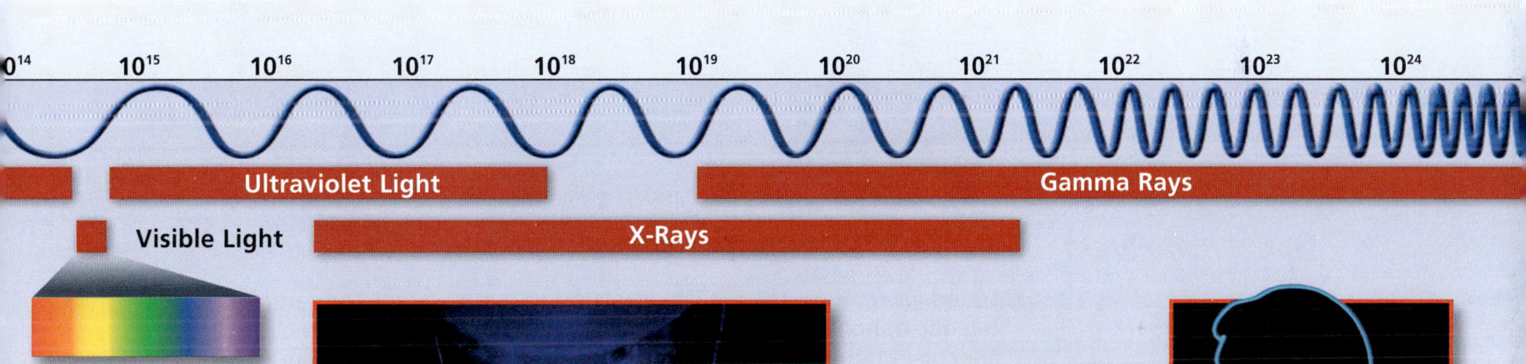

10^{14} 10^{15} 10^{16} 10^{17} 10^{18} 10^{19} 10^{20} 10^{21} 10^{22} 10^{23} 10^{24}

Ultraviolet Light

Gamma Rays

Visible Light

X-Rays

Visible light is the part of the EM spectrum that can be seen with the human eye. This bird's colors come from different wavelengths.

The researcher in this photograph is using **ultraviolet light** in the process of DNA analysis. A chemical in the samples gives off visible pink light when ultraviolet rays are present.

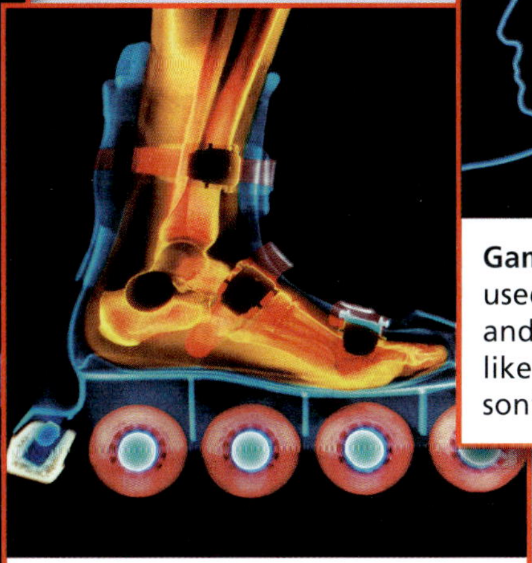

X-rays are useful for showing hard tissues inside the body, such as bones. To make images like the one above, x-ray images have to be displayed using visible light.

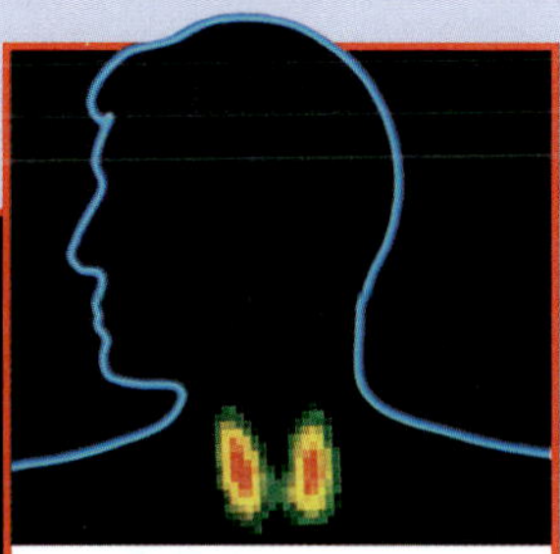

Gamma rays can be used to treat illnesses and to create images like this one of a person's thyroid gland.

Chapter 8: **Electromagnetic Waves** 257

Radio waves and microwaves have long wavelengths and low frequencies.

Radio waves are EM waves that have the longest wavelengths, the lowest frequencies, and the lowest energies. Radio waves travel easily through the atmosphere and many materials. People have developed numerous technologies to take advantage of the properties of radio waves.

VOCABULARY
Make a frame game diagram for *radio waves* and the other types of EM waves.

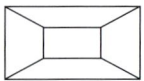

Radio Waves

Radio was the first technology to use EM waves for telecommunication, which is communication over long distances. A radio transmitter converts sound waves into radio waves and broadcasts them in different directions. Radio receivers in many locations pick up the radio waves and convert them back into sound waves.

1 Sound waves enter the microphone and are converted into electrical impulses.

2 The electrical impulses are converted into radio waves and broadcast by the transmitter.

3 The radio waves reach a radio receiver and are converted back into sound.

Different radio stations broadcast radio waves at different frequencies. To pick up a particular station, you have to tune your radio to the frequency for that station. The numbers you see on the radio—such as 670 or 99.5—are frequencies.

Simply transmitting EM waves at a certain frequency is not enough to send music, words, or other meaningful sounds. To do that, the radio transmitter must attach information about the sounds to the radio signal. The transmitter attaches the information by modulating—that is, changing—the waves slightly. Two common ways of modulating radio waves are varying the amplitude of the waves and varying the frequency of the waves. Amplitude modulation is used for AM radio, and frequency modulation is used for FM radio.

You might be surprised to learn that broadcast television also uses radio waves. The picture part of a TV signal is transmitted using an AM signal. The sound part is transmitted using an FM signal.

AM Signal

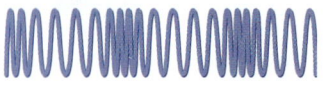

Information is encoded in the signal by varying the radio wave's amplitude.

FM Signal

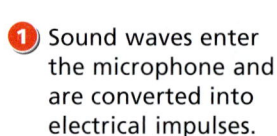

Information is encoded in the signal by varying the radio wave's frequency.

CHECK YOUR READING What two properties of EM waves are used to attach information to radio signals?

258 Unit 2: Waves, Sound, and Light

Microwaves

A type of EM waves called microwaves comes next on the EM spectrum. **Microwaves** are EM waves with shorter wavelengths, higher frequencies, and higher energy than other radio waves. Microwaves get their name from the fact that their wavelengths are generally shorter than those of radio waves. Two important technologies that use microwaves are radar and cell phones.

Radar The term *radar* stands for "radio detection and ranging." Radar came into wide use during World War II (1939–1945) as a way of detecting aircraft and ships from a distance and estimating their locations. Radar works by transmitting microwaves, receiving reflections of the waves from objects the waves strike, and converting these patterns into visual images on a screen. Today, radar technology is used to control air traffic at airports, analyze weather conditions, and measure the speed of a moving vehicle.

Radar led to the invention of the microwave oven. The discovery that microwaves could be used to cook food was made by accident when microwaves melted a candy bar inside a researcher's pocket.

Cell Phones A cell phone is actually a radio transmitter and receiver that uses microwaves. Cell phones depend on an overlapping network of cells, or areas of land several kilometers in diameter. Each cell has at its center a tower that sends and receives microwave signals. The tower connects cell phones inside the cell to each other or to the regular wire-based telephone system. These two connecting paths are shown below.

> **READING TIP**
> As you read about the different categories of EM waves, refer to the diagram on pages 256 and 257.

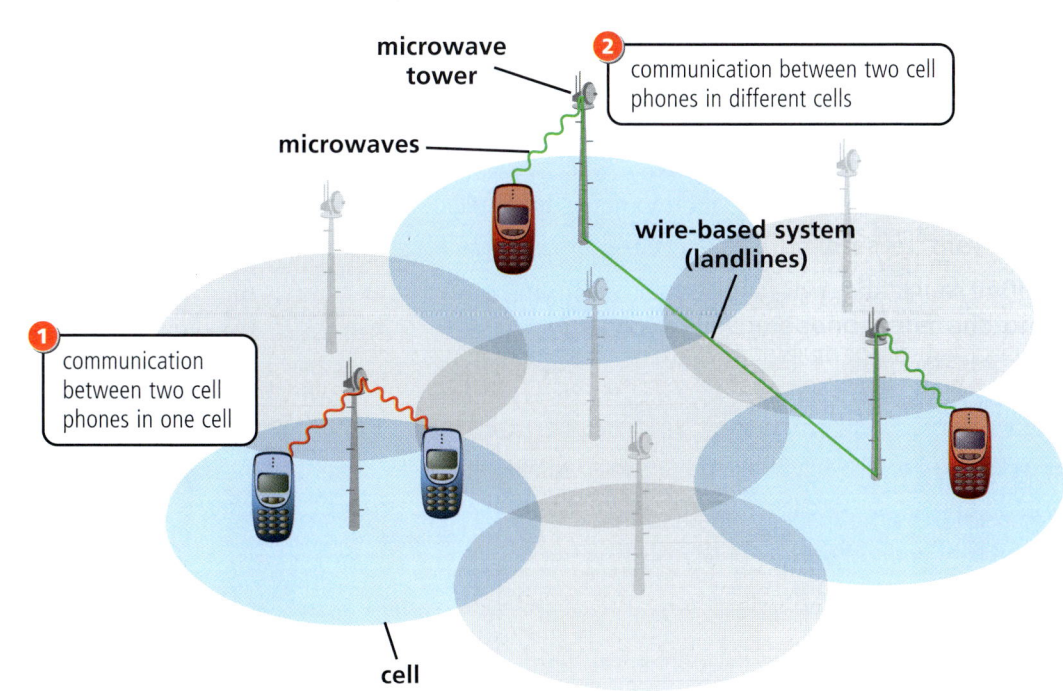

Infrared, visible, and ultraviolet light have mid-range wavelengths and frequencies.

Visible light is the part of the EM spectrum that human eyes can see. It lies between 10^{14} Hz and 10^{15} Hz. We perceive the longest wavelengths of visible light as red and the shortest as violet. This narrow band is very small compared with the rest of the spectrum. In fact, visible light is only about 1/100,000 of the complete EM spectrum. The area below visible light and above microwaves is the infrared part of the EM spectrum. Above visible light is the ultraviolet part of the spectrum. You will read more about visible light in the next section.

READING TIP

Infrared means "below red." *Ultraviolet* means "beyond violet."

Infrared Light

The **infrared light** part of the spectrum consists of EM frequencies between microwaves and visible light. Infrared radiation is the type of EM wave most often associated with heat. Waves in this range are sometimes called heat rays. Although you cannot see infrared radiation, you can feel it as warmth coming from the Sun, a fire, or a radiator. Infrared lamps are used to provide warmth in bathrooms and to keep food warm after it is cooked. Infrared rays also help to cook food—for example, in a toaster or over charcoal.

INVESTIGATE The Electromagnetic Spectrum

How can you detect invisible light?
PROCEDURE

1. Find a place that has both bright sunlight and shade, such as a windowsill. Place the white paper in the shade.
2. Using the marker, color the bulbs of the thermometers black. Place one thermometer on the paper. After three minutes, record the temperature.
3. Position the prism so that it shines a bright color spectrum on the white paper. Place the thermometers so that one bulb is in the blue area, one in the red, and one just outside the red, as shown.
4. After five minutes, record the three temperatures.

WHAT DO YOU THINK?
- How did the temperature in the shade compare to the temperature in the light and just outside of it?
- How might you explain the difference?

CHALLENGE How could you modify the experiment to find the hottest location in the infrared range?

SKILL FOCUS
Drawing conclusions

MATERIALS
- white paper
- black marker
- 3 thermometers
- prism

TIME
30 minutes

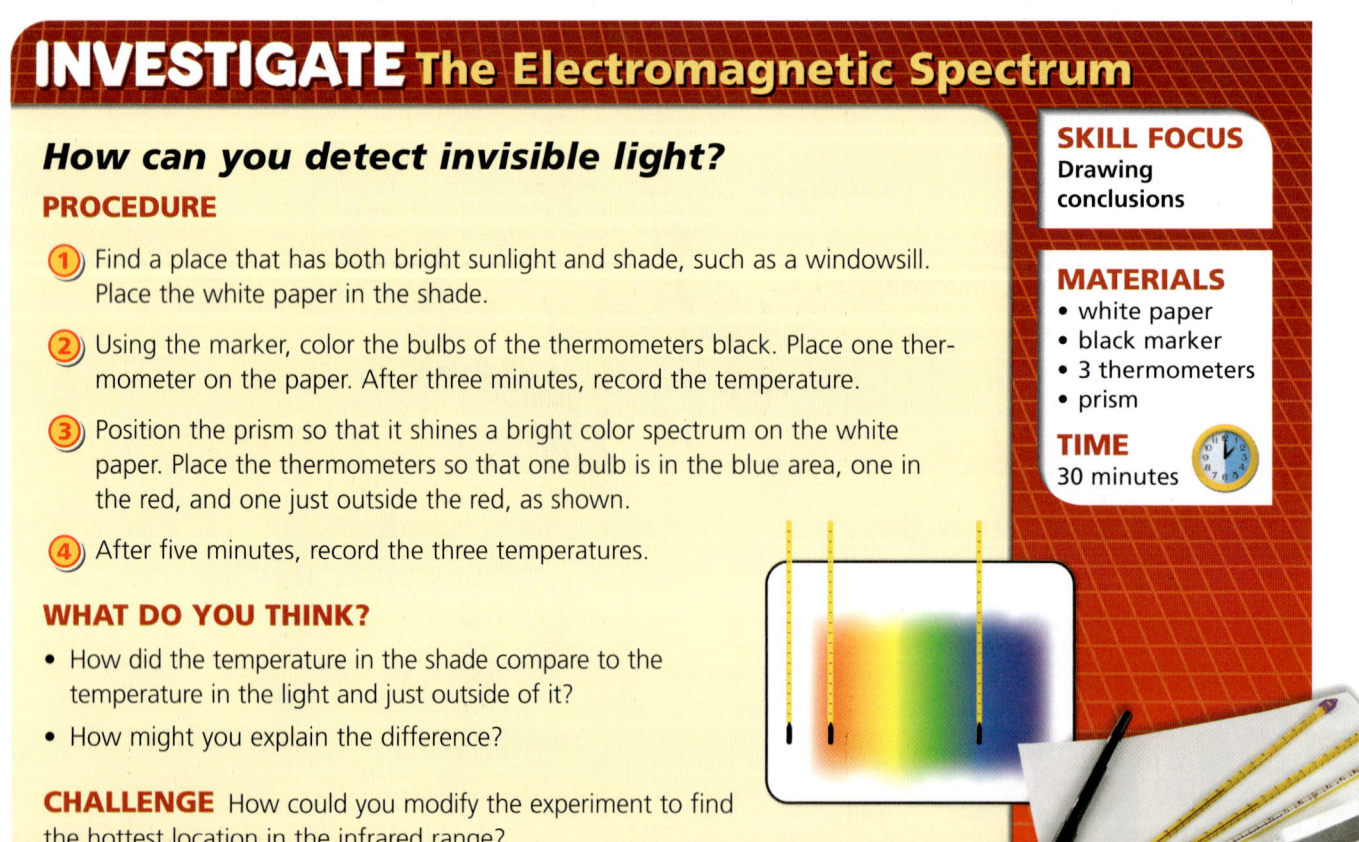

Some animals, such as pit viper snakes, can actually see infrared light. Normally, human beings cannot see infrared light. However, infrared scopes and cameras convert infrared radiation into visible wavelengths. They do this by representing different levels of infrared radiation with different colors of visible light. This technology can create useful images of objects based on the objects' temperatures.

 How do human beings perceive infrared radiation?

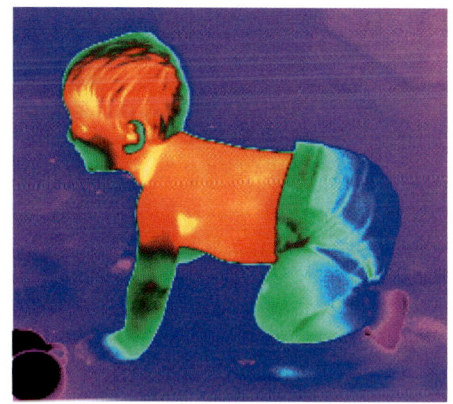

In this infrared image, warmer areas appear red and orange, while cooler ones appear blue, green, and purple.

Ultraviolet Light

The **ultraviolet light** part of the EM spectrum consists of frequencies above those of visible light and partially below those of x-rays. Because ultraviolet (UV) light has higher frequencies than visible light, it also carries more energy. The waves in this range can damage your skin and eyes. Sunblock and UV-protection sunglasses are designed to filter out these frequencies.

Ultraviolet light has beneficial effects as well. Because it can damage cells, UV light can be used to sterilize medical instruments and food by killing harmful bacteria. In addition, UV light causes skin cells to produce vitamin D, which is essential to good health. Ultraviolet light can also be used to treat skin problems and other medical conditions.

Like infrared light, ultraviolet light is visible to some animals. Bees and other insects can see higher frequencies than people can. They see nectar guides—marks that show where nectar is located—that people cannot see with visible light. The photographs below show how one flower might look to a person and to a bee.

This photograph shows the flower as it appears in visible light.

This photograph shows the flower as it might appear to a bee in ultraviolet light. Bees are able to see nectar guides in the UV range.

Chapter 8: **Electromagnetic Waves** 261

X-rays and gamma rays have short wavelengths and high frequencies.

At the opposite end of the EM spectrum from radio waves are x-rays and gamma rays. Both have very high frequencies and energies. **X-rays** have frequencies from about 10^{16} Hz to 10^{21} Hz. **Gamma rays** have frequencies from about 10^{19} Hz to more than 10^{24} Hz. Like other EM waves, x-rays and gamma rays are produced by the Sun and by other stars. People have also developed technologies that use these EM frequencies.

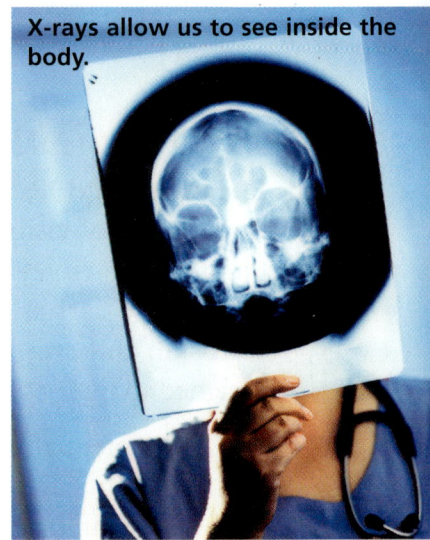

X-rays allow us to see inside the body.

X-rays pass easily through the soft tissues of the body, but many are absorbed by denser matter such as bone. If photographic film is placed behind the body and x-rays are aimed at the film, only the x-rays that pass through the body will expose the film. This makes x-ray images useful for diagnosing bone fractures and finding dense tumors. But too much exposure to x-rays can damage tissue. Even in small doses, repeated exposure to x-rays can cause cancer over time. When you have your teeth x-rayed, you usually wear a vest made out of lead for protection. Lead blocks high-frequency radiation.

Gamma rays have the highest frequencies and energies of any EM waves. Gamma rays are produced by some radioactive substances as well as by the Sun and other stars. Gamma rays can penetrate the soft and the hard tissues of the body, killing normal cells and causing cancer cells to develop. If carefully controlled, this destructive power can be beneficial. Doctors can also use gamma rays to kill cancer cells and fight tumors.

8.2 Review

KEY CONCEPTS

1. What two properties of EM waves change from one end of the EM spectrum to the other?
2. Describe two uses for microwave radiation.
3. How are EM waves used in dentistry and medicine?

CRITICAL THINKING

4. **Infer** Why do you think remote controls for TVs, VCRs, and stereos use infrared light rather than ultraviolet light?
5. **Apply** For a camera to make images of where heat is escaping from a building in winter, what type of EM wave would it need to record?

CHALLENGE

6. **Synthesize** When a person in a car is talking on a cell phone, and the car moves from one cell to another, the conversation continues without interruption. How might this be possible?

Think SCIENCE

SKILL: DETERMINING RELEVANCE

Are Cell Phones Harmful?

In 1993, a man appearing on a popular television talk show claimed that cell phone radiation had caused his wife's brain cancer. Since that time, concerned scientists have conducted more than a dozen studies. None of them have shown clear evidence of a connection between cell phones and cancer. However, researchers have made a number of experimental observations.

▶ Experimental Observations

Here are some results from scientists' investigations.

1. Substances that cause cancer work by breaking chemical bonds in DNA.
2. Only EM radiation at ultraviolet frequencies and above can break chemical bonds.
3. Microwave radiation may make it easier for molecules called free radicals to damage DNA bonds.
4. Other factors such as psychological stress may cause breaks in DNA bonds.
5. Performing multiple tasks like driving and talking on the phone reduces the brain's ability to perform either task.
6. Exposing the brain to microwave radiation may slow reaction times.

▶ Hypotheses

Here are some hypotheses that could be used for further research.

A. Microwaves from cell phones can break DNA bonds.
B. Cell phones may contribute to cancer.
C. Holding and talking into a cell phone while driving increases a person's risk of having an accident.
D. Worrying about cell phones may be a health risk.

▶ Determining Relevance

On Your Own On a piece of paper, write down each hypothesis. Next to the hypothesis write each observation that you think is relevant. Include your reasons.

As a Group Discuss how each observation on your list is or is not relevant to a particular hypothesis.

CHALLENGE Based on the observations listed above, write a question that you think would be a good basis for a further experiment. Then explain how the answer to this question would be helpful.

Talking on a cell phone while driving may increase the risk of accidents.

Chapter 8: Electromagnetic Waves 263

KEY CONCEPT

The Sun is the source of most visible light.

◀ **BEFORE,** you learned

- Visible light is part of the EM spectrum
- EM waves are produced both in nature and by technology

▶ **NOW,** you will learn

- How visible light is produced by materials at high temperatures
- How some living organisms produce light
- How humans produce light artificially

VOCABULARY

incandescence p. 265
luminescence p. 265
bioluminescence p. 265
fluorescence p. 267

THINK ABOUT

Why is light important?

This railroad worm has eleven pairs of green lights on its sides and a red light on its head. The animal probably uses these lights for illumination and to frighten away predators. Almost every living organism, including humans, depends on visible light. Think of as many different ways as you can that plants, animals, and people use light. Then, think of all the sources of visible light that you know of, both natural and artificial. Why is light important to living organisms?

Light comes from the Sun and other natural sources.

Learn more about visible light.

It is hard to imagine life without light. Human beings depend on vision in countless ways, and they depend on light for vision. Light is the only form of EM radiation for which human bodies have specialized sensory organs. The human eye is extremely sensitive to light and color and the many kinds of information they convey.

Most animals depend on visible light to find food and to do other things necessary for their survival. Green plants need light to make their own food. Plants, in turn, supply food directly or indirectly for nearly all other living creatures. With very few exceptions, living creatures depend on light for their existence.

 How is plants' use of light important to animals?

264 Unit 2: Waves, Sound, and Light

Most of the visible light waves in the environment come from the Sun. The Sun's high temperature produces light of every wavelength. The production of light by materials at high temperatures is called **incandescence** (IHN-kuhn-DEHS-uhns). When a material gets hot enough, it gives off light by glowing or by bursting into flames.

Other than the Sun, few natural sources of incandescent light strongly affect life on Earth. Most other stars give off as much light as the Sun, or even more, but little light from stars reaches Earth because they are so far away. Lightning produces bright, short-lived bursts of light. Fire, which can occur naturally, is a lower-level, longer-lasting source of visible light. The ability to make and use fire was one of the first light technologies, making it possible for human beings to see on a dark night or inside a cave.

 Why does little light reach Earth from stars other than the Sun?

Some living things produce visible light.

Many organisms produce their own visible light, which they use in a variety of ways. They produce this light through luminescence. **Luminescence** is the production of light without the high temperatures needed for incandescence. The production of light by living organisms is called **bioluminescence.** Bioluminescent organisms produce light from chemical reactions rather than from intense heat. Bioluminescence enables organisms to produce light inside their tissues without being harmed.

Bioluminescent organisms include insects, worms, fish, squid, jellyfish, bacteria, and fungi. Some of these creatures have light-producing organs that are highly complex. These organs might include light-producing cells but also reflectors, lenses, and even color filters.

The firefly, a type of beetle, uses bioluminescence to attract mates. A chemical reaction in its abdomen allows the firefly to glow at specific intervals. The pattern of glowing helps fireflies of the same species identify each other at night. Most often, the male flashes a signal while flying, and the female responds with a flash. After they have identified each other, the fireflies may continue to exchange flashes until the male has located the female.

> **VOCABULARY**
> Don't forget to make word frames for the terms *luminescence* and *bioluminescence*.
>
>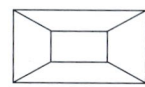

Chapter 8: **Electromagnetic Waves** 265

The process of bioluminescence is very efficient. Almost all of the energy released by the chemical reactions of bioluminescence is converted into light. Very little heat is produced. Researchers in lighting technology wanted for years to imitate this efficiency, and that became possible with the development of light-emitting diodes (LEDs). LEDs produce little heat, converting almost all of the incoming electrical energy into light.

 How is bioluminescence different from incandescence?

A female firefly responds to a male's signal.

Human technologies produce visible light.

Human beings invented the first artificial lighting when they learned to make and control fire. For most of human history, people have made light with devices that use fire in some form, such as oil lamps, candles, and natural gas lamps. After the discovery of electricity, people began to make light through a means other than fire. However, the technique of using a very hot material as a light source stayed the same until the invention of fluorescent lighting. In recent years, "cool" lighting has become much more common.

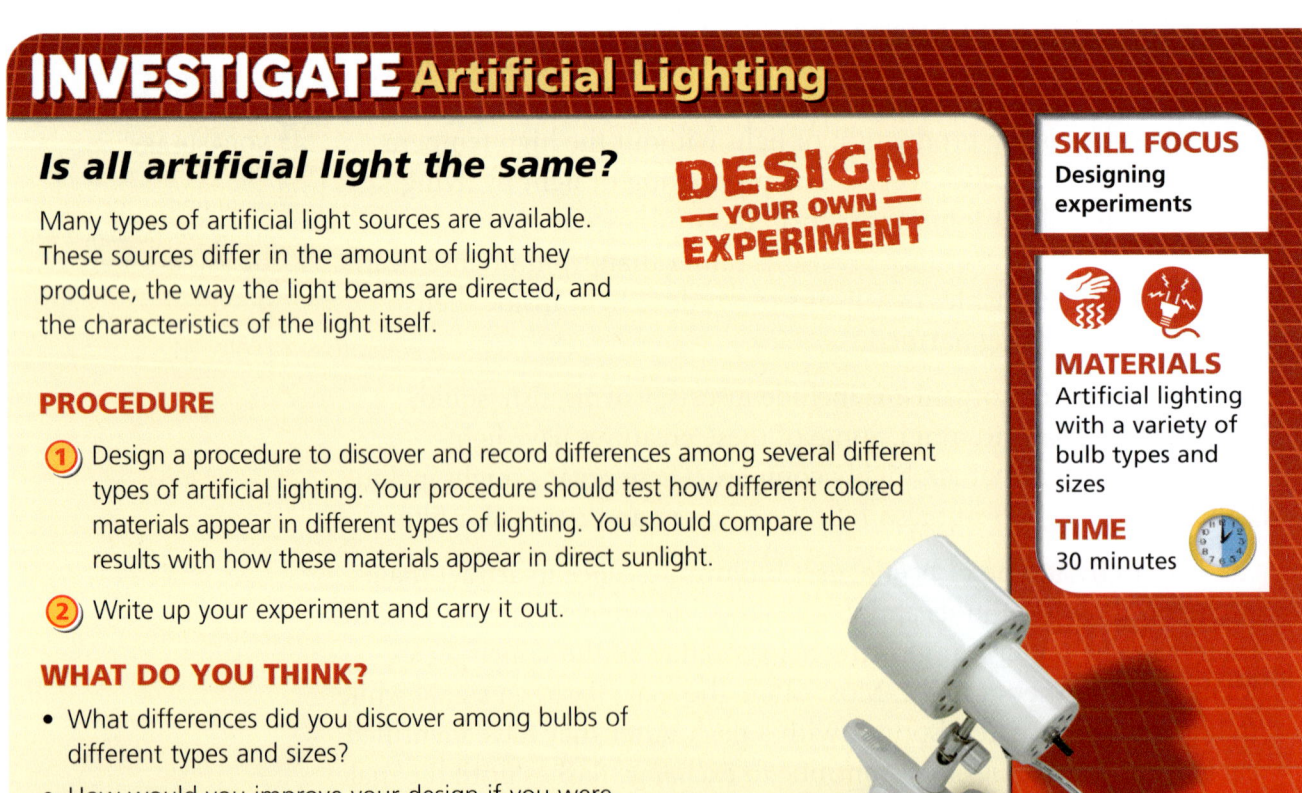

INVESTIGATE Artificial Lighting

Is all artificial light the same? — DESIGN YOUR OWN EXPERIMENT

Many types of artificial light sources are available. These sources differ in the amount of light they produce, the way the light beams are directed, and the characteristics of the light itself.

PROCEDURE

1) Design a procedure to discover and record differences among several different types of artificial lighting. Your procedure should test how different colored materials appear in different types of lighting. You should compare the results with how these materials appear in direct sunlight.

2) Write up your experiment and carry it out.

WHAT DO YOU THINK?

- What differences did you discover among bulbs of different types and sizes?
- How would you improve your design if you were to repeat your experiment?

SKILL FOCUS Designing experiments

MATERIALS Artificial lighting with a variety of bulb types and sizes

TIME 30 minutes

Unit 2: Waves, Sound, and Light

Incandescent and Fluorescent Lighting

The development of the electric light bulb in the late 1800s made light available at a touch. An ordinary light bulb is a sealed glass tube with a thin tungsten wire running through it. This wire is called a filament. When electrical current passes through the filament, the tungsten gets hotter and begins to glow. Because these light bulbs use high temperatures to produce light, they are called incandescent bulbs.

Tungsten can become very hot—about 3500 degrees Celsius (6300°F)—without melting. At such high temperatures, tungsten gives off a bright light. However, the tungsten filament also produces much infrared radiation. In fact, the filament produces more infrared light than visible light. As a result, incandescent bulbs waste a lot of energy that ends up as heat. At such high temperatures, tungsten also slowly evaporates and collects on the inside of the bulb. Eventually, the filament weakens and breaks, and the bulb burns out.

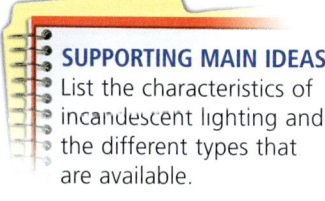

SUPPORTING MAIN IDEAS
List the characteristics of incandescent lighting and the different types that are available.

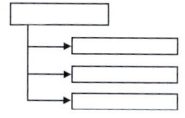

CHECK YOUR READING What causes ordinary light bulbs to burn out?

Since the 1980s, halogen (HAL-uh-juhn) bulbs have come into wide use. Halogen bulbs have several advantages over ordinary incandescent bulbs. They contain a gas from the halogen group. This gas combines with evaporating tungsten atoms and deposits the tungsten back onto the filament. As a result, the filament lasts longer. The filament can also be raised to a higher temperature without damage, so it produces more light. Halogen bulbs, which are made of quartz, resist heat better than glass.

Incandescent Light Bulb

tungsten filament
glass bulb

Halogen Light Bulb
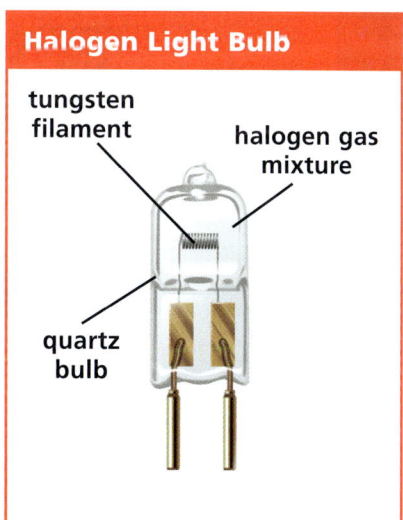
tungsten filament
halogen gas mixture
quartz bulb

Fluorescent Light Bulb
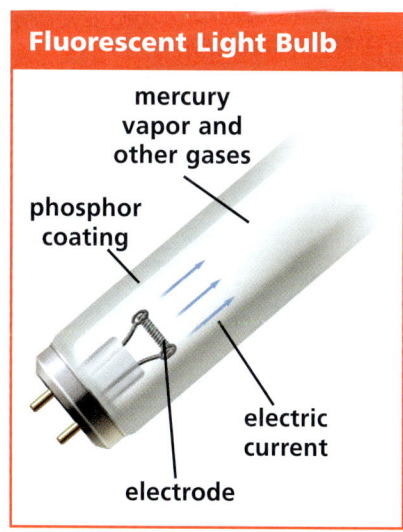
mercury vapor and other gases
phosphor coating
electric current
electrode

Many electric lights in use today are fluorescent. **Fluorescence** (flu-REHS-uhns) occurs when a material absorbs EM radiation of one wavelength and gives off EM radiation of another. Fluorescent bulbs are filled with a mixture of mercury vapor and other gases that give off ultraviolet light when an electric current passes through them.

Chapter 8: **Electromagnetic Waves** 267

The insides of the bulbs are coated with a powder called phosphor that fluoresces. Phosphor absorbs ultraviolet light and gives off visible light. Because fluorescent lighting is cool and does not waste much energy as heat, it is more efficient and more economical than incandescent lighting.

 Why are fluorescent lights more efficient than incandescent lights?

Other Types of Artificial Lighting

Like fluorescent lights, many other artificial light sources use a gas in place of a filament. For example, neon lights use gas-filled tubes to produce light. However, instead of ultraviolet light, the gas gives off visible light directly. The colors of neon lights come from the particular mixtures of gases and filters used. Vapor lights, which are commonly used for street lights, work in a similar way. In a vapor light, a material such as sodium is heated until it becomes a gas, or vapor. The vapor responds to an electric current by glowing brightly.

One of fastest-growing types of artificial lighting is the light emitting diode, or LED. LEDs do not involve bulbs, filaments, or gases. Instead, they produce light electronically. A diode is a type of semiconductor—a device that regulates electric current. An LED is a semiconductor that converts electric energy directly into visible light.

LEDs have many advantages over traditional forms of lighting. They produce a very bright light, do not break easily, use little energy, produce little heat, and can last for decades. Some technologists believe that LEDs will eventually replace most traditional forms of artificial lighting.

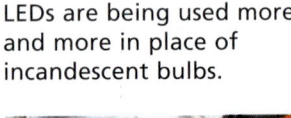
LEDs are being used more and more in place of incandescent bulbs.

8.3 Review

KEY CONCEPTS

1. Describe natural, nonliving sources of incandescent light.
2. What advantages does bioluminescence have over incandescence as a way for living organisms to produce light?
3. What are some advantages and disadvantages of artificial incandescent lighting?

CRITICAL THINKING

4. **Classify** Make a chart summarizing the different types of artificial lighting discussed in this section.
5. **Infer** Why do you think moonlight does not warm you, even though the Moon reflects light from the hot Sun?

CHALLENGE

6. **Compare and Contrast** What does LED lighting have in common with bioluminescence? How are the two different?

KEY CONCEPT

8.4 Light waves interact with materials.

 BEFORE, you learned
- Mechanical waves respond to a change in medium
- Visible light is made up of EM waves
- EM waves interact with a new medium in the same ways that mechanical waves do

 NOW, you will learn
- How the wave behavior of light affects what we see
- How light waves interact with materials
- Why objects have color
- How different colors are produced

VOCABULARY

transmission p. 269
absorption p. 269
scattering p. 271
polarization p. 272
prism p. 273
primary colors p. 274
primary pigments p. 275

EXPLORE Light and Matter

How can a change in medium affect light?

PROCEDURE

1. Fill the container with water.
2. Add 10 mL (2 tsp) of milk to the water. Put on the lid, and gently shake the container until the milk and water are mixed.
3. In a dark room, shine the light at one side of the container from about 5 cm (2 in.) away. Observe what happens to the beam of light.

MATERIALS
- clear plastic container with lid
- water
- measuring spoons
- milk
- flashlight

WHAT DO YOU THINK?
- What happened to the beam of light from the flashlight?
- Why did the light behave in this way?

Light can be reflected, transmitted, or absorbed.

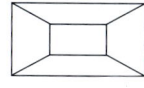

VOCABULARY
Don't forget to make word frames for *transmission* and *absorption*.

You have read that EM waves can interact with a material medium in the same ways that mechanical waves do. Three forms of interaction play an especially important role in how people see light. One form is reflection. Most things are visible because they reflect light. The two other forms of interaction are transmission and absorption.

Transmission (trans-MIHSH-uhn) is the passage of an EM wave through a medium. If the light reflected from objects did not pass through the air, windows, or most of the eye, we could not see the objects. **Absorption** (uhb-SAWRP-shun) is the disappearance of an EM wave into the medium. Absorption affects how things look, because it limits the light available to be reflected or transmitted.

Chapter 8: **Electromagnetic Waves** 269

How Materials Transmit Light

Materials can be classified according to the amount and type of light they transmit.

① Transparent (trans-PAIR-uhnt) materials allow most of the light that strikes them to pass through. It is possible to see objects through a transparent material. Air, water, and clear glass are transparent. Transparent materials are used for items such as windows, light bulbs, thermometers, sandwich bags, and clock faces.

② Translucent (trans-LOO-suhnt) materials transmit some light, but they also cause it to spread out in all directions. You can see light through translucent materials, but you cannot see objects clearly through them. Some examples are lampshades, frosted light bulbs, frosted windows, sheer fabrics, and notepaper.

③ Opaque (oh-PAYK) materials do not allow any light to pass through them, because they reflect light, absorb light, or both. Heavy fabrics, construction paper, and ceramic mugs are opaque. Shiny materials may be opaque mainly because they reflect light. Other materials, such as wood and rock, are opaque mainly because they absorb light.

 **CHECK YOUR READING** What is the difference between translucent and opaque materials?

This stained-glass window contains transparent, translucent, and opaque materials.

A light filter is a material that is transparent to some kinds of light and opaque to others. For example, clear red glass transmits red light but absorbs other wavelengths. Examples of light filters are the colored covers on taillights and traffic lights, infrared lamp bulbs, and UV-protected sunglasses. Filters that transmit only certain colors are called color filters.

Scattering

Sometimes fine particles in a material interact with light passing through the material to cause scattering. **Scattering** is the spreading out of light rays in all directions, because particles reflect and absorb the light. Fog or dust in the air, mud in water, and scratches or smudges on glass can all cause scattering. Scattering creates glare and makes it hard to see through even a transparent material. Making the light brighter causes more scattering, as you might have noticed if you have ever tried to use a flashlight to see through fog.

Fine particles, such as those in fog, scatter light and reduce visibility.

Scattering is what makes the sky blue. During the middle of the day, when the Sun is high in the sky, molecules in Earth's atmosphere scatter the blue part of visible light more than they scatter the other wavelengths. This process makes the sky light and blue. It is too bright to see the faint stars beyond Earth's atmosphere. At dawn and dusk, light from the Sun must travel farther through the atmosphere before it reaches your eyes. By the time you see it, the greens and blues are scattered away and the light appears reddish. At night, because there is so little sunlight, the sky is dark and you can see the stars.

SUPPORTING MAIN IDEAS
Be sure to add to your chart the different ways light interacts with materials.

 How does scattering make the sky blue?

Polarization

Polarizing filters reduce glare and make it easier to see objects. **Polarization** (POH-luhr-ih-ZAY-shuhn) is a quality of light in which all of its waves vibrate in the same direction. Remember that EM waves are made of electric and magnetic fields vibrating at right angles to each other. Polarization describes the electric fields of a light wave. When all of the electric fields of a group of light waves vibrate in the same direction, the light is polarized.

Light can be polarized by a particular type of light filter called a polarizing filter. A polarizing filter acts on a light wave's electric field like the bars of a cage. The filter allows through only waves whose electric fields vibrate in one particular direction. Light that passes through the filter is polarized. In the illustration below, these waves are shown in darker yellow.

Light reflecting off the surface of this pond causes glare.

A polarizing filter reduces glare, making it possible to see objects under the water.

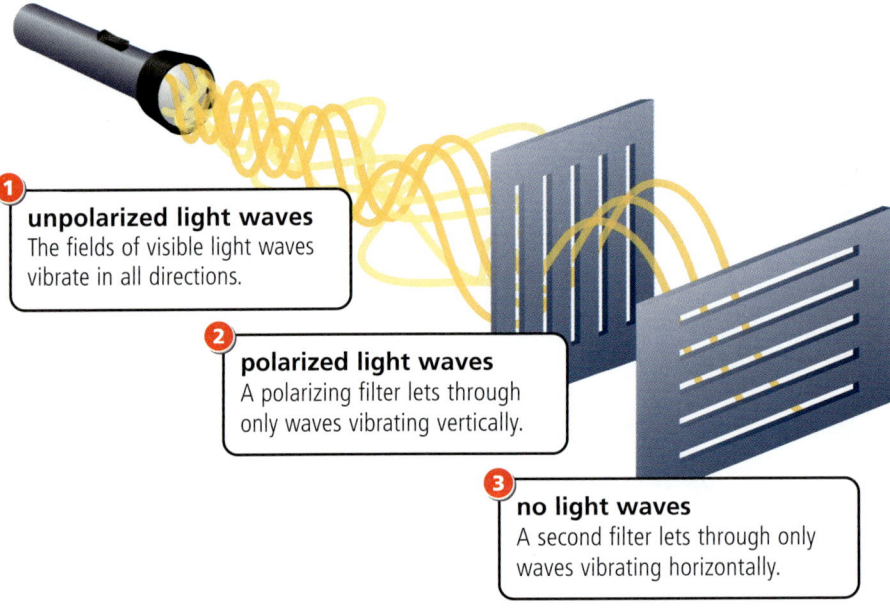

1 **unpolarized light waves**
The fields of visible light waves vibrate in all directions.

2 **polarized light waves**
A polarizing filter lets through only waves vibrating vertically.

3 **no light waves**
A second filter lets through only waves vibrating horizontally.

What do you think happens when polarized light passes into a second polarizing filter? If the direction of the second filter is the same as the first, then all of the light will pass through the second filter. The light will still be polarized. If the second filter is at a right angle to the first, as in the illustration above, then no light at all will pass through the second filter.

Wavelengths determine color.

The section of the EM spectrum called visible light is made up of many different wavelengths. When all of these wavelengths are present together, as in light from the Sun or a light bulb, the light appears white.

Seen individually, different wavelengths appear as different colors of light. This fact can be demonstrated by using a prism. A **prism** is a tool that uses refraction to spread out the different wavelengths that make up white light. The prism bends some of the wavelengths more than others. The lightwaves, bent at slightly different angles, form a color spectrum. The color spectrum could be divided into countless individual wavelengths, each with its own color. However, the color spectrum is usually divided into seven named color bands. In order of decreasing wavelength, the bands are red, orange, yellow, green, blue, indigo, and violet. You see a color spectrum whenever you see a rainbow.

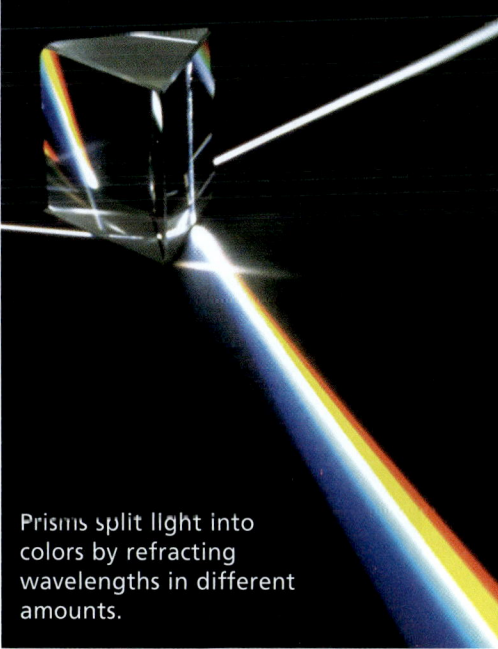

Prisms split light into colors by refracting wavelengths in different amounts.

Color Reflection and Absorption

The color of an object or material is determined by the wavelengths it absorbs and those it reflects. An object has the color of the wavelengths it reflects. A material that reflects all wavelengths of visible light appears white. A material that absorbs all wavelengths of visible light appears black. A green lime absorbs most wavelengths but reflects green, so the lime looks green, as shown below.

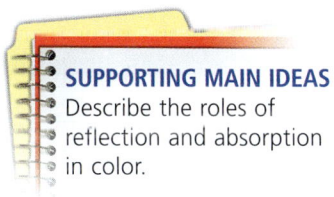

SUPPORTING MAIN IDEAS
Describe the roles of reflection and absorption in color.

① In this simplified diagram, light of all colors strikes the lime.

② The lime absorbs all wavelengths except green.

③ The lime reflects mostly green, so it appears green.

The color that an object appears to the eye depends on another factor besides the wavelengths the object absorbs and reflects. An object can reflect only wavelengths that are in the light that shines on it. In white light, a white object reflects all the wavelengths of visible light and appears white. If you shine only red light on a white piece of paper, however, the paper will appear red, not white, because only red light is available to be reflected.

In summary, two factors determine the color of an object: first, the wavelengths that the object itself reflects or absorbs, and second, the wavelengths present in the light that shines on the object.

 What color band or bands does a red apple absorb? a white flower?

Chapter 8: **Electromagnetic Waves** 273

Primary Colors of Light

The human eye can detect only three color bands: red, green, and blue. Your brain perceives these three colors and various mixtures of them as all the colors. These three colors of light, which can be mixed to produce all possible colors, are called **primary colors.** When all three colors are mixed together equally, they appear white, or colorless. Whenever colored light is added to a mixture, specific wavelengths are added. Mixing colors by adding wavelengths is called additive color mixing.

An example of the practical use of primary colors is a color television or computer monitor. The screen is divided into thousands of tiny bundles of red, green, and blue dots, or pixels. A television broadcast or DVD sends signals that tell the monitor which pixels to light up and when to do so. By causing only some pixels to give off light, the monitor can mix the three colors to create an amazing variety of colorful images.

Primary colors of light combine to make the secondary colors yellow, cyan (light blue), and magenta (dark pink).

CHECK YOUR READING — What does an equal mix of all three primary colors produce?

INVESTIGATE Mixing Colors

What is black ink made of?

PROCEDURE

1. Trim each of the filter papers to a disk about 10 cm (4 in.) in diameter. Make two parallel cuts about 1 cm (.5 in.) apart and 5 cm (2 in.) long from the edge of each disk toward the center. Fold the paper to make a flap at a right angle.

2. Use a different marker to make a dark spot in the middle of the flap on each disk.

3. Fill each of the cups with water. Set one of the disks on top of each cup so that the water covers the end of the flap but does not reach the ink spot.

4. After 15 minutes, examine each of the flaps.

WHAT DO YOU THINK?
- What did you observe about the effects of water on the ink spots?
- How do the three different samples compare?

CHALLENGE Write a hypothesis to explain what you observed about the colors in a black marker.

SKILL FOCUS
Observing

MATERIALS
- 3 coffee filters
- scissors
- 3 brands of black felt-tip marker
- 3 cups
- water

TIME
30 minutes

Primary Pigments

Remember that two factors affect an object's color. One is the wavelengths present in the light that shines on the object. The other is the wavelengths that the object's material reflects or absorbs. Materials can be mixed to produce colors just as light can. Materials that are used to produce colors are called pigments. The **primary pigments** are cyan, yellow, and magenta. You can mix primary pigments just as you can mix primary colors to produce all the colors.

The primary pigment colors are the same as the secondary colors of light. The secondary pigment colors are red, blue, and green—the same as the primary colors of light.

The effect of mixing pigments is different from the effect of mixing light. Remember that a colored material absorbs all wavelengths except those of the color it reflects. Yellow paint absorbs all wavelengths except yellow. Because pigments absorb wavelengths, whenever you mix pigments, you are subtracting wavelengths rather than adding them. Mixing colors by subtracting wavelengths is called subtractive color mixing. When all three primary pigments are mixed together in equal amounts, all wavelengths are subtracted. The result is black—the absence of reflected light.

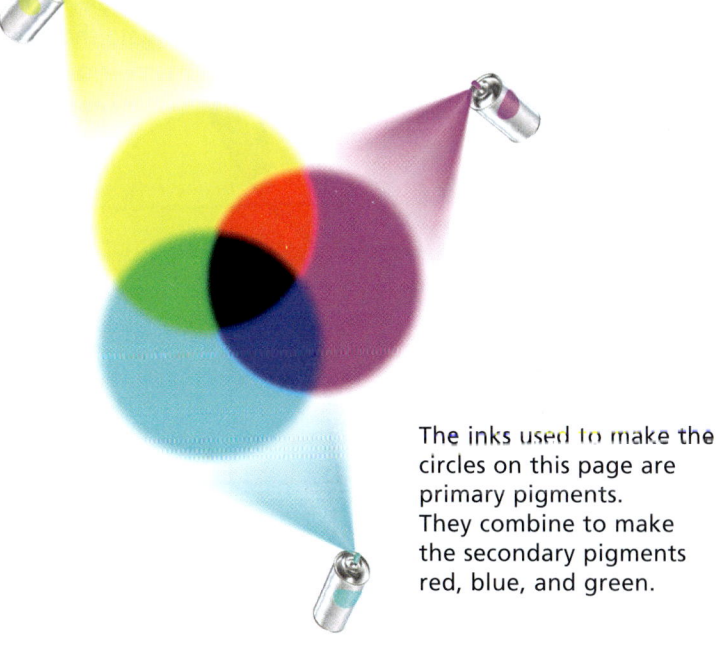

The inks used to make the circles on this page are primary pigments. They combine to make the secondary pigments red, blue, and green.

 How is mixing pigments different from mixing light?

8.4 Review

KEY CONCEPTS

1. What are some ways in which materials affect how light is transmitted?
2. How does a polarizing filter reduce glare?
3. In order for an object to appear white, which wavelengths must the light contain and the object reflect?

CRITICAL THINKING

4. **Apply** Imagine that you are a firefighter searching a smoke-filled apartment. Would using a stronger light help you see better? Explain your answer.
5. **Predict** Higher-energy EM waves penetrate farthest into a dense medium. What colors are more likely to penetrate to the bottom of a lake?

CHALLENGE

6. **Synthesize** If you focus a red light, a green light, and a blue light on the same part of a black curtain, what color will the curtain appear to be? Why?

CHAPTER INVESTIGATION

Wavelength and Color

OVERVIEW AND PURPOSE Lighting directors use color filters to change the look of a scene. The color an object appears depends on both the wavelengths of light shining on it and the wavelengths of light it reflects. In this exercise, you will investigate the factors that affect these wavelengths and so affect the color of an object. You will
- make a light box
- study the effect of different colors of light on objects of different colors

Problem

How does the appearance of objects of different colors change in different colors of light?

Hypothesize

Read the procedure below and look at the sample notebook page. Predict what color each object will appear in each color of light. Give a reason for each prediction.

Procedure

1. Draw a data table like the one in the sample **Science Notebook.**

2. Make 3 color filters by cutting a 10 cm (4 in.) square from each color of acetate.

3. Make a 3 cm (1 in.) wide hole in the middle of the top of the box. This will be the viewing hole.

4. Make an 8 cm (3 in.) hole in one end of the box. This will be the light hole.

5. You will observe each of the four colored objects four times—with no filter and with the red, blue, and green filters. Use masking tape to position the filters in the light hole, as shown.

step 5

MATERIALS
- 3 sheets of acetate (red, blue, and green)
- ruler
- scissors
- shoe box
- masking tape
- light source
- 4 solid-colored objects (white, black, red, and yellow)

276 Unit 2: Waves, Sound, and Light

6 Place the light box on a flat surface near a strong white light source, such as sunlight or a bright lamp. Position the box with the uncovered light hole facing the light source. Place the white object inside the box, look through the eyehole, and observe the object's color. Record your observations.

7 Use the light box to test each of the combinations of object color and filter shown in the table on the sample notebook page. Record your results.

step 7

Observe and Analyze

1. **RECORD OBSERVATIONS** Be sure your data table is complete.

2. **COMPARE** What color did the red object appear to be when viewed with a blue filter? a red filter?

Conclude

1. **INTERPRET** Answer your problem question.

2. **ANALYZE** Compare your results to your predictions. How do the results support your hypothesis?

3. **IDENTIFY VARIABLES** What different variables affected the outcome of your experiment?

4. **INFER** Why do colors of objects appear to change in different types of light?

5. **IDENTIFY LIMITS** What possible limitations or sources of error could have affected your results?

6. **APPLY** If you were going to perform on a stage that was illuminated using several different color filters, what color clothing should you wear in order to look as bright and colorful as possible?

INVESTIGATE Further

CHALLENGE Perform this experiment using different kinds of artificial light. Try it with a low-wattage incandescent bulb, a high-wattage incandescent bulb, a fluorescent bulb, or a full-spectrum bulb. How do different kinds of artificial light affect the colors that objects appear to be?

Wavelength and Color

Problem
How does the appearance of objects of different colors change in different colors of light?

Hypothesize

Observe and Analyze
Table 1. Predicted and Observed Colors of Objects with Different Colored Filters

Predicted	no filter	red filter	blue filter	green filter
white object				
black object				
red object				
yellow object				
Observed	no filter	red filter	blue filter	green filter
white object				

Chapter 8: **Electromagnetic Waves** 277

8 Chapter Review

the BIG idea
Electromagnetic waves transfer energy through radiation.

CONTENT REVIEW
CLASSZONE.COM

KEY CONCEPTS SUMMARY

1 Electromagnetic waves have unique traits.

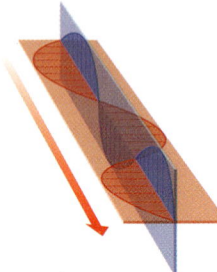

- Electromagnetic (EM) waves are made of vibrating electric and magnetic fields.
- EM waves travel at the speed of light through a vacuum.
- EM waves transfer energy and can interact with matter.

VOCABULARY
electromagnetic wave p. 249
radiation p. 251

2 Electromagnetic waves have many uses.

- EM waves are grouped by frequency on the EM spectrum.
- The EM spectrum is divided into radio waves, microwaves, infrared light, visible light, ultraviolet light, x-rays, and gamma rays.

VOCABULARY
EM spectrum p. 256
radio waves p. 258
microwaves p. 259
visible light p. 260
infrared light p. 260
ultraviolet light p. 261
x-rays p. 262
gamma rays p. 262

3 The Sun is the source of most visible light.

- Most visible light in the environment comes from the Sun.
- Many living organisms produce visible light for their own use.
- Humans produce visible light artificially.

VOCABULARY
incandescence p. 265
luminescence p. 265
bioluminescence p. 265
fluorescence p. 267

4 Light waves interact with materials.

- Reflection, transmission, and absorption affect what light we see.
- Light can be scattered and polarized.
- Visible light is made up of many wavelengths.
- The primary colors are red, blue, and green.
- The primary pigments are yellow, cyan, and magenta.

VOCABULARY
transmission p. 269
absorption p. 269
scattering p. 271
polarization p. 272
prism p. 273
primary colors p. 274
primary pigments p. 275

278 Unit 2: Waves, Sound, and Light

Reviewing Vocabulary

Make a four-square diagram for each of the listed terms. Write the term in the center. Define the term in one square. Write characteristics, examples, and nonexamples in other squares. A sample is shown below.

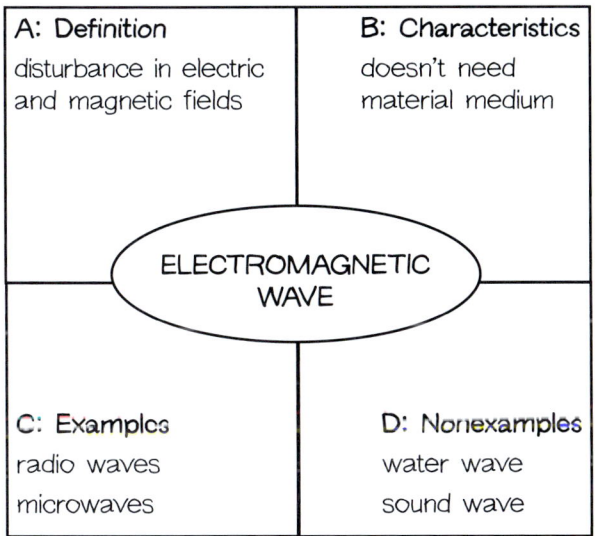

1. gamma rays
2. infrared light
3. transmission
4. absorption
5. pigment
6. radiation
7. bioluminescence
8. EM spectrum
9. incandescence
10. polarization

Reviewing Key Concepts

Multiple Choice *Choose the letter of the best answer.*

11. An electromagnetic wave is a disturbance that transfers energy through a field. In this sense, a disturbance is the same as a
    a. confusion
    b. magnification
    c. vibration
    d. conflict

12. Unlike mechanical waves, EM waves can travel through
    a. a vacuum
    b. water
    c. the ground
    d. air

13. A light year is a measure of
    a. time
    b. distance
    c. speed
    d. wavelength

14. The Sun and a light bulb both produce light through
    a. bioluminescence
    b. incandescence
    c. luminescence
    d. polarization

15. Which of the following types of light bulb converts ultraviolet waves into visible light waves?
    a. incandescent
    b. fluorescent
    c. halogen
    d. tungsten

16. An object seen through translucent material appears less clear than one seen through transparent material because the translucent material
    a. transmits none of the light coming from the object
    b. reflects all the light coming from the object
    c. transmits all the light coming from the object
    d. diffuses some light coming from the object

17. An object appears red because it
    a. reflects light waves of all colors
    b. reflects light waves of red
    c. absorbs light waves of red
    d. transmits light waves of all colors

18. Primary colors of light can combine to make
    a. black light
    b. white light
    c. primary pigments
    d. ultraviolet light

Short Answer *Write a short answer to each question.*

19. What vibrates in an EM wave?

20. How can EM waves be used to measure distance?

21. Describe how microwaves are used in communications.

22. What two properties of an EM wave change as you move from one part of the EM spectrum to another?

23. How does visible light differ from other EM waves? How is it similar?

24. Explain briefly how an incandescent light bulb works.

Chapter 8: **Electromagnetic Waves** 279

Thinking Critically

The diagram below shows how far different wavelengths of visible light penetrate into ocean water. Use information from this diagram to answer the next three questions.

25. **OBSERVE** An EM wave can interact with a material in different ways. Which type of interaction keeps some light waves from reaching the ocean floor?

26. **PREDICT** How would violet light behave in the same water? Think of where violet is on the color spectrum.

27. **SYNTHESIZE** How is the apparent color of objects near the ocean floor affected by the interactions shown in the diagram?

28. **ANALYZE** Under what circumstances can an EM wave begin to convert some of its electromagnetic energy into other forms of energy?

29. **ANALYZE** What two things must be true about the light source and the material of an object for you to see an object as red?

30. **PREDICT** If you shine a blue light on a white object, what color will the object appear to be? What color light would you need to add to make the white object appear white?

31. **APPLY** Why might incandescent lighting become less common in the future? Explain your reasoning.

32. **IDENTIFY CAUSE AND EFFECT** Liquid crystal displays like the ones used in some calculators work by polarizing light. Describe how two polarizing filters could cause the numbers on the display panel to appear black.

33. **COMPARE AND CONTRAST** In what way would a sieve be a good model for a polarizing light filter? In what ways would it not be?

34. **CONTRAST** In what ways is a fluorescent bulb more efficient than incandescent and halogen bulbs?

35. **PREDICT** What color will a white object appear to be if you look at it through a blue filter?

the BIG idea

36. **ANALYZE** Return to the question on page 246. Answer the question again, using what you have learned in the chapter.

37. **SUMMARIZE** Write a summary of this chapter. Use the Big Idea statement from page 246 as the title for your summary. Use the Key Concepts listed on page 246 as the topic sentences for each paragraph. Provide an example for each key concept.

38. **ANALYZE** Describe all of the EM wave behaviors and interactions that occur when a radiator warms a kitten.

UNIT PROJECTS

Check your schedule for your unit project. How are you doing? Be sure that you've placed data or notes from your research in your project folder.

Standardized Test Practice

Interpreting Diagrams

The diagram below shows part of the electromagnetic (EM) spectrum. The lower band shows frequency in hertz. The upper band shows part of the spectrum used by different technologies.

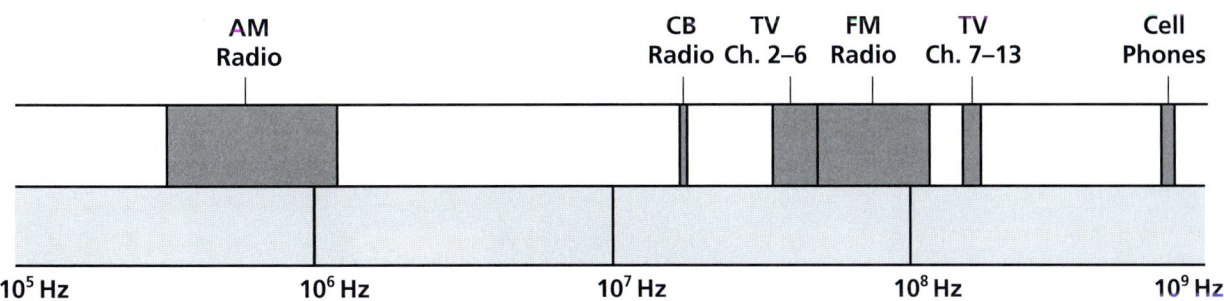

Use the diagram to answer the following questions.

1. Which of the technologies listed below uses the highest frequencies?
   a. AM radio
   b. CB radio
   c. FM radio
   d. TV channels 2–6

2. If you were receiving a signal at a frequency of nearly 10^9 Hz, what would you be using?
   a. a CB radio
   b. an AM radio
   c. an FM radio
   d. a cell phone

3. A television station broadcasts its video signal at 10^6 Hz and its audio signal at 10^8 Hz. To receive the broadcasts, your television would need to use the technologies of
   a. both AM and FM radio
   b. both CB and AM radio
   c. both CB and FM radio
   d. both CB radio and cell phone transmissions

4. Signals with similar frequencies sometimes interfere with each other. For this reason, you might expect interference in which of the following?
   a. lower television channels from cell phones
   b. upper television channels from FM radio
   c. lower television channels from FM radio
   d. upper television channels from cell phones

Extended Response

Answer the two questions below in detail. Include some of the terms from the word box. Underline each term you use in your answer.

| frequency | energy | interaction |
| field | medium | vacuum |

5. What are the similarities and differences between mechanical waves and electromagnetic waves?

6. What are some advantages and disadvantages of different types of artificial lighting?

TIMELINES in Science

THE STORY OF LIGHT

Light has fascinated people since ancient times. The earliest ideas about light were closely associated with beliefs and observations about vision. Over the centuries, philosophers and scientists developed an increasingly better understanding of light as a physical reality that obeyed the laws of physics.

With increased understanding of the nature and behavior of light has come the ability to use light as a tool. Many applications of light technology have led to improvements in human visual abilities. People can now make images of a wide range of objects that were invisible to earlier generations. The study of light has also led to technologies that do not involve sight at all.

This timeline shows just a few of the many steps on the road to understanding light. The boxes below the timeline show how these discoveries have been applied and developed into new technologies.

400 B.C.
Light Travels in a Straight Line
Observing the behavior of shadows, Chinese philosopher Mo-Ti finds that light travels in a straight line. His discovery helps explain why light passing through a small opening forms an upside-down image.

300 B.C.
Reflection Obeys Law
Greek mathematician Euclid discovers that light striking mirrors obeys the law of reflection. The angle at which light reflects off a mirror is equal to the angle at which it strikes the mirror.

EVENTS

450 B.C. 425 B.C. 400 B.C. 375 B.C. 350 B.C. 325 B.C. 300 B.C.

APPLICATIONS AND TECHNOLOGY

APPLICATION
Camera Obscura

The principle described by Mo-Ti in 400 B.C. led to the development of the camera obscura. When light from an object shines through a small hole into a dark room, an image of the object appears on the far wall. The darkened room is called, in Latin, *camera obscura*. Because light travels in a straight line, the highest points on the object appear at the lowest points on the image; thus, the image appears upside down. Room-sized versions of the camera obscura like the one shown here were a popular attraction in the late 1800s.

1666
White Light Is Made of Colors

British scientist Isaac Newton makes a remarkable discovery. After studying the effects of a prism on white light, Newton realizes that white light is actually made up of different colors. This contradicts the long-held belief that white light is pure light, and that colored light gets its color from the impurities of different materials.

A.D. 1000
Eyes Do Not Shoot Rays

Egyptian mathematician and astronomer Ali Alhazen publishes his *Book of Optics*. A diagram of the eye, from this book, is shown below. Alhazen proves that light travels from objects to the eyes, not the other way around. The previously accepted theory, put forth by Greek philosopher Plato centuries ago, claimed that light travels from the eyes to objects.

1676
Light Speeds Into Distance

Looking through a telescope, Danish astronomer Olaus Roemer observes one of Jupiter's moons "setting" earlier and earlier as Earth approaches the planet—and later and later as Earth moves farther away. Roemer infers that distance affects the time it takes light to travel from Jupiter to Earth. He estimates the speed of light as 230,000 kilometers per second.

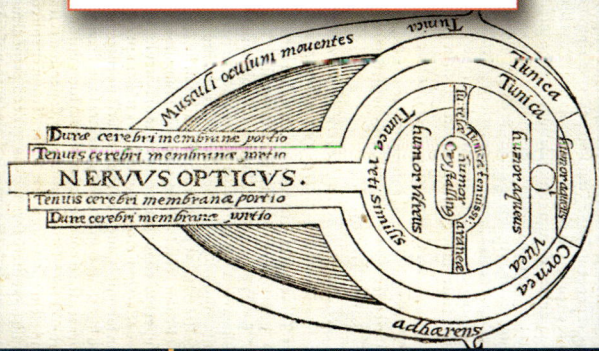

TECHNOLOGY
Reflecting Telescopes

Early astronomers such as Galileo used refracting telescopes. These telescopes, which used a lens to gather light, were difficult to focus because of the uneven refraction of different wavelengths. Isaac Newton built the first reflecting telescope, which overcame this difficulty by using a mirror to gather light and focus an image. All major astronomical telescopes, including the Hubble Space Telescope, now use mirrors.

Timelines in Science 283

1821
Light Waves Move Like Ripples in a Pond
French physicist Augustin-Jean Fresnel confirms the theory that light waves are transverse waves. Like water waves, light waves vibrate at right angles to the direction of their travel. This theory helps to explain many observed behaviors of light, including diffraction fringes like those surrounding this mountain climber.

1801
Light Makes Waves
British scientist Thomas Young finds that beams of light can interact to produce an interference pattern. He aims light through two slits and observes alternating light and dark bands on a screen. Young concludes that light acts as if it were made up of waves, which contradicts the theory put forth by Newton and others that light is made up of particles.

1887
No Medium Needed
U.S. scientists Albert Michelson and Edward Morley disprove the theory that light, like other waves, must have a medium. The men devise an experiment to detect the effect of ether—material that light supposedly uses to move through space—on a light beam. The experiment shows that no ether exists and therefore that light waves need no medium.

1750   1775   1800   1825   1850   1875   1900

APPLICATION
Holograms
Holograms are used today to create images for art, communications, and research. A hologram is an interference pattern created by a collision between the two halves of a split laser beam. One half shines on film, and the other half shines on the object. The object reflects this second beam onto the film, where it creates an interference pattern with the first beam. This interference pattern captures a three-dimensional image of the object, as in this hologram of a shark.

TECHNOLOGY
Gravitational Lenses
As part of his theory of relativity, Albert Einstein predicted that light would bend in a gravitational field. His theory was confirmed in 1919. During a solar eclipse, scientists witnessed the bending of light from more distant stars as that light passed near the Sun. Astronomers take advantage of this effect to get a better look at objects deep in space. Sometimes light from a distant object passes through a closer object's gravitational field on its way to Earth. By analyzing images of the object, scientists can learn more about it.

1960
Light Beams Line Up

U.S. inventor Theodore Harold Maiman builds a working laser by stimulating emission of light in a cylinder of ruby crystal. Laser light waves all have the same wavelength, and their peaks occur together.

2001
Light Is Completely Stopped

After slowing light to the speed of a bicycle, Danish physicist Lene Vestergaard Hau brings it to a complete halt in a supercold medium. Controlling the speed of light could revolutionize computers, communications, and other electronic technology.

 RESOURCE CENTER
CLASSZONE.COM

Learn more about current research involving light.

1925   1950   1975   2000

APPLICATION
Lasers in Eye Surgery

For centuries, people have used corrective lenses to help their eyes focus images more clearly. Today, with the help of lasers, doctors can correct the eye itself. Using an ultraviolet laser, doctors remove microscopic amounts of a patient's cornea to change the way it refracts light. As a result, the eye focuses images exactly on the retina. For many nearsighted people, the surgery results in 20/20 vision or better.

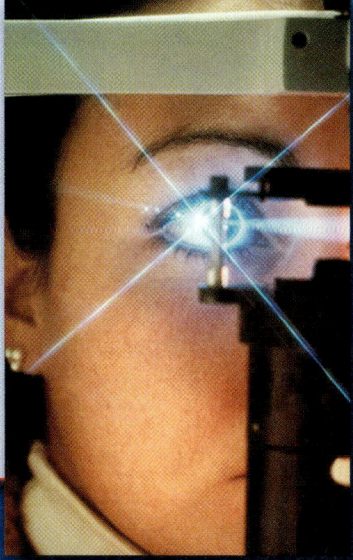

INTO THE FUTURE

Much of our current knowledge in science, from the workings of our bodies to the universe as a whole, is founded upon experiments that used light. Evidence from new light applications will continue to shape our knowledge. In the future, the nature of light, itself, may again come into question as new experiments are performed.

As new light microscopes are developed, scientists will gain more detailed information about how systems within our bodies work, such as how our brain cells interact with each other to perform a complex task. With powerful telescopes, scientists will gain a better understanding of the universe at its beginnings and how galaxies are formed.

Finally, as we continue to study the behavior of light, we may continue to modify its very definition. Sometimes considered a stream of particles, and other times considered waves, light is now understood to have qualities of both particles and waves.

ACTIVITIES

Make a Camera Obscura

Take a small box and paint the interior black. On one side, make a pinhole. On a side next to that one, make a hole about 5 cm in diameter.

On a bright, sunny day, hold the box so that sunlight enters the box through the pinhole. Fit your eye snugly against the larger hole and look inside.

Writing About Science

Lasers are currently used in entertainment, medicine, communication, supermarkets, and so on. Write a prediction about a specific use of lasers in the future. You might describe a new invention.

CHAPTER 9
Light and Optics

the BIG idea

Optical tools depend on the wave behavior of light.

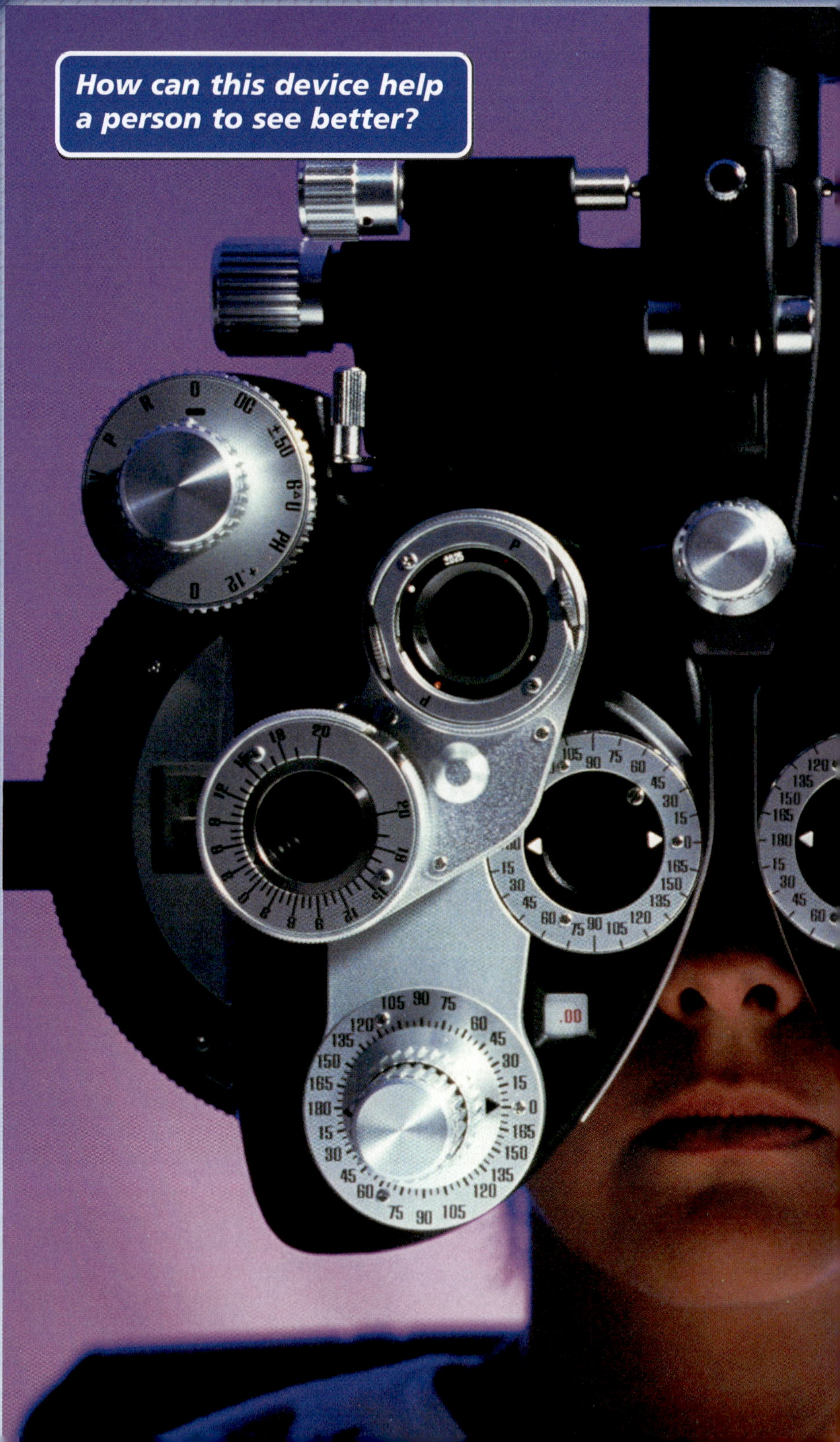

How can this device help a person to see better?

Key Concepts

SECTION 1
Mirrors form images by reflecting light.
Learn how mirrors use reflection to create images.

SECTION 2
Lenses form images by refracting light.
Learn how lenses use refraction to create images.

SECTION 3
The eye is a natural optical tool.
Learn about how eyes work as optical tools.

SECTION 4
Optical technology makes use of light waves.
Learn about complex optical tools.

Internet Preview

CLASSZONE.COM

Chapter 9 online resources: Content Review, Simulation, Visualization, three Resource Centers, Math Tutorial, Test Practice.

286 Unit 2: Waves, Sound, and Light

EXPLORE the BIG idea

How Does a Spoon Reflect Your Face?

Look at the reflection of your face in the bowl of a shiny metal spoon. How does your face look? Is it different from what you would expect? Now turn the spoon over and look at your face in the round side. How does your face look this time?

Observe and Think Why do the two sides of the spoon affect the appearance of your face in these ways?

Why Do Things Look Different Through Water?

Fill a clear, round jar with straight, smooth sides with water. Look through the jar at different objects in the room. Experiment with different distances between the objects and the jar and between yourself and the jar.

Observe and Think How does the jar change the way things look? What do you think causes these changes?

Internet Activity: Optics

Go to **ClassZone.com** to learn more about optics.

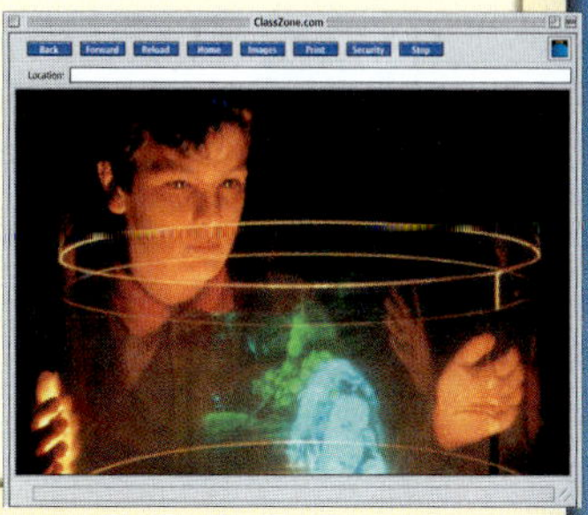

Observe and Think How does research in optics benefit other areas of scientific investigation?

Lenses Code: MDL030

Chapter 9: **Light and Optics** 287

CHAPTER 9

Getting Ready to Learn

CONCEPT REVIEW

- Light tends to travel in a straight line.
- The speed of light is affected by a material medium.
- Reflection and refraction are two ways light interacts with materials.

VOCABULARY REVIEW

reflection p. 201
refraction p. 201
visible light p. 260

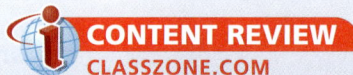

CONTENT REVIEW
CLASSZONE.COM
Review concepts and vocabulary.

TAKING NOTES

COMBINATION NOTES

To take notes about a new concept, first make an informal outline of the information. Then make a sketch of the concept and label it so you can study it later.

SCIENCE NOTEBOOK

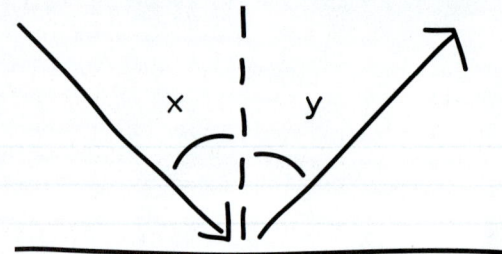

NOTES
The angle of incidence (x) equals the angle of reflection (y).

CHOOSE YOUR OWN STRATEGY

Take notes about new vocabulary terms, using one or more of the strategies from earlier chapters—**four square, description wheel,** or **frame game.** Feel free to mix and match the strategies, or to use an entirely different vocabulary strategy.

FOUR SQUARE

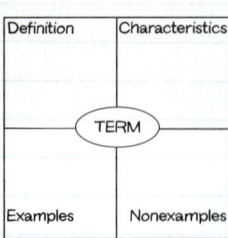

DESCRIPTION WHEEL

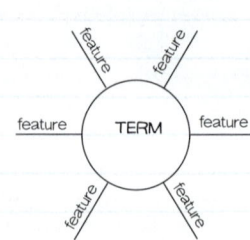

FRAME GAME

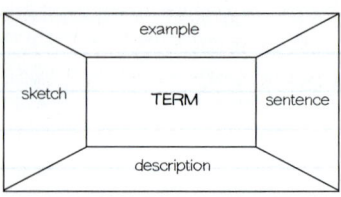

See the Note-Taking Handbook on pages R45–R51.

KEY CONCEPT

Mirrors form images by reflecting light.

 BEFORE, you learned
- EM waves interact with materials
- Light can be reflected

 NOW, you will learn
- About the science of optics
- How light is reflected
- How mirrors form images

VOCABULARY

optics p. 289
law of reflection p. 290
regular reflection p. 290
diffuse reflection p. 290
image p. 291
convex p. 292
concave p. 292
focal point p. 293

EXPLORE Reflection

How does surface affect reflection?

PROCEDURE

1. Tear off a square sheet of aluminum foil. Look at your reflection in the shiny side of the foil.
2. Turn the foil over and look at your reflection in the dull side.
3. Crumple up the piece of foil, then smooth it out again, shiny side up. Again, look at your reflection in the foil.

WHAT DO YOU THINK?
- How did the three reflections differ from one another?
- What might explain these differences?

MATERIALS
aluminum foil

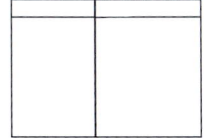 **COMBINATION NOTES** Don't forget to include sketches of important concepts in your notebook.

Optics is the science of light and vision.

Optics (AHP-tihks) is the study of visible light and the ways in which visible light interacts with the eye to produce vision. Optics is also the application of knowledge about visible light to develop tools—such as eyeglasses, mirrors, magnifying lenses, cameras, and lasers—that extend vision or that use light in other ways.

Mirrors, lenses, and other optical inventions are called optical tools. By combining optical tools, inventors have developed powerful instruments to extend human vision. For example, the microscope uses a combination of mirrors and lenses to make very small structures visible. Telescopes combine optical tools to extend vision far into space. As you will see, some of the latest optical technology—lasers—use visible light in ways that do not involve human vision at all.

Mirrors use regular reflection.

You have read that when light waves strike an object, they either pass through it or they bounce off its surface. Objects are made visible by light waves, or rays, bouncing off their surfaces. In section 3 you will see how the light waves create images inside the human eye.

Light rays bounce off objects in a very predictable way. For example, look at the diagram on the left below. Light rays from a flashlight strike a mirror at an angle of 60° as measured from the normal, an imaginary line perpendicular to the surface of the mirror. This angle is called the angle of incidence. The angle at which the rays reflect off the mirror, called the angle of reflection, is also 60° as measured from the normal. The example illustrates the **law of reflection,** which states that the angle of reflection equals the angle of incidence. As you can see in the second diagram, holding the flashlight at a different angle changes both the angle of incidence and the angle of reflection. However, the two angles remain equal.

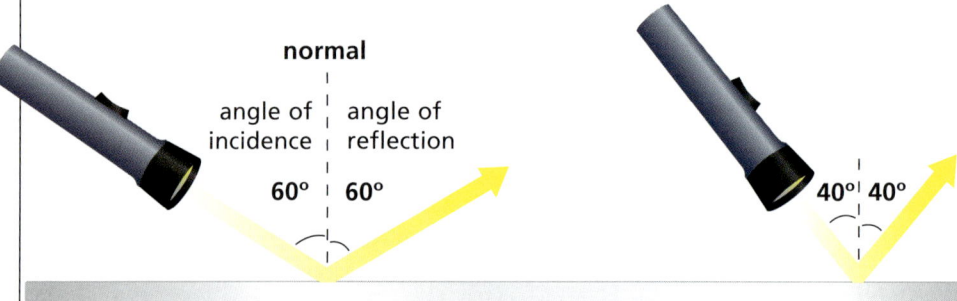

The angle of reflection equals the angle of incidence.

The light rays striking the mirror bounce back by regular reflection. Rays striking everything else bounce back by diffuse reflection.

If the surface of an object is very smooth, like a mirror, light rays that come from the same direction will bounce off in the same new direction. The reflection of parallel light rays all in the same direction is called **regular reflection.**

If the surface is not very smooth—even if it feels smooth to the touch, like a piece of paper—light rays striking it from the same direction bounce off in many new directions. Each light ray follows the law of reflection, but rays coming from the same direction bounce off different bumps and hollows of the irregular surface. The reflection of parallel light rays in many different directions is called **diffuse reflection.**

INVESTIGATE The Law of Reflection

How can you use mirrors to see around a corner?

PROCEDURE

1. To make a periscope, cut two flaps on opposite sides of the carton, one from the top and one from the bottom, as shown in the illustration.
2. Fold each flap inward until it is at a 45-degree angle to the side cuts and tape it into place.
3. Attach a mirror to the outside surface of each of the flaps.
4. Holding the periscope straight up, look through one of the openings. Observe what you can see through the other opening.

WHAT DO YOU THINK?

- Where are the objects you see when you look through the periscope?
- How does the angle of the mirrors affect the path of light through the periscope?

CHALLENGE How would it affect what you see through the periscope if you changed the angle of the mirrors from 45 degrees to 30 degrees? Try it.

SKILL FOCUS
Analyzing

MATERIALS
- paper milk or juice carton
- scissors
- tape
- 2 mirrors slightly smaller than the bottom of the carton
- protractor

TIME
30 minutes

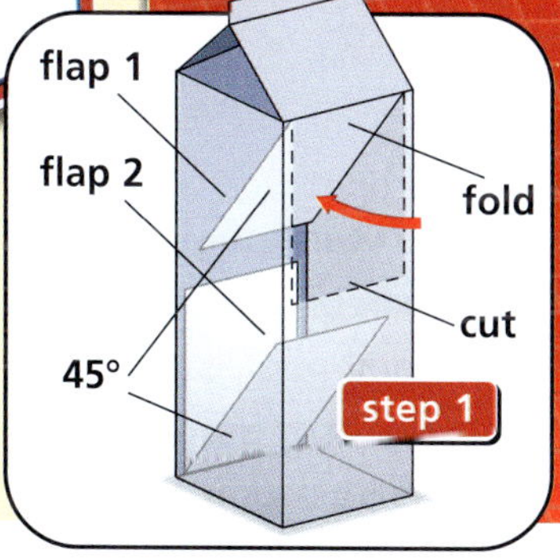

Shape determines how mirrors form images.

When you look in a mirror, you see an image of yourself. An **image** is a picture of an object formed by waves of light. The image of yourself is formed by light waves reflecting off you, onto the mirror, and back toward your eyes. Mirrors of different shapes can produce images that are distorted in certain ways.

See reflection in action.

Flat Mirrors

Your image in a flat mirror looks exactly like you. It appears to be the same size as you, and it's wearing the same clothes. However, if you raise your right hand, the image of yourself in the mirror will appear to raise its left hand. That is because you see the image as a person standing facing you. In fact, your right hand is reflected on the right side of the image, and your left on the left side.

 If you wink your left eye while looking in the mirror, which eye in the image of you will wink?

Chapter 9: **Light and Optics** 291

The solid line shows the actual path of light. The broken line shows where the light appears to be coming from.

If you look closely at your image in a mirror, you will notice that it actually appears to be on the far side of the mirror, exactly as far from the mirror as you are. This is a trick of light. The solid yellow arrows in the photograph above show the path of the light rays from the boy's elbow to the mirror and back to his eyes. The light rays reflect off the mirror. The broken line shows the apparent path of the light rays. They appear to his eyes to be coming through the mirror from a spot behind it.

Concave and Convex Mirrors

VOCABULARY
Try making sketches to help you remember the new terms on this page.

Unlike light rays hitting a flat mirror, parallel light rays reflecting off a curved mirror do not move in the same direction. A **convex** mirror is curved outward, like the bottom of a spoon. In a convex mirror, parallel light rays move away from each other, as you can see in the diagram below on the left. A **concave** mirror is curved inward toward the center, like the inside of a spoon. Parallel light rays reflecting off a concave mirror move toward each other, as shown on the right.

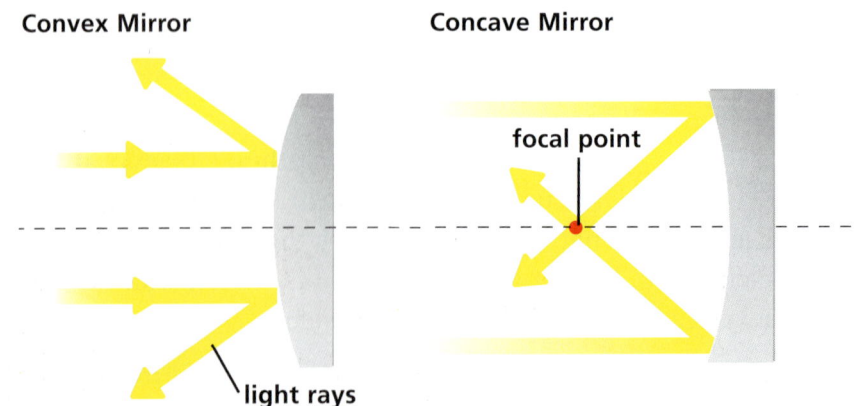

Convex Mirror

Concave Mirror

focal point

light rays

The rays striking a concave mirror cross and then move apart again. The point at which the rays meet is called the **focal point** of the mirror. The distance between the mirror and its focal point depends on the shape of the curve.

The images formed in these mirrors depend on the curve of the mirror's surface and the distance of the object from the mirror. Your image in a curved mirror may appear larger or smaller than you are, and it may even be upside down.

Convex Mirror

Your image in a convex mirror appears smaller than you.

Concave Mirror, Far Away

If you are standing far away, your image in a concave mirror appears upside down and smaller than you.

Concave Mirror, Up Close

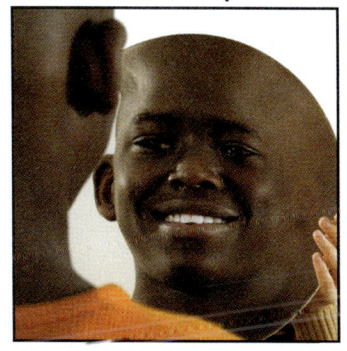

If you are standing inside the focal point, your image in a concave mirror appears right-side up and larger.

All rays parallel to a line through the center of the mirror are reflected off the mirror and pass through the mirror's focal point. Rays from the top of the object are reflected downward and those from the bottom are reflected upward.

CHECK YOUR READING How does your distance from the mirror affect the way your image appears in a concave mirror?

9.1 Review

KEY CONCEPTS

1. Explain the term *optics* in your own words.
2. How is diffuse reflection similar to regular reflection? How is it different?
3. Describe the path that light rays take when they form an image of your smile when you look into a flat mirror.

CRITICAL THINKING

4. **Infer** Imagine seeing your reflection in a polished table top. The image is blurry and hard to recognize. What can you tell about the surface of the table from your observations?
5. **Analyze** Why do images formed by concave mirrors sometimes appear upside down?

CHALLENGE

6. **Synthesize** Draw the letter *R* below as it would appear if you held the book up to (a) a flat mirror and (b) a convex mirror.

R

Chapter 9: **Light and Optics**

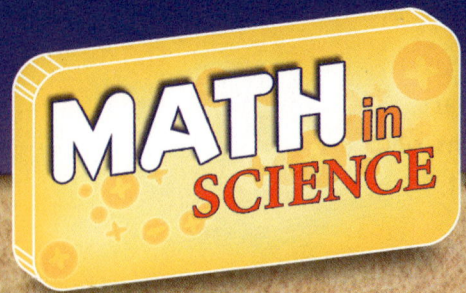

SKILL: MEASURING ANGLES

Send Help!

MATH TUTORIAL
CLASSZONE.COM
Click on Math Tutorial for more help with measuring angles.

Survival kits often contain a small mirror that can be used to signal for help. If you were lost in the desert and saw a search plane overhead, you could use the mirror to reflect sunlight toward the plane and catch the pilot's attention. To aim your signal, you would use the law of reflection. The angle at which a ray of light bounces off a mirror—the angle of reflection—is always equal to the angle at which the ray strikes the mirror—the angle of incidence.

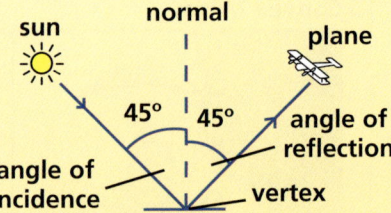

Example

Measure the angle of incidence using a protractor as follows:

(1) Place the center mark of the protractor over the vertex of the angle formed by the incident ray and the normal.

(2) Place the left 0° mark of the protractor on the incident ray.

(3) Read the number where the normal crosses the scale (35°).

(4) The angle of incidence is 35°.

ANSWER Therefore, the angle of reflection will be 35°.

Copy each of the following angles of incidence, extend its sides, and use a protractor to measure it.

1.   2.   3.   4.

CHALLENGE Copy the drawing below. Use a protractor to find the angle of reflection necessary to signal the plane from point A.

A mirror can be used to signal for help.

KEY CONCEPT

9.2 Lenses form images by refracting light.

 BEFORE, you learned

- Waves can refract when they move from one medium to another
- Refraction changes the direction of a wave

 NOW, you will learn

- How a material medium can refract light
- How lenses control refraction
- How lenses produce images

VOCABULARY

lens p. 297
focal length p. 299

EXPLORE Refraction

How does material bend light?

PROCEDURE

1. Place the pencil in the cup, as shown in the photograph. Look at the cup from the side so that you see part of the pencil through the cup.

2. Fill the cup one-third full with water and repeat your observations.

3. Gently add oil until the cup is two-thirds full. After the oil settles into a separate layer, observe.

WHAT DO YOU THINK?
- How did the appearance of the pencil change when you added the water? the oil?
- What might explain these changes?

MATERIALS
- clear plastic cup
- pencil
- water
- mineral oil

A medium can refract light.

When sunlight strikes a window, some of the light rays reflect off the surface of the glass. Other rays continue through the glass, but their direction is slightly changed. This slight change in direction is called refraction. Refraction occurs when a wave strikes a new medium—such as the window—at an angle other than 90° and keeps going forward in a slightly different direction.

Refraction occurs because one side of the wave reaches the new medium slightly before the other side does. That side changes speed, while the other continues at its previous speed, causing the wave to turn.

 How does the motion of a light wave change when it refracts?

Chapter 9: **Light and Optics** 295

Refraction of Light

COMBINATION NOTES
Sketch the ways light is refracted when it moves into a denser medium and into a thinner medium.

Recall that waves travel at different speeds in different mediums. The direction in which a light wave turns depends on whether the new medium slows the wave down or allows it to travel faster. Like reflection, refraction is described in terms of an imaginary line—called the normal—that is perpendicular to the new surface. If the medium slows the wave, the wave will turn toward the normal. If the new medium lets the wave speed up, the wave will turn away from the normal. The wave in the diagram below turns toward the normal as it slows down in the new medium.

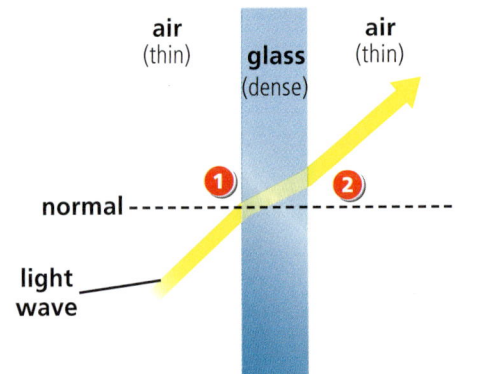

① Waves moving at an angle into a denser medium turn toward the normal.

② Waves moving at an angle into a thinner medium turn away from the normal.

Light from the Sun travels toward Earth through the near vacuum of outer space. Sunlight refracts when it reaches the new medium of Earth's upper atmosphere. Earth's upper atmosphere is relatively thin and refracts light only slightly. Denser materials, such as water and glass, refract light more.

By measuring the speed of light in different materials and comparing this speed to the speed of light in a vacuum, scientists have been able to determine exactly how different materials refract light. This knowledge has led to the ability to predict and control refraction, which is the basis of much optical technology.

READING TIP
A dense medium has more mass in a given volume than a thin medium.

Light passing through a droplet of water is refracted twice, forming a color spectrum.

Refraction and Rainbows

You've seen rainbows in the sky after a rainstorm or hovering in the spray of a sprinkler. Rainbows are caused by refraction and reflection of light through spherical water drops, which act as prisms. Just as a prism separates the colors of white light, producing the color spectrum, each water drop separates the wavelengths of sunlight to produce a spectrum. Only one color reaches your eye from each drop. Red appears at the top of a rainbow because it is coming from higher drops, while violet comes from lower drops.

296 Unit 2: **Waves, Sound, and Light**

Shape determines how lenses form images.

When you look at yourself in a flat mirror, you see your image clearly, without distortions. Similarly, when you look through a plain glass window, you can see what is on the other side clearly. Just as curved mirrors distort images, certain transparent mediums called lenses alter what you see through them. A **lens** is a clear optical tool that refracts light. Different lenses refract light in different ways and form images useful for a variety of purposes.

READING TIP
Distort means to change the shape of something by twisting or moving the parts around.

Convex and Concave Lenses

Like mirrors, lenses can be convex or concave. A convex lens is curved outward; a concave lens is curved inward. A lens typically has two sides that are curved, as shown in the illustration below.

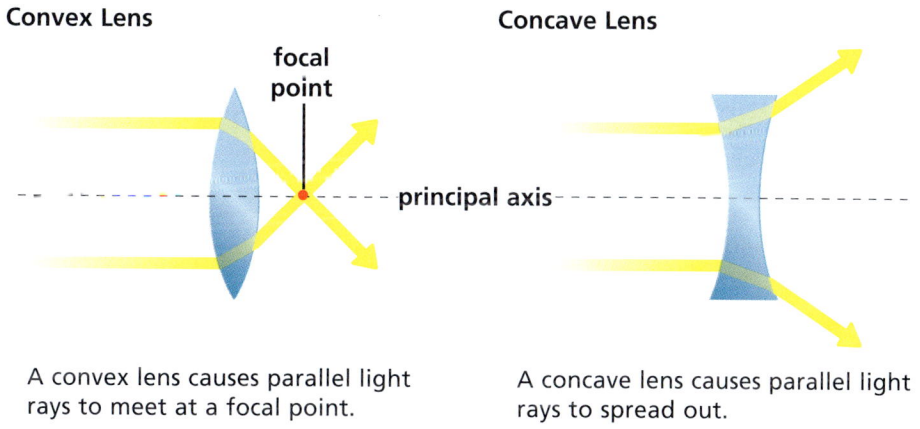

A convex lens causes parallel light rays to meet at a focal point.

A concave lens causes parallel light rays to spread out.

Convex Parallel light rays passing through a convex lens are refracted inward. They meet at a focal point on the other side of the lens. The rays are actually refracted twice—once upon entering the lens and once upon leaving it. This is because both times they are entering a new medium at an angle other than 90 degrees. Rays closest to the edges of the lens are refracted most. Rays passing through the center of the lens—along the principal axis, which connects the centers of the two curved surfaces—are not refracted at all. They pass through to the same focal point as all rays parallel to them.

REMINDER
The focal point is the point at which parallel light rays meet after being reflected or refracted.

Concave Parallel light rays that pass through a concave lens are refracted outward. As with a convex lens, the rays are refracted twice. Rays closest to the edges of the lens are refracted most; rays at the very center of the lens pass straight through without being deflected. Because they are refracted away from each other, parallel light rays passing through a concave lens do not meet.

CHECK YOUR READING Compare what happens to parallel light rays striking a concave mirror with those striking a concave lens.

Chapter 9: **Light and Optics** 297

How a Convex Lens Forms an Image

A convex lens forms an image by refracting light rays. Light rays reflected from an object are refracted when they enter the lens and again when they leave the lens. They meet to form the image.

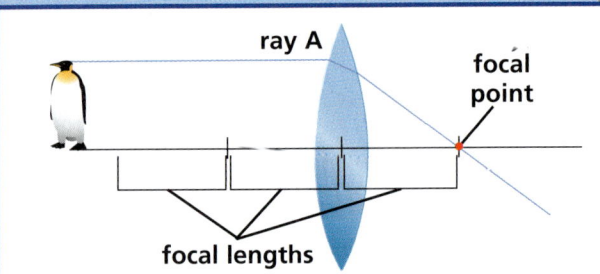

① Light rays reflect off the penguin in all directions, and many enter the lens. Here a single ray (A) from the top of the penguin enters the lens and is refracted downward.

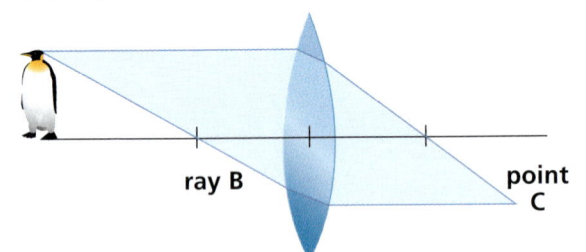

② Another light ray (B) from the top of the penguin passes through the lens at the bottom and meets the first ray at point C. All of the rays from the top of the penguin passing through the lens meet at this point.

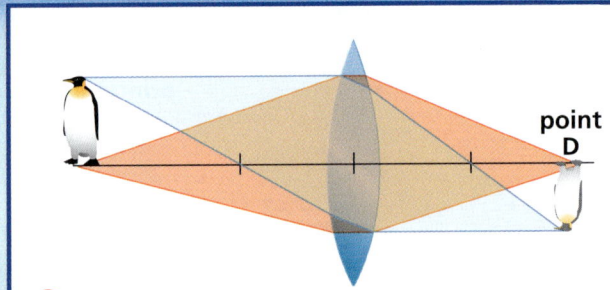

③ All of the light rays from the bottom of the penguin meet at a different point (D). Light rays from all parts of the penguin meet at corresponding points on the image.

READING VISUALS Where do light rays reflected from the middle of the penguin meet?

Images Formed by Lenses

When light rays from an object pass through a lens, an image of the object is formed. The type of image depends on the lens and, for convex lenses, on the distance between the lens and the object.

Work with convex and concave lenses to form images.

Notice the distance between the penguin and the lens in the illustration on page 298. The distance is measured in terms of a **focal length,** which is the distance from the center of the lens to the lens's focal point. The penguin is more than two focal lengths from the camera lens, which means the image formed is upside down and smaller.

If the penguin were between one and two focal lengths away from a convex lens, the image formed would be upside down and larger. Overhead projectors form this type of image, which is then turned right side up by a mirror and projected onto a screen for viewing.

Finally, if an object is less than one focal length from a convex lens, it will appear right side up and larger. In order to enlarge an object so that you can see details, you hold a magnifying lens close to the object. In the photograph, you see a face enlarged by a magnifying lens. The boy's face is less than one focal length from the lens.

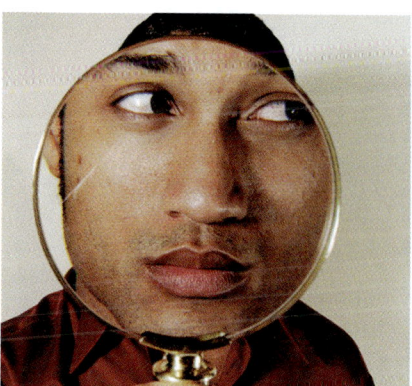

If you look at an object through a concave lens, you'll see an image of the object that is right side up and smaller than the object normally appears. In the case of concave lenses, the distance between the object and the lens does not make a difference in the type of image that is formed. In the next section you'll see how the characteristics of the images formed by different lenses play a role in complex optical tools.

 When will an image formed by a convex lens be upside down?

9.2 Review

KEY CONCEPTS

1. What quality of a material affects how much it refracts light?
2. How does the curve in a lens cause it to refract light differently from a flat piece of glass?
3. How does a camera lens form an image?

CRITICAL THINKING

4. **Infer** You look through a lens and see an image of a building upside down. What type of lens are you looking through?
5. **Make a Model** Draw the path of a light ray moving at an angle from air into water. Write a caption to explain the process.

CHALLENGE

6. Study the diagram on the opposite page. Describe the light rays that would pass through the labeled focal point. Where are they coming from, and how are they related to each other?

CHAPTER INVESTIGATION

Looking at Lenses

OVERVIEW AND PURPOSE Optical tools such as microscopes, telescopes, and eyeglasses use lenses to create images of objects. In this lab, you will use what you have learned about light and lenses to
- experiment with a convex lens to focus images of objects
- determine what makes it possible to focus images of objects.

▶ Procedure

PART A

1. Make a data table like the one shown on the sample notebook page.

2. Draw a stick figure on one index card. Assemble the cards, clay, and lens as shown in the photograph.

3. Position the convex lens so that you can see an enlarged, right-side up image of the stick figure. Measure the distances between the lens and the card, and between the lens and your eye. Record the distances in your data table.

4. Position the lens so that you can see an enlarged, upside down image of the stick figure. Measure the distances between the lens and the object, and between the lens and your eye. Record the distances in your data table.

5. Position the lens so that you can see a reduced, upside down image of the stick figure. Measure the distances between the lens and the object, and between the lens and your eye. Record the distances in your data table.

MATERIALS
- index cards
- marker
- modeling clay
- convex lens
- books
- meter stick
- flashlight
- masking tape
- white poster board

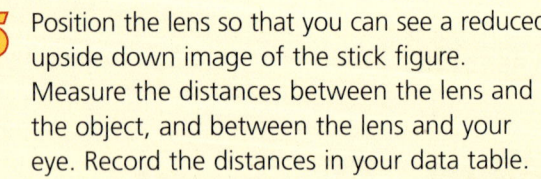

300 Unit 2: **Waves, Sound, and Light**

PART B

6. Put an arrow made of tape on the lens of the flashlight as shown.

7. Assemble poster board and clay to make a screen. Arrange the flashlight, lens, and screen as shown below right.

8. Shine the beam from the flashlight through the lens to form an enlarged, upside down image on the screen. Measure the distances between the lens and the flashlight and between the lens and the screen.

9. Position the light and screen to produce a reduced, upside down image. Measure the distances between the lens and the flashlight and between the lens and the screen.

10. Position the light and screen to produce an enlarged right-side up image.

Observe and Analyze — Write It Up

1. **RECORD OBSERVATIONS** Draw pictures of each setup in steps 3–9 to show what happened. Be sure your data table is complete.

2. **ANALYZE** What was the distance from the lens to the object in step 3? Answer this question for each of the other steps. How do the distances compare?

3. **ANALYZE** What happened when you tried to form the three types of images on the screen? How can you explain these results?

Conclude — Write It Up

1. **ANALYZE** What conclusions can you draw about the relationship between the distances you measured and the type of image that was produced?

2. **IDENTIFY LIMITS** Describe possible sources of error in your procedure or any places where errors might have occurred.

3. **APPLY** What kind of lenses are magnifying glasses? When a magnifying glass produces a sharp clear image, where is the object located in relation to the lens?

step 7

INVESTIGATE Further

CHALLENGE If you were to repeat steps 8 and 9 with a concave lens, you would not be able to focus an image on the screen. Why not?

Looking at Lenses
Observe and Analyze
Table 1. Distances from Lens

Image	Object	Eye
Object enlarged and right-side up		
Object enlarged and upside down		
Object reduced and upside down		
	Flashlight	Screen
Object enlarged and right-side up		
Object enlarged and upside down		
Object reduced and upside down		

Conclude

Chapter 9: **Light and Optics** 301

KEY CONCEPT

The eye is a natural optical tool.

BEFORE, you learned
- Mirrors and lenses focus light to form images
- Mirrors and lenses can alter images in useful ways

NOW, you will learn
- How the eye depends on natural lenses
- How artificial lenses can be used to correct vision problems

VOCABULARY

cornea p. 303
pupil p. 303
retina p. 303

EXPLORE Focusing Vision

How does the eye focus an image?

PROCEDURE

1. Position yourself so you can see an object about 6 meters (20 feet) away.
2. Close one eye, hold up your index finger, and bring it as close to your open eye as you can while keeping the finger clearly in focus.
3. Keeping your finger in place, look just to the side at the more distant object and focus your eye on it.
4. Without looking away from the more distant object, observe your finger.

WHAT DO YOU THINK?
- How does the nearby object look when you are focusing on something distant?
- What might be happening in your eye to cause this change in the nearby object?

The eye gathers and focuses light.

The eyes of human beings and many other animals are natural optical tools that process visible light. Eyes transmit light, refract light, and respond to different wavelengths of light. Eyes contain natural lenses that focus images of objects. Eyes convert the energy of light waves into signals that can be sent to the brain. The brain interprets these signals as shape, brightness, and color. Altogether, these processes make vision possible.

In this section, you will learn how the eye works. You will also learn how artificial lenses can be used to improve vision.

How Light Travels Through the Human Eye

❶ Light enters the eye through the **cornea** (KAWR-nee-uh), a transparent membrane that covers the eye. The cornea acts as a convex lens and does most of the refracting in the eye.

❷ The light then continues through the **pupil,** a circular opening that controls how much light enters the eye. The pupil is surrounded by the iris, which opens and closes to change the size of the pupil.

❸ Next the light passes through the part of the eye called the lens. The lens is convex on both sides. It refracts light to make fine adjustments for near and far objects. Unlike the cornea, the lens is attached to tiny muscles that contract and relax to control the amount of refraction that occurs and to move the focal point.

❹ The light passes through the clear center of the eye and strikes the **retina** (REHT-uhn-uh). The retina contains specialized cells that respond to light. Some of these cells send signals through the optic nerve to the brain. The brain interprets these signals as images.

READING TIP
The word *lens* can refer both to an artificial optical tool and to a specific part of the eye.

How the Human Eye Forms an Image

The cornea and lens together focus a reduced, inverted image on the retina.

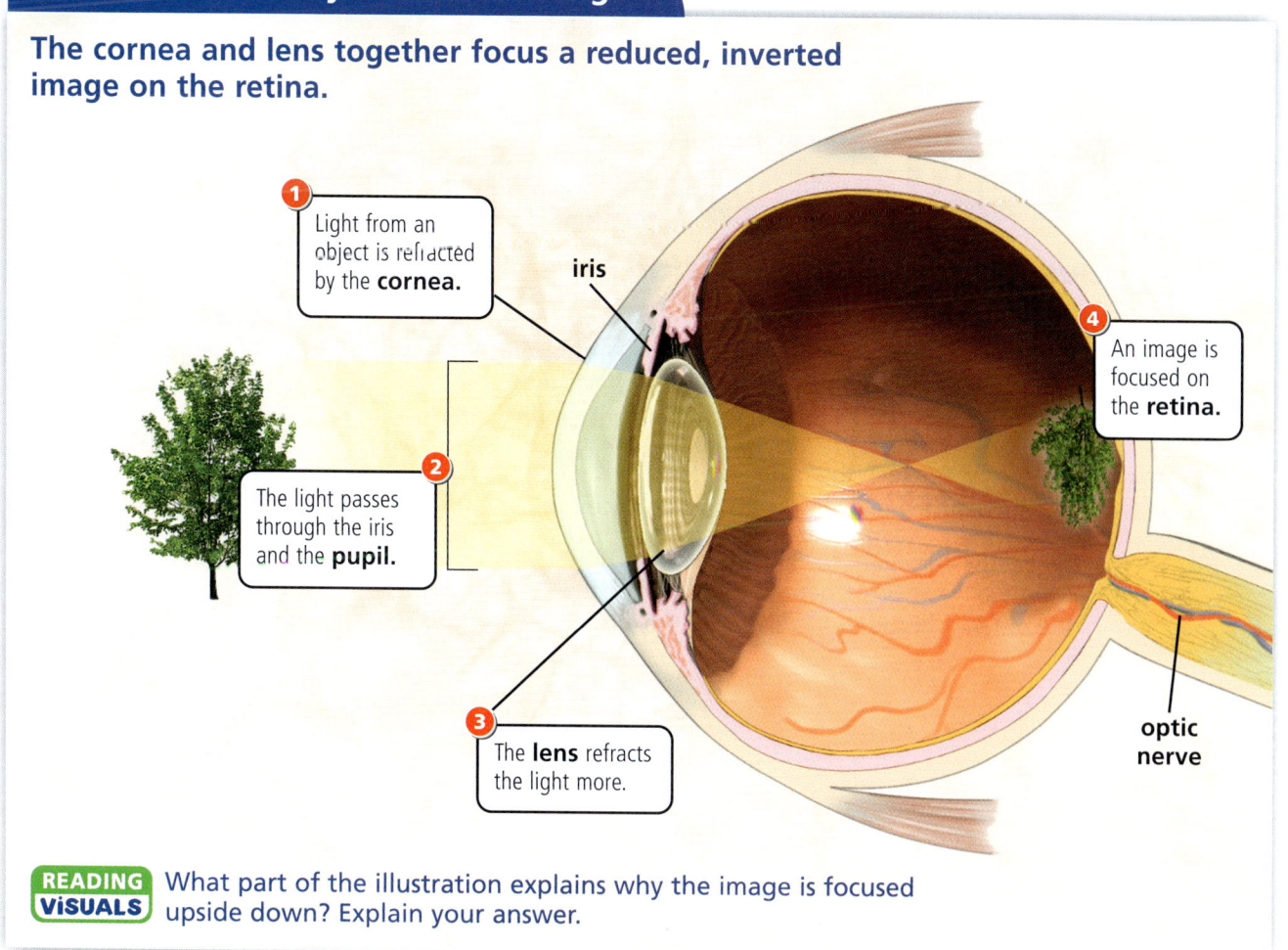

❶ Light from an object is refracted by the **cornea.**

❷ The light passes through the iris and the **pupil.**

❸ The **lens** refracts the light more.

❹ An image is focused on the **retina.**

READING VISUALS What part of the illustration explains why the image is focused upside down? Explain your answer.

Chapter 9: **Light and Optics** 303

How the Eye Forms Images

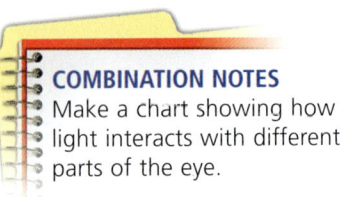

COMBINATION NOTES
Make a chart showing how light interacts with different parts of the eye.

For you to see an object clearly, your eye must focus an image of the object on your retina. The light reflected from each particular spot on the object must converge on a matching point on your retina. Many such points make up an image of an entire object. Because the light rays pass through the lens's focal point, the image is upside down. The brain interprets this upside down image as an object that is right-side up.

For a complete image to be formed in the eye and communicated to the brain, more than the lens and the cornea are needed. The retina also plays an important role. The retina contains specialized cells that detect brightness and color and other qualities of light.

Rod Cells Rod cells distinguish between white and black and shades of gray. Rods respond to faint light, so they help with night vision.

Cone Cells Cone cells respond to different wavelengths of light, so they detect color. There are three types of cones, one for each of the colors red, blue, and green. Cones respond to other colors with combinations of these three, as the screen of a color monitor does. The brain interprets these combinations as the entire color spectrum.

 **CHECK YOUR READING** Which type of cell in the retina detects color?

INVESTIGATE Vision

How does distance affect vision?

PROCEDURE

1. Arrange the materials as shown so that the lamp shines through the lens onto the plate. The lens should be about $\frac{2}{3}$ a meter from the lamp.

2. Adjust the distance between the plate and the lens until you see a focused image of the bulb on the plate. Measure this distance.

3. Move the lens until it is about a meter and a half from the lamp. Adjust the plate once again to get a focused image, then measure the distance between the plate and the lens.

WHAT DO YOU THINK?
- How does the distance needed between the plate and the lens change when the lamp is farther from the lens?
- How is what happens in the eye different from what you did to refocus the image?

CHALLENGE How could you change the model to make it more like what happens in the eye?

SKILL FOCUS
Observing

MATERIALS
- convex lens
- index card
- modeling clay
- white paper plate
- lamp

TIME
10 minutes

Corrective lenses can improve vision.

What happens when the image formed by the lens of the eye does not fall exactly on the retina? The result is that the image appears blurry. This can occur either because of the shape of the eye or because of how the lens works. Artificial lenses can be used to correct this problem.

Corrective Lenses

A person who is nearsighted cannot see objects clearly unless they are near. Nearsightedness occurs when the lens of the eye focuses the image in front of the retina. The farther away the object is, the farther in front of the retina the image forms. This problem can be corrected with glasses made with concave lenses. The concave lenses spread out the rays of light before they enter the eye. The point at which the rays meet then falls on the retina.

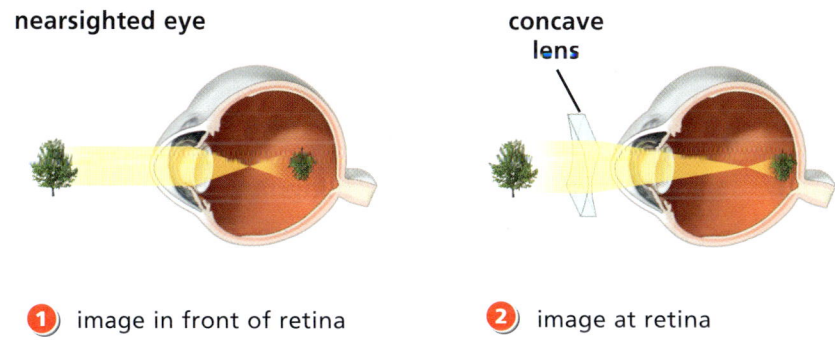

1 image in front of retina   **2** image at retina

Objects are clearer to a farsighted person when the objects are farther away. Farsightedness occurs when the lens of the eye focuses an object's image behind the retina. This condition can result from aging, which may make the lens less flexible. The closer the object is, the farther behind the retina the image forms. Farsightedness can be corrected with glasses made from convex lenses. The convex lenses bend the light rays inward before they enter the eye. The point at which the rays meet then falls on the retina.

READING TIP

Nearsighted people can see objects near to them best. *Farsighted* people can see objects better when the objects are farther away.

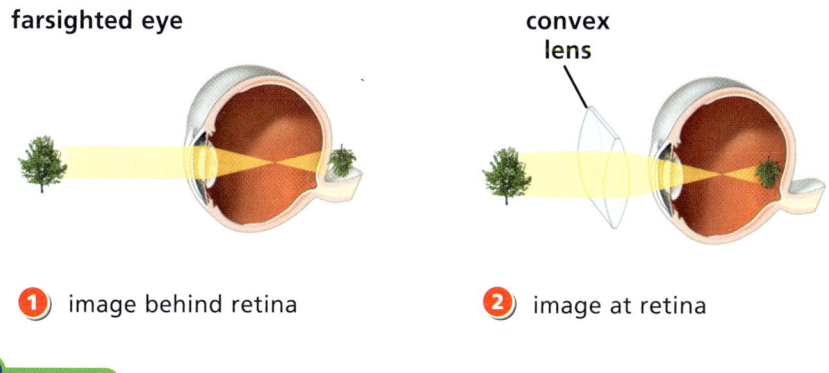

1 image behind retina   **2** image at retina

CHECK YOUR READING What kind of lens is used for correcting nearsightedness?

Chapter 9: **Light and Optics** 305

Surgery and Contact Lenses

Wearing glasses is an effective way to correct vision. It is also possible to change the shape of the cornea to make the eye refract properly. The cornea is responsible for two-thirds of the refraction that takes place inside the eye. As you know, the eye's lens changes shape to focus an image, but the shape of the cornea does not ordinarily change.

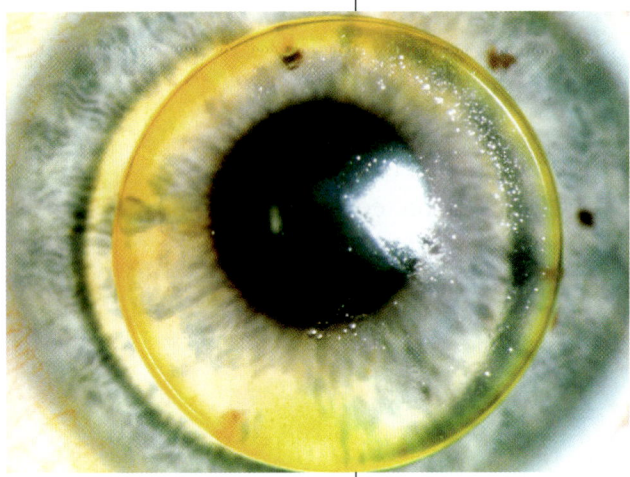

Contact lenses fit directly onto the cornea, changing the way light is refracted as it enters a person's eye.

However, using advanced surgical technology, doctors can change the shape of the cornea. By doing this, they change the way light rays focus in the eye so that the image lines up with the retina. To correct for nearsightedness, surgeons remove tissue from the center of the cornea. This flattens the cornea and makes it less convex so that it will refract less. To correct for farsightedness, surgeons remove tissue from around the edges of the cornea. This increases the cornea's curvature to make it refract more. Surgery changes the shape of the cornea permanently and can eliminate the need for eyeglasses.

Contact lenses also correct vision by changing the way the cornea refracts light. Contact lenses are corrective lenses that fit directly onto the cornea. The lenses actually float on a thin layer of tears. The moisture, the contact lens, and the cornea all function together. The lens of the eye then focuses the light further. Because the change is temporary, contacts, like eyeglasses, can be adapted to new changes in the eye.

 **CHECK YOUR READING** What are two ways of changing the way the cornea refracts light to correct vision?

9.3 Review

KEY CONCEPTS

1. Where are images focused in an eye with perfect vision?
2. What causes people with nearsightedness to see blurry images of objects at a distance?
3. What kind of lens is used for correcting farsightedness? Why?

CRITICAL THINKING

4. **Make a Model** Draw a diagram to answer the following question: How does a convex lens affect the way a nearsighted eye focuses an image?
5. **Analyze** What distance would an eye doctor need to measure to correct a problem with nearsightedness or farsightedness?

CHALLENGE

6. **Apply** A person alternates between wearing glasses and wearing contact lenses to correct farsightedness. Are the contact lenses more or less convex than the lenses of the glasses? Explain the reasoning behind your response.

KEY CONCEPT

9.4 Optical technology makes use of light waves.

◀ BEFORE, you learned

- Mirrors are optical tools that use reflection
- Lenses are optical tools that use refraction
- The eye is a natural optical tool
- Lenses can correct vision

▶ NOW, you will learn

- How mirrors and lenses can be combined to make complex optical tools
- How optical tools are used to extend natural vision
- How laser light is made and used in optical technology

VOCABULARY

laser p. 311
fiber optics p. 313

EXPLORE Combining Lenses

How can lenses be combined?

PROCEDURE

1. Assemble the lenses, clay, and index cards as shown in the photograph.

2. Line the lenses up so that you have a straight line of sight through them.

3. Experiment with different distances between
   - the lenses
   - the far lens and an object
   - the near lens and your eye
   Find an arrangement that allows you to see a clear image of an object through both lenses.

MATERIALS
- 2 convex lenses
- modeling clay
- 2 index cards

WHAT DO YOU THINK?
- What kind of image could you see? What arrangement or arrangements work best to produce an image?
- How do you think the lenses are working together to focus the image?

Mirrors and lenses can be combined to make more powerful optical tools.

COMBINATION NOTES
As you read this section, make a list of optical tools. Add sketches to help you remember important concepts.

If you know about submarines, then you know how much they depend on their periscopes to see above the water. Periscopes are made by combining mirrors. Lenses can also be combined. In the eye, for example, the cornea and the eye's lens work together to focus an image. Mirrors and lenses can be combined with each other, as they are in an overhead projector. Many of the most powerful and complex optical tools are based on different combinations of mirrors and lenses.

Chapter 9: **Light and Optics** 307

Microscopes

Microscopes are used to see objects that are too small to see well with the naked eye. An ordinary microscope works by combining convex lenses. The lens closer to the object is called the objective. The object is between one and two focal lengths from this lens, so the lens focuses an enlarged image of the object inside the microscope.

The other microscope lens—the one you look through—is called the eyepiece. You use this lens to look at the image formed by the objective. Like a magnifying glass, the eyepiece lens forms an enlarged image of the first image.

Very small objects do not reflect much light. Most microscopes use a lamp or a mirror to shine more light on the object.

 Which types of images do the lenses in a microscope form?

Telescopes

Telescopes are used to see objects that are too far away to see well with the naked eye. One type of telescope, called a refracting telescope, is made by combining lenses. Another type of telescope, called a reflecting telescope, is made by combining lenses and mirrors.

Find out more about microscopes and telescopes.

Refracting telescopes combine convex lenses, just as microscopes do. However, the objects are far away from the objective lens instead of near to it. The object is more than two focal lengths from the objective lens, so the lens focuses a reduced image of the object inside the telescope. The eyepiece of a telescope then forms an enlarged image of the first image, just as a microscope does. This second image enlarges the object.

Reflecting telescopes work in the same way that refracting telescopes do. However, there is no objective lens where light enters the telescope. Instead, a concave mirror at the opposite end focuses an image of the object. A small flat mirror redirects the image to the side of the telescope. With this arrangement, the eyepiece does not interfere with light on its way to the concave mirror. The eyepiece then forms an enlarged image of the first image.

Both refracting and reflecting telescopes must adjust for the small amount of light received from distant objects. The amount of light gathered can be increased by increasing the diameter of the objective lens or mirror. Large mirrors are easier and less expensive to make than large lenses. So reflecting telescopes can produce brighter images more cheaply than refracting telescopes.

 How is a reflecting telescope different from a refracting telescope?

Microscopes and Telescopes

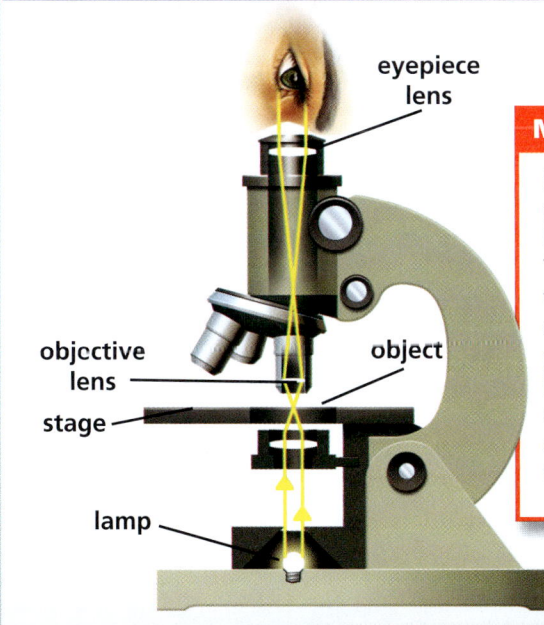

Microscope

Light from an object passes through a convex lens called an objective. The objective lens focuses the light to form an enlarged image. The eyepiece lens enlarges the image even more. The one-celled algae at right, called diatoms, appear 400 times their normal size.

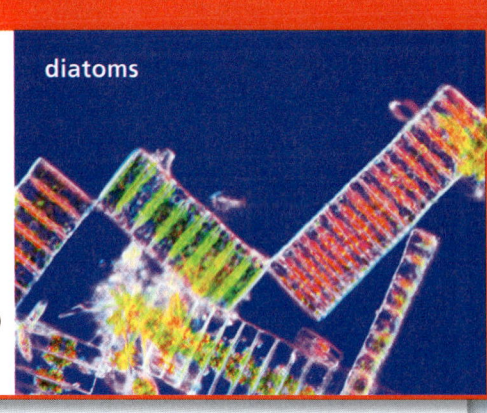
diatoms

Refracting Telescope

The objective lens gathers and focuses light from a distant object to form an image of the object. The eyepiece enlarges the image. The telescope image of the Moon at left shows fine details of the lunar surface.

surface of the Moon

Reflecting Telescope

A concave mirror gathers light through a wide opening and focuses it to form an image of the object. The eyepiece lens enlarges the image. The flat mirror redirects the light so that the eyepiece can be out of the way. The telescope image of Saturn at right shows details of the planet's rings.

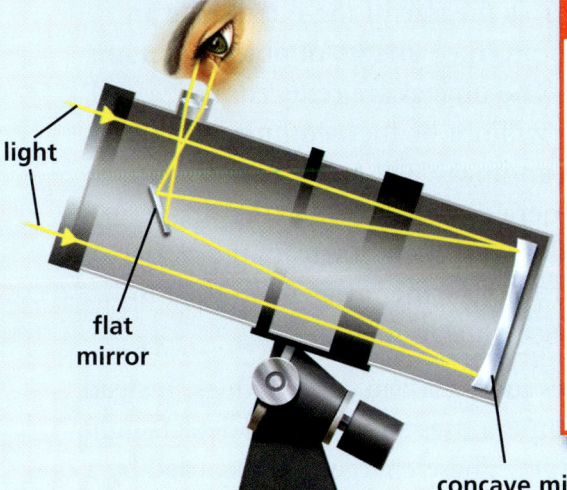

the planet Saturn

READING VISUALS Which type of telescope is similar in construction to a microscope?

Chapter 9: **Light and Optics** 309

INVESTIGATE Optical Tools

How can you make a simple telescope?

Use what you have learned about how a telescope works to build one. Figure out how far apart the two lenses need to be and use that information to construct a working model.

SKILL FOCUS
Making models

MATERIALS
- 2 convex lenses
- 2 cardboard tubes
- duct tape

TIME
30 minutes

PROCEDURE

1. Decide how the lenses should be positioned in relation to an object you select to view.
2. Adjust the lenses until you get a clear image.
3. Use the other materials to fix the lenses into place and to make it possible to adjust the distance between them.

WHAT DO YOU THINK?

- How did you end up positioning the lenses in relation to the object?
- Did your telescope work? Why do you think you got this result?

CHALLENGE Is your telescope image upside down or right-side up? How can you explain this observation?

Cameras

Most film cameras focus images in the same way that the eye does. The iris of a camera controls the size of the aperture, an opening for light, just as the iris of an eye controls the size of the pupil. Like an eye, a camera uses a convex lens to produce images of objects that are more than two focal lengths away. The images are reduced in size and upside down. In the eye, an image will not be focused unless it falls exactly on the retina. In a camera, an image will not be focused unless it falls exactly on the film. The camera does not change the shape of its lens as the eye does to change the focal point. Instead, the camera allows you to move the lens nearer to or farther away from the film until the object you want to photograph is in focus.

A digital camera focuses images just as a film camera does. Instead of using film, though, the digital camera uses a sensor that detects light and converts it into electrical charges. These charges are recorded by a small computer inside the camera. The computer can then reconstruct the image immediately on the camera's display screen.

READING TIP
The term *digital* is often used to describe technology involving computers. Computers process information digitally, that is, using numbers.

How Cameras Work

A camera focuses an image in the same way as an eye.

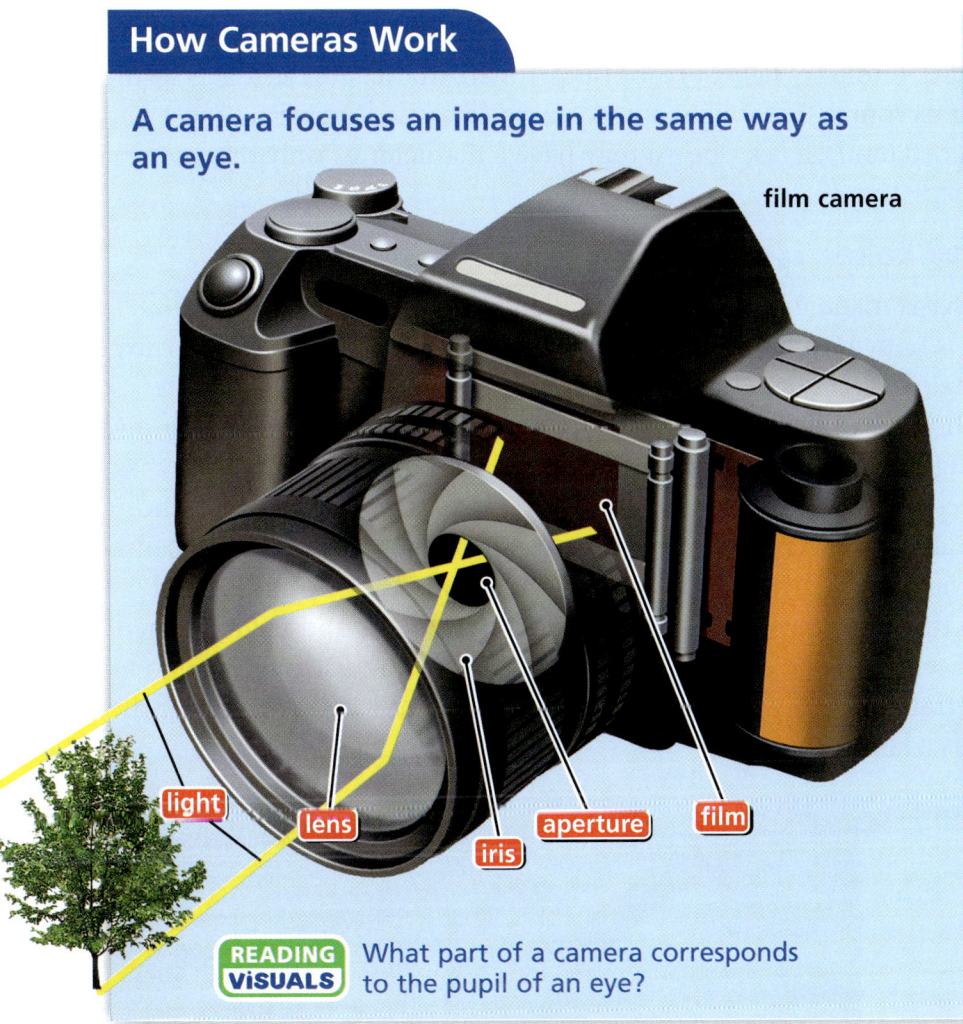

Eye and Camera

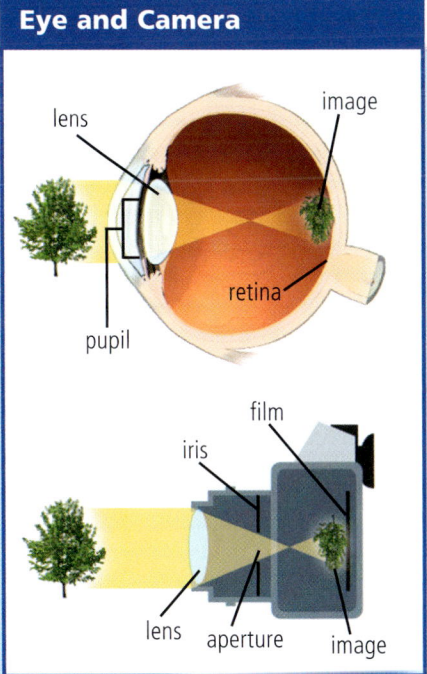

Digital Camera

A **digital camera** records images digitally, that is, using a computer.

READING VISUALS What part of a camera corresponds to the pupil of an eye?

Lasers use light in new ways.

A **laser** (LAY-zuhr) is a device that produces an intense, concentrated beam of light that is brighter than sunlight. The word *laser* means "light amplification by stimulated emission of radiation." Laser light has many uses. It carries a lot of energy and can be controlled precisely.

Ordinary visible light is made up of many different wavelengths. Even colored light usually contains many different wavelengths. But a laser beam is made up of light waves with a single wavelength and a pure color. In addition, the waves are in phase, which means the peaks are lined up so they match exactly.

▼ **REMINDER**

The peak of a wave is where it has the greatest energy.

Visible light waves of different wavelengths

Light waves of a single wavelength

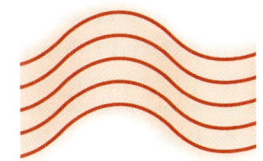
Single wavelength waves in phase

Chapter 9: **Light and Optics** 311

Light waves in a laser beam are highly concentrated and exactly parallel. Ordinary light spreads out, growing more faint as it gets farther from its source. Laser light spreads out very little. After traveling 1 kilometer (0.6 mi), a laser beam may have a diameter of only one meter.

Making Laser Light

A laser is made in a special tube called an optical cavity. A material that is known to give off a certain wavelength of light, such as a ruby crystal, is placed inside the tube. Next, an energy source, such as a bright flash of light, stimulates the material, causing it to emit, or give off, light waves. Both ends of the crystal are mirrored so that they reflect light back and forth between them. One end is mirrored more than the other. As the light waves pass through the crystal, they cause the material to give off more light waves—all perfectly parallel, all with the same wavelength, and all with their crests and troughs lined up. Eventually the beam becomes concentrated and strong enough to penetrate the less-mirrored end of the crystal. What comes out of the end is a laser beam.

RESOURCE CENTER
CLASSZONE.COM
Learn more about lasers.

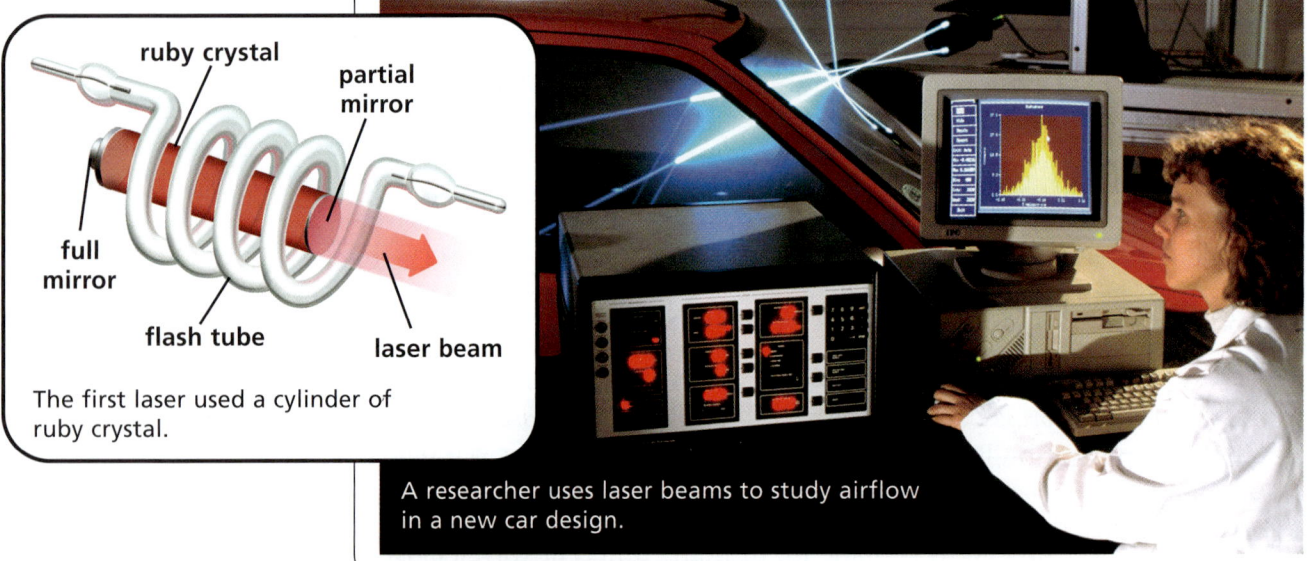

The first laser used a cylinder of ruby crystal.

A researcher uses laser beams to study airflow in a new car design.

Visual Uses of Lasers

Lasers are used today in an amazing variety of ways. One of these ways is to create devices that do the kind of work the human eye does—detecting and interpreting light waves. For example, surveyors once used telescopes to measure distances and angles. Now lasers can be used to take these measurements more precisely. Lasers are used to read bar codes, to scan images and pages of text, and to create holograms—three-dimensional images that appear to hover in the air. Holograms, which are hard to reproduce, are sometimes used in important documents so that the documents cannot be duplicated.

Fiber Optics

Some laser applications use visible light in ways that have nothing to do with vision. One of the fastest growing technologies is fiber optics. **Fiber optics** is technology based on the use of laser light to send signals through transparent wires called optical fibers. Fiber optics makes use of a light behavior called total internal reflection. Total internal reflection occurs when all of the light inside a medium reflects off the inner surface of the medium.

When light strikes the inner surface of a transparent medium, it may pass through the surface or it may be reflected back into the medium. Which one occurs depends on the angle at which the light hits the surface. For example, if you look through the sides of an aquarium, you can see what is behind it. But if you look at the surface of the water from below, it will act like a mirror, reflecting the inside of the aquarium.

Laser light is very efficient at total internal reflection. It can travel long distances inside clear fibers of glass or other materials. Light always travels in a straight line; however, by reflecting off the sides of the fibers, laser light inside fibers can go around corners and even completely reverse direction.

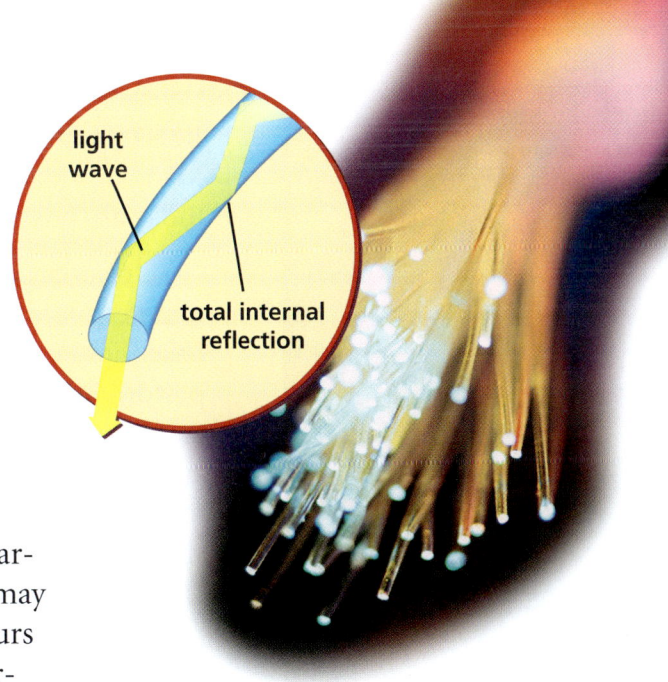

optical fibers

 What is total internal reflection? What questions do you have about this light behavior?

Fiber optics is important in communications, because it can be used to transmit information very efficiently. Optical fibers can carry more signals than a corresponding amount of electrical cable. Optical cables can be used in place of electrical wires for telephone lines, cable television, and broadband Internet connections.

Fiber optics also has visual uses. For example, fiber optics is used in medicine to look inside the body. Using optical cable, doctors can examine organs and diagnose illnesses without surgery or x-rays. Optical fibers can also deliver laser light to specific points inside the body to help surgeons with delicate surgery.

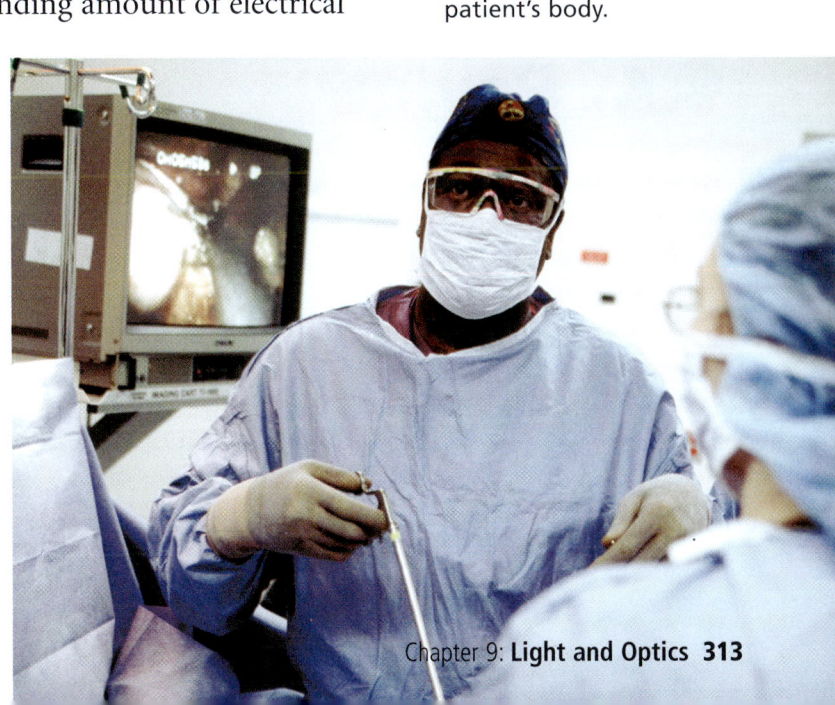

This surgeon uses fiber optics to see inside a patient's body.

Chapter 9: **Light and Optics** 313

In this artist's illustration, a space elevator of the future draws power from a laser beam to climb to an orbiting space station.

Future Uses of Lasers

Research involving new uses of lasers continues at an amazing pace. Many new discoveries and developments in science and technology today are possible only because of lasers.

One area of research in which lasers have made a big impact is nanotechnology—the development of super-tiny machines and tools. Laser light can be controlled very precisely, so scientists can use it to perform extremely fine operations. For example, lasers could be used to cut out parts to make molecule-size motors. Lasers can also be used as "optical tweezers" to handle extremely small objects such as molecules. Scientists are even beginning to use lasers to change the shape of molecules. They do this by varying the laser's wavelength.

Future applications of lasers are also sure to involve new ways of transferring energy. Remember that a wave is a disturbance that transfers energy. Laser light is made up of EM waves. EM waves can move energy over great distances without losing any of it. When EM waves encounter a material medium, their energy can then be converted into other forms and put to use.

One possible future use of lasers is to supply energy to spacecraft. Scientists imagine a day when orbiting space stations will make rockets unnecessary. A cable between the ground and the station will make it possible for a "space elevator" to escape Earth's gravity by climbing up the cable. The elevator will be powered by an Earth-based laser. A device on board the elevator will convert the laser's energy into electrical power.

9.4 Review

KEY CONCEPTS

1. How do refracting and reflecting telescopes use convex lenses and mirrors?
2. What is different about the way a camera focuses images from the way an eye focuses images?
3. How is laser light different from ordinary light?

CRITICAL THINKING

4. **Predict** What would happen to laser light if it passed through a prism?
5. **Analyze** What are two ways reflection is involved in fiber optics?

CHALLENGE

6. **Apply** How could the speed of light and a laser beam be used to measure the distance between two satellites?

SCIENCE on the JOB

PHOTOGRAPHER

Optics in Photography

Photographers use the science of optics to help them make the best photographs possible. For example, a portrait photographer chooses the right equipment and lighting to make each person look his or her best. A photographer needs to understand how light reflects, refracts, and diffuses to achieve just the right effect.

Using Reflection

A gold-colored reflector reflects only gold-colored wavelengths of light onto the subject. Photographers use these to fill in shadows and add warmth.

without gold reflector

with gold reflector

Using Diffusion

When light is directed toward a curved reflective surface, the light scatters in many directions. This diffused light produces a softer appearance than direct light.

direct light   **diffused light**

Using Refraction

Lenses refract light in different ways. A long lens makes the subject appear closer. A wide-angle lens includes more space around the subject.

long lens

wide-angle lens

EXPLORE

1. **COMPARE** Find photos of people and compare them to the photos above. Which would have been improved by the use of a gold reflector? a long lens? diffused light?

2. **CHALLENGE** Using a disposable camera and a desk lamp, experiment with photography yourself. Try using a piece of paper as a reflector and observe its effects on the photograph. What happens if you use more than one reflector? What happens if you use a different color of paper?

Chapter 9: **Light and Optics** 315

Chapter Review

the BIG idea

Optical tools depend on the wave behavior of light.

CONTENT REVIEW
CLASSZONE.COM

KEY CONCEPTS SUMMARY

1 Mirrors form images by reflecting light.

flat mirror

- Light rays obey the law of reflection.
- Mirrors work by regular reflection.
- Curved mirrors can form images that are distorted in useful ways.

VOCABULARY
optics p. 289
law of reflection p. 290
regular reflection p. 290
diffuse reflection p. 290
image p. 291
convex p. 292
concave p. 292
focal point p. 293

2 Lenses form images by refracting light.

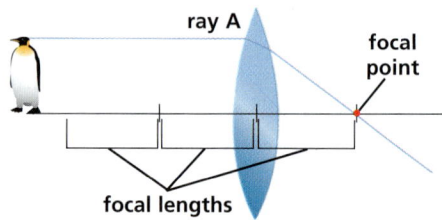
ray A, focal point, focal lengths

- Lenses have curved surfaces that refract parallel light waves in different amounts.
- Convex lenses bend light inward toward a focal point.
- Concave lenses spread light out.
- Lenses form a variety of useful images.

VOCABULARY
lens p. 297
focal length p. 299

3 The eye is a natural optical tool.

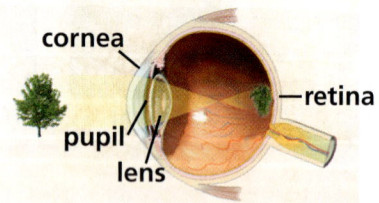
cornea, pupil, lens, retina

- The eyes of humans and many animals use lenses to focus images on the retina.
- The retina detects images and sends information about them to the brain.

VOCABULARY
cornea p. 303
pupil p. 303
retina p. 303

4 Optical technology makes use of light waves.

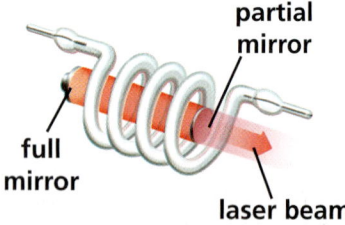
full mirror, partial mirror, laser beam

- Many optical tools are made by combining mirrors and lenses.
- Examples of optical tools include telescopes, microscopes, cameras, and lasers.
- Lasers have a wide variety of uses.

VOCABULARY
laser p. 311
fiber optics p. 313

Reviewing Vocabulary

For each item below, fill in the blank. If the right column is blank, give a brief description or definition. If the left column is blank, give the correct term.

Term	Description
1.	shape like the inside of a bowl
2. convex	
3.	science of light, vision, and related technology
4.	picture of object formed by light rays
5. focal point	
6.	controls the amount of light entering the eye
7.	distance between mirror or lens and place where light rays meet
8. fiber optics	
9. law of reflection	
10.	concentrated, parallel light waves of a single wavelength

Reviewing Key Concepts

Multiple Choice *Choose the letter of the best answer.*

11. What shape is a mirror that reflects parallel light rays toward a focal point?
    a. convex
    b. flat
    c. concave
    d. regular

12. According to the law of reflection, a light ray striking a mirror
    a. continues moving through the mirror in the same direction
    b. moves into the mirror at a slightly different angle
    c. bounces off the mirror toward the direction it came from
    d. bounces off the mirror at the same angle it hits

13. Reflecting telescopes focus images using
    a. several mirrors
    b. several lenses
    c. both mirrors and lenses
    d. either a mirror or a lens, but not both

14. Ordinary light differs from laser light in that ordinary light waves
    a. all have the same wavelength
    b. tend to spread out
    c. stay parallel to one another
    d. all have their peaks lined up

15. Nearsighted vision is corrected when lenses
    a. reflect light away from the eye
    b. allow light rays to focus on the retina
    c. allow light to focus slightly past the retina
    d. help light rays reflect regularly

16. Lasers do work similar to that of human vision when they are used to
    a. perform surgery
    b. send phone signals over optical cable
    c. scan bar codes at the grocery store
    d. change the shape of molecules

Short Answer *Write a short answer to each question.*

17. Name one optical tool, describe how it works, and explain some of its uses.

18. How are the images that are produced by a convex mirror different from those produced by a concave mirror?

19. Describe what typically happens to a ray of light from the time it enters the eye until it strikes the retina.

20. How do lenses correct nearsightedness and farsightedness?

21. What does a refracting telescope have in common with a simple microscope?

22. Describe two ways the distance of an object from a lens can affect the appearance of the object's image.

Thinking Critically

INTERPRET In the four diagrams below, light rays are shown interacting with a material medium. For the next four questions, choose the letter of the diagram that answers the question.

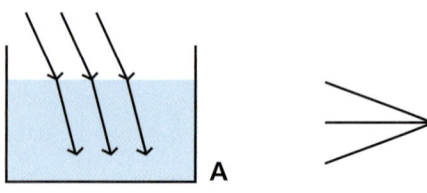

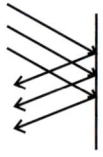

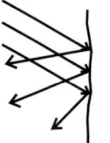

23. Which diagram shows regular reflection?
24. Which diagram shows diffuse reflection?
25. Which diagram shows refraction?
26. Which diagram shows light rays converging at a focal point?

COMPARE AND CONTRAST Copy the chart below. For each pair of terms, write down one way they are alike (compare) and one way they are different (contrast).

Terms	Compare	Contrast
27. flat mirror, curved mirror		
28. convex lens, concave lens		
29. focal point, focal length		
30. nearsighted, farsighted		
31. simple microscope, refracting telescope		
32. regular reflection, total internal reflection		

33. **INFER** What is the approximate focal length of the eye's lens? How do you know?

34. **ANALYZE** Why is laser light used in fiber optics?

35. **APPLY** In order to increase the magnification of a magnifying glass, would you need to make the convex surfaces of the lens more or less curved?

36. **APPLY** Describe a possible use for laser light not mentioned in the chapter. What characteristics of laser light does this application make use of?

the BIG idea

37. **SYNTHESIZE** Using what you have learned in this chapter, describe two possible uses of an optical tool like the one shown on pages 286–287. Explain what wave behaviors of light would be involved in these uses. Then explain how these uses could benefit the person in the photo.

38. **APPLY** Make a sketch of an optical tool that would use three mirrors to make a beam of light return to its source. Your sketch should include:
    - the path of light waves through the tool
    - labels indicating the names of parts and how they affect the light
    - several sentences describing one possible use of the tool

UNIT PROJECTS

Evaluate all the data, results, and information from your project folder. Prepare to present your project.

Standardized Test Practice

Interpreting Diagrams

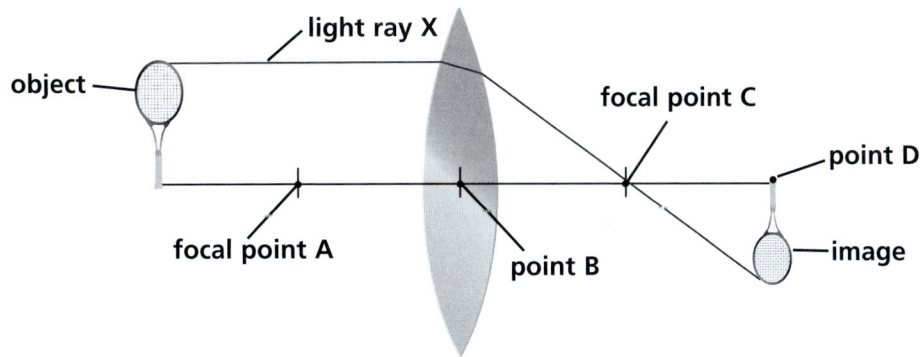

Study the diagram above and then answer the questions that follow.

1. What kind of lens is shown in the diagram?
   a. concave
   b. convex
   c. flat
   d. prism

2. What happens to parallel light rays passing through this type of lens?
   a. They become polarized.
   b. They form a rainbow.
   c. They bend inward.
   d. They bend outward.

3. All light rays parallel to light ray X will pass through what point?
   a. point A
   b. point B
   c. point C
   d. point D

4. How far is the object in the diagram from the lens?
   a. less than one focal length
   b. one focal length
   c. about two focal lengths
   d. more than three focal lengths

5. Where would you position a screen in order to see the image in focus on the screen?
   a. at point A
   b. at point B
   c. at point C
   d. at point D

Extended Response

Answer the two questions below in detail. Include some of the terms from the word box. Underline each term you use in your answer.

concave	focal point	real image
convex	refraction	virtual image
flat mirror	reflection	magnifying glass

6. What kind of mirror would you use to see what is happening over a broad area? Why?

7. Choose one of the following optical tools and explain how it uses mirrors and/or lenses to form an image: camera, telescope, periscope, microscope.

Chapter 9: **Light and Optics** 319

UNIT 3
Chemical Interactions

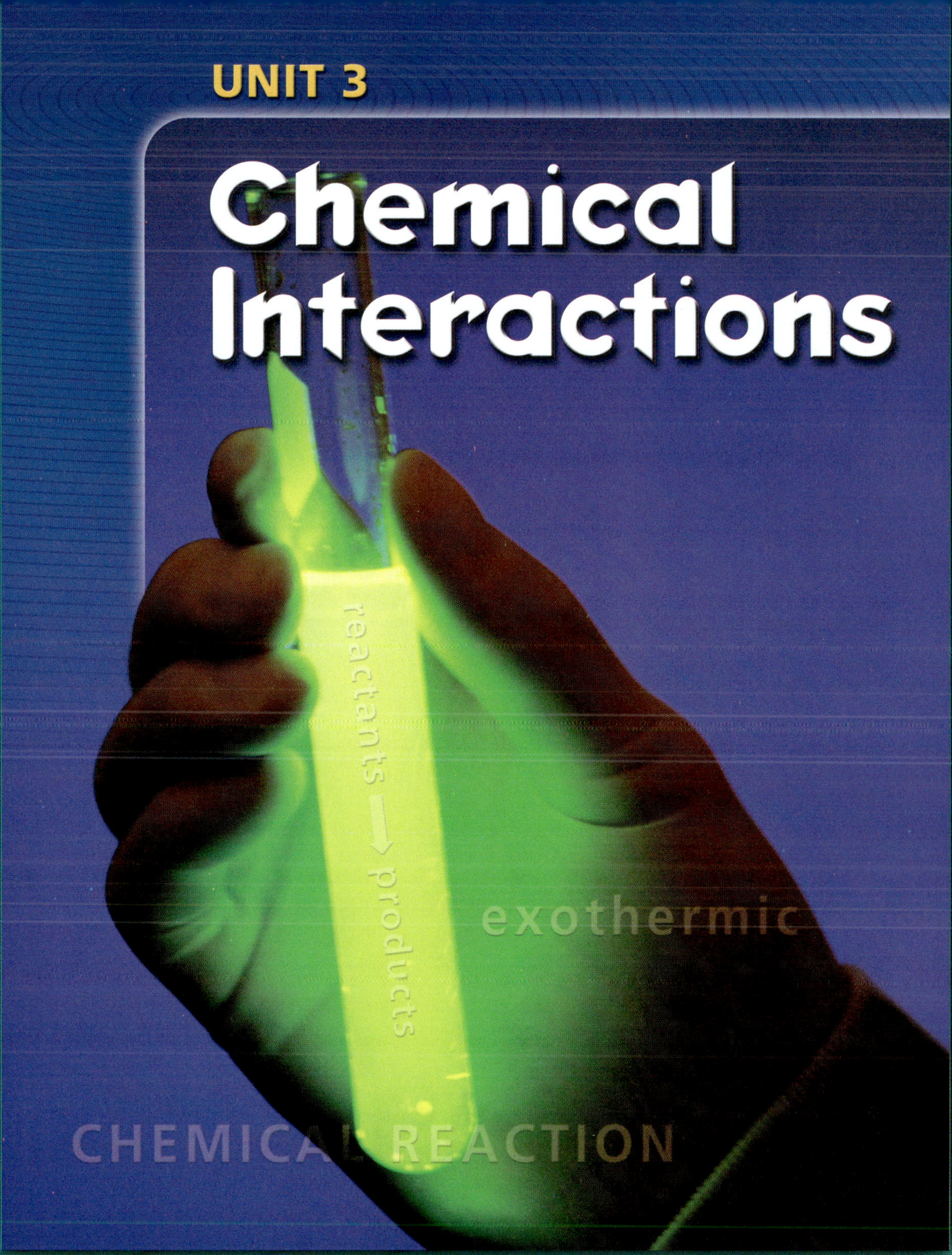

Contents Overview

Frontiers in Science
Medicines from Nature   322

Timelines in Science
The Story of Atomic Structure   386

Chapter 10 Atomic Structure and the Periodic Table   326

Chapter 11 Chemical Bonds and Compounds   358

Chapter 12 Chemical Reactions   390

FRONTIERS in Science

Medicines from Nature

Where have people found medicines?

SCIENTIFIC AMERICAN FRONTIERS

View the "Endangered Wonder Drug" segment of your Scientific American Frontiers video to see how chemicals found in nature can improve the health of people.

322 Unit 3: Chemical Interactions

In Brazil, extracts from plants are used to treat everything from Parkinson's Disease to arthritis.

Finding Natural Remedies

In the 1960s, people were searching desperately for new cancer-fighting agents. Scientists tested over 35,000 compounds, some of which came from the bark of the Pacific yew tree, long known to have strong effects on the body. The tests indicated that something in the bark stopped the growth of cancerous tumors. Scientists eventually derived the drug Taxol from the compounds found in the yew tree.

Natural medicines are much more than simple folk cures, like the sapi karta leaves that the Kuna people of Panama believe increase creativity. Many powerful medicines are based on compounds found in nature. But even though these natural compounds may be very effective at treating diseases, they can be limited in supply and can have harmful side effects. Organic chemists must find ways to make these compounds safer and produce them in greater amounts.

Modeling the Molecule

To make a compound, a chemist must know what its molecule looks like, atom by atom. Many useful drugs have structures that contain many atoms arranged in complicated ways. The chemist must know exactly how many atoms of each kind are in the molecule and how they are arranged. One atom in the wrong place might mean that the drug won't work the way it should.

To study the structures of molecules, chemists use a method called spectroscopy. Spectroscopy is a process that shows how the molecules of a compound respond to certain forms of radiation. Three important types of spectroscopy are

- NMR (nuclear magnetic resonance) spectroscopy, which allows chemists to identify small groups of atoms within larger molecules
- IR (infrared) spectroscopy, which shows the presence of certain types of bonds in molecules
- X-ray studies, which show details such as how much space there is between atoms and what the overall physical shapes of molecules are

Chemists put all this information together to determine the structure of a molecule. They might even build a model of the molecule.

Assembling the Puzzle

Once chemists know the structure of the molecule, they must figure out the starting reactants and the specific sequence of chemical reactions that will produce that molecule as a final product. It is a lot like doing a jigsaw puzzle when you know what the final picture looks like but still have to fit together all the pieces. Only in this case, the chemists may not even be sure what the little pieces look like.

Organic chemists often prefer to complete the process backward. They look at a model of the complete molecule and then figure out how they might build one just like it. How do chemists know what kinds of reactions might produce a certain molecule? Chemists have classified chemical reactions into different types. They determine how combinations of reactions will put the various kinds of atoms into their correct places in the molecule. Chemists may need to combine dozens of reactions to get the desired molecule.

Testing the Medicine

Once chemists have produced the desired drug molecule, the synthetic compound must be carefully tested to make sure it works like the natural substance does. The sequence of reactions must also be tested to make sure they produce the same compound when larger amounts of chemicals are used.

View the "Endangered Wonder Drug" segment of your *Scientific American Frontiers* video to see how modern medicines can be developed from chemical compounds found in nature.

IN THIS SCENE FROM THE VIDEO

A researcher works with a substance found in bark.

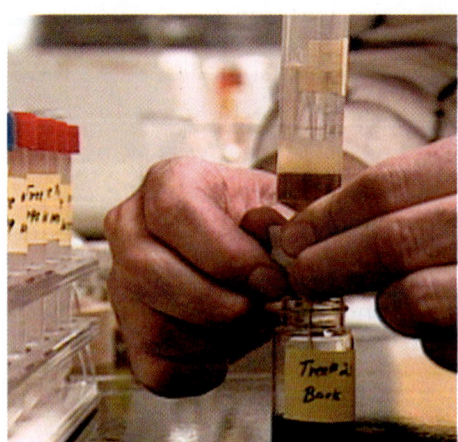

SAVING LIVES THROUGH NATURE AND CHEMISTRY
Medicines from plants and other natural sources have been used by different cultures around the world for thousands of years. The ephedra plant contains the raw material for many decongestants, which help shrink swollen nasal passages. It was used by the Chinese more than 5000 years ago. Today, the bark of the Pacific yew tree is being used as the source of the anticancer drug Taxol. A large amount of bark from the tree, however, is needed to make just one dose of the drug, and very few Pacific yew trees are available. Chemists, therefore, are trying to make this medicine in the laboratory.

Once a potential new drug is found in nature, it may take several years, or even decades, to figure out how to produce the drug synthetically and test it for safety. Only a small percentage of drugs tested ever goes to market, because the drugs must undergo several stages of testing on both animals and humans. Today, chemists routinely search the seas and the forests for marine organisms and rare plants that might have the power to fight cancer, heart disease, or viruses.

Chemists often use computers to make models of drug molecules. Computers allow the chemists to see how the drug molecules will interact with other molecules.

UNANSWERED Questions

The search for new chemical compounds that can be used to treat human illnesses raises many questions. Scientists need to find ways to investigate, produce, and test new, more powerful drugs.

- How might scientists more quickly test the safety and effectiveness of new medicines?
- Can easily synthesized compounds be just as effective as natural medicines?
- Might the processes that produce these drugs in nature be duplicated in a lab?
- Can we discover other new sources of medicines in the natural world?

UNIT PROJECTS

As you study this unit, work alone or with a group on one of these projects.

Medicines Around You

Present a report about a plant in your region that has medicinal properties.

- Collect samples of a plant that has medicinal properties.
- Bring your plant samples into your classroom. Prepare and present a report about the plant and the way it is used in medicine.

Model Medicine

Build a scale model of a molecule that is used to treat a certain illness.

- Using the Internet or an encyclopedia, determine the structure of a compound that interests you.
- Using foam balls, toothpicks, water colors, string, and other materials, construct a model of the molecule. Describe your model to the class.

Remedies

Write a news report about a popular herbal remedy, such as Saint John's Wort.

- To learn more about the herbal remedy, try interviewing a personal fitness trainer or an employee of a health-food store.
- Deliver a news report to the class telling of the advantages of the remedy and warning of its potential dangers.

Learn more about careers in chemistry.

Frontiers in Science 325

CHAPTER 10
Atomic Structure and the Periodic Table

the BIG idea

A substance's atomic structure determines its physical and chemical properties.

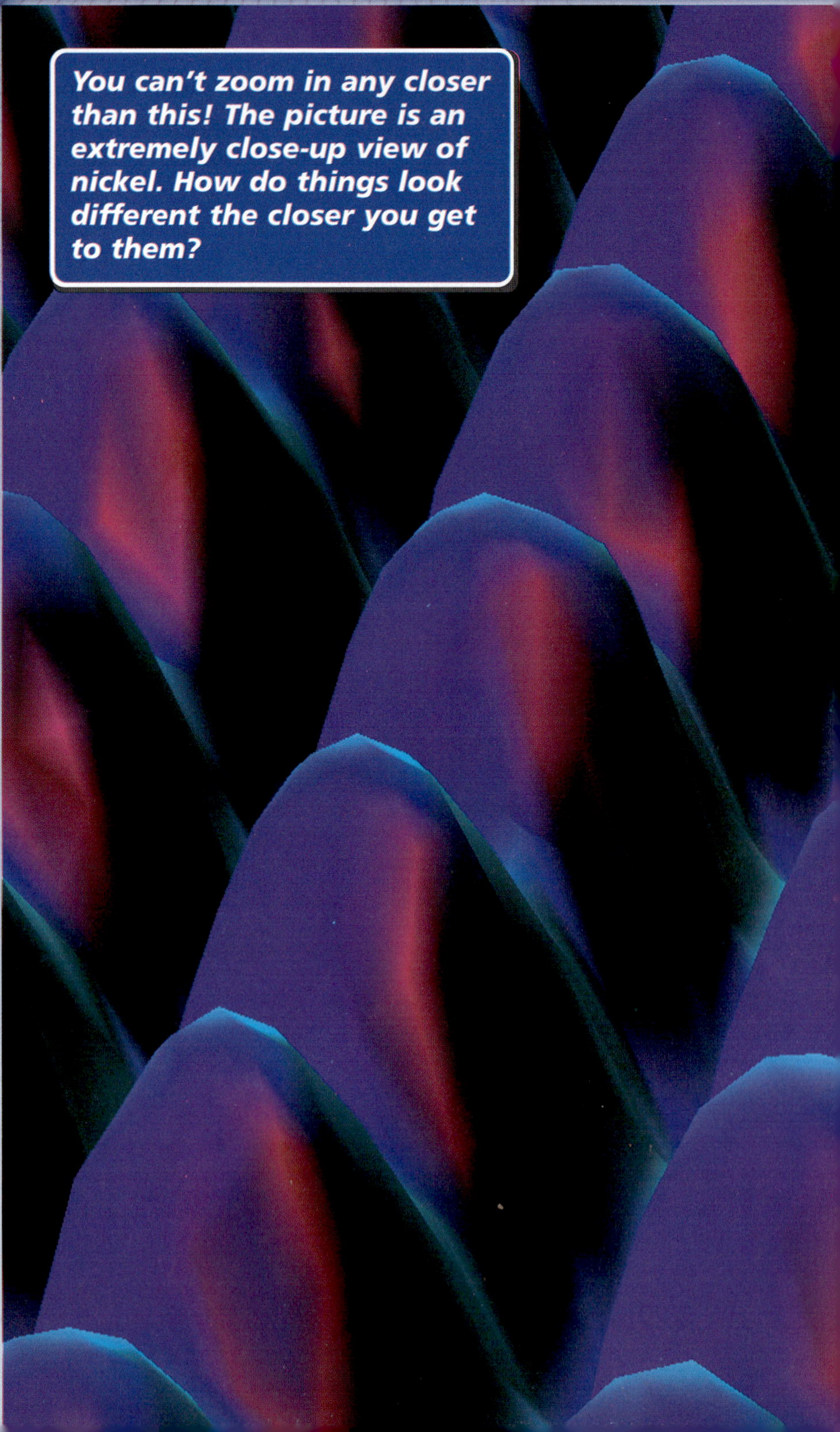

Key Concepts

SECTION 1 **Atoms are the smallest form of elements.**
Learn about the structure of atoms and how each element's atoms are different.

SECTION 2 **Elements make up the periodic table.**
Learn how the periodic table of the elements is organized.

SECTION 3 **The periodic table is a map of the elements.**
Learn more about the groups of elements in the periodic table.

You can't zoom in any closer than this! The picture is an extremely close-up view of nickel. How do things look different the closer you get to them?

Internet Preview

CLASSZONE.COM
Chapter 10 online resources: Content Review, Simulation, Visualization, three Resource Centers, Math Tutorial, Test Practice

EXPLORE the BIG idea

That's Far!

Place a baseball in the middle of a large field. Hold a dime and count off the number of steps from the baseball to the edge of the field. If the baseball were an atom's nucleus and the dime an electron, you would need to go about 6000 steps to walk the distance between the nucleus and the electrons.

Observe and Think How far were you able to go? How much farther would you need to go to model the proportion of an atom? What does this tell you about atomic structure?

Element Safari

Locate the following products in your home or in a grocery store: baking soda, vinegar, cereal flakes, and antacid tablets. You may examine other products if you wish. Look at the labels on the products. Can you recognize the names of any elements? Use your periodic table as a reference.

Observe and Think Which element names did you find?

Internet Activity: Periodic Table

Go to **ClassZone.com** to explore the periodic table. See different ways to set up the table and learn more about the listed elements.

Observe and Think How do atomic number and mass change as you move across the periodic table?

Atomic Theory **Code: MDL022**

Chapter 10: **Atomic Structure and the Periodic Table** 327

CHAPTER 10
Getting Ready to Learn

CONCEPT REVIEW

- Matter is made of particles called atoms that are too small to see with the eyes.
- Matter can be an element, a compound, or a mixture.
- Matter can undergo physical and chemical changes.

VOCABULARY REVIEW

See Glossary for definitions.

atom

compound

element

CONTENT REVIEW CLASSZONE.COM

Review concepts and vocabulary.

TAKING NOTES

MAIN IDEA WEB

Write each new blue heading in a box. Then write notes in boxes around the center box that give important terms and details about that blue heading.

VOCABULARY STRATEGY

Write each new vocabulary term in the center of a **frame game** diagram. Decide what information to frame it with. Use examples, descriptions, parts, sentences that use the term in context, or pictures. You can change the frame to fit each term.

See the Note-Taking Handbook on pages R45–R51.

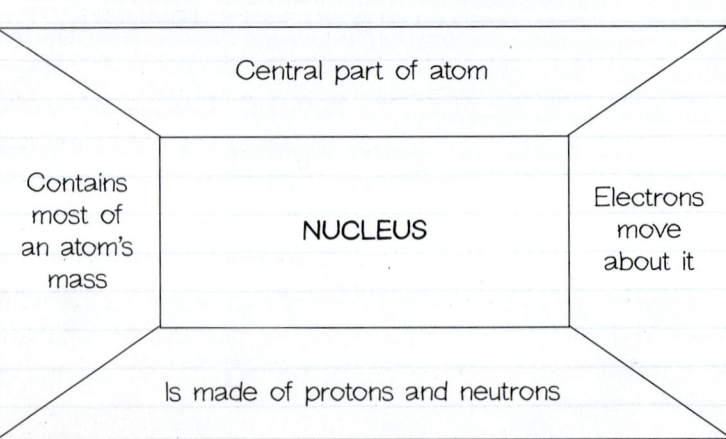

328 Unit 3: Chemical Interactions

KEY CONCEPT
10.1 Atoms are the smallest form of elements.

 BEFORE, you learned
- All matter is made of atoms
- Elements are the simplest substances

 NOW, you will learn
- Where atoms are found and how they are named
- About the structure of atoms
- How ions are formed from atoms

VOCABULARY

proton p. 331
neutron p. 331
nucleus p. 331
electron p. 331
atomic number p. 332
atomic mass number p. 332
isotope p. 332
ion p. 334

EXPLORE The Size of Atoms

How small can you cut paper?

PROCEDURE

1. Cut the strip of paper in half. Cut one of these halves in half.
2. Continue cutting one piece of paper in half as many times as you can.

MATERIALS
- strip of paper about 30 centimeters long
- scissors

WHAT DO YOU THINK?
- How many cuts were you able to make?
- Do you think you could keep cutting the paper forever? Why or why not?

All matter is made of atoms.

Think of all the substances you see and touch every day. Are all of these substances the same? Obviously, the substances that make up this book you're reading are quite different from the substances in the air around you. So how many different substances can there be? This is a question people have been asking for thousands of years.

About 2400 years ago, Greek philosophers proposed that everything on Earth was made of only four basic substances—air, water, fire, and earth. Everything else contained a mixture of these four substances. As time went on, chemists came to realize that there had to be more than four basic substances. Today chemists know that about 100 basic substances, or elements, account for everything we see and touch. Sometimes these elements appear by themselves. Most often, however, these elements appear in combination with other elements to make new substances. In this section, you'll learn about the atoms of the elements that make up the world and how these atoms differ from one another.

READING TIP
The word *element* is related to *elementary*, which means "basic."

Chapter 10: **Atomic Structure and the Periodic Table** 329

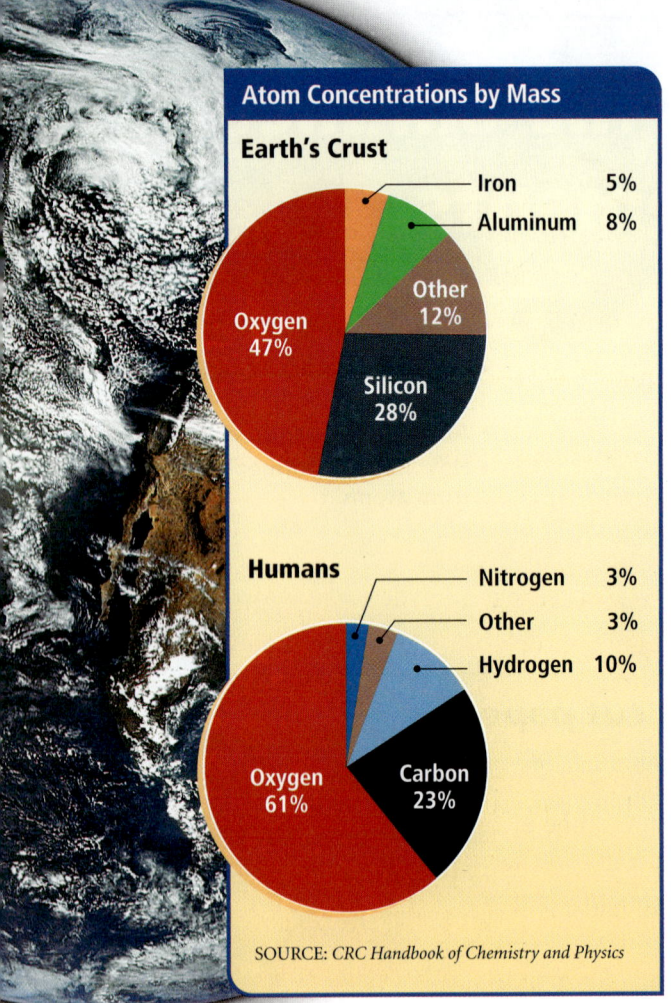

Atom Concentrations by Mass

SOURCE: *CRC Handbook of Chemistry and Physics*

Types of Atoms in Earth's Crust and Living Things

Atoms of the element hydrogen account for about 90 percent of the total mass of the universe. Hydrogen atoms make up only about 1 percent of Earth's crust, however, and most of those hydrogen atoms are combined with oxygen atoms in the form of water. The graph on the left shows the types of atoms in approximately the top 100 kilometers of Earth's crust.

The distribution of the atoms of the elements in living things is very different from what it is in Earth's crust. Living things contain at least 25 types of atoms. Although the amounts of these atoms vary somewhat, all living things—animals, plants, and bacteria—are composed primarily of atoms of oxygen, carbon, hydrogen, and nitrogen. As you can see in the lower graph on the left, oxygen atoms account for more than half your body's mass.

 What is the most common element in the universe?

Names and Symbols of Elements

Elements get their names in many different ways. Magnesium, for example, was named for the region in Greece known as Magnesia. Lithium comes from the Greek word *lithos,* which means "stone." Neptunium was named after the planet Neptune. The elements einsteinium and fermium were named after scientists Albert Einstein and Enrico Fermi.

Each element has its own unique symbol. For some elements, the symbol is simply the first letter of its name.

hydrogen (H)   sulfur (S)   carbon (C)

The symbols for other elements use the first letter plus one other letter of the element's name. Notice that the first letter is capitalized but the second letter is not.

aluminum (Al)   platinum (Pt)   cadmium (Cd)   zinc (Zn)

The origins of some symbols, however, are less obvious. The symbol for gold (Au), for example, doesn't seem to have anything to do with the element's name. The symbol refers instead to gold's name in Latin, *aurum.* Lead (Pb), iron (Fe), and copper (Cu) are a few other elements whose symbols come from Latin names.

Each element is made of a different atom.

In the early 1800s British scientist John Dalton proposed that each element is made of tiny particles called atoms. Dalton stated that all of the atoms of a particular element are identical but are different from atoms of all other elements. Every atom of silver, for example, is similar to every other atom of silver but different from an atom of iron.

Dalton's theory also assumed that atoms could not be divided into anything simpler. Scientists later discovered that this was not exactly true. They found that atoms are made of even smaller particles.

Learn more about the atom.

The Structure of an Atom

A key discovery leading to the current model of the atom was that atoms contain charged particles. The charge on a particle can be either positive or negative. Particles with the same type of charge repel each other—they are pushed apart. Particles with different charges attract each other—they are drawn toward each other.

Atoms are composed of three types of particles—electrons, protons, and neutrons. A **proton** is a positively charged particle, and a **neutron** is an uncharged particle. The neutron has approximately the same mass as a proton. The protons and neutrons of an atom are grouped together in the atom's center. This combination of protons and neutrons is called the **nucleus** of the atom. Because it contains protons, the nucleus has a positive charge. **Electrons** are negatively charged particles that move around outside the nucleus.

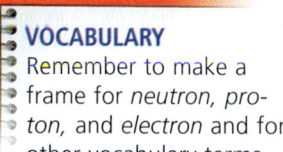

VOCABULARY
Remember to make a frame for *neutron*, *proton*, and *electron* and for other vocabulary terms.

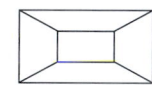

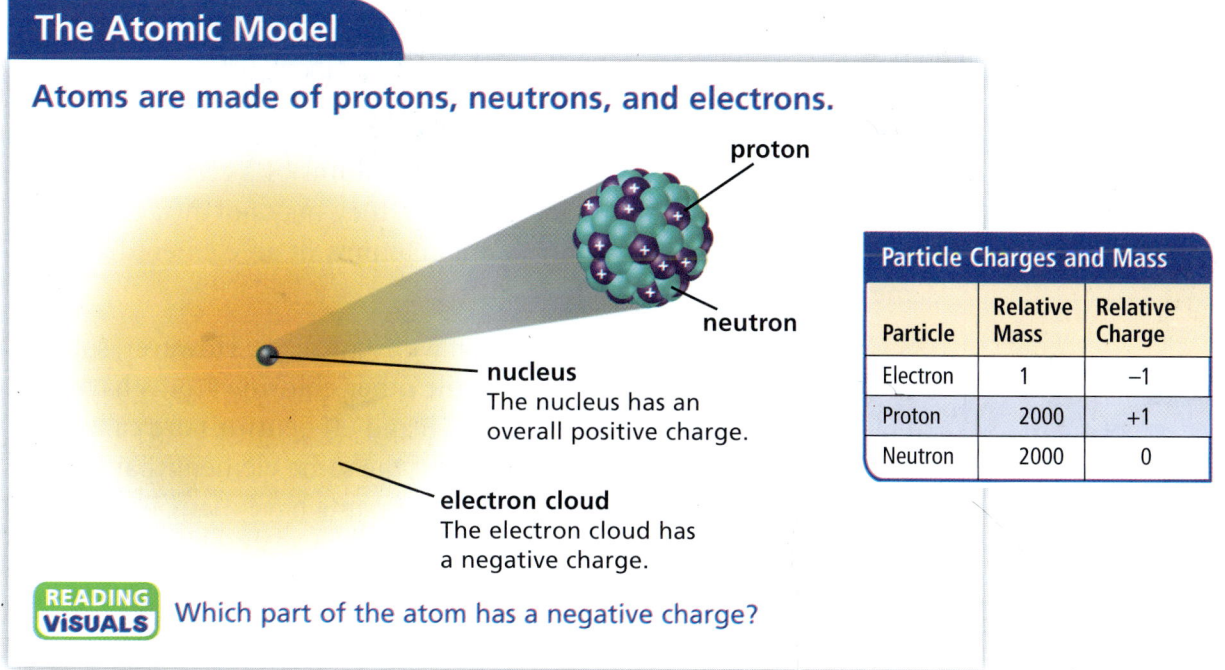

The Atomic Model

Atoms are made of protons, neutrons, and electrons.

- proton
- neutron
- **nucleus** The nucleus has an overall positive charge.
- **electron cloud** The electron cloud has a negative charge.

Particle Charges and Mass		
Particle	Relative Mass	Relative Charge
Electron	1	−1
Proton	2000	+1
Neutron	2000	0

READING VISUALS Which part of the atom has a negative charge?

Build a model of an atom.

Atoms are extremely small, about 10^{-10} meters in diameter. This means that you could fit millions of atoms in the period at the end of this sentence. The diagram on page 331, picturing the basic structure of the atom, is not drawn to scale. In an atom the electron cloud is about 10,000 times the diameter of the nucleus.

Atom Size
Millions of atoms could fit in a space the size of this dot. It would take you 500 years to count the number of atoms in a grain of salt.

Electrons are much smaller than protons or neutrons—about 2000 times smaller. Electrons also move about the nucleus very quickly. Scientists have found that it is not possible to determine their exact positions with any certainty. This is why we picture the electrons as being in a cloud around the nucleus.

The negative electrons remain associated with the nucleus because they are attracted to the positively charged protons. Also, because electrical charges that are alike (such as two negative charges) repel each other, electrons remain spread out in the electron cloud. Neutral atoms have no overall electrical charge because they have an equal number of protons and electrons.

Atomic Numbers

Gold has 79 protons and 79 electrons.

If all atoms are composed of the same particles, how can there be more than 100 different elements? The identity of an atom is determined by the number of protons in its nucleus, called the **atomic number.** Every hydrogen atom—atomic number 1—has exactly one proton in its nucleus. Every gold atom has 79 protons, which means the atomic number of gold is 79.

Atomic Mass Numbers

The total number of protons and neutrons in an atom's nucleus is called its **atomic mass number.** While the atoms of a certain element always have the same number of protons, they may not always have the same number of neutrons, so not all atoms of an element have the same atomic mass number.

All chlorine atoms, for instance, have 17 protons. However, some chlorine atoms have 18 neutrons, while other chlorine atoms have 20 neutrons. Atoms of chlorine with 18 and 20 neutrons are called chlorine isotopes. **Isotopes** are atoms of the same element that have a different number of neutrons. Some elements have many isotopes, while other elements have just a few.

READING TIP
The *iso-* in *isotope* is from the Greek language, and it means "equal."

 How is atomic mass number different from atomic number?

Isotopes

Isotopes have different numbers of neutrons.

Chlorine-35
atomic mass number = 35

- nucleus
- 17 protons
- 18 neutrons
- 17 electrons

Chlorine-37
atomic mass number = 37

- nucleus
- 17 protons
- 20 neutrons
- 17 electrons

A particular isotope is designated by the name of the element and the total number of its protons and neutrons. You can find the number of neutrons in a particular isotope by subtracting the atomic number from the atomic mass number. For example, chlorine-35 indicates the isotope of chlorine that has 18 neutrons. Chlorine-37 has 20 neutrons. Every atom of a given element always has the same atomic number because it has the same number of protons. However, the atomic mass number varies depending on the number of neutrons.

INVESTIGATE Masses of Atomic Particles

How can you model the relative masses of atomic particles?

PROCEDURE

1. Use a paper clip to represent an electron. Determine its mass.
2. Find a substance in the classroom (sand, clay, water) from which you could make a model representing the mass of a proton or neutron. The mass of a proton or neutron is about 2000 times the mass of an electron.
3. Measure out the substance until you have enough of it to make your model.

WHAT DO YOU THINK?

- What substance did you use to make your model?
- What was the model's mass?
- What do you conclude about the masses of atomic particles?

CHALLENGE The diameter of an electron is approximately 1/2000 that of a proton. What two objects could represent each of these to scale?

SKILL FOCUS
Modeling

MATERIALS
- balance
- large paper clip
- other items

TIME
20 minutes

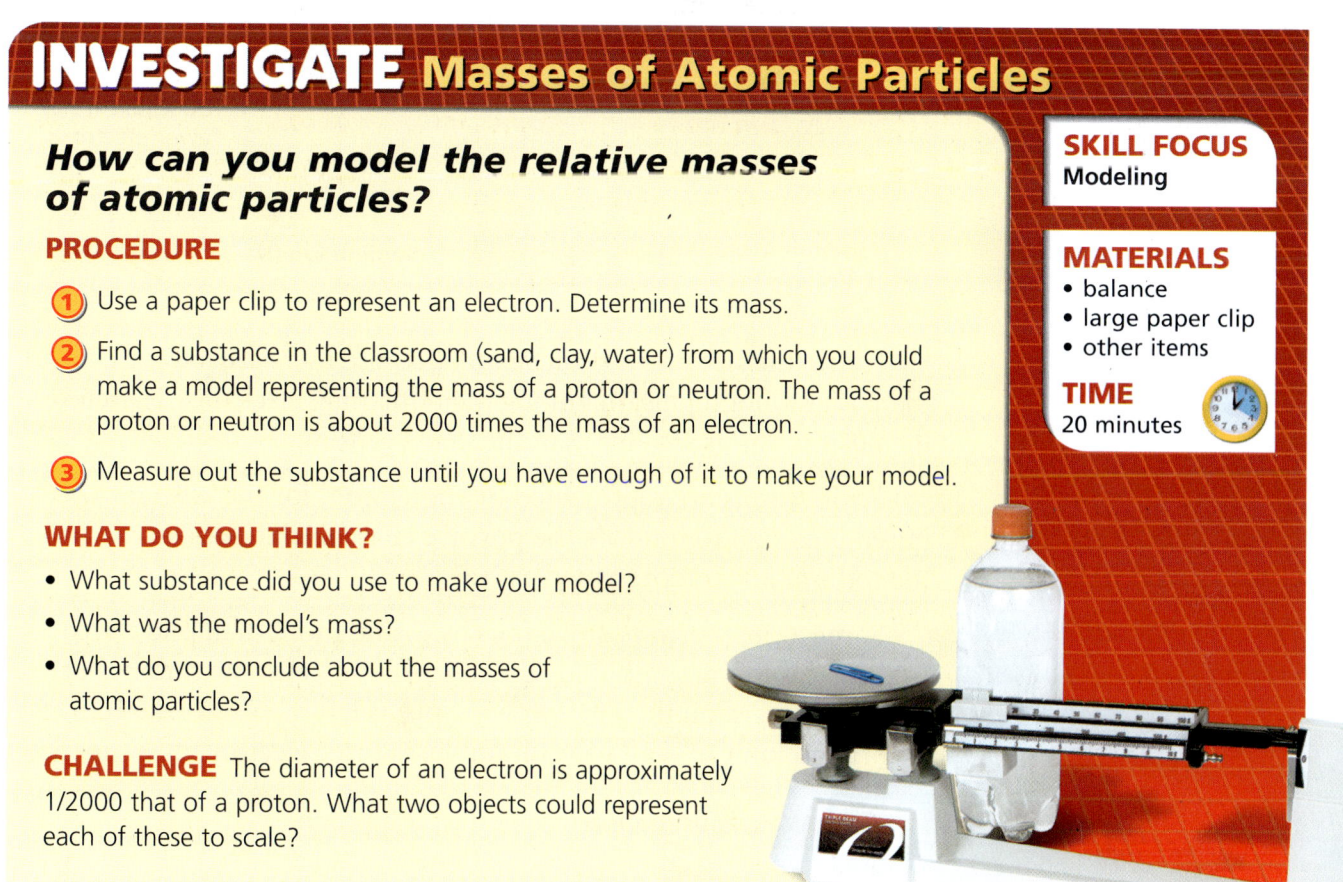

Chapter 10: **Atomic Structure and the Periodic Table** 333

MAIN IDEA WEB
Make a main idea web to organize what you know about ions.

Atoms form ions.

An atom has an equal number of electrons and protons. Since each electron has one negative charge and each proton has one positive charge, atoms have no overall electrical charge. An **ion** is formed when an atom loses or gains one or more electrons. Because the number of electrons in an ion is different from the number of protons, an ion does have an overall electric charge.

Formation of Positive Ions

Consider how a positive ion can be formed from an atom. The left side of the illustration below represents a sodium (Na) atom. Its nucleus contains 11 protons and some neutrons. Because the electron cloud surrounding the nucleus consists of 11 electrons, there is no overall charge on the atom. If the atom loses one electron, however, the charges are no longer balanced. There is now one more proton than there are electrons. The ion formed, therefore, has a positive charge.

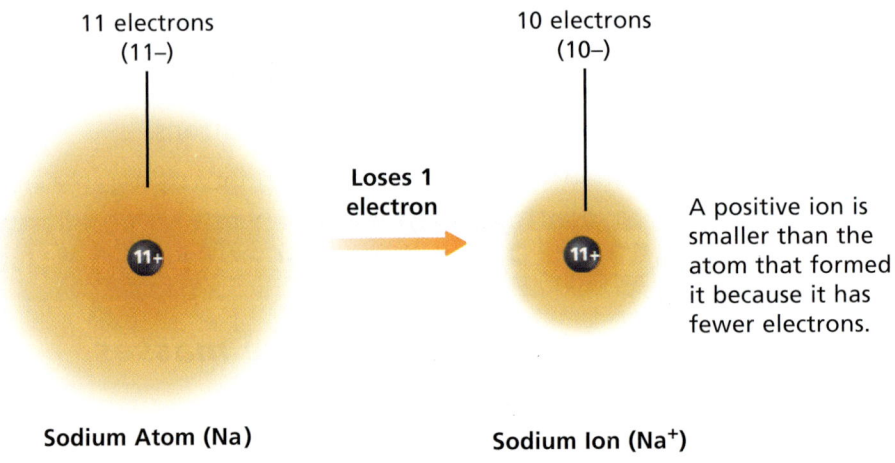

Sodium Atom (Na) → Loses 1 electron → Sodium Ion (Na⁺)

A positive ion is smaller than the atom that formed it because it has fewer electrons.

Notice the size of the positive ion. Because there are fewer electrons, there is less of a repulsion among the remaining electrons. Therefore, the positive ion is smaller than the neutral atom.

Positive ions are represented by the symbol for the element with a raised plus sign to indicate the positive charge. In the above example, the sodium ion is represented as Na^+.

Some atoms form positive ions by losing more than one electron. In those cases, the symbol for the ion also indicates the number of positive charges on the ion. For example, calcium loses two electrons to form an ion Ca^{2+}, and aluminum loses three electrons to form Al^{3+}.

CHECK YOUR READING What must happen to form a positive ion?

Formation of Negative Ions

The illustration below shows how a negative ion is formed. In this case the atom is chlorine (Cl). The nucleus of a chlorine atom contains 17 protons and some neutrons. The electron cloud has 17 electrons, so the atom has no overall charge. When an electron is added to the chlorine atom, a negatively charged ion is formed. Notice that a negative ion is larger than the neutral atom that formed it. The extra electron increases the repulsion within the cloud, causing it to expand.

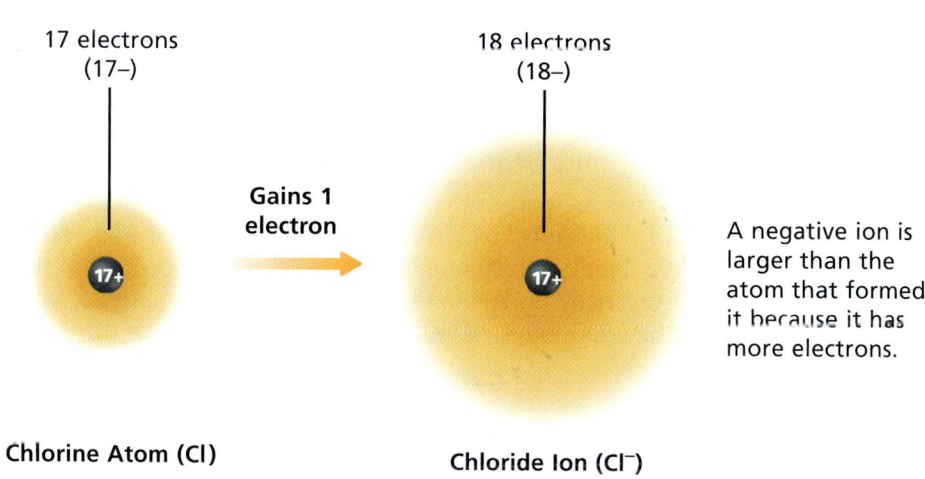

Negative ions are represented by placing a minus sign to the right and slightly above the element's symbol. The negative chloride ion in the example, therefore, would be written as Cl^-. If an ion has gained more than one electron, the number of added electrons is indicated by a number in front of the minus sign. Oxygen (O), for example, gains two electrons when it forms an ion. Its symbol is O^{2-}.

10.1 Review

KEY CONCEPTS

1. Which two atoms are most common in Earth's crust? in the human body?
2. What are the particles that make up an atom?
3. What happens when an atom forms an ion?

CRITICAL THINKING

4. **Infer** Magnesium and sodium atoms are about the same size. How does the size of a magnesium ion with a 2+ charge compare with that of a sodium ion with a single + charge?
5. **Compare** The atomic number of potassium is 19. How does potassium-39 differ from potassium-41?

CHALLENGE

6. **Analyze** When determining the mass of an atom, the electrons are not considered. Why can scientists disregard the electrons?

Connecting Sciences

PHYSICAL SCIENCE AND LIFE SCIENCE

Elements of Life

There are more than 25 different types of atoms in the cells of your body. The table below shows the amount of atoms of some of the elements in a 50-kilogram human. Atoms of the element oxygen account for about 61 percent of a person's mass. Atoms of carbon account for about 23 percent of a person's mass. Although the atoms of some elements are present only in very small amounts, they play an important role in the chemical processes that occur in your cells.

Blood and Other Fluids

Iron ions are part of the hemoglobin that gives your blood its red color and carries oxygen to cells throughout your body. Sodium and potassium ions help regulate the amount and location of the water in your body. Sodium and potassium ions also make up part of the sweat your body produces to regulate temperature.

Bones and Teeth

The sturdier structures of your body get their strength from calcium, magnesium, and phosphorus. You have less than a kilogram of calcium in your body, almost all of which is in your bones and teeth. Fluoride ions make up part of the hard coating on your teeth. This is why you'll often find fluoride ions added to toothpaste.

Elements to Avoid

In some way, the atoms of every element in the periodic table play a role in human lives. Many of them, however, can be hazardous if handled improperly. For example, arsenic and mercury are poisonous.

Mass of Elements in 50 kg Human

Element	Amount (kg)
Oxygen (O)	30.5
Carbon (C)	11.5
Hydrogen (H)	5.0
Nitrogen (N)	1.3
Calcium (Ca)	0.7
Phosphorus (P)	0.6
Potassium (K)	0.1
Sodium (Na)	> 0.1
Chlorine (Cl)	> 0.1

Other elements are in the body in very small amounts.
SOURCE: *CRC Handbook of Chemistry and Physics*

EXPLORE

1. **CALCULATE** What percentage of your body is made up of oxygen, carbon, hydrogen, and nitrogen?
2. **CHALLENGE** Salt, made of sodium ions and chloride ions, is an essential part of your diet. However, too much salt can cause health problems. Use the Internet to find out about the problems caused by too much or too little salt in your diet.

Find out more about the elements important to life.

This photo shows a false color X-ray of the human skull. X-rays show the bones in the human body. Bones contain calcium.

10.2 Elements make up the periodic table.

KEY CONCEPT

 BEFORE, you learned
- Atoms have a structure
- Every element is made from a different type of atom

 NOW, you will learn
- How the periodic table is organized
- How properties of elements are shown by the periodic table

VOCABULARY

atomic mass p. 337
periodic table p. 338
group p. 342
period p. 342

EXPLORE Similarities and Differences of Objects

How can different objects be organized?

PROCEDURE

① With several classmates, organize the buttons into three or more groups.

② Compare your team's organization of the buttons with another team's organization.

MATERIALS
buttons

WHAT DO YOU THINK?
- What characteristics did you use to organize the buttons?
- In what other ways could you have organized the buttons?

Elements can be organized by similarities.

One way of organizing elements is by the masses of their atoms. Finding the masses of atoms was a difficult task for the chemists of the past. They could not place an atom on a pan balance. All they could do was find the mass of a very large number of atoms of a certain element and then infer the mass of a single one of them.

Remember that not all the atoms of an element have the same atomic mass number. Elements have isotopes. When chemists attempt to measure the mass of an atom, therefore, they are actually finding the average mass of all its isotopes. The **atomic mass** of the atoms of an element is the average mass of all the element's isotopes. Even before chemists knew how the atoms of different elements could be different, they knew atoms had different atomic masses.

Mendeleev's Periodic Table

In the early 1800s several scientists proposed systems to organize the elements based on their properties. None of these suggested methods worked very well until a Russian chemist named Dmitri Mendeleev (MENH-duh-LAY-uhf) decided to work on the problem.

In the 1860s, Mendeleev began thinking about how he could organize the elements based on their physical and chemical properties. He made a set of element cards. Each card contained the atomic mass of an atom of an element as well as any information about the element's properties. Mendeleev spent hours arranging the cards in various ways, looking for a relationship between properties and atomic mass.

The exercise led Mendeleev to think of listing the elements in a chart. In the rows of the chart, he placed those elements showing similar chemical properties. He arranged the rows so the atomic masses increased as one moved down each vertical column. It took Mendeleev quite a bit of thinking and rethinking to get all the relationships correct, but in 1869 he produced the first **periodic table** of the elements. We call it the periodic table because it shows a periodic, or repeating, pattern of properties of the elements. In the reproduction of Mendeleev's first table shown below, notice how he placed carbon (C) and silicon (Si), two elements known for their similarities, in the same row.

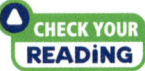

CHECK YOUR READiNG What organizing method did Mendeleev use?

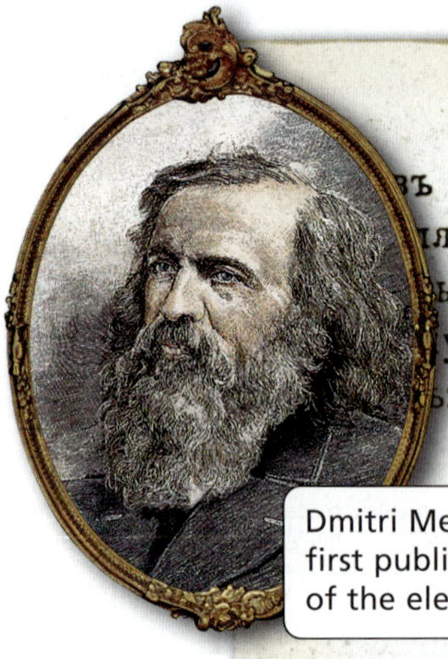

Dmitri Mendeleev (1834–1907) first published a periodic table of the elements in 1869.

— 70 —

ъ ней, мнѣ кажется, уже ясно выражается примѣнимость вы
лемаго мною. начала ко всей совокупности элементовъ, пай
ыхъ извѣстенъ съ достовѣрностію. На этотъ разъ я и желалъ
ущественно найдти общую систему элементовъ. Вотъ этотъ
ъ:

			Ti=50	Zr=90	?=180.
			V=51	Nb=94	Ta=182.
			Cr=52	Mo=96	W=186.
			Mn=55	Rh=104,4	Pt=197,4
			Fe=56	Ru=104,4	Ir=198.
			Ni=Co=59	Pl=106,6,	Os=199.
H=1			Cu=63,4	Ag=108	Hg=200.
	Be=9,4	Mg=24	Zn=65,2	Cd=112	
	B=11	Al=27,4	?=68	Ur=116	Au=197?
	C=12	Si=28	?=70	Sn=118	
	N=14	P=31	As=75	Sb=122	Bi=210
	O=16	S=32	Se=79,4	Te=128?	

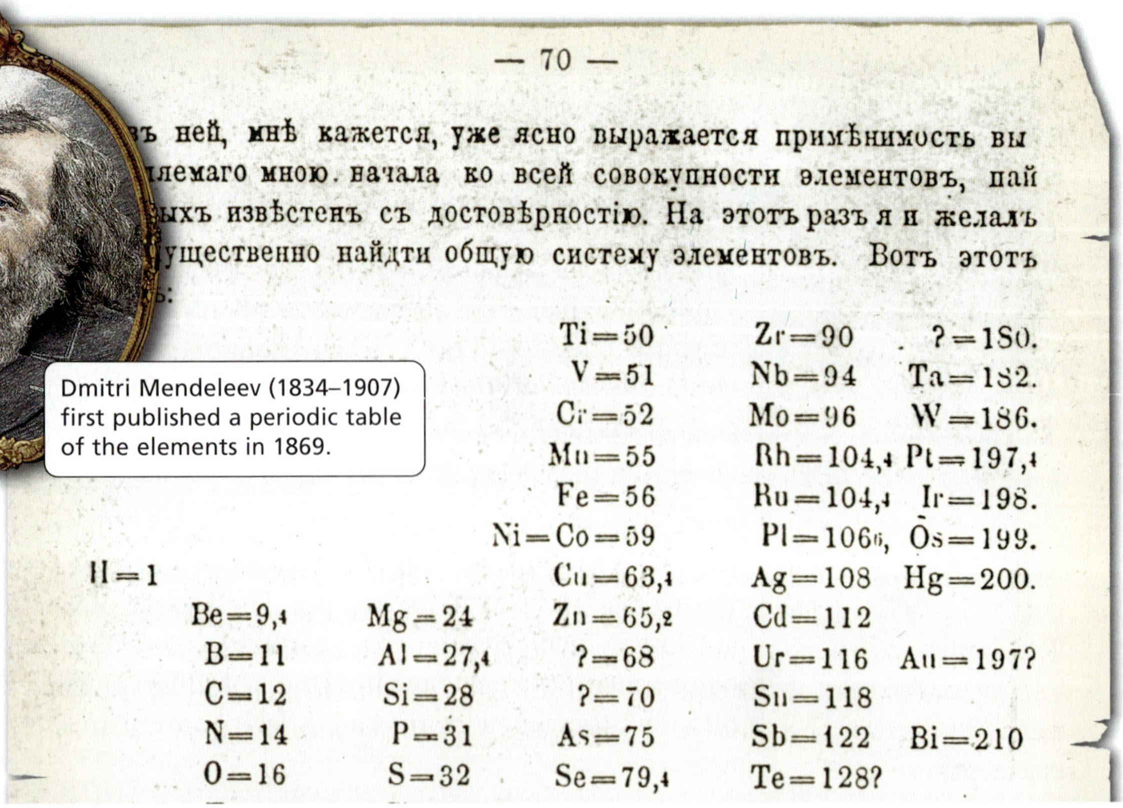

Predicting New Elements

When Mendeleev constructed his table, he left some empty spaces where no known elements fit the pattern. He predicted that new elements that would complete the chart would eventually be discovered. He even described some of the properties of these unknown elements.

At the start, many chemists found it hard to accept Mendeleev's predictions of unknown elements. Only six years after he published the table, however, the first of these elements—represented by the question mark after aluminum (Al) on his table—was discovered. This element was given the name gallium, after the country France (Gaul) where it was discovered. In the next 20 years, two other elements Mendeleev predicted would be discovered.

The periodic table organizes the atoms of the elements by properties and atomic number.

The modern periodic table on pages 340 and 341 differs from Mendeleev's table in several ways. For one thing, elements with similar properties are found in columns, not rows. More important, the elements are not arranged by atomic mass but by atomic number.

MAIN IDEA WEB
Make a main idea web to summarize the information you can learn from the periodic table.

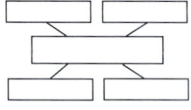

Reading the Periodic Table

Each square of the periodic table gives particular information about the atoms of an element.

① The number at the top of the square is the atomic number, which is the number of protons in the nucleus of an atom of that element.

② The chemical symbol is an abbreviation for the element's name. It contains one or two letters. Some elements that have not yet been named are designated by temporary three-letter symbols.

③ The name of the element is written below the symbol.

④ The number below the name indicates the average atomic mass of all the isotopes of the element.

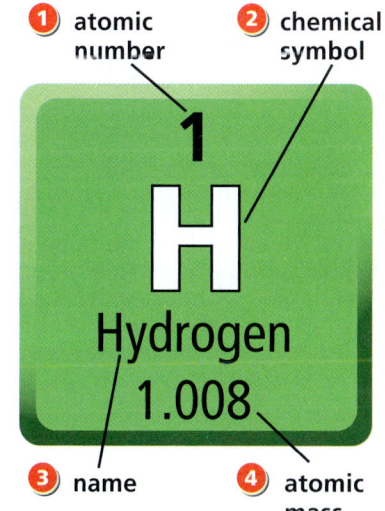

The color of the element's symbol indicates the physical state of the element at room temperature. White letters—such as the *H* for hydrogen in the box to the right—indicate a gas. Blue letters indicate a liquid, and black letters indicate a solid. The background colors of the squares indicate whether the element is a metal, nonmetal, or metalloid. These terms will be explained in the next section.

The Periodic Table of the Elements

Group	1	2	3	4	5	6	7	8	9
1	1 **H** Hydrogen 1.008								
2	3 **Li** Lithium 6.941	4 **Be** Beryllium 9.012							
3	11 **Na** Sodium 22.990	12 **Mg** Magnesium 24.305							
4	19 **K** Potassium 39.098	20 **Ca** Calcium 40.078	21 **Sc** Scandium 44.956	22 **Ti** Titanium 47.87	23 **V** Vanadium 50.942	24 **Cr** Chromium 51.996	25 **Mn** Manganese 54.938	26 **Fe** Iron 55.845	27 **Co** Cobalt 58.933
5	37 **Rb** Rubidium 85.468	38 **Sr** Strontium 87.62	39 **Y** Yttrium 88.906	40 **Zr** Zirconium 91.224	41 **Nb** Niobium 92.906	42 **Mo** Molybdenum 95.94	43 **Tc** Technetium (98)	44 **Ru** Ruthenium 101.07	45 **Rh** Rhodium 102.906
6	55 **Cs** Cesium 132.905	56 **Ba** Barium 137.327	57 **La** Lanthanum 138.906	72 **Hf** Hafnium 178.49	73 **Ta** Tantalum 180.95	74 **W** Tungsten 183.84	75 **Re** Rhenium 186.207	76 **Os** Osmium 190.23	77 **Ir** Iridium 192.217
7	87 **Fr** Francium (223)	88 **Ra** Radium (226)	89 **Ac** Actinium (227)	104 **Rf** Rutherfordium (261)	105 **Db** Dubnium (262)	106 **Sg** Seaborgium (266)	107 **Bh** Bohrium (264)	108 **Hs** Hassium (269)	109 **Mt** Meitnerium (268)

Period

Each row of the periodic table is called a **period**. As read from left to right, one proton and one electron are added from one element to the next.

Group

Each column of the table is called a **group**. Elements in a group share similar properties. Groups are read from top to bottom.

58 **Ce** Cerium 140.116	59 **Pr** Praseodymium 140.908	60 **Nd** Neodymium 144.24	61 **Pm** Promethium (145)	62 **Sm** Samarium 150.36
90 **Th** Thorium 232.038	91 **Pa** Protactinium 231.036	92 **U** Uranium 238.029	93 **Np** Neptunium (237)	94 **Pu** Plutonium (244)

 Metal Metalloid Nonmetal 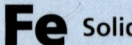 Solid Liquid Gas

Periodic Table

Metals and Nonmetals
This zigzag line separates metals from nonmetals.

13	14	15	16	17	18
					2 **He** Helium 4.003
5 **B** Boron 10.811	6 **C** Carbon 12.011	7 **N** Nitrogen 14.007	8 **O** Oxygen 15.999	9 **F** Fluorine 18.998	10 **Ne** Neon 20.180
13 **Al** Aluminum 26.982	14 **Si** Silicon 28.086	15 **P** Phosphorus 30.974	16 **S** Sulfur 32.066	17 **Cl** Chlorine 35.453	18 **Ar** Argon 39.948

10	11	12	13	14	15	16	17	18
28 **Ni** Nickel 58.69	29 **Cu** Copper 63.546	30 **Zn** Zinc 65.39	31 **Ga** Gallium 69.723	32 **Ge** Germanium 72.61	33 **As** Arsenic 74.922	34 **Se** Selenium 78.96	35 **Br** Bromine 79.904	36 **Kr** Krypton 83.80
46 **Pd** Palladium 106.42	47 **Ag** Silver 107.868	48 **Cd** Cadmium 112.4	49 **In** Indium 114.818	50 **Sn** Tin 118.710	51 **Sb** Antimony 121.760	52 **Te** Tellurium 127.60	53 **I** Iodine 126.904	54 **Xe** Xenon 131.29
78 **Pt** Platinum 195.078	79 **Au** Gold 196.967	80 **Hg** Mercury 200.59	81 **Tl** Thallium 204.383	82 **Pb** Lead 207.2	83 **Bi** Bismuth 208.980	84 **Po** Polonium (209)	85 **At** Astatine (210)	86 **Rn** Radon (222)
110 **Ds** Darmstadtium (269)	111 **Uuu** Unununium (272)	112 **Uub** Ununbium (277)						

Lanthanides & Actinides
The lanthanide series (elements 58–71) and actinide series (elements 90–103) are usually set apart from the rest of the periodic table.

63 **Eu** Europium 151.964	64 **Gd** Gadolinium 157.25	65 **Tb** Terbium 158.925	66 **Dy** Dysprosium 162.50	67 **Ho** Holmium 164.930	68 **Er** Erbium 167.26	69 **Tm** Thulium 168.934	70 **Yb** Ytterbium 173.04	71 **Lu** Lutetium 174.967
95 **Am** Americium (243)	96 **Cm** Curium (247)	97 **Bk** Berkelium (247)	98 **Cf** Californium (251)	99 **Es** Einsteinium (252)	100 **Fm** Fermium (257)	101 **Md** Mendelevium (258)	102 **No** Nobelium (259)	103 **Lr** Lawrencium (262)

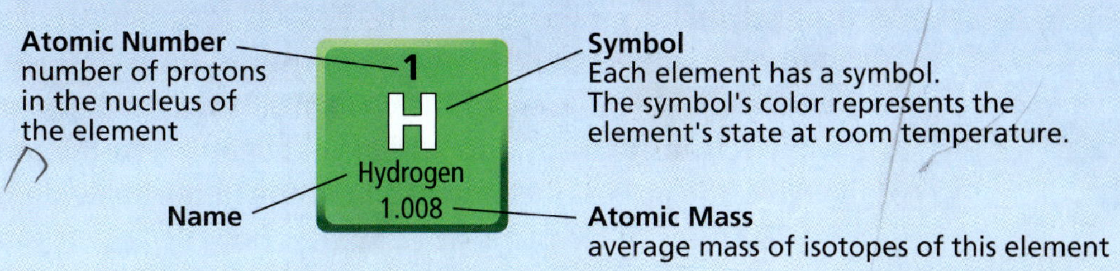

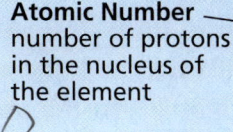

Atomic Number — number of protons in the nucleus of the element

Symbol — Each element has a symbol. The symbol's color represents the element's state at room temperature.

1 **H** Hydrogen 1.008

Name

Atomic Mass — average mass of isotopes of this element

Chapter 10: **Atomic Structure and the Periodic Table**

Groups and Periods

Elements in a vertical column of the periodic table show similarities in their chemical and physical properties. The elements in a column are known as a **group,** and they are labeled by a number at the top of the column. Sometimes a group is called a family of elements, because these elements seem to be related.

The illustration at the left shows Group 17, commonly referred to as the halogen group. Halogens tend to combine easily with many other elements and compounds, especially with the elements in Groups 1 and 2. Although the halogens have some similarities to one another, you can see from the periodic table that their physical properties are not the same. Fluorine and chlorine are gases, bromine is a liquid, and iodine and astatine are solids at room temperature. Remember that the members of a family of elements are related but not identical.

Metals like copper can be used to make containers for water. Some metals—such as lithium, sodium, and potassium—however, react violently if they come in contact with water. They are all in the same group, the vertical column labeled 1 on the table.

Each horizontal row in the periodic table is called a **period.** Properties of elements change in a predictable way from one end of a period to the other. In the illustration below, which shows Period 3, the elements on the far left are metals and the ones on the far right are nonmetals. The chemical properties of the elements show a progression; similar progressions appear in the periods above and below this one.

The elements in Group 17, the halogens, show many similarities.

Period 3 contains elements with a wide range of properties. Aluminum (Al) is used to make drink cans, while argon (Ar) is a gas used in light bulbs.

Trends in the Periodic Table

Because the periodic table organizes elements by properties, an element's position in the table can give information about the element. Remember that atoms form ions by gaining or losing electrons. Atoms of elements on the left side of the table form positive ions easily. For example, Group 1 atoms lose an electron to form ions with one positive charge (1+). Atoms of the elements in Group 2, likewise, can lose two electrons to form ions with a charge of 2+. At the other side of the table, the atoms of elements in Group 18 normally do not form ions at all. Atoms of elements in Group 17, however, often gain one

342 Unit 3: Chemical Interactions

electron to form a negative ion (1−). Similarly, the atoms of elements in Group 16 can gain two electrons to form a 2− ion. The atoms of the elements in Groups 3 to 12 all form positive ions, but the charge can vary.

Other information about atoms can be determined by their position in the table. The illustration to the right shows how the sizes of atoms vary across periods and within groups. An atom's size is important because it affects how the atom will react with another atom.

The densities of elements also follow a pattern. Density generally increases from the top of a group to the bottom. Within a period, however, the elements at the left and right sides of the table are the least dense, and the elements in the middle are the most dense. The element osmium (Os) has the highest known density, and it is located at the center of the table.

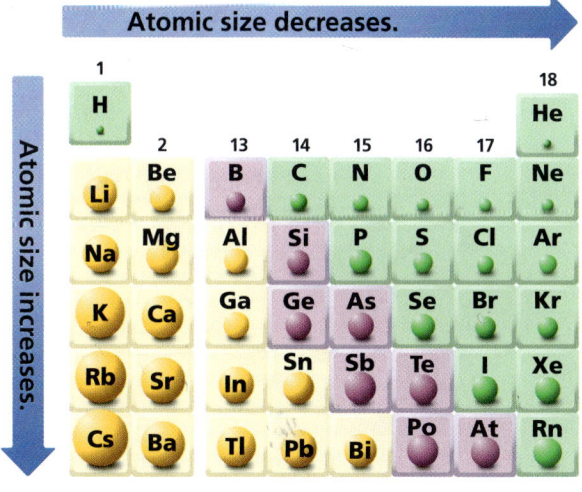

Atomic size is one property that changes in a predictable way across, up, and down the periodic table.

Chemists cannot predict the exact size or density of an atom of one element based on that of another. These trends, nonetheless, are a valuable tool in predicting the properties of different substances. The fact that the trends appeared after the periodic table was organized by atomic number was a victory for all of the scientists like Mendeleev who went looking for them all those years before.

 **CHECK YOUR READING** What are some properties that can be related to position on the periodic table?

10.2 Review

KEY CONCEPTS

1. How is the modern periodic table organized?
2. What information about an atom's properties can you read from the periodic table?
3. How are the relationships of elements in a group different from the relationships of elements in a period?

CRITICAL THINKING

4. **Infer** Would you expect strontium (Sr) to be more like potassium (K) or bromine (Br)? Why?
5. **Predict** Barium (Ba) is in Group 2. Recall that atoms in Group 1 lose one electron to form ions with a 1+ charge. What type of ion does barium form?

CHALLENGE

6. **Analyze** Explain how chemists can state with certainty that no one will discover an element between sulfur (S) and chlorine (Cl).

Chapter 10: **Atomic Structure and the Periodic Table** 343

CHAPTER INVESTIGATION

Modeling Atomic Masses

OVERVIEW AND PURPOSE Atoms are extremely small. They are so small, in fact, that a single drop of water contains more atoms than you could count in a lifetime! Measuring the masses of atoms to discover the patterns in the periodic table was not an easy task for scientists in the past. This investigation will give you some sense of how scientists determined the mass of atoms. You will
- compare the masses of different film can "atoms"
- predict the number of washers in each film can "atom"

Procedure

1. Create a data table similar to the one shown on the sample notebook page.

2. Find the mass of one empty film can. Record this mass in the second row of the table.

3. Collect the four film cans labeled A, B, C, and D in advance by your teacher. Each can contains a different number of washers and represents a different atom. The washers represent the protons and neutrons in an atom's nucleus.

4. Measure the mass of each of the four film cans. Record the masses of the film can atoms in the first row of your data table.

5. Subtract the mass of an empty film can from the mass of each film can atom. Record the differences in the correct spaces in your data table. These masses represent the masses of the washers in your film can atoms. Think of these masses as the masses of the nuclei.

6. Divide the mass of the washers in can B by the mass of the washers in can A. Record the value under the mass of the washers in can B.

MATERIALS
- empty film can
- balance
- 4 filled film cans

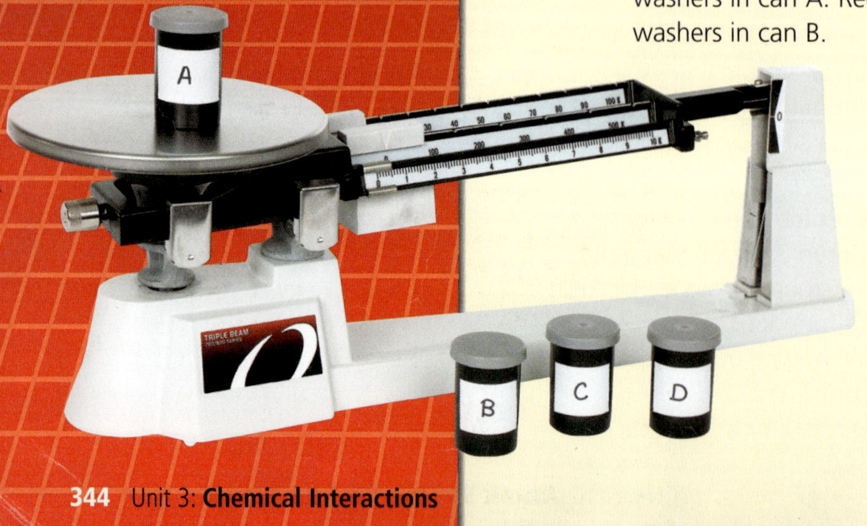

7 Repeat step 6 for film can atoms A, C, and D. Record the value under the masses of the washers in each can.

8 Round the values you obtained in steps 6 and 7 to the nearest whole number. Record the rounded figures in the next row of the table.

Observe and Analyze

1. **RECORD OBSERVATIONS** Be sure your data table and calculations are complete. Double-check your arithmetic.

2. **ANALYZE DATA** Examine your data table. Do you notice any patterns in how the masses increase? Given that all the washers in the film can atoms have identical masses, what might the ratio of the mass of the washers to the smallest mass tell you?

3. **PREDICT** Assume there is only one washer in can A. Estimate the number of washers in the other cans and record your estimates in the last row of the table.

4. **GRAPH DATA** On a sheet of graph paper, plot the masses (in grams) of the washers in the film can atoms on the y-axis and the number of washers in each can on the x-axis. Connect the points on the graph.

5. **INTERPRET DATA** Compare the masses of your film can atoms with the masses of the first four atoms on the periodic table. Which represents which?

Conclude

1. **IDENTIFY LIMITS** What can't this activity tell you about the identity of your film can atoms? (**Hint:** Protons and neutrons in real atoms have about the same mass.)

2. **INFER** Hydrogen has only a single proton in its nucleus. If your film can atoms represent the first four elements in the periodic table, what are the numbers of protons and neutrons in each atom?

3. **APPLY** Single atoms are far too small to place on a balance. How do you think scientists determine the masses of real atoms?

INVESTIGATE Further

CHALLENGE Use a periodic table to find the masses of the next two atoms (boron and carbon). How many washers would you need to make film can atom models for each?

Modeling Atomic Masses

Observe and Analyze

Table 1. Masses of Film Can Atoms

	A	B	C	D
Mass of film can atom (g)				
Mass of empty film can (g)				
Mass of washers (g)				
Mass of washers divided by can A				
Value rounded to nearest whole number				
Estimated number of washers in each can				

KEY CONCEPT

10.3 The periodic table is a map of the elements.

◀ **BEFORE, you learned**
- The periodic table is organized into groups of elements with similar characteristics
- The periodic table organizes elements according to their properties

▶ **NOW, you will learn**
- How elements are classified as metals, nonmetals, and metalloids
- About different groups of elements
- About radioactive elements

VOCABULARY

reactive p. 346
metal p. 347
nonmetal p. 349
metalloid p. 350
radioactivity p. 350
half-life p. 352

THINK ABOUT

How are elements different?

The photograph shows common uses of the elements copper, aluminum, and argon: copper in a penny, aluminum in a pie plate, and argon in a light bulb. Each element is located in a different part of the periodic table, and each has a very different use. Find these elements on the periodic table. What other elements are near these?

The periodic table has distinct regions.

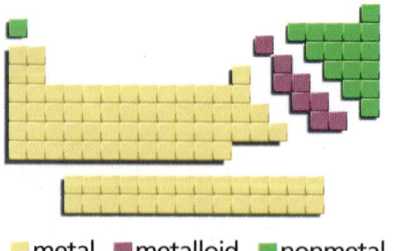

■ metal ■ metalloid ■ nonmetal

The periodic table is a kind of map of the elements. Just as a country's location on the globe gives you information about its climate, an atom's position on the periodic table indicates the properties of its element. The periodic table has three main regions—metals on the left, nonmetals (except hydrogen) on the right, and metalloids in between. The periodic table on pages 340 and 341 indicates these regions with different colors. A yellow box indicates a metal; green, a nonmetal; and purple, a metalloid.

An element's position in the table also indicates how reactive it is. The term **reactive** indicates how likely an element is to undergo a chemical change. Most elements are somewhat reactive and combine with other materials. The atoms of the elements in Groups 1 and 17 are the most reactive. The elements of Group 18 are the least reactive of all the elements.

 How does the periodic table resemble a map?

346 Unit 3: Chemical Interactions

Most elements are metals.

When you look at the periodic table, it is obvious from the color that most of the elements are metals. In general, **metals** are elements that conduct electricity and heat well and have a shiny appearance. Metals can be shaped easily by pounding, bending, or being drawn into a long wire. Except for mercury, which is a liquid, metals are solids at room temperature.

Sodium is a metal that is so soft it can be cut with a knife at room temperature.

You probably can name many uses for the metal **copper**.

Aluminum is often used for devices that must be strong and light.

Reactive Metals

The metals in Group 1 of the periodic table, the alkali metals, are very reactive. Sodium and potassium are often stored in oil to keep them away from air. When exposed to air, these elements react rapidly with oxygen and water vapor. The ions of these metals, Na^+ and K^+, are important for life, and play an essential role in the functioning of living cells.

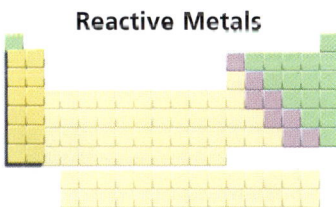

Reactive Metals

The metals in Group 2, the alkaline earth metals, are less reactive than the alkali metals. They are still more reactive than most other metals, however. Calcium ions are an essential part of your diet. Your bones and teeth contain calcium ions. Magnesium is a light, inexpensive metal that is often combined with other metals when a lightweight material is needed, such as for airplane frames.

Transition Metals

The elements in Groups 3–12 are called the transition metals. Among these metals are some of the earliest known elements, such as copper, gold, silver, and iron. Transition metals are generally less reactive than most other metals. Because gold and silver are easily shaped and do not react easily, they have been used for thousands of years to make jewelry and coins. Ancient artifacts made from transition metals can be found in many museums and remain relatively unchanged since the time they were made. Today, dimes and quarters are made of copper and nickel, and pennies are made of zinc with a coating of copper. Transition metal ions even are found in the foods you eat.

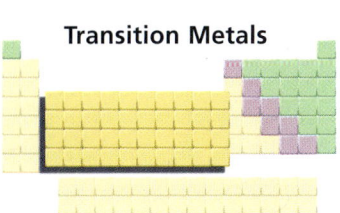

Transition Metals

Chapter 10: **Atomic Structure and the Periodic Table** 347

The properties of the transition metals make them particularly important to industry. Iron is the main part of steel, a material used for bridges and buildings. Most electric wires and many other electrical devices are made of copper. Copper is also used to make water pipes. Indeed, it would be hard to think of an industry that doesn't make use of transition metals.

Although other transition metals may be less familiar, many of them are important for modern technology. The tiny coil of wire inside incandescent light bulbs is made of tungsten. Platinum is in the catalytic converters that reduce pollution from automobile engines.

For many applications, two or more metals are combined to form an alloy. Alloys can be stronger, less likely to corrode, or easier to shape than pure metals. Steel, which is stronger than the pure iron it contains, often includes other transition metals, such as nickel, chromium, or manganese. Brass, an alloy of copper and zinc, is stronger than either metal alone. Jewelry is often made of an alloy of silver and copper, which is stronger than pure silver.

Rare Earth Elements

Rare Earth Elements

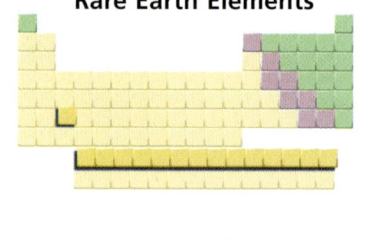

The rare earth elements are the elements in the top row of the two rows of metals that are usually shown outside the main body of the periodic table. Taking these elements out of the main body of the table makes the table more compact. The rare earth elements are often referred to as lanthanides because they follow the element lanthanum (La) on the table. They are called rare earth elements because scientists once thought that these elements were available only in tiny amounts in Earth's crust. As mining methods improved, scientists learned that the rare earths were actually not so rare at all—only hard to isolate in pure form.

More and more uses are being found for the rare earth elements. Europium (Eu), for example, is used as a coating for some television tubes. Praseodymium (Pr) provides a protective coating against harmful radiation in the welder's helmet in the photograph on the right.

Nonmetals and metalloids have a wide range of properties.

The elements to the right side of the periodic table are called **nonmetals.** As the name implies, the properties of nonmetals tend to be the opposite of those of metals. The properties of nonmetals also tend to vary more from element to element than the properties of the metals do. Many of them are gases at room temperature, and one—bromine—is a liquid. The solid nonmetals often have dull surfaces and cannot be shaped by hammering or drawing into wires. Nonmetals are generally poor conductors of heat and electric current.

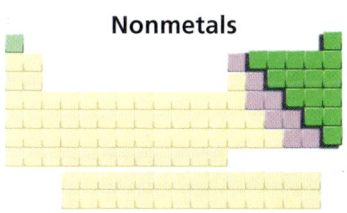
Nonmetals

The main components of the air that you breathe are the nonmetal elements nitrogen and oxygen. Nitrogen is a fairly unreactive element, but oxygen reacts easily to form compounds with many other elements. Burning and rusting are two familiar types of reactions involving oxygen. Compounds containing carbon are essential to living things. Two forms of the element carbon are graphite, which is a soft, slippery black material, and diamond, a hard crystal. Sulfur is a bright yellow powder that can be mined from deposits of the pure element.

Halogens

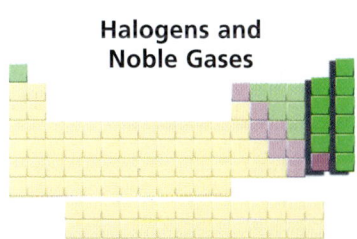
Halogens and Noble Gases

The elements in Group 17 are commonly known as halogens, from Greek words meaning "forming salts." Halogens are very reactive nonmetals that easily form compounds called salts with many metals. Because they are so reactive, halogens are often used to kill harmful microorganisms. For example, the halogen chlorine is used to clean drinking water and to prevent the growth of algae in swimming pools. Solutions containing iodine are often used in hospitals and doctors' offices to kill germs on skin.

Noble gases produce the light for many signs.

Noble Gases

Group 18 elements are called the noble, or inert, gases because they almost never react with other elements. Argon gas makes up about one percent of the atmosphere. The other noble gases are found in the atmosphere in smaller amounts. Colorful lights, such as those in the photograph on the right, are made by passing an electric current through tubes filled with neon, krypton, xenon, or argon gas. Argon gas also is placed in tungsten filament light bulbs, because it will not react with the hot filament.

 Where on Earth can you find noble gases?

Metalloids

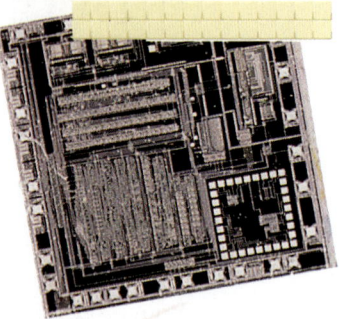

Metalloids

The metalloid silicon is found in sand and in computer microchips.

Metalloids are elements that have properties of both metals and nonmetals. In the periodic table, they lie on either side of a zigzag line separating metals from nonmetals. The most common metalloid is silicon. Silicon atoms are the second most common atoms in Earth's crust.

Metalloids often make up the semiconductors found in electronic devices. Semiconductors are special materials that conduct electricity under some conditions and not under others. Silicon, gallium, and germanium are three semiconductors used in computer chips.

Some atoms can change their identity.

The identity of an element is determined by the number of protons in its nucleus. Chemical changes do not affect the nucleus, so chemical changes don't change one type of atom into another. There are, however, conditions under which the number of protons in a nucleus can change and so change the identity of an atom.

Radioactive Elements

Recall that the nucleus of an atom contains protons and neutrons. Attractive forces between protons and neutrons hold the nucleus together even though protons repel one another. We say an atomic nucleus is stable when these attractive forces keep it together.

Each element has isotopes with different numbers of neutrons. The stability of a nucleus depends on the right balance of protons and neutrons. If there are too few or too many neutrons, the nucleus may become unstable. When this happens, particles are produced from the nucleus of the atom to restore the balance. This change is accompanied by a release of energy.

If the production of particles changes the number of protons, the atom is transformed into an atom of a different element. In the early 1900s, physicist Marie Curie named the process by which atoms produce energy and particles **radioactivity.** Curie was the first person to isolate polonium and radium, two radioactive elements.

An isotope is radioactive if the nucleus has too many or too few neutrons. Most elements have radioactive isotopes, although these isotopes are rare for small atoms. For the heaviest of elements—those beyond bismuth (Bi)—all of the isotopes are radioactive.

Scientists study radioactivity with a device called a Geiger counter. The Geiger counter detects the particles from the breakup of the atomic nucleus with audible clicks. More clicks indicate that more particles are being produced.

CHECK YOUR READING How can an atom of one element change into an atom of a different element?

350 Unit 3: Chemical Interactions

Uses of Radioactivity in Medicine

The radiation produced from unstable nuclei is used in hospitals to diagnose and treat patients. Some forms of radiation from nuclei are used to destroy harmful tumors inside a person's body without performing an operation. Another medical use of radiation is to monitor the activity of certain organs in the body. A patient is injected with a solution containing a radioactive isotope. Isotopes of a given atom move through the body in the same way whether or not they are radioactive. Doctors detect the particles produced by the radioactive isotopes to determine where and how the body is using the substance.

Although radiation has its benefits, in large doses it is harmful to living things and should be avoided. Radiation can damage or kill cells, and the energy from its particles can burn the skin. Prolonged exposure to radiation has been linked to cancer and other health problems.

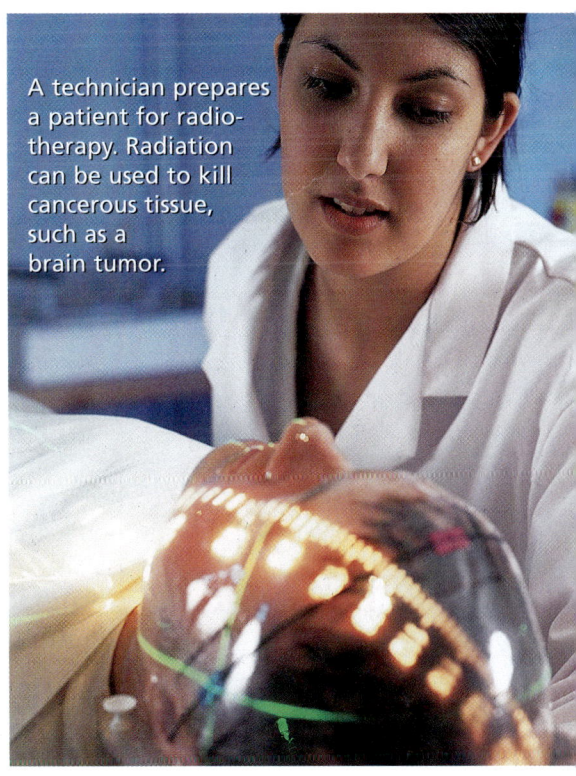

A technician prepares a patient for radiotherapy. Radiation can be used to kill cancerous tissue, such as a brain tumor.

INVESTIGATE Radioactivity

How quickly can atoms change?

PROCEDURE

1. Put 50 pennies in a bag. The pennies represent 50 atoms.
2. Pour out the pennies.
3. Count the number of pennies that landed head side up. These represent atoms whose nuclei changed.
4. Refill the bag with only the pennies that landed tail side up.
5. Repeat steps 2–4 until all of the pennies have landed head side up. Each time you pour out the pennies counts as one turn.
6. Construct a graph with the number of atoms that changed on the y-axis and the number of turns on the x-axis.

WHAT DO YOU THINK?
- After one turn, how many atoms had changed? had not changed?
- In how many turns did all the atoms change?
- From looking at your graph, what can you conclude about the rate of radioactive change?

CHALLENGE If you used a different number of pennies, would your results be different? In what way?

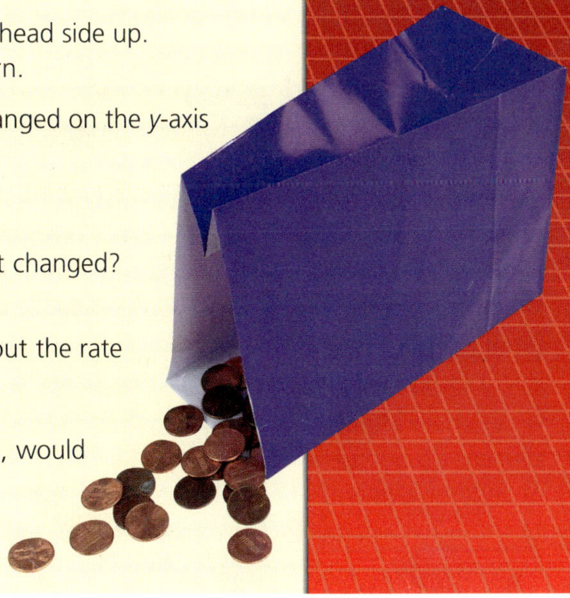

SKILL FOCUS
Modeling

MATERIALS
- 50 pennies
- bag
- graph paper

TIME
30 minutes

Watch how a radioactive element decays over time.

Radioactive Decay

Radioactive atoms produce energy and particles from their nuclei. The identity of these atoms changes because the number of protons changes. This process is known as radioactive decay. Over time, all of the atoms of a radioactive isotope will change into atoms of another element.

Radioactive decay occurs at a steady rate that is characteristic of the particular isotope. The amount of time that it takes for one-half of the atoms in a particular sample to decay is called the **half-life** of the isotope. For example, if you had 1000 atoms of a radioactive isotope with a half-life of 1 year, 500 of the atoms would change into another element over the course of a year. In the next year, 250 more atoms would decay. The illustration to the right shows how the amount of the original isotope would decrease over time.

The half-life is a characteristic of each isotope and is independent of the amount of material. A half-life is also not affected by conditions such as temperature or pressure. Half-lives of isotopes can range from a small fraction of a second to many billions of years.

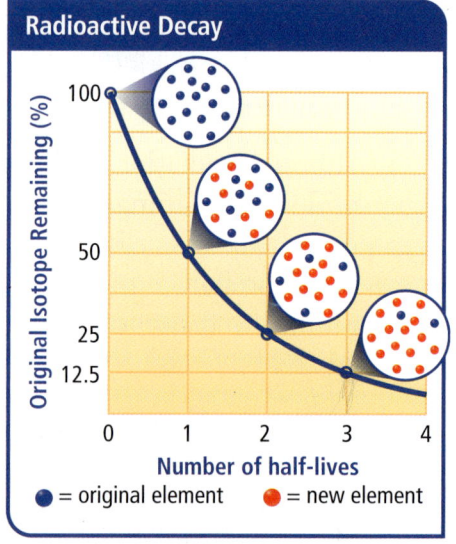

Half-Lives of Selected Elements	
Isotope	Half-Life
Uranium-238	4,510,000,000 years
Carbon-14	5,730 years
Radon-222	3.82 days
Lead-214	27 minutes
Polonium-214	.00016 seconds

10.3 Review

KEY CONCEPTS

1. What are the three main classes of elements in the periodic table?
2. What are the major characteristics of metals?
3. How can an atom of one element change to an atom of another element?

CRITICAL THINKING

4. **Compare** Use the periodic table to determine whether a carbon or a fluorine atom would be more reactive.
5. **Calculate** What fraction of a radioactive sample remains after three half-lives?

CHALLENGE

6. **Analyze** Why do you think the noble gases were among the last of the naturally occurring elements to be discovered?

MATH in SCIENCE

SKILL: USING SCIENTIFIC NOTATION

MATH TUTORIAL
CLASSZONE.COM
Click on Math Tutorial for more help with scientific notation.

Numbers with Many Zeros

Semiconductor devices are at the heart of the modern personal computer. Today tiny chips can contain more than 42,000,000 connections and perform about 3,000,000,000 calculations per second. Computers have little problem working with such large numbers. Scientists, however, use a scientific notation as a shorthand way to write large numbers. Scientific notation expresses a very large or very small number as the product of a number between 1 and 10 and a power of 10.

Example

Large Number How would you express the number 6,400,000,000—the approximate population of the world—in scientific notation?

(1) Look at the number and count how many spaces you would need to move the decimal point to get a number between 1 and 10.

6, 4 0 0, 0 0 0, 0 0 0
    9 8 7   6 5 4   3 2 1

(2) Place the decimal point in the space and multiply the number by the appropriate power of 10. The power of 10 will be equivalent to the number of spaces you moved the decimal point.

ANSWER 6.4×10^9

Small Number How would you express 0.0000023 in scientific notation?

(1) Count the number of places you need to move the decimal point to get a number between 1 and 10. This time you move the decimal point to the right, not the left.

0. 0 0 0 0 0 2 3
    1 2 3 4 5 6

(2) The power of 10 you need to multiply this number by is still equal to the number of places you moved the decimal point. Place a negative sign in front of it to indicate that you moved the decimal point to the right.

ANSWER 2.3×10^{-6}

Answer the following questions.

1. Express the following numbers in scientific notation:
   (a) 75,000   (b) 54,000,000,000   (c) 0.0000064

2. Express these numbers in decimal form:
   (a) 6.0×10^{24} (b) 7.4×10^{22} (c) 5.7×10^{-10}

CHALLENGE What is 2.2×10^{22} subtracted from 4.6×10^{22}?

Chips like the one shown here can be smaller than a fingernail but contain millions of independent components.

Chapter 10: **Atomic Structure and the Periodic Table** 353

Chapter Review

the BIG idea

A substance's atomic structure determines its physical and chemical properties.

KEY CONCEPTS SUMMARY

1 Atoms are the smallest form of elements.

- All matter is made of the atoms of approximately 100 elements.
- Atoms are made of protons, neutrons, and electrons.
- Different elements are made of different atoms.
- Atoms form ions by gaining or losing electrons.

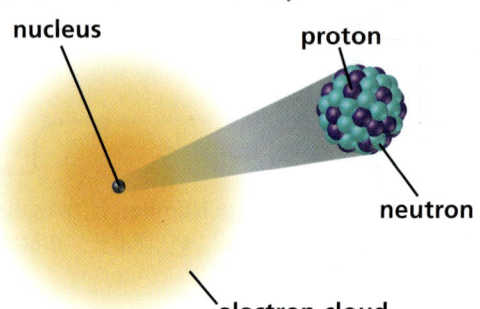

VOCABULARY
proton p. 331
neutron p. 331
nucleus p. 331
electron p. 331
atomic number p. 332
atomic mass number p. 332
isotope p. 332
ion p. 334

2 Elements make up the periodic table.

- Elements can be organized by similarities.
- The periodic table organizes the atoms of the elements by properties and atomic number.

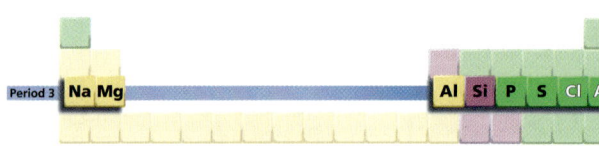

Groups of elements have similar properties.
Elements in a period have varying properties.

VOCABULARY
atomic mass p. 337
periodic table p. 338
group p. 342
period p. 342

3 The periodic table is a map of the elements.

- The periodic table has distinct regions.
- Most elements are metals.
- Nonmetals and metalloids have a wide range of properties.
- Some atoms can change their identity through radioactive decay.

metal metalloid nonmetal

VOCABULARY
reactive p. 346
metal p. 347
nonmetal p. 349
metalloid p. 350
radioactivity p. 350
half-life p. 352

Reviewing Vocabulary

Describe how the vocabulary terms in the following pairs are related to each other. Explain the relationship in a one- or two-sentence answer. Underline each vocabulary term in your answer.

1. isotope, nucleus
2. atomic mass, atomic number
3. electron, proton
4. atomic number, atomic mass number
5. group, period
6. metals, nonmetals
7. radioactivity, half-life

Reviewing Key Concepts

Multiple Choice *Choose the letter of the best answer.*

8. The central part of an atom is called the
    a. electron
    c. proton
    b. nucleus
    d. neutron

9. The electric charge on a proton is
    a. positive
    c. neutral
    b. negative
    d. changing

10. The number of protons in the nucleus is the
    a. atomic mass
    c. atomic number
    b. isotope
    d. half-life

11. Nitrogen has atomic number 7. An isotope of nitrogen containing seven neutrons would be
    a. nitrogen-13
    c. nitrogen-15
    b. nitrogen-14
    d. nitrogen-16

12. How does the size of a negative ion compare to the size of the atom that formed it?
    a. It's smaller.
    b. It's larger.
    c. It's the same size.
    d. It varies.

13. The modern periodic table is organized by
    a. size of atom
    b. atomic mass
    c. number of neutrons
    d. atomic number

14. Elements in a group have
    a. a wide range of chemical properties
    b. the same atomic radius
    c. similar chemical properties
    d. the same number of protons

15. Elements in a period have
    a. a wide range of chemical properties
    b. the same atomic radius
    c. similar chemical properties
    d. the same number of protons

16. From left to right in a period, the size of atoms
    a. increases
    c. remains the same
    b. decreases
    d. shows no pattern

17. The elements in Group 1 of the periodic table are commonly called the
    a. alkali metals
    c. alkaline earth metals
    b. transition metals
    d. rare earth metals

18. The isotope nitrogen-13 has a half-life of 10 minutes. If you start with 40 grams of this isotope, how many grams will you have left after 20 minutes?
    a. 10
    c. 20
    b. 15
    d. 30

Short Answer *Write a short answer to each question. You may need to consult a periodic table.*

19. Rubidium forms the positive ion Rb^+. Is this ion larger or smaller than the neutral atom? Explain.

20. How can you find the number of neutrons in the isotope nitrogen-16?

21. Explain how density varies across and up and down the periodic table.

22. Place these elements in order from least reactive to most reactive: nickel (Ni), xenon (Xe), lithium (Li). How did you determine the order?

Chapter 10: **Atomic Structure and the Periodic Table**

Thinking Critically

The table below lists some properties of six elements. Use the information and your knowledge of the properties of elements to answer the next three questions.

Element	Appearance	Density (g/cm³)	Conducts Electricity
A	dark purple crystals	4.93	no
B	shiny silvery solid	0.97	yes
C	shiny silvery solid	22.65	yes
D	yellow powder	2.07	no
E	shiny gray solid	5.32	semiconductor
F	shiny bluish solid	8.91	yes

23. ANALYZE Based on the listed properties, identify each of the elements as a metal, nonmetal, or metalloid.

24. APPLY Which would weigh more: a cube of element A or a same-sized cube of element D?

25. HYPOTHESIZE Which element(s) do you think you might find in electronic devices? Why?

26. HYPOTHESIZE The thyroid gland, located in your throat, secretes hormones. In 1924 iodine was added to table salt. As more and more Americans used iodized salt, the number of cases of thyroid diseases decreased. Write a hypothesis that explains the observed decrease in thyroid-related diseases.

27. INFER How does the size of a beryllium (Be) atom compare with the size of an oxygen (O) atom?

28. PREDICT Although noble gases do not naturally react with other elements, xenon and krypton have been made to react with halogens such as chlorine in laboratories. Why are the halogens most likely to react with the noble gases?

Below is an element square from the periodic table. Use it to answer the next two questions.

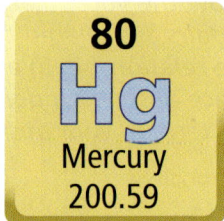

29. CALCULATE One of the more common isotopes of mercury is mercury-200. How many protons and neutrons are in the nucleus of mercury-200?

30. INFER Cadmium occupies the square directly above mercury on the periodic table. Is a cadium atom larger or smaller than a mercury atom?

31. CALCULATE An isotope has a half-life of 40 minutes. How much of a 100-gram sample would remain unchanged after two hours?

32. APPLY When a uranium atom with 92 protons and 146 neutrons undergoes radioactive decay, it produces a particle that consists of two protons and two neutrons from its nucleus. Into which element is the uranium atom transformed?

the BIG idea

33. ANALYZE Look again at the photograph on pages 326–327. Answer the question again, using what you have learned in the chapter.

34. DRAW CONCLUSIONS Suppose you've been given the ability to take apart and assemble atoms. How could you turn lead into gold?

35. ANALYZE Explain how the structure of an atom determines its place in the periodic table.

UNIT PROJECTS

If you are doing a unit project, make a folder for your project. Include in your folder a list of the resources you will need, the date on which the project is due, and a schedule to track your progress. Begin gathering data.

Standardized Test Practice

Interpreting Tables

The table below shows part of the periodic table of elements.

	Group 1	2	13	14	15	16	17	18
Period 1	1 H							2 He
2	3 Li	4 Be	5 B	6 C	7 N	8 O	9 F	10 Ne
3	11 Na	12 Mg	13 Al	14 Si	15 P	16 S	17 Cl	18 Ar
4	19 K	20 Ca	31 Ga	32 Ge	33 As	34 Se	35 Br	36 Kr

Answer the questions based on the information given in the table.

1. What does the number above the symbol for each element represent?
  a. Its number of isotopes
  b. Its atomic number
  c. Its number of neutrons
  d. Its atomic mass

2. The atom of what element is in Period 4, Group 13?
  a. Na
  b. Ga
  c. Al
  d. K

3. What do the elements on the far right of the table (He, Ne, Ar, and Kr) have in common?
  a. They do not generally react with other elements.
  b. They are in liquids under normal conditions.
  c. They are metals that rust easily.
  d. They are very reactive gases.

4. How many electrons does a neutral chlorine (Cl) atom contain?
  a. 16   c. 18
  b. 17   d. 19

5. If a sodium (Na) atom loses one electron to form a positive ion, how many electrons would lithium (Li) lose to form a positive ion?
  a. 0   c. 2
  b. 1   d. 3

6. If a fluorine (F) atom gains one electron to form a negative ion, how many electrons would bromine (Br) gain to form a negative ion?
  a. 0   c. 2
  b. 1   d. 3

Extended Response

Answer the following two questions in detail. Include some of the terms shown in the word box at right. Underline each term you use in your answer.

| electron | nucleus | proton |
| isotope | neutron | radioactivity |

7. Democritus was an ancient Greek philosopher who claimed that all matter was made of tiny particles he called atoms. Democritus said that all atoms were made of the same material. The objects of the world differed because each was made of atoms of different sizes and shapes. How does the modern view of atoms differ from this ancient view? How is it similar?

8. Half-life is a measure of the time it takes half of the radioactive atoms in a substance to decay into other atoms. If you know how much radioactive material an object had to begin with, how could you use half-life to determine its age now?

CHAPTER 11
Chemical Bonds and Compounds

the BIG idea

The properties of compounds depend on their atoms and chemical bonds.

How do these skydivers stay together? How is this similar to the way atoms stay together?

Key Concepts

SECTION 1 — Elements combine to form compounds.
Learn the difference between elements and compounds. Learn how to write and name chemical compounds.

SECTION 2 — Chemical bonds hold compounds together.
Learn about the different types of chemical bonds.

SECTION 3 — Substances' properties depend on their bonds.
Learn how bonds give compounds certain properties.

Internet Preview

CLASSZONE.COM

Chapter 11 online resources: Content Review, two Visualizations, two Resource Centers, Math Tutorial, Test Practice

358 Unit 3: Chemical Interactions

EXPLORE the BIG idea

Mixing It Up

Get some red and yellow modeling compound. Make three red and two yellow balls, each about the diameter of a nickel. Blend one red and one yellow ball together. Blend one yellow and two red balls together.

Observe and Think How different do your combinations look from the original? from each other?

The Shape of Things

Pour some salt onto dark paper. Look at the grains through a hand lens. Try to observe a single grain.

Observe and Think What do you notice about the salt grains? What do you think might affect the way the grains look?

Internet Activity: Bonding

Go to **ClassZone.com** and watch the animation showing ionic and covalent bonding. Observe the differences in the two types of bonding.

Observe and Think What's the difference between an ionic and a covalent bond? Explain how covalent bonding can have different characteristics.

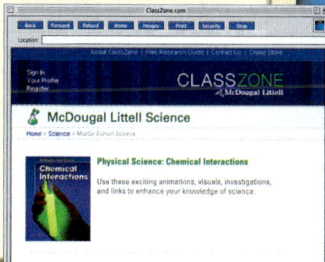

Compounds Code: MDL023

Chapter 11: **Chemical Bonds and Compounds** 359

CHAPTER 11
Getting Ready to Learn

CONCEPT REVIEW

- Electrons occupy a cloud around an atom's nucleus.
- Atoms form ions by losing or gaining electrons.

VOCABULARY REVIEW

electron p. 331
element *See Glossary.*

Review concepts and vocabulary.

TAKING NOTES

MAIN IDEA AND DETAIL NOTES

Make a two-column chart. Write the main ideas, such as those in the blue headings, in the column on the left. Write details about each of those main ideas in the column on the right.

VOCABULARY STRATEGY

Place each vocabulary term at the center of a **description wheel** diagram. Write some words describing it on the spokes.

See the Note-Taking Handbook on pages R45–R51.

SCIENCE NOTEBOOK

MAIN IDEAS	DETAIL NOTES
Atoms combine in predictable numbers.	• Each compound has a specific ratio of atoms. • A ratio is a comparison between two quantities.
Writing chemical formulas	• Find symbols on the periodic table. • Note ratio of atoms with subscripts.

Description wheel for SUBSCRIPT:
- written to the right of a symbol
- slightly below the symbol
- indicates number of atoms per molecule

KEY CONCEPT

Elements combine to form compounds.

 BEFORE, you learned
- Atoms make up everything on Earth
- Atoms react with different atoms to form compounds

 NOW, you will learn
- How compounds differ from the elements that make them
- How a chemical formula represents the ratio of atoms in a compound
- How the same atoms can form different compounds

VOCABULARY

chemical formula p. 363
subscript p. 363

EXPLORE Compounds

How are compounds different from elements?

PROCEDURE

1. Examine the lump of carbon, the beaker of water, and the sugar. Record your observations of each.
2. Light the candle. Pour some sugar into a test tube and heat it over the candle for several minutes. Record your observations.

MATERIALS
- carbon
- water
- sugar
- test tube
- test-tube holder
- candle
- matches

WHAT DO YOU THINK?
- The sugar is made up of atoms of the same elements that are in the carbon and water. How are sugar, carbon, and water different from one another?
- Does heating the sugar give you any clue that sugar contains more than one element?

Compounds have different properties from the elements that make them.

MAIN IDEA AND DETAILS
Make a two-column chart to start organizing information on compounds.

If you think about all of the different substances around you, it is clear that they cannot all be elements. In fact, while there are just over 100 elements, there are millions of different substances. Most substances are compounds. A compound is a substance made of atoms of two or more different elements. Just as the 26 letters in the alphabet can form thousands of words, the elements in the periodic table can form millions of compounds.

The atoms of different elements are held together in compounds by chemical bonds. Chemical bonds can hold atoms together in large networks or in small groups. Bonds help determine the properties of a compound.

Chapter 11: **Chemical Bonds and Compounds** 361

The properties of a compound depend not only on which atoms the compound contains, but also on how the atoms are arranged. Atoms of carbon and hydrogen, for example, can combine to form many thousands of different compounds. These compounds include natural gas, components of automobile gasoline, the hard waxes in candles, and many plastics. Each of these compounds has a certain number of carbon and hydrogen atoms arranged in a specific way.

The properties of compounds are often very different from the properties of the elements that make them. For example, water is made from two atoms of hydrogen bonded to one atom of oxygen. At room temperature, hydrogen and oxygen are both colorless, odorless gases, and they remain gases down to extremely low temperatures. Water, however, is a liquid at temperatures up to 100°C (212°F) and a solid below 0°C (32°F). Sugar is a compound composed of atoms of carbon, hydrogen, and oxygen. Its properties, however, are unlike those of carbon, hydrogen, or oxygen.

calcium + chlorine = calcium chloride

The picture above shows what happens when the elements calcium and chlorine combine to form the compound calcium chloride. Calcium is a soft, silvery metallic solid. Chlorine is a greenish-yellow gas that is extremely reactive and poisonous to humans. Calcium chloride, however, is a nonpoisonous white solid. People who live in cold climates often use calcium chloride to melt the ice that forms on streets in the wintertime.

 **CHECK YOUR READING** How do the properties of a compound compare with the properties of the elements that make it?

Atoms combine in predictable numbers.

A given compound always contains atoms of elements in a specific ratio. For example, the compound ammonia always has three hydrogen atoms for every nitrogen atom—a 3 to 1 ratio of hydrogen to nitrogen. This same 3:1 ratio holds for every sample of ammonia, under all physical conditions. A substance with a different ratio of hydrogen to nitrogen atoms is not ammonia. For example, hydrazoic acid also contains atoms of hydrogen and nitrogen but in a ratio of one hydrogen atom to three nitrogen atoms, or 1:3.

READING TIP

A ratio is a numerical relationship between two values. If you had 3 apples for every 1 orange, you'd have a ratio of 3 to 1.

INVESTIGATE Element Ratios

How can you model a compound?
PROCEDURE

1. Collect a number of nuts and bolts. The nuts represent hydrogen atoms. The bolts represent carbon atoms.
2. Connect the nuts to the bolts to model the compound methane. Methane contains four hydrogen atoms attached to one carbon atom. Make as many of these models as you can.
3. Count the nuts and bolts left over.

WHAT DO YOU THINK?
- What ratio of nuts to bolts did you use to make a model of a methane atom?
- How many methane models did you make? Why couldn't you make more?

CHALLENGE The compound ammonia has one nitrogen atom and three hydrogen atoms. How would you use the nuts and bolts to model this compound?

SKILL FOCUS
Modeling

MATERIAL
- nuts and bolts
- Modeling Compounds Datasheet

TIME
20 minutes

Chemical Formulas

Remember that atoms of elements can be represented by their chemical symbols, as given in the periodic table. A **chemical formula** uses these chemical symbols to represent the atoms of the elements and their ratios in a chemical compound.

Carbon dioxide is a compound consisting of one atom of carbon attached by chemical bonds to two atoms of oxygen. Here is how you would write the chemical formula for carbon dioxide:

- Find the symbols for carbon (C) and oxygen (O) on the periodic table. Write these symbols side by side.
- To indicate that there are two oxygen atoms for every carbon atom, place the subscript 2 to the right of the oxygen atom's symbol. A **subscript** is a number written to the right of a chemical symbol and slightly below it.
- Because there is only one atom of carbon in carbon dioxide, you need no subscript for carbon. The subscript 1 is never used. The chemical formula for carbon dioxide is, therefore,

$$CO_2$$

The chemical formula shows one carbon atom bonded to two oxygen atoms.

VOCABULARY
Remember to create a description wheel for *chemical formula* and other vocabulary words.

READING TIP
The word *subscript* comes from the prefix *sub-*, which means "under," and the Latin word *scriptum*, which means "written." A subscript is something written under something else.

Chapter 11: **Chemical Bonds and Compounds** 363

Chemical Formulas

Chemical formulas show the ratios of atoms in a chemical compound.

Compound Name	Atoms	Atomic Ratio	Chemical Formula
Hydrogen chloride	H Cl	1:1	HCl
Water	H H O	2:1	H_2O
Ammonia	N H H H	1:3	NH_3
Methane	C H H H H	1:4	CH_4
Propane	C C C H H H H H H H H	3:8	C_3H_8

READING VISUALS How many more hydrogen atoms does propane have than methane?

Find out more about chemical formulas.

The chart above shows the names, atoms, ratios, and chemical formulas for several chemical compounds. The subscripts for each compound indicate the number of atoms that combine to make that compound. Notice how hydrogen combines with different atoms in different ratios. Notice in particular that methane and propane are made of atoms of the same elements, carbon and hydrogen, only in different ratios. This example shows why it's important to pay attention to ratios when writing chemical formulas.

 Why is the ratio of atoms in a chemical formula so important?

Same Elements, Different Compounds

Even before chemists devised a way to write chemical formulas, they realized that different compounds could be composed of atoms of the same elements. Nitrogen and oxygen, for example, form several compounds. One compound consists of one atom of nitrogen attached to one atom of oxygen. This compound's formula is NO. A second compound has one atom of nitrogen attached to two atoms of oxygen, so its formula is NO_2. A third compound has two nitrogen atoms attached to one oxygen atom; its formula is N_2O. The properties of these compounds are different, even though they are made of atoms of the same elements.

364 Unit 3: Chemical Interactions

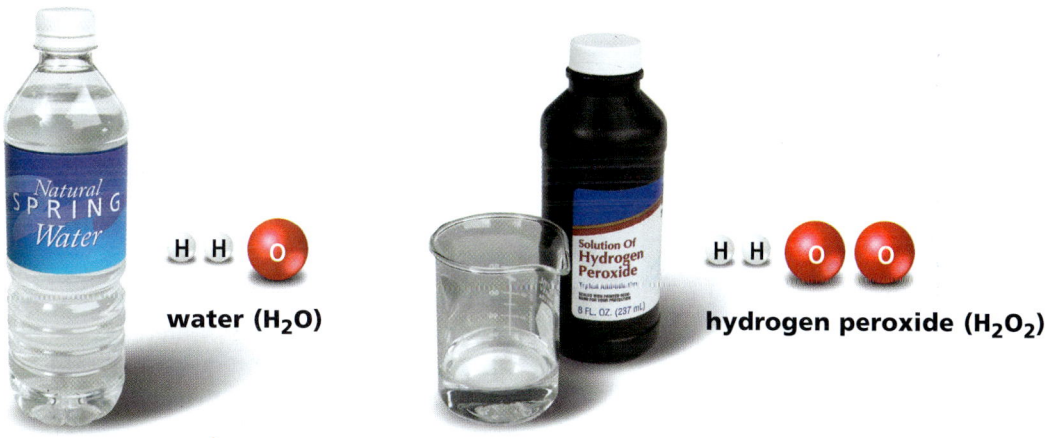

water (H₂O)   hydrogen peroxide (H₂O₂)

There are many other examples of atoms of the same elements forming different compounds. The photographs above show two bottles filled with clear, colorless liquids. You might use the liquid in the first bottle to cool off after a soccer game. The bottle contains water, which is a compound made from two atoms of hydrogen and one atom of oxygen (H_2O). You could not survive for long without water.

You definitely would not want to drink the liquid in the second bottle, although this liquid resembles water. This bottle also contains a compound of hydrogen and oxygen, hydrogen peroxide, but hydrogen peroxide has two hydrogen and two oxygen atoms (H_2O_2). Hydrogen peroxide is commonly used to kill bacteria on skin. One way to tell these two compounds apart is to test them using a potato. A drop of hydrogen peroxide on a raw potato will bubble; a drop of water on the potato will not.

The difference between the two compounds is greater than the labels or their appearance would indicate. The hydrogen peroxide that you buy at a drugstore is a mixture of hydrogen peroxide and water. In its concentrated form, hydrogen peroxide is a thick, syrupy liquid that boils at 150°C (302°F). Hydrogen peroxide can even be used as a fuel.

 **CHECK YOUR READING**   What are the chemical formulas for water and hydrogen peroxide?

11.1 Review

KEY CONCEPTS

1. How do the properties of compounds often compare with the properties of the elements that make them?
2. How many atoms are in the compound represented by the formula $C_{12}H_{22}O_{11}$?
3. How can millions of compounds be made from the atoms of about 100 elements?

CRITICAL THINKING

4. **Apply** If a chemical formula has no subscripts, what can you conclude about the ratio of the atoms in it?
5. **Infer** How might you distinguish between hydrogen peroxide and water?

 CHALLENGE

6. **Analyze** A chemist analyzes two compounds and finds that they both contain only carbon and oxygen. The two compounds, however, have different properties. How can two compounds made from the same elements be different?

MATH in SCIENCE

SKILL: CALCULATING RATIOS

MATH TUTORIAL
CLASSZONE.COM
Click on Math Tutorial for more help with ratios.

A good strikeout-to-walk ratio for a baseball pitcher is 2:1. This means that for every two strikeouts achieved, the pitcher only allows one walk.

Regarding Ratios

No pitcher gets a batter out every time. Sometimes even the worst pitchers have spectacular games. If you're a fan of professional baseball, you've probably seen the quality of certain players rated by using a ratio. A ratio is a comparison of two quantities. For a major league baseball pitcher, for example, one ratio you might hear reported is the number of strikeouts to the number of walks during a season. Chemical formulas are also ratios—ratios that compare the numbers of atoms in a compound.

Example

Consider the chemical formula for the compound glucose:

$$C_6H_{12}O_6$$

From this formula you can write several ratios. To find the ratio of carbon atoms to hydrogen atoms, for instance, do the following:

(1) Find the number of each kind of atom by noting the subscripts.

6 carbon, 12 hydrogen

(2) Write the first number on the left and the second on the right, and place a colon between them.

6:12

(3) Reduce the ratio by dividing each side by the largest number that goes into each evenly, in this case 6.

1:2

ANSWER The ratio of carbon to hydrogen in glucose is 1:2.

Use the table below to answer the following questions.

Compounds and Formulas	
Compound Name	**Chemical Formula**
Carbon dioxide	CO_2
Methane	CH_4
Sulfuric acid	H_2SO_4
Glucose	$C_6H_{12}O_6$
Formic acid	CH_2O_2

1. In carbon dioxide, what is the ratio of carbon to oxygen?

2. What is the ratio of carbon to hydrogen in methane?

3. In sulfuric acid, what is the ratio of hydrogen to sulfur? the ratio of sulfur to oxygen?

CHALLENGE What two chemical compounds in the table have the same ratio of carbon atoms to oxygen atoms?

KEY CONCEPT

Chemical bonds hold compounds together.

◂ BEFORE, you learned

- Elements combine to form compounds
- Electrons are located in a cloud around the nucleus
- Atoms can lose or gain electrons to form ions

▸ NOW, you will learn

- How electrons are involved in chemical bonding
- About the different types of chemical bonds
- How chemical bonds affect structure

VOCABULARY

ionic bond p. 368
covalent bond p. 370
molecule p. 371
polar covalent bond p. 371

THINK ABOUT

How do you keep things together?

Think about the different ways the workers at this construction site connect materials. They may use nails, screws, or even glue, depending on the materials they wish to keep together. Why would they choose the method they do? What factors do you consider when you join two objects?

MAIN IDEA AND DETAILS
Make a two-column chart to organize information on chemical bonds.

Chemical bonds between atoms involve electrons.

Water is a compound of hydrogen and oxygen. The air you breathe, however, contains oxygen gas, a small amount of hydrogen gas, as well as some water vapor. How can hydrogen and oxygen be water sometimes and at other times not? The answer is by forming chemical bonds.

Chemical bonds are the "glue" that holds the atoms of elements together in compounds. Chemical bonds are what make compounds more than just mixtures of atoms.

Remember that an atom has a positively charged nucleus surrounded by a cloud of electrons. Chemical bonds form when the electrons in the electron clouds around two atoms interact. How the electron clouds interact determines the kind of chemical bond that is formed. Chemical bonds have a great effect on the chemical and physical properties of compounds. Chemical bonds also influence how different substances interact. You'll learn more about how substances interact in a later chapter.

Chapter 11: **Chemical Bonds and Compounds** 367

Atoms can transfer electrons.

> **REMINDER**
> Remember that elements in columns show similar chemical properties.

Ions are formed when atoms gain or lose electrons. Gaining electrons changes an atom into a negative ion. Losing electrons changes an atom into a positive ion. Individual atoms do not form ions by themselves. Instead, ions typically form in pairs when one atom transfers one or more electrons to another atom.

An element's location on the periodic table can give a clue as to the type of ions the atoms of that element will form. The illustration to the left shows the characteristic ions formed by several groups. Notice that all metals lose electrons to form positive ions. Group 1 metals commonly lose only one electron to form ions with a single positive charge. Group 2 metals commonly lose two electrons to form ions with two positive charges. Other metals, like the transition metals, also always form positive ions, but the number of electrons they may lose varies.

Nonmetals form ions by gaining electrons. Group 17 nonmetals, for example, gain one electron to form ions with a 1– charge. The nonmetals in Group 16 gain two electrons to form ions with a 2– charge. The noble gases do not normally gain or lose electrons and so do not normally form ions.

CHECK YOUR READING What type of ions do metals form?

Ionic Bonds

What happens when an atom of an element from Group 1, like sodium, meets an atom of an element from Group 17, like chlorine? Sodium is likely to lose an electron to form a positive ion. Chlorine is likely to gain an electron to form a negative ion. An electron, therefore, moves from the sodium atom to the chlorine atom.

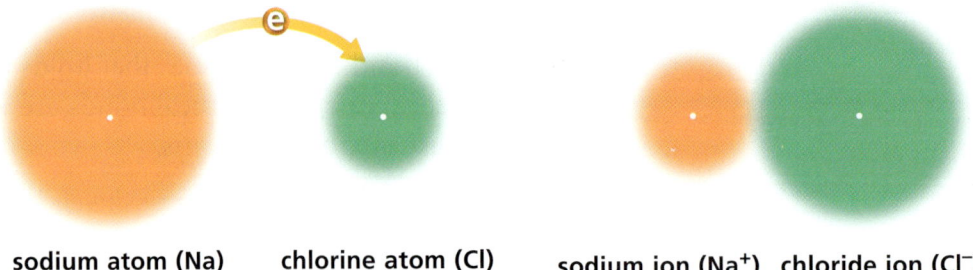

sodium atom (Na)   chlorine atom (Cl)   sodium ion (Na$^+$)   chloride ion (Cl$^-$)

Remember that particles with opposite electrical charges attract one another. When the ions are created, therefore, they are drawn toward one another by electrical attraction. This force of attraction between positive and negative ions is called an **ionic bond.**

Electrical forces act in all directions. Each ion, therefore, attracts all other nearby ions with the opposite charge. The next illustration shows how this all-around attraction produces a network of sodium and chloride ions known as a sodium chloride crystal.

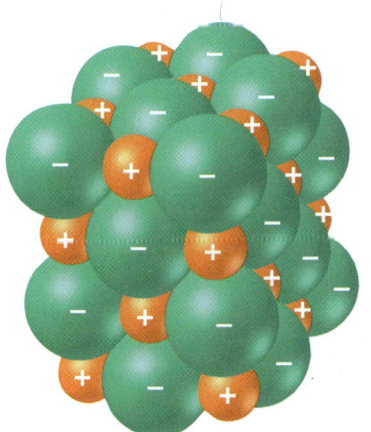

Notice how each positive ion is surrounded by six negative ions, and each negative ion is surrounded by six positive ions. This regular arrangement gives the sodium chloride crystal its characteristic cubic shape. You can see this distinctive crystal shape when you look at table salt crystals through a magnifying glass.

Ionic bonds form between all nearby ions of opposite charge. These interactions make ionic compounds very stable and their crystals very strong. Although sodium chloride crystals have a cubic shape, other ionic compounds form crystals with different regular patterns. The shape of the crystals of an ionic compound depends, in part, on the ratio of positive and negative ions and the sizes of the ions.

The cubic shape of sodium chloride crystals is a result of how the ions form crystals.

Names of Ionic Compounds

The name of an ionic compound is based on the names of the ions it is made of. The name for a positive ion is the same as the name of the atom from which it is formed. The name of a negative ion is formed by dropping the last part of the name of the atom and adding the suffix *-ide*. To name an ionic compound, the name of the positive ion is placed first, followed by the name of the negative ion. For example, the chemical name for table salt is sodium chloride. *Sodium* is the positive sodium ion and *chloride* is the negative ion formed from chlorine.

Therefore, to name the compound with the chemical formula BaI_2

- First, take the name of the positive metal element: barium.
- Second, take the name of the negative, nonmetal element, iodine, and give it the ending *-ide:* iodide.
- Third, combine the two names: barium iodide.

Similarly, the name for KBr is potassium bromide, and the name for MgF_2 is magnesium fluoride.

Atoms can share electrons.

In general, an ionic bond forms between atoms that lose electrons easily to form positive ions, such as metals, and atoms that gain electrons easily to form negative ions, such as nonmetals. Another way in which atoms can bond together is by sharing electrons. Nonmetal atoms usually form bonds with each other by sharing electrons.

Covalent Bonds

VOCABULARY
Make a description wheel for *covalent bond* and other vocabulary words.

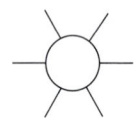

A pair of shared electrons between two atoms is called a **covalent bond.** In forming a covalent bond, neither atom gains or loses an electron, so no ions are formed. The shared electrons are attracted to both positively charged nuclei. The illustrations below show a covalent bond between two iodine atoms. In the first illustration, notice how the electron clouds overlap. A covalent bond is also often represented as a line between the two atoms, as in the second illustration.

Iodine (I_2)

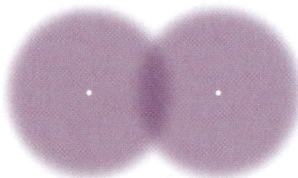 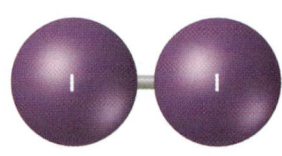

electron cloud model   ball-and-stick model

READING TIP
To help yourself remember that a covalent bond involves a sharing of electrons, remember that the prefix *co-* means "partner."

The number of covalent bonds that an atom can form depends on the number of electrons that it has available for sharing. For example, atoms of the halogen group and hydrogen can contribute only one electron to a covalent bond. These atoms, therefore, can form only one covalent bond. Atoms of Group 16 elements can form two covalent bonds. Atoms of the elements of Group 15 can form three bonds. Carbon and silicon in Group 14 can form four bonds. For example, in methane (CH_4), carbon forms four covalent bonds with four hydrogen atoms, as shown below.

Methane (CH_4)

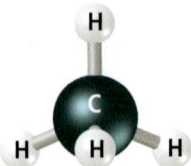   

ball-and-stick model   space-filling model

We don't always show the lines representing the covalent bonds between the atoms. The space-filling model still shows the general shape of the bonded atoms, but occupies far less space on the page.

Each carbon-hydrogen bond in methane is a single bond because one pair of electrons is shared between the atoms. Sometimes atoms may share more than one pair of electrons with another atom. For example, the carbon atom in carbon dioxide (CO_2) forms double bonds with each of the oxygen atoms. A double bond consists of four (two pairs of) shared electrons. Two nitrogen atoms form a triple bond, meaning that they share six (three pairs of) electrons.

Carbon Dioxide (CO_2)

Nitrogen (N_2)

READING TIP

Remember that each line in the model stands for a covalent bond—one shared pair of electrons.

A group of atoms held together by covalent bonds is called a **molecule.** A molecule can contain from two to many thousand atoms. Most molecules contain the atoms of two or more elements. For example, water (H_2O), ammonia (NH_3), and methane (CH_4) are all compounds made up of molecules. However, some molecules contain atoms of only one element. The following elements exist as two-atom molecules: H_2, N_2, O_2, F_2, Cl_2, Br_2, and I_2.

 What is a molecule?

Polar Covalent Bonds

In an iodine molecule, both atoms are exactly the same. The shared electrons therefore are attracted equally to both nuclei. If the two atoms involved in a covalent bond are very different, however, the electrons have a stronger attraction to one nucleus than to the other and spend more time near that nucleus. A covalent bond in which the electrons are shared unequally is called a **polar covalent bond.** The word *polar* refers to anything that has two extremes, like a magnet with its two opposite poles.

READING TIP

To remind yourself that polar covalent bonds have opposite partial charges, remember that Earth has both a North Pole and a South Pole.

Water (H_2O)

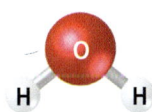

ball-and-stick model

space-filling model

In a water molecule (H_2O), the oxygen atom attracts electrons far more strongly than the hydrogen atoms do. The oxygen nucleus has eight protons, and the hydrogen nucleus has only one proton. The oxygen atom pulls the shared electrons more strongly toward it. In a water molecule, therefore, the oxygen side has a slightly negative charge, and the hydrogen side has a slightly positive charge.

Examine how electrons move in a polar covalent molecule.

Chapter 11: **Chemical Bonds and Compounds** 371

Comparing Bonds

In Salar de Uyuni, Bolivia, salt is mined in great quantities from salt water. The salt is harvested as the water evaporates into the air, leaving the salt behind. All types of chemical bonds are involved.

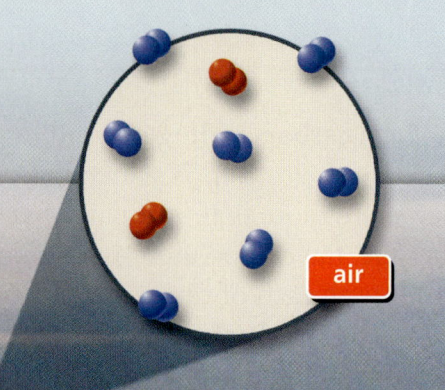
air

salt

water

Ionic Bonds (salt)

Sodium Chloride (NaCl)
A complete transfer of electrons produces the ionic bonds that hold sodium chloride (table salt) crystals together.

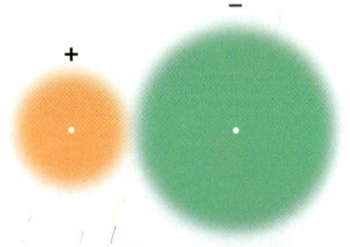

Covalent Bonds (air)

Nitrogen (N_2) and Oxygen (O_2)
Some molecules in air contain multiple covalent bonds. Nitrogen has triple bonds. Oxygen has double bonds.

Polar Covalent Bonds (water)

Water (H_2O)
The covalent bonds in water are very polar because oxygen attracts electrons far more strongly than hydrogen does.

READING VISUALS Atoms of which element are shown both in the air and in the water?

Chemical bonds give all materials their structures.

The substances around you have many different properties. The structure of the crystals and molecules that make up these substances are responsible for many of these properties. For example, crystals bend rays of light, metals shine, and medications attack certain diseases in the body because their atoms are arranged in specific ways.

Ionic Compounds

Most ionic compounds have a regular crystal structure. Remember how the size, shape, and ratio of the sodium ions and chloride ions give the sodium chloride crystal its shape. Other ionic compounds, such as calcium chloride, have different but equally regular structures that depend upon the ratio and sizes of the ions. One consequence of such rigid structures is that, when enough force is applied to the crystal, it shatters rather than bends.

INVESTIGATE Crystals

How does a crystal grow?
PROCEDURE

1. Add a small amount of the crystal-growing substance to a beaker of hot tap water. Stir until it mixes completely with the water. Keep adding the substance and stirring until no more will dissolve.
2. Pour the mixture into another beaker.
3. Tie one end of the string to the paper clip and the other end to a pencil. Lower the paper clip into the solution and lay the pencil across the top of the beaker. The paper clip should hang at about the middle of the beaker.
4. Use a hand lens to observe the paper clip several times a week for three weeks.

WHAT DO YOU THINK?
- Describe the crystals you see forming on the paper clip. Do the crystals look different as they get larger?
- Compare your crystals to those of other groups. What similarities do you see among them? What differences?

CHALLENGE Try growing larger crystals by selecting one of the crystals from your paper clip, tying it to a piece of string, and sinking it into a solution of the same crystal-growing substance.

SKILL FOCUS
Observing

MATERIALS
- crystal-growing substance
- 2 glass beakers
- hot tap water
- stirring stick
- cotton string
- paper clip
- pencil
- hand lens

TIME
30 minutes

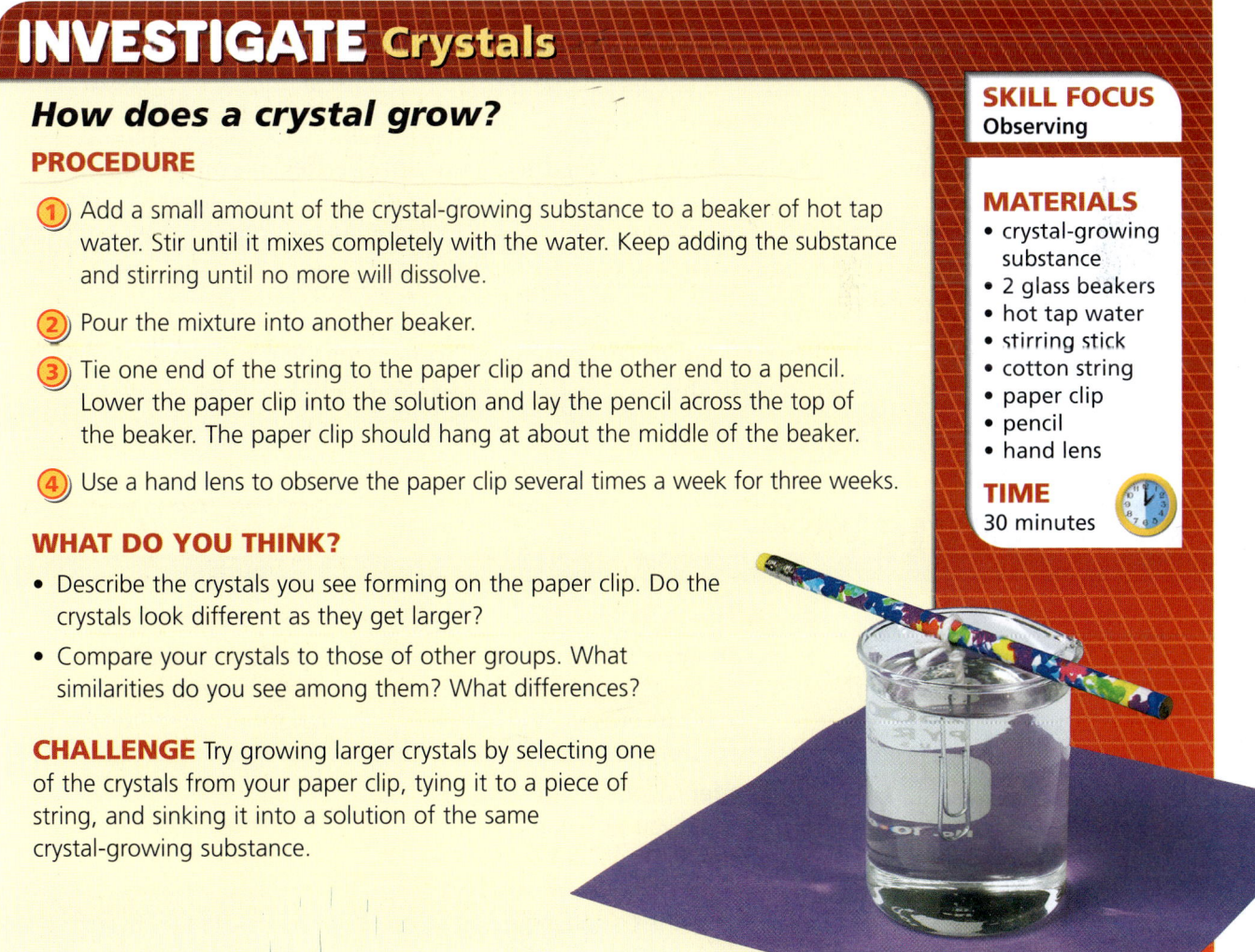

Covalent Compounds

Unlike ionic compounds, covalent compounds exist as individual molecules. Chemical bonds give each molecule a specific, three-dimensional shape called its molecular structure. Molecular structure can influence everything from how a specific substance feels to the touch to how well it interacts with other substances.

A few basic molecular structures are shown below. Molecules can have a simple linear shape, like iodine (I_2), or they can be bent, like a water molecule (H_2O). The atoms in an ammonia molecule (NH_3) form a pyramid, and methane (CH_4) molecules even have a slightly more complex shape. The shape of a molecule depends on the atoms it contains and the bonds holding it together.

READING TIP
To help yourself appreciate the differences among these structures, try making three-dimensional models of them.

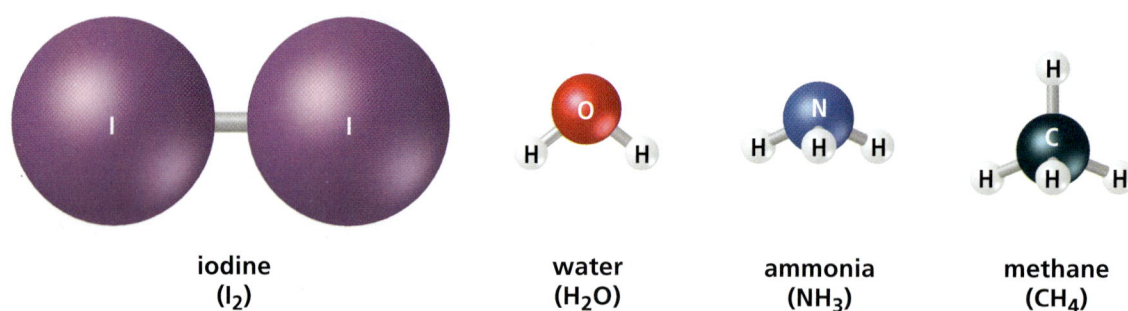

iodine (I_2)   water (H_2O)   ammonia (NH_3)   methane (CH_4)

Molecular shape can affect many properties of compounds. For example, there is some evidence to indicate that we detect scents because molecules with certain shapes fit into certain smell receptors in the nose. Molecules with similar shapes, therefore, should have similar smells. Molecular structure also plays an essential role in how our bodies respond to certain drugs. Some drugs work because molecules with certain shapes can fit into specific receptors in body cells.

11.2 Review

KEY CONCEPTS

1. What part of an atom is involved in chemical bonding?
2. How are ionic bonds and covalent bonds different?
3. Describe two ways that crystal and molecular structures affect the properties of ionic and covalent compounds.

CRITICAL THINKING

4. **Analyze** Would you expect the bonds in ammonia to be polar covalent? Why or why not?
5. **Infer** What kind of bond would you expect atoms of strontium and iodine to form? Why? Write the formula and name the compound.

CHALLENGE

6. **Conclude** Is the element silicon likely to form ionic or covalent bonds? Explain.

Think Science

SKILL: ISOLATING VARIABLES

Stick to It

Glues join objects by forming something like chemical bonds between their surfaces. While glue manufacturers try to make glues as strong as possible, simply being strong does not mean that a glue will join all surfaces equally well. For example, a glue that will hold two pieces of wood together very well may not be able to form a lasting bond between two pieces of plastic piping or two metal sheets.

Variables

When testing a new glue, a scientist wants to know exactly how that glue will perform under all conditions. In any test, however, there are a number of variables that could affect the quality of the bonds formed by the glue. The scientist needs to discover exactly which of these variables most affects the glue's ability to form lasting bonds. Identifying these variables and the effects each has on the glue's strength and lifetime enables glue makers to recommend the best uses for the glue. Following are a few of the variables a glue maker may consider when testing a glue.

- What surfaces the glue is being used to join
- How much glue is used in a test
- How evenly the glue is applied to the surface
- How much force the glue can withstand
- Over how long a time the force is applied
- The environment the glue is used in (wet, dry, or dusty)

Variables to Test

On Your Own You are a scientist at a glue company. You have developed a new type of glue and need to know how specific conditions will affect its ability to hold surfaces together. First, select one variable you wish to test. Next, outline how you would ensure that only that variable will differ in each test. You might start out by listing all the variables you can think of and then put a check by each one and describe how you are controlling it.

As a Group Discuss the outlines of your tests with others. Are there any variables you haven't accounted for?

CHALLENGE Adhesive tapes come in many different types. Outline how you would test how well a certain tape holds in a wet environment and in a dry environment.

The glue on the back of a postage stamp must be activated somehow. This scanning electron microscope photo shows postage stamp glue before (green) and after (blue) it has been activated by moisture.

This highly magnified photograph shows the attachment formed by a colorless, waterproof wood glue.

11.3 Substances' properties depend on their bonds.

KEY CONCEPT

BEFORE, you learned
- Chemical bonds hold the atoms of compounds together
- Chemical bonds involve the transfer or sharing of electrons
- Molecules have a structure

NOW, you will learn
- How metal atoms form chemical bonds with one another
- How ionic and covalent bonds influence substances' properties

VOCABULARY

metallic bond p. 376

EXPLORE Bonds in Metals

What objects conduct electricity?

PROCEDURE

1. Tape one end of a copper wire to one terminal of the battery. Attach the other end of the copper wire to the light bulb holder. Attach a second wire to the holder. Tape a third wire to the other terminal of the battery.

2. Touch the ends of both wires to objects around the classroom. Notice if the bulb lights or not.

MATERIALS
- masking tape
- 3 pieces of copper wire (15 cm)
- D cell (battery)
- light bulb and holder
- objects to test

WHAT DO YOU THINK?
- Which objects make the bulb light?
- How are these objects similar?

Metals have unique bonds.

Metal atoms bond together by sharing their electrons with one another. The atoms share the electrons equally in all directions. The equal sharing allows the electrons to move easily among the atoms of the metal. This special type of bond is called a **metallic bond.**

The properties of metals are determined by metallic bonds. One common property of metals is that they are good conductors of electric current. The electrons in a metal flow through the material, carrying the electric current. The free movement of electrons among metal atoms also means that metals are good conductors of heat. Metals also typically have high melting points. Except for mercury, all metals are solids at room temperature.

REMINDER
Chemical bonds involve the sharing of or transfer of electrons.

376 Unit 3: Chemical Interactions

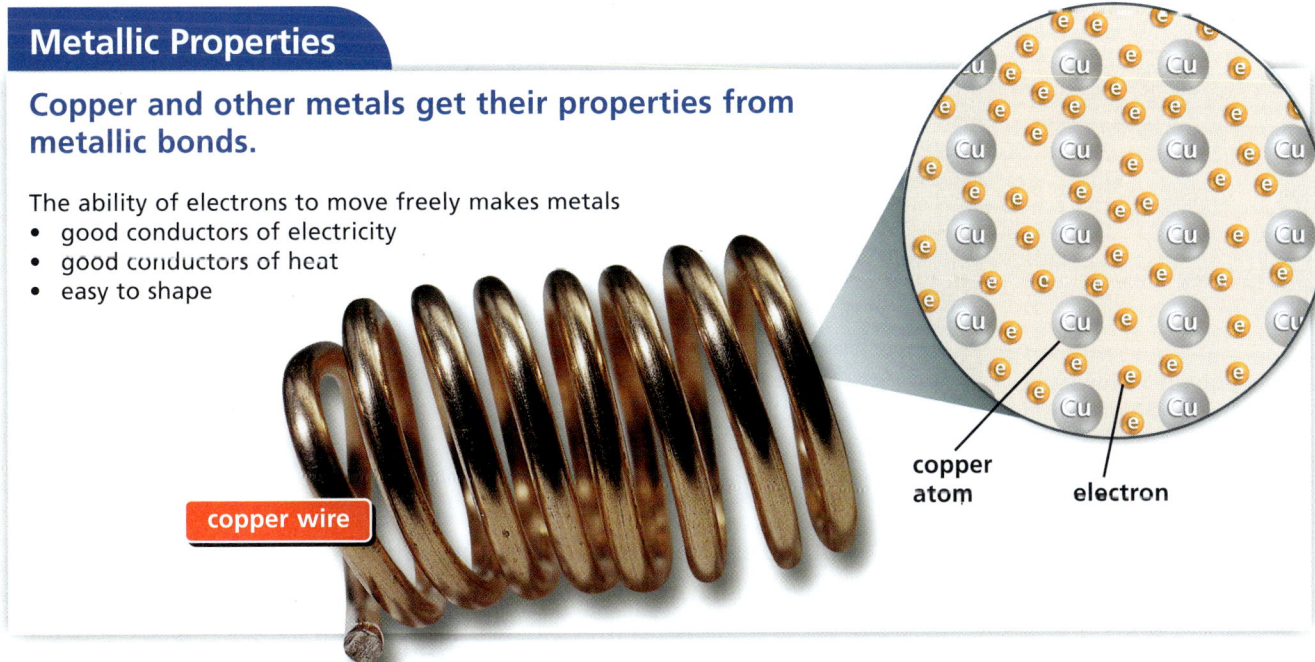

Metallic Properties

Copper and other metals get their properties from metallic bonds.

The ability of electrons to move freely makes metals
- good conductors of electricity
- good conductors of heat
- easy to shape

copper wire

copper atom   electron

Two other properties of metals are that they are easily shaped by pounding and can be drawn into a wire. These properties are also explained by the nature of the metallic bond. In metallic compounds, atoms can slide past one another. It is as if the atoms are swimming in a pool of surrounding electrons. Pounding the metal simply moves these atoms into other positions. This property makes metals ideal for making coins.

 **CHECK YOUR READING** What three properties do metals have because of metallic bonds?

Ionic and covalent bonds give compounds certain properties.

The properties of a compound depend on the chemical bonds that hold its atoms together. For example, you can be pretty certain an ionic compound will be a solid at room temperature. Ionic compounds, in fact, usually have extremely high melting and boiling points because it takes a lot of energy to break all the bonds among all the ions in the crystal. The rigid crystal network also makes ionic compounds hard, brittle, and poor conductors of electricity. No moving electrical charges means no current will flow.

Ionic compounds, however, often dissolve easily in water, separating into positive ions and negative ions. The separated ions can move freely, making solutions of ionic compounds good conductors of electricity. Your body, in fact, uses ionic solutions to help transmit impulses between nerve and muscle cells. Exercise can rapidly deplete these ionic solutions in the body, so sports drinks contain ionic compounds.

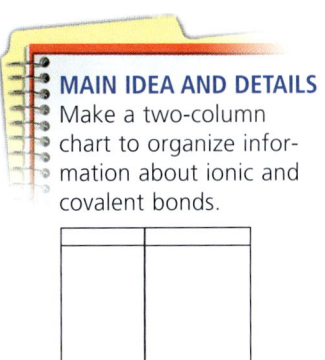

MAIN IDEA AND DETAILS
Make a two-column chart to organize information about ionic and covalent bonds.

A hot pool in Yellowstone Park's Upper Geyser Basin. These pools are often characterized by their striking colors.

Find out more about the properties of ionic and covalent compounds.

These compounds, such as potassium chloride, replace the ions lost during physical activity.

Mineral hot springs, like those found in Yellowstone National Park, are another example of ionic solutions. Many of the ionic compounds dissolved in these hot springs contain the element sulfur, which can have an unpleasant odor. Evidence of these ionic compounds can be seen in the white deposits around the pool's rim.

Covalent compounds have almost the exact opposite properties of ionic compounds. Since the atoms are organized as individual molecules, melting or boiling a covalent compound does not require breaking chemical bonds. Therefore, covalent compounds often melt and boil at lower temperatures than ionic compounds. Unlike ionic compounds, molecules stay together when dissolved in water, which means covalent compounds are poor conductors of electricity. Table sugar, for example, does not conduct an electric current when in solution.

Bonds can make the same element look different.

Covalent bonds do not always form small individual molecules. This explains how the element carbon can exist in three very different forms—diamond, graphite, and fullerene. The properties of each form depend on how the carbon atoms are bonded to each other.

Diamond is the hardest natural substance. This property makes diamond useful for cutting other substances. Diamonds are made entirely of carbon. Each carbon atom forms covalent bonds with four other carbon atoms. The pattern of linked atoms extends throughout the entire volume of a diamond crystal. This three-dimensional structure of carbon atoms gives diamonds their strength—diamond bonds do not break easily.

Another form of carbon is graphite. Graphite is the dark, slippery component of pencil "lead." Graphite has a different structure from diamond, although both are networks of interconnected atoms. Each carbon atom in graphite forms covalent bonds with three other atoms to form two-dimensional layers. These layers stack on top of one another like sheets of paper. The layers can slide past one another easily. Graphite feels slippery and is used as a lubricant to reduce friction between metal parts of machines.

diamond

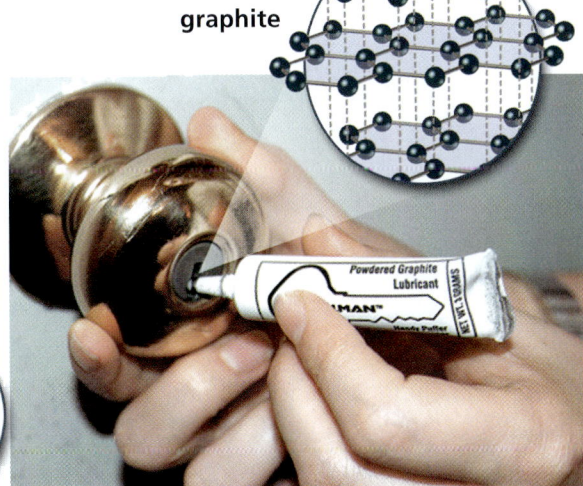
graphite

A third form of carbon, fullerene, contains large molecules. One type of fullerene, called buckminsterfullerene, has molecules shaped like a soccer ball. In 1985 chemists made a fullerene molecule consisting of 60 carbon atoms. Since then, many similar molecules have been made, ranging from 20 to more than 100 atoms per molecule.

buckminsterfullerene

11.3 Review

KEY CONCEPTS

1. How do metal atoms bond together?
2. Why do ionic compounds have high melting points?
3. What are three forms of the element carbon?

CRITICAL THINKING

4. **Apply** A compound known as cubic boron nitride has a structure similar to that of a diamond. What properties would you expect it to have?
5. **Infer** Sterling silver is a combination of silver and copper. How are the silver and copper atoms held together?

CHALLENGE

6. **Infer** Why might the water in mineral springs be a better conductor of electricity than drinking water?

Chapter 11: **Chemical Bonds and Compounds** 379

CHAPTER INVESTIGATION

Chemical Bonds

OVERVIEW AND PURPOSE Chemists can identify the type of bonds in a substance by examining its properties. In this investigation you will examine the properties of different substances and use what you have learned about chemical bonds to identify the type of bond each substance contains. You will
- observe the structure of substances with a hand lens
- test the conductivity of substances
- determine the melting point of substances

Problem

How can you determine the type of chemical bond a substance has?

Hypothesize

Write three hypotheses in "if . . . , then . . . , because . . ." form to answer the problem question for each bond type—ionic, covalent, and metallic.

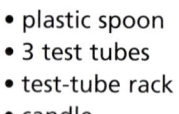

MATERIALS
- 3 wire leads with alligator clips
- battery
- zinc and copper strips
- light bulb and socket
- test compounds
- 3 plastic cups
- distilled water
- beaker
- construction paper
- hand lens
- plastic spoon
- 3 test tubes
- test-tube rack
- candle
- wire test-tube holder

Procedure

1. Create a data table similar to the one shown on the sample notebook page.

2. To build the conductivity tester, connect the first wire to one terminal of the battery and to one of the metal strips. Attach the second wire to the other terminal and to the lamp socket. Finally, connect the lamp socket to the third wire, and connect the other end of this wire to the second metal strip.

3. To make sure your tester works properly, touch the tips of the metal strips together. If the bulb lights, the tester is working properly. If not, check the connections carefully.

4. Get the following test compounds from your teacher: Epsom salts ($MgSO_4$), sugar ($C_{12}H_{22}O_{11}$), and iron filings (Fe). For each substance, put about 20 grams in a cup and label it.

380 Unit 3: **Chemical Interactions**

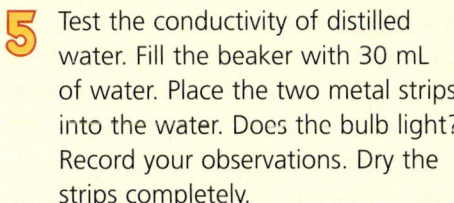

5. Test the conductivity of distilled water. Fill the beaker with 30 mL of water. Place the two metal strips into the water. Does the bulb light? Record your observations. Dry the strips completely.

6. Place dry Epsom salts on dark paper. Observe them with a hand lens. Do you see any kind of patterns in the different grains? Put the salts between the metal strips. Can you get the bulb to light by bringing the strips closer together? Record your observations.

7. Add all but a small amount of the Epsom salts to the beaker of water. Stir well. Repeat the conductivity test. What happens when you put the metal strips into the solution? Record your results.

8. Rinse and dry the beaker. Repeat steps 6–7 with other test substances. Record your results.

9. Put the remainder of each test substance into its own clean, dry test tube. Label the tubes. Light the candle. Use a test tube holder to hold each compound over the candle flame for 2 minutes. Do you notice any signs of melting? Record your observations.

Observe and Analyze *Write It Up*

1. **RECORD OBSERVATIONS** Be sure you have entered all your observations in your data table.

2. **CLASSIFY** Using the periodic table, find the elements these compounds contain. How might consulting the periodic table help you determine what type of bond exists in the compound?

Conclude *Write It Up*

1. **INTERPRET** Review your recorded observations. Classify the compounds as having ionic, covalent, or metallic bonds. Fill in the last row of the data table with your conclusions.

2. **INFER** Compare your results with your hypotheses. Did your results support your hypotheses?

3. **EVALUATE** Describe possible limitations, errors, or places where errors might have occurred.

4. **APPLY** Electrocardiograms are graphs that show the electrical activity of the heart. When an electrocardiogram is made, a paste of sodium chloride is used to hold small metal discs on the patient's skin. What property of ionic compounds does this medical test make use of?

INVESTIGATE Further

CHALLENGE To grow crystals, put about 60 grams of Epsom salts into a baby-food jar that is half full of hot water. Do the same using a second jar containing about 60 grams of sugar. Cover and shake the jars for a count of 60. Line two clean jar lids with dark paper. Brush or spoon a thin coating of each liquid over the paper. Let them stand in a warm place. After several days, observe the crystals that form, using a hand lens.

Chemical Bonds

Problem How can you determine the type of chemical bond a substance has?

Hypothesize

Observe and Analyze

Table 1: Properties of Bonds

Property	Epsom Salts (MgSO4)	Sugar (C12H22O11)	Iron Filings (Fe)
Crystal structure			
Conductivity of solid			
Conductivity in water			
Melting			
Bond type			

Conclude

Chapter 11: **Chemical Bonds and Compounds** 381

Chapter Review

the BIG idea

The properties of compounds depend on their atoms and chemical bonds.

KEY CONCEPTS SUMMARY

1 **Elements combine to form compounds.**
- Compounds have different properties from the elements that made them.
- Atoms combine in predictable numbers.

 +  =

calcium (Ca) + chlorine (Cl_2) = calcium chloride ($CaCl_2$)

VOCABULARY
chemical formula p. 363
subscript p. 363

2 **Chemical bonds hold compounds together.**
- Chemical bonds between atoms involve electrons.
- Atoms can transfer electrons.
- Atoms can share electrons.
- Chemical bonds give all materials their structure.

 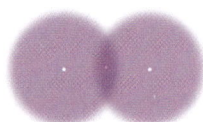

ionic bond   covalent bond

VOCABULARY
ionic bond p. 368
covalent bond p. 370
molecule p. 371
polar covalent bond p. 371

3 **Substances' properties depend on their bonds.**
- Metals have unique bonds.
- Ionic and covalent bonds give compounds certain properties.
- Bonds can make the same element look different.

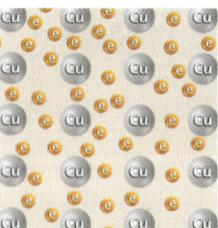  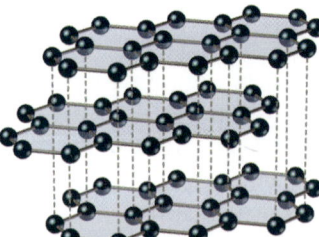

copper   diamond fragment   graphite fragment

VOCABULARY
metallic bond p. 376

Reviewing Vocabulary

Copy and complete the table below. Under each bond type, describe
- how electrons are distributed
- how the compound is structured
- one of the properties of the compound containing this type of bond

Some of the table has been filled out for you.

Ionic Bonds	Covalent Bonds	Metallic Bonds
1.	shared electron pair	2.
3.	4.	close-packed atoms in sea of electrons
have high melting points	5.	6.

Reviewing Key Concepts

Multiple Choice Choose the letter of the best answer.

7. Most substances are
   a. elements
   b. compounds
   c. metals
   d. nonmetals

8. All compounds are made of
   a. atoms of two or more elements
   b. two or more atoms of the same element
   c. atoms arranged in a crystal
   d. atoms joined by covalent bonds

9. The chemical formula for a compound having one barium (Ba) ion and two chloride (Cl) ions is
   a. BCl
   b. BaCl
   c. $BaCl_2$
   d. Ba_2Cl_2

10. The 4 in the chemical formula CH_4 means there are
    a. four carbon atoms to one hydrogen atom
    b. four carbon and four hydrogen atoms
    c. four hydrogen atoms to one carbon atom
    d. four total carbon CH combinations

11. The compound KBr has the name
    a. potassium bromide
    b. potassium bromine
    c. bromide potassium
    d. bromine potassium

12. An atom becomes a positive ion when it
    a. is attracted to all nearby atoms
    b. gains an electron from another atom
    c. loses an electron to another atom
    d. shares an electron with another atom

13. A polar covalent bond forms when two atoms
    a. share one electron equally
    b. share two electrons equally
    c. share one electron unequally
    d. share two electrons unequally

14. Metallic bonds make many metals
    a. poor conductors of heat
    b. liquid at room temperature
    c. difficult to shape
    d. good conductors of electricity

15. Three forms of carbon are
    a. diamond, graphite, and salt
    b. diamond, graphite, and fullerene
    c. graphite, salt, and carbonate
    d. diamond, salt, and fullerene

Short Answer Write a short answer to each question.

16. Why does a mixture of sodium chloride and water conduct electricity but a sodium chloride crystal does not?

17. Describe what makes diamond and graphite, two forms of the element carbon, so different.

Thinking Critically

Use the illustration above to answer the next two questions.

18. **IDENTIFY** Write the chemical formula for the molecule pictured above.

19. **ANALYZE** The nitrogen atom has a far greater attraction for electrons than hydrogen atoms. Copy the molecule pictured above and indicate which parts of the molecule have a slightly positive charge and which parts have a slightly negative charge.

20. **PREDICT** The chemical formula for calcium chloride is $CaCl_2$. What would you predict the formula for magnesium chloride to be? [**Hint:** Find magnesium on the periodic table.]

21. **INFER** When scientists make artificial diamonds, they sometimes subject graphite to very high temperatures and pressures. What do you think happens to change the graphite into diamond?

22. **SYNTHESIZE** Why would seawater be a better conductor of electricity than river water?

23. **ANALYZE** How does the nature of the metallic bond explain the observation that most metals can be drawn into a wire?

24. **EVALUATE** Do you think the types of bonds you've studied occur on the planet Mars? Explain.

25. **INFER** Why don't we use the term *ionic molecule*?

Use the chemical formulas below and a periodic table to answer the next three questions.

Compound
I. K_2SO_4
II. CF_4
III. C_4H_{10}
IV. KCl

26. **APPLY** Name compound IV. Does this compound have ionic or covalent bonds?

27. **ANALYZE** Name the elements in each compound. Tell how many atoms are in each compound.

28. **CALCULATE** Express the ratio of atoms in compounds II, III, and IV. For compound I, express all three ratios.

29. **APPLY** By 1800 Alessandro Volta had made the first electric battery. He placed pieces of cardboard soaked in saltwater in between alternating zinc and silver discs. What properties of the metals and the saltwater made them good materials for a battery?

30. **PREDICT** What is the maximum number of covalent bonds that a hydrogen atom can form? Explain your answer.

the BIG idea

31. **DRAW CONCLUSIONS** Look at the photograph on pages 358–359 again. Can you now recognize any similarities between how the skydivers stay together and how atoms stay together?

32. **APPLY** Phosphorus can be a strange element. Pure phosphorus is sometimes white, black, or red. What can account for the differences in appearance?

UNIT PROJECTS

If you need to create graphs or other visuals for your project, be sure you have graph paper, poster board, markers, or other supplies.

Standardized Test Practice

For practice on your state test, go to...
TEST PRACTICE
CLASSZONE.COM

Interpreting Tables

The table below lists some of the characteristics of substances that contain different types of bonds. Use the table to answer the questions.

Bond Type	Usually Forms Between	Electrons	Properties	Examples
Ionic	an atom of a metal and an atom of a nonmetal	transferred between atoms	• high melting points • conducts electricity when in water	BaS, $BaBr_2$, Ca_3N_2, LiCl, ZnO
Covalent	atoms of nonmetallic elements	shared between atoms but often not equally	• low melting points • does not conduct electricity	C_2H_6, C, Cl_2, H_2, $AsCl_3$
Metallic	atoms of metallic elements	freely moving about the atoms	• high melting points • conducts electricity at all times • easily shaped	Ca, Fe, Na, Cu, Zn

1. Which of these compounds would you expect to have the highest melting point?
    a. C_2H_6
    b. Cl_2
    c. $AsCl_3$
    d. $BaBr_2$

2. Which substance is likely to be easily shaped?
    a. $BaBr_2$
    b. LiCl
    c. Na
    d. C

3. In the compound LiCl, electrons are
    a. shared equally
    b. shared but not equally
    c. transferred between atoms to form ions
    d. freely moving among the atoms

4. Which of the following is an ionic compound?
    a. C_2H_6
    b. Cl_2
    c. $AsCl_3$
    d. ZnO

5. Which of the following compounds has a low melting point?
    a. Cl_2
    b. ZnO
    c. Cu
    d. $BaBr_2$

6. A solid mass of which substance would conduct electricity?
    a. Ca_3N_2
    b. LiCl
    c. Cu
    d. $AsCl_3$

Extended Response

Answer the next two questions in detail. Include some of the terms from the list in the box. Underline each term you use in your answer.

share electron	transfer electron
freely moving electrons	charge
compound	chemical formula

7. Compare how electrons are involved in making the three main types of bonds: ionic, covalent, and metallic.

8. Just about 100 elements occur naturally. There are, however, millions of different materials. How can so few basic substances make so many different materials?

Chapter 11: **Chemical Bonds and Compounds** 385

TIMELINES in Science

THE STORY OF ATOMIC STRUCTURE

About 2500 years ago, certain Greek thinkers proposed that all matter consisted of extremely tiny particles called atoms. The sizes and shapes of different atoms, they reasoned, was what determined the properties of a substance. This early atomic theory, however, was not widely accepted. Many at the time found these tiny, invisible particles difficult to accept.

What everyone could observe was that all substances were liquid, solid, or gas, light or heavy, hot or cold. Everything, they thought, must then be made of only a few basic substances or elements. They reasoned these elements must be water, air, fire, and earth. Different substances contained different amounts of each of these four substances.

The timeline shows a few of the major events that led scientists to accept the idea that matter is made of atoms and agree on the basic structure of atoms. With the revised atomic theory, scientists were able to explain how elements could be basic but different.

1661
Boyle Challenges Concept of the Four Elements
British chemist Robert Boyle proposes that more than four basic substances exist. Boyle also concludes that all matter is made of very tiny particles he calls corpuscles.

EVENTS

1600   1620   1640   1660

APPLICATIONS AND TECHNOLOGY

TECHNOLOGY
Collecting and Studying Gases
Throughout the 1600s, scientists tried to study gases but had difficulty collecting them. English biologist Stephen Hales designed an apparatus to collect gases. The "pneumatic trough" was a breakthrough in chemistry because it allowed scientists to collect and study gases for the first time. The pneumatic trough was later used by such chemists as Joseph Black, Henry Cavendish, and Joseph Priestley to study the gases that make up the air we breathe. The work of these scientists showed that air was made of more than a single gas.

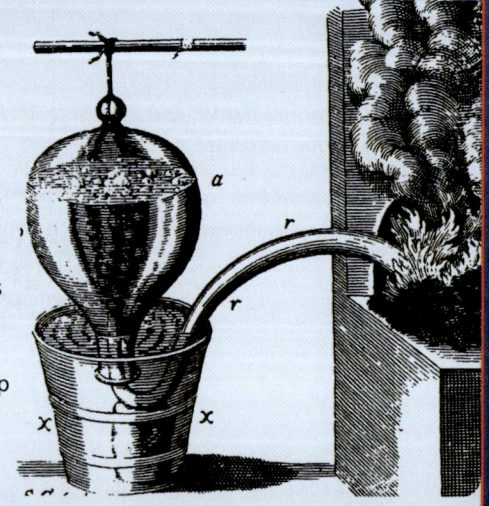

1808
John Dalton Says: "Bring Back the Atom"
English chemist John Dalton revives the ancient Greek idea that all matter is made of atoms. Dalton claims that each element has its own type of atom and that the atoms combine in fixed and predictable ratios with one another in different substances.

1897
It's Smaller Than the Atom!
English physicist Joseph John Thomson discovers the electron—the first subatomic particle to be identified. Thomson concludes that these tiny particles have a negative charge. Thomson will later propose that atoms are made of a great many of these negative particles floating in a sea of positive charge. Thomson suggests that each atom resembles a dish of pudding with raisins in it. The electrons are the raisins and the pudding the positive charge in which they float.

1808
Humphrey Davy Shocks Chemistry
English chemist Humphrey Davy applies an electric current to different materials. He discovers that many materials once thought to be elements break apart into even simpler materials. Davy succeeds in isolating the elements sodium, calcium, strontium, and barium.

1800   1820   1840   1860   1880

TECHNOLOGY
Chemistry and Electric Charge
In 1800 Italian physicist Alessandro Volta announced that he had produced an electric current from a pile, or battery, of alternating zinc and silver discs. Volta's invention was important for the study of atoms and elements in two ways. First, the fact that the contact of two different metals could produce an electric current suggested that electric charge must be part of matter. Second, the powerful electric current produced by the batteries enabled chemists to break apart many other substances, showing that there were more elements than previously thought.

1903
Atoms Release Energy
Polish-born French physicist Marie Curie and her husband, Pierre, have won the Nobel Prize for their isolation of the elements polonium and radium. These elements are unique because they release energy. Marie Curie names this trait "radioactivity." They share the award with Henri Becquerel, who previously observed this trait with the element uranium.

1911
Atoms Have a Center
By aiming a stream of particles at a piece of gold foil, New Zealand-born physicist Ernest Rutherford finds that atoms are not like a dish of pudding filled with raisins, as J. J. Thomson had suggested. Atoms must have a positive center because many of the particles bounce back. He calls the atom's center its nucleus.

1913
Bohr Puts Electrons into Orbit
Building on the work of Rutherford, Danish physicist Niels Bohr claims that electrons move about the nucleus only in certain, well-defined orbits. Bohr also says that electrons can jump to different orbits and emit or absorb energy when doing so.

1919
Atoms Share a Common Bond
U.S. chemists G.N. Lewis and Irving Langmuir suggest that atoms of many elements form bonds by sharing pairs of electrons. The idea that atoms could share electrons leads to a greater understanding of how molecules are structured.

1900   1905   1910   1915   1920   1940

APPLICATION
The Chemistry of Communication
The discovery of the electron resulted in more than a greater understanding of the atom. It also opened new ways of communicating. In 1906, U.S. inventor Lee De Forest invented a device for detecting and amplifying radio signals that he called the audion. The audion worked by producing a beam of electrons inside a vacuum tube. The beam was then made to respond to radio signals that it received from an antenna. The audion helped pave the way for later devices such as the transistor.

1960s
Smaller Particles Discovered
By smashing atoms into one another, scientists discover that protons and neutrons are themselves composed of even smaller particles. In a bit of scientific humor, these smaller particles are named "quarks," a nonsense word taken from a novel. Scientists detect these particles by observing the tracks they make in special detectors.

1980s
Tunneling to the Atomic Level
Scanning tunneling microscopes (STMs) allow scientists to interact with matter at the atomic level. Electrons on the tiny tip of an STM "tunnel" through the gap between the tip and target surface. By recording changes in the tunneling current, researchers get an accurate picture.

 RESOURCE CENTER
CLASSZONE.COM
Explore advances in atomic research.

1960   1980   2000

TECHNOLOGY
Particle Accelerators
Particle accelerators speed up charged particles by passing them through an electric field. By smashing subatomic particles into one another, scientists are able to learn what these particles are made of as well as the forces holding them together. The H1 particle detector in Hamburg, Germany, can accelerate protons to 800 billion volts and is used to study the quarks that make up protons.

INTO THE FUTURE

Humans have gone from hypothesizing atoms exist to being able to see and move them. People once considered only four substances to be true elements; today we understand how there are more than a hundred simple substances. Not only have scientists learned atoms contain electric charges, they have also learned how to use these charges.

As scientists learn more and more about the atom, it is difficult to say what they will find next. Is there something smaller than a quark? Is there one type of particle from which all other particles are made? Will we one day be able to move and connect atoms in any way we want? Are there other kinds of atoms to discover? Maybe one day we will find answers to these questions.

ACTIVITIES

Explore a Model Atom
The discovery of the nucleus was one of the most important discoveries in human history. Rutherford's experiment, however, was a simple one that you can model. Take an aluminum pie plate and place a table tennis ball-sized piece of clay at its center. The clay represents a nucleus. Place the end of a grooved ruler at the edge of the plate. Hold the other end up to form a ramp. Roll a marble down the groove toward the clay. Move the ruler to different angles with each roll. Roll the marble 20 times. How many rolls out of 20 hit the clay ball? How do you think the results would be different if the atoms looked like pudding with raisins in it, as Thomson suggested?

Writing About Science
Suppose you are an atom. Choose one of the events on the timeline and describe it from the atom's point of view.

CHAPTER 12
Chemical Reactions

What changes are happening in this chemical reaction?

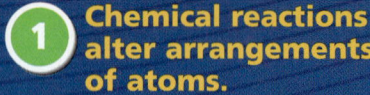

Chemical reactions form new substances by breaking and making chemical bonds.

Key Concepts

SECTION 1
Chemical reactions alter arrangements of atoms.
Learn how chemical reactions are identified and controlled.

SECTION 2
The masses of reactants and products are equal.
Learn how chemical equations show the conservation of mass.

SECTION 3
Chemical reactions involve energy changes.
Learn how energy is absorbed or released by chemical reactions.

SECTION 4
Life and industry depend on chemical reactions.
Learn about some chemical reactions in everyday life.

Internet Preview

CLASSZONE.COM

Chapter 12 online resources: Content Review, two Visualizations, two Resource Centers, Math Tutorial, Test Practice

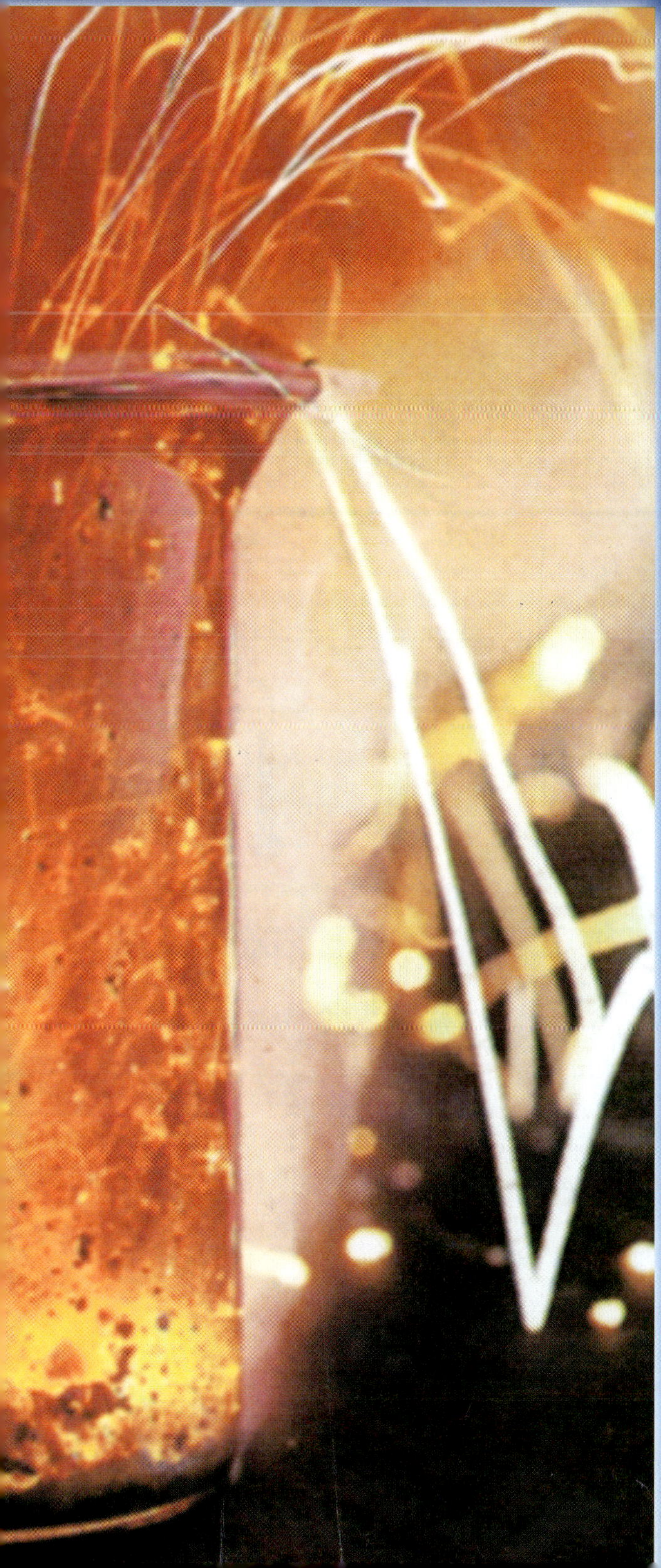

EXPLORE the BIG idea

Changing Steel Wool

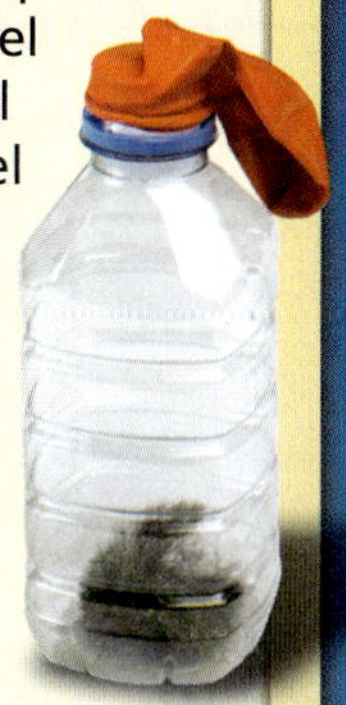

Place a small lump of steel wool in a cup. Pour in enough vinegar to cover the steel wool. After five minutes, take the steel wool out of the vinegar. Shake the steel wool to remove any excess vinegar. Place the steel wool in a small plastic bottle, and cover the mouth of the bottle with a balloon. Observe the steel wool and balloon after one hour.

Observe and Think What happened to the steel wool and balloon? What might have caused this to occur?

A Different Rate

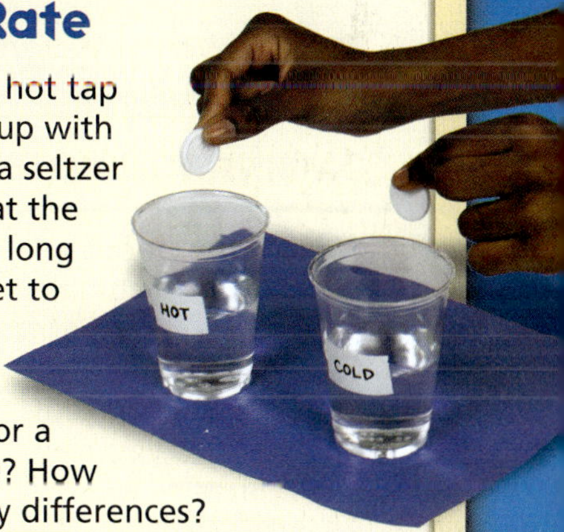

Half fill one cup with hot tap water and a second cup with cold tap water. Drop a seltzer tablet into each cup at the same time. Time how long it takes for each tablet to stop fizzing.

Observe and Think Which tablet fizzed for a longer period of time? How might you explain any differences?

Internet Activity: Reactions

Go to **ClassZone.com** to explore chemical reactions and chemical equations. Learn how a chemical equation can be balanced.

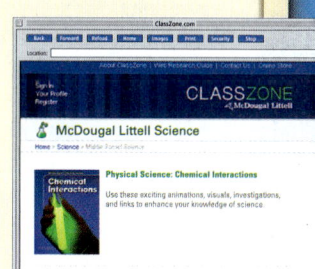

Observe and Think How do chemical equations show what happens during a chemical reaction?

NSTA scilinks.org SCILINKS

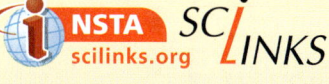

Chemical Reactions **Code: MDL024**

CHAPTER 12
Getting Ready to Learn

CONCEPT REVIEW

- Atoms combine to form compounds.
- Atoms gain or lose electrons when they form ionic bonds.
- Atoms share electrons in covalent bonds.

VOCABULARY REVIEW

electron p. 331
ionic bond p. 368
covalent bond p. 370
See Glossary for definitions.
atom, chemical change

CONTENT REVIEW
CLASSZONE.COM
Review concepts and vocabulary.

TAKING NOTES

COMBINATION NOTES

To take notes about a new concept, first make an informal outline of the information. Then make a sketch of the concept and label it so you can study it later.

VOCABULARY STRATEGY

Write each new vocabulary term in the center of a **four square** diagram. Write notes in the squares around each term. Include a definition, some characteristics, and some examples of the term. If possible, write some things that are not examples of the term.

See the Note-Taking Handbook on pages R45–R51.

SCIENCE NOTEBOOK

NOTES

Chemical reactions
- cause chemical changes
- make new substances
- change reactants into products

Evidence of Chemical Reactions

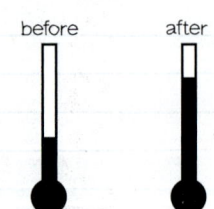

before   after

increase in temperature

Definition	Characteristics
substance present before a chemical reaction occurs	its bonds are broken during a reaction

REACTANT

Examples	Nonexample
oxygen in a combustion reaction	carbon dioxide in a combustion reaction

392 Unit 3: Chemical Interactions

KEY CONCEPT

Chemical reactions alter arrangements of atoms.

BEFORE, you learned
- Atoms of one element differ from atoms of all other elements
- Chemical bonds hold compounds together
- Chemical bonds may be ionic or covalent

NOW, you will learn
- About chemical changes and how they occur
- About three types of chemical reactions
- How the rate of a chemical reaction can be changed

VOCABULARY

chemical reaction p. 393
reactant p. 395
product p. 395
precipitate p. 396
catalyst p. 400

EXPLORE Chemical Changes

How can you identify a chemical change?

PROCEDURE

1. Pour about 3 cm (1 in.) of vinegar into the bowl. Add a spoonful of salt. Stir until the salt dissolves.
2. Put the pennies into the bowl. Wait two minutes, and then put the nail into the bowl.
3. Observe the nail after five minutes and record your observations.

WHAT DO YOU THINK?
- What did you see on the nail? Where do you think it came from?
- Did a new substance form? What evidence supports your conclusion?

MATERIALS
- vinegar
- clear bowl
- plastic spoon
- table salt
- 20 pennies
- large iron nail

COMBINATION NOTES
Use combination notes to organize information about how atoms interact during chemical reactions.

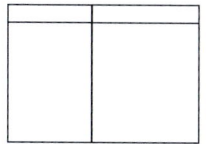

Atoms interact in chemical reactions.

You see substances change every day. Some changes are physical, such as when liquid water changes to water vapor during boiling. Other changes are chemical, such as when wood burns to form smoke and ash, or when rust forms on iron. During a chemical change, substances change into one or more different substances.

A **chemical reaction** produces new substances by changing the way in which atoms are arranged. In a chemical reaction, bonds between atoms are broken and new bonds form between different atoms. This breaking and forming of bonds takes place when particles of the original materials collide with one another. After a chemical reaction, the new arrangements of atoms form different substances.

Chapter 12: **Chemical Reactions** 393

Physical Changes

A change in the state of a substance is an example of a physical change. The substance may have some different properties after a physical change, but it is still the same substance. For example, you know that water can exist in three different physical states: the solid state (ice), the liquid state (water), and the gas state (water vapor). However, regardless of what state water is in, it still remains water, that is, H_2O molecules. As ice melts, the molecules of water move around more quickly, but the molecules do not change. As water vapor condenses, the molecules of water move more slowly, but they are still the same molecules.

Substances can undergo different kinds of physical changes. For example, sugar dissolves in water but still tastes sweet because the molecules that make up sugar do not change when it dissolves. The pressure of helium changes when it is pumped from a high-pressure tank into a balloon, but the gas still remains helium.

CHECK YOUR READING What happens to a substance when it undergoes a physical change?

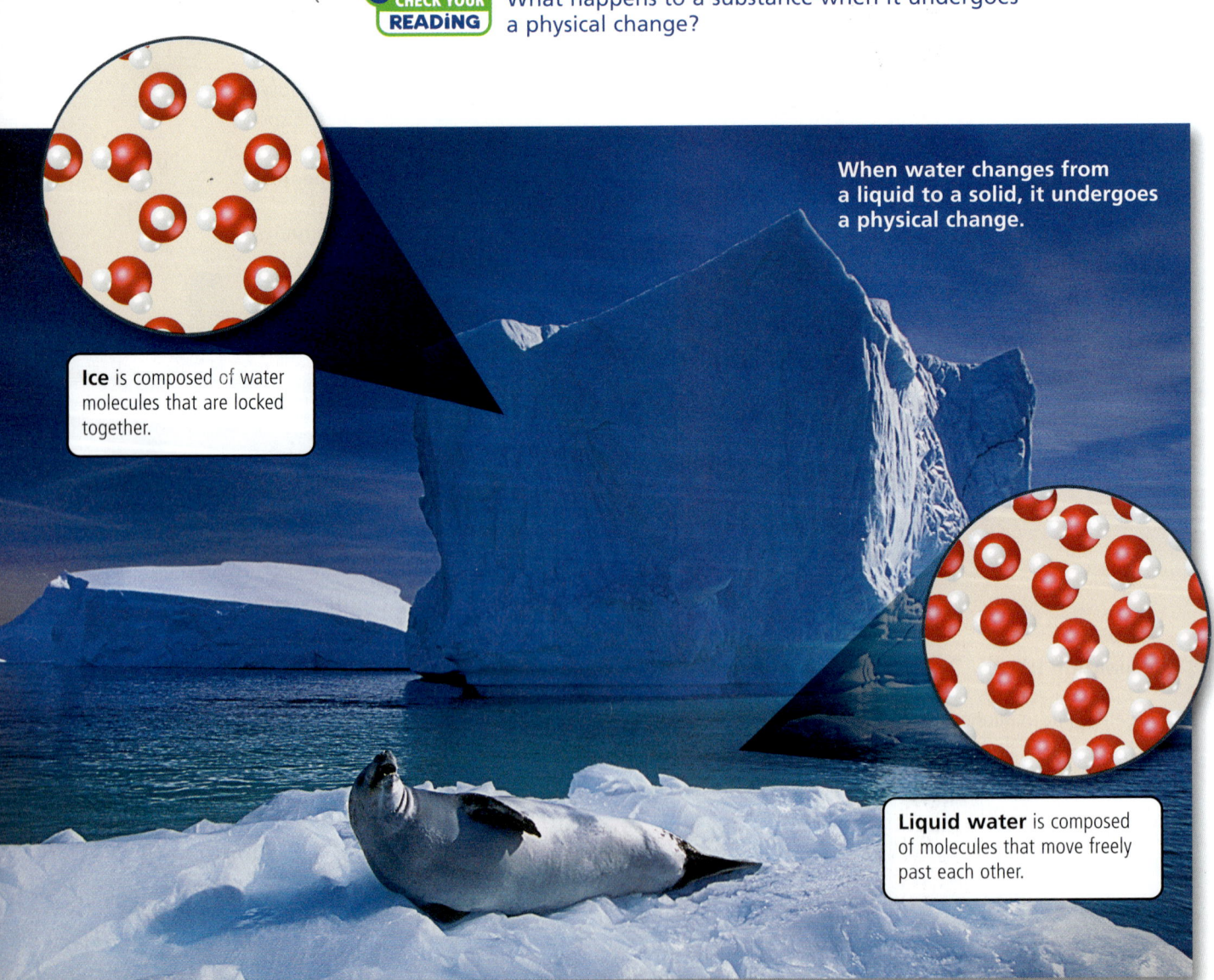

When water changes from a liquid to a solid, it undergoes a physical change.

Ice is composed of water molecules that are locked together.

Liquid water is composed of molecules that move freely past each other.

394 Unit 3: Chemical Interactions

Chemical Changes

Water can also undergo a chemical change. Water molecules can be broken down into hydrogen and oxygen molecules by a chemical reaction called electrolysis. When an electric current is passed through liquid water (H_2O), it changes the water into two gases—hydrogen and oxygen. The molecules of water break apart into individual atoms, which then recombine into hydrogen molecules (H_2) and oxygen molecules (O_2). The original material (water) changes into different substances through a chemical reaction.

Hydrogen and oxygen are used as rocket fuel for the space shuttle. During liftoff, liquid hydrogen and liquid oxygen are combined in a reaction that is the opposite of electrolysis. This reaction produces water and a large amount of energy that helps push the shuttle into orbit.

 How does a chemical change differ from a physical change?

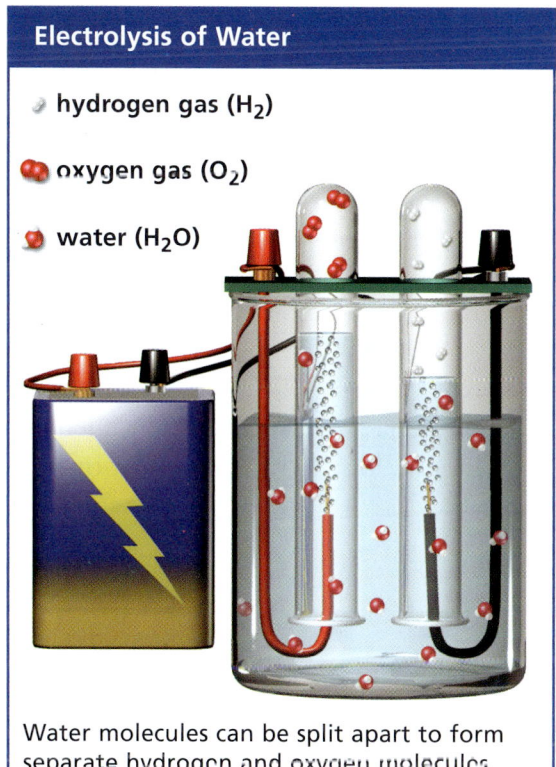

Electrolysis of Water
- hydrogen gas (H_2)
- oxygen gas (O_2)
- water (H_2O)

Water molecules can be split apart to form separate hydrogen and oxygen molecules.

Reactants and Products

Reactants are the substances present at the beginning of a chemical reaction. In the burning of natural gas, for example, methane (CH_4) and oxygen (O_2) are the reactants in the chemical reaction. **Products** are the substances formed by a chemical reaction. In the burning of natural gas, carbon dioxide (CO_2) and water (H_2O) are the products formed by the reaction. Reactants and products can be elements or compounds, depending on the reaction taking place.

During a chemical reaction, bonds between atoms in the reactants are broken and new bonds are formed in the products. When natural gas is burned, bonds between the carbon and hydrogen atoms in methane are broken, as are the bonds between the oxygen atoms in oxygen molecules. New bonds are formed between carbon and oxygen in carbon dioxide gas and between hydrogen and oxygen in water vapor.

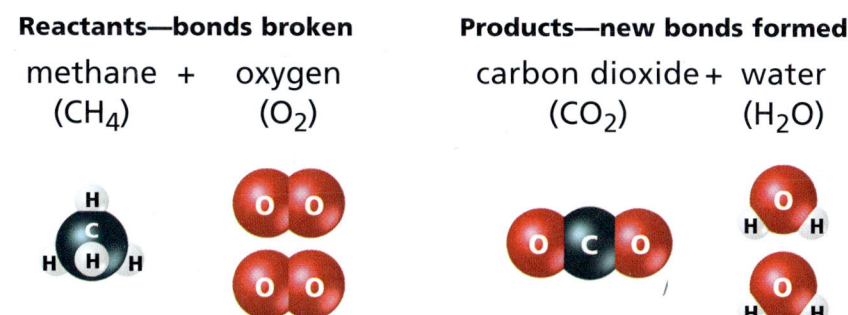

Reactants—bonds broken
methane + oxygen
(CH_4) (O_2)

Products—new bonds formed
carbon dioxide + water
(CO_2) (H_2O)

 What must happen for reactants to be changed into products?

Chapter 12: **Chemical Reactions** 395

Evidence of Chemical Reactions

Some chemical changes are easy to observe—the products formed by the rearrangement of atoms look different than the reactants. Other changes are not easy to see but can be detected in other ways.

Color Change Substances often change color during a chemical reaction. For example, when gray iron rusts, the product that forms is brown, as shown in the photograph below.

Formation of a Precipitate Many chemical reactions form products that exist in a different physical state from the reactants. A solid product called a **precipitate** may form when chemicals in two liquids react, as shown in the photograph below. Seashells are often formed this way when a sea creature releases a liquid that reacts with seawater.

> **VOCABULARY**
> Remember to use a four square diagram for *precipitate* and other vocabulary terms.

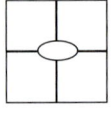

Color Change

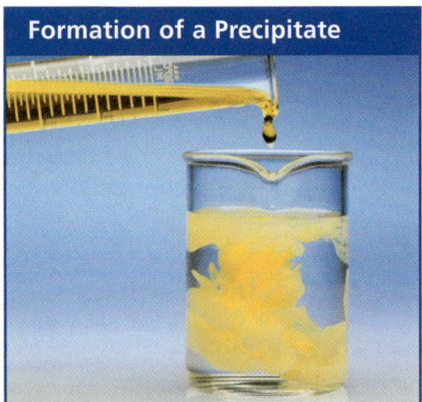
Formation of a Precipitate

Formation of a Gas Chemical reactions may produce a gas, like that often formed when antacid pills are mixed with excess stomach acid. The photograph below shows an example in which carbon dioxide gas is produced by a chemical reaction.

Temperature Change Most chemical reactions involve a temperature change. Sometimes this change can be inferred from the observation of a flame, as in the burning of the metal magnesium in the photograph below. Other temperature changes are not immediately obvious. If you have touched concrete before it hardens, you may have noticed that it felt warm. This warmth is due to a chemical reaction.

Formation of a Gas

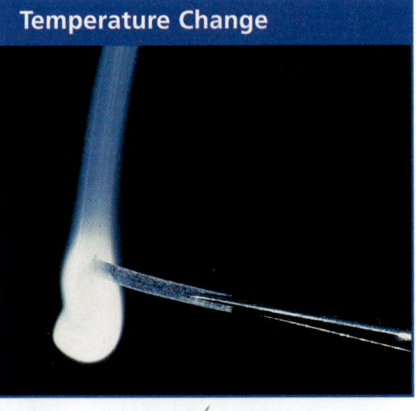
Temperature Change

Chemical reactions can be classified.

Scientists classify chemical reactions in several ways to help make the different types of reactions easier to understand. All reactions form new products, but the ways in which products are made can differ.

Synthesis In a synthesis reaction, a new compound is formed by the combination of simpler reactants. For example, nitrogen dioxide (NO_2), a component of smog, forms when nitrogen and oxygen combine in the air.

> **READING TIP**
> *Synthesis* means "making a substance from simpler substances."

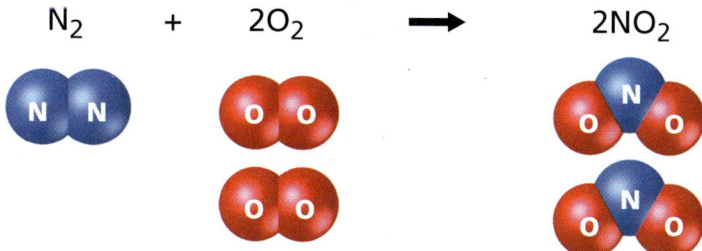

Decomposition In a decomposition reaction, a reactant breaks down into simpler products, which could be elements or other compounds. Decomposition reactions can be thought of as being the reverse of synthesis reactions. For example, water can be decomposed into its elements—hydrogen and oxygen.

> **READING TIP**
> *Decomposition* means "separation into parts."

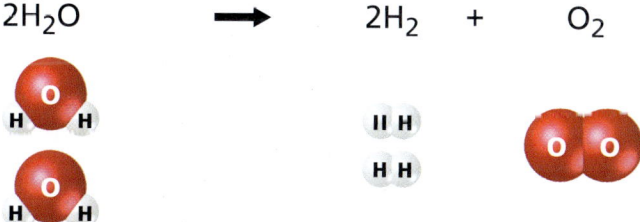

Combustion In a combustion reaction, one reactant is always oxygen and another reactant often contains carbon and hydrogen. The carbon and hydrogen atoms combine with oxygen, producing carbon dioxide and water. The burning of methane is a combustion reaction.

> **READING TIP**
> *Combustion* is the process of burning with oxygen.

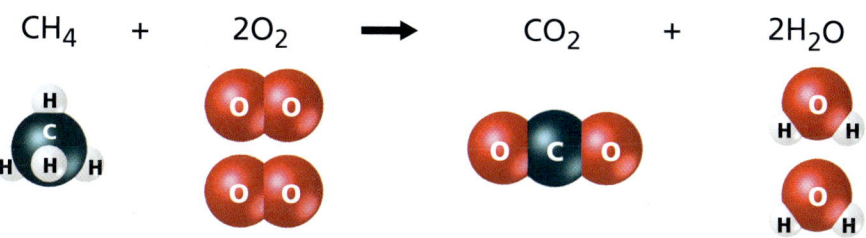

CHECK YOUR READING How are synthesis reactions different from decomposition reactions?

The rates of chemical reactions can vary.

Most chemical reactions take place when particles of reactants collide with enough force to react. Chemical reactions can occur at different rates. Striking a match causes a very quick chemical reaction, while the rusting of an iron nail may take months. However, the rate of a reaction can be changed. For instance, a nail can be made to rust more quickly. Three physical factors—concentration, surface area, and temperature—and a chemical factor—a catalyst—can greatly affect the rate of a chemical reaction.

Concentration

Observe how changing the concentration of a reactant can change the rate of a reaction.

Concentration measures the number of particles present in a certain volume. A high concentration of reactants means that there is a large number of particles that can collide and react. Turning the valve on a gas stove to increase the flow of gas increases the concentration of methane molecules that can combine with oxygen in the air. The result is a bigger flame and a faster combustion reaction.

Surface Area

Suppose one of the reactants in a chemical reaction is present as a single large piece of material. Particles of the second reactant cannot get inside the large piece, so they can react only with particles on the surface. To make the reaction go faster, the large piece of material could be broken into smaller pieces before the reaction starts.

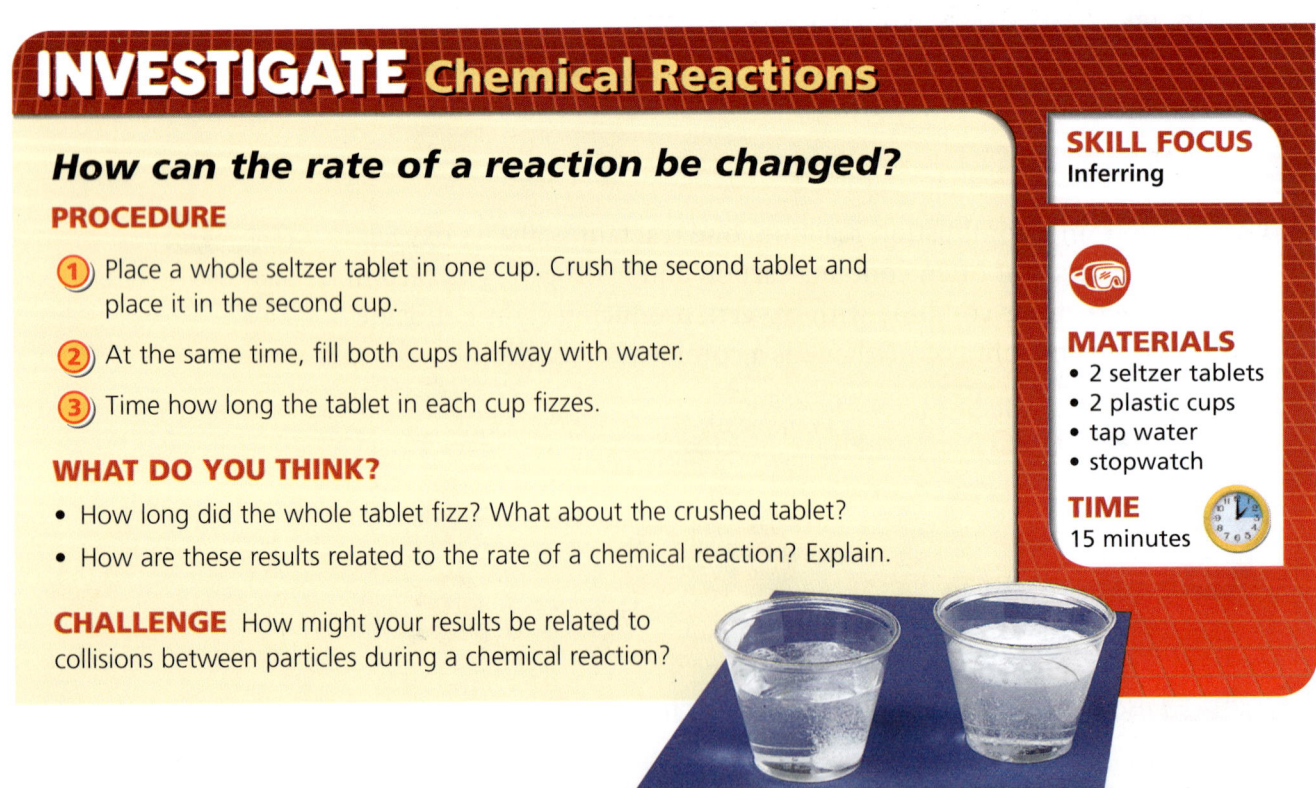

INVESTIGATE Chemical Reactions

How can the rate of a reaction be changed?

PROCEDURE

1. Place a whole seltzer tablet in one cup. Crush the second tablet and place it in the second cup.
2. At the same time, fill both cups halfway with water.
3. Time how long the tablet in each cup fizzes.

WHAT DO YOU THINK?

- How long did the whole tablet fizz? What about the crushed tablet?
- How are these results related to the rate of a chemical reaction? Explain.

CHALLENGE How might your results be related to collisions between particles during a chemical reaction?

SKILL FOCUS
Inferring

MATERIALS
- 2 seltzer tablets
- 2 plastic cups
- tap water
- stopwatch

TIME
15 minutes

Breaking a large piece of material into smaller parts increases the surface area of the material. All of the inner material has no surface when it is inside a larger piece. Each time the large piece is broken, however, more surfaces are exposed. The amount of material does not change, but breaking it into smaller parts increases its surface area. Increasing the surface area increases the rate of the reaction.

 Why does a reaction proceed faster when the reactants have greater surface areas?

Temperature

The rate of a reaction can be increased by making the particles move faster. The result is that more collisions take place per second and occur with greater force. The most common way to make the particles move faster is to add energy to the reactants, which will raise their temperature.

> **REMINDER**
> Temperature is the average amount of kinetic energy of the particles in a substance.

Many chemical reactions during cooking go very slowly, or do not take place at all, unless energy is added to the reactants. Too much heat can make a reaction go too fast, and food ends up burned. Chemical reactions can also be slowed or stopped by decreasing the temperature of the reactants. Again, think about cooking. The reactions that take place during cooking can be stopped by removing the food from the heat source.

Particles and Reaction Rates

Changes in Reactants	Normal Reaction Rate	Increased Reaction Rate
Concentration An increase in concentration of the reactants increases the number of particles that can interact.		
Surface area An increase in the surface area of the reactants increases the number of particles that can interact.		
Temperature Adding energy makes particles move faster and increases temperature. The increase in motion allows reactants to collide and react more frequently.		

Chapter 12: **Chemical Reactions** 399

Learn more about catalysts and how they work in living things.

Catalysts

The rate of a reaction can be changed chemically by adding a catalyst. A **catalyst** is a substance that increases the rate of a chemical reaction but is not itself consumed in the reaction. This means that after the reaction is complete, the catalyst remains unchanged. Catalysts are very important for many industrial and biological reactions. In fact, many chemical reactions would proceed slowly or not take place at all without catalysts.

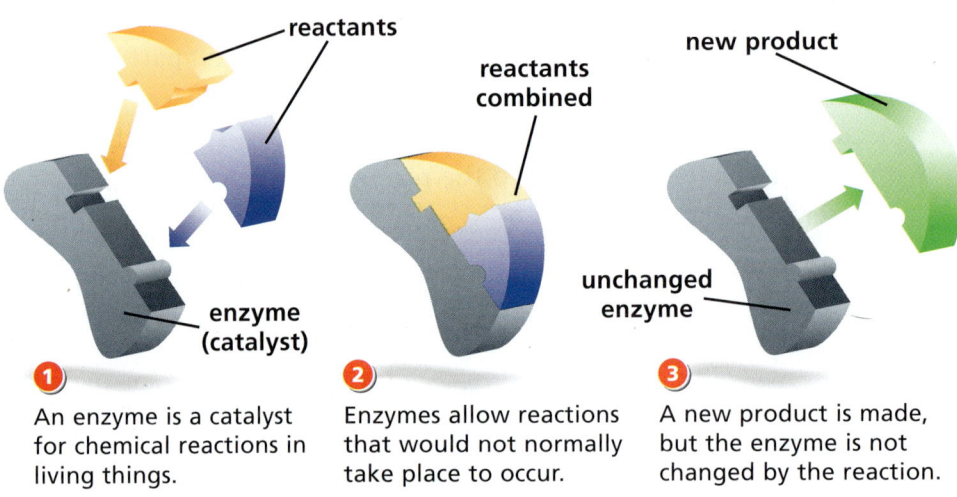

1. An enzyme is a catalyst for chemical reactions in living things.
2. Enzymes allow reactions that would not normally take place to occur.
3. A new product is made, but the enzyme is not changed by the reaction.

In living things, catalysts called enzymes are absolutely necessary for life. Without them, many important reactions could not take place under the conditions within your body. In fact, in 2003, scientists reported that they had discovered the slowest known chemical reaction in living things. This reaction would normally take one trillion years. Enzymes, though, allow the reaction to occur in 0.01 seconds.

 Why are catalysts important in chemical reactions?

12.1 Review

KEY CONCEPTS

1. How do physical changes differ from chemical changes? Explain.
2. Describe four types of evidence of a chemical reaction.
3. Describe the ways in which the rate of a chemical reaction can be changed.

CRITICAL THINKING

4. **Synthesize** What evidence shows that the burning of methane is a chemical reaction?
5. **Compare** What about combustion reactions makes them different from either synthesis or decomposition reactions?

CHALLENGE

6. **Apply** How might the chewing of food be related to the rate of a chemical reaction—digestion—that occurs in your body? Explain.

400 Unit 3: Chemical Interactions

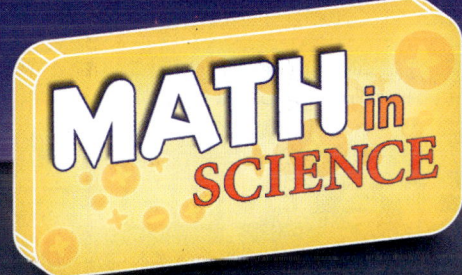

MATH in SCIENCE

MATH TUTORIAL
CLASSZONE.COM

Click on Math Tutorial for more help with interpreting line graphs.

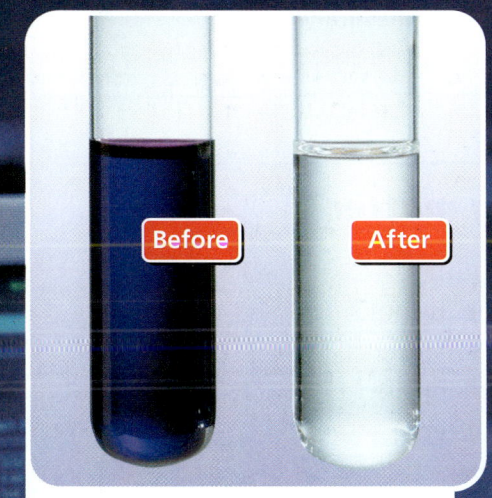

Before | After

The reactants in the iodine clock reaction produce a sudden color change several seconds after the reactants are mixed.

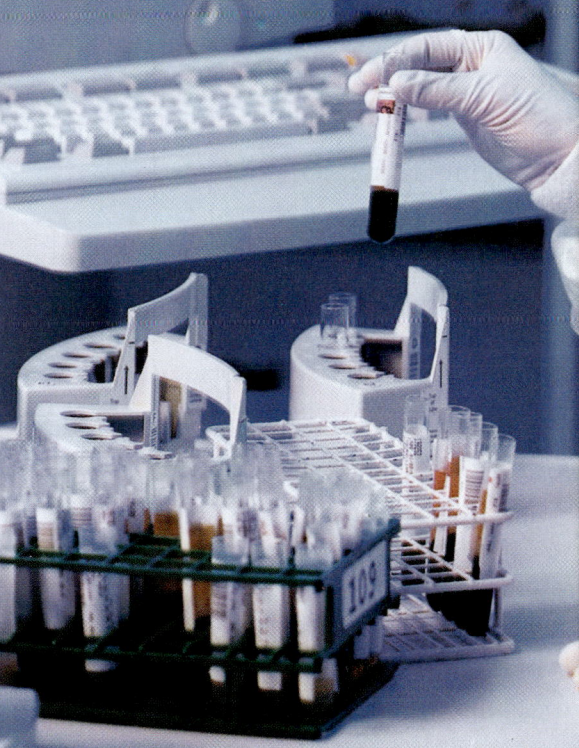

SKILL: ANALYZING LINE GRAPHS

The Iodine Clock

Can a chemical reaction be timed? In the iodine clock reaction, a sudden color change indicates that the reaction has occurred. The length of time that passes before the color changes depends on the concentration ratios of the reactants. As shown in the graph below, the greater the concentration of the reactants, the faster the reaction.

Example

Suppose you are given an unknown iodine concentration to test in the iodine clock reaction. What is the concentration ratio of the iodine if it takes 40 seconds for the color change to occur?

(1) Find 40 seconds on the *x*-axis of the graph below and follow the vertical line up to the plotted data.

(2) Draw a horizontal line from that point on the curve to the *y*-axis to find the iodine concentration ratio in your sample.

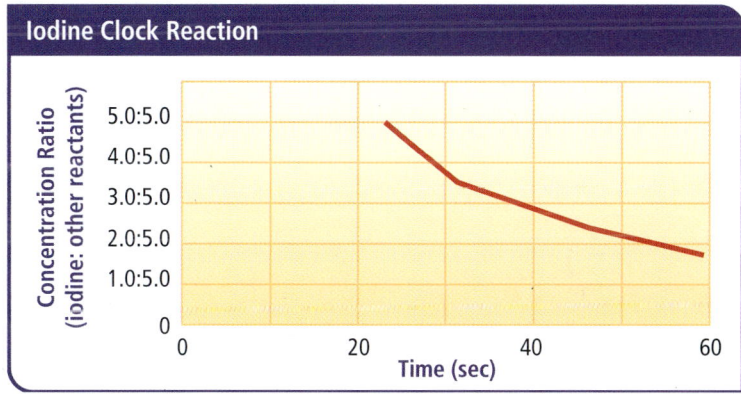

ANSWER The unknown concentration ratio is approximately 3.0:5.0.

Answer the following questions using the information in the graph above.

1. Approximately how long will it take for the reaction to occur if the concentration ratio is 4.0:5.0? 2.0:5.0?

2. Suppose you could extend the curve on the graph. If the reaction took 70 seconds to occur, what would be the approximate iodine concentration ratio?

CHALLENGE Using the following concentration ratios and times for another reactant, draw a reaction rate graph similar to the one shown above.

Concentration Ratios = 5.0:5.0, 4.0:5.0, 3.0:5.0, 2.0:5.0

Times = 24 sec, 25 sec, 43 sec, 68 sec

Chapter 12: **Chemical Reactions** 401

KEY CONCEPT
12.2 The masses of reactants and products are equal.

BEFORE, you learned
- Chemical reactions turn reactants into products by rearranging atoms
- Chemical reactions can be observed and identified
- The rate of chemical reactions can be changed

NOW, you will learn
- About the law of conservation of mass
- How a chemical equation represents a chemical reaction
- How to balance a simple chemical equation

VOCABULARY

law of conservation of mass p. 403
coefficient p. 406

THINK ABOUT

What happens to burning matter?

You have probably watched a fire burn in a fireplace, a campfire, or a candle flame. It looks as if the wood or candle disappears over time, leaving a small pile of ashes or wax when the fire has finished burning. But does matter really disappear? Combustion is a chemical reaction, and chemical reactions involve rearrangements of atoms. The atoms do not disappear, so where do they go?

Careful observations led to the discovery of the conservation of mass.

COMBINATION NOTES
Take notes on the conservation of mass using combination notes.

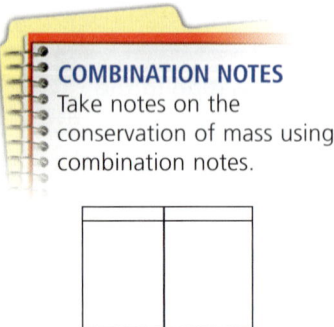

The ashes left over from a wood fire contain less mass than the wood. In many other chemical reactions, mass also appears to decrease. That is, the mass of the products appears to be less than the mass of the reactants. In other reactions, the products appear to gain mass. For example, plants grow through a complex series of reactions, but where does their extra mass come from? At one time, scientists thought that chemical reactions could create or destroy matter.

During the 1780s the French chemist Antoine Lavoisier (luh-VWAH-zee-ay) showed that matter can never be created or destroyed in a chemical reaction. Lavoisier emphasized the importance of making very careful measurements in his experiments. Because of his methods, he was able to show that reactions that seem to gain mass or lose mass actually involve reactions with gases in the air. These gases could not be seen, but their masses could be measured.

An example of Lavoisier's work is his study of the reaction of the metal mercury when heated in air. In this reaction, the reddish-orange product formed has more mass than the original metal. Lavoisier placed some mercury in a jar, sealed the jar, and recorded the total mass of the setup. After the mercury had been heated in the jar, the total mass of the jar and its contents had not changed.

Lavoisier showed that the air left in the jar would no longer support burning—a candle flame was snuffed out by this air. He concluded that a gas in the air, which he called oxygen, had combined with the mercury to form the new product.

Lavoisier conducted many experiments of this type and found in all cases that the mass of the reactants is equal to the mass of the products. This conclusion, called the **law of conservation of mass,** states that in a chemical reaction atoms are neither created nor destroyed. All atoms present in the reactants are also present in the products.

Lavoisier carefully measured both the reactants and the products of chemical reactions.

 How did Lavoisier investigate the conservation of mass?

INVESTIGATE Conservation of Mass

Why is it important to measure the masses of reactants and products?

PROCEDURE

1. Measure 2 tsp of baking soda. Use a funnel to put the baking soda in a balloon.
2. Pour 2 tsp of vinegar into the plastic bottle.
3. Secure the balloon over the mouth of the bottle with the balloon hanging to the side of the bottle. Find and record the mass of the experimental setup.
4. Lift the balloon so that the baking soda drops into the bottle. Observe for five minutes, and then find and record the mass of the setup again.

WHAT DO YOU THINK?

- Did the mass of the experimental setup change?
- How do your observations demonstrate the conservation of mass?

CHALLENGE What do you think you would have observed if you had not used the balloon? Explain.

SKILL FOCUS
Measuring

MATERIALS
- teaspoon
- baking soda
- funnel
- balloon
- vinegar
- plastic bottle
- balance

TIME
35 minutes

Chapter 12: **Chemical Reactions** 403

Chemical reactions can be described by chemical equations.

The law of conservation of mass states that in a chemical reaction, the total mass of reactants is equal to the total mass of products. For example, the mass of sodium plus the mass of chlorine that reacts with the sodium equals the mass of the product sodium chloride. Because atoms are rearranged in a chemical reaction, there must be the same number of sodium atoms and chlorine atoms in both the reactants and products.

Chemical equations represent how atoms are rearranged in a chemical reaction. The atoms in the reactants are shown on the left side of the equation. The atoms in the products are shown on the right side of the equation. Because atoms are rearranged and not created or destroyed, the number of atoms of each different element must be the same on each side of the equation.

 How does a chemical equation show the conservation of mass?

In order to write a chemical equation, the information that you need to know is
- the reactants and products in the reaction
- the atomic symbols and chemical formulas of the reactants and products in the reaction
- the direction of the reaction

Carbon dioxide is a gas that animals exhale.

The following equation describes the formation of carbon dioxide from carbon and oxygen. In words, this equation says "Carbon reacts with oxygen to yield carbon dioxide." Notice that instead of an equal sign, an arrow appears between the reactants and the products. The arrow shows which way the reaction proceeds—from reactants on the left to the product or the products on the right.

reactants	direction of reaction	product
$C + O_2$	$\rightarrow$	CO_2

Remember, the numbers below the chemical formulas for oxygen and carbon dioxide are called subscripts. A subscript indicates the number of atoms of an element in a molecule. You can see in the equation above that the oxygen molecule has two oxygen atoms, and the carbon dioxide molecule also has two oxygen atoms. If the chemical formula of a reactant or product does not have a subscript, it means that only one atom of each element is present in the molecule.

404 Unit 3: Chemical Interactions

Chemical equations must be balanced.

Remember, chemical reactions follow the law of conservation of mass. Chemical equations show this conservation, or equality, in terms of atoms. The same number of atoms of each element must appear on both sides of a chemical equation. However, simply writing down the chemical formulas of reactants and products does not always result in equal numbers of atoms. You have to balance the equation to make the number of atoms equal on each side of an equation.

Balancing Chemical Equations

To learn how to balance an equation, look at the example of the combustion of natural gas, which is mostly methane (CH_4). The reactants are methane and oxygen. The products are carbon dioxide and water. You can write this reaction as the following equation.

REMINDER
Oxygen is always a reactant in a combustion reaction.

Unbalanced Equation

$$CH_4 + O_2 \longrightarrow CO_2 + H_2O$$

  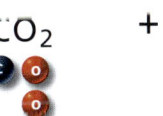

This equation is not balanced. There is one C on each side of the equation, so C is balanced. However, on the left side, H has a subscript of 4, which means there are four hydrogen atoms. On the right side, H has a subscript of 2, which means there are two hydrogen atoms. Also, there are two oxygen atoms on the left and three oxygen atoms on the right. Because of the conservation of mass, you know that hydrogen atoms do not disappear and oxygen atoms do not suddenly appear.

READING TIP
As you read how to balance the equation, look at the illustrations and count the atoms. The number of each type of atom is shown below the formula.

You can balance a chemical equation by changing the amounts of reactants or products represented.

- To balance H first, add another H_2O molecule on the right. Now, both C and H are balanced.
- There are now two oxygen atoms on the left side and four oxygen atoms on the right side. To balance O, add another O_2 molecule on the left.

Balanced Equation

$$CH_4 + O_2 + O_2 \longrightarrow CO_2 + H_2O + H_2O$$

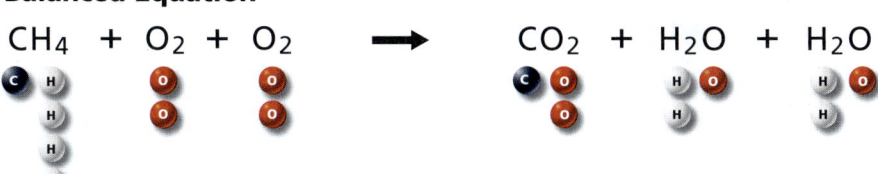

Using Coefficients to Balance Equations

The balanced equation for the combustion of methane shows that one molecule of methane reacts with two molecules of oxygen to produce one molecule of carbon dioxide and two molecules of water. The equation can be simplified by writing $2O_2$ instead of $O_2 + O_2$, and $2H_2O$ instead of $H_2O + H_2O$.

The numbers in front of the chemical formulas are called coefficients. **Coefficients** indicate how many molecules take part in the reaction. If there is no coefficient, then only one molecule of that type takes part in the reaction. The balanced equation, with coefficients, for the combustion of methane is shown below.

> **REMINDER**
> A subscript shows the number of atoms in a molecule. If a subscript is changed, the molecule represented by the formula is changed.

Balanced Equation with Coefficients

$$CH_4 + 2O_2 \longrightarrow CO_2 + 2H_2O$$

coefficient   subscript

Chemical formulas can have both coefficients and subscripts. In these cases, multiply the two numbers together to find the number of atoms involved in the reaction. For example, two water molecules ($2H_2O$) contain $2 \cdot 2 = 4$ hydrogen atoms and $2 \cdot 1 = 2$ oxygen atoms. Remember, coefficients in a chemical equation indicate how many molecules of each type take part in the reaction.

Only coefficients can be changed in order to balance a chemical equation. Subscripts are part of the chemical formula for reactants or products and cannot be changed to balance an equation. Changing a subscript changes the substance represented by the formula.

For example, the equation for the combustion of methane cannot be balanced by changing the formula CO_2 to CO. The formula CO_2 represents carbon dioxide gas, which animals exhale when they breathe. The formula CO represents carbon monoxide gas, which is a very different compound from CO_2. Carbon monoxide gas is poisonous, and breathing too much of it can be fatal.

> **CHECK YOUR READING** Why are coefficients used to balance equations?

The combustion of methane (CH_4) is used to melt glass.

Unit 3: Chemical Interactions

Balancing Equations with Coefficients

The steps below show how to balance the equation for the synthesis reaction between nitrogen (N_2) and hydrogen (H_2), which produces ammonia (NH_3).

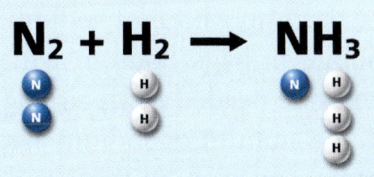

$$N_2 + H_2 \rightarrow NH_3$$

1. Count the atoms. Neither N nor H is balanced. The reactants contain two atoms each of N and H, but the product contains one N atom and three H atoms.

$N_2 + H_2 \rightarrow$	NH_3
N = 2	N = 1
H = 2	H = 3

Tip: Listing the number of atoms of each element makes it easy to see which elements must be balanced.

2. Use a coefficient to add atoms to one side of the equation. A coefficient of 2 on NH_3 balances the number of N atoms.

$N_2 + H_2 \rightarrow$	$2\,NH_3$
N = 2	N = 2
H = 2	H = 6

Tip: When adding coefficients, start with the reactant or product that contains the greatest number of different elements.

3. Add a coefficient to another reactant or product. Adding a coefficient of 3 to H_2 on the left side of the equation balances the number of H atoms on both sides. Now the equation is balanced.

$N_2 + 3\,H_2 \rightarrow$	$2NH_3$
N = 2	N = 2
H = 6	H = 6

Tip: Make sure that the coefficients in your balanced equation are the smallest whole numbers possible—that is, they have no common factor other than 1.

$$N_2 + 3H_2 \rightarrow 2NH_3$$

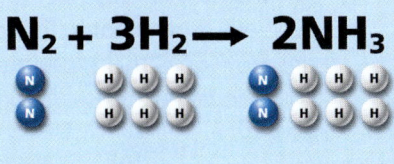

APPLY
Balance the following equations.
1. $Hg + O_2 \rightarrow HgO$
2. $Zn + HCl \rightarrow ZnCl_2 + H_2$

Chapter 12: **Chemical Reactions** 407

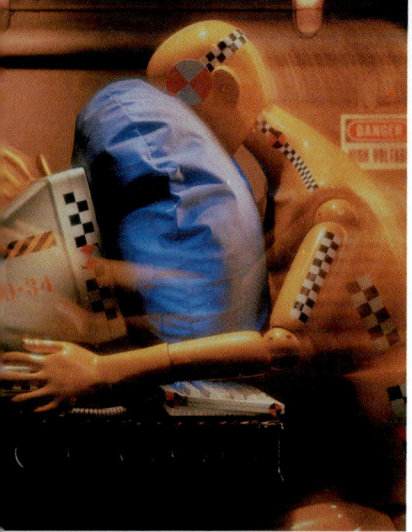

The decomposition of sodium azide is used to inflate air bags in automobiles.

Using the Conservation of Mass

A balanced chemical equation shows that no matter how atoms are rearranged during a chemical reaction, the same number of atoms must be present before and after the reaction. The following example demonstrates the usefulness of chemical equations and the conservation of mass.

The decomposition of sodium azide (NaN_3) is used to inflate automobile air bags. Sodium azide is a solid, and the amount of sodium azide needed in an air bag fills only a small amount of space. In fact, the amount of sodium azide used in air bags is only about 130 grams—an amount that would fit in a large spoon. An inflated air bag, though, takes up much more space even though it contains the same number of atoms that entered the reaction. The reason is illustrated by the chemical equation for this reaction.

Balanced Equation

$$2NaN_3 \rightarrow 2Na + 3N_2$$

According to the balanced equation shown above, three molecules of nitrogen gas are formed for every two molecules of sodium azide that decompose. Because the nitrogen is a gas, it fills a much greater volume than the original sodium azide. In fact, 67 liters of nitrogen gas are produced by the 130 grams of sodium azide in the reaction. This amount of nitrogen is enough to quickly inflate the air bag during a collision—the decomposition of sodium azide to sodium and nitrogen takes 0.03 seconds.

CHECK YOUR READING Why must chemical equations be balanced?

12.2 Review

KEY CONCEPTS

1. State the law of conservation of mass.
2. Write the chemical equation that shows sodium (Na) and chlorine (Cl_2) combining to form table salt (NaCl).
3. Is the following equation balanced? Why or why not?

   $CO \rightarrow C + O_2$

CRITICAL THINKING

4. **Communicate** Describe Lavoisier's experiment with mercury. How does this experiment show the law of conservation of mass?
5. **Synthesize** Suppose a log's mass is 5 kg. After burning, the mass of the ash is 1 kg. Explain what may have happened to the other 4 kg of mass.

CHALLENGE

6. **Synthesize** Suppose a container holds 1000 hydrogen molecules (H_2) and 1000 oxygen molecules (O_2) that react to form water. How many water molecules will be in the container? Will anything else be in the container? If so, what?

408 Unit 3: **Chemical Interactions**

SCIENCE on the JOB

FIREFIGHTER

Chemistry in Firefighting

A firefighter's job may seem simple: to put out fires. However, a firefighter needs to know about chemicals and chemical reactions. A fire is a combustion reaction that requires oxygen as a reactant. Without oxygen, a fire will normally burn itself out, so firefighters try to prevent oxygen from reaching the burning substances. Firefighters often use water or carbon dioxide for this purpose, but these materials make some types of fires more dangerous.

Grease Fires

Some fires can be extinguished by a chemical reaction. In kitchen grease fires, the chemicals that are used to fight the fire react with the grease. The reaction produces a foam that puts out the fire.

Metal Fires

Some fires involve metals such as magnesium. This metal burns at a very high temperature and reacts violently with water. Firefighters try to smother metal fires with a material such as sand.

Hazardous Reactions

Chemicals may react with water to form poisonous gases or acids. Firefighters might use a foam that extinguishes the fire, cools the area around the fire, and traps gases released by the fire. The symbols shown on the left are among several that show firefighters what chemical dangers may be present.

The fire shown above is a magnesium fire in Chicago in 1998. Firefighters used water to protect surrounding buildings, but dumped road salt on the burning magnesium.

EXPLORE

Build a carbon dioxide fire extinguisher.

1. Put 3 tsp of baking soda on a tissue and roll it into a tube. Tie the ends and middle of the tube with thread. Leave extra thread at one end of the tube.
2. Mold clay tightly around a straw.
3. Pour some vinegar into a bottle.
4. Hold the thread to suspend the tissue tube above the vinegar. Place the straw inside the bottle. Use the clay molded around the straw to hold the thread in place. Be sure that the straw is not touching the vinegar.
5. Shake and observe the fire extinguisher.

Chapter 12: **Chemical Reactions**

KEY CONCEPT
12.3 Chemical reactions involve energy changes.

 BEFORE, you learned
- Bonds are broken and made during chemical reactions
- Mass is conserved in all chemical reactions
- Chemical reactions are represented by balanced chemical equations

 NOW, you will learn
- About the energy in chemical bonds between atoms
- Why some chemical reactions release energy
- Why some chemical reactions absorb energy

VOCABULARY
bond energy p. 410
exothermic reaction p. 411
endothermic reaction p. 411
photosynthesis p. 414

EXPLORE Energy Changes

How can you identify a transfer of energy?

PROCEDURE

1. Pour 50 mL of hot tap water into the cup and place the thermometer in the cup.
2. Wait 30 seconds, then record the temperature of the water.
3. Measure 5 tsp of Epsom salts. Add the Epsom salts to the cup and immediately record the temperature while stirring the contents of the cup.
4. Continue to record the temperature every 30 seconds for 2 minutes.

MATERIALS
- graduated cylinder
- hot tap water
- plastic cup
- thermometer
- stopwatch
- plastic spoon
- Epsom salts

WHAT DO YOU THINK?
- What happened to the temperature after you added the Epsom salts?
- What do you think caused this change to occur?

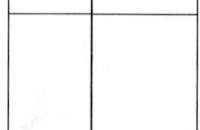

COMBINATION NOTES
Use combination notes to organize information on how chemical reactions absorb or release energy.

Chemical reactions release or absorb energy.

Chemical reactions involve breaking bonds in reactants and forming new bonds in products. Breaking bonds requires energy, and forming bonds releases energy. The energy associated with bonds is called **bond energy**. What happens to this energy during a chemical reaction?

Chemists have determined the bond energy for bonds between atoms. Breaking a bond between carbon and hydrogen requires a certain amount of energy. This amount of energy is different from the amount of energy needed to break a bond between carbon and oxygen, or between hydrogen and oxygen.

410 Unit 3: Chemical Interactions

Energy is needed to break bonds in reactant molecules. Energy is released when bonds are formed in product molecules. By adding up the bond energies in the reactants and products, you can determine whether energy will be released or absorbed.

If more energy is released when the products form than is needed to break the bonds in the reactants, then energy is released during the reaction. A reaction in which energy is released is called an **exothermic reaction.**

If more energy is required to break the bonds in the reactants than is released when the products form, then energy must be added to the reaction. That is, the reaction absorbs energy. A reaction in which energy is absorbed is called an **endothermic reaction.**

These types of energy changes can also be observed in different physical changes such as dissolving or changing state. The state change from a liquid to a solid, or freezing, releases energy—this is an exothermic process. The state change from a solid to a liquid, or melting, absorbs energy—this is an endothermic process.

 How are exothermic and endothermic reactions different?

Exothermic reactions release energy.

Exothermic chemical reactions often produce an increase in temperature. In exothermic reactions, the bond energies of the reactants are less than the bond energies of the products. As a result, less energy is needed to break the bonds in the reactants than is released during the formation of the products. This energy difference between reactants and products is often released as heat. The release of heat causes a change in the temperature of the reaction mixture.

Even though energy is released by exothermic reactions, some energy must first be added to break bonds in the reactants. In exothermic reactions, the formation of bonds in the products releases more energy. Overall, more energy is released than is added.

Some reactions are highly exothermic. These reactions produce a great deal of heat and significantly raise the temperature of their surroundings. One example is the reaction of powdered aluminum metal with a type of iron oxide, a reaction known as the thermite reaction. The equation for this reaction is

$$2Al + Fe_2O_3 \longrightarrow Al_2O_3 + 2Fe$$

This reaction releases enough heat to melt the iron that is produced. In fact, this reaction is used to weld iron rails together.

 What is evidence for an exothermic chemical reaction?

The white clouds of water vapor are formed by the exothermic reaction between hydrogen and oxygen.

$$2H_2 + O_2 \longrightarrow 2H_2O$$

The thermite reaction releases enough heat to weld pieces of iron together.

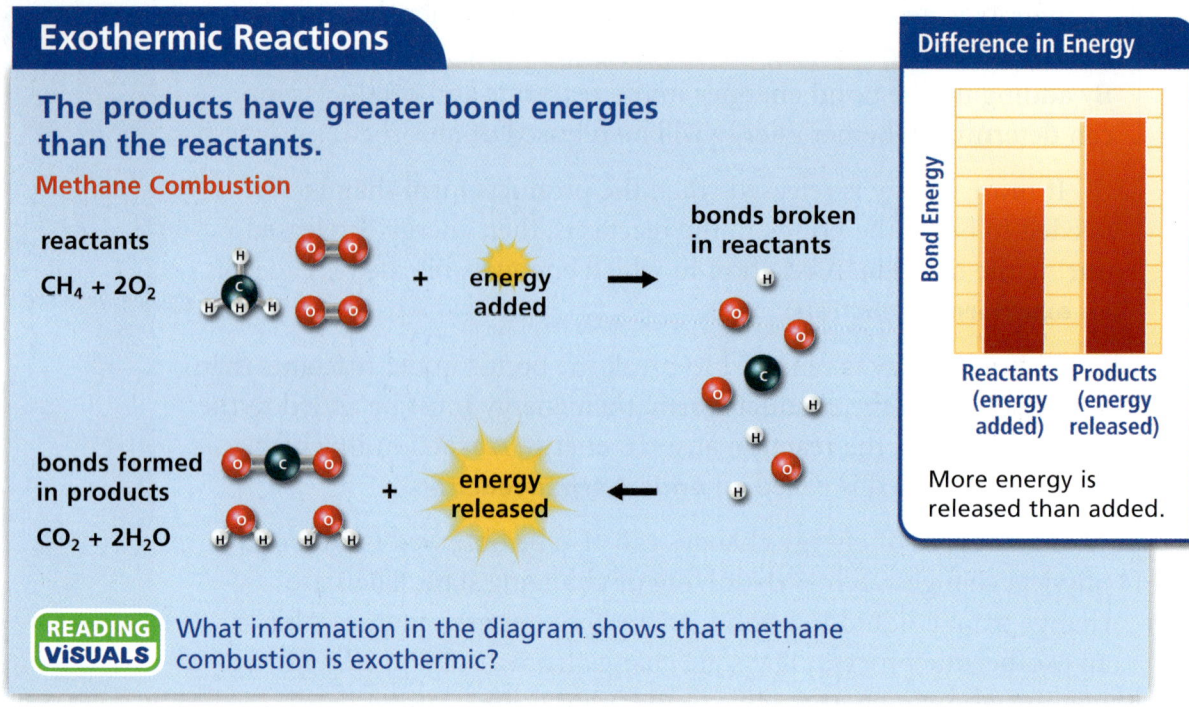

Exothermic Reactions

The products have greater bond energies than the reactants.

Methane Combustion

reactants
$CH_4 + 2O_2$

+ energy added →

bonds broken in reactants

bonds formed in products
$CO_2 + 2H_2O$

+ energy released ←

Difference in Energy

Reactants (energy added) | Products (energy released)

More energy is released than added.

READING VISUALS What information in the diagram shows that methane combustion is exothermic?

All common combustion reactions, such as the combustion of methane, are exothermic. To determine how energy changes in this reaction, the bond energies in the reactants—oxygen and methane—and in the products—carbon dioxide and water—can be added and compared. This process is illustrated by the diagram shown above. The difference in energy is released to the surrounding air as heat.

Some chemical reactions release excess energy as light instead of heat. For example, glow sticks work by a chemical reaction that releases energy as light. One of the reactants, a solution of hydrogen peroxide, is contained in a thin glass tube within the plastic stick. The rest of the stick is filled with a second chemical and a brightly colored dye. When you bend the stick, the glass tube inside it breaks and the two solutions mix. The result is a bright glow of light.

These cup coral polyps glow because of exothermic chemical reactions.

Exothermic chemical reactions also occur in living things. Some of these reactions release energy as heat, and others release energy as light. Fireflies light up due to a reaction that takes place between oxygen and a chemical called luciferin. This type of exothermic reaction is not unique to fireflies. In fact, similar reactions are found in several different species of fish, squid, jellyfish, and shrimp.

CHECK YOUR READING In which ways might an exothermic reaction release energy?

The bombardier beetle, shown in the photograph on the right, uses natural exothermic reactions to defend itself. Although several chemical reactions are involved, the end result is the production of a hot, toxic spray. The most important reaction in the process is the decomposition of hydrogen peroxide into water and oxygen.

$$2H_2O_2 \longrightarrow 2H_2O + O_2$$

When the hydrogen peroxide rapidly breaks down, the hot, toxic mixture made by the series of reactions is pressurized by the oxygen gas from the reaction in the equation above. After enough pressure builds up, the beetle can spray the mixture.

Endothermic reactions absorb energy.

Endothermic reactions often produce a decrease in temperature. In endothermic reactions, the bond energies of the reactants are greater than the bond energies of the products. As a result, more energy is needed to break the bonds in the reactants than is released during the formation of the products. The difference in energy is usually absorbed from the surroundings as heat. This often causes a decrease in the temperature of the reaction mixture.

All endothermic reactions absorb energy. However, they do not all absorb energy as heat. One example of an endothermic reaction of this type is the decomposition of water by electrolysis. In this case, the energy that is absorbed is in the form of electrical energy. When the electric current is turned off, the reaction stops. The change in energy that occurs in this reaction is shown below.

READING TIP
The prefix *endo-* means "inside."

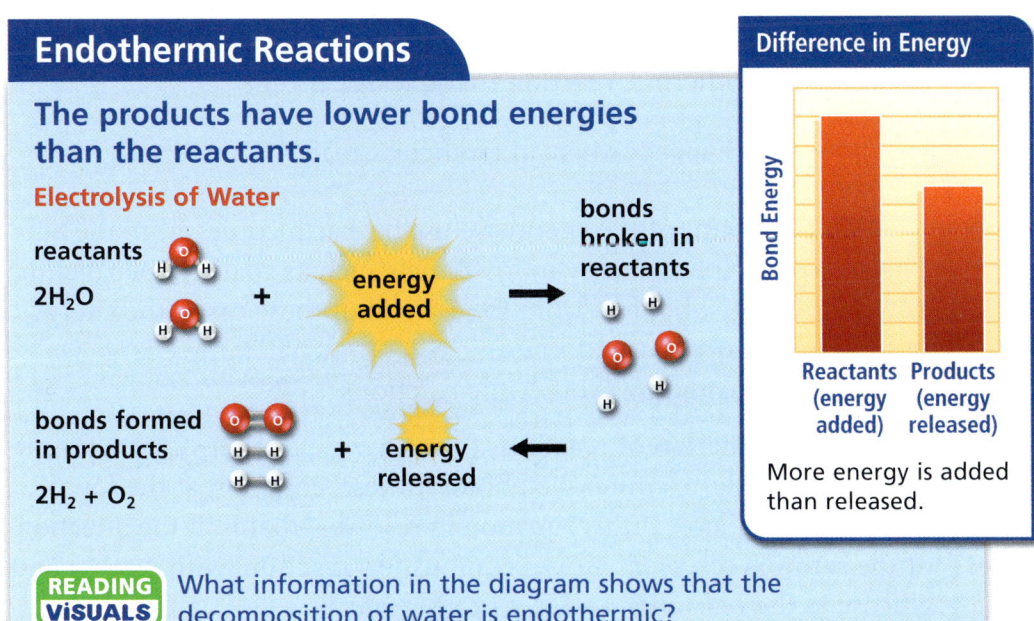

Endothermic Reactions

The products have lower bond energies than the reactants.

Electrolysis of Water

reactants
$2H_2O$ + energy added → bonds broken in reactants

bonds formed in products
$2H_2 + O_2$ + energy released ←

Difference in Energy

Reactants (energy added) | Products (energy released)

More energy is added than released.

READING VISUALS What information in the diagram shows that the decomposition of water is endothermic?

Probably the most important series of endothermic reactions on Earth is photosynthesis. Many steps occur in the process, but the overall chemical reaction is

$$6CO_2 + 6H_2O \longrightarrow C_6H_{12}O_6 + 6O_2$$

Unlike many other endothermic reactions, photosynthesis does not absorb energy as heat. Instead, during **photosynthesis,** plants absorb energy from sunlight to turn carbon dioxide and water into oxygen and glucose, which is a type of sugar molecule. The energy is stored in the glucose molecules, ready to be used when needed.

 How can you determine if a reaction is endothermic?

Exothermic and endothermic reactions work together to supply energy.

When thinking about exothermic and endothermic reactions, it is often useful to consider energy as part of the reaction. An exothermic reaction releases energy, so energy is on the product side of the chemical equation. An endothermic reaction absorbs energy, so energy is on the reactant side of the chemical equation.

Exothermic Reaction
Reactants ⟶ Products + Energy

Endothermic Reaction
Reactants + Energy ⟶ Products

View examples of endothermic and exothermic reactions.

As you can see in the general reactions above, exothermic and endothermic reactions have opposite energy changes. This means that if an exothermic chemical reaction proceeds in the opposite direction, it becomes an endothermic reaction that absorbs energy. Similarly, if an endothermic reaction proceeds in the opposite direction, it becomes an exothermic reaction that releases energy.

 What happens when an exothermic reaction is reversed?

A large amount of the energy we use on Earth comes from the Sun. This energy includes energy in fossil fuels such as coal and petroleum, as well as energy obtained from food. In all of these cases, the energy in sunlight is stored by endothermic reactions. When the energy is needed, it is released by exothermic reactions.

This combination of reactions forms a cycle of energy storage and use. For example, examine the photosynthesis equation at the top of the page. If you look at this equation in reverse—that is, if the direction of the arrow is reversed—it is a combustion reaction, with oxygen and glucose as the reactants, and it is exothermic.

Plants store energy through the endothermic reactions of photosynthesis. Living things can release this energy through a series of exothermic reactions that will be described in the next section.

The energy stored in plants through photosynthesis can also be released in other ways. Consider energy from fossil fuels. Fossil fuels include petroleum, natural gas, and coal. These substances formed from fossilized materials, mainly plants, that had been under high pressures and temperatures for millions of years. When these plants were alive, they used photosynthesis to produce glucose and other molecules from carbon dioxide and water.

The energy stored in the bonds of these molecules remains, even though the molecules have changed over time. The burning of gasoline in a car releases this energy, enabling the car's engine to work. Similarly, the burning of coal in a power plant, or the burning of natural gas in a stove, releases the energy originally stored by the endothermic series of photosynthesis reactions.

Plants such as trees store energy through photosynthesis. Cars and trucks release this energy through combustion.

CHECK YOUR READING How can endothermic and exothermic reactions work together?

12.3 Review

KEY CONCEPTS
1. What are the differences between exothermic and endothermic reactions?
2. Is the combustion of methane an exothermic or endothermic reaction? Explain.
3. Is photosynthesis an exothermic or endothermic reaction? Explain.

CRITICAL THINKING
4. **Synthesize** Describe the connections between the processes of photosynthesis and combustion.
5. **Communicate** Explain how most energy used on Earth can be traced back to the Sun.

CHALLENGE
6. **Synthesize** Electrolysis of water is endothermic. What does this indicate about the bond energy in the reactants and products? What happens when this reaction is reversed?

CHAPTER INVESTIGATION

Exothermic or Endothermic?

OVERVIEW AND PURPOSE A clue that a chemical reaction has taken place is a transfer of energy, often in the form of heat or light. The chemical reaction used to demolish an old building, as shown in the photograph to the left, is a dramatic example of energy release by a reaction. In this investigation, you will use what you have learned about chemical reactions to
- measure and record temperature changes in two processes
- compare temperature changes during the processes in order to classify them as exothermic or endothermic

Procedure

1. Make a data table like the one shown on the sample notebook page.

2. Work with a partner. One should keep track of time. The other should observe the thermometer and report the temperature.

PART 1

3. Pour 30 mL of hydrogen peroxide into a beaker. Put a thermometer into the beaker. Wait 2 minutes to allow the thermometer to reach the temperature of the hydrogen peroxide. During the time you are waiting, measure 1 g of yeast with the balance.

4. Record the starting temperature. Add the yeast to the beaker and immediately record the temperature while gently stirring the contents of the beaker. Continue to record the temperature every 30 seconds as you observe the process for 5 minutes.

MATERIALS
- graduated cylinder
- hydrogen peroxide
- 2 beakers
- 2 thermometers
- stopwatch
- measuring spoons
- yeast
- balance
- plastic spoon
- large plastic cup
- hot tap water
- vinegar
- baking soda

416 Unit 3: **Chemical Interactions**

PART 2

5. Make a hot water bath by filling a large plastic cup halfway with hot tap water.

6. Measure and pour 30 mL of vinegar into a small beaker. Set this beaker in the hot water bath and place a thermometer in the vinegar. Wait until the temperature of the vinegar rises to between 32 and 38°C (90 to 100°F). While waiting for the vinegar's temperature to increase, measure 1 g of baking soda.

step 6

7. Remove the beaker from the hot water bath. Record the starting temperature.

8. Add the baking soda to the vinegar and immediately record the temperature as you swirl the contents of the beaker. Continue to record the temperature every 30 seconds as you observe the reaction for 5 minutes.

Observe and Analyze · Write It Up

1. **RECORD OBSERVATIONS** Remember to complete your data table.

2. **GRAPH** Use the information from your data table to graph your results. Make a double-line graph, plotting your data in a different color for each part of the investigation. Plot temperature in degrees Celsius on the vertical, or y-axis. Plot the time in minutes on the horizontal, or x-axis.

3. **ANALYZE DATA** Examine the graph. When did the temperature change the most in each part of the investigation? When did it change the least? Compare the temperature at the start of each process with the temperature after 5 minutes. How do the temperature changes compare?

Conclude · Write It Up

1. **CLASSIFY** Is the mixture of hydrogen peroxide and yeast endothermic or exothermic? Is the reaction between vinegar and baking soda endothermic or exothermic? Provide evidence for your answers.

2. **EVALUATE** Did you have any difficulties obtaining accurate measurements? Describe possible limitations or sources of error.

3. **APPLY** What does the reaction between baking soda and vinegar tell you about their bond energies?

INVESTIGATE Further

CHALLENGE Repeat Part 2, but instead of using the hot water bath, add the hot water directly to the vinegar before pouring in the baking soda. Does this change in procedure change the results of the experiment? Why might your observations have changed? Explain your answers.

Exothermic or Endothermic?

Observe and Analyze

Table 1. Temperature Measurements

Time (min)	Hydrogen Peroxide and Yeast Temperature (°C)	Vinegar and Baking Soda Temperature (°C)
0		
0.5		
1.0		
....		
5.0		

Conclude

Chapter 12: **Chemical Reactions** 417

KEY CONCEPT

12.4 Life and industry depend on chemical reactions.

◀ **BEFORE, you learned**

- Chemical reactions turn reactants into products by rearranging atoms
- Mass is conserved during chemical reactions
- Chemical reactions involve energy changes

▶ **NOW, you will learn**

- About the importance of chemical reactions in living things
- How chemistry has helped the development of new technology

VOCABULARY

respiration p. 418

THINK ABOUT

How is a glow stick like a firefly?

When a firefly glows in the dark, a chemical reaction that emits light is taking place. Similarly, when you activate a glow stick, a chemical reaction that causes the glow stick to emit light occurs. Many reactions in modern life and technology adapt chemical reactions found in nature. Can you think of other examples?

Living things require chemical reactions.

In section 3, you saw that photosynthesis stores energy from the Sun in forms that can be used later. These forms of stored energy include fossil fuels and the sugar glucose. The glucose molecules produced by photosynthesis make up the basic food used for energy by almost all living things. For example, animals obtain glucose molecules by eating plants or eating other animals that have eaten plants.

Living cells obtain energy from glucose molecules through the process of **respiration,** which is the "combustion" of glucose to obtain energy. This series of chemical reactions is, in general, the reverse of photosynthesis. It produces carbon dioxide and water from oxygen and glucose. The overall reactions for both photosynthesis and respiration are shown on the top of page 419. From a chemical point of view, respiration is the same as any other combustion reaction.

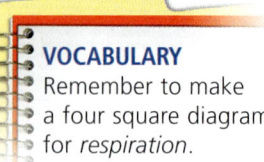

VOCABULARY
Remember to make a four square diagram for *respiration*.

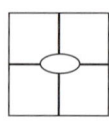

418 Unit 3: Chemical Interactions

Photosynthesis
$6CO_2 + 6H_2O + \text{energy} \longrightarrow C_6H_{12}O_6 + 6O_2$

Respiration
$C_6H_{12}O_6 + 6O_2 \longrightarrow 6CO_2 + 6H_2O + \text{energy}$

The energy released by respiration can be used for growth of new cells, movement, or any other life function. Suppose that you are late for school and have to run to get to class on time. Your body needs to activate nerves and muscles right away, without waiting for you to first eat some food as a source of energy. The glucose molecules in food are stored in your body until you need energy. Then, respiration consumes them in a process that includes several steps.

To make these steps go quickly, the body uses catalysts—enzymes—for each step. Some enzymes break the glucose molecules into smaller pieces, while other enzymes break bonds within each piece. Still other enzymes help form the reaction products—carbon dioxide and water. With the help of enzymes, these reactions take place quickly and automatically. You do not have to think about breaking down glucose when you run—you just start to run and the energy is there.

 **CHECK YOUR READING** How are photosynthesis and respiration opposites?

INVESTIGATE Sugar Combustion

How are catalysts important in the combustion of sugar?

PROCEDURE

1. Using the tongs, hold a sugar cube in a candle flame for 30 seconds. Observe what happens.
2. Rub ashes on the second sugar cube.
3. Using the tongs, hold the second sugar cube in the candle flame for 30 seconds. Observe what happens.

WHAT DO YOU THINK?
- What happened to the first sugar cube? What happened to the second sugar cube?
- What may have caused any differences that you observed?

CHALLENGE
How might the ashes used in this experiment have a similar function to enzymes in your cells? Explain.

SKILL Inferring

MATERIALS
- candle
- matches
- tongs
- 2 sugar cubes
- stopwatch
- ashes

TIME 20 minutes

Chemical reactions are used in technology.

Every time your cells need energy, they essentially complete respiration—the "combustion" of glucose. The series of chemical reactions in respiration involves enzymes, which are catalysts. Every time someone drives a car, another combustion reaction occurs—the combustion of gasoline. While the combustion of gasoline does not require a catalyst, the chemical reactions that change a car's exhaust gases do use a catalyst.

No chemical reaction is ever completely efficient. It does not matter what the reaction is or how the reaction conditions are set up. There are always some reactants that do not change completely into products. Sometimes a chemical reaction makes unwanted waste products.

In the case of gasoline combustion, some of the original carbon compounds, called hydrocarbons, do not burn completely, and carbon monoxide gas (CO) is produced. Also, nitrogen in the air reacts with oxygen in a car's engine to produce compounds of nitrogen and oxygen, including nitric oxide (NO). The production of these gases lowers the overall efficiency of combustion. More importantly, these gases can react with water vapor in the air to form smog and acid rain.

Sometimes, as you can see with gasoline combustion, chemical technology causes a problem. Then, new chemical technology is designed to treat the problem. For example, it was necessary to reduce carbon monoxide and nitric oxide emissions from car exhaust. As a result, engineers in the 1970s developed a device called a catalytic converter. This device causes chemical reactions that remove the unwanted waste products from the combustion of gasoline.

Catalytic converters contain metal catalysts such as platinum, palladium, and rhodium. The products of the reactions in the catalytic converter are nitrogen (N_2), oxygen (O_2), water (H_2O), and carbon dioxide (CO_2), which are all ordinary parts of Earth's atmosphere.

Even though catalytic converters have been used for many years, scientists and engineers are still trying to improve them. One goal of this research is to use less expensive metals, such as magnesium and zinc, inside catalytic converters, while forming the same exhaust products.

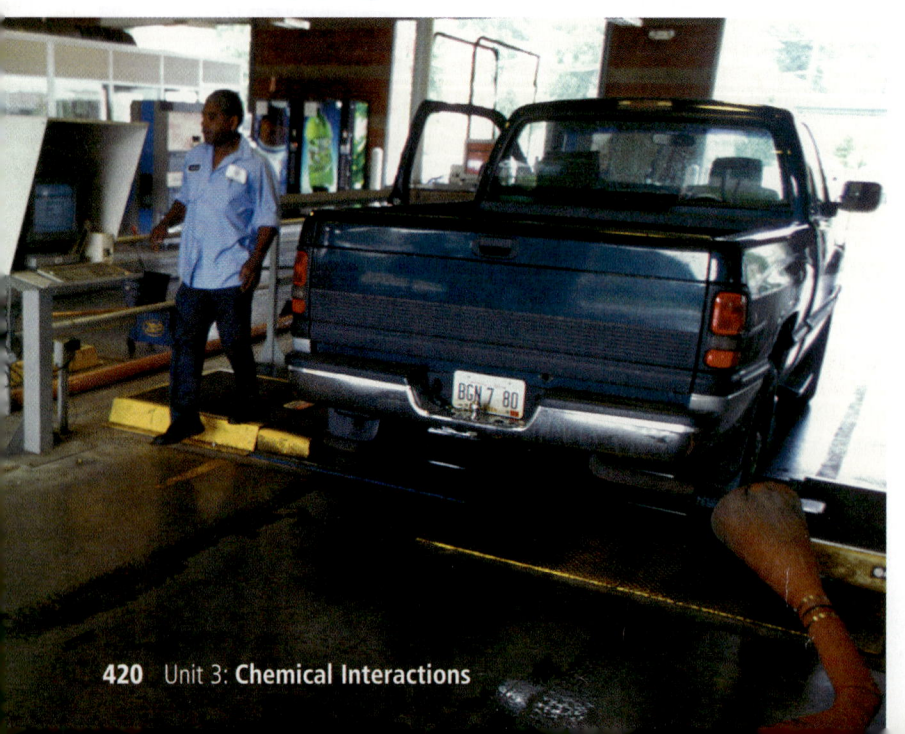

Many states inspect vehicles to test the pollutants in their exhaust gases.

CHECK YOUR READING Why were catalytic converters developed?

Chemical Reactions in Catalytic Converters

The combustion of gasoline makes harmful waste products. Chemical reactions in catalytic converters make these waste products less harmful.

① Into the Catalytic Converter
When gasoline is mixed with air and burned in a car's engine, the reaction produces some unwanted waste products, such as
- carbon monoxide (CO)
- nitric oxide (NO)
- unburned hydrocarbons

② Inside the Catalytic Converter Catalysts in a car's catalytic converter help change these unwanted products into other gases. The catalysts are metals that are bonded to a ceramic structure.

③ Out from the Catalytic Converter
The final products are ordinary parts of Earth's atmosphere.
- nitrogen (N_2)
- oxygen (O_2)
- water (H_2O)
- carbon dioxide (CO_2)

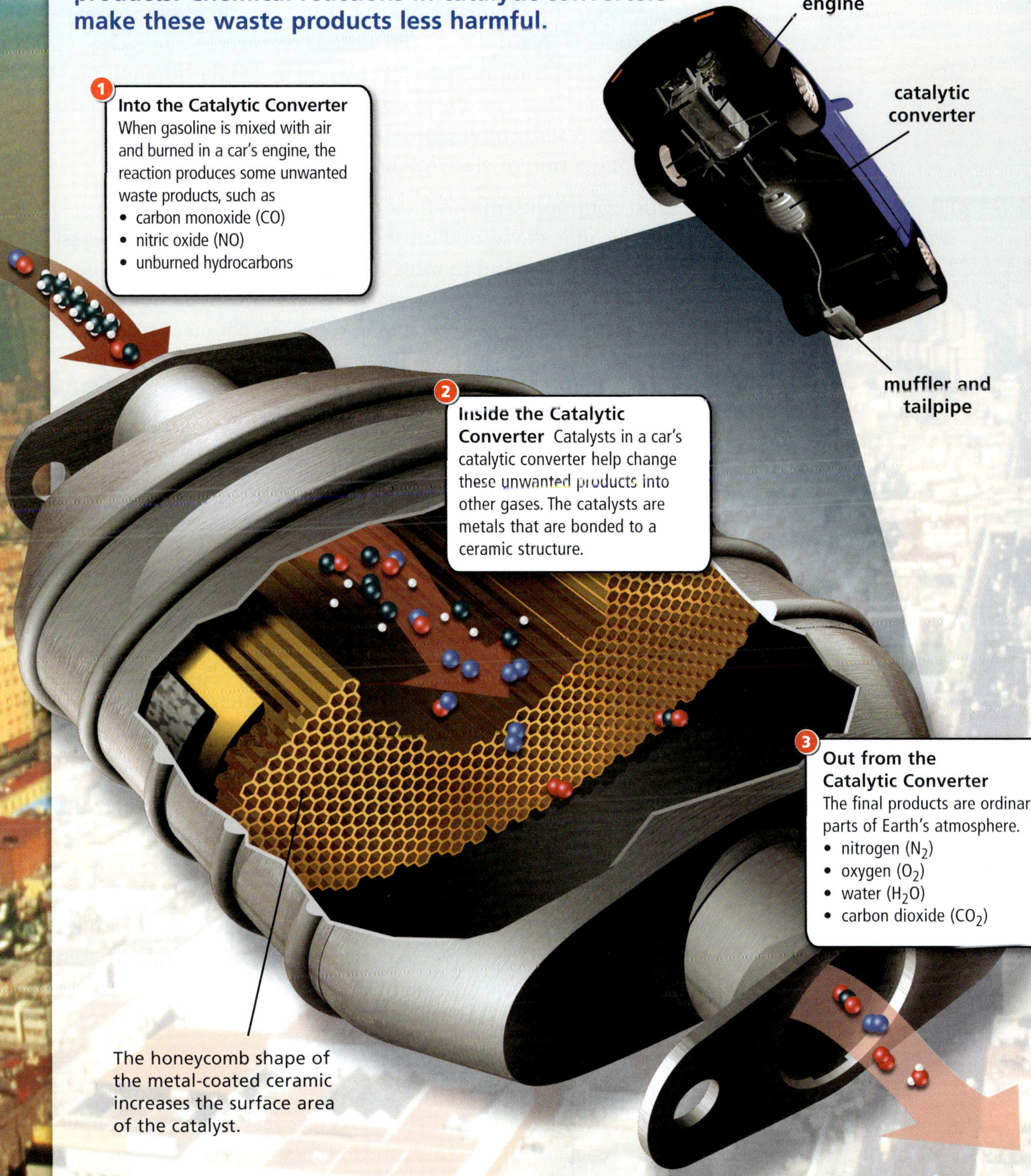

engine
catalytic converter
muffler and tailpipe

The honeycomb shape of the metal-coated ceramic increases the surface area of the catalyst.

READING VISUALS What are CO and NO changed into by a catalytic converter?

Chapter 12: **Chemical Reactions** 421

Industry uses chemical reactions to make useful products.

No area of science and technology has changed today's society as much as the electronics industry has. Just think about all the common electronic products that did not even exist as recently as 30 years ago—from personal computers to CD players to cellular phones. All of these devices are based on the electrical properties of materials called semiconductors. A semiconductor is a material that can precisely control the conduction of electrical signals.

READING TIP
The prefix *semi-* means "partial," so a semiconductor partially conducts electricity.

The most common semiconductor material is the element silicon (Si). Silicon is the second most common element in Earth's crust after oxygen, and it is found in most rocks and sand. Pure silicon is obtained from quartz (SiO_2). The quartz is heated with carbon in an electric furnace at 3000°C. The chemical reaction that takes place is

$$SiO_2 + 2C \longrightarrow Si + 2CO$$

This reaction produces silicon that is about 98 percent pure. However, this silicon is still not pure enough to be used in electronics. Several other refining steps must be used to make silicon that is more than 99.999999999 percent pure.

CHECK YOUR READING   What property makes silicon useful in electronic devices?

Quartz (SiO_2) is the source of silicon for chips.

Early electronic devices had to be large enough to fit various types of glass tubes and connecting wires inside. In the 1950s, however, engineers figured out how to replace all of these different tubes and wires with thin layers of material placed on a piece of silicon. The resulting circuits are often called microchips, or simply chips.

In order to make these chips, another reaction is used. This reaction involves a material called photoresist (FOH-toh-rih-ZIST), whose properties change when it is exposed to ultraviolet light. Silicon wafers are first coated with photoresist. A stencil is placed over the surface, which allows some areas of the wafer to be exposed to ultraviolet light while other areas are protected. A chemical reaction takes place between the ultraviolet light and the coating of photoresist. The exposed areas of photoresist remain on the silicon surface after the rest of the material is washed away.

The entire process is carried out in special clean rooms to prevent contamination by dust. A typical chip has electrical pathways so small that a single particle of smoke or dust can block the path, stopping the chip from working properly. The process is automated, and no human hand ever touches a chip.

From Quartz to Microchips

A chemical reaction makes the tiny circuits that are used to run electronic devices such as cellular phones.

1 After silicon is sliced into very thin wafers, it is coated with photoresist. The silicon is covered with a stencil and exposed to ultraviolet light, which reacts with the photoresist.

2 The entire process takes place in clean rooms, where workers wear special clothing to prevent dust from reaching the chips.

3 The areas of the chip that were exposed to ultraviolet light form tiny circuits used in electronic devices.

One of the many uses of silicon chips is in cellular phones.

The reaction of photoresist with ultraviolet light is an important chemical reaction. The same type of material is used in the printing of books and newspapers. A similar reaction occurs in photocopiers and laser printers. This is an example of how one type of chemical reaction has helped change industry and society in important ways.

 Describe how chemical reactions are important in industry.

12.4 Review

KEY CONCEPTS
1. Explain how respiration and photosynthesis are chemically opposite from each other.
2. Provide an example of how catalysts are used in technology.
3. Describe two chemical reactions used in making silicon chips.

CRITICAL THINKING
4. **Compare and Contrast** How are respiration and the combustion of gasoline similar? How are they different?
5. **Analyze** In microchip manufacture, what would happen if the clean rooms had outside windows? Explain.

CHALLENGE
6. **Infer** The gases released from a catalytic converter include N_2, O_2, H_2O, and CO_2. The original reactants must contain atoms of which elements?

Chapter 12: **Chemical Reactions** 423

Chapter Review

the BIG idea
Chemical reactions form new substances by breaking and making chemical bonds.

CONTENT REVIEW
CLASSZONE.COM

KEY CONCEPTS SUMMARY

1) Chemical reactions alter arrangements of atoms.
- Chemical changes occur through chemical reactions.
- Evidence of a chemical reaction includes a color change, the formation of a precipitate, the formation of a gas, and a change in temperature.
- Chemical reactions change reactants into products.

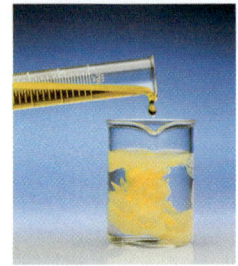

VOCABULARY
chemical reaction p. 393
reactant p. 395
product p. 395
precipitate p. 396
catalyst p. 400

2) The masses of reactants and products are equal.
- Mass is conserved in chemical reactions.
- Chemical equations summarize chemical reactions.
- Balanced chemical equations show the conservation of mass.

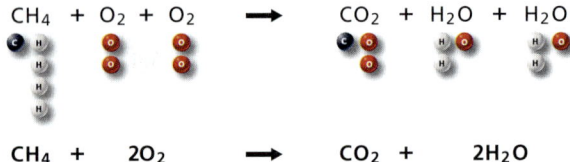

$$CH_4 + 2O_2 \rightarrow CO_2 + 2H_2O$$

VOCABULARY
law of conservation of mass p. 403
coefficient p. 406

3) Chemical reactions involve energy changes.
- Different bonds contain different amounts of energy.
- In an exothermic reaction, more energy is released than added.
- In an endothermic reaction, more energy is added than released.

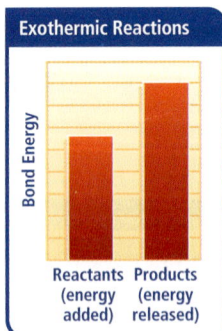
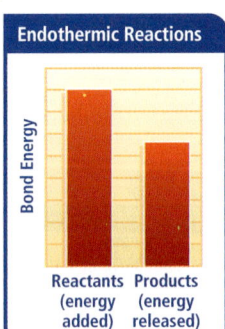

VOCABULARY
bond energy p. 410
exothermic reaction p. 411
endothermic reaction p. 411
photosynthesis p. 414

4) Life and industry depend on chemical reactions.
- Living things rely on chemical reactions that release energy from molecules.
- Different parts of modern society rely on chemical reactions.

VOCABULARY
respiration p. 418

Reviewing Vocabulary

Describe how the vocabulary terms in the following pairs are related to each other. Explain the relationship in a one- or two-sentence answer.

1. reactant, product
2. law of conservation of mass, chemical reaction
3. endothermic, exothermic
4. respiration, photosynthesis

Reviewing Key Concepts

Multiple Choice *Choose the letter of the best answer.*

5. During a chemical reaction, reactants always
   a. become more complex
   b. require catalysts
   c. lose mass
   d. form products

6. The splitting of water molecules into hydrogen and oxygen molecules is an example of a
   a. combination reaction
   b. chemical change
   c. synthesis reaction
   d. physical change

7. Combustion reactions
   a. destroy atoms   c. form precipitates
   b. require glucose   d. require oxygen

8. Which of the following will increase the rate of a reaction?
   a. breaking solid reactants into smaller pieces
   b. removing a catalyst
   c. decreasing the temperature
   d. decreasing the concentration

9. What does a catalyst do in a chemical reaction?
   a. It slows the reaction down.
   b. It speeds the reaction up.
   c. It becomes a product.
   d. It is a reactant.

10. During a chemical reaction, the total amount of mass present
    a. increases
    b. decreases
    c. may increase or decrease
    d. does not change

11. Chemical equations show summaries of
    a. physical changes
    b. changes of state
    c. chemical reactions
    d. changes in temperature

12. A chemical equation must
    a. show energy   c. use subscripts
    b. be balanced   d. use coefficients

13. What type of reaction occurs if the reactants have a greater total bond energy than the products?
    a. an endothermic reaction
    b. a synthesis reaction
    c. an exothermic reaction
    d. a decomposition reaction

14. Endothermic reactions always
    a. absorb energy
    b. make more complex products
    c. release energy
    d. make less complex products

Short Answer *Write a short answer to each question.*

15. Describe the differences between physical and chemical changes. How can each be identified?

16. Compare and contrast the overall chemical reactions of photosynthesis and respiration. How can these reactions be described in terms of bond energy in the reactants and products?

17. Describe an example of an advance in technology that makes use of a chemical reaction.

18. When you balance a chemical equation, why can you change coefficients of reactants or products, but not subscripts?

Thinking Critically

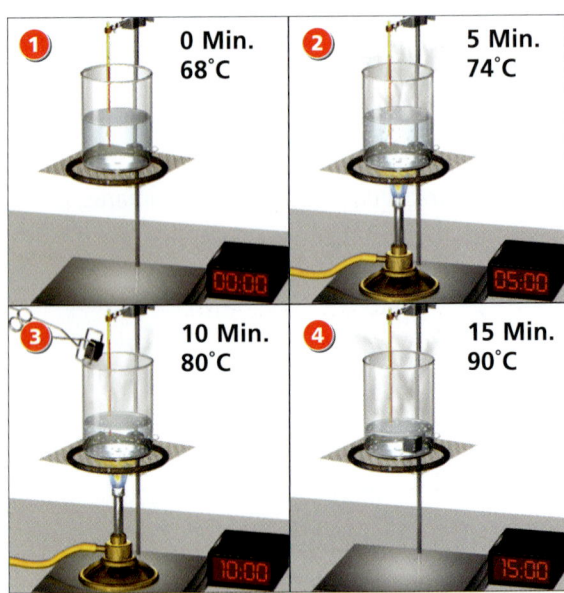

The series of illustrations above shows a chemical reaction at five-minute intervals. Use the information in the illustrations to answer the following six questions.

19. **OBSERVE** What happened to the temperature of the substance in the beaker from the beginning to the end of each five-minute interval?

20. **ANALYZE** Does the reaction appear to continue in step 4? What evidence tells you?

21. **CLASSIFY** Is this an endothermic or exothermic reaction? Explain.

22. **INFER** Suppose the metal cube placed in the beaker in step 3 is a catalyst. What effect did the metal have on the reaction? Why?

23. **PREDICT** If the metal cube is a catalyst, how much of the metal cube will be left in the beaker when the reaction is completed? Explain.

24. **SYNTHESIZE** Assume that the reaction shown is a decomposition reaction. Describe what happens to the reactants.

Using Math Skills in Science

Answer the following ten questions based on the equations below.

Equation 1—$HgO \rightarrow Hg + O_2$

Equation 2—$Al + O_2 \rightarrow Al_2O_3$

Equation 3—$S_8 + O_2 \rightarrow SO_3$

25. Copy and balance equation 1.

26. What coefficients, if any, did you add to equation 1 to balance it?

27. How many Hg atoms take part in the reaction represented by equation 1 when it is balanced?

28. Copy and balance equation 2.

29. What coefficients, if any, did you add to equation 2 to balance it?

30. How many O atoms take part in the reaction represented by equation 2 when it is balanced?

31. Copy and balance equation 3.

32. What coefficients, if any, did you add to equation 3 to balance it?

33. How many S atoms take part in the reaction represented by equation 3 when it is balanced?

34. How many O atoms take part in the reaction represented by equation 3 when it is balanced?

the BIG idea

35. **DRAW CONCLUSIONS** Describe three ways in which chemical reactions are important in your life.

36. **ANALYZE** Look back at the photograph and question on pages 390 and 391. Answer the question in terms of the chapter's Big Idea.

UNIT PROJECTS

Check your schedule for your unit project. How are you doing? Be sure that you have placed data or notes from your research in your project folder.

Standardized Test Practice

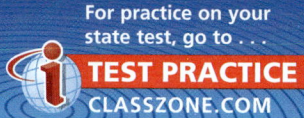

Analyzing Theories

Answer the questions based on the information in the following passage.

During the 1700s, scientists thought that matter contained a substance called phlogiston. According to this theory, wood was made of phlogiston and ash. When wood burned, the phlogiston was released and the ash was left behind.

The ash that remained had less mass than the original wood. This decrease in mass was explained by the release of phlogiston. However, when substances such as phosphorus and mercury burned, the material that remained had more mass than the original substances. This increase in mass did not make sense to some scientists.

The scientists who supported the phlogiston theory said that the phlogiston in some substances had negative mass. So, when the substances burned, they released phlogiston and gained mass. Other scientists disagreed, and their research led to the discovery of a scientific law. Antoine Lavoisier carried out several experiments by burning metals in sealed containers. He showed that mass is never lost or gained in a chemical reaction.

1. What did the phlogiston theory successfully explain?
   a. the presence of ash in unburned wood
   b. the apparent gain of mass in some reactions
   c. the chemical makeup of the air
   d. the apparent decrease in mass in some situations

2. Why did some scientists disagree with the phlogiston theory?
   a. Burning a substance always produced an increase in mass.
   b. Burning a substance always produced a decrease in mass.
   c. Burning could produce either an increase or decrease in mass.
   d. Burning wood produced ash and phlogiston.

3. What law did Lavoisier's work establish?
   a. conservation of energy
   b. conservation of mass
   c. conservation of momentum
   d. conservation of resources

4. To carry out his experiments, what kind of equipment did Lavoisier need?
   a. devices to separate the different elements in the air
   b. machines that could separate wood from ash
   c. microscopes that could be used to study rust and ash
   d. balances that could measure mass very accurately

Extended Response

Answer the following questions in detail. Include some of the terms from the list on the right. Underline each term you use in your answers.

catalyst	coefficient	concentration
temperature	reaction	subscript
surface area		

5. Suppose you wanted to change the rate of a chemical reaction. What might you change in the reaction? Explain each factor.

6. Is the chemical equation shown below balanced? Why or why not? How are balanced chemical equations related to conservation of mass?

$$6CO_2 + 6H_2O \longrightarrow C_6H_{12}O_6 + O_2$$

UNIT 4
Earth's Surface

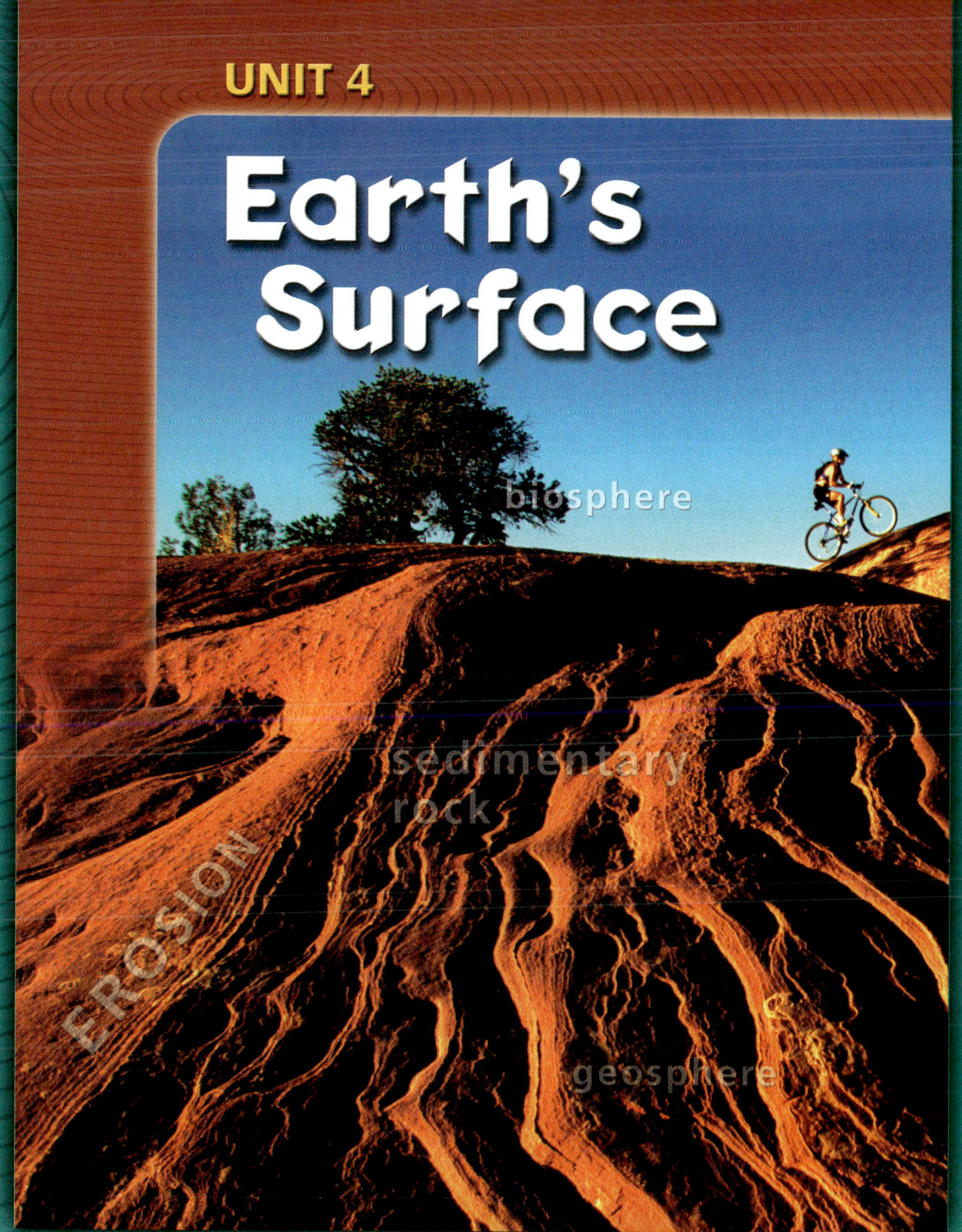

Contents Overview

Frontiers in Science
Remote Sensing — 430

Timelines in Science
History of the Earth System — 536

Chapter 13 Views of Earth Today — 434
Chapter 14 Minerals — 468
Chapter 15 Rocks — 500
Chapter 16 Weathering and Soil Formation — 540
Chapter 17 Erosion and Deposition — 570

FRONTIERS in Science

REMOTE SENSING

Technology high above Earth's surface is giving scientists a whole new look at our planet. This image is of Jasper Ridge, near Palo Alto, California.

SCIENTIFIC AMERICAN FRONTIERS

View the video segment "All That Glitters" to learn how explorers use remote sensing and other methods to find valuable materials.

This research jet aircraft carries instruments to study Earth's land surface, ocean, and atmosphere. It flies at high altitudes, allowing it to collect data and images over large areas during a single flight.

Mapping Earth

You're probably familiar with images of gold prospectors in the Old West. Maybe you've seen them in old movies or read about them in history books. Prospectors wandered through the mountains, looking for signs of ores or gemstones, going here and there in response to rumors or stories, pitching camp in remote canyons on a hunch. People still prospect for minerals today, but they're more likely to fly in airplanes than to ride mules. And stories of fabled mines are just stories and fables. Today's prospectors rely on scientific evidence from remote sensing.

Remote sensing—the use of instruments to gather data from a distance—has two great advantages. The first is that sensors mounted in satellites and airplanes can collect vast amounts of detailed information over large areas. The second is that the sensors can easily collect information about the same area again and again.

For example, scientists use remote sensing to make better and more detailed maps of Earth and to track changes over time. Thanks to remote sensing, scientists now know that Mount Everest, the highest point on Earth, is actually getting higher by about 1 centimeter (0.4 in.) per year. Remote sensors on satellites are also mapping global ocean temperatures and showing how they change over the course of a year.

Uncut diamond

Frontiers in Science 431

Detecting Minerals from Above

One of the many uses of remote sensing is to find new sources of valuable minerals, such as diamonds. To detect minerals from airplanes or satellites, remote sensors make use of the energy in sunlight. Sunlight reaches Earth as radiation, which travels in the form of waves. All objects absorb some types of radiation and reflect others. The particular wavelengths absorbed or reflected depend upon the materials that make up the objects. Each kind of material has a unique "fingerprint" of the wavelengths it absorbs and the wavelengths it reflects.

When sunlight strikes Earth's surface, some of it is reflected back into the sky. Some of the radiation is absorbed by rocks and other objects and then emitted, or given off, in a different form. Remote sensors in airplanes and satellites collect the reflected and emitted radiation and analyze it to determine which types of rocks and minerals lie on the surface. The remote sensing systems collect so much data that computer processing and analysis are difficult and expensive. Still, the data are usually clear enough to show the types of minerals located in the regions scanned. However, minerals that are buried cannot be detected by remote sensing from aircraft or satellites. The sensors receive only energy from or near the surface.

Energy from the Sun reflects at different wavelengths from materials at Earth's surface. Instruments on the jet analyze the reflected energy and map the surface.

SCIENTIFIC AMERICAN FRONTIERS

View the "All that Glitters" segment of your *Scientific American Frontiers* video to see how finding certain common minerals can indicate the presence of a valuable mineral like diamond.

IN THIS SCENE FROM THE VIDEO a mineral prospector searches for diamonds in a cylinder of rock drilled from beneath Earth's surface.

SEARCHING FOR DIAMONDS People used to think that North America did not have many diamonds. However, northern Canada is geologically similar to the world's major diamond-producing areas: southern Africa, Russia, and Australia. A few diamond prospectors kept searching, using remote sensing and other techniques. The prospectors looked for more common minerals that form under the same conditions as diamonds. They made maps showing where these minerals were most plentiful and used the maps to search for diamond-rich rock. Once the prospectors realized that the glaciers of the last ice age had moved the minerals, they looked for and found diamonds farther northward. Canada is now a big producer of diamonds.

Remote sensing can show the presence of minerals that occur with diamonds, but people must still use older methods to collect samples for further analysis.

Prospecting for Diamonds

One of the major regions of mineral exploration in which remote sensing is used is in the Northwest Territories of Canada, where the first diamond mine began operating in 1998. The Canada Centre for Remote Sensing has helped develop sensing equipment that can fit easily onto light airplanes and computer equipment to analyze results quickly. The sensing equipment is used to detect certain types of minerals that are often found along with diamonds.

Using remote sensing to locate minerals associated with diamonds or valuable ores is only a beginning. The data cannot show how far the minerals or ores extend underground. Prospectors must still explore the area and take samples. However, remote sensing gives mineral prospectors an excellent idea of where to start looking.

UNANSWERED Questions

As scientists use remote sensing to study Earth's land surface, ocean, and atmosphere, they work to answer new questions.

- Can remote sensing be used to locate sources of iron, platinum, or gold in areas that are difficult to explore on foot?
- How do changes in water temperature at the ocean surface affect long-range weather patterns and the health of ocean organisms?
- How do different types of clouds affect the amount of sunlight reaching Earth's surface and the average temperature of the surface?

UNIT PROJECTS

As you study this unit, work alone or with a group on one of the projects listed below.

Hiker's Guide Video

Like prospectors, wilderness hikers must be able to read maps that show the shape of the land. Prepare a video to teach hikers how to choose hiking and camping areas by reading maps.

- Obtain a topographic map of a wilderness area in a national or state park.
- Write a script outlining what you will teach and how you will videotape it.
- Present your video and display the maps you used.

Diamond Mine Model

Diamonds can be carried toward Earth's surface by kimberlite pipes. Show how diamonds are mined from kimberlite.

- Build a model of a diamond-mine tunnel that passes through kimberlite.
- Present your model to your class. Explain the relationship between kimberlite and diamonds.

Glacier Photo Essay

Make a photo essay showing how glaciers reshape Earth's surface as they move and melt.

- Find images of areas that are or have been affected by glaciers. Write captions for them.
- Present the images as a photo essay on a poster or in a portfolio.

Learn more about careers in mineralogy.

Frontiers in Science 433

CHAPTER 13
Views of Earth Today

Modern technology has changed the way we view and map Earth.

Key Concepts

SECTION 1
Technology is used to explore the Earth system.
Learn how technology has changed people's view of Earth.

SECTION 2
Maps and globes are models of Earth.
Learn how to locate any place on Earth and how Earth's sphere is portrayed on flat maps.

SECTION 3
Topographic maps show the shape of the land.
Learn about representing the features of Earth's surface on flat maps.

SECTION 4
Technology is used to map Earth.
Learn how satellites and computers are used to provide more detailed maps of Earth.

Internet Preview

CLASSZONE.COM
Chapter 13 online resources: Content Review, Simulation, Visualization, three Resource Centers, Math Tutorial, and Test Practice

What do all these views show about Earth?

Swirling clouds over North and South America: NASA Terra satellite data

EXPLORE the BIG idea

Earth's Changing Surface

Go outside and find evidence of how wind, water, or living things change the surface of Earth. You might look in alleyways, parks, wooded areas, or backyards. For example, you might find a path worn through a grassy area near a parking lot.

Observe and Think What changes do you observe? What do you think caused the changes?

Using Modern Maps

Find a map of a city, a bus or rail system, or a state. Study the names, colors, and symbols on the map and any features of interest.

Observe and Think Which direction on the map is north? What do the symbols mean? How do you measure the distance from one point to another?

Internet Activity: Mapping

Go to **ClassZone.com** to learn more about mapping Earth from space. Find out about a NASA mission to develop the most accurate map of Earth ever made.

Observe and Think Why do you think scientists need different maps produced from satellite data?

Earth's Spheres Code: MDL013

Warm and cool ocean-surface temperatures: NASA satellite image

Chlorophyll levels (green) on land and sea: SeaStar spacecraft image

Earth's rocky surface without the oceans: NASA satellite data

Chapter 13: **Views of Earth Today** 435

CHAPTER 13
Getting Ready to Learn

◀ CONCEPT REVIEW

- Earth, like all planets, is shaped roughly like a sphere.
- Earth supports a complex web of life.
- The planet consists of many parts that interact with one another.

◀ VOCABULARY REVIEW

See Glossary for definitions.

energy

matter

planet

satellite

CONTENT REVIEW
CLASSZONE.COM

Review concepts and vocabulary.

▶ TAKING NOTES

MAIN IDEA AND DETAIL NOTES

Make a two-column chart. Write the main ideas, such as those in the blue headings, in the column on the left. Write details about each of those main ideas in the column on the right.

VOCABULARY STRATEGY

Draw a **word triangle** diagram for each new vocabulary term. On the bottom line write and define the term. Above that, write a sentence that uses the term correctly. At the top, draw a picture to show what the term looks like.

See the Note-Taking Handbook on pages R45–R51.

SCIENCE NOTEBOOK

MAIN IDEAS	DETAIL NOTES
1. The Earth system has four main parts.	1. Atmosphere = mixture of gases surrounding Earth 1. Hydrosphere = all waters on Earth

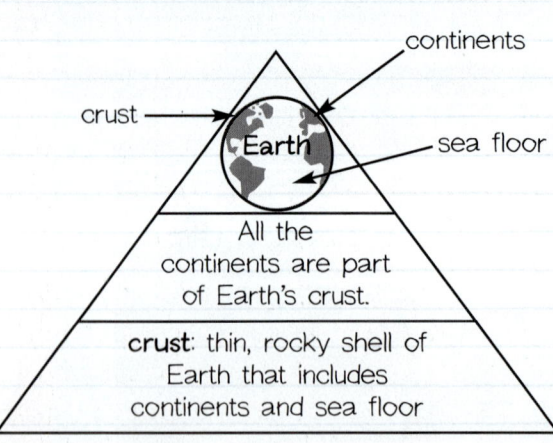

436 Unit 4: Earth's Surface

KEY CONCEPT
Technology is used to explore the Earth system.

 BEFORE, you learned
- Earth has a spherical shape and supports a complex web of life
- Earth's environment is a system with many parts

 NOW, you will learn
- About the Earth system and its four major parts
- How technology is used to explore the Earth system
- How the parts of the Earth system shape the surface

VOCABULARY

system p. 437
atmosphere p. 438
hydrosphere p. 438
biosphere p. 439
geosphere p. 440

THINK ABOUT

How do these parts work together?

Look closely at this terrarium. Notice that the bowl and its cover form a boundary between the terrarium and the outside world. What might happen to the entire terrarium if any part were taken away? What might happen if you placed the terrarium in a dark closet?

VOCABULARY
Remember to draw a word triangle in your notebook for each vocabulary term.

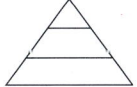

The Earth system has four major parts.

A terrarium is a simple example of a **system**—an organized group of parts that work together to form a whole. To understand a system, you need to see how all its parts work together. This principle is true for a small terrarium, and it is true for planet Earth.

Both a terrarium and Earth are closed systems. They are closed because matter, such as soil or water, cannot enter or leave. However, energy can flow into or out of the system. Just as light and heat pass through the glass of the terrarium, sunlight and heat enter and leave the Earth system through the atmosphere.

Within the Earth system are four connected parts: the atmosphere (Earth's air), the hydrosphere (Earth's waters), the biosphere (Earth's living things), and the geosphere (Earth's interior and its rocks and soils). Each of these parts is an open system because both matter and energy move into and out of it. The four open systems work together to form one large, closed system called Earth.

Chapter 13: **Views of Earth Today** 437

READING TIP

The names of the Earth system's four parts contain Greek prefixes. *Atmo-* refers to vapor or gas. *Hydro-* refers to water. *Bio-* refers to life, and *geo-* refers to earth.

Atmosphere

The **atmosphere** (AT-muh-SFEER) is the mixture of gases and particles that surrounds and protects the surface of Earth. The most abundant gases are nitrogen (about 78%) and oxygen (nearly 21%). The atmosphere also contains carbon dioxide, water vapor, and a few other gases.

Before the 1800s, all studies of the atmosphere had to be done from the ground. Today, scientists launch weather balloons, fly specially equipped planes, and view the atmosphere in satellite images. The data they collect show that the atmosphere interacts with the other parts of the Earth system to form complex weather patterns that circulate around Earth. The more scientists learn about these patterns, the more accurately they can predict local weather.

Hydrosphere

The **hydrosphere** (HY-druh-SFEER) is made up of all the water on Earth in oceans, lakes, glaciers, rivers, and streams and underground. Water covers nearly three-quarters of Earth's surface. Only about 3 percent of the hydrosphere is fresh water. Nearly 70 percent of Earth's fresh water is frozen in glaciers and polar ice caps.

Parts of the Earth System

Atmosphere

Over 400 cones make this weather balloon more stable as it gathers data about the atmosphere.

Hydrosphere

Scientists need special diving equipment to study Earth's oceans.

438 Unit 4: Earth's Surface

In the past 50 years, scientists have used deep-sea vehicles, special buoys, satellite images, and diving suits, such as the one shown on page 438, to study the world's oceans. They have discovered that the oceans contain several layers of cold and warm water. As these layers circulate, they form cold and warm ocean currents. The currents interact with wind patterns in the atmosphere and affect Earth's weather.

 How does the hydrosphere affect the atmosphere?

Biosphere

The **biosphere** (BY-uh-SFEER) includes all life on Earth, in the air, on the land, and in the waters. The biosphere can be studied with a variety of technologies. For example, satellite photos are used to track yearly changes in Earth's plant and animal life. As the photograph below shows, special equipment allows scientists to study complex environments, such as rain forests, without damaging them.

Scientists have learned a lot about how the biosphere interacts with the other parts of the Earth system. For example, large forests act as Earth's "lungs," absorbing carbon dioxide and releasing oxygen into the atmosphere. When dead trees decay, they return nutrients to the soil.

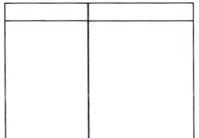 **MAIN IDEA AND DETAILS**
As you read this section, use this strategy to take notes.

Name one way the biosphere and the atmosphere interact.

Biosphere

These platforms, built in the treetops, are used to observe forest plants and animals.

Geosphere

In mines dug deep underground, scientists can explore Earth's minerals and rocks.

Chapter 13: **Views of Earth Today** 439

Geosphere

The **geosphere** (JEE-uh-SFEER) includes all the features on Earth's surface—the continents, islands, and sea floor—and everything below the surface. As the diagram illustrates, the geosphere is made up of several layers: crust, mantle, and outer and inner core.

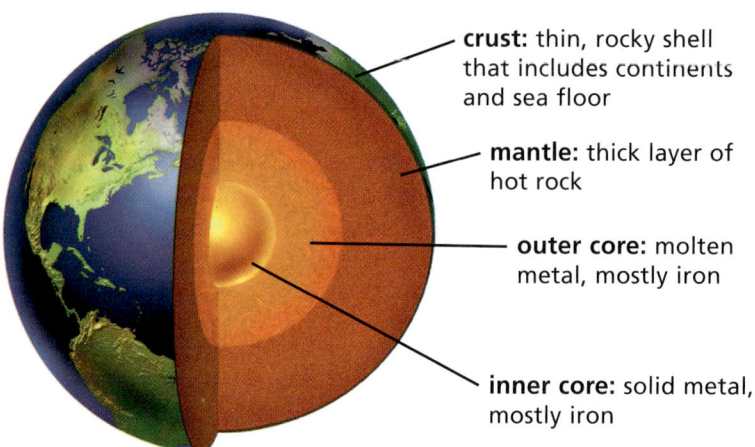

crust: thin, rocky shell that includes continents and sea floor

mantle: thick layer of hot rock

outer core: molten metal, mostly iron

inner core: solid metal, mostly iron

People have studied the surface of the geosphere for centuries. Not until the 1900s, however, were people able to study Earth from space or to explore deep within the planet. Today, scientists use satellite images, sound waves, and computer modeling to develop accurate pictures of features on and below Earth's surface. These images show that Earth constantly changes. Some changes are sudden—a volcano explodes, releasing harmful gases and dust into the air. Other changes, such as the birth of new islands, happen over millions of years.

Earth's continents have many unique landforms such as these rock towers in Cathedral Valley, Utah.

CHECK YOUR READING Give an example of matter moving from the geosphere to the atmosphere.

440 Unit 4: Earth's Surface

INVESTIGATE Geosphere's Layers

How can you model the geosphere's layers?
PROCEDURE

1. To model the layers of the geosphere, you will be using a quarter of an apple that your teacher has cut. Note: NEVER eat food in the science classroom.
2. Hold the apple slice and observe it carefully. Compare it with the diagram of the geosphere's layers on page 440.
3. Draw a diagram of the apple and label it with the names of the layers of the geosphere.

WHAT DO YOU THINK?
- What are the four parts of the apple slice?
- What major layer of the geosphere does each part of the apple resemble?

CHALLENGE What other object do you think would make a good model of the geosphere's layers? What model could you build or make yourself?

SKILL FOCUS
Modeling

MATERIALS
apple slice

TIME
15 minutes

All four parts of the Earth system shape the planet's surface.

Earth's surface is worn away, built up, and reshaped every day by the atmosphere, the hydrosphere, the biosphere, and the geosphere. Here are some of the ways they affect the surface.

Atmosphere and Hydrosphere Not even the hardest stone can withstand wind and water. Over millions of years, rain, wind, and flowing water carve huge formations such as the Grand Canyon in Arizona or the rock towers of Utah, shown on page 440.

Geosphere Landmasses pushing together have set off earthquakes and formed volcanoes and mountain ranges around the world.

Biosphere Plants, animals, and human beings have also changed Earth's surface. For instance, earthworms help make soils more fertile. And throughout human history, people have dammed rivers and cleared forests for farmland.

You are part of this process, too. Every time you walk or ride a bike across open land, you are changing Earth's surface. Your feet or the bike's tires dig into the dirt, wearing away plants and exposing soil to sunlight, wind, and water. If you take the same route every day, over time you will wear a path in the land.

READING TIP

Landmass is a compound word made up of the words *land* and *mass*. Landmass means "a large area of land."

Mudslide in California

Atmosphere and Hydrosphere Heavy winter rains soak the ground until it cannot absorb any more water.

Biosphere People who build on fragile hillsides remove plants whose roots help hold the soil in place.

Geosphere With nothing to hold the water-soaked ground, it slides downhill, leaving a deep trench.

The photograph above shows a good example of how the four parts can suddenly change Earth's surface. A mudslide like this one can happen in a matter of minutes. Sometimes the side of a mountain may collapse, becoming a river of mud that can bury an entire town.

The four parts of the Earth system continue to shape the surface with every passing year. Scientists will continue to record these changes to update maps and other images of the planet's complex system.

 **CHECK YOUR READING** Find three examples on pages 441 and 442 that show how the parts of the Earth system shape the planet's surface.

13.1 Review

KEY CONCEPTS

1. Define *system*. Compare an open and a closed system.
2. Name the four parts of the Earth system. List one fact about each part that scientists learned through modern technology.
3. Give two examples of how the Earth system's four parts can interact with each other.

CRITICAL THINKING

4. **Apply** One day you see that plants are dying in the class terrarium. What part might be missing from its system?
5. **Infer** You visit a state park and see a thin rock wall with a hole, like a window, worn through it. Which of the four parts of the Earth system might have made the hole? Explain.

CHALLENGE

6. **Predict** Imagine that a meteorite 200 meters wide strikes Earth, landing in a wooded area. Describe one way that this event would affect the biosphere or the geosphere. **Hint:** A meteorite is traveling several thousand kilometers per hour when it strikes the ground.

KEY CONCEPT

 Maps and globes are models of Earth.

BEFORE, you learned
- The Earth system has four main parts: atmosphere, hydrosphere, biosphere, and geosphere
- Technology is used to study and map the Earth system
- The Earth system's parts interact to shape Earth's surface

NOW, you will learn
- What information maps can provide about natural and human-made features
- How to find exact locations on Earth
- Why all maps distort Earth's surface

VOCABULARY
relief map p. 444
map scale p. 445
map legend p. 445
equator p. 446
latitude p. 446
prime meridian p. 447
longitude p. 447
projection p. 448

EXPLORE Mapping
What makes a good map?
PROCEDURE

 Draw a map to guide someone from your school to your home or to a point of interest, such as a park, statue, or store, near your school.

② Trade maps with a classmate. Is his or her map easy to understand? Why or why not?

③ Use feedback from your partner to revise your own map.

WHAT DO YOU THINK?
What visual clues make a map easy to understand and use?

MATERIALS
- paper
- pencil or pen

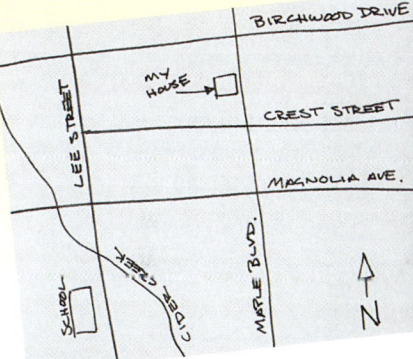

Maps show natural and human-made features.

Have you ever drawn a map to help someone get to your home? If so, your map is actually a rough model of your neighborhood, showing important streets and landmarks. Any map you use is a flat model of Earth's surface, showing Earth's features as seen from above.

On the other hand, a globe represents Earth as if you were looking at it from outer space. A globe is a sphere that shows the relative sizes and shapes of Earth's land features and waters.

In this section you will learn how maps and globes provide different types of information about Earth's surface. They can show everything from city streets to land features to the entire world.

 How are maps and globes alike? How are they different?

Chapter 13: **Views of Earth Today** 443

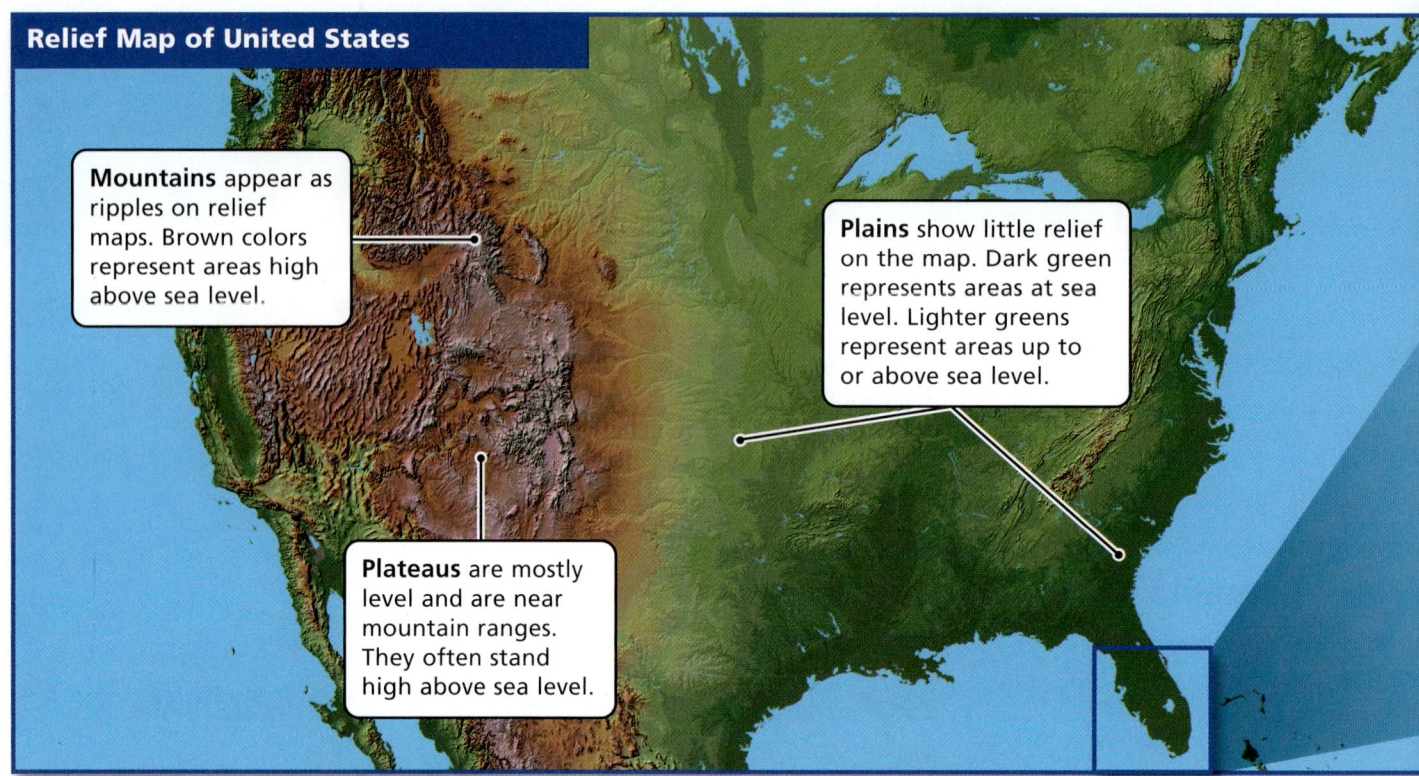

Relief Map of United States

Mountains appear as ripples on relief maps. Brown colors represent areas high above sea level.

Plains show little relief on the map. Dark green represents areas at sea level. Lighter greens represent areas up to or above sea level.

Plateaus are mostly level and are near mountain ranges. They often stand high above sea level.

VOCABULARY
Add a word triangle for *relief map* to your notebook.

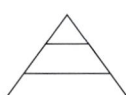

Land Features on Maps

When scientists or travelers want to know what the landscape of an area actually looks like, they will often use a relief map. A **relief map**, such as the one above, shows how high or low each feature is on Earth. A mapmaker uses photographs or satellite images to build a three-dimensional view of Earth's surface. A relief map shows three main types of land features: mountains, plains, and plateaus.

Mountains stand higher than the land around them. A mountain's base may cover several square kilometers. A group of mountains is called a mountain range. Mountain ranges connected in a long chain form a mountain belt. The Rocky Mountains in the United States are part of a huge mountain belt that includes the Canadian Rockies and the Andes Mountains in South America.

Plateaus have fairly level surfaces but stand high above sea level. Plateaus are often found near large mountain ranges. In the United States, the Colorado Plateau is about 3350 meters (11,000 ft) above sea level. This plateau includes parts of Arizona, Colorado, New Mexico, and Utah.

Plains are gently rolling or flat features. The United States has two types of plains—coastal plains near the eastern and southeastern shores, and interior plains in the center of the nation. The interior Great Plains cover the middle third of the United States.

 How is a plateau different from either a mountain or a plain?

444 Unit 4: Earth's Surface

Scale and Symbols on Maps

The maps most people use are road and city maps like the ones above. These maps provide information about human-made features as well as some natural features. To use these maps, you need to know how to read a map scale and a map legend, or key.

① A **map scale** relates distances on a map to actual distances on Earth's surface. Notice that on the map of southern Florida above, the scale is in kilometers and miles. On the Miami Beach map, the scale is in meters and yards. The smaller the area a map shows, the more detail it includes.

The scale can be expressed as a ratio, a bar, or equivalent units of distance. For example, a ratio of 1:25,000 means that 1 centimeter on the map represents 25,000 centimeters (0.25 kilometer) on Earth.

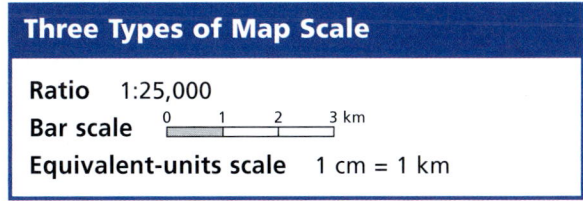

② A **map legend**, also called a key, is a chart that explains the meaning of each symbol used on a map. Symbols can stand for highways, parks, and other features. The legend on the Miami Beach map shows major points of interest for tourists.

READING TIP

As used here, *legend* does not refer to a story. It is based on the Latin word *legenda*, which means "to be read."

③ A map usually includes a compass rose to show which directions are north, south, east, and west. In general, north on a map points to the top of the page.

 What information do map scales and map legends provide?

Chapter 13: **Views of Earth Today** 445

Explore how latitude and longitude help you find locations on Earth's surface.

Latitude and longitude show locations on Earth.

Suppose you were lucky enough to find dinosaur bones in the desert. Would you know how to find that exact spot again? You would if you knew the longitude and latitude of the place. Latitude and longitude lines form an imaginary grid over the entire surface of Earth. This grid provides everyone with the same tools for navigation. Using latitude and longitude, you can locate any place on the planet.

Latitude

Latitude is based on an imaginary line that circles Earth halfway between the north and south poles. This line is called the **equator,** and it divides Earth into northern and southern hemispheres. A hemisphere is one half of a sphere.

READING TIP
Hemi- is a Greek prefix meaning "half."

Latitude is a distance in degrees north or south of the equator, which is 0°. A degree is 1/360 of the distance around a full circle. If you start at one point on the equator and travel all the way around the world back to that point, you have traveled 360 degrees.

The illustration below shows that latitude lines are parallel to the equator and are evenly spaced between the equator and the poles. Also, latitude lines are always labeled north or south of the equator to

Latitude and Longitude

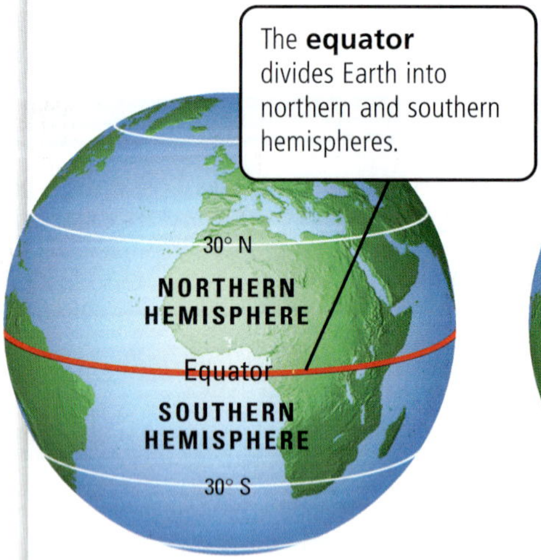

The **equator** divides Earth into northern and southern hemispheres.

The **prime meridian** divides Earth into eastern and western hemispheres.

Latitude is a distance in degrees north or south of the equator.

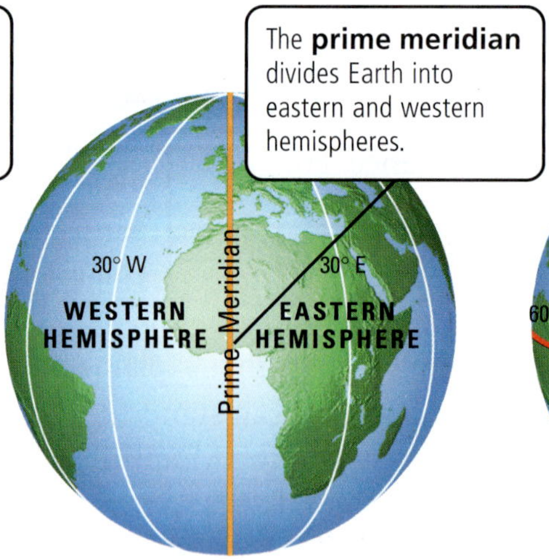

Longitude is a distance in degrees east or west of the prime meridian.

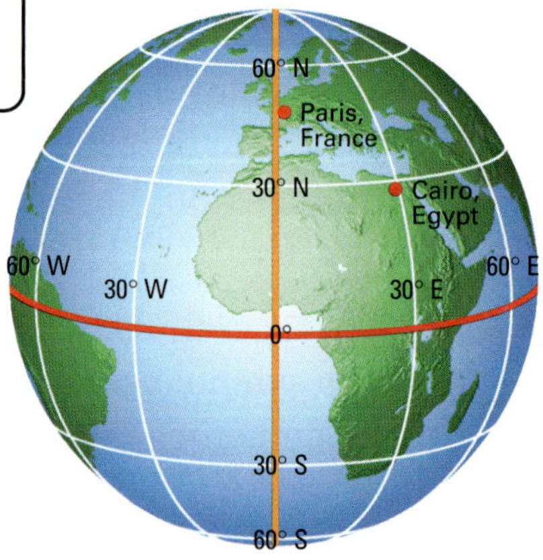

You can find a location by noting where latitude and longitude lines cross.

READING VISUALS What are the approximate latitudes and longitudes of Cairo, Egypt, and Paris, France?

446 Unit 4: Earth's Surface

show whether a location is in the northern or southern hemisphere. For instance, the North Pole is 90° north, or 90°N, while the South Pole is 90° south, or 90°S. Latitude, however, is only half of what you need to locate any spot on Earth. You also need to know its longitude.

Longitude

Longitude is based on an imaginary line that stretches from the North Pole through Greenwich, England, to the South Pole. This line is called the **prime meridian.** Any place up to 180° west of the prime meridian is in the Western Hemisphere. Any place up to 180° east of the prime meridian is in the Eastern Hemisphere.

Longitude is a distance in degrees east or west of the prime meridian, which is 0°. Beginning at the prime meridian, longitude lines are numbered 0° to 180° west and 0° to 180° east.

Longitude lines are labeled east or west to indicate whether a location is in the eastern or western hemisphere. For example, the longitude of Washington, D.C., is about 78° west, or 78°W. The city of Hamburg, Germany, is about 10° east, or 10°E. If you understand latitude and longitude, you can find any spot on Earth's surface.

> **READING TIP**
> There is an easy way to remember the difference between latitude and longitude. Think of longitude lines as the "long" lines that go from pole to pole.

 Why do all cities in the United States have a north latitude and a west longitude?

Global Positioning System

The Global Positioning System (GPS) is a network of satellites that are used to find the latitude, longitude, and elevation, or height above sea level, of any site. Twenty-four GPS satellites circle Earth and send signals that are picked up by receivers on the surface. At least three satellites need to be above the horizon for GPS to work. A computer inside a receiver uses the satellite signals to calculate the user's exact location—latitude, longitude, and elevation. GPS is an accurate, easy method for finding location.

GPS devices are used by many people, including pilots, sailors, hikers, and map makers. Some cars now have GPS receivers and digital road maps stored in their computers. A driver types in an address, and the car's computer finds the best way to get there.

 Explain how GPS can help someone find their exact location.

Never be lost again. This hiker turns on his GPS unit to find out his current latitude and longitude. He then locates these data on his map to pinpoint his exact location.

Chapter 13: **Views of Earth Today** 447

Map projections distort the view of Earth's surface.

The most accurate way to show Earth's surface is on a globe. A globe, however, cannot show much detail, and it is awkward to carry. People use flat maps for their detail and convenience. A **projection** is a way of representing Earth's curved surface on a flat map. Mapmakers use different types of projections, all of which distort, or misrepresent, Earth's surface in different ways.

Cylindrical Projection

The Mercator projection shows Earth as if the map were a large cylinder wrapped around the planet. The outlines of the landmasses and seas are then drawn onto the map. As shown in the diagram on page 449, the cylinder is unrolled to form a flat map. Latitude and longitude appear as straight lines, forming a grid of rectangles.

The Mercator projection is useful for navigating at sea or in the air. It shows the entire world, except for regions near the poles, on one map. Sailors and pilots can draw a straight line from one point to

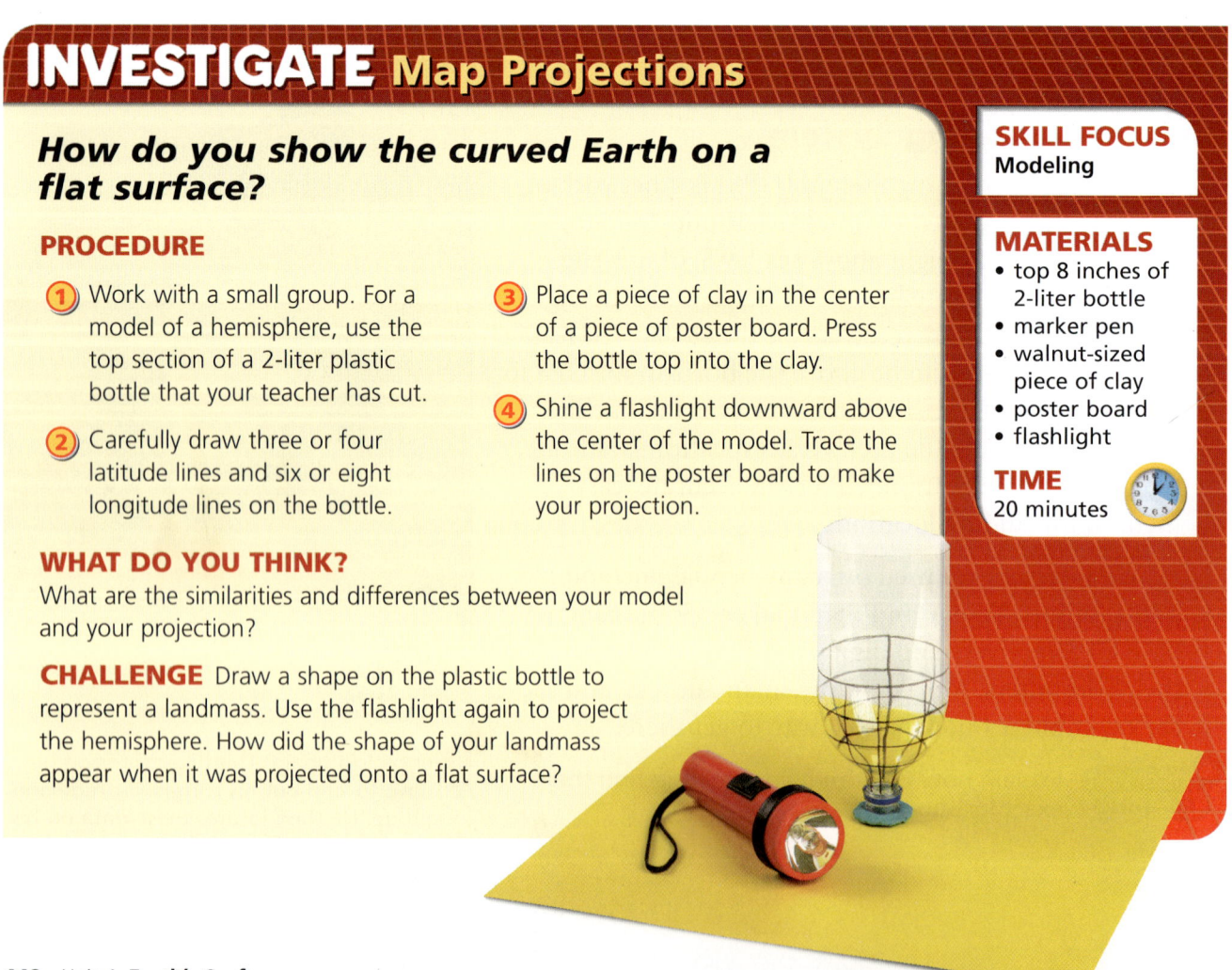

INVESTIGATE Map Projections

How do you show the curved Earth on a flat surface?

PROCEDURE

1. Work with a small group. For a model of a hemisphere, use the top section of a 2-liter plastic bottle that your teacher has cut.

2. Carefully draw three or four latitude lines and six or eight longitude lines on the bottle.

3. Place a piece of clay in the center of a piece of poster board. Press the bottle top into the clay.

4. Shine a flashlight downward above the center of the model. Trace the lines on the poster board to make your projection.

WHAT DO YOU THINK?
What are the similarities and differences between your model and your projection?

CHALLENGE Draw a shape on the plastic bottle to represent a landmass. Use the flashlight again to project the hemisphere. How did the shape of your landmass appear when it was projected onto a flat surface?

SKILL FOCUS
Modeling

MATERIALS
- top 8 inches of 2-liter bottle
- marker pen
- walnut-sized piece of clay
- poster board
- flashlight

TIME
20 minutes

448 Unit 4: Earth's Surface

another to plot a course. The problem with Mercator maps is that areas far away from the equator appear much larger than they really are. On the map below, Greenland looks bigger than South America. In reality, South America is about eight times larger than Greenland.

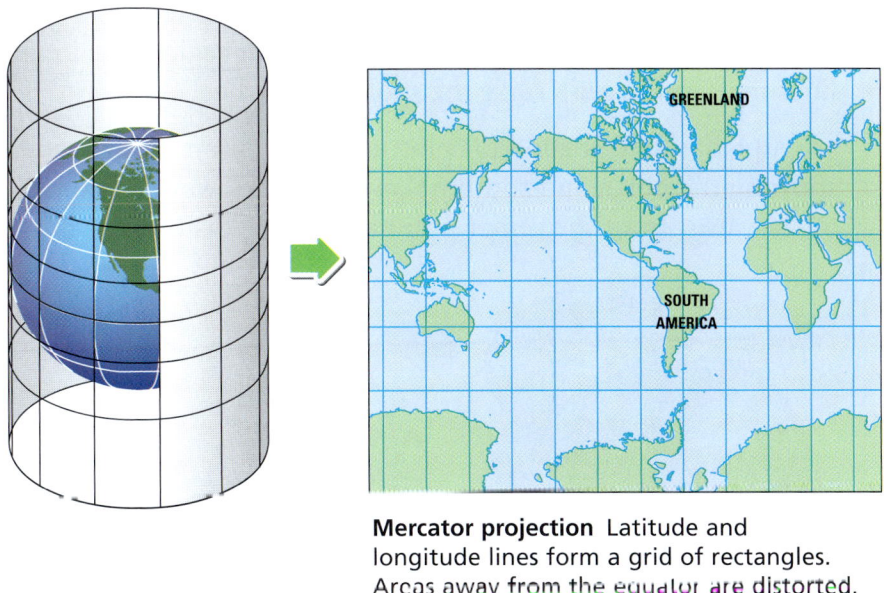

Mercator projection Latitude and longitude lines form a grid of rectangles. Areas away from the equator are distorted.

Conic Projections

Conic projections are based on the shape of a cone. The diagram below shows how a cone of paper might be wrapped around the globe. The paper touches the surface only at the middle latitudes, halfway between the equator and the North Pole.

When the cone is flattened out, the latitude lines are curved slightly. The curved lines represent the curved surface of Earth. This allows the map to show the true sizes and shapes of some landmasses.

Conic projections are most useful for mapping large areas in the middle latitudes, such as the United States. However, landmasses near the equator or near the north or south pole will be distorted.

CHECK YOUR READING What are the main uses of Mercator and conic projections?

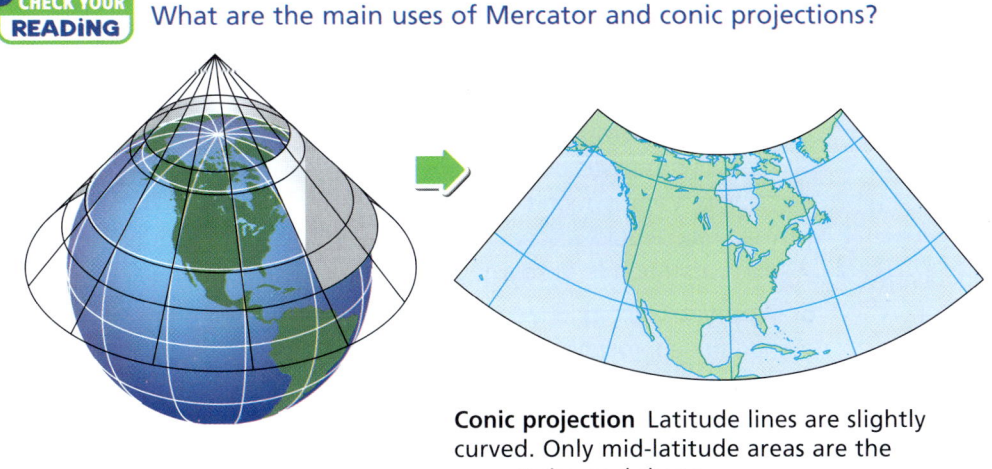

Conic projection Latitude lines are slightly curved. Only mid-latitude areas are the correct size and shape.

Chapter 13: **Views of Earth Today** 449

Find out more about map projections and how they are used.

Planar Projections

Planar projections were developed to help people find the shortest distance between two points. They are drawn as if a circle of paper were laid on a point on Earth's surface. As you look at the diagram below, notice how the shape of the sphere is transferred to the flat map. When a planar map represents the polar region, the longitude lines meet at the center like the spokes of a wheel.

A planar map is good for plotting ocean or air voyages and for showing the north and south polar regions. However, landmasses farther away from the center point are greatly distorted.

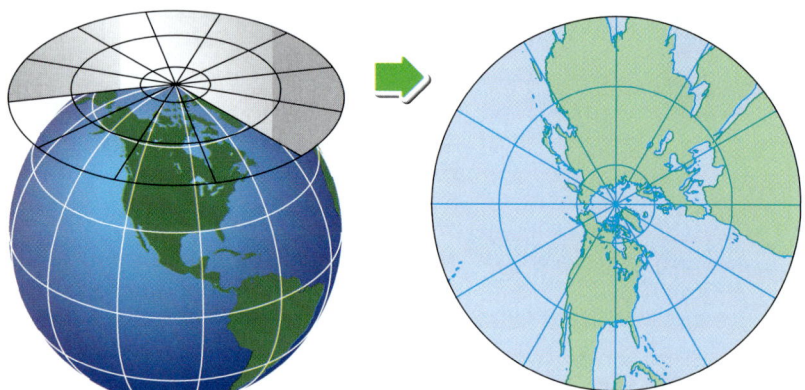

Planar projection Only areas near the center point are the correct size and shape.

The Mercator, conic, and planar projections are all attempts to solve the problem of representing a curved surface on a flat map. Each projection can show certain areas of the world accurately but distorts other areas.

 What areas does the planar projection show accurately?

13.2 Review

KEY CONCEPTS

1. What natural and human-made features can maps show? Give two examples of each.
2. Explain how latitude and longitude can help you locate any place on Earth.
3. Why do all flat maps distort Earth's surface?

CRITICAL THINKING

4. **Provide Examples** Imagine that your family is on a long car trip. What symbols on a road map would you pay the most attention to? Explain.
5. **Apply** Use a world map to find the approximate latitudes and longitudes of Moscow, Russia; Tokyo, Japan; Denver, Colorado; and La Paz, Bolivia.

CHALLENGE

6. **Apply** Working with a partner or with a small group, select the shortest airline route from Chicago to London, using a globe and a Mercator map. Hint: Notice that as you go farther north on the globe, the longitude lines become closer together.

MATH in SCIENCE

SKILL: USING PROPORTIONS

How Far Is It?

A science class is visiting Chicago and is using the map on the left to walk to the lakefront museums. Remember, a map scale shows how distances on the map compare to actual distances on the ground.

Buckingham Fountain

Example

In this case, the map scale indicates that 1 centimeter on the map represents 300 meters on the ground. The map scale shows this as equivalent units. By using these units to write a proportion, you can use cross products to determine actual distances.

What distance does 3 cm on the map represent? Set up the problem like this.

$$\frac{1 \text{ cm}}{300 \text{ m}} = \frac{3 \text{ cm}}{x}$$

(1) $1 \text{ cm} \cdot x = 3 \text{ cm} \cdot 300 \text{ m}$

(2) $x = 3 \cdot 300 \text{ m}$

(3) $x = 900 \text{ m}$

ANSWER 3 centimeters on the map represents 900 meters on the ground.

Use cross products and a metric ruler to answer the following questions.

1. The science class divides into two groups. Each group starts at Buckingham Fountain. How far, in meters, will one group walk to get to the Adler Planetarium if they follow the red dotted line?

2. How far, in meters, will the other group walk to get to the end of Navy Pier if they follow the blue dotted line?

3. The group that walked to Adler decides to take a boat to join the other group at Navy Pier. How far, in meters, is their boat ride along the red dotted line?

CHALLENGE What is the total distance, in kilometers, that the two groups traveled? Set up the problem as a proportion. **Hint:** There are 1000 meters in a kilometer.

Chapter 13: **Views of Earth Today** 451

KEY CONCEPT

13.3 Topographic maps show the shape of the land.

BEFORE, you learned
- Different maps provide information about natural and human-made features
- Latitude and longitude are used to find places on Earth
- All flat maps distort Earth's surface

NOW, you will learn
- How contour lines show elevation, slope, and relief
- What rules contour lines follow
- What common symbols are used on topographic maps

VOCABULARY

topography p. 452
contour line p. 453
elevation p. 453
slope p. 453
relief p. 453
contour interval p. 454

EXPLORE Topographic Maps

How can you map your knuckles?

PROCEDURE

1. Hold your fist closed, knuckles up, as shown in the photo.
2. Draw circles around the first knuckle. Make sure the circles are the same distance from each other.
3. Flatten out your hand. Observe what happens. Write down your observations.

MATERIAL
washable colored pen

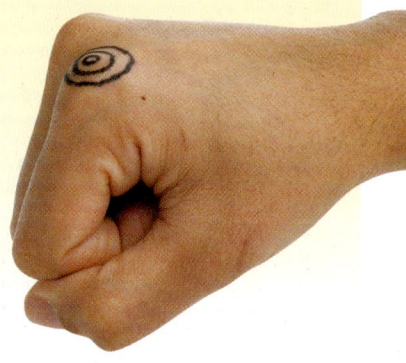

WHAT DO YOU THINK?
- How does the height of your knuckles change when you clench your fist, then flatten out your hand?
- What do you think the circles represent?

Topographic maps use contour lines to show features.

VOCABULARY
Add a word triangle for *topography* to your notebook.

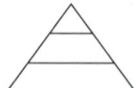

Imagine you are on vacation with your family in a national park. You have a simple trail map that shows you where to hike. But the map does not tell you anything about what the land looks like. Will you have to cross any rivers or valleys? How far uphill or downhill will you have to hike?

To answer these questions, you need to know something about the topography of the area. **Topography** is the shape, or features, of the land. These features can be natural—such as mountains, plateaus, and plains—or human-made—such as dams and roads. To show the topography of an area, mapmakers draw a topographic map.

452 Unit 4: Earth's Surface

A topographic map is a flat map that uses lines to show Earth's surface features. Distance and elevation can be given in feet or meters. Take a look at the topographic map of Mount Hood on this page. The wiggly lines on the map are called **contour lines,** and they show an area's elevation, slope, and relief.

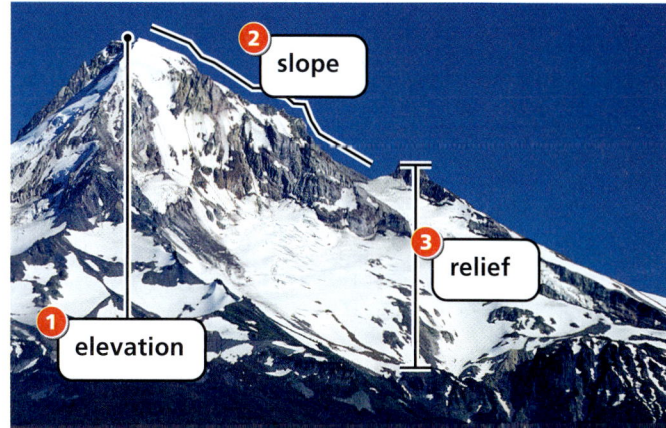

① The **elevation** of a place is how high above sea level it is. An area can range from a few meters to several thousand meters above sea level. The numbers on the contour lines show the elevations of different points in the Mount Hood area.

② The **slope** of a landform or area is how steep it is. The more gradual the slope, the farther apart the contour lines on the map. The steeper the slope, the closer together the contour lines.

③ The **relief** of an area is the difference between its high and low points. For example, subtracting the lowest elevation on the map from the highest gives you a measure of the area's relief.

CHECK YOUR READING What is the difference between elevation and slope?

Mount Hood Topographic Map

A topographic map shows the land as if you were above the land looking down on it.

① Contour lines show the mountain's peak as seen from above. The **elevation** here is given in meters.

② Contour lines close together show a steep **slope**. Lines farther apart show a more gentle slope.

③ The different elevations on a map indicate an area's **relief**.

READING VISUALS What is the elevation of the top of Mount Hood?

MAIN IDEA AND DETAILS Use your main idea and details chart to take notes on the rules for reading a topographic map.

Contour lines follow certain rules.

Contour lines on topographic maps can help you visualize landforms. Think of the following statements as rules for reading such maps:

- **Lines never cross.** Contour lines never cross, because each line represents an exact elevation.
- **Circles show highest and lowest points.** Contour lines form closed circles around mountaintops, hilltops, and the centers of depressions, which are sunken areas in the ground. Sometimes, the elevation of a mountain or hill is written in meters or feet in the middle of the circle.
- **Contour interval is always the same** on a map. The **contour interval** is the difference in elevation from one contour line to the next. For example, the contour interval on the map below is 10 feet. This means that the change in elevation between contour lines is always 10 feet. The contour interval can differ from map to map, but it is always the same on a particular map.

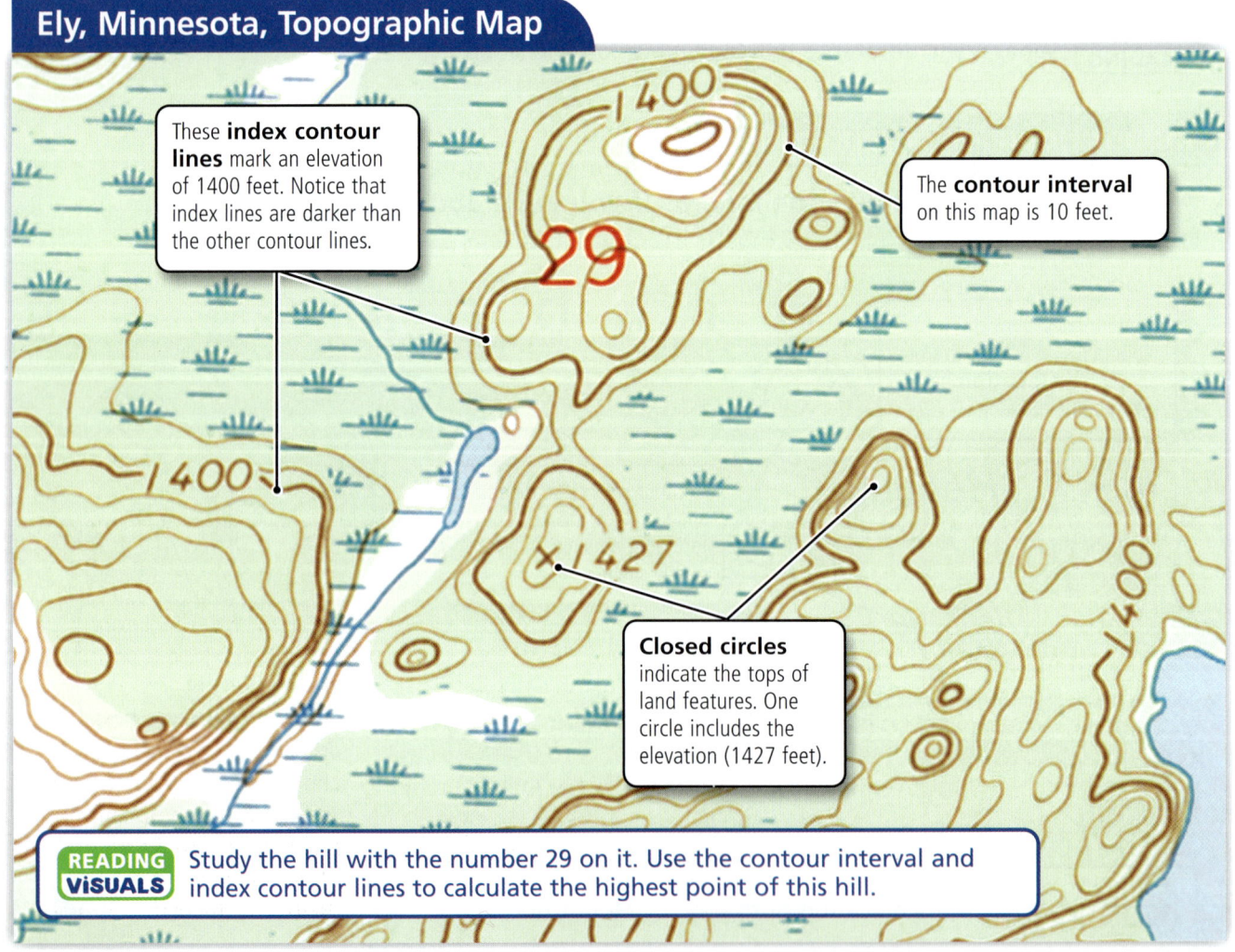

Ely, Minnesota, Topographic Map

These **index contour lines** mark an elevation of 1400 feet. Notice that index lines are darker than the other contour lines.

The **contour interval** on this map is 10 feet.

Closed circles indicate the tops of land features. One circle includes the elevation (1427 feet).

READING VISUALS Study the hill with the number 29 on it. Use the contour interval and index contour lines to calculate the highest point of this hill.

- **Index contour lines mark elevations.** The darker contour lines on a map are called index contour lines. Numbers that indicate elevations are often written on these lines. To calculate higher or lower elevations, simply count the number of lines above or below an index line. Then multiply that number by the contour interval. For instance, on the Ely map, one index line marks 1400 feet. To find the elevation of a point three lines up from this index line, you would multiply 10 feet (the contour interval) by 3. Add the result, 30, to 1400. The point's elevation is 1430 feet.

Discover the relationship between topographic maps and surface features.

 What information do index contour lines provide?

Besides contour lines, topographic maps also contain symbols for natural and human-made features. Below are some common map symbols that the United States Geological Survey (USGS) uses on its topographic maps.

The USGS provides topographic maps for nearly every part of the United States. These maps cover urban, rural, and wilderness areas. Hikers and campers are not the only ones who use topographic maps. Engineers, archaeologists, forest rangers, biologists, and others rely on them as well.

13.3 Review

KEY CONCEPTS

1. How do contour lines show elevation, slope, and relief?
2. Why do contour lines never cross on a topographic map?
3. How would you show the top of a hill, an area of vegetation, or a hiking trail on a topographic map?

CRITICAL THINKING

4. **Apply** For an area with gently sloping hills and little relief, would you draw contour lines close together or far apart? Explain why.
5. **Compare and Contrast** How would a road map and a topographic map of the same area differ? What information would each provide?

CHALLENGE

6. **Synthesize** Work with a group to make a topographic map of the area around your school. First decide how big an area you will include. Then choose a contour interval, a map scale, and symbols for buildings, sports fields, and other features. Let other students test the map's accuracy.

CHAPTER INVESTIGATION

Investigate Topographic Maps

OVERVIEW AND PURPOSE Topographic maps show the shape of the land. In this lab you will use what you have learned about how Earth's three-dimensional surface is represented on maps to
- make a terrain model out of clay
- produce a topographic map of the model

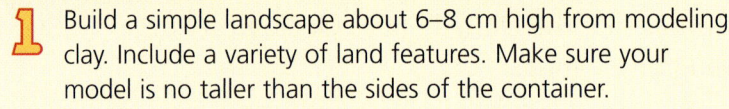

1. Build a simple landscape about 6–8 cm high from modeling clay. Include a variety of land features. Make sure your model is no taller than the sides of the container.

2. Place your model into the container. Stand a ruler upright inside the container and tape it in place.

3. Lay the clear plastic sheet over the container and tape it on one side like a hinge. Carefully trace the outline of your clay model.

step 3

4. Add 2 cm of colored water to the container.

5. Insert spaghetti sticks into the model all around the waterline. Place the sticks about 3 cm apart. Make sure the sticks are vertical and are no taller than the sides of the container.

6. Lower the plastic sheet back over the container. Looking straight down on the container, make a dot on the sheet wherever you see a spaghetti stick. Connect the dots to trace the contour line accurately onto your map.

7. Continue adding water, 2 cm at a time. Each time you add water, insert the sticks into the model at the waterline and repeat step 6. Continue until the model landscape is underwater. Carefully drain the water when finished.

step 5

MATERIALS
- half-gallon cardboard juice container
- scissors
- modeling clay
- clear plastic sheet (transparency or sheet protector)
- cellophane tape
- ruler
- water
- food coloring
- box of spaghetti
- erasable marker pen

456 Unit 4: *Earth's Surface*

Observe and Analyze *Write It Up*

1. Compare your topographic map with the three-dimensional model. Remember that contour lines connect points of equal elevation. What do widely spaced or tightly spaced contour lines mean? What does a closed circle mean?

2. Make a permanent record of your map to keep in your **Science Notebook** by carefully tracing the contour lines onto a sheet of white paper. To make reading the map easier, use a different color for an index contour line.

3. What is the contour interval of your model landscape? For example, each 2 centimeters might represent 20 meters in an actual landscape. Record the elevation of the index contour line on your map.

3. Mark the same elevations on the side of the paper, as shown in the example.

4. Use a ruler to draw a straight line down from each mark to the matching elevation on the side of the paper.

5. Connect the points to draw a profile of the landform.

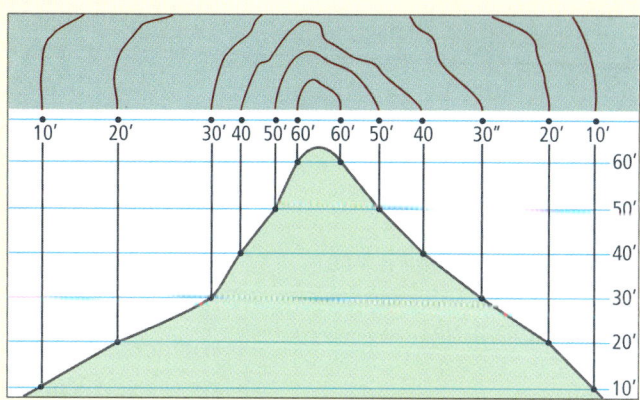

Conclude *Write It Up*

1. **INFER** How would you determine the elevation of a point located halfway between two contour lines?

2. **EVALUATE** Describe any errors that you may have made in your procedure or any places where errors might have occurred.

3. **APPLY** Explain how you would use a topographic map if you were planning a hiking trip or a cross-country bike race.

INVESTIGATE Further

CHALLENGE Choose one feature on a topographic map—such as the map on page 454—to translate into a cross-sectional diagram.

1. Lay a piece of ruled paper across the center of the topographical feature.

2. Mark each of the contour lines on the ruled paper and label each mark with the elevation.

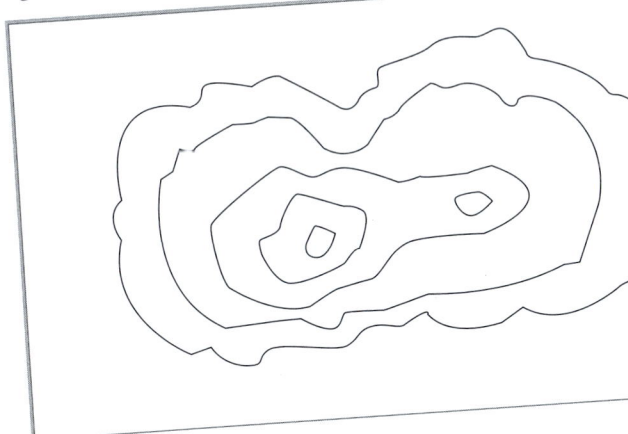

INVESTIGATE TOPOGRAPHIC MAPS
Observe and Analyze
Figure 1. Topographic Map of Model

Conclude

Chapter 13: **Views of Earth Today** 457

KEY CONCEPT
13.4 Technology is used to map Earth.

 BEFORE, you learned
- Contour lines are used on topographic maps to show elevation, slope, and relief
- Contour lines follow certain rules
- Map symbols show many natural and human-made features

 NOW, you will learn
- How remote-sensing images can provide detailed and accurate information about Earth
- How geographic data can be displayed in layers to build maps

VOCABULARY

remote sensing p. 458
sensor p. 459
false-color image p. 460
geographic information systems p. 461

THINK ABOUT

What can you see in this image?

Satellites can record all types of information about Earth's surface. This image shows a section of Washington, D.C. The satellite that collected the data is 680 kilometers (420 mi) above Earth. What familiar items can you see in the picture? How might images like this be useful to scientists, mapmakers, and engineers?

Remote sensing provides detailed images of Earth.

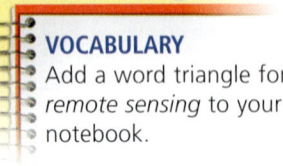
VOCABULARY
Add a word triangle for *remote sensing* to your notebook.

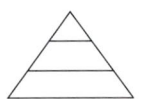

If you have ever looked at an object through a pair of binoculars, you have used remote sensing. **Remote sensing** is the use of scientific equipment to gather information about something from a distance. Remote-sensing technology can be as simple as a camera mounted on an airplane or as complex as a satellite orbiting Earth.

To get an idea of how important remote sensing is, imagine you are a mapmaker in the 1840s. You have been asked to draw a map of a state, but you have no cameras, no photographs from airplanes, and no satellites to help you. To get a good view of the land, you have to climb to the highest points and carefully draw every hill, valley, river, and landform below you. It will take you months to map the state.

458 Unit 4: Earth's Surface

Today, that same map would take far less time to make. Modern mapmakers use remote-sensing images from airplanes and satellites to develop highly detailed and accurate maps of Earth's surface.

Airplane cameras use film to record data, but satellites use sensors to build images of Earth. A **sensor** is a mechanical or electrical device that receives and responds to a signal, such as light. Satellite sensors detect far more than your eyes can see. They collect information about the different types of energy coming from Earth's surface. The satellites then send that information to computers on Earth.

The computers turn the information into images, as shown in the illustration below. Satellite data can be used to build an image of the entire planet, a single continent, or a detail of your area. For example, the image on the right shows a closeup of the Jefferson Memorial in Washington, D.C.

This satellite image includes the Jefferson Memorial, walkways, and roads. See if you can find the memorial in the image on page 458.

 Explain how remote sensing is used to gather information about Earth.

Satellite Imaging

Objects on Earth reflect or emit different types of energy. Satellite sensors can detect and record these energies.

1 As the satellite orbits Earth, its sensors record the energies reflected or emitted by the target area on the surface.

2 The data are transmitted as computer codes, which are turned into electronic dots (called pixels) on a screen.

3 The pixels are used to form an exact image of each section of the target area.

Chapter 13: **Views of Earth Today** 459

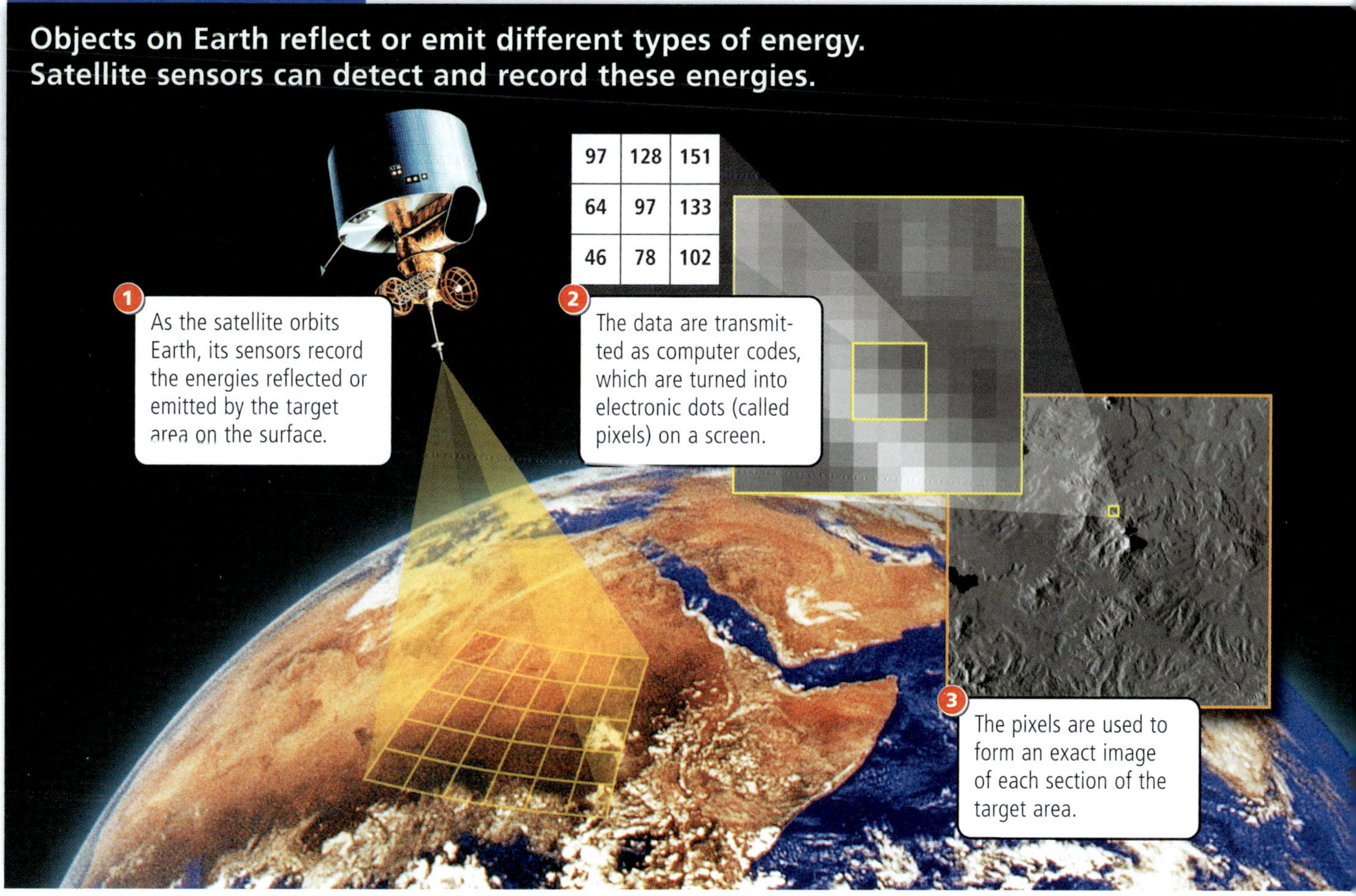

One of the ways scientists study changes is by using false-color images. In one type of **false-color image,** Earth's natural colors are replaced with artificial ones to highlight special features. For example, fire officials used false-color images like the ones below to track the spread of a dangerous wildfire in southern Oregon.

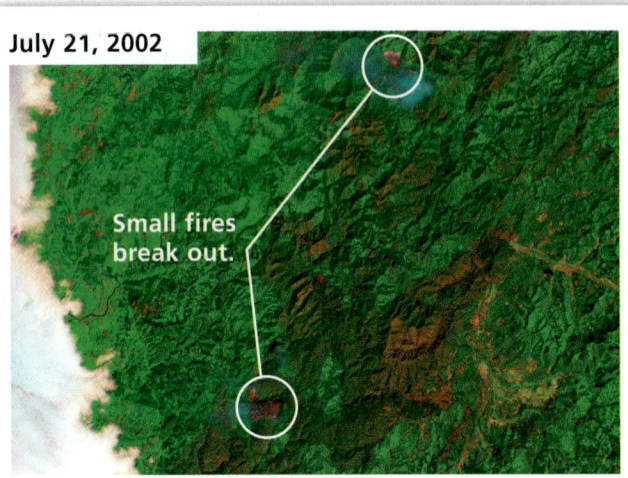

July 21, 2002

Small fires break out.

In this false-color image, vegetation is bright green, burned areas are red, fire is bright pink, and smoke is blue.

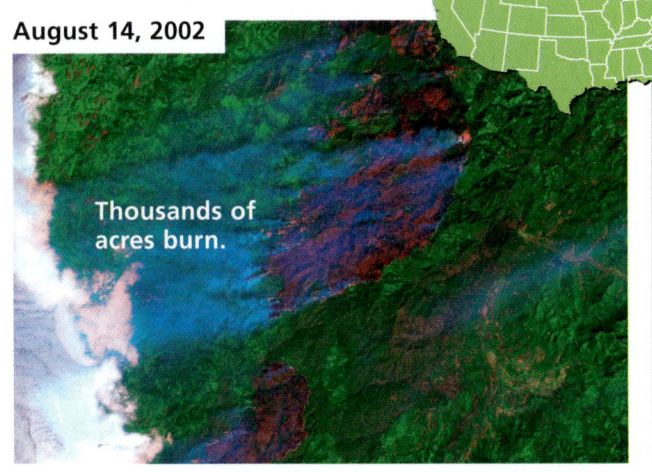

August 14, 2002

Thousands of acres burn.

Three weeks later, as this false-color image clearly shows, the fires had spread over a large area.

INVESTIGATE Satellite Imaging

How do satellites send images to Earth?

PROCEDURE

1. Work with a partner. One of you will be the "sensor," and the other will be the "receiving station."

2. The sensor draws the initials of a famous person on a piece of graph paper. The receiving station does NOT see the drawing.

3. The sensor sends the picture to the receiving station. For blank squares, the sensor says "Zero." For filled-in squares, the sensor says "One." Be sure to start at the top row and read left to right, telling the receiving station when a new row begins.

4. The receiving station transfers the code to the graph paper. At the end, the receiver has three tries to guess whose initials were sent.

WHAT DO YOU THINK?
- What would happen if you accidentally skipped or repeated a row?
- If you increased or decreased the number and size of the squares, how would this affect the picture?

CHALLENGE Use a variety of colors to send other initials or an image. Your code must tell the receiver which color to use for each square.

SKILL FOCUS
Modeling

MATERIALS
- graph paper
- pen or pencil
- *for Challenge:* colored pens or pencils

TIME
25 minutes

Geographic information systems display data in layers.

Find out more about how GIS is used.

Any good city map will show you what is on the surface—buildings, streets, parks, and other features. But suppose you need to know about tunnels under the city. Or maybe you want to know where the most students live. An ordinary map, even one based on remote-sensing images, will not tell you what you want to know.

Instead, you would turn to geographic information systems. **Geographic information systems** (GIS) are computer systems that can store and arrange geographic data and display the data in many different types of maps. Scientists, city planners, and engineers all use GIS maps to help them make decisions. For example, suppose your city wants to build a new airport. It must be away from populated areas and near major highways. The illustration below shows how city officials might use GIS to pick the best site.

Geographic Information Systems

GIS can be used to produce maps that help people make decisions.

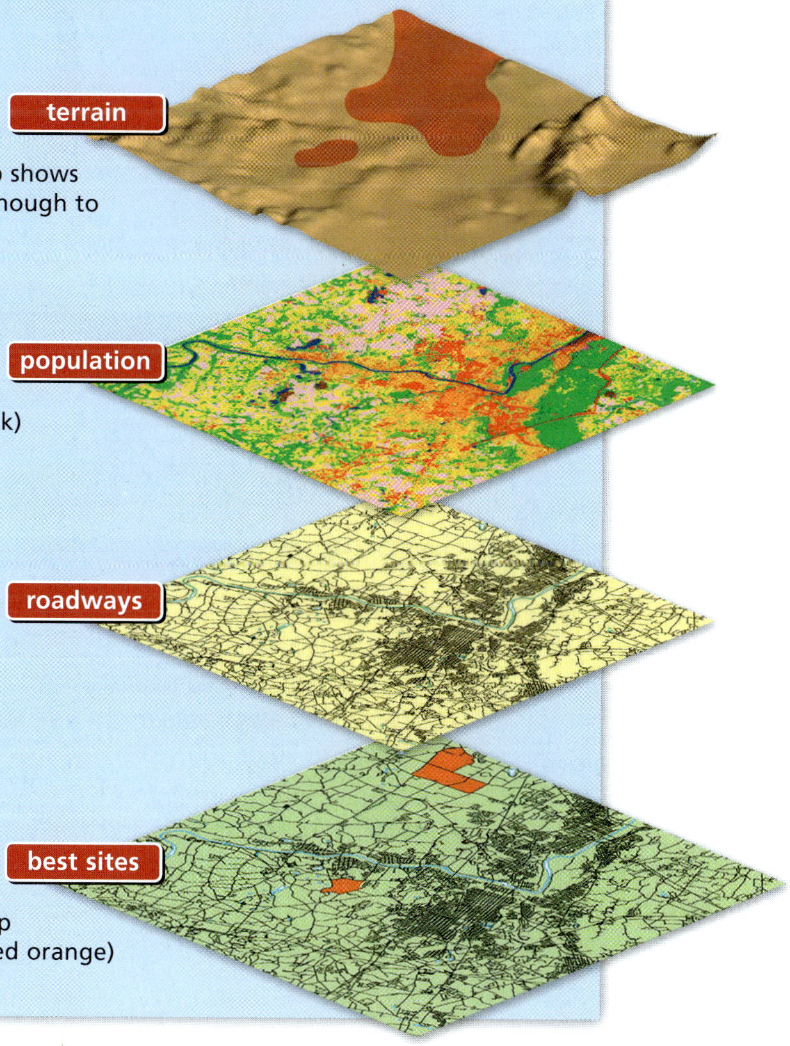

terrain
City officials want to build a new airport. A terrain map shows areas (shaded orange) flat enough to land airplanes.

population
The airport must be built in one of the areas (shaded pink) with the fewest homes.

roadways
The airport must be easily reached by roadways (all areas have good roadways).

best sites
The data are combined by a computer to produce a map showing the best sites (shaded orange) for the airport.

Chapter 13: **Views of Earth Today** 461

Any geographic information can be entered into GIS and converted into a map. These systems are especially useful in displaying information about changes in the environment.

For example, near Long Valley in California, the volcano known as Mammoth Mountain began giving off carbon dioxide, or CO_2. As the gas rose through the soil, it began killing the roots of trees nearby. Scientists measured the flow of CO_2 around Horseshoe Lake and other areas. They used computer software to build the maps shown below.

CHECK YOUR READING Summarize the ways GIS maps can be helpful to engineers, city planners, and scientists.

Mammoth Mountain

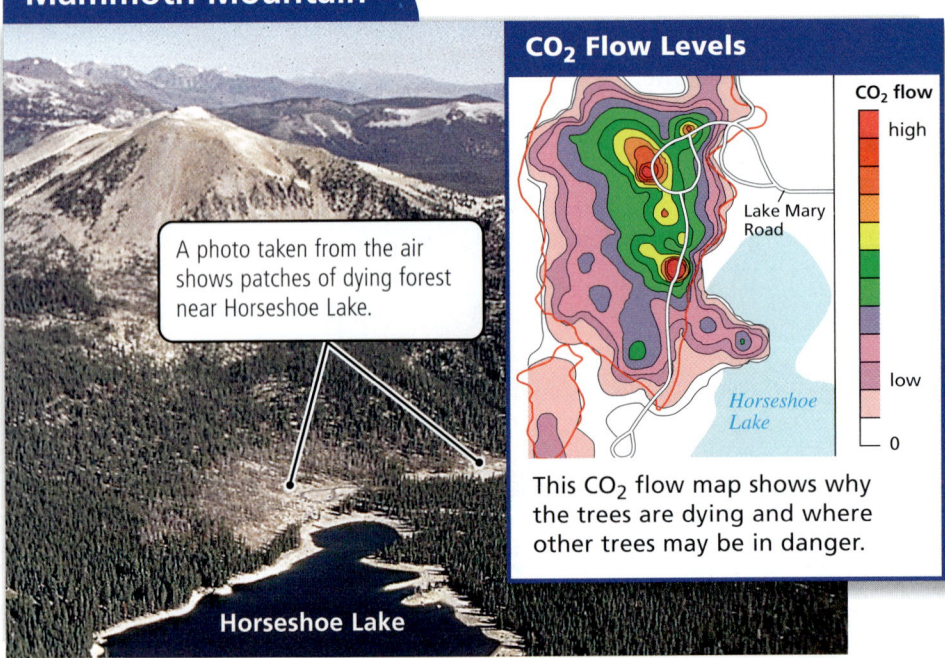

A photo taken from the air shows patches of dying forest near Horseshoe Lake.

Horseshoe Lake

CO_2 Flow Levels

This CO_2 flow map shows why the trees are dying and where other trees may be in danger.

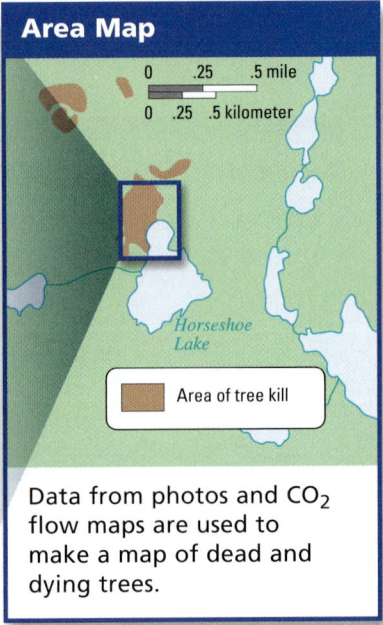

Area Map

Data from photos and CO_2 flow maps are used to make a map of dead and dying trees.

13.4 Review

KEY CONCEPTS

1. How are satellites used to make images of Earth from outer space?
2. What are some of the types of information obtained by remote sensing?
3. Explain in your own words what a GIS map is.

CRITICAL THINKING

4. **Infer** Explain how satellite images might be used to predict what a natural area might look like in 50 or 100 years.
5. **Evaluate** If you wanted to compare a region before and during a flood, how could false-color images help you?

CHALLENGE

6. **Analyze** Work with a small group. Suppose you wanted to ask the city to build a skateboard park. What types of information would you need in order to propose a good site? Draw a map to display each type of information.

Think SCIENCE

SKILL: INTERPRETING DATA

Which Site Is Best for an Olympic Stadium?

Imagine you live in a city that has been chosen to host the Summer Olympics. The only question is where to build the Olympic stadium—in the center of town, in the suburbs, or on the site of an old baseball park. The city government has developed maps to help them decide which is the best site. The planners know that thousands of people will come to see the games. Therefore, they reason, the stadium should be (1) easy to reach by car, (2) close to mass-transit stops, and (3) near restaurants and shops.

Trains and Bus Lines

Train lines
Bus lines

Streets and Freeways

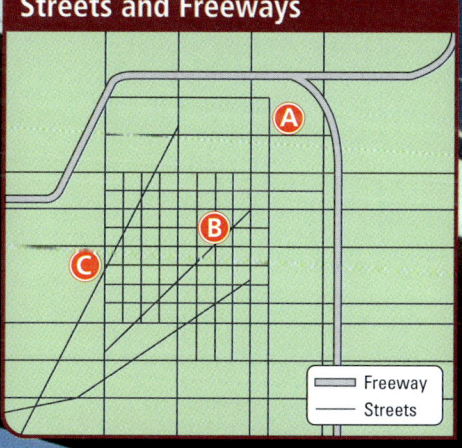

Freeway
Streets

Restaurants and Shopping

Shops and restaurants

▶ Analyzing Map Data

As you study the maps, keep these requirements in mind.

1. Which site(s) is/are easiest to reach by car?
2. Which site(s) is/are closest to bus and train lines?
3. Which site(s) is/are close to shopping areas?

▶ Interpreting Data

In your **Science Notebook,** create a chart like the one below to help you interpret the data displayed on the maps. As you fill in the chart, think about which site offers the greatest benefits to all the people who will attend the Olympic Games.

	Site A		Site B		Site C	
	Yes	No	Yes	No	Yes	No
Near mass transit						
Near highways and roads						
Near shopping areas						

As a group Choose the best site based on your interpretation of the data. Discuss your choice with other groups to see if they agree.

CHALLENGE Once the site is chosen, the planners will start building the stadium. What types of information about the site will they need? Sketch maps displaying the information. **Hint:** The stadium will need electricity, water, and delivery of supplies.

 Chapter Review

the BIG idea

Modern technology has changed the way we view and map Earth.

KEY CONCEPTS SUMMARY

1 Technology is used to explore the Earth system.

The atmosphere, hydrosphere, biosphere, and geosphere work together to form one large system called Earth.

VOCABULARY
system p. 437
atmosphere p. 438
hydrosphere p. 438
biosphere p. 439
geosphere p. 440

2 Maps and globes are models of Earth.

Latitude and longitude are used to locate any point on Earth.
- equator
- prime meridian

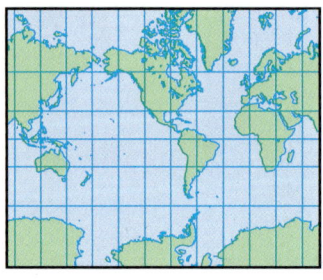

All map projections distort Earth's surface.

VOCABULARY
relief map p. 444
map scale p. 445
map legend p. 445
equator p. 446
latitude p. 446
prime meridian p. 447
longitude p. 447
projection p. 448

3 Topographic maps show the shape of the land.

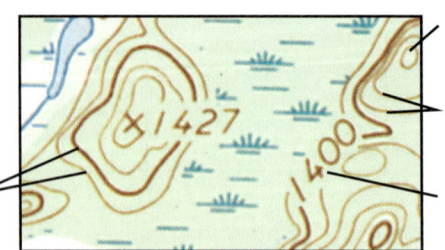

Contour lines show elevation, slope, and relief.

Contour lines never cross.

Closed circles represent hilltops.

Contour lines show steepness of slope.

Index contour lines show elevation.

VOCABULARY
topography p. 452
contour line p. 453
elevation p. 453
slope p. 453
relief p. 453
contour interval p. 454

4 Technology is used to map Earth.

Remote-sensing technology gathers accurate data about Earth.

Geographic information systems are computer programs used to merge layers of information.

VOCABULARY
remote sensing p. 458
sensor p. 459
false-color image p. 460
geographic information systems p. 461

464 Unit 4: Earth's Surface

Reviewing Vocabulary

Copy and complete the chart below, using vocabulary terms from this chapter.

Term	Use	Appearance
map legend	to explain map symbols	chart of symbols
1. latitude	to show distance from the equator	
2. longitude		lines going from pole to pole
3.	to show land features	rippled and smooth areas
4. map scale	to represent distances	
5. equator		line at 0° latitude
6. prime meridian	to separate east and west hemispheres	
7.	to show height above sea level	line showing elevation
8. false-color image	to highlight information	

Reviewing Key Concepts

Multiple Choice Choose the letter of the best answer.

9. Which Greek prefix is matched with its correct meaning?
   a. *hydro* = life
   b. *atmo* = gas
   c. *bio* = earth
   d. *geo* = water

10. What portion of Earth is covered by water?
    a. one-quarter
    b. one-half
    c. three-quarters
    d. nine-tenths

11. The continents and ocean basins are part of Earth's
    a. crust
    b. mantle
    c. outer core
    d. inner core

12. Which Earth system includes humans?
    a. atmosphere
    b. biosphere
    c. hydrosphere
    d. geosphere

13. One way the atmosphere shapes Earth's surface is by
    a. winds
    b. floods
    c. earthquakes
    d. tunnels

14. How are the major parts of the Earth system related to each other?
    a. They rarely can be studied together.
    b. They often are in conflict.
    c. They usually work independently.
    d. They continually affect each other.

15. A flat map shows Earth's curved surface by means of
    a. elevation
    b. topography
    c. relief
    d. projection

16. People use latitude and longitude lines mostly to identify
    a. map scales
    b. country names
    c. exact locations
    d. distances

17. The most accurate way to show Earth's surface is a
    a. globe
    b. conic projection
    c. cylindrical projection
    d. planar projection

18. One example of remote sensing is the use of
    a. contour lines
    b. projections
    c. GIS
    d. binoculars

Short Answer Write a few sentences to answer each question.

19. How does the Global Positioning System work? In your answer use each of the following terms. Underline each term in your answer.

24 satellites	computer	longitude
receiver	latitude	elevation

20. How do Mercator maps distort the view of Earth's surface?

21. How do people use sensors in making maps?

Thinking Critically

Use the topographic map below to answer the next seven questions.

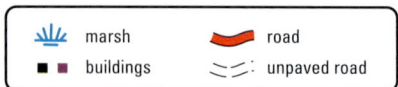
marsh — road
buildings — unpaved road

22. **APPLY** Imagine you are hiking through this area. Which hill—C, D, or E—has the steepest slope? How do you know?

23. **ANALYZE** What is the topography of the land through which the curved road A goes?

24. **IDENTIFY CAUSE** The squares at B represent buildings. Why do you think the buildings were placed here instead of somewhere else in the area?

25. **APPLY** The contour interval is 10 meters. What is the elevation of the highest point on the map?

26. **SYNTHESIZE** Sketch the two hills D and E. What would they look like to someone on the ground?

27. **INFER** Suppose someone wanted to build a road through the terrain on the far left side of the map. What are the advantages and disadvantages of such a route?

28. **EVALUATE** Do you think this area would be a good place to ride mountain bikes? Why or why not?

CHART INFORMATION *On a separate sheet of paper, write a word to fill each blank in the chart.*

Feature	Shown on Topographic Maps?	Belongs to Which Major System?
rivers	yes	hydrosphere
29. slope		
30. winds		
31. plants		
32. lakes		
33. relief		

the BIG idea

34. **APPLY** Look again at the photographs on pages 434–435. Now that you have finished the chapter, reread the question on the main photograph. What would you change in or add to your answer?

35. **SYNTHESIZE** Describe some of the types of information that new technology has provided about Earth.

36. **DRAW CONCLUSIONS** What type of technology do you think has done the most to change the way people view and map Earth? Explain your conclusion.

UNIT PROJECTS

If you are doing a unit project, make a folder for your project. Include in your folder a list of the resources you will need, the date on which the project is due, and a schedule to track your progress. Begin gathering data.

Standardized Test Practice

Analyzing a Diagram

This diagram shows the four major parts of the Earth system. Use it to answer the questions below.

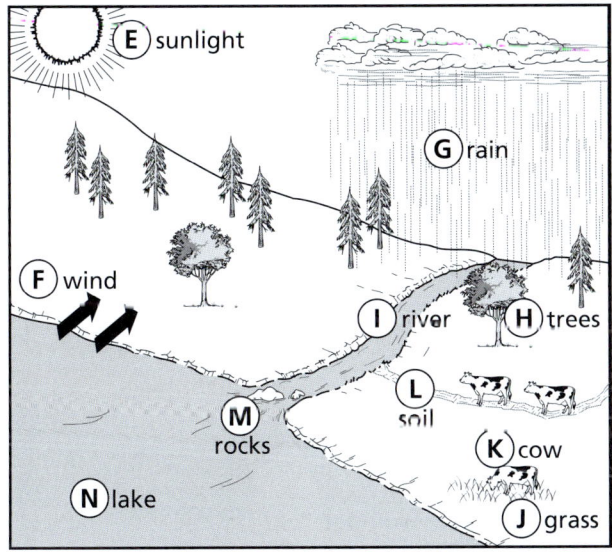

1. Where is the main source of energy for the Earth system?
   - a. E
   - b. F
   - c. G
   - d. L

2. Where is the biosphere shaping the geosphere?
   - a. E
   - b. F
   - c. L
   - d. M

3. Where is matter moving from one part of the hydrosphere to another?
   - a. I to N
   - b. G to H
   - c. J to H
   - d. N to M

4. Which items belong to the geosphere?
   - a. F and G
   - b. H and J
   - c. I and N
   - d. M and L

5. Which process is occurring at M where water is running over the rocks?
   - a. The geosphere is shaping the atmosphere.
   - b. The atmosphere is shaping the biosphere.
   - c. The hydrosphere is shaping the geosphere.
   - d. The biosphere is shaping the geosphere.

6. Where is matter moving from the atmosphere to the biosphere?
   - a. E and F
   - b. F and M
   - c. G and H
   - d. I and G

7. At K, the cow is eating grass. What kind of movement in the Earth system does this represent?
   - a. from the atmosphere to the hydrosphere
   - b. from the hydrosphere to the biosphere
   - c. between two parts of the geosphere
   - d. between two parts of the biosphere

8. Which is an example of how the hydrosphere is supported by the geosphere?
   - a. I, because the river receives the rain
   - b. H, because the trees are rooted in the ground
   - c. M, because the river drains into the lake
   - d. N, because the lake is contained by a basin

Extended Response

Answer the two questions below in detail. Include some of the terms shown in the word box. In your answers, underline each term you use.

| geosphere | surface | system |
| atmosphere | hydrosphere | biosphere |

9. Rain falls and soaks into the soil. Plants and animals use some of the water. More of the water drains into a river, then enters the ocean. Describe this process as movements among the major parts of the Earth system.

10. Describe an example of how people can shape the surface of the geosphere.

Chapter 13: **Views of Earth Today** 467

CHAPTER 14 Minerals

the BIG idea

Minerals are basic building blocks of Earth.

Key Concepts

SECTION 1 — Minerals are all around us.
Learn about the characteristics all minerals share.

SECTION 2 — A mineral is identified by its properties.
Learn how to identify minerals by observing and testing their properties.

SECTION 3 — Minerals are valuable resources.
Learn how minerals form, how they are mined, and how they are used.

Internet Preview

CLASSZONE.COM

Chapter 14 online resources: Content Review, Visualization, three Resource Centers, Math Tutorial, Test Practice

Why can gold be separated from other minerals and rocks in a river?

468 Unit 4: Earth's Surface

EXPLORE the BIG idea

How Do You Turn Water into a Mineral?

Freeze some water into ice cubes. Then compare water, an ice cube, and a penny. Liquid water is not a mineral, but ice is. The surface of the penny is made of the mineral copper.

Observe and Think
How are the water, ice cube, and penny similar? How are they different? What do you think one of the properties of a mineral is?

What Makes Up Rocks?

Find three different rocks near your home or school. Examine them closely with a magnifying glass.

Observe and Think
Describe the rocks. How many materials can you see in each rock? How do you think they got there?

Internet Activity: Minerals

Go to **ClassZone.com** to find out more about minerals that are also precious metals.

Observe and Think
In addition to jewelry, how many different uses can you find for gold?

Identifying Minerals Code: MDL014

Chapter 14: **Minerals** 469

CHAPTER 14
Getting Ready to Learn

CONCEPT REVIEW

- Earth has four main layers: crust, mantle, outer core, and inner core.
- Matter exists in the forms of gas, liquid, and solid.
- People use maps to show many different features of Earth.

VOCABULARY REVIEW

atom See Glossary.
geosphere p. 440

CONTENT REVIEW
CLASSZONE.COM
Review concepts and vocabulary.

TAKING NOTES

SUPPORTING MAIN IDEAS

Make a chart to show each main idea and the information that supports it. Copy each blue heading. Below each heading, add supporting information, such as reasons, explanations, and examples.

VOCABULARY STRATEGY

Place each vocabulary term at the center of a **description wheel**. On the spokes write some words explaining it.

See the Note-Taking Handbook on pages R45–R51.

SCIENCE NOTEBOOK

Minerals have four characteristics.
→ Minerals form naturally.
→ All minerals are solids.
→ Each mineral is always made of the same element or elements.
→ All minerals have crystal structures.

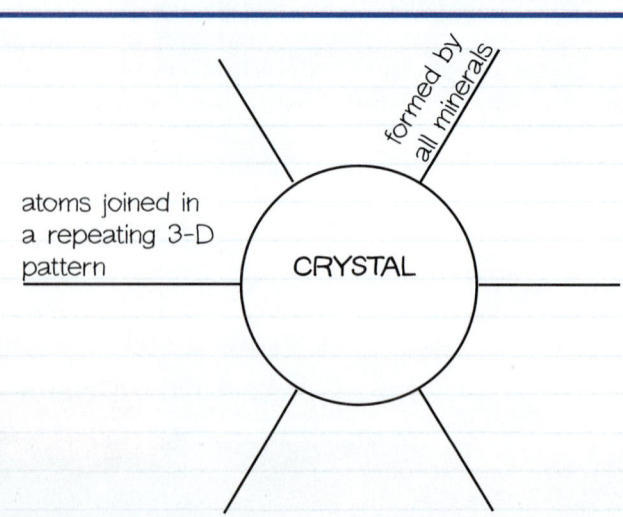

atoms joined in a repeating 3-D pattern
formed by all minerals
CRYSTAL

KEY CONCEPT

14.1 Minerals are all around us.

BEFORE, you learned
- Earth is made of layers
- Earth's outermost rocky layer is the crust

NOW, you will learn
- What the characteristics of minerals are
- How minerals are classified into groups
- Which mineral group is most common

VOCABULARY

mineral p. 471
element p. 473
crystal p. 474

EXPLORE Minerals

What are some characteristics of a mineral?

PROCEDURE

1. Sprinkle some table salt on a sheet of colored paper. Look at a few grains of the salt through a magnifying glass. Then rub a few grains between your fingers.

2. In your notebook, describe all the qualities of the salt that you observe.

3. Examine the rock salt in the same way and describe its qualities in your notebook. How do the two differ?

MATERIALS
- colored paper
- table salt
- rock salt
- magnifying glass

WHAT DO YOU THINK?
Salt is a mineral. From your observations of salt, what do you think are some characteristics of minerals?

Minerals have four characteristics.

You use minerals all the time. Every time you turn on a microwave oven or a TV, you depend on minerals. The copper in the wires that carry electricity to the device is a mineral. Table salt, or halite (HAYL-yt), is another mineral that you use in your everyday life.

Minerals have four characteristics. A **mineral** is a substance that

- forms in nature
- is a solid
- has a definite chemical makeup
- has a crystal structure

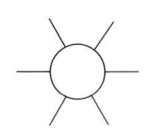

VOCABULARY
Add a description wheel for *mineral* in your notebook.

Chapter 14: **Minerals** 471

Minerals in Rocks

Most rocks are made up of minerals.

This piece of granite contains the minerals quartz, feldspar, and mica.

You might think that minerals and rocks are the same things. But a mineral must have the four characteristics listed on page 471. A rock has only two of these characteristics—it is a solid and it forms naturally. A rock usually contains two or more types of minerals.

Two samples of the same type of rock may vary greatly in the amounts of different minerals they contain. Minerals, however, are always made up of the same materials in the same proportions. A ruby is a mineral. Therefore, a ruby found in India has the same makeup as a ruby found in Australia.

READING TIP

Proportions show relationships between amounts. For example, a quartz crystal always has two oxygen atoms for every silicon atom.

CHECK YOUR READING How are minerals different from rocks?

Formed in Nature

Minerals are formed by natural processes. Every type of mineral can form in nature by processes that do not involve living organisms. As you will read, a few minerals can also be produced by organisms as part of their shells or bones.

Minerals form in many ways. The mineral halite, which is used as table salt, forms when water evaporates in a hot, shallow part of the ocean, leaving behind the salt it contained. Many types of minerals, including the ones in granite, develop when molten rock cools. Talc, a mineral that can be used to make baby powder, forms deep in Earth as high pressure and temperature cause changes in solid rock.

READING TIP

Molten rock refers to rock that has become so hot that it has melted.

472 Unit 4: Earth's Surface

Solid

A mineral is a solid—that is, it has a definite volume and a rigid shape. Volume refers to the amount of space an object takes up. For example, a golf ball has a smaller volume than a baseball, and a baseball has a smaller volume than a basketball.

A substance that is a liquid or a gas is not a mineral. However, in some cases its solid form is a mineral. For instance, liquid water is not a mineral, but ice is.

Definite Chemical Makeup

Each mineral has a definite chemical makeup: it consists of a specific combination of atoms of certain elements. An **element** is a substance that contains only one type of atom. In turn, an atom is the smallest particle an element can be divided into.

Everything you can see or touch is made up of atoms. Some substances, including the minerals gold and copper, consist of just one element. All the atoms in gold or copper are of the same type. However, most substances contain atoms of more than one element. Most minerals are compounds, substances consisting of several elements in specific proportions. Halite, for example, has one atom of sodium for every atom of chlorine.

The types of atoms that make up a mineral are part of what makes the mineral unique. The way in which the atoms are bonded, or joined together, is also important. As you will read, many properties of minerals are related to how strong or weak the bonds are.

READING TIP

You may remember *compound* from compound words—words formed by joining together smaller words: *note* + *book* = *notebook*. Likewise, a chemical compound has two or more elements joined together.

Atoms in Minerals

copper

The mineral copper is made up only of copper atoms.

Atoms in Copper

copper

halite

The mineral halite is made up of equal numbers of sodium and chlorine atoms.

Atoms in Halite

chlorine

sodium

READING VISUALS How do the diagrams show that copper consists of only one element and halite is a compound?

VISUALIZATION
CLASSZONE.COM

Explore an animation of crystal growth.

Crystal Structure

If you look closely at the particles of ice that make up frost, you will notice that they have smooth, flat surfaces. These flat surfaces form because of the arrangement of atoms in the ice, which is a mineral. Such an internal arrangement is a characteristic of minerals. It is the structure of a **crystal,** a solid in which the atoms are arranged in an orderly, repeating three-dimensional pattern.

Each mineral has its own type of crystal structure. In some cases, two minerals have the same chemical composition but different crystal structures. For example, both diamond and graphite consist of just one element—carbon. But the arrangements of the carbon atoms in these two minerals are not the same, so they have different crystal structures and very different properties. Diamonds are extremely hard and have a brilliant sparkle. Graphite is soft, gray, and dull.

In nature, a perfect crystal is rare. One can grow only when a mineral is free to form in an open space—a condition that rarely exists within Earth's crust. The photographs on page 475 show examples of nearly perfect crystals. The amount of space available for growth influences the shape and size of crystals. Most crystals have imperfect shapes because their growth was limited by other crystals forming next to them.

INVESTIGATE Crystal Shape

How do crystals differ in shape?
PROCEDURE

1. Cut sheets of paper so that they fit inside the pie plates as shown. Place one sheet in each pie plate.
2. Add the table salt to 30 mL of water in the cup. Stir the water until the salt has dissolved.
3. Pour enough salt solution into one of the pie plates to completely cover the paper with a small film of liquid. Be careful not to pour into the plate any undissolved salt that may be in the bottom of the cup.
4. Repeat steps 2 and 3 with the Epsom salts. Let the plates dry overnight.

WHAT DO YOU THINK?
- Compare and describe the shapes of the crystals.
- What do you think accounts for any differences you observe?

CHALLENGE
Why are the shapes of the crystals the same as or different from the shapes in the materials you started with?

SKILL FOCUS
Observing

MATERIALS
- tablespoon
- 2 mixing cups
- 2 stirring rods
- 1 tbs table salt
- 1 tbs Epsom salts
- 60 mL water
- 2 pie plates
- 2 sheets black paper
- scissors

TIME
20 minutes for setup

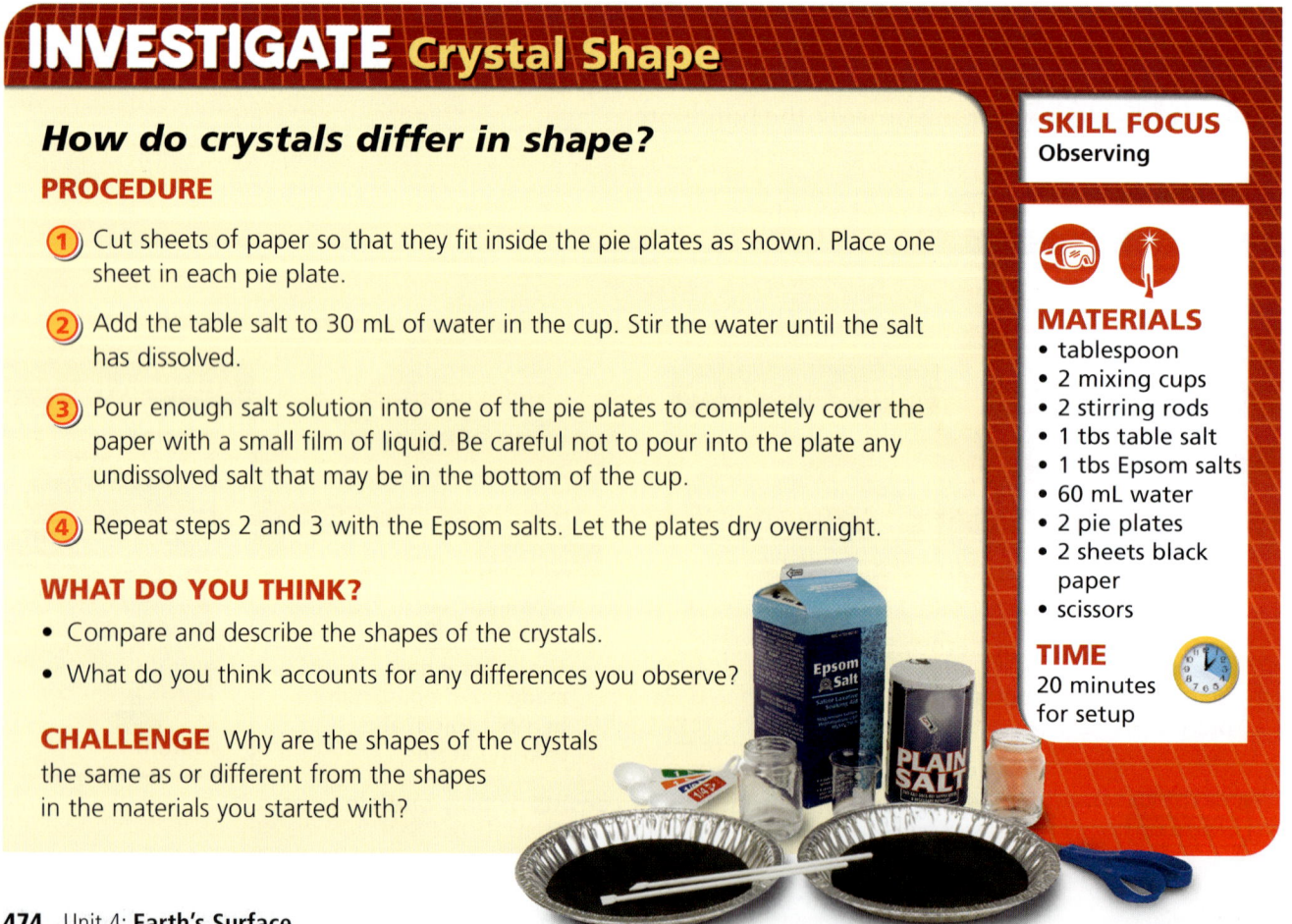

474 Unit 4: Earth's Surface

Crystal Groups

Crystal groups are named by their shapes and the angles formed by imaginary lines through their centers. Crystals take many shapes, but all belong to these six groups.

Cubic — galena

Tetragonal — wulfenite

Hexagonal — beryl

Orthorhombic — topaz

Monoclinic — gypsum

Triclinic — microcline

Minerals are grouped according to composition.

Scientists classify minerals into groups on the basis of their chemical makeups. The most common group is the silicates. All the minerals in this group contain oxygen and silicon—the two most common elements in Earth's crust—joined together.

Though there are thousands of different minerals, only about 30 are common in Earth's crust. These 30 minerals make up most rocks in the crust. For that reason, they are called rock-forming minerals. Silicates, which make up about 90 percent of the rocks in Earth's crust, are the most common rock-forming minerals. Quartz, feldspar, and mica (MY-kuh) are common silicates.

SUPPORTING MAIN IDEAS
Enter this blue heading in a chart and record supporting information.

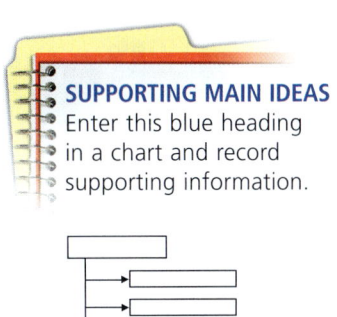

 Which mineral group do most rock-forming minerals belong to?

Chapter 14: **Minerals** 475

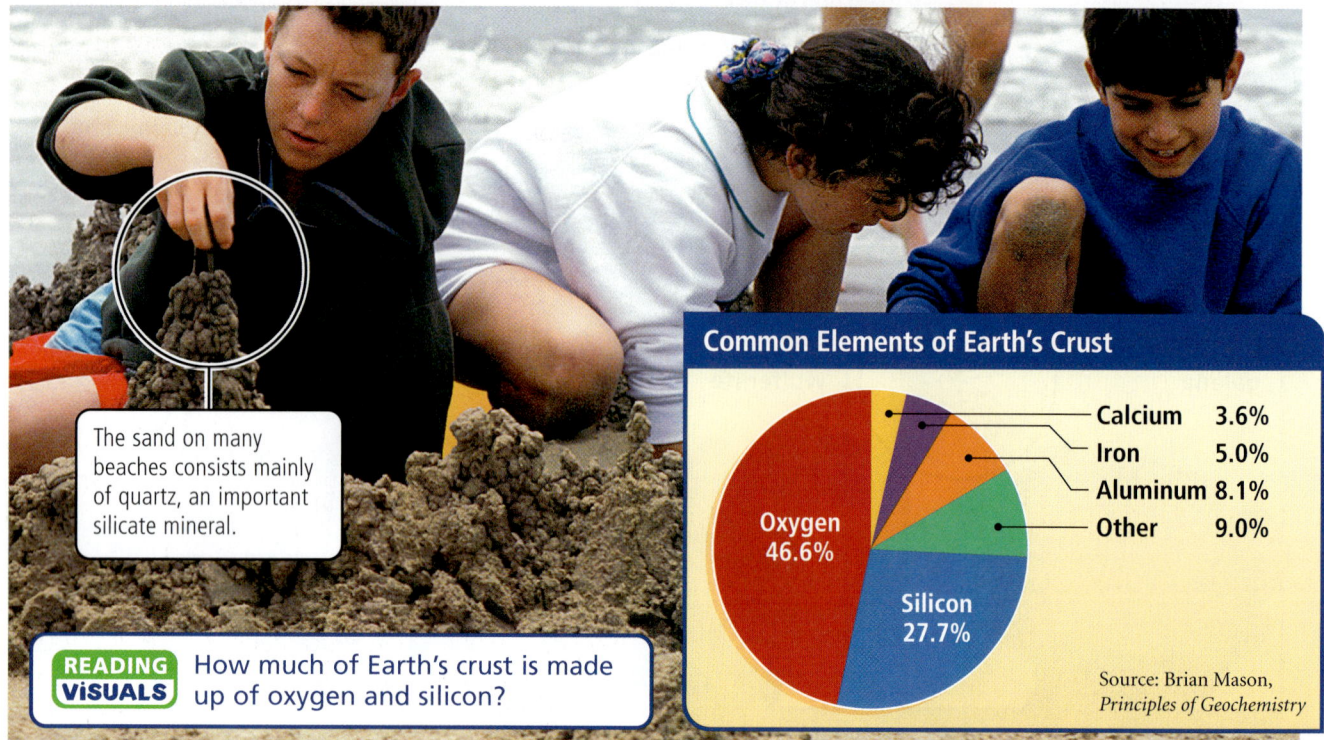

The sand on many beaches consists mainly of quartz, an important silicate mineral.

Common Elements of Earth's Crust

- Oxygen 46.6%
- Silicon 27.7%
- Calcium 3.6%
- Iron 5.0%
- Aluminum 8.1%
- Other 9.0%

Source: Brian Mason, *Principles of Geochemistry*

READING VISUALS How much of Earth's crust is made up of oxygen and silicon?

Find information on minerals.

The second most common group of rock-forming minerals is the carbonates. All the minerals in this group contain carbon and oxygen joined together. Calcite (KAL-syt), which is common in seashells, is a carbonate mineral.

There are many other mineral groups. All are important, even though their minerals may not be as common as rock-forming minerals. For instance, the mineral group known as oxides contains the minerals from which most metals, such as tin and copper, are refined. An oxide consists of an element, usually a metal, joined to oxygen. This group includes hematite (HEE-muh-tyt), a source of iron.

CHECK YOUR READING Why is the oxide mineral group important?

14.1 Review

KEY CONCEPTS

1. What are the four characteristics of a mineral?
2. On what basis do scientists classify minerals?
3. What is the most common group of minerals? What percentage of the crust do they make up?

CRITICAL THINKING

4. **Classify** Can oil and natural gas be classified as minerals? Why or why not?
5. **Apply** When a piece of quartz is heated to a very high temperature, it melts into a liquid. Is it still a mineral? Why or why not?

CHALLENGE

6. **Interpret** You can see perfect crystals lining the inside of certain rocks when they are broken open. How do you think the crystals were able to form?

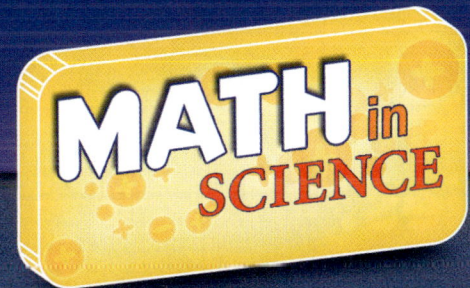

MATH in SCIENCE

MATH TUTORIAL
CLASSZONE.COM
Click on Math Tutorial for more help with percents and fractions.

SKILL: WRITING FRACTIONS AS PERCENTS

Minerals in Rocks

Like most rocks, granite is a mixture of several minerals. Each mineral makes up a certain proportion, or fraction, of the granite. You can compare mineral amounts by expressing each mineral's fraction as a percentage.

Granite

Example

To change a fraction to a percentage, you must find an equivalent fraction with 100 as the denominator. Suppose, for example, you want to change the fraction $\frac{1}{5}$ to a percentage. First, divide 100 by the denominator 5, which gives you 20. Then, multiply both the numerator and denominator by 20 to find the percentage.

$$\frac{1}{5} \cdot \frac{20}{20} = \frac{20}{100} \text{ or } 20\% \qquad \frac{1}{5} \text{ is } 20\%$$

The table below shows the fraction of each mineral in a granite sample.

Minerals in Granite Sample

Mineral	Fraction of Granite Sample	Percentage of Granite
Quartz	$\frac{1}{4}$	?
Feldspar	$\frac{13}{20}$	?
Mica	$\frac{3}{50}$	?
Dark minerals	$\frac{1}{25}$	?

Answer the following questions.

1. On your paper, copy the table and fill in the percentage of each mineral in the granite sample above.

2. Which minerals make up the greatest and smallest percentages of the granite?

3. In another granite sample, feldspar makes up $\frac{3}{5}$ and mica makes up $\frac{2}{25}$. What is the percentage of each mineral in the rock?

CHALLENGE The mineral hornblende is often one of the dark minerals in granite. If hornblende makes up $\frac{1}{32}$ of a granite sample, what percentage of the rock is hornblende?

Chapter 14: **Minerals** 477

KEY CONCEPT

14.2 A mineral is identified by its properties.

BEFORE, you learned
- All minerals have four characteristics
- Most minerals in Earth's crust are silicates

NOW, you will learn
- Which mineral properties are most important in identification
- How minerals are identified by their properties

VOCABULARY
streak p. 479
luster p. 480
cleavage p. 481
fracture p. 481
density p. 482
hardness p. 483

THINK ABOUT

What can you tell by looking at a mineral?

The photographs at the right show five pieces of the mineral fluorite (FLUR-YT). As you can see, the pieces are very different in color and size. Fluorite occurs in many colors, even in colorless forms. Its crystals can be well formed or poorly formed. Also, the sides of the crystals may be smooth or rough.

If you came across fluorite while hiking, would you know what it was by just looking at it? Probably not. Read on to find out how you could identify it.

A mineral's appearance helps identify it.

READING TIP
The word *characteristic* is used for a feature that is typical of a person or thing. It can be used as a noun or an adjective.

To identify a mineral, you need to observe its properties—characteristic features that identify it. You might begin by looking at the mineral's color. However, many minerals occur in more than one color, so you would need to examine other properties as well. You might also notice how the mineral reflects light, which determines how shiny or dull it is. Most minerals reflect light in characteristic ways. In this section you will read about how the properties of a mineral—including its appearance—are used to identify it.

CHECK YOUR READING Why do you need to look at properties other than color to identify a mineral?

478 Unit 4: Earth's Surface

Color and Streak

Some minerals can be almost any color, but most minerals have a more limited color range. For example, a particular mineral may almost always be brown to black.

Three main factors cause minerals to vary in color. First, a mineral may get its color from tiny amounts of an element that is not part of its normal chemical makeup. For example, a sample of pure quartz is clear and colorless, but tiny amounts of iron can give quartz a violet color. This violet variety of quartz is called amethyst. Second, a mineral's color can change when it is at or near Earth's surface and is in contact with the atmosphere or water. Third, mineral crystals can have defects in their crystal structures that change their color.

Some minerals have a different color when they are ground into a fine powder than when they are left whole. A mineral's **streak** is the color of the powder left behind when the mineral is scraped across a surface. Geologists use a tile of unglazed porcelain, called a streak plate, as a tool to identify minerals by their streaks. Streak is a better clue to a mineral's identity than surface color is. Look at the photographs of hematite below. Even though the mineral samples are different colors, both leave a reddish brown streak when scraped across a streak plate. All samples of the same mineral have the same streak.

READING TIP
A geologist is a scientist who studies Earth.

CHECK YOUR READING What is the difference between color and streak?

Streak

These samples are of the mineral hematite. They are different colors, but they have the same streak.

This hematite looks dull because it has tiny crystals that reflect light in all directions.

This hematite looks shiny because it has larger crystals.

READING VISUALS What is a clue that both samples are of the same mineral?

Chapter 14: **Minerals** 479

Luster

READING TIP
Luster comes from the Latin *lūstrāre*, "to make bright." But luster isn't always bright or shiny. Some minerals have lusters that are waxlike or dull.

A mineral's **luster** is the way in which light reflects from its surface. The two major types of luster are metallic and nonmetallic. The mineral pyrite has a metallic luster. It looks as if it were made of metal. A mineral with a nonmetallic luster can be shiny, but it does not appear to be made of metal. An example of a nonmetallic luster is the glassy luster of garnet. Compare the lusters of pyrite and garnet in the photographs below.

Pyrite has a metallic luster.

Garnet crystals in this rock have a nonmetallic luster.

Like a mineral's color, its luster may vary from sample to sample. If a mineral has been exposed to the atmosphere or to water, its surface luster can become dull. However, if the mineral is broken to reveal a fresh surface, its characteristic luster can be seen.

The way a mineral breaks helps identify it.

SUPPORTING MAIN IDEAS
Enter this blue heading in a chart and record supporting information.

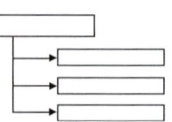

If you hit a piece of calcite with a hammer, the calcite will break into tilted blocks. You can peel off layers of mica because it splits into thin, flat sheets. Each kind of mineral always breaks in the same way, and this property can help identify a mineral. In fact, the way a mineral breaks is a better clue to its identity than are its color and luster.

Cleavage

Cleavage is a tendency to break along flat surfaces.

Calcite has cleavage.

It breaks along flat surfaces because the bonds between its atoms are less strong in some directions than in others.

480 Unit 4: *Earth's Surface*

Cleavage

Cleavage is the tendency of a mineral to break along flat surfaces. The way in which a mineral breaks depends on how its atoms are bonded, or joined together. In a mineral that displays cleavage, the bonds of the crystal structure are weaker in the directions in which the mineral breaks.

When geologists describe the cleavage of a mineral, they consider both the directions in which the mineral breaks and the smoothness of the broken surfaces. Mica has cleavage in one direction and breaks into sheets. The photographs on page 480 show that calcite has cleavage in three directions and breaks into tilted blocks. Because the broken surfaces of both mica and calcite are smooth, these minerals are said to have perfect cleavage.

Carbon Bonds in Graphite

strong bonds within layers

weak bonds between layers

carbon atoms

In graphite, carbon atoms are arranged in layers. Graphite has cleavage because the weak bonds between the layers break easily.

Fracture

Fracture is the tendency of a mineral to break into irregular pieces. Some minerals such as quartz break into pieces with curved surfaces, as shown below. Other minerals may break differently—perhaps into splinters or into rough or jagged pieces.

In a mineral that displays fracture, the bonds that join the atoms are fairly equal in strength in all directions. The mineral does not break along flat surfaces because there are no particular directions of weakness in its crystal structure.

VOCABULARY
Add a description wheel for *fracture* in your notebook.

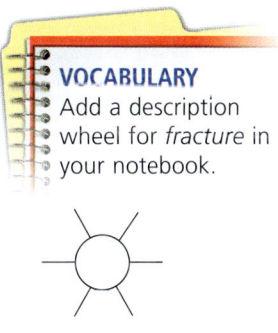

CHECK YOUR READING How does the strength of the bonds between atoms determine whether a mineral displays cleavage or fracture?

Fracture

Fracture is a tendency to break into irregular pieces.

Quartz does not have cleavage. It breaks by fracturing.

It breaks along irregular surfaces because the bonds between its atoms are about the same strength in every direction.

Chapter 14: **Minerals** 481

A mineral's density and hardness help identify it.

A tennis ball is not as heavy or as hard as a baseball. You would be able to tell the two apart even with your eyes closed by how heavy and hard they feel. You can identify minerals in a similar way.

Density

Even though a baseball and a tennis ball are about the same size, the baseball has more mass and so is more dense. A substance's **density** is the amount of mass in a given volume of the substance. For example, 1 cubic centimeter of the mineral pyrite has a mass of 5.1 grams, so pyrite's density is 5.1 grams per cubic centimeter.

Density is very helpful in identifying minerals. For example, gold and pyrite look very similar. Pyrite is often called fool's gold. However, you can tell the two minerals apart by comparing their densities. Gold is much denser than pyrite. The mass of a piece of gold is almost four times the mass of a piece of pyrite of the same size. A small amount of a very dense mineral, such as gold, can have more mass and be heavier than a larger amount of a less dense mineral, such as pyrite. A mineral's density is determined by the kinds of atoms that make up

> **READING TIP**
> The unit of density is grams per cubic centimeter and is abbreviated as g/cm^3.

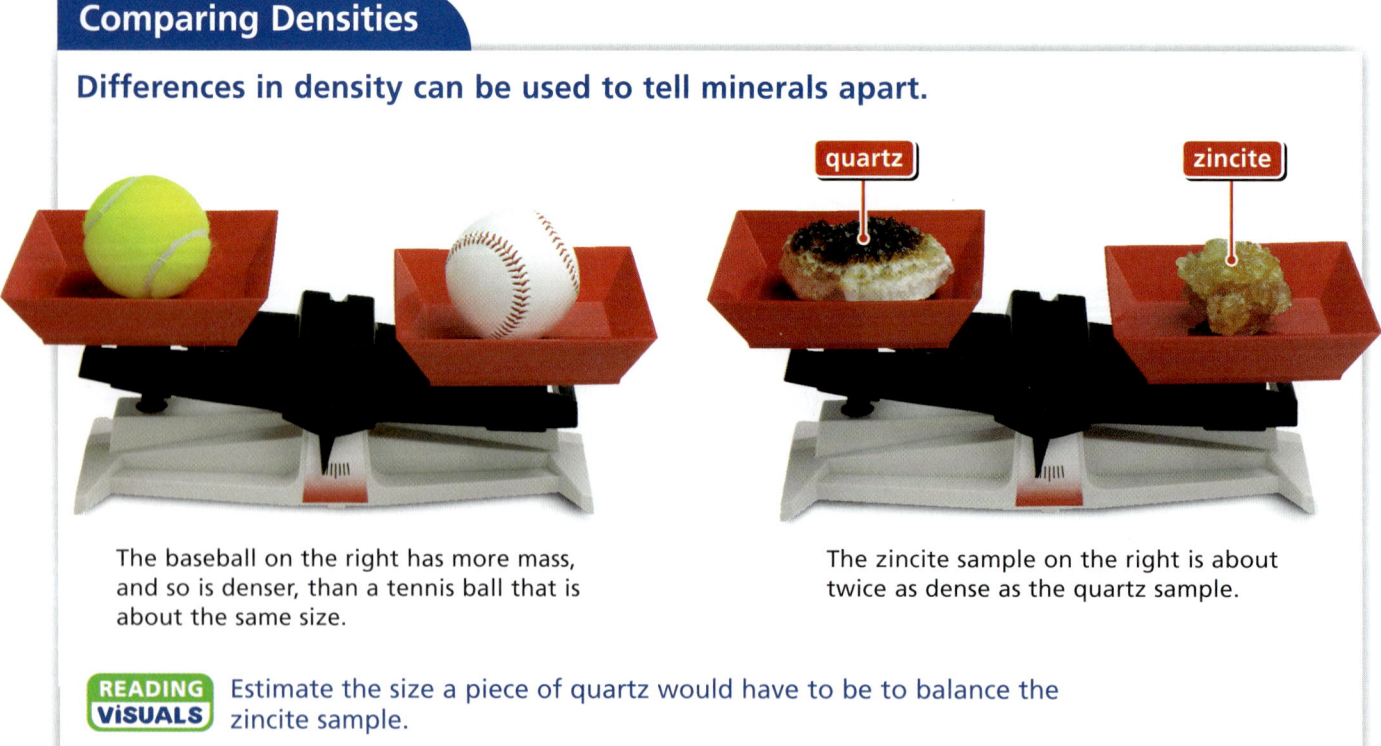

Comparing Densities

Differences in density can be used to tell minerals apart.

The baseball on the right has more mass, and so is denser, than a tennis ball that is about the same size.

The zincite sample on the right is about twice as dense as the quartz sample.

READING VISUALS Estimate the size a piece of quartz would have to be to balance the zincite sample.

482 Unit 4: Earth's Surface

the mineral, as well as how closely the atoms are joined together. An experienced geologist can estimate the density of a mineral by lifting it. But to get an exact measurement, geologists use special scales.

 Why does a piece of gold weigh much more than a piece of pyrite that is the same size?

Hardness

One way to tell a tennis ball from a baseball without looking at them is to compare their densities. Another way is to test which one is harder. Hardness is another dependable clue to a mineral's identity.

A mineral's **hardness** is its resistance to being scratched. Like a mineral's cleavage, a mineral's hardness is determined by its crystal structure and the strength of the bonds between its atoms. Harder minerals have stronger bonds.

A scale known as the Mohs scale is often used to describe a mineral's hardness. This scale is based on the fact that a harder mineral will scratch a softer one. As you can see in the chart at the right, ten minerals are numbered in the scale, from softest to hardest. Talc is the softest mineral and has a value of 1. Diamond, the hardest of all minerals, has a value of 10.

A mineral can be scratched only by other minerals that have the same hardness or are harder. To determine the hardness of an unknown mineral, you test whether it scratches or is scratched by the minerals in the scale. For example, if you can scratch an unknown mineral with apatite but not with fluorite, the mineral's hardness is between 4 and 5 in the Mohs scale.

In place of minerals, you can use your fingernail, a copper penny, and a steel file to test an unknown mineral. To avoid damage to the minerals, you can test whether the mineral scratches these items. When using a penny to test hardness, make sure its date is 1982 or earlier. Only older pennies are made mainly of copper, which has a hardness of about 3.

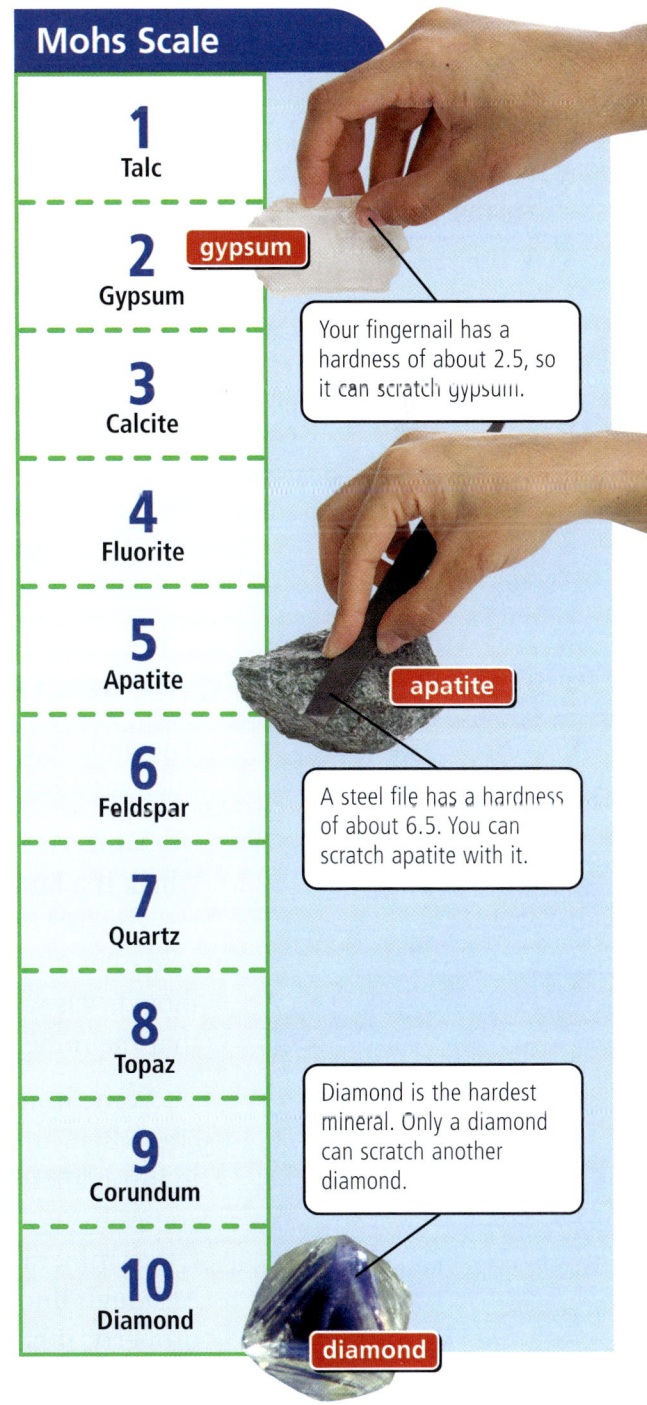

Chapter 14: **Minerals** 483

INVESTIGATE Hardness of Minerals

How hard are some common minerals?

PROCEDURE

1. Try to scratch each mineral with your fingernail, the penny, and the steel file. Record the results in a chart.
2. Assign a hardness range to each mineral.
3. In the last column of your chart, rank the minerals from hardest to softest.

WHAT DO YOU THINK?

- Use your results to assign a hardness range in the Mohs scale to each sample.
- If two minerals have the same hardness range according to your tests, how could you tell which is harder?

CHALLENGE If you had a mineral that could not be scratched by the steel file, what else might you test it with to estimate its hardness?

SKILL FOCUS
Classifying

MATERIALS
- samples of 5 minerals
- copper penny (1982 or earlier)
- steel file

TIME
20 minutes

Some minerals have special properties.

The photographs on page 485 show how geologists test some minerals. Such tests help them identify minerals that have unusual properties.

Minerals in the carbonate group, such as calcite, react with acid. Chalk is a familiar item that is made up of carbonate minerals. The test consists of putting a drop of a weak solution of hydrochloric acid on a mineral sample. If the acid reacts with the mineral, carbon dioxide gas will form and bubble out of the acid. The bubbles show that the mineral is a carbonate.

Some minerals have a property known as fluorescence (flu-REHS-uhns). Fluorescent minerals glow when they are exposed to ultraviolet (UHL-truh-VY-uh-liht) light. The word *fluorescence* comes from the name of the mineral fluorite, which has this property. Other minerals that display fluorescence include calcite and willemite. Although fluorescence is an interesting and sometimes dramatic property, it has limited value in mineral identification. Different samples of the same mineral may or may not display fluorescence, and they may glow in different colors.

 To identify calcite, why would it be more useful to test with dilute hydrochloric acid than to check for fluorescence?

484 Unit 4: Earth's Surface

Special Properties

Fluorescence

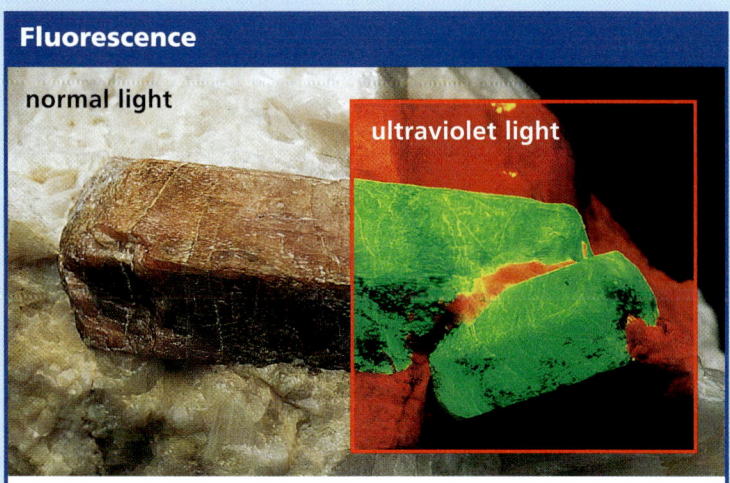

These minerals look ordinary in normal light but display red and green fluorescence under ultraviolet light.

Acid Test

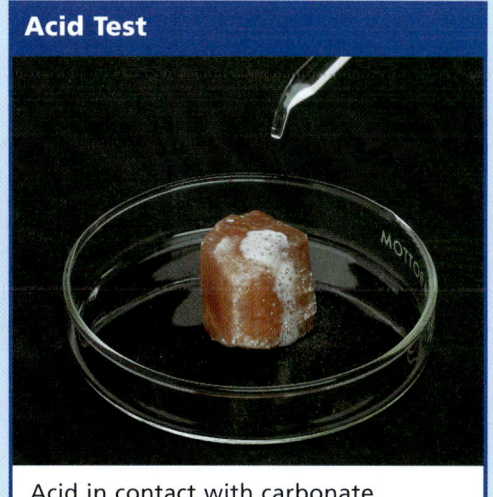

Acid in contact with carbonate minerals, such as calcite, forms bubbles.

A few minerals respond to magnets. A magnet is pulled toward these minerals. The mineral magnetite strongly attracts magnets, and some other minerals weakly attract magnets. To test a mineral, hold a magnet loosely and bring it close to the mineral. You will be able to notice if there is even a small pull of the magnet toward the mineral. Magnets are commonly used in laboratories and industries to separate magnetic minerals from other minerals.

Some rare minerals have a property known as radioactivity. They contain unstable elements that change into other elements over time. As this happens, they release energy. Geologists can measure this energy and use it to identify minerals that contain unstable elements.

14.2 Review

KEY CONCEPTS

1. Why is color not a reliable clue to the identity of a mineral?
2. What is the difference between cleavage and fracture?
3. Describe what would happen if you rubbed a mineral with a Mohs hardness value of 7 against a mineral with a value of 5.

CRITICAL THINKING

4. **Analyze** Which mineral-identification tests would be easy for a person to perform at home? Which would be difficult?
5. **Draw Conclusions** Diamond and graphite contain only carbon atoms. How can you tell which mineral's atoms are bonded more closely?

CHALLENGE

6. **Apply** The mineral topaz has perfect cleavage in one direction. It also displays fracture. Explain why a mineral such as topaz can display both cleavage and fracture.

Chapter 14: **Minerals** 485

CHAPTER INVESTIGATION

Mineral Identification

OVERVIEW AND PURPOSE In this activity, you will observe and perform tests on minerals. Then you will compare your observations to a mineral identification key.

▶ Procedure

1. Make a data table like the one shown in the notebook on the next page.

2. You will examine and identify five minerals. Get a numbered mineral sample from the mineral set. Record the number of your sample in your table.

3. First, observe the sample. Note the color and the luster of the sample. Write your observations in your table. In the row labeled "Luster," write *metallic* if the mineral appears shiny like metal. Write *nonmetallic* if the sample does not look like metal. For example, it may look glassy, pearly, or dull.

4. Observe the sample through the hand lens. Look to see any signs of how the crystals in the mineral broke. If it appears that the crystals have broken along straight lines, put a check in the row labeled "Cleavage." If it appears that the sample has fractured, put a check in the appropriate row of your table.

5. **CAUTION: Keep the streak plate on your desktop or table while you are doing the streak test. A broken streak plate can cause serious cuts.** Rub the mineral sample on the streak plate. If the sample does not leave a mark, the mineral is harder than the streak plate. Write *no* in the row labeled "Streak." If the sample does leave a mark on the streak plate, write the color of the streak in that row.

MATERIALS
- numbered mineral samples
- hand lens
- streak plate
- copper penny
- steel file
- magnet
- dilute hydrochloric acid
- eyedropper
- Mohs scale
- Mineral Identification Key

step 3

step 4

step 5

486 Unit 4: Earth's Surface

6. Test each sample for its hardness on the Mohs scale. Try to scratch the sample with each of these items in order: a fingernail, a copper penny, and a steel file. In the Mohs scale, find the hardness number of the object that first scratches the sample. Write in the table that the mineral's hardness value is between that of the hardest item that did not scratch the sample and that of the item that did scratch it.

7. Test the sample with the magnet. If the magnet is attracted to the sample, put a check in the row labeled "Magnetic."

step 7

8. Repeat steps 2 through 7 for each of the other numbered samples.

Observe and Analyze — Write It Up

1. **INTERPRET DATA** Use the Mineral Identification Key and the information in your data table to identify your samples. Write the names of the minerals in your table.

2. **COLLECT DATA CAUTION: Before doing the acid test, put on your safety glasses, protective gloves, and lab apron. Acids can cause burns.** If you identified one of the samples as a carbonate mineral, such as calcite, you can check your identification with the acid test. Use the eyedropper to put a few drops of dilute hydrochloric acid on the mineral. If the acid bubbles, the sample is a carbonate.

Conclude — Write It Up

1. **COMPARE AND CONTRAST** How are the minerals calcite and halite alike? Which property can you use to test whether a sample is calcite or halite?

2. **INTERPRET** Look at the data in your table. Name any minerals that you could identify on the basis of a single property.

3. **APPLY** Examine a piece of granite rock. On the basis of your examination of granite and your observations of the samples, try to determine what the light-colored, translucent mineral in the granite is and what the flaky, darker mineral is.

INVESTIGATE Further

Specific gravity is another property used to identify minerals. The specific gravity of a mineral is determined by comparing the mineral's density with the density of water.

Find the specific gravity of an unknown mineral chosen from your teacher's samples. Attach your mineral with a string to a spring scale. Record its mass and label this value $M1$. Then suspend the mineral in a beaker of water. Record the measurement of the mineral's mass in water. Label this value $M2$. To determine the mineral's specific gravity, use the following equation:

$$\frac{M1}{M1 - M2} = \text{specific gravity}$$

Do all the other steps to identify the sample. Does the specific gravity you measured match the one listed for that mineral in the identification key?

Mineral Identification
Table 1. Mineral Properties

Property	Sample Number				
	1	2	3	4	5
Color					
Luster					
Cleavage					
Fracture					
Streak					
Hardness					
Magnetic					
Acid test					
Name of mineral					

Chapter 14: **Minerals** 487

KEY CONCEPT

 Minerals are valuable resources.

 **BEFORE, you learned**

- Minerals are classified according to their compositions and crystal structures
- A mineral can be identified by its properties

 NOW, you will learn

- How minerals are used in industry and art
- How minerals form
- How minerals are mined

VOCABULARY

magma p. 490
lava p. 490
ore p. 492

EXPLORE Minerals at Your Fingertips

What is an everyday use of minerals?

PROCEDURE

① Observe the core of a wooden pencil. Even though it is called lead, it is made of a mixture of minerals—clay and graphite. A No. 4 pencil has more clay in its lead.

② Use each pencil to draw something, noticing how each marks the page.

MATERIALS

- No. 2 wooden pencil
- No. 4 wooden pencil
- paper

WHAT DO YOU THINK?
- How is using a pencil similar to a streak test?
- When would a No. 4 pencil be more useful than a No. 2 pencil?

Minerals have many uses in industry.

Minerals are necessary to our modern way of life. Mineral deposits are sources of

- metals for cars and airplanes
- quartz and feldspar for glass
- fluorite and calcite for toothpaste
- silver compounds for photographic film
- mica and talc for paint

These examples illustrate just a few of the many ways we depend on minerals.

 Give three examples of the use of minerals in familiar products.

488 Unit 4: Earth's Surface

Minerals have many uses in the arts.

No matter what month you were born in, there is a mineral associated with it—your birthstone. The tradition of birthstones is hundreds of years old. It is one example of the value that people place on the particularly beautiful minerals known as gemstones. In fact, the ancient Egyptians used gems in necklaces and other jewelry at least 4000 years ago.

When gemstones are found, they are usually rough and irregularly shaped. Before a gemstone is used in jewelry, a gem cutter grinds it into the desired shape and polishes it. This process increases the gemstone's beauty and sparkle. The material used to shape and polish a gemstone must be at least as hard as the gemstone itself. Metals, such as gold and silver, also are used in jewelry making and other decorative arts. Both gold and silver are usually combined with copper to increase their hardness.

RESOURCE CENTER
CLASSZONE.COM
Learn more about gemstones.

READING TIP
Corundum and diamond are the two hardest minerals in the Mohs scale. They are often used to grind and polish gemstones.

CHECK YOUR READING How are minerals prepared for use in jewelry? What other questions do you have about how minerals are used?

Uses of Minerals

Common Uses of Minerals	
Mineral	**Products**
Quartz (source of silicon)	Optics, glass, abrasives, gems
Hematite (source of iron)	Machines, nails, cooking utensils
Gibbsite (source of aluminum)	Soda cans, shopping carts
Dolomite (source of magnesium)	Insulators, medicines
Chromite (source of chromium)	Automobile parts, stainless steel
Galena (source of lead)	Batteries, fiber optics, weights
Kaolinite (found in clay)	Ceramics, paper, cosmetics
Beryl (source of beryllium)	Aircraft frames, gems (green form is emerald)

Technology
A clear quartz crystal was sliced to make this computer chip. Minerals such as copper, silver, and gold are commonly used in electronics.

Industry
Diamonds are used as abrasives, as in this drill tip. Minerals are also used in such products as insulators and water filters.

Arts
Cinnabar is ground up to make the pigment known as vermilion. Other minerals are also used as pigments in dyes and paints. Gemstones are used in jewelry, as are platinum and gold.

Chapter 14: **Minerals** 489

> **REMINDER**
>
> An element is a substance that contains only one type of atom. For instance, oxygen is an element. Pure oxygen contains only oxygen atoms.

Minerals form in several ways.

Minerals form within Earth or on Earth's surface by natural processes. Minerals develop when atoms of one or more elements join together and crystals begin to grow. Recall that each type of mineral has its own chemical makeup. Therefore, what types of minerals form in an area depends in part on which elements are present there. Temperature and pressure also affect which minerals form.

Water evaporates. Water usually has many substances dissolved in it. Minerals can form when the water evaporates. For example, when salt water evaporates, the atoms that make up halite, which is used as table salt, join to form crystals. Other minerals form from evaporation too, depending on the substances dissolved in the water. The mineral gypsum often forms as water evaporates.

Hot water cools. As hot water within Earth's crust moves through rocks, it can dissolve minerals. When the water cools, the dissolved minerals separate from the water and become solid again. In some cases, minerals are moved from one place to another. Gold can dissolve in hot water that moves through the crust. As the water cools and the gold becomes solid again, it can fill cracks in rocks. In other cases, the minerals that form are different from the ones that dissolved. Lead from the mineral galena can later become part of the mineral wulfenite as atoms join together into new minerals.

Molten rock cools. Many minerals grow from magma. **Magma**—molten rock inside Earth—contains all the types of atoms that are found in minerals. As magma cools, the atoms join together to form different minerals. Minerals also form as lava cools. **Lava** is molten rock that has reached Earth's surface. Quartz is one of the many minerals that crystallize from magma and lava.

Heat and pressure cause changes. Heat and pressure within Earth cause new minerals to form as bonds between atoms break and join again. The mineral garnet can grow and replace the minerals chlorite and quartz as their atoms combine in new ways. The element carbon is present in some rocks. At high temperatures carbon forms the mineral graphite, which is used in pencils.

Organisms produce minerals. A few minerals are produced by living things. For example, ocean animals such as oysters and clams produce calcite and other carbonate minerals to form their shells. Even you produce minerals. Your body produces one of the main minerals in your bones and teeth—apatite.

 **CHECK YOUR READING** How is the formation of minerals as molten rock cools similar to the formation of minerals as water evaporates?

Mineral Formation

Minerals form at Earth's surface and within Earth.

Water evaporates.

As water evaporates along a shoreline, it leaves behind substances that were dissolved in it. Here, gypsum is forming.

Hot water cools.

Gold dissolved in hot water can fill cracks in rocks as the water cools.

Molten rock cools.

Minerals such as quartz grow as molten rock cools.

Heat and pressure cause changes.

Graphite forms inside Earth when carbon is subjected to great heat.

READING VISUALS Each of the four processes shown involves heat. What is the heat source for rapid evaporation of water at Earth's surface?

Minerals and Ores Around the World

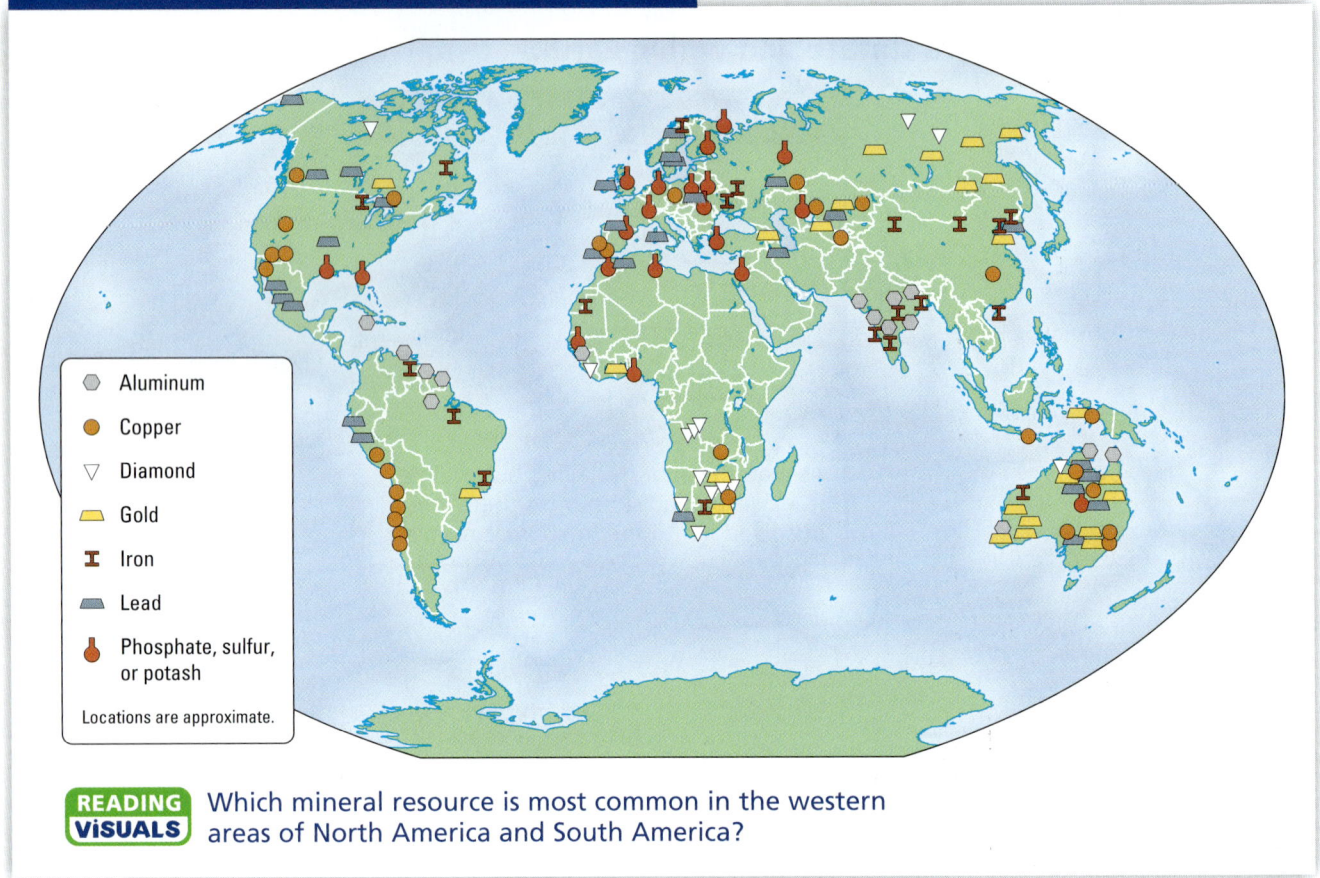

READING VISUALS Which mineral resource is most common in the western areas of North America and South America?

Many minerals are mined.

Before minerals can be used to make products, they must be removed from the ground. Some minerals are found near Earth's surface, while others lie deep underground. Some minerals are found at a wide range of depths, from the surface to deep within Earth.

Most minerals are combined with other minerals in rocks. For any mineral to be worth mining, there must be a fairly large amount of the mineral present in a rock. Rocks that contain enough of a mineral to be mined for a profit are called **ores.**

READING TIP
To make a profit, mine owners must be able to sell ores for more than it cost them to dig the ores out.

Surface Mining

Minerals at or near Earth's surface are recovered by surface mining. Some minerals, such as gold, are very dense. These minerals can build up in riverbeds as less dense minerals are carried away by the water. In a method called panning, a miner uses a pan to wash away unwanted minerals that are less dense. The gold and other dense minerals stay in the bottom of the pan and can then be further separated. In bigger riverbed mining operations, miners use machines to dig out and separate the valuable minerals.

492 Unit 4: Earth's Surface

Another method of surface mining is strip mining. Miners strip away plants, soil, and unwanted rocks from Earth's surface. Then they use special machines to dig out an ore.

Like strip mining, open-pit mining involves removing the surface layer of soil. Miners then use explosives to break up the underlying rock and recover the ore. As they dig a deep hole, or pit, to mine the ore, they build roads up the sides of the pit. Trucks carry the ore to the surface. Ores of copper and of iron are obtained by open-pit mining.

If an Olympic-sized swimming pool were filled with rock from this mine, it might contain enough copper to make a solid "beach ball" 146 cm (60 in.) in diameter.

 **CHECK YOUR READING** How are strip mining and open-pit mining similar? How are they different?

INVESTIGATE Mining

What are the benefits and costs of mining ores?

PROCEDURE

1. Put the birdseed into a pan. Add the beads to the birdseed and mix well.
2. Search through the seeds and separate out the beads and sunflower seeds, placing each kind in a different pile. Take no more than 3 minutes.
3. Assign a value to each of the beads and seeds: red bead, $5; green bead, $4; blue bead, $3; sunflower seed, $2. Count up the value of your beads and seeds. For every yellow bead, subtract $100, which represents the cost of restoring the land after mining.

WHAT DO YOU THINK?

- How does the difficulty of finding the red beads relate to the difficulty of finding the most valuable ores?
- How does the total value of the blue beads and the sunflower seeds compare to the total value of the red and green beads? What can you conclude about deciding which materials to mine?

CHALLENGE The sunflower seeds and the red, green, and blue beads could represent minerals that contain copper, gold, iron, and silver. Which bead or seed is most likely to represent each mineral? Explain your choices.

SKILL FOCUS
Drawing conclusions

MATERIALS
- 1 pound wild-birdseed mix with sunflower seeds
- shallow pan
- 2 small red beads
- 4 small green beads
- 8 small blue beads
- 3 medium yellow beads

TIME
25 minutes

Chapter 14: **Minerals** 493

Deep Mining

Deep-mining methods are needed when an ore lies far below Earth's surface. These methods are used to obtain many minerals. Miners dig an opening to reach a deep ore. When the ore is inside a mountain or hill, miners can cut a level passage to reach the mineral they want. Miners dig a vertical passage to reach an ore that lies underground in a flat area or under a mountain.

From the main passage, miners blast, drill, cut, or dig the ore. If the passage is horizontal, they keep digging farther and farther into the hill or mountain. If it is vertical, they remove the ore in layers.

These gold miners are working underground near Carlin, Nevada. The world's deepest gold mine is in South Africa and extends almost 3 km (2 mi) underground.

14.3 Review

KEY CONCEPTS

1. Give two examples of the use of minerals in industry and two examples of the use of minerals in the arts.
2. What are the five ways in which minerals form?
3. What is required for rocks to be considered ores?

CRITICAL THINKING

4. **Infer** Would an ore at Earth's surface or an ore deep underground be more expensive to mine? Explain.
5. **Apply** The mineral quartz has been used as a gemstone for thousands of years. What minerals could jewelry makers use to grind and polish quartz?

CHALLENGE

6. **Analyze** Both strip mining and open-pit mining are types of surface mining. When might miners choose to use open-pit mining rather than strip mining to obtain an ore?

494 Unit 4: **Earth's Surface**

SCIENCE on the JOB

GEM CUTTER

Geometry for Gems

If you found a gemstone in nature, it would probably look dull and rough. You might want to take it to a gem cutter, who would use a grinding wheel to shape and polish your rough stone into a beautiful gem. You would also discover that a lot of the rough gemstone is ground away into powder.

Gem cutters use geometry to help them choose the best final shapes of gems. Geometry also helps them to shape gems with many small, flat surfaces at specific angles. These surfaces are called facets, and they make the gems sparkle.

Starred Gems

Some gems—such as certain rubies, sapphires, and forms of quartz—show a six-pointed star when cut in a rounded shape instead of facets. These gems contain tiny flaws aligned at 120-degree angles. When light hits the flaws, it scatters in a star-shaped pattern. The star ruby shown here is a good example of these beautiful gems.

Sparkling Gems

How much a gem sparkles depends on the geometric angles at which it is cut. If the overall angle of the bottom part of a gem is too shallow **(A)** or too steep **(C)**, light will go through the gem.

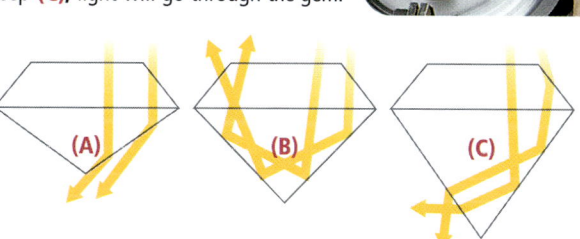

However, if the angles are correct **(B)**, light will bounce around inside the gem as it is reflected to the viewer's eye. The more facets a gem has, the more the light will bounce, and the more the gem will sparkle.

Deeply Colored Gems

Some gems are shaped to show off their rich colors rather than their sparkle. These gems have fewer and larger facets. Also, many brightly colored gems contain lighter and darker areas of color. The gems are shaped so that the richest color is toward the bottom. Light entering one of these gems strikes the bottom and reflects the rich color to the viewer's eye.

EXPLORE

1. **COMPARE** Table salt, which is the mineral halite, sparkles as light is reflected from its crystal faces. Snow, which is the mineral ice, also sparkles in sunlight. How are the crystal faces of salt and snow similar to facets? How are they different?

2. **CHALLENGE** When would it be best for a gem cutter to split an irregularly shaped crystal into two or more smaller stones before grinding them into finished gems? Remember, one larger stone is usually more valuable than two smaller ones.

14 Chapter Review

the BIG idea
Minerals are basic building blocks of Earth.

CONTENT REVIEW
CLASSZONE.COM

KEY CONCEPTS SUMMARY

1 Minerals are all around us.

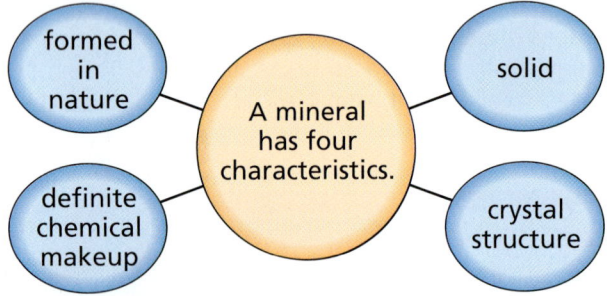

VOCABULARY
mineral p. 471
element p. 473
crystal p. 474

2 A mineral is identified by its properties.

Mineral Properties	wulfenite
color	orange
streak	white
luster	nonmetallic
cleavage	yes
density	6.9
hardness	3

VOCABULARY
streak p. 479
luster p. 480
cleavage p. 481
fracture p. 481
density p. 482
hardness p. 483

3 Minerals are valuable resources.

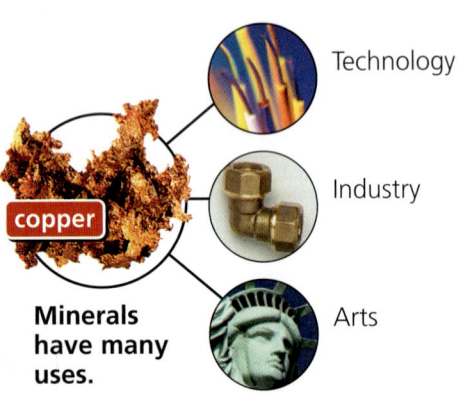

Minerals have many uses.
- Technology
- Industry
- Arts
- copper

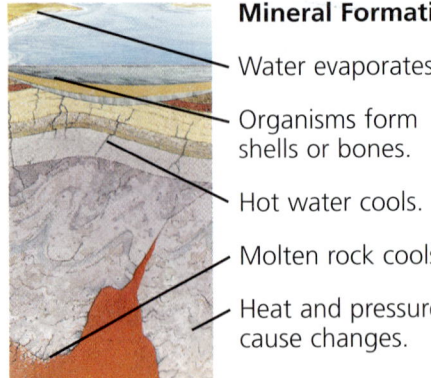

Mineral Formation
- Water evaporates.
- Organisms form shells or bones.
- Hot water cools.
- Molten rock cools.
- Heat and pressure cause changes.

VOCABULARY
magma p. 490
lava p. 490
ore p. 492

496 Unit 4: Earth's Surface

Reviewing Vocabulary

On a separate sheet of paper, write a sentence describing the relationship between the two vocabulary terms.

1. mineral, crystal
2. cleavage, fracture
3. magma, lava
4. element, density
5. mineral, ore
6. element, magma

Reviewing Key Concepts

Multiple Choice *Choose the letter of the best answer.*

7. A mineral is a substance that forms
   a. from rocks
   b. in nature
   c. from one element
   d. in liquid

8. A crystal structure is characteristic of
   a. an element
   b. a rock
   c. magma
   d. a mineral

9. A mineral is made up of one or more
   a. ores
   b. rocks
   c. compounds
   d. elements

10. How is it possible for two different minerals to have the same chemical composition?
    a. They have different crystal structures.
    b. One is formed only by organisms.
    c. Only one is a rock-forming mineral.
    d. They have different appearances.

11. Most minerals in Earth's crust belong to the silicate mineral group because this group contains the
    a. rarest elements on Earth
    b. most common elements on Earth
    c. most valuable metals on Earth
    d. largest crystals on Earth

12. Which of the following is the least reliable clue to a mineral's identity?
    a. color
    b. density
    c. hardness
    d. luster

13. Many properties of a mineral are related to the
    a. number of elements of which it is made
    b. other types of minerals present as it formed
    c. strength of bonds between its atoms
    d. speed at which it formed

14. What types of minerals form in an area depends in part on
    a. which elements are present
    b. the types of rock present
    c. the density of rocks present
    d. whether crystals can form

15. Open-pit mining is used to obtain ores that lie
    a. under flat land
    b. deep in Earth's crust
    c. near the surface of Earth
    d. in riverbeds

16. Gemstones are used in
    a. building materials
    b. paper products
    c. automobile parts
    d. jewelry making

Short Answer *Write a short answer for each question.*

17. Why aren't all solids minerals? Include the term *crystal structure* in your answer.

18. Why is a mineral's streak more useful in identifying it than its color?

19. If you drop dilute hydrochloric acid on the mineral aragonite, it bubbles. What mineral group do you think aragonite belongs to? Why?

20. Describe how the strength of the bonds between atoms in a mineral determines whether the mineral displays cleavage or fracture.

Chapter 14: **Minerals** 497

Thinking Critically

Properties such as hardness and density are used to identify minerals. Use the information from the chart to answer the next five questions.

Mineral	Hardness	Density (g/cm^3)
platinum	4.5	19.0
aragonite	4	3
topaz	8	3.5
quartz	7	2.7
arsenic	3.5	5.7

21. COMPARE Platinum can combine with arsenic to form the mineral sperrylite. How do you think the density of sperrylite compares with the densities of platinum and arsenic?

22. APPLY Gems made of topaz are much more valuable than those made of quartz, even though the two minerals can look similar. Describe two methods you could use to identify quartz.

23. APPLY Would a miner be more likely to use the method of panning to find platinum or to find topaz? Why?

24. INFER Aragonite forms very attractive crystals, yet this common mineral is rarely used in jewelry. Why do you think this is?

25. DEDUCE About how many times heavier than a piece of quartz would you expect a piece of platinum of the same size to be? Show your work.

26. HYPOTHESIZE *Halite* is the mineral name for table salt. Thick layers of halite are mined near Detroit, Michigan. At one time, an ocean covered the area. Write a hypothesis that explains how the halite formed there.

27. PREDICT The mineral chromite is the main ore of the metal chromium. What might happen after all the chromite on Earth is mined?

28. PREDICT The mineral apatite is a compound in your bones and teeth. Apatite contains the elements phosphorus and calcium. How might your bones be affected if you do not have enough of these elements in your diet?

29. DRAW CONCLUSIONS You live on the surface of Earth's crust. The average density of the crust is about 2.8 grams per cubic centimeter. Most metal ores have densities greater than 5 grams per cubic centimeter. How common do you think metal ores are in the crust? Why?

the BIG idea

30. ANALYZE Minerals are basic components of planets such as Earth and Mars. Other planets in our solar system, such as Jupiter and Saturn, are called gas giants because they are composed mainly of the gases hydrogen and helium. They do not have solid surfaces. Do you think that minerals are basic components of gas giants? Why or why not?

Mars

Jupiter

31. INFER Minerals make up much of Earth. People use minerals as sources of many materials, such as metals. Some metals are used to make machine parts or build houses. How would your life be different if minerals that contain metals were rare in Earth's crust?

UNIT PROJECTS

If you need to do an experiment for your unit project, gather the materials. Be sure to allow enough time to observe results before the project is due.

Standardized Test Practice

For practice on your state test, go to...
TEST PRACTICE
CLASSZONE.COM

Analyzing a Table

This table shows characteristics of four minerals. Use it to answer the questions below.

Sample	Cleavage or Fracture	Density (g/cm³)	Hardness (in Mohs scale)	Magnetic
E	cleavage	3.7	8.5	no
F	fracture	5.2	5.5	yes
G	fracture	2.7	7.0	no
H	cleavage	2.7	3.0	no

1. Which sample is most dense?
   a. E
   b. F
   c. G
   d. H

2. Which sample is hardest?
   a. E
   b. F
   c. G
   d. H

3. What will happen if G is rubbed against each of the other samples?
   a. It will scratch only E.
   b. It will scratch only F.
   c. It will scratch only H.
   d. It will scratch F and H.

4. Which statement accurately describes how one of the samples will affect a magnet?
   a. E will attract the magnet.
   b. F will attract the magnet.
   c. G will be pushed away from the magnet.
   d. H will be pushed away from the magnet.

5. Which sample or samples have a crystal structure?
   a. E, F, G, and H
   b. only F
   c. E and H
   d. F and G

6. Which samples are likely to break along flat surfaces?
   a. E and G
   b. F and G
   c. G and H
   d. E and H

7. An unidentified mineral sample has a density of 2.9 grams per cubic centimeter and a hardness of 6.7. Which mineral is it most like?
   a. E
   b. F
   c. G
   d. H

8. Which is true about one-cubic-centimeter pieces of these samples?
   a. Each would have the same weight.
   b. E would be heaviest.
   c. F would be heaviest.
   d. H would be heaviest.

Extended Response

Answer the two questions below in detail. Include some of the terms shown in the word box. In your answers underline each term you use.

| chemical makeup | element | compound |
| crystal structure | Mohs scale | hardness |

9. Describe the characteristics of minerals that make them different from rocks.

10. Describe the type of mineral that would work best on the tip of a drill designed to make holes in hard materials.

Chapter 14: **Minerals** 499

CHAPTER 15 Rocks

Rocks change into other rocks over time.

> How long will these rocks remain as they are?

Key Concepts

SECTION 1 The rock cycle shows how rocks change.
Learn the types of rock and how they change over time.

SECTION 2 Igneous rocks form from molten rock.
Learn how igneous rocks form within Earth and at Earth's surface.

SECTION 3 Sedimentary rocks form from earlier rocks.
Learn how layers of loose materials develop into sedimentary rocks.

SECTION 4 Metamorphic rocks form as existing rocks change.
Learn how one type of rock can change into another.

Internet Preview

CLASSZONE.COM
Chapter 15 online resources: Content Review, Simulation, Visualization, four Resource Centers, Math Tutorial, Test Practice

500 Unit 4: Earth's Surface

EXPLORE the BIG idea

How Can Rocks Disappear?

Chalk is made of carbonate minerals, as is a type of rock called limestone. Put a piece of chalk in a cup. Pour vinegar over the chalk.

Observe and Think Describe what happens to the chalk. How do you think this change could happen to limestone in nature? **Hint:** Think about the amount of time it might take.

What Causes Rocks to Change?

Make two balls out of modeling clay and freeze them. Take the clay balls out of the freezer and put them on paper. Cover one ball with plastic wrap and stack books on top of it.

Observe and Think Observe how the clay balls change over time. How might rocks respond to changes in temperature, pressure, or both?

Internet Activity: Rocks

Go to **ClassZone.com** to explore how rocks form and change.

Observe and Think Give three examples of the ways in which rocks are continually changing.

The Rock Cycle **Code: MDL015**

CHAPTER 15
Getting Ready to Learn

CONCEPT REVIEW

- Every mineral has a specific chemical composition.
- A mineral's atoms are arranged in a crystal structure.
- Minerals form under a variety of conditions.

VOCABULARY REVIEW

mineral p. 471
crystal p. 474
magma p. 490
lava p. 490

CONTENT REVIEW
CLASSZONE.COM
Review concepts and vocabulary.

TAKING NOTES

MAIN IDEA WEB

Write each new blue heading in the center box. In the boxes around it, take notes about important terms and details that relate to the main idea.

VOCABULARY STRATEGY

Draw a **magnet word** diagram for each new vocabulary term. Around the "magnet" write words and ideas related to the term.

See the Note-Taking Handbook on pages R45–R51.

SCIENCE NOTEBOOK

- Rocks are not the same as minerals.
- Different types of rocks contain different minerals.
- Most rocks are made of minerals.
- A rock may be made up of only one mineral.
- A few kinds of rocks contain no minerals at all.

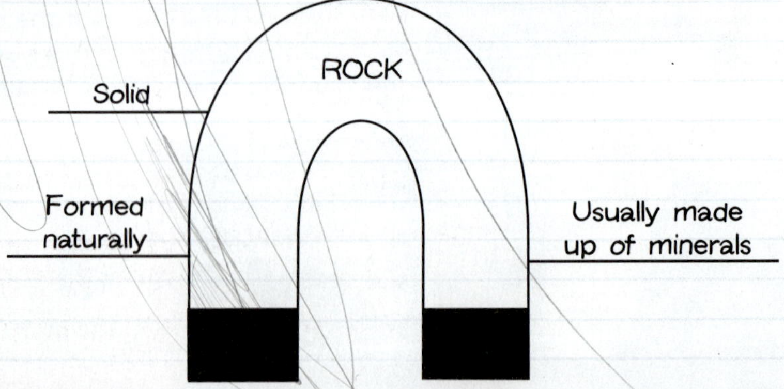

ROCK
- Solid
- Formed naturally
- Usually made up of minerals

502 Unit 4: Earth's Surface

KEY CONCEPT

15.1 The rock cycle shows how rocks change.

 BEFORE, you learned
- Minerals are basic components of Earth
- Minerals form in many different ways

 NOW, you will learn
- What the three types of rocks are
- How one type of rock can change into another
- How common each rock type is in Earth's crust

VOCABULARY

rock p. 503
rock cycle p. 506
igneous rock p. 506
sedimentary rock p. 506
metamorphic rock p. 506

EXPLORE Rocks and Minerals

How do rocks differ from minerals?

PROCEDURE

1. Closely examine the rock and mineral samples. What do you notice about the forms, shapes, colors, and textures of the rock and the mineral?

2. In your notebook, make lists of the characteristics of the rock and of the mineral.

MATERIALS
- mineral sample
- rock sample
- magnifying glass

WHAT DO YOU THINK?
- What are the similarities and differences between the rock and the mineral?
- What additional observations or tests might help you determine other differences between rocks and minerals?

Most rocks are made of minerals.

If you have ever put together a jigsaw puzzle, you know that each piece is an important part of the final picture. Just as the pieces combine to form the picture, minerals combine to form most rocks. Another way to consider the relationship between minerals and rocks is to compare rocks to words. Just as letters combine to make up words, minerals combine to make up rocks. A **rock** is a naturally formed solid that is usually made up of one or more types of minerals.

The structure of rocks is different from that of minerals. A mineral is always made of the same elements in the same proportions. All minerals have an orderly crystal structure. In contrast, the proportion of different minerals in a particular kind of rock may vary. In addition, the minerals in a rock can be all jumbled together.

Chapter 15: **Rocks** 503

A few types of rocks are made up of one kind of mineral, and a few contain no minerals at all. Limestone, for example, can be composed entirely of the mineral calcite. Obsidian (ahb-SIHD-ee-uhn) is a rock that contains no minerals. It consists of natural glass, which is not a mineral because it does not have a crystal structure. Coal is another rock that is not composed of minerals. It is made up of the remains of ancient plants that have been buried and pressed into rock.

Gabbro, like most rocks, is made up of several types of minerals.

Obsidian is an unusual rock because it contains no minerals.

MAIN IDEA WEB
As you read, write each blue heading in a central box and record important details in boxes around it.

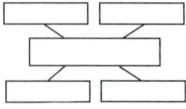

These huge cliffs on the coast of the Hawaiian island of Kauai show only a tiny part of the rock that makes up Earth.

Our world is built of rocks.

Earth is built almost entirely of rock. When you look at Earth's surface, you can see soil, plants, rivers, and oceans. These surface features, however, form only a very thin covering on the planet. Between this thin layer and Earth's metallic core, Earth is made of solid and molten rock.

Because rocks are so common, it is not surprising that people use them for many different purposes, including

- the building of houses and skyscrapers
- the sources of metals, such as iron, aluminum, and copper
- the carving of statues and other works of art
- as a base for pavement for roads and highways

People value rocks because rocks last a long time and because some are beautiful. Ancient rock structures and carvings give us a link to our distant past. Many famous monuments and sculptures are made from rocks. Granite blocks form part of the Great Wall of China. Limestone blocks make up the Great Pyramid in Egypt. The faces of four U.S. presidents are carved in the granite of Mount Rushmore.

CHECK YOUR READING Why do people use rocks for many different purposes?

This sculptor in Indonesia, like artists throughout the world, shapes rocks into lasting works of art.

People study rocks to learn how areas have changed through time. For example, rocks show that North America, as well as most of the rest of the world, has been buried under thick layers of ice many times. You could learn about the types of rocks in your area by collecting and identifying them. You could also examine a map that shows types of rocks and where they are located. This type of map is called a geologic map. The map may be of a large area, such as your state, or a smaller area, such as your county.

INVESTIGATE Classification of Rocks

How can rocks be classified?

Geologists classify rocks by their physical characteristics. Design your own system for classifying rocks, as a scientist might.

PROCEDURE

1. Examine the rock samples. Look at their physical characteristics.
2. Make a list of the differences in the physical characteristics of the rocks.
3. Use your list to decide which characteristics are most important in classifying the rocks into different types. Make a chart in which these characteristics are listed and used to classify the rocks into types.

WHAT DO YOU THINK?

- Which physical characteristic is most helpful in classifying the rocks?
- Which physical characteristic is least helpful in classifying the rocks?

CHALLENGE Is it possible to classify rocks only by the characteristics you can see?

SKILL FOCUS
Classifying

MATERIALS
6 rock samples

TIME
20 minutes

Rocks change as they move through the rock cycle.

VOCABULARY
Add a magnet word diagram for *rock cycle* to your notebook. Then add diagrams for the names of the rock types.

When you want to describe a person you can depend on, you may say that he or she is "like a rock." That's the way people think of rocks—as solid and unchanging. Nevertheless, rocks do change. But the changes usually occur over a huge span of time—thousands to millions of years. The **rock cycle** is the set of natural processes that form, change, break down, and re-form rocks.

A cycle is made up of repeating events that happen one after another. This does not mean that rocks move through the rock cycle in a particular order. As the illustration shows on page 507, a rock at any point in the cycle can change in two or three different ways. Like all cycles, the rock cycle has no beginning or ending but goes on continually.

Rock Types

The three types of rocks are classified by how they form.

- **Igneous rock** (IHG-nee-uhs) forms when molten rock cools and becomes solid. Igneous rock can form within Earth, or it can form on Earth's surface. Igneous rocks that originally formed at great depths can reach Earth's surface over time. Deep rocks may be raised closer to the surface when mountains are pushed up. At the same time, other processes can wear away the rocks that cover the deeper rocks.

- Most **sedimentary rock** (SEHD-uh-MEHN-tuh-ree) forms when pieces of older rocks, plants, and other loose material get pressed or cemented together. Loose material is carried by water or wind and then settles out, forming layers. The lower layers of material can get pressed into rock by the weight of the upper layers. Also, new minerals can grow in the spaces within the material, cementing it together. Some sedimentary rocks form in other ways, as when water evaporates, leaving behind minerals that were dissolved in it.

- **Metamorphic rock** (MEHT-uh-MAWR-fihk) forms when heat or pressure causes older rocks to change into new types of rocks. For example, a rock can get buried deeper in the crust, where pressure and temperature are much greater. The new conditions cause the structure of the rock to change and new minerals to grow in place of the original minerals. The rock becomes a metamorphic rock. Like igneous rocks, metamorphic rocks can be raised to Earth's surface over time.

READING TIP
When material dissolves in water, it breaks into many tiny parts. When the water evaporates, the parts join together and the material becomes solid again.

 **CHECK YOUR READING** What are the three rock types? What questions do you have about how rocks move through the rock cycle?

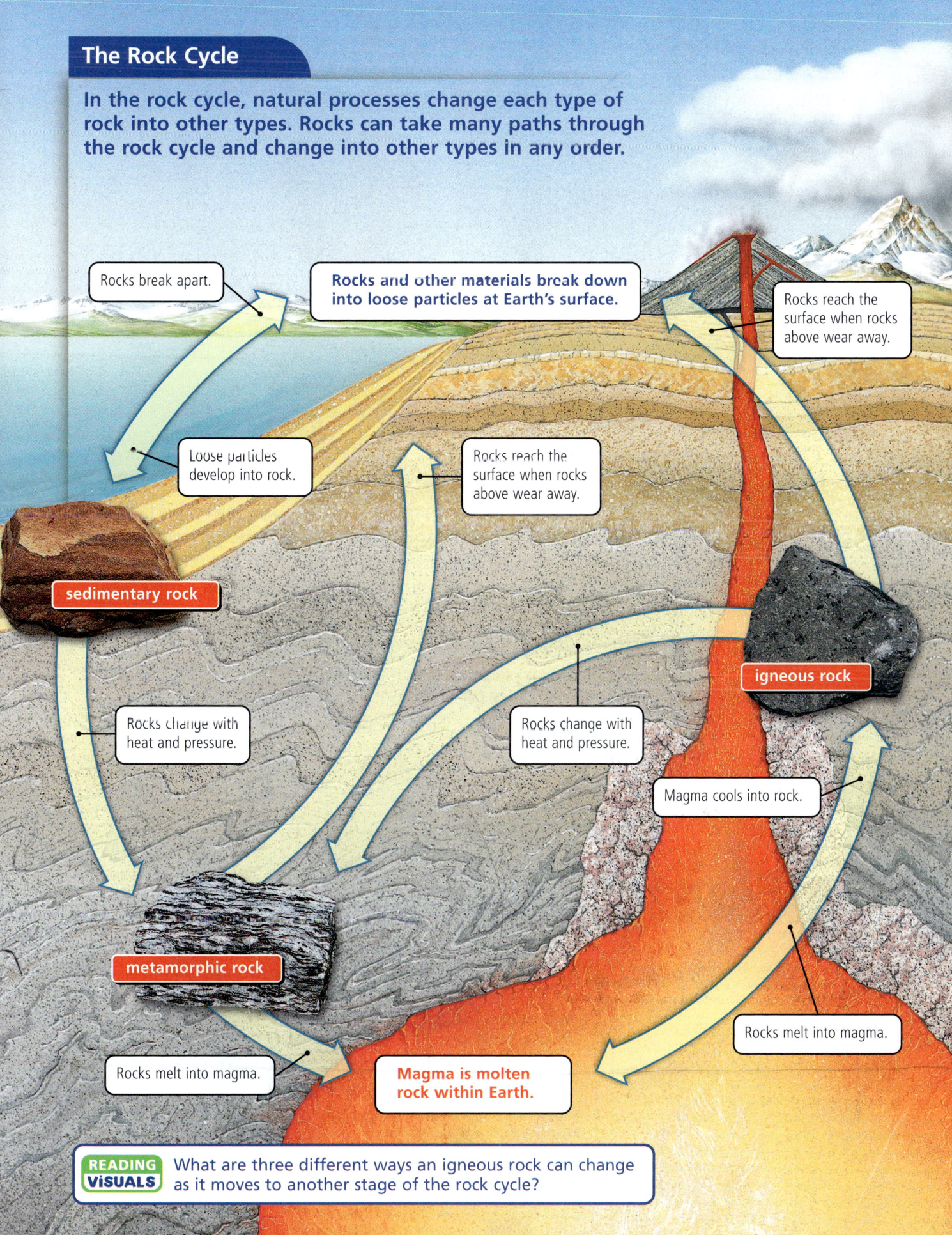

Rocks in the Crust

Even though sedimentary rock is common at Earth's surface, as a whole the crust consists mainly of igneous and metamorphic rock.

Rocks in the Crust

Igneous, sedimentary, and metamorphic rocks are all found in Earth's crust. But these rock types are not evenly distributed. Most of Earth's crust—95 percent of it—consists of igneous rock and metamorphic rock. Sedimentary rock, which forms a thin covering on Earth's surface, makes up only 5 percent of the crust.

The distribution of rock types is a reflection of the rock cycle. Sedimentary rocks are most common at the surface because they are formed by processes that occur at the surface. Most igneous rocks and metamorphic rocks are formed by processes that occur deeper within Earth.

CHECK YOUR READING Would you expect to find sedimentary rock deep in Earth's crust? Why or why not?

15.1 Review

KEY CONCEPTS

1. How are rocks and minerals different?
2. What are the three types of rock?
3. Which rock types are most common within Earth's crust? Which type is most common at Earth's surface?

CRITICAL THINKING

4. **Analyze** Why is the set of natural processes by which rocks change into other types of rocks called a cycle?
5. **Infer** Which type of rock would you expect to be common on the floor of a large, deep lake? Why?

CHALLENGE

6. **Synthesize** Draw a diagram showing how an igneous rock could change into a metamorphic rock and how the metamorphic rock could change into a sedimentary rock.

508 Unit 4: Earth's Surface

EXTREME SCIENCE

Rocks from Space

Earth makes its own rocks. But some rocks come from space and land on Earth's surface. About 30,000 rocks with masses greater than 100 grams (3.5 oz) fall to Earth's surface every year. That's a rate of more than 80 rocks per day!

- A rock from space that reaches Earth's surface after passing through its atmosphere is called a meteorite.
- Most meteorites go unnoticed when they strike Earth. Either they fall in areas where there are few people, or they fall into the ocean.
- The largest rock from space ever found on Earth is called the Hoba meteorite. It weighs 60 tons! It landed in what is now Namibia, Africa, about 80,000 years ago.

This rock is a piece of the meteorite that formed Barringer Crater.

Meteorite Hunters Search Ice

Meteorite hunters search the icy wastes of Antarctica for these rocks. Do more meteorites fall there? No. But they are easy to see against the ice. The cold also helps preserve them in their original condition. In addition, the movements of the ice gather meteorites together in certain locations.

Meteorites Blast Earth

Large meteorites are very rare. This is fortunate, because they hit with great power. About 50,000 years ago, a meteorite that was about 45 meters (150 ft) in diameter slammed into what is now Arizona and blasted a crater 1.2 kilometers (0.75 mi) wide. Craters from ancient impacts may be hard to recognize because the land has been reshaped by geological processes. Evidence can still be found, though. The energy of an impact is so high that some minerals, such as quartz, are permanently altered.

A meteorite impact formed Barringer Crater, which is located in the Arizona desert.

EXPLORE

1. **PREDICT** Oceans cover about 71 percent of Earth's surface. Calculate how many meteorites with masses greater than 100 grams are likely to fall into the ocean each year. How many are likely to fall on land?
2. **CHALLENGE** Use information from the Resource Center to describe how a meteorite impact could have helped cause the dinosaurs to become extinct.

RESOURCE CENTER
CLASSZONE.COM
Learn more about meteorites and meteorite impacts.

A streak of light marks the path of a rock from space through Earth's atmosphere. The rock probably burned up completely before it could land.

Chapter 15: **Rocks** 509

KEY CONCEPT
15.2 Igneous rocks form from molten rock.

▶ **BEFORE, you learned**
- Earth's interior is very hot
- Most minerals in Earth's crust are silicates

▶ **NOW, you will learn**
- Why igneous rocks formed at Earth's surface are different from those formed within Earth
- Why silica content is important in classifying igneous rocks
- Why igneous rocks can make long-lasting landforms

VOCABULARY

intrusive igneous rock p. 511
extrusive igneous rock p. 511

THINK ABOUT

Why do two rocks made of the same minerals look very different?

Look at a sample of granite and a sample of rhyolite (RY-uh-LYT). These two igneous rocks contain the same minerals, so their chemical compositions are very similar. Yet granite and rhyolite look very different. What do you think might cause this difference?

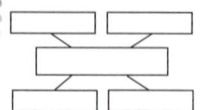

MAIN IDEA WEB
Remember to make a web for each main idea.

Magma and lava form different types of igneous rocks.

Igneous rocks form from molten rock, but where does molten rock come from? The temperature inside Earth increases with depth. That is, the farther down you go, the hotter it gets. Deep within Earth, temperatures are hot enough—750°C to 1250°C (about 1400°F to 2300°F)—to melt rock. This molten rock is called magma. Molten rock that reaches Earth's surface is called lava.

An igneous rock is classified on the basis of its mineral composition and the size of its mineral crystals. A rock formed from magma can have the same composition as a rock formed from lava. The rocks, though, will have different names, because the sizes of their crystals will be very different. You will read why later in this section.

People's decisions about how to use igneous rocks are based in part on the rocks' crystal sizes. For example, rocks with large mineral crystals are often used as building stones because they are attractive.

510 Unit 4: Earth's Surface

Origin of Igneous Rocks

Depending on where they form, igneous rocks are classified as intrusive (ihn-TROO-sihv) or extrusive (ihk-STROO-sihv). An **intrusive igneous rock** is one that forms when magma cools within Earth. An **extrusive igneous rock** is one that forms when lava cools on Earth's surface.

Granite is a common intrusive rock in continents. If magma with the same composition reaches the surface, it forms extrusive rocks such as rhyolite and pumice (PUHM-ihs). Basalt (buh-SAWLT) is an extrusive igneous rock that forms the ocean floor. Gabbro is an intrusive rock that has the same composition as basalt.

VOCABULARY
Add magnet word diagrams for *intrusive igneous rock* and *extrusive igneous rock* to your notebook.

CHECK YOUR READING How are gabbro and basalt similar? How are they different?

You can see extrusive igneous rocks at Earth's surface. But intrusive igneous rocks form within Earth. How do they reach the surface? Forces inside Earth can push rocks up, as when mountains form. Also, water and wind break apart and carry away surface rocks. Then deeper rocks are uncovered at the surface.

Types of Igneous Rocks

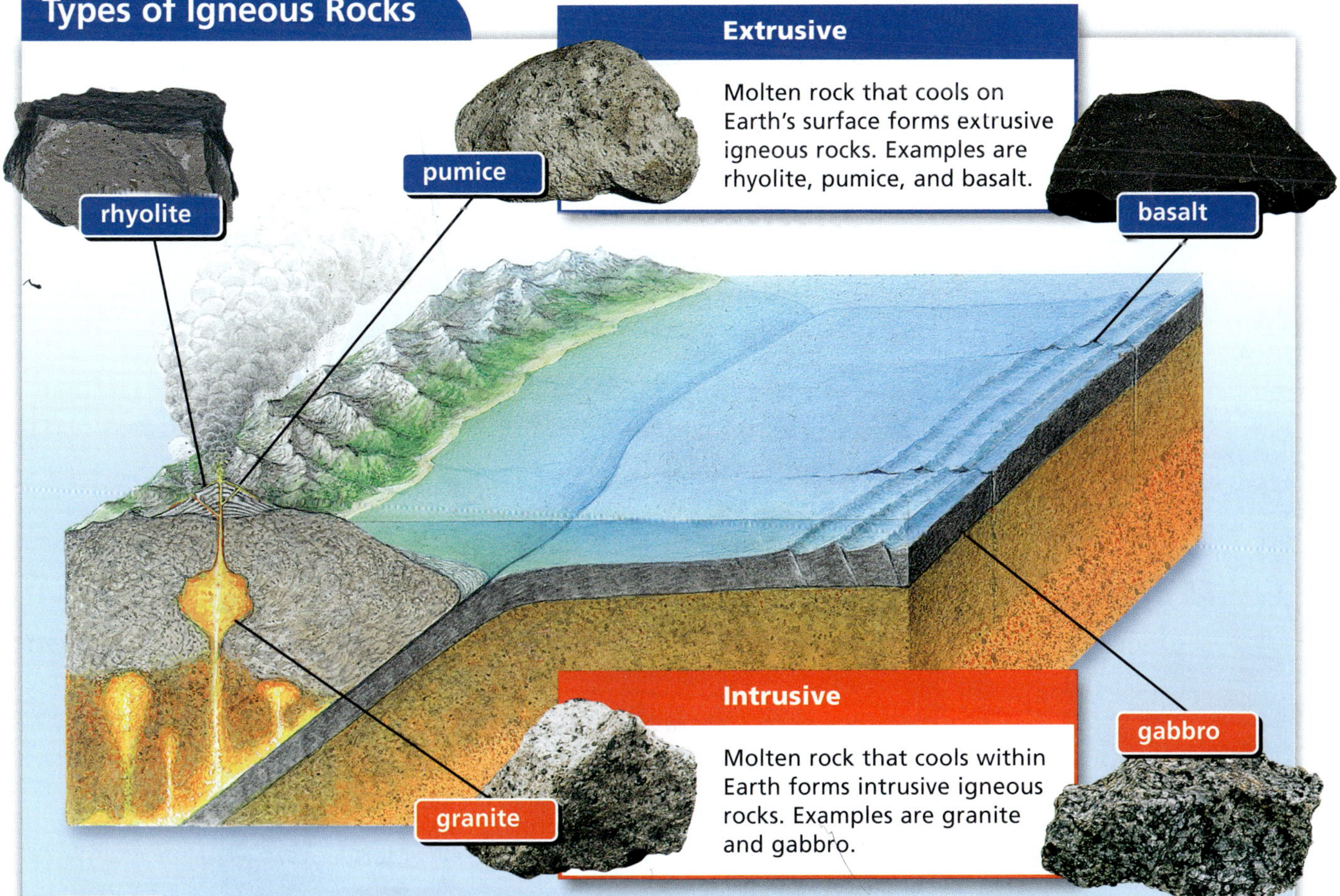

Extrusive
Molten rock that cools on Earth's surface forms extrusive igneous rocks. Examples are rhyolite, pumice, and basalt.

- rhyolite
- pumice
- basalt

Intrusive
Molten rock that cools within Earth forms intrusive igneous rocks. Examples are granite and gabbro.

- granite
- gabbro

READING VISUALS Is the volcano in the illustration built of layers of intrusive or extrusive igneous rock? Explain your answer.

Chapter 15: **Rocks** 511

Textures of Igneous Rocks

VISUALIZATION
CLASSZONE.COM

Explore an animation showing how crystals form as molten rock cools.

The texture of an igneous rock—that is, the size of its mineral crystals—depends on how quickly magma or lava cooled to form it. In an icemaker, crystals form as water freezes into ice. In a similar way, mineral crystals form as molten rock freezes into solid rock.

The magma that forms intrusive igneous rocks stays below the surface of Earth. Large crystals can form in intrusive rocks because

- the interior of Earth is very hot
- the high temperatures allow magma to cool slowly
- slow cooling allows time for large mineral crystals to form

The lava that forms extrusive igneous rocks reaches Earth's surface. Very small crystals form in extrusive rocks because

- the surface of Earth is cooler than Earth's interior
- the lower temperatures cause the lava to cool quickly
- there is no time for large mineral crystals to form

Some igneous rocks contain crystals of very different sizes. These rocks formed from magma that started cooling within Earth and then erupted onto the surface. The large crystals grew as the magma cooled slowly. The small crystals grew as the lava cooled quickly.

CHECK YOUR READING How does an igneous rock that has both large and small mineral crystals form?

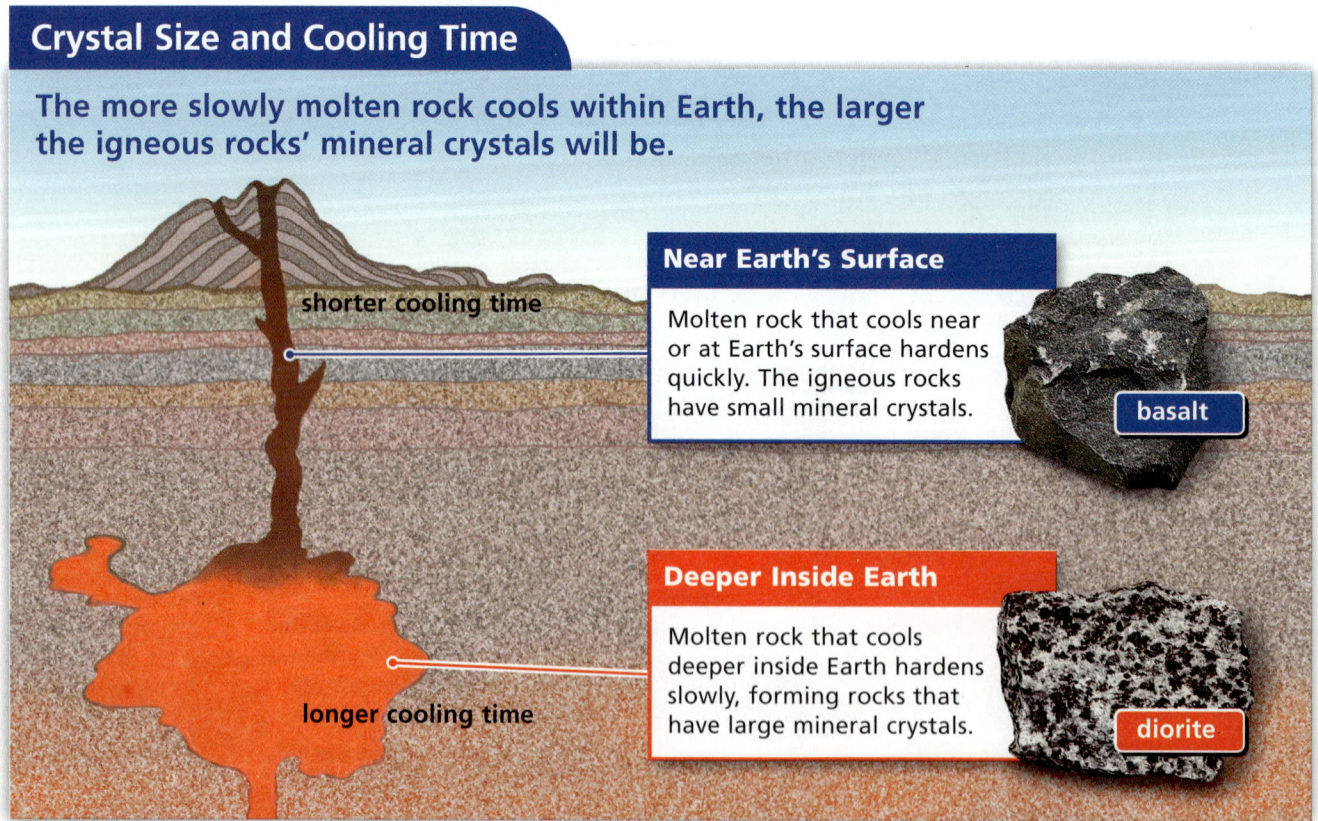

Crystal Size and Cooling Time

The more slowly molten rock cools within Earth, the larger the igneous rocks' mineral crystals will be.

shorter cooling time

Near Earth's Surface
Molten rock that cools near or at Earth's surface hardens quickly. The igneous rocks have small mineral crystals.

basalt

longer cooling time

Deeper Inside Earth
Molten rock that cools deeper inside Earth hardens slowly, forming rocks that have large mineral crystals.

diorite

INVESTIGATE Crystal Size

How does cooling time affect crystal size?

PROCEDURE

1. Look at the Mineral Crystal Diagrams datasheet.
2. Describe your observations of the crystals in each of the igneous-rock diagrams A–C on the lines provided.
3. Describe what is shown in each of graphs 1–3 on the lines provided.
4. Match each igneous-rock diagram with its corresponding graph.
5. On the back of the paper, explain why you matched each crystal diagram with a particular graph.

WHAT DO YOU THINK?

- Which diagram shows an intrusive igneous rock, such as gabbro?
- Where do you think the rock shown in diagram B formed? Explain your answer.

CHALLENGE Write a hypothesis to explain why the rock shown in diagram C might be found at a shallow depth in Earth's crust.

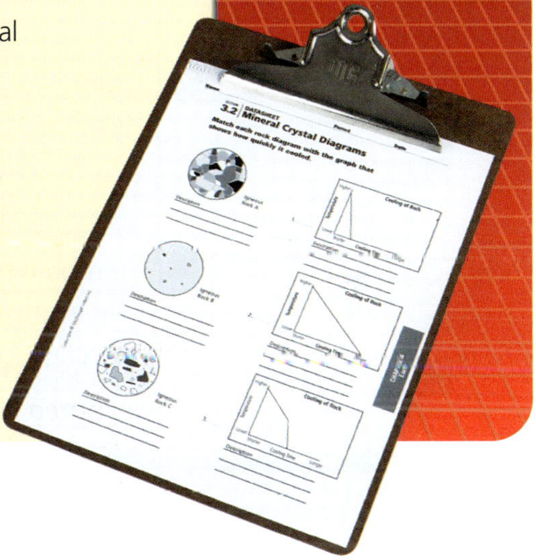

SKILL FOCUS
Analyzing

MATERIALS
Mineral Crystal Diagrams datasheet

TIME
20 Minutes

Composition of Igneous Rocks

Texture is not enough to identify an igneous rock. Think about substances that have similar textures, such as sugar and salt. A spoonful of sugar and a spoonful of salt both consist of small white grains. However, sugar and salt are different materials—that is, they have different compositions. Likewise, different igneous rocks might have similar textures. To identify them, you must also consider their compositions.

Most igneous rocks are mainly made up of silicate minerals, which you read about in the last chapter. The silicate mineral group is the most common group in Earth's crust. Silicate minerals contain varying amounts of silica, a compound of silicon and oxygen. After identifying the texture of an igneous rock, geologists classify the rock on the basis of how rich it is in silica.

Special equipment must be used to determine a rock's exact composition, but you can estimate the level of silica in an igneous rock by looking at its color. Igneous rocks with high levels of silica, such as granite and rhyolite, are typically light in color. Those with low levels of silica, such as gabbro and basalt, are dark in color.

 Would you expect a light gray igneous rock to be rich or poor in silica? Why?

Chapter 15: **Rocks** 513

Find out more about igneous rocks.

Igneous rocks make long-lasting landforms.

In northwestern New Mexico, a great peak rises out of a flat, barren desert. The Navajo call the peak Tsé Bit'a'í (tseh biht-ah-ih), meaning "rock with wings." In English, it's called Ship Rock, because it looks something like a sailing ship. Ship Rock is an example of the kinds of landforms that are made of igneous rocks. A landform is a natural feature on Earth's land surface.

Intrusive Rock Formations

Ship Rock actually formed about one kilometer below the surface of Earth 30 million years ago. It is all that remains of magma that once fed a volcano. The magma cooled slowly and formed intrusive igneous rock.

As magma pushes up toward Earth's surface, it makes channels and other formations underground. Formations of intrusive igneous rock can be harder and more lasting than other types of rock. Notice in the illustration below how igneous rock has been left at the surface as other, weaker types of rock have been worn away.

Intrusive Rock Formation

Wind and water wear away surrounding, weaker rock to reveal intrusive rock formations, such as Ship Rock.

Ancient Land Surface

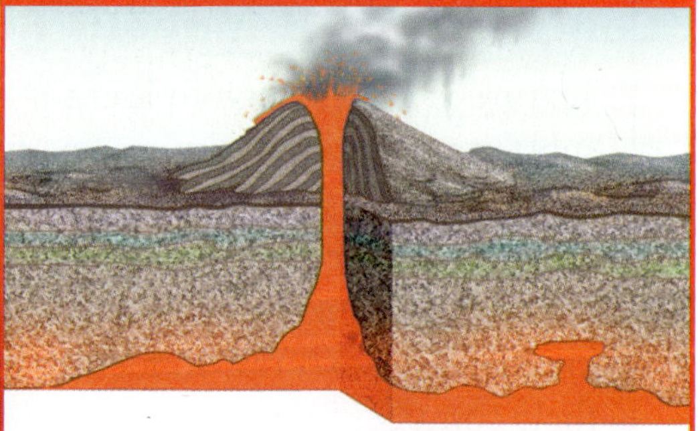

Magma that remains below the surface will later become intrusive igneous rock.

Present-Day Land Surface

Surface rock has worn away to reveal some of the intrusive rock.

READING VISUALS Where in the bottom illustration is more intrusive rock likely to be uncovered next?

514 Unit 4: Earth's Surface

Extrusive Rock Formations

When magma makes its way to Earth's surface through a volcano or crack, the lava may erupt in different ways. Some lava can build huge plateaus when it erupts from long cracks in Earth's surface. Lava that is low in silica, such as basalt lava, flows easily and spreads out in thin sheets over great distances. The Columbia Plateau in Oregon and Washington is made of basalt. When lava that is low in silica erupts at a single point, it can build up a huge volcano with gently sloping sides. The Hawaiian Islands are a chain of volcanoes that are built of basalt lava. The volcanoes started erupting on the sea floor and over a very long time grew tall enough to rise above the surface of the ocean as islands.

> **READING TIP**
> Notice what properties of basalt lava allow it to build large plateaus.

Lava that contains a greater amount of silica does not flow easily. Silica-rich lava tends to build cone-shaped volcanoes with steep sides. Volcanoes fed by silica-rich magma tend to erupt explosively. Because the magma is thick and sticky, pressure can build up in volcanoes until they explode. An example is Mount St. Helens in the state of Washington. Its 1980 eruption reduced the volcano's height by 400 meters (about 1300 ft). Lava flows are adding new extrusive igneous rock. At the current rate it will take more than 200 years for the volcano to reach its pre-1980 height.

Basalt lava can flow long distances. Here it is spreading over a road in Hawaii.

CHECK YOUR READING Why does silica-rich lava tend to build steep volcanoes instead of spreading out?

15.2 Review

KEY CONCEPTS

1. What is the main difference between intrusive and extrusive igneous rocks?
2. What are the two major properties used to classify igneous rocks?
3. Why can intrusive igneous rocks be left behind when surrounding rocks are worn away?

CRITICAL THINKING

4. **Draw Conclusions** If granite within Earth melts and then erupts at the surface, what type of extrusive rock is likely to form?
5. **Analyze** Would you expect extrusive rocks produced by an explosive volcano to be light or dark in color? Why?

CHALLENGE

6. **Synthesize** Why are the names *intrusive* and *extrusive* appropriate for the two types of igneous rocks?

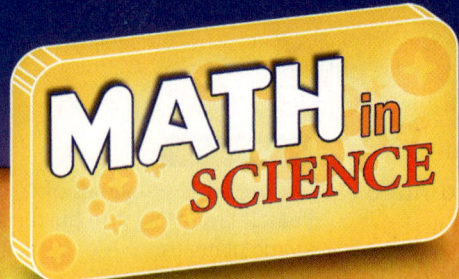

MATH in SCIENCE

SKILL: ESTIMATING AREA

**MATH TUTORIAL
CLASSZONE.COM**

Click on Math Tutorial for more help with estimating areas.

Resurfacing Earth

Lava flows from volcanoes are common on the island of Hawaii. The map below shows lava flows from the Kilauea volcano. The flow shown in blue destroyed more than 180 homes and covered the region in a layer of lava up to 25 meters thick.

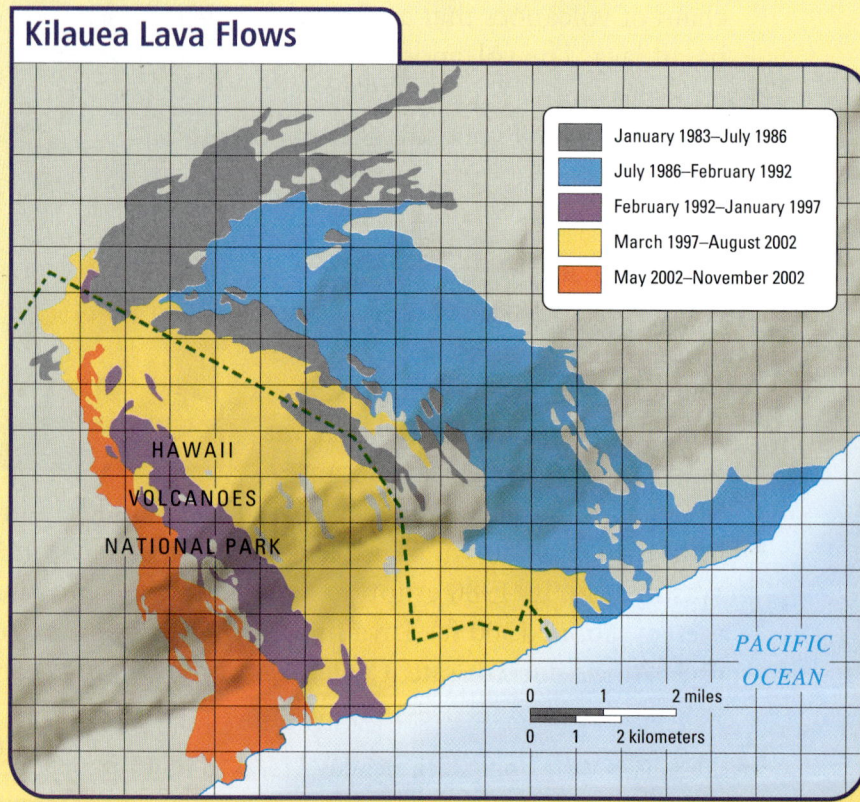

Kilauea Lava Flows

- January 1983–July 1986
- July 1986–February 1992
- February 1992–January 1997
- March 1997–August 2002
- May 2002–November 2002

Use the map to answer the following questions.

1. How many squares does the lava flow shown in yellow cover? First, count the complete grid squares covered by the lava flow shown in yellow. Next, think of partially covered grid squares as fractions, and add them together to get whole squares. Finally, add the number of these squares to the number of complete squares.

2. What is the area of the flow in square kilometers?

3. Use the same method to estimate the areas of the flows shown in purple and blue.

CHALLENGE To estimate the area covered by all the lava flows shown on the map, would it be better to estimate the area of each flow separately and then add the results together? Or would it be better to estimate the total area of the flows in one step? Explain your reasoning.

KEY CONCEPT

15.3 Sedimentary rocks form from earlier rocks.

 BEFORE, you learned
- Most rocks are made of minerals
- Some ocean organisms build their shells from minerals
- Dissolved minerals re-form as water evaporates

 NOW, you will learn
- What kinds of materials make up sedimentary rocks
- What the processes that form sedimentary rocks are
- How sedimentary rocks record past conditions

VOCABULARY

sediment p. 517

EXPLORE Particle Layers

What happens as rock particles settle in water?

PROCEDURE

1. Pour 2 cups of water into the jar.
2. Add the gravel and sand to the water.
3. Shake the jar for a few seconds and then set it down on a counter. Observe and record what happens to the materials in the water.

MATERIALS
- jar
- measuring cup
- water
- 1/3 cup gravel
- 1/3 cup sand

WHAT DO YOU THINK?
- What determines how the materials settle to the bottom of the jar?
- In a lake, how would a mixture of different-sized rock particles settle to the bottom?

Some rocks form from rock particles.

If the sand grains on a beach become naturally cemented together, they form a sedimentary rock called sandstone. Most sedimentary rock forms as sandstone does—from loose material that gets pressed together or cemented into rock. Sedimentary rock forms in other ways, too.

Sedimentary rock takes its name from the word *sediment*, which means "something that settles." **Sediments** are materials that settle out of water or air. In addition to loose pieces of rocks and minerals, pieces of plant and animal remains can also make up sediments. Sedimentary rocks develop from layers of sediments that build up on land or underwater.

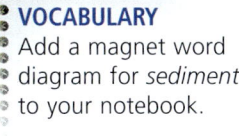

VOCABULARY
Add a magnet word diagram for *sediment* to your notebook.

 What types of material can make up sediments?

Chapter 15: **Rocks** 517

Forming and Transporting Rock Particles

A sandy ocean beach, a gravel bar in a river, and a muddy lake bottom all consist mainly of rock particles. These particles were broken away from rocks by the action of water or wind or a combination of both. Such particles may vary in size from boulders to sand to tiny bits of clay.

Just as water washes mud off your hands as it runs over them, rainwater washes away rock particles as it flows downhill. The water carries these rock particles to streams and rivers, which eventually empty into lakes or oceans. Strong winds also pick up sand and rock dust and carry them to distant places.

RESOURCE CENTER
CLASSZONE.COM
Find information on sedimentary rocks.

As winds or water currents slow down, rock particles settle on the land or at the bottom of rivers, lakes, and oceans. The sediments form layers as larger particles settle first, followed by smaller ones.

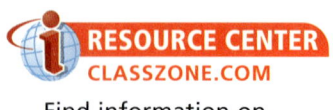

Forming Loose Sediments into Rocks

If you have ever watched workers building a road, you know that they first put down layers of gravel and other materials. Then they press the layers together, using a huge roller. In a similar way, layers of sediments

Sorting Sediments by Size

Fast-moving water can move large particles of sediment. As the water slows, the sediment particles settle from it by size.

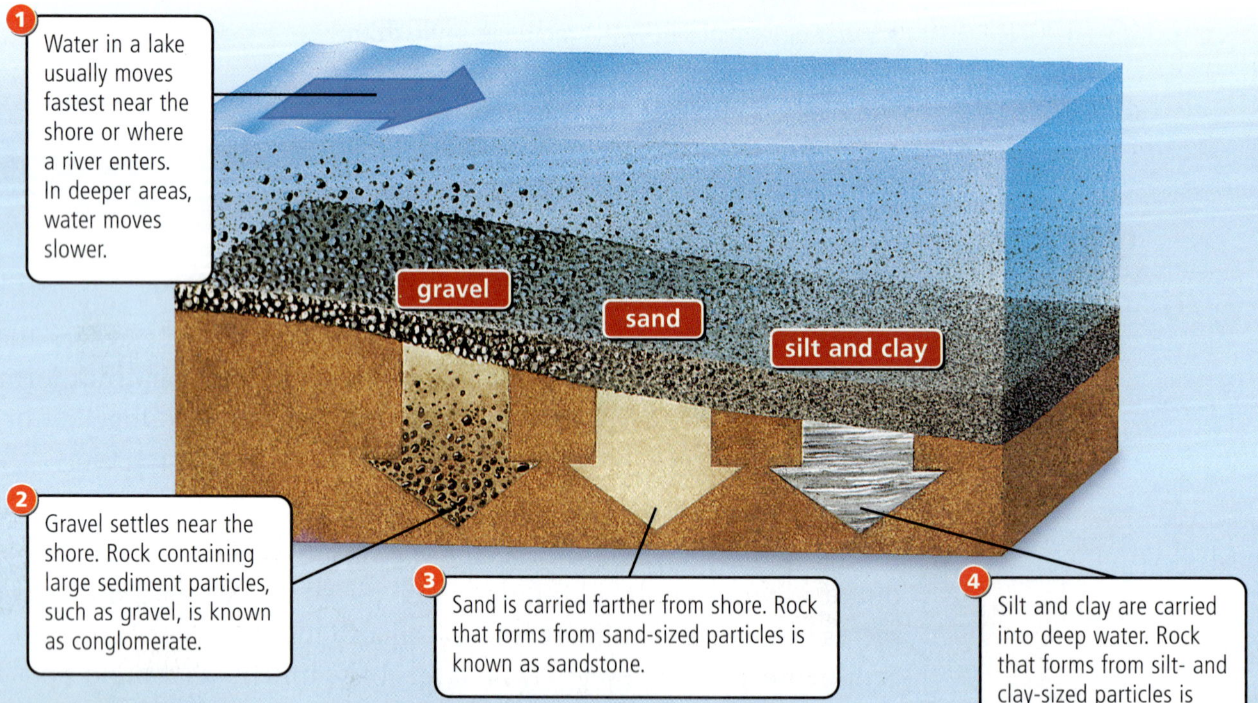

1 Water in a lake usually moves fastest near the shore or where a river enters. In deeper areas, water moves slower.
gravel
sand
silt and clay
2 Gravel settles near the shore. Rock containing large sediment particles, such as gravel, is known as conglomerate.
3 Sand is carried farther from shore. Rock that forms from sand-sized particles is known as sandstone.
4 Silt and clay are carried into deep water. Rock that forms from silt- and clay-sized particles is known as shale.

READING VISUALS Is shale more likely to form near the shore or near the middle of a big lake or ocean?

composed of rock particles may get pressed together to form rock. One layer gets buried by another, and then another. The overlying layers apply pressure to, or press down on, the sediments underneath.

Small particles of sediment, such as silt and clay, may be formed into rock by pressure alone. In other sedimentary rocks the particles are held together by minerals that have crystallized between them, acting as cement. Over a long time, these processes transform loose sediments into sedimentary rocks.

 What are two processes that can change sediments into rocks?

Some rocks form from plants or shells.

Processes similar to the ones that produce sedimentary rocks from rock particles also produce rocks from shells or plant remains. These remains are fossils. A fossil is the remains or trace of an organism from long ago.

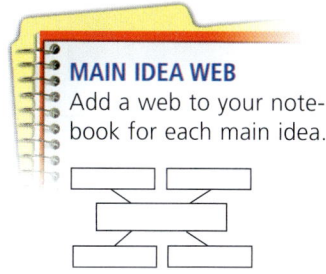

MAIN IDEA WEB
Add a web to your notebook for each main idea.

Coal

If you look at a piece of coal through a magnifying glass, you may be able to make out the shapes of bits of wood or leaves. That is because coal is made up of remains of plants—dead wood, bark, leaves, stems, and roots. Coal is an unusual sedimentary rock because it forms from plants instead of earlier rocks.

The coal people use today started forming millions of years ago in swamps. As plants died, their remains fell upon the remains of earlier plants. Then layers of other sediments buried the layers of plant remains. The weight of the sediments above pressed the plant material into coal.

The dark layer in these rocks is coal.

Here, you can see fossils of ancient plants preserved in coal.

Chapter 15: **Rocks** 519

Limestone

Limestone is made up of carbonate minerals, such as calcite. The shells and skeletons of ocean organisms are formed of these minerals. When the organisms die, the shells and skeletons settle on the ocean floor as layers of sediment. Over time, the layers become buried, pressed together, and cemented to form limestone. The photographs below show how loose shells can become limestone.

These shells were made by ocean organisms.

READING TIP
Notice that limestone made up of cemented shells and the limestone in coral reefs were both formed by ocean organisms.

1 The shells get cemented together into limestone as some of their minerals dissolve and re-form.

2 Individual shells become harder to see as minerals in the limestone continue to dissolve and re-form.

3 Over time, what was once loose sediment becomes limestone with no recognizable shells.

The famous white cliffs of Dover, England, consist of a type of limestone called chalk. The limestone began to form millions of years ago, when the land was under the ocean. The rock developed from shells of tiny organisms that float in the ocean. Most limestone comes from shells and skeletons of ocean organisms. The materials the organisms use to build their shells and skeletons are present in ocean water because they were dissolved from earlier rocks. Like almost all sedimentary rock, limestone forms from material that came from older rocks.

Coral reefs also consist of limestone that comes from organisms. However, in the case of reefs, the limestone is produced directly as coral organisms build their skeletons one on top of another. In the formation of coral, the rock does not go through a loose-sediment stage.

The skeletons of these tiny coral organisms eventually make huge coral reefs.

Some rocks form when dissolved minerals re-form from water.

If you have grown crystals in a container, you know that some substances can dissolve in water and then re-form as the water evaporates. The same process happens in nature. Some sedimentary rocks are made up of minerals that crystallized as water dried up.

The water in oceans, lakes, rivers, and streams contains minerals that came from rocks. Some of these minerals are in solid form. As rainwater washes over rocks, it picks up pieces of minerals and rock particles and carries them into streams and rivers, where many of them settle to the bottom. However, some of the minerals dissolve in the water and are carried along with it.

Water often flows through cracks in rock that is near Earth's surface. As water moves through limestone, some of the rock dissolves. A large open space, or cave, can be left in the rock. As the water flows and drips through the cave, some of it evaporates. The new limestone that forms can take many odd and beautiful shapes.

Sometimes minerals crystallize along the edges of lakes and oceans where the climate is dry and a lot of water evaporates quickly. Over time, the minerals build up and form layers of sedimentary rock. Rock salt and gypsum form in this way. Under the city of Detroit, for example, is a large bed of rock salt that developed when part of an ancient ocean dried up.

Water is shaping this limestone cavern. Water dissolves and transports minerals, then leaves the minerals behind as it evaporates.

CHECK YOUR READING How are the origins of rock salt and some limestone similar?

These limestone towers in Mono Lake, California, formed underwater. They are now above the surface because the lake level has dropped.

INVESTIGATE Rock Layers

How do sedimentary rocks form in layers?
PROCEDURE

1. Prepare the plaster of Paris by mixing it with the water.
2. Mix 2 tablespoons of the gravel with 2 tablespoons of the plaster of Paris and pour the mixture into the paper cup.
3. Mix the sand with 2 tablespoons of the plaster of Paris and the food coloring. Add the mixture to the paper cup, on top of the gravel mixture.
4. Mix the rest of the gravel with the rest of the plaster of Paris. Add the mixture to the paper cup, on top of the sand mixture.
5. After the mixtures harden for about 5 minutes, tear apart the paper cup and observe the layers.

WHAT DO YOU THINK?
- How is the procedure you used to make your model similar to the way sedimentary rock forms?
- Describe how similar layers of real rock could form.

CHALLENGE How would you create a model to show the formation of fossil-rich limestone?

SKILL FOCUS
Modeling

MATERIALS
- 1 paper cup
- 3 mixing cups
- 6 tbs plaster of Paris
- 3 tbs water
- 4 tbs gravel
- 2 tbs sand
- 3 drops food coloring

TIME
20 minutes

Sedimentary rocks show the action of wind and water.

READING TIP
Notice that sedimentary rocks are laid down in layers. As conditions in an area change, so do the characteristics of the layers.

Sedimentary rocks are laid down in layers, with the oldest layers on the bottom. A geologist studying layers of sedimentary rocks can tell something about what conditions were like in the past. For instance, fossils of fish or shells in a layer of rock show that the area was covered by a lake or an ocean long ago.

Fossils are not the only way to tell something about what past conditions were like. The sediments themselves contain a great deal of information. For example, a layer of sedimentary rock may contain sediment particles of different sizes. The largest particles are at the very bottom of the layer. Particles higher in the layer become increasingly smaller. A layer like this shows that the water carrying the sediment was slowing down. The largest particles dropped out when the water was moving quickly. Then smaller and smaller particles dropped out

522 Unit 4: Earth's Surface

Crossbeds	Ripples	Mud Cracks
 The tilted layers in these sandstone rocks are called crossbeds. The layers were once moving sand dunes.	Ripples image. The surface of this sandstone preserves ancient sand ripples.	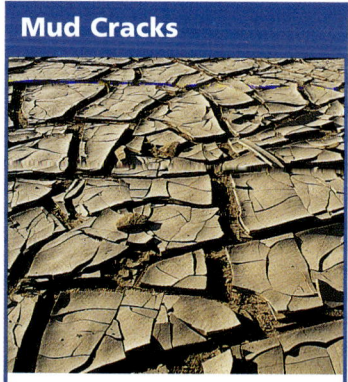 As wet silt and clay dry out, cracks develop on the surface of the sediment.

as the water slowed. This type of layer is often created by a flood, when a large amount of water is at first moving quickly.

Sedimentary rocks can give information about the directions in which long-ago wind or water currents were traveling when sediments settled from them. Sand can be laid down in tilted layers on the slopes of sand dunes or sandbars. Sand can also form ripples as water or wind moves over its surface. If the sand has been buried and cemented into sandstone, a geologist can examine it and tell the direction in which the water or wind was moving.

Some rocks made of clay or silt have cracks that developed when the mud from which they formed dried out. Mud cracks show that the rocks formed in areas where wet periods were followed by dry periods.

CHECK YOUR READING What could a geologist learn by finding rocks that have ripples or mud cracks?

15.3 Review

KEY CONCEPTS

1. What types of material can make up sediments?
2. Describe the three processes by which sedimentary rocks form.
3. Describe how a sedimentary rock can show how fast water was flowing when its sediments were laid down.

CRITICAL THINKING

4. **Infer** Why is coal called a fossil fuel?
5. **Analyze** How could the speed of flowing water change to lay down alternating layers of sand and mud?

CHALLENGE

6. **Synthesize** How is it possible for a single sedimentary rock to contain rock particles, animal shells, and minerals that crystallized from water?

Chapter 15: **Rocks** 523

KEY CONCEPT
15.4 Metamorphic rocks form as existing rocks change.

◀ **BEFORE, you learned**
- Igneous rocks form as molten rock cools
- Sedimentary rocks form from earlier rocks

▶ **NOW, you will learn**
- How a rock can change into another type of rock
- How new minerals can grow in existing rocks

VOCABULARY
metamorphism p. 524
recrystallization p. 525
foliation p. 528

THINK ABOUT

How does a rock change into another kind of rock?

Examine a sample of shale and a sample of schist (shihst). Shale, a sedimentary rock, can change into schist. Think about how this change could occur without the shale's melting or breaking apart. Make a prediction about what process changes shale into schist.

Heat and pressure change rocks.

When you cook popcorn, you use heat to increase the pressure within small, hard kernels until they explode into a fluffy snack. Cooking popcorn is just one example of the many ways in which heat and pressure can change the form of things—even things like rocks.

The process in which an existing rock is changed by heat or pressure—or both—is called **metamorphism** (MEHT-uh-MAWR-FIHZ-uhm). The original sedimentary or igneous rock is called the parent rock. The resulting rock is a metamorphic rock. Even a metamorphic rock can be a parent rock for another type of metamorphic rock.

Many of the metamorphic rocks people use were once sedimentary rocks. Limestone is the parent rock of marble, which is used by builders and artists. Shale can be the parent rock of schist, which can be a source of the gemstone garnet. Some schists are a source of the mineral graphite, which is used in pencils.

READING TIP

Rocks change into other rocks by the process of metamorphism. A similar word, *metamorphosis*, refers to what happens when a caterpillar changes into a butterfly.

 Give an example of a way people use metamorphic rocks.

During metamorphism, rocks undergo many changes. One type of change occurs when pressure causes a rock's minerals to flatten out in one direction. Other changes can occur in a rock's minerals, but the rock remains solid. Rocks do not melt when they undergo metamorphism. If the temperature gets high enough to melt the rock, the end result is an igneous rock, not a metamorphic rock.

Heat and pressure can break the bonds that join atoms in minerals. Then the atoms can join together differently as new bonds form. This process is called **recrystallization.** It has two main results. First, individual mineral crystals can grow larger as more atoms join their crystal structures. Second, atoms can combine in different ways, and new minerals can form in place of older ones. For example, shale is a sedimentary rock that is formed from silt and clay. During recrystallization, garnet can form from these materials.

How Rocks Change

Because pressure and temperature increase with depth, rocks change when they are buried deeper in the crust.

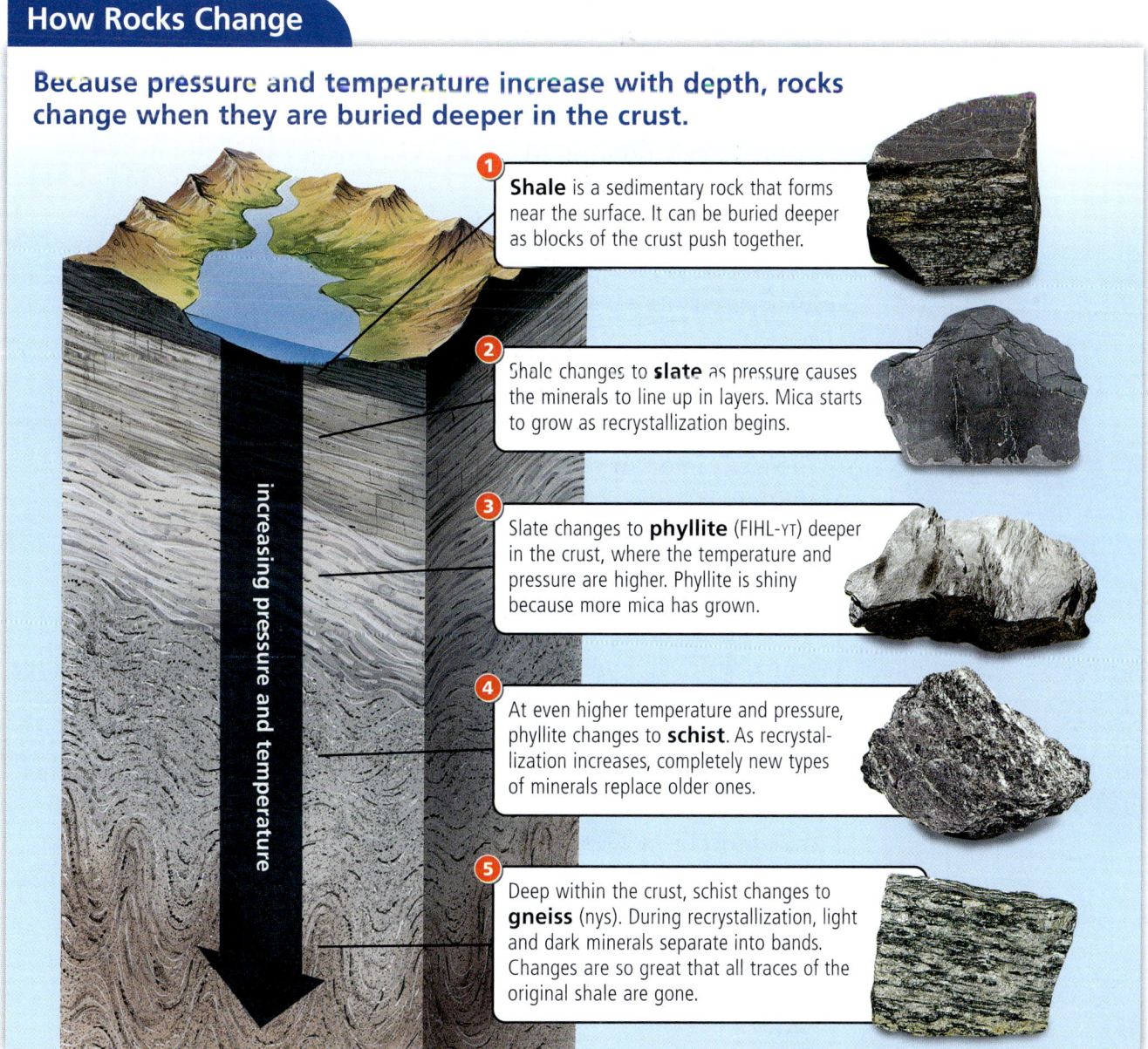

1. **Shale** is a sedimentary rock that forms near the surface. It can be buried deeper as blocks of the crust push together.

2. Shale changes to **slate** as pressure causes the minerals to line up in layers. Mica starts to grow as recrystallization begins.

3. Slate changes to **phyllite** (FIHL-yt) deeper in the crust, where the temperature and pressure are higher. Phyllite is shiny because more mica has grown.

4. At even higher temperature and pressure, phyllite changes to **schist**. As recrystallization increases, completely new types of minerals replace older ones.

5. Deep within the crust, schist changes to **gneiss** (nys). During recrystallization, light and dark minerals separate into bands. Changes are so great that all traces of the original shale are gone.

Chapter 15: **Rocks** 525

INVESTIGATE Metamorphic Changes

How can pressure and temperature change a solid?

PROCEDURE

1. Use a vegetable peeler to make a handful of wax shavings of three different colors. Mix the shavings.
2. Use your hands to warm the shavings, and then squeeze them into a wafer.

WHAT DO YOU THINK?

- Describe what happened to the wax shavings.
- How do the changes you observed resemble metamorphic changes in rocks?

CHALLENGE What changes that occur in metamorphic rocks were you unable to model in this experiment?

SKILL FOCUS
Modeling

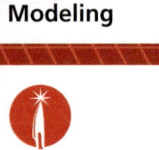

MATERIALS
- 3 candles of different colors
- vegetable peeler

TIME
10 minutes

Metamorphic changes occur over large and small areas.

The types of metamorphic changes that occur depend on the types of parent rocks and the conditions of temperature and pressure. When both high temperature and high pressure are present, metamorphic changes can occur over very large areas. When only one of these conditions is present, changes tend to occur over smaller areas.

Change over Large Areas

Most metamorphic changes occur over large areas in which both temperature and pressure are high. An example is a region where large blocks of rock are pressing together and pushing up mountain ranges. This process can affect an area hundreds of kilometers wide and tens of kilometers deep. In such an area, rocks are buried, pressed together, bent, and heated. The pressure and heat cause the rocks to undergo metamorphism. Generally, the deeper below the surface the rocks are, the greater the metamorphic changes that occur in them. For example, a sedimentary rock may change to slate near the surface but become gneiss deep inside a mountain.

 Where can metamorphic changes occur over large areas?

526 Unit 4: Earth's Surface

Change over Small Areas

Some metamorphic changes occur over small areas. For example, magma can push into rocks underground, or surface rock can be covered by a lava flow. The magma or lava heats the rock it is in contact with, causing recrystallization. These changes are mainly due to high temperature, not pressure. The rocks get roasted but not squeezed. The thickness of rock changed by the heat can range from less than one meter to several hundred meters, depending on the amount and temperature of the molten rock.

Small areas of metamorphic rock can also be formed by high pressure alone. At or near Earth's surface, rocks move and grind past one another during earthquakes. Rocks that grind together in this way can be subjected to high pressures that cause metamorphic changes.

Find information on metamorphic rocks.

Metamorphic Changes

Changes can occur over hundreds of kilometers or over just a few centimeters.

Changes over Large Areas

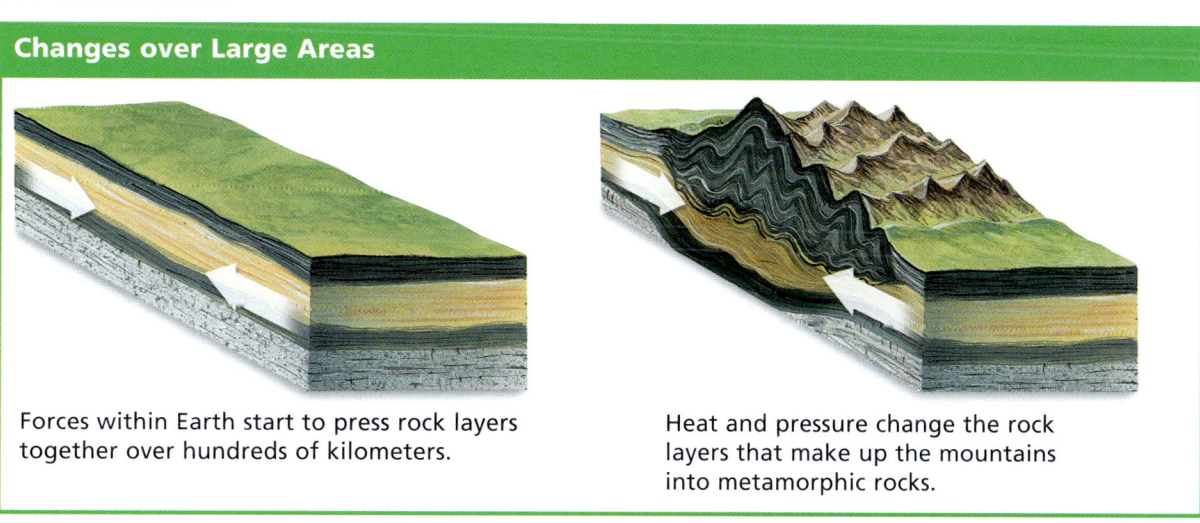

Forces within Earth start to press rock layers together over hundreds of kilometers.

Heat and pressure change the rock layers that make up the mountains into metamorphic rocks.

Changes over Small Areas

Magma can push into rock layers and cause changes over areas ranging from a few centimeters to tens of meters.

The magma is hot enough to bake the surrounding rocks into metamorphic rocks.

READING VISUALS Compare how heat and pressure cause changes over the large and small areas shown above.

Chapter 15: **Rocks** 527

Most metamorphic rocks develop bands of minerals.

VOCABULARY
Add a magnet word diagram for *foliation* to your notebook.

Some buildings have floors covered with tiles of the metamorphic rock slate. This rock is especially useful for tiles because it displays foliation, a common property of metamorphic rocks. **Foliation** is an arrangement of minerals in flat or wavy parallel bands. Slate can be split into thin sheets along the boundaries between its flat bands of minerals.

You may be familiar with the word *foliage*. Both *foliage* and *foliation* come from the Latin word *folium*, meaning "leaf." Foliated rocks either split easily into leaflike sheets or have bands of minerals that are lined up and easy to see.

Foliated Rocks

Foliation develops when rocks are under pressure. Foliation is common in rocks produced by metamorphic changes that affect large areas. However, as you will see, a metamorphic rock that consists almost entirely of one type of mineral does not show foliation.

Foliation in Metamorphic Rocks

Metamorphic rocks that contain several minerals develop foliation under pressure.

phyllite

Phyllite is a foliated metamorphic rock that contains several types of minerals.

marble

Marble is a nonfoliated metamorphic rock that consists almost entirely of only one mineral.

Foliated

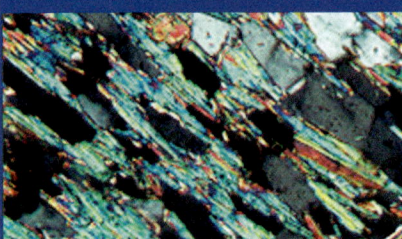

Using a microscope, you can see that the minerals are lined up in bands.

Nonfoliated

The mineral crystals in this rock are not lined up.

READING VISUALS Compare the pictures of the minerals in the foliated rock and the nonfoliated rock. What is different about their arrangements?

Foliation develops when minerals flatten out or line up in bands. At low levels of metamorphism, the bands are extremely thin, as in slate. With higher pressure and temperature, the mineral mica can grow and make the rock look shiny, as is common in phyllite and schist. At even higher levels of metamorphism, the minerals in the rock tend to separate into light and dark bands, like those in gneiss.

 How do rocks change as foliation develops?

Nonfoliated Rocks

Metamorphic rocks that do not show foliation are called nonfoliated rocks. One reason a metamorphic rock may not display foliation is that it is made up mainly of one type of mineral, so that different minerals cannot separate and line up in layers. One common nonfoliated metamorphic rock is marble, which develops from limestone. Marble is used as a decorative stone. It is good for carving and sculpting. Because marble is nonfoliated, it does not split into layers as an artist is working with it. Another example of a nonfoliated rock is quartzite. It forms from sandstone that is made up almost entirely of pieces of quartz.

Another reason that a metamorphic rock may lack foliation is that it has not been subjected to high pressure. Hornfels is a metamorphic rock that can form when a rock is subjected to high temperatures. Hornfels, which often forms when magma or lava touches other rock, is nonfoliated.

 What are two reasons a metamorphic rock might not show foliation?

KEY CONCEPTS

1. What conditions can cause a sedimentary or igneous rock to change into a metamorphic rock?
2. How do new minerals grow within existing rocks?
3. Why do bands of minerals develop in most metamorphic rocks?

CRITICAL THINKING

4. **Draw Conclusions** Would gneiss be more likely to form at shallow depths or at great depths where mountains are being pushed up? Why?
5. **Infer** Would you expect to find foliated or nonfoliated metamorphic rocks next to a lava flow? Why?

CHALLENGE

6. **Synthesize** What features of sedimentary rocks are unlikely to be found in metamorphic rocks? What features of metamorphic rocks do not occur in sedimentary rocks?

CHAPTER INVESTIGATION

Rock Classification

OVERVIEW AND PURPOSE In this activity you will examine rock samples and refer to a rock classification key. You will classify each sample as igneous, sedimentary, or metamorphic.

▶ Procedure

1. Make a data table like the one shown on the **Science Notebook** page.

2. Get a numbered rock sample. Record its number in your data table.

3. Observe the sample as a whole. Then closely examine it with the hand lens. Record in your table all visible properties of the sample. For example, include properties such as mineral or sediment size, layering, or banding.

step 3

4. Look at the Rock Classification Key. Each item in the key consists of paired statements. Start with item 1 of the key. Choose the statement that best describes the rock you are examining. Look at the end of the statement and then go to the item number indicated.

MATERIALS
- magnifying glass
- 6–8 rock samples
- Rock Classification Key

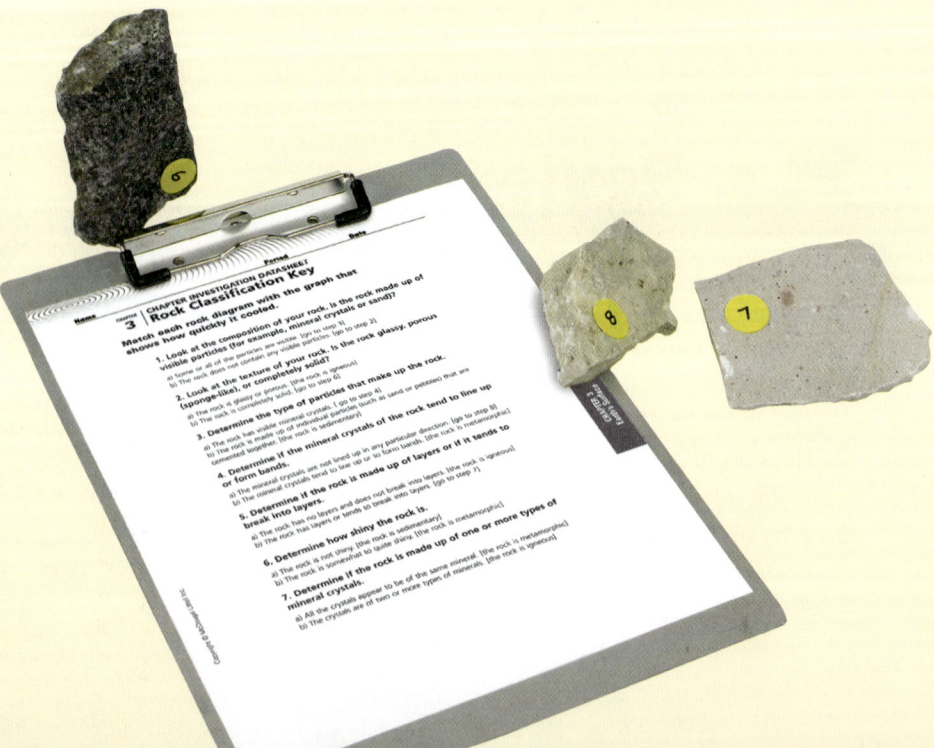

530 Unit 4: Earth's Surface

5 Examine the rock sample again and choose the statement that best describes the rock.

6 Continue to work through the key until your choices lead you to a classification that fits your rock. Repeat steps 2–5 for each of the numbered samples.

Observe and Analyze — Write It Up

1. **INTERPRET** Referring to the Rock Classification Key and the observations you recorded, write the type of each rock in your data table.

2. **IDENTIFY LIMITS** What problems, if any, did you experience in applying the key? Which samples did not seem to fit easily into a category? How could you improve the key?

Conclude — Write It Up

1. **COMPARE AND CONTRAST** How are igneous and metamorphic rocks similar? How can you tell them apart?

2. **ANALYZE** Examine a sample of sedimentary rock in which visible particles are cemented together. In addition to sight, what other sense could help you classify this sample?

3. **APPLY** What have you learned from this investigation that would help you make a classification key that someone else could follow? How might you make a key to classify the recordings in a music collection? Write two pairs of numbered statements that would start the classification process.

INVESTIGATE Further

CHALLENGE Make a rock classification key to distinguish between rocks from Earth and rocks from the Moon. Here are some facts to consider. The surface of the Moon was once covered by a thick layer of magma. The Moon has no running water and almost no atmosphere. Minerals on Earth often contain tiny amounts of water. Minerals on the Moon almost never contain any water. The Moon does not have processes that can cause a rock to change into another type of rock.

An astronaut photographed this rock on the Moon. The rock sits in a valley that formed 4 billion years ago. The rock may not have changed or moved since that time.

Rock Classification
Observe and Analyze
Table 1. Rock Sample Properties

Sample Number	Description of Visible Properties	Rock Type

Conclude

Chapter 15: **Rocks** 531

Chapter Review

the BIG idea

Rocks change into other rocks over time.

KEY CONCEPTS SUMMARY

1 The rock cycle shows how rocks change.

Processes at Earth's surface and heat within Earth cause rocks to change into other types of rocks.

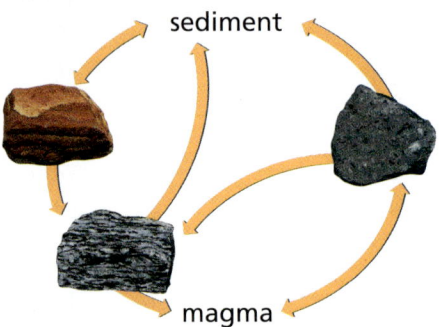

VOCABULARY
rock p. 503
rock cycle p. 506
igneous rock p. 506
sedimentary rock p. 506
metamorphic rock p. 506

---

2 Igneous rocks form from molten rock.

As molten rock cools, minerals crystallize and form igneous rocks.

Extrusive igneous rocks cool quickly at Earth's surface.

Intrusive igneous rocks cool slowly within Earth.

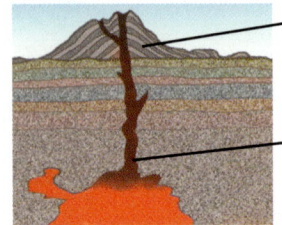

VOCABULARY
intrusive igneous rock p. 511
extrusive igneous rock p. 511

---

3 Sedimentary rocks form from earlier rocks.

Layers of sedimentary rocks form as
• sediments are pressed or cemented together
• dissolved minerals re-form as water evaporates

Larger particles of sediment settle faster.

VOCABULARY
sediment p. 517

---

4 Metamorphic rocks form as existing rocks change.

Metamorphic rocks form as the structures of the parent rocks change and as their minerals recrystallize.

shale

heat and pressure

schist

VOCABULARY
metamorphism p. 524
recrystallization p. 525
foliation p. 528

532 Unit 4: Earth's Surface

Reviewing Vocabulary

Copy and complete the chart below. There may be more than one correct response.

Rock Type	Forms From	Example / Identifying characteristic
intrusive igneous rock	magma	1.
		large mineral crystals
extrusive igneous rock	2.	basalt
		3.
sedimentary rock	4.	conglomerate
		contains large pieces of earlier rocks
sedimentary rock	ancient plant remains	5.
		may contain plant fossils
sedimentary rock	6.	limestone
		7.
foliated metamorphic rock	parent rock that has several types of minerals	8.
		minerals are lined up
nonfoliated metamorphic rock	9.	10.
		11.

Reviewing Key Concepts

Multiple Choice *Choose the letter of the best answer.*

12. The three groups of rock are sedimentary, metamorphic, and
    a. limestone
    b. granite
    c. igneous
    d. coal

13. The rock cycle shows how rocks continually
    a. increase in size
    b. increase in number
    c. become more complex
    d. change over time

14. Which kind of rock forms when molten rock cools?
    a. metamorphic
    b. sedimentary
    c. igneous
    d. extrusive

15. An existing rock can change into another type of rock when it is subjected to great
    a. pressure
    b. winds
    c. flooding
    d. foliation

16. Which kind of rock forms by recrystallization?
    a. intrusive igneous
    b. extrusive igneous
    c. sedimentary
    d. metamorphic

17. Geologists classify an igneous rock on the basis of its crystal size and the amount of _____ its minerals contain.
    a. carbon
    b. silica
    c. sediment
    d. foliation

18. Pieces of rock can settle from water and get cemented into
    a. metamorphic rock
    b. sedimentary rock
    c. igneous rock
    d. extrusive rock

19. Rock salt is an example of a sedimentary rock that develops from dissolved minerals as
    a. water evaporates
    b. magma cools
    c. sediments break down
    d. sand settles in water

Short Answer *Write a short answer to each question.*

20. What is the difference between a rock and a mineral?

21. Compare the distribution of rock types at Earth's surface to their distribution in the entire crust. How are any differences related to processes occurring in the rock cycle?

22. How is the texture of an igneous rock related to the rate at which it cooled?

Thinking Critically

Use the photograph below to answer the next four questions.

23. **INFER** What are the dark markings on the rock?

24. **OBSERVE** Which of the three groups of rocks does this rock belong to? How do you know?

25. **SUMMARIZE** Describe the process by which this rock most likely formed.

26. **PREDICT** If this rock were subjected to metamorphism, how might it change?

27. **APPLY** Copy and complete the concept map below.

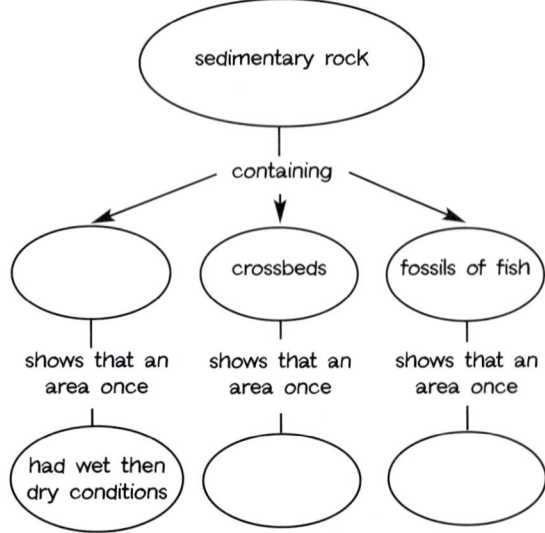

PREDICT Which of the three rock types—igneous, sedimentary, or metamorphic—would you be most likely to find in each area?

Area	Rock Type
28. the bottom of a large lake	
29. older rock surrounding an igneous intrusion	
30. a lava flow from a volcano	
31. a part of the surface that was once deep within a mountain range	
32. the sides of a cave	

the BIG idea

33. **ANALYZE** Look again at the photograph on pages 500–501. Using your knowledge of the rock cycle, draw a diagram showing how sedimentary rocks can form cliffs at Earth's surface. Then add to the diagram by showing how the rocks are likely to change over time.

34. **CONNECT** Describe how material in a rock near the top of a mountain can later be used by an ocean organism in forming its shell.

UNIT PROJECTS

Check your schedule for your unit project. How are you doing? Be sure that you've placed data or notes from your research in your project folder.

Standardized Test Practice

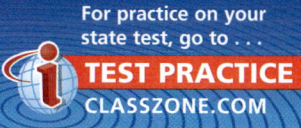

Analyzing a Diagram

This diagram shows a simple version of the rock cycle. Use it to answer the questions below.

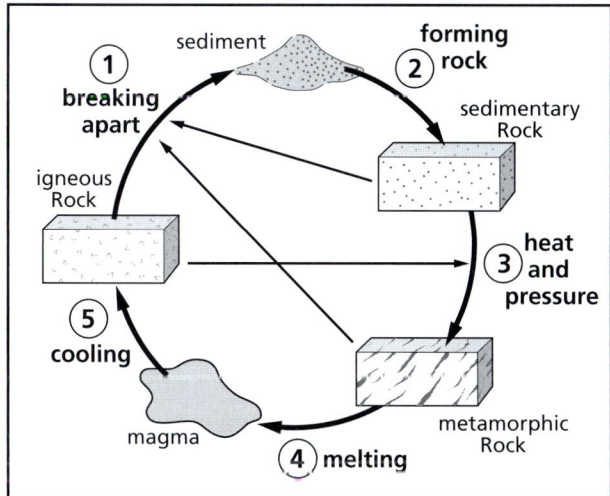

1. Where are loose materials developing into rock?
   a. 1   c. 4
   b. 2   d. 5

2. Where are sand and other small particles forming from rock?
   a. 1   c. 4
   b. 2   d. 5

3. Where is magma developing into rock?
   a. 1   c. 4
   b. 3   d. 5

4. Where is molten rock forming?
   a. 1   c. 4
   b. 3   d. 5

5. Where are heat and pressure changing solid rock into another type of rock without melting it?
   a. 1   c. 4
   b. 3   d. 5

6. According to the diagram, what can happen to sedimentary rock?
   a. It can become sediment or magma.
   b. It can become igneous rock or magma.
   c. It can become sediment or metamorphic rock.
   d. It can become sediment, metamorphic rock, or magma.

7. How could you change the diagram to show that igneous rock can become magma again?
   a. Add an arrow from igneous rock to metamorphic rock.
   b. Add an arrow from heat and pressure to igneous rock.
   c. Add an arrow from igneous rock to melting.
   d. Add an arrow from melting to igneous rock.

8. What must happen to rock that formed inside Earth before it can become sediment?
   a. It must reach the surface as rock above it wears away.
   b. It must become magma and erupt from a volcano.
   c. Heat and pressure must change it into sediment.
   d. It must become sedimentary rock while inside Earth.

Extended Response

Answer the two questions below in detail. Include some of the terms shown in the word box. In your answers underline each term you use.

| pressed together   buried   mineral crystals |
| cooling time |

9. Most sedimentary rock forms from pieces of existing rocks. Explain why coal is an unusual sedimentary rock and how coal forms.

10. Melba is trying to decide whether an igneous rock formed deep inside Earth or at the surface. What should she look for? Why?

Chapter 15: **Rocks** 535

TIMELINES in Science

HISTORY OF THE EARTH SYSTEM

Systems of air, water, rocks, and living organisms have developed on Earth during the planet's 4.6 billion years of history. More and more scientists have become curious about how these parts of Earth work together. Today, scientists think of these individual systems as part of one large Earth system.

The timeline shows a few events in the history of the Earth system. Scientists have developed special tools and procedures to study this history. The boxes below the timeline show how technology has led to new knowledge about the Earth system and how that knowledge has been applied.

4.6 BYA
Earth Forms in New Solar System
The Sun and nine planets, one of which is Earth, form out of a cloud of gas and dust. Earth forms and grows larger as particles collide with it. While Earth is still young, a slightly smaller object smashes into it and sends huge amounts of material flying into space. Some of this material forms a new object—the Moon.

EVENTS

5 BYA
Billion Years Ago

APPLICATIONS AND TECHNOLOGY

TECHNOLOGY
Measuring Age of Solar System
In 1956, Clair C. Patterson published his estimate that the solar system was 4.55 billion years old. Previously, scientists had learned how to use radioactive elements present in rocks to measure their ages. Patterson used this technology to determine the ages of meteorites that were formed along with the solar system and later fell to Earth. Since 1956, scientists have studied more samples and used new technologies. These studies have generally confirmed Patterson's estimate.

This iron meteorite fell in Siberia in 1947. Data from such meteorites are clues to how and when the solar system formed.

4.4 BYA
Earth Gains Atmosphere, Ocean
Earth's atmosphere forms as volcanoes release gases, including water vapor. Though some gases escape into space, Earth's gravity holds most of them close to the planet. The atmosphere contains no free oxygen. As Earth starts to cool, the water vapor becomes water droplets and falls as rain. Oceans begin to form.

3.5 BYA
Organisms Affect Earth System
Tiny organisms use energy from sunlight to make their food, giving off oxygen as a waste product. The oxygen combines with other gases and with minerals. It may be another billion years before free oxygen starts to build up in the atmosphere.

1.8 BYA
First Supercontinent Forms
All of Earth's continents come together to form one huge supercontinent. The continents and ocean basins are still moving and changing. This supercontinent will break apart in the future. New supercontinents will form and break apart as time goes on.

4 BYA   **3** BYA   **2** BYA   **1** BYA

APPLICATION
Measuring Ozone Levels
In 1924, scientists developed the first instrument to measure ozone, the Dobson spectrophotometer. Ozone is a molecule that consists of three oxygen atoms. In the 1970s, scientists realized that levels of ozone in the upper atmosphere were falling. Countries have taken action to preserve the ozone layer, which protects organisms—including humans—from dangerous ultraviolet radiation. Today, computers process ozone data as they are collected and make them quickly available to researchers around the world.

A Dobson spectrophotometer measures the total amount of ozone in the atmosphere above it.

600 MYA
New Animals Appear
The first multi-celled animals appear in the ocean. Some types of these animals are fastened to the sea floor and get food from particles in water flowing past them. Worms are the most complex type of animals to appear so far.

480 MYA
Plants Appear on Land
The earliest plants appear. These plants, perhaps similar to mosses, join the lichens that already live on land. Through photosynthesis, plants and lichens decrease the amount of carbon dioxide in the air and increase the amount of oxygen. These changes may lead to the eventual development of large, complex animals.

200 MYA
Atlantic Ocean Forms
Earth's continents, which have been combined into the supercontinent Pangaea, start to separate. As what are now the continents of North America and Africa spread apart, the Atlantic Ocean forms.

| 800 MYA | 600 MYA | 400 MYA | 200 MYA |

Million Years Ago

TECHNOLOGY
Ocean-Floor Core Samples
In the 1960s, scientists began drilling holes into the sea floor to collect long cores, or columns, of sediment and rock. The cores give clues about Earth's climate, geology, and forms of life for millions of years.

The research ship *JOIDES Resolution* has a drilling rig built into it. Equipment attached to the rig is lowered to the sea floor to collect core samples.

12,000 years ago
Earth Emerges from Ice—Again
Earth's temperature warms slightly. Kilometers-thick ice sheets that formed during the latest of Earth's many ice ages start to melt. Forests and grasslands expand. Sea level rises about 100 meters (330 ft), and the ocean floods the edges of the continents.

1972
New View of Earth
Harrison "Jack" Schmitt, an astronaut traveling 24,000 kilometers (15,000 mi) above Earth, takes a photograph. It is the first to show Earth fully lit by the Sun, and the image is sometimes called the Blue Marble. It helps people see the planet as one system.

 RESOURCE CENTER
CLASSZONE.COM
Learn more about the Earth system.

100 MYA   Today

INTO THE FUTURE

In almost every area of life, from music to food to sports, the world has become more connected. Science is no exception. In the past century, scientists have begun to monitor the ozone layer. They have realized that the processes that cause continents to change positions also cause earthquakes and volcanic eruptions to occur.

Changes in technology are likely to help scientists increase their understanding of the Earth system. For example, instruments on artificial satellites measure changes in clouds, ocean life, and land temperatures. These types of data help scientists understand how changes in one part of Earth affect other parts.

ACTIVITIES

Taking a Core Sample
Add layers of damp sand of different colors to a paper cup. Switch cups with a partner. Press a clear straw through the sand, put your finger over the top of the straw, and pull the straw out. Determine the order in which your partner added the sand layers. How would you know if there was a layer of sand that did not go across the entire cup?

Writing About Science
Imagine you are living in microgravity like the astronauts on the International Space Station. Write a detailed description of two hours of your day.

APPLICATION
International Space Station
The International Space Station has laboratories in which scientists study Earth, the solar system, and the universe. Also, scientists are doing research to better understand the effects of very low gravity on people. This work is part of an effort to develop the life-support systems needed for people to remain in space a long time. Eventually it might aid in the further exploration of space by humans.

CHAPTER 16 Weathering and Soil Formation

Natural forces break rocks apart and form soil, which supports life.

How is rock related to soil?

Key Concepts

SECTION 1 Mechanical and chemical forces break down rocks.
Learn about the natural forces that break down rocks.

SECTION 2 Weathering and organic processes form soil.
Learn about the formation and properties of soil.

SECTION 3 Human activities affect soil.
Learn how land use affects soil and how soil can be protected and conserved.

Internet Preview

CLASSZONE.COM

Chapter 16 online resources: Content Review, two Visualizations, two Resource Centers, Math Tutorial, Test Practice

EXPLORE the BIG idea

Ice Power

Fill a plastic container to the top with water and seal the lid tightly. Place it in the freezer overnight. Check on your container the next morning.

Observe and Think What happened to the container? Why?

Getting the Dirt on Soil

Remove the top and bottom of a tin can. Be careful of sharp edges. Measure and mark 2 cm from one end of the can. Insert the can 2 cm into the ground, up to the mark. Fill the can with water and time how long it takes for the can to drain. Repeat the procedure in a different location.

Observe and Think What do you think affects how long it takes for soil to absorb water?

Internet Activity: Soil Formation

Go to **ClassZone.com** to watch how soil forms. Learn how materials break down and contribute to soil buildup over time.

Observe and Think What do rocks and soil have in common? What do organic matter and soil have in common?

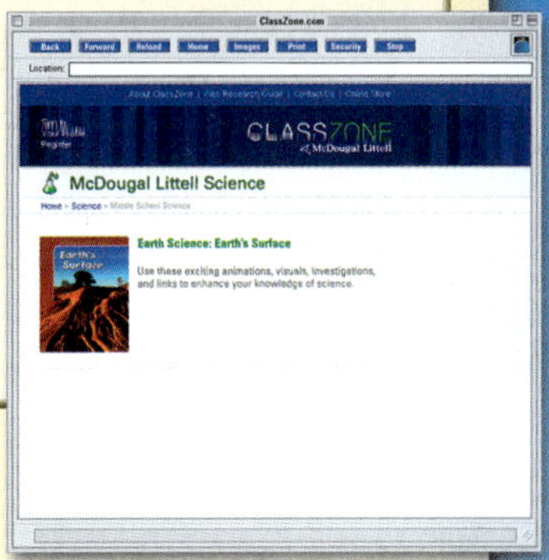

Soil Conservation Code: MDL016

Chapter 16: **Weathering and Soil Formation** 541

CHAPTER 16
Getting Ready to Learn

◁ CONCEPT REVIEW

- The atmosphere, hydrosphere, biosphere, and geosphere interact to shape Earth's surface.
- Natural processes form, change, break down, and re-form rocks.

◁ VOCABULARY REVIEW

cleavage p. 481
fracture p. 481
rock p. 503
rock cycle p. 506
sediment p. 517

CONTENT REVIEW
CLASSZONE.COM
Review concepts and vocabulary.

▷ TAKING NOTES

COMBINATION NOTES

To take notes about a new concept, first make an informal outline of the information. Then make a sketch of the concept and label it so that you can study it later.

CHOOSE YOUR OWN STRATEGY

Take notes about new vocabulary terms, using one or more of the strategies from earlier chapters—**magnet word, word triangle,** or **description wheel.** Feel free to mix and match the strategies, or use an entirely different vocabulary strategy.

See the Note-Taking Handbook on pages R45–R51.

SCIENCE NOTEBOOK

NOTES

Causes of Mechanical Weathering
- Ice
- Pressure Release
- Plant Roots
- Moving Water

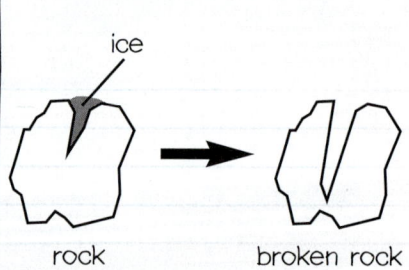
rock → broken rock

Description Wheel
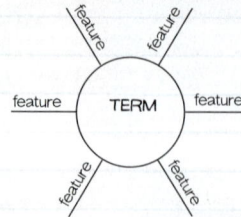

Word Triangle
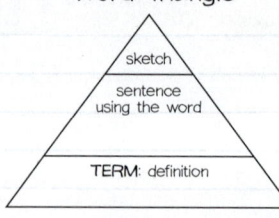

Magnet Word
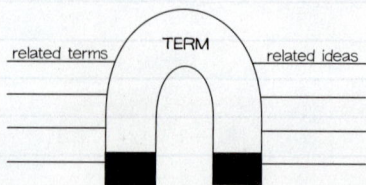

542 Unit 4: Earth's Surface

KEY CONCEPT

Mechanical and chemical forces break down rocks.

 BEFORE, you learned
- Minerals make up most rocks
- Different minerals have different properties
- Rocks are broken down to form sediments

 NOW, you will learn
- How mechanical weathering breaks down rocks
- How chemical weathering changes rocks
- What factors affect the rate at which weathering occurs

VOCABULARY

weathering p. 543
mechanical weathering p. 544
exfoliation p. 544
abrasion p. 544
chemical weathering p. 546

EXPLORE Mechanical Weathering

What causes rocks to break down?

PROCEDURE

1. Place a handful of rocks on a piece of dark-colored construction paper. Observe the rocks and take notes on their appearance.

2. Place the rocks in a coffee can. Put the lid on the can and shake the can forcefully for 2 minutes, holding the lid tightly shut.

3. Pour the rocks onto the construction paper. Observe them and take notes on any changes in their appearance.

MATERIALS
- coffee can with lid
- rocks
- dark-colored construction paper

WHAT DO YOU THINK?
- What happened to the rocks and why?
- What forces in nature might affect rocks in similar ways?

Weathering breaks rocks into smaller pieces.

Think about the tiniest rock you have ever found. How did it get so small? It didn't start out that way! Over time, natural forces break rocks into smaller and smaller pieces. If you have ever seen a concrete sidewalk or driveway that has been cracked by tree roots, you have seen this process. The same thing can happen to rocks.

Weathering is the process by which natural forces break down rocks. In this section you will read about two kinds of weathering. One kind occurs when a rock is physically broken apart—like the cracked sidewalk. Another kind occurs when a chemical reaction changes the makeup of a rock.

VOCABULARY
Remember to add *weathering* to your notebook, using the vocabulary strategy of your choice.

Chapter 16: **Weathering and Soil Formation** 543

Mechanical weathering produces physical changes in rocks.

If you smash a walnut with a hammer, you will break it into a lot of small pieces, but you will not change what it is. Even though the pieces of the walnut are no longer connected together, they are still composed of the same materials. **Mechanical weathering**—the breaking up of rocks by physical forces—works in much the same way. In this natural process, physical forces split rocks apart but do not change their composition—what they are made of. Ice wedging, pressure release, plant root growth, and abrasion can all cause mechanical weathering.

❶ Ice Wedging When water freezes, it expands. When water freezes in the cracks and pores of rocks, the force of its expansion is strong enough to split the rocks apart. This process, which is called ice wedging, can break up huge boulders. Ice wedging is common in places where temperatures rise above and fall below the freezing point for water, which is 0°C (32°F).

❷ Pressure Release Rock deep within Earth is under great pressure from surrounding rocks. Over time, Earth's forces can push the rock up to the surface, or the overlying rocks and sediment can wear away. In either case, the pressure inside the rock is still high, but the pressure on the surface of the rock is released. This release of pressure causes the rock to expand. As the rock expands, cracks form in it, leading to exfoliation. **Exfoliation** (ehks-FOH-lee-AY-shuhn) is a process in which layers or sheets of rock gradually break off. This process is sometimes called onion-skin weathering, because the rock surface breaks off in thin layers similar to the layers of an onion.

❸ Plant Root Growth Trees, bushes, and other plants may take root in cracks in rocks. As the roots of these plants grow, they wedge open the cracks. The rock—even if it is large—can be split completely apart.

❹ Abrasion Water can wear down rocks on riverbeds and along shorelines by abrasion. **Abrasion** (uh-BRAY-zhuhn) is the process of wearing down by friction, the rubbing of one object or surface against another. The force of moving water alone can wear away particles of rock. Water also causes rocks to tumble downstream. The tumbling rocks wear down as they grind against the riverbed and against each other. Ocean waves beating against a rocky shore also wear down rocks by abrasion.

△ CHECK YOUR READING How does moving water weather rocks?

RESOURCE CENTER CLASSZONE.COM
Learn more about weathering.

READING TiP
The word *expand* means "to increase in size or volume."

Mechanical Weathering

Ice wedging, pressure release, plant root growth, and abrasion can all break apart rocks.

1 Ice Wedging

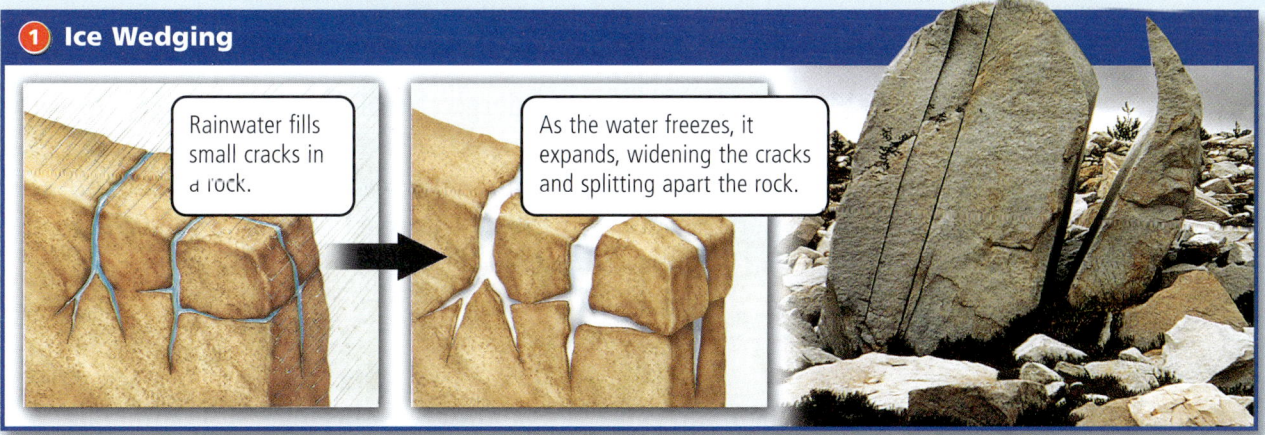

Rainwater fills small cracks in a rock.

As the water freezes, it expands, widening the cracks and splitting apart the rock.

2 Pressure Release

Earth's forces can push rock that formed deep underground up to the surface.

The release of pressure causes the rock to expand and crack.

3 Plant Root Growth

When plants grow in cracks in a rock, their roots can widen the cracks and force the rock apart.

4 Abrasion

Flowing water can move rocks, causing them to rub together and wear down into rounded shapes.

READING VISUALS What evidence of mechanical weathering can you see in each photograph above?

Chemical weathering changes the mineral composition of rocks.

Watch chemical weathering in action.

If you have seen an old rusty nail, you have witnessed the result of a chemical reaction and a chemical change. The steel in the nail contains iron. Oxygen in air and water react with the iron to form rust.

Minerals in rocks also undergo chemical changes when they react with water and air. **Chemical weathering** is the breakdown of rocks by chemical reactions that change the rocks' makeup, or composition. When minerals in rocks come into contact with air and water, some dissolve and others react and are changed into different minerals.

Dissolving

Water is the main cause of chemical weathering. Some minerals completely dissolve in ordinary water. The mineral halite, which is the same compound as table salt, dissolves in ordinary water. Many more minerals dissolve in water that is slightly acidic—like lemonade. In the atmosphere, small amounts of carbon dioxide dissolve in rainwater. The water and carbon dioxide react to form a weak acid. After falling to Earth, the rainwater moves through the soil, picking up additional

INVESTIGATE Chemical Weathering

What is necessary for rust to form?
PROCEDURE

1. Place a piece of steel wool in a cup filled to the top with water. Place a second piece of steel wool in a cup with a small amount of water. The water should touch but not cover the steel wool. Place a third piece in a cup with no water.

2. Allow the three cups to sit overnight. Observe the appearance of the steel wool in each container the next day.

WHAT DO YOU THINK?
- What happened to the steel wool in each cup?
- Judging by the appearance of the pieces of steel wool, what do you think is necessary for rusting to occur?

CHALLENGE Tear the steel wool that rusted most apart and compare the appearances of the inside and the outside. Why might the inside and the outside look different?

SKILL FOCUS
Identifying variables

MATERIALS
- steel wool
- 3 cups
- water

TIME
15 minutes

546 Unit 4: Earth's Surface

About 100 Years Ago | **Today**

READING VISUALS — **INFER** This ancient stone monument was moved from a desert in Egypt to New York City in 1881. How and why has it changed?

carbon dioxide from decaying plants. The slightly acidic water breaks down minerals in rocks. In the process, the rocks may also break apart into smaller pieces.

Air pollution can make rainwater even more acidic than it is naturally. Power plants and automobiles produce gases such as sulfur dioxide and nitric oxide, which react with water vapor in the atmosphere to form acid rain. Acid rain causes rocks to weather much faster than they would naturally. The photographs above show how acid rain can damage a granite column in just a hundred years.

Rusting

The oxygen in the air is also involved in chemical weathering. Many common minerals contain iron. When these minerals dissolve in water, oxygen in the air and the water combines with the iron to produce iron oxides, or rust. The iron oxides form a coating that colors the weathered rocks like those you see in the photograph of Oak Creek Canyon in Arizona.

CHECK YOUR READING — How is air involved in chemical weathering?

The rocks in Oak Creek Canyon are reddish because iron in the rocks reacted with water and air to produce iron oxides.

Chapter 16: **Weathering and Soil Formation** 547

COMBINATION NOTES
Record in your notes three factors that affect the rate at which rock weathers.

Weathering occurs at different rates.

Most weathering occurs over long periods of time—hundreds, thousands, or even millions of years. It can take hundreds or thousands of years for a very hard rock to wear down only a few millimeters—a few times the thickness of your fingernail. But the rate of weathering is not the same for all rocks. Factors such as surface area, rock composition, and location influence the rate of weathering.

Surface Area The more of a rock's surface that is exposed to air and water, the faster the rock will break down. A greater surface area allows chemical weathering to affect more of a rock.

① Over time, mechanical weathering breaks a rock into smaller pieces.

② As a result, more of the rock's surface is exposed to chemical weathering.

Rock Composition Different kinds of rock break down at different rates. Granite, for example, breaks down much more slowly than limestone. Both of these rocks are often used for tombstones and statues.

Climate Water is needed for chemical weathering to occur, and heat speeds up chemical weathering. As a result, chemical weathering occurs faster in hot, wet regions than it does in cold, dry regions. However, mechanical weathering caused by freezing and thawing occurs more in cold regions than in hot regions.

16.1 Review

KEY CONCEPTS
1. What is weathering?
2. What are four causes of mechanical weathering?
3. How do water and air help cause chemical weathering?
4. Describe three factors that affect the rate at which weathering occurs.

CRITICAL THINKING
5. **Infer** How does mechanical weathering affect the rate of chemical weathering?
6. **Predict** Would weathering affect a marble sculpture inside a museum? Explain your answer.

⚠ CHALLENGE
7. **Infer** The word *weather* is most commonly used to refer to the state of the atmosphere at a certain time. Why do you think the same word is used to refer to the breakdown of rocks?

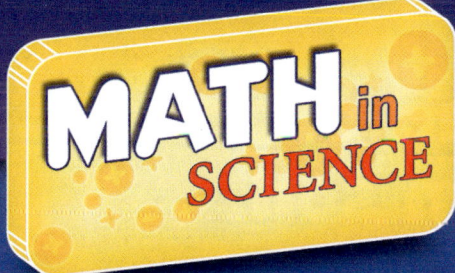

MATH in SCIENCE

MATH TUTORIAL
CLASSZONE.COM

Click on Math Tutorial for more help with finding the surface areas of rectangular prisms.

Weathering has broken apart these rocks in the Isles of Scilly, England.

SKILL: FINDING THE SURFACE AREA OF A RECTANGULAR PRISM

Rock Weathering

How quickly a rock weathers depends, in part, on its surface area. The greater the surface area, the more quickly the rock weathers. Do you think a rock will weather more quickly if you break it in half? You can find out by using a rectangular prism to represent the rock.

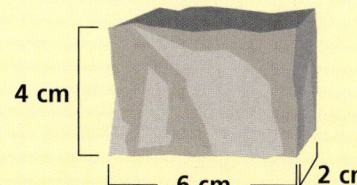

Example

To find the surface area of the prism, add the areas of its faces.

(1) Find the area of each face.

Area of top (or bottom) face: 6 cm × 2 cm = 12 cm²
Area of front (or back) face: 6 cm × 4 cm = 24 cm²
Area of right (or left) face: 4 cm × 2 cm = 8 cm²

(2) Add the areas of all six faces to find the surface area.

Surface area = 12 cm² + 12 cm² + 24 cm² + 24 cm² + 8 cm² + 8 cm²
= 88 cm²

ANSWER The surface area of the prism is 88 cm².

For the rock broken in half, you can use two smaller rectangular prisms to represent the two halves.

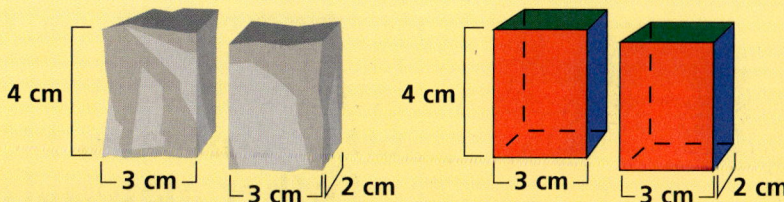

Answer the following questions.

1. What is the surface area of each of the smaller rectangular prisms?

2. How does the total surface area of the two smaller prisms compare with the surface area of the larger prism?

3. Will the rock weather more quickly in one piece or broken in half?

CHALLENGE If the two smaller prisms both broke in half, what would be the total surface area of the resulting four prisms?

 KEY CONCEPT
Weathering and organic processes form soil.

◀ **BEFORE, you learned**
- Weathering processes break down rocks
- Climate influences the rate of weathering

▶ **NOW, you will learn**
- What soil consists of
- How climate and landforms affect a soil's characteristics
- How the activities of organisms affect a soil's characteristics
- How the properties of soil differ

VOCABULARY

humus p. 551
soil horizon p. 552
soil profile p. 552

EXPLORE Soil Composition
What makes soils different?

PROCEDURE

1. Spread some potting soil on a piece of white paper. Spread another type of soil on another piece of white paper.
2. Examine the two soil samples with a hand lens. Use the tweezers to look for small pieces of rock or sand, humus, and clay. Humus is brown or black, and clay is lighter in color. Record your observations.

WHAT DO YOU THINK?
- How do the two soil samples differ? How are they alike?
- What might account for the differences between the two soils?

MATERIALS
- potting soil
- local soil sample
- white paper (2 pieces)
- hand lens
- tweezers

Soil is a mixture of weathered rock particles and other materials.

Soil may not be the first thing you think of when you wake up in the morning, but it is a very important part of your everyday life. You have spent your whole life eating food grown in soil, standing on soil, and living in buildings built on soil. Soil is under your feet right now—or at least there used to be soil there before the building you are in was constructed. In this section you will learn more about the world of soil beneath your feet.

 Why is soil important?

550 Unit 4: Earth's Surface

Soil Composition

Soil is a mixture of four materials: weathered rock particles, organic matter, water, and air. Weathered rock particles are the main ingredient of soil. Soils differ, depending on what types of rock the rock particles came from—for example, granite or limestone.

Water and air each make up about 20 to 30 percent of a soil's volume. Organic matter makes up about 5 percent. The word *organic* (awr-GAN-ihk) means "coming from living organisms." Organic matter in soil comes from the remains and waste products of plants, animals, and other living organisms. For example, leaves that fall to a forest floor decay and become part of the soil. The decayed organic matter in soil is called **humus** (HYOO-muhs).

All soils are not the same. Different soils are made up of different ingredients and different amounts of each ingredient. In the photographs below, the black soil contains much more decayed plant material than the red soil. The black soil also contains more water. The kind of soil that forms in an area depends on a number of factors, including

- the kind of rock in the area
- the area's climate, or overall weather pattern over time
- the landforms in the area, such as mountains and valleys
- the plant cover in the area
- the animals and other organisms in the area
- time

The composition of a soil determines what you can grow in it, what you can build on it, and what happens to the rainwater that falls on it.

VOCABULARY
A description wheel would be a good choice for taking notes about the term *humus*.

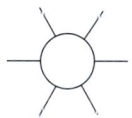

READING VISUALS **COMPARE AND CONTRAST** These two soils look different because they contain different ingredients. How would you describe their differences?

Chapter 16: **Weathering and Soil Formation** 551

Soil Horizons

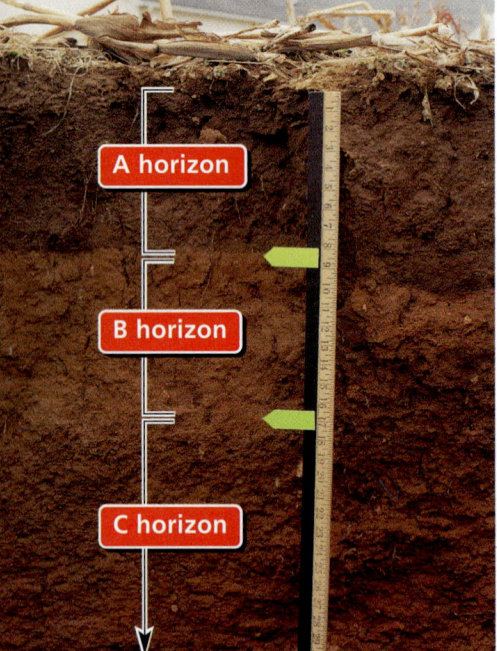

This soil profile in Hagerstown, Maryland, shows distinct A, B, and C horizons.

If you dig a deep hole in the ground, you might notice that the deeper soil looks different. As you dig down, you will find larger rock particles that are less weathered. There is also less organic matter in deeper soil.

Soil develops in a series of horizontal layers called soil horizons. A **soil horizon** is a layer of soil with properties that differ from those of the layer above or below it. Geologists label the main horizons A, B, and C. In some places there may also be a layer of dead leaves and other organic matter at the surface of the ground.

- **The A horizon** is the upper layer of soil and is commonly called topsoil. It contains the most organic matter of the three horizons. Because of the humus the A horizon contains, it is often dark in color.

- **The B horizon** lies just below the A horizon. It has little organic matter and is usually brownish or reddish in color. It contains clay and minerals that have washed down from the A horizon.

- **The C horizon** is the deepest layer of soil. It consists of the largest and least-weathered rock particles. Its color is typically light yellowish brown.

The soil horizons in a specific location make up what geologists call a **soil profile.** Different locations can have very different soil profiles. The A horizon, for example, may be very thick in some places and very thin in others. In some areas, one or more horizons may even be missing from the profile. For example, a soil that has had only a short time to develop might be missing the B horizon.

 **CHECK YOUR READING** What are soil horizons?

Climate and landforms affect soil.

COMBINATION NOTES Record in your notes four categories of soil that form in different climate regions.

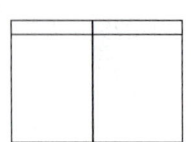

Different kinds of soils form in different climates. The soil that forms in a hot, wet climate is different from the soil of a cold, dry climate. Climate also influences the characteristics and thickness of the soil that develops from weathered rock. Tropical, desert, temperate, and arctic soils are four types of soil that form in different climate regions.

The shape of the land also affects the development of soil. For example, mountain soils may be very different from the soils in nearby valleys. The cold climate on a mountain results in slow soil formation, and the top layer of soil continually washes down off the slopes. As a result, mountain slopes have soils with thin A horizons that cannot support large plants. The soil that washes down the slopes builds up in the surrounding valleys, so the valleys may have soils with thick A horizons that can support many plants.

552 Unit 4: Earth's Surface

World Soil Types

Different types of soils form in different climates.

Tropical Soils

Tropical soils form in warm, rainy regions. Heavy rains wash away minerals, leaving only a thin surface layer of humus. Tropical soils are not suitable for growing most crops.

Desert Soils

Desert soils form in dry regions. These soils are shallow and contain little organic matter. Because of the low rainfall, chemical weathering and soil formation occur very slowly in desert regions.

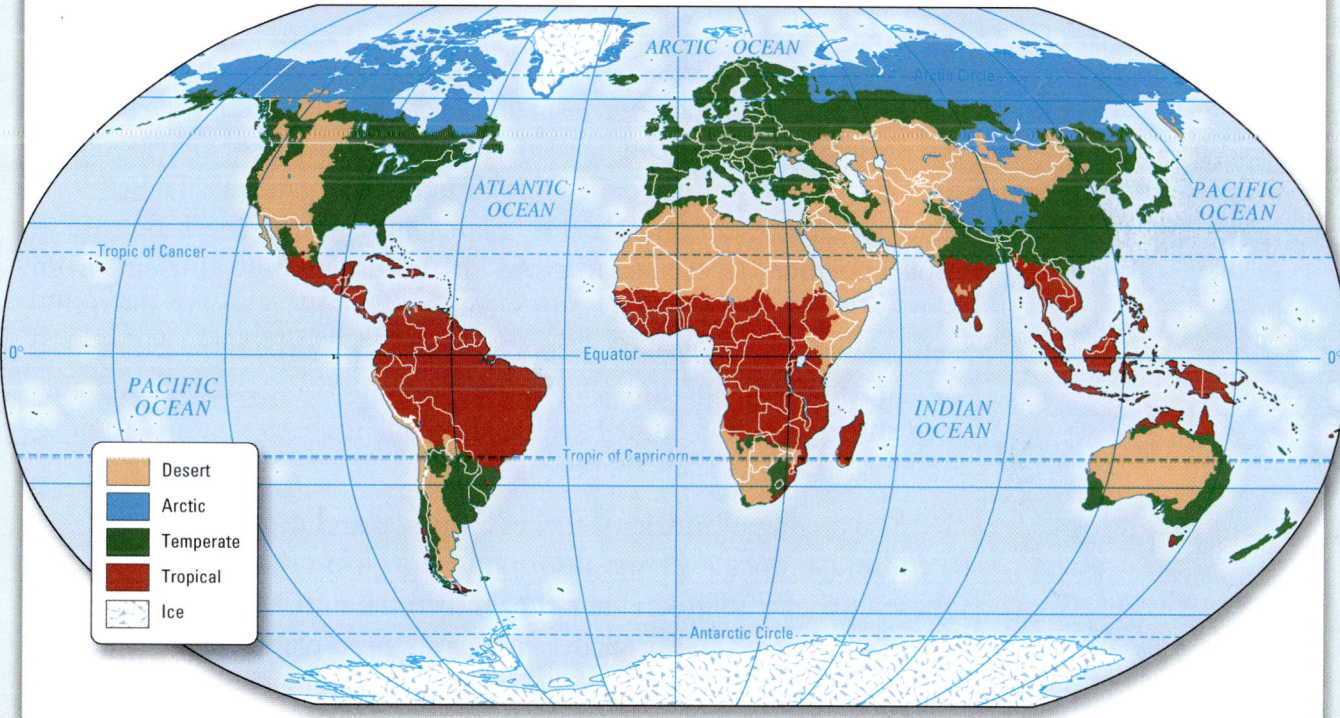

Legend:
- Desert
- Arctic
- Temperate
- Tropical
- Ice

Temperate Soils

Temperate soils form in regions with moderate rainfall and temperatures. Some temperate soils are dark-colored, rich in organic matter and minerals, and good for growing crops.

Arctic Soils

Arctic soils form in cold, dry regions where chemical weathering is slow. They typically do not have well-developed horizons. Arctic soils contain a lot of rock fragments.

The activities of organisms affect soil.

COMBINATION NOTES
Record in your notes three types of organisms that affect soil characteristics.

Under the ground beneath your feet is a whole world of life forms that are going about their daily activities. The living organisms in a soil have a huge impact on the soil's characteristics. In fact, without them, the soil would not be able to support the wide variety of plants that people depend on to live. The organisms that affect the characteristics of soils include plants, microorganisms (MY-kroh-AWR-guh-NIHZ-uhmz), and animals.

Plants, such as trees and grasses, provide most of the organic matter that gets broken down to form humus. Trees add to the organic matter in soil as they lose their branches and leaves. Trees and other plants also contribute to humus when they die and decompose, or break down.

 How are plants and humus related?

READING TIP
A decomposer is an organism that decomposes, or breaks down, dead plants and animals.

Microorganisms include decomposers such as bacteria and fungi (FUHN-jy). The prefix *micro-* means "very small." Microorganisms are so small that they can be seen only with a microscope. A spoonful of soil may contain more than a million microorganisms! These microorganisms decompose dead plants and animals and produce nutrients that plants need to grow. Plants absorb these nutrients from the soil through their roots. Nitrogen, for example, is one of the nutrients plants need to grow. Microorganisms change the nitrogen in dead organic matter—and nitrogen in the air—into compounds that plants can absorb and use. Some bacteria also contribute to the formation of soil by producing acids that break down rocks.

The cycling of nutrients through the soil and through plants is a continual process. Plants absorb nutrients from the soil and use those nutrients to grow. Then they return the nutrients to the soil when they die or lose branches and leaves. New plants then absorb the nutrients from the soil and start the cycle over again.

Animals such as earthworms, ants, termites, mice, gophers, moles, and prairie dogs all make their homes in the soil. All of these animals loosen and mix the soil as they tunnel through it. They create spaces in the soil, thereby adding to its air content and improving its ability to absorb and drain water. Burrowing animals also bring partly weathered rock particles to the surface of the ground, where they become exposed to more weathering. Just like plants, animals return nutrients to the soil when their bodies decompose after death.

 How do animals affect soil? Name at least three ways.

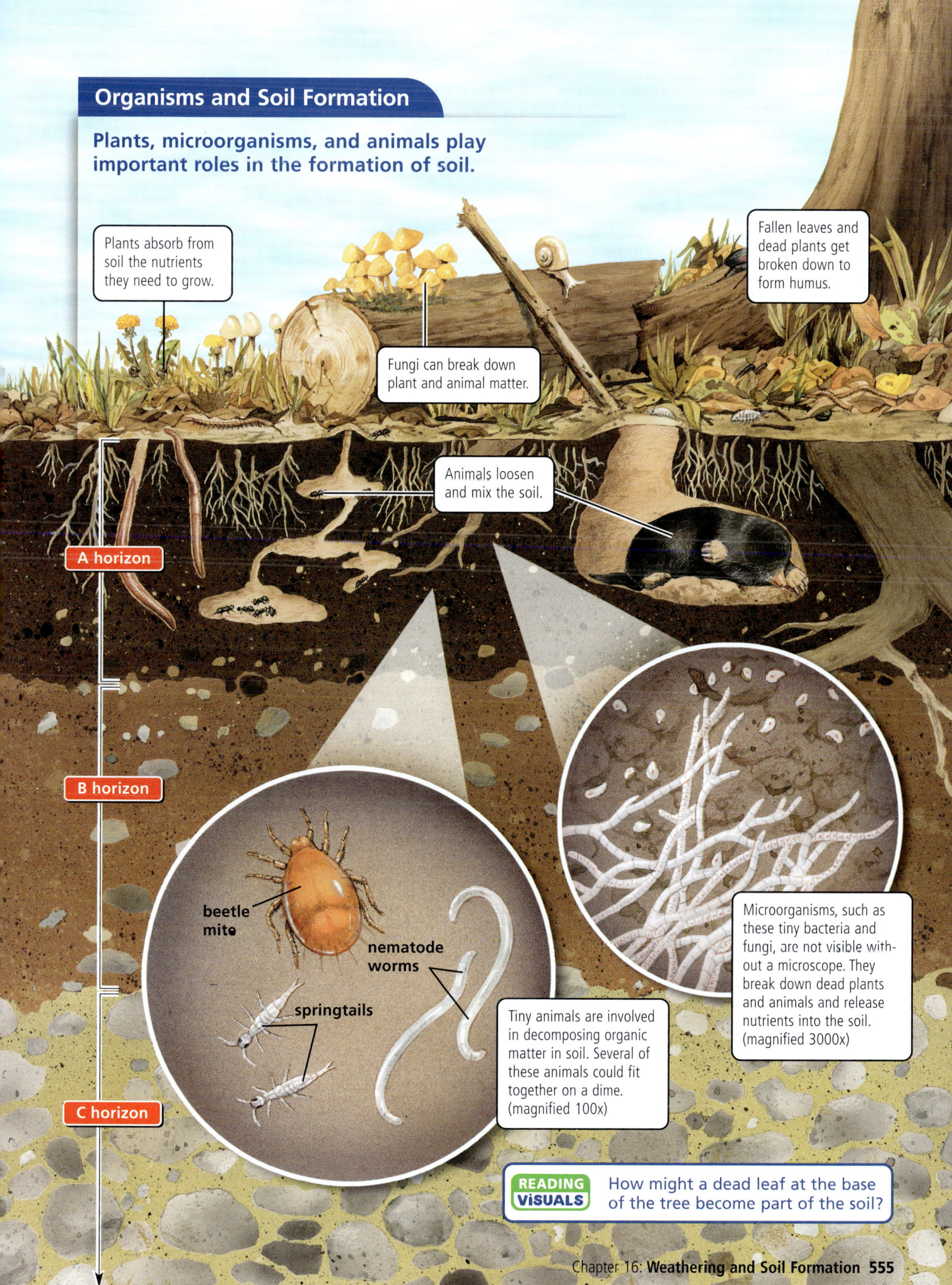

Properties of soil can be observed and measured.

Observations and tests of soil samples reveal what nutrients the soils contain and therefore what kinds of plants will grow best in them. Farmers and gardeners use this information to improve the growth of crops and other plants. Soil scientists study many soil properties, including texture, color, pore space, and chemistry.

Texture

The texture of a soil is determined by the size of the weathered rock particles it contains. Soil scientists classify the rock particles in soils into three categories, on the basis of size: sand, silt, and clay. Sand particles are the largest and can be seen without a microscope. Silt particles are smaller than sand particles—too small to be seen without a microscope. Clay particles are the smallest. Most soils contain a mixture of sand, silt, and clay. The texture of a soil influences how easily air and water move through the soil.

Soil Texture

The texture of a soil is determined by the amounts of sand, silt, and clay it contains.

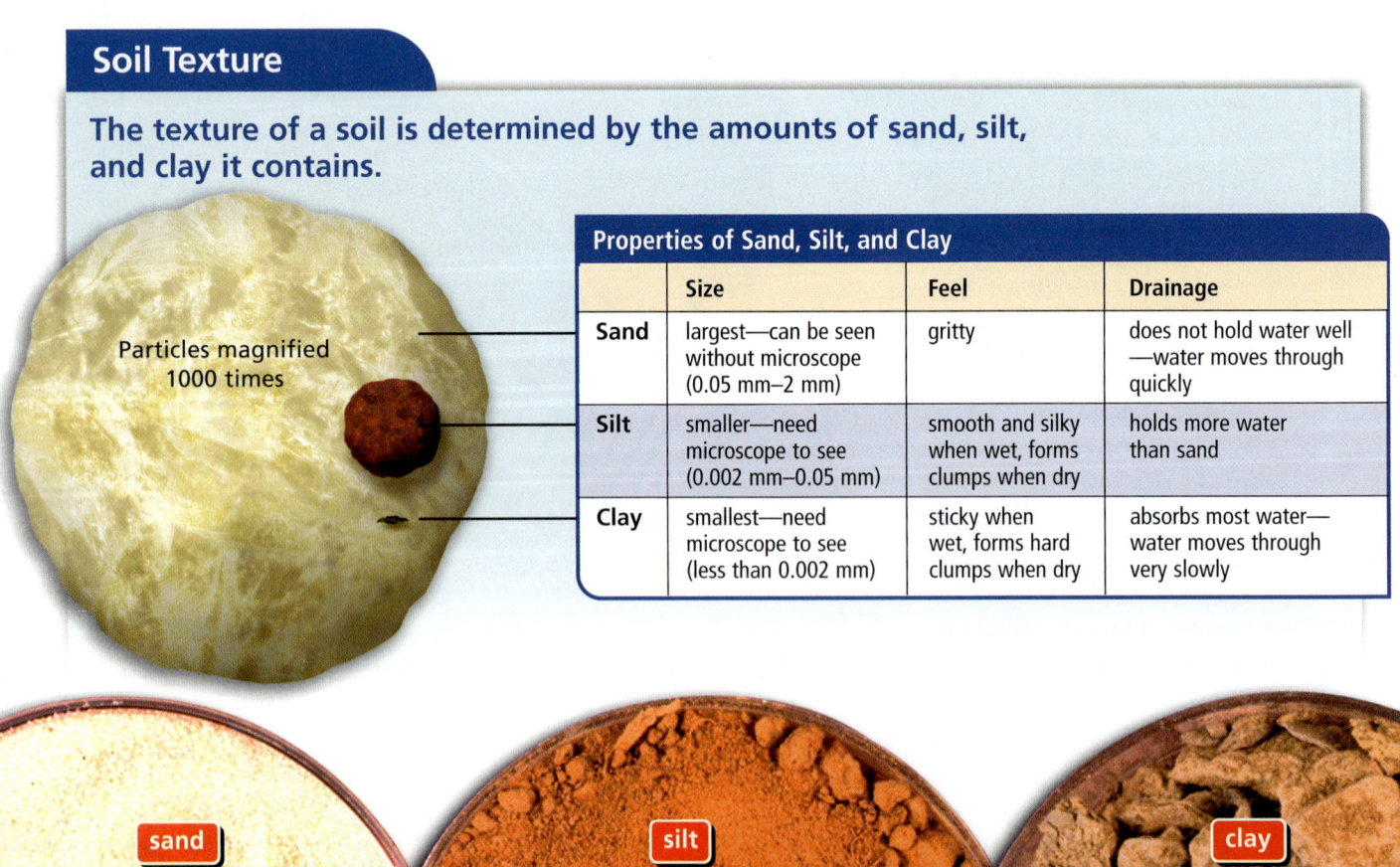

Particles magnified 1000 times

Properties of Sand, Silt, and Clay			
	Size	Feel	Drainage
Sand	largest—can be seen without microscope (0.05 mm–2 mm)	gritty	does not hold water well—water moves through quickly
Silt	smaller—need microscope to see (0.002 mm–0.05 mm)	smooth and silky when wet, forms clumps when dry	holds more water than sand
Clay	smallest—need microscope to see (less than 0.002 mm)	sticky when wet, forms hard clumps when dry	absorbs most water—water moves through very slowly

sand

silt

clay

Color

The color of a soil is a clue to its other properties. Soil colors include red, brown, yellow, green, black, and even white. Most soil colors come from iron compounds and humus. Iron gives soil a reddish color. Soils with a high humus content are usually black or brown. Besides indicating the content of a soil, color may also be a clue to how well water moves through the soil—that is, how well the soil drains. Bright-colored soils, for instance, drain well.

Investigate soil.

Pore Space

Pore space refers to the spaces between soil particles. Water and air move through the pore spaces in a soil. Plant roots need both water and air to grow. Soils range from about 25 to 60 percent pore space. An ideal soil for growing plants has 50 percent of its volume as pore space, with half of the pore space occupied by air and half by water.

This gardener is adding lime to the soil to make it less acidic.

Chemistry

Plants absorb the nutrients they need from the water in soil. These nutrients may come from the minerals or the organic matter in the soil. To be available to plant roots, the nutrients must be dissolved in water. How well nutrients dissolve in the water in soil depends on the water's pH, which is a measure of acidity. Farmers may apply lime to make soil less acidic. To make soil more acidic, an acid may be applied.

 How does soil acidity affect whether the nutrients in soil are available to plants?

16.2 Review

KEY CONCEPTS
1. What are the main ingredients of soil?
2. How do climate and landforms affect soils' characteristics?
3. How do the activities of organisms affect the characteristics of soil?
4. Describe four properties of soil.

CRITICAL THINKING
5. **Compare and Contrast** How would a soil containing a lot of sand differ from a soil with a lot of clay?
6. **Infer** Which would you expect to be more fertile, the soil on hilly land or the soil on a plain? Why?

CHALLENGE
7. **Synthesize** What kinds of roots might you expect to find on plants that grow in arctic soils? Why?

Chapter 16: **Weathering and Soil Formation** 557

CHAPTER INVESTIGATION

Testing Soil

OVERVIEW AND PURPOSE Soil is necessary for life. Whether a soil is suitable for farming or construction, and whether it absorbs water when it rains, depends on the particular properties of that soil. In this investigation you will
- test a soil sample to measure several soil properties
- identify the properties of your soil sample

▶ Procedure

PORE-SPACE TEST

1. Measure 200 mL of the dried soil sample in a graduated cylinder. Pour it into the jar.

2. Rinse the graduated cylinder, then fill it with 200 mL of water. Slowly pour the water into the jar until the soil is so soaked that any additional water would pool on top.

3. Record the amount of water remaining in the graduated cylinder. Then determine by subtraction the amount you added to the soil sample. Make a soil properties chart in your **Science Notebook** and record this number in it.

4. Discard the wet soil according to your teacher's instructions, and rinse the jar.

pH TEST AND DRAINAGE TEST

5. Cut off the top of a plastic bottle and use a rubber band to attach a piece of window screening over its mouth. Place the bottle top, mouth down, into the jar.

6. Use the graduated cylinder to measure 200 mL of soil, and pour the soil into the inverted bottle top.

7. Rinse the graduated cylinder, and fill it with 100 mL of water. Test the water's pH, using a pH test strip. Record the result in the "before" space in your soil properties chart.

8. Pour the water into the soil. Measure the amount of time it takes for the first drips to fall into the jar. Record the result in your soil properties chart.

step 5 — top of plastic bottle, jar, window screening

MATERIALS
- dried soil sample
- 250 mL graduated cylinder
- 1 qt jar, with lid
- water
- 2 L plastic bottle
- scissors
- window screening
- rubber band
- pH test strips
- clock with second hand
- *for Challenge:* Texture Flow Chart

558 Unit 4: Earth's Surface

9. Once the water stops dripping, remove the bottle top. Use a new pH strip to measure the pH of the water in the jar. Record this measurement in the "after" space in your soil properties chart and note any differences in the appearance of the water before and after its filtering through the soil.

10. Discard the wet soil according to your teacher's instructions, and rinse the jar.

PARTICLE-TYPE TEST

11. Add water to the jar until it is two-thirds full. Pour in soil until the water level rises to the top of the jar, then replace the lid. Shake the jar, and set it to rest undisturbed on a countertop overnight.

12. The next day, observe the different soil layers. The sample should have separated into sand (on the bottom), silt (in the middle), and clay (on the top). Measure the height of each layer, as well as the overall height of the three layers. Record your measurements in your soil properties chart.

13. Use the following formula to calculate the percentage of each kind of particle in the sample:

$$\frac{\text{height of layer}}{\text{total height of all layers}} \times 100$$

Record your results and all calculations in your soil properties chart.

Observe and Analyze [Write It Up]

1. **RECORD** Complete your soil properties chart.

2. **IDENTIFY** How did steps 1–3 test your soil sample's pore space?

3. **IDENTIFY** How did steps 5–9 test your soil sample's drainage rate?

Conclude [Write It Up]

1. **EVALUATE** In step 3 you measured the amount of space between the soil particles in your sample. In step 8 you measured how quickly water passed through your sample. Are these two properties related? Explain your answer.

2. **EVALUATE** Would packing down or loosening up your soil sample change any of the properties you tested? Explain your answer.

3. **INTERPRET** What happened to the pH of the water that passed through the soil? Why do you think that happened?

4. **ANALYZE** Look at the percentages of sand, silt, and clay in your sample. How do the percentages help to explain the properties you observed and measured?

INVESTIGATE Further

CHALLENGE Soil texture depends on the size of the weathered rock particles the soil contains. Use the Texture Flow Chart to determine the texture of your soil sample.

Testing Soil
Observe and Analyze
Table 1. Soil Properties Chart

Property	Result	Notes and Calculations
Pore space	__ mL water added	
pH	before: pH = __ after: pH = __	
Drainage	__ seconds	
Particle type	height of sand = __ cm height of silt = __ cm height of clay = __ cm total height = __ cm	

Conclude

16.3 Human activities affect soil.

KEY CONCEPT

BEFORE, you learned
- Soils consist mainly of weathered rock and organic matter
- Soils vary, depending on climate
- Organisms affect the characteristics of soil
- Soil properties can be measured

NOW, you will learn
- Why soil is a necessary resource
- How people's use of land affects soil
- How people can conserve soil

VOCABULARY

desertification p. 561

THINK ABOUT

How does land use affect soil?

Look outside for evidence of ways that people have affected the soil. Make a list of all the things that you can see or think of. Use your list to make a two-column table with the headings "Activity" and "Effects."

Soil is a necessary resource.

Soil helps sustain life on Earth—including your life. You already know that soil supports the growth of plants, which in turn supply food for animals. Therefore, soil provides you with nearly all the food you eat. But that's not all. Many other items you use, such as cotton clothing and medicines, come from plants. Lumber in your home comes from trees. Even the oxygen you breathe comes from plants.

Besides supporting the growth of plants, soil plays other life-sustaining roles. Soil helps purify, or clean, water as it drains through the ground and into rivers, lakes, and oceans. Decomposers in soil also help recycle nutrients by breaking down the remains of plants and animals, releasing nutrients that living plants use to grow. In addition, soil provides a home for a variety of living things, from tiny one-celled organisms to small mammals.

CHECK YOUR READING Why is soil a necessary resource?

Land-use practices can harm soil.

The way people use land can affect the levels of nutrients and pollution in soil. Any activity that exposes soil to wind and rain can lead to soil loss. Farming, construction and development, and mining are among the main activities that impact soil resources.

Farming

Farming is very important to society because almost all of the world's food is grown on farms. Over the 10,000 years humans have been farming, people have continually improved their farming methods. However, farming has some harmful effects and can lead to soil loss.

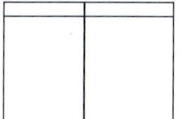

COMBINATION NOTES
Remember to take notes about how farming affects soil.

Farmers often add nutrients to soil in the form of organic or artificial fertilizers to make their crops grow better. However, some fertilizers can make it difficult for microorganisms in the soil to produce nutrients naturally. Fertilizers also add to water pollution when rainwater draining from fields carries the excess nutrients to rivers, lakes, and oceans.

Over time, many farming practices lead to the loss of soil. All over the world, farmers clear trees and other plants and plow up the soil to plant crops. Without its natural plant cover, the soil is more exposed to rain and wind and is therefore more likely to get washed or blown away. American farmers lose about five metric tons of soil for each metric ton of grain they produce. In many other parts of the world, the losses are even higher.

Another problem is overgrazing. Overgrazing occurs when farm animals eat large amounts of the land cover. Overgrazing destroys natural vegetation and causes the soil to wash or blow away more easily. In many dry regions of the world, overgrazing and the clearing of land for farming have led to desertification. **Desertification** (dih-ZUR-tuh-fih-KAY-shuhn) is the expansion of desert conditions in areas where the natural plant cover has been destroyed.

Exposed soil can be blown away by wind or washed away by rain.

The top of this hill in San Bernardino County, California, was cleared for a housing development. A house will be built on each flat plot of land.

Construction and Development

To make roads, houses, shopping malls, and other buildings, people need to dig up the soil. Some of the soil at construction sites washes or blows away because its protective plant cover has been removed. The soil that is washed or blown away ends up in nearby low-lying areas, in rivers and streams, or in downstream lakes or reservoirs. This soil can cause problems by making rivers and lakes muddy and harming the organisms that live in them. The buildup of soil on riverbeds raises the level of the rivers and may cause flooding. The soil can also fill up lakes and reservoirs.

Mining

Some methods of mining cause soil loss. For example, the digging of strip mines and open-pit mines involves the removal of plants and soil from the surface of the ground.

By exposing rocks and minerals to the air and to rainwater, these forms of mining speed up the rate of chemical weathering. In mining operations that expose sulfide minerals, the increased chemical weathering causes a type of pollution known as acid drainage. Abandoned mines can fill with rainwater. Sulfide minerals react with the air and the water to produce sulfuric acid. Then the acid water drains from the mines, polluting the soil in surrounding areas.

CHECK YOUR READING How do some methods of mining affect the soil?

To make this open-pit mine in Cananea, Mexico, plants and soil were removed from the surface of the ground.

562 Unit 4: Earth's Surface

Soil can be protected and conserved.

Soil conservation is very important, because soil can be difficult or impossible to replace once it has been lost. Soil takes a very long time to form. A soil with well-developed horizons may take hundreds of thousands of years to form! Most soil conservation methods are designed to hold soil in place and keep it fertile. Below are descriptions of a few of the many soil conservation methods that are used by farmers around the world.

Crop rotation is the practice of planting different crops on the same field in different years or growing seasons. Grain crops, such as wheat, use up a lot of the nitrogen—a necessary plant nutrient—in the soil. The roots of bean crops, such as soybeans, contain bacteria that restore nitrogen to the soil. By rotating these crops, farmers can help maintain soil fertility.

Conservation tillage includes several methods of reducing the number of times fields are tilled, or plowed, in a year. The less soil is disturbed by plowing, the less likely it is to be washed or blown away. In one method of conservation tillage, fields are not plowed at all. The remains of harvested crops are simply left on the fields to cover and protect the soil. New seeds are planted in narrow bands of soil.

INVESTIGATE Soil Conservation

How can you model Earth's soil with an apple?
PROCEDURE

1. Fill in a row of the Apple Chart as you complete each step.
2. Cut the apple into quarters. Set aside three of the quarters.
3. Cut the remaining quarter in half. Set aside one of these pieces.
4. Cut the remaining piece from step 3 into four pieces. Set aside three of them.
5. Peel the skin off the remaining piece from step 4.

WHAT DO YOU THINK?
- How does the amount of fertile soil on Earth compare with what you expected?
- Do you think that the amount of fertile soil on Earth is increasing or decreasing? Explain your answer.

CHALLENGE Invent a method of soil conservation other than the ones you have read about. How would your method help keep soil in place?

SKILL FOCUS
Making models

MATERIALS
- Apple Chart
- apple
- plastic knife

TIME
20 minutes

Terracing

Contour Plowing

READING VISUALS **COMPARE** Both terracing and contour plowing are soil conservation methods used on sloping land. How does each method help conserve soil?

Terraces are flat, steplike areas built on a hillside to hold rainwater and prevent it from running downhill. Crops are planted on the flat tops of the terraces.

Contour plowing is the practice of plowing along the curves, or contours, of a slope. Contour plowing helps channel rainwater so that it does not run straight downhill, carrying away soil with it. A soil conservation method called strip-cropping is often combined with contour plowing. Strips of grasses, shrubs, or other plants are planted between bands of a grain crop along the contour of a slope. These strips of plants also help slow the runoff of water.

Windbreaks are rows of trees planted between fields to "break," or reduce, the force of winds that can carry off soil.

16.3 Review

KEY CONCEPTS

1. Why is soil a necessary resource?
2. How do land-use practices in farming, construction and development, and mining affect soil?
3. Describe at least three methods of soil conservation.

CRITICAL THINKING

4. **Compare and Contrast** How might the problem of soil loss on flat land be different from that on sloping land?
5. **Apply** If you were building a new home in an undeveloped area, what steps would you take to reduce the impact of construction on the soil?

CHALLENGE

6. **Apply** You have advised an inexperienced farmer to practice strip-cropping, but the farmer wants to plant all the land in wheat in order to grow as much as possible. What argument would you use to convince the farmer?

SCIENCE on the JOB

LANDSCAPE ARCHITECT

Soil, Water, and Architecture

Landscape architects design the landscapes around buildings and in parks. For example, they decide where to build sidewalks and where to place benches. Since flowing water can wash away soil, they try to control how water moves. They select plants, modify the slope of the land, and install drainage systems that will control the water. The plan below was used to build the park shown in the photographs.

Existing Plants
Large oak trees were already growing on the land. The trees were left in place to provide shade and help protect the soil.

Retaining Wall
The landscape architect added mounds of soil planted with bushes to help divide the inside of the park from the roads around it. Stone walls hold the soil of the mounds in place. Without the walls, the soil would wash down onto the walkways.

Plan for New Park
A landscape architect used a computer program to draw this plan for a park. The program is designed to make the plan look as if it were drawn by hand.

EXPLORE

1. ANALYZE Examine the soil, drainage, plants, and other elements of the landscape of a park or the area around a building. Describe any areas where soil may wash away.

2. CHALLENGE Design a landscape surrounding a new school, stadium, or other building. Draw a sketch and add notes to explain your choices of locations for trees, sidewalks, and other features.

Chapter 16: **Weathering and Soil Formation** 565

16 Chapter Review

the BIG idea

Natural forces break rocks apart and form soil, which supports life.

CONTENT REVIEW
CLASSZONE.COM

KEY CONCEPTS SUMMARY

1 Mechanical and chemical forces break down rocks.

Over time, **mechanical weathering** breaks a rock into smaller pieces.

Chemical weathering affects exposed rock surfaces.

VOCABULARY
weathering p. 543
mechanical weathering p. 544
exfoliation p. 544
abrasion p. 544
chemical weathering p. 546

2 Weathering and organic processes form soil.

Soil has measurable properties, such as color, texture, pore space, and chemistry.

Soil is a mixture of weathered rock, organic matter, water, and air.

Plants, microorganisms, and animals affect soil characteristics.

VOCABULARY
humus p. 551
soil horizon p. 552
soil profile p. 552

3 Human activities affect soil.

Soil is essential to life and takes a long time to form. It is difficult or impossible to replace soil that has been lost.

Soil Loss
Farming, construction and development, and mining are three human activities that affect soil.

Soil Conservation
Soil conservation practices help keep soil from blowing or washing away.

VOCABULARY
desertification p. 561

566 Unit 4: Earth's Surface

Reviewing Vocabulary

Copy the three-column chart below. Complete the chart for each term. The first one has been done for you.

Term	Definition	Example
EXAMPLE chemical weathering	the breakdown of rocks by chemical reactions that change the rocks' mineral composition	Iron reacts with air and water to form iron oxides or rust.
1. mechanical weathering		
2. abrasion		
3. exfoliation		
4. desertification		

Reviewing Key Concepts

Multiple Choice *Choose the letter of the best answer.*

5. The force of expanding water in the cracks and pores of a rock is an example of
   a. chemical weathering
   b. mechanical weathering
   c. oxidation
   d. desertification

6. The breakdown of a rock by acidic water is an example of
   a. chemical weathering
   b. mechanical weathering
   c. oxidation
   d. desertification

7. Soil is a mixture of what four materials?
   a. granite, limestone, nitrogen, and air
   b. plant roots, iron oxides, water, and air
   c. rock particles, plant roots, humus, and nitrogen
   d. rock particles, humus, water, and air

8. What is the main component of soil?
   a. humus   c. air
   b. water   d. rock particles

9. What is humus?
   a. the decomposed rock particles in soil
   b. the decomposed organic matter in soil
   c. the material that makes up the B horizon
   d. the material that makes up the C horizon

10. Three factors that affect the rate of weathering are
    a. microorganisms, plants, and animals
    b. weather, landforms, and rainfall
    c. surface area, rock composition, and climate
    d. texture, color, and pore space

11. Microorganisms affect the quality of soil by
    a. decomposing organic matter
    b. creating tunnels
    c. absorbing water
    d. increasing mechanical weathering

12. The movement of air and water through a soil is influenced most by the soil's
    a. color and chemistry
    b. texture and pore space
    c. pH and nitrogen content
    d. microorganisms

13. Contour plowing, strip-cropping, and terracing are conservation methods designed to reduce the
    a. runoff of water
    b. activity of microorganisms
    c. acidity of soil
    d. pore space of soil

Short Answer *Write a few sentences to answer each question.*

14. How do farming, construction and development, and mining affect soil?

15. How do ice wedging, pressure release, plant root growth, and abrasion cause mechanical weathering?

16. How do air and water cause chemical weathering?

Thinking Critically

Use the photograph to answer the next three questions.

17. APPLY Make a sketch of the soil profile above, labeling the A, B, and C horizons.

18. OBSERVE What does the color of the top layer indicate about this soil?

19. APPLY Which part of the profile is most affected by chemical and mechanical weathering? Why?

20. APPLY Suppose that you own gently sloping farmland. Describe the methods that you would use to hold the soil in place and maintain its fertility.

21. SYNTHESIZE Describe the composition, color, texture, and amount of pore space of a soil that would be good for growing crops.

22. COMPARE AND CONTRAST How does mechanical weathering differ from chemical weathering? How are the two processes similar?

23. PREDICT What effect will the continued growth of the world's population likely have on soil resources?

24. ANALYZE Soil loss is a problem all over the world. Where might lost soil end up?

25. ANALYZE Can lost soil be replaced? Explain.

26. ANALYZE Copy the concept map below and fill it in with the following terms and phrases.

acidic water	chemical weathering
damaged statue	exfoliation
mechanical weathering	moving water
oxygen and water	pressure release
rounded rocks	rust

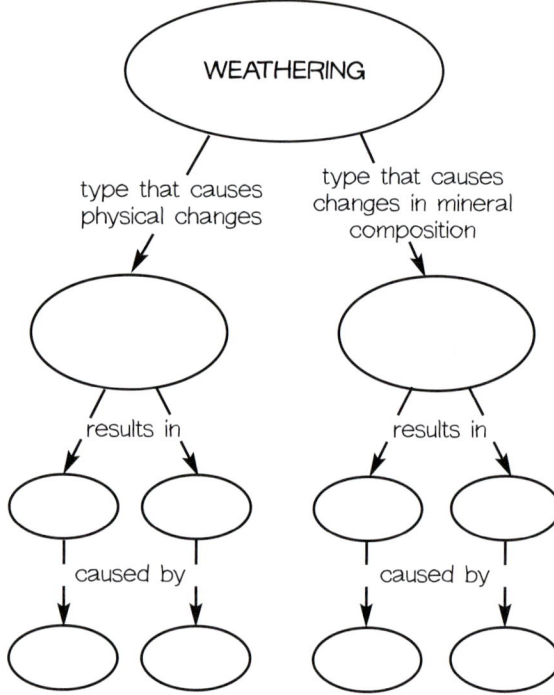

27. ANALYZE Add to the concept map to show the three factors that affect the rate of weathering.

the BIG idea

28. MODEL Draw a diagram that shows an example of a natural force breaking rocks apart to form soil that supports life.

29. SYNTHESIZE A cycle is a series of events or actions that repeats regularly. Describe a cycle that involves soil and living things.

UNIT PROJECTS

If you need to create graphs or other visuals for your project, be sure you have grid paper, poster board, markers, or other supplies.

Standardized Test Practice

Analyzing a Table

The table indicates some of the characteristics of four soil samples. Use the table to answer the questions below.

Sample	Color	Ability to Hold Water	Percentage of Pore Space	Percentage of Humus
1	black	average	50%	9%
2	yellowish brown	low	70%	3%
3	reddish brown	average	60%	3%
4	very red	average to low	65%	2%

1. Soils that contain a lot of sand do not hold water very well. Which sample probably contains the most sand?
   a. 1
   b. 2
   c. 3
   d. 4

2. Iron gives soil a reddish color. Which sample probably contains the most iron?
   a. 1
   b. 2
   c. 3
   d. 4

3. Crops grow best in soils with about half of their volume consisting of pore space. Which soil has an ideal amount of pore space for growing crops?
   a. 1
   b. 2
   c. 3
   d. 4

4. What soil color might indicate a high level of organic matter?
   a. black
   b. yellow
   c. red-brown
   d. red

5. Imagine you have an additional soil sample. The sample is dark brown, has an average ability to hold water, and has 55% pore space. What percentage of humus would this soil most likely contain?
   a. 1%
   b. 2%
   c. 3%
   d. 8%

Extended Response

Answer the two questions below in detail. Include some of the terms shown in the word box. In your answers, underline each term you use.

abrasion	moving water
chemical weathering	plant roots
ice	rusting
mechanical weathering	

6. Jolene is comparing a rock from a riverbed and a rock from deep underground. One is very smooth. The other has very sharp edges. Explain which rock was probably found in each location.

7. In a museum, Hank sees two iron knives that were made in the early 1800s. One has spent 200 years on the top of a fortress wall. The other one has been stored in the museum for 200 years. Why might the two knives look different?

CHAPTER 17
Erosion and Deposition

the BIG idea

Water, wind, and ice shape Earth's surface.

Key Concepts

SECTION 1 Forces wear down and build up Earth's surface.
Learn how natural forces shape and change the land.

SECTION 2 Moving water shapes land.
Learn about the effects of water moving over land and underground.

SECTION 3 Waves and wind shape land.
Discover how waves and wind affect land.

SECTION 4 Glaciers carve land and move sediments.
Learn about the effect of ice moving over land.

Internet Preview

CLASSZONE.COM
Chapter 17 online resources: Content Review, two Visualizations, three Resource Centers, Math Tutorial, Test Practice

How can ice carve a valley?

570 Unit 4: Earth's Surface

EXPLORE the BIG idea

Where Has Water Been?

Think about what water does when it falls and flows on the ground. Go outside your school or home and look at the ground and pavement carefully. Look in dry places for evidence of where water has been.

Observe and Think What evidence did you find? How does it show that water was in a place that is now dry?

How Do Waves Shape Land?

Pile a mixture of sand and gravel on one side of a pie tin to make a "beach." Slowly add water away from the beach until the tin is about one-third full. Use your hand to make waves in the tin and observe what happens.

Observe and Think What happened to the beach? How did the waves affect the sand and gravel?

Internet Activity: Wind Erosion

Go to **ClassZone.com** to learn about one type of wind erosion. See how wind can form an arch in rock.

Observe and Think How long do you think it would take for wind to form an arch?

Wind Erosion Code: MDL017

Chapter 17: **Erosion and Deposition** 571

CHAPTER 17
Getting Ready to Learn

CONCEPT REVIEW

- Weathering breaks down rocks.
- Water and ice are agents of weathering.
- Soil contains weathered rock and organic material.

VOCABULARY REVIEW

sediment p. 517
weathering p. 543
abrasion p. 544

CONTENT REVIEW
CLASSZONE.COM
Review concepts and vocabulary.

TAKING NOTES

CHOOSE YOUR OWN STRATEGY

Take notes using one or more of the strategies from earlier chapters—**main idea and detail notes, supporting main ideas, main idea web,** or **combination notes.** Feel free to mix and match the strategies, or use an entirely different note-taking strategy.

VOCABULARY STRATEGY

Write each new vocabulary term in the center of a **four square** diagram. Write notes in the squares around each term. Include a definition, some characteristics, and some examples of the term. If possible, write some things that are not examples of the term.

See the Note-Taking Handbook on pages R45–R51.

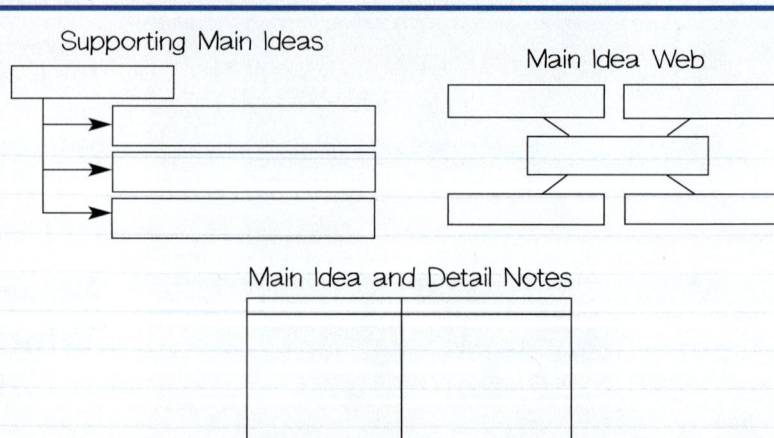

KEY CONCEPT

Forces wear down and build up Earth's surface.

BEFORE, you learned
- Weathering breaks rocks apart
- Weathering forms soil

NOW, you will learn
- How erosion moves and deposits rock and soil
- How gravity causes movement of large amounts of rock and soil

VOCABULARY

erosion p. 573
deposition p. 573
mass wasting p. 575

THINK ABOUT

How did natural forces shape this landform?

This valley in Iceland was formed by the action of water. How long might it have taken to form? Where did the material that once filled the valley go?

VOCABULARY
Use four square diagrams to take notes about the terms *erosion* and *deposition*.

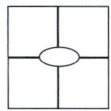

Natural forces move and deposit sediments.

The valley in the photograph was formed by the movement of water. The water flowed over the land and carried away weathered rock and soil, shaping a valley where the water flows. In this section you will learn about the processes that shape landscapes.

The process in which weathered particles are picked up and moved from one place to another is called **erosion** (ih-ROH-zhuhn). Erosion has a constant impact on Earth's surface. Over millions of years, it wears down mountains by removing byproducts of weathering and depositing them elsewhere. The part of the erosion process in which sediment is placed in a new location, or deposited, is called **deposition** (DEHP-uh-ZIHSH-uhn).

The force of gravity is an important part of erosion and deposition. Gravity causes water to move downward, carrying and depositing sediment as it flows. Gravity can pull huge masses of ice slowly down mountain valleys. And gravity causes dust carried by the wind to fall to Earth.

Chapter 17: **Erosion and Deposition** 573

Erosion of weathered rock by the movement of water, wind, and ice occurs in three major ways:

- **Water** Rainwater and water from melting snow flow down sloping land, carrying rock and soil particles. The water makes its way to a river, which then carries the sediment along. The sediment gets deposited on the river's bottom, banks, or floodplain, or near its mouth. Waves in oceans and lakes also carry sediment and deposit it to form beaches and other features.

- **Wind** Strong winds lift tiny particles of dust and carry them long distances. When the wind dies down, the particles drop to the ground. Wind can also push larger particles of sand along the ground.

- **Ice** As ice moves slowly downhill, it transports rock and soil particles that are embedded in it.

 What are the three major ways in which erosion moves sediment?

INVESTIGATE Erosion

How does the effect of rainwater on sloping land differ from its effect on flat land?

DESIGN YOUR OWN EXPERIMENT

Streams are one of the main agents of erosion on Earth. Design an experiment to show the effect that rainwater has on sloping land.

PROCEDURE

1. Figure out how to use the soil, water, and trays to test the effects of rainwater on sloping land and on flat land.
2. Write up your procedure.
3. Carry out your experiment.

WHAT DO YOU THINK?

- What were the results of your experiment? Did it work? Why or why not?
- What were the variables in your experiment?
- What does your experiment demonstrate about erosion and running water?

CHALLENGE How would you design an experiment to demonstrate the relationship between floods and erosion?

SKILL FOCUS
Designing experiments

MATERIALS
- soil
- 2 large trays
- pitcher of water

TIME
25 minutes

Gravity can move large amounts of rock and soil.

Along the California coast many homes are built atop beautiful cliffs, backed by mountains and looking out to the sea. These homes may seem like great places to live. They are, however, in a risky location.

The California coast region and other mountainous areas have many landslides. A landslide is one type of **mass wasting**—the downhill movements of masses of rock and soil.

In mass wasting, gravity pulls material downward. A triggering event, such as heavy rain or an earthquake, might loosen the rock and soil. As the material becomes looser, it gives way to the pull of gravity and moves downward.

Mass wasting can occur suddenly or gradually. It can involve tons of rock sliding down a steep mountain slope or moving little by little down a gentle hillside. One way to classify an occurrence of mass wasting is by the type of material that is moved and the speed of the movement. A sudden, fast movement of rock and soil is called a landslide. Movements of rock are described as slides or falls. Movement of mud or soil is described as a mudflow.

> **VOCABULARY**
> Be sure to make a four square diagram for *mass wasting* in your notebook.
>
>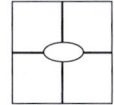

Mass Wasting of Rock

Mass wasting of rock includes rockfalls and rockslides:

- In a rockfall, individual blocks of rock drop suddenly and fall freely down a cliff or steep mountainside. Weathering can break a block of rock from a cliff or mountainside. The expansion of water that freezes in a crack, for example, can loosen a block of rock.

- In a rockslide, a large mass of rock slides as a unit down a slope. A rockslide can reach a speed of a hundred kilometers per hour. Rockslides can be triggered by earthquakes.

Mass wasting of rock often takes place in high mountains. In some places, rocks can fall or slide onto roads. You might also see evidence of rockfalls and rockslides at the base of steep cliffs, where piles of rock slope outward.

Rockslides, such as this one in California, can drop huge amounts of rock onto highways.

Chapter 17: **Erosion and Deposition** 575

Mudflows in 1999 in Venezuela happened very quickly and took as many as 30,000 lives.

Learn more about mudflows.

Mudflow

Sometimes a mountain slope collapses. Then a mixture of rock, soil, and plants—called debris (duh-BREE)—falls or slides down. Like mass wasting of rock, mass movements of debris are common in high mountains with steep slopes.

A major type of mass wasting of debris is a mudflow. A mudflow consists of debris with a large amount of water. Mudflows often happen in mountain canyons and valleys after heavy rains. The soil becomes so heavy with water that the slope can no longer hold it in place. The mixture of soil, water, and debris flows downward, picking up sediment as it rushes down. When it reaches a valley, it spreads in a thin sheet over the land.

Mudflows also occur on active volcanoes. In 1985, a huge mudflow destroyed the town of Armero, Colombia, and killed more than 20,000 people. When a volcano erupted there, the heat caused ice and snow near the top of the volcano to melt, releasing a large amount of water that mixed with ash from the volcano. The mixture of ash and water rushed down the volcano and picked up debris. It formed gigantic mudflows that poured into all the surrounding valleys.

Mount St. Helens, a volcanic mountain in the state of Washington, is a place where large mudflows have occurred. During an eruption in 1980, some mudflows from the volcano traveled more than 90 kilometers (56 mi) from the mountain.

 What causes a mudflow to occur?

Slumps and Creep

Slumps and creep are two other main types of mass wasting on hilly land. These forms of mass wasting can be much less dramatic than rockslides or mudflows. But they are the types of mass movement that you are most likely to see evidence of.

In this example of slump, at Mesa Verde National Park in Colorado, a huge mass of rock and soil moved downward.

A slump is a slide of loose debris that moves as a single unit. Slumps can occur along roads and highways where construction has made slopes unstable. They can cover sections of highway with debris. Like other types of mass movement, slumps can be triggered by heavy rain.

The slowest form of mass movement of soil or debris is creep. The soil or debris moves at a rate of about 1 to 10 millimeters a year—a rate too slow to actually be seen. But evidence of creep can be seen on hillsides that have old fences or telephone poles. The fences or poles may lean downward, or some may be out of line. They have been moved by the creeping soil. The soil closer to the surface moves faster than the soil farther down, which causes the fences or poles to lean.

1 Originally, the fence posts stand vertically in the ground.

2 Over many years, the soil holding the posts slowly shifts downhill, and the posts lean.

Even the slight slope of this land in Alberta, Canada, caused these posts to tilt because of creep.

Creep can affect buildings as well. The weight of a heavy mass of soil moving slowly downhill can be great enough to crack a building's walls. Creep affects all hillsides covered with soil, but its rate varies. The wetter the soil, the faster it will creep downhill.

17.1 Review

KEY CONCEPTS

1. How does erosion change landscapes?
2. Describe why weathering is important in erosion.
3. How can gravity move large amounts of rock and soil?

CRITICAL THINKING

4. **Compare and Contrast** What is the main difference between erosion and mass wasting?
5. **Infer** What force and what cause can contribute to both erosion and mass wasting?

⚠ CHALLENGE

6. **Rank** Which of the four locations would be the best and worst places to build a house? Rank the four locations and explain your reasoning.

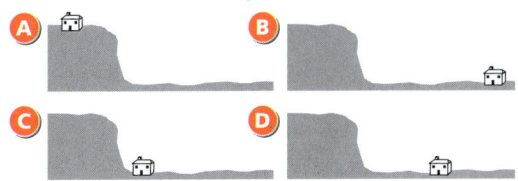

Chapter 17: **Erosion and Deposition** 577

KEY CONCEPT
17.2 Moving water shapes land.

BEFORE, you learned
- Erosion is the movement of rock and soil
- Gravity causes mass movements of rock and soil

NOW, you will learn
- How moving water shapes Earth's surface
- How water moving underground forms caves and other features

VOCABULARY
drainage basin p. 579
divide p. 579
floodplain p. 580
alluvial fan p. 581
delta p. 581
sinkhole p. 583

EXPLORE Divides

How do divides work?

PROCEDURE
1. Fold the sheet of paper in thirds and tape it as shown to make a "ridge."
2. Drop the paper clips one at a time directly on top of the ridge from a height of about 30 cm. Observe what happens and record your observations.

MATERIALS
- sheet of paper
- tape
- paper clips

WHAT DO YOU THINK?
How might the paper clips be similar to water falling on a ridge?

Streams shape Earth's surface.

If you look at a river or stream, you may be able to notice something about the land around it. The land is higher than the river. If a river is running through a steep valley, you can easily see that the river is the low point. But even in very flat places, the land is sloping down to the river, which is itself running downhill in a low path through the land.

Running water is the major force shaping the landscape over most of Earth. From the broad, flat land around the lower Mississippi River to the steep mountain valleys of the Himalayas, water running downhill changes the land. Running water shapes a variety of landforms by moving sediment in the processes of erosion and deposition. In this section, you will learn how water flows on land in systems of streams and rivers and how water shapes and changes landscapes. You also will learn that water can even carve out new features underground.

NOTE-TAKING STRATEGY
A main idea and detail notes chart would be a good strategy to use for taking notes about streams and Earth's surface.

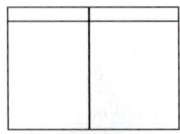

578 Unit 4: Earth's Surface

Drainage Basins and Divides

When water falls or ice melts on a slope, some of the water soaks into the ground and some of it flows down the slope in thin sheets. But within a short distance this water becomes part of a channel that forms a stream. A stream is any body of water—large or small—that flows down a slope along a channel.

Streams flow into one another to form complex drainage systems, with small streams flowing into larger ones. The area of land in which water drains into a stream system is called a **drainage basin.** In most drainage basins, the water eventually drains into a lake or an ocean. For example, in the Mississippi River drainage basin, water flows into the Mississippi, and then drains into the Gulf of Mexico, which is part of the ocean.

Drainage basins are separated by ridges called divides, which are like continuous lines of high land. A **divide** is a ridge from which water drains to one side or the other. Divides can run along high mountains. On flatter ground, a divide can simply be the highest line of land and can be hard to see.

Divides are the borders of drainage basins. A basin can be just a few kilometers wide or can drain water from a large portion of a continent. The Continental Divide runs from Alaska to Mexico. Most water that falls west of the Continental Divide ends up draining into the Pacific Ocean. Most water that falls east of it drains into the Gulf of Mexico and Atlantic Ocean.

Divides and Drainage Basins

Divides are ridges that form the borders of drainage basins.

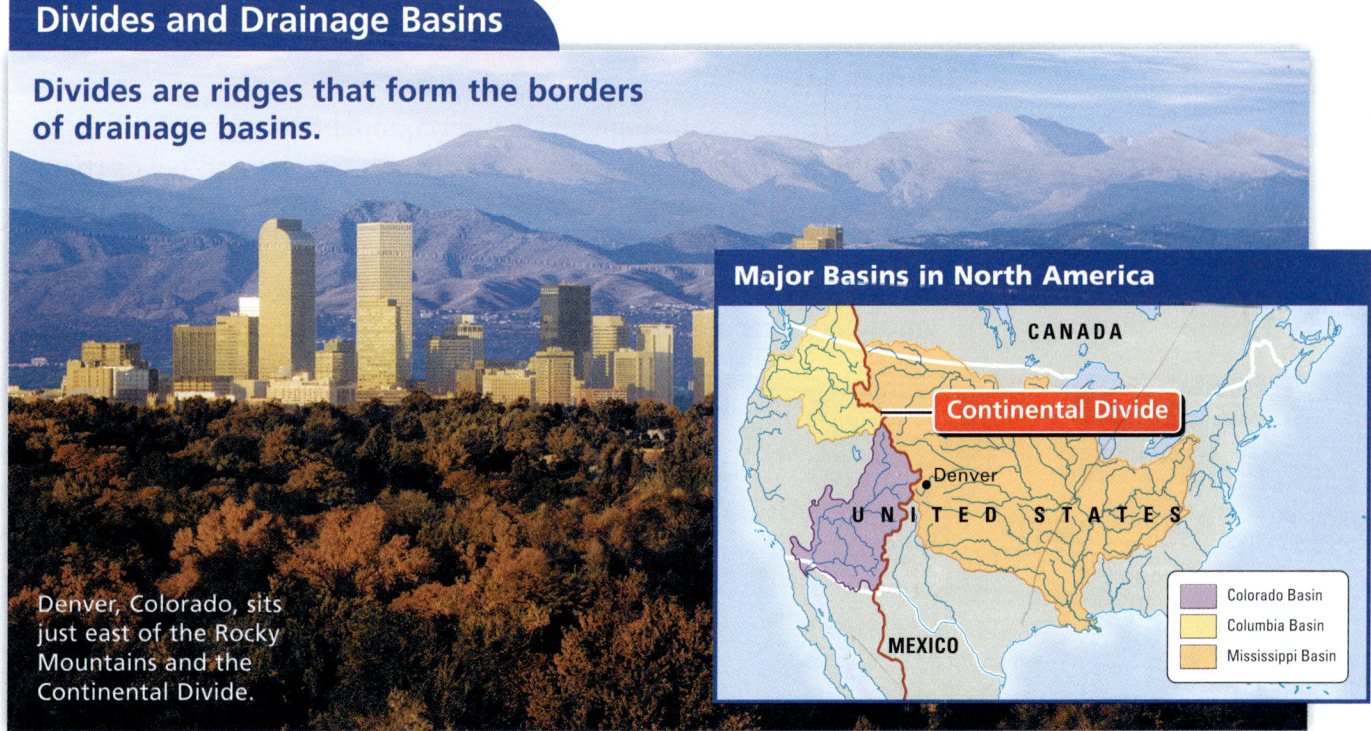

Denver, Colorado, sits just east of the Rocky Mountains and the Continental Divide.

Major Basins in North America
- Colorado Basin
- Columbia Basin
- Mississippi Basin

Downtown Davenport, Iowa, sits in the floodplain of the Mississippi River and was covered with water when the river flooded in 1993.

Valleys and Floodplains

As streams flow and carry sediment from the surface of the land, they form valleys. In high mountains, streams often cut V-shaped valleys that are narrow and steep walled. In lower areas, streams may form broad valleys that include floodplains. A **floodplain** is an area of land on either side of a stream that is underwater when the stream floods. The floodplain of a large river may be many kilometers wide.

When a stream floods, it deposits much of the sediment that it carries onto its floodplain. This sediment can make the floodplain very fertile—or able to support a lot of plant growth. In the United States, the floodplains of the Mississippi River are some of the best places for growing crops.

Find out more about rivers and erosion.

CHECK YOUR READING Why is fertile land often found on flat land around rivers?

Stream Channels

As a stream flows through a valley, its channel may run straight in some parts and curve around in other parts. Curves and bends that form a twisting, looping pattern in a stream channel are called meanders (mee-AN-duhrz). The moving water erodes the outside banks and deposits sediment along the inside banks. Over many years, meanders shift position.

The meanders of this river and oxbow lakes formed as the river deposited sediment and changed course.

During a flood, the stream may cut a new channel that bypasses a meander. The cut-off meander forms a crescent-shaped lake, which is called an oxbow lake. This term comes from the name of a U-shaped piece of wood that fits under the neck of an ox and is attached to its yoke.

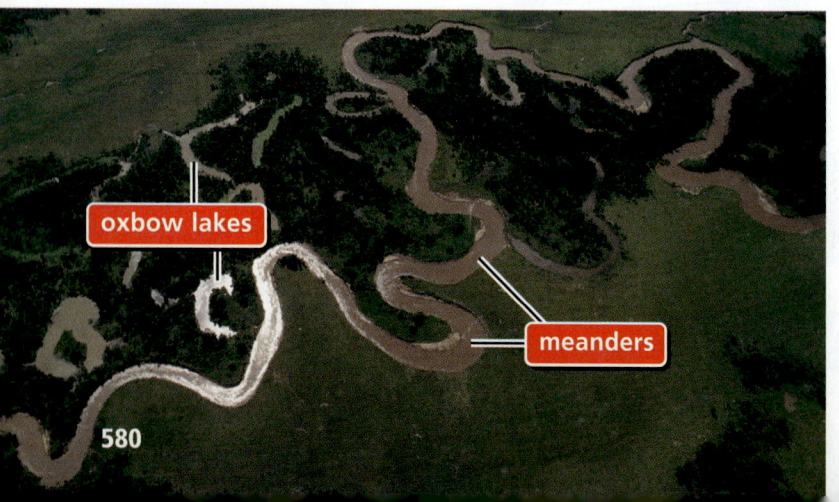

Alluvial Fans and Deltas

Besides shaping valleys and forming oxbow lakes, streams also create landforms called alluvial fans and deltas. Both of these landforms are formed by the deposition of sediment.

An **alluvial fan** (uh-LOO-vee-uhl) is a fan-shaped deposit of sediment at the base of a mountain. It forms where a stream leaves a steep valley and enters a flatter plain. The stream slows down and spreads out on the flatter ground. As it slows down, it can carry less sediment. The slower moving water drops some of its sediment, leaving it at the base of the slope.

A **delta** is an area of land formed by the buildup of sediment at the end, or mouth, of a river. When a river enters the ocean, the river's water slows down, and the river drops much of its sediment. This sediment gradually builds up to form a plain. Like alluvial fans, deltas tend to be fan-shaped. Over a very long time, a river may build up its delta far out into the sea. A large river, such as the Mississippi, can build up a huge delta. Like many other large rivers on Earth, the Mississippi has been building up its delta out into the sea for many thousands of years.

This alluvial fan was formed by a stream flowing into the Jago River in Alaska.

From Divide to Delta

On their path to the ocean, streams and rivers slow down and flatten out.

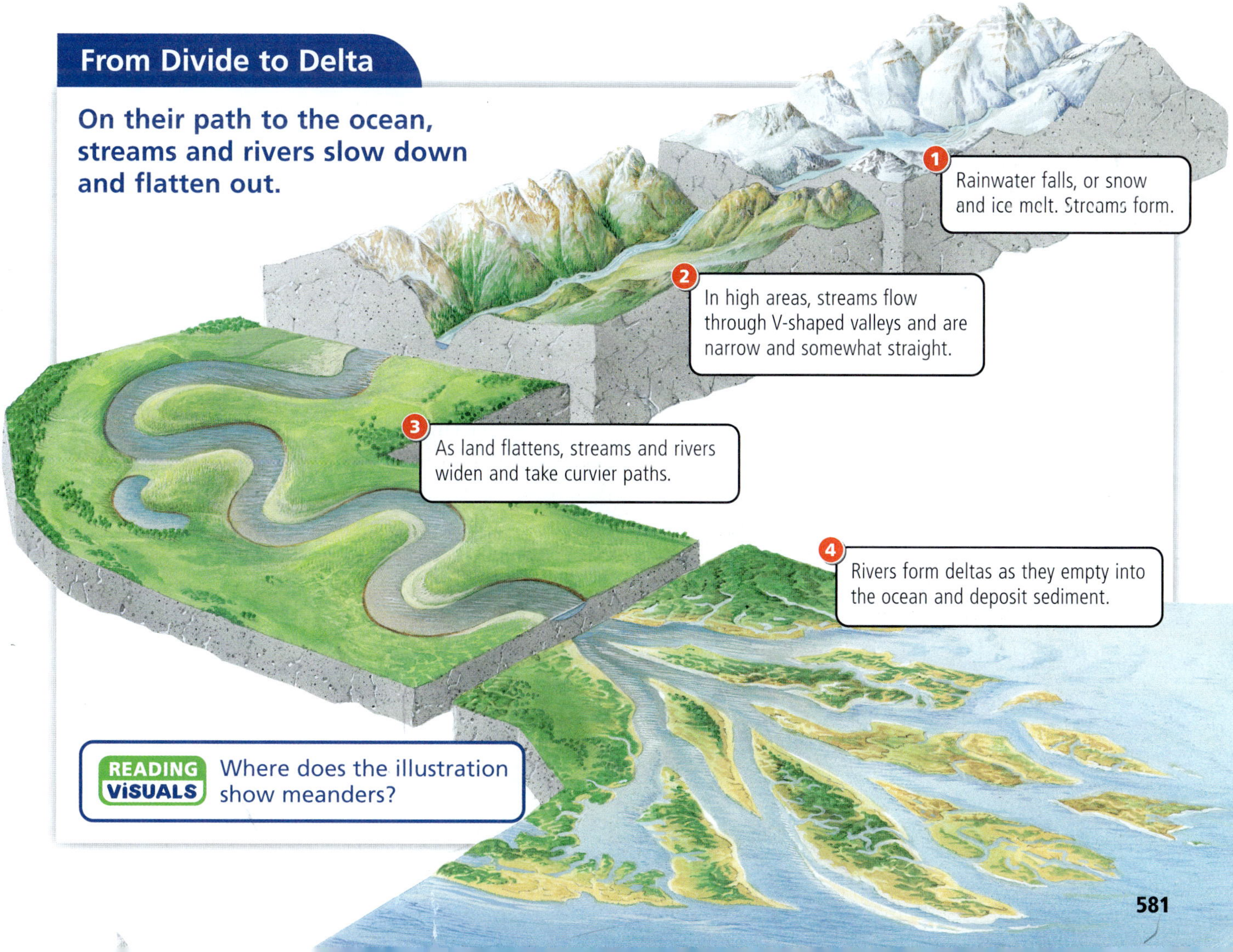

1. Rainwater falls, or snow and ice melt. Streams form.
2. In high areas, streams flow through V-shaped valleys and are narrow and somewhat straight.
3. As land flattens, streams and rivers widen and take curvier paths.
4. Rivers form deltas as they empty into the ocean and deposit sediment.

READING VISUALS Where does the illustration show meanders?

Water moving underground forms caverns.

Not all rainwater runs off the land and flows into surface streams. Some of it evaporates, some is absorbed by plants, and some soaks into the ground and becomes groundwater. At a certain depth below the surface, the spaces in soil and rock become completely filled with water. The top of this water-filled region is called the water table. The water below the water table is called groundwater.

The water table is at different distances below the surface in different places. Its level also can change over time in the same location, depending on changes in rainfall. Below the water table, groundwater flows slowly through underground beds of rock and soil, where it causes erosion to take place.

You have read that chemicals in water and air can break down rock. As you read in Chapter 16, rainwater is slightly acidic. This acidic water can dissolve certain rocks, such as limestone. In some areas, where the underground rock consists of limestone, the groundwater can dissolve some of the limestone and carry it away. Over time, this

Observe the process of cave formation.

Cavern Formation

Caves form as water underground dissolves limestone, leaving open spaces.

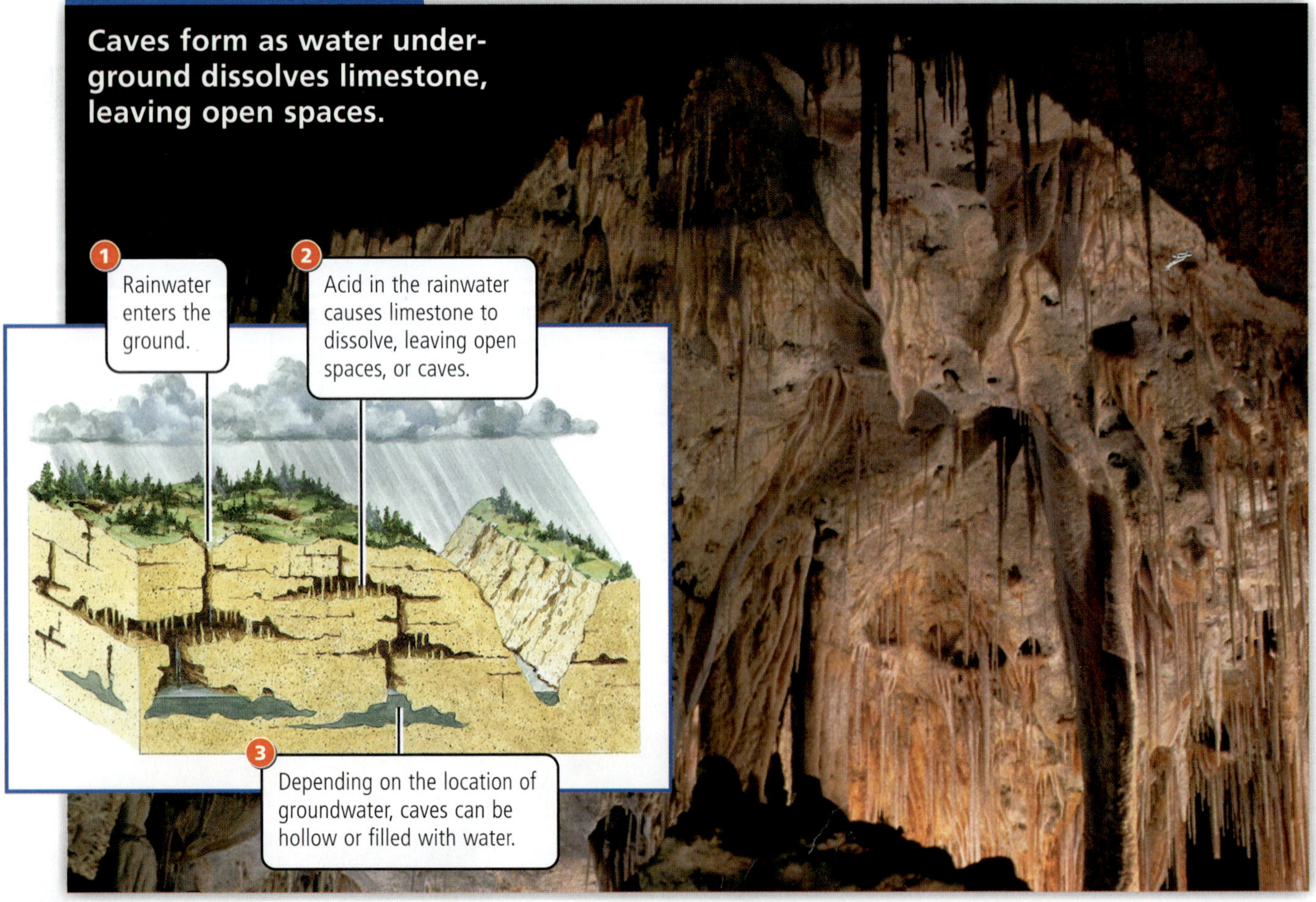

1. Rainwater enters the ground.
2. Acid in the rainwater causes limestone to dissolve, leaving open spaces, or caves.
3. Depending on the location of groundwater, caves can be hollow or filled with water.

582 Unit 4: Earth's Surface

This sinkhole took down a large part of a parking lot in Atlanta, Georgia.

process produces open spaces, or caves. Large caves are called caverns. If the water table drops, a cavern may fill with air.

Some caverns have huge networks of rooms and passageways. Mammoth Cave in Kentucky, for example, is part of a cavern system that has more than 560 kilometers (about 350 mi) of explored passageways. Within the cavern are lakes and streams.

A surface feature that often occurs in areas with caverns is a sinkhole. A **sinkhole** is a basin that forms when the roof of a cave becomes so thin that it suddenly falls in. Sometimes it falls in because water that supported the roof has drained away. Landscapes with many sinkholes can be found in southern Indiana, south central Kentucky, and central Tennessee. In Florida, the collapse of shallow underground caverns has produced large sinkholes that have destroyed whole city blocks.

 Why do caverns form in areas with limestone?

17.2 Review

KEY CONCEPTS
1. What is the difference between a drainage basin and a divide?
2. How do streams change as they flow from mountains down to plains?
3. How do caverns form?

CRITICAL THINKING
4. **Sequence** Draw a cartoon with three panels showing how a sinkhole forms.
5. **Compare and Contrast** Make a Venn diagram to compare and contrast alluvial fans and deltas.

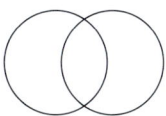

CHALLENGE
6. **Apply** During a flood, a river drops the largest pieces of its sediment on the floodplain close to its normal channel. Explain why. (**Hint:** Think about the speed of the water.)

Chapter 17: **Erosion and Deposition** 583

CHAPTER INVESTIGATION

Creating Stream Features

OVERVIEW AND PURPOSE A view from the sky reveals that a large river twists and bends in its channel. But as quiet as it might appear, the river constantly digs and dumps Earth materials along its way. This erosion and deposition causes twists and curves called meanders, and forms a delta at the river's mouth. In this investigation you will

- create a "river" in a stream table to observe the creation of meanders and deltas
- identify the processes of erosion and deposition

▶ Problem

Write It Up

How does moving water create meanders and deltas?

▶ Procedure

1. Arrange the stream table on a counter so that it drains into a sink or bucket. If possible, place a sieve beneath the outlet hose to keep sand out of the drain. You can attach the inlet hose to a faucet if you have a proper adapter. Or you can gently pour water in with a pitcher or use a recirculating pump and a bucket.

2. Place wood blocks beneath the inlet end of the stream table so that the table tilts toward the outlet at about a 20 degree angle. Fill the upper two-thirds of the stream table nearly to the top with sand. Pack the sand a bit, and level the surface with the edge of a ruler. The empty bottom third of the stream table represents the lake or bay into which the river flows.

3. Using the end of the ruler, dig a gently curving trench halfway through the thickness of the sand from its upper to its lower end.

MATERIALS
- stream table, with hose attachment or recirculating pump
- sieve (optional)
- wood blocks
- sand
- ruler
- water
- sink with drain
- pitcher (optional)
- bucket (optional)

584 Unit 4: Earth's Surface

4. Direct a gentle flow of tap water into the upper end of the trench. Increase the flow slightly when the water begins to move through the trench. You may have to try this several times before you find the proper rate of flow to soak the sand and fill the stream channel. Avoid adding so much water that it pools at the top before moving into the channel. You can also change the stream table's tilt.

5. Once you are successful in creating a river, observe its shape and any movement of the sand. Continue until the top part of the sand is completely washed away and your river falls apart. Scrape the sand back into place with the ruler and repeat the procedure until you thoroughly understand the stream and sand movements.

Observe and Analyze   *Write It Up*

1. **RECORD** Diagram your stream-table setup, and make a series of drawings showing changes in your river over time. Be sure to label the river's features, as well as areas of erosion and deposition. Be sure to diagram the behavior of the sand at the river's mouth.

2. **RECORD** Write a record of the development of your river from start to finish. Include details such as the degree of tilt you used, your method of introducing water into the stream table, and features you observed forming.

Conclude   *Write It Up*

1. **EVALUATE** How do you explain the buildup of sand at the mouth of your river? Use the words *speed*, *erosion*, and *deposition* in your answer. Did the slope of the stream change over time?

2. **INTERPRET** Where in your stream table did you observe erosion occurring? Deposition? What features did each process form?

3. **INFER** What might have occurred if you had increased the amount or speed of the water flowing into your river?

4. **IDENTIFY LIMITS** In what ways was your setup a simplified version of what would actually occur on Earth? Describe the ways in which an actual stream would be more complex.

5. **APPLY** Drawing on what you observed in this investigation, make two statements that relate the age of a stream to (1) the extent of its meanders and (2) to the size of its delta or alluvial fan.

INVESTIGATE Further

CHALLENGE Revise this activity to test a problem statement about a specific stream feature. You could choose to vary the stream's slope, speed, or volume to test the changes' effects on meanders and deltas, for example. Or you could vary the sediment size and observe the movements of each size. Write a hypothesis and design an experimental procedure. Identify the independent and dependent variables.

Creating stream features
Observe and Analyze
1. Before adding water

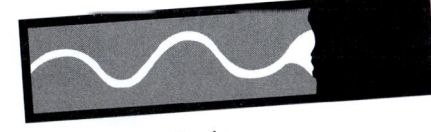

2. After one minute

Chapter 17: **Erosion and Deposition** 585

17.3 Waves and wind shape land.

KEY CONCEPT

 **BEFORE, you learned**
- Stream systems shape Earth's surface
- Groundwater creates caverns and sinkholes

 NOW, you will learn
- How waves and currents shape shorelines
- How wind shapes land

VOCABULARY

longshore drift p. 587
longshore current p. 587
sandbar p. 588
barrier island p. 588
dune p. 589
loess p. 590

THINK ABOUT

How did these pillars of rock form?

The rock formations in this photograph stand along the shoreline near the small town of Port Campbell, Australia. What natural force created these isolated stone pillars? What evidence of this force can you see in the photograph?

NOTE-TAKING STRATEGY
Remember to organize your notes in a chart or web as you read.

Waves and currents shape shorelines.

The stone pillars, or sea stacks, in the photograph above are a major tourist attraction in Port Campbell National Park. They were formed by the movement of water. The constant action of waves breaking against the cliffs slowly wore them away, leaving behind pillarlike formations. Waves continue to wear down the pillars and cliffs at the rate of about two centimeters (one inch) a year. In the years to come, the waves will likely wear away the stone pillars completely.

The force of waves, powered by wind, can wear away rock and move thousands of tons of sand on beaches. The force of wind itself can change the look of the land. Moving air can pick up sand particles and move them around to build up dunes. Wind can also carry huge amounts of fine sediment thousands of kilometers.

In this section, you'll read more about how waves and wind shape shorelines and a variety of other landforms.

586 Unit 4: Earth's Surface

Shorelines

Some shorelines, like the one near Port Campbell, Australia, are made up of steep, rock cliffs. As waves crash against the rock, they wear away the bottom of the cliffs. Eventually, parts of the cliffs above break away and fall into the water, where they are worn down and carried away by the water.

While high, rocky coasts get worn away, low coastlines often get built up. As you read earlier, when a stream flows into an ocean or a lake, it deposits its sediment near its mouth. This sediment mixes with the sediment formed by waves beating against the coast. Waves and currents move this sediment along the shore, building up beaches. Two terms are used to describe the movement of sediment and water along a shore: *longshore drift* and *longshore current*.

- **Longshore drift** is the zigzag movement of sand along a beach. Waves formed by wind blowing across the water far from shore may hit a shoreline at an angle. These angled waves carry sand up onto the shore, and then gravity pulls the water and sand directly back into the water. The sand gradually moves down the beach. The illustration below shows longshore drift.

- A **longshore current** is movement of water along a shore as waves strike the shore at an angle. The direction of the longshore current can change from day to day as the direction of the waves striking the shore changes.

Longshore drift moves large amounts of sand along beaches. It can cause a beach to shrink at one location and grow at another.

Walls of rock extend out into the ocean at Cape May, New Jersey. They were built to keep beaches from being lost to longshore drift.

Longshore Drift

1. Incoming waves push sand up the beach at an angle.
2. The sand washes back straight down the beach.

longshore current

wave direction

INVESTIGATE Longshore Drift

How does sand move along a beach?

PROCEDURE

1. Prop up a book as shown.
2. Hold a coin with your finger against the bottom right corner of the book.
3. Gently flick the coin up the slope of the book at an angle. The coin should slide back down the book and fall off the bottom. If necessary, readjust the angle of the book and the strength with which you are flicking the coin.
4. Repeat step 3 several times. Observe the path the coin takes. Record your observations. Include a diagram that shows the general path the coin takes as it slides up and down the book.

WHAT DO YOU THINK?

- What path did the coin take on its way up? On its way down?
- In this model of longshore drift, what represents the beach, what represents the sand, and what represents a wave?

CHALLENGE In this model, in which direction will the longshore current move? How could you change the model to change the direction of the current?

SKILL FOCUS
Observing

MATERIALS
- 2 or 3 books
- coin

TIME
15 minutes

Sandbars and Barrier Islands

As they transport sand, ocean waves and currents shape a variety of coastal landforms. Longshore currents, for example, often deposit sand along shorelines. The sand builds up to form sandbars. A **sandbar** is a ridge of sand built up by the action of waves and currents. A sandbar that has built up above the water's surface and is joined to the land at one end is called a spit. The tip of Cape Cod, Massachusetts, is a spit.

Strong longshore currents that mostly move in one direction may produce sandbars that build up over time into barrier islands. A **barrier island** is a long, narrow island that develops parallel to a coast.

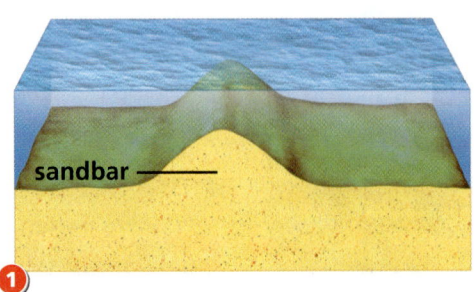

1 Waves and currents move and build up sand deposits to form a sandbar under the water surface.

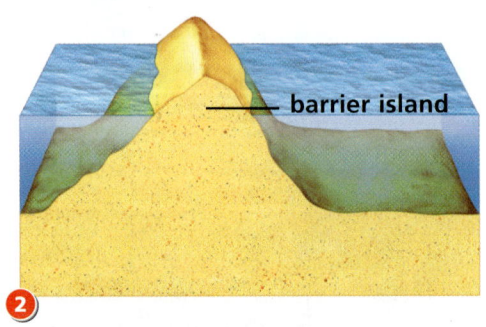

2 As more sand is deposited, the sandbar rises above the surface to become a barrier island.

A barrier island gets its name from the fact that it forms a barrier between the ocean waves and the shore of the mainland. As a barrier island builds up, grasses, bushes, and trees begin to grow on it.

Barrier islands are common along gently sloping coasts around the world. They occur along the coasts of New Jersey and North Carolina and along the coastline of the Gulf of Mexico. Padre Island in Texas is a barrier island about 180 kilometers (110 mi) in length.

Barrier islands constantly change shape. Hurricanes or other storms can speed up the change. During large storms, waves can surge across the land, carrying away huge amounts of sediment and depositing it elsewhere. Houses on beaches can be destroyed in storms.

This lighthouse on a barrier island in North Carolina had to be moved because of beach erosion. The photograph shows the lighthouse before it was moved.

 **CHECK YOUR READING** How and where do barrier islands form?

Wind shapes land.

At Indiana Dunes National Lakeshore, not far from the skyscrapers of Chicago, you can tumble or slide down huge sand dunes. First-time visitors to the Indiana dunes find it hard to believe that sand formations like these can be found so far from a desert or an ocean. What created this long stretch of dune land along the southern shore of Lake Michigan? The answer: wind. A **dune** is a mound of sand built up by wind.

Like water, wind has the power to transport and deposit sediment. Although wind is a less powerful force of erosion than moving water, it can still shape landforms, especially in dry regions and in areas that have few or no plants to hold soil in place. Wind can build up dunes, deposit layers of dust, or make a land surface as hard as pavement.

Chapter 17: **Erosion and Deposition** 589

Wind makes sand particles build up and tumble down, causing a dune to migrate, or move.

These hills of sand are at the Great Sand Dunes National Monument in Colorado.

Dune Formation

Even a light breeze can carry dust. A moderate wind can roll and slide grains of sand along a beach or desert, creating ripples. Only a strong wind, however, can actually pick up and carry sand particles. When the wind dies down or hits something—such as a cliff or a hill—it drops the sand. Over time, the deposits of sand build up to create dunes.

Some dunes start out as ripples that grow larger. Others form as wind-carried sand settles around a rock, log, or other obstacle. In climates with enough rainfall, plants begin to grow on dunes a short distance from beaches.

Dunes form only where there are strong winds and a constant supply of loose sand. They can be found on the inland side of beaches of oceans and large lakes, on the sandy floodplains of large rivers, and in sandy deserts.

Dunes can form in a variety of sizes and shapes. They can reach heights of up to 300 meters (about 1000 ft). Some dunes are curved; others are long, straight ridges; still others are mound-shaped hills. A dune usually has a gentle slope on the side that faces the wind and a steeper slope on the side sheltered from the wind.

Loess

Besides forming dunes, wind also changes the soil over large regions of Earth by depositing dust. A strong windstorm can move millions of tons of dust. As the wind dies down, the dust drops to the ground. Deposits of fine wind-blown sediment are called **loess** (LOH-uhs).

In some regions, deposits of loess have built up over thousands and even millions of years. Loess is a valuable resource because it forms good soil for growing crops.

This loess deposit in Iowa built up over many thousands of years.

Loess covers about 10 percent of the land surface of Earth. China has especially large deposits of loess, covering hundreds of thousands of square kilometers. Some of the deposits are more than 300 meters (about 1000 ft) thick. Such thick deposits take a long time to develop. Some of the loess deposits in China are 2 million years old. Winds blowing over the deserts and dry regions of central Asia carried the dust that formed these deposits.

Parts of east central Europe and the Mississippi Valley in the United States also contain significant loess deposits. In the central United States, loess deposits are between 8 and 30 meters (25 and 100 ft) thick.

Desert Pavement

Not only does wind shape land surfaces by depositing dust; it also shapes land surfaces by removing dust. When wind blows away all the smallest particles from a mixture of sand, silt, and gravel, it leaves behind just a layer of stones and gravel. This stony surface is called desert pavement because it looks like a cobblestone pavement. The coarse gravel and rocks are too large to be picked up by wind.

CHECK YOUR READING How are both loess and desert pavement formed by wind?

Desert pavement is made up of particles too large to be picked up by wind.

17.3 Review

KEY CONCEPTS

1. What kinds of landforms do longshore drift and longshore currents produce?
2. How do dunes form?
3. How does loess form, and why is it important?

CRITICAL THINKING

4. **Identify Cause and Effect** Is longshore drift the cause or effect of a longshore current? Explain.
5. **Predict** What effect would a barrier island have on the shoreline of the mainland?

CHALLENGE

6. **Hypothesize** The south and east shores of Lake Michigan have large areas of sand dunes, but the north and west shores do not. Write a hypothesis that explains why. You might want to use a map and draw the shape of Lake Michigan to explain.

Chapter 17: **Erosion and Deposition** 591

Connecting Sciences

EARTH SCIENCE AND LIFE SCIENCE

The leaves of American beach grass contain silica, the main component of sand. The leaves are therefore very tough. Why is this important on a dune?

Life on Dunes

Sand dunes are a difficult environment for most organisms. For example, few plants can gather enough nutrition from sand to grow quickly. However, any plant that grows slowly is likely to be buried by the shifting sand. Plants and animals that thrive on dunes generally have unusual traits that help them survive in dune conditions.

American Beach Grass

Among the first plants to grow on new coastal dunes is American beach grass. It grows faster as sand begins to bury it, and it can grow up to 1 meter (more than 3 ft) per year. Its large root system—reaching down as much as 3 meters (about 10 ft)—helps it gather food and water. The roots also help hold sand in place. As the grass's roots make the dunes stable, other plants can begin to grow there.

Sand Food

One of the most unusual plants in desert dunes is called sand food. It is one of the few plants that cannot convert sunlight into energy it can use. Instead, its long underground stem grabs onto the root of another plant and sucks food from it. Most of the plant is the stem. Sand food plants may be more than 2 meters (almost 7 ft) long.

Fowler's Toad

Fowler's toad is one of the animals that can live in coastal dunes. During the day, sunlight can make the top layer of the sand very hot and dry. These toads dig down into the sand, where they are safe, cool, and moist. They are most active at night.

Fowler's toads have a brownish or greenish color that makes them hard to see against a sandy background. How would this help protect them from animals that want to eat them?

In spring, sand food produces a small head of purple flowers that barely comes out of the ground. How does growing mostly underground help sand food survive?

EXPLORE

1. **GENERALIZE** Dune plants often have long roots. Propose an explanation for this.
2. **CHALLENGE** Use library or Internet resources to learn about another plant or animal that lives on dunes. Describe how it has adapted to the conditions in which it lives.

KEY CONCEPT

17.4 Glaciers carve land and move sediments.

◀ **BEFORE, you learned**
- Running water shapes landscapes
- Wind changes landforms

▶ **NOW, you will learn**
- How moving ice erodes land
- How moving ice deposits sediment and changes landforms

VOCABULARY

glacier p. 593
till p. 596
moraine p. 596
kettle lake p. 597

EXPLORE Glaciers

How do glaciers affect land?

PROCEDURE

1. Flatten the clay on top of a paper towel.
2. Drag the ice cube across the clay as shown. Record your observations.
3. Leave the ice cube to melt on top of the clay.

WHAT DO YOU THINK?
- What happened when you dragged the ice cube across the clay?
- What happened to the sand and gravel in the ice cube as it melted?

MATERIALS
- modeling clay
- paper towel
- ice cube containing sand and gravel

VOCABULARY
Remember to add a four square diagram for *glacier* to your notebook.

Glaciers are moving bodies of ice.

You might not think of ice as something that moves. But think about what happens to an ice cube on a table. The cube begins to melt, makes a small puddle, and may slide a little. The water under the cube makes the table surface slippery, which allows the ice cube to slide.

A similar process happens on a much larger scale with glaciers. A **glacier** is a large mass of ice that moves over land. A glacier forms in a cold region when more snow falls than melts each year. As the snow builds up, its weight presses the snow on the bottom into ice. On a mountain, the weight of a heavy mass of ice causes it to flow downward, usually slowly. On flatter land, the ice spreads out as a sheet. As glaciers form, move, and melt away, they shape landscapes.

Chapter 17: **Erosion and Deposition** 593

Extent of Glaciers

Glaciers can exist only in places where it is cold enough for water to stay frozen year round. Glaciers are found in mountain ranges all over the world and in land regions near the north and south poles.

Today, glaciers cover about 10 percent of Earth's land surface. However, the amount of land surface covered by glaciers has varied greatly over Earth's history. Glaciers have expanded during long cold periods called ice ages and have disappeared during long warm periods. About 30,000 years ago—during the last major ice age—glaciers extended across the northern parts of North America and Eurasia. They covered nearly 30 percent of the present land surface of Earth.

There are two major types of glaciers: alpine glaciers and continental glaciers.

Learn more about the movement and effects of glaciers.

Alpine Glaciers

Alpine glaciers, also called valley glaciers, form in mountains and flow down through valleys. As these glaciers move, they cause erosion, breaking up rock and carrying and pushing away the resulting sediment. Over time, an alpine glacier can change a V-shaped mountain valley into a U-shaped valley with a wider, flatter bottom.

Some glaciers extend all the way down into the lower land at the bases of mountains. At an alpine glacier's lower end, where temperatures are warmer, melting can occur. The melting glacier drops sediment, and streams flowing from the glacier carry some of the sediment away. If an alpine glacier flows into the ocean, big blocks may break off and become icebergs.

Continental Glaciers

Continental glaciers, also called ice sheets, are much larger than alpine glaciers. They can cover entire continents, including all but the highest mountain peaks. An ice sheet covered most of Canada and the northern United States during the last ice age. This ice sheet melted and shrank about 10,000 years ago.

Today, ice sheets cover most of Greenland and Antarctica. Each of these glaciers is shaped like a wide dome over the land. The ice on Antarctica is as much as 4500 meters (15,000 ft) thick.

 What are the two major types of glaciers and where do they form?

Types of Glaciers and Movement

A glacier is a large mass of ice that moves over land.

Alpine Glaciers

A glacier, such as this one in Alaska, changes the landscape as it moves down a mountain valley.

Continental Glaciers

Huge sheets of ice cover the continent of Antarctica and other land regions.

Glacier Movement

Gravity causes the ice in a glacier to move downhill. Two different processes cause glaciers to move: flowing and sliding.

Flowing The ice near the surface of a glacier is brittle, and cracks often form in it. However, deep inside a glacier, ice does not break as easily because it is under great pressure from the weight of the ice above it. Instead of breaking, ice inside a glacier flows like toothpaste being squeezed in its tube.

As a glacier moves, it breaks up rock and pushes and carries sediment.

Sliding The weight of a glacier and heat from Earth cause ice at the bottom of a glacier to melt. A layer of water forms under the glacier. The glacier slides along on this layer of water just as an ice cube might slide on a countertop.

READING VISUALS In the illustration, why are cracks shown near the surface of the glacier and not at the bottom?

Chapter 17: **Erosion and Deposition** 595

A moving glacier left visible abrasion lines on this rock.

Glaciers deposit large amounts of sediment.

As glaciers have melted and retreated, they have shaped the landscapes of many places on Earth. As a glacier moves or expands, it transports a vast amount of sediment—a mix of boulders, small rocks, sand, and clay. It acts like a plow, pushing rock and soil and plucking out big blocks of rock. As a glacier moves over rock, it scratches and scrapes the rock in a process called abrasion. Abrasion leaves visible grooves on rock surfaces.

Moraines

When glaciers expand and advance and then melt and retreat, they affect both the land underneath them and the land around them. A glacier pushes huge amounts of sediment to its sides and front. When the glacier retreats, the deposits of sediment remain as visible evidence that ice once moved through. The sediment left directly on the ground surface by a retreating glacier is called **till.**

A deposit of till left behind by a retreating glacier is called a **moraine** (muh-RAYN). The ridges of till deposited at the sides of a glacier are called lateral moraines. The till that marks the farthest advance of a glacier forms a deposit called an end moraine. Moraines formed by continental glaciers, such as those in North America during the ice age, can be huge—many kilometers long.

The blanket of till that a glacier deposits along its bottom is called a ground moraine. Rock deposits from glaciers can often be identified as till because the till rocks are different, in type or age, from the rock that was present before the glacier formed.

CHECK YOUR READING Draw a sketch of a glacier and label where lateral, end, and ground moraines would form.

A glacier scooped out this valley in California and left behind lateral moraines.

Lateral moraines

Lakes

Besides ridges, hills, and blankets of till, melting glaciers also leave behind depressions of various sizes that can become lakes. Landscapes shaped by glaciers are often dotted with small kettle lakes as well as larger lakes. A **kettle lake** is a bowl-shaped depression that was formed by a block of ice from a glacier and then became filled with water.

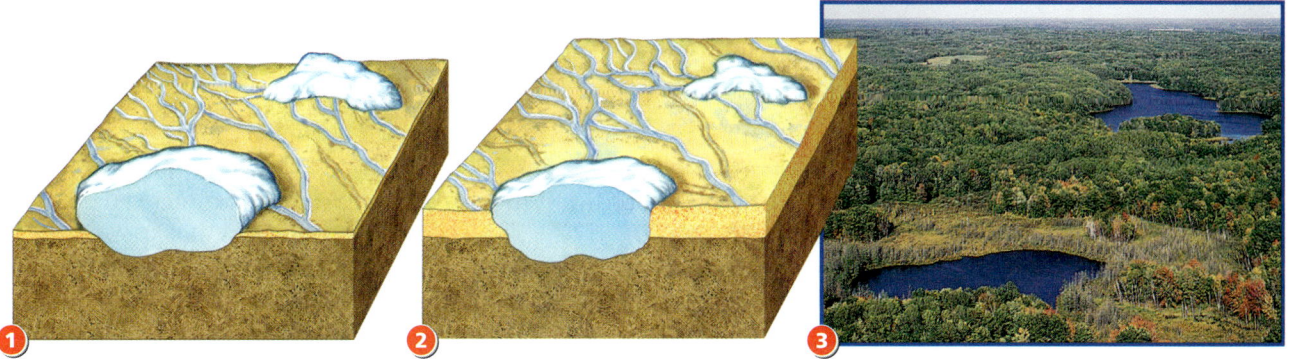

① As a glacier moves away, it leaves huge blocks of ice.

② Over time, sediment builds up around the ice.

③ The ice melts, leaving behind bowls that become kettle lakes. These lakes are in Wisconsin.

The last ice sheet in North America formed many kettle lakes in some regions. Kettle lakes are common in Michigan, Wisconsin, and Minnesota.

INVESTIGATE Kettle Lake Formation

How do kettle lakes form?

Kettle lakes form when sediment builds up around blocks of ice left behind by a retreating glacier. Use what you know about kettle lake formation to design a model of the process.

DESIGN YOUR OWN

PROCEDURE

① Use the tray, the ice cubes, and the other materials to model how sediment builds up around ice blocks.

② Write a description of the process you used to make your model.

WHAT DO YOU THINK?

- Describe how your model worked. What did you do first? What happened next?
- Did your model accurately represent the formation of kettle lakes? Did it work? Why or why not?
- What were the limitations of your model? Are there any aspects of kettle lake formation that are not represented? If so, what are they?

SKILL FOCUS
Designing models

MATERIALS
- shallow tray
- ice cubes
- modeling clay
- sand
- gravel
- water

TIME
30 minutes

Great Lakes Formation

① 14,000 Years Ago

The ice sheet covering a land of river valleys began to retreat.

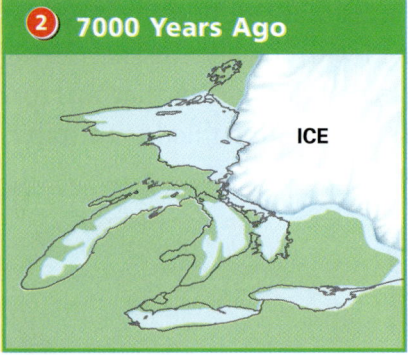

② 7000 Years Ago

Water filled the bowls carved out by the ice.

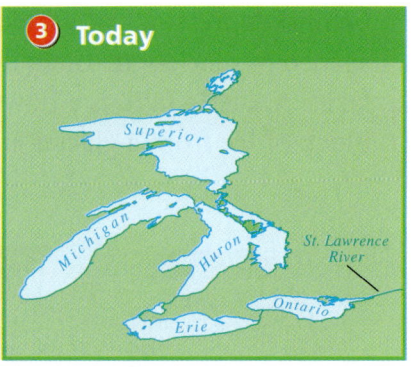

③ Today

The Great Lakes contain 20 percent of the world's fresh lake water.

Many large lakes are the result of ice ages. In some places, lakes formed after glaciers in valleys melted and left behind moraines that dammed the valleys. Many of these lakes are long and narrow, like the Finger Lakes in New York, which are named for their slender shape.

The Great Lakes were formed thousands of years ago as an ice sheet moved over the land and then melted. A million years ago, the region of the Great Lakes had many river valleys. The ice sheet gouged out large depressions in the land and left piles of rock and debris that blocked water from draining out. In some areas, where the deepest Great Lakes are now, the enormous weight of the glacier actually caused the land to sink as much as one kilometer.

The ice sheet started to melt about 14,000 years ago. By about 7000 years ago, it had melted past what would become Lake Erie and Lake Ontario, the lakes farthest to the east.

 **CHECK YOUR READING** What are two ways the ice sheet formed the Great Lakes?

17.4 Review

KEY CONCEPTS

1. Describe the two processes that cause glaciers to move.
2. What are the two major types of glaciers, and where are they found?
3. Describe the land features left behind by glaciers that have melted and shrunk.

CRITICAL THINKING

4. **Compare and Contrast** Identify two ways in which the erosion effects of glaciers differ from those of rivers.
5. **Predict** How would glaciers be affected by changes in climate, such as global warming and global cooling?

CHALLENGE

6. **Infer** Regions near the equator are generally the warmest on Earth. However, in one small area of Africa, there are glaciers close to the equator. Form a hypothesis to explain why these glaciers exist.

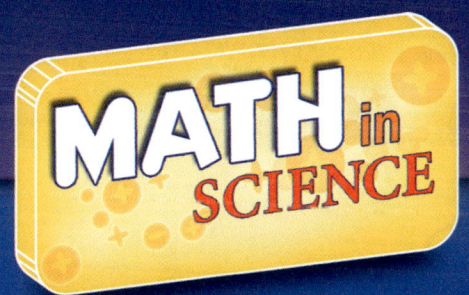

Math in Science

MATH TUTORIAL
CLASSZONE.COM
Click on Math Tutorial for more help with making line graphs.

SKILL: CREATING A LINE GRAPH

Snow Line Elevation and Latitude

Glaciers form above the snow line, the lowest elevation at which there is permanent snow in the summer. The snow line elevation depends on temperature and precipitation. In the hot tropics the snow line is high in the mountains, while at the poles it is near sea level. The table shows the snow line elevations at different locations on Earth. The latitude of each location indicates how far the location is from the equator; the latitude of the equator is 0 degrees, and the latitude of the North Pole is 90 degrees.

Location	Latitude (degrees north)	Snow Line Elevation (meters)
North Pole	90	0
Juneau, Alaska	58	1050
Glacier National Park	49	2600
Sierra Nevada	37	3725
Himalayas (East Nepal)	28	5103
Ecuador	0	4788

Follow the steps below to make a line graph of the data.

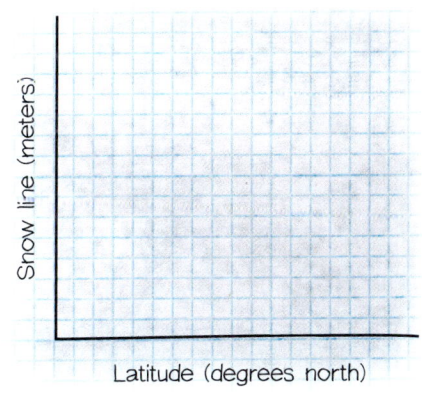

(1) On a sheet of graph paper, draw and label axes. Put latitude on the horizontal axis and snow line elevation on the vertical axis.

(2) Choose and mark a scale for each axis.

(3) Graph each point.

(4) Draw line segments to connect the points.

Use your graph to answer the following questions.

1. Mount Kenya is very close to the equator. Estimate the snow line elevation on Mount Kenya.

2. Mount Rainier is at 47 degrees north latitude and is 4389 meters tall. Can there be glaciers on Mount Rainier? If so, estimate the elevation above which the glaciers form.

3. Mount Washington in New Hampshire is at 45 degrees north latitude and is 1917 meters tall. Can there be glaciers on Mount Washington? If so, estimate their lowest elevation.

CHALLENGE Temperatures are hotter at the equator than at 28 degrees north latitude. Why is the snow line lower at the equator in Ecuador? (**Hint:** The answer involves precipitation.)

Chapter 17: **Erosion and Deposition** 599

17 Chapter Review

the BIG idea
Water, wind, and ice shape Earth's surface.

CONTENT REVIEW
CLASSZONE.COM

KEY CONCEPTS SUMMARY

1 Forces wear down and build up Earth's surface.

Water, wind, and ice move sediment in the process called **erosion**. The placement of sediment in a new location is **deposition**, part of the erosion process.

VOCABULARY
erosion p. 573
deposition p. 573
mass wasting p. 575

2 Moving water shapes land.

Water drains from land in **drainage basins**, which are separated by **divides**. As water flows over land and underground, it moves sediment and changes land features.

VOCABULARY
drainage basin p. 579
divide p. 579
floodplain p. 580
alluvial fan p. 581
delta p. 581
sinkhole p. 583

3 Waves and wind shape land.

The action of water moves sand and builds up new landforms, such as **sandbars** and **barrier islands**. Wind forms **dunes**.

VOCABULARY
longshore drift p. 587
longshore current p. 587
sandbar p. 588
barrier island p. 588
dune p. 589
loess p. 590

4 Glaciers carve land and move sediments.

Glaciers are large bodies of ice that change landscapes as they move.

VOCABULARY
glacier p. 593
till p. 596
moraine p. 596
kettle lake p. 597

600 Unit 4: Earth's Surface

Reviewing Vocabulary

Copy and complete the chart below. Explain how each landscape feature is formed.

Feature	How It Forms
EXAMPLE delta	A river deposits sediment as it enters the ocean.
1. alluvial fan	
2. sinkhole	
3. sandbar	
4. barrier island	
5. dune	
6. loess	
7. moraine	
8. kettle lake	

Reviewing Key Concepts

Multiple Choice *Choose the letter of the best answer.*

9. The first stage in the erosion process is
   a. deposition
   b. mass wasting
   c. drainage
   d. weathering

10. The main natural force responsible for mass movements of rocks and debris is
    a. rainwater   c. gravity
    b. wind   d. fire

11. A sinkhole is formed by the collapse of
    a. an alluvial fan
    b. a cavern
    c. a moraine
    d. a kettle lake

12. Rivers transport sediment to
    a. drainage basins
    b. oceans and lakes
    c. the water table
    d. moraines

13. Drainage basins are separated by a
    a. moraine   c. tributary
    b. divide   d. barrier island

14. In high mountains, a valley carved by a stream has the shape of a
    a. U   c. plate
    b. crescent   d. V

15. An oxbow lake is formed by the cutting off of a
    a. meander   c. sinkhole
    b. drainage basin d. glacier

16. Sandbars, spits, and barrier islands can all be built up by
    a. glaciers   c. wind
    b. ocean waves   d. mass wasting

17. A dune is a sand mound built up primarily by
    a. gravity   c. glaciers
    b. running water d. wind

18. Strong winds can transport large quantities of
    a. gravel   c. dry sand
    b. wet sand   d. clay

19. A mountain valley carved by a glacier has the shape of a
    a. U   c. bowl
    b. crescent   d. V

Short Answer *Answer each of the following questions in a sentence or two.*

20. How is deposition part of the erosion process?
21. How can rainwater in the Rocky Mountains end up in the ocean?
22. What is the effect of a longshore current on a beach?
23. Why is a mass movement of mud called a flow?
24. What visual evidence is a sign of creep?
25. What is the connection between icebergs and glaciers?

Chapter 17: **Erosion and Deposition** 601

Thinking Critically

This photograph shows two glaciers joining to form one (A). Make a sketch of the glaciers to answer the next three questions.

26. APPLY Place an arrow to show in which direction the main glacier (A) is moving.

27. ANALYZE Mark the places where you think till would be found.

28. APPLY Mark the location of a lateral moraine.

29. ANALYZE Why does the main glacier not have an end moraine?

30. COMPARE AND CONTRAST Compare the main glacier valley in the photograph with the valley at the far right (B). How are the valleys different? Explain why they might be different.

31. APPLY In exploring an area of land, what clues would you look for to determine whether glaciers were once there?

32. COMPARE AND CONTRAST How is a deposit of till from a glacier similar to a river delta? How is it different?

33. EVALUATE If you were growing crops on a field near a slow-moving, curvy river, what would an advantage of the field's location be? What might be a disadvantage?

34. COMPARE AND CONTRAST How are mudflows and mass wasting of rock similar? How are they different? Include references to speed and types of material in your answer.

35. INFER If the wind usually blows from west to east over a large area of land, and the wind usually slows down over the eastern half of the area, where would you be likely to find loess in the area? Explain your answer.

36. APPLY If you were considering a location for a house and were concerned about creep, what two factors about the land would you consider?

37. SYNTHESIZE Describe how the processes of erosion and deposition are involved in the formation of kettle lakes.

the BIG idea

38. SYNTHESIZE Describe how snow falling onto the Continental Divide in the Rocky Mountains can be part of the process of erosion and deposition. Include the words *divide*, *glacier*, *stream*, and *ocean* in your answer.

39. PROVIDE EXAMPLES Choose three examples of erosion processes—one each from Sections 17.2, 17.3, and 17.4. Explain how gravity is involved in each of these processes.

UNIT PROJECTS

Evaluate all the data, results, and information in your project folder. Prepare to present your project. Be ready to answer questions posed by your classmates about your results.

Standardized Test Practice

For practice on your state test, go to...
TEST PRACTICE
CLASSZONE.COM

Analyzing a Diagram

Use the diagram to answer the questions below.

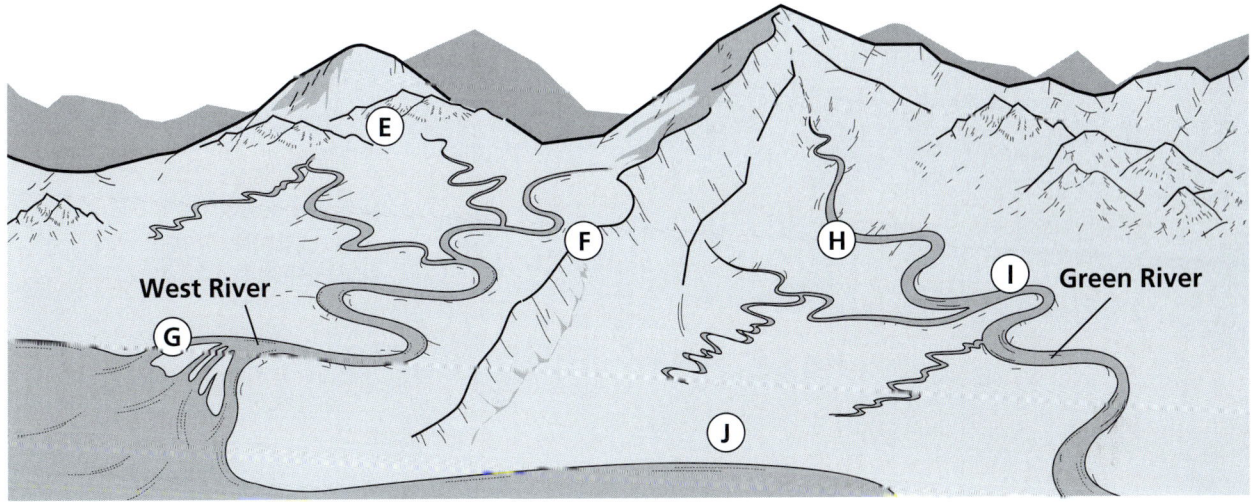

1. Where would a glacier be most likely to form?
   a. E
   b. F
   c. G
   d. H

2. Where is a divide?
   a. E
   b. F
   c. H
   d. I

3. Where is a delta?
   a. E
   b. F
   c. G
   d. J

4. Which process could move sediment from point E to point G?
   a. weathering
   b. erosion
   c. deposition
   d. drifting

5. Which word best describes the building up of sediment at point G?
   a. weathering
   b. erosion
   c. deposition
   d. drifting

6. Why might the water in the Green River move faster at point H than at point I?
   a. The river at point H is warmer.
   b. The river at point H is smaller.
   c. The slope at point H is steeper.
   d. More rain falls at point H.

Extended Response

Answer the two questions below in detail. Include some of the terms shown in the word box. In your answers, underline each term you use.

| ocean waves | currents | barrier island |
| grass | glaciers | kettle lakes |

7. Each year, Clark and his family visit the ocean. Clark notices that a sandbar near the coast is slightly larger each year. Predict what will happen if this trend continues.

8. Annika often goes fishing at one of several small, round lakes that are within 20 miles of her house in Minnesota. How might these lakes have formed?

Chapter 17: **Erosion and Deposition** 603

UNIT 5

The Changing Earth

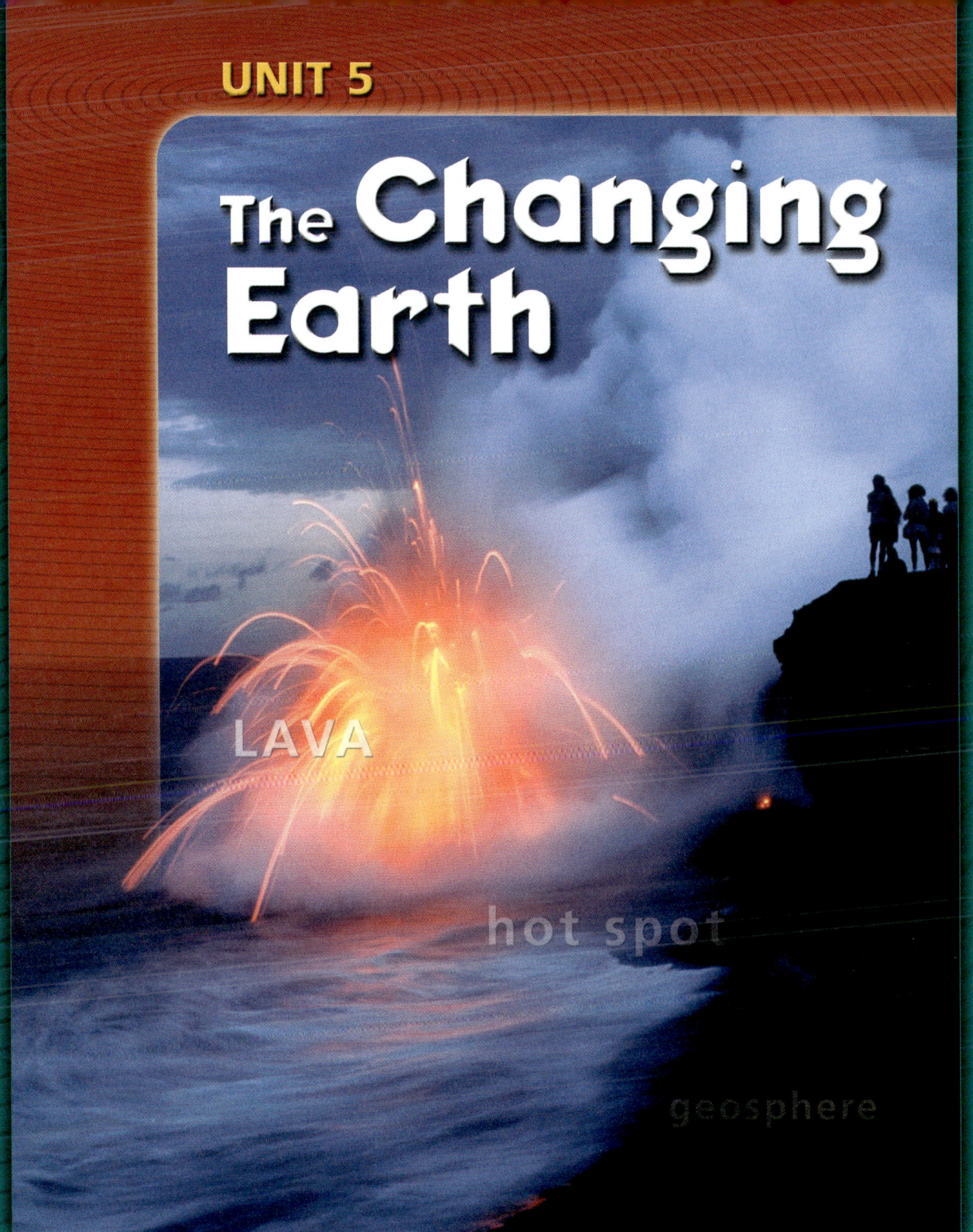

LAVA

hot spot

geosphere

Contents Overview

Frontiers in Science
Studying Volcanoes with Satellites — 606

Timelines in Science
The Story of Fossils — 744

Chapter 18	Plate Tectonics	610
Chapter 19	Earthquakes	646
Chapter 20	Mountains and Volcanoes	678
Chapter 21	Views of Earth's Past	712
Chapter 22	Natural Resources	748

FRONTIERS in Science

Studying VOLCANOES with Satellites

New ways of viewing Earth are giving scientists powerful tools for learning about and predicting volcanic eruptions.

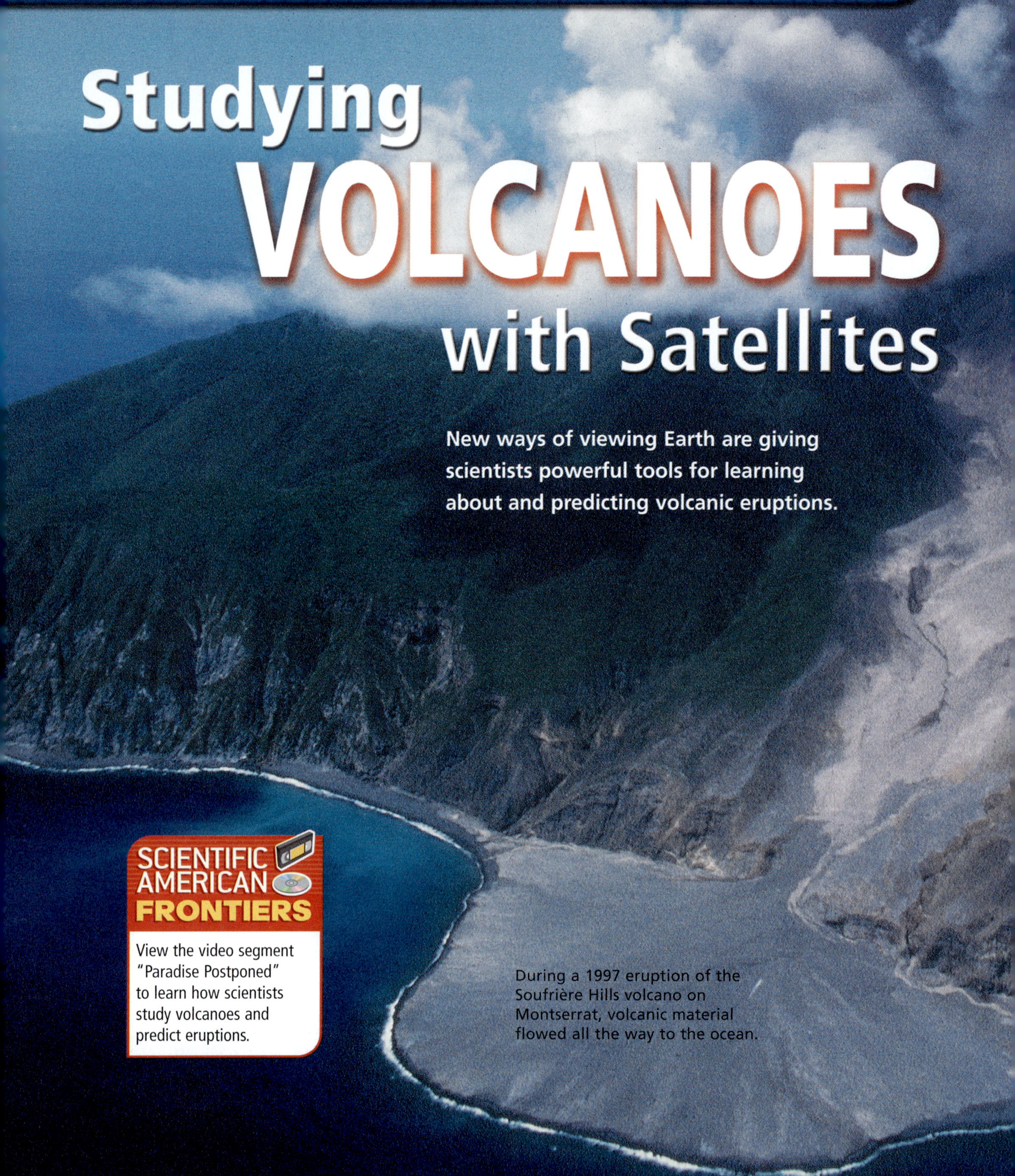

SCIENTIFIC AMERICAN FRONTIERS
View the video segment "Paradise Postponed" to learn how scientists study volcanoes and predict eruptions.

During a 1997 eruption of the Soufrière Hills volcano on Montserrat, volcanic material flowed all the way to the ocean.

A plume of volcanic ash and gases rises from Soufrière Hills volcano, Montserrat, in this photograph taken from a satellite on October 29, 2002.

Deadly Eruptions

On the island of Montserrat in the West Indies, small eruptions of the Soufrière Hills volcano began in 1995. These early warnings gave people time to move away several months before the first of the large explosions.

People living in the towns near Nevado del Ruiz volcano in Colombia were not so fortunate. On a night in November 1985, a storm hid the snow-covered volcano. No one could see the start of an eruption. Huge amounts of snow and ice melted and mixed with volcanic ash to form mudflows that killed 25,000 people. The flow that buried much of the town of Armero traveled 74 kilometers in just two and one-half hours.

Throughout history volcanic eruptions have caused some of the world's worst disasters. Warnings might have saved hundreds of thousands of lives. But in most cases people had no idea that a rain of rock, a cloud of toxic gases, or other deadly effects of an erupting volcano would soon engulf their area. By the time people realized that a volcano was erupting, it was too late to get away. Today, scientists monitor volcanoes around the world to help avoid such tragedies.

A 1996 eruption of Alaska's Pavlof volcano was the first to be predicted with the use of data from space. The satellite image recorded during the eruption shows an area of hot ground on the volcano in red.

Predicting Volcanic Eruptions

Scientists who study volcanoes paid close attention when an instrument on a weather satellite unexpectedly "saw" hot ground in 1996. The instrument's usual function is to measure cloud temperatures, but it detected an area of increased heat on Alaska's Pavlof volcano. The scientists predicted that the volcano would soon erupt. Three days later, it did. This eruption was the first to be predicted with information from space. Now computers check satellite data as they receive the data. Any unusually hot areas trigger an automatic e-mail alert to scientists.

In 1999, NASA launched the *Terra* satellite as part of a program to study Earth's surface and atmosphere. Among *Terra's* instruments is one that detects heat given off by the planet's surface. When scientists observe an unusual increase in surface temperature, they determine whether magma is rising underground. In some cases unusual heat has been the first sign that a volcano is building toward an eruption.

After an Eruption

Satellites are also used to monitor eruptions as they happen. Lava flows show up clearly, as you can see in the *Terra* image on page 609. In addition, satellites are used to track the locations of volcanic ash and gas clouds. Airplanes flying into this material can be severely damaged, so pilots need to know where it is. Volcanic material in

SCIENTIFIC AMERICAN FRONTIERS

View the "Paradise Postponed" segment of your *Scientific American Frontiers* video to learn how scientists monitor volcanic eruptions.

IN THIS SCENE FROM THE VIDEO
Scientist Barry Voigt examines the effects of a powerful eruption that occurred a few days earlier.

STUDYING VOLCANOES Until 1995, the Caribbean island of Montserrat was a peaceful tourist destination. Then, the island's volcano began to erupt. Over the next two years, the volcano erupted dozens of times, spewing out hot ash, rocks, and gases. These eruptions destroyed most of the island's towns and drove away many residents.

Scientists from around the world have come to Montserrat to find out how well they can predict eruptions. Seismic stations buried near the volcano detect earthquakes, which can be a sign that the volcano is about to erupt. Scientists can also predict an eruption by studying changes in the lava dome that has built up on the volcano. When an eruption does occur, scientists visit the site to collect rocks and measure the volcanic ash flow.

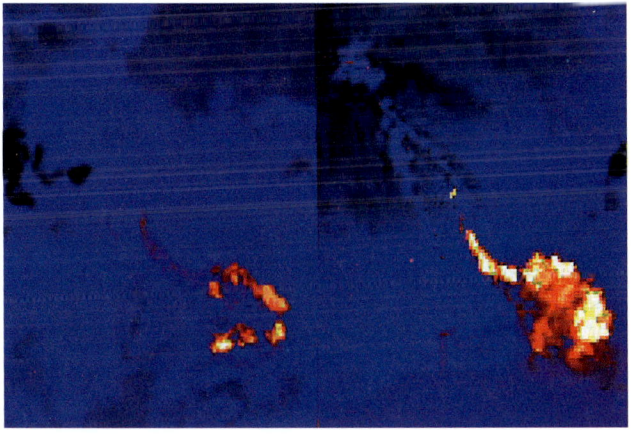

Data collected by the *Terra* satellite show the progress of a Hawaiian lava flow as it enters the ocean on May 13, 2000 (left), and on August 1, 2000 (right).

the air can be difficult to see or to distinguish from normal clouds, especially at night. Satellites are particularly helpful in identifying and tracking eruptions in remote areas where there are few or no observers.

Explosive Neighbors

Satellites such as *Terra* are among the tools scientists use to monitor restless volcanoes near urban areas. Mount Rainier, a volcano in Washington, looms near the large cities of Seattle and Tacoma. In the past, heat from eruptions has melted large amounts of the ice and snow at the top of the volcano, creating mudflows that destroyed everything in their path. Another extremely dangerous volcano is Mount Vesuvius, near Naples, Italy. Timely warnings before eruptions of such volcanoes can allow authorities to safely evacuate the millions of people who live near them.

UNANSWERED Questions

Even when scientists predict that a volcano will erupt soon, many questions still cannot be answered.

- How powerful will the next eruption be?
- On what day (or even during what week) will the volcano erupt?
- How much magma is rising under the volcano, and how fast is it rising? Will it stop?

UNIT PROJECTS

As you study this unit, work alone or with a group on one of the projects listed below.

Review Movie Science

Review a movie that features a volcanic eruption to evaluate how accurate the movie's depiction of a volcano is.

- Visit the U.S. Geological Survey Web site for a list of movies about volcanoes, such as *Dante's Peak*.
- Evaluate one movie and prepare a report on it for a radio or TV spot.

Earthquake Report

Make a map of the volcanic eruptions and earthquakes that occur around the world while you are studying this unit.

- Write a news script and create a graphic to show the events' locations and intensities.
- Present your findings as a special TV report for an evening news program.

Ash-Fall Fossil Exhibit

Prepare an exhibit showing how volcanic ash can preserve fossils of the organisms it buries. You could begin by researching Ashfall Fossil Beds State Historical Park in Nebraska.

- Create a poster that shows the major steps in the formation of fossils of creatures in volcanic ash.
- Make models or tracings of some ash-fall fossils.
- Display the poster and models as a classroom or Web-site exhibit.

CAREER CENTER
CLASSZONE.COM

Learn more about careers in volcanology.

CHAPTER 18

Plate Tectonics

the BIG idea

The movement of tectonic plates causes geologic changes on Earth.

What might have made this huge crack in the Earth?

Key Concepts

SECTION 1 Earth has several layers.
Learn about Earth's interior and its rigid surface plates.

SECTION 2 Continents change position over time.
Learn how continental drift and plate tectonics changed the way people view Earth.

SECTION 3 Plates move apart.
Learn about the three types of plate boundaries and what happens when plates move apart.

SECTION 4 Plates converge or scrape past each other.
Learn what geologic events occur at these plate boundaries.

Internet Preview

CLASSZONE.COM
Chapter 18 online resources: Content Review, two Visualizations, one Resource Center, Math Tutorial, and Test Practice

EXPLORE the BIG idea

Watching a Pot Boil

Put a medium-sized pot of water on to boil. Place a small wet sponge on the water. Watch the water and sponge as the water heats.

Observe and Think
What happened to the water as it heated? What happened to the sponge as the water became hotter?

Earth's Moving Surface

Place two halves of a peanut butter and jelly sandwich side by side. Very slowly push them together. Then take one half and very slowly tear it into two pieces.

Observe and Think
What happened when you pushed and pulled on the sandwich halves? What might this activity tell you about the movements of Earth's surface?

Internet Activity: Earth's Interior

Go to **ClassZone.com** to explore the makeup of Earth's layers. Find out how scientists learned what the interior of Earth is like.

Observe and Think
Science fiction books and movies show people traveling to the center of Earth. Do you think this can happen any time soon? Why or why not?

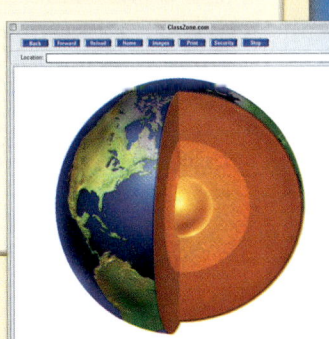

Plates **Code: MDL052**

Chapter 18: **Plate Tectonics** 611

CHAPTER 18
Getting Ready to Learn

CONCEPT REVIEW

- Most rocks are made of minerals.
- Different types of rocks are formed under different temperatures and pressures.
- Earth's surface has changed over millions of years.

VOCABULARY REVIEW

See Glossary for definitions.

density
mineral
rock

CONTENT REVIEW
CLASSZONE.COM
Review concepts and vocabulary.

TAKING NOTES

SUPPORTING MAIN IDEAS

Make a chart to show main ideas and the information that supports them. Copy each blue heading. Below each heading, add supporting information, such as reasons, explanations, and examples.

VOCABULARY STRATEGY

Place each vocabulary term at the center of a **description wheel** diagram. Write some words describing it on the spokes.

See the Note-Taking Handbook on pages R45–R51.

SCIENCE NOTEBOOK

Earth is made up of materials with different densities.
→ Dense materials—such as iron and nickel—sink toward center
→ Less dense materials rise toward surface

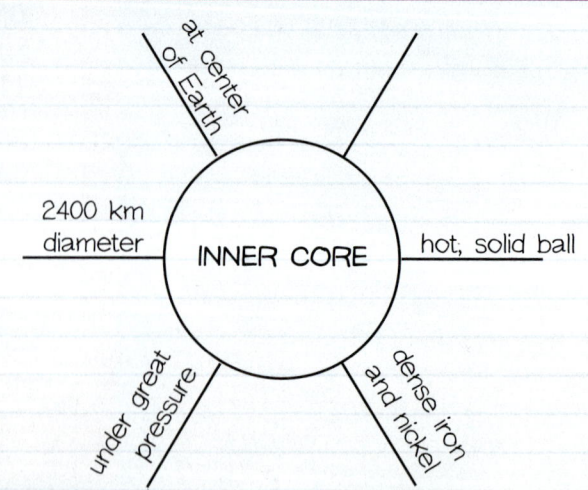

INNER CORE
- at center of Earth
- hot, solid ball
- dense iron and nickel
- under great pressure
- 2400 km diameter

612 Unit 5: The Changing Earth

KEY CONCEPT
Earth has several layers.

 BEFORE, you learned
- Minerals and rocks are the building blocks of Earth
- Different types of rocks make up Earth's surface

 NOW, you will learn
- About the different properties of Earth's layers
- About the plates that make up Earth's outermost layers

VOCABULARY

inner core p. 614
outer core p. 614
mantle p. 615
crust p. 615
lithosphere p. 615
asthenosphere p. 615
tectonic plate p. 616

EXPLORE Density

Will a denser material sink or float?

PROCEDURE

1. Add equal amounts of water to 2 cups. Add 3 spoonfuls of salt to one of the cups and stir until the salt is dissolved.

2. Add 10 drops of food coloring to the same cup in which you dissolved the salt.

3. Gently pour about a third of the colored salt water into the cup of fresh water. Observe what happens.

WHAT DO YOU THINK?
- What did you observe when the two types of water were mixed?
- What does this activity tell you about materials of different density?

MATERIALS
- 2 clear plastic cups
- tap water
- table salt
- plastic spoon
- food coloring

SUPPORTING MAIN IDEAS
Support the main ideas about Earth's layers with details and examples.

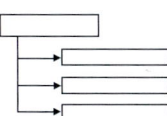

Earth is made up of materials with different densities.

Scientists think that about 4.6 billion years ago, Earth formed as bits of material collided and stuck together. The planet grew larger as more and more material was added. These impacts, along with radioactive decay and Earth's gravity, produced intense heat. The young planet became a glowing ball of melted rock.

In time, denser materials, such as iron and nickel, sank toward the center of Earth. Less dense materials moved toward the surface. Other materials settled between the planet's center and its surface. Slowly, Earth's main layers formed—the core, the mantle, and the crust.

Chapter 18: **Plate Tectonics** 613

VOCABULARY
Draw a description wheel in your notebook for each term. You might want to include the pronunciation of some terms.

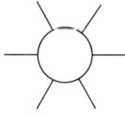

Earth's layers have different properties.

How do scientists know what Earth's deep interior is like? After all, no one has seen it. To explore the interior, scientists study the energy from earthquakes or underground explosions they set off. The energy travels through Earth somewhat like ripples move through a pond. The energy moves slower through less dense materials or liquids and faster through denser materials or solids. In this way, scientists infer what each layer is made of and how thick the layers are, as shown in the diagram below.

Core, Mantle, Crust

The core is Earth's densest region and is made up of two parts. The **inner core** is a ball of hot, solid metals. There is enormous pressure at the center of Earth. This squeezes the atoms of the metals so closely together that the core remains solid despite the intense heat.

The **outer core** is a layer of liquid metals that surrounds the inner core. The temperature and pressure in the outer core are lower than in the inner core. The lower pressure allows the metals to remain liquid.

Earth's Layers

Earth's layers formed as denser materials sank toward the center and less dense materials rose toward the surface.

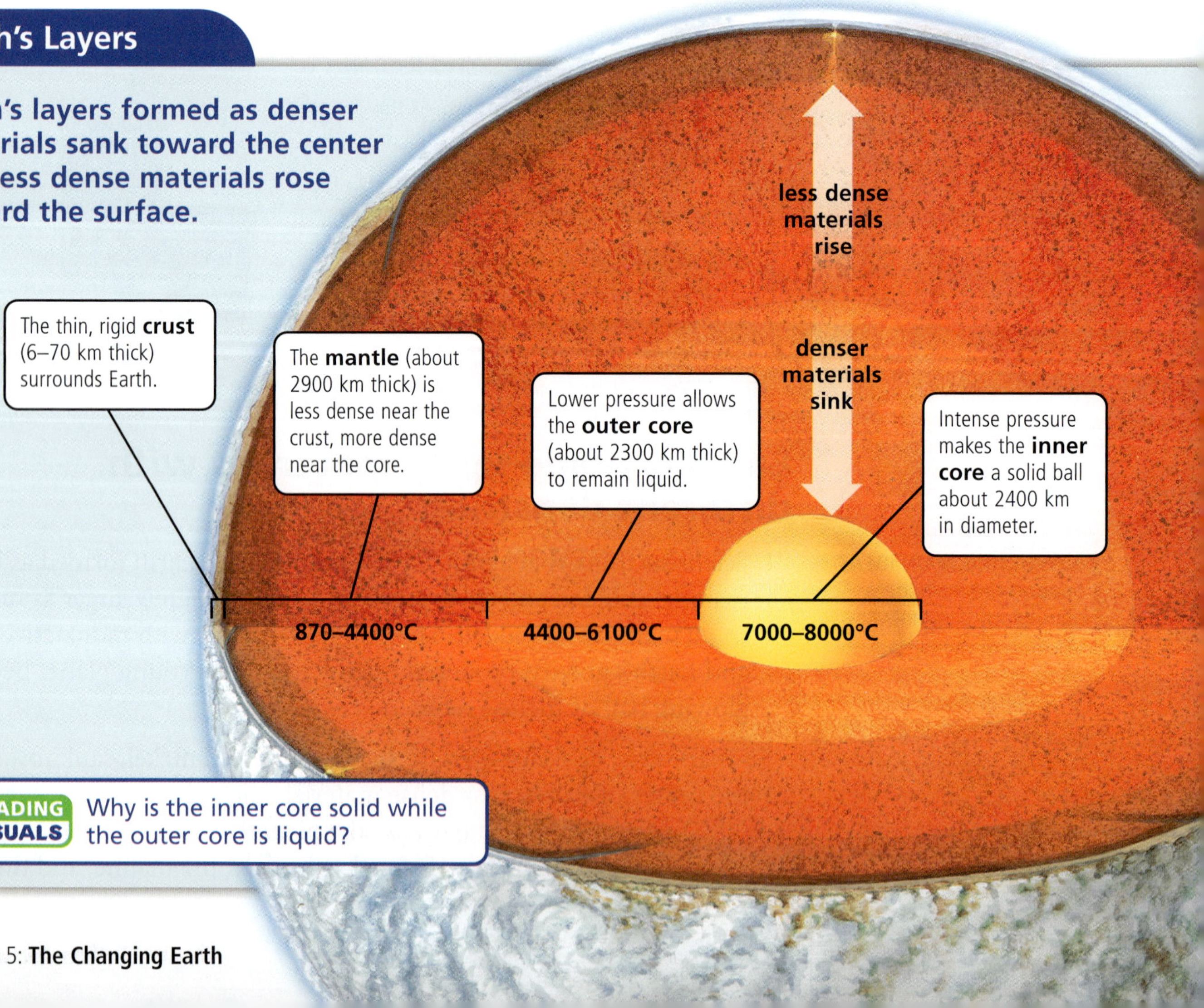

- The thin, rigid **crust** (6–70 km thick) surrounds Earth.
- The **mantle** (about 2900 km thick) is less dense near the crust, more dense near the core.
- Lower pressure allows the **outer core** (about 2300 km thick) to remain liquid.
- Intense pressure makes the **inner core** a solid ball about 2400 km in diameter.

less dense materials rise

denser materials sink

870–4400°C   4400–6100°C   7000–8000°C

READING VISUALS Why is the inner core solid while the outer core is liquid?

614 Unit 5: The Changing Earth

The **mantle** is Earth's thickest layer, measuring nearly 2900 kilometers (1700 mi). It is made of hot rock that is less dense than the metallic core. The very top part of the mantle is cool and rigid. Just below that, the rock is hot and soft enough to move like a thick paste.

The **crust** is a thin layer of cool rock. It surrounds Earth somewhat like a shell surrounds an egg. There are two basic types of crust. Continental crust includes all continents and some major islands. Oceanic crust includes all the ocean floors. As the diagram below shows, Earth's crust is thinnest under the oceans and thickest under continental mountain ranges. The crust is home to all life on Earth.

Lithosphere and Asthenosphere

Earth's crust and the very top of the mantle together form the **lithosphere** (LIHTH-uh-SFEER). The Greek prefix *litho-* means "stone" or "rock." This layer is the most rigid of all the layers. The lithosphere sits on top of the **asthenosphere** (as-THEHN-uh-SFEER), a layer of hotter, softer rock in the upper mantle. The Greek word *asthenés* means "weak." This layer is not actually weak, but it is soft enough to flow slowly like hot tar. You can imagine the lithosphere as solid pieces of pavement resting on hot tar.

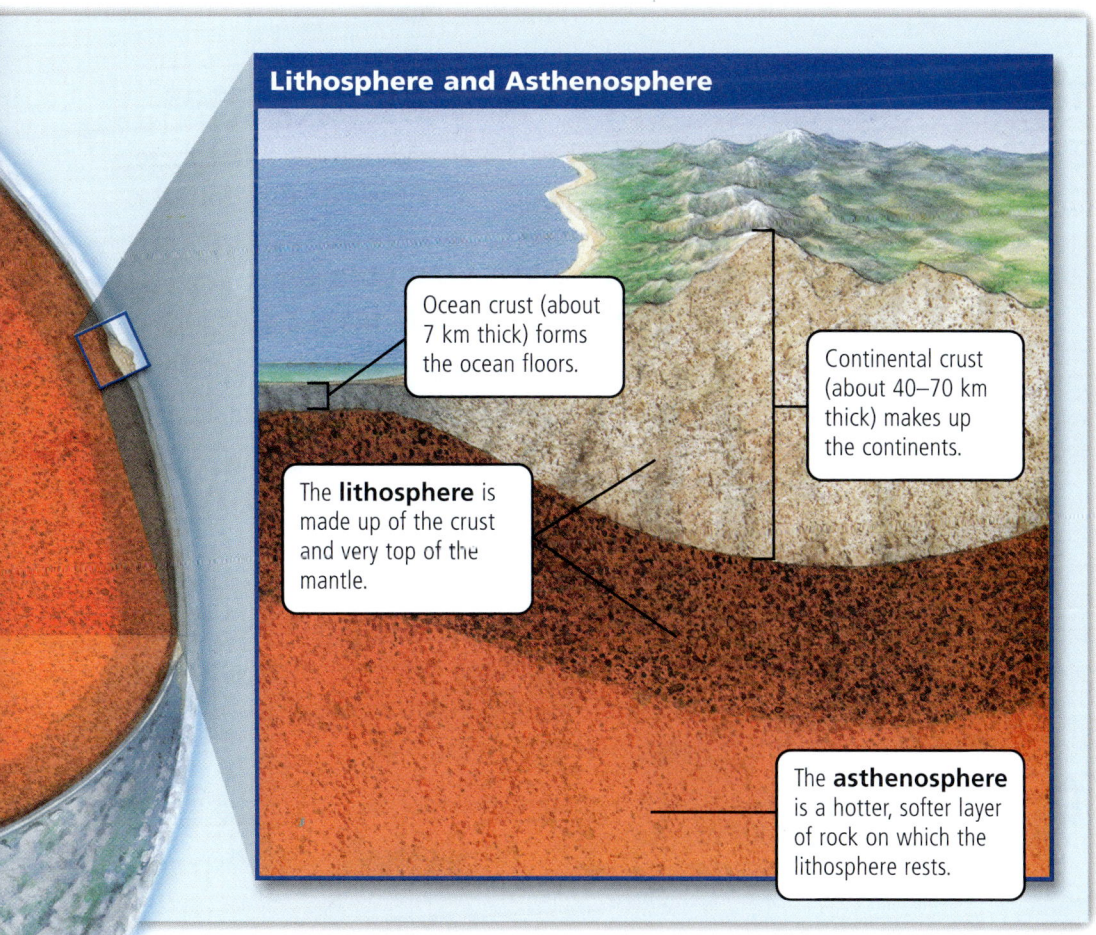

Lithosphere and Asthenosphere

Ocean crust (about 7 km thick) forms the ocean floors.

Continental crust (about 40–70 km thick) makes up the continents.

The **lithosphere** is made up of the crust and very top of the mantle.

The **asthenosphere** is a hotter, softer layer of rock on which the lithosphere rests.

Chapter 18: **Plate Tectonics**

INVESTIGATE Earth's Different Layers

How can you model Earth's layers?

PROCEDURE

1. Put a layer of wooden beads about 1 centimeter thick at the bottom of a clear plastic cup or small jar.
2. Put a layer of gravel about 2 centimeters thick on top of the wooden beads. Stir the beads and gravel until they are well mixed.
3. Put another layer of gravel about 1 centimeter thick on top of the mix. Do NOT mix this layer of gravel.
4. SLOWLY fill the cup about two-thirds full of water. Be sure not to disturb the layers in the cup.
5. Stir the beads and gravel with the stick. Observe what happens.

WHAT DO YOU THINK?

- What happened to the materials when you stirred them?
- How do you think this model represents the layers of Earth?

CHALLENGE What could you add to the model to represent Earth's solid core?

SKILL FOCUS
Modeling

MATERIALS
- clear plastic cup
- small colored wooden beads
- gravel
- stirring stick
- tap water

TIME
15 minutes

The lithosphere is made up of many plates.

READING TiP
The word *tectonic* comes from the Greek *tektōn*, which means "builder." Tectonic plates are constantly building and changing landforms and oceans around Earth.

As scientists studied Earth's surface, they discovered that the lithosphere does not form a continuous shell around Earth. Instead, they found that the lithosphere is broken into many large and small slabs of rock called **tectonic plates** (tehk-TAHN-ihk). Scientists do not know exactly how or when in Earth's history these giant plates formed.

Tectonic plates fit together like a jigsaw puzzle that makes up the surface of Earth. You could compare the lithosphere to the cracked shell of a hard-boiled egg. The shell may be broken into many pieces, but it still forms a "crust" around the egg itself.

Most large tectonic plates include both continental crust and oceanic crust, as shown in the diagram on page 617. Most of the thicker continental crust rises above the ocean. The rest of the plate is thin oceanic crust, or sea floor, and is underwater. The next time you look at the continents on a world map, remember you are seeing only the part of Earth's crust that rises above the ocean.

 Why do you see only the dry land areas of tectonic plates on a typical world map?

616 Unit 5: The Changing Earth

African Plate

Most tectonic plates have both continental and oceanic crust.

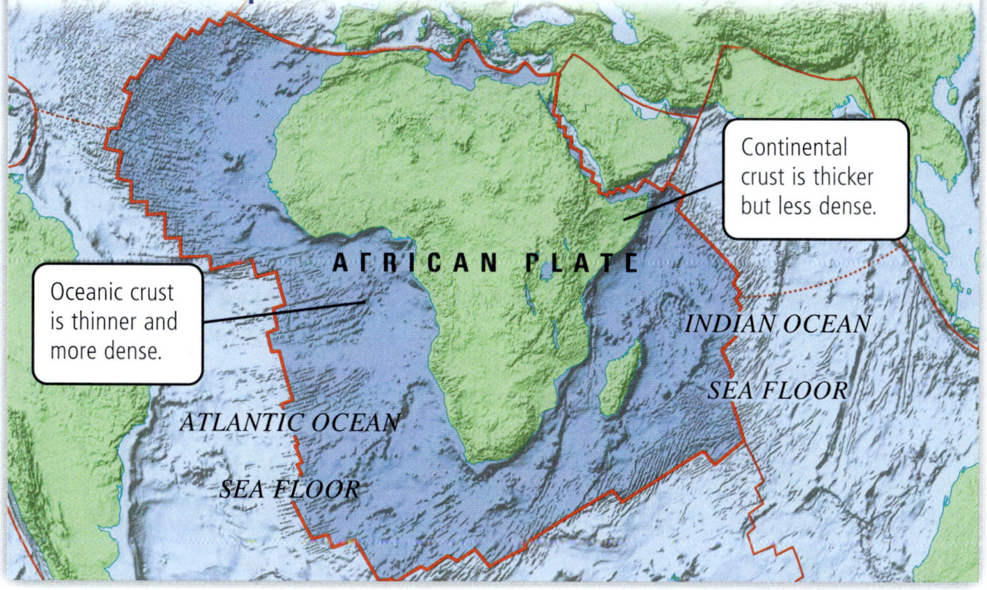

- Oceanic crust is thinner and more dense.
- Continental crust is thicker but less dense.

ATLANTIC OCEAN SEA FLOOR
AFRICAN PLATE
INDIAN OCEAN SEA FLOOR

In the diagram above, notice how much of the African Plate, shaded darker blue, lies underwater. The continent of Africa, which looks large on a world map, is actually about half the size of the entire plate. The plate's oceanic crust forms part of the sea floor of the Atlantic and Indian oceans and of the Mediterranean Sea. The ocean crusts of other plates make up the rest of the sea floors.

Earth's layers and tectonic plates are two of the most important discoveries in geology. They helped solve a mystery that had puzzled people for nearly 400 years. The mystery involved two questions. Have the continents always been where they are today? If not, how did they move to their present positions? In Section 18.2, you will find out how scientists are answering these questions.

18.1 Review

KEY CONCEPTS
1. Briefly describe the inner and outer cores, the mantle, and the crust.
2. In what ways is the lithosphere different from the asthenosphere?
3. Describe the structure of most tectonic plates.

CRITICAL THINKING
4. **Draw Conclusions** Suppose you are looking at a scene that has mountains near an ocean. Where do you think the crust would be the thickest? Why?
5. **Hypothesize** What would Earth look like if most of its crust was above sea level?

CHALLENGE
6. **Predict** You have learned that Earth's lithosphere is made up of many plates. How do you think this fact might help scientists solve the mystery of the moving continents?

KEY CONCEPT
Continents change position over time.

◀ **BEFORE, you learned**
- Earth's main layers are the core, the mantle, and the crust
- The lithosphere and asthenosphere are the topmost layers of Earth
- The lithosphere is made up of tectonic plates

▶ **NOW, you will learn**
- How the continental drift hypothesis was developed
- About evidence for plate movement from the sea floor
- How scientists developed the theory of plate tectonics

VOCABULARY

continental drift p. 618
Pangaea p. 620
mid-ocean ridge p. 620
convection p. 621
convection current p. 621
theory of plate tectonics p. 622

EXPLORE Movements of Continents

How do you put together a giant continent?

PROCEDURE

1. Work with a small group. Draw the outline of a large landmass. Fill in mountains, rivers, lakes, and any other features you like.

2. Cut out your landmass, then tear the drawing into several pieces and mix the pieces up. Ask another group to put the puzzle together.

MATERIALS
- sheet of paper
- colored marking pens
- scissors

WHAT DO YOU THINK?
- What clues helped you fit the pieces together?
- Do any lands on a world map seem to fit together?

Continents join together and split apart.

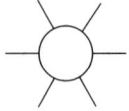

VOCABULARY
Draw a description wheel in your notebook for *continental drift*.

The idea that Earth's surface might be moving is not new. As far back as the 1500s, when mapmakers started including North and South America in their world maps, they noticed something curious. The western coast of Africa and the eastern coast of South America seemed to fit together like pieces in a puzzle. Were these continents joined at one time?

In the late 1800s, German scientist Alfred Wegener (VAY-guh-nuhr) began studying this question. In 1912, he proposed a hypothesis known as **continental drift**. According to Wegener's hypothesis, Earth's continents were once joined in a single landmass and gradually moved, or drifted, apart. For many years, people did not accept Wegener's ideas. Not until the mid-1900s did scientists find new evidence that made them consider continental drift more seriously.

Evidence for Continental Drift

Wegener gathered evidence for his hypothesis from fossils, from studies of ancient climate, and from the geology of continents.

Fossils Wegener learned that the fossils of an ancient reptile, *Mesosaurus* (MEHZ-uh-SAWR-uhs), had been discovered in South America and western Africa. This small reptile lived about 270 million years ago. Its fossils were not found anywhere else in the world. Wegener said this fact could easily be explained if South America and Africa were once joined, as shown in the map below.

Climate Evidence of climate change also supported Wegener's hypothesis. For example, Greenland today lies near the Arctic Circle and is mostly covered in ice. Yet fossils of tropical plants can be found on its shores. In contrast, South Africa today has a warm climate. Yet its rocks were deeply scratched by ice sheets that once covered the area.

Wegener suggested that these continents had moved, carrying their fossils and rocks with them. Greenland, for example, had once been near the equator and had slowly moved to the Arctic Circle. South Africa, once closer to the South Pole, had moved slowly north to a warmer region.

Geology Wegener's best evidence for continental drift came from the kinds of rocks that make up the continents. He showed that the type of rock found in Brazil matched the rock found in western Africa. Also, limestone layers in the Appalachian Mountains of North America were exactly like the limestone in Scotland's Highlands.

> **READING TIP**
> *Climate* refers to a pattern of wind, temperature, and rain or snow that occurs in a region over time. Earth's climates have changed many times in the planet's long history.

CHECK YOUR READING Which evidence for continental drift do you think is the most convincing? Explain your answer.

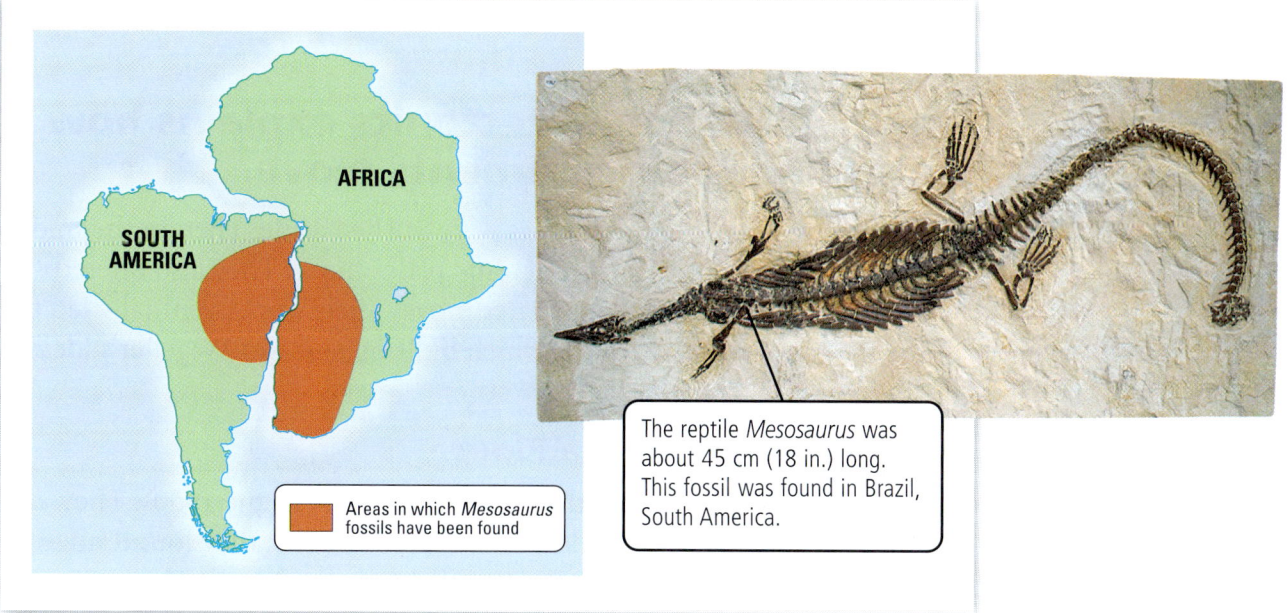

Areas in which *Mesosaurus* fossils have been found

The reptile *Mesosaurus* was about 45 cm (18 in.) long. This fossil was found in Brazil, South America.

Chapter 18: **Plate Tectonics** 619

Pangaea and Continental Drift

VISUALIZATION
CLASSZONE.COM
Examine continental movement over the past 150 million years.

For Wegener, all the evidence pointed to a single conclusion. The continents had once been joined in a huge supercontinent he called **Pangaea** (pan-JEE-uh). *Pangaea* comes from the Greek word meaning "all lands." This giant continent reached from pole to pole and was centered over the area where Africa lies today.

Pangaea began to split apart some 200 million years ago. In time, the continents moved to where they are today. Yet Wegener could not explain *how* the continents moved. Because of this, his critics called continental drift "a fairy tale" and rejected his hypothesis.

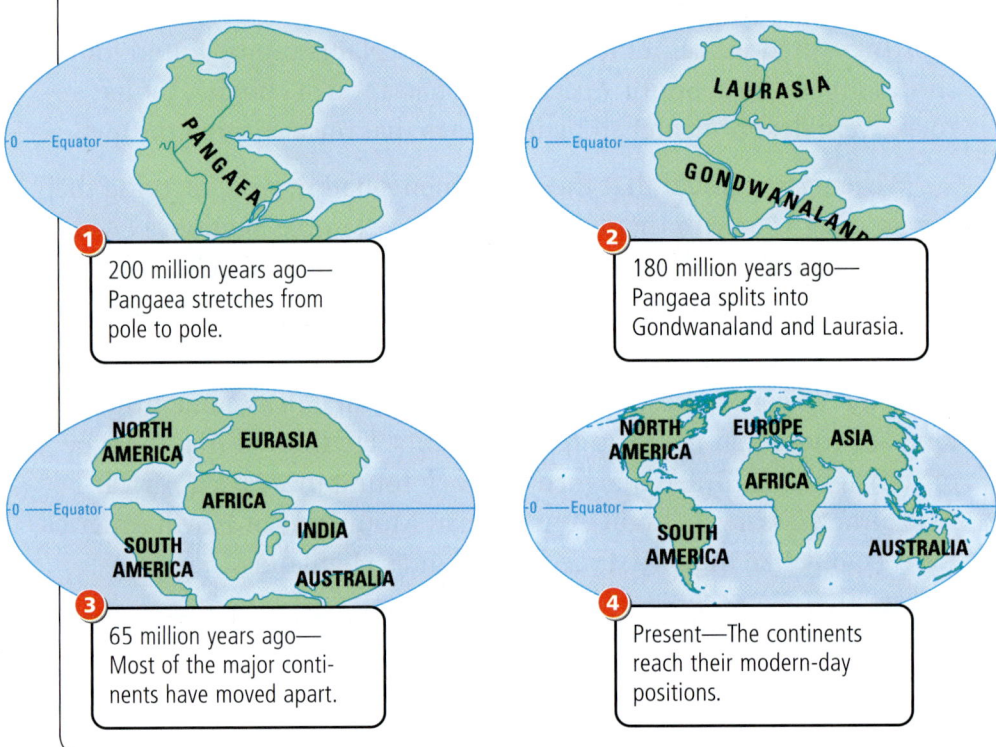

1. 200 million years ago— Pangaea stretches from pole to pole.
2. 180 million years ago— Pangaea splits into Gondwanaland and Laurasia.
3. 65 million years ago— Most of the major continents have moved apart.
4. Present—The continents reach their modern-day positions.

The theory of plate tectonics explains how plates and their continents move.

For many years, Wegener's ideas were pushed aside. Then in the mid-1900s, scientists proved that tectonic plates move. They also offered explanations about how the plates move. Their work eventually led to the theory of plate tectonics, which built on some of Wegener's ideas.

Evidence from the Sea Floor

Scientists began mapping the sea floor in detail in the 1950s. They expected the floor to be smooth and level. Instead, they found huge underwater mountain ranges, called **mid-ocean ridges.** These ridges appeared in every ocean, circling Earth like seams in a baseball.

Sea-Floor Spreading Scientists learned that the ridges form along cracks in the crust. Molten rock rises through these cracks, cools, and forms new oceanic crust. The old crust is pulled away to make room for new material. In this way, the sea floor slowly spreads apart. Scientists call these areas spreading centers. You will read more about spreading centers in Section 18.3.

Age of the Sea Floor Further evidence that the sea floor is spreading apart came from the age of the rocks in the crust. Scientists drilled into the sea floor from a specially equipped vessel called the *Glomar Challenger*. The rock samples revealed that the youngest rock is closest to the ridge, while the oldest rock is farthest away.

The samples also showed that even the oldest ocean floor is young—only 160 to 180 million years old. Continental crust is much older—up to 4 billion years old. These data confirmed that the ocean floor is constantly forming and moving away from the mid-ocean ridges like a conveyor belt. As the sea floor moves, so do the tectonic plates and their continents.

Ocean Trenches Yet, if the sea floor has been spreading for millions of years, why is Earth not getting larger? Scientists discovered the answer when they found huge trenches, like deep canyons, in the sea floor. At these sites, dense oceanic crust is sinking into the asthenosphere. Old crust is being destroyed at the same rate that new crust is forming. Thus, Earth remains the same size.

Scientists now had proof that tectonic plates move. But the same question remained. *How* could the plates move thousands of kilometers around the planet? The asthenosphere provided a possible answer.

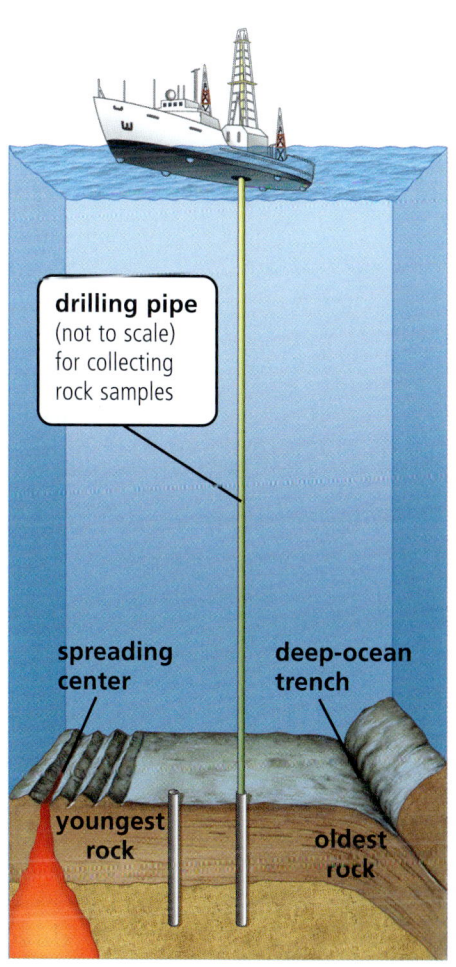

Scientists drill into the sea floor to obtain rock samples. The different ages of the rocks prove that plates move.

 How does the age of the sea floor show that plates move?

Causes of Plate Movement

Tectonic plates rest on the asthenosphere, a layer of soft, hot rock. Rock in this layer and in the mantle just below it moves by convection. **Convection** is energy transfer by the movement of a material. You have seen convection if you have ever boiled a pot of water. The water at the bottom of the pot heats up, becomes less dense, and rises. At the surface, it cools, becomes denser, and sinks, only to be heated and rise again.

The rock in the asthenosphere acts in a similar way. The hot, soft rock rises, cools, and sinks, then is heated and rises again. If this sinking and rising motion continues, it is called a **convection current**—a motion that transfers heat energy in a material.

Convection currents in the mantle are much slower than those in boiling water. The rock creeps only a few centimeters a year. The diagram below shows convection currents circulating. The tectonic plates in the lithosphere are carried on the asthenosphere like long, heavy boxes moved on huge rollers. Over millions of years, convection currents carry the plates thousands of kilometers.

Scientists suspect that two other motions—slab pull and ridge push—help move these huge plates. Slab pull occurs where gravity pulls the edge of a cool, dense plate into the asthenosphere, as shown in the diagram below. Because plates are rigid, the entire plate is dragged along. Ridge push occurs when material from a mid-ocean ridge slides downhill from the ridge. The material pushes the rest of the plate.

Putting the Theory Together

Geologists combined their knowledge of Earth's plates, the sea floor, and the asthenosphere to develop the **theory of plate tectonics.** The theory states that Earth's lithosphere is made up of huge plates that move over the surface of the Earth.

The map on page 623 shows Earth's major tectonic plates and the directions in which they move. They are the African, the Antarctic, the Australian, the Indian, the Eurasian, the Nazca, the North and South American, and the Pacific plates.

REMINDER
A scientific theory is a well-tested explanation that is consistent with all available evidence.

Causes of Plate Movement

Convection currents, slab pull, and ridge push move Earth's huge tectonic plates.

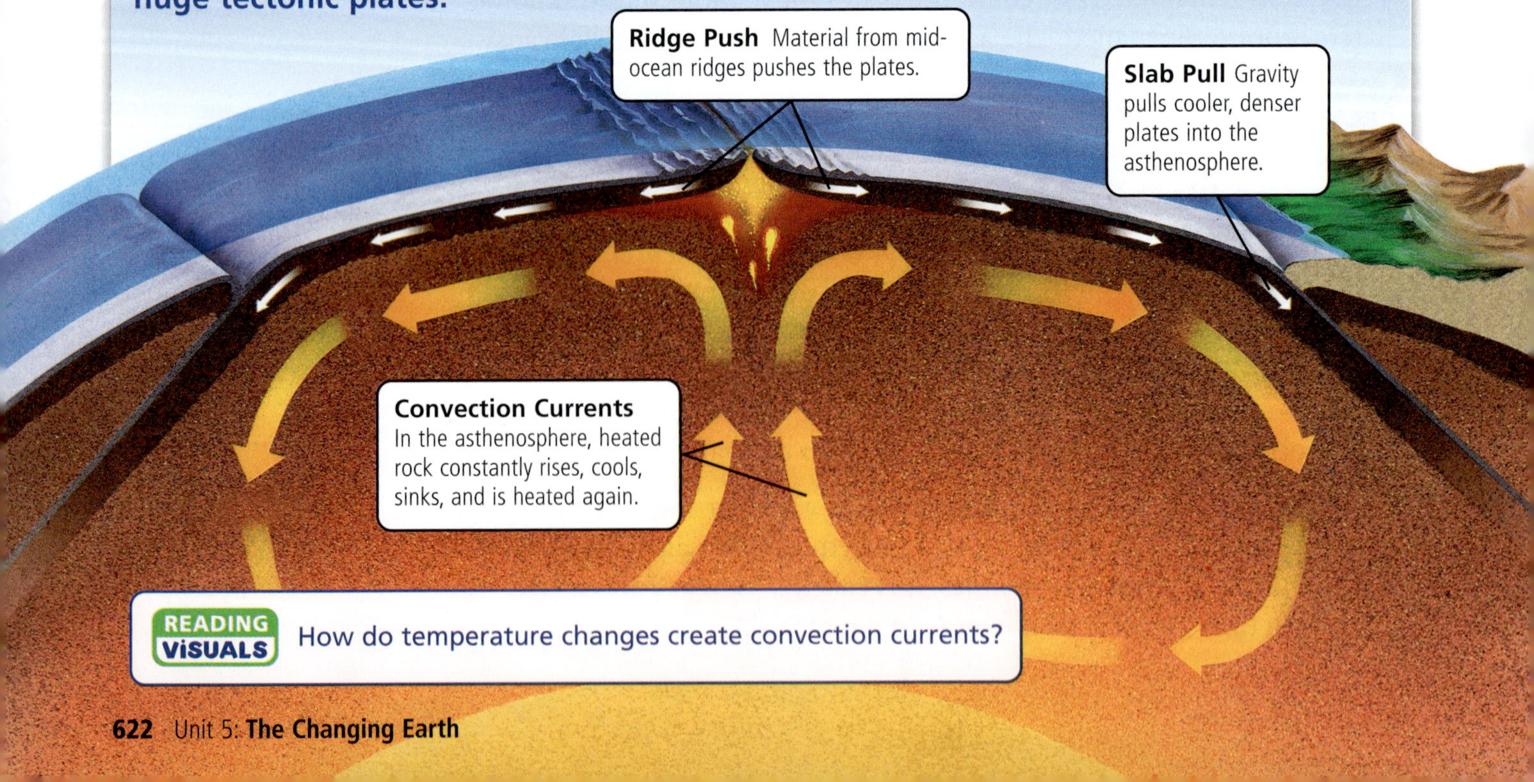

Ridge Push Material from mid-ocean ridges pushes the plates.

Slab Pull Gravity pulls cooler, denser plates into the asthenosphere.

Convection Currents In the asthenosphere, heated rock constantly rises, cools, sinks, and is heated again.

READING VISUALS How do temperature changes create convection currents?

Tectonic Plates

Earth's lithosphere is made up of moving plates.

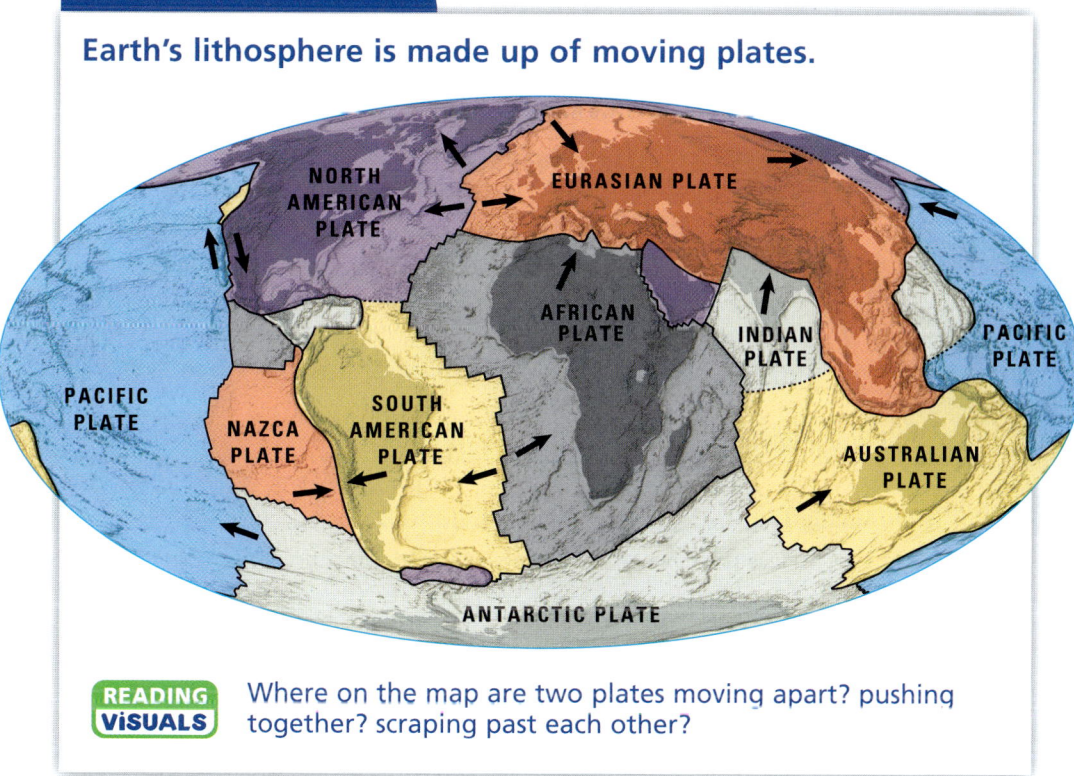

READING VISUALS Where on the map are two plates moving apart? pushing together? scraping past each other?

As scientists studied the plates, they realized that one plate could not shift without affecting the others nearby. They found that plates can move apart, push together, or scrape past each other. The arrows on the map above show each type of plate motion.

Plate movements cause great changes in Earth's crust. Most major earthquakes, volcanoes, and mountain ranges appear where tectonic plates meet. You will learn why as you read more about plate movements.

18.2 Review

KEY CONCEPTS

1. What evidence did Wegener gather to support his continental drift hypothesis?
2. Give three types of evidence from the sea floor that prove Earth's tectonic plates move.
3. Explain how motions in the asthenosphere can move tectonic plates around Earth.

CRITICAL THINKING

4. **Apply** A friend tells you he read on a Web site that Earth is getting smaller. What can you tell him that shows Earth's size is not changing?
5. **Evaluate** What other types of scientists, besides geologists, would find the theory of plate tectonics useful in their work?

CHALLENGE

6. **Infer** Use the arrows on the map above and your knowledge of sea-floor spreading and ocean trenches to answer these questions: What is happening to the size of the Atlantic Ocean? What can you infer is happening to the size of the Pacific Ocean? Explain your answers.

Chapter 18: **Plate Tectonics** 623

CHAPTER INVESTIGATION

Convection Currents and Plate Movement

OVERVIEW AND PURPOSE South America and Africa are drifting slowly apart. What powerful force could be moving these two plates? In this investigation you will
- observe the movement of convection currents
- determine how convection currents in Earth's mantle could move tectonic plates

▶ Problem

How do convection currents in a fluid affect floating objects on the surface?

▶ Hypothesize

Write a hypothesis to explain how convection currents affect floating objects. Your hypothesis should take the form of an "If . . . , then . . . , because . . ." statement.

▶ Procedure

MATERIALS
- oven-glass lasagna pan
- 2 bread pans or 2 bricks
- water
- liquid food coloring
- 2 small candles
- matches
- 2 sponges
- scissors
- 3–4 pushpins

1. Use two overturned bread pans or two bricks to raise and support the glass lasagna pan. Fill the pan with water to a depth of 4 cm.

2. Hold the food coloring over the middle of the pan. Squeeze several drops into the water. Be careful not to touch or disturb the water with the plastic tip or your hands. Write down your observations.

3. Light the two candles and place them beneath the center of the pan. Then squeeze several more drops of food coloring into the middle of the pan.

4. Observe what happens for a few minutes, then write down your observations. After you have finished, blow out the candles and wait until the water cools.

5. Moisten the two sponges. Cut one into the shape of South America and the other into the shape of Africa. Insert the pushpins as shown in the photo.

624 Unit 5: The Changing Earth

6. Place the sponges on top of the water in the center of the pan. Fit the two sponges together along their coastlines.

7. Gently hold the sponges together until the water is still, then let go. Observe them for a few minutes and record what you saw.

8. Light the candles again. Place them under the pan and directly beneath the two sponges.

9. Gently hold the sponges together again until the water heats up. Then carefully let go of the sponges, trying not to disturb the water.

10. Observe the sponges for a few minutes, and then record your observations.

Observe and Analyze

1. **RECORD** Draw diagrams to show how the food coloring and the sponges moved in cold water and in heated water. Use arrows to indicate any motion.

2. **ANALYZE** Did the food coloring and the sponges move more with or without the candles? Use what you have learned about convection to explain the role of the candles.

Conclude

1. **EVALUATE** Water is a fluid, but the asthenosphere is not. What properties of the asthenosphere allow it to move like a fluid and form convection currents?

2. **COMPARE AND CONTRAST** In what ways is your setup like Earth's asthenosphere and lithosphere? In what ways is your setup different?

3. **ANALYZE** Compare your results with your hypothesis. Do your observations support your hypothesis? Why or why not?

4. **INTERPRET** Write an answer to your problem statement.

5. **IDENTIFY CONTROLS** Did your experiment include controls? If so, what purpose did they serve here?

6. **APPLY** In your own words, explain how the African continent and the South American continent are drifting apart.

7. **APPLY** Suppose you own an aquarium. You want to make sure your fish are warm whether they swim near the top or near the bottom of the aquarium. The pet store sells two types of heaters. One heater extends 5 cm below the water's surface. The other heater rests on the bottom of the aquarium. Based on what you learned in this activity, which heater would you choose, and why?

INVESTIGATE Further

CHALLENGE Design a new version of this experiment that you think would be a better model of the movements in Earth's asthenosphere and lithosphere. What materials will you need? What changes would you make to the procedure? Sketch your version of the lab, and explain what makes it better.

Convection Currents and Plate Movement
Problem How do convection currents in a fluid affect floating objects on the surface?
Hypothesize
Observe and Analyze
Diagram 1. Sponges on Unheated Water

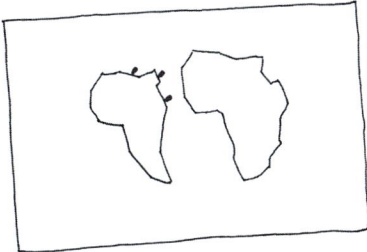

Conclude

Chapter 18: **Plate Tectonics** 625

KEY CONCEPT
Plates move apart.

 BEFORE, you learned
- The continents join and break apart
- The sea floor provides evidence that tectonic plates move
- The theory of plate tectonics helps explain how the plates move

 NOW, you will learn
- About different plate boundaries
- What happens when plates move apart
- How the direction and speed of plates can be measured

VOCABULARY

divergent boundary p. 626
convergent boundary p. 626
transform boundary p. 626
rift valley p. 627
magnetic reversal p. 628
hot spot p. 631

EXPLORE Divergent Boundaries

What happens when plates move apart?

PROCEDURE

1. Cut the piece of striped paper into two symmetrical pieces slightly less wide than the slit in the oatmeal box.

2. Match up the lines of the two pieces and tape the pieces together at one edge. Push the taped edge into the box until only a few centimeters of the free edges show at the top.

3. Grasp each piece of paper, one in each hand. Slowly pull the two pieces horizontally out of the cylinder, pulling them in opposite directions.

MATERIALS
- scissors
- piece of striped paper
- tape
- small oatmeal box with slit cut in side

WHAT DO YOU THINK?
How is your model similar to the process of sea-floor spreading?

READING TIP

Use word meanings to help remember science terms.

diverge = to go in different directions
converge = to come together from different directions
transform = to change

Tectonic plates have different boundaries.

A plate boundary is where the edges of two plates meet. After studying the way plates move, geologists identified three types of boundaries.

- A **divergent boundary** (dih-VUR-juhnt) occurs where plates move apart. Most divergent boundaries are found in the ocean.

- A **convergent boundary** (kuhn-VUR-juhnt) occurs where plates push together.

- A **transform boundary** occurs where plates scrape past each other.

In this section, you will discover what happens at divergent boundaries in the ocean and on land. You will read more about convergent and transform boundaries in Section 18.4.

The sea floor spreads apart at divergent boundaries.

In the ocean, divergent boundaries are also called spreading centers. Mid-ocean ridges mark these sites where the ocean floor is spreading apart. As the ridges continue to widen, a gap called a **rift valley** forms. Here molten material rises to build new crust.

Mid-Ocean Ridges and Rift Valleys

Mid-ocean ridges are the longest chain of mountains on Earth. Most of these ridges contain a rift valley along their center, as shown in the diagram below. When molten material rises from the asthenosphere, cold ocean water cools the rock until it becomes solid. As the plates move apart, new cracks open in the solid rock. More molten material rises and hardens. The growing ridge stands high above the sea floor.

The world's longest ridge, the Mid-Atlantic Ridge, runs the length of the Atlantic Ocean. Here the North and South American plates are moving away from the Eurasian and African plates. The ridge extends nearly 11,000 kilometers (6214 mi) from Iceland to near Antarctica. The rift valley is 24 kilometers (15 mi) wide and 9 kilometers (6 mi) deep—about 7 kilometers (4 mi) deeper than the Grand Canyon!

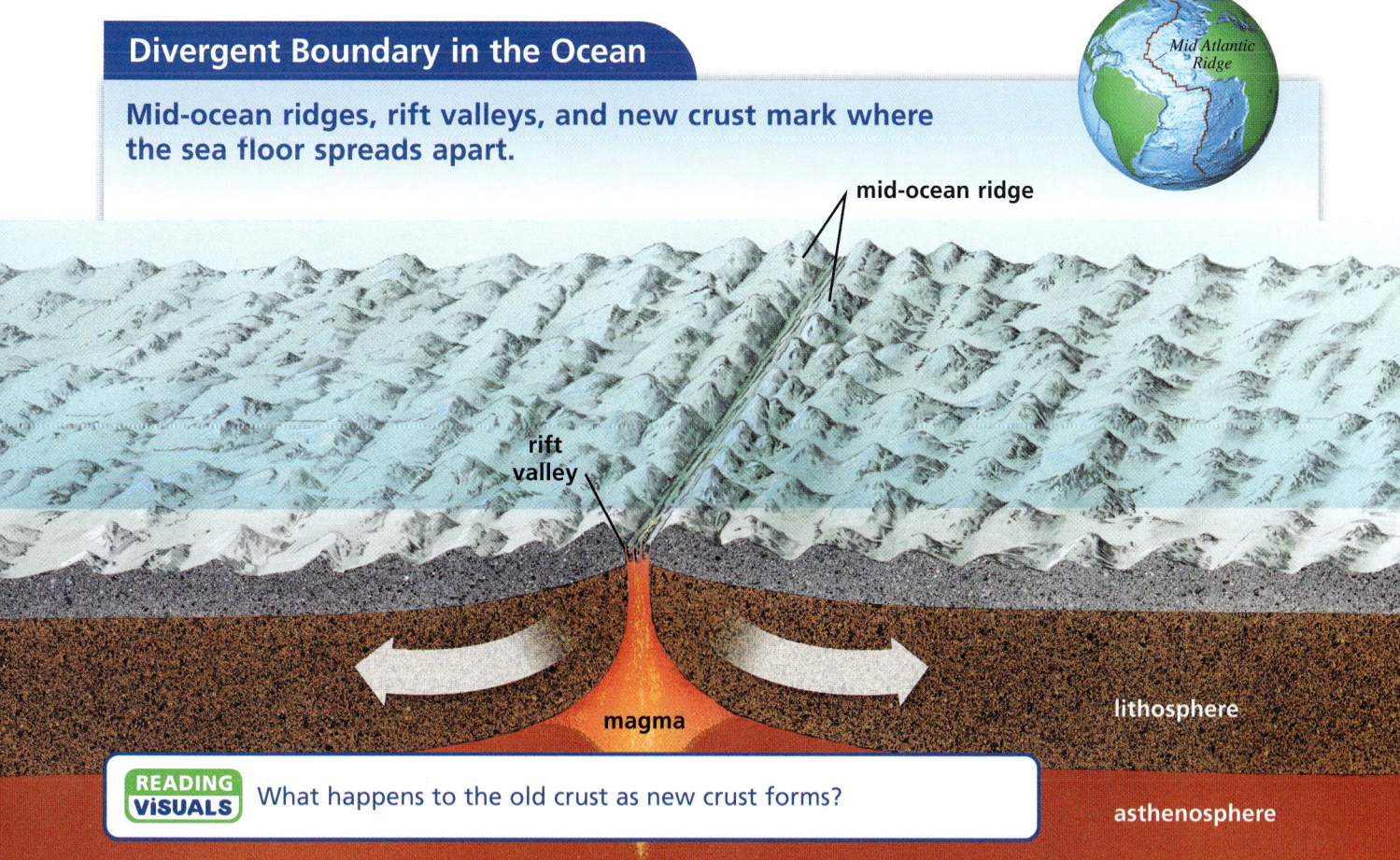

Divergent Boundary in the Ocean

Mid-ocean ridges, rift valleys, and new crust mark where the sea floor spreads apart.

READING VISUALS What happens to the old crust as new crust forms?

Sea-Floor Rock and Magnetic Reversals

You read earlier that the sea floor is younger near a mid-ocean ridge and older farther away. As scientists continued to study the sea-floor rock, they made a surprising discovery about Earth's magnetic field.

To understand Earth's magnetic field, you can compare the planet to a bar magnet, which has a north and a south pole. Earth's magnetic field affects the entire planet, as shown in the diagram below. Notice that Earth's geographic and magnetic poles are not in the same place.

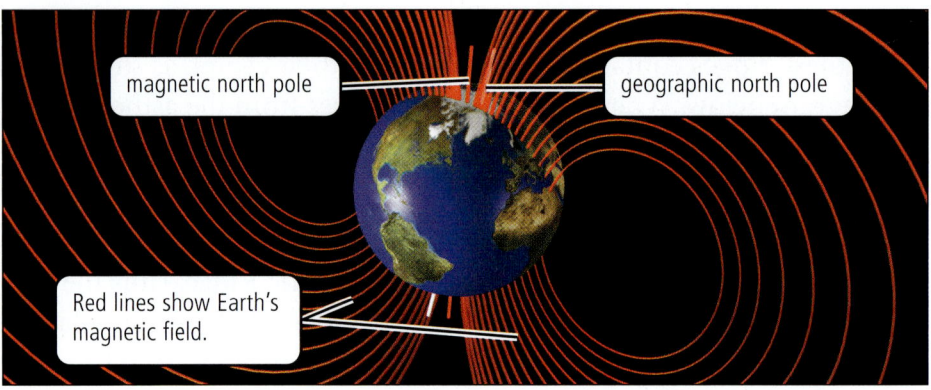

Unlike a bar magnet, however, Earth's magnetic poles switch places every so often. The north pole becomes the south pole and the south pole becomes the north pole. This switch in direction is called a **magnetic reversal.** Such reversals are caused by changes in Earth's magnetic field. As yet, no one knows why these changes happen. In contrast, Earth's geographic poles never change places.

Magnetic Reversals

Rocks moving away from a mid-ocean ridge carry records of magnetic reversals.

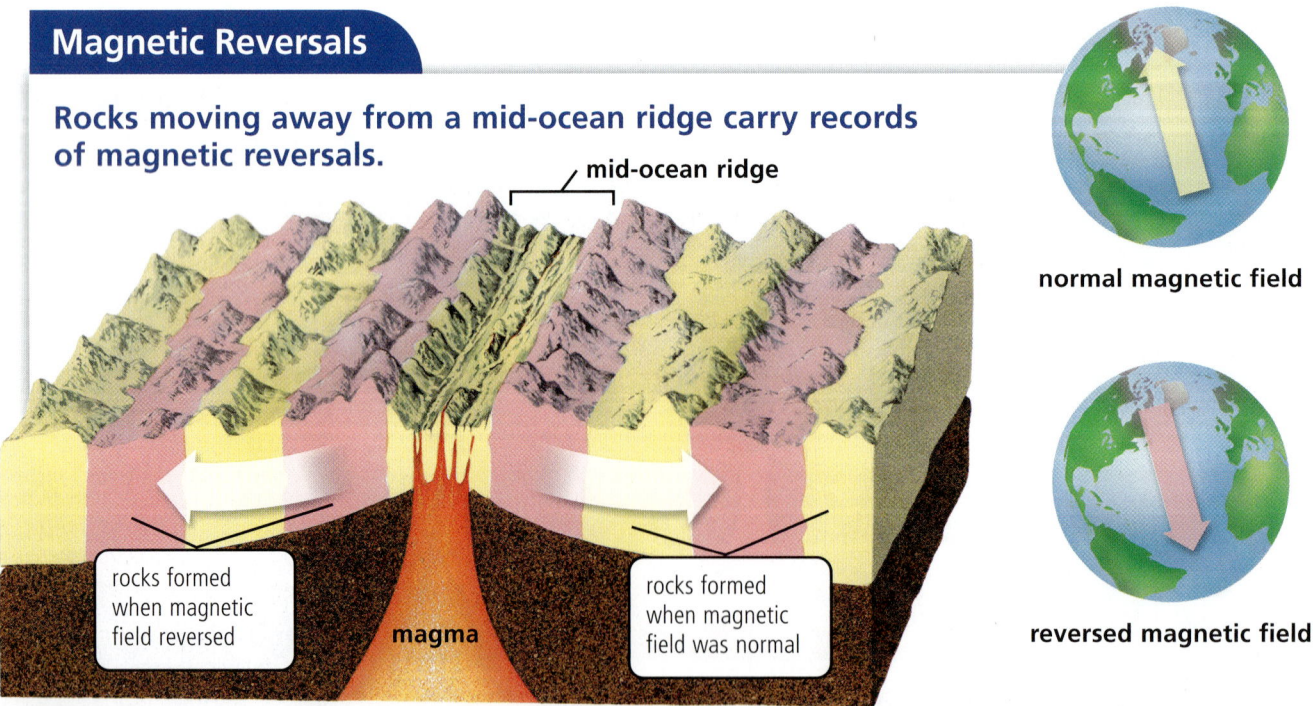

628 Unit 5: **The Changing Earth**

Scientists found that each magnetic reversal is recorded in the sea-floor rock. These records are especially clear at some mid-ocean ridges. As the molten material rises and cools, some magnetic minerals line up with the Earth's magnetic field. When the material hardens, these minerals are permanently fixed like tiny compass needles pointing north and south. Whenever the magnetic field reverses, the cooling minerals record the change.

As shown in the diagram on page 628, the records of magnetic reversals line up like stripes in the rock. As the two plates move away from a mid-ocean ridge, each plate carries a record of magnetic reversals with it. The records are the same on either side of the ridge.

As scientists continued to map the ocean floor, they found more records of these reversals. By dating the rock, scientists had further evidence of plate movement. The youngest rock records the most recent reversal, which happened only about 760,000 years ago. The oldest rock, farthest from the mid-ocean ridge, records reversals that happened more than 150 million years ago.

 **CHECK YOUR READING** Explain how records of magnetic reversals show that plates move apart.

INVESTIGATE Magnetic Reversals

How can you map magnetic reversals?

PROCEDURE

1) Wrap one end of the string around the middle of the bar magnet. Tape the string in place as shown.

2) Place a small piece of tape on one end of the magnet. Label the tape "N" to represent north.

3) Hold the bar magnet over one end of the sea-floor model as shown. Move the magnet SLOWLY toward the other end of the sea-floor model. Record your observations.

WHAT DO YOU THINK?

- What did the magnet reveal about the sea-floor model? Draw a diagram showing any pattern that you might have observed.
- Which part of the model represents the youngest sea floor? Which part represents the oldest sea floor?

CHALLENGE If Earth's magnetic field had never reversed in the past, how would the sea-floor model be different?

SKILL FOCUS
Modeling

MATERIALS
- string
- bar magnet
- masking tape
- marking pen
- sea-floor model

TIME
20 minutes

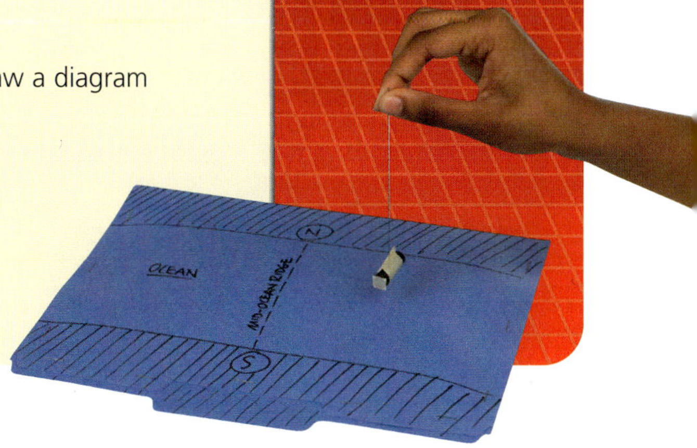

Chapter 18: **Plate Tectonics** 629

Continents split apart at divergent boundaries.

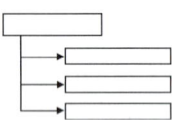

SUPPORTING MAIN IDEAS
Use this diagram to help you take notes on how continents split apart.

Like the sea floor, continents also spread apart at a divergent boundary. The boundary begins to form when hot material rises from deep in the mantle. This heat causes the crust to bulge upward. The crust cracks as it is stretched, and a rift valley forms, as shown in the diagram below. Magma rises through the cracked, thinned crust, forming volcanoes. As the rift valley grows wider, the continent begins to split apart.

If the rift valley continues to widen, the thinned valley floor sinks lower and lower until it is below sea level. Water from nearby oceans or rivers may fill the valley and form a sea or a lake. In the Middle East, for example, the Arabian Plate and African Plate have been moving apart for several million years. Over time, the waters of the Indian Ocean gradually filled the rift valley, forming the Red Sea. This sea is slowly getting wider as the plates continue to move apart.

CHECK YOUR READING What happens when the floor of a rift valley sinks below sea level?

Divergent Boundary on Land

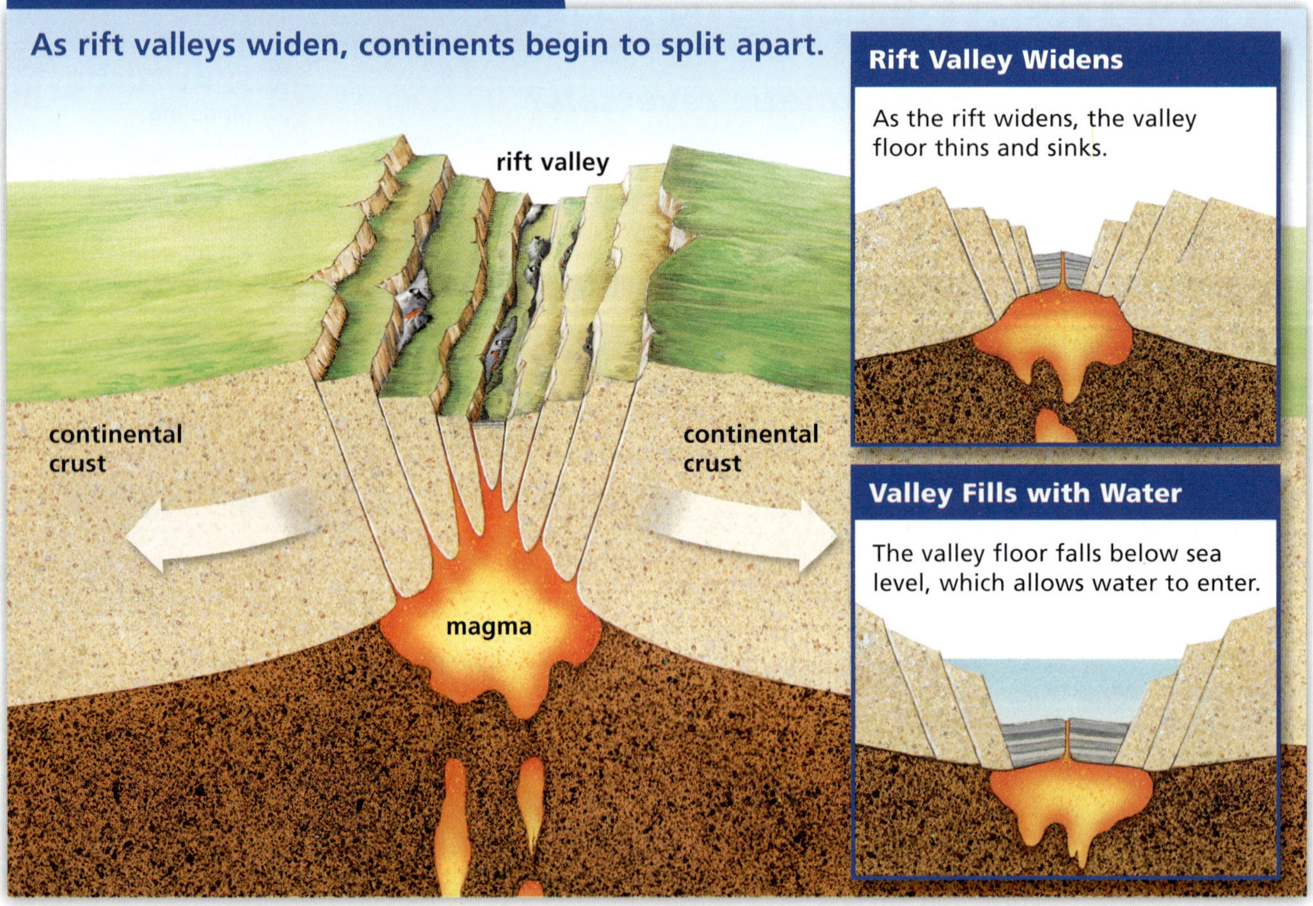

As rift valleys widen, continents begin to split apart.

rift valley

continental crust

continental crust

magma

Rift Valley Widens
As the rift widens, the valley floor thins and sinks.

Valley Fills with Water
The valley floor falls below sea level, which allows water to enter.

630 Unit 5: The Changing Earth

The Great Rift Valley in eastern Africa, shown in the photograph above, is a good example of a continental rift valley. It is getting wider as the African Plate splits apart. This huge valley is thousands of kilometers long and as much as 1800 meters (5900 ft) deep.

PREDICT Rift valleys, like the Great Rift Valley in Africa, occur where plates are moving apart. What will happen to the Rift Valley when it gets low enough?

Hot spots can be used to track plate movements.

In some places, called **hot spots,** heated rock rises in plumes, or thin columns, from the mantle. Volcanoes often develop above the plume. Although most hot spots occur far from plate boundaries, they offer a way to measure plate movement. This is because a hot spot generally stays in one place while the tectonic plate above it keeps moving.

At a hot spot, the heat from the plume partly melts some of the rock in the tectonic plate above it. It is like holding a candle under a wax tablet. Eventually, the wax above the flame will melt. Likewise, if the plate stays over the hot spot long enough, the rock above it will melt.

In time, a volcano will form at the surface of the plate. The volcano may become high enough to rise above the sea as an island. For example, the Hawaiian Islands are being built as the Pacific Plate moves slowly over a hot spot.

The Hawaiian islands are located in the middle of the Pacific Plate. The largest island, Hawaii, is still over the hot spot.

Hot Spots

Tectonic plates move over hot spots in the mantle.

Oceanic Hot Spot

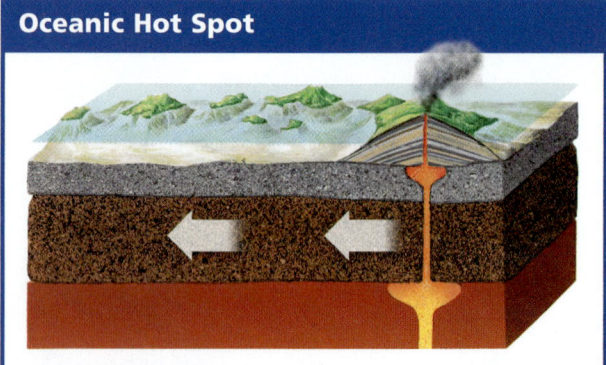

The Pacific Plate carries each Hawaiian island away from the hot spot. Eventually, a new volcano forms over the plume.

Continental Hot Spot

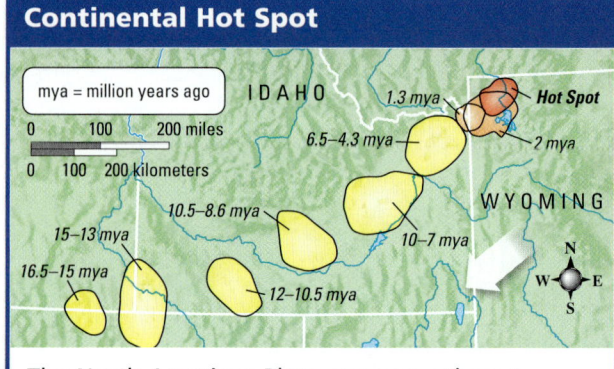

The North American Plate moves southwest, carrying each inactive volcano away from the Yellowstone hot spot.

 Which island or landform in each diagram was formed first? How do you know?

When the plate moves on, it carries the first volcano away from the hot spot. Heat from the mantle plume will then melt the rock at a new site, forming a new volcano. The diagram on the left shows this process.

Many hot spots provide a fixed point that scientists can use to measure the speed and direction of plate movements. For example, the Yellowstone hot spot under the North American Plate has formed a chain of inactive volcanoes, as shown in the diagram on the right. Scientists estimate that the North American Plate is moving southwest at about 2.3 cm (1 in.) per year.

 How does a hot-spot volcano form?

18.3 Review

KEY CONCEPTS

1. Name and describe the three types of plate movements.
2. Create a two-column chart with the headings: Divergent boundary; Features. Fill in the chart for divergent boundaries at sea and on land.
3. How are hot spots used to track plate motion?

CRITICAL THINKING

4. **Predict** Suppose a magnetic reversal occurred today. How would new rocks at mid-ocean ridges differ from rocks that formed last year?
5. **Infer** A huge crack runs through Iceland, an island that lies above the Mid-Ocean Ridge. What do you think is happening to this country?

CHALLENGE

6. **Hypothesize** Look carefully at the diagram above and the Hawaiian Islands picture on page 631. Notice that some hot spot islands or landforms are larger than other islands or landforms in the same chain. Develop a hypothesis, based on plate movement, that might explain this fact.

MATH in SCIENCE

SKILL: CALCULATING EQUIVALENT RATES

Tracking Tectonic Plates

Scientists use lasers to track the movements of tectonic plates. They bounce laser light off satellites and measure the distance from each satellite to the ground. As the plates move, the distance changes. With this tracking system, scientists know exactly how much tectonic plates move each year.

You can use equivalent rates to predict how far two divergent plates will move over a given time. A rate is a ratio of two measures expressed in different units, such as

$$\frac{10 \text{ cm}}{4 \text{ yr}}$$

This 0.61-meter-wide satellite is covered with mirrors to reflect laser light back to Earth.

MATH TUTORIAL
CLASSZONE.COM
Click on Math Tutorial for more help with rates.

Example

If Boston, Massachusetts, and Lisbon, Portugal, are moving apart at an average rate of 10 cm every 4 years, how much farther apart will they move in 20 years?

Solution
Write an equivalent rate.

$$\frac{10 \text{ cm}}{4 \text{ yr}} = \frac{?}{20 \text{ yr}}$$

$$20 \div 4 = 5$$

$$10 \times 5 = 50$$

$$\frac{10 \text{ cm}}{4 \text{ yr}} = \frac{50 \text{ cm}}{20 \text{ yr}}$$

Divide 20 yr by 4 yr to get 5, then multiply 10 cm by 5.

ANSWER Boston and Lisbon will move 50 centimeters farther apart in 10 years.

Answer the following questions.

1. If New York, New York, and London, England, are moving apart at an average rate of 5 cm every 2 years, how much farther apart will they move in 8 years?

2. If Miami, Florida, and Casablanca, Morocco, are moving apart at an average rate of 25 cm every 10 years, how much farther apart will they move in 30 years?

3. If Portland, Maine, and Dublin, Ireland, are moving apart at an average rate of 50 cm every 20 years, how much farther apart will they move in 10 years?

CHALLENGE If Halifax, Nova Scotia, and Birmingham, England, are moving apart at an average rate of 5 cm every 2 years, how long will it take them to move 35 cm farther apart?

Arabian Plate

Red Sea

African Plate

This satellite photograph shows where the Arabian Plate and the African Plate are moving apart. As a result, the Red Sea is slowly growing wider.

Chapter 18: **Plate Tectonics** 633

KEY CONCEPT

18.4 Plates converge or scrape past each other.

BEFORE, you learned
- Plates move apart at divergent boundaries
- In the oceans, divergent boundaries mark where the sea floor spreads apart
- On land, continents split apart at divergent boundaries

NOW, you will learn
- What happens when two continental plates converge
- What happens when an oceanic plate converges with another plate
- What happens when one plate scrapes past another plate

VOCABULARY
subduction p. 634
continental-continental collision p. 635
oceanic-oceanic subduction p. 636
oceanic-continental subduction p. 637

EXPLORE Tectonic Plates

What happens when tectonic plates collide?

PROCEDURE

 Arrange six square napkins in two rows.

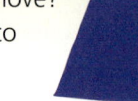 Slowly push the two rows of napkins together. Observe what happens.

MATERIALS
6 square napkins

WHAT DO YOU THINK?
- In what ways did the napkin edges move?
- How might your observations relate to the movement of tectonic plates?

Tectonic plates push together at convergent boundaries.

You read earlier that new crust forms at divergent boundaries where plates move apart. At convergent boundaries, where plates push together, crust is either folded or destroyed.

When two plates with continental crust collide, they will crumple and fold the rock between them. A plate with older, denser oceanic crust will sink beneath another plate. The crust melts in the asthenosphere and is destroyed. When one plate sinks beneath another, it is called **subduction.** The word is based on the Latin prefix *sub-*, meaning "under," and the Latin *ducere,* meaning "to lead." Therefore, subduction is a process in which one plate is "led under" another.

There are three types of convergent boundaries: where two continental plates meet, where two oceanic plates meet, or where an oceanic plate and a continental plate meet. Major geologic events occur at all three types of boundaries.

VOCABULARY
Remember to make a description wheel for the terms in this section.

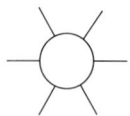

634 Unit 5: The Changing Earth

Continental-Continental Collision

A **continental-continental collision** occurs where two plates carrying continental crust push together. Because both crusts are the same density, neither plate can sink beneath the other. If the plates keep moving, their edges crumple and fold, as in the diagram below.

You can see the same effect if you put two blocks of clay on a table and push them together. If you push hard enough, one or both of the blocks will buckle. One cannot sink under the other, so the clay folds under the pressure.

In some cases, the folded crust can be pushed up high enough to form mountains. Some of the world's largest mountains appear along continent-continent boundaries. For instance, the European Alps, shown in the photograph at right, are found where the African and European plates are colliding. The tallest mountains in the world, the Himalayas, first formed when the Indian Plate began colliding with the European Plate.

The Himalayas and the Alps are still forming today. As long as the plates keep moving, these mountains will keep rising higher.

The European Alps began rising nearly 40 million years ago as a section of the African Plate collided with the European Plate.

CHECK YOUR READING Explain how colliding plates form mountain ranges.

Convergent Boundary—Collision

Rocks crumple and fold to form mountains.

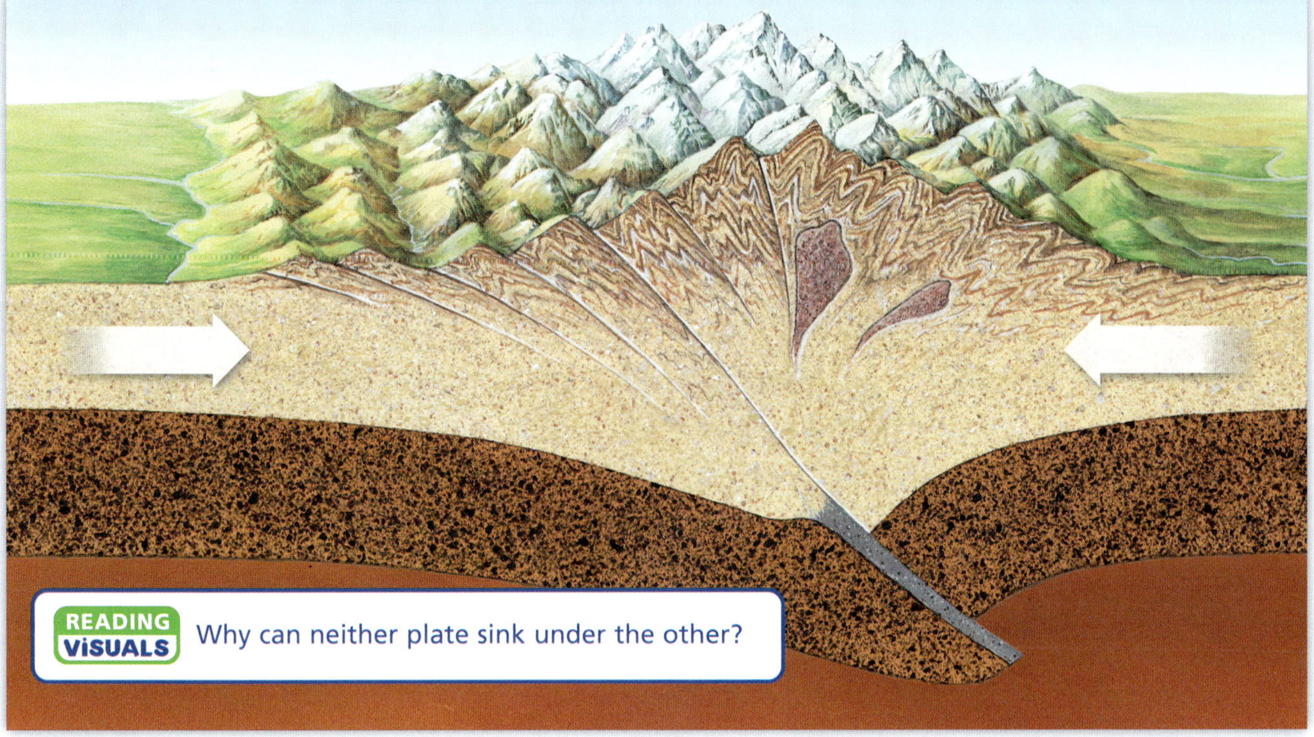

READING VISUALS Why can neither plate sink under the other?

Chapter 18: **Plate Tectonics** 635

Oceanic-Oceanic Subduction

An **oceanic-oceanic subduction** occurs where one plate with oceanic crust sinks, or subducts, under another plate with oceanic crust. The older plate sinks because it is colder and denser than the younger plate. When the older crust reaches the asthenosphere, it melts in the intense heat. Two main features form at oceanic-oceanic subductions: deep-ocean trenches and island arcs.

Deep-Ocean Trenches These trenches are like deep canyons that form in the ocean floor as a plate sinks. Most deep-ocean trenches are found in the Pacific Ocean. For example, at the Mariana Trench, the Pacific Plate is sinking under the Philippine Plate. This trench is the deepest place in the world's oceans, extending nearly 11,000 meters (36,000 ft) into the sea floor.

Island Arcs There are chains of volcanic islands that form on the top plate, parallel to a deep-ocean trench. As oceanic crust of the sinking plate melts, magma rises through the top plate. Over time, the flows build up a series of islands. Island arcs include the Philippine Islands, the Aleutian Islands of Alaska, and the islands of Japan.

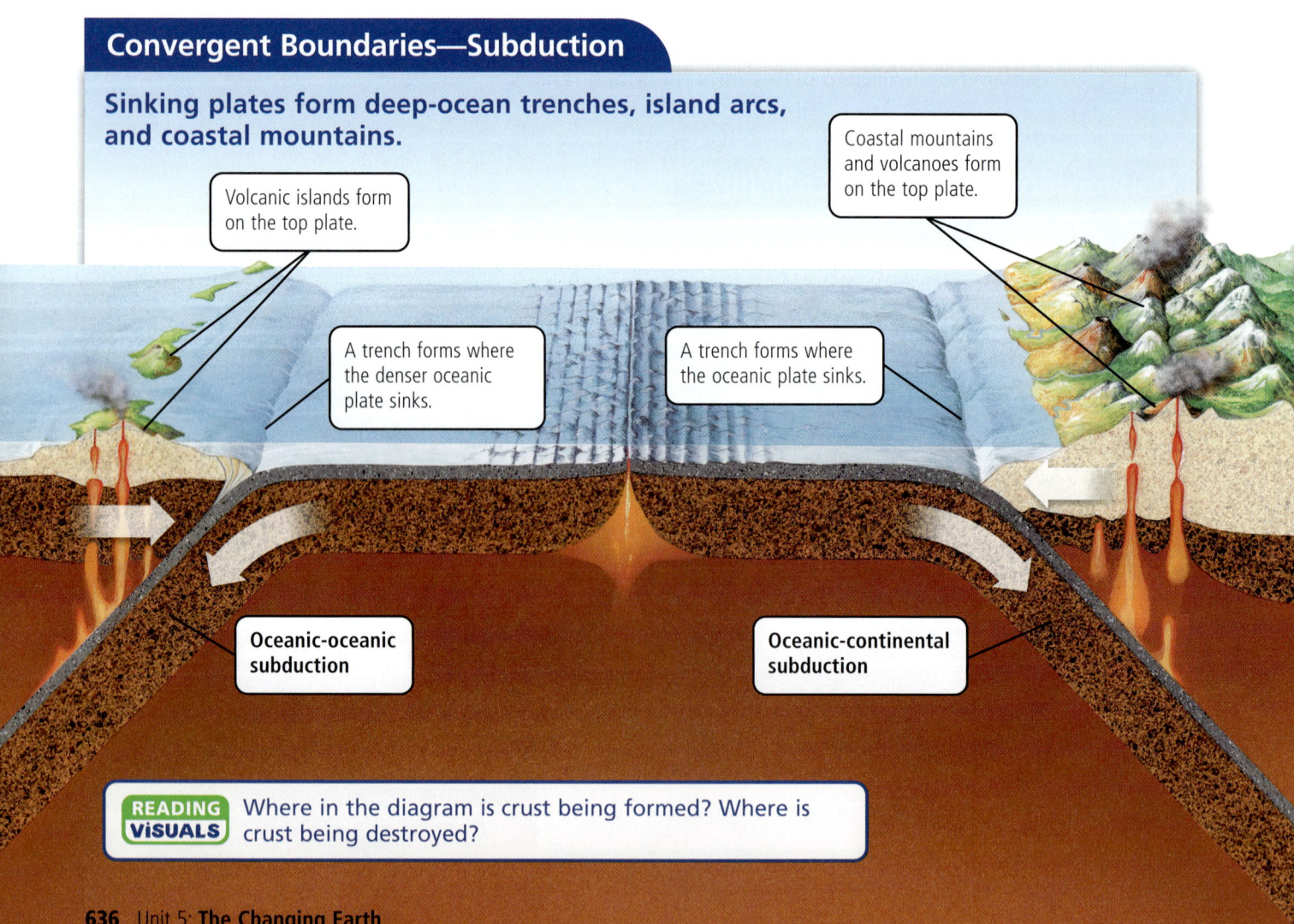

Convergent Boundaries—Subduction

Sinking plates form deep-ocean trenches, island arcs, and coastal mountains.

- Volcanic islands form on the top plate.
- A trench forms where the denser oceanic plate sinks.
- A trench forms where the oceanic plate sinks.
- Coastal mountains and volcanoes form on the top plate.
- Oceanic-oceanic subduction
- Oceanic-continental subduction

READING VISUALS Where in the diagram is crust being formed? Where is crust being destroyed?

Oceanic-Continental Subduction

An **oceanic-continental subduction** occurs when ocean crust sinks under continental crust, as shown in the diagram on page 636. The oceanic crust sinks because it is colder and denser than the continental crust. At these sites, deep-ocean trenches also form, along with coastal mountains.

Deep-Ocean Trenches Some of the world's youngest trenches are in the eastern Pacific Ocean. Here, for example, the Pacific Plate is sinking under the North American Plate. As the oceanic crust moves, it often causes underwater earthquakes.

Coastal Mountains As oceanic crust sinks under a continent, the continental crust buckles to form a range of mountains. These mountains, like island arcs, parallel a deep-ocean trench. As the diagram on page 636 shows, some of these mountains are volcanoes, which form as melted oceanic crust rises through the top plate.

The Cascade Mountains in Oregon and Washington are an example of coastal mountains. They began forming as the Juan de Fuca Plate began sinking under the North American Plate. Some of these peaks, such as Mount St. Helens in Washington, are active volcanoes.

Explore what happens along plate boundaries.

 Why do deep-ocean trenches form at both types of subduction?

INVESTIGATE Convergent Boundaries

How can you model converging plates?

Tectonic plates move so slowly and are so large that it may be hard to visualize exactly how they move. Use what you know to design models showing how converging plates collide and subduct.

PROCEDURE

1. Design your models using the materials listed. You can use the diagrams on pages 635–636 as a guide.
2. Add more clay to your models if you need it.

WHAT DO YOU THINK?

- Describe how your models worked. You can draw a picture of each model to go along with your description.
- How well did your models represent each type of zone? Did each model work? Why or why not?
- How would you modify your designs now that you have seen the results?

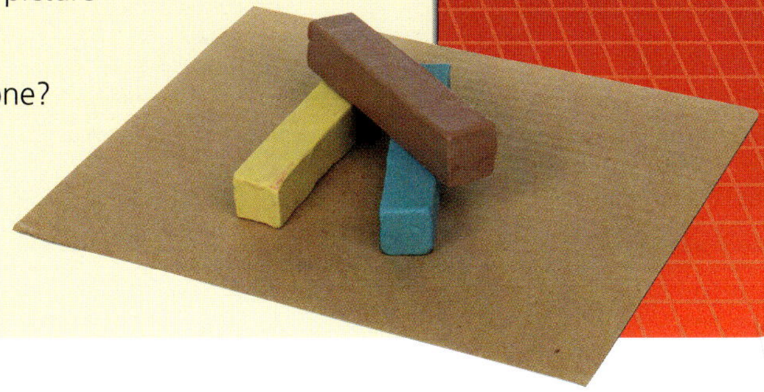

SKILL FOCUS
Designing models

MATERIALS
- clay in three or more colors
- poster board
- marker pens

TIME
30 minutes

Tectonic plates scrape past each other at transform boundaries.

You learned that crust is formed at a divergent boundary and folded or destroyed at a convergent boundary. However, at a transform boundary, crust is neither formed nor destroyed. Here, two plates move past each other in opposite directions, as shown in the diagram below. As the plates move, their edges scrape and grind against each other.

Transform boundaries occur mostly on the sea floor near mid-ocean ridges. They also occur on land, where some are clearly visible as long cracks in Earth's surface. The San Andreas Fault in California is a transform boundary that runs from the Gulf of California through the San Francisco area. It marks where the Pacific Plate and part of the North American Plate are moving in opposite directions. If the plates keep moving at their present rate, Los Angeles will be a suburb of San Francisco in about 10 million years.

This long crack in the earth reveals the transform boundary known as the San Andreas Fault.

CHECK YOUR READING What makes the San Andreas Fault a transform boundary?

Transform Boundary

Plate edges grind and scrape past each other. Crust is neither formed nor destroyed.

valley

riverbed offset as plates move

Tectonic Plate Boundaries

There are three types of plate boundaries: transform, divergent, and convergent. Major geologic events occur at all three types.

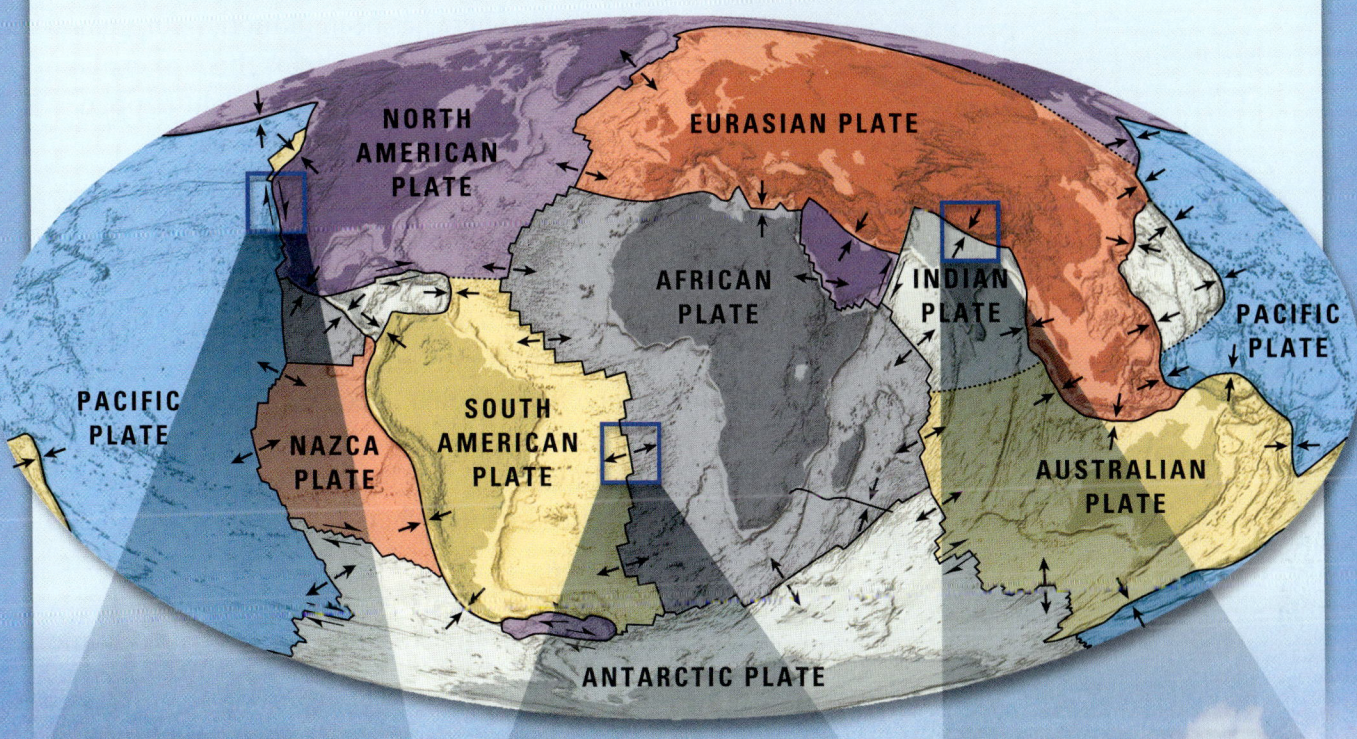

Transform Boundaries
Plates scrape horizontally past each other. Crust is neither formed nor destroyed.

Divergent Boundaries
As plates move apart, new crust is built, forming mid-ocean ridges and rift valleys.

Convergent Boundaries
Crust is destroyed where plates subduct. It is folded where plates collide.

READING VISUALS Where else on the map above can you find a transform, divergent, and convergent boundary?

Chapter 18: **Plate Tectonics** 639

Current U. S. Eastern Coastline

The Appalachian Mountains formed along an ancient collision boundary.

The theory of plate tectonics helps geologists today.

The theory of plate tectonics changed the way that scientists view Earth. They learned that the planet's lithosphere has been in motion for millions of years. Today, the theory helps them to explain Earth's past and to predict what might happen along plate boundaries in the future.

By studying rock layers and using the theory, geologists can uncover the history of any region on Earth. For example, in the eastern United States, the deformed and folded rocks in the Appalachian Mountains are evidence of an ancient convergent boundary. Geologists discovered that these rocks are the same type and age as rocks in northwest Africa. These facts reveal that the mountains formed when North America collided with Africa and Eurasia as part of Pangaea. Where the plates eventually pulled apart, the rift valleys formed part of the current U. S. eastern coastline.

The theory of plate tectonics also gives scientists a way to study and predict geologic events. Scientists can predict, for example, that there are likely to be more earthquakes where plates slide past each other. They can look for volcanic activity where plates are sinking beneath other plates. And they can predict that mountains will continue to rise where plates push together.

CHECK YOUR READING What future events can scientists predict using the theory of plate tectonics? Give two examples.

18.4 Review

KEY CONCEPTS

1. What are the three types of convergent boundaries?
2. Describe what happens at a transform boundary.
3. Why is the theory of plate tectonics so important to geologists?

CRITICAL THINKING

4. **Compare and Contrast** Use a Venn diagram to compare and contrast oceanic-oceanic and oceanic-continental subduction boundaries.
5. **Interpreting Visuals** Look again at the map on page 639. Identify the plates and type of boundary that formed the Andes Mountains on the west coast of South America.

CHALLENGE

6. **Synthesize** Sketch a diagram of the following landscape and label all the features. A plate with oceanic crust is sinking beneath a plate with continental crust. Further inland on the continent, a transform boundary can be seen in Earth's crust.

Think SCIENCE

SKILL: EVALUATING CONCLUSIONS

What on Earth Is Happening Here?

When tectonic plates move, they cause major changes in Earth's surface. Among other things, the earth shakes, magma erupts on the surface, crust is built or destroyed, and mountains or islands form. Read the observations about plate movements below, then evaluate the conclusions given.

▶ Observations

Scientists made these observations about a region known for the movement of two major tectonic plates.

a. The region is on the coast of a landmass.
b. Along the coast is a deep-ocean trench.
c. The mountains on the coast are volcanic.
d. A line connecting these mountains is fairly straight.
e. The mountains are getting higher.
f. Far out at sea, a mid-ocean ridge is forming.

▶ Conclusions

Here are three possible conclusions about the movement of tectonic plates in the region.

- One plate is pulling away from the other.
- One plate is sinking under the other.
- One plate is scraping past the other.

▶ Evaluate Each Conclusion

On Your Own Decide how well the observations support each conclusion. Note any observations that indicate that a conclusion is not justified.

As a Group Decide which conclusion is most reasonable. Discuss your ideas in a small group, and see if the group can agree.

CHALLENGE What further observations would support or weaken each conclusion? How could you make these observations? What other phenomena might this conclusion help explain?

A volcanic coastal mountain spews out ash.

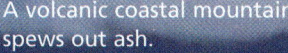

Learn more about the effects of plate movement.

Chapter 18: **Plate Tectonics** 641

18 Chapter Review

the BIG idea
The movement of tectonic plates causes geologic changes on Earth.

CONTENT REVIEW
CLASSZONE.COM

KEY CONCEPTS SUMMARY

1 Earth has several layers.

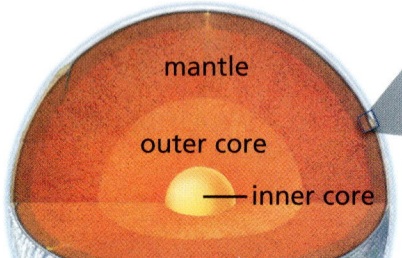
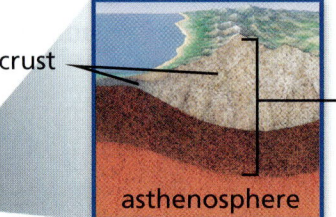

The lithosphere is made up of tectonic plates, which rest on the asthenosphere.

VOCABULARY
inner core p. 614
outer core p. 614
mantle p. 615
crust p. 615
lithosphere p. 615
asthenosphere p. 615
tectonic plate p. 616

2 Continents change position over time.

Gravity and motions in the asthenosphere move tectonic plates over Earth's surface.

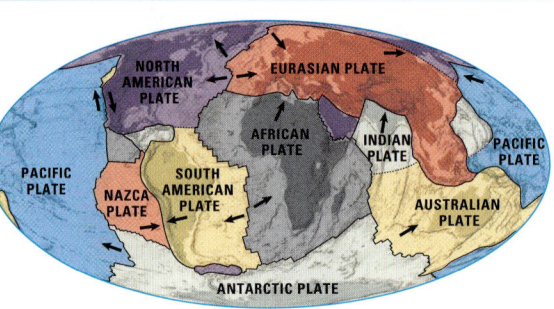

VOCABULARY
continental drift p. 618
Pangaea p. 620
mid-ocean ridge p. 620
convection p. 621
convection current p. 621
theory of plate tectonics p. 622

3 Plates move apart.

New crust is formed at divergent boundaries. Features include:
- mid-ocean ridges
- records of magnetic reversals
- rift valleys

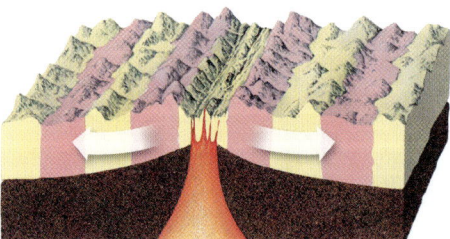

VOCABULARY
divergent boundary p. 626
convergent boundary p. 626
transform boundary p. 626
rift valley p. 627
magnetic reversal p. 628
hot spot p. 631

4 Plates converge or scrape past each other.

Crust is destroyed or folded at convergent boundaries.
- Subduction boundaries form island arcs, deep-ocean trenches, and coastal mountains.
- Collision boundaries can form mountains.

Crust is neither formed nor destroyed at transform boundaries.

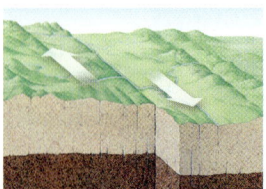

VOCABULARY
subduction p. 634
continental-continental collision p. 635
oceanic-oceanic subduction p. 636
oceanic-continental subduction p. 637

Reviewing Vocabulary

Make a magnet word diagram for each of the vocabulary terms listed below. Write the term in the magnet. Write other terms or ideas related to it on the lines around the magnet.

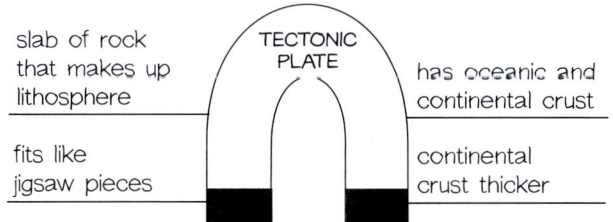

1. mantle
2. lithosphere
3. mid-ocean ridge
4. convection current
5. divergent boundary
6. convergent boundary

Reviewing Key Concepts

Multiple Choice *Choose the letter of the best answer.*

7. Which of the following best describes Earth's mantle?
   a. the densest of Earth's layers
   b. the home of all life on Earth
   c. the thickest layer of hot rock
   d. the thinnest and hottest layer

8. Tectonic plates make up Earth's
   a. lower mantle
   b. lithosphere
   c. asthenosphere
   d. inner core

9. Why did many scientists reject Wegener's continental drift hypothesis?
   a. He could not explain how the continents moved.
   b. The geology of continents did not support his hypothesis.
   c. Fossil evidence showed that the continents were never joined.
   d. The climates of the continents have remained the same.

10. What evidence from the sea floor shows that tectonic plates move?
    a. The sea floor is much older than any of the continents.
    b. The sea floor is youngest near a mid-ocean ridge and older farther away.
    c. Mid-ocean ridges circle Earth like seams in a baseball.
    d. The sea floor is thinner than continental crust.

11. A mid-ocean ridge forms where plates
    a. move apart
    b. push together
    c. scrape past each other
    d. subduct

12. Plate motion is caused partly by
    a. magnetic reversals
    b. convection currents
    c. continental drift
    d. volcanic hot spots

13. Which of the following is formed at a collision zone?
    a. mountain range
    b. volcanic island chain
    c. deep-ocean trench
    d. continental rift valley

14. What happens when two oceanic plates meet?
    a. Both plates sink into the asthenosphere.
    b. The colder, denser plate sinks.
    c. Both plates fold the rock between them.
    d. One plate slides past the other.

15. Where is crust neither formed nor destroyed?
    a. mid-ocean ridge
    b. continental rift valley
    c. transform boundary
    d. subduction zone

Short Answer *Write a short answer to each question.*

16. How does the theory of plate tectonics help geologists predict future geologic events?

17. How do rocks record changes in Earth's magnetic field?

18. Explain what happens when a continental plate splits apart.

Thinking Critically

Use the diagram to answer the questions below.

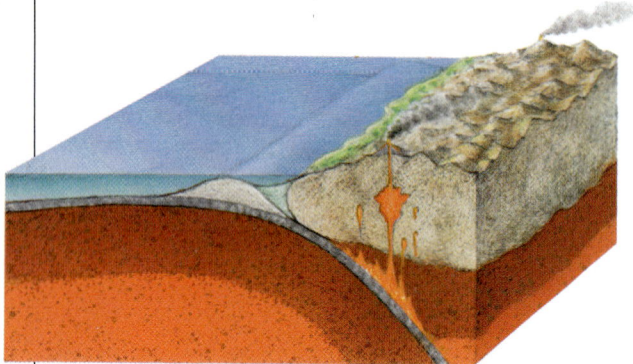

19. **ANALYZE** Write your own explanation of how the coastal mountains formed.

20. **PREDICT** Would you expect the volcanoes on this coastline to continue to be active? Why or why not?

21. **APPLY** Looking at the map above, why do you think the coastal mountains are in a fairly straight line?

22. **APPLY** On the map above, where would you expect to find a deep ocean trench? Why?

23. **APPLY** A friend looks at the diagram and tells you that there should be an island arc forming off the coast. Use your own knowledge and the map above to support or reject your friend's statement.

24. **SYNTHESIZE** On a separate piece of paper, extend the diagram to the left. Draw the type of plate boundary that someone might find far out at sea.

25. **PREDICT** Will the Andes Mountains on the west coast of South America become taller or shorter in the future? Use the theory of plate tectonics to explain your answer.

APPLY Copy the chart below. Fill in the type of boundary—divergent, convergent, or transform—where each formation is likely to appear.

Formation	Type of Boundary
26. Mid-ocean ridge	
27. Volcanic island arc	
28. Rift valley on land	
29. Mountains	
30. Deep-ocean trench	
31. Hot-spot volcano	

the BIG idea

32. **IDENTIFY CAUSE AND EFFECT** Look again at the photograph on pages 610–611. Now that you have finished the chapter, explain what may be forming this crack in Earth's surface.

33. **PREDICT** Use the map on page 623, which shows Earth's tectonic plates and the directions in which they are moving. Based on the plate movements, where do you think the continents might be in a few million years? Draw a map that illustrates your prediction. You might want to give your landmasses names.

UNIT PROJECTS

If you are doing a unit project, make a folder for your project. Include in your folder a list of the resources you will need, the date on which the project is due, and a schedule to keep track of your progress. Begin gathering data.

Standardized Test Practice

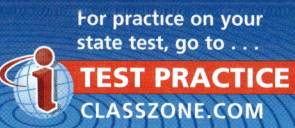

Analyzing a Diagram

The diagram shows several tectonic plates. The arrows indicate the direction each plate is moving. Study the diagram and answer the questions below.

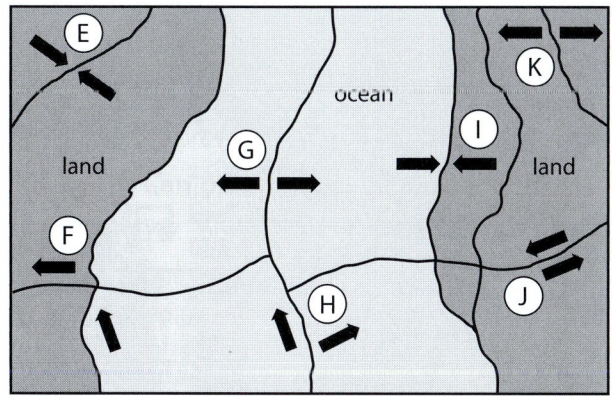

1. Where is an ocean trench most likely to form?
   a. F
   b. G
   c. H
   d. I

2. Where is a continental rift valley most likely to form?
   a. E
   b. F
   c. J
   d. K

3. Where would you find a convergent boundary?
   a. E
   b. F
   c. H
   d. K

4. Where is a mid-ocean ridge most likely to form?
   a. G
   b. H
   c. I
   d. F

5. What is a good example of a transform boundary?
   a. E
   b. I
   c. J
   d. K

6. Which is most likely to happen at I?
   a. Island arcs will form parallel to a trench.
   b. A spreading center will create a rift valley.
   c. Continental crust will be destroyed.
   d. Subduction will cause oceanic crust to melt.

7. Why are earthquakes likely to occur at J?
   a. Two plates are spreading away from each other.
   b. Two plates are colliding with each other.
   c. Two plates are scraping past each other.
   d. One plate is sliding under another plate.

8. Why are mountains likely to form at E?
   a. A rift valley is forming.
   b. Two plates are colliding.
   c. Magma is flowing upward.
   d. One plate is sinking.

9. Which is most likely to happen at G?
   a. Rising magma will create new crust.
   b. Subduction will cause a deep trench.
   c. Colliding plates will cause rocks to crumple.
   d. Moving plates will create island arcs.

Extended Response

Answer the two questions below in detail. Include some of the terms shown in the word box. In your answer, underline each term you use.

| tectonic plates | subduction | magma | crust |
| continental drift | hot spot | mantle | |

10. Two island chains are separated by a deep ocean trench. Although they are close to each other, the islands have very different fossils and types of rock. Explain why these island chains have such different geologic features.

11. Andrea lives near a chain of mountains located far from plate boundaries. The closest mountain is an active volcano. The other mountains used to be volcanoes. The farther away a mountain is in the chain, the older it is. Explain these facts.

Chapter 18: **Plate Tectonics** 645

CHAPTER 19 Earthquakes

the BIG idea

Earthquakes release stress that has built up in rocks.

Key Concepts

SECTION 1 Earthquakes occur along faults.
Learn how rocks move along different kinds of faults.

SECTION 2 Earthquakes release energy.
Learn how energy from an earthquake is used to determine its location and size.

SECTION 3 Earthquake damage can be reduced.
Learn how structures are built to better withstand earthquakes.

Internet Preview

CLASSZONE.COM
Chapter 19 online resources: Content Review, two Visualizations, three Resource Centers, Math Tutorial, Test Practice

What caused these rails to bend, and how long did it take?

EXPLORE the BIG idea

Can You Bend Energy?

Put a clear glass filled with water on a table. Holding a flashlight at an angle to the glass, shine light through the water so that an oval of light forms on the table.

Observe and Think Did the light, which is a form of energy, travel in a straight line through the layers of air and water? Do you think other forms of energy travel in straight lines through layers inside Earth?

How Can Something Move Forward, Yet Sideways?

Put a stack of cards on a table and hold them as shown in the photograph. Slide the entire stack forward, tilting your fingers from side to side to fan the cards back and forth.

Observe and Think Compare the direction of movement of the entire stack of cards with the directions of movement of individual cards. How might this be similar to how energy can travel in waves?

Internet Activity: Earthquakes

Go to **ClassZone.com** to see maps of recent earthquakes around the world, in the United States, and in your own area.

Observe and Think
Where and when did the largest earthquakes occur?

Earthquakes Code: MDL053

Chapter 19: **Earthquakes** 647

CHAPTER 19
Getting Ready to Learn

◁ CONCEPT REVIEW

- Earth's lithosphere is broken into tectonic plates.
- Tectonic plates pull apart, push together, and scrape past one another.
- Major geologic events occur along tectonic plate boundaries.

◁ VOCABULARY REVIEW

lithosphere p. 615
tectonic plate p. 616
mid-ocean ridge p. 620
subduction p. 634

CONTENT REVIEW
CLASSZONE.COM
Review concepts and vocabulary.

▷ TAKING NOTES

MAIN IDEA AND DETAIL NOTES

Make a two-column chart. Write the main ideas, such as those in the blue headings, in the column on the left. Write details about each of those main ideas in the column on the right.

VOCABULARY STRATEGY

For each vocabulary term, make a **magnet word** diagram. Write other terms or ideas related to that term around it.

See the Note-Taking Handbook on pages R45–R51.

SCIENCE NOTEBOOK

MAIN IDEAS	DETAIL NOTES
1. Rocks move along faults.	1. Blocks of rock can move past one another slowly and constantly.
	1. Blocks of rock can get stuck and then break free, causing earthquakes.
2. Most faults are located along tectonic plate boundaries.	2.
	2.
	2.

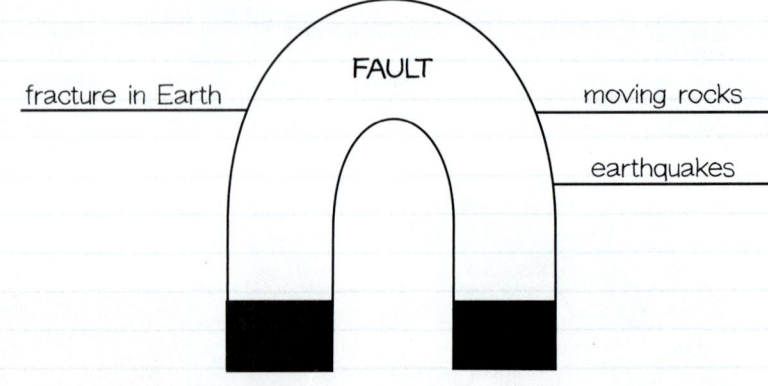

648 Unit 5: The Changing Earth

KEY CONCEPT

Earthquakes occur along faults.

◀ **BEFORE, you learned**
- The crust and uppermost mantle make up the lithosphere
- The lithosphere is cold and rigid
- Tectonic plates move over hotter, weaker rock in the asthenosphere

▶ **NOW, you will learn**
- Why earthquakes occur
- Where most earthquakes occur
- How rocks move during earthquakes

VOCABULARY

fault p. 649
stress p. 649
earthquake p. 649

EXPLORE Pressure

How does pressure affect a solid material?

PROCEDURE

1. Hold a wooden craft stick at each end.
2. Bend the stick very slowly. Continue to put pressure on the stick until it breaks.

WHAT DO YOU THINK?
- How did the stick change before it broke?
- How might rocks react to pressure?

MATERIALS
wooden craft stick

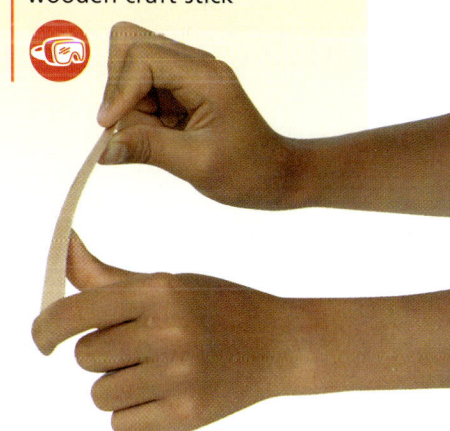

Rocks move along faults.

Sometimes when you pull on a drawer, it opens smoothly. At other times, the drawer sticks shut. If you pull hard enough, the drawer suddenly flies open. Rocks along faults behave in a similar way. A **fault** is a fracture, or break, in Earth's lithosphere, along which blocks of rock move past each other.

Along some parts of a fault, the rock on either side may slide along slowly and constantly. Along other parts of the fault, the rocks may stick, or lock together. The rocks bend as stress is put on them. **Stress** is the force exerted when an object presses on, pulls on, or pushes against another object. As stress increases, the rocks break free. A sudden release of stress in the lithosphere causes an earthquake. An **earthquake** is a shaking of the ground caused by the sudden movement of large blocks of rock along a fault.

VOCABULARY
Add magnet word diagrams for *fault*, *stress*, and *earthquake* to your notebook.

Most faults are located along tectonic plate boundaries, so most earthquakes occur in these areas. However, the blocks of rock that move during an earthquake are much smaller than a tectonic plate. A plate boundary can be many thousands of kilometers long. During even a very powerful earthquake, blocks of rock might move only a few meters past each other along a distance of several hundred kilometers. The strength of an earthquake depends in part on

- how much stress builds up before the rocks move
- the distance the rocks move along the fault

About 80 percent of all earthquakes occur in a belt around the edges of the Pacific Ocean. In the United States, the best-known fault in this belt is the San Andreas (san an-DRAY-uhs) Fault in California. It forms part of the boundary between the North American Plate and the Pacific Plate. Unlike many other faults, parts of the San Andreas Fault can be seen on the surface of the ground.

A small percentage of earthquakes occur along faults within plates. As you read in Chapter 18, a tectonic plate is rigid. Therefore, stress along a plate's boundary can cause rocks to break and move along weak areas toward the middle of the plate.

Where Earthquakes Occur

This map shows the locations of moderate to intense earthquakes from 1993 through 2002.

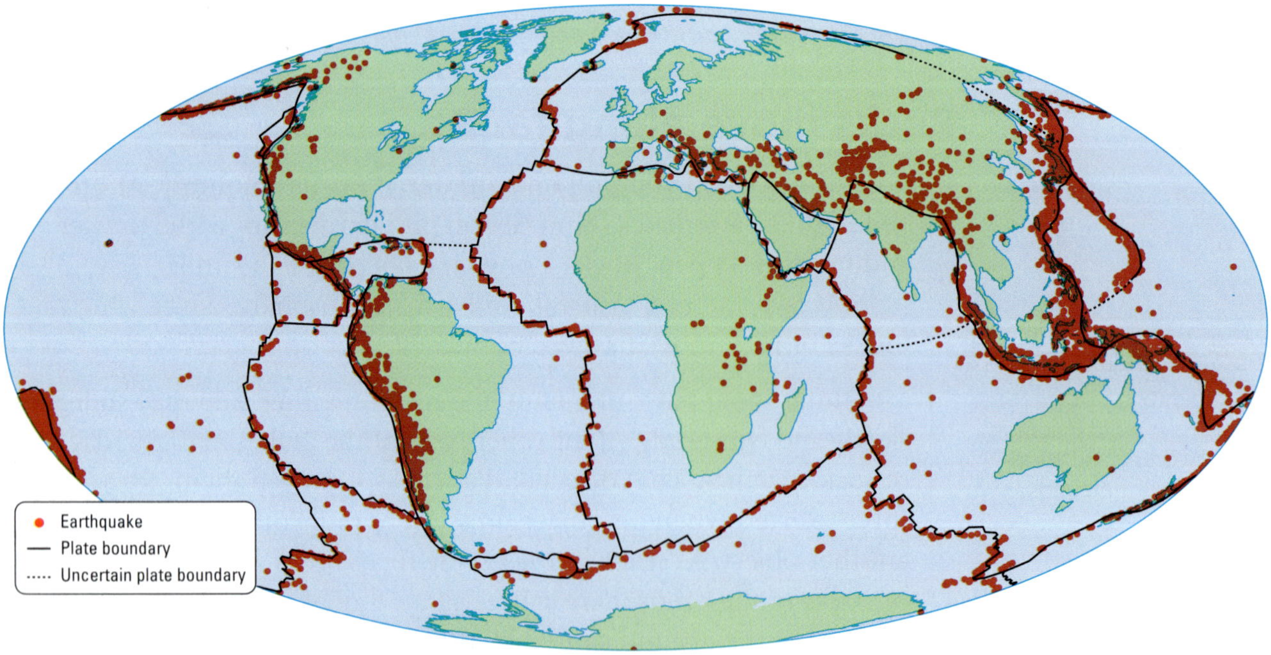

- Earthquake
- — Plate boundary
- ····· Uncertain plate boundary

READING VISUALS Why do most earthquakes in North America and South America occur near the continents' western coasts?

All earthquakes occur in the lithosphere. To understand why, you might compare a tectonic plate to a piece of cold, hard caramel. Like cold caramel, the plate is rigid and brittle. The rocks can break and move suddenly, causing an earthquake. Now compare the asthenosphere below the plate to warm, soft caramel. In the asthenosphere, hot rock bends and flows rather than breaks. A few earthquakes occur far below the normal depth of the lithosphere only because tectonic plates sinking in subduction zones are still cold enough to break.

 Why don't earthquakes occur in the asthenosphere?

Faults are classified by how rocks move.

The blocks of rock along different types of faults move in different directions, depending on the kinds of stress they are under. Scientists classify a fault according to the way the rocks on one side move with respect to the rocks on the other side.

The three main types of faults are normal faults, reverse faults, and strike-slip faults. More than one type of fault may be present along the same plate boundary. However, the type of fault that is most common along a boundary depends on whether plates are pulling apart, pushing together, or scraping past one another at that boundary.

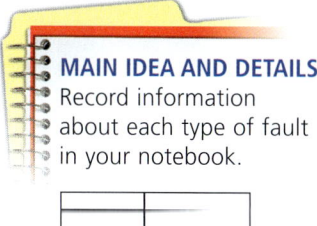

MAIN IDEA AND DETAILS
Record information about each type of fault in your notebook.

INVESTIGATE Faults

How can rocks move along faults?
PROCEDURE

1. Place one triangular block of wood against the other to form a rectangle.
2. Put two pieces of masking tape across both blocks. Draw a different pattern on each piece of tape. Break the tape where it crosses the blocks.
3. Keep the blocks in contact and slide one block along the other.
4. Repeat step 3 until you find three different ways the blocks can move relative to each other. Draw diagrams showing how the blocks moved. Include the tape patterns.

WHAT DO YOU THINK?
- How can you use the tape patterns to find the relative directions in which the blocks were moved?
- In each case, what sort of stress (such as pulling) did you put on the blocks?

CHALLENGE Compare the ways you moved the blocks with the ways tectonic plates move at their boundaries.

SKILL FOCUS
Modeling

MATERIALS
- 2 triangular blocks of wood
- masking tape
- marker

TIME
15 minutes

Chapter 19: **Earthquakes** 651

READING TIP
The word *plane* comes from the Latin word *planum*, which means "flat surface."

The illustrations on this page and page 653 show that a fault forms a plane that extends both horizontally and vertically. Blocks of rock move along the fault plane during an earthquake. Along a normal or reverse fault, the movement of the blocks is mainly vertical—the blocks move up or down. Along a strike-slip fault, the movement is horizontal—the blocks move sideways.

Normal Faults

Along a normal fault, the block of rock above the fault plane slides down relative to the other block. Stress that pulls rocks apart causes normal faults. Earthquakes along normal faults are common near boundaries where tectonic plates are moving apart, such as in the Great Rift Valley of Africa.

READING TIP
Compare the directions of the arrows in the diagrams with the directions of the arrows on the photographs.

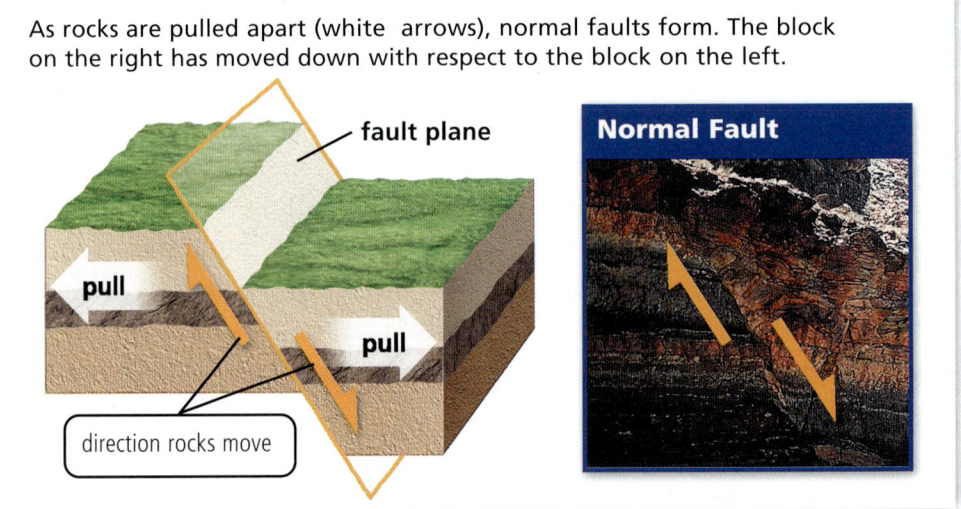

As rocks are pulled apart (white arrows), normal faults form. The block on the right has moved down with respect to the block on the left.

Reverse Faults

Along a reverse fault, the block of rock above the fault plane moves up relative to the other block. Stress that presses rocks together causes reverse faults. These faults can occur near collision-zone boundaries

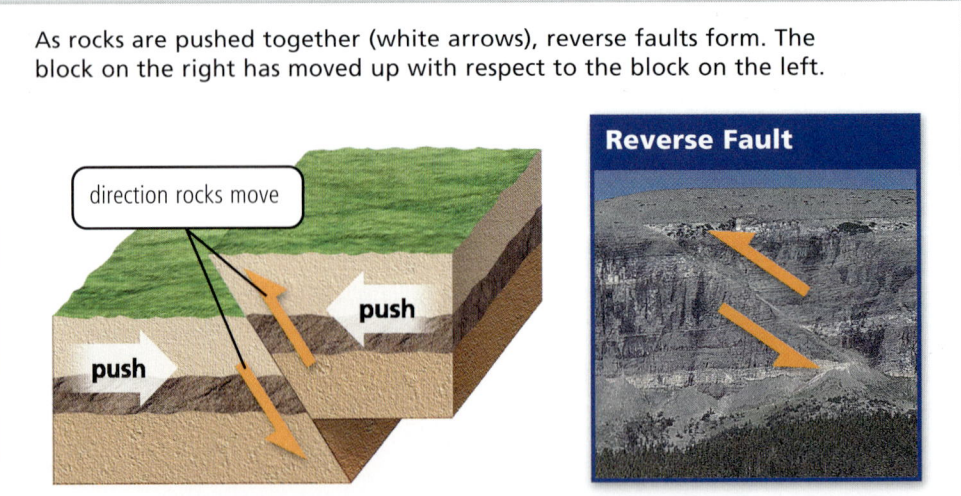

As rocks are pushed together (white arrows), reverse faults form. The block on the right has moved up with respect to the block on the left.

between plates. The Himalaya Mountains, which rise in the area where the Indian Plate is pushing into the Eurasian Plate, have many earthquakes along reverse faults.

 **CHECK YOUR READING** What type of stress produces reverse faults?

Strike-Slip Faults

Along a strike-slip fault, blocks of rock move sideways on either side of the fault plane. Stresses that push blocks of rock horizontally cause earthquakes along strike-slip faults. These faults can occur where plates scrape past each other. The San Andreas Fault is a strike-slip fault.

Explore animations showing fault motion.

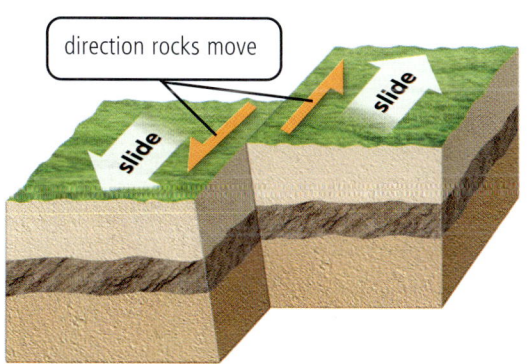

As rocks are pushed horizontally in opposite directions, strike-slip faults form. The block on the right has moved to the right with respect to the block on the left.

direction rocks move

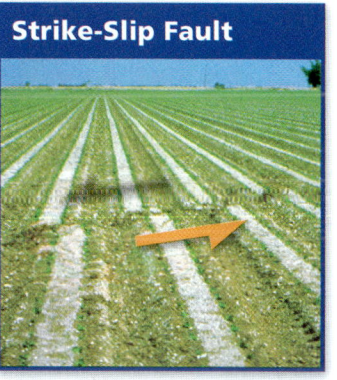

Strike-Slip Fault

Over time, movement of rocks along normal and reverse faults can push up mountains and form deep valleys. As rocks move along strike-slip faults, rocks that were once in continuous layers can become separated by hundreds of kilometers.

19.1 Review

KEY CONCEPTS

1. What causes earthquakes?
2. Why do most earthquakes occur along tectonic plate boundaries?
3. What is the main direction of stress on blocks of rock at normal faults, reverse faults, and strike-slip faults?

CRITICAL THINKING

4. **Compare and Contrast** Make a chart showing the similarities and differences between normal and reverse faults.
5. **Connect** Japan is near a subduction zone. What type of faults would you expect to be responsible for many of the earthquakes there? Explain.

CHALLENGE

6. **Analyze** What evidence from rock layers could show a scientist that earthquakes had occurred in an area before written records were kept?

Chapter 19: **Earthquakes** 653

INCREDIBLE EARTHQUAKES

When Earth Shakes

Alaskan Earthquake Sinks Louisiana Boats

The most powerful earthquake ever recorded in the United States struck Prince William Sound in Alaska on March 27, 1964. Plates that had been moving a few centimeters per year lurched 9 meters (30 ft), causing the ground to shake for more than three minutes. When energy from the earthquake reached Louisiana, more than 5000 kilometers (3000 mi) away, it caused waves high enough to sink fishing boats in a harbor.

Wall of Water Higher than 20-Story Building

The 1964 Alaskan earthquake caused buildings to crumble and collapse. It also produced tsunamis—water waves caused by a sudden movement of the ground during an earthquake, landslide, or volcanic eruption. In Alaska's Valdez Inlet, a landslide triggered by the earthquake produced a tsunami 67 meters (220 ft) high—taller than a 20-story building.

Missouri Earthquakes Ring Massachusetts Bells

Earthquakes near New Madrid, Missouri, in 1811 and 1812 caused church bells in Boston, Massachusetts—nearly 1600 kilometers (1000 mi) away—to ring.

A landslide caused by the 1964 Alaskan earthquake tore this school in Anchorage apart. Fortunately, school was not in session.

In Anchorage, almost 120 km from the center of the earthquake, the ground shook for about three minutes, causing severe damage.

Five Largest Earthquakes Since 1900		
Location	Date	Moment Magnitude
Off the coast of Chile	1960	9.5
Prince William Sound, Alaska	1964	9.2
Andreanof Islands, Alaska	1957	9.1
Kamchatka Peninsula, Russia	1952	9.0
Off the coast of Sumatra	2004	9.0

Largest Earthquake Ever

The most powerful earthquake ever recorded hit Chile in 1960. This earthquake released almost 10 times as much energy as the 1964 earthquake in Alaska—and about 600 times the energy of the earthquake that destroyed much of San Francisco in 1906.

EXPLORE

1. **EXPLAIN** How were the 1964 Alaskan earthquake and the 1960 Chilean earthquake related to movements along tectonic plate boundaries?
2. **CHALLENGE** An inlet is a narrow body of water connected to a lake or ocean. Why might a tsunami be higher in an inlet than along the coastline around it?

KEY CONCEPT
 Earthquakes release energy.

BEFORE, you learned
- Most earthquakes occur along tectonic plate boundaries
- Different directions of stress cause normal, reverse, and strike-slip faults

NOW, you will learn
- How energy from an earthquake travels through Earth
- How an earthquake's location is determined

VOCABULARY

seismic wave p. 655
focus p. 656
epicenter p. 656
seismograph p. 660

EXPLORE Movement of Energy

How does energy travel?

PROCEDURE

1. On a flat surface, hold one end of a spring toy while a partner holds the other end. Stretch the spring, then squeeze some coils together and release them.

2. Again, hold one end of the spring while your partner holds the other end. Shake your end of the spring back and forth.

WHAT DO YOU THINK?
- How did energy travel along the spring when you gathered and released some coils?
- How did energy travel along the spring when you shook one end back and forth?

MATERIALS
spring toy

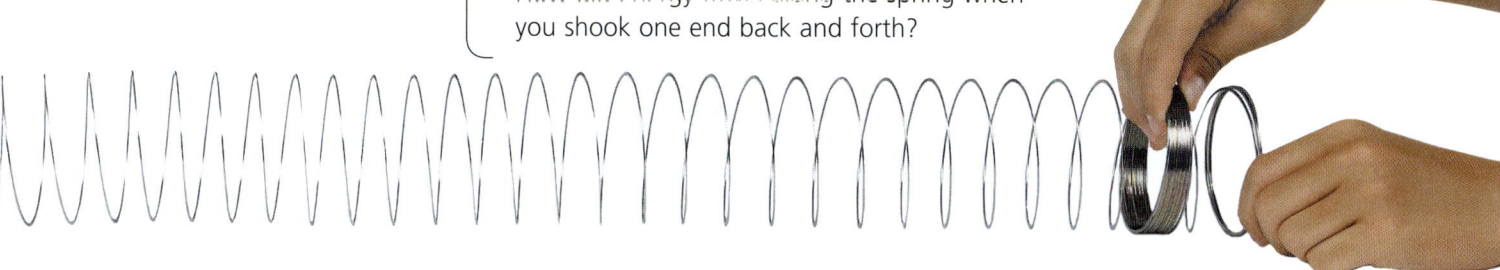

MAIN IDEA AND DETAILS
Record information about the energy released by earthquakes.

Energy from earthquakes travels through Earth.

When you throw a rock into a pond, waves ripple outward from the spot where the rock hits the water. The energy released by an earthquake travels in a similar way through Earth. Unlike the pond ripples, though, earthquake energy travels outward in all directions—up, down, and to the sides. The energy travels as **seismic waves**, (SYZ-mihk) which are vibrations caused by earthquakes. Seismic waves from even small earthquakes can be recorded by sensitive instruments around the world.

Chapter 19: **Earthquakes** 655

READING TIP

The prefix *epi-* comes from a Greek word meaning "on top of." An earthquake's epicenter is directly over its focus.

All earthquakes start beneath Earth's surface. The **focus** of an earthquake is the point underground where rocks first begin to move. Seismic waves travel outward from the earthquake's focus. The **epicenter** (EHP-ih-SEHN-tuhr) is the point on Earth's surface directly above the focus. Scientists often name an earthquake after the city that is closest to its epicenter.

In general, if two earthquakes of equal strength have the same epicenter, the one with the shallower focus causes more damage. Seismic waves from a deep-focus earthquake lose more of their energy as they travel farther up to Earth's surface.

The depths of earthquakes along tectonic plate boundaries are related to the directions in which the plates move. For example, an earthquake along a mid-ocean spreading center has a shallow focus. There, the plates are pulling apart, and the new crust that forms is thin. Subduction zones have a wide range of earthquake depths, from shallow to very deep. Earthquakes can occur anywhere along the sinking plates.

Focus and Epicenter

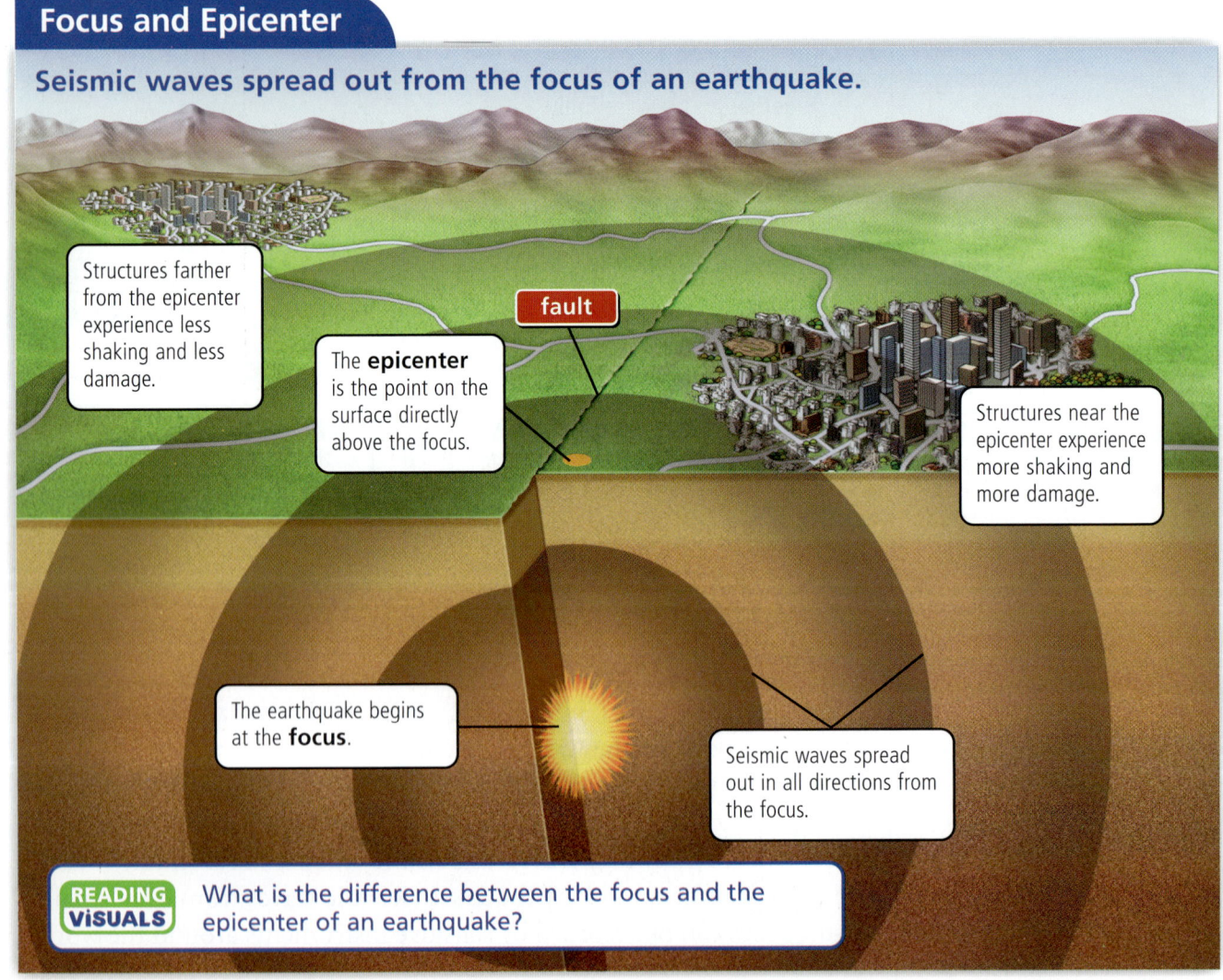

Seismic waves spread out from the focus of an earthquake.

- Structures farther from the epicenter experience less shaking and less damage.
- The **epicenter** is the point on the surface directly above the focus.
- fault
- Structures near the epicenter experience more shaking and more damage.
- The earthquake begins at the **focus**.
- Seismic waves spread out in all directions from the focus.

READING VISUALS What is the difference between the focus and the epicenter of an earthquake?

INVESTIGATE Subduction-Zone Earthquakes

Why are some earthquakes deeper than others?

PROCEDURE

1. Cut the first string into 4 pieces that are 4 cm long. Cut the second string into 3 pieces that are 8 cm long, and the third string into 4 pieces that are 15 cm long.

2. Use the key on the Earthquake Map to match string lengths with earthquake depths.

3. Tape one end of the pieces of string to the map at the earthquake locations, as shown in the photograph. Always cover the same amount of string with tape.

4. Hold the map upside down, with the strings hanging down. Observe the patterns of earthquake locations and depths.

WHAT DO YOU THINK?

- What patterns among the strings do you observe? How do you explain them?
- How might the earthquake depths relate to the sinking of a tectonic plate in a subduction zone?

CHALLENGE Draw a line on the map, showing where the subduction zone might be at Earth's surface. How might the depths of the earthquakes be different if the subduction zone were on the other side of the island?

SKILL FOCUS
Analyzing

MATERIALS
- different colors of string
- ruler
- scissors
- Earthquake Map
- tape

TIME
20 minutes

Waves and Energy

Waves are part of your everyday life. For example, music reaches your ears as sound waves. All waves, including seismic waves, carry energy from place to place. As a wave moves through a material, particles of the material move out of position temporarily, causing the particles next to them to move. After each particle moves, it returns to its original position. In this way, energy moves through the material, but matter does not.

On October 17, 1989, an earthquake stopped baseball's World Series at Candlestick Park in San Francisco. As the seismic waves arrived, fans heard a low rumble; then for about 15 seconds the stadium shook from side to side and up and down. About 20 minutes after the earthquake was felt at the stadium, the seismic waves had traveled to the other side of Earth. There, the waves did not shake the ground hard enough for people to notice. The waves could be detected only by scientific instruments.

Chapter 19: **Earthquakes** 657

Earthquakes produce three types of seismic waves: primary waves, secondary waves, and surface waves. Each type moves through materials differently. In addition, the waves can reflect, or bounce, off boundaries between different layers. The waves can also bend as they pass from one layer into another. Scientists learn about Earth's layers by studying the paths and speeds of seismic waves traveling through Earth.

Primary Waves

READING TIP
One meaning of *primary* is "first." Primary waves arrive before secondary waves.

The fastest seismic waves are called primary waves, or P waves. These waves are the first to reach any particular location after an earthquake occurs. Primary waves travel through Earth's crust at an average speed of about 5 kilometers per second (3 mi/s). Primary waves can travel through solids, liquids, and gases. As they pass through a material, the particles of the material are slightly pushed together and pulled apart. Buildings also experience this push and pull as primary waves pass through the ground they are built on.

Secondary Waves

Explore primary-wave and secondary-wave motion.

Secondary waves are the second seismic waves to arrive at any particular location after an earthquake, though they start at the same time as primary waves. Secondary waves travel through Earth's interior at about half the speed of primary waves. Secondary waves are also called S waves. As they pass through a material, the material's particles are shaken up and down or from side to side. Secondary waves rock small buildings back and forth as they pass.

Secondary waves can travel through rock, but unlike primary waves they cannot travel through liquids or gases. Look at the illustrations on page 659. As a primary wave passes through a material, the volume and density of the material change slightly. But as a secondary wave passes, the material changes slightly in shape. Liquids and gases do not have definite shapes. These materials flow—that is, particles in them do not return to their original positions after being moved. When scientists learned that secondary waves cannot pass through Earth's outer core, they realized that the outer core is not solid.

 Why can't secondary waves travel through liquids or gases?

Surface Waves

Surface waves are seismic waves that move along Earth's surface, not through its interior. They make the ground roll up and down or shake from side to side. Surface waves cause the largest ground movements and the most damage. Surface waves travel more slowly than the other types of seismic waves.

Seismic Waves

Earthquakes produce three types of seismic waves.

Primary Waves

In primary waves, the particles of materials are slightly pushed together and pulled apart in the direction of the waves' travel.

Secondary Waves

In secondary waves, the particles of materials move at a right angle to the direction of the waves' travel.

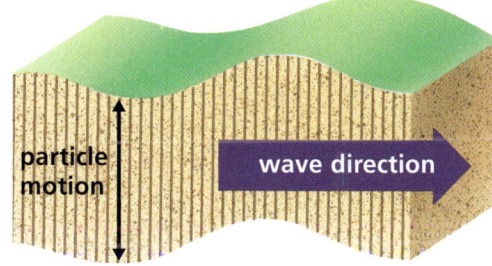

Surface Waves

Surface waves are seismic waves trapped near Earth's surface. As depth within Earth increases, motion due to surface waves decreases, then stops.

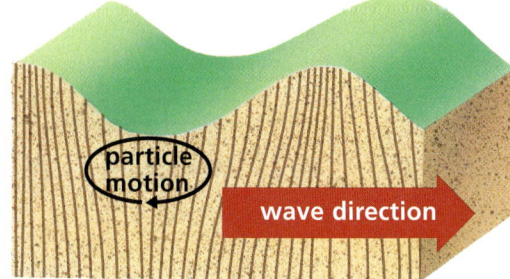

READING VISUALS How do particles move as primary waves and secondary waves pass through materials?

Seismic waves can be measured.

VOCABULARY
Add a magnet word diagram for *seismograph* to your notebook.

Without listening to the news, scientists at seismic stations all over the world know when an earthquake occurs. Seismic stations are places where ground movements are measured. A **seismograph** (SYZ-muh-GRAF) is an instrument that constantly records ground movements. The recording of an earthquake looks like a group of wiggles in a line. The height of the wiggles indicates the amount of ground movement produced by seismic waves at the seismograph's location.

Using Seismographs

Separate seismographs are needed to record side-to-side movements and up-and-down movements. A seismograph that measures side-to-side movements has a heavy weight hanging from a wire. The weight remains almost still as the ground moves back and forth beneath it. A pen attached to the weight records the movements. A seismograph that records up-and-down movements has a heavy weight hanging from a spring. As the ground moves, the weight stays almost still as the spring absorbs the movement by getting longer or shorter. A pen attached to the weight records the changes in distance between the ground and the weight.

Learn more about seismology.

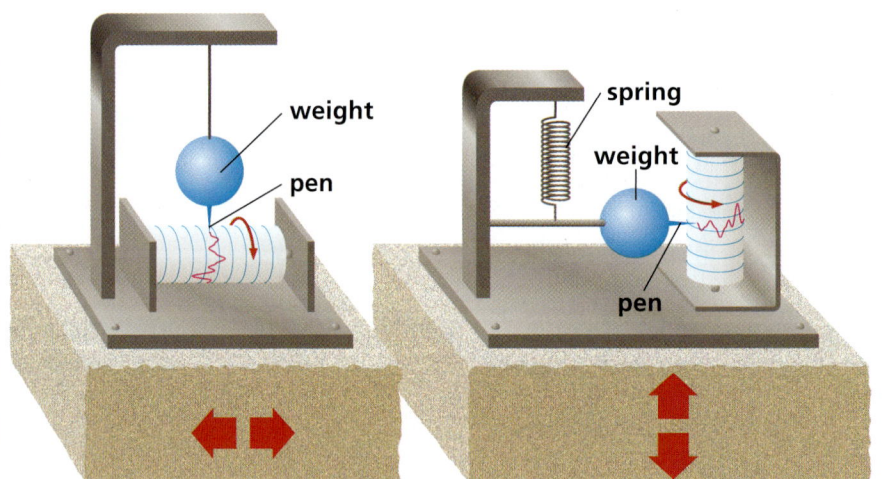

This seismograph records side-to-side movements.

This seismograph records up-and-down movements.

CHECK YOUR READING Why is more than one kind of seismograph needed to record all the movements of the ground during an earthquake?

Scientists use seismographs to measure thousands of earthquakes, large and small, every year. Some seismographs can detect ground movements as small as one hundred-millionth of a centimeter. The recording produced by a seismograph is called a seismogram. By studying seismograms, scientists can determine the locations and strengths of earthquakes.

Locating an Earthquake

To locate the epicenter of an earthquake, scientists must have seismograms from at least three seismic stations. The procedure for locating an epicenter has three steps:

① Scientists find the difference between the arrival times of the primary and the secondary waves at each of the three stations.

② The time difference is used to determine the distance of the epicenter from each station. The greater the difference in time, the farther away the epicenter is.

③ A circle is drawn around each station, with a radius corresponding to the epicenter's distance from that station. The point where the three circles meet is the epicenter.

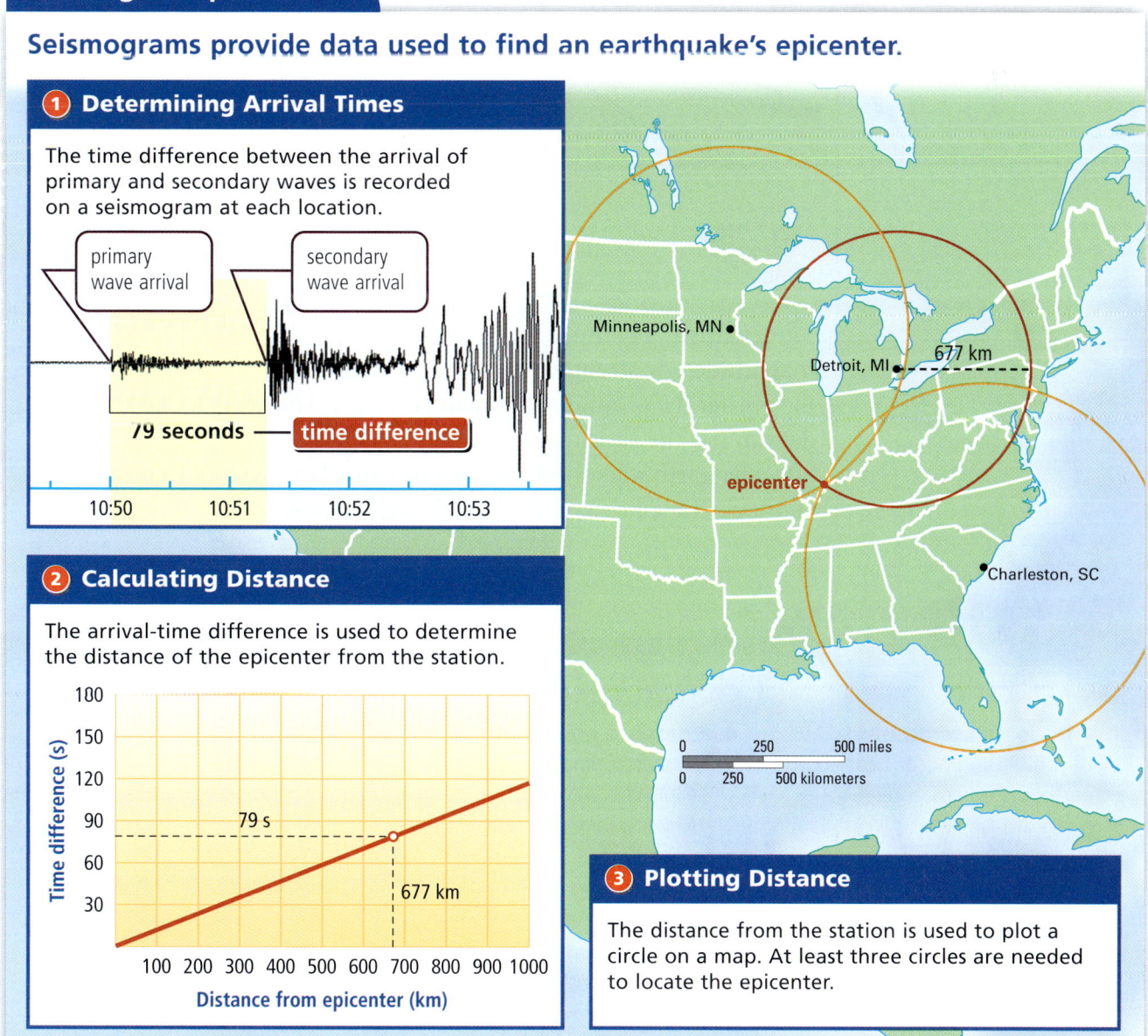

Finding an Epicenter

Seismograms provide data used to find an earthquake's epicenter.

① Determining Arrival Times

The time difference between the arrival of primary and secondary waves is recorded on a seismogram at each location.

79 seconds — time difference

② Calculating Distance

The arrival-time difference is used to determine the distance of the epicenter from the station.

79 s → 677 km

③ Plotting Distance

The distance from the station is used to plot a circle on a map. At least three circles are needed to locate the epicenter.

Chapter 19: **Earthquakes** 661

Scientists can also use seismograph data to locate the focus of an earthquake. They study seismograms to identify waves that have reflected off boundaries inside Earth. Some of these waves help the scientists to determine the earthquake's depth.

A seismogram records the time when the first primary wave arrives. This wave travels by a direct path. The data also show when the first reflected primary wave arrives. After leaving the focus, this wave reflects from Earth's surface and then travels to the seismic station. The reflected wave takes a longer path, so it arrives slightly later. The difference in arrival times indicates the depth of the focus. Scientists can make the necessary calculations, but more commonly a computer is used to calculate the location of an earthquake's epicenter and focus.

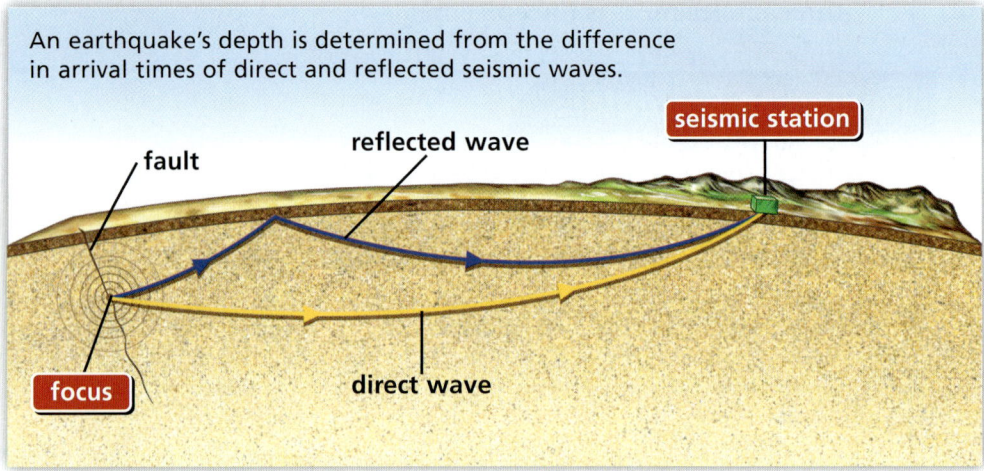

An earthquake's depth is determined from the difference in arrival times of direct and reflected seismic waves.

READING TIP
The word *magnitude* comes from the Latin word *magnitudo*, meaning "greatness."

Scientists also use seismograms to determine earthquakes' magnitudes, or strengths. The more energy an earthquake releases, the greater the ground movement recorded. The greatest movement determines the earthquake's strength on a magnitude scale. Stronger earthquakes get higher numbers. You will read more about earthquake magnitude scales in the next section.

19.2 Review

KEY CONCEPTS

1. Why does the greatest shaking of the ground occur near an earthquake's epicenter?
2. What information do you need to completely describe where an earthquake started?
3. What types of information can a scientist get by studying seismograms?

CRITICAL THINKING

4. **Compare and Contrast** How are primary and secondary waves similar? How are they different?
5. **Apply** What information could you get about an earthquake's location from only two seismic stations' data? Explain.

CHALLENGE

6. **Apply** Why might an earthquake's primary waves, but not its secondary waves, reach a location on the other side of the world from the epicenter?

MATH in SCIENCE

MATH TUTORIAL
CLASSZONE.COM
Click on Math Tutorial for more help with multiplication.

SKILL: MULTIPLICATION

Earthquake Energy

Seismologists use the moment magnitude scale to describe the energies of earthquakes. Because earthquakes vary from quite weak to very strong, the scale is designed to cover a wide range of energies. Each whole number increase in magnitude represents the release of about 32 times as much energy. For example, a magnitude 5 earthquake releases about 32 times as much energy as a magnitude 4 earthquake.

Magnitude	1	2	3	4	5	6	7	8	9	10
Energy		×32	×32	×32	×32	×32	×32	×32	×32	×32

Similarly, a magnitude 6 earthquake releases about 32 times as much energy as a magnitude 5 earthquake, and a magnitude 7 earthquake releases about 32 times as much energy as a magnitude 6 earthquake. You can use multiplication to compare the energies of earthquakes.

Example

Compare the energy of a magnitude 4 earthquake to the energy of a magnitude 7 earthquake. Give your answer to the nearest 1000.

SOLUTION

Magnitude	1	2	3	4	5	6	7	8	9	10
Energy		×32	×32	×32	×32	×32	×32	×32	×32	×32

(1) Multiply: $32 \times 32 \times 32 = 32{,}768$

(2) Round your answer to the nearest 1000: **33,000**

ANSWER A magnitude 7 earthquake releases about 33,000 times as much energy as a magnitude 4 earthquake.

Compare the energies of two earthquakes:

1. Magnitude 4 and magnitude 6; give your answer to the nearest 100

2. Magnitude 5 and magnitude 9; give your answer to the nearest 100,000

3. Magnitude 3.3 and magnitude 4.3

CHALLENGE What is the magnitude of an earthquake that releases about 1000 times the energy of a magnitude 2 earthquake?

Chapter 19: **Earthquakes** 663

KEY CONCEPT
 Earthquake damage can be reduced.

BEFORE, you learned
- Seismic waves travel through Earth
- An earthquake's location and magnitude can be determined

NOW, you will learn
- How an earthquake's magnitude is related to the damage it causes
- How structures are built to withstand most earthquakes
- How scientists estimate the earthquake risk in an area

VOCABULARY
aftershock p. 666
liquefaction p. 666
tsunami p. 666

EXPLORE Shaking
What happens as materials are shaken?

PROCEDURE

① Pour a pile of sand on a newspaper. Place a metal washer on top of the sand. Shake the paper and observe what happens to the sand and the washer.

② Now place the washer on top of a flat rock. Shake the rock and observe what happens.

WHAT DO YOU THINK?
- How did the washer, the sand, and the rock react differently to shaking?
- How might the washer, the sand, and the rock model what happens to buildings and land during earthquakes?

MATERIALS
- sand
- newspaper
- flat rock
- washer

Earthquakes can cause severe damage and loss of life.

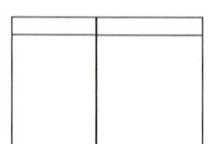

MAIN IDEA AND DETAILS Record information about the effects of earthquakes in your notebook.

Every year, on average, an extremely powerful earthquake—one with a magnitude of 8 or higher—strikes somewhere on Earth. Such an earthquake can destroy almost all the buildings near its epicenter and cause great loss of life.

Earthquakes are most dangerous when they occur near areas where many people live. Most injuries and deaths due to earthquakes are not directly caused by the movement of the ground. They are caused by collapsing buildings and other structures and by fires. After an earthquake, fires may start due to broken natural-gas lines, broken electrical power lines, or overturned stoves.

664 Unit 5: The Changing Earth

Earthquake Magnitude

A very powerful earthquake can release more energy than 1 million weak earthquakes combined. Earthquake magnitude scales give scientists and engineers a simple way to describe this huge range in energy.

The first scale of earthquake magnitude was developed in California during the 1930s by the scientists Charles Richter (RIHK-tuhr) and Beno Gutenberg. In this scale, called the Richter scale, an earthquake's magnitude is based on how fast the ground moves at a seismic station. However, most scientists today prefer to use a newer, more accurate scale: the moment magnitude scale. This scale is based on the total amounts of energy released by earthquakes. The moment magnitude scale is used for all earthquake magnitudes given in this chapter.

Both the Richter scale and the moment magnitude scale are often shown with a top value of 10, but neither actually has a maximum value. On each scale, an increase of one whole number indicates an increase of 32 times more energy. For example, a magnitude 5 earthquake releases 32 times as much energy as a magnitude 4 earthquake and about 1000 times as much energy as a magnitude 3 earthquake.

Magnitude and Effects Near Epicenter

More powerful earthquakes have higher magnitude values.

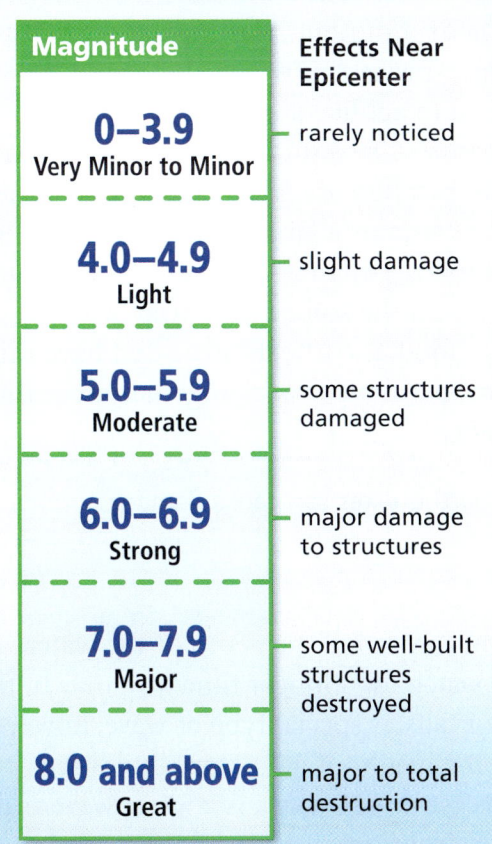

Magnitude	Effects Near Epicenter
0–3.9 Very Minor to Minor	rarely noticed
4.0–4.9 Light	slight damage
5.0–5.9 Moderate	some structures damaged
6.0–6.9 Strong	major damage to structures
7.0–7.9 Major	some well-built structures destroyed
8.0 and above Great	major to total destruction

Damage from Powerful Earthquake

This road collapsed during a magnitude 6.9 earthquake in California on October 17, 1989. About 140 earthquakes with magnitudes of 6 or higher occur each year around the world.

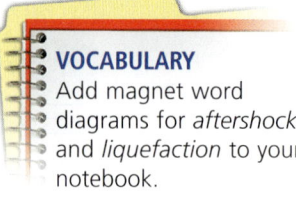

VOCABULARY
Add magnet word diagrams for *aftershock* and *liquefaction* to your notebook.

The moment magnitude scale is more accurate for larger earthquakes than the Richter scale. Another advantage of the moment magnitude scale is that it can be used for earthquakes that occurred before seismographs were invented. Geologists can measure the strength of the rocks and the length they moved along a fault to calculate a past earthquake's magnitude. This information is important for geologists to know when they determine an area's earthquake risk.

 What are two advantages of the moment magnitude scale over the Richter scale?

Damage from Earthquakes

Movement of the blocks of rock on either side of a fault can crack roads, buildings, dams, and any other structures on the fault. As blocks of rock move, they can also raise, lower, or tilt the ground surface. Sometimes structures weakened by an earthquake collapse during shaking caused by aftershocks. An **aftershock** is a smaller earthquake that follows a more powerful earthquake in the same area. Also, fires that break out can cause great damage if broken water pipes keep firefighters from getting water. In the 1906 San Francisco earthquake, fires caused more than 90 percent of the building damage.

Earthquakes can cause major damage by affecting the soil and other loose materials. For example, landslides often occur as a result of earthquakes. A landslide is a movement of soil and rocks down a hill or mountain. Earthquakes can cause soil **liquefaction,** a process in which shaking of the ground causes soil to act like a liquid. For a short time the soil becomes like a thick soup. Liquefaction occurs only in areas where the soil is made up of loose sand and silt and contains a large amount of water. As the shaking temporarily changes the wet soil, structures either sink down into the soil or flow away with it. Shaking of the ground also affects areas that have mixtures of soils. Some soil types pack together more than others when shaken.

This building in Venezuela tilted and sank as the ground beneath it collapsed during an earthquake in 1967.

 List five ways in which earthquakes can cause damage.

Damage from Tsunamis

If you sit on an ocean beach, you can watch the depth of the water change as waves come in. If you watch for a longer time, you may notice bigger changes as the tide rises or falls. A special type of wave, however, can make water rise more than the height of a 20-story building. This wave, known as a **tsunami** (tsu-NAH-mee), is a water wave triggered by an earthquake, volcanic eruption, or landslide. Tsunamis are sometimes called tidal waves, but they are not caused by the forces that produce tides. A tsunami may not be a single wave but several waves that can have different heights and can arrive hours apart.

Explore tsunamis.

Tsunamis move quickly and can travel thousands of kilometers without weakening. In deep water, they can reach speeds of about 700 kilometers per hour (430 mi/h). A tsunami in the deep water of the open ocean may be less than one meter (3 ft) in height at the surface. As a tsunami reaches shallow water around an island or continent, however, it slows down, and its height greatly increases.

A 1946 earthquake on Alaska's coast caused a tsunami that swept across the entire Pacific Ocean. In Alaska the tsunami destroyed a new U.S. Coast Guard lighthouse that otherwise would have been able to send warnings to other areas. In less than five hours, the tsunami reached Hawaii as a series of waves. The highest wave was about 17 meters (55 ft) tall. Because people did not know of the danger, no one had evacuated, and 159 people were killed.

In 1993, a tsunami from a powerful earthquake in Japan threw boats onto land.

Many earthquakes occur around the edges of the Pacific Ocean. Therefore, Hawaii and other areas in and around this ocean are likely to be hit by tsunamis. The Pacific Tsunami Warning Center, located in Hawaii, was established in 1949. The center monitors earthquakes and issues warnings to areas that could be struck by tsunamis.

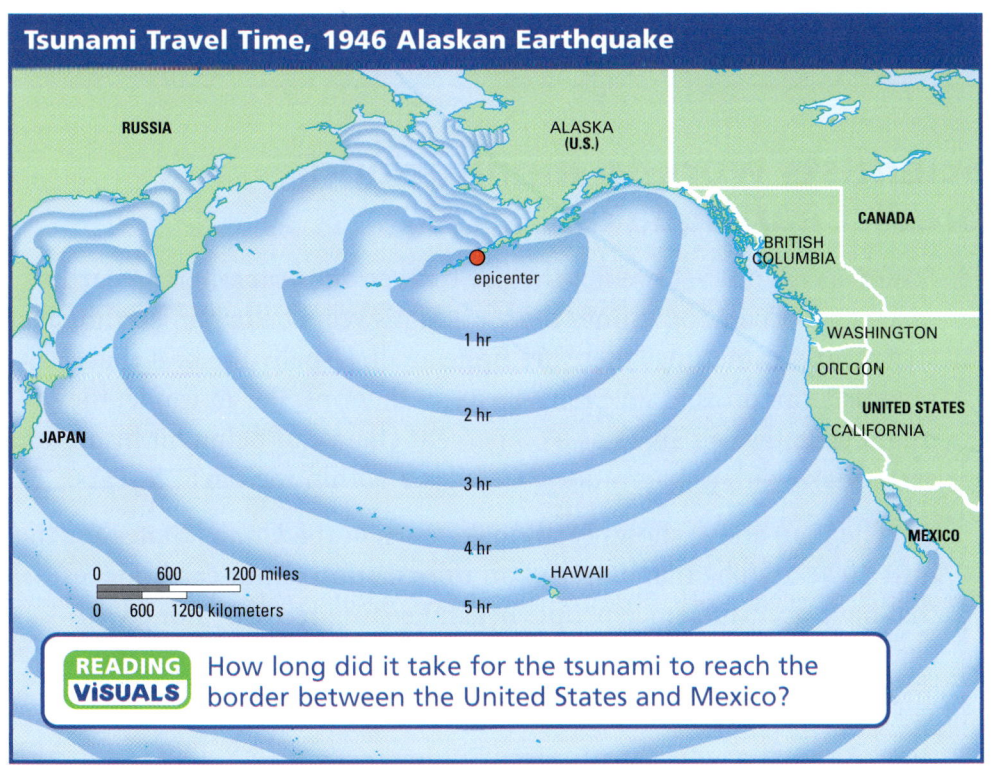

READING VISUALS How long did it take for the tsunami to reach the border between the United States and Mexico?

Chapter 19: **Earthquakes** 667

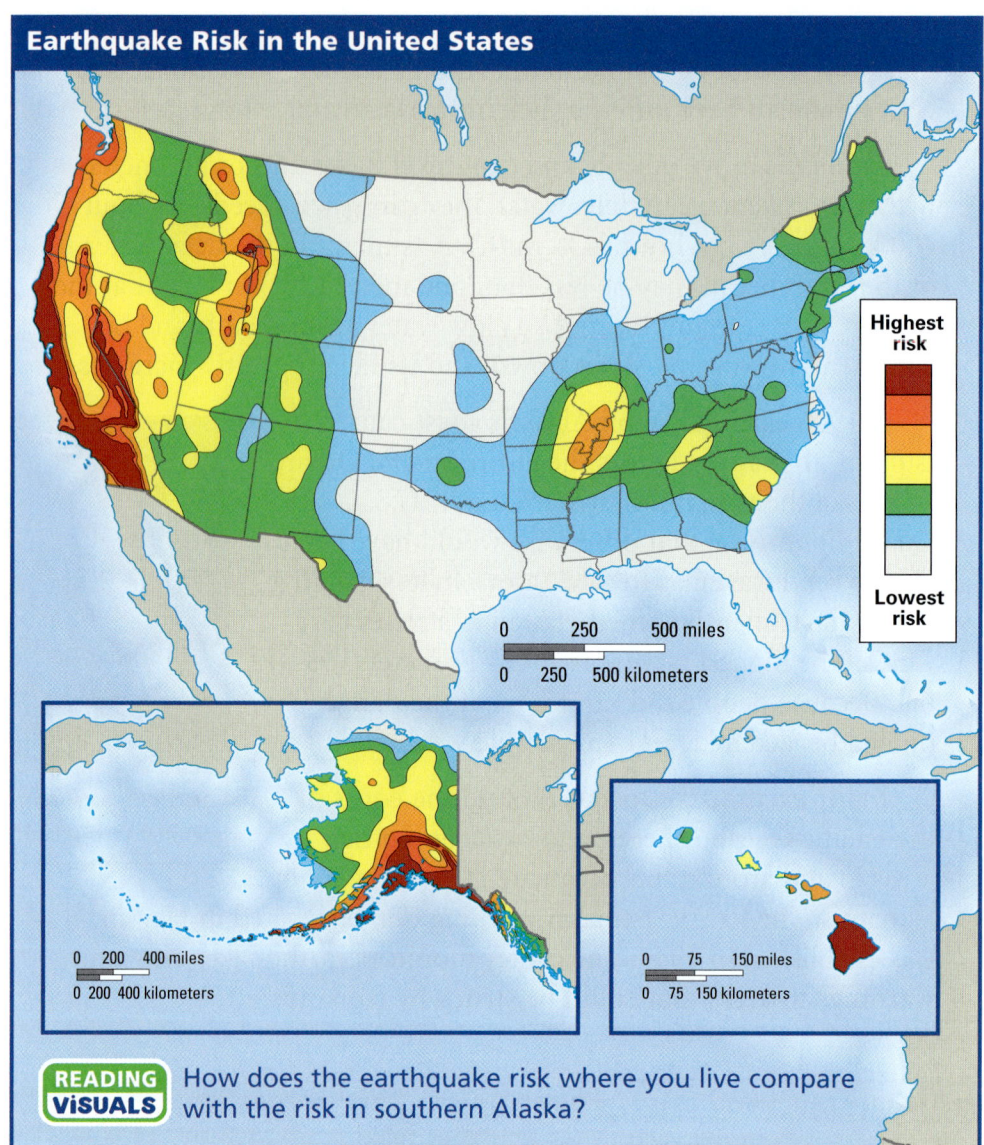

Earthquake Risk in the United States

READING VISUALS — How does the earthquake risk where you live compare with the risk in southern Alaska?

Scientists work to monitor and predict earthquakes.

READING TIP

A prediction is a statement about an event before it occurs. Scientists use their knowledge to make predictions about when earthquakes might occur.

Scientists cannot yet predict the day or even the year when an earthquake will occur. Sometimes there are signs years before an earthquake strikes, and sometimes there are none at all. Usually the best that scientists can do is to give long-term predictions. For example, they might state that an area has a 60 percent chance of being hit by an earthquake with a magnitude 7 or higher within the next 25 years.

The map above shows earthquake risks in the United States for the next 50 years. The map is based on information about earthquakes that have occurred since people began keeping records, along with evidence of earlier earthquakes preserved in rocks. Note that most areas with the highest earthquake risks are near the Pacific Ocean.

To learn more about earthquakes and to find ways of predicting them, scientists all over the world study seismic activity along faults. They monitor whether stress is building up in the rocks along faults. Such signs include

- tilts or changes in the elevation of the ground
- slow movements or stretching in rock
- the development of small cracks in the ground

An increase in small earthquakes can be a sign that stress is building up along a fault and that a large earthquake is likely to occur. But an increase in small earthquakes can also be a sign that a fault is releasing stress bit by bit, decreasing the likelihood of a major earthquake.

Scientists also look for areas where earthquakes have not occurred along an otherwise active fault. They make diagrams in which they plot the locations where earthquakes have started, as shown below. Sometimes such a diagram shows an area of few or no earthquakes that is surrounded by many earthquakes. This area is called a seismic gap. A seismic gap can indicate a location where a fault is stuck. Movement along other parts of the fault can increase stress along the stuck part. This stress could be released by a major earthquake.

CHECK YOUR READING Why can a lack of earthquakes in an area near an active fault cause concern?

Seismic Gaps

A seismic gap is a section of a fault with few earthquakes compared with sections of the fault on either side of the gap.

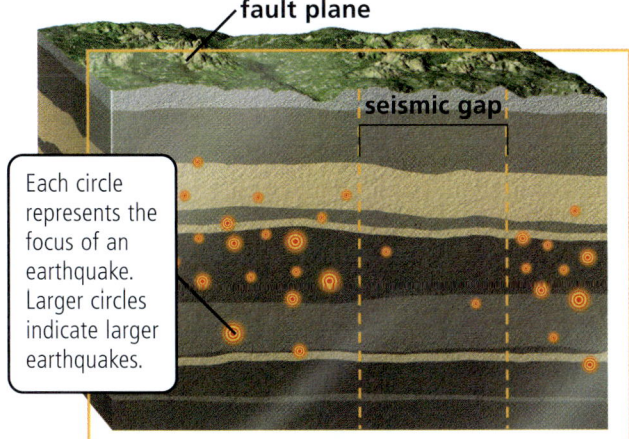

① Over several years many earthquakes have occurred along this fault. However, one section of the fault has had little earthquake activity. Stress is building up along this section.

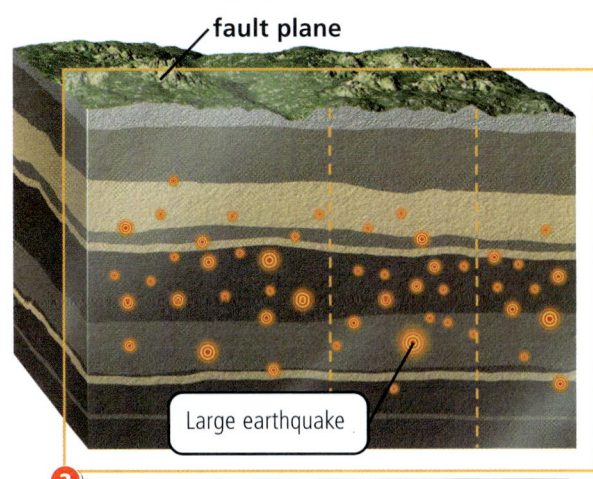

② A large earthquake and its aftershocks have occurred, releasing built-up stress. Over just a few weeks the seismic gap has been filled in.

Chapter 19: **Earthquakes** 669

Structures can be designed to resist earthquake damage.

READING TIP
Here, the term *structure* refers to office buildings, homes, bridges, dams, factories—all the things that people build.

For safety, it might be best to be outdoors, far from any buildings, during an earthquake. But there is no way to tell just when or where an earthquake will occur. For this reason, the best way to reduce deaths, injuries, and damage from earthquakes is to build structures able to withstand strong ground shaking. The first step is to understand what the risks from earthquakes are in an area. The second step is to build structures that are appropriate for the area.

Scientists make maps of areas to show the locations of fault zones, past earthquakes, and areas likely to experience flooding, landslides, or liquefaction. In Japan, California, and other areas that have many earthquakes, planners use these maps to develop rules for building new structures and strengthening older ones. The maps are also used to select building locations that are stable—unlikely to experience landslides or liquefaction.

Earthquake damage to small buildings, such as most houses, often occurs when the buildings are shaken off their foundations. Small buildings are better protected when they are firmly fastened to their foundations. Also, their walls need to be strong. Some houses were built before modern safety rules were in place. The walls of these houses can be made stronger by adding supports. Supports are particularly important in brick walls, which can easily collapse in an earthquake. A special type of steel is commonly used for the supports because it is strong and is able to bend, then return to its original shape.

SAFETY TIPS

Earthquakes

Before
- Fasten heavy objects, such as bookcases, to floors or walls to keep them from falling.
- Put latches on cabinets to keep dishes from falling out.
- Identify safe spots in every room, such as the space under a strong table.
- Keep an emergency supply of bottled water.

During and After
- If you are inside a building, stay inside until the shaking stops. Objects falling from buildings cause many injuries.
- If you are outdoors, move away from buildings, poles, and trees.
- Make a family plan for contacting a person who lives in another town. As people call to say they are safe, this person can pass on the information.

Many of the methods used to make larger buildings and other structures safer are designed to reduce the amount they shake during an earthquake. One method is to use devices called base isolators, as shown in the illustration. Base isolators are placed between a building and its foundation. The isolators are made of flexible materials that are stacked in layers like pancakes. When an earthquake occurs, the isolators absorb much of the ground motion. Any shaking that does reach the building is slower and smoother.

A building may also have an open space, or moat, around it. The moat, which may be covered at the surface with sidewalks and landscaping, lets the building shake more gently than the ground during an earthquake.

Special walls, called shear walls, add strength to a structure. These walls contain steel supports. Shear walls in the center of a building are often built around a stairwell or an elevator shaft. These walls make up a part of the building known as the shear core.

Walls can also be made stronger by adding braces. Pairs of braces that form an **X** shape are called cross braces. They help a structure keep its shape while it is being shaken.

 Describe two methods used to make buildings stronger.

KEY CONCEPTS

1. How is an earthquake magnitude scale related to the amounts of energy released by earthquakes?
2. What are the major dangers to people from an earthquake?
3. Name three methods of improving a building's safety before an earthquake.

CRITICAL THINKING

4. **Apply** What might people living next to the ocean do to protect themselves if they were given a two-hour warning of an approaching tsunami?
5. **Connect** If you lived in an area where earthquakes were common, what could you do to make your room safer?

CHALLENGE

6. **Analyze** Earthquakes release stress that has built up in rocks. Why do you think aftershocks occur?

CHAPTER INVESTIGATION

How Structures React in Earthquakes

DESIGN YOUR OWN

OVERVIEW AND PURPOSE

In 1989 a magnitude 6.9 earthquake struck the San Francisco Bay area, killing 62 people and leaving 12,000 homeless. In 1988 a magnitude 6.9 earthquake occurred near Spitak, Armenia. There, nearly 25,000 people died and 514,000 lost their homes. The difference in the effects of these two earthquakes was largely due to differences in construction methods. In this investigation you will

- build a structure and measure how long it can withstand shaking on a shake table provided by your teacher
- explore methods of building earthquake-resistant structures

MATERIALS
- modeling clay
- stirrer straws
- piece of thin cardboard 15 cm on each side
- scissors
- ruler
- shake table

▶ Problem
Write It Up

How can structures be built to withstand most earthquakes?

▶ Hypothesize
Write It Up

Write a hypothesis to explain how structures can be built to withstand shaking. Your hypothesis should take the form of an "If . . . , then . . . , because . . ." statement.

▶ Procedure

1. Make a data table like the one shown on the next page.

2. Use stirrers joined with clay to build a structure at least 20 cm tall on top of the cardboard. Cut the stirrers if necessary.

3. Make a diagram of your structure.

step 2

672 Unit 5: The Changing Earth

4. Lift your structure by its cardboard base and place it on the shake-table platform. Pull the platform 2 centimeters to one side and release it.

5. Repeat step 4 until the structure begins to collapse.

step 4

5. **COMPARE** Examine the diagrams of the three structures that lasted longest in your class. What characteristics, if any, did they have in common?

6. **APPLY** Based on your results, write a list of recommendations for building earthquake-resistant structures.

Observe and Analyze *Write It Up*

1. **RECORD** Complete your data table and make notes about the collapse, including areas of possible weakness in your structure.

2. **INFER** Use your observations to design a structure that will better withstand shaking.

Conclude *Write It Up*

1. **INTERPRET** Compare your results with your hypothesis. Do your observations support your hypothesis?

2. **INFER** How would you use the shake table to model earthquakes of different magnitudes?

3. **IDENTIFY VARIABLES** How might your results differ if you always pulled the platform to the same side or if you pulled it to different sides?

4. **IDENTIFY LIMITS** In what ways might a building's behavior during an earthquake differ from the behavior of your structure on the shake table?

INVESTIGATE Further

CHALLENGE Have a contest to see who can build the most earthquake-resistant structure. Design your structure as if you were an earthquake engineer. Make a model of your structure at least 30 centimeters tall, using the types of materials you used in this investigation. Test the structure on the shake table. What design features helped the winning structure to resist shaking the longest?

How Structures React in Earthquakes

Problem How can structures be built to withstand most earthquakes?

Hypothesize

Observe and Analyze

Table 1. Number of Trials Until Collapse of Structure

Trial	Distance Platform Pulled to Side (cm)	Notes
1	2	
2	2	
3	2	
4	2	

Conclude

Chapter 19 Review

the BIG idea
Earthquakes release stress that has built up in rocks.

CONTENT REVIEW
CLASSZONE.COM

KEY CONCEPTS SUMMARY

1 Earthquakes occur along faults.

Normal faults form as rocks are pulled apart.

Reverse faults form as rocks are pushed together.

Strike-slip faults form as rocks are pushed horizontally in opposite directions.

VOCABULARY
fault p. 649
stress p. 649
earthquake p. 649

2 Earthquakes release energy.

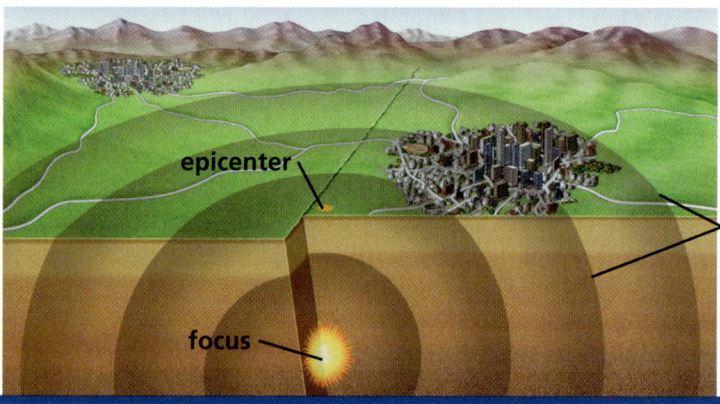

Seismic waves move out from the focus in all directions.

VOCABULARY
seismic wave p. 655
focus p. 656
epicenter p. 656
seismograph p. 660

3 Earthquake damage can be reduced.

A powerful earthquake releases more energy and causes more shaking of the ground than does a weak earthquake.

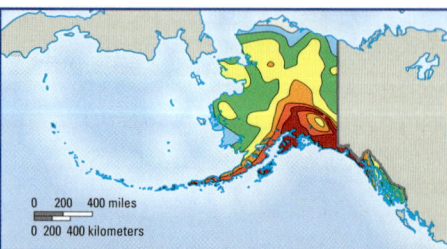

An area's risk of earthquakes can be predicted.

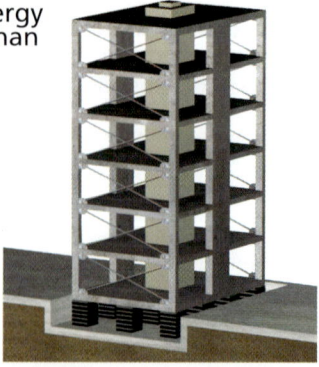

Structures can be designed for greater safety in an earthquake.

VOCABULARY
aftershock p. 666
liquefaction p. 666
tsunami p. 666

674 Unit 5: The Changing Earth

Reviewing Vocabulary

On a separate sheet of paper, draw a diagram to show the relationships among each set of words. One set has been done as an example.

seismograph, seismic waves, seismogram

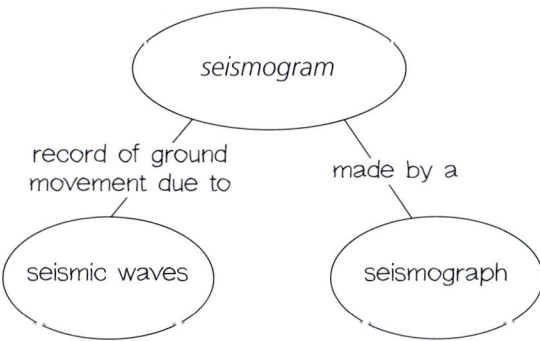

1. earthquake, epicenter, focus
2. earthquake, tsunami, liquefaction
3. fault, stress, earthquake, aftershock
4. tsunami, epicenter, seismogram

Reviewing Key Concepts

Multiple Choice *Choose the letter of the best answer.*

5. What causes an earthquake?
   a. a rise of magma in the mantle
   b. a sudden movement of blocks of rock
   c. a buildup of seismic waves
   d. a change in Earth's magnetic poles

6. Earthquakes release energy in the form of
   a. seismic waves
   b. faults
   c. stress lines
   d. seismograms

7. Most damage from an earthquake usually occurs
   a. below the focus
   b. far from the epicenter
   c. at the focus
   d. near the epicenter

8. To locate the epicenter of an earthquake, scientists need seismograms from at least _____ seismic stations.
   a. two
   b. three
   c. four
   d. five

9. The seismic waves that usually cause the most damage are
   a. surface waves
   b. tsunami waves
   c. primary waves
   d. secondary waves

10. Earthquakes release _____ that has built up in rocks.
    a. water
    b. magnetism
    c. stress
    d. electricity

11. About 80 percent of all earthquakes occur in a belt around the
    a. Pacific Ocean
    b. San Andreas Fault
    c. North American Plate
    d. African Rift Valley

12. In a strike-slip fault, blocks of rock move _____ along the fault plane.
    a. up
    b. down
    c. sideways
    d. up and down

13. One method of making a building earthquake resistant is to
    a. add sand under the foundation
    b. reduce the use of steel
    c. make the walls of brick
    d. use cross braces

Short Answer *Write a short answer to each question.*

14. Why do most earthquakes occur at or near tectonic plate boundaries?

15. How do data from seismic waves indicate that Earth's outer core is liquid?

16. What causes most of the injuries and deaths due to earthquakes?

Thinking Critically

Study the illustration below, showing the epicenter and focus of an earthquake, then answer the following six questions.

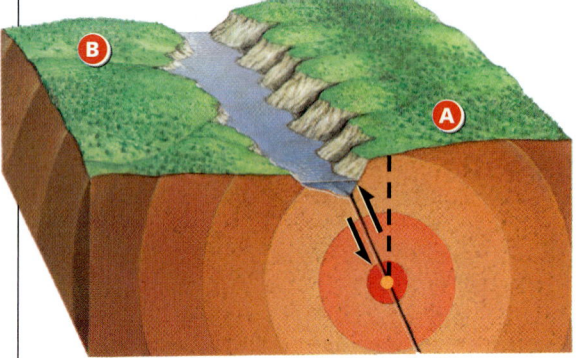

17. APPLY What type of fault is shown in the illustration? How do you know?

18. APPLY Where on the surface is the greatest shaking likely to occur?

19. INFER What does the set of circles around the focus represent?

20. EXPLAIN In what ways would the times of arrival of primary and secondary waves be different at points *A* and *B*?

21. IDENTIFY EFFECTS The land surface to the left of the fault is lower than the land surface to the right. How might this be related to movements along the fault?

22. ANALYZE What are the main directions of stress on the blocks of rock on either side of the fault?

23. APPLY A builder is planning to construct a new house near a fault along which earthquakes are common. Write a list of guidelines that the builder might use to decide where and how to build the house.

24. ANALYZE Identify two areas of the United States where earthquakes are most likely to occur. Explain your choices in terms of plate tectonics.

25. IDENTIFY EFFECTS A town has been struck by an earthquake with a magnitude of 5.8. The epicenter was 10 kilometers (6 mi) away, and the focus was shallow. What sort of damage would you expect to find in the town?

26. ANALYZE What role do earthquakes play in shaping Earth's surface?

27. CALCULATE If primary waves travel at a speed of about 5 kilometers per second, how long would it take them to arrive at a seismic station located 695 kilometers from an earthquake's focus?

the BIG idea

28. CONNECT Look again at the photograph of earthquake damage on pages 646–647. Explain how energy released by an earthquake can travel through rock and cause damage at Earth's surface.

29. SYNTHESIZE The illustration below shows convection in Earth's mantle. What are the relationships among the heat inside Earth, the movements of tectonic plates, and the occurrences of earthquakes?

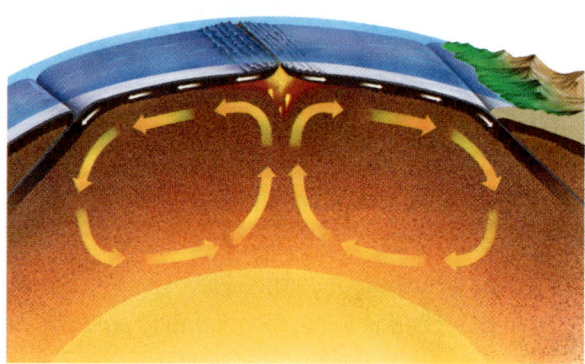

UNIT PROJECTS

If you need to do an experiment for your unit project, gather the materials. Be sure to allow enough time to observe results before the project is due.

Standardized Test Practice

Analyzing Data

The following tables show magnitudes and average numbers of earthquakes in the world per year, and states in which two or more major earthquakes have been recorded. Use the information in the tables to answer the questions below.

Earthquakes in the World per Year

Classification	Magnitude	Average Number per Year
Great	8.0 and higher	1
Major	7.0–7.9	18
Strong	6.0–6.9	120
Moderate	5.0–5.9	800
Light	4.0–4.9	6200
Minor	3.0–3.9	49,000

States That Have Recorded Two or More Major Earthquakes

State	Number of Major Earthquakes
Alaska	74
Arkansas	2
California	16
Hawaii	4
Missouri	2
Nevada	3

1. A major earthquake can have a magnitude of
   a. 6.0–6.9
   b. 6.0 and higher
   c. 7.4
   d. 8.2

2. The most major earthquakes have been recorded in which state?
   a. Arkansas
   b. Hawaii
   c. Missouri
   d. Nevada

3. A magnitude 3.2 earthquake is classified as
   a. major
   b. strong
   c. moderate
   d. minor

4. The world's most powerful earthquakes occur along reverse faults. In which state are reverse faults most likely to be common?
   a. Alaska
   b. California
   c. Hawaii
   d. Nevada

5. In which state is a tectonic plate boundary most likely to be located?
   a. Arkansas
   b. California
   c. Hawaii
   d. Nevada

6. Compared to the number of major earthquakes each year, the number of moderate earthquakes is
   a. about 40 times greater
   b. about 4 times greater
   c. about equal
   d. smaller

7. Alaska has recorded a total of 82 earthquakes with magnitudes of 7.0 and higher. How many of these earthquakes are classified as "great"?
   a. 0
   b. 8
   c. 56
   d. 74

8. An earthquake of which classification releases the most energy?
   a. great
   b. major
   c. strong
   d. minor

Extended Response

Answer the two questions below in detail. Include some of the terms shown in the word box. In your answers underline each term you use.

| seismic waves | primary | secondary | surface |
| stress | fault | plate boundary | |

9. During an earthquake, Dustin felt a small amount of shaking. About 15 seconds later, he felt some more shaking. Then about 45 seconds later he felt the strongest shaking. Explain what happened.

10. The island of Sumatra is located in an area where the Pacific Plate sinks under the Eurasian Plate. Explain why Sumatra has many earthquakes.

Chapter 19: **Earthquakes** 677

CHAPTER 20: Mountains and Volcanoes

the BIG idea

Mountains and volcanoes form as tectonic plates move.

How does new land form from molten rock?

Key Concepts

SECTION 1: Movement of rock builds mountains.
Learn how different types of mountains form.

SECTION 2: Volcanoes form as molten rock erupts.
Learn why there are different types of volcanoes and volcanic eruptions.

SECTION 3: Volcanoes affect Earth's land, air, and water.
Learn how volcanic eruptions affect land, air, and water.

Internet Preview

CLASSZONE.COM
Chapter 20 online resources: Content Review, Simulation, Visualization, two Resource Centers, Math Tutorial, Test Practice

678 Unit 5: The Changing Earth

EXPLORE the BIG idea

Making Mountains

Line up and hold a row of about ten checkers or coins on a table. Tilt the row, then let it go.

Observe and Think What happened to the height, length, and shape of the row? How do you think these changes might be similar to the processes by which some mountains and valleys form?

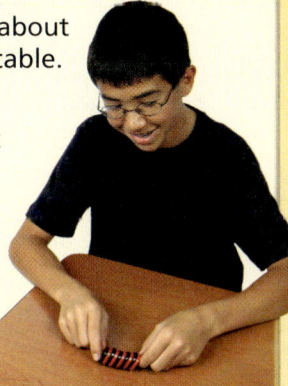

Under Pressure

Half fill two empty plastic bottles with a fresh carbonated beverage. Screw the caps on the bottles tightly. Put one bottle in hot tap water and one in ice water. Wait three minutes.

Observe and Think Slowly unscrew the caps from the bottles and observe how quickly gas bubbles form and escape. What is the role of pressure? How might gas bubbles cause pressure to build up in magma as they form?

Internet Activity: Volcanoes

Go to **ClassZone.com** to make a volcano erupt.

Observe and Think Why are some volcanic eruptions much more violent than others?

Explore Volcanoes Code: MDL054

Chapter 20: **Mountains and Volcanoes**

CHAPTER 20
Getting Ready to Learn

◀ CONCEPT REVIEW

- Earthquakes occur as blocks of rock move along faults.
- Tectonic plates pull apart, push together, or scrape past one another along their boundaries.

◀ VOCABULARY REVIEW

convergent boundary p. 626
subduction p. 634
fault p. 649
earthquake p. 649
magma *See Glossary.*

CONTENT REVIEW
CLASSZONE.COM
Review concepts and vocabulary.

▶ TAKING NOTES

CONTENT FRAME

Organize your notes into a **content frame** for mountains. Make categories at the top that describe their types, features, and how they form. Then fill in the boxes for each type of mountain. Later in the chapter you will make content frames for other topics.

VOCABULARY STRATEGY

Draw a **word triangle** diagram for each new vocabulary term. On the bottom line, write and define the term. Above that, write a sentence that uses the term correctly. At the top, draw a small picture to show what the term looks like.

See the Note-Taking Handbook on pages R45–R51.

SCIENCE NOTEBOOK

TYPE OF MOUNTAINS	CHARACTERISTIC	WHERE THEY FORM	EXAMPLES
folded	rocks bent and folded	at convergent plate boundaries	Appalachians Himalayas
fault-block			

Fault-block mountains form as continental crust is pulled apart.

fault-block mountain: a mountain pushed up or tilted along a fault

680 Unit 5: The Changing Earth

KEY CONCEPT

Movement of rock builds mountains.

 BEFORE, you learned

- Major geologic events occur at tectonic plate boundaries
- Most faults are located along plate boundaries

 NOW, you will learn

- How the folding of rock can form mountains
- How movement along faults can form mountains

VOCABULARY

folded mountain p. 684
fault-block mountain p. 686

EXPLORE Folding

How does rock fold?

PROCEDURE

1. Make three flat layers of clay on top of a sheet of newspaper. Put a block at either end of the clay.
2. Hold one block still. Push on the other block to slowly bring the blocks closer together.

WHAT DO YOU THINK?

- What happened to the clay when you pushed on the block?
- What shape did the middle layer of clay form?
- If a large block of rock reacted to pressure in a similar way, what kind of landform would result?

MATERIALS

- 2 or 3 colors of modeling clay
- 2 blocks
- newspaper

Most mountains form along plate boundaries.

A shallow sea once covered the area that is now Mount Everest, Earth's tallest mountain. If you were to climb Mount Everest, you would be standing on rocks containing the remains of ocean animals. Mount Everest also contains rocks that formed far away at a spreading center on the sea floor. How can rocks from the sea floor be on top of a mountain on a continent? Plate tectonics provides the answer.

Recall that an oceanic plate sinks when it collides with a continental plate. Some sea-floor material scrapes off the sinking plate and onto the continent. As continental mountains form, material once at the bottom of an ocean can be pushed many kilometers high.

Chapter 20: **Mountains and Volcanoes** 681

Mountain Ranges and Belts

A mountain is an area of land that rises steeply from the land around it. A single mountain is rare. Most mountains belong to ranges—long lines of mountains that were formed at about the same time and by the same processes. Ranges that are close together make up mountain belts. For example, the Rocky Mountain belt in western North America contains about 100 ranges.

1 Mountains rise high above the land around them.

2 Most mountains are in groups called mountain ranges.

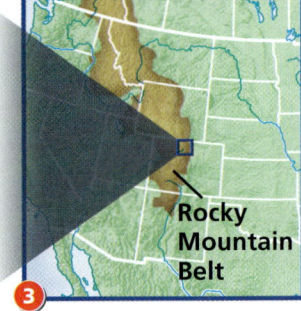

3 Closely spaced mountain ranges make up mountain belts.

Most of the world's major mountain belts are located along tectonic plate boundaries. But mountain belts like the Appalachians (AP-uh-LAY-chee-uhnz) in eastern North America are in the interior of plates. Mountains such as these were formed by ancient plate collisions that assembled the present-day continents.

Major Mountain Belts

Major mountain belts mark the locations of present or past plate boundaries.

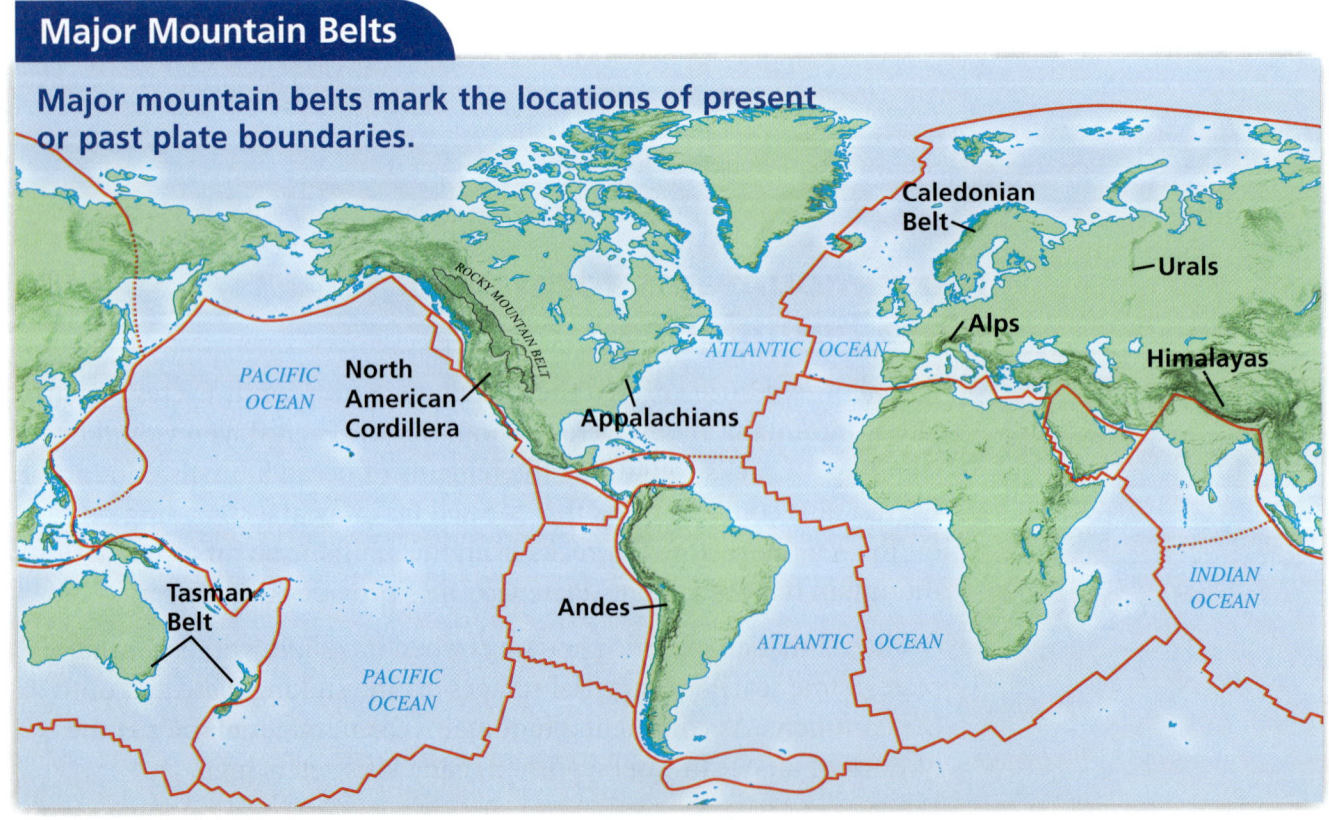

682 Unit 5: The Changing Earth

Mountains, Rocks, and Sediment

At the same time that some processes push mountains up, other processes wear them down. At Earth's surface, water and wind break rocks apart and move the pieces away. As long as mountains are pushed up faster than they wear down, they grow taller. For this reason, young mountains tend to be tall and steep. But eventually mountain-building processes slow, then end. Water and wind take over. Given enough time, all mountains become rounded hills, and then they are gone. Countless mountains have formed and worn away throughout Earth's long history.

Rocks break down into loose pieces that can be carried by water or wind. These pieces are called sediments. For example, sand on a beach is sediment. Thick layers of sediments can build up in low-lying areas, such as valleys, lakes, or the ocean. Pieces of sediments form sedimentary rock as they are pressed together or joined by natural cement.

The land becomes flatter as mountains wear down and valleys fill with sediments. If tectonic plates were to stop moving, eventually the surfaces of all the continents would be completely flat.

Mountains Wear Down

Mountains wear down as water and wind break their rocks into sediments and carry them away.

Young Mountains

Most young mountains are rugged. But even as they form, their rocks are being broken apart.

Old Mountains

Most old mountains are rounded. Lower areas around them contain thick layers of sediments.

READING VISUALS How do mountains wear away?

Mountains can form as rocks fold.

Though people usually do not think of rocks as being able to bend and fold, they can. Think of a wax candle. If you bend a candle quickly, it will break. If you leave a candle propped up at an angle, over many days it will bend. If the candle is in a warm area, it will bend more quickly. Rocks also bend when stress is applied slowly. Rocks deep in the crust are at high temperatures and pressures. They are particularly likely to bend rather than break.

CHECK YOUR READING Under what conditions are rocks likely to bend and fold?

VOCABULARY
Make a word triangle for *folded mountain* in your notebook.

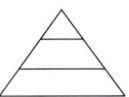

READING TIP
Eurasia is the landmass consisting of Europe and Asia.

Remember that tectonic plates move only a few centimeters each year. The edge of a continent along a convergent boundary is subjected to stress for a very long time as another plate pushes against it. Some of the continent's rocks break, and others fold. As folding continues, mountains are pushed up. A **folded mountain** is a mountain that forms as continental crust crumples and bends into folds.

Folded mountains form as an oceanic plate sinks under the edge of a continent or as continents collide. One example is the Himalaya (HIHM-uh-LAY-uh) belt, which formed by a collision between India and Eurasia. Its formation is illustrated on page 685.

① Convergent Boundary Develops At one time an ocean separated India and Eurasia. As India moved northward, oceanic lithosphere sank in a newly formed subduction zone along the Eurasian Plate. Along the edge of Eurasia, folded mountains formed. Volcanoes also formed as magma rose from the subduction zone to the surface.

② Continental Collision Begins Eventually the sea floor was completely destroyed, and India and Eurasia collided. Subduction ended. The volcanoes stopped erupting because they were no longer supplied with magma. Sea-floor material that had been added to the edge of Eurasia became part of the mountains pushed up by the collision.

③ Collision Continues India and Eurasia continue to push together. Their collision has formed the Himalayas, the world's tallest mountains. They grow even higher as rock is folded and pushed up for hundreds of kilometers on either side of the collision boundary.

Earthquakes can also be important to the upward growth of folded mountains. A great deal of rock in the Himalaya belt has been pushed up along reverse faults, which are common at convergent boundaries.

Formation of Himalayas

The Himalayas are being pushed higher by an ongoing continental collision.

① Convergent Boundary Develops

As India began moving toward Eurasia 200 million years ago, a convergent boundary developed along the edge of Eurasia. The oceanic lithosphere between the two continents sank into a subduction zone.

Folded mountains formed as oceanic and continental plates pushed together.

Volcanoes formed as magma rose from the subduction zone to the surface.

② Continental Collision Begins

The sea floor was completely destroyed about 50 million years ago, and India and Eurasia collided.

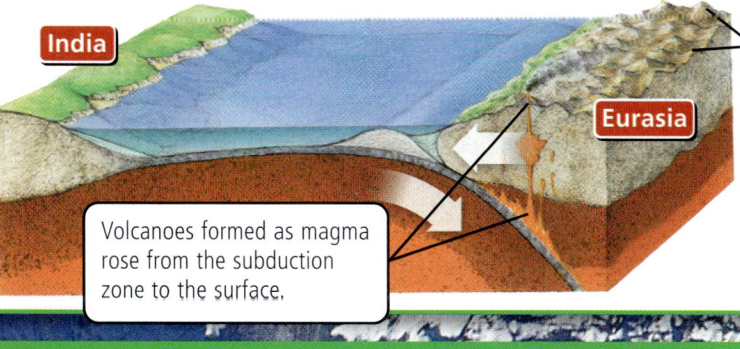

Crust along the edges of both continents was crumpled and folded into mountains.

Subduction stopped after the continents collided. No more magma formed.

③ The Collision Continues

Currently, the Himalayas are growing more than one centimeter higher each year.

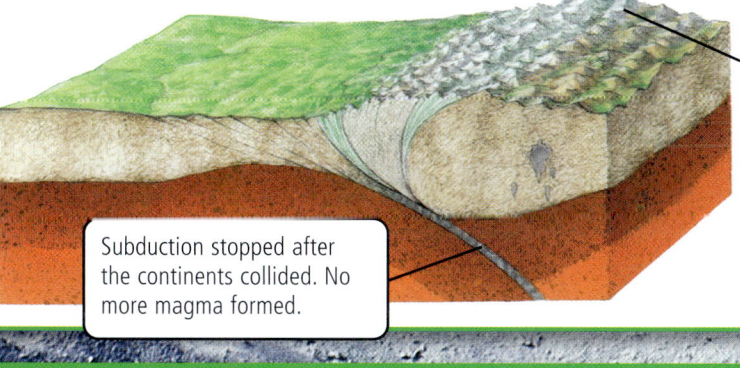

As the collision continues, the crust keeps folding. Also, earthquakes are common.

A remnant of sea floor crust remains deep under the mountains.

READING VISUALS In each illustration, where is the boundary between India and Eurasia?

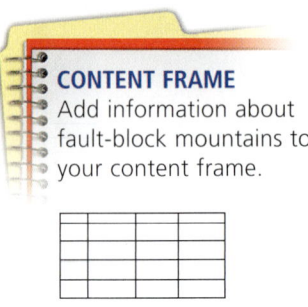

CONTENT FRAME
Add information about fault-block mountains to your content frame.

Mountains can form as rocks move along faults.

In the southwestern United States and northwestern Mexico, hundreds of mountain ranges line up in rows. The ranges, as well as the valleys between them, formed along nearly parallel normal faults. Mountains that form as blocks of rock move up or down along normal faults are called **fault-block mountains.**

CHECK YOUR READING How can the movement of rocks along faults lead to the formation of mountains?

Fault-block mountains form as the lithosphere is stretched and pulled apart by forces within Earth. The rocks of the crust are cool and rigid. As the lithosphere begins to stretch, the crust breaks into large blocks. As stretching continues, the blocks of rock move along the faults that separate them. The illustrations on page 687 show how this process forms fault-block mountains.

INVESTIGATE Fault-Block Mountains

How do fault-block mountains form?

Fault-block mountains form along normal faults as blocks of continental crust are pulled apart. In this activity, you will use wooden blocks to demonstrate the processes that form fault-block mountains.

PROCEDURE

1. Use the triangular blocks to demonstrate how movements along normal faults form two mountains separated by a valley. Start with the blocks arranged as shown. Move the outer blocks apart to form two mountains separated by a valley. Draw a diagram of your results.

2. Use the rectangular blocks to demonstrate how a row of tilted fault-block mountains forms along normal faults. (**Hint:** You can tilt the blocks as they move.) Draw a diagram of your results.

WHAT DO YOU THINK?
- How do your diagrams show that fault-block mountains form as the crust is being stretched?
- Along which type of plate boundary would fault-block mountains be most likely to form—divergent, convergent, or transform? Explain.

CHALLENGE Why do fault-block mountains not form at strike-slip faults?

SKILL FOCUS
Modeling

MATERIALS
- 3 triangular blocks
- 3 rectangular blocks

TIME
15 minutes

686 Unit 5: The Changing Earth

① An area of the lithosphere can arch upward when, for example, it is heated by material rising in the mantle beneath it. As the crust stretches, it breaks into many blocks separated by faults.

② As the lithosphere is pulled apart, some blocks tilt. The edges of the blocks that tilt upward form mountains, and the edges that tilt downward form valleys. Other blocks drop down between faults, forming valleys. The edges of the blocks next to blocks that drop down are left standing high above the valleys as mountains.

Fault-block mountains form as stress repeatedly builds up in the crust and then is released during earthquakes. Even the most powerful earthquakes can move blocks of rock only a few meters up or down at one time. Fault-block mountains can be kilometers high. Millions of years and countless earthquakes are needed for them to form.

 Describe two ways that blocks of rock can move along faults and form mountains.

Fault-Block Mountains

Fault-block mountains form as the crust stretches and breaks into blocks that move along faults.

① **Stretching Begins**

The crust breaks into blocks as it is stretched.

② **Blocks Tilt or Drop Down**

As the crust is stretched more, the blocks move along the normal faults between them.

This block has dropped down.

This block has tilted.

The Sierra Nevada moved up along one side of the fault.

Approximate location of fault

The land on the other side of the fault dropped down.

The Sierra Nevada in California is a fault-block mountain range. The range moved up along a normal fault along its eastern edge. The block on the other side of the fault dropped down. This combination of upward and downward movement formed the steep eastern side of the Sierra Nevada. The western side of the range tilts down gently toward California's Central Valley.

In summary, both folded mountains and fault-block mountains form over millions of years. Folded mountains are pushed up by slow, continual stress that causes rock to gradually bend. Fault-block mountains form, earthquake by earthquake, as stress built up in the crust is released by the movement of rock. Folded mountains form where continental crust is being compressed, and fault-block mountains form where it is being stretched.

20.1 Review

KEY CONCEPTS

1. How is the formation of mountain belts related to tectonic plate boundaries?
2. How do folded mountains form?
3. How do fault-block mountains form?

CRITICAL THINKING

4. **Analyze** The Ural Mountain belt is no longer along the edge of a tectonic plate. Would you expect the Urals to be tall and steep or low and rounded? Why?
5. **Synthesize** How could it be possible for a mountain range to be continually pushed up but not get any higher?

CHALLENGE

6. **Analyze** This graph shows how the heights of two mountains changed as they formed. Which line shows the formation of a folded mountain? a fault-block mountain? Explain.

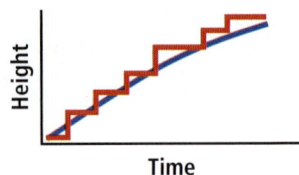

MATH in SCIENCE

MATH TUTORIAL
CLASSZONE.COM
Click on Math Tutorial for more help finding the mean.

SKILL: CALCULATING THE MEAN OF A DATA SET

Comparing Mountain Heights

How do the tallest mountains in the United States compare with the tallest mountains in the world? The table shows the heights of the five tallest mountains in the world. All five are in Asia.

Mountain	Height (meters)
Everest	8850
K2	8611
Kanchenjunga	8586
Lhotse	8516
Makalu	8463

To describe data, you can find their average, or mean. The **mean** of a data set is the sum of the values divided by the number of values.

Example

To find the mean height of the five tallest mountains in the world, first add the heights.

```
  8,850
  8,611
  8,586
  8,516
 +8,463
 ------
 43,026
```

Then divide by 5, the number of mountains.

$$\frac{43{,}026}{5} = 8605.2$$

Round your result to a whole number.

ANSWER The mean height of the five tallest mountains is 8605 meters.

Mountain	Height (meters)
McKinley	6194
St. Elias	5489
Foraker	5304
Bona	5029
Blackburn	4996

Mount McKinley, Alaska, is the tallest mountain in North America.

Answer the following questions.

1. The table to the left shows the heights of the five tallest mountains in the United States. All five are in Alaska. Find the mean of the data.

2. What is the difference between the mean height of the three tallest mountains in the world and the mean height of the three tallest mountains in the United States?

3. Suppose Mount Everest were in the United States. What would the mean of the three tallest mountains in the United States then be?

CHALLENGE The mean height of all the land in the United States is 763 meters. Does knowing the mean height help you describe the shape of the land in the United States? Explain why or why not.

Chapter 20: **Mountains and Volcanoes** 689

KEY CONCEPT
20.2 Volcanoes form as molten rock erupts.

 **BEFORE, you learned**
- Magma is molten rock inside Earth
- Magma forms as a plate sinking in a subduction zone starts to melt
- Volcanoes can form over hot spots far from plate boundaries

 NOW, you will learn
- Where most volcanoes are located
- How volcanoes erupt
- What types of volcanoes there are

VOCABULARY

volcano p. 690
lava p. 691
pyroclastic flow p. 692

EXPLORE Eruptions

What happens when a volcano erupts?

PROCEDURE

1. Add water to an empty film canister until it is three-fourths full.
2. Drop an antacid tablet in the water and put the lid on the canister. Observe what happens.

WHAT DO YOU THINK?
- What happened to the water and to the canister lid?
- What caused the changes you observed?
- How might the events you observed be similar to the eruption of a volcano?

MATERIALS
- empty film canister
- effervescent antacid tablet
- water

VOCABULARY
Make a word triangle for *volcano* in your notebook.

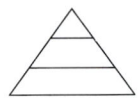

Volcanoes erupt many types of material.

Earth's thin outer layer is made of cool rock, but most of Earth is made of extremely hot rock and molten metal. Some of the heat inside Earth escapes to the surface through volcanoes. A **volcano** is an opening in Earth's crust through which molten rock, rock fragments, and hot gases erupt. A mountain built up from erupted material is also called a volcano.

A volcano may erupt violently or gently. A violent eruption can cause tremendous destruction even if not much molten rock reaches the surface. For example, a volcano might throw out huge amounts of rock fragments that start fires where they land or fall in thick layers on roofs, causing them to collapse. A volcano can erupt gently yet pour out rivers of molten rock that flow long distances. The violence of an eruption depends mainly on the type of magma feeding the volcano.

Magma

A major portion of all magma is silica, which is a compound of silicon and oxygen. Magma also contains gases, which expand as the magma rises. Magma that is high in silica resists flowing, so expanding gases are trapped in it. Pressure builds up until the gases blast out in a violent, dangerous explosion. Magma that is relatively poor in silica flows easily, so gas bubbles move up through it and escape fairly gently. Though an eruption of silica-poor magma can throw lava high into the air, forming lava fountains, visitors can usually watch safely nearby.

Magma rises toward Earth's surface as long as it is less dense than the surrounding rock. Once magma stops rising, it can collect in areas called magma chambers. Magma can remain in a chamber until it cools, forming igneous rock, or it can erupt. Volcanic eruptions occur when, for example, a chamber is not large enough to hold additional magma that pushes in. When magma erupts, it is called lava. **Lava** is magma that has reached Earth's surface.

CONTENT FRAME
Make a content frame for volcanic materials. Add categories across the top for what they are made of and how they are erupted.

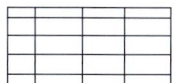

Structure of a Volcano

Magma collects in a magma chamber before erupting through a volcano.

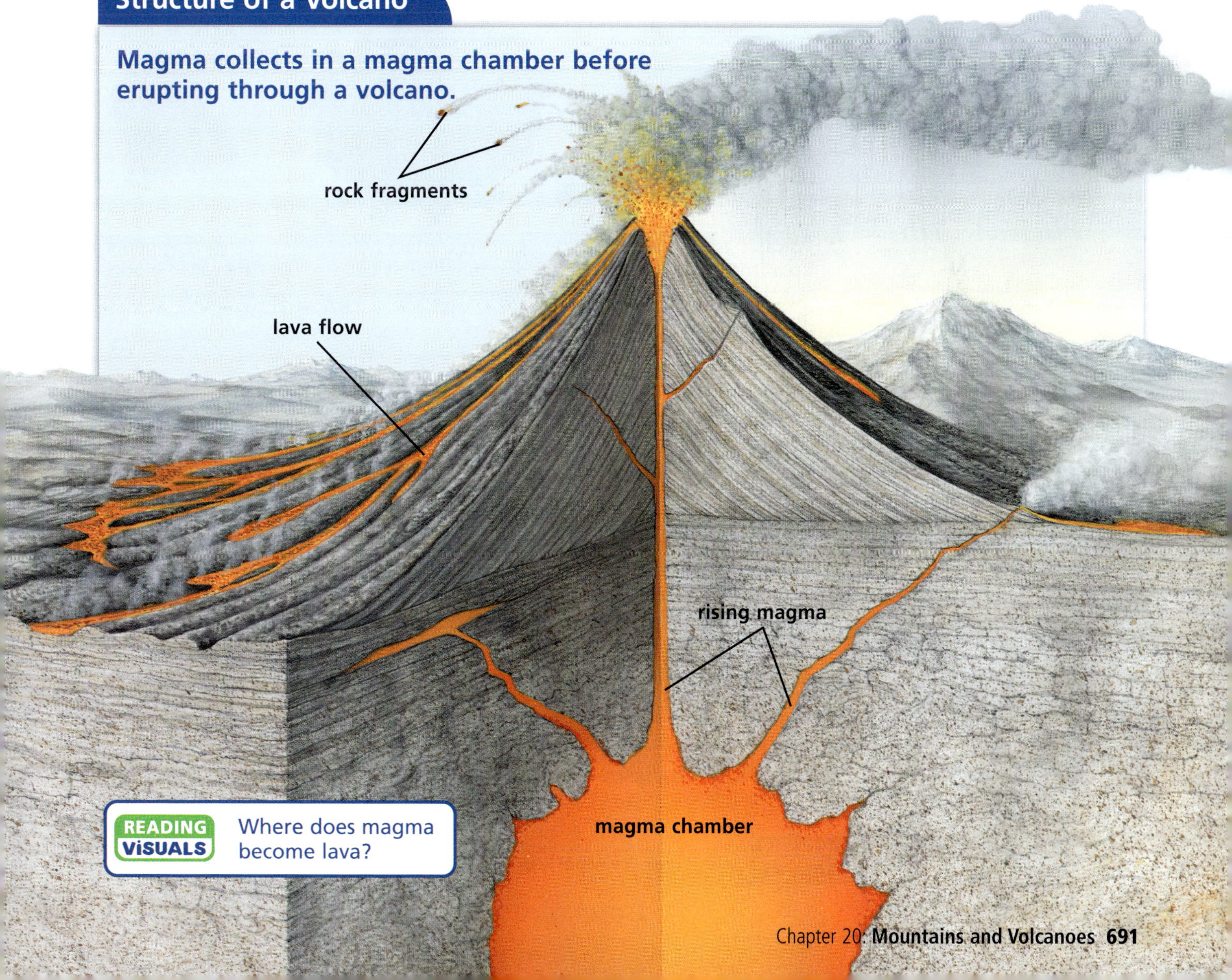

- rock fragments
- lava flow
- rising magma
- magma chamber

READING VISUALS Where does magma become lava?

Watch clips of erupted volcanic material.

Rock Fragments

A great deal of material erupts from volcanoes as rock fragments. The fragments form as

- escaping gas bubbles pop, tearing magma apart
- larger pieces of lava are thrown into the air, cooling and hardening during their flight
- rocks of all sizes rip loose from volcanoes' walls during eruptions

Tiny rock fragments form volcanic ash, which consists of particles ranging from the size of dust to about the size of rice grains. Volcanic cinders are somewhat larger. The largest fragments are volcanic bombs and blocks. Bombs are molten when they are thrown out and often have streamlined shapes. Blocks, which can be the size of houses, erupt as solid pieces of rock. Large rock fragments fall quickly, but ash can be carried long distances by winds—even all the way around Earth.

Volcanic ash is made up of rock fragments less than 2 millimeters in diameter.

Cinders contain holes and tunnels left by escaping gases.

Large fragments are called blocks or bombs.

Volcanic Gases

What looks like smoke rising from a volcano is actually a mixture of ash and gases. The main gases in magma are water vapor and carbon dioxide. Some volcanic gases combine with water in the air to form acids—you will read about these in the next section.

During an eruption, volcanic gases can mix with rock fragments and stay near the ground. The mixture forms a **pyroclastic flow** (PY-roh-KLAS-tihk), which is a dense cloud of superhot gases and rock fragments that races downhill. Such a flow can be as hot as 800°C (1500°F) and can travel faster than 160 kilometers per hour (100 mi/h). Pyroclastic flows are the most dangerous type of volcanic eruption.

READING TIP

The prefix *pyro-* means "heat," and *clastic* means "made up of rock fragments."

 What are two reasons why pyroclastic flows are dangerous?

Most volcanoes form along plate boundaries.

Volcanoes are common along tectonic plate boundaries where oceanic plates sink beneath other plates. As a plate sinks deep into a subduction zone, it heats and begins to melt, forming magma. If the magma reaches the surface it can build tall volcanic mountains.

Volcanoes are also common along tectonic boundaries where plates pull apart, allowing magma to rise from the mantle. Some of these volcanoes are in Africa's Great Rift Valley. However, much of Earth's volcanic activity takes place underwater. Magma erupts along spreading centers in the ocean and cools to form new lithosphere.

Less commonly, a volcano can form over a hot spot far from a plate boundary. Heat carried by material rising from deep in the mantle melts some of the rock in the lithosphere above it. Eruptions over a hot spot built the Hawaiian Islands.

More than 400 volcanoes—about 80 percent of all active volcanoes above sea level—are along subduction zones in the Pacific Ocean. An active volcano is one that is erupting or has erupted in recorded history. The volcanoes around the Pacific Ocean form a belt called the Ring of Fire. Some of these volcanoes are in the western United States.

Ring of Fire

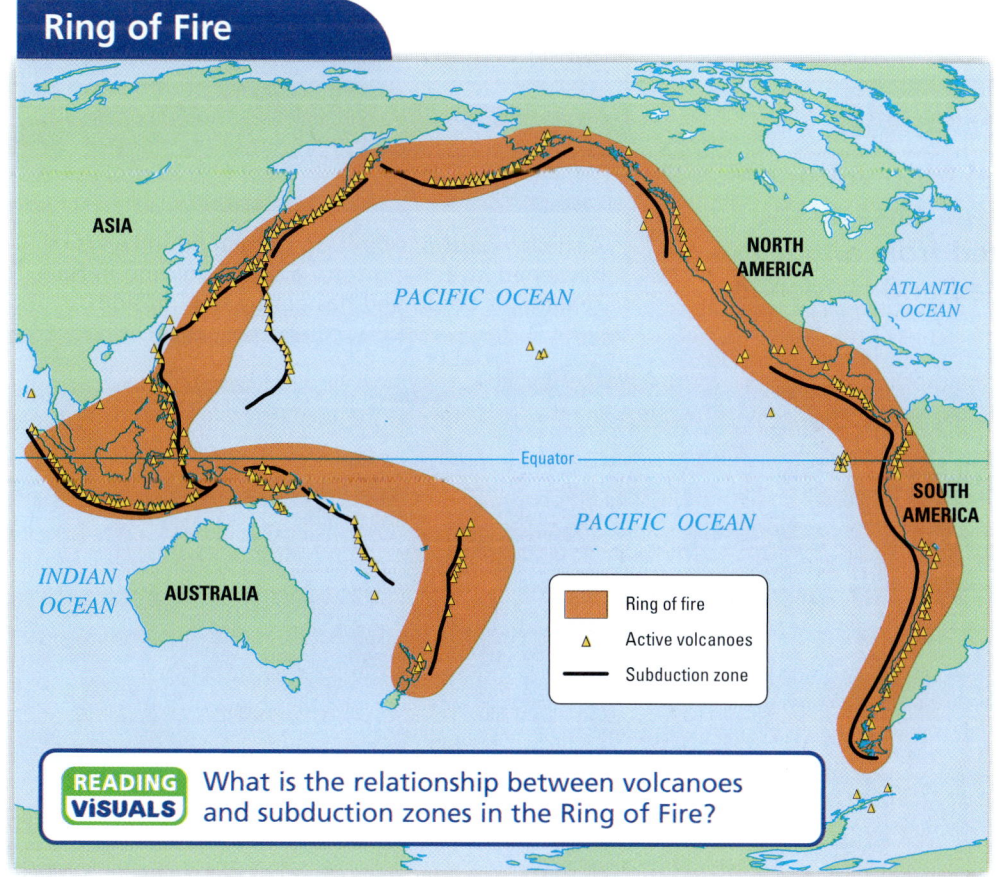

READING VISUALS What is the relationship between volcanoes and subduction zones in the Ring of Fire?

Chapter 20: **Mountains and Volcanoes** 693

CONTENT FRAME Make a content frame for types of volcanoes. Add categories for shape, size, makeup, and examples.

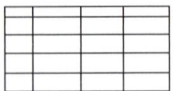

Learn more about historic and current volcanic eruptions.

Volcanoes can have many shapes and sizes.

Mount St. Helens is a cone-shaped volcano in Washington. Its eruption in 1980 killed 57 people. One side of the volcano exploded, blasting out a mixture of hot rock, ash, and gases that destroyed trees tens of kilometers away. Since 1980, this volcano has had many smaller eruptions.

Volcanoes can have many shapes, including steep cones and nearly flat land. Most volcanoes erupt from openings in bowl-shaped pits called craters. Some volcanoes erupt from long cracks in the ground. The type of magma feeding a volcano determines its shape.

❶ Shield Volcano A shield volcano is shaped like a broad, flat dome. It is built up by many eruptions of lava that is relatively low in silica and therefore flows easily and spreads out in thin layers. The largest volcano on Earth, Mauna Loa (MOW-nuh LOH-uh), is a shield volcano. It makes up much of the island of Hawaii. The total height of this volcano is about 17 kilometers (10.5 mi), but only about 4 kilometers (2.5 mi) are above sea level. At the top of Mauna Loa is a crater that is 5 kilometers (3 mi) across at its widest point. Mauna Loa is one of Earth's most active volcanoes.

❷ Cinder Cone A cinder cone is a steep, cone-shaped hill formed by the eruption of cinders and other rock fragments that pile up around

Three Types of Volcanoes

Two types of material form volcanoes: rock fragments that fall close to the openings they erupted from and lava flows that have cooled and hardened.

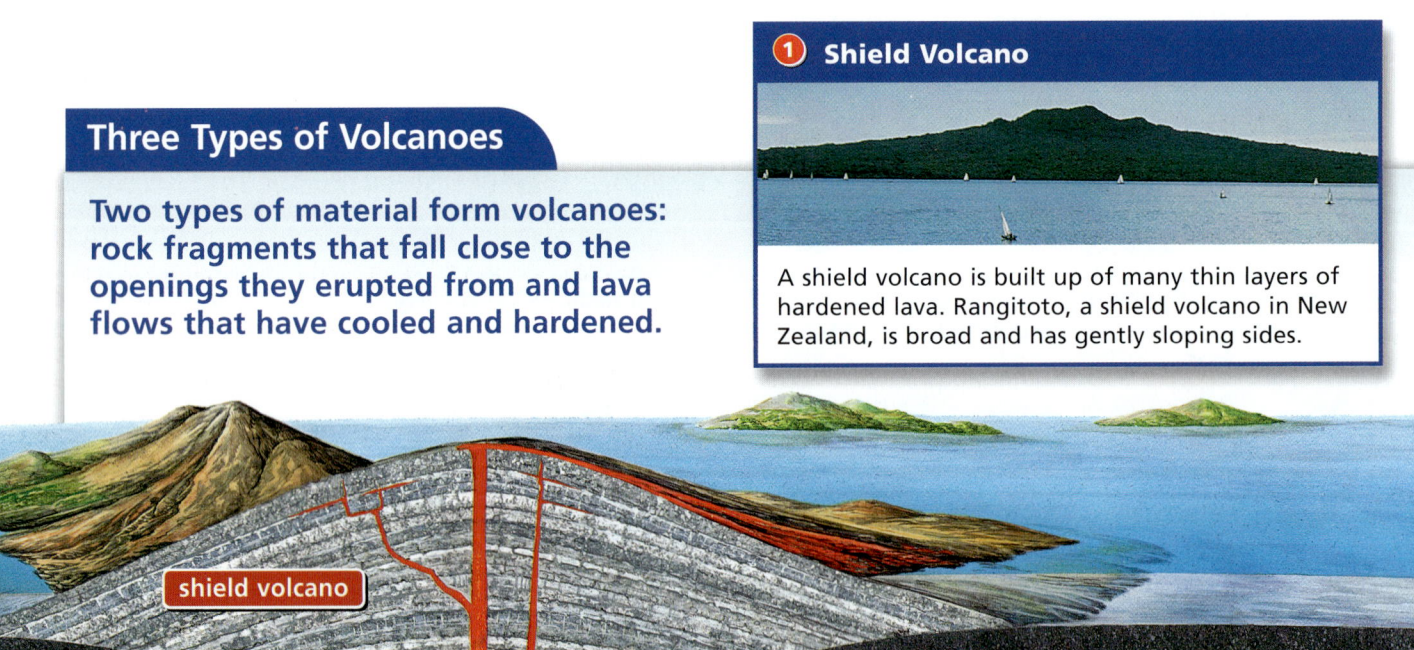

❶ Shield Volcano

A shield volcano is built up of many thin layers of hardened lava. Rangitoto, a shield volcano in New Zealand, is broad and has gently sloping sides.

694 Unit 5: The Changing Earth

a single crater. Cinders form as gas-rich magma erupts. Escaping gases throw small chunks of lava into the air, where they harden before landing. Cinder cones are tens to hundreds of meters tall. Many of them form on the sides of other types of volcanoes.

❸ **Composite Volcano** A composite volcano is a cone-shaped volcano built up of layers of lava and layers of rock fragments. Its magma is high in silica, and therefore is pasty. A composite volcano is steep near the top and flattens out toward the bottom. Because hardened lava flows add strength to the structure of a composite volcano, it can grow much larger than a cinder cone.

READING TIP
The word *composite* comes from a Latin word meaning "put together." Something that is composite is made of distinct parts.

Composite volcanoes have violent eruptions for two reasons. First, expanding gases trapped in rising magma tend to cause explosions. Second, hardened lava from earlier eruptions often plugs openings in these volcanoes. This rock must be blown out of the way before any more magma can escape. Mount St. Helens is a composite volcano. Though its 1980 eruption was devastating, many composite volcanoes have exploded with much greater power.

CHECK YOUR READING List the three main types of volcanoes. What questions do you have about how they form?

❷ **Cinder Cone**

A cinder cone, like this one in Arizona, has steep sides and is a loose pile of volcanic rock fragments.

❸ **Composite Volcano**

A composite volcano is usually cone-shaped and is built up of layers of hardened lava and of rock fragments. Mount St. Helens is a typical composite volcano.

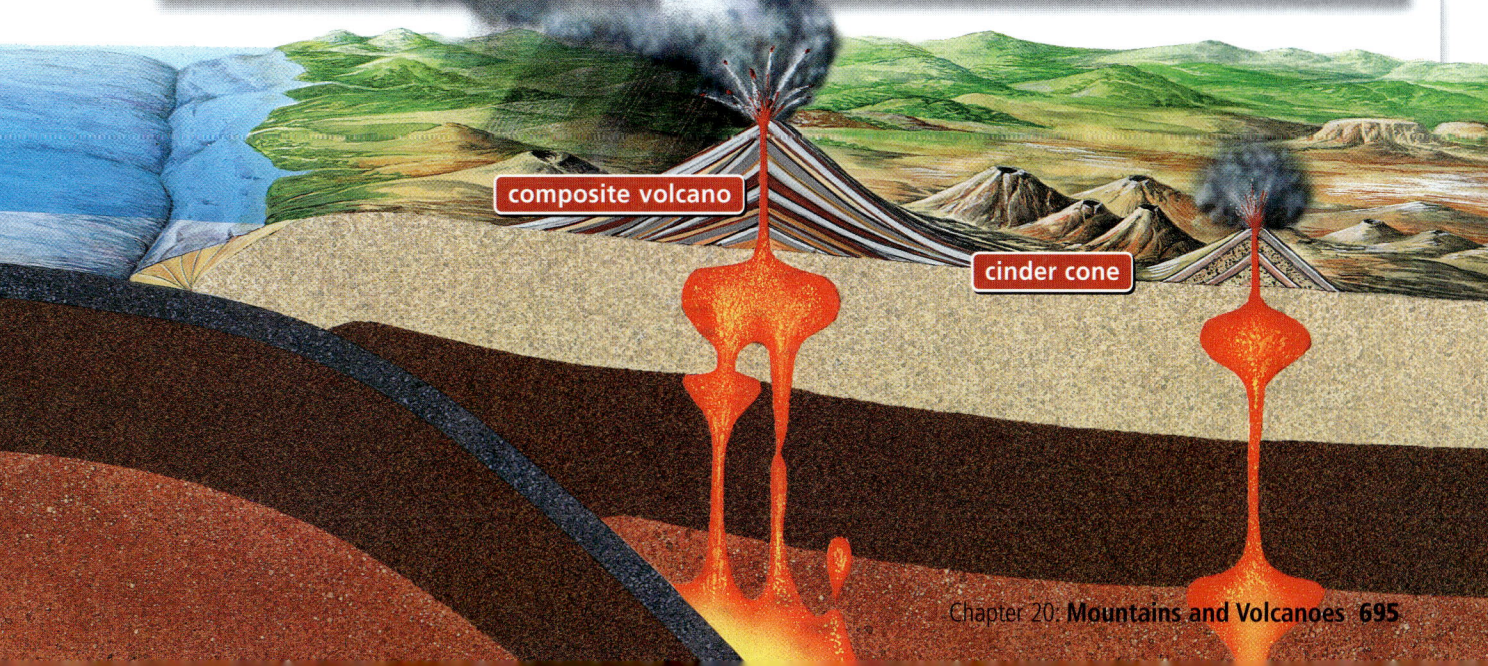

Chapter 20: **Mountains and Volcanoes** 695

Formation of Crater Lake

Crater Lake fills the caldera of a composite volcano.

A huge eruption removed much of the magma from the magma chamber.

The volcano collapsed, creating a caldera 8 kilometers in diameter and 1.6 kilometers deep.

New eruptions built a small cone in the caldera. The caldera filled with water from rain and snow.

Both shield volcanoes and composite volcanoes can form features called calderas (kal-DAIR-uhz). A caldera is a huge crater formed by the collapse of a volcano when magma rapidly erupts from underneath it. The crater at the top of Mauna Loa in Hawaii is a caldera. Crater Lake in Oregon fills a caldera formed by a composite volcano about 7700 years ago. A violent eruption emptied much of its magma chamber, and the top of the volcano collapsed into it. The caldera now holds the deepest lake in the United States.

Scientists monitor volcanoes.

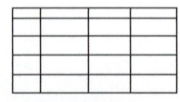

CONTENT FRAME
Make a content frame for types of data used to predict eruptions. Include categories for current activity and history.

Before Mount Pinatubo (PIHN-uh-TOO-boh) in the Philippines erupted in 1991, most people living in the area did not realize that it was a composite volcano. It had not erupted in about 500 years, and erosion had changed its shape. Fortunately, scientists in the Philippines knew that the volcano was becoming active months before it exploded. They were able to warn the government and ask people to leave the area. Their efforts probably saved tens of thousands of lives.

As the 1991 eruption of Mount Pinatubo shows, volcanoes can go hundreds of years between eruptions. Before Pinatubo's eruption, scientists noticed warning signs that included the occurrence of many small earthquakes followed by explosions of steam near the volcano's top. Researchers brought in equipment to monitor the volcano's activity. Although they could not stop the eruption, they were able to tell when people should leave.

Scientists monitor volcanoes around the world for signs of eruptions. Indications that magma is moving underneath a volcano include earthquake activity and changes in the tilt of the ground. Scientists also monitor the temperatures at openings, springs, and lakes on volcanoes, as well as the amounts and types of gases given off by the volcanoes. Rising temperatures and changes in volcanic gases can indicate that fresh magma has moved into a shallow magma chamber.

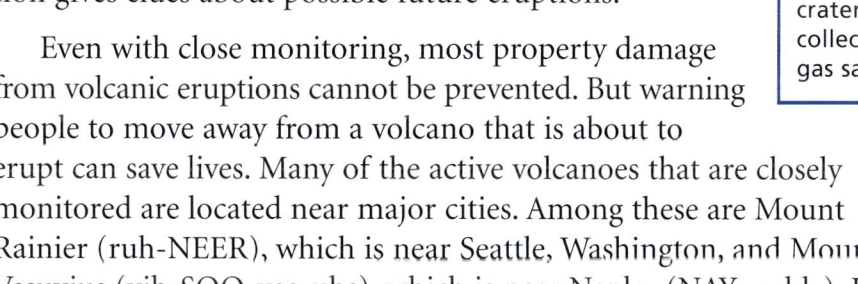

The robot Dante II is about to enter the crater of Mt. Spurr, Alaska, where it will collect video data as well as water and gas samples.

Scientists study the ages and types of volcanic rocks around a volcano to understand the volcano's history, including how much time has passed between eruptions and how violent the eruptions have been. This information gives clues about possible future eruptions.

Even with close monitoring, most property damage from volcanic eruptions cannot be prevented. But warning people to move away from a volcano that is about to erupt can save lives. Many of the active volcanoes that are closely monitored are located near major cities. Among these are Mount Rainier (ruh-NEER), which is near Seattle, Washington, and Mount Vesuvius (vih-SOO-vee-uhs), which is near Naples (NAY-puhlz), Italy.

 **CHECK YOUR READING** What is the purpose of monitoring volcanoes?

20.2 Review

KEY CONCEPTS

1. Where are most volcanoes located, and why are they located there?
2. How does the type of material that erupts from a volcano determine the shape of the volcano?
3. What conditions do scientists examine when they monitor volcanoes?

CRITICAL THINKING

4. **Compare and Contrast** How do the three main types of volcanoes differ?
5. **Infer** Volcanic ash can be deposited in areas many kilometers away from the volcano that produced it. What are two ways in which the ash can reach these areas?

CHALLENGE

6. **Analyze** Draw diagrams showing how a composite volcano might change in shape by getting larger or smaller with repeated eruptions.

Chapter 20: **Mountains and Volcanoes** 697

CHAPTER INVESTIGATION

Make Your Own Volcanoes

OVERVIEW AND PURPOSE Scientists who have never been to a particular volcano can estimate how steep a climb it would be to its top. All they need to know is what type of volcano it is. Volcanoes vary not only in size but also in slope, or the steepness of their sides. The three main types of volcanoes—cinder cones, shield volcanoes, and composite volcanoes—are very different in size and shape. In this activity you will
- make models of volcanoes and measure their slopes
- determine how the types of materials that form a volcano affect how steep it can get

MATERIALS
- 375 mL plaster of Paris
- 180 mL water
- 500 mL gravel
- 3 cardboard pieces
- two 250 mL paper cups
- stirrer
- ruler
- protractor

▶ Problem *Write It Up*

What does a volcano's slope reveal about the materials that formed it?

▶ Hypothesize *Write It Up*

Write a hypothesis to explain how a volcano's slope is related to the materials it is made of. Your hypothesis should take the form of an "If . . . , then . . . , because . . ." statement.

▶ Procedure

1. Make a data table like the one shown in the sample notebook on page 699.

2. Mix 125 mL of plaster of Paris with 60 mL of water in a paper cup. Stir the mixture well. Work quickly with the mixture, because it will harden quickly.

3. Pour the mixture onto a piece of cardboard from a height of 2–3 cm. Write "cone A" on the cardboard and set it aside.

4. Fill another paper cup with gravel. Slowly pour the gravel onto a second piece of cardboard from a height of about 10 cm. Label this model "cone B" and set it aside.

step 3

698   Unit 5: **The Changing Earth**

5 In a cup, mix the rest of the plaster of Paris with the rest of the water. Fill the other paper cup with gravel. Pour a small amount of the plaster mixture onto the third piece of cardboard, then pour some gravel on top. Repeat until all the plaster mixture and gravel have been used. Label this model "cone C" and set it aside until the plaster in both cone A and cone C has hardened (about 20 min).

Observe and Analyze

1. **MEASURE** Use the protractor to measure the approximate slope of each cone.
2. **RECORD** Complete your data table.
3. **OBSERVE** Compare the appearances of the cone. Record your observations in your **Science Notebook.**
4. **COMPARE** How different are the slopes of the cones?

Conclude

1. **CONNECT** Which volcanic materials do the plaster mixture and the gravel represent?
2. **IDENTIFY VARIABLES** What is the relationship between the cones' slopes and the materials they are made of?
3. **ANALYZE** Compare your results with your hypothesis. Do your data support your hypothesis?
4. **INTERPRET** Which type of volcano does each model represent?
5. **DRAW CONCLUSIONS** Which of your models represents a volcano that cannot grow as large as the others? Explain.
6. **APPLY** What factors might cause the slopes of real volcanoes to be different from those of your models?
7. **APPLY** If you were a scientist, what information, in addition to slope, might you need in order to determine a volcano's type?
8. **APPLY** How could the method you used to make a model of a cinder cone be used to show how the slope of a hill or mountain contributes to a landslide?

INVESTIGATE Further

CHALLENGE Calculate the slopes of your models using the formula $y = mx + b$. In this formula, y and x are graph coordinates of a point on a straight line. The slope of the line is m. The intersection of the line with the y-axis of the graph is b. For example, if the height of a model is 1.6 cm, and the distance from its edge to its center is 4 cm, then the equation becomes $1.6 = m4 + 0$.

The slope is $\frac{1.6}{4}$, or 0.4.

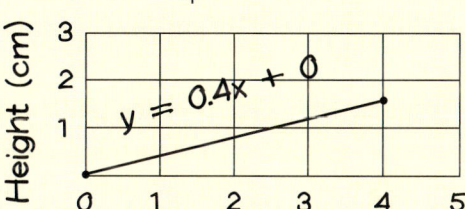

Make Your Own Volcanoes
Table 1. Volcano Model and Slope

Cone	Drawing of Cone	Slope (degrees)
A.		
B.		
C.		

KEY CONCEPT

20.3 Volcanoes affect Earth's land, air, and water.

◀ **BEFORE, you learned**
- Rock fragments, lava, and gases erupt from volcanoes
- Some volcanoes have explosive eruptions

▶ **NOW, you will learn**
- How volcanic eruptions affect Earth's surface
- How volcanic gases affect the atmosphere
- How volcanic activity affects water

VOCABULARY

acid rain p. 704
geyser p. 705

THINK ABOUT

Which volcano is more dangerous?

Mauna Loa is a shield volcano that forms a large part of the island of Hawaii. It is one of the most active volcanoes on Earth, frequently producing large amounts of lava that flow long distances. Mount Shasta is a composite volcano in California. It has erupted at least once every 600 to 800 years for the past 10,000 years. Mount Shasta can erupt with devastating violence. Which volcano do you think it is more dangerous to live near. Why?

Mauna Loa

Mount Shasta

CONTENT FRAME
Add a content frame for how eruptions affect Earth's land and air. Include categories for what dangers are caused and how long the dangers last.

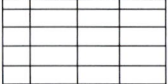

Volcanic eruptions affect the land.

A volcanic eruption can knock down forests and clog rivers with volcanic ash. Damage can occur far from the volcano. But volcanoes build as well as destroy. Material erupted from volcanoes can form new land. Over time, lava flows can form new, rich soil.

Many towns and cities are located close to volcanoes. The people of Goma in the eastern Democratic Republic of the Congo experienced an eruption of a nearby volcano in 2002. A lava flow cut the city in half and destroyed the homes of tens of thousands of people, either by flowing into the homes or by starting fires. Hilo (HEE-loh), the largest city on the island of Hawaii, is built in part on young lava flows. The city is at high risk from future volcanic activity.

700 Unit 5: The Changing Earth

Immediate Effects

The effects of a volcanic eruption largely depend on how much material and what types of material the volcano ejects. Near a volcano, lava flows can cover the land with new rock. A much larger area can be affected by events such as ash falls, landslides, mudflows, pyroclastic flows, and steam explosions.

Lava Flows Most lava moves slowly enough that people can move away and not be hurt. But even a slow-moving lava flow will knock down, cover, or burn nearly everything in its path.

Volcanic Ash Near a volcanic eruption, the weight of fallen volcanic ash can cause the roofs of buildings to collapse. Volcanic ash is heavy because it is made of tiny pieces of rock. Ash makes roads slippery, and it clogs up machinery, including cars and airplanes. Large amounts of falling ash can suffocate plants, animals, and people.

Mudflows Mudflows are landslides that occur when loose rocks and soil are mixed with water. Heat from an eruption melts any ice and snow on the volcano very quickly. Mudflows form as the water mixes with volcanic ash and other loose particles. Mudflows also form as ash mixes into rivers flowing from a volcano. Fast-moving mudflows have buried entire towns tens of kilometers from an eruption.

Pyroclastic flows As a pyroclastic flow rushes downhill, it can knock down or burn everything in its way. Pyroclastic flows tend to follow valleys. However, a particularly fast-moving flow can sweep up and over hills, then race down a neighboring valley. As a flow passes, it can leave a thick layer of volcanic rock fragments. Pyroclastic flows are extremely dangerous. In 1902, a pyroclastic flow from an eruption in the West Indies completely destroyed the city of Saint Pierre (SAYNT PEER). Almost 30,000 people were killed within a few minutes.

Landslides Part of a volcano can collapse and start a landslide—a rapid downhill movement of rock and soil. The collapse may be caused by magma moving underground, an eruption, an earthquake, or even heavy rainfall. A landslide can cause a tsunami if a large amount of material falls into the ocean.

Lava Flow

Trees catch fire as a lava flow moves through a forest in Hawaii in 1999.

Volcanic Ash

Large piles of volcanic ash from the 1991 eruption of Mt. Pinatubo line a street in Olongapo, Philippines, at the start of the cleanup effort.

> **REMINDER**
> A tsunami is a water wave caused by an earthquake, a volcanic eruption, or a landslide.

Find out more about the effects of volcanic eruptions.

Steam Explosions Though relatively uncommon, steam explosions can be devastating. They occur when magma comes near water or into contact with it. A steam explosion may have caused the destruction of a volcanic island in Indonesia. The entire island of Krakatau (KRACK-uh-TOW) exploded in 1883, causing a tsunami that destroyed hundreds of towns and killed more than 36,000 people.

 What are two ways a volcanic eruption can result in damage to areas hundreds of kilometers away?

Long-term Effects

Volcanic eruptions can be tremendously destructive. But even after an eruption ends, a volcano can remain dangerous for many years.

The explosive eruption of Mount Pinatubo in 1991 threw out huge amounts of volcanic ash and rock fragments. The area the volcano is in gets heavy rains each year. Mudflows have formed as large amounts of rainwater mixed with ash and other loose material on the sides of the volcano. Since the eruption, mudflows have destroyed the homes of more than 100,000 people.

This school bus was partly buried by a mudflow from Mount St. Helens. No one was in the bus when the mudflow hit.

Another possible source of water for mudflows was a lake that began filling the volcano's crater. The upper part of the crater is weak, and the lake level was rising. A collapse of the crater could have emptied the lake of much of its water. In 2001, people dug a channel to lower the level of the lake, greatly decreasing the chance of a collapse.

 Why can volcanic ash be dangerous for years after an eruption?

Even though volcanoes are dangerous, over time they can have positive effects. When a lava flow cools, it forms a layer of hard rock on which no plants can grow. However, over many years, this rock can break down to form rich soil. Volcanic ash can smother plants, but the tiny pieces of rock break down quickly and make soil richer. Highly productive farmland surrounds some active volcanoes.

Over time, repeated volcanic eruptions can build a magnificent landscape of mountains and valleys. People may choose to live in a volcanic area in part for its natural beauty. Many other people may visit the area, supporting a tourist industry.

INVESTIGATE Mudflows

How does the shape of the land affect mudflows?
PROCEDURE

1. Look at the map of Mount Rainier mudflows. Observe the relationship between the paths of rivers and the paths of the mudflows.

2. Write the number of towns shown within the boundaries of mudflow areas.

3. Write the differences in elevation between the following locations: the top of Mount Rainier and the point where the West Fork joins the White River, the point where the rivers join and the town of Buckley, and the towns of Buckley and Auburn. Where is the land steepest?

4. On the back of the paper, explain why in some areas mudflows have followed rivers and in other areas mudflows have spread out.

WHAT DO YOU THINK?

- What three factors are most important in causing mudflows to start near the top of Mount Rainier and flow long distances?
- How likely are future mudflows to follow the same paths as earlier mudflows?

CHALLENGE The largest mudflow starting on Mount Rainier moved at about 22 kilometers per hour (14 mi/h) and covered the land to an average depth of 6 meters (20 ft). Describe the steps you would take to protect people from a similar mudflow in the same area.

SKILL FOCUS
Analyzing

MATERIAL
Map of Mount Rainier Mudflows

TIME
25 minutes

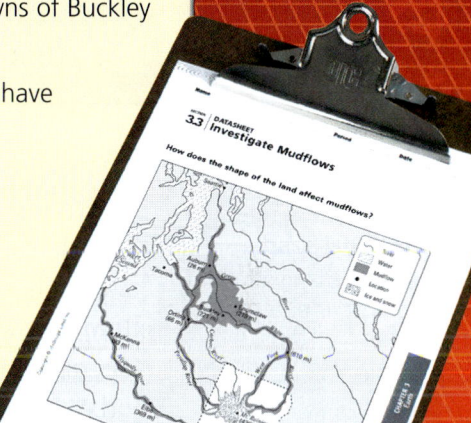

Volcanic gases and ash affect the air.

If you visit a volcano, you might notice some unpleasant odors. These odors come from gases released into the air from magma. Some of these gases contain the element sulfur. Hydrogen sulfide gas smells like rotten eggs. Sulfur dioxide gas is what you smell when you strike a match. The volcano might also be releasing carbon dioxide, a gas you would not notice because it has no color or odor. Volcanoes release gases before, during, and after eruptions.

Many gases from volcanoes are dangerous. They can make breathing difficult and damage the lungs of people and animals. Carbon dioxide can be fatal. In West Africa, a sudden release of carbon dioxide killed 1700 people in 1986. The gas came from a volcano at the bottom of a lake. Carbon dioxide built up in the water until a large amount escaped at once. Pipes are now being used to release carbon dioxide from the bottom of the lake so that the gas will not build up again.

READING TIP

An element is a substance that contains only one type of atom.

A cloud of hot gases and ash rises high into the atmosphere during an eruption of Mount Etna in Italy.

VOCABULARY
Make a word triangle for *acid rain* in your notebook.

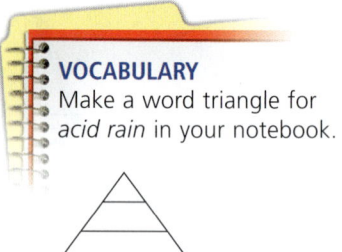

Some gases, such as sulfur dioxide, form acids when they mix with water in the air. These acids fall to Earth's surface in rain, snow, or sleet. Rain that contains large amounts of acid is called **acid rain.** Volcanoes are sources of acid-forming gases, but a bigger source is human activity. For example, the burning of coal in electrical power plants adds acid-forming gases to the air. In some areas, acid rain has damaged forests and killed fish in lakes.

Large amounts of volcanic gases in the atmosphere can change weather worldwide. The 1991 eruption of Mount Pinatubo released enough sulfur dioxide to form a haze high in the atmosphere around the entire planet. The haze decreased the amount of sunlight reaching Earth's surface and lowered average world temperatures in 1992 and 1993.

Volcanic gases can lift ash high above an erupting volcano. Winds can then carry the ash far away. During the May 1980 eruption of Mount St. Helens, ash falling 400 kilometers (250 mi) away in Spokane, Washington, blocked so much sunlight that nighttime streetlights were turned on during the day. The smallest ash particles can remain in the air for years, circling Earth many times. These particles also reflect sunlight and can lower Earth's temperature.

 **CHECK YOUR READING** Describe two ways sulfur dioxide can affect the atmosphere.

Volcanic activity affects water.

Yellowstone National Park in the western United States is famous for its hot springs—places where heated water flows to Earth's surface. Yellowstone is a volcanic region, and its hot springs sit in a huge caldera. The springs' heat comes from a hot spot under the North American Plate.

Geysers

Rainwater can sink through cracks in rock. If it is heated within Earth, it can rise to form hot springs and geysers.

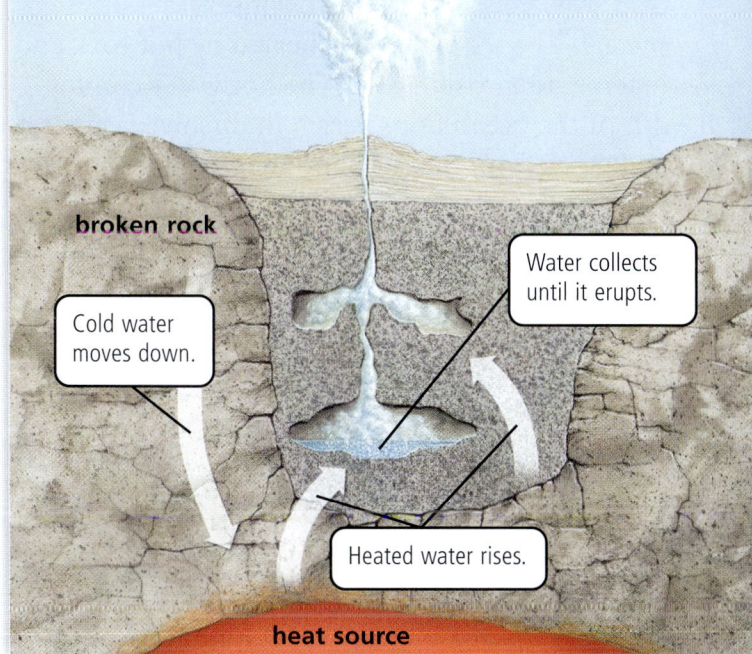

- broken rock
- Cold water moves down.
- Water collects until it erupts.
- Heated water rises.
- heat source

Old Faithful geyser in Yellowstone National Park erupts more often than any other large geyser. Heated water is forced up into the air through a narrow channel.

Hot Springs, Geysers, and Fumaroles

Most hot springs are in areas where magma or hot rock is near Earth's surface. Water moves down through the ground, gets heated, and rises at a hot spring. At most hot springs, the water flows out into a calm pool. But at a type of hot spring called a **geyser**, water shoots into the air. A geyser forms where water collects in an underground chamber, then erupts through a narrow channel. Old Faithful, a geyser in Yellowstone National Park, erupts every 35 minutes to 2 hours. Most geysers erupt less predictably.

In addition to the United States, countries with many hot springs and geysers include New Zealand and Iceland. Beneath Iceland, which sits on an ocean spreading center, is magma that rises as plates pull apart. People in Iceland use hot underground water as an energy source to heat their capital city, Reykjavík (RAY-kyuh-VEEK).

A feature known as a fumarole (FYOO-muh-ROHL) is similar to a hot spring. Instead of liquid water, though, a fumarole releases steam and other gases. Changes in hot springs and fumaroles located on the sides of a volcano can show that the volcano is becoming more active. As magma moves close to the surface, water temperatures get higher, and fumaroles can release more or different gases.

CONTENT FRAME
Make a content frame for features formed by heated water. Include categories for how they form and where they form.

CHECK YOUR READING Why might fumaroles and hot springs be monitored?

Chapter 20: **Mountains and Volcanoes** 705

Deep-Sea Vents

Deep-sea vents are hot springs that form at spreading centers in the ocean. In these places, the ocean floor has many cracks through which cold seawater sinks to depths of several kilometers. The sea water gets heated by hot rock and magma, then rises again. The hot water coming out of the ocean floor is rich in dissolved minerals and gases from the rock and magma.

At some deep-sea vents, warm water flows gently from cracks in the ocean floor. At others, water at temperatures that can be higher than 350°C (660°F) shoots out of chimney-like vents. The water looks black because it contains large amounts of dissolved minerals. As the hot water mixes with cold water, dissolved minerals form into solid minerals again, building up the vent chimneys.

This deep-sea vent is more than 3 kilometers (2 mi) below the surface of the Atlantic Ocean. A black cloud of mineral-rich water rises from the vent.

Deep-sea vents support such unusual life forms as blind crabs and tubeworms that measure up to 3 meters (10 ft) long. These animals feed on one-celled organisms that get their energy from chemicals in the vent water. Unlike other one-celled organisms, these organisms do not need sunlight to make their food.

 **CHECK YOUR READING** Why do chimneys form around some deep-sea vents?

20.3 Review

KEY CONCEPTS

1. Describe how a heavy ash fall from a volcanic eruption can affect Earth's surface.
2. Describe how large amounts of volcanic gases can affect weather around Earth.
3. Why do hot springs occur in volcanic areas?

CRITICAL THINKING

4. **Compare and Contrast** What do geysers and deep-sea vents that form chimneys have in common? How are they different?
5. **Evaluate** Which is more dangerous, a pyroclastic flow or a mudflow? Explain.

CHALLENGE

6. **Analyze** Ice in Greenland and Antarctica contains layers of ash from eruptions that occurred many thousands of years ago. How do you think the ash reached the ice, and why is it preserved?

SCIENCE on the JOB

PARK RANGER

Rangers at Yellowstone

Rangers at Yellowstone National Park help monitor volcanic activity. The hot spot that is now under Yellowstone has powered some of the largest volcanic eruptions on Earth. The amount of volcanic ash and lava produced by Yellowstone's three giant eruptions could fill the Grand Canyon. The last giant eruption occurred 640,000 years ago. At least 30 smaller eruptions have occurred since. Most of Yellowstone's hot springs and geysers sit in the caldera produced by the last giant eruption.

Beware Volcanic Gases

Park rangers must be aware of the effects of volcanic gases given off by hot springs. Here, volcanic gases are bubbling up through mud. Carbon dioxide, a common volcanic gas, is heavier than air. It sinks and fills low areas. Rangers sometimes find the body of a small animal that entered a shallow cave and died for lack of oxygen.

On Thin Ground

It is dangerous to walk up to the edge of Yellowstone's springs, some of which contain scalding hot water. The ground might be a layer of rock too thin to support a person's weight. Park rangers make sure visitors know to stay on safe walkways, and they inform the public about the science of hot springs.

Tracking Yellowstone's Temperature

Park rangers measure the temperatures of hot springs every month. Increases in temperatures or in hot-spring and geyser activity might indicate increasing volcanic activity.

EXPLORE

1. **ANALYZE** Why do you think Yellowstone is sometimes called a supervolcano? What do you think the characteristics of supervolcanoes might be?
2. **CHALLENGE** A geyser's activity often changes after an earthquake. Draw diagrams showing how changes to a geyser's underground system could cause its water to shoot higher when it erupts.

Chapter 20: **Mountains and Volcanoes** 707

20 Chapter Review

the BIG idea

Mountains and volcanoes form as tectonic plates move.

CONTENT REVIEW
CLASSZONE.COM

KEY CONCEPTS SUMMARY

① Movement of rock builds mountains.

Folded mountains form as plates push together.

Fault-block mountains form as the lithosphere is stretched.

VOCABULARY
folded mountain p. 684
fault-block mountain p. 686

② Volcanoes form as molten rock erupts.

Volcanoes erupt molten rock, rock fragments, and gases. Different types of erupted materials build up different types of volcanoes.

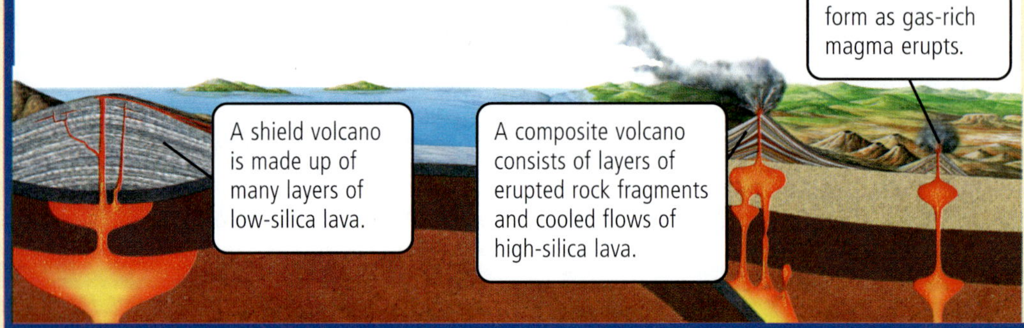

A shield volcano is made up of many layers of low-silica lava.

A composite volcano consists of layers of erupted rock fragments and cooled flows of high-silica lava.

A cinder cone is made up of loose rock fragments and cinders that form as gas-rich magma erupts.

VOCABULARY
volcano p. 690
lava p. 691
pyroclastic flow p. 692

③ Volcanoes affect Earth's land, air, and water.

Materials erupted from volcanoes, as well as heat from molten rock underground, affect Earth's surface.

VOCABULARY
acid rain p. 704
geyser p. 705

Land	Air	Water
• lava • volcanic ash • landslides • mudflows • pyroclastic flows	• poisonous gases • adds to acid rain • haze • lower temperatures	• hot springs • geysers • fumaroles • deep-sea vents

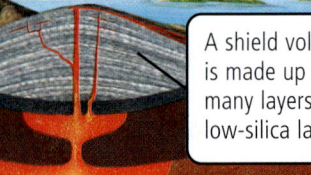
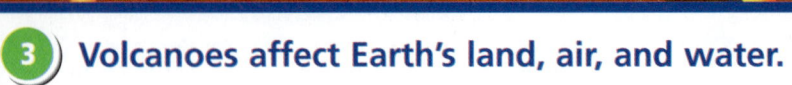
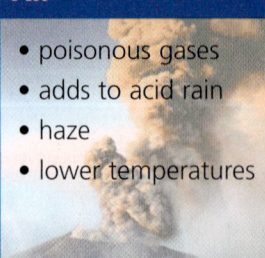

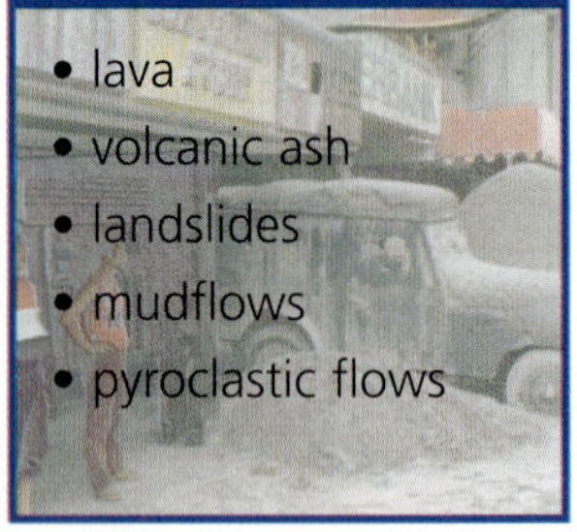

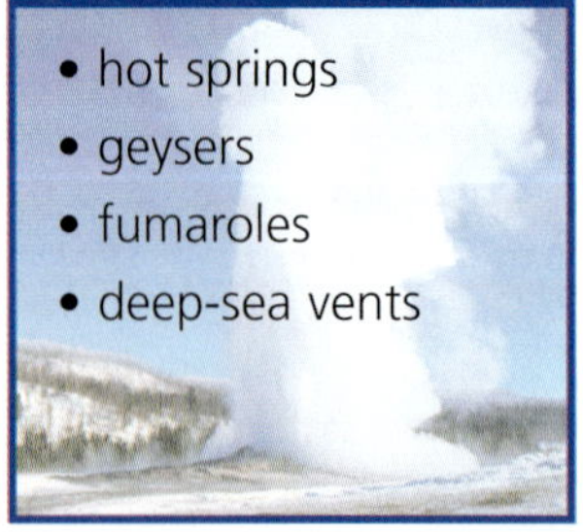

708 Unit 5: The Changing Earth

Reviewing Vocabulary

Draw a Venn diagram to compare and contrast each pair of features. Example:

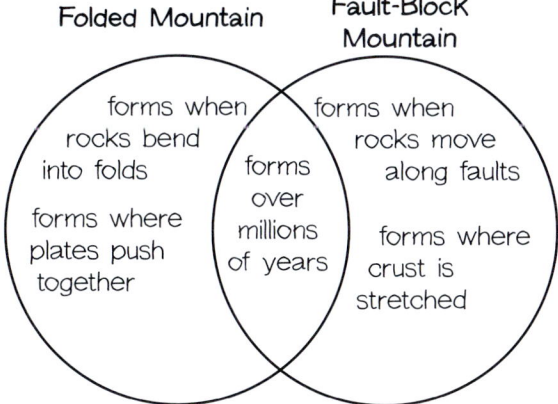

1. folded mountain, volcano
2. lava, pyroclastic flow
3. volcano, geyser

Reviewing Key Concepts

Multiple Choice *Choose the letter of the best answer.*

4. In areas where the lithosphere is being pulled apart, the crust
   a. folds and crumples into mountains
   b. breaks into blocks separated by faults
   c. slides down into the mantle
   d. develops a subduction zone

5. When two plates carrying continental crust collide, the rock of the continents
   a. folds   c. expands
   b. melts   d. stretches

6. The movement of huge blocks of rock along a fault can produce
   a. lava plugs   c. fault-block mountains
   b. volcanoes   d. folded mountains

7. Volcanoes in the Ring of Fire are supplied with magma rising from
   a. spreading centers   c. rift valleys
   b. hot spots   d. subduction zones

8. Before magma erupts it collects under a volcano in a
   a. chamber   c. crater
   b. caldera   d. vent

9. The explosiveness of a volcanic eruption depends mostly on the _____ of the magma.
   a. gas content   c. amount
   b. silica content d. temperature

10. The type of magma erupting from a volcano determines the volcano's
    a. size   c. shape
    b. age   d. location

11. Volcanic ash can be carried thousands of kilometers from an eruption by
    a. lava flows   c. landslides
    b. pyroclastic flows d. winds

12. In a volcanic region, water moving through the ground gets _____ by magma or hot rock.
    a. melted   c. erupted
    b. dissolved d. heated

Short Answer *Write a short answer to each question.*

13. Describe how an old mountain belt located in the center of a continent most likely formed.

14. How are the locations of volcanoes related to tectonic plate boundaries?

15. What causes a shield volcano to be shaped like a broad dome?

16. By what processes can a volcanic eruption affect temperatures around the world?

Thinking Critically

This photograph shows a volcanic eruption. The volcano produces rivers of lava that flow long distances. Use the photograph to answer the next six questions.

17. **INFER** What kind of volcano is shown in the photograph? How do you know?

18. **APPLY** Is this eruption likely to produce large amounts of ash that could lead to dangerous mudflows for many years afterward? Why or why not?

19. **IDENTIFY EFFECTS** How might volcanic gases affect the health of people and animals living near the volcano?

20. **ANALYZE** What would be likely to happen if a large amount of water reached the volcano's magma chamber?

21. **COMPARE AND CONTRAST** How could this volcano affect nearby farmland during the eruption? many years after the eruption?

22. **SYNTHESIZE** What types of changes would let scientists monitoring the volcano know that an eruption was likely to occur?

23. **COMPARE AND CONTRAST** How does the stress on continental crust in areas where folded mountains form differ from that in areas where fault-block mountains form?

24. **APPLY** Draw a diagram showing how one magma chamber can supply magma to a shield volcano and to a cinder cone on the side of the shield volcano.

25. **INFER** Many of the volcanoes in the Ring of Fire erupt explosively. Would you expect these volcanoes to be cinder cones, shield volcanoes, or composite volcanoes? Explain your answer.

26. **PREDICT** How might an area with many hot springs and geysers be affected as magma and hot rock near the surface cooled?

27. **ANALYZE** Why do volcanoes form along boundaries where oceanic plates are pushing into other plates but not along boundaries where continents are pushing together?

28. **APPLY** Explain why shield volcanoes, composite volcanoes, and cinder cones have different sizes and shapes.

the BIG idea

29. **INFER** How would you expect tectonic plates to be moving at a plate boundary where folded mountains are being pushed up and volcanoes are erupting?

30. **PREDICT** If tectonic plates continue to move as they are moving today, the continents of Australia and Antarctica will collide in the far future. What will happen after the sea floor that is now between the continents is destroyed?

UNIT PROJECTS

Check your schedule for your unit project. How are you doing? Be sure that you have placed data or notes from your research in your project folder.

Standardized Test Practice

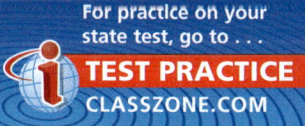

Analyzing Data

The graph below shows the amounts of lava, rock, and other materials released in four large volcanic eruptions. Study the graph, then answer the questions below.

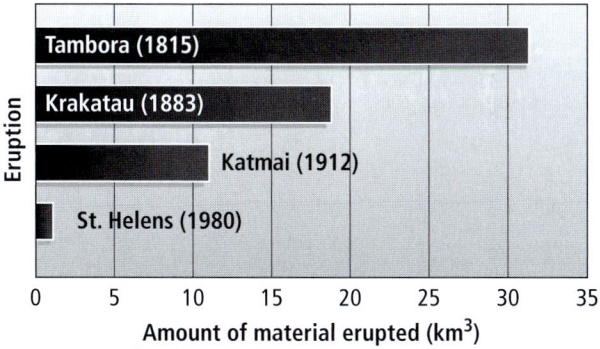

1. How much material did the eruption of Katmai release in 1912?
   a. 12 km³
   b. 17 km³
   c. 29 km³
   d. 41 km³

2. After 1850, which of these eruptions released the greatest amount of material?
   a. Krakatau
   b. Tambora
   c. Katmai
   d. St. Helens

3. About how much more material erupted from Krakatau in 1883 than from Katmai in 1912?
   a. 28 km³
   b. 12 km³
   c. 6 km³
   d. 2 km³

4. Katmai, a large mountain built of layers of hardened lava flows and of rock fragments, is a
   a. cinder cone
   b. shield volcano
   c. pyroclastic cone
   d. composite volcano

5. How much material did the 1815 eruption of Tambora produce compared with the 1883 eruption of Krakatau?
   a. less than one-half the amount
   b. a nearly equal amount
   c. almost two times the amount
   d. almost four times the amount

6. All of the eruptions shown in the graph created calderas—craters formed by the collapse of volcanoes—because the eruptions were large enough to
   a. mostly empty the volcanoes' magma chambers
   b. produce lava that flowed long distances
   c. produce lava that had a low silica content
   d. form dangerous pyroclastic flows and mudflows

7. The average temperature of Earth can decrease for several years when a huge volcanic eruption adds to the atmosphere large amounts of
   a. acid rain
   b. energy
   c. volcanic cinders
   d. volcanic gases

8. A thick layer of volcanic ash can be heavy enough to collapse the roofs of buildings because ash
   a. is produced as rocks burn
   b. is made up of tiny pieces of rock
   c. becomes heavier as it cools
   d. can hold large amounts of water

Extended Response

Answer the two questions below in detail. Include some of the terms shown in the word box. In your answers, underline each term you use.

boundaries	hot spots	rising
subduction	magma	heat
spreading centers		

9. Petra is marking the locations of active volcanoes on a map of the world. Explain how the locations of the volcanoes are related to the locations of tectonic plates.

10. Scientists regularly check the temperature of a lake on a volcano. Explain how this information might help them learn whether the volcano is becoming more active.

Chapter 20: **Mountains and Volcanoes** 711

CHAPTER

Views of Earth's Past

Rocks, fossils, and other types of natural evidence tell Earth's story.

What does this footprint tell you about the animal that left it?

Key Concepts

SECTION 1 — Earth's past is revealed in rocks and fossils.
Learn about different kinds of fossils and what they tell about Earth's past.

SECTION 2 — Rocks provide a timeline for Earth.
Learn how information from rocks tells about Earth's past.

SECTION 3 — The geologic time scale shows Earth's past.
Learn about 4.6 billion years of Earth's history.

 Internet Preview

CLASSZONE.COM
Chapter 21 online resources: Content Review, two Visualizations, three Resource Centers, Math Tutorial, Test Practice

712 Unit 5: The Changing Earth

EXPLORE the BIG idea

How Do You Know What Happened?

Observe an area around your neighborhood to find evidence of a past event. For example, you might see tracks from tires or a stump from a tree. Record your observations.

Observe and Think What evidence did you find? What does the evidence suggest about the past?

How Long Has That Been There?

Look inside a cabinet or refrigerator and choose one item to investigate. See if you can tell where the item was made, where it was purchased, how long it has been in the cabinet or refrigerator, and when it was last used.

Observe and Think How did you figure out the history of the item?

Internet Activity: Earth's History

Go to **ClassZone.com** to discover how scientists pieced together information to figure out the story of the dinosaurs.

Observe and Think What kinds of evidence did scientists use?

Earth's Story Code: MDL055

CHAPTER 21
Getting Ready to Learn

CONCEPT REVIEW

- Earth has layers that change over time.
- Movement of rock builds mountains.
- Volcanoes form as molten rock erupts.

VOCABULARY REVIEW

crust p. 615
continental drift p. 618
lava p. 691

CLASSZONE.COM
Review concepts and vocabulary.

TAKING NOTES

OUTLINE

As you read, copy the headings on your paper in the form of an outline. Then add notes in your own words that summarize what you read.

CHOOSE YOUR OWN STRATEGY

Take notes about new vocabulary terms, using one or more of the strategies from earlier chapters—**description wheel, word magnet,** and **word triangle**. Mix and match the strategies, or use an entirely different strategy.

See the Note-Taking Handbook on pages R45–R51.

SCIENCE NOTEBOOK

I. Earth's past is revealed in rocks and fossils.
  A. Rocks, fossils, and original remains give clues about the past.
    1. Original Remains
      a.
      b.
      c.
    2. Fossil Formation
      a.
      b.
      c.

Description Wheel
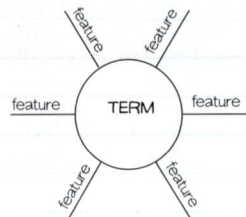

Word Triangle
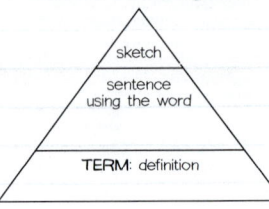

Magnet Word
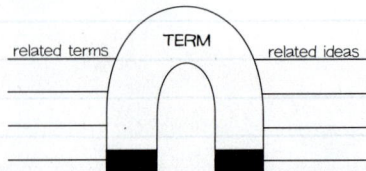

KEY CONCEPT

Earth's past is revealed in rocks and fossils.

 BEFORE, you learned

- The slow, continuous movement of tectonic plates causes large changes over time
- Molten rock cools to form solid rock

 NOW, you will learn

- How different kinds of fossils show traces of life from Earth's past
- How ice cores and tree rings reveal conditions and changes in the environment

VOCABULARY

fossil p. 715
original remains p. 716
ice core p. 721

EXPLORE Rocks

What can we learn from a rock?

PROCEDURE

1. Use a hand lens to examine the rock sample.
2. Make a sketch of any shapes you see in the rock.

WHAT DO YOU THINK?
- What do you think those shapes are?
- How did they get there?

MATERIALS
- rock sample
- hand lens
- paper and pencil

OUTLINE
Remember to take notes on this section in outline form.

I. Main idea
   A. Supporting idea
      1. Detail
      2. Detail
   B. Supporting idea

Rocks, fossils, and original remains give clues about the past.

You have read about mountain formation, earthquakes, and other ways in which Earth changes over time. Scientists have learned about these changes—even changes that happened long ago—by studying rocks, fossils, and other natural evidence. Two hundred million years ago, for example, huge dinosaurs walked on Earth. These giant reptiles were a major form of animal life on the planet for millions of years. Then, about 65 million years ago, the dinosaurs became extinct, or died out. What happened?

To solve the mystery of why dinosaurs disappeared, scientists look for clues. Fossils, for example, are important clues about past events. **Fossils** are traces or remains of living things from long ago. Dinosaur bones and footprints preserved in stone are examples of fossils.

Chapter 21: **Views of Earth's Past** 715

Using fossils and other natural evidence, scientists have formed a theory about why the dinosaurs disappeared. They now think that some major event, such as the crashing of one or more giant asteroids into Earth, led to rapid changes that caused the dinosaurs to become extinct.

Fossils also tell us about organisms, such as dinosaurs, that are now extinct. Even though no one has ever seen a dinosaur, people have some idea about what dinosaurs looked like and how they behaved because of fossils.

Fossils exist in many different forms. Most fossils are hardened animal remains such as shells, bones, and teeth. Minerals replace the remains, forming a fossil of the hard skeletal body parts. Other fossils are impressions or other evidence of an organism preserved in rock. Sometimes, an actual organism—or part of an organism—can be preserved and become a fossil.

Original Remains

Fossils that are the actual bodies or body parts of organisms are called **original remains.** Usually, soft parts of dead animals and plants decay and disappear. But soft parts can become fossil evidence if they are sealed in a substance that keeps out air and tiny organisms. Original remains are found in places where conditions prevent the decomposition, or breakdown, that normally occurs. Original remains are important because they give direct evidence of forms of life that lived long ago.

Original Remains

① Ice

This frozen mammoth body was found in Siberia.

② Amber

These insects, which are related to flies and mosquitoes, were trapped and preserved in amber 40 million years ago.

③ Tar

This skull of a saber-toothed cat, found in the La Brea Tar Pits in California, was preserved in the tar for 10,000 to 40,000 years.

① Ice Ice is one of the best preservers of the remains of prehistoric life. Huge ice fields in Siberia and Alaska contain the bodies of 10,000-year-old mammoths and prehistoric rhinos, with bones, muscle, skin, and even hair still in place. The ice preserved the animals after they died.

② Amber Another natural substance that preserves the remains of some living things is amber. Amber forms from resin, a sticky substance inside trees that flows like syrup and protects the tree by trapping insects. If the tree gets buried after it dies, the resin can harden into amber. Amber can contain the remains of insects and other small organisms.

③ Tar The original remains of animals have also been found in places where there were pools of tar—a thick, oily liquid. Saber-toothed cats and other animals were trapped in the tar and preserved.

Fossil Formation

Conditions have to be just right for a fossil to form in rock. The organism or trace of the organism must be preserved before it decomposes or disappears. Usually, the soft parts of an organism decay too quickly to be preserved in rock. For that reason, many rock fossils reveal traces or shapes of only the hard parts of animals or plants. Hard parts, such as shells, bones, teeth, and stems or tree trunks, decompose slowly, so they are more likely to be preserved as fossil evidence. Most organisms that lived in the past died and decomposed without leaving any traces. An organism that has no hard parts, such as a mushroom or a slug, rarely leaves fossil evidence.

Rock fossils form in sedimentary rock. Sedimentary rock forms from layers of sediment, such as sand or mud. Sometimes, the sediment builds up around animal and plant remains, which can leave fossils in the rock. If sedimentary rocks are changed by heat or pressure, their fossils can be destroyed. Igneous rocks never contain fossils. The heat of the molten rock—from which igneous rock cools—destroys any traces of plants or animals.

VISUALIZATION CLASSZONE.COM
Explore how fossils form.

CHECK YOUR READING Why do rock fossils form in sedimentary rock rather than in igneous rock?

Theropod Fossil

Artist's Drawing of Theropod

This 130-million-year-old skeleton of a small theropod dinosaur, found between two slabs of rock in China, contains well-preserved featherlike structures. The fossil is about a meter (3 ft) long.

Fossils in Rocks

If an organism is covered by or buried in sediment, it may become a fossil as the sediments become rock. Many rock fossils are actual body parts, such as bones or teeth, that were buried in sediment and then replaced by minerals and turned to stone.

Some fossils are not original remains or actual body parts that have turned to stone. Instead, these fossils are impressions or traces made of rock and provide indirect evidence that the organisms were there, just as a shoeprint can reveal much about the shoe that made it. Rocks can contain detailed shapes or prints of plants, animals, and even organisms too small to see without a microscope. Fossils in rock include molds and casts, petrified wood, carbon films, and trace fossils.

Learn more about fossils.

❶ **Molds and Casts** Some fossils that form in sedimentary rock are mold fossils. A mold is a visible shape that was left after an animal or plant was buried in sediment and then decayed away. In some cases, a hollow mold later becomes filled with minerals, producing a cast fossil. The cast fossil is a solid model in the shape of the organism. If you think of the mold as a shoeprint, the cast would be what would result if sand filled the print and hardened into stone.

❷ **Petrified Wood** The stone fossil of a tree is called petrified wood. In certain conditions, a fallen tree can become covered with sediments. Over time, water passes through the sediments and into the tree's cells. Minerals that are carried in the water take the place of the cells, producing a stone likeness of the tree.

These ancient logs in the Painted Desert Wilderness in Arizona have been preserved as petrified wood for around 225 million years. Minerals replaced the wood to make the stone logs.

❸ **Carbon Films** Carbon is an element that is found in every living thing. Sometimes when a dead plant or animal decays, its carbon is left behind as a visible layer. This image is called a carbon film. Carbon films can show details of soft parts of animals and plants that are rarely seen in other fossils.

❹ **Trace Fossils** Do you want to know how fast a dinosaur could run? Trace fossils might be able to tell you. These are not parts of an animal or impressions of it, but rather evidence of an animal's presence in a given location. Trace fossils include preserved footprints, trails, animal holes, and even feces. By comparing these clues with what is known about modern animals, scientists can learn how prehistoric animals may have lived, what they ate, and how they behaved. For instance, dinosaur tracks can be studied to learn how fast dinosaurs ran.

CHECK YOUR READING What do carbon film fossils show that trace fossils do not show?

Fossils in Rocks

Rock fossils show shapes and traces of past life.

① Molds and Casts

A mold and cast are formed in the steps below.

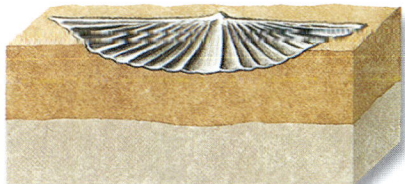

An organism dies and falls into soft sediment.

Over time, the sediment becomes rock and the organism decays, leaving a mold.

Minerals fill the mold and make a cast of the organism.

② Petrified Wood

In this close-up, you can see the minerals that replaced the wood, forming petrified wood.

③ Carbon Films

This carbon film of a moth is about 10 million years old. Carbon films are especially useful because they can show details of the soft parts of organisms.

④ Trace Fossils

A trace fossil, such as this footprint of a dinosaur in rock, can provide important information about where an animal lived and how it walked and ran.

READING VISUALS What is similar about mold-and-cast fossils and petrified wood?

Fossils and other natural evidence show changes in life and the environment.

Fossils reveal that Earth has undergone many changes over billions of years. Scientists study fossils to learn what organisms and animals once lived in places where the fossils were found. Today the land around the South Pole is mostly covered by ice, but fossils show that crocodiles, dinosaurs, and palm trees once lived on that land. The land was once much closer to the equator.

The earliest fossils are of tiny one-celled organisms that lived in an environment without oxygen. Three billion years ago, humans or the land animals we know today could not have breathed the air on Earth. Fossils also record the disappearance of many species.

Tree Rings

The rings in tree trunks are also a tool for studying the past. The width of tree rings varies, depending on how much the tree grows in various years. In dry years, a tree does not grow very much and the rings for those years are thin. A thick ring is a sign of a good year for growth, with enough rainfall. By analyzing the tree rings of many old trees, scientists can develop an accurate history of overall weather patterns over time.

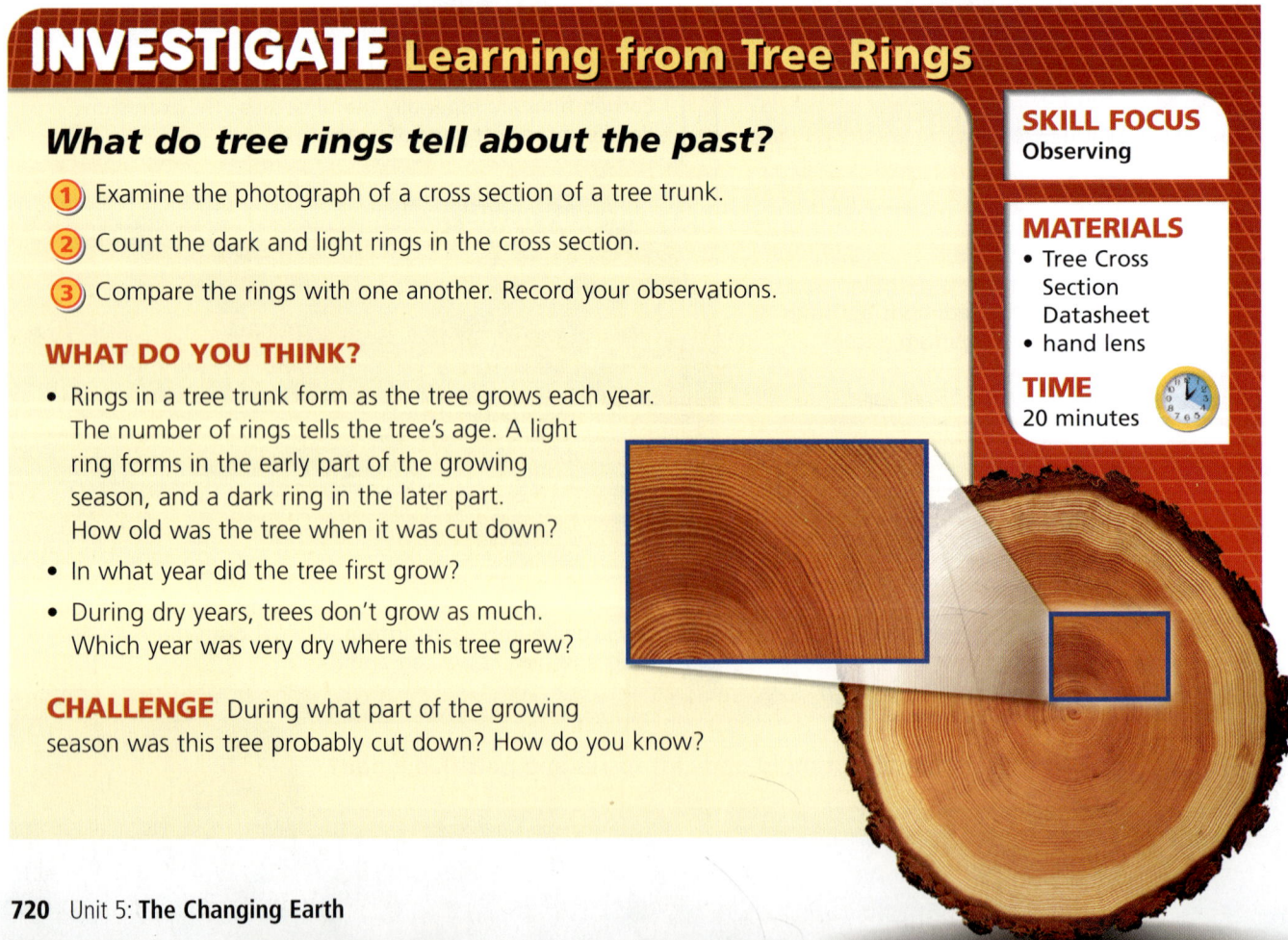

INVESTIGATE Learning from Tree Rings

What do tree rings tell about the past?

1. Examine the photograph of a cross section of a tree trunk.
2. Count the dark and light rings in the cross section.
3. Compare the rings with one another. Record your observations.

WHAT DO YOU THINK?

- Rings in a tree trunk form as the tree grows each year. The number of rings tells the tree's age. A light ring forms in the early part of the growing season, and a dark ring in the later part. How old was the tree when it was cut down?
- In what year did the tree first grow?
- During dry years, trees don't grow as much. Which year was very dry where this tree grew?

CHALLENGE During what part of the growing season was this tree probably cut down? How do you know?

SKILL FOCUS
Observing

MATERIALS
- Tree Cross Section Datasheet
- hand lens

TIME
20 minutes

These scientists are removing an ice core from a thick ice sheet in Antarctica. Ice at the bottom end is oldest.

Scientists study tiny specks of dirt in the ice, looking for signs of past microscopic organisms.

Ice Cores

In Greenland and Antarctica, snowfall has built up gigantic layers of ice that can be much deeper than the height of skyscrapers and as much as 530,000 years old at the bottom. Scientists drill into the ice and remove ice cores for study. An **ice core** is a tubular sample that shows the layers of snow and ice that have built up over thousands of years. The layers serve as a vertical timeline of part of Earth's past.

Scientists analyze air trapped in the ice to learn how the atmosphere has changed. Increases in dust or ash in the ice show when major volcanic eruptions occurred somewhere on Earth. Differences in the air content at different levels of the ice indicate how much temperatures went up and down, showing how long ice ages and warm periods lasted. This information can help scientists understand how Earth's climate might be changing now and how it might change in the future.

CHECK YOUR READING How does an ice core provide information about Earth's history?

21.1 Review

KEY CONCEPTS

1. What can rock fossils and original remains show about Earth's past?
2. Why do rock fossils form in sedimentary rock and not in igneous rock?
3. How do tree rings and ice cores help scientists understand how Earth has changed over time?

CRITICAL THINKING

4. **Infer** If you uncovered fossils of tropical fish and palm trees, what could you say about the environment at the time the fossils formed?
5. **Synthesize** Why might ancient lake and sea beds be rich sources of fossils?

CHALLENGE

6. **Rank** Which evidence—a fossil, a tree ring, or an ice core—would be most helpful to a historian studying how the Pilgrims grew food at Plymouth Colony in 1620? Explain your reasoning.

Chapter 21: **Views of Earth's Past** 721

Connecting Sciences

EARTH SCIENCE AND LIFE SCIENCE

Could *T. Rex* Win a Race?

If you want to know how fast a dinosaur ran, study a chicken. Two scientists, John Hutchinson and Mariano Garcia, did just that. They wanted to know if *Tyrannosaurus rex* was actually as fast on its feet as some people said it was.

To find the answer, the scientists worked to figure out how strong the dinosaur's legs were. What they needed to know was how much muscle the giant dinosaur had in its legs. Yet they couldn't study *T. rex's* muscle mass directly, because there are no complete remains of dinosaur muscle, just bones. This is where the chicken comes in.

Fossils and Fowls

The bone fossils of dinosaurs suggest that birds and dinosaurs have some similarities. Using the chicken as a model for *T. rex*, the scientists found that a chicken needs at least one-tenth of its body mass to be leg muscle. They measured chickens and found they have even more than that, about one-fifth.

The scientists used a computer program to learn if a chicken the size of a 5900 kilogram (10,000 lb) *T. rex* would be able to run. The computer model showed that a chicken that size would need 90 percent of its body mass in its legs to run fast. By connecting their knowledge of dinosaur fossils and chickens, the two scientists showed that *T. rex* was not a fast runner.

Still, the giant dinosaur was not exactly a slowpoke. The scientists also calculated that with its 2.5 meter (8 ft) legs *T. rex* could travel at a rate of about 24 kilometers per hour (15 mi/h). For many people, that's running speed.

EXPLORE

1. **SYNTHESIZE** Based on what you have read, what might be the relationship between the size of an animal and its speed?
2. **DRAW CONCLUSIONS** Why do you think some scientists think that *T. rex*, a meat eater, mostly ate animals already dead instead of live prey?

KEY CONCEPT

21.2 Rocks provide a timeline for Earth.

 BEFORE, you learned

- Fossils contain information about the past
- Fossils, ice cores, and tree rings record conditions and changes in the environment

 NOW, you will learn

- What the relative ages of rock layers reveal about Earth
- How index fossils are used to determine the ages of rock layers
- How the absolute ages of rocks are determined

VOCABULARY

relative age p. 723
index fossil p. 725
absolute age p. 727
half-life p. 727

THINK ABOUT

How old are these bicycles?

You might not know exactly when each of the bicycles shown was made, but you can probably tell which is the oldest. How could you arrange these bikes in order of their ages without knowing how old each is?

VOCABULARY
Remember to add *relative age* to your notebook, using the vocabulary strategy of your choice.

Layers of sedimentary rocks show relative age.

Fossils are clues in the story of Earth's past. But for the story to make sense, the clues need to be arranged in order. **Relative age** is the age of an event or object in relation to other events or objects. You probably know relative ages for many things in your life. For example, if a friend tells you she has an older brother and a younger brother, you know the relative ages of her brothers even if you don't know their exact ages.

Until the beginning of the 1900s, geologists didn't have a way to determine the exact ages of objects that existed in Earth's past. Instead, they reconstructed Earth's story based on the relative ages of different clues. Today there are still many parts of Earth's history that cannot be given exact ages. Determining relative age continues to be an important way of piecing together the puzzle of Earth's past.

Chapter 21: **Views of Earth's Past** 723

READING TIP
- *Vertical* means "straight up and down."
- *Horizontal* means "level."

Sedimentary rock layers contain information about the relative ages of events and objects in Earth's history. As you read earlier, sedimentary rocks form from the sediments that fall to the bottom of lakes, rivers, and seas. Over time, the sediments pile up to form horizontal layers of sedimentary rocks. The bottom layer of rock forms first, which means it is oldest. Each layer above that is younger, and the top layer is youngest of all. This ordering is relative because you cannot be sure exactly when each layer formed, only that each layer is younger then the one below it.

When horizontal layers of sedimentary rock are undisturbed, the youngest layer is always on top, as shown in the photograph on the left below. But over millions of years, the movement of tectonic plates can disturb rock layers. A whole set of layers can get turned on its side. Rock layers can get bent, or even folded over, like taco shells that begin as flat tortillas. If a set of rock layers has been disturbed, the youngest layer may no longer be on top. One way scientists determine the original order is to compare the disturbed rock layers with a similar but undisturbed stack of layers.

CHECK YOUR READING When might the youngest layer in a set of sedimentary rock layers not be on top?

Rock Layers

Undisturbed Layers

Because sedimentary rock forms in layers, the oldest layer of undisturbed sedimentary rock will be on the bottom and the youngest on top.

Disturbed Layers

If the rock layers are bent, they may no longer be in order from oldest to youngest.

READING VISUALS Where are the youngest layers in each photo?

Igneous Rock and Sedimentary Layers

Sedimentary rock layers can also be disturbed by igneous rock. Molten rock from within Earth can force its way up through the layers above it, cooling and forming igneous rock. Because the sedimentary rock layers have to be present before the molten rock cuts through them, the igneous rock must be younger than the layers it cuts through.

Watch molten rock cut through layers of sedimentary rock.

1 Over time, sand and silt form horizontal layers of sedimentary rock.

2 Deep underground, molten rock cuts through the sedimentary rock layers.

3 A river gradually wears away the rock, exposing the younger igneous rock.

If the molten rock erupts and flows onto the surface, it forms a layer of igneous rock on top of the layers of sedimentary rock. Over time, more sedimentary rock layers may form on top of the igneous rock. The igneous rock layer is younger than the sedimentary layers under it and older than the sedimentary layers that form on top of it.

 Why is igneous rock always younger than any rock it cuts through?

Index Fossils

Fossils contained within sedimentary rock can offer clues about the age of the rock. An organism that was fossilized in rock must have lived during the same time span in which the rock formed. Using information from rocks and other natural evidence, scientists have determined when specific fossilized organisms existed. If people know how long ago a fossilized organism lived, then they can figure out the age of the rock in which the fossil was found.

Fossils of organisms that were common, that lived in many areas, and that existed only during specific spans of time are called **index fossils.** These characteristics of index fossils make them especially useful for figuring out when rock layers formed.

This rock contains the index fossil *Arnioceras semicostatum*, an organism that lived between 206 million and 144 million years ago.

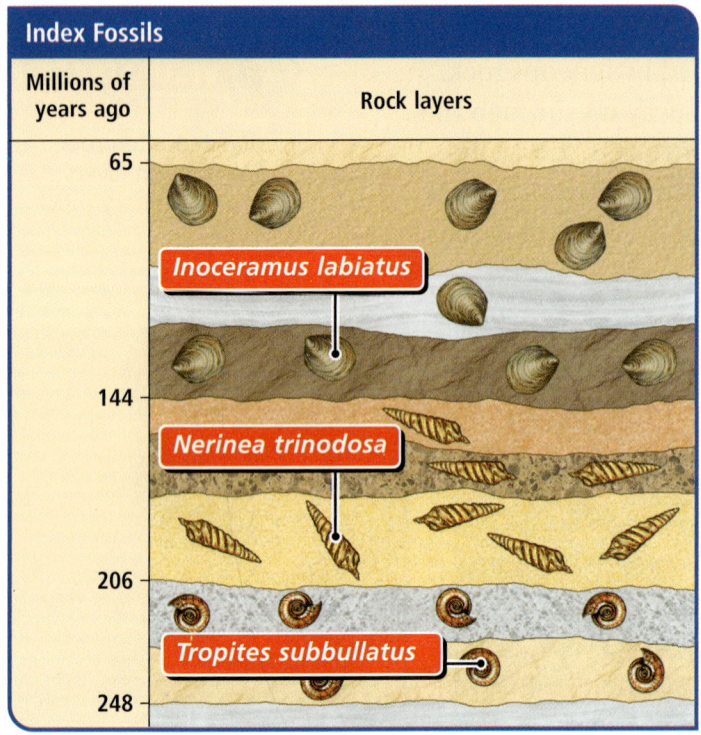

Index fossils can be used to estimate the ages of the rocks in which they are found.

The mollusk *Inoceramus labiatus*, for example, is a kind of sea animal that appeared 144 million years ago and went extinct 65 million years ago. So, if you find a rock that contains a fossil of this mollusk, the rock must be between 144 million and 65 million years old because this mollusk lived during that time span.

The chart shows a cross section of rock layers in which *Inoceramus labiatus* and two other index fossils are found. *Nerinea trinodosa* is a kind of sea animal that lived between 206 million and 144 million years ago. *Tropites subbullatus* is a kind of sea animal that lived between 248 million and 206 million years ago.

Remember that one characteristic of index fossils is that they are widespread—they are found in many different parts of the world. Because they are widespread, index fossils can be used to compare the ages of rock layers in different parts of the world.

INVESTIGATE Relative and Absolute Age

How can newspapers model rock layers?

PROCEDURE

1. Have one person in your group arrange the newspapers in a pile with the oldest newspaper on the bottom and the newest on top.

2. After the newspapers are stacked, place one pencil between two newspapers and the other pencil between two different newspapers. Use the model to answer the questions below.

WHAT DO YOU THINK?

- If the newspapers were really placed on the stack on the days they were published, which pencil has probably been there longer?
- Look at the dates on the newspapers. Now what can you say about when the pencils were placed on the stack?

CHALLENGE How does what you could tell about the "ages" of the pencils before looking at the dates differ from what you could tell after looking?

SKILL FOCUS
Making models

MATERIALS
- 5 or more newspapers with different dates
- 2 pencils

TIME
20 minutes

Radioactive dating can show absolute age.

Think again about the friend who tells you that she has two brothers, one older than she is and one younger. You know the order in which they were born—that is, their relative ages. The older brother, however, might be 1 year older or 20 years older. The exact age of the younger brother is also still a mystery. To find out how much older or younger your friend's brothers are, you need to know their actual ages. The actual age of an event or object is called its **absolute age.**

 **CHECK YOUR READING** What is the difference between relative age and absolute age? Use an example in your explanation.

Half-Life

Because scientists can't ask a rock its age, they have had to find a different way of determining the absolute ages of rocks. The solution lies in the smallest unit of matter, the atom. Atoms make up everything on Earth, including you and rocks. The atoms of many chemical elements exist in various forms. Some of these forms are unstable and break down over time into another form. This breakdown—called radioactivity—is a very useful clock because a particular unstable form of an element always breaks down at the same rate into the same other form.

The rate of change of a radioactive element is measured in half-lives. A **half-life** is the length of time it takes for half of the atoms in a sample of a radioactive element to change from an unstable form into another form. Different elements have different half-lives, ranging from fractions of a second to billions of years.

Just as a ruler is not a very useful tool for measuring the distance between planets, elements with very short half-lives are not very useful for measuring the ages of rocks. Instead, elements with half-lives of millions to billions of years are used to date rocks. For example, uranium 235 has a half-life of 704 million years. Uranium 235 is an unstable element found in some igneous rocks. Over time, uranium 235 breaks down into lead 207. Using information from radioactive dating of rocks, scientists estimate that Earth is around 4.6 billion years old.

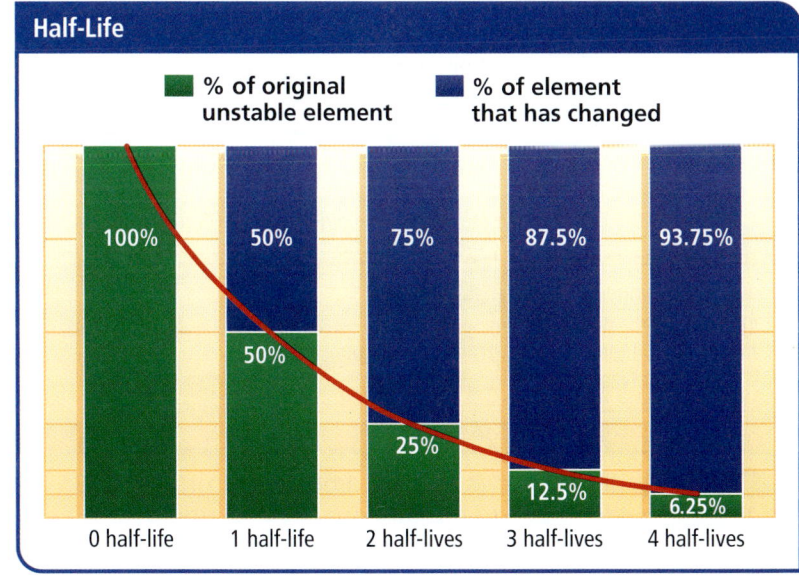

Over time, a radioactive element breaks down at a constant rate into another form.

Radioactive Breakdown and Dating Rock Layers

Igneous rocks contain radioactive elements that break down over time. This breakdown can be used to tell the ages of the rocks.

① 1408 Million Years Ago

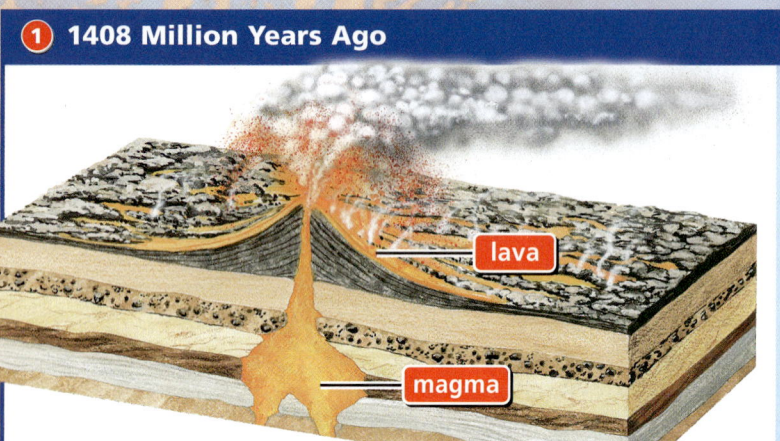

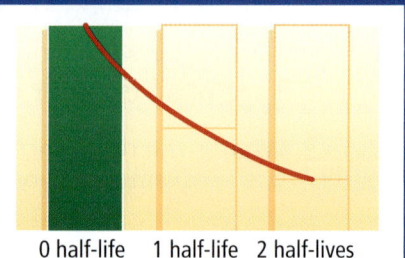

When magma first hardens into rock, it contains some uranium 235 and no lead 207.

② 704 Million Years Ago

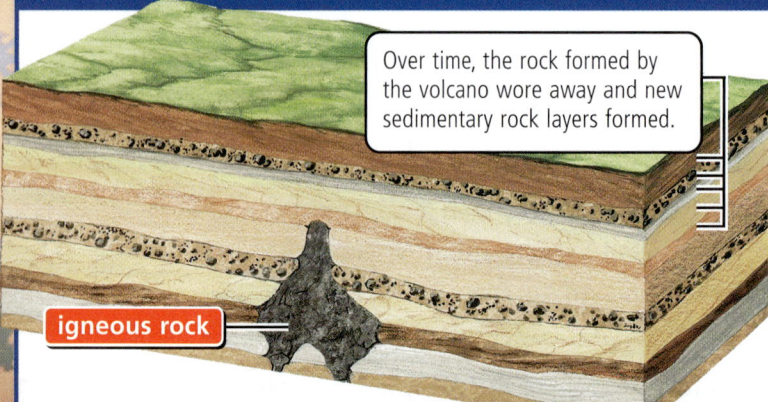

Over time, the rock formed by the volcano wore away and new sedimentary rock layers formed.

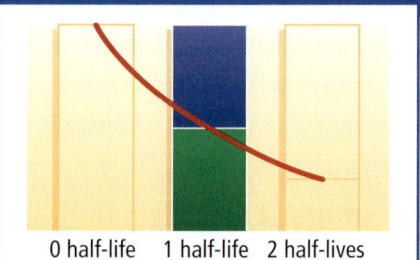

After 704 million years, or one half-life, half of the uranium 235 in the igneous rock has broken down into lead 207.

③ Today

Radioactive dating shows that this igneous rock is about 1408 million years old.

These layers formed before the magma cut through, so they must be older than 1408 million years.

The layers that formed on top of the igneous rock must be younger than 1408 million years.

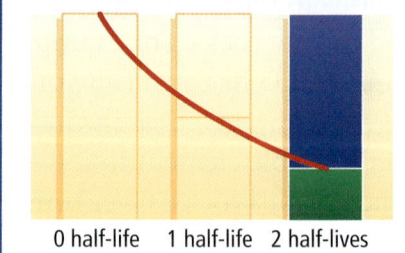

After 1408 million years, or 2 half-lives, only one-fourth of the uranium 235 in the igneous rock remains.

READING VISUALS How do the relative amounts of uranium 235 and lead 207 in the igneous rock change over time?

Radioactive dating works best with igneous rocks. Sedimentary rocks are formed from material that came from other rocks. For this reason, any measurements would show when the original rocks were formed, not when the sedimentary rock itself formed.

Just as uranium 235 can be used to date igneous rocks, carbon 14 can be used to find the ages of the remains of some things that were once alive. Carbon 14 is an unstable form of carbon, an element found in all living things. Carbon 14 has a half-life of 5730 years. It is useful for dating objects between about 100 and 70,000 years old, such as the wood from an ancient tool or the remains of an animal from the Ice Age.

RESOURCE CENTER
CLASSZONE.COM
Find out more about how scientists date rocks.

Using Absolute and Relative Age

Scientists must piece together information from all methods of determining age to figure out the story of Earth's past.

- Radioactive dating of igneous rocks reveals their absolute age.
- Interpreting layers of sedimentary rock shows the relative order of events.
- Fossils help to sort out the sedimentary record.

You have read that it is not possible to date sedimentary rocks with radioactivity directly. Geologists, however, can date any igneous rock that might have cut through or formed a layer between sedimentary layers. Then, using the absolute age of the igneous rock, geologists can estimate the ages of nearby sedimentary layers.

 How might the absolute age of an igneous rock layer help scientists to determine the ages of nearby sedimentary rock layers?

21.2 Review

KEY CONCEPTS

1. What can you tell from undisturbed rock layers? Discuss the concept of relative age in your answer.
2. How can index fossils help scientists determine the ages of rock layers?
3. What property of radioactive elements makes them useful for determining absolute age?

CRITICAL THINKING

4. **Provide Examples** What are some things in your life for which you know only their relative ages?
5. **Apply** In your daily life are there index events (like index fossils) that tell you approximate times even when you can't see a clock? What are they?

CHALLENGE

6. **Apply** A rock contains a radioactive element with a half-life of 100 million years. Tests show that the element in the rock has gone through three half-lives. How old is the rock?

Chapter 21: **Views of Earth's Past** 729

Math in Science

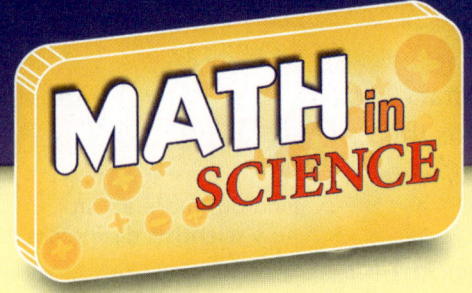

SKILL: INTERPRETING GRAPHS

Dating Mammoth Bones

Imagine that scientists find an ancient lakebed with hundreds of well-preserved mammoth bones in it. They are able to measure the amount of carbon 14 that remains in the bones. Carbon 14 has a half-life of approximately 5700 years. How could you use the half-life of carbon 14 to determine how old the bones are?

MATH TUTORIAL
CLASSZONE.COM
Click on Math Tutorial for more help with reading line graphs and multiplying whole numbers.

Example

Mammoth bone A has $\frac{1}{4}$ of its original carbon 14. How old is mammoth bone A? Use the half-life of carbon 14 and the graph below.

(1) Find $\frac{1}{4}$ on the vertical axis and follow the line out to the red curved line.

(2) Then follow the line down to the horizontal axis to determine that the carbon 14 in the bone has been through 2 half-lives.

(3) $5700 \times 2 = 11{,}400$
    ↑   ↑
  years per   number of
  half-life   half-lives

ANSWER Bone A is 11,400 years old.

Mammoths were close relatives of today's elephants. Mammoths lived earlier in the Cenozoic era and are now extinct.

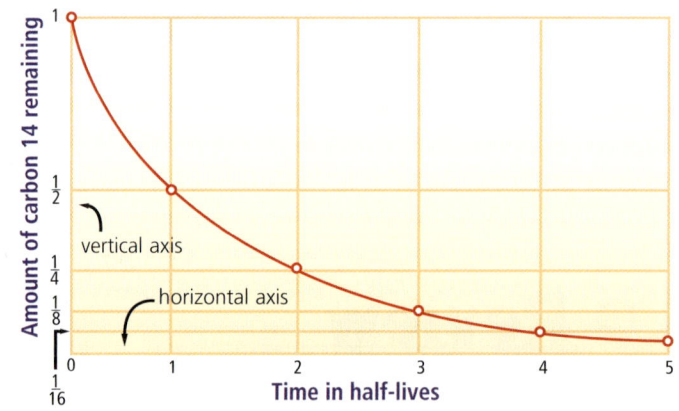

Half-Lives

Amount of carbon 14 remaining vs. Time in half-lives

Answer the following questions.

1. Mammoth bone B has $\frac{1}{8}$ of its original carbon 14. How old is mammoth bone B?

2. Mammoth bone C has $\frac{1}{16}$ of its original carbon 14. How old is mammoth bone C?

CHALLENGE Mammoth bone D is 28,500 years old. What fraction of the original carbon 14 remains in bone D?

KEY CONCEPT
21.3 The geologic time scale shows Earth's past.

BEFORE, you learned
- Rocks and fossils give clues about life on Earth
- Layers of sedimentary rocks show relative ages
- Radioactive dating of igneous rocks gives absolute ages

NOW, you will learn
- That Earth is always changing and has always changed in the past
- How the geologic time scale describes Earth's history

VOCABULARY

uniformitarianism p. 732
geologic time scale p. 733

EXPLORE Time Scales

How do you make a time scale of your year?

PROCEDURE

1. Divide your paper into three columns.
2. In the last column, list six to ten events in the school year in the order they will happen. For example, you may include a particular soccer game or a play.
3. In the middle column, organize those events into larger time periods, such as soccer season, rehearsal week, or whatever you choose.
4. In the first column, organize those time periods into even larger ones.

MATERIALS
- pen
- sheet of paper

WHAT DO YOU THINK?
How does putting events into categories help you to see the relationship among events?

OUTLINE
Remember to start an outline in your notebook for this section.

I. Main idea
   A. Supporting idea
      1. Detail
      2. Detail
   B. Supporting idea

Earth is constantly changing.

In the late 1700s a Scottish geologist named James Hutton began to question some of the ideas that were then common about Earth and how Earth changes. He found fossils and saw them as evidence of life forms that no longer existed. He also noticed that different types of fossilized creatures were found in different layers of rocks. Based on his observations of rocks and other natural evidence, Hutton came up with a new theory to explain the story told in the rocks. He was the first to present a hypothesis about Earth's changing over time.

Chapter 21: **Views of Earth's Past** 731

Gradual Change

This line shows how the Adirondack Mountains may have looked several hundred million years ago.

Over hundreds of millions of years, natural forces wore down the jagged peaks to form the rounded hills seen today.

Adirondack Mountain Range

Hutton recognized that Earth is a constantly changing place. Wind, water, heat, and cold break down rocks. Other processes, such as volcanic eruptions and the building up of sediment, continue to form new rock. Earth's interior is constantly churning with powerful forces that move, fold, raise, and swallow the surface of the planet.

The same processes that changed Earth in the past continue to occur today. A billion years ago a river would have carried particles of rock just as a river does today. Similarly, volcanoes in the past would have erupted just as volcanoes do today. Hutton's theory of **uniformitarianism** (YOO-nuh-fawr-mih-TAIR-ee-uh-nihz-uhm) is the idea that

- Earth is an always-changing place
- the same forces of change at work today were at work in the past

Although this idea may seem simple, it is very important. The theory of uniformitarianism is the basis of modern geology.

Some changes on Earth are gradual. Mountains form and are worn down over many millions of years. Climate and the amount of ice on land can change over hundreds or thousands of years. Other changes are fast. A volcanic eruption, an earthquake, or a flood can cause huge changes over a period of minutes or days. Fast or slow, Earth is always changing.

> **READING TIP**
> To remember what *uniformitarianism* means, think of the word *uniform*, which means "same."

CHECK YOUR READING What was the new idea that Hutton had about Earth? Describe the idea in your own words.

Fast Change

READING VISUALS **COMPARE AND CONTRAST** These photos show Mount St. Helens before and after it erupted in 1980. What rapid changes occurred during the eruption?

The geologic time scale divides Earth's history.

From a person's point of view, 4.6 billion years is a tremendous amount of time. To help make sense of it, scientists have organized Earth's history in a chart called the geologic time scale. The **geologic time scale** divides Earth's history into intervals of time defined by major events or changes on Earth.

Scientists use information from fossils and radioactive dating to figure out what happened over the 4.6 billion years of Earth's history. The oldest evidence of life is from about 3.8 billion years ago, but life may be even older. Organisms with more than one cell appeared around 1 billion years ago, and modern humans appeared only 100,000 years ago.

Imagine Earth's history compressed into one year. If Earth forms on January 1, the first life we have evidence for appears in the beginning of March. Life with more than one cell appears months later, in the middle of October. Humans do not show up until 11 minutes before midnight on the last day of the year, and they do not understand how old Earth is until about a second before midnight.

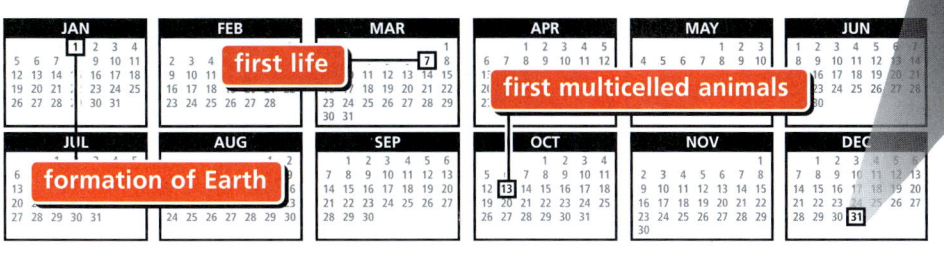

If Earth's history is compared to a calendar year, humans appear just before midnight on December 31.

Chapter 21: **Views of Earth's Past** 733

READING TIP
As you read, find the eons, eras, and periods on the chart below.

Divisions of Geologic Time

The geologic time scale is divided into eons, eras, periods, and epochs (EHP-uhks). Unlike divisions of time such as days or minutes, the divisions of the geologic time scale have no fixed lengths. Instead, they are based on changes or events recorded in rocks and fossils.

Eon The largest unit of time is an eon. Earth's 4.6-billion-year history is divided into four eons.

Era Eons may be divided into eras. The most recent eon is divided into three eras: the Paleozoic, the Mesozoic, and the Cenozoic.

Period Each era is subdivided into a number of periods.

Epoch The periods of the Cenozoic, the most recent era, are further divided into epochs.

Geologic Time Scale

The geologic time scale divides Earth's history into eons, eras, periods, and epochs.

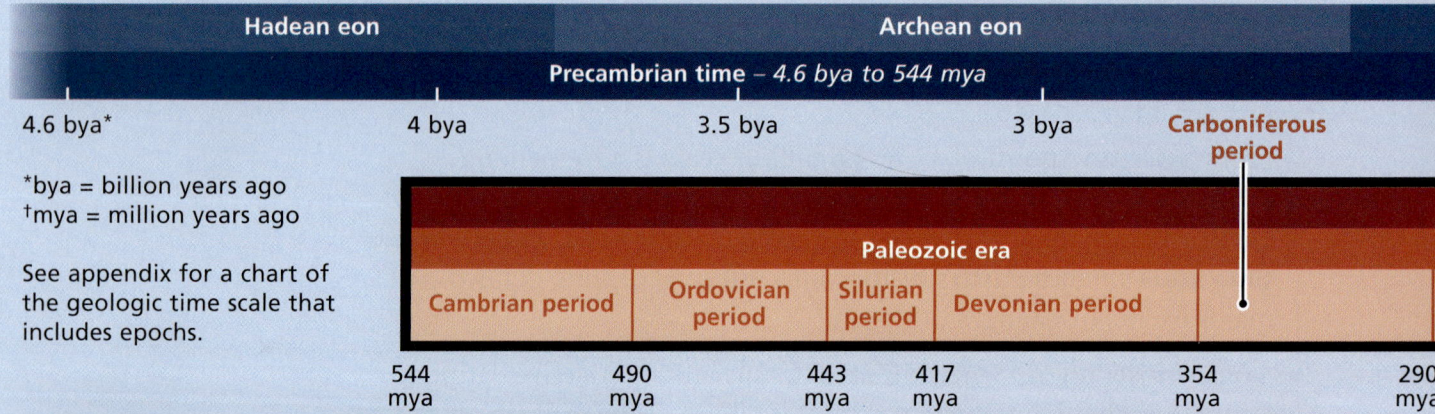

*bya = billion years ago
†mya = million years ago

See appendix for a chart of the geologic time scale that includes epochs.

Precambrian Time at 3.6 Billion Years Ago
For nearly 4 billion years, during most of Precambrian time, no plants or animals existed.

Paleozoic Era at 544 Million Years Ago
At the beginning of the Paleozoic era, all life lived in the oceans.

The Hadean, Archean, and Proterozoic eons together are called Precambrian time and make up almost 90 percent of Earth's history. The fossil record for Precambrian time consists mostly of tiny organisms that cannot be seen without a microscope. Other early forms of life had soft bodies that rarely formed into fossils.

The Phanerozoic eon stretches from the end of Precambrian time to the present. Because so many more changes are recorded in the fossil record of this eon, it is further divided into smaller units of time. The smaller time divisions relate to how long certain conditions and life forms on Earth lasted and how quickly they changed or became extinct.

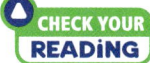

CHECK YOUR READING What part of geologic time makes up most of Earth's history?

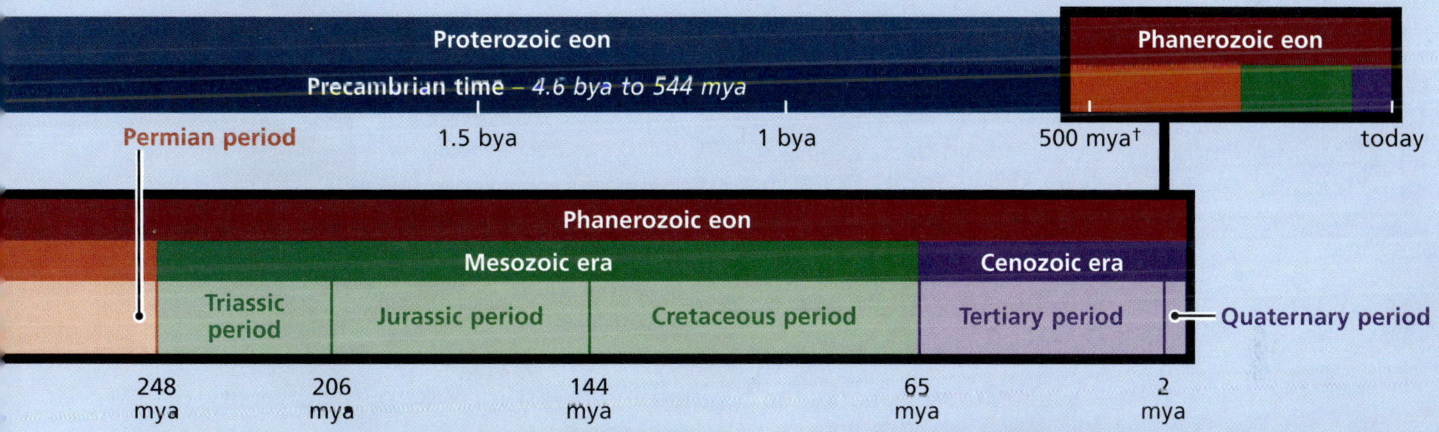

Mesozoic Era at 195 to 65 Million Years Ago

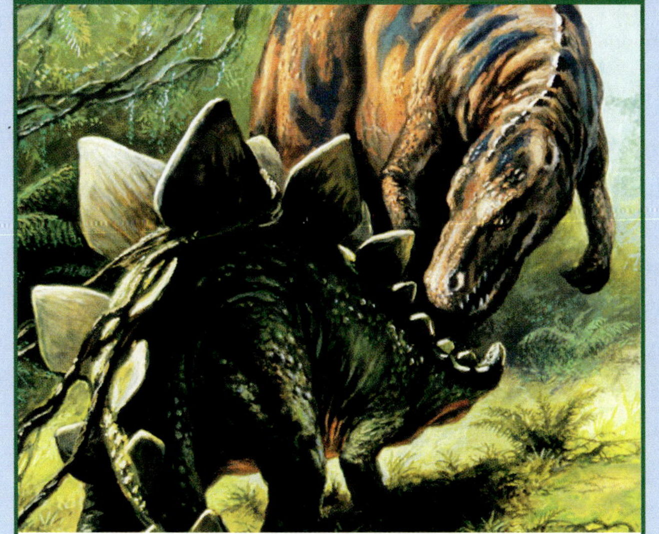

During the Mesozoic era, dinosaurs lived along with the first mammals, birds, and flowering plants.

Cenozoic Era at Present Day

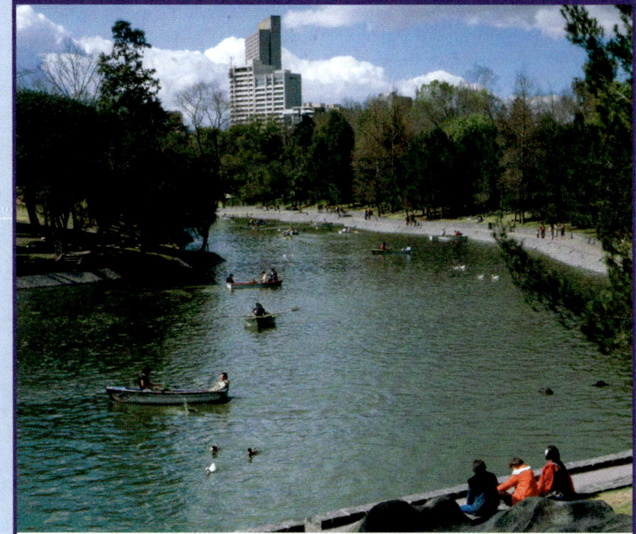

The first humans appeared in the later part of the Cenozoic era, which continues today.

Rock Layers in the Grand Canyon

Rock layers offer clues about conditions on Earth when the layers formed.

Hermit Shale: formed about 265 million years ago, during the Permian period

Supai Group: formed about 285 million years ago, near the beginning of the Permian period

Redwall Limestone: formed about 335 million years ago, during the Carboniferous period

Bright Angel Shale: formed about 530 million years ago, during the Cambrian period

READING VISUALS During which period did the oldest rock layer shown form?

Phanerozoic Eon

The most recent eon, the Phanerozoic, began around 544 million years ago. Its start marks the beginning of a fast increase in the diversity, or variety, of life. The Phanerozoic eon is divided into three eras:

- the Paleozoic, whose name means "ancient life"
- the Mesozoic, whose name means "middle life"
- the Cenozoic, whose name means "recent life"

The Paleozoic era is the first era of the Phanerozoic eon. At the start of the Paleozoic, all life lived in the ocean. Fish, the first animals with backbones, developed during this time. Toward the end of this era, life moved onto land. Reptiles, insects, and ferns were common. A mass extinction occurred at the end of the Paleozoic era, 248 million years ago. A mass extinction is when many different life forms all die out, or become extinct, at once. The cause of this extinction is not completely understood.

The Mesozoic era spans the next 183 million years and is best known for the dinosaurs that ruled Earth. Mammals, birds, and flowering plants also first appeared during the Mesozoic. For some of this time, parts of North America were covered by a vast sea. The end of the

READING TIP
As you read, find each era in the geologic time scale on pages 734–735.

Mesozoic marks the end of the dinosaurs and many other animals in another mass extinction. This extinction may have been caused by one or more giant asteroids that slammed into Earth, throwing huge amounts of dust into the air. The dust blocked the sunlight, causing plants to die and, along with them, many animals.

The Cenozoic era, the most recent era, began 65 million years ago and continues today. The Cenozoic is often called the Age of Mammals because it marks the time when mammals became a main category of life on Earth.

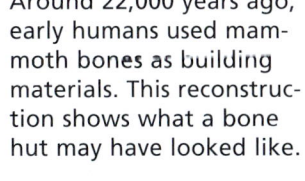

Around 22,000 years ago, early humans used mammoth bones as building materials. This reconstruction shows what a bone hut may have looked like.

The Cenozoic era is divided into two periods: the Tertiary and the Quaternary. The Quaternary period stretches from about 2 million years ago to the present. Most of the Quaternary has been a series of ice ages, with much of Europe, North America, and Asia covered in thick sheets of ice. Mammoths, saber-toothed cats, and other giant mammals were common during the first part of the Quaternary. Fossils of the first modern humans are also from this period; they are about 100,000 years old.

As the amount of ice on land shrank and grew, the ocean levels rose and fell. When the ocean levels fell, exposed land served as natural bridges that connected continents previously separated by water. The land bridges allowed humans and other animals to spread around the planet. It now seems that the end of Quaternary may be defined by the rise of human civilization.

 How did falling ocean levels lead to the spread of humans and other animals on Earth?

21.3 Review

KEY CONCEPTS
1. Describe the concept of uniformitarianism.
2. What does the geologic time scale measure?
3. What was life like on Earth for most of its history?

CRITICAL THINKING
4. **Apply** What period, era, and eon do you live in?
5. **Evaluate** Some cartoons have shown early humans keeping dinosaurs as pets. From what you know about Earth's history, is this possible? Why or why not?

CHALLENGE
6. **Infer** How might the geologic time scale be different if the event that caused the mass extinction 65 million years ago had never occurred?

CHAPTER INVESTIGATION

Geologic Time

OVERVIEW AND PURPOSE Geologists use information from rocks, fossils, and other natural evidence to piece together the history of Earth. The geologic time scale organizes Earth's history into intervals of time called eons, eras, periods, and epochs. In this investigation you will
- construct a model of the geologic time scale
- place fossil organisms and geologic events in the correct sequence on the timeline

Procedure

MATERIALS
- geologic time scale conversion chart
- adding-machine paper 5 meters long
- scissors
- colored markers, pens, or pencils
- metric tape measure or meter stick
- sticky notes

1. Complete the geologic time scale conversion chart. Use the conversion 1 mm = 1 million years to change the number of years for each eon, era, period, and epoch on the chart into metric measurements (millimeters, centimeters, and meters).

2. Lay the adding-machine paper out in front of you. At the far right end of the strip write "TODAY" lengthwise along the edge.

3. Starting from the TODAY mark, measure back 4.6 meters, or 4600 million years. Label this point "AGE OF EARTH." Cut off excess paper.

4. Fold the paper in half lengthwise and then fold it in half lengthwise again. Unfold the paper. The creases should divide your paper into four rows.

5. At the far left end of the strip, label each of the four rows as shown.

6. Using the numbers from your chart, measure each eon. Start each measurement from the TODAY line and measure back in time. For example, the Archean eon started 3800 million years ago, so measure back 3.8 meters from today. Mark that distance and write "ARCHEAN EON." Do the same for the other eons.

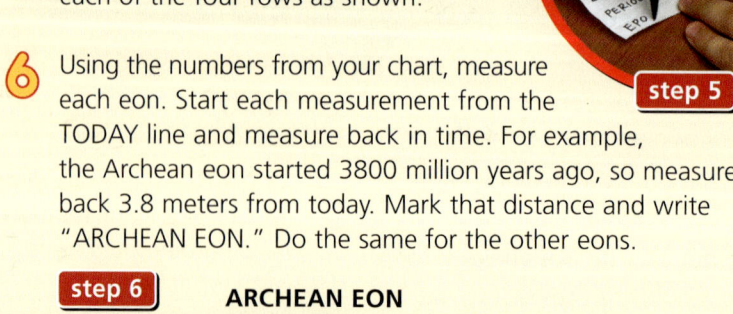

step 6 ARCHEAN EON
3800 million years ago (3.8 meters)

AGE OF EARTH

TODAY

738 | Unit 5: The Changing Earth

7 Repeat step 6 to measure and label the eras, periods, and epochs.

8 After all the eons, eras, periods, and epochs are measured and labeled, use the same measuring technique to add the fossils and events from the table below.

Table 1. Important Events in Earth's History

Fossils and Events	Time (millions of years ago)
First trilobite	554
First mammal	210
Greatest mass extinction	248
First green algae	1000
Early humans	2
Extinction of dinosaurs	65
First life forms	3800
Flowering plants	130

9 Draw pictures of the fossils and events or write the names of the fossils and events on the timeline. If you do not have space to write directly on the timeline, write on sticky notes and then place the sticky notes at the correct positions on the timeline.

Observe and Analyze

1. **COMPARE AND CONTRAST** The time from 4.6 billion years ago up until the beginning of the Phanerozoic eon is called Precambrian time. Find the part of your timeline that represents Precambrian time. How does Precambrian time compare in length with the rest of the geologic time scale?

2. **COMPARE AND CONTRAST** The Cenozoic era is the most recent era, and it includes the present. How does the Cenozoic era compare in length with the other eras?

3. **INTERPRET** Where on the timeline are the two major extinction events?

4. **INFER** What does the location of the two major extinction events suggest about how geologists divided the time scale into smaller units?

Conclude

1. **INTERPRET** Where are most of the life forms that you placed on your time line grouped?

2. **INFER** Judging by the locations of most of the life forms on your timeline, why do you think the shortest era on the timeline—the Cenozoic era—has been divided into so many smaller divisions?

3. **EVALUATE** What limitations or difficulties did you experience in constructing or interpreting this model of the geologic time scale?

4. **APPLY** Think about the relationships among fossils, rock layers, and the geologic time scale. Why do you think the geologists who first constructed the geologic time scale found it difficult to divide the first three eons into smaller time divisions?

INVESTIGATE Further

CHALLENGE Choose several more events or life forms mentioned in the chapter. For each, find either an absolute date or a relative date that will allow you to place it in the correct position in the geologic sequence. Draw or label these new items on your timeline. What new patterns or connections did adding these events or life forms to the timeline reveal?

Geologic Time Scale Conversion Chart

Division of Geologic Time	Millions of Years Ago It Began	Measurement
Eons		
Hadean	4600	4.6 meters
Archean	3800	
Proterozoic	2500	
Phanerozoic	544	
Eras	544	

Chapter Review

the BIG idea

Rocks, fossils, and other types of natural evidence tell Earth's story.

CONTENT REVIEW
CLASSZONE.COM

KEY CONCEPTS SUMMARY

1 Earth's past is revealed in rocks and fossils.

Fossils are traces or remnants of past life. Many fossils are found in rock. Rocks, fossils, and other natural evidence provide information about how Earth and life on Earth have changed over time.

A cast fossil is formed when minerals take the shape of a decayed organism.

VOCABULARY
fossil p. 715
original remains p. 716
ice core p. 721

2 Rocks provide a timeline for Earth.

Sedimentary rock layers show the order in which rocks formed. The order of the layers is used to determine the **relative ages** of fossils found in the rock.

Radioactive dating can be used to determine the **absolute age** of igneous rock.

Scientists combine information about the relative and absolute ages of rocks and fossils to construct a timeline of Earth.

VOCABULARY
relative age p. 723
index fossil p. 725
absolute age p. 727
half-life p. 727

3 The geologic time scale shows Earth's past.

The **geologic time scale** divides Earth's history into eons, eras, periods, and epochs. The divisions are based on major changes or events that occurred in Earth's history.

■ Phanerozoic eon ■ Paleozoic era ■ Mesozoic era ■ Cenozoic era

Hadean eon	Archean eon	Proterozoic eon		
		Precambrian time		
4.6 bya*	3 bya	2 bya	1 bya	500 mya† — today

*bya = billion years ago   †mya = million years ago

EON → ERA → PERIOD → EPOCH

VOCABULARY
uniformitarianism p. 732
geologic time scale p. 733

740 Unit 5: The Changing Earth

Vocabulary

Make a concept definition map for each of the vocabulary terms listed below. Write the term in the center box. Fill in the other boxes by answering the questions. A sample is shown below.

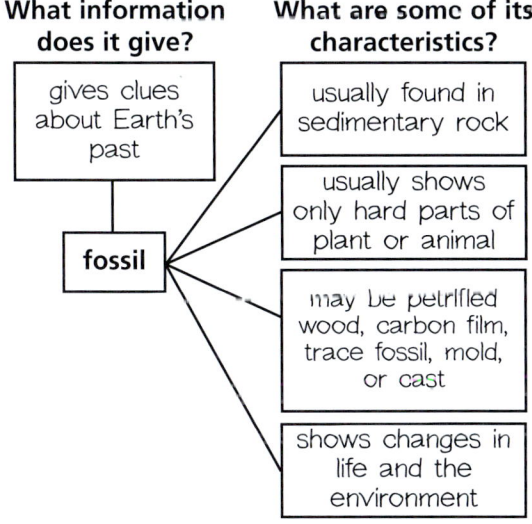

1. index fossil
2. ice core
3. original remains

Reviewing Key Concepts

Multiple Choice *Choose the letter of the best answer.*

4. Which of the following might show evidence of a year with low rainfall?
    a. tree rings   c. original remains
    b. index fossils   d. sedimentary rock

5. In which time span did dinosaurs live?
    a. Cenozoic era   c. Paleozoic era
    b. Mesozoic era   d. Precambrian time

6. Half-life is a measurement of
    a. fossil age
    b. radioactive breakdown
    c. cold climates
    d. relative age

7. What is the age of Earth?
    a. 570 million years   c. 4.6 billion years
    b. 1.1 billion years   d. 9.5 billion years

8. What was the earliest form of life?
    a. a fish   c. a one-celled organism
    b. a fern   d. a reptile

9. Which statement best describes the theory of uniformitarianism?
    a. Earth continues to change as it always has.
    b. Earth is changing, but not as quickly as it used to.
    c. Earth is changing, but faster than it used to.
    d. Earth is no longer changing.

10. How does petrified wood form?
    a. A log falls into water that freezes.
    b. Sedimentary rock forms over a log.
    c. Igneous rock covers a log and heats it.
    d. Water seeps through a log, replacing its cells with minerals.

11. A cast fossil is formed from
    a. igneous rock   c. amber
    b. a mold   d. wood

12. Which of these substances best preserves soft parts of an organism?
    a. sedimentary rock   c. amber
    b. igneous rock   d. air

13. Which part of an ancient reptile would you expect to see in a rock fossil?
    a. eye   c. heart
    b. bone   d. muscle

14. Which type of fossil would be most likely to show the complete outline of a leaf?
    a. petrified wood   c. cast fossil
    b. carbon film   d. trace fossil

Short Answer *Write a few sentences to answer each question.*

15. Why are no fossils found in igneous rocks?

16. Why is radioactive dating not useful for determining the ages of sedimentary rocks?

Chapter 21: **Views of Earth's Past** 741

Thinking Critically

APPLY Refer to the illustration below to answer the next four questions.

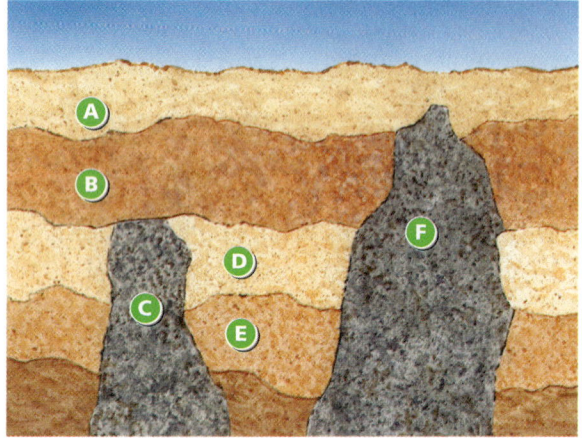

The illustration above is a side view of formations of sedimentary and igneous rock. C and F are igneous rock.

17. For which of the labeled rock formations could the absolute age be determined? Why?

18. Which of the labeled rock formations is the youngest? How do you know?

19. Which rock is younger, C or D? Why?

20. Which of the labeled rock layers is the oldest? Why?

21. **INFER** Why do you think the Hadean, Archean, and Proterozoic eons are not divided into eras, periods, or epochs?

22. **COMPARE AND CONTRAST** How is the geologic time scale like a calendar? How is it different?

23. **CONNECT** Copy the concept map below. Use the geologic time scale on pages 734–735 to complete the map.

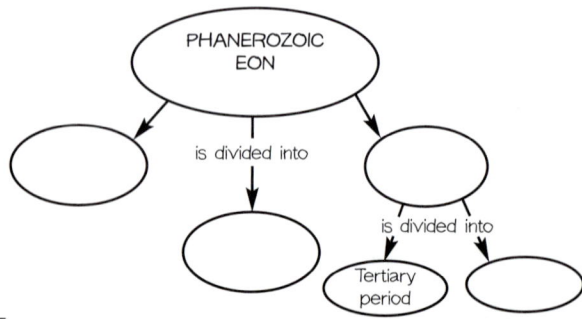

24. **APPLY AND GRAPH** Copy the graph below on your paper. Plot a point on the graph above each of the half-life numbers to show what percentage of the original unstable element remains. Note that the first point has been placed on the graph to show that all of the original element remains at the beginning, when no half-lives have passed.

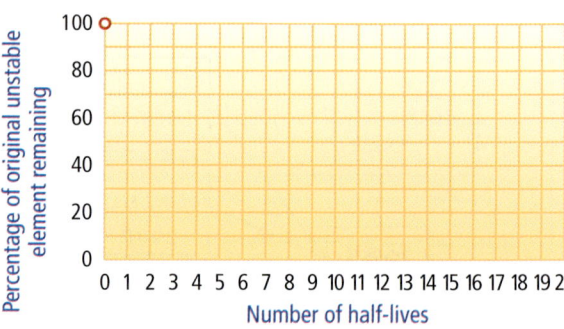

the BIG idea

25. **SYNTHESIZE** Look at the geologic time scale and think about the major events in the history of Earth and the changes in life forms that it shows. How do rocks, fossils, and other natural evidence tell Earth's story?

26. **PREDICT** What do you think will remain as evidence of today's world 100,000 years from now? How will the types of evidence differ from those that remain from 100,000 years ago?

UNIT PROJECTS

If you need to create graphs or other visuals for your project, be sure you have grid paper, poster board, markers, or other supplies.

Standardized Test Practice

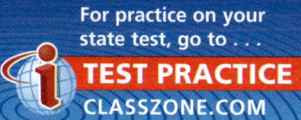

For practice on your state test, go to...
TEST PRACTICE
CLASSZONE.COM

Analyzing a Diagram

This diagram shows a cross section of rock layers. All of the layers are sedimentary, except for the area marked as igneous. Use the diagram to answer the questions below.

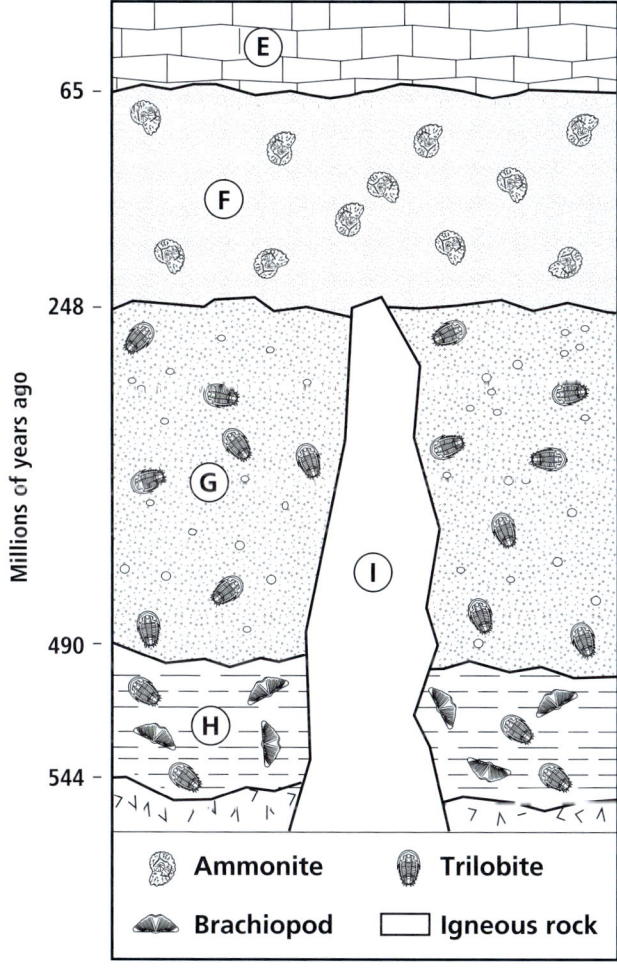

1. What is the approximate age of the oldest ammonite fossil shown in the diagram?
   a. 65 million years
   b. 248 million years
   c. 480 million years
   d. 540 million years

2. When did trilobites live on Earth?
   a. within the last 65 million years
   b. between 65 million years ago and 248 million years ago
   c. between 248 million years ago and 544 million years ago
   d. more than 544 million years ago

3. Which fossils are most common in the rock that is 500 million years old?
   a. brachiopods
   b. trilobites
   c. ammonites
   d. theropods

4. What is the best estimate of the age of rock I?
   a. less than 300 million years old
   b. 300 million years old
   c. more than 300 million years old
   d. more than 544 million years old

5. Which point shows where a fossil that is 500 million years old would most likely be found?
   a. E
   b. F
   c. G
   d. H

Extended Response

Answer the two questions below in detail. Include some of the terms shown in the word box. In your answers, underline each term you use.

index fossils	original remains	igneous rock
layers	folded	bent
ice core	tree ring	trilobite

6. Azeem is part of a team of scientists studying the natural history of a region. What types of natural evidence might he and his team look for? Why?

7. In studying fossils found in her community, Yvette noticed a pattern in their ages. People found older fossils close to the surface and younger fossils at greater depths. Explain how that might be.

Chapter 21: **Views of Earth's Past** 743

TIMELINES in Science

THE STORY OF FOSSILS

Fossils are an important source of information about the history of life on Earth. The first observer to suggest that fossils provided clues to the past was Xenophanes. He lived in Greece around 500 B.C. Today, knowledge about fossils helps people find deposits of oil and understand changes in weather patterns. Above all, fossils reveal information about plants and animals that lived in the past.

The timeline shows a few events in the history of the study of fossils. Tools, such as radar and CT scanners that were invented for other purposes have helped scientists learn more from fossils. The boxes below the timeline highlight the role of technology, along with applications of knowledge about fossils.

1669
Scientist Notes Importance of Rock Layers

Danish-born scientist Nicolaus Steno recognizes that sediments form new layers of rock on top of old layers. Therefore, digging down provides a way to move back in time. Scientists plan to build on Steno's discovery to determine the ages of fossils found in rock layers.

EVENTS

1640   1660   1680   1700

APPLICATIONS AND TECHNOLOGY

This sandstone formation in Utah displays layers of sediment that were laid down one on top of another.

1799
Siberian Discovers Frozen Mammoth
While hunting for ivory tusks in Siberia, a man discovers a 37,000-year-old mammoth frozen in ice. Unfortunately, before scientists can study the five-ton animal, it thaws and wild animals eat most of it. However, the skeleton and bits of hair still provide clues to Earth's past.

1785
New Theory Suggests Naturalness of Change
James Hutton of Scotland revolutionizes geology with his theory of uniformitarianism. He argues that volcanoes, erosion, and other forces shaped Earth's landscape slowly over a very long period and continue to do so. Hutton's ideas challenge the belief that the landscape is the result of sudden changes and one-time events. His theory leads to a better understanding of the vast ages of Earth and fossils.

1824
Geologist Identifies Bones from Extinct Animal
English geologist William Buckland concludes that a fossilized jawbone comes from an enormous reptilelike animal that is extinct. He names the animal *Megalosaurus*. This is the first dinosaur to be given a scientific name.

1720 1740 1760 1780 1800 1820 1840

APPLICATION
Mapping Earth's Layers
In the late 1700s, the geologist William Smith helped survey land for canals throughout England and Wales. As workers dug deeper into the ground, Smith noticed that fossils always appeared in the same order. He used this information to create the first map showing the locations of rock layers under surface soil. It was published in 1815. As people began to understand the importance of rock layers, they collected more information from projects that required digging. Maps showing this type of information became more detailed and more useful. Today, geologists combine information collected in the field with data from satellite images to create precise maps of rock layers.

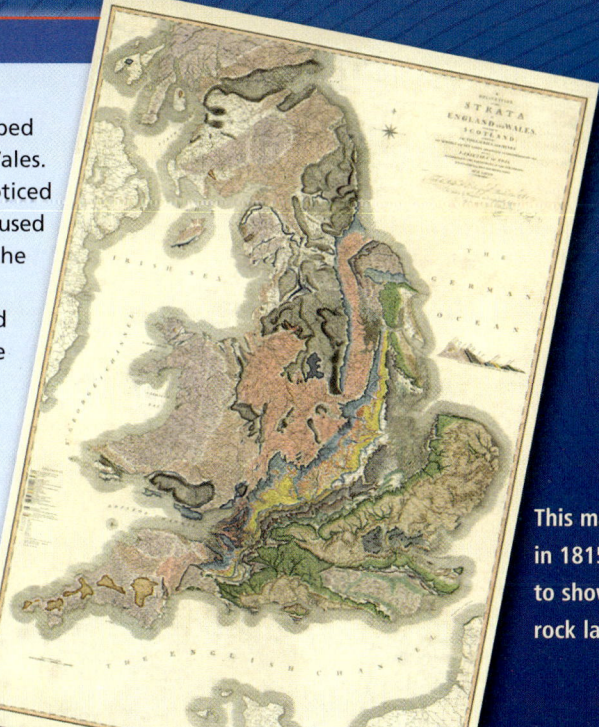

This map, hand-painted in 1815, was the first to show locations of rock layers.

1861
Workers Uncover Bird Fossil
Laborers digging up limestone rock in southern Germany find a fossil that looks like a lizard with wings. The fossil is about 150 million years old—the oldest known one of a bird.

1923
Dinosaur Eggs Show Link with Birds
Researchers in Mongolia find a nest of fossilized dinosaur eggs. The eggs are in a circle. This fact suggests that dinosaurs, like modern birds, moved their eggs and arranged their nests.

1965
Microfossils Cause Sensation
Two new scientific papers focus attention on Earth's earliest life forms. In these papers scientists describe rocks from Canada that contain microfossils of algae and fungi—traces of life vastly older than any others yet found. These findings trigger huge new efforts in scientific research on ancient life.

| 1860 | 1880 | 1900 | 1920 | 1940 | 1960 | 1980 |

TECHNOLOGY
Chemist Creates New Time Scale
In the 1890s, scientists studying radiation began to understand the idea of half-life. The chemist B. B. Boltwood used half-life data to identify the ages of various rocks and create a new geologic time scale. The ages he calculated were in the hundreds of millions or even billions of years—far greater than the ages many scientists had been using. The time scale continues to be modified as new technologies allow for ever more precise measurements.

The half-life of carbon 14 will be used to calculate the ages of the samples this researcher is preparing.

2000
Dinosaur Heart Surprises Many

North Carolina scientists use a medical device called a CT scanner to identify the first known fossilized dinosaur heart. The heart surprises those who thought all dinosaurs were cold-blooded. Its structure suggests that the dinosaur was warm-blooded.

2001
Researchers Find Earliest Mammal

Scientists in China find the oldest known mammal fossil. The 195-million-year-old skull is from an animal that weighed just 2 grams—less than the weight of a penny.

RESOURCE CENTER
CLASSZONE.COM
Learn more about fossils.

2000

TECHNOLOGY
CT Scans Show That *T. Rex* Could Smell

Computerized tomography (CT) scans are commonly used in medicine to search inside human bodies without surgery. A CT scan of the skull of a *Tyrannosaurus rex* known as Sue showed that it had a large area in its brain for smelling. Its sharp sense of smell, combined with its size and strength, made the tyrannosaur an effective hunter and scavenger.

This skull is part of Sue's skeleton—the largest and most complete *T. rex* yet found.

INTO THE FUTURE

When did life begin on Earth? Fossils have helped scientists answer this question. Many think that the oldest fossils date from 3.5 billion years ago. This date might be pushed back if new techniques identify even older fossils. Or the date might be pushed forward. Some scientists argue that the 3.5-billion-year-old traces in rocks are not really fossils at all. Rather, they argue, the traces are just signs of chemical reactions that did not involve any living organisms.

Research on fossils also helps people evaluate the impact of human activity on the environment. For example, the fossil record shows a pattern of warming and cooling in Earth's history. Human activity, such as burning of coal and oil, has helped cause Earth to get warmer over the past century. Further studies of fossils will help people understand how much of this warming is normal and how much is a result of human action.

ACTIVITIES

Reliving History

Get permission to dig a hole outside. Dig down two feet or more. Draw a sketch showing the layers of soil. Add notes to describe any variations that are not clear in the sketch. Try to explain the differences you notice in the layers.

Writing About Science

Suppose you are an archaeologist who has made one of the fossil discoveries on the timeline. Write a speech to your fellow scientists explaining the importance of your discovery.

CHAPTER 22

Natural Resources

Society depends on natural resources for energy and materials.

Key Concepts

SECTION 1 — Natural resources support human activity. Learn about the costs and benefits of using natural resources to obtain energy and to make products.

SECTION 2 — Resources can be conserved and recycled. Learn about efforts to conserve and recycle natural resources.

SECTION 3 — Energy comes from other natural resources. Learn how nuclear power and renewable resources can provide energy to the world.

Internet Preview

CLASSZONE.COM
Chapter 22 online resources: Content Review, Simulation, Visualization, three Resource Centers, Math Tutorial, Test Practice

How do people obtain energy from Earth's resources?

EXPLORE the BIG idea

Sunlight as an Energy Source

Tape black paper around two plastic cups. Half fill the cups with water. Fasten plastic wrap over each top with rubber bands. Place one cup in sunlight and one cup in shade. Wait half an hour. Remove the plastic wrap. Place a thermometer in each cup to measure the water temperature.

Observe and Think
What happened to the water temperature in each cup? How do you think people might use sunlight as a source of energy?

Saving Water as You Brush

Time how long it takes you to brush your teeth. Then set aside a bucket or large container and a measuring cup. Close the sink's drain; run the water for the same length of time you brushed your teeth. How many cups of water can you bail out of the sink?

Observe and Think
Estimate how much water you could save in a week by turning the water off as you brush.

Internet Activity: Resources

Go to **ClassZone.com** to learn more about natural resources and energy.

Observe and Think
What are the most important natural resources in your state?

Nonrenewable Resources Code: MDL056

Chapter 22: **Natural Resources** 749

CHAPTER 22

Getting Ready to Learn

CONCEPT REVIEW

- Fossils preserve the remains of living things from long ago.
- Fossils and half-lives of elements can be used to determine the age of Earth's rock layers.
- The same forces that have changed Earth in the past are still at work today.

VOCABULARY REVIEW

fossil p. 715
half-life p. 727
See glossary for definitions.
geosphere, mineral

CONTENT REVIEW
CLASSZONE.COM
Review concepts and vocabulary.

TAKING NOTES

CHOOSE YOUR OWN STRATEGY

As you read, take notes, using one or more of the strategies from earlier chapters—**main idea and detail notes, supporting main ideas, content frame,** or **outline**. Mix and match these strategies, or use an entirely different one.

VOCABULARY STRATEGY

Write each new vocabulary term in the center of a **four-square** diagram. Write notes in the squares around the term. Include a definition, some characteristics, and some examples. If possible, write some things that are not examples.

See the Note-Taking Handbook on pages R45–R51.

SCIENCE NOTEBOOK

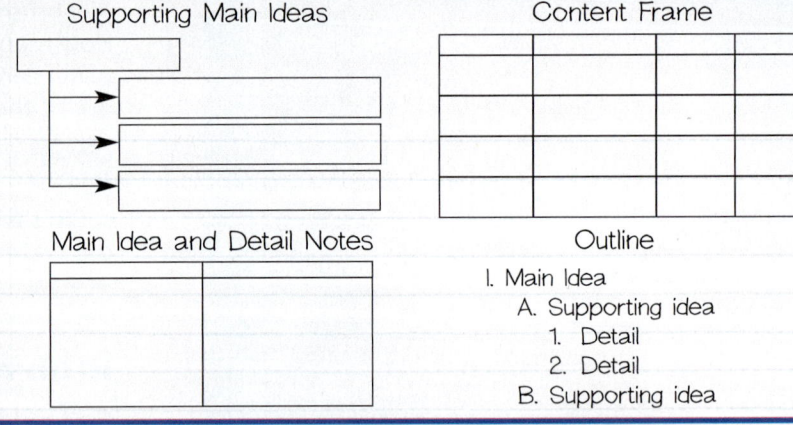

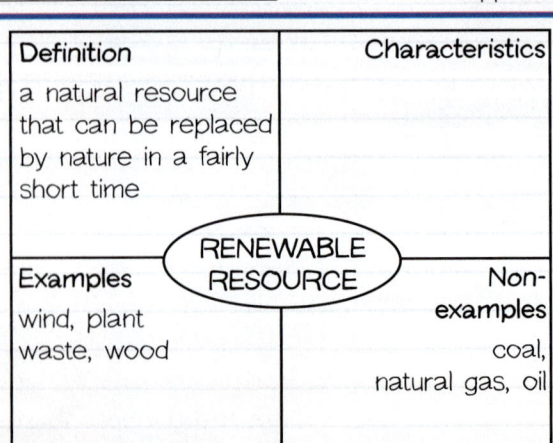

Definition: a natural resource that can be replaced by nature in a fairly short time
Characteristics:
RENEWABLE RESOURCE
Examples: wind, plant waste, wood
Non-examples: coal, natural gas, oil

750 Unit 5: The Changing Earth

KEY CONCEPT

 Natural resources support human activity.

BEFORE, you learned

- Earth's distant past is revealed in rocks and fossils
- Layers of sedimentary rock show relative ages
- Living things have inhabited Earth for over 3 billion years

NOW, you will learn

- What makes a natural resource renewable or nonrenewable
- About benefits and costs of using fossil fuels
- How people use natural resources in modern life

VOCABULARY

natural resource p. 751
renewable resource p. 752
nonrenewable resource p. 752
fossil fuel p. 754

THINK ABOUT

What resources do you need the most?

Think about all the products you use at school and at home—clothing, books, video games, CDs, backpacks, and other items.

Which ones do you use the most often? What materials are these products made of? Plastic? Cloth? Metal? What would you lose if one of these materials, such as plastic, vanished from Earth overnight?

VOCABULARY
Use a four-square diagram for the term *natural resource* in your notebook.

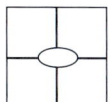

Natural resources provide materials and energy.

For thousands of years, people have used natural resources to make tools, build cities, heat their homes, and in general make their lives more comfortable. A **natural resource** is any energy source, organism, or substance found in nature that people use.

The four parts of the Earth system—atmosphere, hydrosphere, biosphere, and geosphere—provide all the materials needed to sustain human life. The atmosphere, for instance, provides the air you breathe and the rain that helps living things grow. The hydrosphere contains all of Earth's waters in rivers, lakes, oceans, and underground. The biosphere and the geosphere are sources of food, fuel, clothing, and shelter.

Chapter 22: **Natural Resources** 751

NOTE TAKING
A content frame can help you take notes about the costs and benefits of using natural resources.

However, people also know that there are costs as well as benefits in using natural resources. For example, burning coal produces heat but also releases smoke that pollutes the air. When forests are cut down, the soil beneath is exposed to the air. Wind and rain can strip away valuable topsoil, making it harder for new trees to grow. The soil can choke streams and rivers and kill fish and other animals living in the waters. As you can see, using resources from one part of Earth's system affects all the other parts.

People are also concerned about saving natural resources. Some resources, such as the water in a river or the wind used to turn a windmill, are constantly being replaced. But others, such as oil, take millions of years to form. If these resources are used faster than they are replaced, they will run out. Today people are more aware of which resources are renewable and which are nonrenewable.

 Summarize the costs and benefits of using natural resources.

Renewable Resources

The charts on page 753 list some of the most common resources people use in modern life. As you might have guessed, sunlight, wind, water, and trees and other plants are renewable. A **renewable resource** is a natural resource that can be replaced in nature at about the same rate it is used.

For example, a lumber company might plant a new tree for each mature tree it cuts down. Over time, the forest will continue to have the same number of trees. However, if the trees are cut down faster than they can be replaced, even a renewable resource will run out.

Nonrenewable Resources

A **nonrenewable resource** is a natural resource that exists in a fixed amount or that is used up faster than it can be replaced in nature. This means the supply of any nonrenewable resource is limited. In general, all resources produced by geologic forces—coal, natural gas, oil, uranium—are nonrenewable. These resources form over millions of years.

Today people are using coal, oil, and natural gas much faster than they are forming in nature. As a result, these resources are becoming more scarce and expensive. Many countries realize that they must conserve their nonrenewable resources. Some, like the United States, are developing alternative energy sources, such as solar and wind energy.

 Compare and contrast renewable and nonrenewable resources.

752 Unit 5: **The Changing Earth**

Natural Resources

Natural resources can be classified as renewable and nonrenewable resources.

Renewable Resources

Resource	Common Uses
Sunlight	power for solar cells and batteries, heating of homes and businesses, and generating electricity
Wind	power to move windmills that pump water, grind grain, and generate electricity
Water	power to generate electricity, transportation with boats and ships, drinking and washing
Trees and other plants	materials for furniture, clothing, fuel, dyes, medicines, paper, cardboard, and generating electricity
Animal waste	material for fuels

Nonrenewable Resources

Resource	Common Uses
Coal	fuel to generate electricity, chemicals for medicines and consumer products
Oil	fuel for cars, airplanes, and trucks; fuel for heating and generating electricity; chemicals for plastics, synthetic fabrics, medicines, grease, and wax
Natural gas	fuel for heating, cooking, and generating electricity
Uranium	fuel to generate electricity
Minerals and rocks	materials for coins, jewelry, building, computer chips, lasers, household products, paint, and dyes

READING VISUALS Read the common uses of each resource. Which of these resources are used to generate electricity?

Chapter 22: **Natural Resources** 753

Fossil fuels supply most of society's energy.

When you turn on the air conditioner, a computer, or a microwave oven, you may use energy from fossil fuels. Millions of people depend on these fuels—coal, oil, and natural gas—for electricity, heat, and fuel.

A **fossil fuel** is a nonrenewable energy source formed from ancient plants and animals buried in Earth's crust for millions of years. The energy in such a fuel represents a form of stored sunlight, since ancient organisms depended on the sun. The buried organisms form layers at the bottom of oceans, ponds, and swamps. Over a long time, this material is compressed and pushed deeper into Earth's crust. High heat and pressure change it chemically into coal, oil, and natural gas.

 Explain how fossil fuels are formed from ancient organisms.

Fossil Fuel Power Station

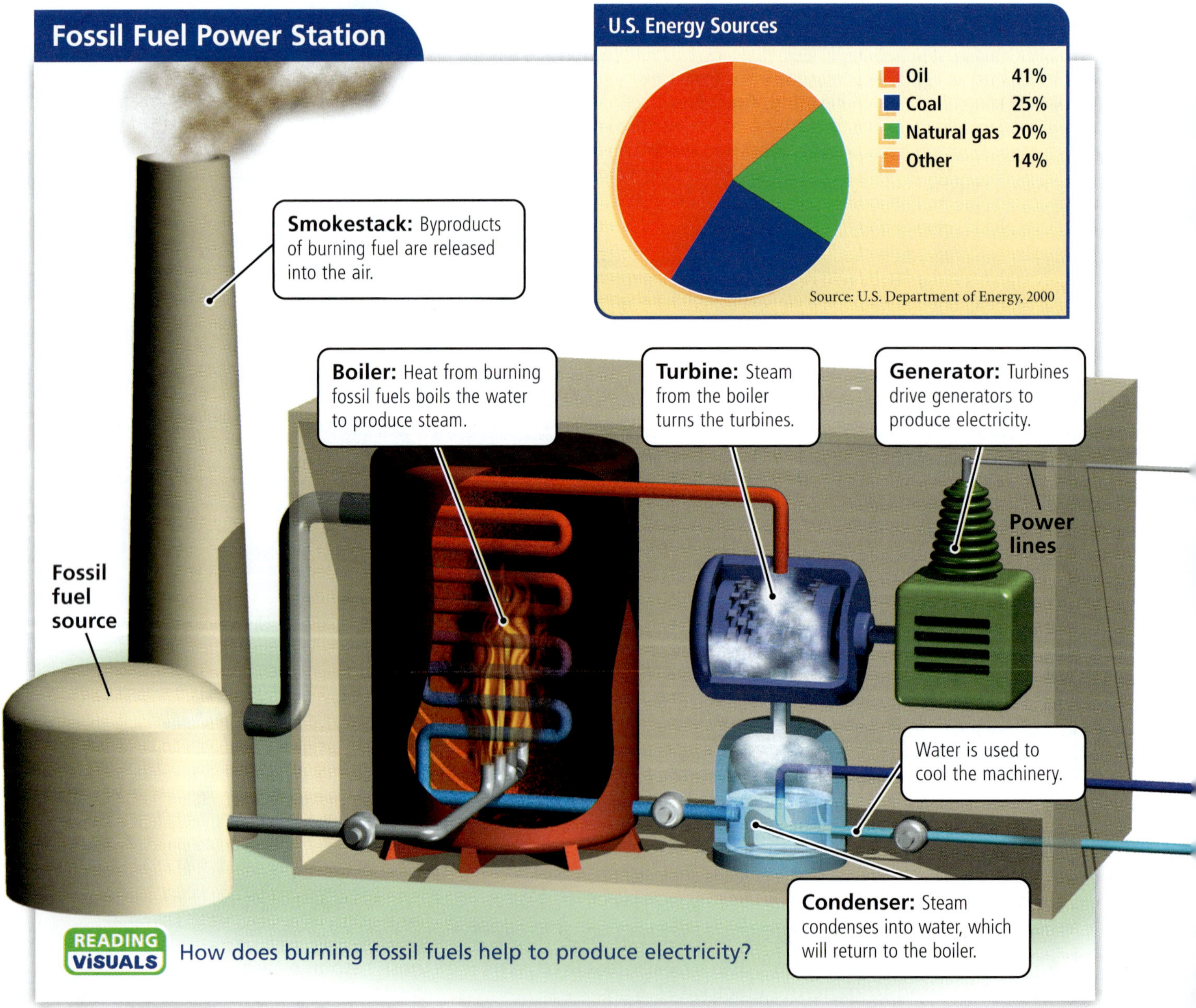

U.S. Energy Sources
- Oil 41%
- Coal 25%
- Natural gas 20%
- Other 14%

Source: U.S. Department of Energy, 2000

Smokestack: Byproducts of burning fuel are released into the air.

Fossil fuel source

Boiler: Heat from burning fossil fuels boils the water to produce steam.

Turbine: Steam from the boiler turns the turbines.

Generator: Turbines drive generators to produce electricity.

Power lines

Water is used to cool the machinery.

Condenser: Steam condenses into water, which will return to the boiler.

READING VISUALS How does burning fossil fuels help to produce electricity?

Fossil fuels burn easily and produce a lot of heat. They are used to run most of the power plants that generate electricity. As shown in the diagram on page 754, heat from a burning fuel is used to change water into steam. The steam turns a turbine. The turbine drives a generator to produce electricity, which is carried through power lines to towns and cities. Electricity runs nearly everything in modern life, from giant factories to the smallest light in your home.

But these resources also harm the environment. Burning fossil fuels produces excess carbon dioxide, harmful acids, and other forms of pollution. Most of this pollution comes from power plants and fossil fuels burned by cars and other vehicles.

READING TIP

Turbine is based on the Latin *turbo,* which means "spinning top." *Generator* is based on the Latin *generāre,* which means "to produce."

Coal

Coal is a solid fossil fuel formed underground from buried and decayed plant material. As shown below, heat and pressure determine the type of coal formed. The hardest coal makes the best energy source. It burns hotter and much cleaner than softer coals. At one time, coal was the main source of energy in the United States.

① Swamp plants decay and are compressed to form peat.

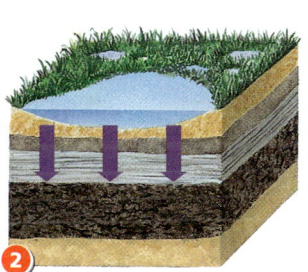
② Sediments bury the peat, and rising pressure and heat change it into soft coal.

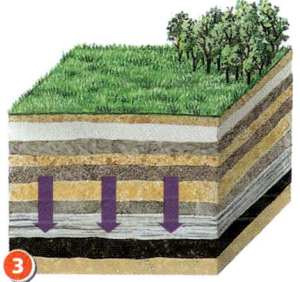
③ Over millions of years, increasing pressure and heat form harder coal.

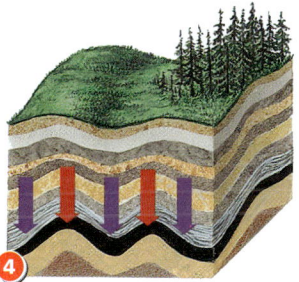
④ It takes the longest time and the greatest heat and pressure to form the hardest coal.

The world's largest coal deposits are in the United States, Russia, and China. People use surface mining and deep mining to obtain coal. In surface mines, overlying rock is stripped away to expose the coal. In deep mines, miners must go underground to dig out the coal. Most of the world's coal is used to fuel power plants and to run factories that produce steel and cement.

When burned as a fuel, however, coal produces byproducts that pollute air and water. Also, surface mining can destroy entire landscapes. Coal dust in deep mines damages miners' lungs. Yet reducing pollution, restoring landscapes, and protecting miners cost millions of dollars. Society faces a difficult choice—keep the cost of energy low or raise the price to protect the environment and human health.

 **CHECK YOUR READING** What is the main use of coal?

Chapter 22: **Natural Resources** 755

Oil and Natural Gas

READING TIP
Non- is a Latin prefix meaning "not." Porous rock is full of tiny cracks or holes. Therefore, *nonporous* rock is rock that does not have tiny cracks or holes.

Most oil and natural gas is trapped underground in porous rock. Heat and pressure can push the oil and natural gas upward until they reach a layer of nonporous rock, where they collect. As shown in the illustration below, wells can be drilled through the nonporous rock to bring the oil and natural gas to the surface. Major oil and natural gas deposits are found under the oceans as well as on land.

 How is oil removed from layers of rock?

Recovered oil is transported by ships, trucks, and pipelines from the wells to refineries. Refineries use heat to break down the oil into its different parts. Each part is used to make different products, from gasoline and jet fuel to cleaning supplies and plastics. Oil and natural gas burn at high temperatures, releasing energy. They are easily transported, which makes them ideal fuels to heat homes and to power vehicles.

There are costs in using oil. When ships that transport oil are damaged, they can spill millions of gallons into the environment. These spills pollute coastlines and waterways, killing many plants and animals. Cleaning up these spills costs governments millions of dollars each year. Even after the cleanup, some of the oil will remain in the environment for years.

Air pollution is another problem. Waste products from the burning of gasoline, jet fuels, and diesel fuels react with sunlight to produce smog—a foglike layer of air pollution. Some countries have passed clean air laws to reduce this pollution. Yet smog continues to be a problem in most large cities.

 What are the benefits and costs of using oil?

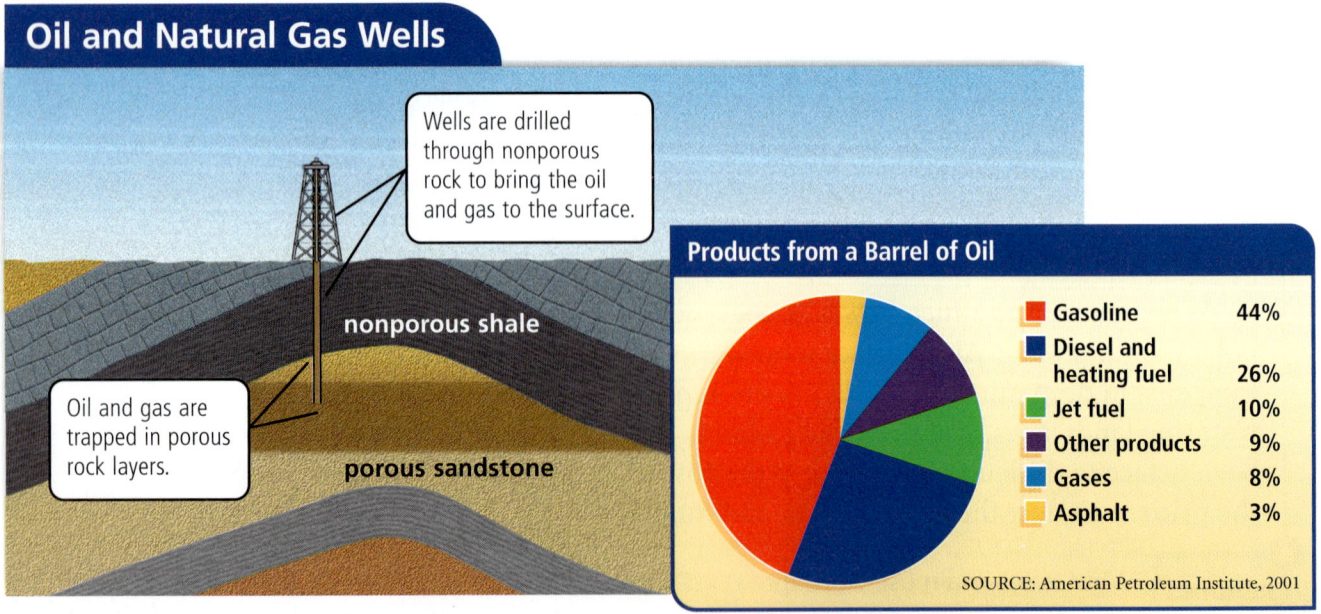

Oil and Natural Gas Wells

Wells are drilled through nonporous rock to bring the oil and gas to the surface.

Oil and gas are trapped in porous rock layers.

nonporous shale

porous sandstone

Products from a Barrel of Oil

Gasoline	44%
Diesel and heating fuel	26%
Jet fuel	10%
Other products	9%
Gases	8%
Asphalt	3%

SOURCE: American Petroleum Institute, 2001

INVESTIGATE Fossil Fuels

Why does an oil spill do so much harm?

PROCEDURE

1. Fill the pan about halfway with water. Using an eyedropper, carefully add 10 drops of oil in the middle of the pan. Rock the pan gently.

2. Observe what happens to the drops of oil over the next 2 min. Record your observations in your **Science Notebook.**

3. Place the plastic-foam ball in the oil slick, wait a few seconds, then carefully lift the ball out again. Examine it and record your observations.

WHAT DO YOU THINK?

- What happened when the drops of oil came in contact with the water?
- What might happen to an animal that swims through spilled oil?

CHALLENGE Think of a way to clean up the oil slick on the water. Discuss your ideas with your teacher before you test your cleaning method.

SKILL FOCUS
Modeling

MATERIALS
- water
- vegetable oil
- large pan (at least 22 cm)
- plastic-foam ball (about 5 cm)
- eyedropper

TIME
20 minutes

Fossil fuels, minerals, and plants supply materials for modern products.

Many of the products you use come from fossil fuels. For example, oil is broken down into different chemicals used to make plastics. Plastic materials can be easily shaped, colored, and formed. They are used in electronic and computer equipment, in packaging, in cars and airplanes, and in such personal items as your shoes, toothbrush, and comb.

Minerals are found in cars and airplanes, tools, wires, computer chips, and probably your chair. Minerals such as limestone, gypsum, sand, and salt are used to make building materials and cement. In the United States, it takes 9,720 kilograms (20,000 lbs) of minerals every year to make the products used by just one person.

Plants are used to make another large group of products. For centuries people have used wood to build homes and to make furniture, household utensils, and different types of paper. Plants are also rich sources of dyes, fibers, and medicines. The plant indigo, for example, has been used to dye fabrics since Roman times.

These products benefit people's lives in many important ways, but they also have drawbacks. Fossil fuels must be burned to generate power for the factories and businesses that produce these products.

Chapter 22: **Natural Resources** 757

Consumer Products

Thousands of everyday products are made from natural resources.

Fossil Fuels

Fossil fuels are used to make thousands of products from aspirin to zippers. For example, oil-based plastics are used to make this motocross rider's safety helmet, suit, gloves, and boots. Gasoline powers the motorbike.

Minerals and Rocks

The U.S. Treasury uses zinc, copper, and nickel to mint over 14 billion coins a year. Gold and silver are used in special coins.

Trees and Other Plants

Each year, the United States produces about 400 billion square feet of corrugated cardboard used to make boxes of all sizes.

Factory waste can pollute air, water, and soil. Even making computer chips can be a problem. So much water is needed to clean the chips during manufacture that local water supplies may be reduced.

To maintain modern life and to protect the planet, people must use natural resources wisely. In the next section you will read about ways for every person to conserve resources and reduce pollution.

22.1 Review

KEY CONCEPTS

1. Define *renewable resource* and *nonrenewable resource*. Give four examples of each type of resource.
2. List three advantages and three disadvantages of using fossil fuels.
3. In what ways are natural resources used to make people's lives more comfortable?

CRITICAL THINKING

4. **Infer** Why do you think people are willing to accept the costs as well as the benefits of using fossil fuels?
5. **Predict** If supplies of coal, oil, and natural gas ran out tomorrow, what are some of the ways your life would change?

CHALLENGE

6. **Apply** Suppose you are lost in the woods, miles from any city or town. You have some dried food and matches but no other supplies. What natural resources might you use to survive until you are found?

CONNECTING SCIENCES

EARTH SCIENCE AND LIFE SCIENCE

Got Oil Spills? Call in the Microbes!

You have seen the photographs. A beautiful coastline is fouled by dark, sticky oil. The oil slick coats birds and other animals the same dark color. Hundreds of experts and volunteers appear with buckets, chemicals, shovels, and brooms to clean up the mess.

But did you know that seawater and the world's beaches contain their own natural cleanup crews? These crews consist of tiny microbes that digest oil and other waste products and turn them into gases such as carbon dioxide.

Nature's Disposal Units Do a Great Job . . .

Scientists learned how effective oil-digesting microbes are during the 1989 *Exxon Valdez* oil spill in Alaska. Since then, cleanup crews have been using bacteria and other microbes to help clean up oil spills around the world. Scientists find that areas treated with microbes recover faster than areas treated with chemicals.

. . . But It Is Not All That Simple

Cleaning up oil spills is not as simple as watching millions of microbes munch their way through the mess. Scientists have had to solve a few problems.

- **Problem:** Microbes cannot multiply fast enough to handle a large oil spill. **Solution:** Add nutrients to help them multiply faster.
- **Problem:** There are not enough of the right types of microbes to digest oil. **Solution:** Grow the desired microbes in a laboratory, and add them into the polluted area.
- **Problem:** There is not enough oxygen in the water for all the microbes. **Solution:** Pump in more oxygen to help them work.

Who would have imagined that a partnership between people and microbes would be the best way to clean up oil spills?

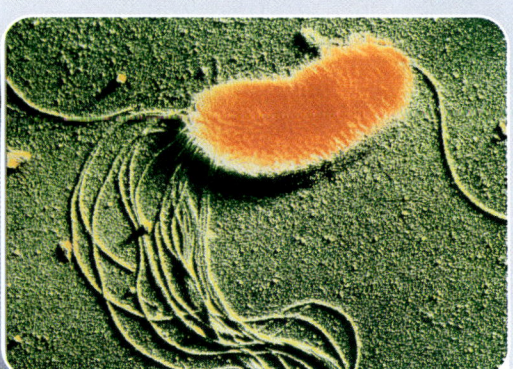

Above is the oil eating microbe *Pseudomonas fluorescens,* magnified 17,300 times. Millions of microbes like this swim in the water layer that surrounds soil particles. They digest oil clinging to the particles.

This otter swam through a spill and was covered in black, sticky oil. Animals who try to clean their fur will swallow the oil, which is poisonous.

EXPLORE

1. **COLLECT DATA** Go to the EPA Web site to learn how the agency uses microbes to clean up different types of pollution. Look under the word *bioremediation,* which means "the correction of a problem through biological means."

2. **CHALLENGE** Do research on bioremediation and find out whether there are any drawbacks to using microbes to clean up pollution.

 **RESOURCE CENTER** CLASSZONE.COM Read about microbes that eat pollutants for lunch.

KEY CONCEPT

22.2 Resources can be conserved and recycled.

◀ **BEFORE, you learned**
- Natural resources are either renewable or nonrenewable
- Fossil fuels are used to supply most of society's energy and products, but at a cost to the environment

▶ **NOW, you will learn**
- How conservation can help people to reduce waste and reuse natural resources
- How recycling can help people to recover and extend natural resources

VOCABULARY
conservation p. 761
recycling p. 762

EXPLORE Energy Use

What is your EQ (energy quotient)?

PROCEDURE

 Think about the electrical appliances you use every day at home (TV, computer, room lights, microwave, hair curler, hair dryer). Draw a usage chart like the one in the photo.

② Estimate the number of hours you use each item every day. Add up all the hours in each column.

③ Multiply the total of each column by 2.5 kilowatts. This is your energy quotient.

MATERIALS
- paper
- pen or pencil
- calculator

WHAT DO YOU THINK?
- Which item(s) do you use the most? How much of the use is necessary?
- What ways can you think of to conserve electricity each day?

Conservation involves reducing waste and reusing natural resources.

In the 1960s, each person in the United States produced 1.2 kilograms (2.7 lb) of trash a day. Today, that number has doubled. All together, the nation's households produce nearly 180 million tons of trash each year! Over half of this amount is buried in landfills.

Conservation programs can be used to extend natural resources, to protect human health, and to slow the growing mountain of trash. Read on to find out how much your efforts count.

NOTE TAKING
You might want to take main idea and details notes as you read this section.

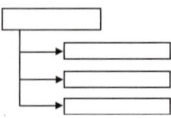

Conservation means protecting, restoring, and managing natural resources so that they last as long as possible. Conserving resources can also reduce the amount of pollution released into the air, water, and soil. There are two ways every person can help: reducing and reusing.

Reduce You can reduce waste at the source, whether the source is a local retail store or your own home. Here are a few suggestions:

- When choosing between two similar products, choose the one with less packaging. Product packaging is a major source of paper and plastic waste.
- When brushing your teeth or washing your face, turn the water off until you are ready to rinse. You can save 8 to 23 liters (2 to 6 gal.) of water a day, or 2920 to 8395 liters (730 to 2190 gal.) per year.
- When eating in a restaurant or cafeteria, use only the napkins and ketchup and mustard packets that you really need. The less you throw away, the less garbage will be buried in a landfill.
- Where possible, use energy-efficient light bulbs in your home. Turn off lights and appliances when you are not using them.

Reuse Many products can be used more than once. Reusable products and containers conserve materials and resources. Here are some things that you can do:

- Refill plastic water bottles instead of buying new bottles.
- Donate old clothes and other items instead of throwing them away.
- Rinse and reuse plastic sandwich and storage bags.
- Cut the top off a half-gallon container to make a watering can.

VOCABULARY
Add a four-square diagram for the term *conservation* in your notebook.

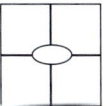

Reducing Waste

You can reduce paper and plastic waste by choosing products with the least packaging.

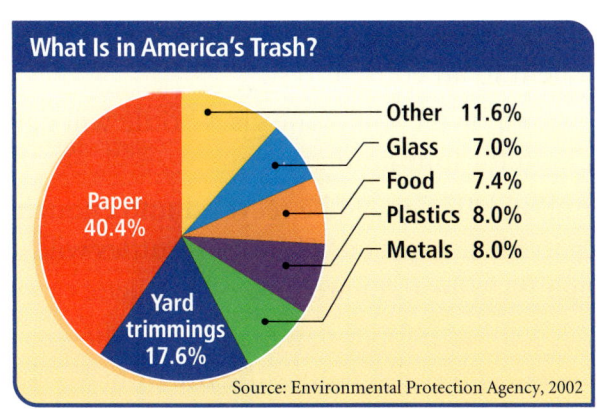

What Is in America's Trash?
- Paper 40.4%
- Yard trimmings 17.6%
- Other 11.6%
- Glass 7.0%
- Food 7.4%
- Plastics 8.0%
- Metals 8.0%

Source: Environmental Protection Agency, 2002

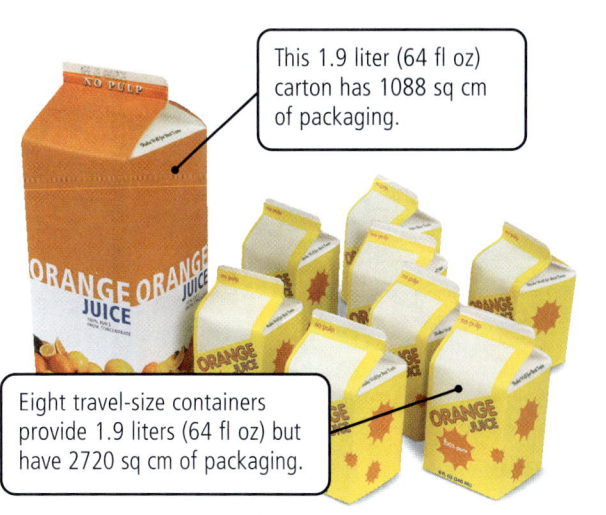

This 1.9 liter (64 fl oz) carton has 1088 sq cm of packaging.

Eight travel-size containers provide 1.9 liters (64 fl oz) but have 2720 sq cm of packaging.

INVESTIGATE Conservation

How can you tell which bulb wastes less energy?

The more heat a light bulb gives off, the more energy it wastes. Use what you know about how to measure the temperature of an object to design an experiment that confirms which type of light bulb wastes less energy.

DESIGN YOUR OWN EXPERIMENT

PROCEDURE

1. Figure out how you are going to test which light bulb—incandescent or fluorescent—wastes less energy.
2. Write up your procedure.
3. Conduct your experiment and record your results.

WHAT DO YOU THINK?

- What were the variables in your experiment?
- What were the results of your experiment?
- How does your experiment demonstrate which light bulb is less wasteful?

SKILL FOCUS
Designing experiments

MATERIALS
- 2 table lamps
- incandescent light bulb
- fluorescent light bulb
- 2 thermometers
- pen or pencil

Recycling involves recovering and extending natural resources.

Did you know that recycling one aluminum can saves enough energy to run a television set for three hours? **Recycling** involves recovering materials that people usually throw away. Some common materials you can recycle are glass, aluminum cans, certain plastics, paper, scrap iron, and such metals as gold, copper, and silver. Here are a few statistics that might encourage you to recycle:

- Recycling 90 percent of the newspapers printed in the United States on just one Sunday would save 500,000 trees, equivalent to an entire forest.
- The energy saved by recycling one glass bottle will light a 100-watt bulb for four hours.
- Five 2-liter plastic bottles can be recycled into enough plastic fiber to fill a ski jacket. Thirty-six bottles will make enough fiber for a square yard of synthetic carpet.
- If you recycled all household newspapers, cardboard, glass, and metal, you could reduce the use of fossil fuels. It takes less energy to make products from recycled materials than to make new products.

With every item you recycle, you help to recover and extend limited resources.

Recycled: 500 kilograms (1,102 lb) of cans, glass, plastic, and paper

Buried in landfill: 2500 kilograms (5,512 lb) of garbage

The average family of four generates about 3,000 kilograms (6614 lb) of trash per year. Recycling is catching on, but there is still a long way to go.

It is important to remember that not every item can be recycled or reused. In the photograph above, for instance, only about one-fifth of the family's trash is being recycled. Even some types of plastic and glass items must be thrown away because they cannot be recovered. All the trash in the family's plastic bags will be buried in landfills. You can see why it is important to recycle the items you can and to avoid using items that cannot be recycled.

Recycling is only part of the solution to our resource problems. It takes time, energy, and money to collect waste materials, sort them, remove what can be used, and form new objects. Even with these limitations, however, recycling can help extend available resources and protect human health and the environment.

 What are some of the benefits and drawbacks of recycling?

22.2 Review

KEY CONCEPTS

1. Give examples of ways people can reduce waste and conserve natural resources.
2. Explain how recycling can help people recover and extend natural resources.
3. What are some of the limitations of conservation and recycling programs?

CRITICAL THINKING

4. **Evaluate** How can conserving or recycling materials help protect the environment?
5. **Calculate** Your city pays $115 per ton to bury an average of 13 tons of garbage a month in a landfill. A recycling program could reduce that number to 8 tons a month. How much would the city save in landfill fees per month? per year?

CHALLENGE

6. **Synthesize** Work with a group of classmates to list some of the ways in which you could conserve and recycle resources in your home and at school. Create a graphic—such as a poster or advertisement—to present your ideas to the rest of the class.

Chapter 22: **Natural Resources** 763

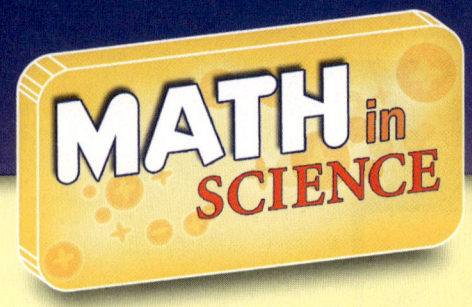

MATH in SCIENCE

SKILL: COMPARING DECIMALS

Gas Mileage

An automobile engineer ran tests on new cars to determine their gas mileage in miles per gallon. Her results were in decimals. You can compare two decimals by looking at their place values to determine which is greater.

MATH TUTORIAL
CLASSZONE.COM
Click on Math Tutorial for more help with comparing decimals.

Steps for comparing decimals

(1) Write the decimals in a column, lining up the decimal points.

(2) If necessary, write zeros to the right of one decimal so that both decimals have the same number of decimal places.

(3) Compare the place values from left to right.

Examples

Example A
For two mid-size sedans, she calculated the following mileages:

The tens digits are the same.
The ones digits are the same.

Car A: 28.**4**50 mi/gal
Car B: 28.**5**02 mi/gal

The tenths digits are different: 5 > 4.

ANSWER:
28.450 mi/gal < 28.502 mi/gal

Example B
For two sport utility vehicles (SUVs), she calculated the following mileages:

The tens digits are the same.
The ones digits are the same.

SUV A: 12.9**4** mi/gal
SUV B: 12.9**0** mi/gal

The tenths digits are the same.
The hundredths digits are different: 4 > 0.

ANSWER:
12.94 mi/gal > 12.90 mi/gal

Copy each statement and complete it with <, >, or =.

1. 34.75 mi/gal ___ 34.56 mi/gal
2. 50.5 mi/gal ___ 50.50 mi/gal
3. 52.309 mi/gal ___ 52.311 mi/gal
4. 26.115 mi/gal ___ 26.106 mi/gal
5. 41.75 mi/gal ___ 41.750 mi/gal

CHALLENGE Find a value of n that makes the following statement true:

38.0894 mi/gal > n > 38.08925 mi/gal

KEY CONCEPT
22.3 Energy comes from other natural resources.

◁ **BEFORE, you learned**
- Conservation helps people reduce waste and reuse natural resources
- Recycling helps people recover and extend natural resources

▷ **NOW, you will learn**
- About the benefits and costs of nuclear power
- How renewable resources are used to generate energy

VOCABULARY
nuclear fission p. 765
hydroelectric energy p. 768
solar cell p. 769
geothermal energy p. 770
biomass p. 772
hydrogen fuel cell p. 772

EXPLORE Nuclear Energy

How can you model splitting atoms?

PROCEDURE

1. Work in a small group for this activity. Draw a large circle on a piece of paper. Set the paper on the floor or on a countertop.

2. Put a handful of marbles in the circle (see the photograph). Imagine the circle is an atom and the marbles are particles in its nucleus.

3. Take turns shooting one marble into the others. Put the marbles back in the circle after each shot. Record your observations.

MATERIALS
- marbles
- large piece of paper
- pen or marker

WHAT DO YOU THINK?
- How many marbles were moved by each shot?
- What does this activity suggest will happen when the center of an atom is struck?

NOTE TAKING
As you read this section, pick a note-taking strategy that will help you list the benefits and limits of each type of energy source.

Nuclear power is used to produce electricity.

Fossil fuels are the most commonly used sources of energy, but they are not the only ones. The United States and many other countries use nuclear power to produce electricity. In the United States, nuclear power plants generate about 10 percent of the total energy used.

You learned that in fossil fuel power plants, water is boiled to make steam that turns a turbine, which drives a generator. In a nuclear power plant, the same process happens. However, the source of energy used to heat the water is nuclear fission. In the process of **nuclear fission,** the nucleus of a radioactive atom is split, forming lighter elements and releasing a huge amount of energy.

Chapter 22: **Natural Resources** 765

A uranium nucleus splits, forming lighter elements and releasing neutrons and a great deal of energy.

Nuclear power plants use uranium atoms as fuel. When a uranium nucleus splits, it forms two smaller nuclei. It also releases two or three neutrons and a large amount of energy in the form of light and heat. The neutrons split other uranium nuclei in a process called a chain reaction. This process is similar to shooting one marble into a group of marbles. Every marble that is hit will strike others nearby.

The power-plant diagram below shows the reactor vessel where the chain reaction takes place. Control rods are used to limit the reaction to provide a safe amount of energy. The chain reaction creates enough heat to produce steam in the reactor vessel. The steam heats a coiled pipe, which is used to boil water in the heat exchanger.

Steam from the exchanger turns the turbines, which drive the generators that produce electricity. The steam condenses into water and is pumped back into the heat exchanger. Water from the cooling tower keeps the equipment from overheating. As you can see, nuclear power plants require an abundant water supply to produce steam and to stay cool.

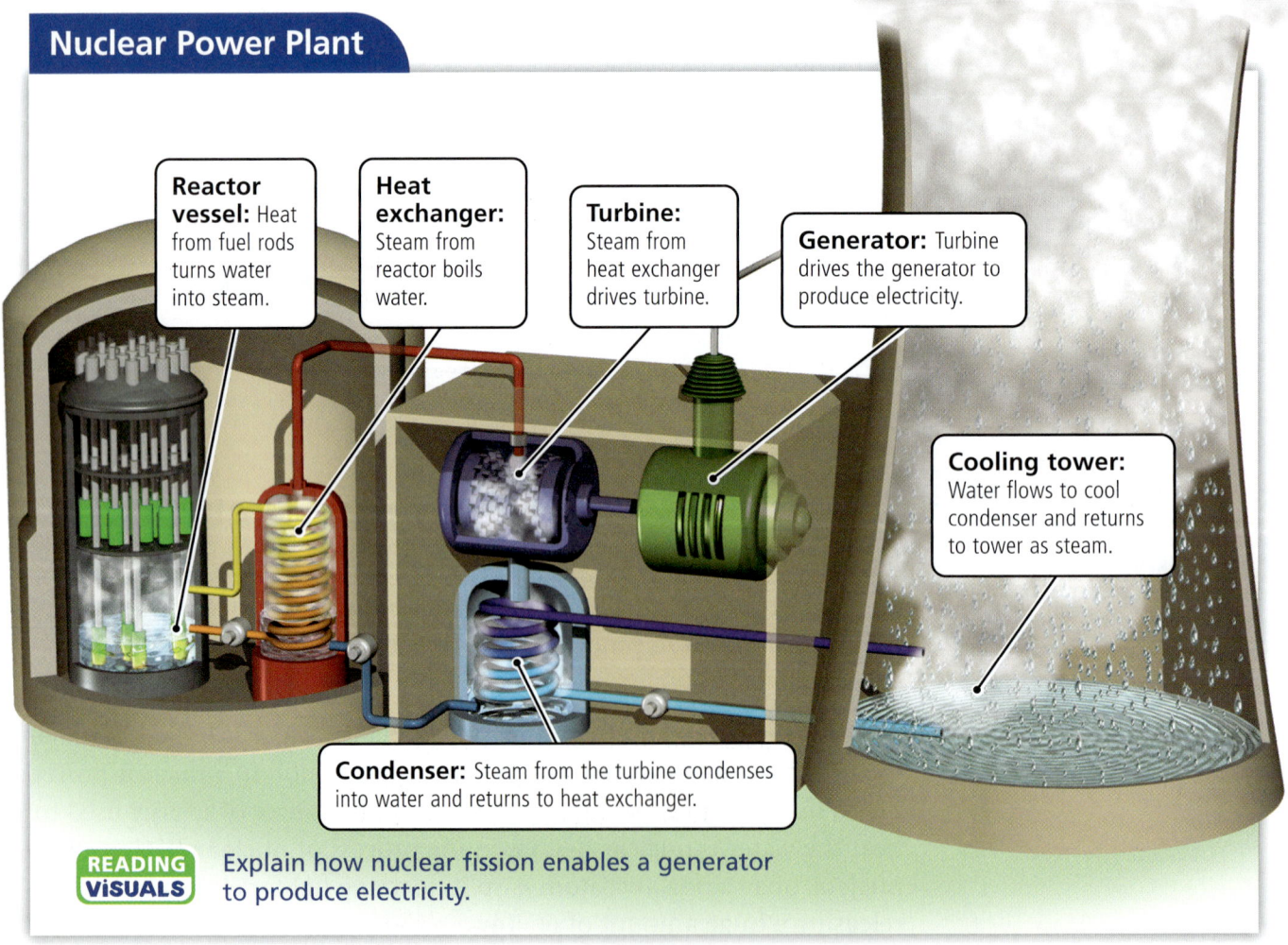

Nuclear Power Plant

Reactor vessel: Heat from fuel rods turns water into steam.

Heat exchanger: Steam from reactor boils water.

Turbine: Steam from heat exchanger drives turbine.

Generator: Turbine drives the generator to produce electricity.

Cooling tower: Water flows to cool condenser and returns to tower as steam.

Condenser: Steam from the turbine condenses into water and returns to heat exchanger.

READING VISUALS Explain how nuclear fission enables a generator to produce electricity.

766 Unit 5: **The Changing Earth**

Splitting just one atom of uranium releases 20 million times more energy than does burning one molecule of natural gas. However, nuclear fission also produces radioactive waste. Radioactivity is a form of energy that can cause death and disease if living things are exposed to it long enough. Nuclear waste from a power plant will remain radioactive for thousands of years. Countries that use nuclear energy face the challenge of storing this waste safely. The storage sites must keep any radioactivity from escaping until the waste material becomes harmless.

A nuclear power plant usually has three main sections: reactor buildings, turbine buildings, and cooling towers.

 Explain how fission is used to generate energy.

Explore how a nuclear power plant produces energy.

Renewable resources are used to produce electricity and fuel.

Moving water, wind, Earth's internal heat, sunlight, living matter, and hydrogen are all sources of renewable energy. Unlike fossil fuels, many of these sources of energy are in unlimited supply. They usually produce electricity or fuel with little or no pollution. Using these clean energy sources helps preserve the environment and protect human health.

So far, however, these resources cannot produce enough energy to pay for the cost of developing them on a large scale. As a result, renewable resources provide only a small percentage of the energy used in the world. In the United States, only about 6 percent of the total energy used comes from these resources.

Scientists and engineers must improve the necessary technologies before renewable resources can supply clean energy to more of the world's people. Imagine if everyone's car ran on hydrogen and produced only water as a byproduct. Or think of solar panels generating enough electricity to light a major city. These visions could come true in your lifetime.

 What makes renewable resources attractive as energy sources?

Chapter 22: **Natural Resources** 767

Hydroelectric Energy

Hydroelectric energy is electricity produced by moving water. If you have ever stood near a waterfall or even just turned on a faucet, you have felt the force of moving water. People can use flowing water to generate electricity.

Learn more about the benefits and costs of renewable energy resources.

In most cases, a dam is built across a large river, blocking the river's flow and creating an artificial lake, or reservoir. As the illustration below shows, water from the lake enters the dam through intake gates and flows down a tunnel. The fast flowing water turns turbines that drive generators, which produce electricity. Because hydroelectric power does not burn any fuel, it produces no pollution. Dams in the United States generate enough electricity to save 500 million barrels of oil a year.

However, building dams poses problems for the environment. By flooding land to create reservoirs, dams destroy wildlife habitats. In some rivers, such as the Snake and Columbia rivers in the United States, dams interfere with the annual migration of salmon and other fish. Also, areas near the end of the river may receive less water than before, making it harder to raise crops and livestock.

Areas with large rivers can use their power to produce electricity. The dam in the photo was built on the Yukon River in Alaska.

Hydroelectric Dam

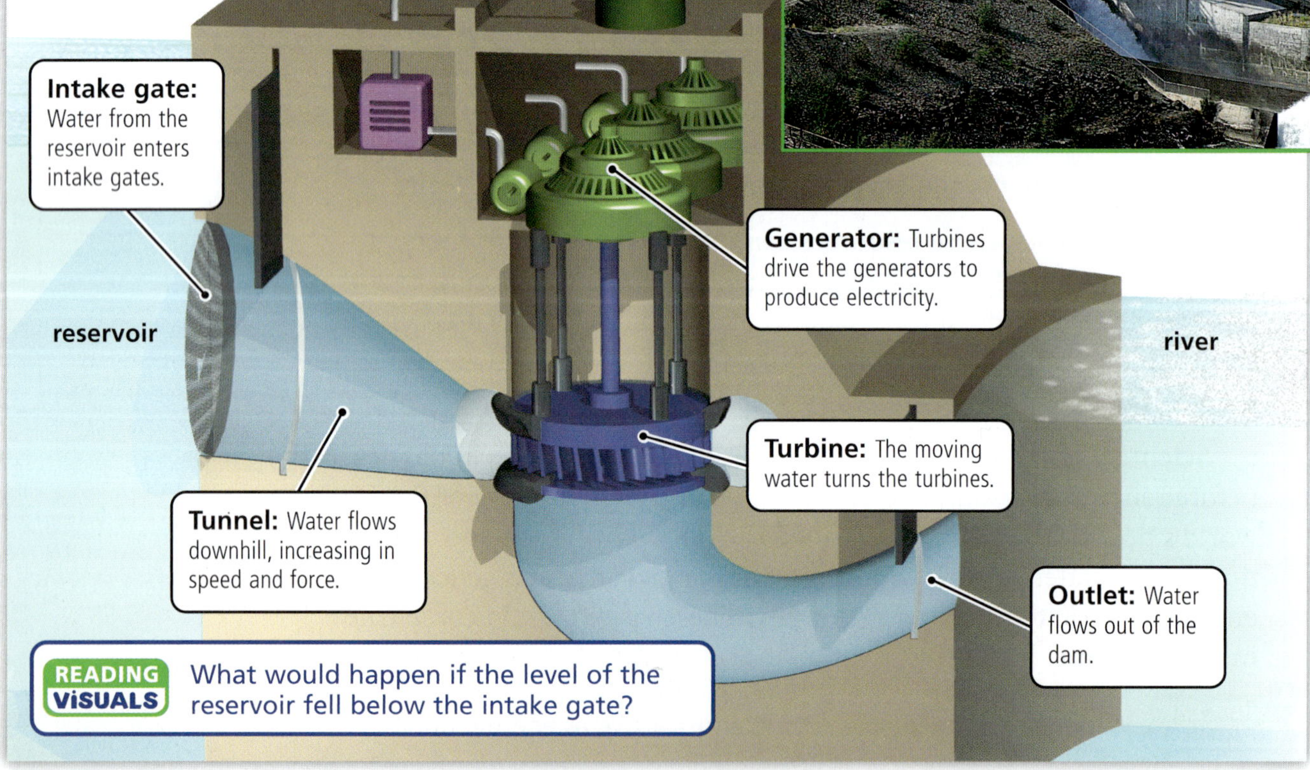

Intake gate: Water from the reservoir enters intake gates.

Generator: Turbines drive the generators to produce electricity.

Turbine: The moving water turns the turbines.

Tunnel: Water flows downhill, increasing in speed and force.

Outlet: Water flows out of the dam.

reservoir

river

READING VISUALS What would happen if the level of the reservoir fell below the intake gate?

768 Unit 5: **The Changing Earth**

Solar Energy

Only a small fraction of the sun's energy falls on Earth. Yet even this amount is huge. Every day enough energy from the sun strikes the United States to supply all the nation's energy needs for one and a half years. The problem is how to use this abundant resource to produce electricity.

In an effort to solve the problem, scientists developed solar cells. A **solar cell** is a specially constructed sandwich of silicon and other materials that converts light energy to electricity. As shown in the diagram below, when sunlight strikes the cell, electrons move from the lower to the upper layer, producing an electric current. Individual solar cells can power small appliances, such as calculators and lights.

Solar cells can be wired together in solar panels, which provide heat and electricity for homes and businesses. Solar panels are also used to power some spacecraft and space stations once they are in orbit. To meet the energy needs of some cities, hundreds or even thousands of solar panels are built into large structures called arrays. Many western cities like Barstow, California, receive part of their electricity from solar arrays.

Sunlight is an unlimited source of clean energy. But current methods of collecting sunlight are expensive and somewhat inefficient. As solar technology improves, sunlight is likely to become an important energy source for the world.

VOCABULARY
Add a four-square diagram for the term *solar cell* in your notebook.

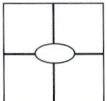

READING TIP
Array refers to an arrangement of objects in rows and columns.

CHECK YOUR READING How can people use sunlight to produce electricity?

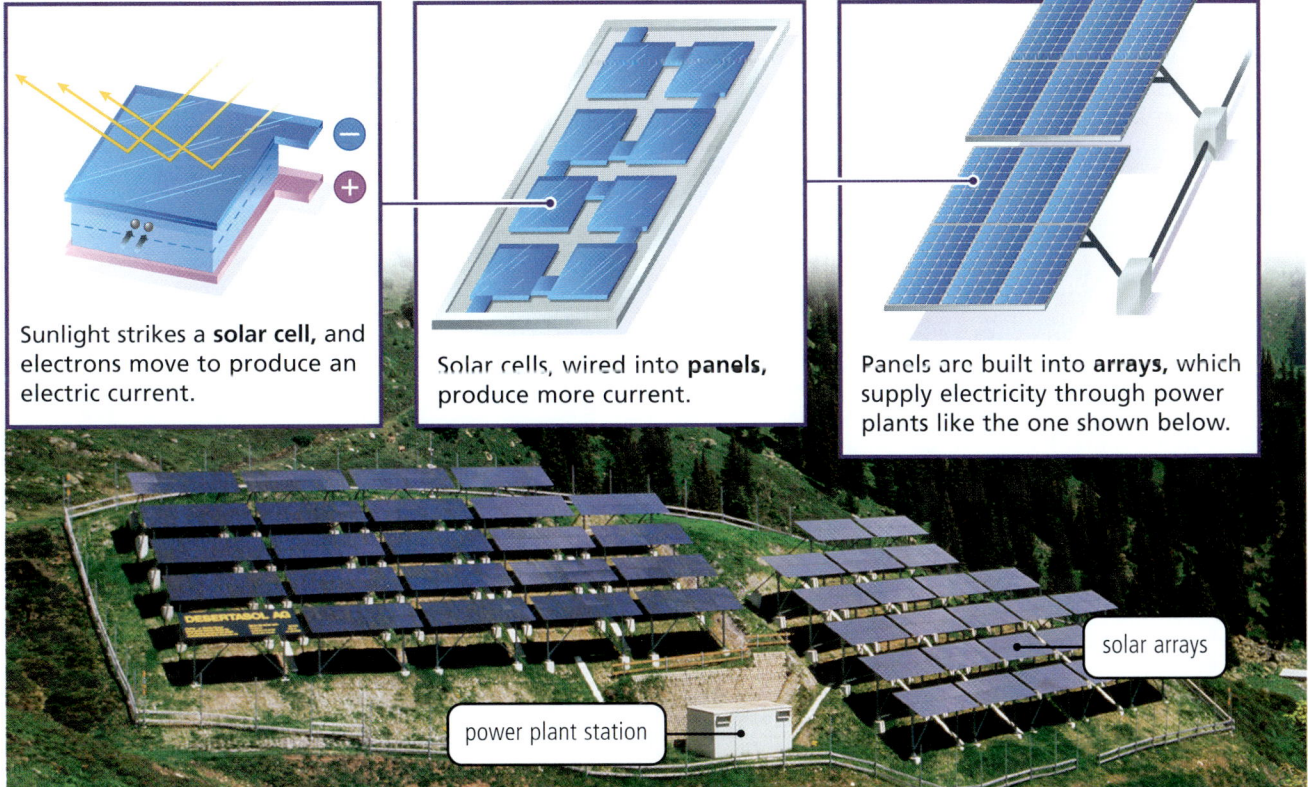

Sunlight strikes a **solar cell,** and electrons move to produce an electric current.

Solar cells, wired into **panels,** produce more current.

Panels are built into **arrays,** which supply electricity through power plants like the one shown below.

solar arrays

power plant station

Chapter 22: **Natural Resources** 769

Geothermal Energy

READING TIP
Geothermal combines the Greek prefix *geo-*, meaning "earth," and the Greek word *thermē*, meaning "heat."

Imagine tapping into Earth's heat to obtain electricity for your home. In some places, that is exactly what people do. They use **geothermal energy,** or energy produced by heat within Earth's crust.

Geothermal energy comes from underground water that is heated by hot rock. The illustration below shows how hot water is piped from a well into a power plant. This superheated water enters a flash tank and produces enough steam to run turbines, which power generators. Excess water is then pumped back into the ground. Some plants also pipe hot water into homes and businesses for heating.

In the United States, geothermal energy provides electricity for nearly 3.5 million homes. Other major geothermal power plants are in New Zealand and Iceland.

Geothermal energy is clean and renewable. So far, its use is limited to areas where hot water is fairly close to the surface. However, some companies are experimenting with pumping cold water into underground areas of hot rock found in all parts of Earth's crust. The rock heats the water, which is then pumped back to the surface and used

In Iceland, geothermal power plants like the one in the photograph supply nearly all of the country's electricity.

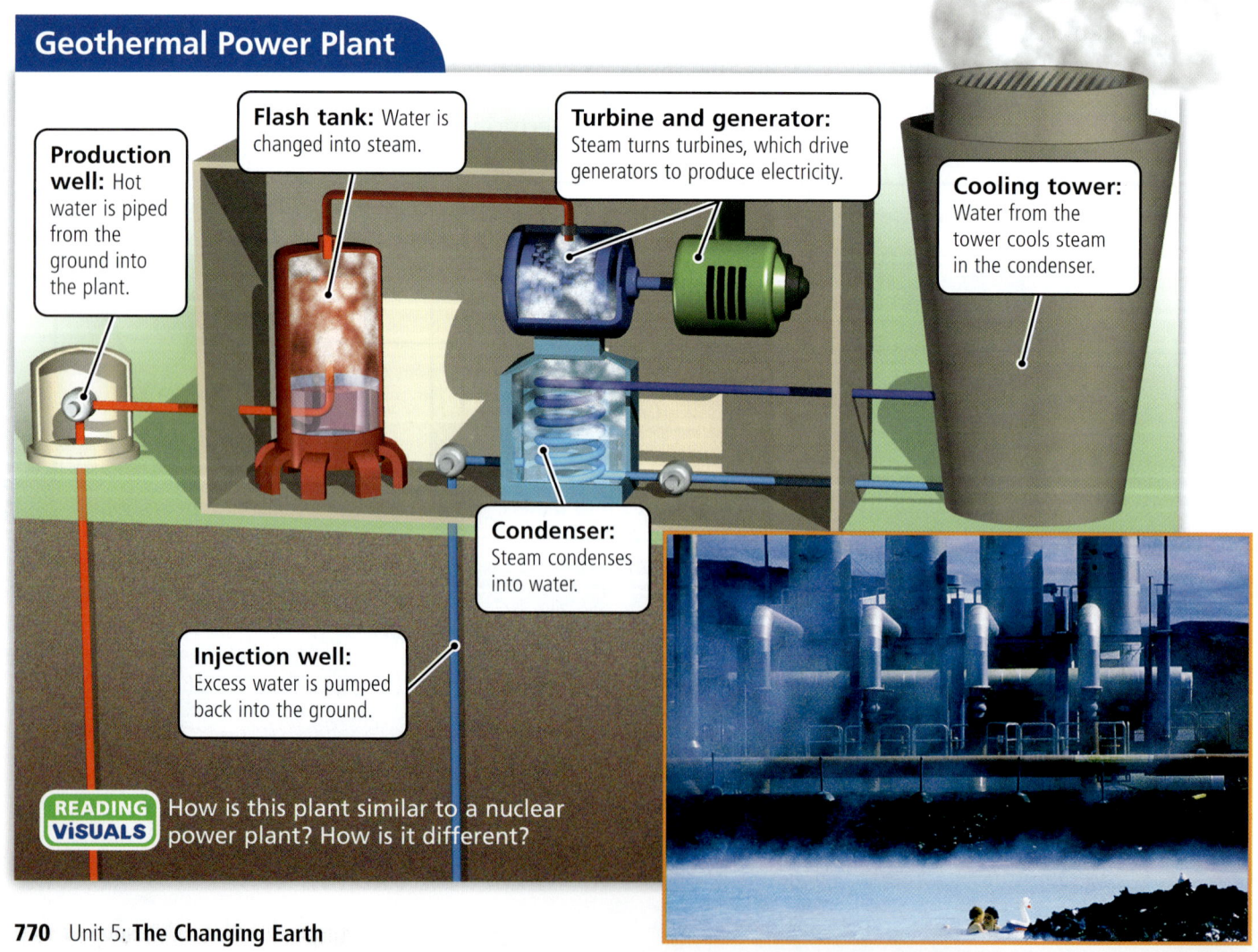

Geothermal Power Plant

Production well: Hot water is piped from the ground into the plant.

Flash tank: Water is changed into steam.

Turbine and generator: Steam turns turbines, which drive generators to produce electricity.

Cooling tower: Water from the tower cools steam in the condenser.

Condenser: Steam condenses into water.

Injection well: Excess water is pumped back into the ground.

READING VISUALS How is this plant similar to a nuclear power plant? How is it different?

to generate electricity. This new technique may allow more countries to make use of geothermal energy.

 What is the source of geothermal energy?

Wind Energy

For thousands of years, people have captured the tremendous energy of wind to move ships, grind grain, and pump water from underground. Today, people also use wind energy—from the force of moving air—to generate electricity.

The modern windmill is made of metal and plastic and can stand as tall as a 40-story building. The blades act as a turbine, turning a set of gears that drives the generator. The amount of electricity a windmill produces depends on the speed and angle of the wind across its blades. The faster the blades turn, the more power the windmill produces.

REMINDER
The generator is the part that produces the electric current, whether it is driven by turbines or gears.

To supply electricity to an area, hundreds of windmills are built on a "wind farm." Wind farms, like the one in the photograph below, are already producing electricity in California, Hawaii, New Hampshire, and several other states. Other countries, such as Denmark and Germany, also use wind farms to supply electricity to some of their cities.

Although wind energy is clean and renewable, it has certain drawbacks. It depends on steady, strong winds blowing most of the time, which are found only in a few places. Wind farms take up a great deal of land, and the turning blades can be noisy. There is also a limit to how much power each windmill can produce. However, in the future, wind farms may become more productive and more widely used.

 What factor determines how much electricity a windmill produces?

The blades turn the gears, which drive the generator to produce electricity. The controller points the windmill's head into the wind to keep the blades turning rapidly.

Biomass Energy

Biomass is organic matter, such as plant and animal waste, that can be used as fuel. The U.S. Department of Energy works with state and local groups to find ways of converting biomass materials into energy sources.

Each year biomass power stations in the United States burn about 60 million tons of wood and other plant material to generate 37 billion kilowatt hours of electricity. That is more electricity than the state of Colorado uses in an entire year. Small biomass stations are used in rural areas to supply power to farms and towns. Fast-growing trees, grasses, and other crops can be planted to supply a renewable energy source that is cheaper than fossil fuels.

Some plant and animal waste can be converted into liquid fuels. The sugar and starch in corn and potatoes, for example, are made into a liquid fuel called ethanol. Ethanol can be added to gasoline to form gasohol. This fuel can power small cars, farm machinery, and buses. A liquid fuel made from animal waste is used for heating and cooking in many rural areas around the world.

This wood-burning biomass plant sends electrical energy at a rate of 21 million watts to the San Francisco Bay area. Wood waste products are collected from farms and industries as fuel for the plant.

Although biomass is a renewable resource, certain problems limit its use. Burning wood and crops can release as much carbon dioxide into the air as burning fossil fuels does. Biomass crops take up land that could be used to raise food. Also, plant fuels such as ethanol are still too expensive to produce on a large scale. For now, biomass materials provide only a small part of the world's energy.

 **CHECK YOUR READING** What are the advantages and disadvantages of biomass fuels?

Hydrogen Fuel Cells

Watch a hydrogen fuel cell in action.

Scientists are also exploring the use of hydrogen gas as a renewable energy source. Hydrogen is the simplest atom, made up of one proton—the nucleus—and one electron. Scientists have found ways to separate hydrogen from water and from fossil fuels. It is a flammable gas and must be handled with care

Hydrogen is used in a **hydrogen fuel cell,** a device that produces electricity by separating hydrogen into protons and electrons. The diagram on page 773 shows hydrogen fuel entering on one side of the cell while oxygen from the air enters on the other side. Once in the cell, electrons flow out of the cell through wires, forming an electric current that powers the motor. The protons pass through a membrane and combine with oxygen to form water as a byproduct.

Hydrogen fuel cells are used to supply electrical energy on spacecraft and space stations. Fuel-cell buses are being tested in several countries.

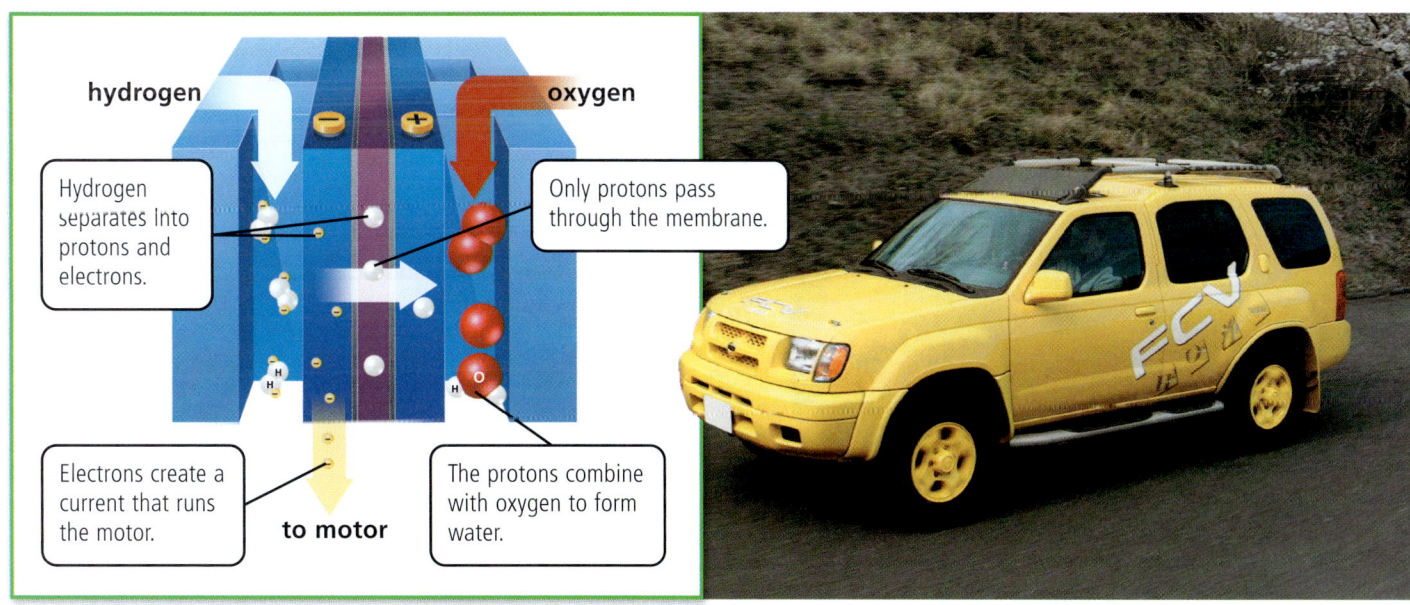

Also, some fuel-cell cars are now available to the public. Storage tanks in these vehicles carry hydrogen fuel for the cells.

Fuel-cell technology holds great promise for the future. Hydrogen is a clean source of energy, producing only water and heat as byproducts. If every vehicle in the world were powered by hydrogen, the level of air pollution would drop sharply.

However, hydrogen fuel cells are still too expensive to produce in large numbers. Separating hydrogen from water or from fossil fuels takes a great deal of energy, time, and money. Also, there are only a few fueling stations to supply cars and other vehicles that run on hydrogen. The U.S. Department of Energy is working with the automotive industry and other industries to solve these problems.

A storage tank in the back of this SUV holds hydrogen fuel. Electrical energy from fuel cells powers the motor and a backup battery.

 **CHECK YOUR READING** Why is hydrogen considered a promising alternative energy source?

22.3 Review

KEY CONCEPTS

1. List the main advantages and disadvantages of nuclear energy as a power source.
2. Describe the advantages of using sunlight, water, and Earth's heat energy to produce electrical power.
3. What are some factors that limit the use of biomass, wind, and hydrogen as energy sources?

CRITICAL THINKING

4. **Evaluate** Do you think people would use a clean, renewable fuel that cost twice as much as gasoline? Explain.
5. **Calculate** One acre of corn yields 20 gallons of ethanol. A bus gets 20 miles per gallon and travels 9000 miles in one year. How many acres of corn are needed to fuel the bus for a year?

CHALLENGE

6. **Synthesize** Review the energy sources discussed in this section. Then think of ways in which one or more of them could be used to supply electricity to a house in Florida and a house in Alaska. Which energy sources would be suitable in each environment? Describe your ideas in writing, or make sketches of the houses.

CHAPTER INVESTIGATION

Wind Power

OVERVIEW AND PURPOSE Early windmills were used mainly to pump water and grind flour. In this lab, you will use what you have learned about renewable resources to
- build a model windmill and use it to lift a small weight
- improve its performance by increasing the strength of the wind source

Problem

What effect will increasing the wind strength have on the lifting power of a model windmill?

Hypothesize

After completing step 8 of the procedure, write a hypothesis to explain what you think will happen in the next two sets of trials. Your hypothesis should take the form of an "If . . . , then . . . , because . . ." statement.

MATERIALS
- half of a file folder
- metric ruler
- quarter
- scissors
- paper punch
- brass paper fastener
- drinking straw
- pushpin
- masking tape
- small paper clip
- pint carton
- 30 cm of string
- clock or stopwatch
- small desktop fan

Procedure

1. Make a data table in your **Science Notebook,** like the one on page 775.

2. Cut a 15 cm square from a manila file folder. With a ruler, draw lines from the corners toward the center, forming an X. Where the lines cross, use a quarter to draw a circle. Cut inward along the lines from the four corners, stopping at the small circle. Punch a hole in each corner and in the center of the circle.

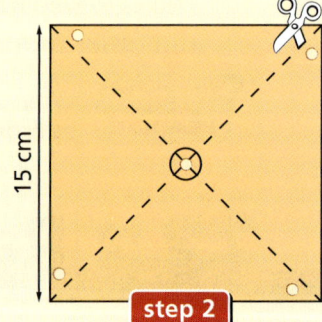
step 2

3. Bend the cardboard to align the holes. Push a brass paper fastener through the holes toward the back of the pinwheel. Do not flatten the metal strips of the fastener.

4. Use a pushpin to poke a hole through a straw, about 4 cm from the end. Then push the metal strips through the hole and flatten them at right angles to the straw. Fold the tip of the straw over and tape it to the rest of the straw.

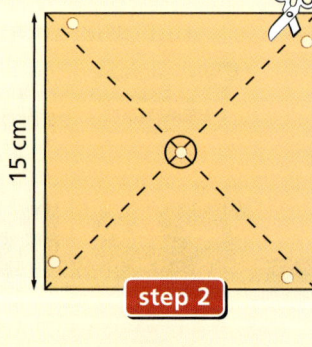
step 4

774 Unit 5: **The Changing Earth**

5. Cut the spout portion off the top of the pint carton. Punch two holes on opposite sides of the carton. Make sure the holes line up and are large enough for the straw to turn easily.

6. Slide the straw through the holes. Tape the string to the end of the straw. Tie a small paper clip (weight) to the other end of the string.

7. Test the model by blowing on the blades. Describe what happens to the weight.

step 6

8. Run three trials of the lifting power of the model windmill as you blow on the blades. Keep the amount of force you use constant. Have a classmate use a stopwatch or clock with a second hand to time the trials. Record the results in your data table. Average your results.

9. Vary the strength of the wind by using a desktop fan at different speeds to turn the windmill's blades. Remember to record your hypothesis explaining what you think will happen in the next two sets of trials.

Observe and Analyze
Write It Up

1. **MODEL** Draw a picture of the completed windmill. What happens to the weight when the blades turn?

2. **IDENTIFY VARIABLES** What method did you use to increase the wind strength? Add a sketch of this method to your picture to illustrate the experimental procedure.

3. **RECORD OBSERVATIONS** Make sure your data table is completed.

4. **COMPARE** How did the average times it took to raise the weight at different wind strengths differ?

Conclude

1. **INTERPRET** Answer the question under "problem" on page 774.

2. **ANALYZE** Did your results support your hypothesis?

3. **IDENTIFY LIMITS** What limitations or sources of error could have affected your experimental results?

4. **APPLY** Wind-powered turbines are used to generate electricity in some parts of the country. What might limit the usefulness of wind power as an energy source?

INVESTIGATE Further

CHALLENGE How you can get your model windmill to do more work? You might try different weights, or you might build a larger windmill and compare it with your original. Create a new data table. Use a bar graph to compare different weights and wind strengths. How much wind power is needed to lift the additional weight?

Wind Power

Problem

Hypothesize

Observe and Analyze

Table 1. Time to Lift Weight

Wind Force Used	Trial Number	Time (sec)
Student powered	1	
	2	
	3	
	Average	
Fan on low speed	1	
	2	
	3	
	Average	
Fan on high speed	1	
	2	
	3	
	Average	

Conclude

Chapter 22: **Natural Resources** 775

Chapter Review

the BIG idea

Society depends on natural resources for energy and materials.

CONTENT REVIEW
CLASSZONE.COM

KEY CONCEPTS SUMMARY

1 Natural resources support human activity.

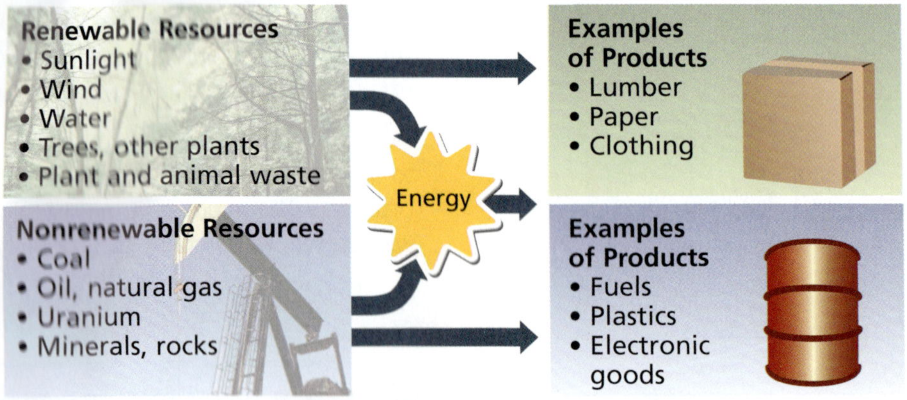

Renewable Resources
- Sunlight
- Wind
- Water
- Trees, other plants
- Plant and animal waste

→ Energy →

Examples of Products
- Lumber
- Paper
- Clothing

Nonrenewable Resources
- Coal
- Oil, natural gas
- Uranium
- Minerals, rocks

Examples of Products
- Fuels
- Plastics
- Electronic goods

VOCABULARY
natural resource p. 751
renewable resource p. 752
nonrenewable resource p. 752
fossil fuel p. 754

2 Resources can be conserved and recycled.

People can **conserve** natural resources by reducing waste at the source and reusing products.

Recycling helps people recover materials, reduce the use of fossil fuels, and protect the environment and human health.

VOCABULARY
conservation p. 761
recycling p. 762

3 Energy comes from other natural resources.

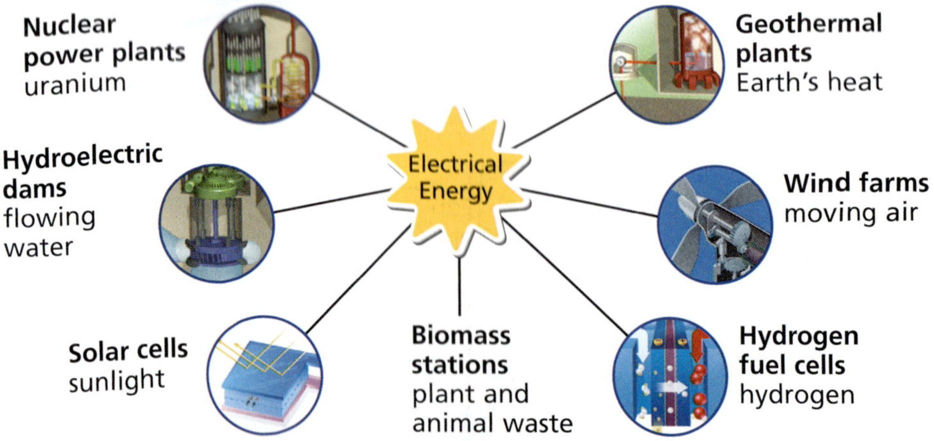

Nuclear power plants uranium

Hydroelectric dams flowing water

Solar cells sunlight

Biomass stations plant and animal waste

Geothermal plants Earth's heat

Wind farms moving air

Hydrogen fuel cells hydrogen

Electrical Energy

VOCABULARY
nuclear fission p. 765
hydroelectric energy p. 768
solar cell p. 769
geothermal energy p. 770
biomass p. 772
hydrogen fuel cell p. 772

776 Unit 5: The Changing Earth

Reviewing Vocabulary

Copy the chart below, and write each word's definition. Use the meaning of the underlined word part to help you.

Word	Meaning of Part	Definition
1. Natural resource	to rise again	
2. Renewable resource	to refresh	
3. Nonrenewable resource	not to refresh	
4. Fossil fuel	material that burns	
5. Nuclear energy	nut or kernel	
6. Geothermal energy	heat	

Reviewing Key Concepts

Multiple Choice *Choose the letter of the best answer.*

7. What makes wind a renewable resource?
   a. no pollution
   b. varied speeds
   c. no waste products
   d. unlimited supply

8. Which of the following is a nonrenewable resource?
   a. trees
   b. oil
   c. sunlight
   d. geothermal energy

9. Fossil fuels provide most of the energy used in the United States because they
   a. are found everywhere in the world
   b. have no harmful byproducts
   c. are easy to transport and burn
   d. can be quickly replaced in nature

10. Which part of a power plant actually produces electricity?
    a. boiler
    b. generator
    c. turbine
    d. power lines

11. Which of the following is not a problem associated with the use of fossil fuels?
    a. air pollution
    b. explosions
    c. limited supply
    d. radiation

12. Which category of products is the most dependent on oil?
    a. pottery
    b. coins
    c. plastics
    d. paper

13. How do nuclear power plants generate the heat energy to turn water into steam?
    a. by drawing hot water from Earth's crust
    b. by producing an electric current
    c. by turning a turbine
    d. by splitting uranium atoms

14. Hydroelectric energy is produced by using the force of
    a. wind
    b. sunlight
    c. moving water
    d. living matter

15. Solar cells produce which of the following?
    a. heat energy
    b. steam
    c. radiation
    d. electricity

16. What limits the use of biomass liquid fuels?
    a. not enough plant material
    b. too expensive to mass-produce
    c. not enough energy generated
    d. too many harmful byproducts

17. Hydrogen fuel cells produce electricity when
    a. electrons from hydrogen leave the cell
    b. hydrogen is separated from fossil fuels
    c. protons from hydrogen combine with oxygen
    d. hydrogen fuel flows into the cell

Short Answer *Write a few sentences to answer each question.*

18. Why is it important to find renewable sources of energy?

19. Why is conservation of natural resources important?

20. How can recycling help reduce the use of fossil fuels?

Chapter 22: **Natural Resources** 777

Thinking Critically

Use the circle graphs below to answer the following questions.

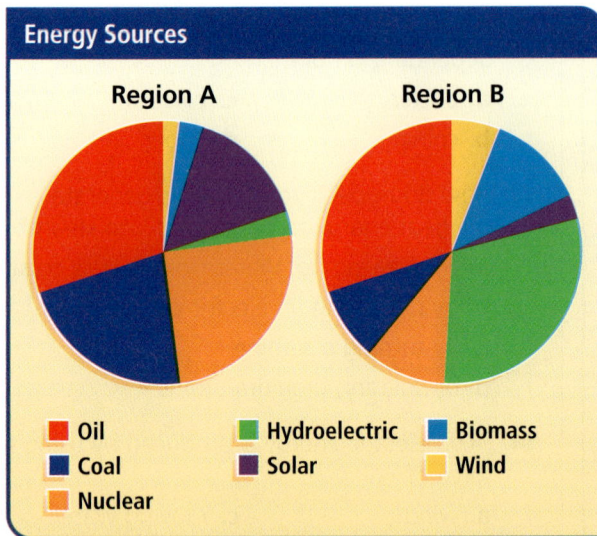

Energy Sources
- Oil
- Coal
- Nuclear
- Hydroelectric
- Solar
- Biomass
- Wind

21. INTERPRET Which colors represent nonrenewable resources and which ones represent renewable resources?

22. CALCULATE Fossil fuels and nuclear energy together represent about what percentage of the total energy resources in region A? in region B?

23. PREDICT If the price of nonrenewable energy sources rises sharply, which region is likely to be affected more? Why?

24. DRAW CONCLUSIONS What might be one reason that region A uses a greater percentage of fossil fuels and nuclear energy than region B does?

25. INFER Look at the renewable energy sources used in each region. What can you infer about the climate in region A compared with the climate in region B?

26. IDENTIFY CAUSES Why might region B use so much more hydroelectric energy?

27. SYNTHESIZE Region C gets half of its electrical energy from fossil fuels. The region has only 100 days of clear sunlight a year but has abundant plant crops and strong, steady winds. Draw a circle graph for region C, showing the percentage of fossil fuels and the percentage of each renewable energy source the region might use. Explain your choices.

Charting Information

Copy and fill in this chart.

Type of Energy	Produces Energy From	Byproducts
28. uranium		radioactive waste
29. fossil fuel	burning oil, coal	
30.	moving air	none
31. river		
32. sunlight		
33.	burning wood	carbon dioxide
34. hydrogen		

the BIG idea

35. APPLY Look again at the photograph on pages 748–749. Reread the question on the photograph. Now that you have finished the chapter, what would you add to or change about your answer?

36. SYNTHESIZE Imagine that you are a scientist or engineer who is developing a new energy source. What characteristics would you want your energy source to have? List your choices in order of importance, with the most important first—for instance, nonpolluting, inexpensive to mass-produce, and so on.

37. APPLY If you were in charge of your town or city, what measures would you take to conserve natural resources?

UNIT PROJECTS

Evaluate all the data, results, and information in your project folder. Prepare to present your project.

Standardized Test Practice

Analyzing a Graph

This graph shows what happens to fuels consumed for energy in the United States. Some of this energy is used and some is lost as heat. Use the graph to answer the questions below.

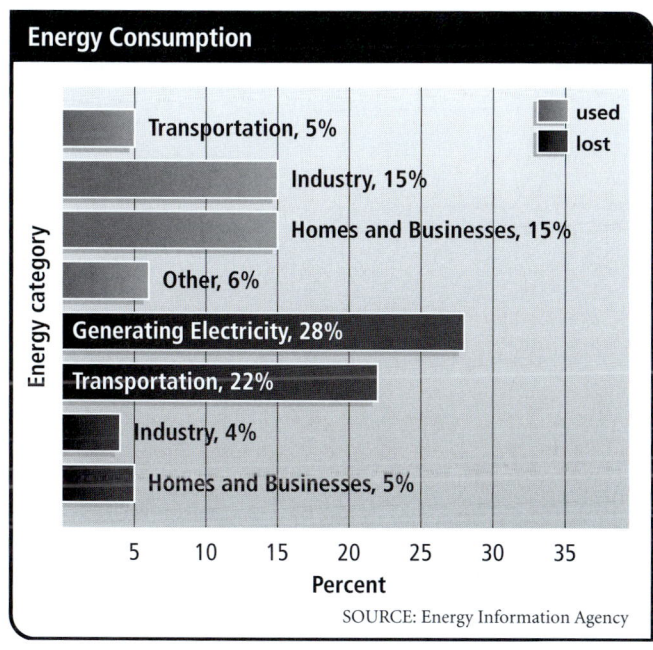

SOURCE: Energy Information Agency

1. How much energy is used for transportation and industry?
   a. 15 percent
   b. 20 percent
   c. 30 percent
   d. 35 percent

2. What is the total amount of energy used and lost in industry?
   a. 4 percent
   b. 15 percent
   c. 19 percent
   d. 28 percent

3. What is the largest category of lost energy?
   a. transportation
   b. homes and businesses
   c. generating electricity
   d. industry

4. Which category would include energy used to heat a grocery store?
   a. used in homes and businesses
   b. used in industry
   c. used in transportation
   d. used in other ways

5. If cars burned fuel more efficiently, which category would probably be smaller?
   a. used in homes and businesses
   b. used in other ways
   c. lost in transportation
   d. lost in industry

6. Which statement is true about energy used and lost in transportation?
   a. The amount lost is greater than the amount used.
   b. The amount used is greater than the amount lost.
   c. The amounts used and lost are about the same.
   d. The amounts used and lost are very low in comparison to the other categories.

Extended Response

Answer the two questions below in detail. Include some of the terms in the word box. In your answers, underline each term you use.

| reusing | recycling | conserve | extends |
| electricity | hot water | factories | |

7. Explain the difference between reusing and recycling products. How does each activity help to reduce the use of natural resources?

8. Give three or more examples of ways in which people in the United States use or rely on energy resources every day.

Chapter 22: **Natural Resources** 779

UNIT 6
Life Over Time

Contents Overview

Frontiers in Science
Life by Degrees 782

Timelines in Science
Life Unearthed 854

Chapter 23 The History of Life on Earth 786

Chapter 24 Classification of Living Things 820

Chapter 25 Population Dynamics 858

FRONTIERS in Science

Life By Degrees

What happens when Earth's climate changes? Scientists are studying how climate change has influenced the evolution of life on Earth.

SCIENTIFIC AMERICAN FRONTIERS

Learn about how climate change affected life on Earth. See the video "Noah's Snowball."

Climate and Life

Throughout its history, Earth's climate has changed many times. Often the changes are gradual. They may seem small. However, an average global temperature change of just a few degrees can have a large impact on climate. Small changes in climate then cause big changes for plants and animals.

Before there were humans to record events, Earth recorded its changes in its rocks and fossils. For example, scientists get a sense for Earth's climate at different times in the distant past by looking at fossils, the remains and traces of living things. If scientists find fossils of tropical plants in places near the arctic circle, then they may conclude that the climate in those places was different in the past.

Scientists have found that warmer climates lead to a greater diversity of organisms. One researcher examined fossils of tiny organisms called phytoplankton (FY-toh-PLANK-tuhn). During cooler climate periods, there were fewer types of phytoplankton than during warmer periods. The same is true for other organisms. Peter Wilf and Conrad Labandeira studied fossil plants. They were especially interested in the marks they found on the plants. The marks were left by plant-eating animals who bit the leaves. The warmer the climate was, the more types of plants there were—and the more kinds of animals were eating the plants.

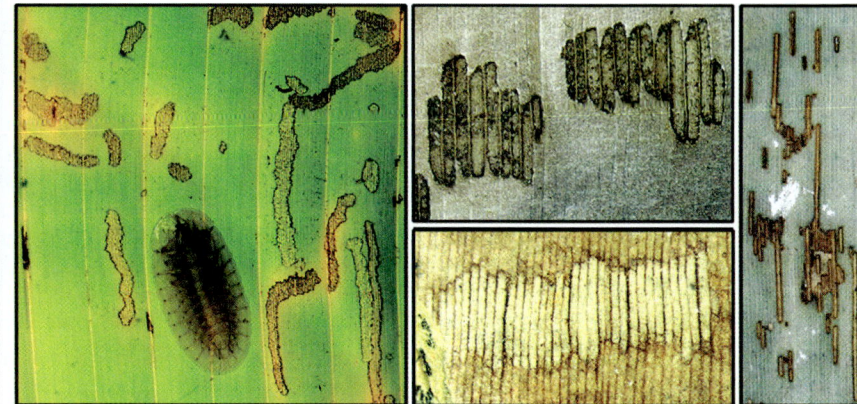

SOURCE: Images © 2000 AAAS

The chew marks of the hispine beetle larva on living ginger in Panama (left) look similar to fossilized chew marks found in Wyoming (three photos right).

Before and after photographs of the sky show that distinct bands appeared due to dust and ash from the 1991 volcanic eruption of Mt. Pinatubo.

Mass Extinction

Several times in Earth's past, many kinds of animals and plants have disappeared in a relatively short time. These events are called mass extinctions. While we don't know for sure what causes them, most scientists think climate change plays a role in mass extinctions.

The largest mass extinction in Earth's history happened at the end of the Permian (PER-mee-uhn) Period about 248 million years ago. Scientists estimate that 90–95 percent of animal species that lived in the water died out. About three quarters of the vertebrates, or animals with backbones, living on land died out too.

Turn of Events

What caused this extinction? Using fossils, scientists have concluded that Earth's climate became cooler. Material from erupting volcanoes may have blocked sunlight long enough to cool the Earth. The cool temperatures and lack of sunlight may have killed plants and animals.

Scientist Peter Ward has been studying the Permian extinction. He looked at ancient African rivers and found evidence that rivers had became clogged with soil. Plants normally holding soil in place may have been wiped out, causing the soil on the riverbanks to loosen. The plant extinction would also have led to animal extinction.

SCIENTIFIC AMERICAN FRONTIERS

View the "Noah's Snowball" segment of your Scientific American Frontiers video to learn about another theory of how climate change affected life on Earth.

IN THIS SCENE FROM THE VIDEO Fossil hunters examine evidence of early life in China.

DEEP FREEZE Can you imagine what Earth would be like if it were completely covered in ice? Geologists Paul Hoffman and Dan Schrag suggest Earth was frozen solid until about 600 million years ago. They think Earth's climate changed by just a few degrees, but it was enough to make the ice caps cover the planet. The only life that survived was bacteria that were kept warm by volcanoes. And it was the volcanoes that changed the climate again, say Hoffman and Schrag. Suddenly eruptions melted the ice. Ocean levels rose. The scientists think this change might have taken only a hundred years. Not everyone agrees with the snowball hypothesis, but it could explain why new forms of life began to appear.

What Hit Them?

Not all scientists agree about what caused the Permian extinction. If an asteroid hit Earth, it would push massive amounts of dirt and dust into the air. This could block sunlight and create a cooler climate. An increase in volcanic eruptions is another possible cause.

The most famous extinction of all took place at the end of the Cretaceous Period. The extended winter that may have followed a meteor impact caused many large land animals—including dinosaurs—to become extinct.

In a new climate some species thrive and survive. They spread out and, over time, evolve to fill empty niches or unique roles in the environment. For example, before the Cretaceous extinction, the only mammals were small. After the dinosaurs became extinct, large mammals could fill the roles of large plant-eaters and meat-eaters.

Even today, climate change continues. Earth's average temperature rose about half a degree Celsius in the twentieth century. Studying how past climate changes shaped life helps scientists predict how it may affect us in the future.

A large plant-eating mammal, *Chalicotherium grande*, roamed Asia millions of years ago.

❓ UNANSWERED Questions

Scientists have learned a lot about climate change and mass extinctions by studying fossils. There are many questions still to be answered.

- What caused changes in Earth's climate?
- What else might have caused mass extinctions?
- How might climate change affect life on Earth in the future?

UNIT PROJECTS

As you study this unit, work alone or with a group on one of the projects listed below. Use the bulleted steps to guide your project.

Museum Display

What organisms survived the Permian extinction? What organisms went extinct?

- Create a museum display using art and text.
- Use visuals to show the organisms and the modern relatives that have close connections to them.

Design a Robot

Often, scientists design robots to study dangerous or distant locations.

- Design an artificial robot that would be well-adapted to survive an event that causes a mass extinction.
- Explain why the design would help the robot remain in operation.

Species over Time

Find out more about species that have gone extinct during recorded history.

- Choose one species that is now extinct.
- Present a timeline giving a history of that species.
- Describe what some of its ancestors and surviving related organisms are.
- Describe when it was last seen. Include some of the possible reasons for why it died out.

CAREER CENTER
CLASSZONE.COM

Learn more about careers in paleontology.

CHAPTER 23
The History of Life on Earth

Living things, like Earth itself, change over time.

Key Concepts

SECTION 1 Earth has been home to living things for about 3.8 billion years.
Learn how fossils help explain the development of life on Earth.

SECTION 2 Species change over time.
Learn how species develop and change.

SECTION 3 Many types of evidence support evolution.
Learn about the evidence scientists use to support evolution.

How do scientists learn about the history of life on Earth?

Internet Preview
CLASSZONE.COM
Chapter 23 online resources: Content Review, Simulation, Visualization, three Resource Centers, Math Tutorial, Test Practice

EXPLORE the BIG idea

What Can Rocks Show About Earth's History?

Look closely at two rocks from different places or at the two rocks below. What are the characteristics of each rock? Can you see evidence of living things in one of them?

Observe and Think
How could the evidence you gathered from your observations help you describe Earth's history?

Which One of These Things Is Not Like the Others?

Observe a handful of beans. Measure the length of each bean, observe the color, and note how many seeds are in each bean.

Observe and Think
What variety do you observe in the beans?

Investigate Activity: Matching Finch Beaks

Go to **Classzone.com** to match different finch beaks with the foods they eat. Learn how each type of beak functions.

Observe and Think
Can you think of any other beak types birds may have and how they relate to the food they eat?

The Fossil Record **Code: MDL036**

Chapter 23: **History of Life** 787

CHAPTER 23
Getting Ready to Learn

CONCEPT REVIEW

- Earth was formed over 4 billion years ago.
- Living things interact with their environment.

VOCABULARY REVIEW

See Glossary for definitions.

cell	organism
DNA	species
genetic material	theory

CONTENT REVIEW
CLASSZONE.COM
Review concepts and vocabulary.

TAKING NOTES

MAIN IDEA AND DETAILS

Make a two-column chart. Write the main ideas, such as those in the blue headings, in the column on the left. Write details about each of those main ideas in the column on the right.

VOCABULARY STRATEGY

Write each new vocabulary term in the center of a **frame game** diagram. Decide what information to frame it with. Use examples, descriptions, and parts of sentences that use the term in context or pictures. You can change the frame to fit each item.

See the Note-Taking Handbook on pages R45–R51.

SCIENCE NOTEBOOK

MAIN IDEAS	DETAILS
1. Fossils provide evidence of earlier life	1. Bones, prints, minerals
	1. Relative dating compares fossils
	1. Absolute dating uses the level of radioactivity

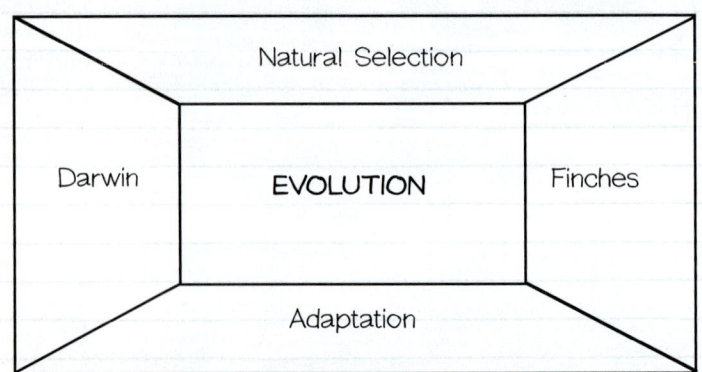

788 Unit 6: Life Over Time

KEY CONCEPT

Earth has been home to living things for about 3.8 billion years.

BEFORE, you learned
- Living things are diverse
- Living things share common characteristics
- A species is a group of living things that can breed with one another

NOW, you will learn
- How scientists use fossils to learn about the history of life
- About patterns in the fossil record
- About mass extinctions

VOCABULARY

fossil p. 789
unicellular organism p. 792
multicellular organism p. 793
mass extinction p. 794

EXPLORE Fossils

What can you infer from the marks an object leaves behind?

PROCEDURE

1. Press a layer of clay into the petri dish.
2. Choose a small object and press it into the clay to make an imprint of your object.
3. Remove the object carefully and trade your imprint with a classmate.

MATERIALS
- clay
- petri dish
- small object

WHAT DO YOU THINK?
- What object made the imprint?
- What do your observations indicate to you about how the imprint was formed?

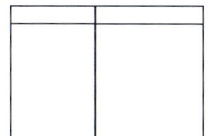

MAIN IDEA AND DETAILS
As you read this section, continue filling in the chart begun on page 788

Fossils provide evidence of earlier life.

Imagine watching a movie about the history of life on Earth. The beginning of the movie is set 3.8 billion years ago. At that time, the ocean would have been the setting. All living things lived in the sea. The end of the movie would show Earth today—a planet that is home to millions of species living on land as well as in water and air.

Of course, learning about the history of life isn't as easy as watching a movie. Modern ideas about life's history involve careful observation of the available evidence. Much of this evidence is provided by fossils. **Fossils** are the remains of organisms preserved in the earth. Fossils provide a glimpse of a very long story. In some ways, observing a fossil is like hitting the pause button on your video machine or looking at a snapshot of another time.

Chapter 23: **History of Life** 789

Fossils

Bones, such as this jawbone, are a common type of fossil.

This fossil trilobite formed as minerals replaced the remains of the organism.

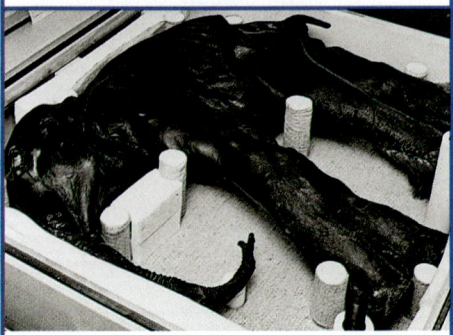
The preserved remains of ancient mammals, like the woolly mammoth, are rare.

Explore how a fossil can form.

Types of Fossils

You may have learned that fossils are the imprints or remains of once-living things. Most fossils are hard body parts such as bone. Perhaps you have seen displays of dinosaur skeletons in museums. These displays include fossil bones, such as the jawbone to the left. Other fossils form when minerals replace the remains of organisms or parts of organisms. The trilobite fossil shown in the middle photograph is an example of this type of fossil. Fossils also include prints made by organisms.

Very rarely, people find fossils that are the original remains of entire organisms. Explorers have found the frozen bodies of animals called woolly mammoths that lived about 10,000 years ago. The bodies of insects can be preserved in sap from plants.

Finding the Age of Fossils

How can scientists tell that the first organisms lived in oceans, or that dinosaurs lived on land and that they disappeared 65 million years ago? These questions and others can be addressed by determining the age of fossils. There are two approaches to dating fossils—relative dating and absolute dating. In relative dating, one fossil is compared with another fossil. The relative age tells you whether a fossil formed before or after another fossil.

The places where fossils are discovered provide information about their relative ages. Much of Earth's crust is rock, and rock forms over long periods of time. Understanding when and how rock forms gives scientists information about the sequence of events in Earth's history.

Materials such as sand and mud may settle to the bottom of a body of water. Over many millions of years, layers harden into rock. Shells and other remains of organisms can be trapped in those layers, forming fossils. Newer fossils are usually found in the top layers of rock, while older fossils are in the lower layers.

The absolute age of a fossil tells you when it was formed. To find the absolute age, scientists study the radioactive elements found in rocks and fossils. Some of these elements, such as uranium, decay at a very precise rate into more stable elements, such as lead. Thus, by measuring the amount of uranium and the amount of lead in an object, scientists can determine the object's age. The more lead it has, the older it is.

 What are the two ways scientists can determine the age of fossils?

INVESTIGATE Fossil Records

How do scientists interpret fossil evidence?
PROCEDURE

1. Individually examine each of your group's puzzle pieces. Consider the shape and size of each piece.
2. Arrange the pieces so that they fit together in the best possible way.
3. On the basis of your pieces, try to interpret what the overall puzzle picture may be.
4. Combine your puzzle pieces with another group's. Repeat steps 2 and 3.

WHAT DO YOU THINK?

- How did your interpretation of the puzzle picture change once you had more pieces to work with?
- Explain whether the gaps in the puzzle picture influenced your interpretation.
- Was it easier or more difficult to study the record with more "scientists" in your group?

CHALLENGE Brainstorm other ways scientists could learn about early life on Earth.

SKILL FOCUS
Analyzing

MATERIALS
puzzle pieces

TIME
15 minutes

Assembling the Fossil Record

By combining absolute dating with relative dating, scientists can estimate the age of most fossils. The information about the fossils found in a particular location is called the fossil record. By assembling a fossil record, scientists can identify the periods of time during which different species lived and died. Scientists have used the fossil record to develop an overview of Earth's history.

READING TIP
A species is a group of organisms with similar characteristics that can interbreed.

Information from fossils helps scientists and artists describe wooly mammoths.

More complex organisms developed over time.

One of the most striking patterns that scientists find when they study the fossil record involves the development of more complex organisms. Below you will see how scientists have reconstructed the history of a modern city to show how life has developed over time. Recall that the first organisms were made up of single cells. Most organisms living today are single-celled. However, more and more species have developed more and more complex cells and structures over time.

Unicellular Organisms

READING TIP
Uni- means "single" and *multi-* means "several" or "many."

Unicellular organisms are organisms made up of a single cell. The organisms in the ocean 3.8 billion years ago were made of simple, single cells. Some of these organisms are responsible for the oxygen that now makes up our atmosphere. The early atmosphere did not contain as much oxygen as it now does. As the atmosphere changed, so did life on Earth.

Different types of single cells developed over time. Over millions of years the cells of organisms became more complex. Today, there are different species of life that include organisms made up of many cells.

Reconstructing the Past

Digging deep into the city of Denver, scientists have been able to reconstruct the ancient past.

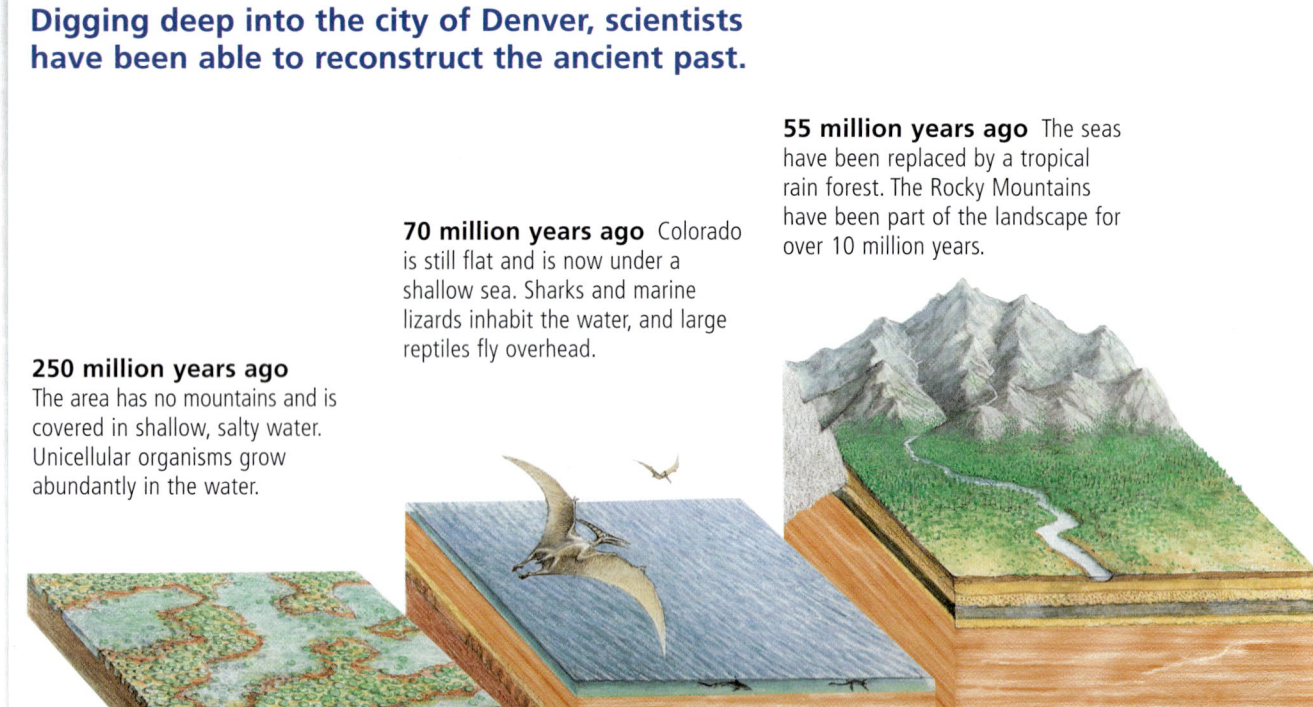

250 million years ago The area has no mountains and is covered in shallow, salty water. Unicellular organisms grow abundantly in the water.

70 million years ago Colorado is still flat and is now under a shallow sea. Sharks and marine lizards inhabit the water, and large reptiles fly overhead.

55 million years ago The seas have been replaced by a tropical rain forest. The Rocky Mountains have been part of the landscape for over 10 million years.

Multicellular Organisms

Around 1.2 billion years ago, organisms made up of many cells began to live in Earth's oceans. **Multicellular organisms** are living things made up of many cells. Individual cells within multicellular organisms often perform specific tasks. For example, some cells may capture energy. Other cells might store materials. Still others might carry materials from one part of the organism to another. The most complex species of multicellular organisms have cells that are organized into tissues, organs, and systems.

Recall that all organisms have similar needs for energy, water, materials, and living space. For almost 3 billion years, these needs were met only in oceans. According to fossil records, the earliest multicellular organisms were tiny seaweeds. The earliest animals were similar to today's jellyfish.

Scientists learn about early life by studying different layers of rock

 Explain how unicellular and multicellular organisms differ.

Life on Land

Consider the importance of water. Without it, you and most other living things would not be able to live. About 500 million years ago, the first multicellular organisms moved from water to land.

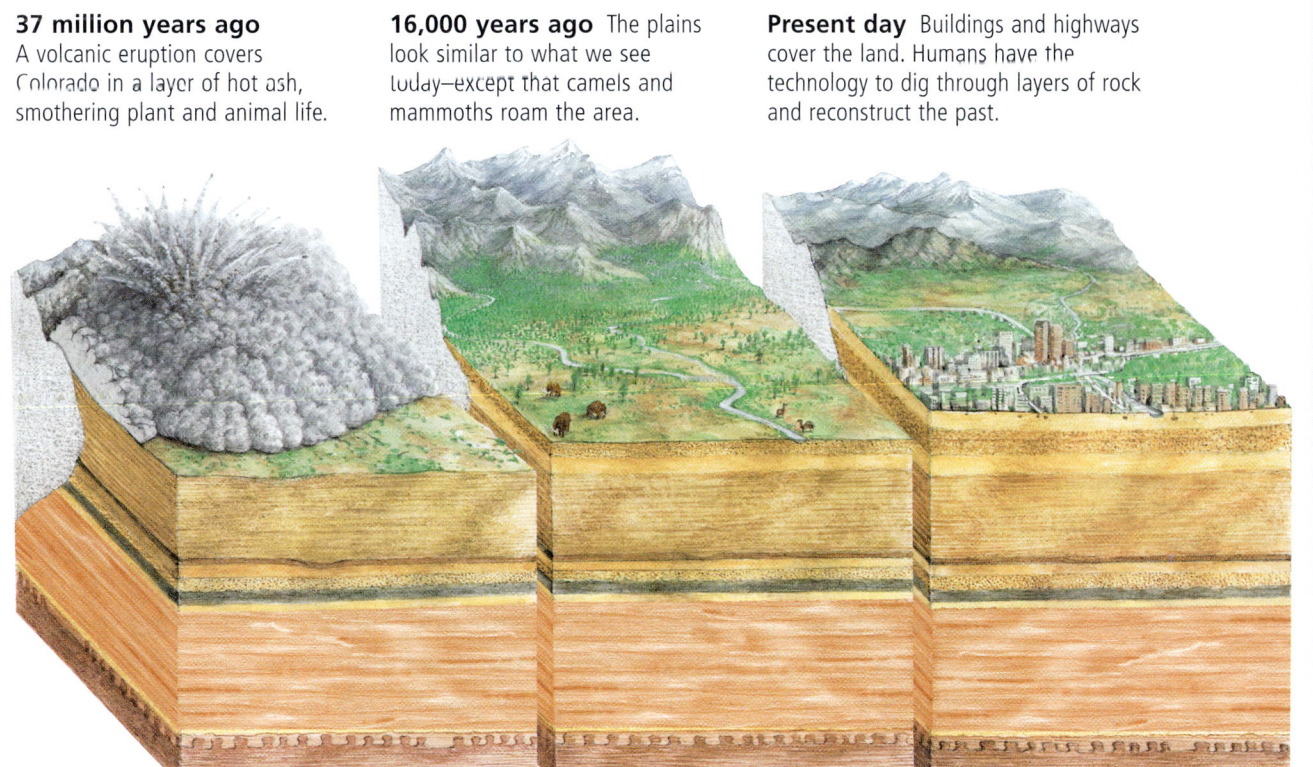

37 million years ago A volcanic eruption covers Colorado in a layer of hot ash, smothering plant and animal life.

16,000 years ago The plains look similar to what we see today—except that camels and mammoths roam the area.

Present day Buildings and highways cover the land. Humans have the technology to dig through layers of rock and reconstruct the past.

Chapter 23: **History of Life** 793

Find out more about mass extinctions.

In order to survive, these living things needed structures to help them get water. The first land-dwelling organisms were simple plants and fungi. Plants were able to obtain water from the soil through structures called roots. Fungi absorbed water from plants as well as from the soil. Insects were also probably among the first living things to inhabit land. Plants provided insects with food and shelter. After insects, animals such as amphibians and reptiles began living on land. They were followed by birds and mammals.

Earth's history includes mass extinctions.

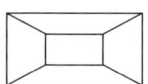
VOCABULARY Remember to make a frame game for the term *mass extinction*.

About 10,000 years ago, the last woolly mammoth died without any offspring. At that time, the species became extinct, which means it disappeared. The only way that we know that some species, such as woolly mammoths, ever existed is through the fossil record. During Earth's history, there have been several periods when huge numbers of species have died or become extinct in a very short time. These events are called **mass extinctions.**

Although the fossil record shows a pattern of mass extinctions, two of these extinctions are particularly interesting. These are the Permian Extinction and the Cretaceous Extinction. The causes of these mass extinctions are not fully known.

Permian Extinction

About 250 million years ago, approximately 90 percent of the species living in the ocean became extinct. At the same time, many land-dwelling animals disappeared. Scientists who have studied Earth's history think that Earth's landmasses joined together, forming one enormous continent. This event would have changed the climate on land and the conditions within Earth's waters.

The largest mass extinction, the Permian Extinction, affected many different living things but it was the most devastating to organisms that lived in oceans.

Cretaceous Extinction

Fossils show that around 140 million years ago, animals called dinosaurs lived all over the planet. However, the fossil record for dinosaurs ends about 65 million years ago. At the same time, more than half of the other species living on Earth became extinct.

How do scientists explain the extinction of so many species? One possibility is that a very large meteorite from space collided with Earth. The collision and its aftereffects wiped out most of the existing species. The remains of such a collision, the Chicxulub crater, can be found off the coast of Mexico. The computer graphic on page 795 shows the area of impact.

Chicxulub Crater

Scientists think the impact of a meteorite off the coast of Mexico caused the Cretaceous extinction.

The meteorite left a 200 km-wide crater off the Yucatán peninsula in Mexico.

Fragments from the meteorite have been found in the area.

The pattern in the fossil record shows that mass extinctions were followed by periods during which increasing numbers of new species developed. There may be a connection between the extinction of one species and the development of new species. For example, the extinction of dinosaurs may have made it possible for new species of mammals to develop.

 **CHECK YOUR READING** What do scientists think caused the most recent mass extinction?

23.1 Review

KEY CONCEPTS
1. How do fossils help scientists understand the history of life?
2. How do scientists know that the first organisms were simple, unicellular organisms?
3. What is extinction? Give an example of a mass extinction and its results.

CRITICAL THINKING
4. **Synthesize** How do absolute dating and relative dating help scientists assemble a fossil record for an area?
5. **Sequence** Draw a timeline showing the sequence of three major events in the history of life. Include the following terms on your timeline: *unicellular, multicellular, ocean, land.*

CHALLENGE
6. **Predict** Using the Denver reconstruction as your model, explain how you would reconstruct the history of the environment in your town.

Chapter 23: **History of Life** 795

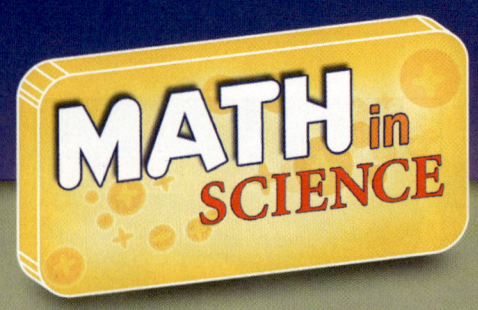

MATH in SCIENCE

SKILL: USING PROPORTIONS

Click on Math Tutorial for more help writing and solving proportions.

This fossil is very similar to the modern snail shown above.

A Span of Time

The history of planet Earth spans from the present to about 5 billion years back. By comparison, the history of life on the planet spans about 4/5 of that time. Such a comparison is called a proportion.

Example

To compare time spans in the history of Earth, you could make a meter-long timeline. Follow these steps:

(1) Measure and cut a piece of paper longer than 1 meter. Draw a straight line that is 1 meter long on your paper.

(2) Mark "0" at the far left to show the present day. Mark "5,000,000,000" at the right to show 5 billion years.

(3) Mark each centimeter along the line with a short stroke.

(4) Make a longer stroke at every 10 pencil marks. Your 5-billion-year span is now divided into 500-million-year sections. Each section is 1/10 in proportion to the total.

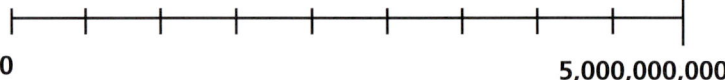

0   5,000,000,000

Label the timeline by answering the questions below.

1. Each short pencil stroke, or tick, represents 1/100 of the total span. How many years will each centimeter represent?

2. Each of the 10 long pencil marks should have its own label for the amount of time before the present day. The label for the first long pencil mark should be "500 million years." What numbers should label the others?

3. What fractions of the total span do the numbers in Question 2 represent?

CHALLENGE Copy and complete the table.

Event	Years Before Present Time	Number of cm from 0	Fraction of Total Time Span
Life appears on Earth.	3,800,000,000		
Multicellular life appears.	1,500,000,000		
First animals appear on land.	420,000,000		

KEY CONCEPT
Species change over time.

BEFORE, you learned
- Fossils are evidence of earlier life
- More complex organisms have developed over time
- Mass extinctions contributed to the development of Earth's history

NOW, you will learn
- About early ideas and observations on evolution
- How Darwin developed his theory of natural selection
- How new species arise from older species

VOCABULARY
evolution p. 797
natural selection p. 801
adaptation p. 802
speciation p. 804

THINK ABOUT

How have telephones changed over time?

Today people across the world can communicate in many different ways. One of the most common ways is over the telephone. Looking at the two pictures, can you describe how this form of communication has changed over time?

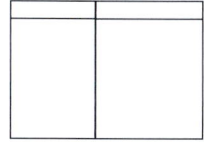

MAIN IDEA AND DETAILS
Make a chart for the main idea *scientists explore the concept of evolution*. Include details about scientists' observations.

Scientists explore the concept of evolution.

In a general sense, evolution involves a change over time. You could say that the way humans communicate has evolved. Certainly telephones have changed over time. The first telephones were the size of a shoebox. Today a telephone can fit in the palm of your hand and can send images as well as sound.

In biology, **evolution** refers to the process though which species change over time. The change results from a change in the genetic material of an organism and is passed from one generation to the next.

 What is evolution?

Chapter 23: **History of Life** 797

READING TIP
The word *acquire* comes from the root meaning "to add to." Acquired traits are those that are "added" after an organism is born.

Early Ideas

In the early 1800s, a French scientist named Jean Baptiste de Lamarck was the first scientist to propose a model of how life evolves. He became convinced that the fossil record showed that species had changed over time. He proposed an explanation for evolution based on the idea that an individual organism can acquire a new trait during its lifetime and then pass that trait on to its offspring. For example, Lamarck suggested that when giraffes stretched their necks to reach the leaves of tall trees, they passed the result of this stretching—a longer neck—to the next generation. Lamarck was a highly respected scientist, but he was unable to provide any evidence to support his idea.

CHECK YOUR READING How did Lamarck explain the process of evolution?

Darwin's Voyage

The *Beagle*
Darwin traveled with a crew of over 70 people on this 90-foot-long vessel. 

Glyptodon fossil 
Darwin hiked in the **Andes Mountains** and found a glyptodon fossil that resembles the modern armadillo.

Darwin left **England** on December 27, 1836. He returned 5 years later.

NORTH AMERICA · ENGLAND · EUROPE · ATLANTIC OCEAN · AFRICA · Galápagos Islands · Equator · ANDES MOUNTAINS · SOUTH AMERICA · Cape of Good Hope

798 Unit 6: Life Over Time

Darwin's Observations

About 50 years after Lamarck, the British naturalist Charles Darwin published what would become the basis of the modern theory of evolution. As a young adult, Darwin spent 5 years as a naturalist aboard the *Beagle,* a ship in the British navy. The map below shows the route Darwin traveled. As he sailed along the coast of South America, he studied rock formations and collected fossils. He also began to compare the new animals he was seeing with ones from his own country.

The differences he saw in animals became more obvious when he visited the Galápagos Islands, a chain of volcanic islands about 950 kilometers (600 mi) off the South American coast. On the Galápagos Islands, plants and animals not only differed from those he saw on the mainland, but some differed from island to island.

Darwin was only 20 in 1831 when he joined H.M.S. *Beagle*.

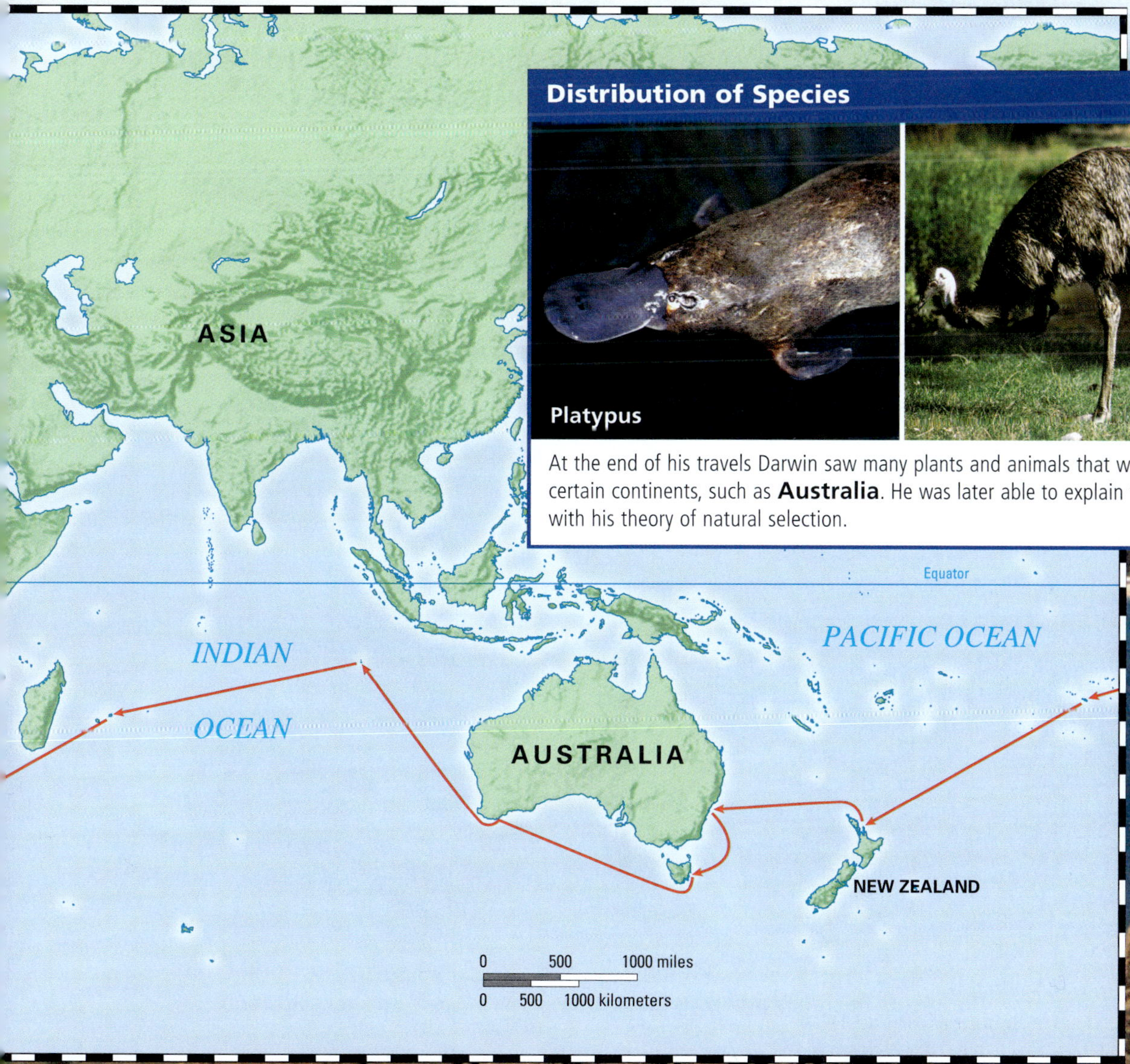

Distribution of Species

Platypus

Emu

At the end of his travels Darwin saw many plants and animals that were specific to certain continents, such as **Australia**. He was later able to explain this pattern with his theory of natural selection.

Darwin observed several types of tortoises on the islands. Tortoises with short necks were living in damp areas with abundant plant life that grew close to the ground. Longer-necked tortoises were living in dry areas with cacti. He considered whether the length of their necks made it possible for the tortoises to live in different environments.

Darwin also found many different types of birds called finches living on the islands. Some finches were common in the treetops, while others lived in the lower shrubs of a neighboring island. Among the different islands he noticed a variety of beak shapes and sizes. Some finches had heavy, short beaks useful for pecking trees or seeds, while others had small, thin beaks that could be used for capturing insects. These observations caused Darwin to wonder if the birds had evolved from similar species.

Darwin's Finches

On the Galápagos Islands, Darwin observed similar-looking birds with very different beaks. These birds are closely related finch species that are suited to different habitats on the island.

Woodpecker Finch

Vegetarian Finch

The woodpecker finch is able to hold a twig in its long pointed beak, which it uses to pull the larvas of insects from a tree. The vegetarian finch has a curved beak, ideal for taking large berries from a branch.

Large Ground Finch

Cactus Finch

The large ground finch has a large beak that it uses to crack open the hard shells of the seeds it feeds on. The cactus finch has a narrow beak that it uses to cut into a cactus and eat the tissue inside.

Natural selection explains how living things evolve.

After Darwin returned home to England in 1836, he spent several years analyzing the observations and specimens he had collected on his voyage. He struggled to develop an explanation that would account for the amazing diversity of species he saw and for the relationships between them. By 1844 he had developed a hypothesis based in part on an insight from one of his hobbies—breeding pigeons.

Darwin knew from personal experience that breeders can produce new varieties of an animal over time. The process breeders use is called artificial selection. For example, breeders produce a new breed of dog by selecting dogs that have certain desired traits and then allowing only those individuals to mate. From the resulting litters, they again selectively breed only the individual dogs with the desired traits. By repeating this process generation after generation, a new breed is produced.

Learn more about natural selection.

 **CHECK YOUR READING** What is artificial selection?

Artificial Selection

Cairne | Airedale | Tibetan

COMPARE AND CONTRAST These dogs are all terriers, but they have been bred through artificial selection to show very specific traits. How are the dogs similar? How are they different?

Darwin's insight was that a similar process might be going on in nature. He proposed that, through a process he called **natural selection,** members of a species that are best suited to their environment survive and reproduce at a higher rate than other members of the species. Darwin based this idea on a few key principles. These are overproduction, variation, adaptation, and selection.

Chapter 23: **History of Life** 801

Overproduction

Take a look at how Darwin's ideas are useful for the study of salmon. When a plant or an animal reproduces, it usually makes more offspring than the environment can support, as you can see in the diagram on page 803. A female salmon may lay several thousand fertile eggs, but not all of them will hatch. Only a few hundred of the salmon that hatch from the eggs will survive disease and avoid fish-eating predators. Several dozen of these survivors will live to adulthood. An even smaller number will successfully reproduce.

Variation

Within a species there are natural differences, or variations, in traits. For example, if you looked very closely at thousands of salmon, you might see slight differences among individuals. Some might have larger fins. Others might have distinct patterns of spots on their scales. Many of the differences among individuals result from differences in the genetic material of the fish.

Sometimes the genetic material itself changes, causing a new variation to come about. A change in the genetic material is referred to as a mutation. As the fish with the new variation reproduces, the trait gets passed on to its offspring. Therefore, genetic variations are passed on from one generation to the next.

Adaptation

Sometimes a mutation occurs that makes an individual better able to survive than other members of the group. An **adaptation** is any inherited trait that gives an organism an advantage in its particular environment. For example, a slight change in the shape of a tail fin may increase a fish's chance of survival by helping it swim faster and avoid predators.

Selection

Darwin reasoned that individual organisms with a particular adaptation are most likely to survive long enough to reproduce. As a result, the adaptation becomes more common in the next generation of offspring. As this process repeats from generation to generation, more members of a species show the adaptation. Consider the shape of the salmon. If a change in the tail fin makes the salmon better able to move upstream and lay eggs, scientists say this trait has been selected for in this environment. In other words, the species is evolving through natural selection.

> **READING TIP**
> As you read about the principles of natural selection, refer to the diagrams on page 803.

Natural Selection

Certain traits become more common in a group of organisms through the process of natural selection.

Overproduction

A fish may lay hundreds of eggs, but only a small number will survive to reach adulthood.

Variation

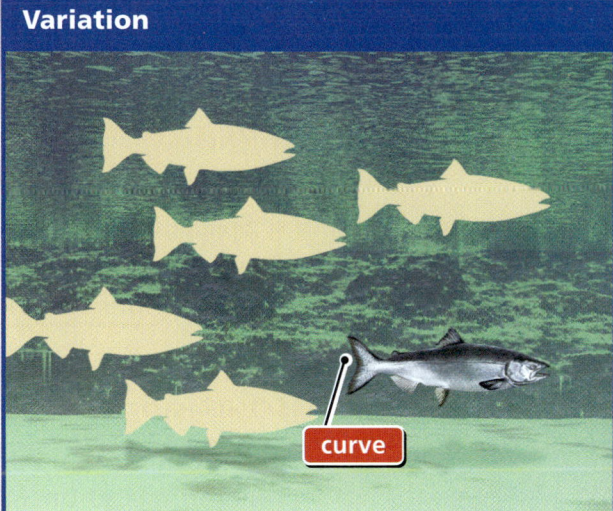

A mutation may cause a slight curve to develop in a fish's tail.

Adaptation

The fish with the curved tail is able to swim more quickly and so escapes predators. The fish reproduces.

Selection

With each generation, more fish with a curved tail survive to reproduce. Over time, they make up a larger part of the group.

READING VISUALS How does natural selection occur for an individual salmon?

New species develop from earlier species.

Darwin's personal observations and the work of another scientist, Alfred Wallace, led Darwin to write about this new concept of evolution. In 1859, after more than twenty years of work, Darwin published his ideas in his book *On the Origin of Species.* This work led the way for our modern understanding of how new species arise.

Speciation

Speciation is the evolution of new species from an existing species. Speciation may occur when the environment changes dramatically, or when the environment changes gradually. The Galápagos finch populations Darwin studied showed evidence of speciation.

Isolation

Darwin's trip to the Galápagos Islands showed him an important point about speciation. Many new species had evolved after populations were separated from the mainland and were not able to breed with their mainland relatives. Darwin reasoned that isolation of populations by geographical or other barriers could contribute to the process of speciation. A species of fish called cichlids shows how a physical barrier contributes to speciation.

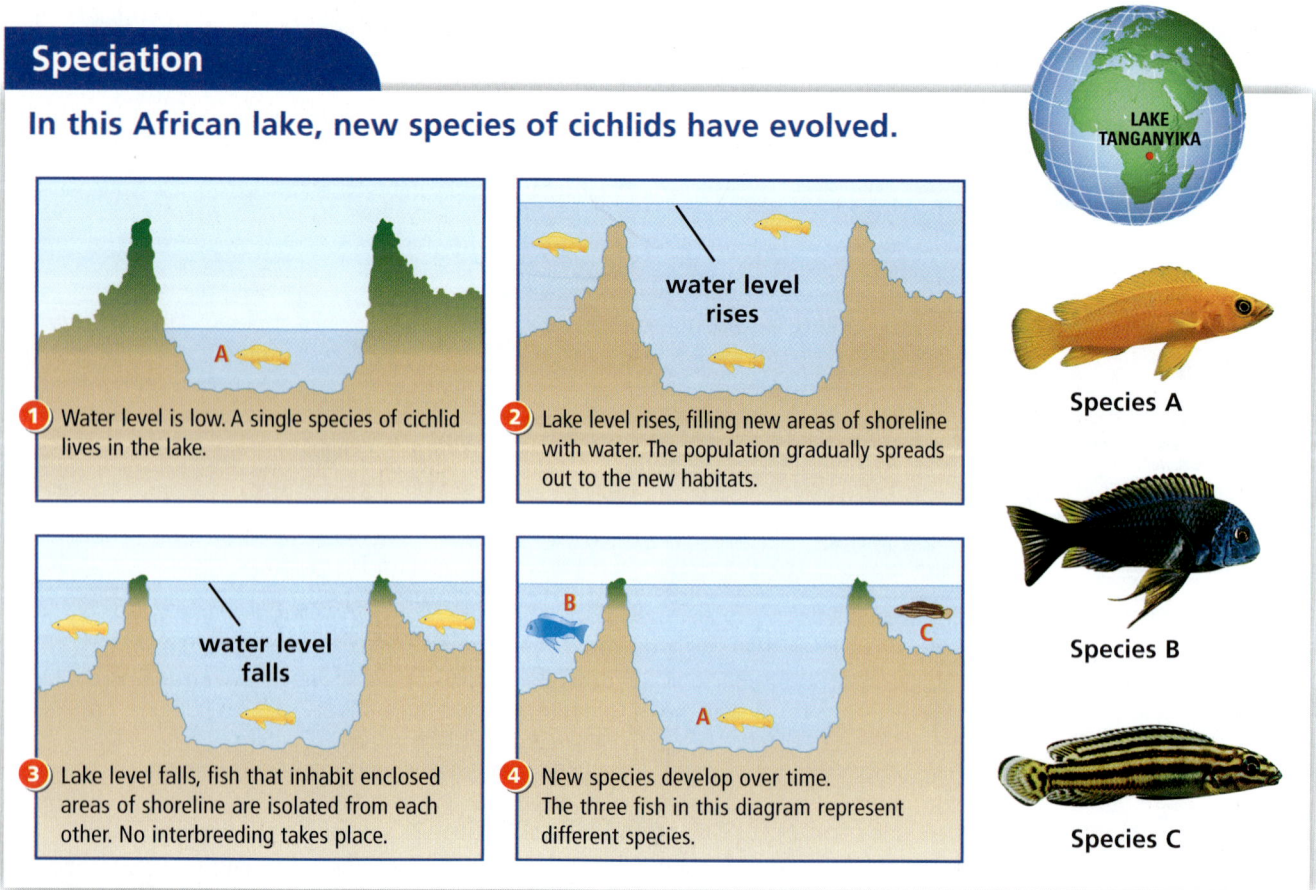

Speciation

In this African lake, new species of cichlids have evolved.

LAKE TANGANYIKA

1. Water level is low. A single species of cichlid lives in the lake.
2. Lake level rises, filling new areas of shoreline with water. The population gradually spreads out to the new habitats.
3. Lake level falls, fish that inhabit enclosed areas of shoreline are isolated from each other. No interbreeding takes place.
4. New species develop over time. The three fish in this diagram represent different species.

Species A

Species B

Species C

804 Unit 6: Life Over Time

In Lake Tanganyika, one of the largest lakes in the world, there are over 150 species of cichlids. Members of one particular genus, *tropheus*, originally lived along the rocky shore and couldn't cross the open water. The climate and geology of the area caused the lake's water level to rise and fall many times over thousands of years. As the water level changed, a new, rocky habitat was formed, and some populations of cichlids became isolated from each other.

The isolated populations were unable to interact with each other because they couldn't cross open waters. As a result, genetic differences began to add up in these populations. The cichlid populations now represent distinct species. They have developed unique characteristics and cannot breed with each other. See diagram on page 804.

Today scientists understand that isolation is essential to speciation. For a species to separate, two populations must be prevented from reproducing with each other. A geographic boundary like an ocean or mountain range can result in isolation. Two populations of a species can also be isolated if they feed on different things or reproduce at different times of the year.

As the cichlids in Lake Tanganyika show, the mutations in one isolated group may differ from another. Two or more populations may evolve differently from each other. The result is speciation, which has contributed to the biodiversity on Earth.

The Rocky Mountains are an example of a barrier that can isolate populations.

CHECK YOUR READING What is a key factor that can lead to speciation?

23.2 Review

KEY CONCEPTS

1. How did Lamarck's ideas differ from Darwin's?
2. What did Darwin observe in the finch populations that supported his idea of natural selection?
3. Explain how isolation helps speciation.

CRITICAL THINKING

4. **Hypothesize** Two species of grasses are separated by a tall mountain range. A third species of grass shares some characteristics with each of the other two species. It inhabits a small valley, surrounded on all sides by mountains. Form a hypothesis for the origin of the third species.

CHALLENGE

5. **Predict** The Arctic hare lives in snow-covered mountains in Canada. The hare is hunted by foxes, wolves, and owls. Which trait is more likely to be inherited by new generations of hares: white fur or black fur?

Chapter 23: **History of Life** 805

CHAPTER INVESTIGATION

Modeling Natural Selection

OVERVIEW AND PURPOSE Organisms that are best adapted to their environment tend to survive and reproduce. In this lab you will
- play a game that models the effect of natural selection in an environment
- determine what happens to a group of organisms as a result of natural selection

❯ Question

Write It Up

As you read the steps to the game, think about what makes a population successful in an environment. How will the game model natural selection?

MATERIALS
- pair of number cubes
- 16 red paper clips
- 16 blue paper clips
- 16 yellow paper clips

❯ Procedure

1 Make a game board like the one shown below. In your **Science Notebook** make a table like the one on page 807 to record your data.

	1	2	3	4
1				
2				
3				
4				

2 Count out 10 red paper clips, 4 blue paper clips, and 2 yellow paper clips. Randomly place the paper clips on the board. Keep the rest of the paper clips in a reserve pile.

806 Unit 6: Life Over Time

3. Each color represents a different population of a single species. The board represents the environment. Roll the number cubes to determine which paper clips "live," or remain on the board, and which paper clips "die," or are removed from the board. Predict which color paper clip you think will be the last remaining color. Write down your prediction.

4. Roll the number cubes to determine which square, or part of the environment, will be affected. For example, 2,3 indicates the paper clip in column 2, row 3. If the numbers 5 or 6 come up, roll again until you have a number between 1 and 4 for each cube.

5. Now roll one cube to see what will happen to the paper clip or organism in that square. Use the chart below to determine if the paper clip "lives" or "dies." If the paper clip lives, repeat steps 4 and 5 until one paper clip dies, or is removed from the board. In your table, record which colors live and die.

Red	Remove if you roll a 1, 2, 3, 4, or 5.
Blue	Remove if you roll a 1, 2, or 3.
Yellow	Remove if you roll a 1 or 2.

6. Now that a paper clip has been removed, you need to see what population will reproduce to fill that space. Roll both cubes to choose another square. The color of the paper clip in that square represents the population that will "reproduce." Pick the same color paper clip from your reserve pile and place it on the empty square. All squares on the board should always have a paper clip.

7. Continue playing the game by repeating steps 4–6 until all the paper clips on the board are the same color.

Observe and Analyze

1. **OBSERVE** Which color paper clip filled the board at the end of the game?

2. **PREDICT** Compare the results with your prediction. Do the results support your prediction?

Conclude

1. **INFER** What does the random selection by rolling both number cubes represent? Explain.

2. **INFER** If the individual paper clips represent different members of a single species, then what might the different colors represent?

3. **LIMITATIONS** What problems or sources of error exist in this model? Give examples.

4. **APPLY** How does this game model natural selection?

INVESTIGATE Further

CHALLENGE Occasionally mutations occur in a population that can either help or damage the population's chance of survival. Add another step to the game that would account for mutations.

Modeling Natural Selection

Table 1. Patterns in a Population

Paper Clip Color	Live	Die

KEY CONCEPT
23.3 Many types of evidence support evolution.

BEFORE, you learned
- Natural selection explains part of the process of evolution
- New species develop from earlier species

NOW, you will learn
- How scientists develop theories
- About the evidence Darwin used to support evolution
- About additional evidence most scientists use today

VOCABULARY
ancestor p. 809
vestigial organ p. 810
gene p. 813

EXPLORE Evidence

How can observations supply evidence?

PROCEDURE

1. Consider the following statement: It rained last night.

2. Look at the following observations and determine which pieces of evidence support the statement.
   - There are puddles on the ground.
   - The weather report says there will be scattered showers today.
   - Your sister tells you there was a rain delay during last night's tennis match.

MATERIALS
- paper
- pencil

WHAT DO YOU THINK?
- What other observations can you come up with that would supply evidence for the first statement?
- Could any of the evidence be misleading?

Observations provide evidence for theories.

MAIN IDEA AND DETAILS
Don't forget to make a chart of details supporting the main idea that observations provide evidence for theories. Include a definition of *theory* in your chart.

In this chapter, you've learned about important observations that scientists have used to understand the history of living things. These observations provided Darwin with information he used to describe his ideas about evolution.

Darwin, like all good scientists, was skeptical about his observations and conclusions. Although the historic trip on the *Beagle* took place between 1831 and 1836, Darwin didn't publish the book explaining his theory until 1859. In order to understand the importance of Darwin's work, it is also important to understand the meaning of the term *theory*.

808 Unit 6: Life Over Time

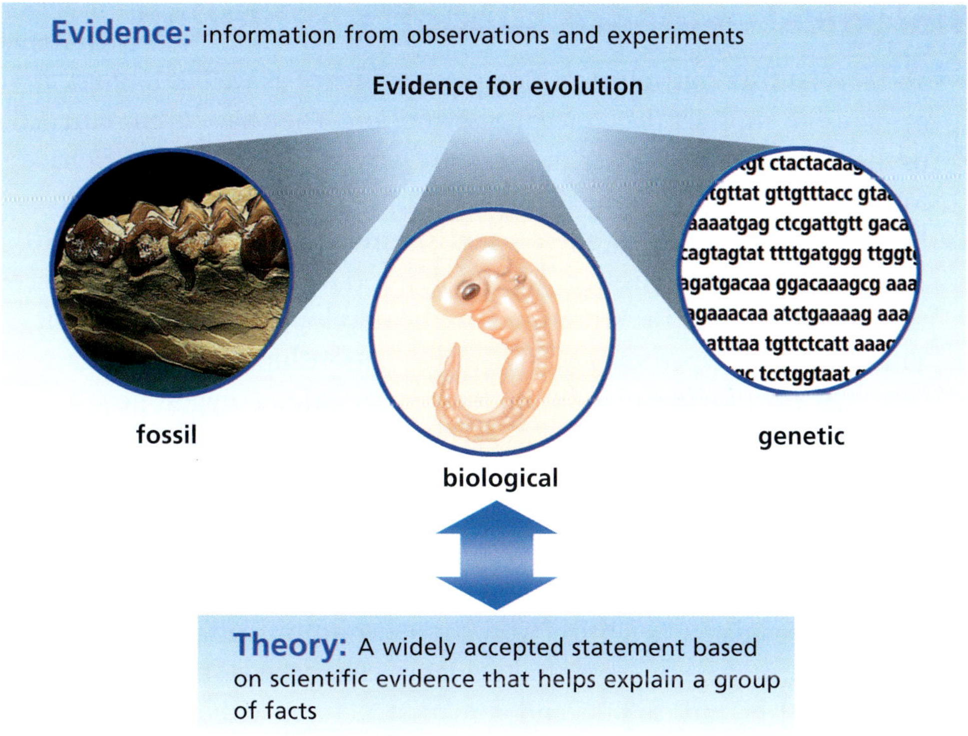

Examine evidence to support evolution.

Evidence: information from observations and experiments

Evidence for evolution

fossil

biological

genetic

Theory: A widely accepted statement based on scientific evidence that helps explain a group of facts

A scientific theory is a statement based on observation and experiment. If continued observation and experiment support the statement, it may become widely accepted. A theory that has been widely accepted is used to explain and predict natural phenomena. The chart above will help give you an idea of how a theory works and what evidence has been used to support evolution and the theory of natural selection.

 How do scientists support theories?

Fossil evidence supports evolution.

You have read that Darwin collected many specimens of fossils on his trip. These specimens provided evidence that species existing in the past were very similar to species living during Darwin's time. For example, the fossil of an extinct animal called the glyptodon resembles the modern armadillo, an animal found today in South America.

The geographic information about many fossils provides evidence that two species with a common ancestor can develop differently in different locations. An **ancestor** is an early form of an organism from which later forms descend. The idea of common ancestors is important to the theory of natural selection and to the evidence that supports the theory. Scientists comparing modern plants and modern algae to fossil algae can tell that they all share a common ancestor.

 What is a common ancestor?

Chapter 23: **History of Life** 809

Biological evidence supports evolution.

Today scientists continue to study fossil evidence as well as biological evidence to support the concept of evolution. They have even returned to the Galápagos to further investigate Darwin's work. What they have found gives strength to the theory he proposed nearly 150 years ago. Returning year after year, these scientists are able to follow and record evolutionary changes as they are unfolding. The biological evidence they study includes the structure and the development of living things. This work has helped scientists identify relationships between organisms that exist today. In addition, their observations suggest how modern organisms are related to earlier species.

Similarities in Structure

Evidence for evolution can be observed within the physical structures of adult organisms. Scientists who study evolution and development consider two types of structural evidence. They are vestigial (veh-STIHJ-ee-uhl) organs and similar structures with different functions.

 **CHECK YOUR READING** What are two types of structural evidence?

READING TIP
The root of the word vestigial means "footprint." A vestige refers to visible evidence that is left behind—such as a footprint.

Vestigial organs are physical structures that were fully developed and functional in an ancestral group of organisms but are reduced and unused in the later species. In the bodies of whales there are small leg bones that are vestigial. The skeletons of snakes also have traces of leglike structures that are not used. These vestigial organs help researchers see how some modern organisms are related to ancestors that had similar structures.

Similar structures with different functions Scientists studying the anatomy of living things have also noticed that many different species share similar structures. But these structures are used differently by each species. For example, lizards, bats, and manatees have forelimbs that have a similar bone structure. As you can see from the diagram on page 811, there is one short bone and one long bone that go from a shoulder structure to a wrist structure. But obviously, a lizard, a bat, and a manatee use this structure in different ways.

This similarity in structure indicates that these organisms shared a common ancestor. The process of natural selection caused the variations in form and function that can be observed today. These organisms lived in different environments and so were under different pressures. For lizards the environment was land, for bats it was the air, and for manatees the water. The environment influenced the selection of traits.

Biological Evidence for Evolution

Scientists learn about common ancestors by looking at physical structures.

Vestigial Structures

The small, leglike bones in modern whales indicate that an early ancestor may have had legs.

Ambulocetus, an extinct whalelike animal with four legs

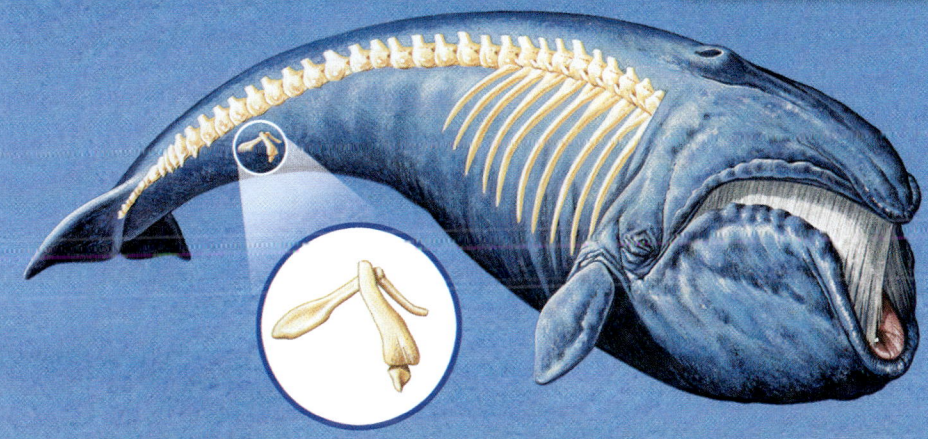

modern whale

Similar Structures, Different Functions

gecko lizard

little brown myotis bat

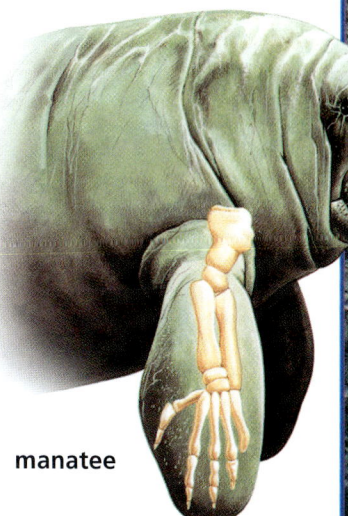

manatee

These animals share a similar bone structure that they use in very different ways. The presence of this similar structure indicates a common ancestor.

Similarities in Development

READING TIP
As you read about the development of a chicken, rabbit, and salamander, study the diagram below.

Scientists in the 1700s were fascinated by the fact that various animals looked similar in their earliest stages of life. They noted that as the organisms developed, they became less and less alike. Today's scientists continue to compare the developmental stages of different species.

The adult stages of many species do not look similar. For example, a rabbit does not look anything like a chicken. However, study reveals that the early life stages of a chicken and a rabbit are similar. An organism that is in an early stage of development is called an embryo.

In the diagram below, notice the development of three different species: a chicken, a rabbit, and a salamander. In the early stages of development, the embryos of all three organisms look similar. As they continue to develop, they begin to take on distinct characteristics. The chicken has a structure that starts to resemble a beak. The salamander begins to look as if it is adapted for life near water. In their adult stages, these three species no longer look similar.

Similarities in Development

The study of embryos shows that animals that appear to be very different as adults are similar during early development.

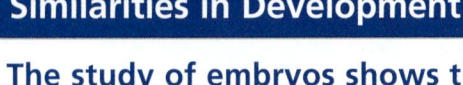

Early Development: Embryos

Adults

812 Unit 6: Life Over Time

INVESTIGATE Genes

How can a sequence communicate information?

PROCEDURE

1. From your pile of letters (A, D, E, R), spell out the word RED.
2. Working with a partner, use the letters to spell two more words having three letters.

WHAT DO YOU THINK?

How does rearranging the letters change the meaning of the words?

CHALLENGE Cut out words from a newspaper. Arrange these words to form different phrases. How do these phrases communicate different messages?

SKILL FOCUS
Sequencing

MATERIALS
letter cards

TIME
20 minutes

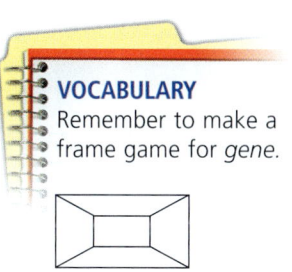

Genetic evidence supports evolution.

The key to understanding how traits are passed from one generation to the next lies in the study of DNA, the genetic material found in all organisms. DNA contains the information all organisms need to grow and to maintain themselves. When organisms reproduce, they pass on their genetic material to their offspring.

DNA contains a code that a cell uses to put together all the materials it needs to function properly. The code is made up of four different chemical subunits called bases. The bases are symbolized by the four letters A, T, C, and G. Located within DNA are individual genes. A **gene** is a segment of DNA that relates to a specific trait or function of an organism. Each gene has a particular sequence of bases. The cell takes this sequence and translates it into the chemicals and structures the organism needs.

Scientists studying genes have identified a gene called the clock gene in many mammals. This particular gene relates to the function of sleeping and waking. As scientists learn more they can identify patterns of behavior in different organisms. The chart on page 814 compares the DNA sequence of part of the clock gene in both humans and mice.

VOCABULARY
Remember to make a frame game for *gene*.

 What is a gene?

Chapter 23: **History of Life** 813

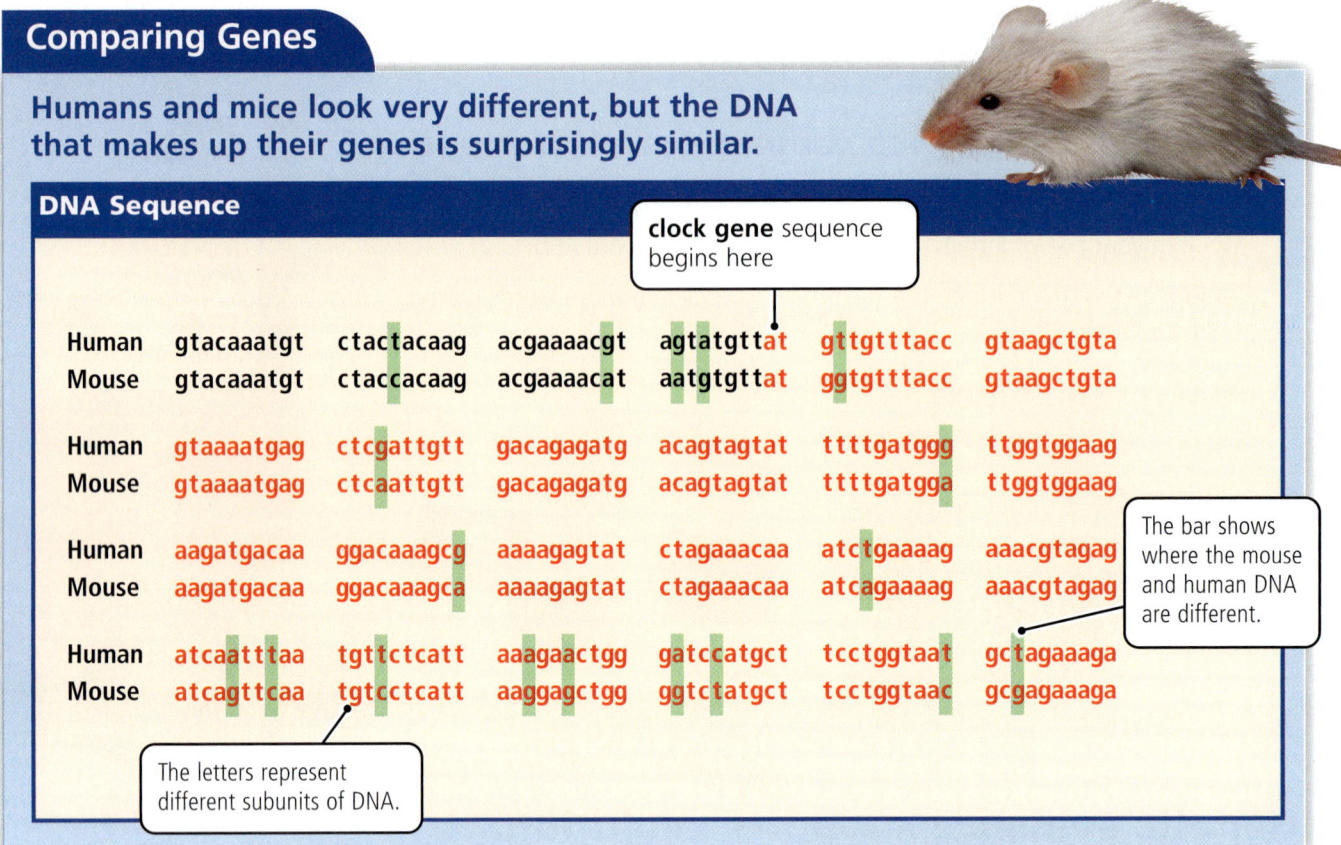

Scientists can tell how closely organisms are related by comparing their DNA. The more matches there are in the sequence of bases between two organisms, the more closely related they are. For example, almost all the genes found in a mouse are also found in a human. Even though the two organisms appear so different, much of the functioning of their cells is similar.

23.3 Review

KEY CONCEPTS

1. Describe in your own words how scientists use the word *theory*.
2. What type of evidence did Darwin use to support his theory of evolution?
3. Identify three different types of evidence that today's scientists use to support the theory of evolution.

CRITICAL THINKING

4. **Analyze** Describe three characteristics of a scientific theory. Explain how Darwin's theory of evolution is an example of a scientific theory.

CHALLENGE

5. **Predict** If you were looking at the sequence within the genes of two species, how would you predict that the two species are related?

Think SCIENCE

SKILL: EVALUATING HYPOTHESES

How Did the Deep-Sea Angler Get Its Glow?

A fish that uses a fishing pole to catch food might seem odd. However, anglerfish do just that. The fish have a modified spine that extends from their head, almost like a fishing pole. At the end is a small piece of tissue that is similar in shape to a small worm. The tissue functions like a lure that a fisherman uses to catch fish. The anglerfish wiggles its "lure" to attract prey. If the prey fish moves in close enough, the anglerfish opens its mouth and swallows the prey whole. The "fishing poles" of abyssal anglerfish, anglerfish that live in the deep sea, have an interesting adaptation. The "lure" actually glows in the dark—it is bioluminescent.

▶ Observations

From laboratory research and field studies, scientists made these observations.

> There are more than 200 species of anglerfish. Many of these live in deep water.
>
> Shallow-water species do not have glow-in-the-dark "lures."
>
> Only female abyssal anglerfish have a "pole." They do not have pelvic fins and are not strong swimmers.
>
> Other deep-sea organisms, including bacteria, jellyfish, even some squid, are bioluminescent.

▶ Hypotheses

Consider these hypotheses.

> The ancestors of abyssal anglerfish lived in shallow waters. Some of these fish drifted into deep waters. A bioluminescent lure helped some survive.
>
> Light does not reach down to the bottom of the deep sea. Bioluminescence provides an advantage for the anglerfish because it makes its lure noticeable.
>
> A bioluminescent lure is more valuable to a female abyssal anglerfish than the ability to swim.

▶ Evaluate Each Hypothesis

On Your Own For each hypothesis, think about whether all the observations support it. Some facts may rule out some hypotheses. Others may support them.

As a Group Decide which hypothesis is the most reasonable. Discuss your thinking and conclusions in a small group and see if the group can agree.

Chapter 23: **History of Life** 815

23 Chapter Review

the BIG idea

Living things, like Earth itself, change over time.

CONTENT REVIEW
CLASSZONE.COM

KEY CONCEPTS SUMMARY

1 Earth has been home to living things for about 3.8 billion years.

Fossil records inform humans about the development of life on Earth. Information from fossils can help scientists reconstruct Earth's history.

VOCABULARY
fossil p. 789
unicellular organism p. 792
multicellular organism p. 793
mass extinction p. 794

2 Species change over time.

Darwin's theory of natural selection explains evolution.

Four principles of natural selection
- overproduction
- variation
- adaptation
- selection

The beak of this cactus finch provides an example of an adaptation.

VOCABULARY
evolution p. 797
natural selection p. 801
adaptation p. 802
speciation p. 804

3 Many types of evidence support evolution.

Three different types of evidence provide a bigger picture of evolution

fossil

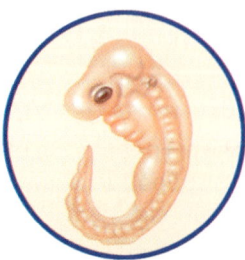
biological

genetic

VOCABULARY
ancestor p. 809
vestigial organ p. 810
gene p. 813

816 Unit 6: Life Over Time

Reviewing Vocabulary

Draw a triangle for each of the terms below. On the wide bottom of the triangle, write the term and your own definition of it. Above that, write a sentence in which you use the term correctly. At the top of the triangle, draw a small picture to show what the term looks like.

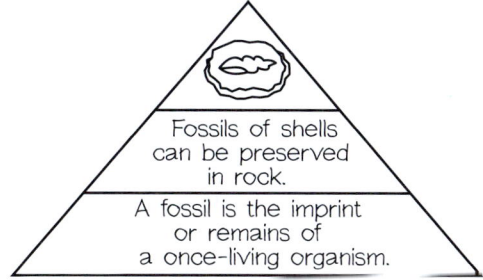

1. unicellular organism
2. multicellular organism
3. adaptation
4. vestigial structure

Reviewing Key Concepts

Multiple Choice *Choose the letter of the best answer.*

5. Which is *not* part of the fossil record?
   a. fossil bones
   b. preserved remains
   c. living unicellular organisms
   d. imprints

6. Whether a fossil formed before or after another fossil is described by its
   a. relative age
   b. absolute age
   c. fossil record
   d. radioactive age

7. The earliest multicellular organisms were
   a. jellyfish
   b. simple plants
   c. fungi
   d. tiny seaweeds

8. Which is a possible explanation for mass extinctions?
   a. Earth had no water.
   b. A meteorite collided with Earth.
   c. The continents separated.
   d. Woolly mammoths left no offspring.

9. Darwin's theory that species develop new traits and change over time is known as
   a. natural selection   c. speciation
   b. evolution   d. adaptation

10. Which describes Lamarck's explanation for changes in the fossil record?
    a. Species best suited to their environments survive better than others.
    b. Variation within a species can be passed on to offspring.
    c. Acquired traits are passed on from one generation to another.
    d. Giraffes adapted to their environment.

11. A slight change in a rabbit's ability to hear its predators better and help it survive is
    a. an adaptation
    b. a vestigial structure
    c. an aquired trait
    d. an isolation

12. Which is necessary for speciation to occur?
    a. adaptation
    b. mass extinction
    c. isolation
    d. acquired traits

13. Which of the following statements explain why the theory of evolution is widely accepted by the scientific community?
    a. It has been proven by experiments.
    b. The fossil record is complete.
    c. It is supported by genetic evidence.
    d. Lamarck's theory was correct.

14. Genetic evidence is based on the study of
    a. embryonic development
    b. mutations
    c. common ancestors
    d. DNA sequences

15. Genetic information that cells use to control the production of new cells is located in
  a. embryos
  b. genes
  c. the environment
  d. vestigial structures

Short Answer *Write a short answer to each question.*

16. Describe how the relative age of a fossil is determined by studying layers of rock.

17. Explain the difference between artificial selection and natural selection.

18. How does common ancestry between two species support evolution?

Thinking Critically

19. COMMUNICATE What have scientists learned about past life on Earth from the fossil record?

20. PROVIDE EXAMPLES Explain the principle of overproduction. Give an example.

21. SYNTHESIZE How might the mass extinction of dinosaurs enable many new species of mammals to develop?

22. EVALUATE How would natural selection have led to the development of giraffes with long necks as opposed to giraffes with short necks?

23. PROVIDE EXAMPLES How are variation and adaptations related to natural selection? Give an example.

24. PREDICT In Africa's Lake Tanganyika different populations of cichlids became isolated from each other. Based on what you already learned, predict how the changing water level helped the cichlid population to change. How do you think the development of new cichlid species affected other living things in the lake?

25. ANALYZE How is geographic isolation related to the formation of a new species?

26. EVALUATE Pandas were once considered to be closely related to raccoons and red pandas because of their physical similarities. Today, scientists have learned that pandas are more closely related to bears than to raccoons and red pandas. What evidence might scientists have used to draw this conclusion? Explain.

27. INFER What does the presence of similar structures in two organisms—such as a dolphin's flipper and a lizard's forelimb—indicate?

the BIG idea

28. INFER Look again at the picture on pages 786–787. Now that you have finished the chapter, how would you change or add details to your answer to the question on the photograph?

29. SYNTHESIZE The beaks of hummingbirds are adapted to fit into long, thin flowers. Hummingbirds can feed on the nectar inside the flower. Write an explanation for this adaptation that Lamarck might have proposed. Then write an explanation for this adaptation based on Darwin's ideas. Use the terms acquired traits and natural selection in your answer.

UNIT PROJECTS

If you are doing a unit project, make a folder for your project. Include in your folder a list of the resources you will need, the date on which the project is due, and a schedule to track your progress. Begin gathering data.

Standardized Test Practice

Interpreting Diagrams

Choose the letter of the best answer.

This diagram shows how groups of carnivores are related to one another. Each Y in the diagram indicates a common ancestor.

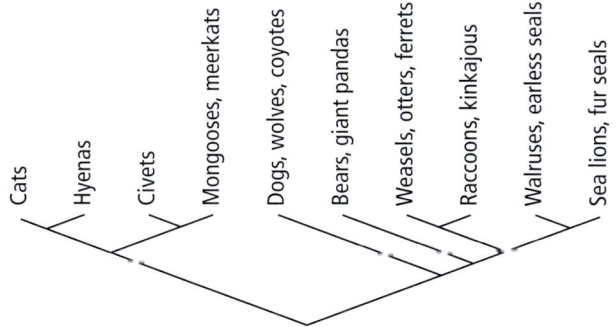

1. Hyenas are most closely related to which group?
   a. cats
   b. civets
   c. mongooses and meerkats
   d. raccoons and kinkajous

2. Weasels, otters, and ferrets are most closely related to
   a. bears and giant pandas
   b. sea lions and fur seals
   c. raccoons and kinkajous
   d. mongooses and meerkats

3. Sea lions and fur seals share their closest common ancestor with
   a. walruses and earless seals
   b. raccoons and kinkajous
   c. mongoose and muskrats
   d. civets

4. Which statement is true based on the information in the diagram?
   a. Dogs, wolves, and coyotes do not share a common ancestor with any of the groups.
   b. Raccoons are more closely related to weasels than they are to giant pandas.
   c. None of the groups shown in the diagram share a common ancestor.
   d. Mongooses and meerkats are the same as civets.

5. The branches on the diagram indicate where
   a. mass extinctions might have occurred
   b. speciation took place
   c. groups acquired traits and passed them onto their offspring
   d. there are gaps in the line of evolution

Extended Response

6. A scientist has discovered a new type of animal in the tundra area near the North Pole. Write a paragraph describing the type of evidence the scientist might use to classify the animal by its evolutionary history in the chart shown. Use these terms in your paragraph. Underline each term in your answer.

   | embryo | DNA sequences |
   | vestigial structures | common ancestor |

7. Write a paragraph in which you describe the traits of one of the animals named in the diagram. Choose several traits and describe how these traits might help the animal survive. Then describe how these might have been the result of adaptations and natural selection.

Chapter 23: History of Life 819

CHAPTER

24 Classification of Living Things

the BIG idea

Scientists have developed a system for classifying the great diversity of living things.

Key Concepts

SECTION 1 Scientists develop systems for classifying living things.
Learn about why scientists classify living things and about taxonomy.

SECTION 2 Biologists use seven levels of classification.
Learn about scientific names, how to classify organisms in seven levels, and dichotomous keys.

SECTION 3 Classification systems change as scientists learn more.
Learn how classification systems have changed based on features of cells.

Internet Preview

CLASSZONE.COM
Chapter 24 online resources: Content Review, Simulation, 3 Resource Centers, Math Tutorial, Test Practice

How many different types of organisms do you see and how would you group them?

EXPLORE the BIG idea

How Are Fingerprints Different?

Make fingerprints of your thumb and the thumbs of several classmates on separate index cards.

Observe and Think What traits do all fingerprints have in common? What traits of fingerprints allow you to tell them apart?

How Would You Sort Pennies?

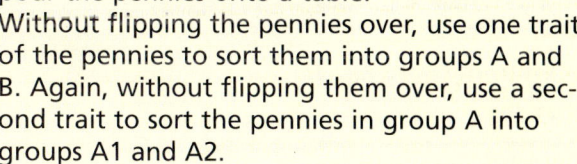

Place 20 pennies in a plastic cup. Place your hand over the cup and shake it. Gently pour the pennies onto a table. Without flipping the pennies over, use one trait of the pennies to sort them into groups A and B. Again, without flipping them over, use a second trait to sort the pennies in group A into groups A1 and A2.

Observe and Think What traits do the pennies in each group share? Which group has the largest numbers of pennies?

Internet Activity: Linnaeus

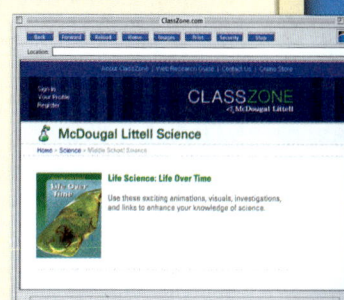

Go to Classzone.com to learn more about Carolus Linnaeus, who, over 200 years ago, laid the groundwork for how today's scientists classify things.

Observe and Think What evidence did Linnaeus use to classify organisms?

NSTA
scilinks.org
SCLINKS

Classification Systems **Code: MDL037**

Chapter 24: **Classification of Living Things** 821

CHAPTER 24
Getting Ready to Learn

CONCEPT REVIEW

- Species change over time.
- Fossils and other evidence show that species change.
- New species develop from ancestral species.

VOCABULARY REVIEW

evolution p. 797
ancestor p. 809

See Glossary for definitions.
species, trait, DNA

CLASSZONE.COM
Review concepts and vocabulary.

TAKING NOTES

SUPPORTING MAIN IDEAS

Make a chart to show main ideas and the information that supports them. Copy each blue heading. Below each heading, add supporting information, such as reasons, explanations, and examples.

VOCABULARY STRATEGY

Place each vocabulary term at the center of a **description wheel** diagram. Write some words describing it on the spokes.

See the Note-Taking Handbook on pages R45–R51.

SCIENCE NOTEBOOK

Scientists classify millions of species.
- Taxonomy is the science of classifying and naming organisms.
- Classification is the process of arranging organisms in groups.
- To classify organisms, scientists compare their characteristics.

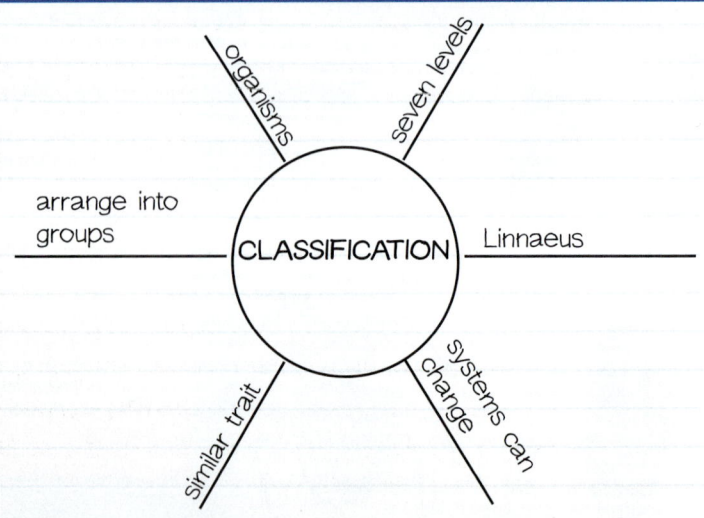

822 Unit 6: Life Over Time

KEY CONCEPT
Scientists develop systems for classifying living things.

BEFORE, you learned
- Natural selection helps explain how new species develop
- Evidence indicates that species change over time
- New species develop from ancestral species

NOW, you will learn
- Why scientists classify living things
- That taxonomists study biological relationships
- About evidence used to classify organisms

VOCABULARY
classification p. 824
taxonomy p. 824

THINK ABOUT

How are these organisms similar?

Both a worm and a caterpillar share many characteristics. Both have long, skinny bodies that are divided into segments. But an earthworm moves underground, has no legs or eyes, and can grow back segments that are lost. A caterpillar crawls aboveground and is just one part of a butterfly's life cycle. As you read this chapter, think about whether you would classify these animals together or separately.

Scientists classify millions of species.

About 400 years ago, scientists who studied insects classified them based upon their appearance and behavior. If animals looked alike, researchers concluded that they were related. In the last few centuries scientists have realized that appearances can suggest false connections. Although caterpillars look like worms, they are actually an earlier stage of a butterfly's life.

For some people, the world seemed to grow larger during the 1600s. Travelers sailed to distant lands and oceans. Scientists went on many of these trips, observing and collecting samples of living things they had never seen before. In addition, the microscope allowed scientists to see tiny organisms that had been invisible before. But how could scientists organize and talk about this wonderful new knowledge?

Chapter 24: **Classification of Living Things** 823

VOCABULARY
Add a description wheel for *classification* to your notebook. Include the word *group* in your diagram.

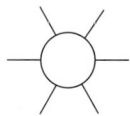

Classification and Taxonomy

Two scientific processes deal with classifying and naming living things. **Classification** is the process of arranging organisms into groups based on similarities. **Taxonomy** is the science of naming and classifying organisms. A good system of classification allows you to organize a large amount of information so that it is easy to find and to understand. The system should provide a tool for comparing very large groups of organisms as well as smaller groups. Large groups might include all animals. Smaller groups might include birds, reptiles, or mammals.

A good system of taxonomy allows people to communicate about organisms. Before the 1700s, scientists had not agreed on a system of naming and grouping organisms. Take, for example, the common wild briar rose. Some scientists called it *Rosa sylvestris inodora seu canina* (odorless woodland dog rose). Others used the name *Rosa sylvestris alba cum rubore, folio glabro* (pinkish-white woodland rose with hairless leaves). Plus, any scientist studying a species could change the name.

These long Latin names may sound confusing, but even common names can be confusing. In England the bird called a robin—Britain's national bird—is only distantly related to the bird called a robin in the United States, even though they both have red feathers on their chests. A daddy longlegs could be either a long-legged relative of spiders (in the United States) or a long-legged relative of mosquitoes (in England).

British Daddy Longlegs

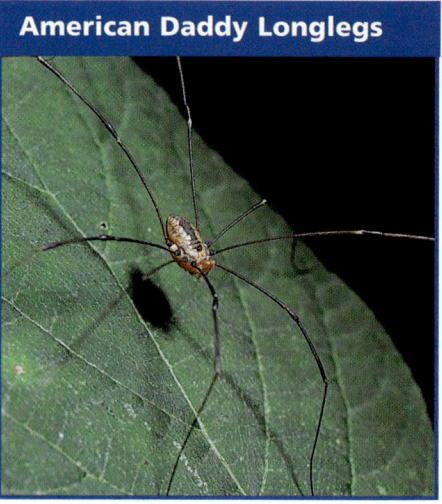
American Daddy Longlegs

Find out more about taxonomy.

Clearly, biologists need both a system for organizing and a system for naming. Each name should refer to one specific type of organism. That way, scientists can use the species name and be sure that everybody knows exactly which organism they are talking about.

CHECK YOUR READING What is the difference between classification and taxonomy?

Using Classification

To classify organisms, scientists use similarities and differences among species. Sometimes these differences are easy to see, such as whether an animal has fur, feathers, or scales. Other times, seeing the differences requires special laboratory equipment, such as equipment to study DNA.

A classification system can help you identify unfamiliar organisms. For example, if you had never heard of a caracal but were told that it was a kind of cat, you already would know many things about it. It has fur, fangs, and sharp claws. It's a meat eater, not a plant eater. You would know these things because the caracal shares those characteristics with all of the members of the cat family.

If you looked up *caracal* in an encyclopedia, you'd find that your guesses were right. The caracal is a small wildcat native to Africa, the Middle East, and India. It weighs about 13 to 19 kilograms (29 to 42 pounds). The name *caracal* comes from a Turkish word meaning "black-eared."

The more characteristics two organisms share, the more similar their names should be in the classification system. The caracal, a pet cat, and all the cats below are different in size, habitat, and other characteristics. But they also have many similarities, and all belong to the cat family, Felidae.

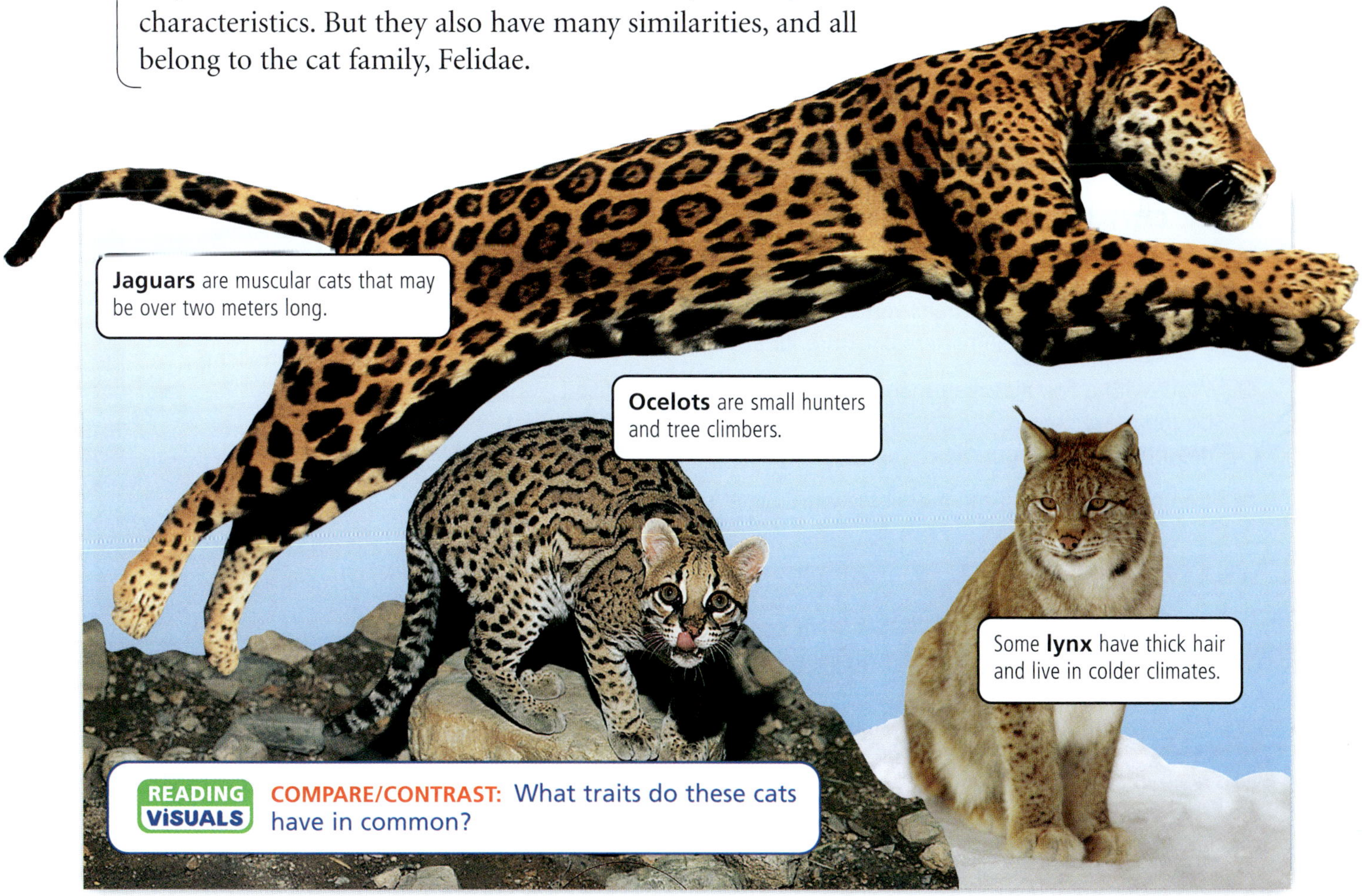

Like other cats, a caracal has fur, sharp fangs, and is a meat eater.

Jaguars are muscular cats that may be over two meters long.

Ocelots are small hunters and tree climbers.

Some **lynx** have thick hair and live in colder climates.

READING VISUALS **COMPARE/CONTRAST:** What traits do these cats have in common?

Chapter 24: **Classification of Living Things** 825

Taxonomists study biological relationships.

READING TIP
Taxonomy, taxonomist, and *taxon* all share the same root.

Scientists need a simple, standard way of arranging all of the different species. The science of taxonomy is related to the Greek word *taxis*, which means "arrangement." Taxonomists are the scientists who classify and name organisms based on their similarities and differences. A taxon is a group of organisms that share certain traits. Taxons can be broad, like animals and plants, or more specific, like cats and roses.

As you learned in Chapter 23, living things evolve over time. A single species found in a fossil record might be the ancestor of many different species found on Earth today. Taxonomists study the relationships between species, trying to discover how one species evolved as compared with another species. Species that share ancestors are grouped together.

To determine how to classify organisms, scientists compare a variety of characteristics, or traits. A trait is a characteristic or behavior that can be used to tell two species apart, such as size or bone structure. If two organisms share a trait, taxonomists try to determine if they share the trait because they share an ancestor.

CHECK YOUR READING How do taxonomists use biological relationships to classify organisms?

INVESTIGATE Classifying Leaves

How can you classify leaves?
PROCEDURE

1. Decide, as a class, what traits you will use to classify leaves. You may use size, shape, color, vein patterns, texture, or anything else that you observe.
2. Work with a few classmates. Sort your leaves into four or five taxons, based on the characteristics chosen in step 1. Give each taxon a name that describes its common traits.
3. Compare your classification scheme with those of other groups.

WHAT DO YOU THINK?
- How did you arrange the leaves into groups?
- Did your methods of classifying leaves match those of other student groups?

CHALLENGE How does your group's classification scheme compare with the scheme scientists use for classification?

SKILL FOCUS
Classifying

MATERIALS
- leaves
- hand lens

TIME
20 minutes

826 Unit 6: Life Over Time

Biological Relationships

The **sargassum fish** and the sea dragon are both fish with wavy fronds.

This **sargassum seaweed** and the sea dragon both have leafy fronds.

Both the **sea horse** and sea dragon have the same basic body shape.

Look at the photographs and try to determine to which organism a leafy sea dragon is more closely related. The leafy sea dragon shares traits with all of the other organisms pictured. For example, the sea dragon and the sargassum seaweed look similar, with greenish wavy fronds. But the sea dragon is an animal that moves, gets food from other organisms, and breathes oxygen. The sargassum seaweed is not an animal, it is a type of algae.

The sargassum fish shares more traits with the sea dragon, but its body is a much different shape and has scales. In fact, the leafy sea dragon is an animal that is closely related to a sea horse. Both have heads and bodies with similar shapes, and neither has scales. The sea horse shares more traits with the leafy sea dragon than with the other two organisms.

Taxonomists take evidence and try to reconstruct the evolution of a species. Then they place the species in the classification system. Scientists use physical evidence, such as fur, bones, and teeth. They also use genetic evidence, which is found within an organism's DNA.

Physical Evidence

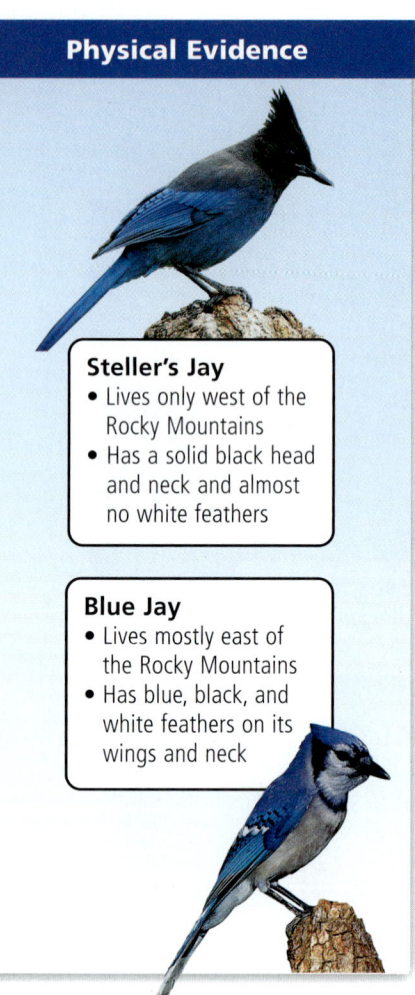

Steller's Jay
- Lives only west of the Rocky Mountains
- Has a solid black head and neck and almost no white feathers

Blue Jay
- Lives mostly east of the Rocky Mountains
- Has blue, black, and white feathers on its wings and neck

The primary tools early scientists used for taxonomy were their eyes and measuring devices. They collected examples of organisms and noted characteristics, such as color, size, weight, and how groups of organisms obtain energy. Scientists who studied animals observed the internal structure, as well as outward appearances. These physical features are still important today.

Individuals of two species, such as the two jays shown to the left, can have many similarities as well as some differences. One obvious difference is the color pattern. Another is the area of the world in which they live. Blue jays live east of the Rocky Mountains, and steller's jays live west of the Rockies. The common names and the scientific names reflect the differences and the common ancestor: blue jay, *Cyanocitta cristata* and steller's jay, *Cyanocitta stelleri*.

Skeletons, shells, and other hard parts of organisms become fossilized more easily than soft parts do. Scientists can observe and measure fossilized bones or pieces of bones and compare them with each other. They can also compare bones of species that are extinct with bones of modern species. From such studies, scientists can determine many things about the organism. Physical evidence provides clues about how an organism may have lived, how it moved, or what type of food it ate.

All of this physical evidence helps scientists see that all living organisms are related by evolution. Some are more closely related than others. This means they share a more recent ancestor.

 **CHECK YOUR READING** How could comparing fossilized bones with a modern animal's bones help you see the modern animal's evolutionary history?

Genetic Evidence

In the early 20th century scientists discovered that organisms inherit their traits through structures called genes. In the mid-1950s they observed that genes are made of DNA and that DNA stores coded information.

Today scientists can use laboratory machines to catalog each component of an organism's DNA. With that information stored on a computer, scientists can compare the components of a gene from one organism with the components of the same gene from another organism.

Genetic evidence usually supports physical evidence, but not always. Consider the example shown on page 829. For years, taxonomists argued about how to classify this small, reddish animal from China. Its scientific name is *Ailurus fulgens*, and the common name is red panda.

Genetic Evidence

Both of these pandas live in the same habitat, have similar faces, and eat bamboo. But genetic evidence shows that red pandas and giant pandas are only distant relatives.

Later, scientists discovered a larger, bearlike animal in China, which they called the giant panda. Both pandas ate only bamboo, shared a common name, and their faces looked similar. Scientists concluded they were related to each other and to raccoons. However, molecular evidence has shown that the red panda is more closely related to raccoons and the giant panda is more closely related to bears.

24.1 Review

KEY CONCEPTS

1. Describe the benefits of classifying species.
2. Why do taxonomists study biological relationships?
3. How do scientists use genetic evidence when classifying organisms?

CRITICAL THINKING

4. **Analyze** Why do people need a universal system of naming organisms?
5. **Predict** The animal called a marbled godwit is a bird. What traits would you predict it has?

CHALLENGE

6. **Synthesize** Suppose you found two species of cave-dwelling lizards without eyes living on opposite sides of the world. Explain how you would try to determine if the two species were closely related.

Chapter 24: **Classification of Living Things** 829

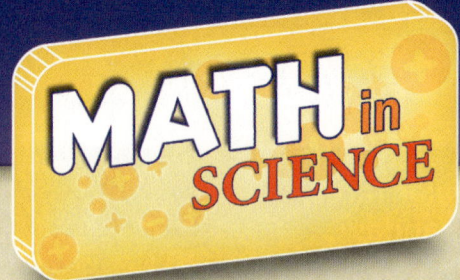

MATH in SCIENCE

SKILL: WRITING PERCENTS

MATH TUTORIAL
CLASSZONE.COM
Click on Math Tutorial for more help with percents and fractions.

Differences Between Species

Does it surprise you to learn that roughly 50 percent of the DNA in your cells is nearly identical to the DNA in the cells of a banana? You probably know from experience that 50 percent is the same as one half. But you can also convert any percent to a fraction by using the number 100 to represent the whole. Fifty parts out of 100 is the same as one half. Another example is shown below.

Example

Comparing the cells of two species, scientists find 40 percent of the DNA is identical. How can you show what fraction that is?

(1) Rewrite the percent as a numerator with a denominator of 100.
$$\frac{40}{100}$$

(2) Reduce the fraction. Use the greatest common factor (GCF) to write the numerator and the denominator as products.
$$\frac{40}{100} = \frac{2 \cdot 20}{5 \cdot 20}$$

(3) Divide the GCF by itself to get $\frac{1}{1}$, or 1.
$$\frac{2}{5} \cdot \frac{20}{20} = \frac{2}{5} \cdot 1 = \frac{2}{5}$$

ANSWER: 40 percent = $\frac{2}{5}$

Rewrite each sentence, changing the percent to a fraction.

1. About 85 percent of the DNA in human cells is similar to the DNA in mouse cells.

2. The tooth of a modern great white shark can be 34 percent of the length of a fossil tooth from a prehistoric shark.

3. There are about 20 percent as many penguin species as there are pine tree species in the world today.

4. There are about 8 percent as many bear species as pine tree species.

CHALLENGE Choose one example or exercise on this page. Tell whether the comparison works better as a fraction or a percent. Explain why.

KEY CONCEPT

24.2 Biologists use seven levels of classification.

 BEFORE, you learned
- Classification is a system of organization
- Evidence is used to classify organisms

 NOW, you will learn
- About scientific names
- About seven levels of classification
- How to use a dichotomous key

VOCABULARY

genus p. 832
binomial nomenclature p. 832
dichotomous key p. 836

EXPLORE Classification

What data do you need to identify objects?

PROCEDURE

1. Have one student in your group think of a secret object. The student should then tell the group one characteristic (shape, color, size, type, and so on) of that object.

2. The rest of the group guesses the object's identity. Each time someone guesses incorrectly, another characteristic of the object should be given. Record the characteristics and guesses as you go.

3. When the secret object is guessed correctly, begin again with a different student picking a different secret object.

WHAT DO YOU THINK?
- How many characteristics did it usually take to guess an object's identity?
- How does this exercise relate to identifying organisms?

Linnaeus named about 4000 species.

Scientists name species and arrange them into groups. One scientist named Carolus Linnaeus developed systems for both naming species and organizing them into groups. All 4000 species that Linnaeus named were plants or animals. Today, scientists have named over a million species. Linnaeus used appearance to group species. As you have read, modern scientists also use appearance, along with other types of evidence, to arrange species into groups.

SUPPORTING MAIN IDEAS
Make a chart to show information that supports the first main idea presented: *Linnaeus named about 4000 species.*

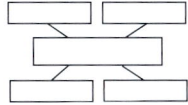

Chapter 24: **Classification of Living Things** 831

Naming Species

Sometimes using only one word to name an organism isn't specific enough. If you are telling a friend about your favorite writer, you might name Mary Oliver or Mary Whitebird or Mary Shelley. Using only "Mary" won't help your friend know the author you name, so you use two words. In a similar way, scientists use two words to name organisms.

A **genus** (JEE-nuhs) is a group of species that have similar characteristics. For example, the genus *Ursus* groups all of the animals known as bears. Included in this genus are *Ursus arctos* (grizzly bears), and *Ursus maritimus* (polar bears). Members of the same genus are closely related.

The system for naming species developed by Linnaeus is the basis of modern taxonomy. We call this system **binomial nomenclature** (by-NOH-mee-uhl NOH-muhn-KLAY-chuhr). *Binomial* means "two names" and *nomenclature* means "list of names." So binomial nomenclature describes a system of naming something using two names, or words. Most scientific names are Latin terms.

INVESTIGATE Binomial Nomenclature

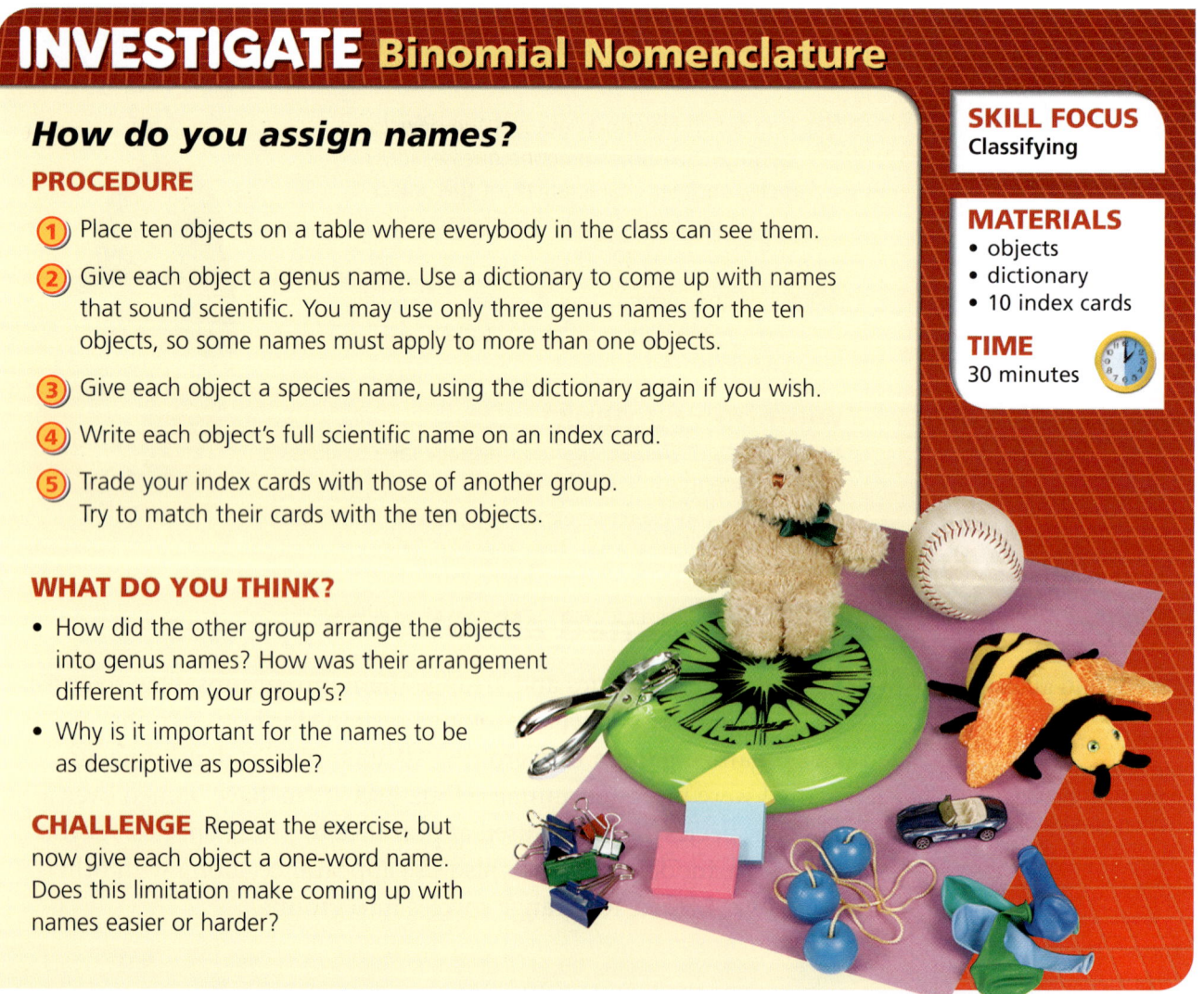

How do you assign names?

PROCEDURE

1. Place ten objects on a table where everybody in the class can see them.
2. Give each object a genus name. Use a dictionary to come up with names that sound scientific. You may use only three genus names for the ten objects, so some names must apply to more than one objects.
3. Give each object a species name, using the dictionary again if you wish.
4. Write each object's full scientific name on an index card.
5. Trade your index cards with those of another group. Try to match their cards with the ten objects.

SKILL FOCUS
Classifying

MATERIALS
- objects
- dictionary
- 10 index cards

TIME
30 minutes

WHAT DO YOU THINK?
- How did the other group arrange the objects into genus names? How was their arrangement different from your group's?
- Why is it important for the names to be as descriptive as possible?

CHALLENGE Repeat the exercise, but now give each object a one-word name. Does this limitation make coming up with names easier or harder?

Binomial Nomenclature

All organisms are given a unique two-part name. Some organisms have the same species names: *gracilis* means "slender" or "graceful." Without the genus name, the species name is unclear.

Aubrieta gracilis
(false rockcress)

Chameleo gracilis
(gracile chameleon)

Mammillaria gracilis
(thimble cactus)

Using Scientific Names

Linnaeus's system of binomial nomenclature made communication about certain species much easier. When naming an organism, the use of a genus name as well as a species name is necessary.

If the genus name is not included in the scientific name, the identity of a species can be a mystery. For example, the species name of the three different species shown above is *gracilis*. The word *gracilis* means "graceful" or "slender" in Latin.

- *Aubrieta gracilis* is a type of flower found in a rock garden.
- *Chameleo gracilis* is a type of lizard called a chameleon.
- *Mammillaria gracilis* is a type of cactus.

People follow certain rules when they write scientific names. The genus name comes first; the first letter is capitalized and the entire name is in italics. The species name is also written in italics, it follows the genus name, and the first letter is lowercased.

 What is the difference between a genus and a species?

In addition to species and genus, the classification system includes several larger groups. Each larger group includes one or more smaller groups. Turn to page 834 to read about the larger groups in our modern system of classification.

SUPPORTING MAIN IDEAS
Make a chart to show information that supports the main idea that *organisms can be classified into seven levels.*

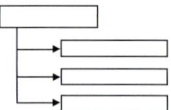

READING TIP
Phyla is the plural form of *phylum*.

Organisms can be classified into seven levels.

You've read about species and genus, the most specific levels of the classification system most scientists use today. There are seven levels that describe a species. The largest level is the kingdom, the group containing the most species. The seven levels of classification for a spotted turtle and a housecat are listed below.

1. Kingdom (Animalia—the animals)
2. Phylum (Chordata—animals with backbones)
3. Class (Mammalia—mammals, or furry animals that nurse their young)
4. Order (Carnivora—carnivores, or animals that kill and eat other animals)
5. Family (Felidae—the cat family)
6. Genus (*Felis*—housecats, cougars, and many others)
7. Species (*catus*—all housecats, no matter what their breed)

Like the cat, the turtle is also classified into seven levels. However, only the two largest levels, Animalia and Chordata, are the same as the classification for a housecat. The more names an organism shares with another organism, the more closely related the two organisms are. Cats and turtles are both animals with backbones, but are otherwise different. Spotted turtles have more traits in common with snakes and lizards than with cats. Lizards, snakes, and turtles all belong in the class Reptilia. Phyla are more specific than kingdoms, classes are more specific than phyla, and so on. The illustration on page 835 shows how kingdom is the broadest grouping of organisms, and species is the most specific.

Classification Hierarchy		
	Spotted turtle	**Cat**
Kingdom	Animalia	Animalia
Phylum	Chordata	Chordata
Class	Reptilia	Mammalia
Order	Testudines	Carnivora
Family	Emydidae	Felidae
Genus	*Clemmys*	*Felis*
Species	*guttata*	*catus*

Clemmys guttata

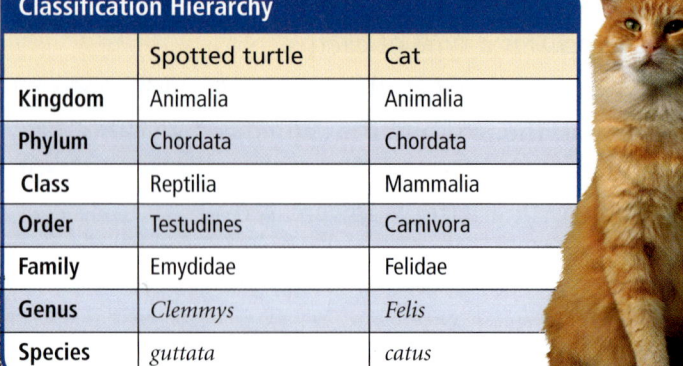

Felis catus

834 Unit 6: Life Over Time

Scientists can compare very broad categories of organisms, such as kingdoms and phyla. Or they can compare very specific categories, such as species. If scientists wish to compare all the different types of turtles to one another, then they will compare the organisms in the order Testudines. But if scientists want to compare turtles that live in or near water, then they will compare only organisms in the family Emydidae.

You can remember the classification levels and their order with this memory aid: Kings Play Chess On Fat Green Stools. The first letter of each word is the same as the first letter in each level of classification: *kingdom, phylum, class, order, family, genus,* and *species*. A complete classification of humans goes like this: kingdom Animalia, phylum Chordata, class Mammalia, order Primates, family Hominidae, genus *Homo,* species *sapiens.*

 Which level of classification in the seven-level system includes the most species?

Dichotomous keys and field guides help people identify organisms.

With millions of organisms on Earth, how could a specific one be identified? Even if you know some of the larger categories, it can be difficult to find the species, genus, or even family name of many organisms from a long list of possibilities.

Take a beetle, for example. Even if you knew that it is in the kingdom Animalia, phylum Arthropoda (animals with jointed legs), class Insecta (insects), and order Coleoptera (hard-winged insects), you'd still have to choose among 300,000 known species of beetles that have been discovered around the world.

Taxonomists have come up with a tool to identify organisms such as this beetle. A **dichotomous key** (dy-KAHT-uh-muhs) asks a series of questions that can be answered in only two ways. Your answer to each question leads you to another question with only two choices. After a number of such questions, you will identify the organism. One example of a dichotomous key for trees is shown on page 837.

The questions in a dichotomous key gradually narrow down the list of possible organisms. The questions can ask about any trait. The idea is simply to make identifying an organism as easy as possible. The dichotomous key for trees, for example, asks a set of questions that only ask about the traits of the leaves. Leaves are usually easy to get from a tree that needs to be identified, and they include many characteristics that can be used to tell different trees apart.

The prefix *di-* means "two."

Use an interactive dichotomous key.

- A bird's **scientific name** is shown next to its common name. The first name is the genus, and the second name is the species.
- **Range maps** show where a bird can be found in each season.
- **Body shape and body size** give clues to determining if you have identified the right bird.

Another tool for identifying organisms is a field guide. Field guides include paintings or photographs of familiar species. Flower guides may start with the flower's color. Bird guides are arranged by orders and families. Field guides also include maps showing where organisms live.

CHECK YOUR READING What two tools have taxonomists developed to identify organisms?

24.2 Review

KEY CONCEPTS

1. What is binomial nomenclature?
2. Write the names of the seven levels of classification. Which level contains the most organisms?
3. What makes a dichotomous key easy to use?

CRITICAL THINKING

4. **Summarize** What were Carolus Linnaeus's main contributions to taxonomy?
5. **Compare and Contrast** Compare a dichotomous key with a typical field guide. What are the strengths and weaknesses of each?

CHALLENGE

6. **Synthesize** Predict what differences you might find among organisms in the same species.

EXTREME SCIENCE

NEW INSECT SPECIES

The Undiscovered

Everyone agrees that insects are the largest group of animals on Earth, but nobody knows exactly how many insect species exist. Some estimates predict that there are as many as 30 million. However, only about 900,000 have been classified. Twenty-nine million insect species may be waiting to be discovered!

Where in the World?

Many of the new insect species are found in tropical forests of South America and Asia. But plenty may be hiding close to your own home.

- The most massive bug in Southern California went undiscovered until April 4, 2002. This wingless relative of the Jerusalem cricket looks something like a puffed-up 3-inch-long ant.
- While studying for her graduate degree, Christina Sandoval captured insects in Santa Barbara, California. She caught an unidentified species of walking stick insect, which she named after herself: *Timema cristinae*.
- The Hanford Nuclear Reservation, in Washington state, was closed to the public for about 50 years. After it opened for cleanup, the Nature Conservancy found 27 new insect species in just 4 years, including a new micromoth less than 1/8 inch long.

Scientists think that over one third of the estimated 164,000 insect species in the United States have yet to be discovered and named. Start looking. Who knows where they'll be!

A Whole New Order

In March 2002, for the first time in 87 years, a whole new order of insects was discovered. Insects in this order look like a cross between stick insects, praying mantises, and grasshoppers. Upon its discovery, the order was nicknamed *gladiators*. Now called *Mantophasmatodea*, the "gladiator bugs" raised the total number of insect orders to 31.

EXPLORE

1. **ANALYZE** List some things about an insect that could be included in its species name. Tell why each is important.
2. **CHALLENGE** Scientists recently discovered a new centipede in New York's Central Park, the first new species in the park in over 100 years. Centipedes are related to insects. Find out what centipedes and insects have in common and how they differ.

An adult Jerusalem cricket can reach 2 inches in length.

RESOURCE CENTER
CLASSZONE.COM
Learn more about newly discovered insects.

Chapter 24: **Classification of Living Things** 839

KEY CONCEPT
Classification systems change as scientists learn more.

◀ **BEFORE, you learned**
- Scientists give each species a unique scientific name
- There are seven levels of classification
- Dichotomous keys help us identify organisms

▶ **NOW, you will learn**
- About the connection between new discoveries and taxonomy
- About three domains
- About six kingdoms

VOCABULARY

domain p. 841
Plantae p. 843
Animalia p. 843
Protista p. 843
Fungi p. 843
Archaea p. 843
Bacteria p. 843

THINK ABOUT

How do scientists define kingdoms?

Look at this photograph of a sea urchin. It lives its life buried in or slowly moving across the ocean floor. The sea urchin's mouth is located on its underside. It feeds on food particles that settle on or are buried in the ocean floor. The sea urchin doesn't appear to have much in common with a tiger, an alligator, even a human. Yet all of these organisms belong in the same kingdom, called Animalia. Why do you think scientists would group these organisms together?

Taxonomy changes as scientists make discoveries.

The list of species continues to grow as scientists discover new species. In addition, taxonomists are learning more about the evolutionary history of species. As you read in Section 24.1, new knowledge resulted in the reclassification of species such as the giant panda. Both the names of species and the groups into which they are arranged may change as a result of discoveries about the evolution of these species.

Early scientists described two large groups of organisms—plants and animals. Plants were described as green and nonmoving. Animals moved. Most scientists today use a system that includes six kingdoms. In addition, taxonomists have added a level of organization above the kingdom level.

840 Unit 6: Life Over Time

Three Domains

Microscopes and other advances in technology have allowed scientists to observe that there are three fundamentally different types of cells. On the basis of this observation, scientists have arranged kingdoms into larger groups called **domains.** For example, the domain Eukarya contains the protists, fungi, plants, and animals.

The table below summarizes the relationships among the six kingdoms and the three domains. You will learn more about kingdoms in the rest of this section.

Find out more about modern classification.

Domains and Kingdoms						
Domain	Bacteria	Archaea	Eukarya			
Kingdom	Bacteria	Archaea	Protista	Fungi	Plantae	Animalia
Cell type	No nucleus	No nucleus	With nucleus	With nucleus	With nucleus	With nucleus
Cell number	Unicellular	Unicellular	Unicellular	Mostly multicellular	Multicellular	Multicellular
How organisms get energy	Varies	Varies	Varies	Absorbs materials	Uses sunlight	Consumes food

The photographs below show examples of cells from each domain. One of the traits that distinguishes cells of Eukarya from cells of Bacteria and Archaea is the presence of a nucleus. Cells that contain a nucleus are called eukaryotic cells, and cells that do not contain a nucleus are called prokaryotic cells. The domains Bacteria and Archaea include only organisms with prokaryotic cells. The domain Eukarya includes only organisms with eukaryotic cells.

 How are prokaryotic cells different from eukaryotic cells?

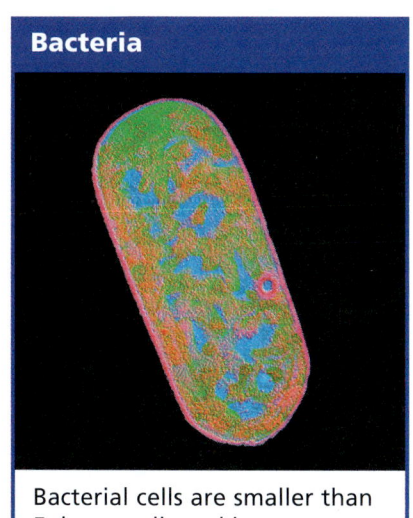

Bacteria

Bacterial cells are smaller than Eukarya cells and have no nucleus.

Archaea

Archaea cells have a distinctive chemistry and can survive extreme environments.

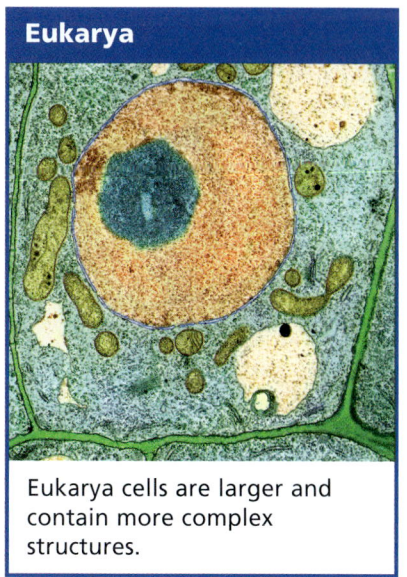

Eukarya

Eukarya cells are larger and contain more complex structures.

Chapter 24: **Classification of Living Things** 841

Six Kingdoms

All living things on Earth can be classified in six kingdoms.

Plantae
- Plants are multicellular and live on land.
- Plants obtain energy from sunlight.
- A plant cell has a nucleus, a cell wall, and chloroplasts.

Animalia
- Animals are multicellular and able to move.
- Animals obtain energy by eating food.
- An animal cell has a nucleus but no cell wall or chloroplasts.

Protista
- Most protists are single-celled.
- Multicellular protists lack complex structure.
- A protist cell has a nucleus.

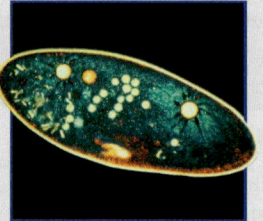

Fungi
- All fungi except yeasts are multicellular.
- Fungi obtain energy by absorbing materials.
- A fungus cell has a nucleus and a cell wall, but no chloroplasts.

Archaea
- Archaea are unicellular organisms without nuclei.
- Archaea cells have different chemicals than bacteria.
- Archaea can live in extreme conditions.

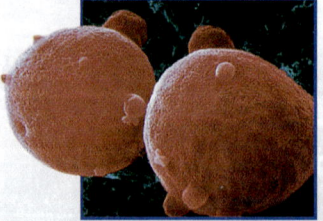

Bacteria
- Bacteria are unicellular organisms.
- A bacterial cell has no nucleus.
- Bacteria reproduce by dividing in two.

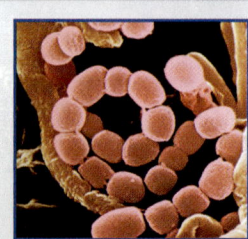

Six Kingdoms

The classification system that many scientists use today has six kingdoms. Every known species on Earth is included in one of these six kingdoms.

- Kingdom **Plantae** (PLAN-TEE) includes plants such as trees, grass, and moss.
- Kingdom **Animalia** (AN-uh-MAL-yuh) includes animals, from lions and tigers and bears to bugs and multicellular microbes.
- Kingdom **Protista** (pruh-TIHS-tuh) includes organisms that don't fit easily into animals, plants, or fungi. They are either unicellular organisms or have a simple multicellular structure.
- Kingdom **Fungi** (FUHN-jy) includes mushrooms, molds, and yeasts.
- Kingdom **Archaea** (AHR-kee-uh) contains organisms that are similar to bacteria, but have a cell structure that is so different that scientists separate them into their own kingdom.
- Kingdom **Bacteria** (bak-TIHR-ee-uh) are unicellular organisms with no nucleus.

> **VOCABULARY**
> Add description wheels for *Plantae, Animalia, Protista, Fungi, Archaea,* and *Bacteria* to your notebook. You may want to add to your diagrams as you read the section.
>
>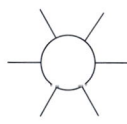

This system may change as scientists learn more about the species in each kingdom. Before 1990, most scientists preferred a five-kingdom system that combined Archaea and Bacteria into a single kingdom. However, as scientists learned of chemical differences between the cells of the species, they arranged them into two kingdoms. Today, some scientists suggest that the kingdom Protista should be arranged into smaller kingdoms because of the many differences among its species. Many scientists agree on a three domain and six kingdom system similar to the one summarized on pages 841–843.

 Which of the six kingdoms include unicellular organisms?

The two most familiar kingdoms are plants and animals.

Carolus Linnaeus divided all of the species he identified into two large groups: plants and animals. People still use these groups to describe most living things today. But these two kingdoms also include unfamiliar organisms.

It might seem odd that living things that are so different from each other—humans, elephants, termites, ducks, fish, worms—are all part of the same group. However, all of these organisms share some general traits, just as all plants share another set of general traits.

Chapter 24: **Classification of Living Things** 843

Clematis viticella
(Italian clematis)

Plantae

About 250,000 plant species live on Earth. They range from tiny mosses to the largest organisms on the planet, giant sequoia trees. The oldest living organism on our planet is a plant called the bristlecone pine. Some living bristlecone pines were growing when the Egyptians built the pyramids, about 4000 years ago.

All plants are multicellular and are eukaryotes, which means their DNA is stored in the nucleus of their cells. All plants are able to make sugars using the Sun's energy. Plants cannot move from place to place, but they can grow around objects, turn toward light, and grow upward. Plant cells are different from animal cells, because plant cells have tough walls outside their cell membranes.

 Animalia

Scientists have already named a million species in the kingdom Animalia. Many different types of animals inhabit the planet, but more than 90 percent of the named species are insects. The animal kingdom also includes familiar animals such as whales, sharks, humans, bears, dogs, and fish.

All animals get their energy by eating other organisms or by eating food made by other organisms. Animals have the ability to move around for at least part of their life. Most animals have mouths and some type of nervous system. Plant and animal cells are both eukaryotic, but animal cells have no cell walls.

CHECK YOUR READING What is the most abundant type of species in the animal kingdom?

Abracadabrella birdsville
(jumping spider)

Giraffa camelopardalis
(giraffe)

Octopus cyanea
(day octopus)

Other organisms make up four more kingdoms.

Carolus Linnaeus's classification systems included the organisms he knew about in the late 1700s. Some of the organisms Linnaeus called plants—the mushrooms, molds, and their relatives—turned out to have some characteristics very different from those of plants. Biologists now put fungi in a kingdom of their own.

Three other kingdoms consist mainly of microscopic organisms. These are Protista, Archaea, and Bacteria. Most organisms on Earth are classified as bacteria or archaea. These are prokaryotic organisms, which have small, simple cells and no nuclei.

 What are the four kingdoms besides Plantae and Animalia?

Protista

The kingdom Protista includes a wide variety of organisms. Most protists are unicellular. Protists that are multicellular have structures that are too simple to be classified as animals, plants, or fungi. All protists have large, complex cells with a true nucleus (eukaryotes). Some eat other organisms as animals do; some get energy from sunlight as plants do. Some protists resemble fungi. However, protists that are multicellular do not have as many specialized cells or structures as plants, animals, and fungi.

Many protists live in pond water or sea water. The largest of the unicellular species are barely visible without a microscope. However, large organisms such as seaweeds are also classified as Protista. Some seaweeds can grow hundreds of feet in a single year.

Different groups of protists evolved from different ancestors. Scientists still debate whether kingdom Protista should be classified as one kingdom or should be split into several kingdoms.

Macrocystis pyrifera (giant kelp)

Chapter 24: **Classification of Living Things** 845

Fungi

Every time a loaf of bread is baked, a fungus is responsible for the rising dough. One group of fungi called yeasts makes it possible for us to make bread and many other food products. Another type of fungi that people eat includes some mushrooms. A mushroom grows in thin threads underground, and only the small cap breaks above the ground.

READING TIP
Fungi is the plural form of *fungus*.

Fungi are usually divided into three categories: mushrooms, molds, and yeasts. The trait that separates fungi from other organisms is that fungi take in nutrients from their surroundings instead of eating other organisms or using sunlight. Both plants and fungi remain rooted in one place. Most fungi have cell walls similar to the cell walls of plants. Unlike plants, however, many fungi act as decomposers, breaking down dead or decaying material into simpler parts that can be absorbed or recycled by other organisms.

Penicillium (bread mold)

Lepiota procera (parasol mushroom)

Archaea

In the mid-1990s a researcher studying the genes of some bacteria discovered that although they resembled bacteria in size and cell type, some species had very specific genetic differences. After more study, scientists decided to call these organisms archaea. They differ so much that scientists now classify archaea in the separate kingdom or domain of Archaea.

In some ways, archaea appear to be more related to eukaryotes—organisms with complex cells containing nuclei—than to bacteria. Archaea do not have nuclei, but their cell structure is different from that of bacteria. Like bacteria, archaea live in many environments, especially in the ocean. But they also live in some very extreme environments, such as boiling mud near geysers, hot vents at the bottom of the ocean, salty ponds, and deep under the sand.

Methanococcoides burtonii

CHECK YOUR READING
Which traits classify an organism as part of the kingdom Archaea?

Bacteria

Bacteria live nearly everywhere on Earth. This kingdom includes organisms that cause human disease and spoil food, but most of these organisms are helpful members of biological communities.

All bacteria are unicellular organisms. They have small, simple cells without a nucleus. Most bacteria have a cell wall outside the cell membrane, but this wall is not the same as the cell wall of plants. Bacteria reproduce by dividing in two, and can produce many new generations in a short period of time.

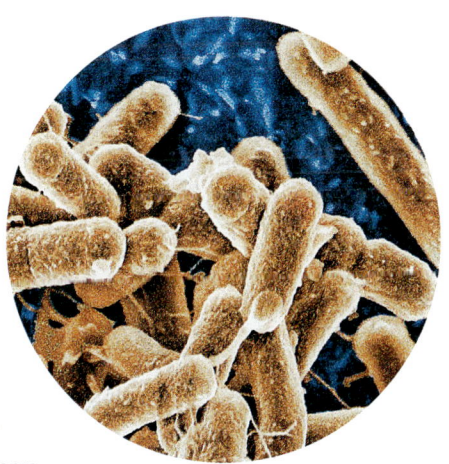

Escherichia coli (E. coli)

Species and environments change.

In the last chapter you read about the ways species change over time. You have also read how the evolutionary history of species helps scientists classify living things.

Scientists have named over a million species and placed them into six kingdoms. In addition, scientists estimate that there are millions maybe tens of millions—more species that haven't been discovered. Scientists have also discovered forms of life preserved in the fossil record. Some of those organisms are the ancestors of organisms that live today.

Species evolve over time as individual organisms and environments change. Individual organisms are faced with many other pressures that affect daily lives. These pressures may come from changes in their living space, in the availability of food or other resources, or from other organisms. In the next chapter, you will read about how groups of species are affected by changes in their surroundings.

24.3 Review

KEY CONCEPTS

1. What are the names of the six kingdoms used in the classification system?
2. How are species sorted into the various kingdoms?

CRITICAL THINKING

3. **Communicate** Make a table with columns headed Characteristics, Animalia, and Plantae. Using as many rows as needed, list characteristics that differ between these two kingdoms.
4. **Analyze** Explain how fungi differ from plants.

CHALLENGE

5. **Analyze** One bacterium has a membrane surrounding its DNA. Should this organism be classified with the eukaryotes? Why or why not?

CHAPTER INVESTIGATION

Making a Field Guide

OVERVIEW AND PURPOSE A field guide is an illustrated book that shows the differences and similarities among plant or animal organisms. In this activity you will
- observe and classify leaves
- prepare a field guide based on your observations

Question

A field guide helps scientists identify organisms. Can you successfully prepare such a field guide? What would you like to know about how field guides are used and made? Write a question that begins with *Which, How, Why, When,* or *What.*

Procedure

MATERIALS
- plastic gloves
- shoebox
- hand lens
- pencil
- paper
- tracing paper
- crayons

1. Make 5 or more tables like the one shown on the sample science notebook on page 849. Gather at least 5 samples of different leaves from an area that your teacher chooses. **CAUTION: Wear protective gloves when handling plants. Be aware of any poisonous plants in your area.** Place your samples in a shoebox and bring them back to the classroom for observation.

2. **CAUTION: Wear plastic gloves when handling leaf samples.** Use the hand lens to study the leaves that you gathered. Make a sketch of each of the leaves. Create leaf rubbings by placing each leaf between two sheets of tracing paper and rubbing the top paper with the side of a pencil or crayon. Record your observations about each leaf in one of the data tables.

848 Unit 6: **Life Over Time**

3 Use the information in your table to prepare your field guide. Start by dividing your leaves into two groups on the basis of one of the characteristics you observed. Then compare the leaves in each group. How are they similar or different? Continue to observe and divide the samples in each group until each leaf is in a classification by itself.

4 Use scientific field guides or other sources to identify your sample leaves. Find out the common and scientific name for each leaf and add that information to your table.

5 Describe the location of each sample and what effect the plant it represents has on its environment. For example, does the plant provide food or shelter for animals? Does it have a commercial use, or is it an important part of the environment?

6 Use your data tables, sketches, and leaf rubbings to prepare your field guide for the chosen area.

▶ Observe and Analyze   *Write It Up*

1. CLASSIFY What characteristics did you choose for classifying your leaf samples? Explain why you grouped the leaves the way you did.

2. ANALYZE Which characteristics of the leaves you gathered were most useful in finding their scientific names and in identifying them?

▶ Conclude   *Write It Up*

1. INFER Could you use the same characteristics you used to group your samples to classify leaves of other species?

2. LIMITATIONS Were there any leaves you could not classify? What would help you classify them?

3. APPLY How are field guides useful to scientists working on environmental studies? How are field guides useful to tourists or others who are exploring an environment?

▶ INVESTIGATE Further

CHALLENGE Combine your field guide with those made by all the other members of your class to make one large field guide. Use all the sketches and observations to classify leaves into several large groups.

Making a Field Guide: Leaf 1

Characteristic	Observations
Simple leaf or several leaflets	
Number of lobes	
Texture	
Leaf edge	
Vein patterns	

Common name

Scientific name

Location where found

Uses/role in environment

Chapter 24: **Classification of Living Things** 849

24 Chapter Review

the BIG idea
Scientists have developed a system for classifying the great diversity of living things.

CONTENT REVIEW
CLASSZONE.COM

KEY CONCEPTS SUMMARY

1 Scientists develop systems for classifying living things.

- Living things are arranged in groups based on similarities.
- Classification is the process of arranging organisms into groups.
- Taxonomy involves classifying as well as naming species.

VOCABULARY
classification p. 824
taxonomy p. 824

2 Biologists use seven levels of classification.

Spotted turtle
Clemmys guttata

Classification: Spotted turtle	
Kingdom	Animalia
Phylum	Chordata
Class	Reptilia
Order	Testudines
Family	Emydidae
Genus	Clemmys
Species	guttata

VOCABULARY
genus p. 832
binomial nomenclature p. 832
dichotomous key p. 836

3 Classification systems change as scientists learn more.

The most popular system of classification in use today is a three-domain system that includes six kingdoms of organisms.

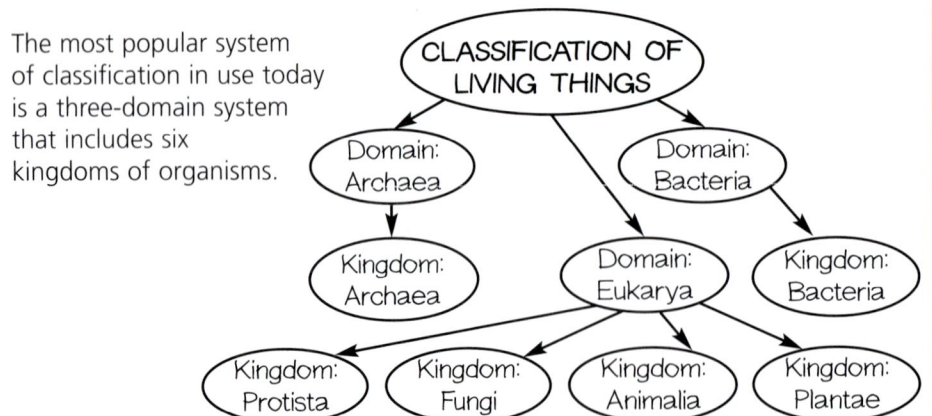

VOCABULARY
domain p. 841
Plantae p. 843
Animalia p. 843
Protista p. 843
Fungi p. 843
Archaea p. 843
Bacteria p. 843

Reviewing Vocabulary

Make a frame like the one shown for each vocabulary word listed below. Write the word in the center. Decide what information to frame it with. Use definitions, examples, descriptions, parts, or pictures.

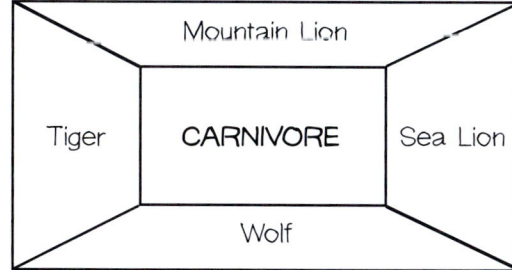

1. Plantae
2. Animalia
3. Protista
4. Fungi

Reviewing Key Concepts

Multiple Choice *Choose the letter of the best answer.*

5. The scientific process of arranging organisms into groups based on similarities is
   a. observation
   b. classification
   c. binomial nomenclature
   d. dichotomy

6. The system of naming organisms developed by Carolus Linnaeus is called
   a. binomial nomenclature
   b. taxonomy
   c. dichotomous nomenclature
   d. classification

7. Which group includes the most species?
   a. kingdom
   b. family
   c. domain
   d. phylum

8. The science of taxonomy allows scientists to
   a. identify unfamiliar organisms
   b. classify and name organisms
   c. refer to one specific type of organism
   d. determine similar traits of organisms

9. Which allows scientists to use genetic information to classify organisms?
   a. physical traits
   b. DNA
   c. fossil evidence
   d. habitats

10. A dichotomous key contains a series of questions that people use to
    a. find similar organisms
    b. identify organisms
    c. name organisms
    d. describe organisms

11. What are the names of the three domains?
    a. Plantae, Animalia, Protista
    b. Bacteria, Protista, Fungi
    c. Bacteria, Archaea, Eukarya
    d. Protista, Archaea, Eukarya

12. Which is an example of a trait?
    a. bone structure
    b. DNA information
    c. fossil records
    d. habitat

13. A group of species that have similar characteristics is called
    a. an order
    b. a family
    c. a phylum
    d. a genus

14. Which characteristic is common to animals, plants, protists, and fungi?
    a. ability to make their own food
    b. eukaryotic cells
    c. ability to move
    d. multicellular structure

Chapter 24: **Classification of Living Things** 851

Short Answer *Write a short answer to each question.*

15. What are the rules for creating a scientific name for an organism?

16. How is a field guide different from a dichotomous key?

17. What types of information caused scientists to add the level of domain to the system of classification?

Thinking Critically

18. **ANALYZE** How do scientists use fossils to classify organisms?

19. **APPLY** Scientists once classified American vultures and African vultures together in the falcon family. Now, scientists know that American vultures are more closely related to storks. What type of evidence might scientists have used to come to this conclusion? Explain your answer.

20. **EVALUATE** Which two of these species are more closely related: *Felis catus, Felis concolor, Picea concolor?* How do you know?

21. **INFER** A scientist is studying the following organisms. What conclusions can you draw about the organisms based on their scientific names?
    - *Ursus americanus*
    - *Ursus arctos*
    - *Ursus maritimus*

22. **ANALYZE** Two organisms you are studying are in the same class, but in a different order. What does this information tell you about the two organisms?

23. **RANK** Which of these have more groups of organisms: phylum or family? Explain your answer.

24. **SUMMARIZE** Describe how you would use a dichotomous key to identify this leaf.

25. **SYNTHESIZE** Why was it necessary for scientists to create groups for classifying organisms other than the groups of plants and animals described by Linnaeus?

26. **CLASSIFY** Suppose you discover a new organism that is single celled, has a nucleus, lives in the water, and uses sunlight to produce its energy. In which kingdom would you classify this organism? Explain.

the BIG idea

27. **INFER** Look again at the picture on pages 820–821. Now that you have finished the chapter, how would you change or add details to your answer to the question on the photograph?

28. **PROVIDE EXAMPLES** Imagine that you are a scientist studying a variety of organisms in a South American rain forest. You have classified one organism in the kingdom Animalia and another organism in the kingdom Plantae. Give examples of the characteristics that would enable you to classify each organism in those kingdoms.

UNIT PROJECTS

Check your schedule for your unit project. How are you doing? Be sure that you've placed data or notes from your research in your project folder.

Standardized Test Practice

Analyzing Graphics

Choose the letter of the best response.

By following the steps in this chart, it is possible to find the type of tree to which a leaf belongs.

Step 1
1a) Leaves are needlelike..................Go to step 2
1b) Leaves are flat and scalelike.........Go to step 5
Step 2
2a) Needles are clustered...................Go to step 3
2b) Needles are not clustered..............Go to step 4
Step 3
3a) Clusters of 2–5 needles................Pine
3b) Clusters greater than 10.............Go to step 4
Step 4
4a) Needles soft...............................Larch
4b) Needles stiff..............................True cedar
Step 5
5a) Needles are short and sharp........Giant sequoia
5b) Some needles are not sharp..........Go to Step 6

1. Which has leaves with clusters of 2–5 needles?
   a. pine tree
   b. larch tree
   c. true cedar tree
   d. giant sequoia

2. If a tree has clusters of needles greater than 10, you would go to
   a. step 1
   b. step 2
   c. step 3
   d. step 4

3. Each step on the key compares two
   a. species
   b. animals
   c. traits
   d. trees

4. A tree with soft needles that are not clustered is most likely a
   a. pine tree
   b. larch tree
   c. true cedar tree
   d. giant sequoia

5. Which statement best describes the characteristics of a giant sequoia?
   a. flat, scalelike needles that are short and sharp
   b. flat, scalelike needles that are stiff
   c. clustered needles that are soft
   d. clustered needles that are short and sharp

Extended Response

6. A biologist has discovered and collected a number of unknown plant species from a rain-forest environment. Explain what type of evidence a biologist would rely on to determine if the plant species were new. Give specific examples of what a biologist would look for. What process would scientists go through to name the new species?

7. As you learned in the chapter, there are scientists who classify and name organisms. Explain why it is important for these taxonomists to study biological relationships. What may these relationships indicate about early life and modern life?

Chapter 24: **Classification of Living Things** 853

TIMELINES in Science

LIFE Unearthed

How do scientists know about life on Earth millions of years ago? They dig, scratch, and hunt. The best clues they find are hidden in layers of rock. The rock-locked clues, called fossils, are traces or remains of living things from long ago. Some fossils show the actual bodies of organisms, while others, such as footprints, reveal behavior.

Before 1820, most fossil finds revealed the bodies of ocean life. Then large bones of lizardlike walking animals began turning up, and pictures of a new "terrible lizard," or dinosaur, took shape. Later, discoveries of tracks and nests showed behaviors such as flocking and caring for young. Even today, discoveries of "living fossils," modern relatives of prehistoric species, have offered us a rare glimpse of the activity of early life.

1824
Giant Lizards from Fragments
William Buckland describes *Megalosaurus*, a giant crocodilelike animal he studies from only a few bits of jaw, teeth, ribs, pelvis, and one leg. A year later Gideon Mantell assembles *Iguanodon*, a similar animal, from fossil bones.

EVENTS

1800   1810   1820

APPLICATIONS AND TECHNOLOGY

TECHNOLOGY

Removing Fossils with Care

The technology for removing fossils from rock beds has not changed much since the 1820s. Collectors still work by hand with hammers, chisels, trowels, dental picks, and sieves. Gideon Mantell used these when he chiseled out *Iguanodon* bones embedded in one large rock called the "Mantle piece."

Fossil hunters also use hand lenses and microscopes. Sometimes a protective layer is built up with glue, varnish, or another finish. For larger samples, a plaster cast often supports the fossil. Most fossils are packed using a technology found in any kitchen—a sealable plastic bag.

1909
Burgess Shale Shows Soft Bodies

In the Burgess Pass of the Canadian Rocky Mountains, Charles Walcott finds fossils preserved in shale, a soft rock that preserves lacelike details such as the soft tissues of the Marella. The glimpse of life 505 million years ago is the earliest yet seen.

1944
New Dawn for the Dawn Redwood

Beside a small temple, a Chinese scientist discovers the dawn redwood, or metasequoia, growing. Common in fossil specimens 100 million years old, the tree had not been seen alive in recorded history. The 1944 find starts a search, and in 1948, scientists find a small wild grove in China as well.

1938
African Fisherman Hauls in History

A South African fisherman pulls up a five-foot fish he has never seen. He calls the local museum, whose curator, a naturalist, has also never seen the species. To her surprise, biologists identify it as a coelacanth, a prehistoric fish thought to be extinct for more than 50 million years.

APPLICATION

Protecting Fossils and Dig Sites

The United States Antiquities Act of 1906 preserves and protects historic and prehistoric sites. The act requires collectors to have a permit to dig for or to pick up fossils on public lands such as national parks. It also requires that any major find be publicly and permanently preserved in a museum.

The United Nations also now designates World Heritage sites. For example, the original Burgess Shale find in Yoho National Park in Canada is now protected by international law. Since 1906, many states and provinces in Canada have enacted their own laws about land rights and the excavation and transport of fossils.

1974
"Lucy" and Upright Kin Found

Digging in Ethiopia, Donald Johanson finds an almost complete hominid skeleton. He names the fossil "Lucy," after a Beatles song. Lucy is over 3 million years old, is three and one-half feet tall, and has an upright stance or posture. A year later, Johanson's crew finds "The First Family," a group of 13 skeletons of the same species as Lucy.

1990
Largest *Tyrannosaurus*, "Sue"

Out on a walk with her dog in the South Dakota badlands, amateur fossil hunter Sue Hendrickson discovers three huge bones jutting out of a cliff. Hendrickson finds the largest and most complete *T. rex* skeleton yet. The 67-million-year-old "Sue" is now on display in the Field Museum in Chicago, Illinois.

1953
Piltdown Man No Neanderthal

Scientists once applauded the discovery in 1912 of a "Neanderthal skull" in the Piltdown gravel pit, but a few had their doubts. In 1953, radioactive potassium dating proves the Piltdown man to be nothing more than the jaw of an orangutan placed beside human skull fragments.

1950   1960   1970   1980   1990

TECHNOLOGY
How Old Is a Fossil?

Before 1947, scientists used a method of fossil dating called relative dating. They assigned a date to a fossil according to the rock layer in which it was found. The deeper, or older, the layer, the older the fossil.

The discovery of radiometric dating in 1947 marked the first time a fossil's date could be pinpointed. Organic matter decays at a constant rate. So, by measuring the rate of decay, you can tell the age of the matter. Radiocarbon 14 is used to tell the age of a fossil that is less than 10,000 years old. Since most fossils are older than that, scientists use other methods.

Potassium-argon decays more slowly than carbon. It is a more common method of dating. All types of fossil dating have margins of error, or limits to accuracy.

1993
Oldest Fossils Are Too Small to See

Fossils discovered up to this point date back about 550 million years, to the dawn of the Cambrian Period. J. William Schopf identifies fossils of microorganisms scientifically dated to 3.4 billion years ago. This startling find near Australia's Marble Bar opens up a vast period of time and once again reshapes theories about life's beginnings.

 RESOURCE CENTER
CLASSZONE.COM
Discover more about the latest fossil and living-fossil finds.

2000

TECHNOLOGY
Fossil Classification and DNA

There are many ways to classify fossils. Scientists look at bone structure, body posture, evidence of behavior, and environment. Microscopes are used to identify organisms too small for the eye to see. Study of DNA molecules helps to identify species when soft tissues remain intact, such as in fossils formed in amber or crystallized tree sap. In 1985, polymerase chain reaction (PCR) became the simplest method to study the DNA extracted from fossils. In PCR, parts of DNA can be copied billions of times in a few hours.

INTO THE FUTURE

Technology is sure to play a role in future fossil finds. Scientists can communicate via laptop computers and satellites, which allow the public to follow excavations as they occur.

Computer modeling helps scientists determine what incomplete skeletons looked like. It also helps them determine how dinosaurs and other living things once moved. Fossil finds can be combined with digitized information about modern living organisms and about environmental conditions. The model can test hypotheses or even help to formulate them.

Another area of technology that may become increasingly applied to fossils is DNA testing to identify and help date fossils. This is more complicated in fossilized bone, as the genetic material can be fragmented. But with time, scientists may discover new techniques to extract better genetic information. DNA is also the basis for cloning, which as yet can only be applied to living organisms. Perhaps in the future it can be applied to preserved remains.

ACTIVITIES

Writing About Science: Film Script

Write your own version of the story of life on Earth. Include drawings, photographs, or video clips to illustrate your story.

Reliving History

Think about the equipment archaeologists and paleontologists use on excavations. Think about their goals. Write a proposal to a local university or museum asking them to fund your excavation.

CHAPTER 25
Population Dynamics

the BIG idea

Populations are shaped by interactions between organisms and the environment.

Key Concepts

SECTION 1 — Populations have many characteristics.
Learn about the stages and factors that all populations have in common.

SECTION 2 — Populations respond to pressures.
Learn how change can affect populations.

SECTION 3 — Human populations have unique responses to change.
Learn how the responses of human populations are different from responses of other populations.

Internet Preview

CLASSZONE.COM
Chapter 25 online resources: Content Review, Visualization, three Resource Centers, Math Tutorial, Test Practice

This image was created by combining satellite shots of parts of Earth. What does it suggest about Earth's populations?

EXPLORE the BIG idea

How Does Population Grow?

For every three human births there is one death. Use a bucket and water to represent the human population. For every 3 cups of water you add to the bucket, take away one cup.

Observe and Think
How did the water level rise—quickly, slowly, or steadily?

How Do Populations Differ?

Put about 40 marbles in a bowl. Remove any 10 marbles from the bowl and put them in another dish. Each dish of marbles represents a population.

Observe and Think
How would a chance event such as a fire affect these two populations differently?

Internet Activity: Population Dynamics

Go to **ClassZone.com** to learn more about the factors that describe a population. Find out how change in each of the factors can affect the population.

Observe and Think
How would a change in one factor affect the dynamics of a population?

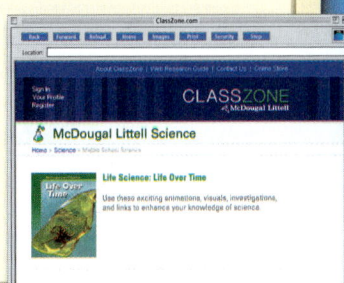

Limiting Factors Code: MDL038

Chapter 25: **Population Dynamics** 859

CHAPTER 25
Getting Ready to Learn

CONCEPT REVIEW

- Living things change over time.
- Species adapt to their environment or become extinct.

VOCABULARY REVIEW

See Glossary for definition.
species

CONTENT REVIEW
CLASSZONE.COM
Review concepts and vocabulary.

TAKING NOTES

CHOOSE YOUR OWN STRATEGY

Take notes using one or more strategies from earlier chapters—**main idea and details** or **supporting main ideas**. You can also use other note-taking strategies that you might already know.

VOCABULARY STRATEGY

Think about a vocabulary term as a **magnet word** diagram. Write the other terms or ideas related to that term around it.

See the Note-Taking Handbook on pages R45–R51.

SCIENCE NOTEBOOK

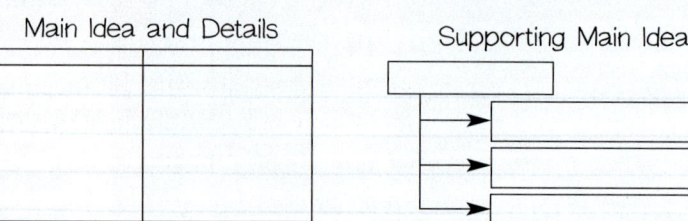

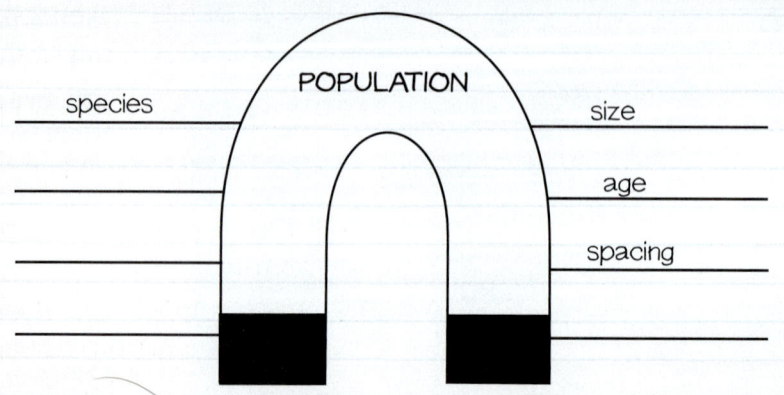

860 Unit 6: **Life Over Time**

KEY CONCEPT
25.1 Populations have many characteristics.

BEFORE, you learned
- Species change over time
- Evolution is a process of change
- A habitat is an area that provides organisms with resources

NOW, you will learn
- About stages in population dynamics
- About variables that define a population
- About changes that affect populations

VOCABULARY
population dynamics p. 861
carrying capacity p. 862
population size p. 864
population density p. 865

THINK ABOUT

How fast can a population grow?

How big can a population grow? Suppose you started with a pair of fruit flies. That single pair can produce 200 eggs. In three weeks, each pair from that batch could produce 200 flies of its own—producing up to 20,000 flies. Assume all eggs hatch—an event highly unlikely in the real world. After three weeks, 2 million fruit flies would be buzzing around the area. After just 17 generations, given ideal conditions (for the fruit fly, that is), the mass of fruit flies would exceed the mass of planet Earth.

CHOOSE YOUR OWN STRATEGY
Begin taking notes on the three stages of populations. Use a strategy from an earlier chapter or one that you already know.

Populations go through three stages.

Look closely at the fruit flies above. As a group of the same species living together in a particular area, they represent a population. The particular area in which a scientist studies a population may be as large as a mountain range or as small as a puddle. Scientists study how populations of organisms change as they interact with each other and the environment. Over time, the number of individuals in a population changes by increasing or decreasing. **Population dynamics** is the study of why populations change and what causes them to change. In this chapter you will learn about some of the important observations scientists have made about populations.

CHECK YOUR READING What is population dynamics?

Chapter 25: **Population Dynamics** 861

One species of iguana may have several populations living on different islands. As a result, these iguana populations don't interact with each other. Yet there may be other populations of iguanas living on the islands made up of a different species.

Growth, Stability, and Decline

As different as populations may be—whether cacti, finches, dragonflies, or iguanas—all populations go through the same three stages of change: growth, stability, and decline.

All living things need resources such as water, energy, and living space. Populations get their resources from the environment. However, the area a population occupies can support only so many individuals. **Carrying capacity** is the maximum number of individuals an ecosystem can support.

When a habitat contains enough resources to meet the needs of a population, the population grows rapidly. This growth stage of a population tends to be brief. On a graph, it looks like a sharp rise. The growth stage is followed by a period of stability, when the size of a population remains constant. For most populations, the stability stage is the longest stage of a population's existence. The stability stage is often followed by a decline in population size.

READING TIP As you read about growth, stability, and decline, refer to the explanations on the graph.

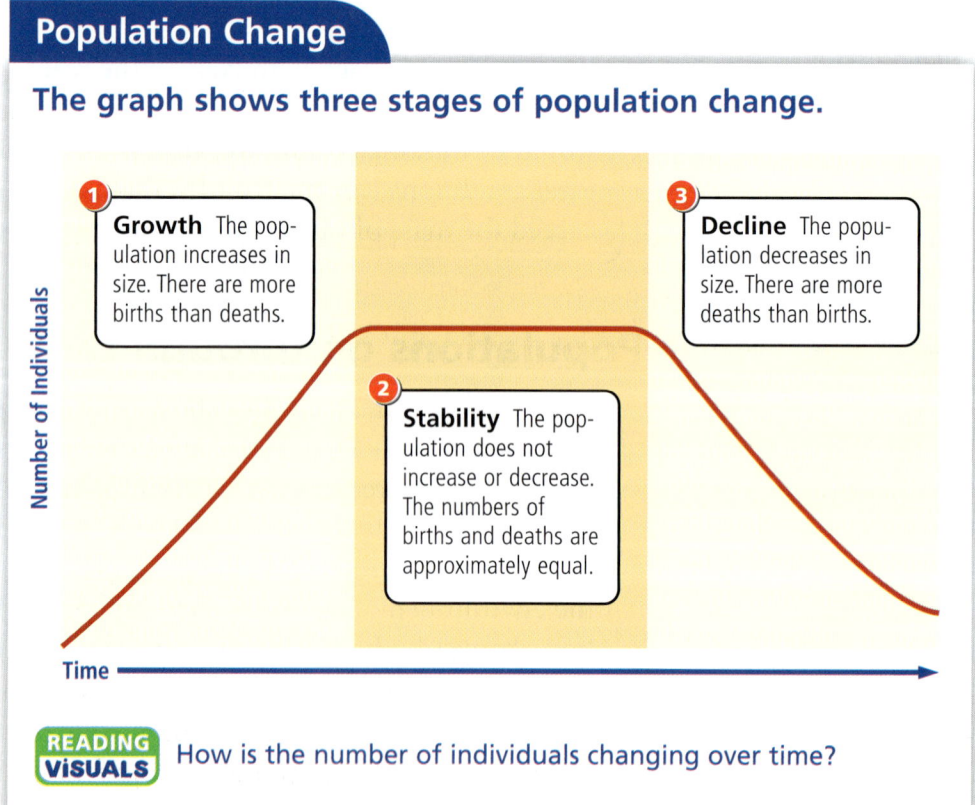

Population Change

The graph shows three stages of population change.

① Growth The population increases in size. There are more births than deaths.

② Stability The population does not increase or decrease. The numbers of births and deaths are approximately equal.

③ Decline The population decreases in size. There are more deaths than births.

READING VISUALS How is the number of individuals changing over time?

During the growth stage, populations can increase according to two general patterns. One pattern is rapid growth, which increases at a greater and greater rate. Another pattern is gradual growth, which increases at a fairly steady rate. The two graphs below show the two different types of growth.

Population Growth

The graphs show two patterns of population growth.

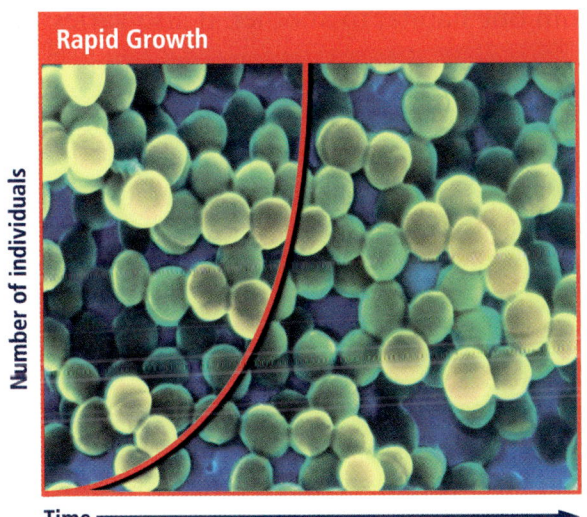

Rapid Growth

Gradual Growth

Darwin's Observations of Population Growth

In Chapter 23 you read about the observations and conclusions made by the naturalist Charles Darwin. In his book *On the Origin of Species* Darwin included important observations about population growth.

> **REMINDER**
> A species that is no longer living is considered extinct.

- All populations are able to grow rapidly.
- Populations tend to remain constant in size.
- There are limits to natural resources.
- Within a given population there is genetic variation.

Darwin recognized that organisms in most species have the ability to produce more than two surviving offspring. He knew that if there were no limits to growth, then populations would grow rapidly. However, Darwin also observed that in the real world there are natural limits to growth, so populations tend to stabilize. In order for a species to continue, individuals must be replaced as they die. This means that, on average, one member of a population must produce one surviving offspring. If the birth rate doesn't match the death rate, a population can decline until it becomes extinct.

Four characteristics define a population.

When scientists think about population dynamics, they consider four major characteristics. These characteristics include population size, population density, population spacing, and age structure.

Population Size

Population size is the number of individuals in a population at a given time. Even when the population size appears to be stable over time, changes can occur from year to year or from place to place. Population size varies from one habitat to another. It also varies within a single habitat.

An area where the summers are hot and the winters are cold is a good place to observe how population size might change at different times of year. For example, the population sizes of many insects change within a year. Mosquitoes that are all around you on warm summer evenings are nowhere in sight when the temperatures fall below freezing.

The size of plant populations can also change during the year. In the spring and summer you can see flowering plants across the deserts, woods, and mountains of North America. However, by fall and early winter, when there is less rainfall and temperatures drop, many of these plants die. Below is a picture of a southwestern desert in full bloom. During the springtime months of March through May, many deserts in the United States experience a change. There is a period of rapid growth as a variety of wildflowers begins to bloom.

When there is little rainfall a desert seems empty. After a rain, there is a brief time when plants bloom.

The availability of resources, such as water, increases plant growth. By summer the change in season brings higher temperatures and less rainfall. As a result, desert wildflowers experience a rapid decline in their population size.

 What are two factors that affect population size?

Population Density

Population density is a measure of the number of individuals in a certain space at a particular time. Population density is related to population size. If a population's size increases and all of the individuals remain in the same area, then population density increases, too. There are more individuals living in the same amount of space. If the size of a population in a particular area decreases, density also decreases. Some species, such as bumblebees or mice, live in populations with high densities. Other species, such as blue herons or wolves, live in populations with low densities.

 What is the difference between low density and high density?

Population Density

Density can change over time and over the entire area of the population.

Low Density

Herons are usually found alone or in pairs in marshy areas. Herons are an example of a low-density population.

High Density

Bees in a beehive are an example of a high-density population—many individuals are packed into a small area.

READING VISUALS **COMPARE** How does the number of herons in an area compare with the number of bees?

The distribution of a population across a large geographic area is its range. Within that range, population density may vary. For example, there may be more grasshoppers in the middle of a prairie than there are at the edges. The population density tends to be higher where more resources are available. Habitats located in the middle of a population range tend to have a greater population density than habitats located at the edges.

CHECK YOUR READING How might population density vary within a range?

Population Spacing

Take a look around you as you walk through a local park. You might notice many flowers growing in open, sunny spots but few beneath the shade of large trees. The pattern in which the flowers grow is an example of population spacing. Scientists have observed three distinct patterns of spacing: clumped, uniform, and random.

In clumped spacing, individuals form small groups within a habitat. Animals like elephants clump because of their social nature. Clumping can also result from the way resources are distributed throughout a habitat. Salamanders that prefer moist, rotten logs may be clumped where logs have fallen in their habitat.

Population Spacing

Population spacing describes how individuals arrange themselves within a population.

Clumped

Individuals that clump themselves often gather around resources.

Uniform

Individuals that are uniformly arranged often compete for resources.

Random

Random patterns are rare and occur without regard to other individuals.

READING VISUALS Compare and contrast the way populations are spaced.

866 Unit 6: Life Over Time

Some individuals live at a distance from each other. These individuals are uniformly spaced. Many plants that grow too close together become evenly spaced as individuals die out. Uniform spacing can protect saguaro cacti from competing for important resources in the desert. Individuals that aren't uniform or clumped space themselves randomly. Dandelions, for instance, grow no matter where other dandelions are growing.

Age Structure

Scientists divide a population into three groups based on age.

- postreproductive: organisms can no longer reproduce
- reproductive: organisms capable of reproduction
- prereproductive: organisms not yet able to reproduce

The age structure of a population affects how much it can grow. On the graph below, the postreproductive age range for humans is over 45, reproductive is 14 to 44 years of age, and prereproductive is 0 to 14.

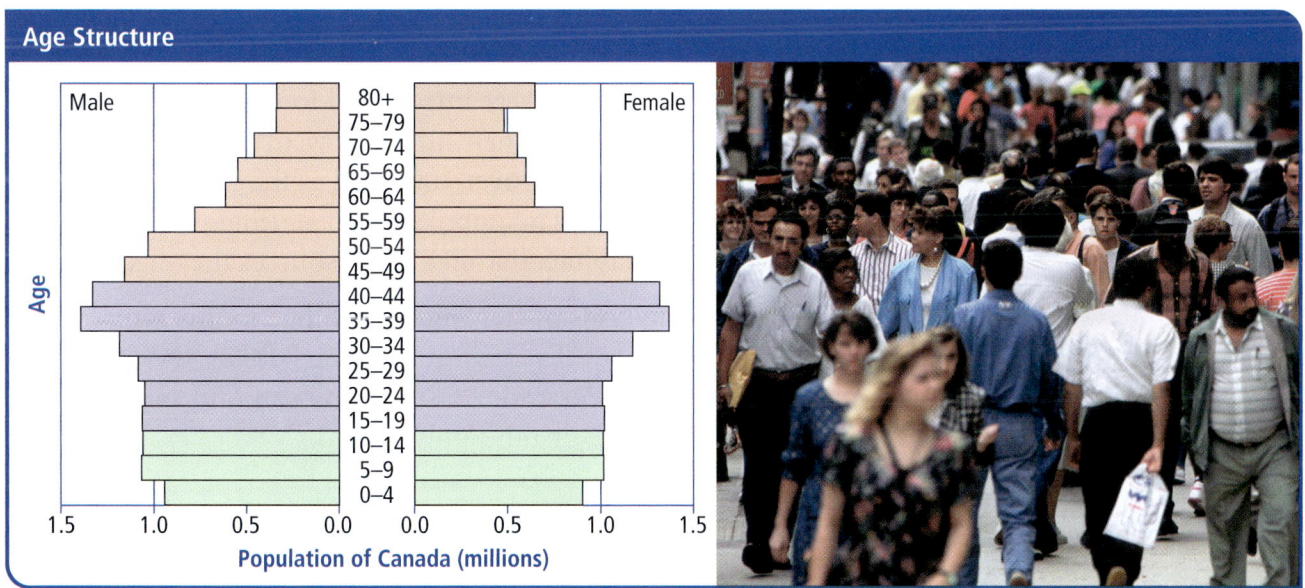

Age Structure

Scientists can predict population change.

Scientists use these four factors—size, density, spacing, and age structure—to describe a population and to predict how it might change over time. Sometimes a population changes when a particular factor changes.

A population can change in response to its surroundings. Suppose a population of frogs is living in a pond where the water becomes saltier. Only those frogs that can survive in an environment with more salt will survive. Thus the population size of frogs will probably decrease as a result of the changing conditions. By looking at population size, scientists can predict how changes affect the population.

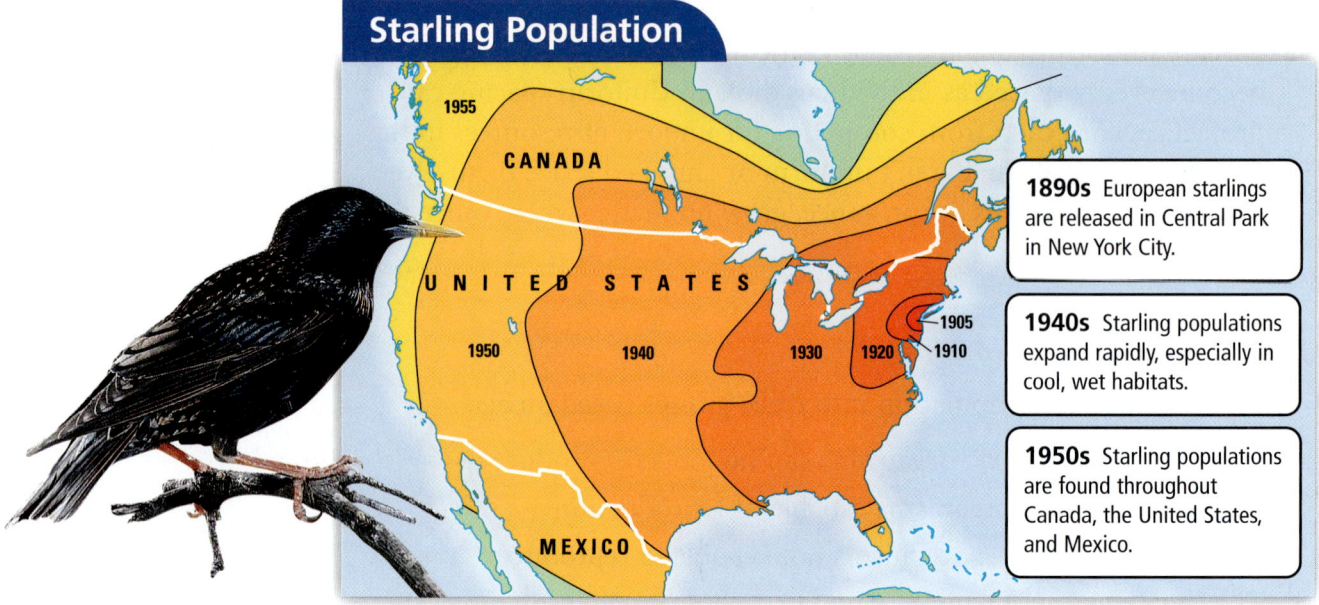

Starling Population

1890s European starlings are released in Central Park in New York City.

1940s Starling populations expand rapidly, especially in cool, wet habitats.

1950s Starling populations are found throughout Canada, the United States, and Mexico.

Scientists can also predict change by looking at the distribution of population. The story of the European starling provides a dramatic example of how the movement of organisms into or out of an area affects a population.

In 1890, the first starlings were introduced to the United States in New York City's Central Park. Their numbers went from 60 individuals to about 200 million in just over 100 years as they expanded on the North American continent. The population of starlings rose as starlings moved into new habitats that had the resources they needed.

Today large populations of starlings can still be found across the North American continent. Even within a given habitat, the population can vary. In Central Park, for example, you can find starlings in clumps, uniformly spaced, or randomly spaced.

Watch how a change in the environment can affect a population.

25.1 Review

KEY CONCEPTS

1. Describe the three stages of population growth.
2. Make a chart showing the four factors that affect population dynamics and an example of each.
3. Give an example of how a shift in age distribution can affect population growth.

CRITICAL THINKING

4. **Apply** Choose a population in your neighborhood. Describe its population spacing. Is it clumped, uniformly spaced, or randomly spaced?
5. **Compare/Contrast** How is population size related to population density? Your answer should mention area.

CHALLENGE

6. **Predict** Explain how a heavy thunderstorm might affect the population density of birds living in the area.

868 Unit 6: Life Over Time

Math in Science

**MATH TUTORIAL
CLASSZONE.COM**
Click on Math Tutorial for more help finding the mean.

SKILL: FINDING AVERAGES

Making Sense of Samples

In a pond study, a biologist takes samples of water from four locations in one pond every three months. Using a microscope, she examines the samples and calculates the protist population for each location. The data table shows the number of protists found per milliliter in each sample of pond water.

Data Table: Number of protists per milliliter (mL) of pond water

Location	Fall	Winter	Spring	Summer
Under the pier	150	50	120	410
Among the water lilies	200	80	180	500
Shallow area	220	90	200	360
Deepest area	80	60	100	390
Seasonal Average				

Example

Suppose you want to find the average number of protists per milliliter of pond water for that fall.

Step 1. Find the sum of all the data given above for "Fall."

Step 2. Divide this total by the number of data entries for "Fall."

Step 3. Round to nearest whole number.

```
  150
  200
  220
+  80
  650
```

$650 \div 4 = 162.5$

$162.5 \rightarrow 163$

ANSWER 163 protists per mL of pond water

For each season or location give the average number of protists.

1. Winter
2. Spring
3. Summer
4. Under the pier
5. Among the water lilies
6. Shallow area
7. Deepest area
8. Whole pond, yearlong

CHALLENGE Suppose the biologist only took samples from three areas in the pond. Which missing area would throw off the averages the most?

KEY CONCEPT
Populations respond to pressures.

 BEFORE, you learned
- Four characteristics are used to describe a population
- Scientists study these four characteristics to predict population change

 NOW, you will learn
- About limits to population growth
- How population density affects limiting factors
- About two reproductive strategies found within populations

VOCABULARY
immigration p. 871
emigration p. 871
limiting factor p. 872
opportunist p. 875
competitor p. 876

EXPLORE Population Density

How does population density vary?
PROCEDURE

1. Choose three different locations in your school where you can observe how many people enter and leave an area during a specific time period.
2. Position three people at each location a counter, a timekeeper, and a recorder.
3. Count the number of people who pass through the area for at least 2 minutes. Record the number.
4. Compare your data with the data collected by other groups.

MATERIALS
- stopwatch
- notebook

WHAT DO YOU THINK?
- Where was the number of people the highest? the lowest?
- Explain what may have affected population density at each location.

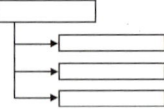

CHOOSE YOUR OWN STRATEGY
Use a strategy from an earlier chapter or one of your own to take notes on the main idea: *Population growth is limited.*

Population growth is limited.

No population can grow forever. Every population has a limit to its growth. For example, the cockroach has been around for more than 300 million years. This insect has outlived the dinosaurs and may persist long after humans have become extinct. Yet even if cockroaches became the only species on the planet, several factors would limit their population size.

870 Unit 6: Life Over Time

Birth, Death, Immigration, and Emigration

When scientists study how a population changes, they must consider four things: birth, death, immigration, and emigration. There is even a simple formula to help scientists track population change.

Population change = (birth + immigration) − (death + emigration)

It is too simple to say that a high birth rate means population growth, or that many deaths mean population decline. **Immigration** is the movement of individuals into a population. For example, if a strong wind blows the seeds of a plant from one area into another, the new plant would be said to immigrate into the new area. Immigration can increase a population or help stabilize a declining population. Birth and immigration introduce individuals into a population.

Emigration is the movement of individuals out of a population. If resources become scarce within a habitat, some of the individuals might move to areas with greater supplies. Others may even die. Death and emigration remove individuals from a population.

CHECK YOUR READING List two factors that lead to population growth and two that lead to population decline.

Consider, for example, a flock of seagulls that flies inland during a storm. They stop at a city dump, where food is plentiful. These incoming seagulls become part of the seagull population that is already living at the dump. A raccoon population living in the same area has been eating the seagulls' eggs, causing the number of seagull births to decrease. If enough seagulls immigrate to the dump, the seagull population would increase, making up for the decrease in births. Immigration would help keep the population stable. The seagull population would also increase if part of the raccoon population moved away.

Limiting Factors

When a population is growing at a rapid rate, the birth rate is much higher than the death rate. That means that more individuals are being born than are dying during a particular time period. There are plenty of resources available, and the population size is increasing rapidly. Eventually, however, the population will stop growing, because a habitat can support only a limited number of organisms.

A **limiting factor** is a factor that prevents the continuing growth of a population in an ecosystem. Abiotic, or nonliving, limiting factors include air, light, and water. Other limiting factors can be living things, such as other organisms in the same population or individuals belonging to different species within the same area.

CHECK YOUR READING   What are two limiting factors?

Competition can occur between different populations sharing the same habitat. Competition can also occur among individuals of the same population. Suppose, for example, that a population of deer in a forest preserve were to increase, either through births or immigration. Population density at the forest preserve would go up. More and more deer in that area would be competing for the same amount of food.

Density-Dependent Factors

Density-dependent factors have a greater effect on populations with many individuals in a small area.

Factors may include
- Competition
- Disease
- Parasitism
- Predation

Effects of Population Density

In the situation described above, the seagull population could decrease as a result of competition for food. Competition is an example of a density-dependent factor—that is, a limiting factor that affects a population when density is high. Disease is another density-dependent factor. The more crowded an area becomes, the easier it is for disease to spread, so more individuals are affected. If population density is low, there is less contact between individuals, which means that disease will spread more slowly. Density-dependent factors have a greater effect on the population as it grows. They can bring a population under control, because they apply more pressure to a growing population.

There are also density-independent factors. These limiting factors have the same effect on a population, whether it has a high density or a low density. Freezing temperatures could be considered a density-independent factor. A freeze might kill all of the flowering plants in an area, whether or not the population density is high. A natural event such as a wildfire is another example of a density-independent factor. When a wildfire occurs in a forest, it can wipe out an entire ecosystem.

CHECK YOUR READING How are limiting factors that are density-dependent different from limiting factors that are density-independent?

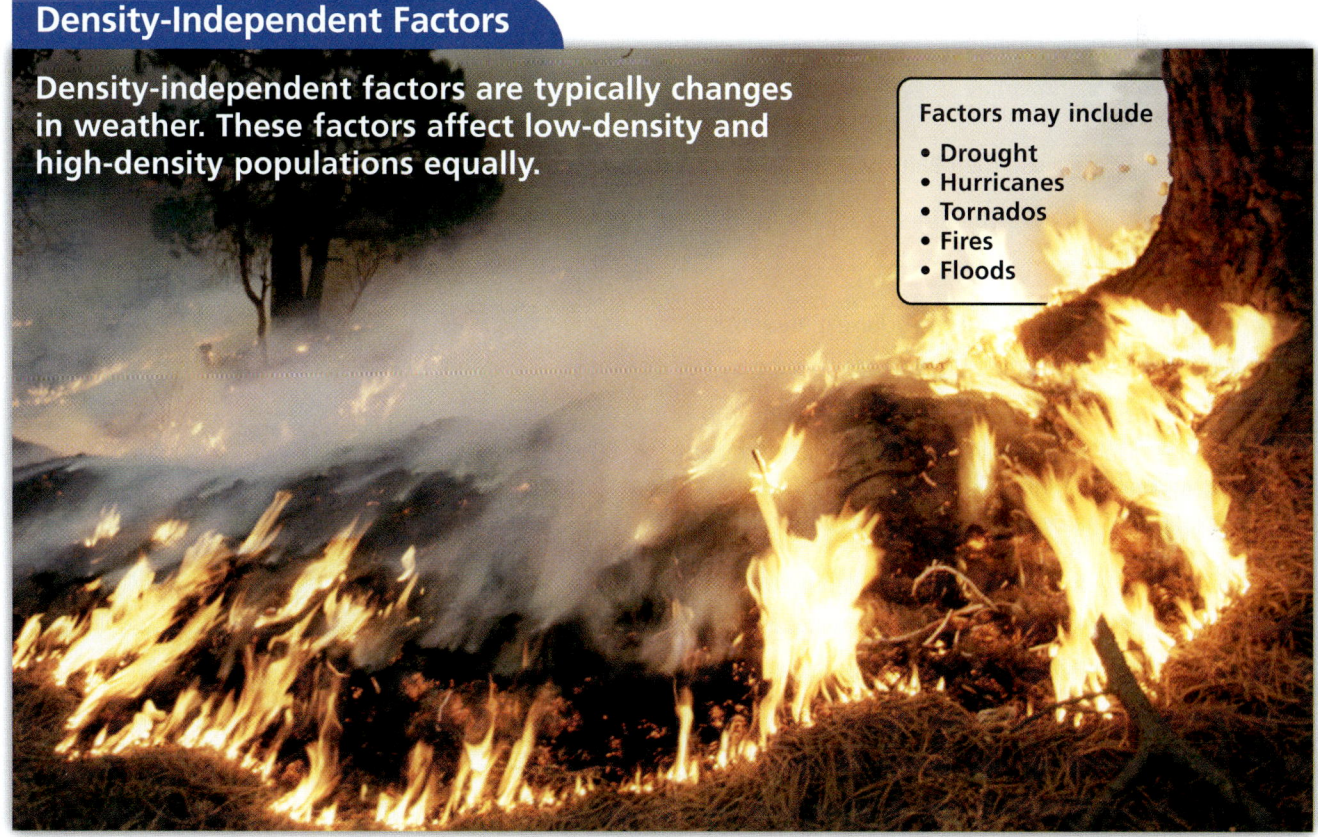

Density-Independent Factors

Density-independent factors are typically changes in weather. These factors affect low-density and high-density populations equally.

Factors may include
- Drought
- Hurricanes
- Tornados
- Fires
- Floods

Chapter 25: **Population Dynamics** 873

Limiting factors include nonliving factors in the environment and natural events such as earthquakes, fires, and storms. During times of drought, there may not be enough food to meet the needs of all the organisms in an area. The quality of the food declines as well. For example, a lack of water may cause a population of trees to produce fewer pieces of fruit, and the fruit itself may be smaller. If there is little food available, a condition called famine arises. If the famine is severe, and if death rates exceed birth rates, then the population size will fall dramatically.

CHECK YOUR READING How do limiting factors affect populations? Remember: a summary includes only the most important information.

Limiting factors affect human populations as well. However, humans have found different ways to help overcome many of these limits. In Section 25.3 you will read about how the human response to limits differs from that of other biological populations.

INVESTIGATE Limiting Factors

What limiting factors determine plant growth?

Using the materials below, design an experiment to test how limiting factors such as sunlight or water can determine how well a plant population will grow.

DESIGN YOUR OWN EXPERIMENT

PROCEDURE

1. Decide how to use the beans, soil, and water.
2. Write up your experimental procedure. Include any safety tips.

WHAT DO YOU THINK?

- What variables did you use in your experiment?
- What evidence do you expect to see to support the goal of your experiment?

CHALLENGE Conduct your experiment. Be sure to observe your beans daily and note which ones are most healthy. Make a chart and record your observations. The beans should grow for at least two weeks before you make your conclusion.

SKILL FOCUS
Designing experiments

MATERIALS
- 6 paper cups
- potting soil
- beans
- water

TIME
20 minutes

Populations have distinct reproductive survival strategies.

Although reproduction of offspring is not necessary for the survival of an individual organism, it is necessary for the survival of a species. Scientists studying populations observe patterns in the reproductive strategies used among species. There are two main strategies that many species use. There are also many species whose strategies fit somewhere in between.

Strategies of Opportunists

Opportunists are species that reproduce rapidly if their population falls below carrying capacity. They share many characteristics, including a short life span and the ability to reproduce large quantities of offspring. Their population size tends to change often, and opportunists live across many areas. Opportunists include algae, dandelions, bacteria, and insects. These species can reproduce and move across an area quickly. In addition, they can adapt quickly to environmental changes. Populations of opportunists often grow rapidly.

> **VOCABULARY**
> Remember to make a word magnet for the term *opportunist*. Include examples in your diagram.

Opportunists

Pine trees are opportunists that can spread across an area quickly.

Pine cones release huge amounts of pollen into the air.

Chapter 25: **Population Dynamics** 875

Competitors

Wolves are examples of competitor species. These cubs will be cared for by adults until they are able to hunt.

Strategies of Competitors

You might be familiar with the term *competitor* as meaning an organism that struggles with another to get resources. Scientists who study population growth use the term *competitor* in another way. **Competitors** are species with adaptations that allow them to remain at or near their carrying capacity for long periods of time. Competitors have many characteristics that differ from those of opportunists.

Species that have a competitive reproductive strategy often live longer and have fewer offspring. Elephants and saguaro cacti are two examples of competitors. The offspring of competitors take longer to develop than those of opportunists. Also, animals with this strategy tend to take care of their young for a longer period of time. Competitors are not distributed across areas as widely as opportunists, but greater numbers of their offspring survive to reproductive age.

25.2 Review

KEY CONCEPTS

1. What four factors do scientists consider when they measure population change?
2. Give two examples of density-dependent factors and two examples of density-independent factors.
3. Other than life span, how do opportunists and competitors differ?

CRITICAL THINKING

4. **Analyze** Why would it be a mistake to predict population growth based on birth rate alone?
5. **Apply** Give an example of a factor that limits a population near you.

CHALLENGE

6. **Synthesize** There has been an oil spill along a waterway famous for its populations of seals, dolphins, and sea birds. Six months later, all populations show a decline. Explain what factors might have caused such a change and whether the oil spill was a density-dependent or density-independent factor or both.

Extreme Science

Forest Fires release jackpine seeds from their pinecones to sprout after the fire stops.

AMAZING SEEDS

Seed Survivors

Not only can seeds survive harsh conditions, but sometimes harsh conditions actually make it possible for seeds to grow into new plants.

Forest Fires

Jackpine seeds are locked inside pinecones by a sticky resin. The pinecones survive hot forest fires that melt the resin and release the seeds. In fact, without the high temperatures from fires, the seeds would never get the chance to germinate and grow into jackpine trees.

Bomb Damage

In 1940, during World War II, the British Museum was firebombed. People poured water over the burning museum and its contents. In the museum were silk-tree seeds collected in China and brought to the museum in 1793. After the firebombing 147 years later, the seeds sprouted.

Dodo Digestion

Seeds of Calvaria trees, which live on the island of Mauritius have very hard outer shells. The outer shell must be softened before the seeds can sprout. Hundreds of years ago, dodo birds ate the Calvaria fruits. Stones and acids in the birds' digestive tract helped soften the seed. After the dodo birds deposited them, the softened seeds would sprout. Dodo birds went extinct in 1681, and no young Calvaria trees grew. In 1975, only about 13 Calvaria trees remained. Recently, scientists have used artificial means to grind and break down the Calvaria seed cover and foster new tree growth.

EXPLORE

1. **INFER** Why do you think the silk tree seeds sprouted? Think about how the seeds' environment changed.
2. **CHALLENGE** If you were a scientist who wanted to help the Calvaria trees make a comeback, what methods might you try for softening the seeds?

RESOURCE CENTER
CLASSZONE.COM
Find out more about extreme seeds.

KEY CONCEPT
25.3 Human populations have unique responses to change.

◀ BEFORE, you learned
- Over time, all populations stop growing
- All populations are affected by limiting factors
- Reproductive strategies include opportunism and competition

▶ NOW, you will learn
- How human populations differ from other populations
- How humans adapt to the environment
- How human populations affect the environment

VOCABULARY

pollution p. 884

EXPLORE Population Change

How can you predict human population growth?

PROCEDURE

 Copy the graph on the right. The graph shows population growth expected in the United States with an increase in both birth and death rates and with steady immigration.

 The graph shows a medium rate of growth. Draw another line to show what low population growth might look like. Label it.

 Explain the patterns of birth rates, death rates, and immigration that might be likely to result in low population growth.

WHAT DO YOU THINK?
- How would the projected U.S. population size change if there were no immigration?
- How might an increase in immigration affect expected birth rates?

MATERIALS
- graph paper
- colored pencils

Human populations differ from populations of other species.

CHOOSE YOUR OWN STRATEGY
Begin taking notes on the differences between human populations and populations of other species.

Humans are not the fastest or the largest organisms on Earth. They must get food from other organisms. Humans have a limited sense of smell, and the vision of a human is inferior to that of a hawk. However, the human population now dominates our planet. Why? Humans are able to shape their environment. Humans are also able to determine their own biological reproduction. Because humans can control many factors that limit growth, Earth's carrying capacity for humans has increased. Two key factors that have increased Earth's carrying capacity for humans are habitat expansion and technology.

878 Unit 6: Life Over Time

Habitat Expansion

Individuals who study the history of ancient peoples know that populations of humans have spread throughout the world. Discoveries of ancient human tools and skeletons indicate that the first human populations lived on the continent now known as Africa. Over time, human populations have spread over nearly the entire planet.

The word *habitat* refers to a place where an organism can live. Humans have expanded their habitats, and thus the population has grown. Humans can survive in many different environments by adding air conditioning or heat to regulate indoor temperature. They can design and build shelters that protect them from harsh environments.

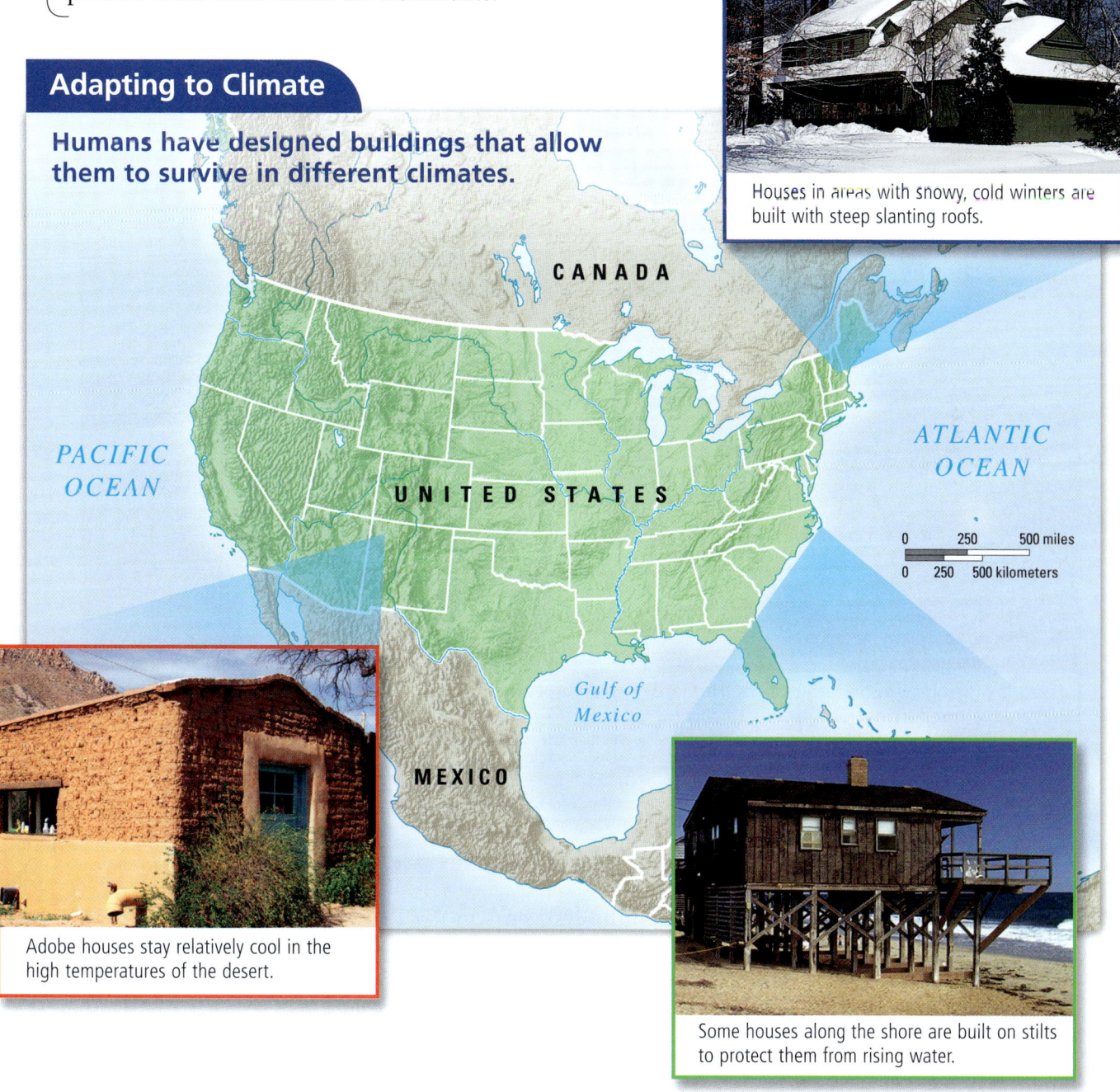

Adapting to Climate

Humans have designed buildings that allow them to survive in different climates.

Houses in areas with snowy, cold winters are built with steep slanting roofs.

Adobe houses stay relatively cool in the high temperatures of the desert.

Some houses along the shore are built on stilts to protect them from rising water.

Chapter 25: **Population Dynamics**

Technology

Limited resources and environmental conditions such as climate do not affect human population growth the way they do the growth of other biological populations. Humans have found ways to fit themselves into almost every climate by altering their clothing, shelter, diet, and means of transportation.

Scientific discoveries and the advances of technology—such as improved sanitation and medical care—have increased the standard of living and the life expectancy of many humans. Important goods such as food and shelter are manufactured and shipped around the world. Water, which is a limited resource, can be transported through pipes and dams to irrigate fields or reach normally dry areas. Water can also be purified for drinking or treated before it is released back into the environment.

 How does technology help humans get resources they need for survival?

Technology

Transporting Water
Food is often grown on large farms. Humans have developed irrigation systems to carry water to the fields.

Purifying Water
Water that has been used by humans contains wastes that can be removed at large watertreatment plants.

Human populations are growing.

As you've read, humans have developed solutions to many limits on growth. These solutions have allowed the human population to grow rapidly. Scientists are studying the history of this growth and trying to predict whether it will continue or change.

History of Human Population Growth

Until about 300 years ago, the human population grew slowly. Disease, climate, and the availability of resources limited population size. Most offspring did not survive to adulthood. Even though birthrates were high, death rates were also high.

Notice the human population on the graph below. Many historical events have affected its growth. For example, the development of agriculture provided humans with a more stable food source. This in turn helped support human population growth. Today, populations across many parts of the world are increasing rapidly. Scientists identify three conditions that allow for rapid growth: the availability of resources, lack of predators, and survival of offspring to reproductive age. As these conditions change, so does the population.

Learn more about world-wide human population growth.

Population Projections

To help prepare for the future, scientists make predictions called population projections. Population projections forecast how a population will change, based on its present size and age structure. Population projections provide a picture of what the future might look like. Using population projections, government agencies, resource managers, and economists can plan to meet the future needs of a population.

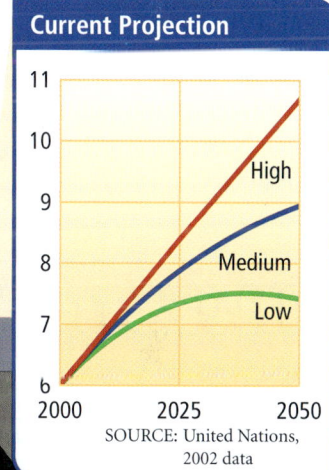

The blowout of the graph shows three projections for the human population size. Experts disagree about the rate at which the population will grow.

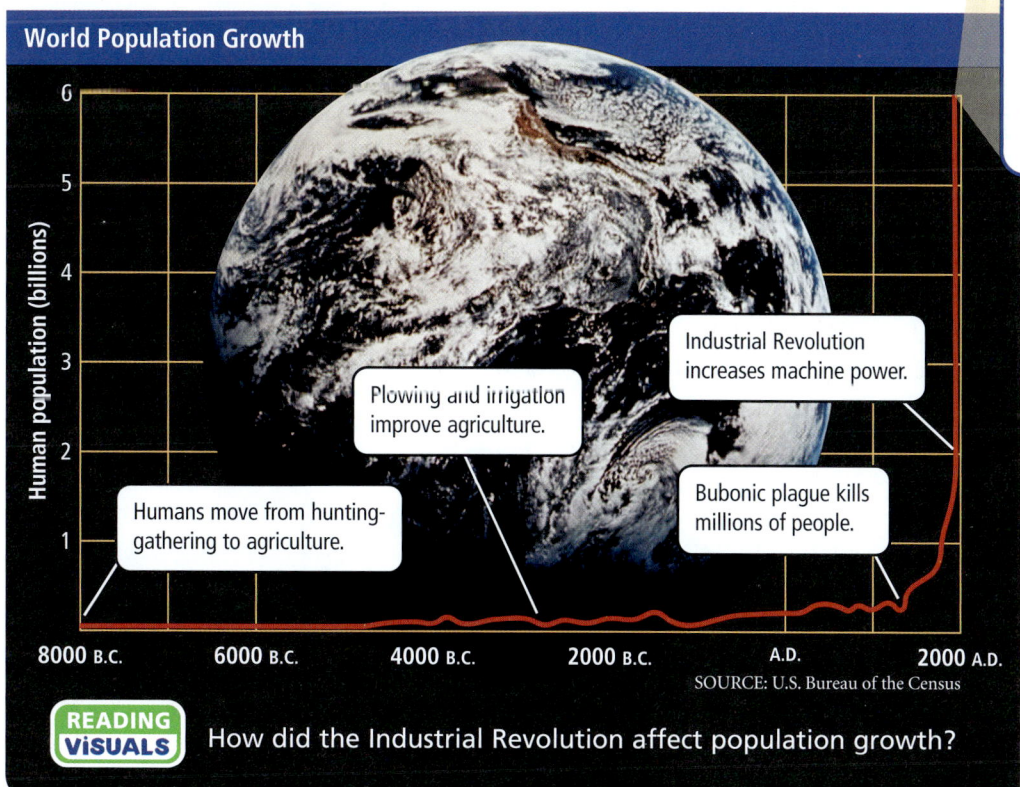

READING VISUALS How did the Industrial Revolution affect population growth?

In addition to population size and age structure, scientists making population projections consider other factors. These factors include the ages of individuals having children. The average number of offspring produced by an individual also affects projections. In addition, life expectancy and health in a particular population affect population growth.

The factors affecting population growth vary from society to society. The human population in the African country Botswana provides an example of how disease and health can affect population growth.

In some African countries, death rates due to HIV/AIDS have lowered population projections for the year 2015 by almost 18 percent. Botswana's population will decline, because more than 30 percent of adults are infected with HIV/AIDS. So many people in Botswana have already died of HIV/AIDS that the average life expectancy has dropped from 63 years of age in the late 1980s to 32 years in 2003. Consider the impact this will have on the population's age structure. Because many people who die from HIV/AIDS are in their reproductive years, the long-term effects on population growth will be significant.

 What factors do scientists consider when they make population projections?

INVESTIGATE Population

How can you graph population growth data for your area?

PROCEDURE

1. Use local population data taken from each census over five decades.
2. On graph paper, mark off five decades along the x–axis. Make a y–axis to show population size.
3. Plot the census information for each decade as a line graph.

WHAT DO YOU THINK?

- How did the local population change over time?
- What do you think accounted for the change?

CHALLENGE Based on the trend you see so far, how might the population change in the future? Use another color to extend the line on your graph to project population change over the next five decades. Explain why you think the population will change as you have predicted.

SKILL FOCUS
Graphing data

MATERIALS
- graph paper
- census data
- 2 colored pencils

TIME
30 minutes

Human population growth affects the environment.

You have read that extinction of species is a part of the history of life on Earth. The ways a population uses and disposes of resources have a great impact on local and global environments. As the human population continues to grow and use more resources, it contributes to the decline and extinction of other populations.

Some scientists estimate that over 99 percent of the species that have ever existed on Earth are now extinct. Most of these species vanished long before humans came on the scene. However, some experts are concerned that human activity is causing other species to become extinct at a much higher rate than they would naturally. Human populations put pressure on the environment in many ways, including

- introduction of new species
- pollution
- overfishing

Find out more on introduced species in the United States.

Introduction of New Species

Travelers have introduced new species to areas both on purpose and by accident. Many species introduced to an area provide benefits, such as food or beauty. Some species, however, cause harm to ecosystems. One example of an introduced species is the zebra mussel. An ocean vessel accidentally released zebra mussels from Europe into the Great Lakes region of the United States. With no natural predators that consume them, the mussels have reproduced quickly, invading all of the Great Lakes, the Mississippi River, and the Hudson River. The mussels compete with native species for food and affect water quality, endangering the ecosystem.

Kudzu is another introduced species. In the 1930s, kudzu was used in the southeastern United States to keep soil from being washed away. The plants, which have beautiful purple flowers, were imported from Japan. Starch made from kudzu is also a popular ingredient in some Asian recipes. However, populations of the kudzu vines planted in the United States have grown too far and too fast. Kudzu grows as much as 0.3 meters (about a foot) per day, killing trees and other plants living in the same area.

The kudzu plant, though at one time considered beautiful, is threatening other species.

Pollution

While human activities might cause some populations to decline, they can also cause other populations to grow. Sometimes this population growth causes pollution and habitat disturbance. **Pollution** is the addition of harmful substances to the environment. One example of such an activity is large-scale hog farming.

Human demands for pork combined with a growing human population have caused the hog farming industry to expand. Between 1987 and 2001, the hog population in North Carolina grew from 2.6 million to 10 million. These 10 million hogs produced more than 50,000 tons of waste each day. Wastes from large populations of hogs affect water supplies, soil, and air quality.

Pollution has also affected the Salton Sea in southeastern California. The growing demand for goods and agriculture has led to chemical dumping from industries and pesticide runoff from nearby farms. The rivers that run into the lake carry high levels of harmful chemicals such as DDT. Local birds that live and feed in this area have weakened shells that cannot support baby birds. Pollution has also caused fish to become deformed.

Large-scale hog farms affect water, soil, and air quality.

Pollution

The Salton Sea in California is surrounded by farm fields and industries that contribute to pollution.

Used water from irrigation drains into the Salton Sea.

Overfishing

Fish and crustaceans such as shrimp and lobsters have long been an important food source for many people. In the 1900s, the techniques and equipment that fishers used allowed them to catch so many fish that fish populations began to decrease. As the human population has continued to grow, so has the demand for fish. However, if fish do not survive long enough in the wild, they do not have the chance to reproduce. Many species have been so overfished that their populations may not recover.

Lobster fishing in particular has supported coastal communities in the northeastern United States for generations. But the demand for this food source has caused populations to decline. Areas that fishers trapped for years may now have only a small population of lobsters. And the lobsters fishers are catching may not be as large as those from earlier decades.

In order to help lobster populations recover, laws have been enforced to protect their life cycle and reproduction. Today, people who trap lobsters are required to release females with eggs. They are also allowed to keep only mature lobsters. Younger lobsters are returned to the waters to mature and reproduce. Efforts like these help protect the lobster population and secure the jobs of fishers by helping fish populations remain stable.

Fishers harvesting lobster measure the tails of the animals they catch. A lobster that is too small is returned to the sea to allow it to grow.

CHECK YOUR READING Describe how overfishing would affect resources.

25.3 Review

KEY CONCEPTS

1. What factors—other than birth, death, immigration, and emigration—must scientists consider when making projections of human population?
2. Give an example of how Earth's carrying capacity for humans has increased.
3. What are three ways that humans affect other populations?

CRITICAL THINKING

4. **Infer** Consider the effect of HIV/AIDS on Botswana's human population. How might age structure affect Botswana's population growth?
5. **Analyze** Do you think it is possible to predict the maximum number of humans that Earth can support? Why or why not?

CHALLENGE

6. **Apply** Identify a challenge faced by the human population in your state. Explain how the challenge is related to pollution, introduction of new species, habitat disturbance, or overfishing.

CHAPTER INVESTIGATION

Sustainable Resource Management

OVERVIEW AND PURPOSE Wood is a renewable resource, but the demand for wood is continuing to grow worldwide. Humans are harvesting trees more quickly than trees have the ability to grow and replace themselves. The result is a forest in decline. In this activity you will
- model what happens when trees are harvested to meet the needs of a growing population
- calculate the rate at which the population of a renewable resource declines

▶ Question

How can people meet the ongoing human demand for wood without using all the trees? You will use the increasing human demand for wood to determine how overuse of a resource might affect a population. What would you like to discover about resource management? Write a question that begins with *Which, How, Why, When,* or *What.*

MATERIALS
- coffee can with 120 craft sticks
- bundle of 32 craft sticks
- stopwatch

▶ Procedure

1. Copy the data table on page 887 into your **Science Notebook.**

2. In your group of classmates, decide who will fill each of the following roles: forest, timer, forest manager, harvester/record keeper.

3. **Forest:** Get a coffee can of 120 craft sticks. These sticks represent the available tree supply.

4. **Timer:** Sound off each 15-second interval and each minute.

886 Unit 6: **Life Over Time**

5 **Forest Manager:** Get 32 sticks from the teacher. You will add 1 new tree every 15 seconds by putting a stick in the coffee can.

6 **Harvester:** At the end of the first minute, cut down 1 tree by removing 1 stick from the coffee can. At the end of the second minute, cut down 2 trees; at the end of the third, cut down 4 trees. At the end of each additional minute cut down twice as many trees as you did before. This represents the doubling of the demand for trees based on human population growth.

Observe and Analyze

1. **CALCULATE** At the end of each minute, add 4 trees, but subtract twice as many trees as you subtracted the minute before.

2. **RECORD AND CALCULATE** Complete the chart. How many trees are left in the forest after 8 minutes of harvesting?

Conclude

1. **INFER** What effect does increasing human population growth have on forests?

2. **EVALUATE** Was the forest always shrinking?

3. **EVALUATE** How does this investigation help you to answer or change your question about resource management?

4. **IDENTIFY LIMITS** What aspects of this investigation fail to model the natural habitat?

5. **APPLY** What other renewable resources need sustainable management?

INVESTIGATE Further

CHALLENGE Explain how you could use the data gathered in this investigation to develop methods of sustainable resource management.

Sustainable Resource Management

Table 1. Rate of Harvest

Minutes	Number of Trees at Start of Minute	Number of New Trees	Number of Trees Harvested	Number of Trees at End of Minute
1	120	+4	−1	123
2				
3				
4				
5				
6				
7				
8				

Chapter Review

the BIG idea
Populations are shaped by interactions between organisms and the environment.

KEY CONCEPTS SUMMARY

1 Populations have many characteristics.

- Populations go through three stages:
  growth
  stability
  decline
- Four characteristics define a population:
  size
  density
  spacing
  age structure
- Scientists can predict population changes.

VOCABULARY
population dynamics p. 861
carrying capacity p. 862
population size p. 864
population density p. 865

2 Populations respond to pressures.

Populations change as they respond to pressures from limiting factors.

Two types of limiting factors are density dependent and density independent.

VOCABULARY
immigration p. 871
emigration p. 871
limiting factor p. 872
opportunist p. 875
competitor p. 876

3 Human populations have unique responses to change.

Humans can control many factors that limit most biological populations.

VOCABULARY
pollution p. 884

Reviewing Vocabulary

Describe how the vocabulary terms in the following pairs are related to each other. Explain the relationship in a one- or two-sentence answer. Underline each vocabulary term in your answers.

1. population dynamics and carrying capacity
2. immigration and emigration
3. limiting factor and population density
4. opportunists and competitors

Reviewing Key Concepts

Multiple Choice *Choose the letter of the best answer.*

5. The study of changes in a population over time and the factors that affect these changes is called population
    a. stability
    b. dynamics
    c. spacing
    d. density

6. A population that has reached its maximum size in a given area is said to have reached its
    a. population range
    b. gradual growth
    c. carrying capacity
    d. population projection

7. Assuming there is no immigration or emigration, a population size will remain constant if
    a. the birth rate equals the death rate
    b. the birth rate exceeds the death rate
    c. the death rate exceeds the birth rate
    d. the birth rate increases constantly

8. Distinct patterns in a population such as clumped, uniform, or random populations are examples of population
    a. density
    b. spacing
    c. growth
    d. dynamics

9. Which factors affect the size and growth of a population?
    a. number of births and deaths
    b. emigration and immigration
    c. competition between populations
    d. all of the above

10. A limiting factor that depends on the size of the population in a given area is a
    a. density-dependent factor
    b. density-independent factor
    c. reproduction survival strategy
    d. carrying capacity

11. Density-independent limiting factors include
    a. predators
    b. parasites
    c. floods
    d. competition

12. Which are abiotic factors in an environment?
    a. disease and parasites
    b. air, light, and water
    c. pollution and overfishing
    d. competition and predators

13. Which is an example of competition for resources?
    a. individuals in a population feeding on the same food sources
    b. movement of seagulls into a population of other seagulls
    c. an increase in the population of raccoons in a particular environment at a steady rate
    d. a population of fruit trees producing less fruit because of drought

14. Two factors that have increased Earth's carrying capacity for humans are habitat expansion, and
    a. habitat disturbance
    b. strategies of competitors
    c. strategies of opportunists
    d. technology

Short Answer *Write a short answer to each question.*

15. What factors might affect the density of a population?

16. What is the age structure of a population?

17. Describe three factors that account for the rapid growth of the human population during the past 500 years.

Thinking Critically

18. **ANALYZE** Under what conditions does gradual growth in a population occur?

19. **COMMUNICATE** Describe four observations that Darwin made about population growth.

20. **PREDICT** The graph below shows the exponential growth rate of a colony of unicellular organisms. If the population continues to grow at the same rate during the next 2 hours, what will the population be after 10 hours? Explain your answer.

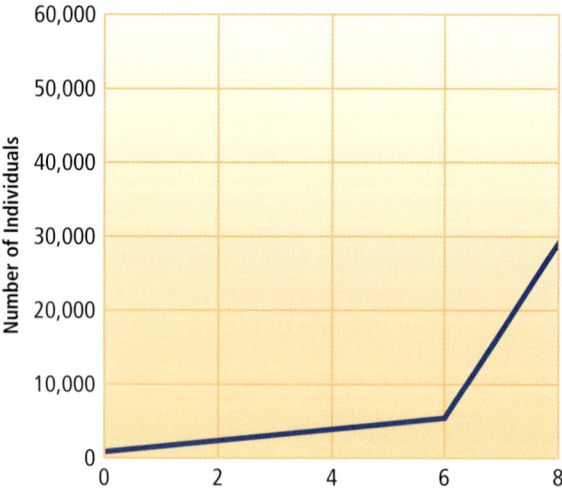

21. **PREDICT** In a certain population 35 percent of the individuals are under the age of 20. What predictions might you make about the size of the population in 10 years?

22. **PROVIDE EXAMPLES** What limiting factors might cause the carrying capacity of a population to change? Provide at least three examples. Describe how the population might change.

23. **SYNTHESIZE** What is an example of a density-independent factor that has affected a human population? Describe how this factor changed the population.

24. **INFER** Wolves are the natural predators of moose. Both populations are found on an island in the middle of Lake Superior. During one season, the population of moose increased dramatically. What could have caused the increase in the moose population?

25. **EVALUATE** Why do you suppose that the growth rate of human populations differs dramatically in different countries?

26. **SYNTHESIZE** Human activity has resulted in the decline of many populations of other species. Choose one example of how humans have put pressure on species around the world and describe ways that humans can avoid causing continued decreases in these populations.

the BIG idea

27. **INFER** Look again at the picture on pages 858–859. Now that you have finished the chapter, how would you change or add details to your answer to the question on the photograph?

28. **SUMMARIZE** Write one or more paragraphs describing the factors that affect population size, density, and age structure. Use the following terms in your descriptions.

immigration	density-dependent factors
emigration	density-independent factors
limiting factors	

UNIT PROJECTS

If you need to do an experiment for your unit project, gather the materials. Be sure to allow enough time to observe results before the project is due.

Standardized Test Practice

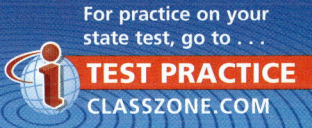

Analyzing Data

The graph below is an example of a population growth curve.

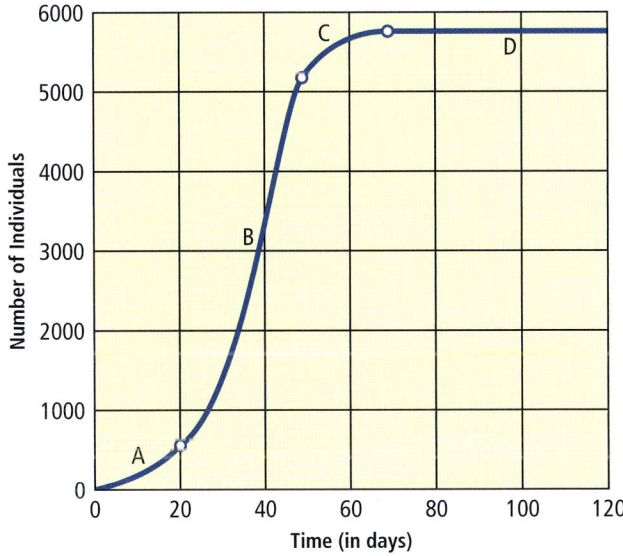

Use the graph to answer the questions below.

1. What does the time interval marked *D* represent?
   a. Population is decreasing.
   b. Carrying capacity has been reached.
   c. Birth rates exceed death rates.
   d. Population is growing.

2. Which time interval on the graph represents gradual growth?
   a. interval A and interval B
   b. interval C and interval D
   c. interval C only
   d. interval D only

3. During which time interval do limiting factors in a population begin to have an effect on the population growth?
   a. interval A only
   b. interval B only
   c. interval C only
   d. interval C and interval D

4. This graph represents a typical
   a. gradual curve
   b. rapid curve
   c. slow curve
   d. flat curve

5. What conclusion can you draw from the information in the graph?
   a. Density-dependent factors have had no effect on the population shown on the graph.
   b. The graph indicates an absence of disease and a supply of unlimited resources.
   c. Resources have become more available, so the population continues to increase exponentially.
   d. As resources become less available, the population rate slows or stops.

Extended Response

6. What part of the graph above shows the growth of the human population during the last 500 years? Explain. What are some factors that might allow the human population to reach its carrying capacity?

7. Choose a population of organisms in your area. Describe the limiting factors that may affect the growth of that population. Make sure you include both density-dependent and density-independent factors in your discussion.

Student Resource Handbooks

Scientific Thinking Handbook — R2

Making Observations	R2
Predicting and Hypothesizing	R3
Inferring	R4
Identifying Cause and Effect	R5
Recognizing Bias	R6
Identifying Faulty Reasoning	R7
Analyzing Statements	R8

Lab Handbook — R10

Safety Rules	R10
Using Lab Equipment	R12
The Metric System and SI Units	R20
Precision and Accuracy	R22
Making Data Tables and Graphs	R23
Designing an Experiment	R28

Math Handbook — R36

Describing a Set of Data	R36
Using Ratios, Rates, and Proportions	R38
Using Decimals, Fractions, and Percents	R39
Using Formulas	R42
Finding Areas	R43
Finding Volumes	R43
Using Significant Figures	R44
Using Scientific Notation	R44

Note-Taking Handbook — R45

Note-Taking Strategies	R45
Vocabulary Strategies	R50

Scientific Thinking Handbook

Making Observations

An **observation** is an act of noting and recording an event, characteristic, behavior, or anything else detected with an instrument or with the senses.

Observations allow you to make informed hypotheses and to gather data for experiments. Careful observations often lead to ideas for new experiments. There are two categories of observations:

- **Quantitative observations** can be expressed in numbers and include records of time, temperature, mass, distance, and volume.
- **Qualitative observations** include descriptions of sights, sounds, smells, and textures.

EXAMPLE

A student dissolved 30 grams of Epsom salts in water, poured the solution into a dish, and let the dish sit out uncovered overnight. The next day, she made the following observations of the Epsom salt crystals that grew in the dish.

Table 1. Observations of Epsom Salt Crystals

Quantitative Observations	Qualitative Observations
• mass = 30 g	• Crystals are clear.
• mean crystal length = 0.5 cm	• Crystals are long, thin, and rectangular.
• longest crystal length = 2 cm	• White crust has formed around edge of dish.

To determine the mass, the student found the mass of the dish before and after growing the crystals and then used subtraction to find the difference.

The student measured several crystals and calculated the mean length. (To learn how to calculate the mean of a data set, see page R36.)

Photographs or sketches are useful for recording qualitative observations.

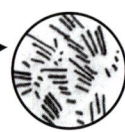 Epsom salt crystals

MORE ABOUT OBSERVING

- Make quantitative observations whenever possible. That way, others will know exactly what you observed and be able to compare their results with yours.
- It is always a good idea to make qualitative observations too. You never know when you might observe something unexpected.

Predicting and Hypothesizing

A **prediction** is an expectation of what will be observed or what will happen. A **hypothesis** is a tentative explanation for an observation or scientific problem that can be tested by further investigation.

EXAMPLE

Suppose you have made two paper airplanes and you wonder why one of them tends to glide farther than the other one.

1. Start by asking a question.
2. Make an educated guess. After examination, you notice that the wings of the airplane that flies farther are slightly larger than the wings of the other airplane.
3. Write a prediction based upon your educated guess, in the form of an "If . . . , then . . ." statement. Write the independent variable after the word *if,* and the dependent variable after the word *then*.
4. To make a hypothesis, explain why you think what you predicted will occur. Write the explanation after the word *because*.

---

1. Why does one of the paper airplanes glide farther than the other?

2. The size of an airplane's wings may affect how far the airplane will glide.

3. Prediction: If I make a paper airplane with larger wings, then the airplane will glide farther.

   To read about independent and dependent variables, see page R30.

4. Hypothesis: If I make a paper airplane with larger wings, then the airplane will glide farther, because the additional surface area of the wing will produce more lift.

   Notice that the part of the hypothesis after because *adds an explanation of why the airplane will glide farther.*

MORE ABOUT HYPOTHESES

- The results of an experiment cannot prove that a hypothesis is correct. Rather, the results either support or do not support the hypothesis.
- Valuable information is gained even when your hypothesis is not supported by your results. For example, it would be an important discovery to find that wing size is not related to how far an airplane glides.
- In science, a hypothesis is supported only after many scientists have conducted many experiments and produced consistent results.

Scientific Thinking Handbook **R3**

Inferring

An **inference** is a logical conclusion drawn from the available evidence and prior knowledge. Inferences are often made from observations.

EXAMPLE

A student observing a set of acorns noticed something unexpected about one of them. He noticed a white, soft-bodied insect eating its way out of the acorn.

The student recorded these observations.

Observations
- There is a hole in the acorn, about 0.5 cm in diameter, where the insect crawled out.
- There is a second hole, which is about the size of a pinhole, on the other side of the acorn.
- The inside of the acorn is hollow.

Here are some inferences that can be made on the basis of the observations.

Inferences
- The insect formed from the material inside the acorn, grew to its present size, and ate its way out of the acorn.
- The insect crawled through the smaller hole, ate the inside of the acorn, grew to its present size, and ate its way out of the acorn.
- An egg was laid in the acorn through the smaller hole. The egg hatched into a larva that ate the inside of the acorn, grew to its present size, and ate its way out of the acorn.

When you make inferences, be sure to look at all of the evidence available and combine it with what you already know.

MORE ABOUT INFERENCES

Inferences depend both on observations and on the knowledge of the people making the inferences. Ancient people who did not know that organisms are produced only by similar organisms might have made an inference like the first one. A student today might look at the same observations and make the second inference. A third student might have knowledge about this particular insect and know that it is never small enough to fit through the smaller hole, leading her to the third inference.

Identifying Cause and Effect

In a **cause-and-effect relationship,** one event or characteristic is the result of another. Usually an effect follows its cause in time.

There are many examples of cause-and-effect relationships in everyday life.

Cause	Effect
Turn off a light.	Room gets dark.
Drop a glass.	Glass breaks.
Blow a whistle.	Sound is heard.

Scientists must be careful not to infer a cause-and-effect relationship just because one event happens after another event. When one event occurs after another, you cannot infer a cause-and-effect relationship on the basis of that information alone. You also cannot conclude that one event caused another if there are alternative ways to explain the second event. A scientist must demonstrate through experimentation or continued observation that an event was truly caused by another event.

EXAMPLE

Make an Observation

Suppose you have a few plants growing outside. When the weather starts getting colder, you bring one of the plants indoors. You notice that the plant you brought indoors is growing faster than the others are growing. You cannot conclude from your observation that the change in temperature was the cause of the increased plant growth, because there are alternative explanations for the observation. Some possible explanations are given below.

- The humidity indoors caused the plant to grow faster.
- The level of sunlight indoors caused the plant to grow faster.
- The indoor plant's being noticed more often and watered more often than the outdoor plants caused it to grow faster.
- The plant that was brought indoors was healthier than the other plants to begin with.

To determine which of these factors, if any, caused the indoor plant to grow faster than the outdoor plants, you would need to design and conduct an experiment.

See pages R28–R35 for information about designing experiments.

Scientific Thinking Handbook R5

Recognizing Bias

Television, newspapers, and the Internet are full of experts claiming to have scientific evidence to back up their claims. How do you know whether the claims are really backed up by good science?

Bias is a slanted point of view, or personal prejudice. The goal of scientists is to be as objective as possible and to base their findings on facts instead of opinions. However, bias often affects the conclusions of researchers, and it is important to learn to recognize bias.

When scientific results are reported, you should consider the source of the information as well as the information itself. It is important to critically analyze the information that you see and read.

SOURCES OF BIAS

There are several ways in which a report of scientific information may be biased. Here are some questions that you can ask yourself:

1. **Who is sponsoring the research?**

   Sometimes, the results of an investigation are biased because an organization paying for the research is looking for a specific answer. This type of bias can affect how data are gathered and interpreted.

2. **Is the research sample large enough?**

   Sometimes research does not include enough data. The larger the sample size, the more likely that the results are accurate, assuming a truly random sample.

3. **In a survey, who is answering the questions?**

   The results of a survey or poll can be biased. The people taking part in the survey may have been specifically chosen because of how they would answer. They may have the same ideas or lifestyles. A survey or poll should make use of a random sample of people.

4. **Are the people who take part in a survey biased?**

   People who take part in surveys sometimes try to answer the questions the way they think the researcher wants them to answer. Also, in surveys or polls that ask for personal information, people may be unwilling to answer questions truthfully.

SCIENTIFIC BIAS

It is also important to realize that scientists have their own biases because of the types of research they do and because of their scientific viewpoints. Two scientists may look at the same set of data and come to completely different conclusions because of these biases. However, such disagreements are not necessarily bad. In fact, a critical analysis of disagreements is often responsible for moving science forward.

Identifying Faulty Reasoning

Faulty reasoning is wrong or incorrect thinking. It leads to mistakes and to wrong conclusions. Scientists are careful not to draw unreasonable conclusions from experimental data. Without such caution, the results of scientific investigations may be misleading.

EXAMPLE

Scientists try to make generalizations based on their data to explain as much about nature as possible. If only a small sample of data is looked at, however, a conclusion may be faulty. Suppose a scientist has studied the effects of the El Niño and La Niña weather patterns on flood damage in California from 1989 to 1995. The scientist organized the data in the bar graph below.

The scientist drew the following conclusions:

1. The La Niña weather pattern has no effect on flooding in California.
2. When neither weather pattern occurs, there is almost no flood damage.
3. A weak or moderate El Niño produces a small or moderate amount of flooding.
4. A strong El Niño produces a lot of flooding.

Flood and Storm Damage in California

SOURCE: *Governor's Office of Emergency Services, California*

For the six-year period of the scientist's investigation, these conclusions may seem to be reasonable. However, a six-year study of weather patterns may be too small of a sample for the conclusions to be supported. Consider the following graph, which shows information that was gathered from 1949 to 1997.

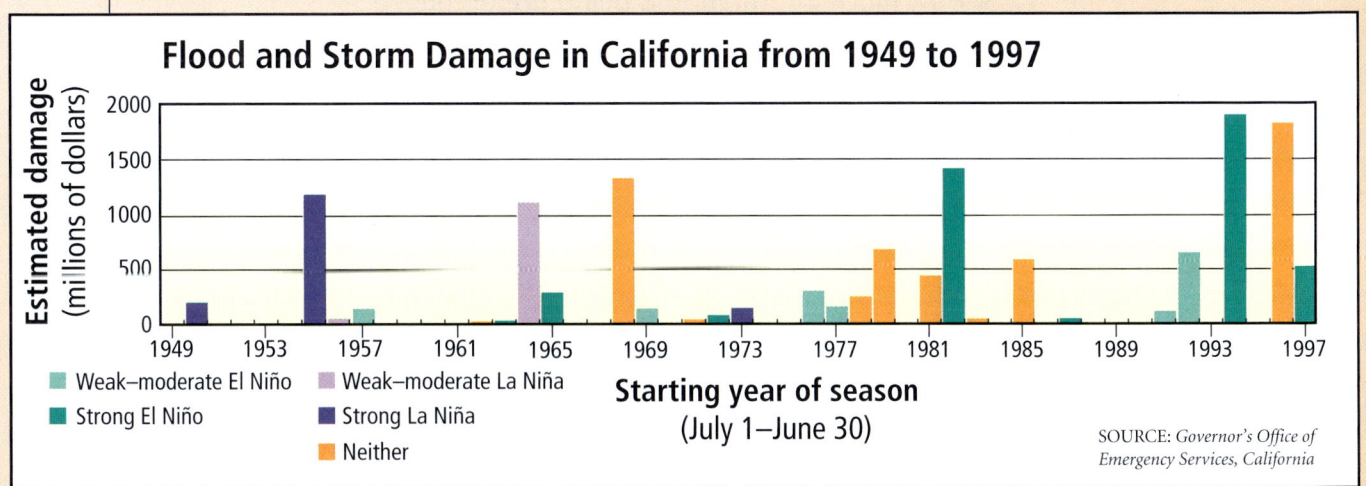

Flood and Storm Damage in California from 1949 to 1997

- Weak–moderate El Niño
- Weak–moderate La Niña
- Strong El Niño
- Strong La Niña
- Neither

SOURCE: *Governor's Office of Emergency Services, California*

The only one of the conclusions that all of this information supports is number 3: a weak or moderate El Niño produces a small or moderate amount of flooding. By collecting more data, scientists can be more certain of their conclusions and can avoid faulty reasoning.

Scientific Thinking Handbook **R7**

Analyzing Statements

To **analyze** a statement is to examine its parts carefully. Scientific findings are often reported through media such as television or the Internet. A report that is made public often focuses on only a small part of research. As a result, it is important to question the sources of information.

Evaluate Media Claims

To **evaluate** a statement is to judge it on the basis of criteria you've established. Sometimes evaluating means deciding whether a statement is true.

Reports of scientific research and findings in the media may be misleading or incomplete. When you are exposed to this information, you should ask yourself some questions so that you can make informed judgments about the information.

1. **Does the information come from a credible source?**

    Suppose you learn about a new product and it is stated that scientific evidence proves that the product works. A report from a respected news source may be more believable than an advertisement paid for by the product's manufacturer.

2. **How much evidence supports the claim?**

    Often, it may seem that there is new evidence every day of something in the world that either causes or cures an illness. However, information that is the result of several years of work by several different scientists is more credible than an advertisement that does not even cite the subjects of the experiment.

3. **How much information is being presented?**

    Science cannot solve all questions, and scientific experiments often have flaws. A report that discusses problems in a scientific study may be more believable than a report that addresses only positive experimental findings.

4. **Is scientific evidence being presented by a specific source?**

    Sometimes scientific findings are reported by people who are called experts or leaders in a scientific field. But if their names are not given or their scientific credentials are not reported, their statements may be less credible than those of recognized experts.

Differentiate Between Fact and Opinion

Sometimes information is presented as a fact when it may be an opinion. When scientific conclusions are reported, it is important to recognize whether they are based on solid evidence. Again, you may find it helpful to ask yourself some questions.

1. **What is the difference between a fact and an opinion?**

   A **fact** is a piece of information that can be strictly defined and proved true. An **opinion** is a statement that expresses a belief, value, or feeling. An opinion cannot be proved true or false. For example, a person's age is a fact, but if someone is asked how old they feel, it is impossible to prove the person's answer to be true or false.

2. **Can opinions be measured?**

   Yes, opinions can be measured. In fact, surveys often ask for people's opinions on a topic. But there is no way to know whether or not an opinion is the truth.

HOW TO DIFFERENTIATE FACT FROM OPINION

Human Activities and the Environment

Unfortunately, human use of fossil fuels is one of the most significant developments of the past few centuries. Humans rely on fossil fuels, a non-renewable energy resource, for more than 90 percent of their energy needs.

This careless misuse of our planet's resources has resulted in pollution, global warming, and the destruction of fragile ecosystems. For example, oil pipelines carry more than one million barrels of oil each day across tundra regions. Transporting oil across such areas can only result in oil spills that poison the land for decades.

Opinions
Notice words or phrases that express beliefs or feelings. The words *unfortunately* and *careless* show that opinions are being expressed.

Opinion
Look for statements that speculate about events. These statements are opinions, because they cannot be proved.

Facts
Statements that contain statistics tend to be facts. Writers often use facts to support their opinions.

Lab Handbook

Safety Rules

Before you work in the laboratory, read these safety rules twice. Ask your teacher to explain any rules that you do not completely understand. Refer to these rules later on if you have questions about safety in the science classroom.

Directions

- Read all directions and make sure that you understand them before starting an investigation or lab activity. If you do not understand how to do a procedure or how to use a piece of equipment, ask your teacher.
- Do not begin any investigation or touch any equipment until your teacher has told you to start.
- Never experiment on your own. If you want to try a procedure that the directions do not call for, ask your teacher for permission first.
- If you are hurt or injured in any way, tell your teacher immediately.

Dress Code

goggles

apron

gloves

- Wear goggles when
  — using glassware, sharp objects, or chemicals
  — heating an object
  — working with anything that can easily fly up into the air and hurt someone's eye
- Tie back long hair or hair that hangs in front of your eyes.
- Remove any article of clothing—such as a loose sweater or a scarf—that hangs down and may touch a flame, chemical, or piece of equipment.
- Observe all safety icons calling for the wearing of eye protection, gloves, and aprons.

Heating and Fire Safety

fire safety

heating safety

- Keep your work area neat, clean, and free of extra materials.
- Never reach over a flame or heat source.
- Point objects being heated away from you and others.
- Never heat a substance or an object in a closed container.
- Never touch an object that has been heated. If you are unsure whether something is hot, treat it as though it is. Use oven mitts, clamps, tongs, or a test-tube holder.
- Know where the fire extinguisher and fire blanket are kept in your classroom.
- Do not throw hot substances into the trash. Wait for them to cool or use the container your teacher puts out for disposal.

Electrical Safety

electrical safety

- Never use lamps or other electrical equipment with frayed cords.
- Make sure no cord is lying on the floor where someone can trip over it.
- Do not let a cord hang over the side of a counter or table so that the equipment can easily be pulled or knocked to the floor.
- Never let cords hang into sinks or other places where water can be found.
- Never try to fix electrical problems. Inform your teacher of any problems immediately.
- Unplug an electrical cord by pulling on the plug, not the cord.

Chemical Safety

chemical safety

poison

fumes

Wafting

- If you spill a chemical or get one on your skin or in your eyes, tell your teacher right away.
- Never touch, taste, or sniff any chemicals in the lab. If you need to determine odor, waft. Wafting consists of holding the chemical in its container 15 centimeters (6 in.) away from your nose, and using your fingers to bring fumes from the container to your nose.
- Keep lids on all chemicals you are not using.
- Never put unused chemicals back into the original containers. Throw away extra chemicals where your teacher tells you to.
- Pour chemicals over a sink or your work area, not over the floor.
- If you get a chemical in your eye, use the eyewash right away.
- Always wash your hands after handling chemicals, plants, or soil.

Glassware and Sharp-Object Safety

sharp objects

- If you break glassware, tell your teacher right away.
- Do not use broken or chipped glassware. Give these to your teacher.
- Use knives and other cutting instruments carefully. Always wear eye protection and cut away from you.

Animal Safety

- Never hurt an animal.
- Touch animals only when necessary. Follow your teacher's instructions for handling animals.
- Always wash your hands after working with animals.

Cleanup

disposal

- Follow your teacher's instructions for throwing away or putting away supplies.
- Clean your work area and pick up anything that has dropped to the floor.
- Wash your hands.

Using Lab Equipment

Different experiments require different types of equipment. But even though experiments differ, the ways in which the equipment is used are the same.

Beakers

- Use beakers for holding and pouring liquids.
- Do not use a beaker to measure the volume of a liquid. Use a graduated cylinder instead. (See page R16.)
- Use a beaker that holds about twice as much liquid as you need. For example, if you need 100 milliliters of water, you should use a 200- or 250-milliliter beaker.

Test Tubes

- Use test tubes to hold small amounts of substances.
- Do not use a test tube to measure the volume of a liquid.
- Use a test tube when heating a substance over a flame. Aim the mouth of the tube away from yourself and other people.
- Liquids easily spill or splash from test tubes, so it is important to use only small amounts of liquids.

Test-Tube Holder

- Use a test-tube holder when heating a substance in a test tube.
- Use a test-tube holder if the substance in a test tube is dangerous to touch.
- Make sure the test-tube holder tightly grips the test tube so that the test tube will not slide out of the holder.
- Make sure that the test-tube holder is above the surface of the substance in the test tube so that you can observe the substance.

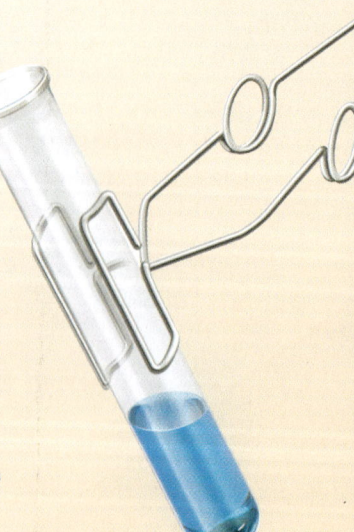

Test-Tube Rack

- Use a test-tube rack to organize test tubes before, during, and after an experiment.
- Use a test-tube rack to keep test tubes upright so that they do not fall over and spill their contents.
- Use a test-tube rack that is the correct size for the test tubes that you are using. If the rack is too small, a test tube may become stuck. If the rack is too large, a test tube may lean over, and some of its contents may spill or splash.

Forceps

- Use forceps when you need to pick up or hold a very small object that should not be touched with your hands.
- Do not use forceps to hold anything over a flame, because forceps are not long enough to keep your hand safely away from the flame. Plastic forceps will melt, and metal forceps will conduct heat and burn your hand.

Hot Plate

- Use a hot plate when a substance needs to be kept warmer than room temperature for a long period of time.
- Use a hot plate instead of a Bunsen burner or a candle when you need to carefully control temperature.
- Do not use a hot plate when a substance needs to be burned in an experiment.
- Always use "hot hands" safety mitts or oven mitts when handling anything that has been heated on a hot plate.

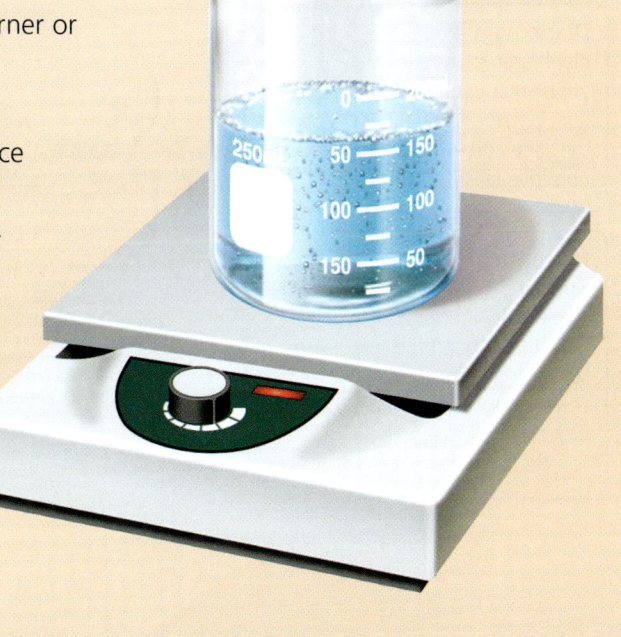

Lab Handbook R13

Microscope

Scientists use microscopes to see very small objects that cannot easily be seen with the eye alone. A microscope magnifies the image of an object so that small details may be observed. A microscope that you may use can magnify an object 400 times—the object will appear 400 times larger than its actual size.

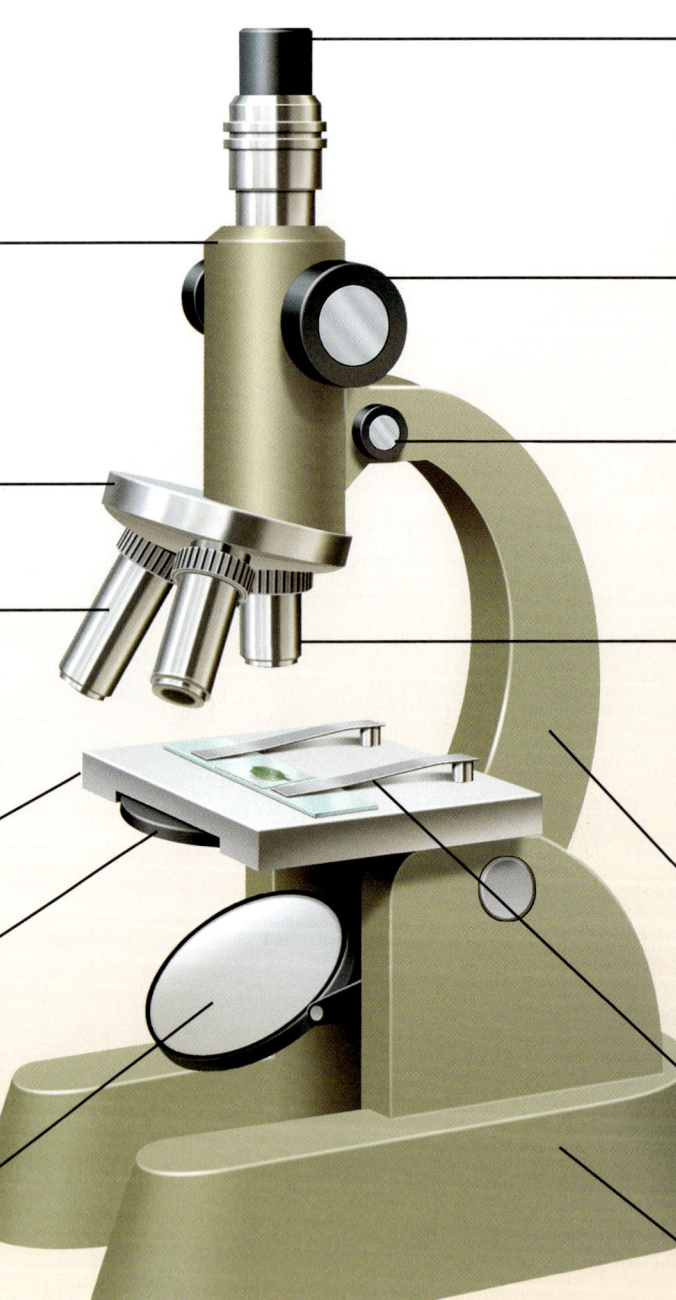

Eyepiece Objects are viewed through the eyepiece. The eyepiece contains a lens that commonly magnifies an image 10 times.

Body The body separates the lens in the eyepiece from the objective lenses below.

Coarse Adjustment This knob is used to focus the image of an object when it is viewed through the low-power lens.

Nosepiece The nosepiece holds the objective lenses above the stage and rotates so that all lenses may be used.

Fine Adjustment This knob is used to focus the image of an object when it is viewed through the high-power lens.

High-Power Objective Lens This is the largest lens on the nosepiece. It magnifies an image approximately 40 times.

Low-Power Objective Lens This is the smallest lens on the nosepiece. It magnifies an image approximately 10 times.

Stage The stage supports the object being viewed.

Arm The arm supports the body above the stage. Always carry a microscope by the arm and base.

Diaphragm The diaphragm is used to adjust the amount of light passing through the slide and into an objective lens.

Stage Clip The stage clip holds a slide in place on the stage.

Mirror or Light Source Some microscopes use light that is reflected through the stage by a mirror. Other microscopes have their own light sources.

Base The base supports the microscope.

VIEWING AN OBJECT

1. Use the coarse adjustment knob to raise the body tube.
2. Adjust the diaphragm so that you can see a bright circle of light through the eyepiece.
3. Place the object or slide on the stage. Be sure that it is centered over the hole in the stage.
4. Turn the nosepiece to click the low-power lens into place.
5. Using the coarse adjustment knob, slowly lower the lens and focus on the specimen being viewed. Be sure not to touch the slide or object with the lens.
6. When switching from the low-power lens to the high-power lens, first raise the body tube with the coarse adjustment knob so that the high-power lens will not hit the slide.
7. Turn the nosepiece to click the high-power lens into place.
8. Use the fine adjustment knob to focus on the specimen being viewed. Again, be sure not to touch the slide or object with the lens.

MAKING A SLIDE, OR WET MOUNT

1 Place the specimen in the center of a clean slide.

2 Place a drop of water on the specimen.

3 Place a cover slip on the slide. Put one edge of the cover slip into the drop of water and slowly lower it over the specimen.

4 Remove any air bubbles from under the cover slip by gently tapping the cover slip.

5 Dry any excess water before placing the slide on the microscope stage for viewing.

Lab Handbook R15

Spring Scale (Force Meter)

- Use a spring scale to measure a force pulling on the scale.
- Use a spring scale to measure the force of gravity exerted on an object by Earth.
- To measure a force accurately, a spring scale must be zeroed before it is used. The scale is zeroed when no weight is attached and the indicator is positioned at zero.
- Do not attach a weight that is either too heavy or too light to a spring scale. A weight that is too heavy could break the scale or exert too great a force for the scale to measure. A weight that is too light may not exert enough force to be measured accurately.

Graduated Cylinder

- Use a graduated cylinder to measure the volume of a liquid.
- Be sure that the graduated cylinder is on a flat surface so that your measurement will be accurate.
- When reading the scale on a graduated cylinder, be sure to have your eyes at the level of the surface of the liquid.
- The surface of the liquid will be curved in the graduated cylinder. Read the volume of the liquid at the bottom of the curve, or meniscus (muh-NIHS-kuhs).
- You can use a graduated cylinder to find the volume of a solid object by measuring the increase in a liquid's level after you add the object to the cylinder.

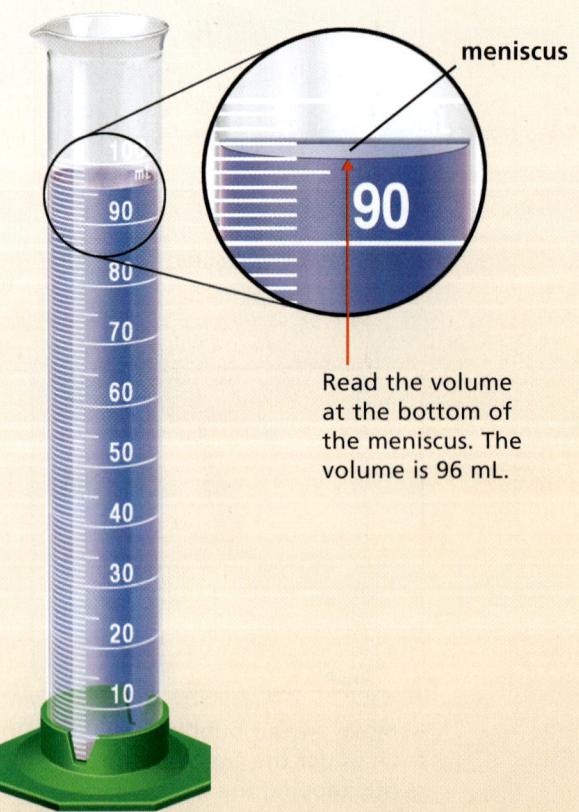

meniscus

Read the volume at the bottom of the meniscus. The volume is 96 mL.

Metric Rulers

- Use metric rulers or meter sticks to measure objects' lengths.
- Do not measure an object from the end of a metric ruler or meter stick, because the end is often imperfect. Instead, measure from the 1-centimeter mark, but remember to subtract a centimeter from the apparent measurement.
- Estimate any lengths that extend between marked units. For example, if a meter stick shows centimeters but not millimeters, you can estimate the length that an object extends between centimeter marks to measure it to the nearest millimeter.
- **Controlling Variables** If you are taking repeated measurements, always measure from the same point each time. For example, if you're measuring how high two different balls bounce when dropped from the same height, measure both bounces at the same point on the balls—either the top or the bottom. Do not measure at the top of one ball and the bottom of the other.

EXAMPLE

How to Measure a Leaf

1. Lay a ruler flat on top of the leaf so that the 1-centimeter mark lines up with one end. Make sure the ruler and the leaf do not move between the time you line them up and the time you take the measurement.
2. Look straight down on the ruler so that you can see exactly how the marks line up with the other end of the leaf.
3. Estimate the length by which the leaf extends beyond a marking. For example, the leaf below extends about halfway between the 4.2-centimeter and 4.3-centimeter marks, so the apparent measurement is about 4.25 centimeters.
4. Remember to subtract 1 centimeter from your apparent measurement, since you started at the 1-centimeter mark on the ruler and not at the end. The leaf is about 3.25 centimeters long (4.25 cm – 1 cm = 3.25 cm).

Triple-Beam Balance

This balance has a pan and three beams with sliding masses, called riders. At one end of the beams is a pointer that indicates whether the mass on the pan is equal to the masses shown on the beams.

1. Make sure the balance is zeroed before measuring the mass of an object. The balance is zeroed if the pointer is at zero when nothing is on the pan and the riders are at their zero points. Use the adjustment knob at the base of the balance to zero it.
2. Place the object to be measured on the pan.
3. Move the riders one notch at a time away from the pan. Begin with the largest rider. If moving the largest rider one notch brings the pointer below zero, begin measuring the mass of the object with the next smaller rider.
4. Change the positions of the riders until they balance the mass on the pan and the pointer is at zero. Then add the readings from the three beams to determine the mass of the object.

300 g	position of largest rider
90 g	position of middle rider
+ 3 g	position of smallest rider
393 g	mass of beaker

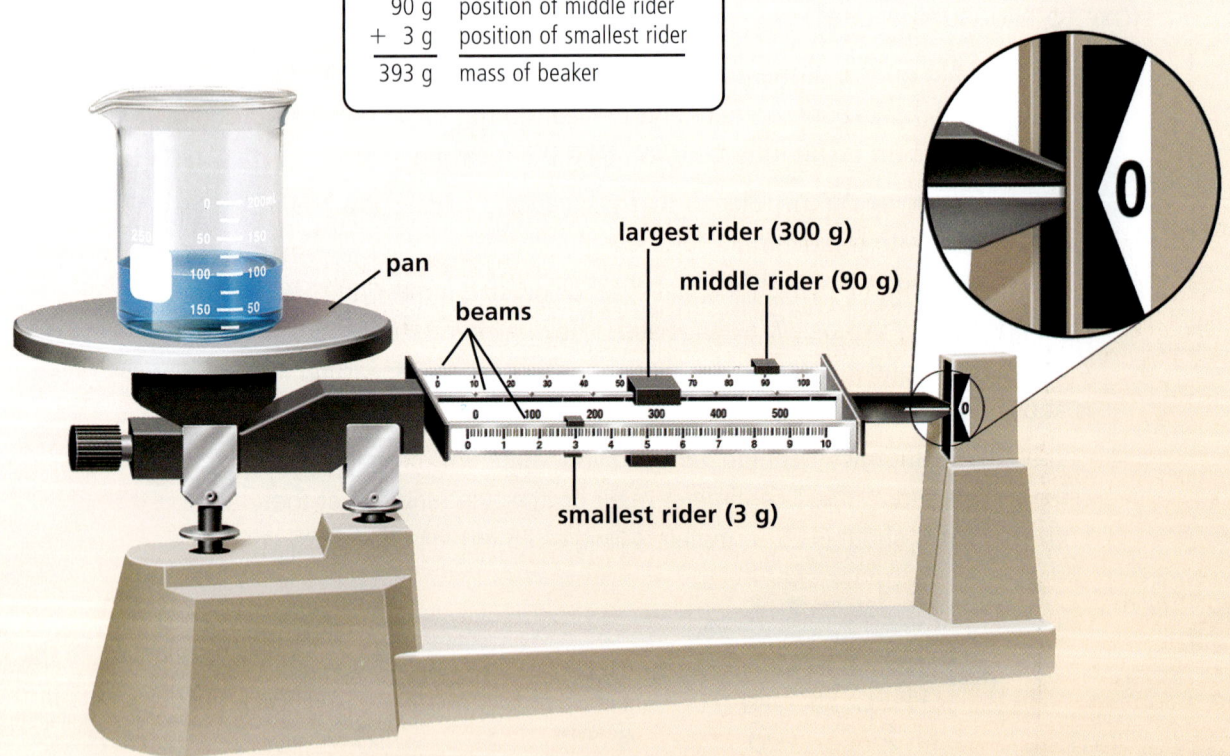

Double-Pan Balance

This type of balance has two pans. Between the pans is a pointer that indicates whether the masses on the pans are equal.

1. Make sure the balance is zeroed before measuring the mass of an object. The balance is zeroed if the pointer is at zero when there is nothing on either of the pans. Many double-pan balances have sliding knobs that can be used to zero them.

2. Place the object to be measured on one of the pans.

3. Begin adding standard masses to the other pan. Begin with the largest standard mass. If this adds too much mass to the balance, begin measuring the mass of the object with the next smaller standard mass.

4. Add standard masses until the masses on both pans are balanced and the pointer is at zero. Then add the standard masses together to determine the mass of the object being measured.

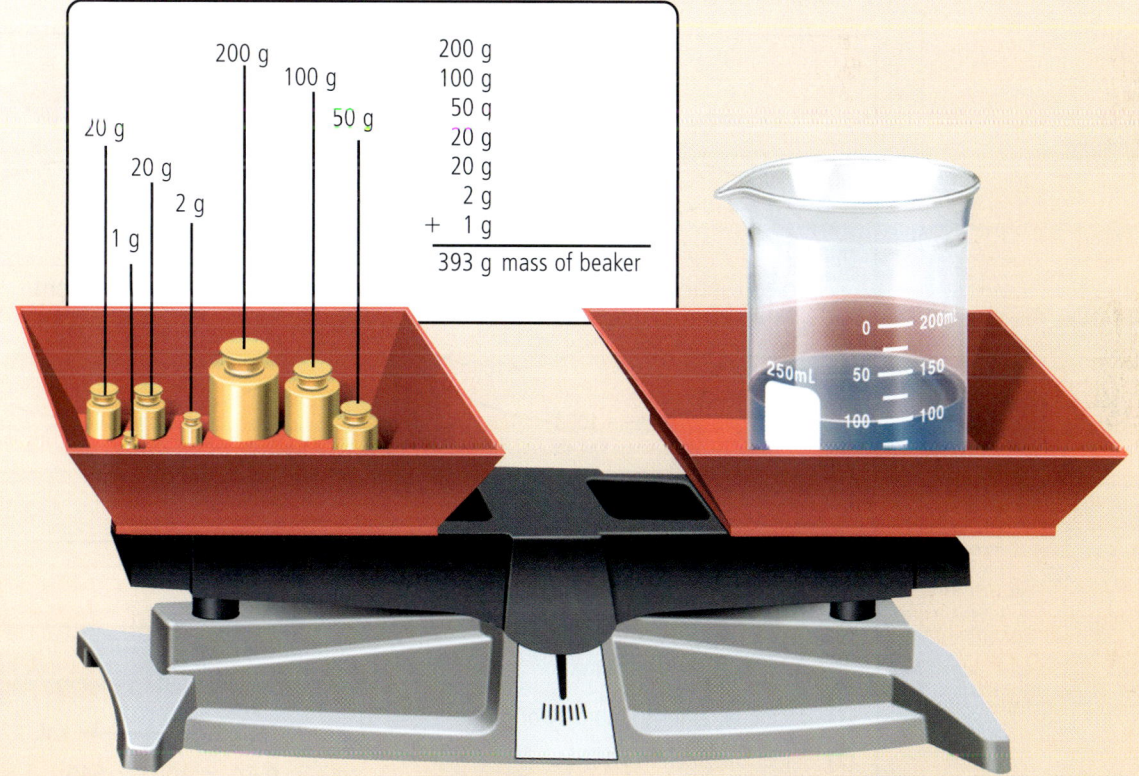

```
         200 g
         100 g
          50 g
          20 g
          20 g
           2 g
       +   1 g
       ─────────
       393 g mass of beaker
```

Never place chemicals or liquids directly on a pan. Instead, use the following procedure:

① Determine the mass of an empty container, such as a beaker.

② Pour the substance into the container, and measure the total mass of the substance and the container.

③ Subtract the mass of the empty container from the total mass to find the mass of the substance.

Lab Handbook **R19**

The Metric System and SI Units

Scientists use International System (SI) units for measurements of distance, volume, mass, and temperature. The International System is based on multiples of ten and the metric system of measurement.

Basic SI Units		
Property	Name	Symbol
length	meter	m
volume	liter	L
mass	kilogram	kg
temperature	kelvin	K

SI Prefixes		
Prefix	Symbol	Multiple of 10
kilo-	k	1000
hecto-	h	100
deca-	da	10
deci-	d	0.1 ($\frac{1}{10}$)
centi-	c	0.01 ($\frac{1}{100}$)
milli-	m	0.001 ($\frac{1}{1000}$)

Changing Metric Units

You can change from one unit to another in the metric system by multiplying or dividing by a power of 10.

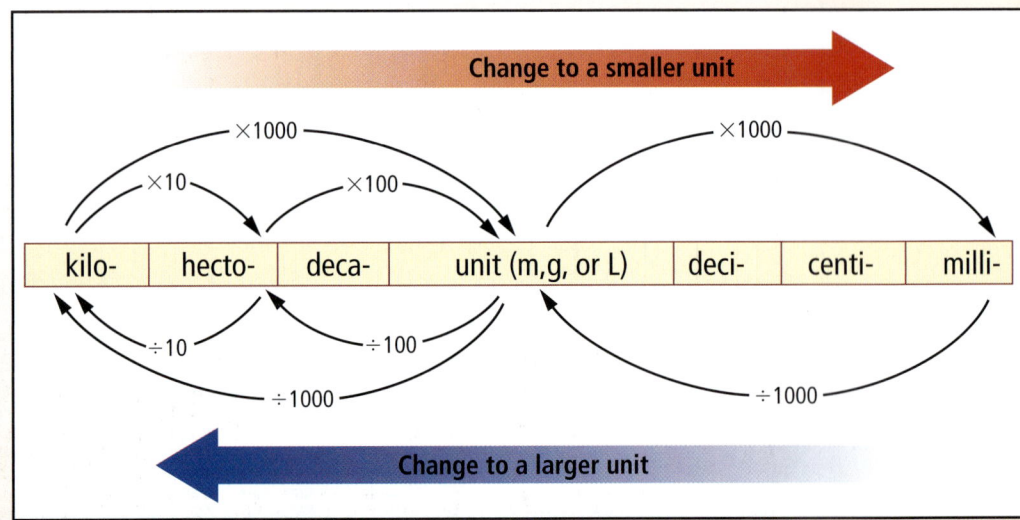

Example

Change 0.64 liters to milliliters.

(1) Decide whether to multiply or divide.
(2) Select the power of 10.

ANSWER 0.64 L = 640 mL

Change to a smaller unit by multiplying.

L ———×1000——→ mL

0.64 × 1000 = 640.

Example

Change 23.6 grams to kilograms.

(1) Decide whether to multiply or divide.
(2) Select the power of 10.

ANSWER 23.6 g = 0.0236 kg

Change to a larger unit by dividing.

kg ←——÷ 1000 ——— g

23.6 ÷ 1000 = 0.0236

Temperature Conversions

Even though the kelvin is the SI base unit of temperature, the degree Celsius will be the unit you use most often in your science studies. The formulas below show the relationships between temperatures in degrees Fahrenheit (°F), degrees Celsius (°C), and kelvins (K).

$$°C = \frac{5}{9}(°F - 32)$$

$$°F = \frac{9}{5}°C + 32$$

$$K = °C + 273$$

See page R42 for help with using formulas.

Examples of Temperature Conversions		
Condition	Degrees Celsius	Degrees Fahrenheit
Freezing point of water	0	32
Cool day	10	50
Mild day	20	68
Warm day	30	86
Normal body temperature	37	98.6
Very hot day	40	104
Boiling point of water	100	212

Converting Between SI and U.S. Customary Units

Use the chart below when you need to convert between SI units and U.S. customary units.

SI Unit	From SI to U.S. Customary			From U.S. Customary to SI		
Length	When you know	multiply by	to find	When you know	multiply by	to find
kilometer (km) = 1000 m	kilometers	0.62	miles	miles	1.61	kilometers
meter (m) = 100 cm	meters	3.28	feet	feet	0.3048	meters
centimeter (cm) = 10 mm	centimeters	0.39	inches	inches	2.54	centimeters
millimeter (mm) = 0.1 cm	millimeters	0.04	inches	inches	25.4	millimeters
Area	When you know	multiply by	to find	When you know	multiply by	to find
square kilometer (km²)	square kilometers	0.39	square miles	square miles	2.59	square kilometers
square meter (m²)	square meters	1.2	square yards	square yards	0.84	square meters
square centimeter (cm²)	square centimeters	0.155	square inches	square inches	6.45	square centimeters
Volume	When you know	multiply by	to find	When you know	multiply by	to find
liter (L) = 1000 mL	liters	1.06	quarts	quarts	0.95	liters
	liters	0.26	gallons	gallons	3.79	liters
	liters	4.23	cups	cups	0.24	liters
	liters	2.12	pints	pints	0.47	liters
milliliter (mL) = 0.001 L	milliliters	0.20	teaspoons	teaspoons	4.93	milliliters
	milliliters	0.07	tablespoons	tablespoons	14.79	milliliters
	milliliters	0.03	fluid ounces	fluid ounces	29.57	milliliters
Mass	When you know	multiply by	to find	When you know	multiply by	to find
kilogram (kg) = 1000 g	kilograms	2.2	pounds	pounds	0.45	kilograms
gram (g) = 1000 mg	grams	0.035	ounces	ounces	28.35	grams

Precision and Accuracy

When you do an experiment, it is important that your methods, observations, and data be both precise and accurate.

low precision

precision, but not accuracy

precision and accuracy

Precision

In science, **precision** is the exactness and consistency of measurements. For example, measurements made with a ruler that has both centimeter and millimeter markings would be more precise than measurements made with a ruler that has only centimeter markings. Another indicator of precision is the care taken to make sure that methods and observations are as exact and consistent as possible. Every time a particular experiment is done, the same procedure should be used. Precision is necessary because experiments are repeated several times and if the procedure changes, the results will change.

EXAMPLE

Suppose you are measuring temperatures over a two-week period. Your precision will be greater if you measure each temperature at the same place, at the same time of day, and with the same thermometer than if you change any of these factors from one day to the next.

Accuracy

In science, it is possible to be precise but not accurate. **Accuracy** depends on the difference between a measurement and an actual value. The smaller the difference, the more accurate the measurement.

EXAMPLE

Suppose you look at a stream and estimate that it is about 1 meter wide at a particular place. You decide to check your estimate by measuring the stream with a meter stick, and you determine that the stream is 1.32 meters wide. However, because it is hard to measure the width of a stream with a meter stick, it turns out that you didn't do a very good job. The stream is actually 1.14 meters wide. Therefore, even though your estimate was less precise than your measurement, your estimate was actually more accurate.

Making Data Tables and Graphs

Data tables and graphs are useful tools for both recording and communicating scientific data.

Making Data Tables

You can use a **data table** to organize and record the measurements that you make. Some examples of information that might be recorded in data tables are frequencies, times, and amounts.

EXAMPLE

Suppose you are investigating photosynthesis in two elodea plants. One sits in direct sunlight, and the other sits in a dimly lit room. You measure the rate of photosynthesis by counting the number of bubbles in the jar every ten minutes.

1. Title and number your data table.
2. Decide how you will organize the table into columns and rows.
3. Any units, such as seconds or degrees, should be included in column headings, not in the individual cells.

Table 1. Number of Bubbles from Elodea

Time (min)	Sunlight	Dim Light
0	0	0
10	15	5
20	25	8
30	32	7
40	41	10
50	47	9
60	42	9

Always number and title data tables.

The data in the table above could also be organized in a different way.

Table 1. Number of Bubbles from Elodea

Light Condition	Time (min)						
	0	10	20	30	40	50	60
Sunlight	0	15	25	32	41	47	42
Dim light	0	5	8	7	10	9	9

Put units in column heading.

Lab Handbook R23

Making Line Graphs

You can use a **line graph** to show a relationship between variables. Line graphs are particularly useful for showing changes in variables over time.

EXAMPLE

Suppose you are interested in graphing temperature data that you collected over the course of a day.

Table 1. Outside Temperature During the Day on March 7

	Time of Day						
	7:00 A.M.	9:00 A.M.	11:00 A.M.	1:00 P.M.	3:00 P.M.	5:00 P.M.	7:00 P.M.
Temp (°C)	8	9	11	14	12	10	6

1. Use the vertical axis of your line graph for the variable that you are measuring—temperature.
2. Choose scales for both the horizontal axis and the vertical axis of the graph. You should have two points more than you need on the vertical axis, and the horizontal axis should be long enough for all of the data points to fit.
3. Draw and label each axis.
4. Graph each value. First find the appropriate point on the scale of the horizontal axis. Imagine a line that rises vertically from that place on the scale. Then find the corresponding value on the vertical axis, and imagine a line that moves horizontally from that value. The point where these two imaginary lines intersect is where the value should be plotted.
5. Connect the points with straight lines.

Be sure to add a number and a title to your graph.

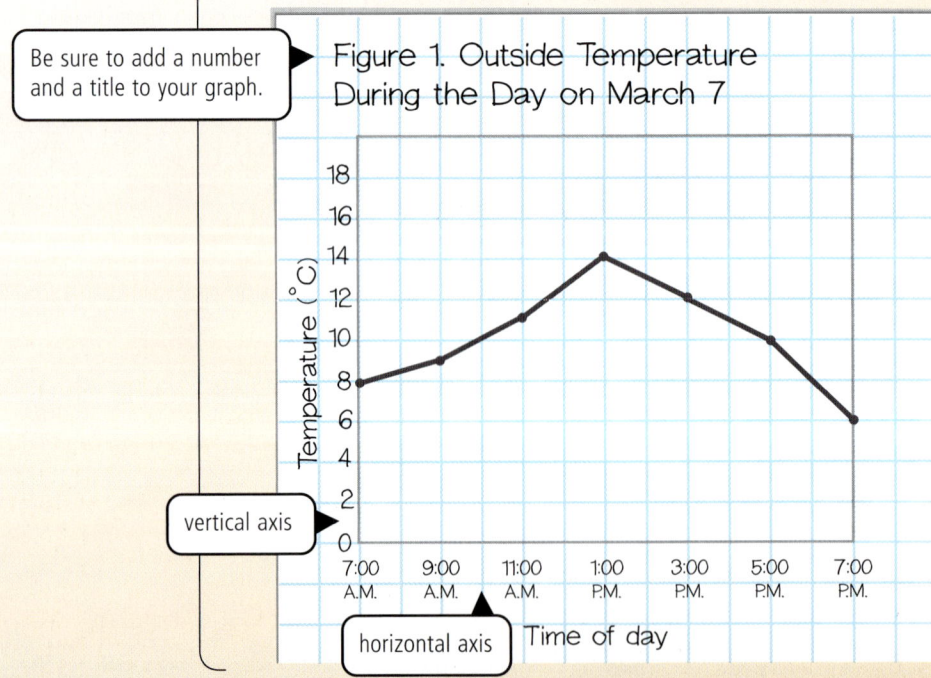

Figure 1. Outside Temperature During the Day on March 7

Making Circle Graphs

You can use a **circle graph,** sometimes called a pie chart, to represent data as parts of a circle. Circle graphs are used only when the data can be expressed as percentages of a whole. The entire circle shown in a circle graph is equal to 100 percent of the data.

EXAMPLE

Suppose you identified the species of each mature tree growing in a small wooded area. You organized your data in a table, but you also want to show the data in a circle graph.

1. To begin, find the total number of mature trees.

   $56 + 34 + 22 + 10 + 28 = $ 150

2. To find the degree measure for each sector of the circle, write a fraction comparing the number of each tree species with the total number of trees. Then multiply the fraction by 360°.

   Oak: $\frac{56}{150} \times 360° = 134.4°$

3. Draw a circle. Use a protractor to draw the angle for each sector of the graph.

4. Color and label each sector of the graph.

5. Give the graph a number and title.

Table 1. Tree Species in Wooded Area

Species	Number of Specimens
Oak	56
Maple	34
Birch	22
Willow	10
Pine	28

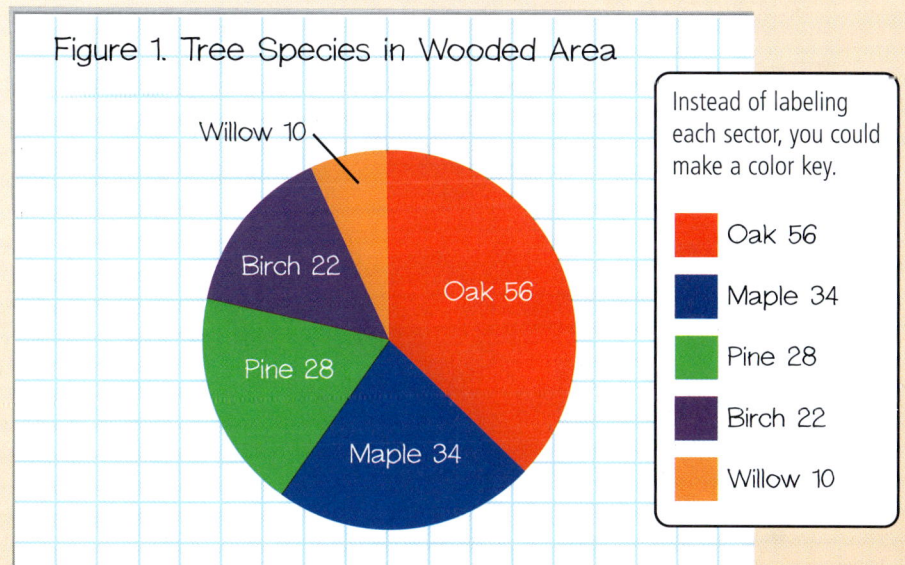

Figure 1. Tree Species in Wooded Area

Instead of labeling each sector, you could make a color key.

- Oak 56
- Maple 34
- Pine 28
- Birch 22
- Willow 10

Lab Handbook **R25**

Bar Graph

A **bar graph** is a type of graph in which the lengths of the bars are used to represent and compare data. A numerical scale is used to determine the lengths of the bars.

EXAMPLE

To determine the effect of water on seed sprouting, three cups were filled with sand, and ten seeds were planted in each. Different amounts of water were added to each cup over a three-day period.

Table 1. Effect of Water on Seed Sprouting

Daily Amount of Water (mL)	Number of Seeds That Sprouted After 3 Days in Sand
0	1
10	4
20	8

1. Choose a numerical scale. The greatest value is 8, so the end of the scale should have a value greater than 8, such as 10. Use equal increments along the scale, such as increments of 2.
2. Draw and label the axes. Mark intervals on the vertical axis according to the scale you chose.
3. Draw a bar for each data value. Use the scale to decide how long to make each bar.

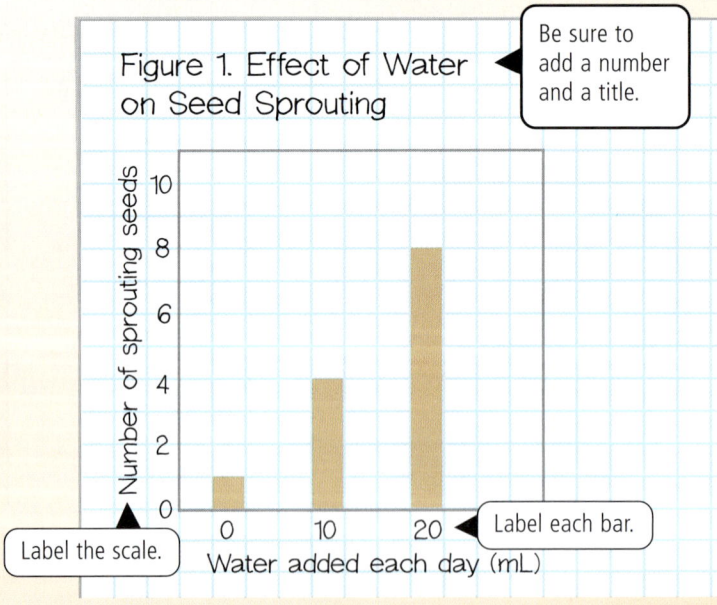

Double Bar Graph

A **double bar graph** is a bar graph that shows two sets of data. The two bars for each measurement are drawn next to each other.

EXAMPLE

The seed-sprouting experiment was done using both sand and potting soil. The data for sand and potting soil can be plotted on one graph.

1. Draw one set of bars, using the data for sand, as shown below.
2. Draw bars for the potting-soil data next to the bars for the sand data. Shade them a different color. Add a key.

Table 2. Effect of Water and Soil on Seed Sprouting

Daily Amount of Water (mL)	Number of Seeds That Sprouted After 3 Days in Sand	Number of Seeds That Sprouted After 3 Days in Potting Soil
0	1	2
10	4	5
20	8	9

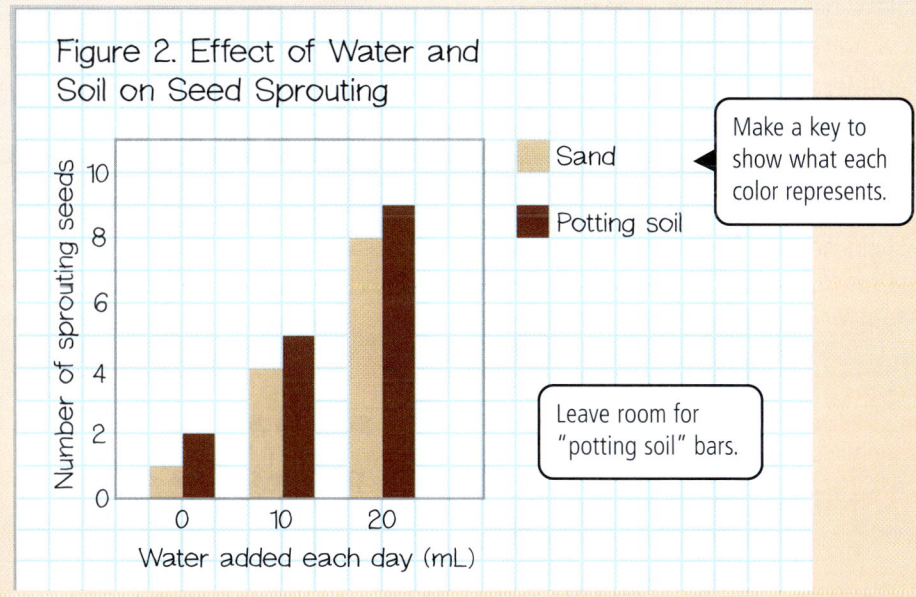

Figure 2. Effect of Water and Soil on Seed Sprouting

Make a key to show what each color represents.

Leave room for "potting soil" bars.

Lab Handbook R27

Designing an Experiment

Use this section when designing or conducting an experiment.

Determining a Purpose

You can find a purpose for an experiment by doing research, by examining the results of a previous experiment, or by observing the world around you. An **experiment** is an organized procedure to study something under controlled conditions.

1. Write the purpose of your experiment as a question or problem that you want to investigate.
2. Write down research questions and begin searching for information that will help you design an experiment. Consult the library, the Internet, and other people as you conduct your research.

> Don't forget to learn as much as possible about your topic before you begin.

EXAMPLE

Middle school students observed an odor near the lake by their school. They also noticed that the water on the side of the lake near the school was greener than the water on the other side of the lake. The students did some research to learn more about their observations. They discovered that the odor and green color in the lake

came from algae. They also discovered that a new fertilizer was being used on a field nearby. The students inferred that the use of the fertilizer might be related to the presence of the algae and designed a controlled experiment to find out whether they were right.

Problem
How does fertilizer affect the presence of algae in a lake?

Research Questions
- Have other experiments been done on this problem? If so, what did those experiments show?
- What kind of fertilizer is used on the field? How much?
- How do algae grow?
- How do people measure algae?
- Can fertilizer and algae be used safely in a lab? How?

> **Research**
> As you research, you may find a topic that is more interesting to you than your original topic, or learn that a procedure you wanted to use is not practical or safe. It is OK to change your purpose as you research.

Writing a Hypothesis

A **hypothesis** is a tentative explanation for an observation or scientific problem that can be tested by further investigation. You can write your hypothesis in the form of an "If . . . , then . . . , because . . ." statement.

> Hypothesis
>
> If the amount of fertilizer in lake water is increased, then the amount of algae will also increase, because fertilizers provide nutrients that algae need to grow.

Hypotheses For help with hypotheses, refer to page R3.

Determining Materials

Make a list of all the materials you will need to do your experiment. Be specific, especially if someone else is helping you obtain the materials. Try to think of everything you will need.

> Materials
> - 1 large jar or container
> - 4 identical smaller containers
> - rubber gloves that also cover the arms
> - sample of fertilizer-and-water solution
> - eyedropper
> - clear plastic wrap
> - scissors
> - masking tape
> - marker
> - ruler

Determining Variables and Constants

EXPERIMENTAL GROUP AND CONTROL GROUP

An experiment to determine how two factors are related always has two groups—a control group and an experimental group.

1. Design an experimental group. Include as many trials as possible in the experimental group in order to obtain reliable results.
2. Design a control group that is the same as the experimental group in every way possible, except for the factor you wish to test.

Experimental Group: two containers of lake water with one drop of fertilizer solution added to each
Control Group: two containers of lake water with no fertilizer solution added

> Go back to your materials list and make sure you have enough items listed to cover both your experimental group and your control group.

VARIABLES AND CONSTANTS

Identify the variables and constants in your experiment. In a controlled experiment, a **variable** is any factor that can change. **Constants** are all of the factors that are the same in both the experimental group and the control group.

1. Read your hypothesis. The **independent variable** is the factor that you wish to test and that is manipulated or changed so that it can be tested. The independent variable is expressed in your hypothesis after the word *if*. Identify the independent variable in your laboratory report.
2. The **dependent variable** is the factor that you measure to gather results. It is expressed in your hypothesis after the word *then*. Identify the dependent variable in your laboratory report.

Hypothesis
If the amount of fertilizer in lake water is increased, then the amount of algae will also increase, because fertilizers provide nutrients that algae need to grow.

Table 1. Variables and Constants in Algae Experiment

Independent Variable	Dependent Variable	Constants
Amount of fertilizer in lake water	Amount of algae that grow	• Where the lake water is obtained • Type of container used • Light and temperature conditions where water will be stored

> Set up your experiment so that you will test only one variable.

MEASURING THE DEPENDENT VARIABLE

Before starting your experiment, you need to define how you will measure the dependent variable. An **operational definition** is a description of the one particular way in which you will measure the dependent variable.

Your operational definition is important for several reasons. First, in any experiment there are several ways in which a dependent variable can be measured. Second, the procedure of the experiment depends on how you decide to measure the dependent variable. Third, your operational definition makes it possible for other people to evaluate and build on your experiment.

EXAMPLE 1

An operational definition of a dependent variable can be qualitative. That is, your measurement of the dependent variable can simply be an observation of whether a change occurs as a result of a change in the independent variable. This type of operational definition can be thought of as a "yes or no" measurement.

Table 2. Qualitative Operational Definition of Algae Growth

Independent Variable	Dependent Variable	Operational Definition
Amount of fertilizer in lake water	Amount of algae that grow	Algae grow in lake water

A qualitative measurement of a dependent variable is often easy to make and record. However, this type of information does not provide a great deal of detail in your experimental results.

EXAMPLE 2

An operational definition of a dependent variable can be quantitative. That is, your measurement of the dependent variable can be a number that shows how much change occurs as a result of a change in the independent variable.

Table 3. Quantitative Operational Definition of Algae Growth

Independent Variable	Dependent Variable	Operational Definition
Amount of fertilizer in lake water	Amount of algae that grow	Diameter of largest algal growth (in mm)

A quantitative measurement of a dependent variable can be more difficult to make and analyze than a qualitative measurement. However, this type of data provides much more information about your experiment and is often more useful.

Writing a Procedure

Write each step of your procedure. Start each step with a verb, or action word, and keep the steps short. Your procedure should be clear enough for someone else to use as instructions for repeating your experiment.

> If necessary, go back to your materials list and add any materials that you left out.

> **Controlling Variables**
> The same amount of fertilizer solution must be added to two of the four containers.

> **Controlling Variables**
> All four containers must receive the same amount of light.

Procedure

1. Put on your gloves. Use the large container to obtain a sample of lake water.

2. Divide the sample of lake water equally among the four smaller containers.

3. Use the eyedropper to add one drop of fertilizer solution to two of the containers.

4. Use the masking tape and the marker to label the containers with your initials, the date, and the identifiers "Jar 1 with Fertilizer," "Jar 2 with Fertilizer," "Jar 1 without Fertilizer," and "Jar 2 without Fertilizer."

5. Cover the containers with clear plastic wrap. Use the scissors to punch ten holes in each of the covers.

6. Place all four containers on a window ledge. Make sure that they all receive the same amount of light.

7. Observe the containers every day for one week.

8. Use the ruler to measure the diameter of the largest clump of algae in each container, and record your measurements daily.

Recording Observations

Once you have obtained all of your materials and your procedure has been approved, you can begin making experimental observations. Gather both quantitative and qualitative data. If something goes wrong during your procedure, make sure you record that too.

Observations For help with making qualitative and quantitative observations, refer to page R2.

For more examples of data tables, see page R23.

Table 4. Fertilizer and Algae Growth

	Experimental Group		Control Group		
Date and Time	Jar 1 with Fertilizer (diameter of algae in mm)	Jar 2 with Fertilizer (diameter of algae in mm)	Jar 1 without Fertilizer (diameter of algae in mm)	Jar 2 without Fertilizer (diameter of algae in mm)	Observations
5/3 4:00 P.M.	0	0	0	0	condensation in all containers
5/4 4:00 P.M.	0	3	0	0	tiny green blobs in jar 2 with fertilizer
5/5 4:15 P.M.	4	5	0	3	green blobs in jars 1 and 2 with fertilizer and jar 2 without fertilizer
5/6 4:00 P.M.	5	6	0	4	water light green in jar 2 with fertilizer
5/7 4:00 P.M.	8	10	0	6	water light green in jars 1 and 2 with fertilizer and in jar 2 without fertilizer
5/8 3:30 P.M.	10	18	0	6	cover off jar 2 with fertilizer
5/9 3:30 P.M.	14	23	0	8	drew sketches of each container

Notice that on the sixth day, the observer found that the cover was off one of the containers. It is important to record observations of unintended factors because they might affect the results of the experiment.

Use technology, such as a microscope, to help you make observations when possible.

Drawings of Samples Viewed Under Microscope on 5/9 at 100x

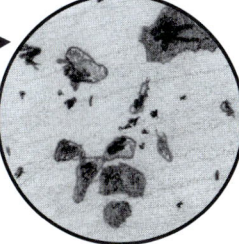 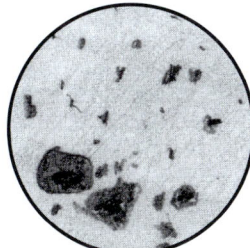 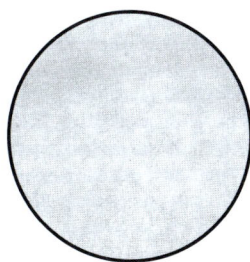 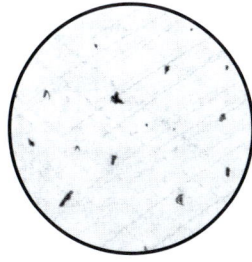

Jar 1 with Fertilizer | Jar 2 with Fertilizer | Jar 1 without Fertilizer | Jar 2 without Fertilizer

Summarizing Results

To summarize your data, look at all of your observations together. Look for meaningful ways to present your observations. For example, you might average your data or make a graph to look for patterns. When possible, use spreadsheet software to help you analyze and present your data. The two graphs below show the same data.

EXAMPLE 1

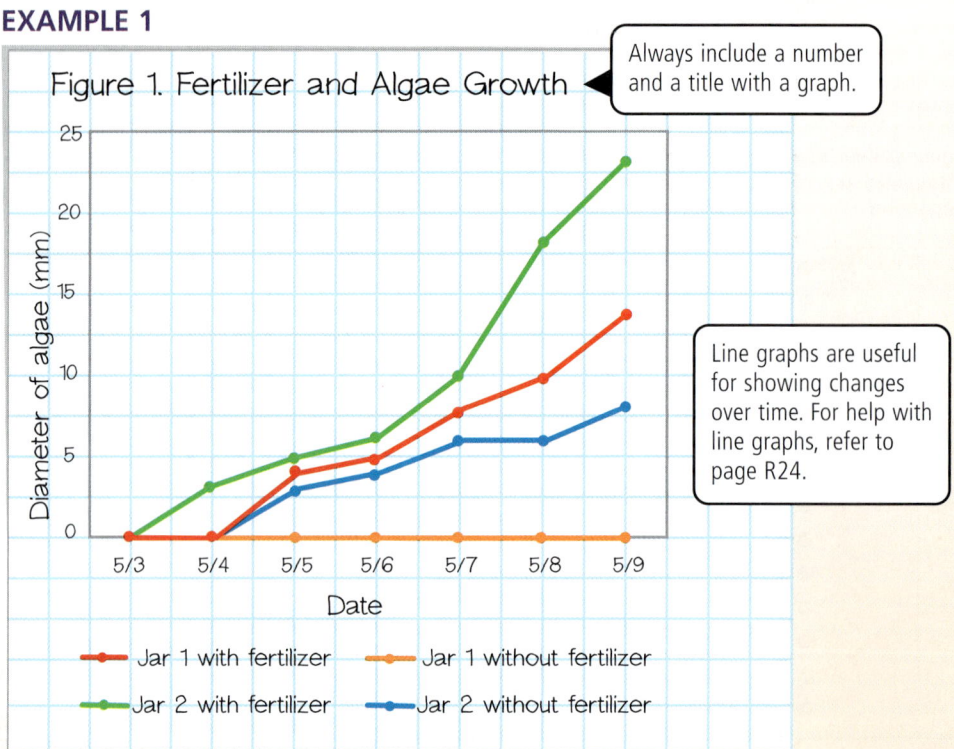

Always include a number and a title with a graph.

Line graphs are useful for showing changes over time. For help with line graphs, refer to page R24.

EXAMPLE 2

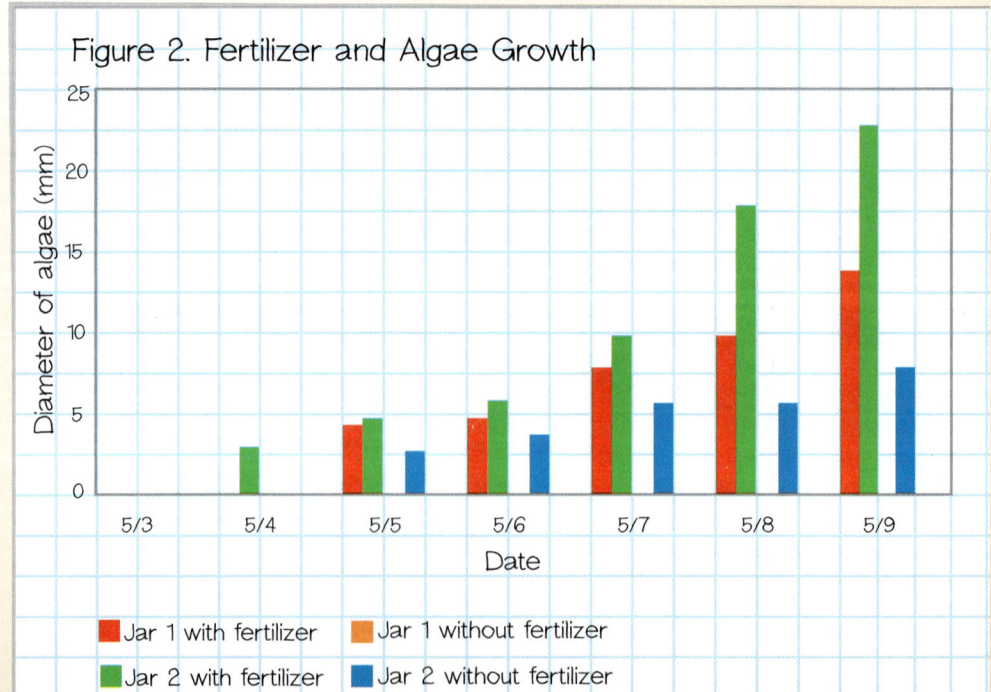

Bar graphs are useful for comparing different data sets. This bar graph has four bars for each day. Another way to present the data would be to calculate averages for the tests and the controls, and to show one test bar and one control bar for each day.

Drawing Conclusions

RESULTS AND INFERENCES

To draw conclusions from your experiment, first write your results. Then compare your results with your hypothesis. Do your results support your hypothesis? Be careful not to make inferences about factors that you did not test.

> For help with making inferences, see page R4.

Results and Inferences
The results of my experiment show that more algae grew in lake water to which fertilizer had been added than in lake water to which no fertilizer had been added. My hypothesis was supported. I infer that it is possible that the growth of algae in the lake was caused by the fertilizer used on the field.

> Notice that you cannot conclude from this experiment that the presence of algae in the lake was due only to the fertilizer.

QUESTIONS FOR FURTHER RESEARCH

Write a list of questions for further research and investigation. Your ideas may lead you to new experiments and discoveries.

Questions for Further Research
- What is the connection between the amount of fertilizer and algae growth?
- How do different brands of fertilizer affect algae growth?
- How would algae growth in the lake be affected if no fertilizer were used on the field?
- How do algae affect the lake and the other life in and around it?
- How does fertilizer affect the lake and the life in and around it?
- If fertilizer is getting into the lake, how is it getting there?

Math Handbook

Describing a Set of Data

Means, medians, modes, and ranges are important math tools for describing data sets such as the following widths of fossilized clamshells.

13 mm   25 mm   14 mm   21 mm   16 mm   23 mm   14 mm

Mean

The **mean** of a data set is the sum of the values divided by the number of values.

Example

To find the mean of the clamshell data, add the values and then divide the sum by the number of values.

$$\frac{13 \text{ mm} + 25 \text{ mm} + 14 \text{ mm} + 21 \text{ mm} + 16 \text{ mm} + 23 \text{ mm} + 14 \text{ mm}}{7} = \frac{126 \text{ mm}}{7} = 18 \text{ mm}$$

ANSWER The mean is 18 mm.

Median

The **median** of a data set is the middle value when the values are written in numerical order. If a data set has an even number of values, the median is the mean of the two middle values.

Example

To find the median of the clamshell data, arrange the values in order from least to greatest. The median is the middle value.

13 mm   14 mm   14 mm   16 mm   21 mm   23 mm   25 mm

ANSWER The median is 16 mm.

Mode

The **mode** of a data set is the value that occurs most often.

> **Example**
>
> To find the mode of the clamshell data, arrange the values in order from least to greatest and determine the value that occurs most often.
>
> 13 mm   14 mm   14 mm   16 mm   21 mm   23 mm   25 mm
>
> **ANSWER** The mode is 14 mm.

A data set can have more than one mode or no mode. For example, the following data set has modes of 2 mm and 4 mm:

  2 mm   2 mm   3 mm   4 mm   4 mm

The data set below has no mode, because no value occurs more often than any other.

  2 mm   3 mm   4 mm   5 mm

Range

The **range** of a data set is the difference between the greatest value and the least value.

> **Example**
>
> To find the range of the clamshell data, arrange the values in order from least to greatest.
>
> 13 mm   14 mm   14 mm   16 mm   21 mm   23 mm   25 mm
>
> Subtract the least value from the greatest value.
>
>   13 mm is the least value.
>   25 mm is the greatest value.
>   25 mm − 13 mm = 12 mm
>
> **ANSWER** The range is 12 mm.

Math Handbook R37

Using Ratios, Rates, and Proportions

You can use ratios and rates to compare values in data sets. You can use proportions to find unknown values.

Ratios

A **ratio** uses division to compare two values. The ratio of a value a to a nonzero value b can be written as $\frac{a}{b}$.

Example

The height of one plant is 8 centimeters. The height of another plant is 6 centimeters. To find the ratio of the height of the first plant to the height of the second plant, write a fraction and simplify it.

$$\frac{8 \text{ cm}}{6 \text{ cm}} = \frac{4 \times \cancel{2}}{3 \times \cancel{2}} = \frac{4}{3}$$

ANSWER The ratio of the plant heights is $\frac{4}{3}$.

You can also write the ratio $\frac{a}{b}$ as "a to b" or as $a:b$. For example, you can write the ratio of the plant heights as "4 to 3" or as $4:3$.

Rates

A **rate** is a ratio of two values expressed in different units. A unit rate is a rate with a denominator of 1 unit.

Example

A plant grew 6 centimeters in 2 days. The plant's rate of growth was $\frac{6 \text{ cm}}{2 \text{ days}}$. To describe the plant's growth in centimeters per day, write a unit rate.

Divide numerator and denominator by 2: $\quad \frac{6 \text{ cm}}{2 \text{ days}} = \frac{6 \text{ cm} \div 2}{2 \text{ days} \div 2}$

Simplify: $\quad = \frac{3 \text{ cm}}{1 \text{ day}}$

You divide 2 days by 2 to get 1 day, so divide 6 cm by 2 also.

ANSWER The plant's rate of growth is 3 centimeters per day.

Proportions

A **proportion** is an equation stating that two ratios are equivalent. To solve for an unknown value in a proportion, you can use cross products.

Example

If a plant grew 6 centimeters in 2 days, how many centimeters would it grow in 3 days (if its rate of growth is constant)?

Write a proportion: $\dfrac{6 \text{ cm}}{2 \text{ days}} = \dfrac{x}{3 \text{ days}}$

Set cross products: $6 \text{ cm} \cdot 3 = 2x$

Multiply 6 and 3: $18 \text{ cm} = 2x$

Divide each side by 2: $\dfrac{18 \text{ cm}}{2} = \dfrac{2x}{2}$

Simplify: $9 \text{ cm} = x$

ANSWER The plant would grow 9 centimeters in 3 days.

Using Decimals, Fractions, and Percents

Decimals, fractions, and percentages are all ways of recording and representing data.

Decimals

A **decimal** is a number that is written in the base-ten place value system, in which a decimal point separates the ones and tenths digits. The values of each place is ten times that of the place to its right.

Example

A caterpillar traveled from point A to point C along the path shown.

A —— 36.9 cm —— B —— 52.4 cm —— C

ADDING DECIMALS To find the total distance traveled by the caterpillar, add the distance from A to B and the distance from B to C. Begin by lining up the decimal points. Then add the figures as you would whole numbers and bring down the decimal point.

```
  36.9 cm
+ 52.4 cm
  89.3 cm
```

ANSWER The caterpillar traveled a total distance of 89.3 centimeters.

Math Handbook R39

Example continued

SUBTRACTING DECIMALS To find how much farther the caterpillar traveled on the second leg of the journey, subtract the distance from A to B from the distance from B to C.

$$\begin{array}{r} 52.4 \text{ cm} \\ -\ 36.9 \text{ cm} \\ \hline 15.5 \text{ cm} \end{array}$$

ANSWER The caterpillar traveled 15.5 centimeters farther on the second leg of the journey.

Example

A caterpillar is traveling from point D to point F along the path shown. The caterpillar travels at a speed of 9.6 centimeters per minute.

D   E   33.6 cm   F

MULTIPLYING DECIMALS You can multiply decimals as you would whole numbers. The number of decimal places in the product is equal to the sum of the number of decimal places in the factors.

For instance, suppose it takes the caterpillar 1.5 minutes to go from D to E. To find the distance from D to E, multiply the caterpillar's speed by the time it took.

$$\begin{array}{r} 9.6 \\ \times\ 1.5 \\ \hline 480 \\ 96 \\ \hline 14.40 \end{array} \quad \begin{array}{l} 1 \text{ decimal place} \\ +\ 1 \text{ decimal place} \\ \\ \\ \\ 2 \text{ decimal places} \end{array}$$

Align as shown.

ANSWER The distance from D to E is 14.4 centimeters.

DIVIDING DECIMALS When you divide by a decimal, move the decimal points the same number of places in the divisor and the dividend to make the divisor a whole number.

For instance, to find the time it will take the caterpillar to travel from E to F, divide the distance from E to F by the caterpillar's speed.

$9.6\overline{)33.6}$ ◀ Move each decimal point one place to the right.

$$\begin{array}{r} 3.5 \\ 96\overline{)336.} \\ \underline{288} \\ 480 \\ \underline{480} \\ 0 \end{array}$$

◀ Line up decimal points.

ANSWER The caterpillar will travel from E to F in 3.5 minutes.

Fractions

A **fraction** is a number in the form $\frac{a}{b}$, where b is not equal to 0. A fraction is in **simplest form** if its numerator and denominator have a greatest common factor (GCF) of 1. To simplify a fraction, divide its numerator and denominator by their GCF.

Example

A caterpillar is 40 millimeters long. The head of the caterpillar is 6 millimeters long. To compare the length of the caterpillar's head with the caterpillar's total length, you can write and simplify a fraction that expresses the ratio of the two lengths.

Write the ratio of the two lengths: $\quad \frac{\text{Length of head}}{\text{Total length}} = \frac{6 \text{ mm}}{40 \text{ mm}}$

Write numerator and denominator as products of numbers and the GCF: $\quad = \frac{3 \times 2}{20 \times 2}$

Divide numerator and denominator by the GCF: $\quad = \frac{3 \times \cancel{2}^1}{20 \times \cancel{2}_1}$

Simplify: $\quad = \frac{3}{20}$

ANSWER In simplest form, the ratio of the lengths is $\frac{3}{20}$.

Percents

A **percent** is a ratio that compares a number to 100. The word *percent* means "per hundred" or "out of 100." The symbol for *percent* is %.

For instance, suppose 43 out of 100 caterpillars are female. You can represent this ratio as a percent, a decimal, or a fraction.

Percent	Decimal	Fraction
43%	0.43	$\frac{43}{100}$

Example

In the preceding example, the ratio of the length of the caterpillar's head to the caterpillar's total length is $\frac{3}{20}$. To write this ratio as a percent, write an equivalent fraction that has a denominator of 100.

Multiply numerator and denominator by 5: $\quad \frac{3}{20} = \frac{3 \times 5}{20 \times 5}$

$\quad = \frac{15}{100}$

Write as a percent: $\quad = 15\%$

ANSWER The caterpillar's head represents 15 percent of its total length.

Using Formulas

A **formula** is an equation that shows the general relationship between two or more quantities.

In science, a formula often has a word form and a symbolic form. The formula below expresses Ohm's law.

Word Form

Current = $\dfrac{\text{voltage}}{\text{resistance}}$

Symbolic Form

$I = \dfrac{V}{R}$

In this formula, *I*, *V*, and *R* are variables. A mathematical **variable** is a symbol or letter that is used to represent one or more numbers.

> The term *variable* is also used in science to refer to a factor that can change during an experiment.

Example

Suppose that you measure a voltage of 1.5 volts and a resistance of 15 ohms. You can use the formula for Ohm's law to find the current in amperes.

Write the formula for Ohm's law: $\quad I = \dfrac{V}{R}$

Substitute 1.5 volts for V and 15 ohms for R: $\quad I = \dfrac{1.5 \text{ volts}}{15 \text{ ohms}}$

Simplify: $\quad I = 0.1$ amp

ANSWER The current is 0.1 ampere.

If you know the values of all variables but one in a formula, you can solve for the value of the unknown variable. For instance, Ohm's law can be used to find a voltage if you know the current and the resistance.

Example

Suppose that you know that a current is 0.2 amperes and the resistance is 18 ohms. Use the formula for Ohm's law to find the voltage in volts.

Write the formula for Ohm's law: $\quad I = \dfrac{V}{R}$

Substitute 0.2 amp for I and 18 ohms for R: $\quad 0.2 \text{ amp} = \dfrac{V}{18 \text{ ohms}}$

Multiply both sides by 18 ohms: $\quad 0.2 \text{ amp} \cdot 18 \text{ ohms} = V$

Simplify: $\quad 3.6 \text{ volts} = V$

ANSWER The voltage is 3.6 volts.

Finding Areas

The area of a figure is the amount of surface the figure covers.

Area is measured in square units, such as square meters (m^2) or square centimeters (cm^2). Formulas for the areas of three common geometric figures are shown below.

Area = (side length)^2
$A = s^2$

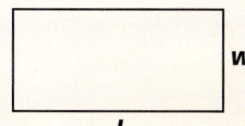

Area = length × width
$A = lw$

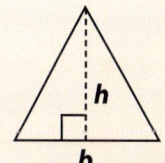

Area = $\frac{1}{2}$ × base × height
$A = \frac{1}{2} bh$

Example

Each face of a halite crystal is a square like the one shown. You can find the area of the square by using the steps below.

Write the formula for the area of a square:	$A = s^2$
Substitute 3 mm for s:	$= (3 \text{ mm})^2$
Simplify:	$= 9 \text{ mm}^2$

ANSWER The area of the square is 9 square millimeters.

Finding Volumes

The volume of a solid is the amount of space contained by the solid.

Volume is measured in cubic units, such as cubic meters (m^3) or cubic centimeters (cm^3). The volume of a rectangular prism is given by the formula shown below.

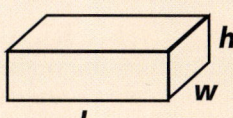

Volume = length × width × height
$V = lwh$

Example

A topaz crystal is a rectangular prism like the one shown. You can find the volume of the prism by using the steps below.

Write the formula for the volume of a rectangular prism:	$V = lwh$
Substitute dimensions:	$= 20 \text{ mm} \times 12 \text{ mm} \times 10 \text{ mm}$
Simplify:	$= 2400 \text{ mm}^3$

ANSWER The volume of the rectangular prism is 2400 cubic millimeters.

Using Significant Figures

The **significant figures** in a decimal are the digits that are warranted by the accuracy of a measuring device.

When you perform a calculation with measurements, the number of significant figures to include in the result depends in part on the number of significant figures in the measurements. When you multiply or divide measurements, your answer should have only as many significant figures as the measurement with the fewest significant figures.

Example

Using a balance and a graduated cylinder filled with water, you determined that a marble has a mass of 8.0 grams and a volume of 3.5 cubic centimeters. To calculate the density of the marble, divide the mass by the volume.

Write the formula for density: $\text{Density} = \dfrac{\text{mass}}{\text{Volume}}$

Substitute measurements: $= \dfrac{8.0 \text{ g}}{3.5 \text{ cm}^3}$

Use a calculator to divide: $\approx 2.285714286 \text{ g/cm}^3$

ANSWER Because the mass and the volume have two significant figures each, give the density to two significant figures. The marble has a density of 2.3 grams per cubic centimeter.

Using Scientific Notation

Scientific notation is a shorthand way to write very large or very small numbers. For example, 73,500,000,000,000,000,000,000 kg is the mass of the Moon. In scientific notation, it is 7.35×10^{22} kg.

Example

You can convert from standard form to scientific notation.

Standard Form	Scientific Notation
720,000	7.2×10^5
5 decimal places left	Exponent is 5.
0.000291	2.91×10^{-4}
4 decimal places right	Exponent is −4.

You can convert from scientific notation to standard form.

Scientific Notation	Standard Form
4.63×10^7	46,300,000
Exponent is 7.	7 decimal places right
1.08×10^{-6}	0.00000108
Exponent is −6.	6 decimal places left

Note-Taking Handbook

Note-Taking Strategies

Taking notes as you read helps you understand the information. The notes you take can also be used as a study guide for later review. This handbook presents several ways to organize your notes.

Content Frame

1. Make a chart in which each column represents a category.
2. Give each column a heading.
3. Write details under the headings.

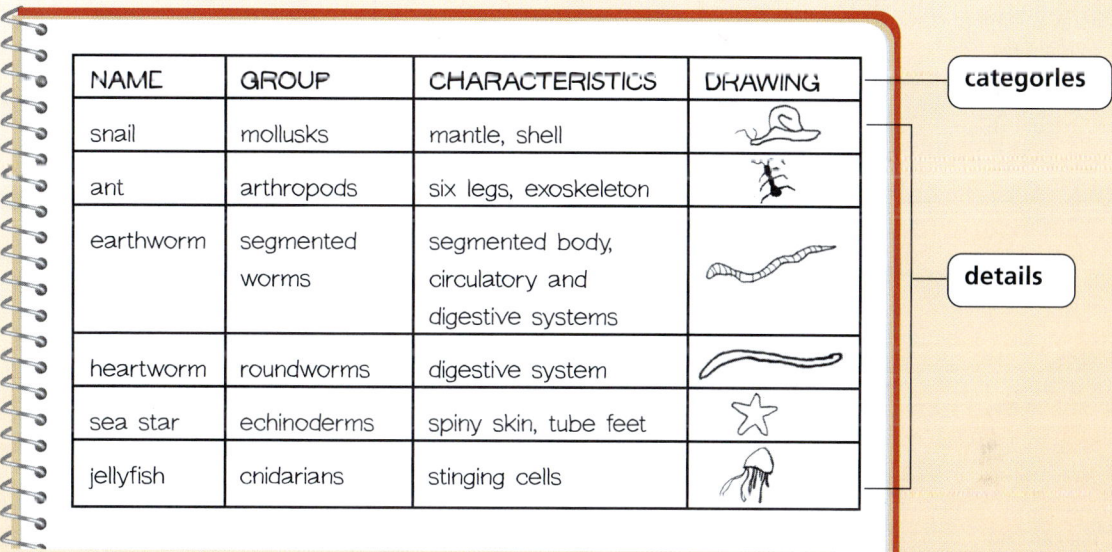

Combination Notes

1. For each new idea or concept, write an informal outline of the information.
2. Make a sketch to illustrate the concept, and label it.

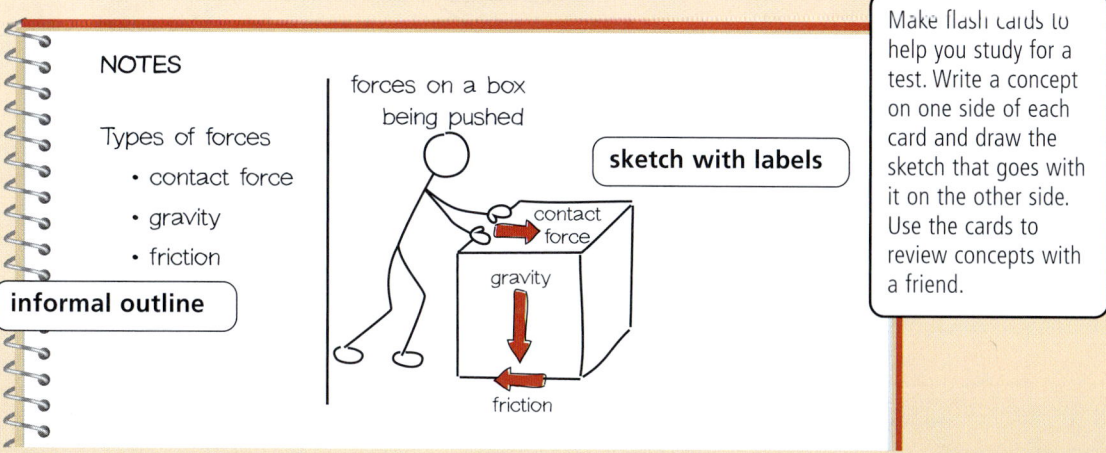

Make flash cards to help you study for a test. Write a concept on one side of each card and draw the sketch that goes with it on the other side. Use the cards to review concepts with a friend.

Note-Taking Handbook R45

Main Idea and Detail Notes

1. In the left-hand column of a two-column chart, list main ideas. The blue headings express main ideas throughout this textbook.
2. In the right-hand column, write details that expand on each main idea.

You can shorten the headings in your chart. Be sure to use the most important words.

When studying for tests, cover up the detail notes column with a sheet of paper. Then use each main idea to form a question—such as "How does latitude affect climate?" Answer the question, and then uncover the detail notes column to check your answer.

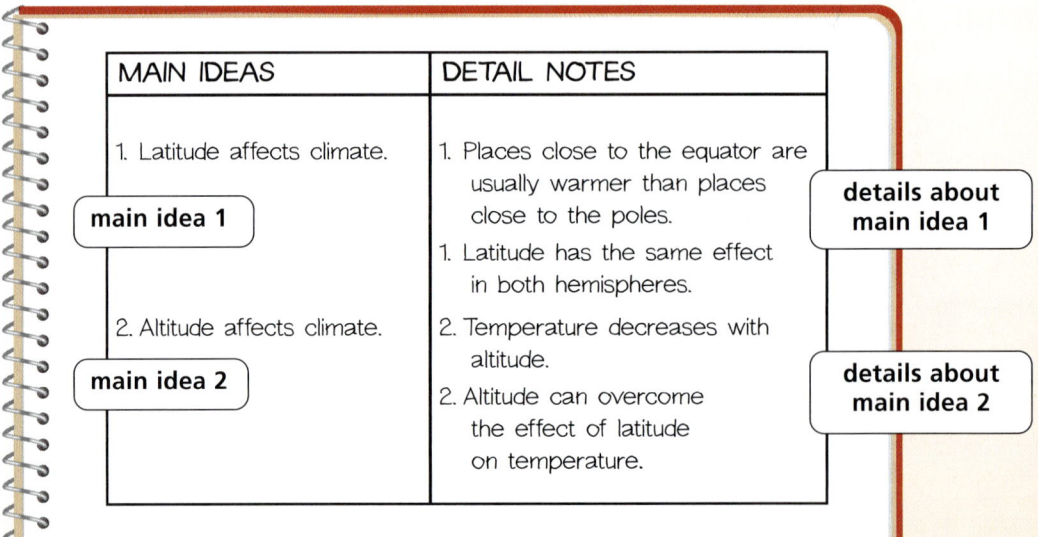

Main Idea Web

1. Write a main idea in a box.
2. Add boxes around it with related vocabulary terms and important details.

You can find definitions near highlighted terms.

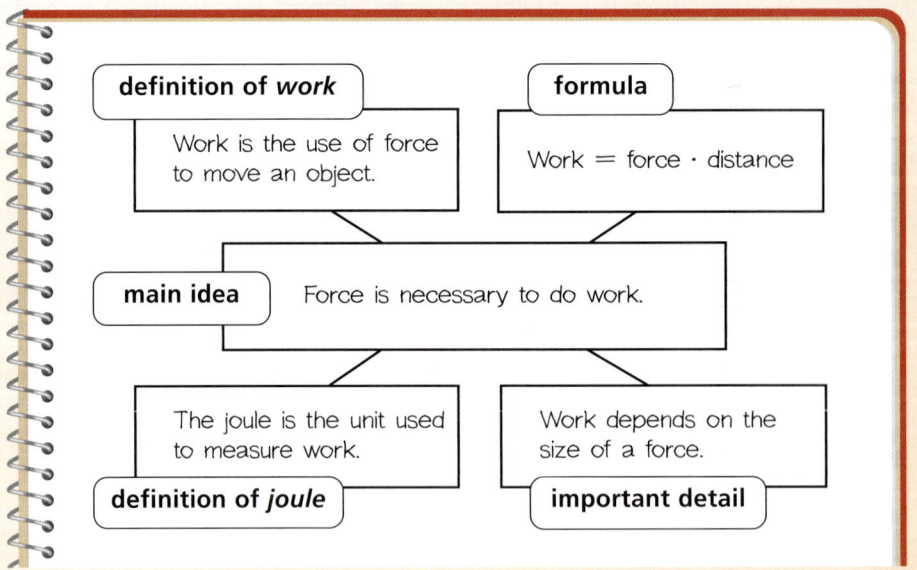

R46 Student Resources

Mind Map

1. Write a main idea in the center.
2. Add details that relate to one another and to the main idea.

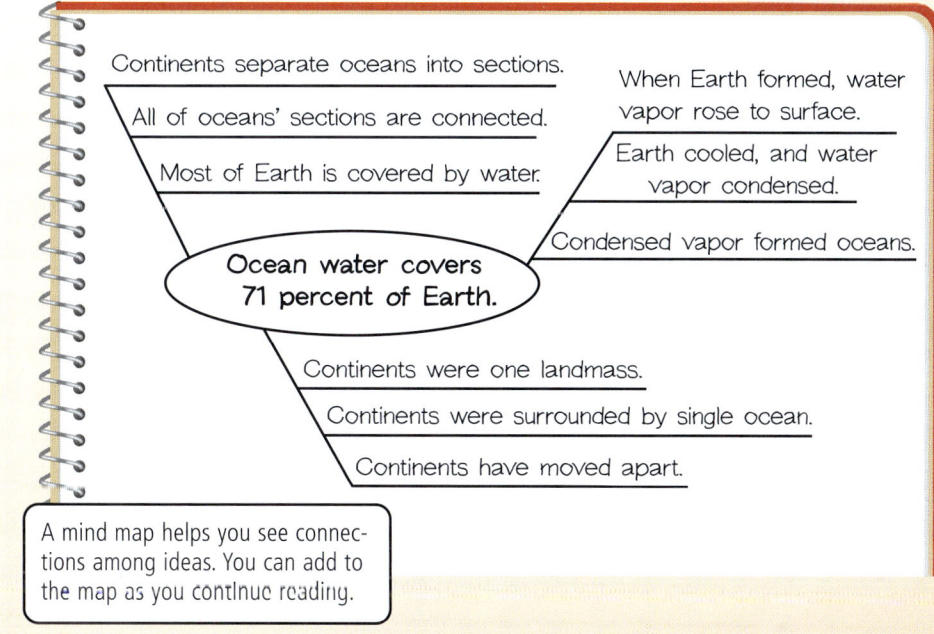

A mind map helps you see connections among ideas. You can add to the map as you continue reading.

Supporting Main Ideas

1. Write a main idea in a box.
2. Add boxes underneath with information—such as reasons, explanations, and examples—that supports the main idea.

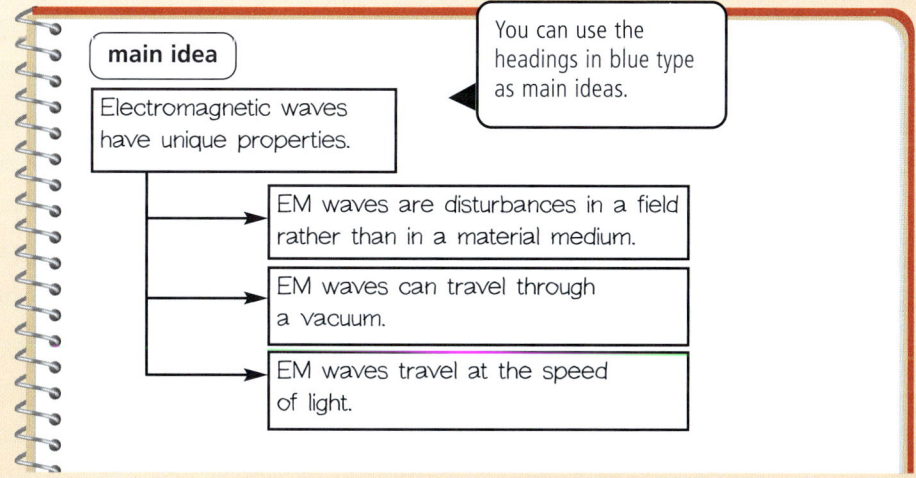

You can use the headings in blue type as main ideas.

Note-Taking Handbook R47

Outline

1. Copy the chapter title and headings from the book in the form of an outline.
2. Add notes that summarize in your own words what you read.

Cell Processes — **1st key idea**
I. Cells capture and release energy. — **1st subpoint of I**
   A. All cells need energy.
   B. Some cells capture light energy. — **2nd subpoint of I**
      1. Process of photosynthesis — **1st detail about B**
      2. Chloroplasts (site of photosynthesis) — **2nd detail about B**
      3. Carbon dioxide and water as raw materials
      4. Glucose and oxygen as products
   C. All cells release energy.
      1. Process of cellular respiration
      2. Fermentation of sugar to carbon dioxide
      3. Bacteria that carry out fermentation
II. Cells transport materials through membranes.
   A. Some materials move by diffusion.
      1. Particle movement from higher to lower concentrations
      2. Movement of water through membrane (osmosis)
   B. Some transport requires energy.
      1. Active transport
      2. Examples of active transport

Correct Outline Form
Include a title.

Arrange key ideas, subpoints, and details as shown.

Indent the divisions of the outline as shown.

Use the same grammatical form for items of the same rank. For example, if A is a sentence, B must also be a sentence.

You must have at least two main ideas or subpoints. That is, every A must be followed by a B, and every 1 must be followed by a 2.

Concept Map

1. Write an important concept in a large oval.
2. Add details related to the concept in smaller ovals.
3. Write linking words on arrows that connect the ovals.

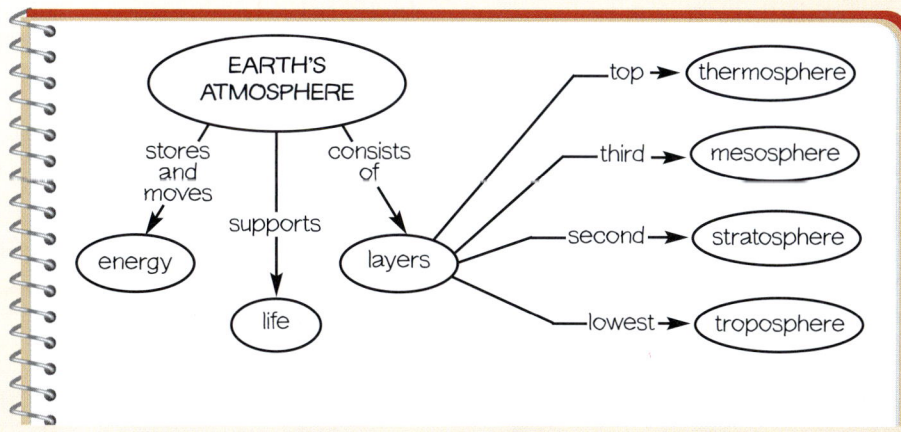

The main ideas or concepts can often be found in the blue headings. An example is "The atmosphere stores and moves energy." Use nouns from these concepts in the ovals, and use the verb or verbs on the lines.

Venn Diagram

1. Draw two overlapping circles, one for each item that you are comparing.
2. In the overlapping section, list the characteristics that are shared by both items.
3. In the outer sections, list the characteristics that are peculiar to each item.
4. Write a summary that describes the information in the Venn diagram.

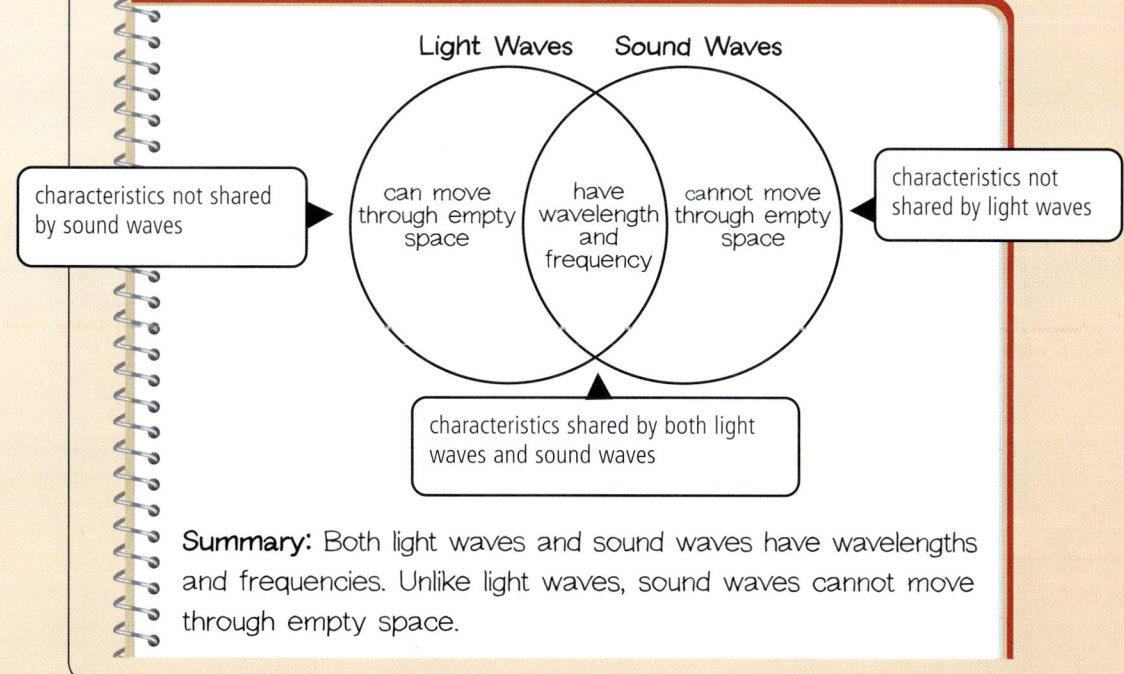

Summary: Both light waves and sound waves have wavelengths and frequencies. Unlike light waves, sound waves cannot move through empty space.

Note-Taking Handbook **R49**

Vocabulary Strategies

Important terms are highlighted in this book. A definition of each term can be found in the sentence or paragraph where the term appears. You can also find definitions in the Glossary. Taking notes about vocabulary terms helps you understand and remember what you read.

Description Wheel

1. Write a term inside a circle.
2. Write words that describe the term on "spokes" attached to the circle.

> When studying for a test with a friend, read the phrases on the spokes one at a time until your friend identifies the correct term.

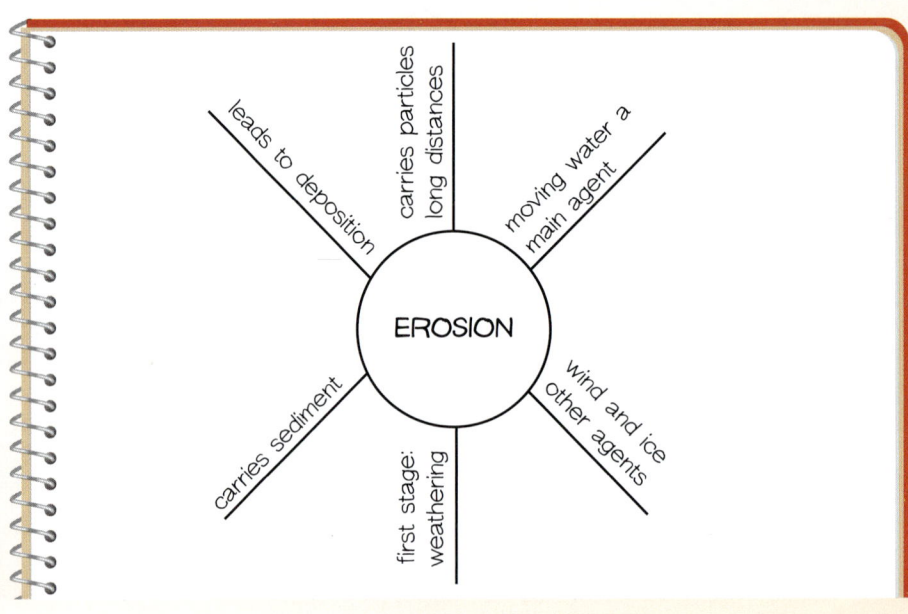

Four Square

1. Write a term in the center.
2. Write details in the four areas around the term.

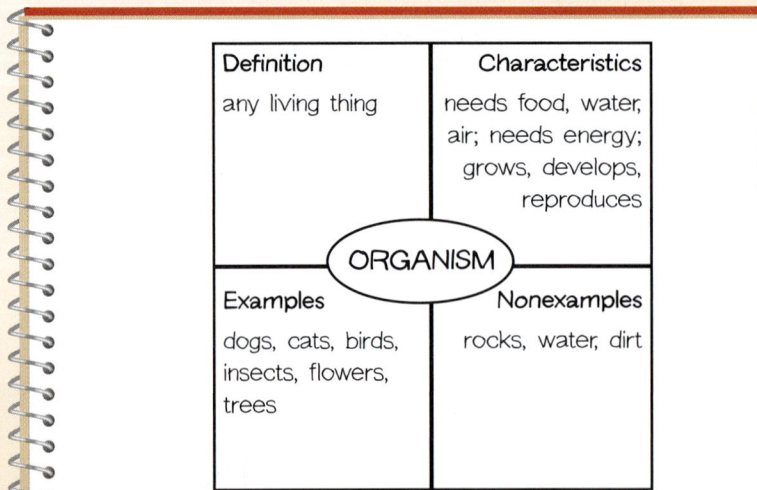

> Include a definition, some characteristics, and examples. You may want to add a formula, a sketch, or examples of things that the term does *not* name.

Frame Game

1. Write a term in the center.
2. Frame the term with details.

Include examples, descriptions, sketches, or sentences that use the term in context. Change the frame to fit each new term.

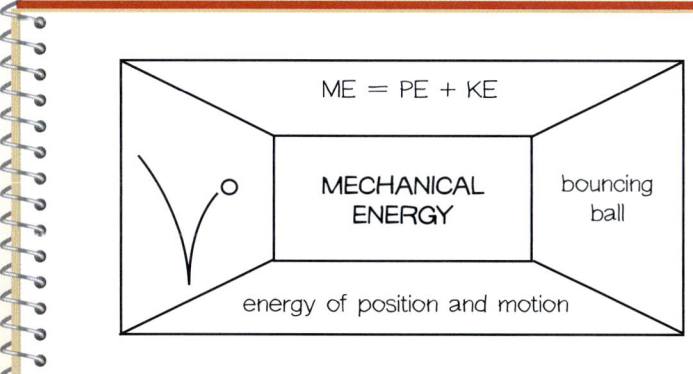

Magnet Word

1. Write a term on the magnet.
2. On the lines, add details related to the term.

You can also use phrases or sentences on the lines.

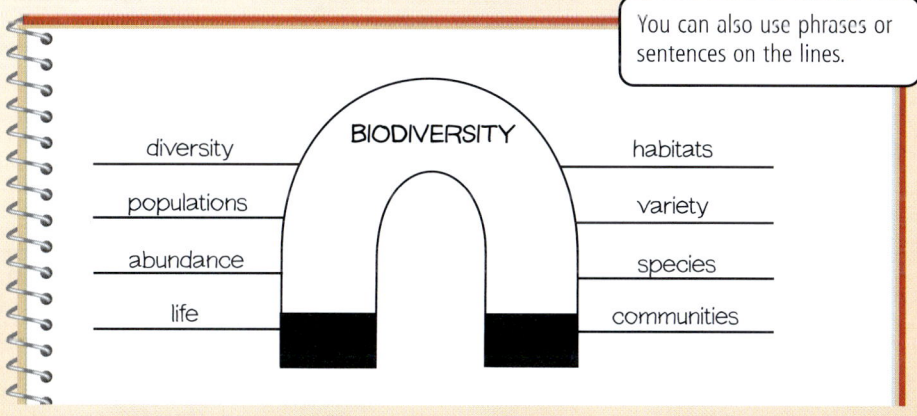

Word Triangle

1. Write a term and its definition in the bottom section.
2. In the middle section, write a sentence in which the term is used correctly.
3. In the top section, draw a small picture to illustrate the term.

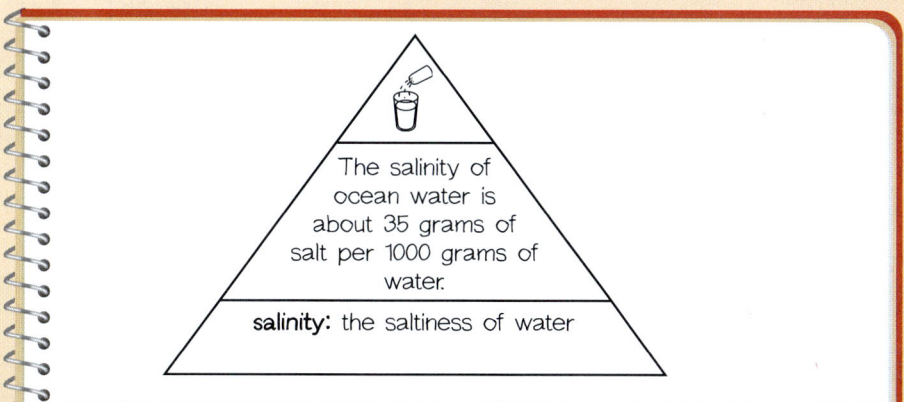

Appendix

Properties of Common Minerals

In this table, minerals are arranged alphabetically, and the most useful properties for identification are printed in *italic* type. Most minerals can be identified by means of two or three of the properties listed below. For some minerals, density is important; for others, cleavage is characteristic; and for others, the crystal shapes identify the minerals. The colors listed are the most common for each mineral.

Name	Hardness	Color	Streak	Cleavage	Remarks
Apatite	5	Green, brown	White	Poor in one direction	Nonmetallic (glassy) luster. Sp. gr. 3.1 to 3.2.
Augite	5–6	Dark green to black	Greenish	*Two directions, nearly at 90°*	Nonmetallic (glassy) luster. *Stubby four- or eight-sided crystals.* Common type of pyroxene. Sp. gr. 3.2 to 3.4.
Beryl	7.5–8	*Bluish-green, yellow, pink, colorless*	White	Imperfect in one direction	Nonmetallic (glassy) luster. *Hardness, greenish color, six-sided crystals.* Aquamarine and emerald are gem varieties. Sp. gr. 2.6 to 2.8.
Biotite mica	2.5–3	Black, brown, dark green	White	*Perfect in one direction*	Nonmetallic (glassy) luster. *Thin elastic films peel off easily.* Sp. gr. 2.8 to 3.2.
Calcite	3	White, colorless	White	*Perfect, three directions, not at 90° angles*	Nonmetallic (glassy to dull) luster. *Fizzes in dilute hydrochloric acid.* Sp. gr. 2.7.
Chalcopyrite	3.5–4	*Golden yellow*	Greenish black	Poor in one direction	Metallic luster. *Hardness distinguishes from pyrite.* Sp. gr. 4.1 to 4.3.
Chlorite	2–2.5	*Greenish*	Pale green to gray or brown	Perfect in one direction	Nonmetallic (glassy to pearly) luster. *Nonelastic flakes.* Sp. gr. 2.6 to 3.3.
Copper	2.5–3	*Copper red*	Copper	None	*Metallic luster on fresh surface. Dense.* Sp. gr. 8.9.
Corundum	9	Brown, pink, blue	White	None, parting resembles cleavage	Nonmetallic (glassy to brilliant) luster. *Barrel-shaped, six-sided crystals with flat ends.* Sp. gr. 4.0.
Diamond	10	Colorless to pale yellow	White	Perfect, four directions	Nonmetallic (brilliant to greasy) luster. *Hardest of all minerals.* Sp. gr. 3.5.

Sp. gr. = specific gravity

Name	Hardness	Color	Streak	Cleavage	Remarks
Dolomite	3.5–4	Pinkish, colorless, white	White	Perfect, three directions, not at 90° angles	Nonmetallic luster. *Scratched surface fizzes in dilute hydrochloric acid. Cleavage surfaces curved.* Sp. gr. 2.8 to 2.9.
Feldspar (Orthoclase)	6	*Salmon pink, red,* white, *light gray*	White	Good, two directions, 90° intersection	Nonmetallic (glassy) luster. *Hardness, color, and cleavage taken together are diagnostic.* Sp. gr. 2.6.
Feldspar (Plagioclase)	6	*White to light gray,* can be salmon pink	White	Good, two directions, about 90°	Nonmetallic (glassy to pearly) luster. *If striations are visible, they are diagnostic.* Sp. gr. 2.6 to 2.8.
Fluorite	4	Varies	White	Perfect, four directions	Nonmetallic (glassy) luster. *In cubes or octahedrons as crystals.* Sp. gr. 3.2.
Galena	2.5	*Lead gray*	Lead gray	Perfect, three directions, at 90° angles	*Metallic luster.* Occurs as crystals and masses. *Dense.* Sp. gr. 7.4 to 7.6.
Gold	2.5–3	*Gold*	Gold	None	Metallic luster. *Dense.* Sp. gr. 15.0 to 19.3.
Graphite	1–2	*Dark gray to black*	Grayish black	Perfect in one direction	Metallic or nonmetallic (earthy) luster. *Greasy feel, marks paper.* This is the "lead" in a pencil (mixed with clay). Sp. gr. 2.2.
Gypsum	2	Colorless, white, gray, yellowish, reddish	White	Perfect in one direction	Nonmetallic (glassy to silky) luster. *Can be scratched easily by a fingernail.* Sp. gr. 2.3.
Halite	2–2.5	Colorless, white	White	Perfect, three directions, at 90° angles	Nonmetallic (glassy) luster. *Salty taste.* Sp. gr. 2.2.
Hematite	5–6 (may appear softer)	*Reddish-brown,* gray, black	Reddish	None	Metallic or nonmetallic (earthy) luster. *Dense.* Sp. gr. 5.3.
Hornblende	5–6	*Dark green to black*	Brown to gray	Perfect, two directions at angles of 56° and 124°	Nonmetallic (glassy to silky) luster. Common type of amphibole. Long, slender, six-sided crystals. Sp. gr. 3.0 to 3.4.
Kaolinite	2	White, gray, yellowish	White	Perfect in one direction	Nonmetallic (dull, earthy) luster. Claylike masses. Sp. gr. 2.6.
Limonite group	4–5.5	*Yellow, brown*	Yellowish brown	None	Nonmetallic (earthy) luster. Rust stains. Sp. gr. 2.9 to 4.3.
Magnetite	5.5–6.5	*Black*	Black	None	Metallic luster. Occurs as eight-sided crystals and granular masses. *Magnetic. Dense.* Sp. gr. 5.2.

Sp. gr. = specific gravity

Properties of Common Minerals *continued*

Name	Hardness	Color	Streak	Cleavage	Remarks
Muscovite mica	2–2.5	Colorless in thin films; silvery, yellowish, and greenish in thicker pieces	White	Perfect in one direction	Nonmetallic (glassy to pearly) luster. *Thin elastic films peel off readily.* Sp. gr. 2.8 to 2.9.
Olivine	6.5–7	Yellowish, greenish	White	None	Nonmetallic (glassy) luster. *Granular.* Sp. gr. 3.3 to 4.4.
Opal	5–6.5	Varies	White	None	Nonmetallic (glassy to pearly) luster. *Conchoidal fracture.* Sp. gr. 2.0 to 2.2.
Pyrite	6–6.5	Brass yellow	Greenish black	None	Metallic luster. *Cubic crystals and granular masses. Dense.* Sp. gr. 5.0 to 5.1.
Quartz	7	Colorless, white; varies	White	None	Nonmetallic (glassy) luster. *Conchoidal fracture. Six-sided crystals common. Many varieties.* Sp. gr. 2.6.
Serpentine	3–5	Greenish (variegated)	White	None or good in one direction, depending on variety	Nonmetallic (greasy, waxy, or silky) luster. *Conchoidal fracture.* Sp. gr. 2.5 to 2.6.
Sphalerite	3.5–4	Yellow, brown, black	Yellow to light brown	Perfect, six directions	Nonmetallic (brilliant to resinous) luster. Sp. gr. 3.9 to 4.1.
Sulfur	1.5–2.5	Yellow	Yellow	Poor, two directions	Nonmetallic (glassy to earthy) luster. *Granular.* Sp. gr. 2.0 to 2.1.
Talc	1	Apple-green, gray, white	White	Perfect in one direction	Nonmetallic (pearly to greasy) luster. *Nonelastic flakes, greasy feel.* Sp. gr. 2.7 to 2.8.
Topaz	8	Varies	White	Perfect in one direction	Nonmetallic (brilliant to glassy) luster. *Crystals commonly striated lengthwise.* Sp. gr. 3.4 to 3.6.
Tourmaline	7–7.5	Black; varies	White	None	Nonmetallic (glassy) luster. *Crystals often have triangular cross sections. Conchoidal fracture.* Sp. gr. 3.0 to 3.3.

Sp. gr. = specific gravity

Topographic Map Symbols

The U.S. Geological Survey uses the following symbols to mark human-made and natural features on all of the topographic maps the USGS produces.

Primary highway, hard surface	
Secondary highway, hard surface	
Light-duty road, hard or improved surface	
Unimproved road	
Trail	
Railroad: single track	
Railroad: multiple track	
Bridge	
Drawbridge	
Tunnel	
Footbridge	
Overpass—Underpass	
Power transmission line with located tower	
Landmark line (labeled as to type)	TELEPHONE

Dam with lock	
Canal with lock	
Large dam	
Small dam: masonry—earth	
Buildings (dwelling, place of employment, etc.)	
School—Church—Cemeteries	
Buildings (barn, warehouse, etc.)	
Tanks, oil, water, etc. (labeled only if water)	Water Tank
Wells other than water (labeled as to type)	Oil Gas
U.S. mineral or location monument—Prospect	
Quarry—Gravel pit	
Mine shaft—Tunnel or cave entrance	
Campsite—Picnic area	
Located or landmark object—Windmill	
Exposed wreck	
Rock or coral reef	
Foreshore flat	
Rock: bare or awash	

Benchmarks	BM ×671 ×672
Road fork—Section corner with elevation	429 +58
Checked spot elevation	×5970
Unchecked spot elevation	×5970

Boundary: national	
State	
county, parish, municipio	
civil township, precinct, town, barrio	
incorporated city, village, town, hamlet	
reservation, national or state	
small park, cemetery, airport, etc.	
land grant	
Township or range line, U.S. land survey	
Section line, U.S. land survey	
Township line, not U.S. land survey	
Section line, not U.S. land survey	
Fence line or field line	
Section corner: found—indicated	
Boundary monument: land grant—other	

Index contour	Intermediate contour
Supplementary cont	Depression contours
Cut—Fill	Levee
Mine dump	Large wash
Dune area	Distorted surface
Sand area	Gravel beach

Glacier	Intermittent streams
Seasonal streams	Aqueduct tunnel
Water well—Spring	Falls
Rapids	Intermittent lake
Channel	Small wash
Sounding—Depth curve	Marsh (swamp)
Dry lake bed	Land subject to controlled flooding

Woodland	Mangrove
Submerged marsh	Scrub
Orchard	Wooded marsh
Vineyard	Many buildings
Areas revised since previous edition	

Source: U.S. Geological Survey

Properties of Rocks and Earth's Interior

Scheme for Sedimentary Rock Identification

TEXTURE	GRAIN SIZE	COMPOSITION	COMMENTS	ROCK NAME	MAP SYMBOL
Clastic (fragmental)	Pebbles, cobbles, and/or boulders embedded in sand, silt, and/or clay	Mostly quartz, feldspar, and clay minerals; may contain fragments of other rocks and minerals	Rounded fragments	Conglomerate	
			Angular fragments	Breccia	
	Sand (0.2 to 0.006 cm)		Fine to coarse	Sandstone	
	Silt (0.006 to 0.0004 cm)		Very fine grain	Siltstone	
	Clay (less than 0.0004 cm)		Compact; may split easily	Shale	

CHEMICALLY AND/OR ORGANICALLY FORMED SEDIMENTARY ROCKS

TEXTURE	GRAIN SIZE	COMPOSITION	COMMENTS	ROCK NAME	MAP SYMBOL
Crystalline	Varied	Halite	Crystals from chemical precipitates and evaporites	Rock Salt	
	Varied	Gypsum		Rock Gypsum	
	Varied	Dolomite		Dolostone	
Bioclastic	Microscopic to coarse	Calcite	Cemented shell fragments or precipitates of biologic origin	Limestone	
	Varied	Carbon	From plant remains	Coal	

Scheme for Metamorphic Rock Identification

TEXTURE		GRAIN SIZE	COMPOSITION	TYPE OF METAMORPHISM	COMMENTS	ROCK NAME	MAP SYMBOL
FOLIATED	MINERAL ALIGNMENT	Fine	MICA / QUARTZ / FELDSPAR / AMPHIBOLE / GARNET / PYROXENE	Regional (Heat and pressure increase with depth)	Low-grade metamorphism of shale	Slate	
		Fine to medium			Foliation surfaces shiny from microscopic mica crystals	Phyllite	
		Fine to medium			Platy mica crystals visible from metamorphism of clay or feldspars	Schist	
	BANDING	Medium to coarse			High-grade metamorphism; some mica changed to feldspar; segregated by mineral type into bands	Gneiss	
NONFOLIATED		Fine	Variable	Contact (Heat)	Various rocks changed by heat from nearby magma/lava	Hornfels	
		Fine to coarse	Quartz	Regional or Contact	Metamorphism of quartz sandstone	Quartzite	
		Fine to coarse	Calcite and/or dolomite		Metamorphism of limestone or dolostone	Marble	
		Coarse	Various minerals in particles and matrix		Pebbles may be distorted or stretched	Metaconglomerate	

Scheme for Igneous Rock Identification

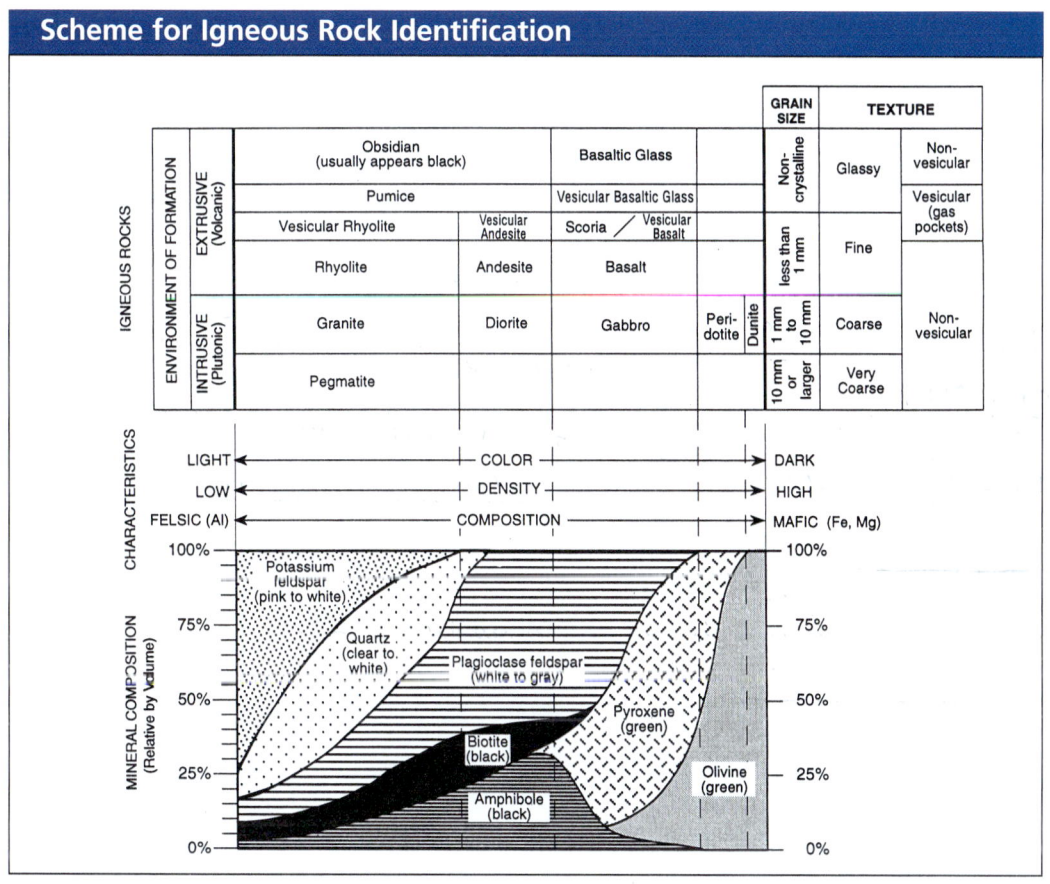

Inferred Properties of Earth's Interior

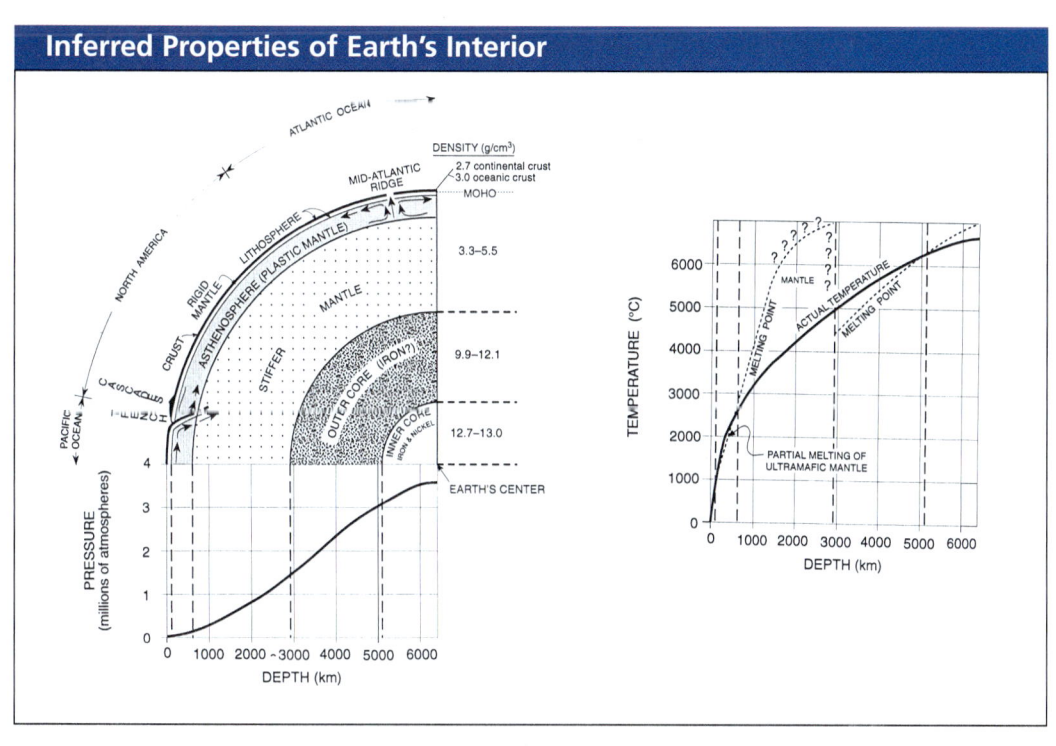

United States Physical Map

World Physical Map

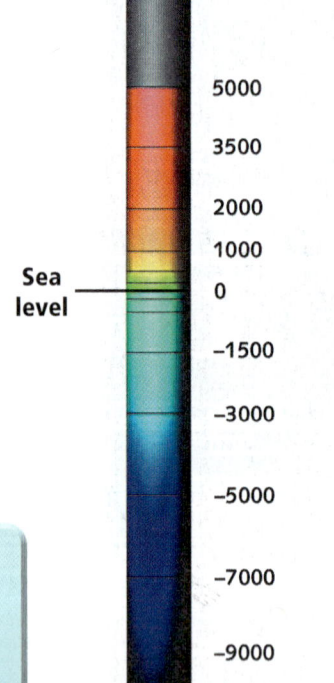

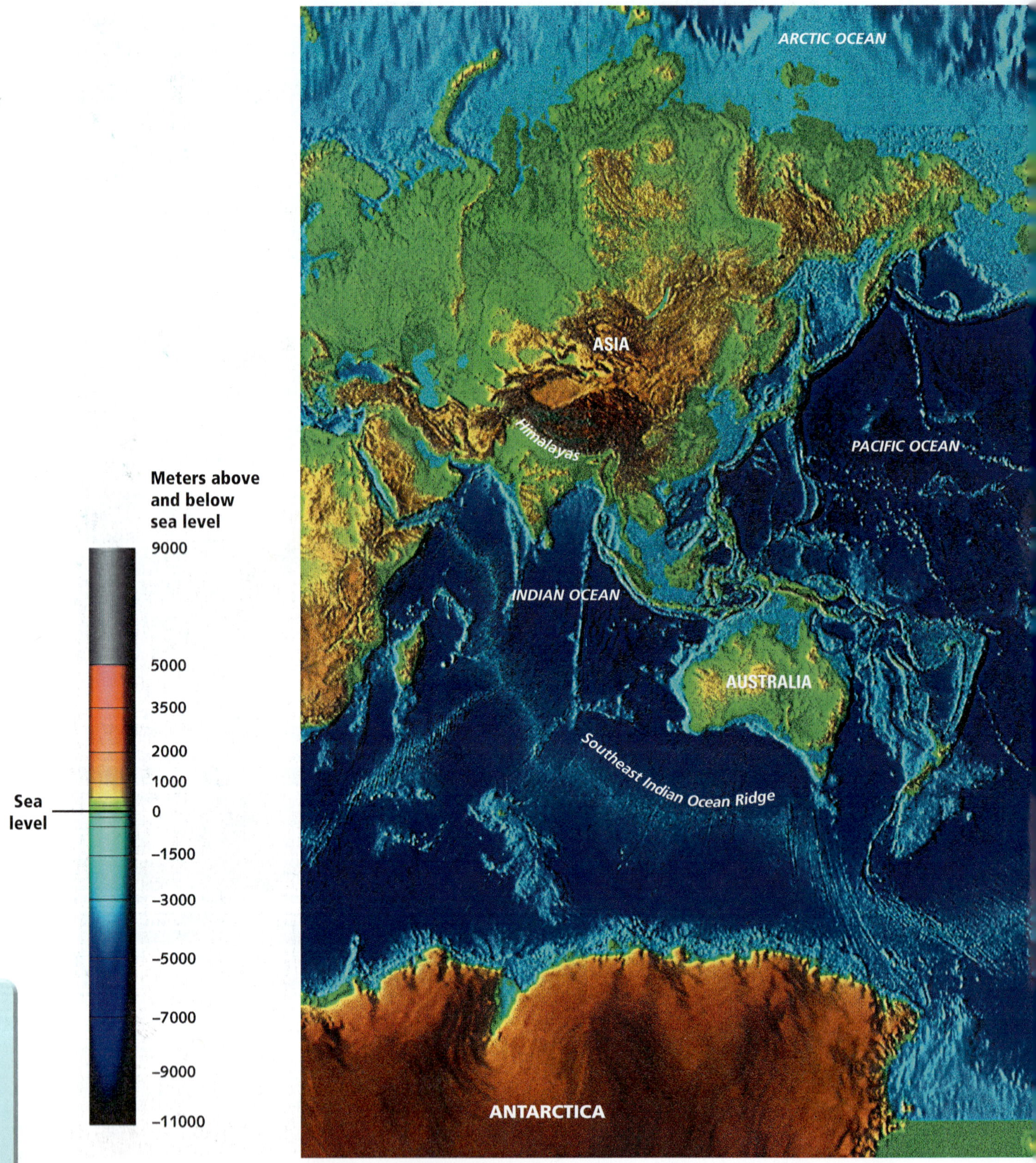

This image was generated from a combination of satellite altimetry data, ship-based data, and land-based data.

Tectonic Plates

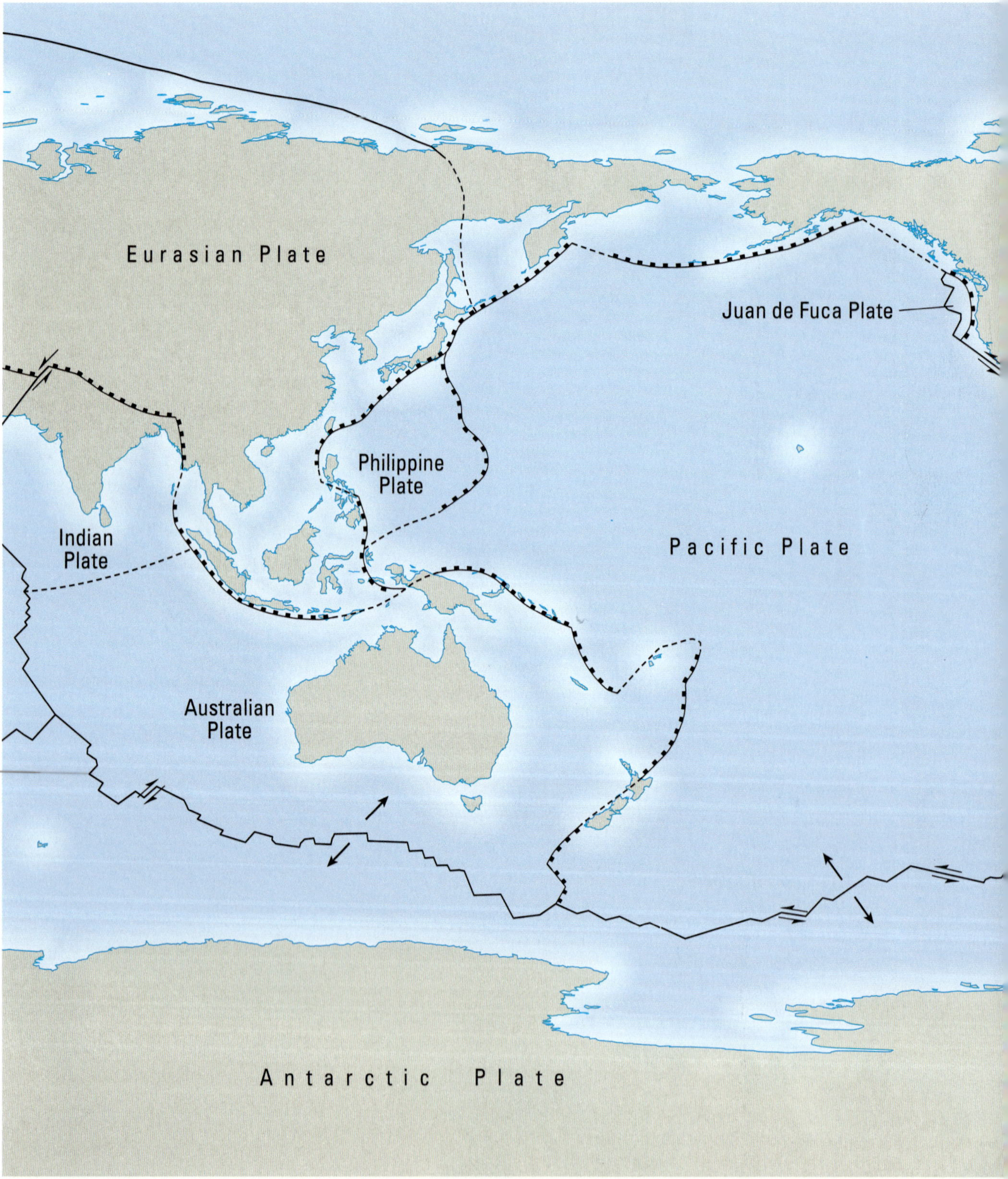

Eurasian Plate

Juan de Fuca Plate

Philippine Plate

Indian Plate

Pacific Plate

Australian Plate

Antarctic Plate

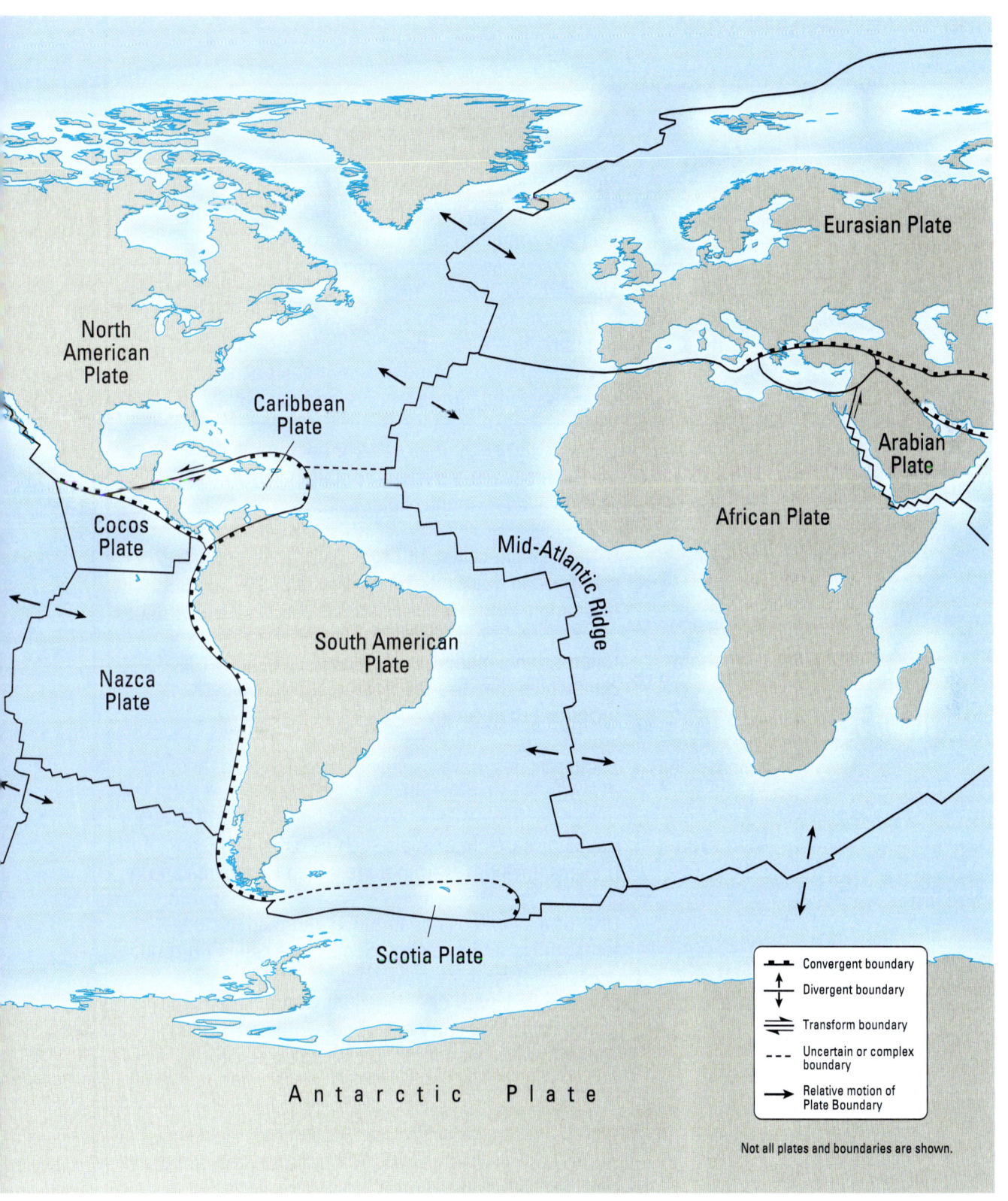

Classification of Living Things

Living things are classified into three domains. These domains are further divided into kingdoms, and then phyla. Major phyla are described in the table below, along with important features that are used to distinguish each group.

Classification of Living Things

Domain	Kingdom	Phylum	Common Name and Description
Archaea	Archaea		Single-celled, with no nucleus. Live in some of Earth's most extreme environments, including salty, hot, and acid environments, and the deep ocean.
Bacteria	Bacteria		Single-celled, with no nucleus, but chemically different from Archaea. Live in all types of environments, including the human body; reproduce by dividing from one cell into two. Includes blue-green bacteria (cyanobacteria), *Streptococcus*, and *Bacillus*.
Eukarya			Cells are larger than archaea or bacteria and are eukaryotic (have a nucleus containing DNA). Single-celled or multicellular.
	Protista		Usually single-celled, but sometimes multicellular. DNA contained in a nucleus. Many phyla resemble plants, fungi, or animals but are usually smaller or simpler in structure.
	Animal-like protists	Ciliophora	Ciliates; have many short, hairlike extensions called cilia, which they use for feeding and movement. Includes paramecium.
		Zoomastigina	Zooflagellates; have usually one or two long, hairlike extensions called flagella.
		Sporozoa	Cause diseases in animals such as birds, fish, and humans. Includes *Plasmodium*, which causes malaria.
		Sarcodina	Use footlike extensions to move and feed. Includes foraminifers and amoebas. Sometimes called Rhizopoda.
	Plantlike protists	Euglenozoa	Single-celled, with one flagellum. Some have chloroplasts that carry out photosynthesis. Includes euglenas and *Trypanosoma*, which causes African sleeping sickness.
		Dinoflagellata	Dinoflagellates; usually single-celled; usually have chloroplasts and flagellum. In great numbers, some species can cause red tides along coastlines.

Classification of Living Things (cont.)

Domain	Kingdom	Phylum	Common Name and Description
		Chrysophyta	Yellow algae, golden-brown algae, and diatoms; single-celled; named for the yellow pigments in their chloroplasts (*chrysophyte,* in Greek, means "golden plant").
		Chlorophyceae	Green algae; have chloroplasts and are chemically similar to land plants. Unicellular or forms simple colonies of cells. Includes *Chlamydomonas, Ulva* (sea lettuce), and *Volvox.*
		Phaeophyta	Brown seaweed; contain a special brown pigment that gives these organisms their color. Multicellular, live mainly in salt water; includes kelp.
		Rhodophyta	Red algae; contain a red pigment that makes these organisms red, purple, or reddish-black. Multicellular, live in salt water.
	Funguslike protists	Acrasiomycota	Cellular slime molds; live partly as free-living single-celled organisms, then fuse together to form a many-celled mass. Live in damp, nutrient-rich environments; decomposers.
		Myxomycota	Acellular slime molds; form large, slimy masses made of many nuclei but technically a single cell.
		Oomycota	Water molds and downy mildews; produce thin, cottonlike extensions called hyphae. Feed off of dead or decaying material, often in water.
	Fungi		Usually multicellular; eukaryotic; cells have a thick cell wall. Obtain nutrients through absorption; often function as decomposers.
		Chytridiomycota	Oldest and simplest fungi; usually aquatic (fresh water or brackish water); single-celled or multicellular.
		Basidiomycota	Multicellular; reproduce with a club-shaped structure that is commonly seen on forest floors. Includes mushrooms, puffballs, rusts, and smuts.
		Zygomycota	Mostly disease-causing molds; often parasitic.
		Ascomycota	Includes single-celled yeasts and multicellular sac fungi. Includes *Penicillium.*

Classification of Living Things (cont.)

Domain	Kingdom	Phylum	Common Name and Description
	Plantae		Multicellular and eukaryotic; make sugars using energy from sunlight. Cells have a thick cell wall of cellulose.
		Bryophyta	Mosses; small, grasslike plants that live in moist, cool environments. Includes sphagnum (peat) moss. Seedless, nonvascular plants.
		Hepatophyta	Liverworts; named for the liver-shaped structure of one part of the plant's life cycle. Live in moist environments. Seedless, nonvascular plants.
		Anthoceratophyta	Hornworts; named for the visible hornlike structures with which they reproduce. Live on forest floors and other moist, cool environments. Seedless, nonvascular plants.
		Psilotophyta	Simple plant, just two types. Includes whisk ferns found in tropical areas, a common greenhouse weed. Seedless, vascular plants.
		Lycophyta	Club mosses and quillworts; look like miniature pine trees; live in moist, wooded environments. Includes *Lycopodium* (ground pine). Seedless vascular plants.
		Sphenophyta	Plants with simple leaves, stems, and roots. Grow about a meter tall, usually in moist areas. Includes *Equisetum* (scouring rush). Seedless, vascular plants.
		Pterophyta	Ferns; fringed-leaf plants that grow in cool, wooded environments. Includes many species. Seedless, vascular plants.
		Cycadophyta	Cycads; slow-growing palmlike plants that grow in tropical environments. Reproduce with seeds.
		Ginkgophyta	Includes only one species: *Ginkgo biloba,* a tree that is often planted in urban environments. Reproduce with seeds in cones.
		Gnetophyta	Small group includes desert-dwelling and tropical species. Includes *Ephedra* (Mormon tea) and *Welwitschia,* which grows in African deserts. Reproduce with seeds.
		Coniferophyta	Conifers, including pines, spruces, firs, sequoias. Usually evergreen trees; tend to grow in cold, dry environments; reproduce with seeds produced in cones.

Classification of Living Things (cont.)

Domain	Kingdom	Phylum	Common Name and Description
		Anthophyta	Flowering plants; includes grasses and flowering trees and shrubs. Reproduce with seeds produced in flowers, becoming fruit.
	Animalia		Multicellular and eukaryotic; obtain energy by consuming food. Usually able to move around.
		Porifera	Sponges; spend most of their lives fixed to the ocean floor. Feed by filtering water (containing nutrients and small organisms) through their body.
		Cnidaria	Aquatic animals with a radial (spokelike) body shape; named for their stinging cells (cnidocytes). Includes jellyfish, hydras, sea anemones, and corals.
		Ctenophora	Comb jellies; named for the comblike rows of cilia (hairlike extensions) that are used for movement.
		Platyhelminthes	Flatworms; thin, flattened worms with simple tissues and sensory organs. Includes planaria and tapeworms, which cause diseases in humans and other hosts.
		Nematoda	Roundworms; small, round worms; many species are parasites, causing diseases in humans, such as trichinosis and elephantiasis.
		Annelida	Segmented worms; body is made of many similar segments. Includes earthworms, leeches, and many marine worms.
		Mollusca	Soft-bodied, aquatic animals that usually have an outer shell. Includes snails, mussels, clams, octopus, and squid.
		Arthropoda	Animals with an outer skeleton (exoskeleton) and jointed appendages (for example, legs or wings). Very large group that includes insects, spiders and ticks, centipedes, millipedes, and crustaceans.
		Echinodermata	Marine animals with a radial (spokelike) body shape. Includes feather stars, sea stars (starfish), sea urchins, sand dollars, and sea cucumbers.
		Chordata	Mostly vertebrates (animals with backbones) that share important stages of early development. Includes tunicates (sea squirts), fish, sharks, amphibians, reptiles, birds, and mammals.

Glossary

A

abrasion (uh-BRAY-zhuhn)
The process of wearing something down by friction. (p. 544)

abrasión El proceso de desgaste de algo por efecto de la fricción.

absolute age
The actual age in years of an event or object. (p. 727)

edad absoluta La edad real en años de un evento u objeto.

absorption (uhb-SAWRP-shuhn)
The disappearance of a wave into a medium. When a wave is absorbed, the energy transferred by the wave is converted into another form of energy, usually thermal energy. (p. 269)

absorción La desaparición de una onda dentro de un medio. Cuando se absorbe una onda, la energía transferida por la onda se convierte a otra forma de energía, normalmente a energía térmica.

acceleration
The rate at which velocity changes over time. (p. 25)

aceleración La razón a la cual la velocidad cambia con respecto al tiempo.

acid rain
Rain that has become more acidic than normal due to pollution. (p. 704)

lluvia ácida Lluvia que se ha vuelto más ácida de lo normal debido a la contaminación.

acoustics (uh-KOO-stihks)
The scientific study of sound; the behavior of sound waves inside a space. (p. 231)

acústica El estudio científico del sonido; el comportamiento de las ondas sonoras dentro de un espacio.

adaptation
A characteristic, a behavior, or any inherited trait that makes a species able to survive and reproduce in a particular environment. (p. 802)

adaptación Una característica, un comportamiento o cualquier rasgo heredado que permite a una especie sobrevivir o reproducirse en un medio ambiente determinado.

aftershock
A smaller earthquake that follows a more powerful earthquake in the same area. (p. 666)

réplica Un terremoto más pequeño que ocurre después de uno más poderoso en la misma área.

air resistance
The fluid friction due to air. (p. 89)

resistencia del aire La fricción fluida debida al aire.

alluvial fan (uh-LOO-vee-uhl)
A fan-shaped deposit of sediment at the base of a slope, formed as water flows down the slope and spreads at the bottom. (p. 581)

abanico aluvial Un depósito de sedimentos en forma de abanico situado en la base de una pendiente; se forma cuando el agua baja por la pendiente y se dispersa al llegar al pie de la misma.

amplification
The strengthening of an electrical signal, often used to increase the intensity of a sound wave. (p. 231)

amplificación El fortalecimiento de una señal eléctrica, a menudo se usa para aumentar la intensidad de una onda sonora.

amplitude
The maximum distance that a disturbance causes a medium to move from its rest position; the distance between a crest or trough of a wave and line through the center of a wave. (p. 193)

amplitud La distancia máxima que se mueve un medio desde su posición de reposo debido a una perturbación; la distancia entre una cresta o valle de una onda y una línea que pasa por el centro de la onda.

ancestor
A distant or early form of an organism from which later forms descend. (p. 809)

ancestro Una forma distante o temprana de un organismo a partir de la cual descienden formas posteriores.

Animalia (AN-uh-MAL-yuh)
Part of a classification system that divides all living things into six kingdoms. Kingdom Animalia includes multicellular organisms, from humans and lions to insects and microbes, that rely on food for energy. (p. 843)

Animalia Parte de un sistema de clasificación que divide a todos los organismos vivos en seis reinos. El reino Animalia incluye a organismos multicelulares, desde humanos y leones hasta insectos y microbios, que dependen del alimento como fuente de energía.

Archaea (AHR-kee-uh)
Part of a classification system that divides all living things into six kingdoms. Kingdom Archaea includes microscopic single-celled organisms with a distinctive cell structure that allows them to live in extreme environments. (p. 843)

Archaea Parte de un sistema de clasificación que divide a todos los organismos vivos en seis reinos. El reino Archaea incluye a organismos microscópicos de una sola célula con una estructura celular distintiva que les permite vivir en medios ambientes extremosos.

asthenosphere (as-THEHN-uh-SFEER)
The layer in Earth's upper mantle and directly under the lithosphere in which rock is soft and weak because it is close to melting. (p. 615)

astenosfera La capa del manto superior de la Tierra situada directamente bajo la litosfera en la cual la roca es blanda y débil por encontrarse próxima a su punto de fusión.

atmosphere (AT-muh-SFEER)
The outer layer of gases of a large body in space, such as a planet or star; the mixture of gases that surrounds the solid Earth; one of the four parts of the Earth system. (p. 438)

atmósfera La capa externa de gases de un gran cuerpo que se encuentra en el espacio, como un planeta o una estrella; la mezcla de gases que rodea la Tierra sólida; una de las cuatro partes del sistema terrestre.

atom
The smallest particle of an element that has the chemical properties of that element. (p. xxxvii)

átomo La partícula más pequeña de un elemento que tiene las propiedades químicas del elemento.

atomic mass
The average mass of the atoms of an element. (p. 337)

masa atómica La masa promedio de los átomos de un elemento.

atomic mass number
The total number of protons and neutrons in an atom's nucleus.

número de masa atómica El número total de protones y neutrones que hay en el núcleo de un átomo.

atomic number
The number of protons in the nucleus of an atom. (p. 332)

número atómico El número de protones en el núcleo de un átomo.

B

Bacteria (bak-TIHR-ee-uh)
Part of a classification system that divides all living things into six kingdoms. Kingdom Bacteria includes microscopic single-celled organisms found in many environments. Bacteria can be associated with disease in other organisms. (p. 843)

Bacteria Parte de un sistema de clasificación que divide a todos los organismos vivos en seis reinos. El reino Bacteria incluye a organismos microscópicos de una sola célula que se encuentran en muchos medios ambientes. Las bacterias pueden estar asociadas a enfermedades en otros organismos.

barrier island
A long, narrow island that develops parallel to a coast as a sandbar builds up above the water's surface. (p. 588)

isla barrera Una isla larga y angosta que se desarrolla paralelamente a la costa al crecer una barra de arena hasta rebasar la superficie del agua.

Bernoulli's principle
A statement that describes the effects of movement on fluid pressure. According to this principle, an increase in the speed of the motion of a fluid decreases the pressure within the fluid. (p. 100)

principio de Bernoulli Un enunciado que describe los efectos del movimiento sobre la presión de un líquido. De acuerdo a este principio, un aumento en la velocidad del movimiento de un fluido disminuye la presión dentro del líquido.

binomial nomenclature
(by-NOH-mee-uhl NOH-muhn-KLAY-chuhr)
The two-part naming system used to identify species. The first part of the name is the genus, and the second part of the name is the species. (p. 832)

nomenclatura biológica El sistema de denominación de dos partes que se usa para identificar a las especies. La primera parte del nombre es el género y la segunda parte del nombre es la especie.

Glossary **R69**

biodiversity
The number and variety of living things found on Earth or within an ecosystem. (p. xxxiii)
biodiversidad La cantidad y variedad de organismos vivos que se encuentran en la Tierra o dentro de un ecosistema.

bioluminescence
The production of light by living organisms. (p. 265)
bioluminiscencia La producción de luz por parte de organismos vivos.

biomass
Organic matter that contains stored energy from sunlight and that can be burned as fuel. (p. 772)
biomasa Materia orgánica que contiene energía almacenada proveniente de la luz del Sol y que puede ser usada como combustible.

biosphere (BY-uh-SFEER)
All living organisms on Earth in the air, on the land, and in the waters; one of the four parts of the Earth system. (p. 439)
biosfera Todos los organismos vivos de la Tierra, en el aire, en la tierra y en las aguas; una de las cuatro partes del sistema de la Tierra.

bond energy
The amount of energy in a chemical bond between atoms.
energía de enlace La cantidad de energía que hay en un enlace químico entre átomos.

buoyant force
The upward force on objects in a fluid; often called buoyancy. (p. 98)
fuerza flotante La fuerza hacia arriba que ejerce un fluido sobre un objeto inmerso en él, a menudo llamada flotación.

carbohydrate
A type of carbon-based molecule in living things. Carbohydrates include sugars and starches used for energy or as structural materials. Carbohydrate molecules contain carbon, hydrogen, and oxygen atoms.
carbohidrato Un tipo de molécula de los organismos vivos basada en el carbono. Los carbohidratos incluyen los azúcares y los almidones usados como fuente de energía o como materiales estructurales. Las moléculas de los carbohidrato contienen átomos de carbono, hidrógeno y oxígeno.

carrying capacity
The maximum size that a population can reach in an ecosystem. (p. 862)
capacidad de carga El tamaño máximo que una población puede alcanzar en un ecosistema.

catalyst
A substance that increases the rate of a chemical reaction but is not consumed in the reaction. (p. 400)
catalizador Una sustancia que aumenta lel a ritmo velocidad de una reacción química pero que no es consumida en la reacción.

cell
The smallest unit that is able to perform the basic functions of life. (p. xxxiii)
célula La unidad más pequeña capaz de realizar las funciones básicas de la vida.

centripetal force (sehn-TRIHP-ih-tuhl)
Any force that keeps an object moving in a circle. (p. 54)
fuerza centrípeta Cualquier fuerza que mantiene a un objeto moviéndose en forma circular.

chemical change
A change of one substance into another substance.
cambio químico Un cambio de una sustancia a otra sustancia.

chemical formula
An expression that shows the number and types of atoms joined in a compound. (p. 363)
fórmula química Una expresión que muestra el número y los tipos de átomos unidos en un compuesto.

chemical reaction
The process by which chemical changes occur. In a chemical reaction, atoms are rearranged, and chemical bonds are broken and formed. (p. 393)
reacción química El proceso mediante el cual ocurren cambios químicos. En una reacción química, los átomos se reorganizan y los enlaces químicos se rompen y se vuelven a formar.

chemical weathering
The breakdown or decomposition of rock that takes place when minerals change through chemical processes. (p. 546)
meteorización química La descomposición de las rocas que ocurre cuando los minerales cambian mediante procesos químicos.

classification
The systematic grouping of different types of organisms by their shared characteristics. (p. 824)

clasificación La agrupación sistemática de diferentes tipos de organismos en base a las características que comparten.

cleavage
The property of a mineral that describes its tendency to break along flat surfaces. (p. 481)

clivaje La propiedad de un mineral que describe su tendencia a romperse a lo largo de una superficie plana.

climate
The characteristic weather conditions in an area over a long period of time.

clima Las condiciones meteorológicas características de un lugar durante un largo período de tiempo.

coefficient
The number before a chemical formula that indicates how many molecules are involved in a chemical reaction.

coeficiente El número anterior a una fórmula química que indica cuántas moléculas están involucradas en una reacción química.

collision
A situation in which two objects in close contact exchange energy and momentum. (p. 66)

colisión Situación en la cual dos objetos en contacto cercano intercambian energía y momento.

competitor
A species characterized by a relatively longer life span, with relatively few offspring, when compared with an opportunist species. (p. 876)

competidor Una especie caracterizada por una vida relativamente larga, con relativamente pocas crías, en comparación con una especie oportunista.

compound
A substance made up of two or more different types of atoms bonded together.

compuesto Una sustancia formada por dos o más diferentes tipos de átomos enlazados.

compound machine
A machine that is made up of two or more simple machines. (p. 164)

máquina compuesta Una máquina que está hecha de dos o más máquinas simples.

concave
Curved inward toward the center, like the inside of a spoon. (p. 292)

cóncavo Dicho de una superficie con curvatura hacia dentro, como la parte interna de una cuchara.

concentration
The amount of solute dissolved in a solvent at a given temperature.

concentración La cantidad de soluto disuelta en un solvente a una temperatura determinada.

conservation
The process of saving or protecting a natural resource. (p. 761)

conservación El proceso de salvar o proteger un recurso natural.

continental drift
The hypothesis that Earth's continents move on Earth's surface. (p. 618)

deriva continental La hipótesis que postula que los continentes de la Tierra se mueven sobre la superficie del planeta.

continental-continental collision
A boundary along which two plates carrying continental crust push together. (p. 635)

colisión continente-continente Un límite a lo largo del cual dos placas de corteza continental empujan contra sí.

contour interval
On a topographic map, the difference in elevation from one contour line to the next. (p. 454)

equidistancia entre curvas de nivel En un mapa topográfico, la diferencia en elevación de una curva de nivel a la siguiente.

contour line
A line on a topographic map that joins points of equal elevation. (p. 453)

curva de nivel Una línea en un mapa topográfico que une puntos de igual elevación.

convection
The transfer of energy from place to place by the motion of heated gas or liquid; in Earth's mantle, convection is thought to transfer energy by the motion of solid rock, which when under great heat and pressure can move like a liquid. (p. 621)

convección La transferencia de energía de un lugar a otro por el movimiento de un líquido o gas calentado; se piensa que en el manto terrestre la convección transfiere energía mediante el movimiento de roca sólida, la cual puede moverse como un líquido cuando está muy caliente y bajo alta presión.

convection current
A circulation pattern in which material is heated and rises in one area, then cools and sinks in another area, flowing in a continuous loop. (p. 621)

corriente de convección Un patrón de circulación en el cual el material se calienta y asciende en un área, luego se enfría y se hunde en otra área, fluyendo en un circuito continuo.

convergent boundary (kun-VUR-juhnt)
A boundary along which two tectonic plates push together, characterized either by subduction or a continental collision. (p. 626)

límite convergente Un límite a lo largo del cual dos placas tectónicas se empujan mutuamente; este límite se caracteriza por una zona de subducción o una colisión entre continentes.

convex
Curved outward, like the underside of a spoon. (p. 292)

convexo Dicho de una superficie con curvatura hacia afuera, como la parte externa de una cuchara.

cornea (KAWR-nee-uh)
A transparent membrane that covers the eye. (p. 303)

córnea Una membrana transparente que cubre el ojo.

covalent bond
A pair of electrons shared by two atoms. (p. 370)

enlace covalente Un par de electrones compartidos por dos átomos.

crest
The highest point, or peak, of a wave. (p. 193)

cresta El punto más alto, o el pico, de una onda.

crust
A thin outer layer of rock above a planet's mantle, including all dry land and ocean basins. Earth's continental crust is 40 kilometers thick on average and oceanic crust is 7 kilometers thick on average. (p. 615)

corteza Una delgada capa exterior de roca situada sobre el manto de un planeta que incluye toda la tierra seca y todas las cuencas oceánicas. La corteza continental de la Tierra tiene un grosor promedio de 40 kilómetros y la corteza oceánica tiene un grosor promedio de 7 kilómetros.

crystal
A solid substance in which the atoms are arranged in an orderly, repeating, three-dimensional pattern. (p. 474)

cristal Una sustancia sólida en la cual los átomos están organizados en un patrón tridimensional y ordenado que se repite.

cycle
n. A series of events or actions that repeat themselves regularly; a physical and/or chemical process in which one material continually changes locations and/or forms. Examples include the water cycle, the carbon cycle, and the rock cycle.
v. To move through a repeating series of events or actions.

ciclo *s.* Una serie de eventos o acciones que se repiten regularmente; un proceso físico y/o químico en el cual un material cambia continuamente de lugar y/o forma. Ejemplos: el ciclo del agua, el ciclo del carbono y el ciclo de las rocas.

D

data
Information gathered by observation or experimentation that can be used in calculating or reasoning. *Data* is a plural word; the singular is *datum*.

datos Información reunida mediante observación o experimentación y que se puede usar para calcular o para razonar.

decibel dB
The unit used to measure the intensity of a sound wave. (p. 228)

decibel La unidad que se usa para medir la intensidad de una onda sonora.

delta
An area of land at the end, or mouth, of a river that is formed by the buildup of sediment. (p. 581)

delta Un área de tierra al final, o en la desembocadura, de un río y que se forma por la acumulación de sedimentos.

density
A property of matter representing the mass per unit volume. (pp. 99, 482)

densidad Una propiedad de la materia que representa la masa por unidad de volumen.

deposition (DEHP-uh-ZISH-uhn)
The process in which transported sediment is laid down. (p. 573)

sedimentación El proceso mediante el cual se deposita sedimento que ha sido transportado.

desertification (dih-ZUR-tuh-fih-KAY-shuhn)
The expansion of desert conditions in areas where the natural plant cover has been destroyed. (p. 561)

desertificación La expansión de las condiciones desérticas en áreas donde la vegetación natural ha sido destruida.

dichotomous key (dy-KAHT-uh-muhs)
A series of questions, each with only two answers, that can be used to help identify an organism's genus and species. (p. 836)

clave dicotómica Una serie de preguntas, cada una con solo dos respuestas, que puede usarse para ayudar a identificar el género y especie de un organismo.

diffraction
The spreading out of waves as they pass through an opening or around the edges of an obstacle. (p. 202)

difracción La dispersión de las ondas al pasar por una apertura o alrededor de los bordes de un obstáculo.

diffuse reflection
The reflection of parallel light rays in many different directions. (p. 290)

reflexión difusa La reflexión de rayos de luz paralelos en muchas direcciones diferentes.

divergent boundary (dih-VUR-juhnt)
A boundary along which two tectonic plates move apart, characterized by either a mid-ocean ridge or a continental rift valley. (p. 626)

límite divergente Un límite a lo largo del cual dos placas tectónicas se separan; este límite se caracteriza por una dorsal oceánica o un valle de rift continental.

divide
A continuous high line of land—or ridge—from which water drains to one side or the other. (p. 579)

línea divisoria de aguas Una línea continua de tierra alta, o un cerro, desde donde el agua escurre hacia un lado o hacia el otro.

DNA
The genetic material found in all living cells that contains the information needed for an organism to grow, maintain itself, and reproduce. Deoxyribonucleic acid (dee-AHK-see-RY-boh-noo-KLEE-ihk).

ADN El material genético que se encuentra en todas las céulas vivas y que contiene la información necesaria para que un organismo crezca, se mantenga a sí mismo y se reproduzca. Ácido desoxiribunucleico.

domain
One of three divisions in a classification system based on different types of cells. The six kingdoms of living things are grouped into three domains: Archaea, Bacteria, and Eukarya. (p. 841)

dominio Una de las tres divisiones en un sistema de clasificación basado en los diferentes tipos de células. Los seis reinos de los organismos vivos esta agrupados en tres dominios: Archaea, Bacteria y Eukarya.

Doppler effect
The change in perceived pitch that occurs when the source or the one who hears the sound is moving. (p. 226)

efecto Doppler El cambio en el tono percibido que ocurre cuando la fuente o el receptor de un sonido está en movimiento.

drainage basin
An area of land in which water drains into a stream system. The borders of a drainage basin are called divides. (p. 579)

cuenca tributaria Un área de tierra en la cual el agua escurre a un sistema de corrientes. Los límites de una cuenca tributaria se denominan líneas divisorias de aguas.

dune
A mound of sand built up by wind. (p. 589)

duna Un montículo de arena formado por el viento.

E

earthquake
A shaking of the ground caused by the sudden movement of large blocks of rocks along a fault. (p. 649)

terremoto Un temblor del suelo ocasionado por el movimiento repentino de grandes bloques de rocas a lo largo de una falla.

echolocation
The sending out of high-pitched sound waves and the interpretation of the returning echoes. (p. 235)

ecolocación El envío de ondas sonoras de tono alto y la interpretación de los ecos que regresan.

efficiency
The percentage of the input work done on a machine that the machine can return in output work. A machine's output work divided by its input work and multiplied by 100. (p. 150)

eficiencia El porcentaje del trabajo de entrada suministrado a una máquina que la máquina puede devolver como trabajo de salida. El trabajo de salida de una máquina dividido por su trabajo de entrada y multiplicado por cien.

electromagnetic spectrum EM spectrum
The range of all electromagnetic frequencies, including the following types (from lowest to highest frequency): radio waves, microwaves, infrared light, visible light, ultraviolet light, x-rays, and gamma rays. (p. 256)

espectro electromagnético La escala de todas las frecuencias electromagnéticas, incluyendo los siguientes tipos (de la frecuencia más baja a la más alta): ondas de radio, microondas, luz infrarroja, luz visible, luz ultravioleta, rayos X y rayos gamma.

electromagnetic wave EM wave
A type of wave, such as a light wave or radio wave, that does not require a medium to travel; a disturbance that transfers energy through a field. (p. 249)

onda electromagnética Un tipo de onda, como una onda luminosa o de radio, que no requiere un medio para propagarse; una perturbación que transfiere energía a través de un campo.

electron
A negatively charged particle located outside an atom's nucleus. An electron is about 2000 times smaller than either a proton or neutron. (p. 331)

electrón Una partícula con carga negativa localizada fuera del núcleo de un átomo. Un electrón es como aproximadamente 2000 veces más pequeño que un protón o un neutrón.

element
A substance that cannot be broken down into a simpler substance by ordinary chemical changes. An element consists of atoms of only one type. (p. 473)

elemento Una sustancia que no puede descomponerse en otra sustancia más simple por medio de cambios químicos normales. Un elemento consta de átomos de un solo tipo.

elevation
A measure of how high something is above a reference point, such as sea level. (p. 453)

elevación Una medida de lo elevado que está algo sobre un punto de referencia, como el nivel del mar.

emigration
In population studies, the movement of individuals out of an ecosystem. (p. 871)

emigración En estudios poblacionales, el movimiento de individuos fuera de un ecosistema.

endothermic reaction
A chemical reaction that absorbs energy. (p. 411)

reacción endotérmica Una reacción química que absorbe energía.

energy
The ability to do work or to cause a change. For example, the energy of a moving bowling ball knocks over pins; energy from food allows animals to move and to grow; and energy from the Sun heats Earth's surface and atmosphere, which causes air to move. (p. xxxv)

energía La capacidad para trabajar o causar un cambio. Por ejemplo, la energía de una bola de boliche en movimiento tumba los pinos; la energía proveniente de su alimento permite a los animales moverse y crecer; la energía del Sol calienta la superficie y la atmósfera de la Tierra, lo que ocasiona que el aire se mueva.

environment
Everything that surrounds a living thing. An environment is made up of both living and nonliving factors. (p. xxxiii)

medio ambiente Todo lo que rodea a un organismo vivo. Un medio ambiente está compuesto de factores vivos y factores sin vida.

epicenter (EHP-ih-SEHN-tuhr)
The point on Earth's surface directly above the focus of an earthquake. (p. 656)

epicentro El punto en la superficie de la Tierra situado directamente sobre el foco sísmico.

equator
An imaginary east-west line around the center of Earth that divides the planet into the Northern Hemisphere and the Southern Hemisphere; a line set at 0° latitude. (p. 446)

ecuador Una línea imaginaria de este a oeste alrededor del centro de la Tierra y que divide al planeta en hemisferio norte y hemisferio sur; la línea está fijada a latitud 0°.

erosion
The process in which sediment is picked up and moved from one place to another. (p. 573)

erosión El proceso en el cual el sedimento es recogido y transportado de un lugar a otro.

evaporation
The process by which liquid changes into gas.

evaporación El proceso por el cual un líquido se transforma en gas.

evolution
The process through which species change over time; can refer to the changes in a particular population or to the formation and extinction of species over the course of Earth's history. (p. 797)

evolución El proceso mediante el cual las especies cambian con el tiempo; puede referirse a cambios en una población en particular o a la formación y extinción de especies en el curso de la historia de la Tierra.

exfoliation (ex-FOH-lee-AY-shuhn)
In geology, the process in which layers or sheets of rock gradually break off. (p. 544)

exfoliación En geología, el proceso en el cual capas u hojas de roca se desprenden gradualmente.

exothermic reaction
A chemical reaction that releases energy. (p. 411)

reacción exotérmica Una reacción química que libera energía.

experiment
An organized procedure to study something under controlled conditions. (p. xl)

experimento Un procedimiento organizado para estudiar algo bajo condiciones controladas.

extinction
The permanent disappearance of a species. (p. xxxiii)

extinción La desaparición permanente de una especie.

extrusive igneous rock (ihk-STROO-sihv)
Igneous rock that forms as lava cools on Earth's surface. (p. 511)

roca ígnea extrusiva Roca ígnea que se forma al enfriarse la lava sobre la superficie de la Tierra.

F

false-color image
A computer image in which the colors are not what the human eye would see. A false-color image can assign different colors to different types of radiation coming from an object to highlight its features. (p. 460)

imagen de color falso Una imagen computacional en la cual los colores no son los que el ojo humano observaría. Una imagen de color falso puede asignar diferentes colores a los diferentes tipos de radiación que provienen de un objeto para hacer destacar sus características.

fault
A fracture in Earth's lithosphere along which blocks of rock move past each other. (p. 649)

falla Una fractura en la litosfera de la Tierra a lo largo de la cual bloques de roca se mueven y pasan uno al lado de otro.

fault-block mountain
A mountain that forms as blocks of rock move up or down along normal faults in areas where the lithosphere is being pulled apart. (p. 686)

montaña de bloques de falla Una montaña que se forma cuando bloques de roca se mueven hacia arriba o hacia abajo a lo largo de fallas normales en las áreas donde la litosfera está siendo separada.

fiber optics
Technology based on the use of laser light to send signals through transparent wires called optical fibers. This technology is often used in communications. (p. 313)

fibra óptica Tecnología basada en el uso de luz de láser para mandar señales por alambres transparentes llamados fibras ópticas. Esta tecnología se usa a menudo en comunicaciones.

field
An area around an object where the object can apply a force—such as gravitational force, magnetic force, or electrical force—on another object without touching it.

campo Un área alrededor de un objeto donde el objeto puede aplicar una fuerza, como fuerza gravitacional, fuerza magnética o fuerza eléctrica, sobre otro objeto sin tocarlo.

floodplain
A flat area of land on either side of a stream that becomes flooded when a river overflows its banks. (p. 580)

planicie de inundación Un área plana de tierra en cualquier costado de un arroyo que se inunda cuando un río se desborda.

fluid
A substance that can flow easily, such as a gas or a liquid. (p. 88)

fluido Una sustancia que fluye fácilmente, como por ejemplo un gas o un líquido.

fluorescence (flu-REHS-uhns)
A phenomenon in which a material absorbs electromagnetic radiation of one wavelength and gives off electromagnetic radiation of a different wavelength. (p. 267)

fluorescencia Un fenómeno en el cual un material absorbe radiación electromagnética de una longitud de onda y emite radiación electromagnética de longitud de onda diferente.

focal length
The distance from the center of a convex lens to its focal point. (p. 299)

distancia focal La distancia del centro de un lente convexo a su punto focal.

focal point
The point at which parallel light rays reflected from a concave mirror come together; the point at which parallel light rays refracted by a convex lens come together. (p. 293)

punto focal El punto en el cual se unen los rayos paralelos de luz reflejados por un espejo cóncavo; el punto en el cual se unen los rayos paralelos de luz refractados por un lente convexo.

focus
In an earthquake, the point underground where the rocks first begin to move. (p. 656)

foco sísmico En un terremoto, el punto subterráneo donde comienza el movimiento de las rocas.

folded mountain
A mountain that forms as continental crust is compressed and rocks bend into large folds. (p. 684)

montaña plegada Una montaña que se forma cuando la corteza continental es comprimida y las rocas se doblan en grandes pliegues.

foliation
The arrangement of minerals within rocks into flat or wavy parallel bands; a characteristic of most metamorphic rocks. (p. 528)

foliación La organización de minerales en bandas paralelas planas u onduladas en las rocas; una característica de la mayoría de las rocas metamórficas.

force
A push or a pull; something that changes the motion of an object. (p. 41)

fuerza Un empuje o un jalón; algo que cambia el movimiento de un objeto.

fossil
A trace or the remains of a once-living thing from long ago. (pp. 715, 789)

fósil Un rastro o los restos de un organismo que vivió hace mucho tiempo.

fossil fuels
Fuels formed from the remains of prehistoric organisms that are burned for energy. (p. 754)

combustibles fósiles Combustibles formados a partir de los restos de organismos prehistóricos que son consumidos para obtener energía.

fracture
The tendency of a mineral to break into irregular pieces. (p. 481)

fractura La tendencia de un mineral a romperse en pedazos irregulares.

frequency
The number of wavelengths (or wavecrests) that pass a fixed point in a given amount of time, usually one second; the number of cycles per unit time. (p. 193)

frecuencia El número de ondas que pasan un punto fijo en un período de tiempo determinado, normalmente un segundo; el número de ciclos por unidad de tiempo.

friction
A force that resists the motion between two surfaces in contact. (p. 85)

fricción Una fuerza que resiste el movimiento entre dos superficies en contacto.

fulcrum
A fixed point around which a lever rotates. (p. 155)

fulcro Un punto fijo alrededor del cual gira una palanca.

Fungi (FUHN-jy)
Part of a classification system that divides all living things into six kingdoms. Kingdom Fungi includes multicellular mushrooms and molds and single-celled yeasts. (p. 843)

Fungi Parte de un sistema de clasificación que divide a todos los organismos vivos en seis reinos. El reino Fungi incluye a los hongos multicelulares, a los mohos y a las levaduras unicelulares.

gamma rays
Part of the electromagnetic spectrum that consists of waves with the highest frequencies; electromagnetic waves with frequencies ranging from more than 10^{19} hertz to more than 10^{24} hertz. (p. 262)

rayos gamma Parte del espectro electromagnético que consiste de ondas con las frecuencias más altas; las ondas electromagnéticas con frecuencias de más de 10^{19} hertzios hasta más de 10^{24} hertzios.

gene
The basic unit of heredity that consists of a segment of DNA on a chromosome. (p. 813)

gen La unidad básica de herencia que consiste en un segmento de ADN en un cromosoma.

genetic material
The nucleic acid DNA that is present in all living cells and contains the information needed for a cell's growth, maintenance, and reproduction.

material genético El ácido nucleico ADN, que está presente en todas las células vivas y que contiene la información necesaria para el crecimiento, el mantenimiento y la reproducción celular.

genus
The first part of a binomial name that groups together closely related species. The genus Felis includes all species of small cats. (p. 832)

género La primera parte de un nombre biológico que agrupa a especies muy relacionadas entre sí. El género Felis incluye a todas las especies de gatos pequeños.

geographic information systems
Computer systems that can store, arrange, and display geographic data in different types of maps. (p. 461)

sistemas de información geográfica Sistemas computarizados que pueden almacenar, organizar y mostrar datos geográficos en diferentes tipos de mapas.

geologic time scale
The summary of Earth's history, divided into intervals of time defined by major events or changes on Earth. (p. 733)

escala de tiempo geológico El resumen de la historia de la Tierra, dividido en intervalos de tiempo definidos por los principales eventos o cambios en la Tierra.

geosphere (JEE-uh-SFEER)
All the features on Earth's surface—continents, islands, and seafloor—and everything below the surface—the inner and outer core and the mantle; one of the four parts of the Earth system. (p. 440)

geosfera Todas las características de la superficie de la Tierra, es decir, continentes, islas y el fondo marino, y de todo bajo la superficie, es decir, el núcleo externo e interno y el manto; una de las cuatro partes del sistema de la Tierra.

geothermal energy
Heat energy that originates from within Earth and drives the movement of Earth's tectonic plates. Geothermal energy can be used to generate electricity. (p. 770)

energía geotérmica Energía calorífica que se origina en el interior de la Tierra y que impulsa el movimiento de las placas tectónicas de planeta. La energía geotérmica puede usarse para generar electricidad.

geyser
A type of hot spring that shoots water into the air. (p. 704)

géiser Un tipo de fuente termal que dispara agua al aire.

glacier (GLAY-shuhr)
A large mass of ice that exists year-round and moves over land. (p. 593)

glaciar Una gran masa de hielo que existe durante todo el año y se mueve sobre la tierra.

gravity
The force that objects exert on each other because of their masses. (p. 77)

gravedad La fuerza que los objetos ejercen entre sí debido a sus masas.

group
A vertical column in the periodic table of the elements. Elements in a group have similar properties. (p. 342)

grupo Una columna vertical en la tabla periódica de los elementos. Los elementos en un grupo tienen propiedades similares.

H

half-life
The amount of time it takes for half of the nuclei of a radioactive isotope to decay into atoms of another element. (pp. 352, 727)
  vida media La cantidad de tiempo que se necesita para que le toma a la mitad del núcleo de un isótopo radioactivo se en descomponganerse en átomos de otro elemento.

hardness
The resistance of a mineral or other material to being scratched. (p. 483)
  dureza La resistencia de un mineral o de otro material a ser rayado.

hertz Hz
The unit used to measure frequency. One hertz is equal to one complete cycle per second. (p. 222)
  hercio La unidad usada para medir frecuencia. un hercio es igual a un ciclo completa por segundo.

horizontal
Parallel to the horizon; level.
  horizontal Paralelo al horizonte; nivelado.

horsepower hp
The unit of measurement of power for engines and motors. One horsepower equals 745 watts. (p. 132)
  caballos de fuerza La unidad de medición de potencia para máquinas y motores. Un caballo de fuerza es igual a 745 vatios.

hot spot
An area where a column of hot material rises from deep within a planet's mantle and heats the lithosphere above it, often causing volcanic activity at the surface. (p. 631)
  punto caliente Un área donde una columna de material caliente surge del interior del manto de un planeta y calienta la litosfera situada sobre él, con frecuencia ocasionando actividad volcánica en la superficie.

humus (HYOO-muhs)
The decayed organic matter in soil. (p. 551)
  humus La materia orgánica en descomposición del suelo.

hydroelectric energy
Electricity that is generated by the conversion of the energy of moving water. (p. 768)
  energía hidroeléctrica Electricidad que se genera por la conversión de la energía del agua en movimiento.

hydrogen fuel cell
A device that uses hydrogen and oxygen to produce electricity. The byproducts are heat and water. (p. 772)
  celda de combustible de hidrógeno Un aparato que usa hidrógeno y oxígeno para producir electricidad. Los subproductos son calor y agua.

hydrosphere (HY-druh-SFEER)
All water on Earth—in the atmosphere and in the oceans, lakes, glaciers, rivers, streams, and underground reservoirs; one of the four parts of the Earth system. (p. 438)
  hidrosfera Toda el agua de la Tierra: en la atmósfera y en los océanos, lagos, glaciares, ríos, arroyos y depósitos subterráneos; una de las cuatro partes del sistema de la Tierra.

hypothesis
A tentative explanation for an observation or phenomenon. A hypothesis is used to make testable predictions. (p. xxxv)
  hipótesis Una explicación provisional de una observación o de un fenómeno. Una hipótesis se usa para hacer predicciones que se pueden probar.

I

ice core
A tubular sample that shows the layers of snow and ice that have built up over the years. (p. 721)
  núcleo de hielo Una muestra tubular que presenta las capas de nieve y hielo que se han acumulado con los años.

igneous rock (IHG-nee-uhs)
Rock that forms as molten rock cools and becomes solid. (p. 506)
  roca ígnea Roca que se forma al enfriarse la roca fundida y hacerse sólida.

image
A picture of an object formed by rays of light. (p. 291)
  imagen Reproducción de la figura de un objeto formada por rayos de luz.

immigration
In population studies, the movement of an organism into a range inhabited by individuals of the same species. (p. 871)
  inmigración En estudios poblacionales, el movimiento de un organismo hacia un territorio habitado por individuos de la misma especie.

incandescence (IHN-kuhn-DEHS-uhns)
1. The production of light by materials having high temperatures. 2. Light produced by an incandescent object. (p. 265)

incandescencia 1. La producción de luz por parte de materiales a altas temperaturas. 2. La luz producida por un objeto incandescente.

inclined plane
A simple machine that is a sloping surface, such as a ramp. (p. 158)

plano inclinado Una máquina simple que es una superficie en pendiente, como por ejemplo una rampa.

index fossil
A fossil of an organism that was common, lived in many areas, and existed only during a certain span of time. Index fossils are used to help determine the age of rock layers. (p. 725)

fósil indicador Un fósil de un organismo que era común, vivió en muchas áreas y existió sólo durante cierto período de tiempo. Los fósiles indicadores se usan para ayudar a determinar la edad de las capas de roca.

inertia (ih-NUR-shuh)
The resistance of an object to a change in the speed or the direction of its motion. (p. 46)

inercia La resistencia de un objeto al cambio de la velocidad o de la dirección de su movimiento.

infrared light
Part of the electromagnetic spectrum that consists of waves with frequencies between those of microwaves and visible light. (p. 260)

luz infrarroja Parte del espectro electromagnético que consiste de ondas con frecuencias entre las de las microondas y las de la luz visible.

inner core
A solid sphere of metal, mainly nickel and iron, at Earth's center. (p. 614)

núcleo interno Una esfera sólida de metal, principalmente níquel y hierro, que se encuentra en el centro de la Tierra.

intensity
The amount of energy of a wave, per wavelength. Intensity is associated with the amplitude of a sound wave and with the quality of loudness produced by the sound wave. (p. 228)

intensidad La cantidad de energía de una onda sonora, por longitud de onda. La intensidad está asociada con la amplitud de una onda sonora y con la calidad del volumen producido por la onda sonora.

interaction
The condition of acting or having an influence upon something. Living things in an ecosystem interact with both the living and nonliving parts of their environment. (p. xxxiii)

interacción La condición de actuar o influir sobre algo. Los organismos vivos en un ecosistema interactúan con las partes vivas y las partes sin vida de su medio ambiente.

interference
The meeting and combining of waves; the adding or subtracting of wave amplitudes that occurs as waves overlap. (p. 203)

interferencia El encuentro y la combinación de ondas; la suma o la resta de amplitudes de onda que ocurre cuando las ondas se traslapan.

intrusive igneous rock (ihn-TROO-sihv)
Igneous rock that forms as magma cools below Earth's surface. (p. 511)

roca ígnea intrusiva Roca ígnea que se forma al enfriarse el magma bajo la superficie de la Tierra.

ion
An atom or group of atoms that has a positive or negative electric charge. (p. 334)

ión Un átomo o un grupo de átomos que tiene una carga eléctrica positiva o negativa.

ionic bond
The electrical attraction between a negative ion and a positive ion. (p. 368)

enlace iónico La atracción eléctrica entre un ión negativo y un ión positivo.

isotope
An atom of one element that has a different number of neutrons than another atom of the same element. (p. 332)

isótopo Un átomo de un elemento que tiene un número diferente de neutrones que otro átomo del mismo elemento.

J, K

joule (jool) J
A unit used to measure energy and work. One calorie is equal to 4.18 joules of energy; one joule of work is done when a force of one newton moves an object one meter. (p. 117)

julio Una unidad que se usa para medir la energía y el trabajo. Una caloría es igual a 4.18 julios de energía; se hace un joule de trabajo cuando una fuerza de un newton mueve un objeto un metro.

kettle lake
A bowl-shaped lake that was formed as sediment built up around a block of ice left behind by a glacier. (p. 597)

lago kettle Un lago en forma de tazón que se formó al acumularse sedimento alrededor de un bloque de hielo que quedó tras el paso de un glaciar.

kinetic energy (kuh-NEHT-ihk)
The energy of motion. A moving object has the most kinetic energy at the point where it moves the fastest. (p. 122)

energía cinética La energía de movimiento. Un objeto en movimiento tiene la mayor energía cinética en el punto en donde se mueve más rápidamente.

L

laser (LAY-zuhr)
A device that produces an intense, concentrated beam of light that can be brighter than sunlight. Lasers are often used in medicine and communications. (p. 311)

láser Un aparato que produce un intenso rayo de luz concentrado que es más brillante que la luz del Sol. Los láseres se usan a menudo en la medicina y las comunicaciones.

latitude
The distance in degrees north or south from the equator. (p. 446)

latitud La distancia en grados norte o sur a partir del ecuador.

lava
Molten rock that reaches a planet's surface through a volcano. (pp. 490, 691)

lava Roca fundida que llega a la superficie de un planeta a través de un volcán.

law
In science, a rule or principle describing a physical relationship that always works in the same way under the same conditions. The law of conservation of energy is an example.

ley En las ciencias, una regla o un principio que describe una relación física que siempre funciona de la misma manera bajo las mismas condiciones. La ley de la conservación de la energía es un ejemplo.

law of conservation of energy
A law stating that no matter how energy is transferred or transformed, it continues to exist in one form or another.

ley de la conservación de la energía Una ley que establece que no importa cómo se transfiere o transforma la energía, toda la energía sigue presente en alguna forma u otra.

law of conservation of mass
A law stating that atoms are not created or destroyed in a chemical reaction. (p. 403)

ley de la conservación de la masa Una ley que establece que los átomos ni se crean ni se destruyen en una reacción química.

law of conservation of momentum
A law stating that the amount of momentum a system of objects has does not change as long as there are no outside forces acting on that system. (p. 67)

ley de la conservación del momento Una ley que establece que la cantidad de momento que tiene un sistema de objetos no cambia mientras no haya fuerzas externas actuando sobre el sistema.

law of reflection
A law of physics stating that the angle at which light strikes a surface (the angle of incidence) equals the angle at which it reflects off the surface (the angle of reflection). (p. 290)

ley de la reflexión Una ley de la física que establece que el ángulo al cual la luz incide sobre una superficie (el ángulo de incidencia) es igual al ángulo al cual se refleja (ángulo de reflexión) de la superficie.

lens
A transparent optical tool that refracts light. (p. 297)

lente Una herramienta óptica transparente que refracta la luz.

lever
A solid bar that rotates, or turns, around a fixed point (fulcrum); one of the six simple machines. (p. 155)

palanca Una barra sólida que da vueltas o gira alrededor de un punto fijo (el fulcro); una de las seis máquinas simples.

limiting factor
A factor or condition that prevents the continuing growth of a population in an ecosystem. (p. 872)

factor limitante Un factor o una condición que impide el crecimiento continuo de una población en un ecosistema.

liquefaction
A process in which the shaking of ground causes loose, wet soil to act like a liquid. (p. 666)

licuación Un proceso en el cual el temblor del suelo ocasiona que la tierra húmeda y suelta actúe como un líquido.

lithosphere (LIHTH-uh-SFEER)
The layer of Earth made up of the crust and the rigid rock of the upper mantle, averaging about 40 kilometers thick and broken into tectonic plates. (p. 615)

litosfera La capa de la Tierra compuesta por la corteza y la roca rígida del manto superior, con un promedio de 40 kilómetros de grosor y fracturada en placas tectónicas.

loess (LOH-uhs)
Deposits of fine-grained, wind-blown sediment. (p. 590)

loes Depósitos de sedimento de grano fino transportado por el viento.

longitude
The distance in degrees east or west of the prime meridian. Longitude lines are numbered from 0° to 180°. (p. 447)

longitud La distancia en grados al este o al oeste del primer meridiano. Las líneas de longitud están numeradas de 0° a 180°.

longitudinal wave (LAHN-jih-TOOD-uhn-uhl)
A type of wave in which the disturbance moves in the same direction that the wave travels. (p. 190)

onda longitudinal Un tipo de onda en la cual la perturbación se mueve en la misma dirección en la que viaja la onda.

longshore current
The overall direction and movement of water as waves strike the shore at an angle. (p. 587)

corriente litoral La dirección y el movimiento general del agua conforme las olas golpean la costa en ángulo.

longshore drift
The zigzag movement of sand along a beach, caused by the action of waves. (p. 587)

deriva litoral El movimiento en zigzag de la arena a lo largo de una playa, ocasionado por la acción de las olas.

luminescence
The production of light without the high temperatures needed for incandescence. (p. 265)

luminiscencia La producción de luz sin las altas temperaturas necesarias para la incandescencia.

luster
The property of a mineral that describes the way in which light reflects from its surface. Major types of luster are metallic and nonmetallic. (p. 480)

brillo La propiedad de un mineral que describe la manera en la cual la luz se refleja en su superficie. Los principales tipos de brillo son metálico y no metálico.

machine
Any device that makes doing work easier. (p. 145)

máquina Cualquier aparato que facilita el trabajo.

magma
Molten rock beneath Earth's surface. (p. 490)

magma Roca fundida que se encuentra bajo la superficie de la Tierra.

magnetic reversal
A switch in the direction of Earth's magnetic field so that the magnetic north pole becomes the magnetic south pole and the magnetic south pole becomes the magnetic north pole. (p. 628)

inversión magnética Un cambio en la dirección del campo magnético de la Tierra, de modo que el polo norte magnético se convierte en el polo sur magnético y el polo sur magnético se convierte en el polo norte magnético.

mantle
The layer of rock between Earth's outer core and crust, in which most rock is hot enough to flow in convection currents; Earth's thickest layer. (p. 615)

manto La capa de roca situada entre el núcleo externo y la corteza de la Tierra, en la cual la mayor parte de la roca es lo suficientemente caliente para fluir en corrientes de convección; la capa más gruesa de la Tierra.

map legend
A chart that explains the meaning of each symbol used on a map; also called a key. (p. 445)

clave del mapa Una tabla que explica el significado de cada símbolo usado en un mapa.

map scale
The comparison of distance on a map with actual distance on what the map represents, such as Earth's surface. Map scale may be expressed as a ratio, a bar scale, or equivalent units. (p. 445)

escala del mapa La comparación de la distancia en un mapa con la distancia real en lo que el mapa representa, como la superficie de la Tierra. La escala del mapa puede expresarse como una azón, una barra de escala o en unidades equivalentes.

mass
A measure of how much matter an object is made of.

masa Una medida de la cantidad de materia de la que está compuesto un objeto.

mass extinction
One of several periods in Earth's history when large numbers of species became extinct at nearly the same time. (p. 794)

extinción masiva Uno de varios períodos en la historia de la Tierra cuando grandes números de especies se extinguieron casi al mismo tiempo.

mass wasting
The downhill movement of loose rock or soil. (p. 575)

movimiento de masa El desplazamiento cuesta abajo de suelo o de roca suelta.

matter
Anything that has mass and volume. Matter exists ordinarily as a solid, a liquid, or a gas. (p. xxxv)

materia Todo lo que tiene masa y volumen. Generalmente la materia existe como sólido, líquido o gas.

mechanical advantage
The number of times a machine multiplies the input force; output force divided by input force. (p. 147)

ventaja mecánica El número de veces que una máquina multiplica la fuerza de entrada; la fuerza de salida dividida por la fuerza de entrada.

mechanical energy
A combination of the kinetic energy and potential energy an object has. (p. 125)

energía mecánica La combinación de la energía cinética y la energía potencial que tiene un objeto.

mechanical wave
A wave, such as a sound wave or a seismic wave, that transfers kinetic energy through matter. (p. 187)

onda mecánica Una onda, como una onda sonora o una onda sísmica, que transfiere energía cinética a través de la materia.

mechanical weathering
The breakdown of rock into smaller pieces of the same material without any change in its composition. (p. 544)

meteorización mecánica El desmoronamiento de las rocas en pedazos más pequeños del mismo material, sin ningún cambio en su composición.

medium
A substance through which a wave moves. (p. 187)

medio Una sustancia a través de la cual se mueve una onda.

metal
An element that tends to be shiny, easily shaped, and a good conductor of electricity and heat. (p. 347)

metal Un elemento que tiende a ser brilloso, fácilmente deformable moldeado y buen conductor de electricidad y calor.

metallic bond
A certain type of bond in which nuclei float in a sea of electrons. (p. 376)

enlace metálico Cierto tipo de enlace en el cual los núcleos flotan en un mar de electrones.

metalloid
An element that has properties of both metals and nonmetals. (p. 350)

metaloide Un elemento que tiene propiedades de los metales así como de los no metales.

metamorphic rock (MEHT-uh-MAWR-fihk)
Rock formed as heat or pressure causes existing rock to change in structure, texture, or mineral composition. (p. 506)

roca metamórfica Roca formada cuando el calor o la presión ocasionan que la roca existente cambie de estructura, textura o composición mineral.

metamorphism (MEHT-uh-MAWR-FIHZ-uhm)
The process by which a rock's structure or mineral composition is changed by pressure or heat. (p. 524)

metamorfismo El proceso mediante el cual la estructura o la composición mineral de una roca cambia debido a la presión o al calor.

meter m
The international standard unit of length, about 39.37 inches.

metro La unidad estándar internacional de longitud, aproximadamente 39.37 pulgadas.

microwaves
Part of the electromagnetic spectrum that consists of waves with higher frequencies than radio waves, but lower frequencies than infrared waves. (p. 259)

microondas Parte del espectro electromagnético que consiste de ondas con frecuencias mayores a las ondas de radio, pero menores a las de las ondas infrarrojas.

mid-ocean ridge
A long line of sea-floor mountains where new ocean crust is formed by volcanic activity along a divergent boundary. (p. 620)

dorsal oceánica Una larga línea de montañas en el fondo marino donde se forma nueva corteza oceánica debido a la actividad volcánica a lo largo de un límite divergente.

mineral
A substance that forms in nature, is a solid, has a definite chemical makeup, and has a crystal structure. (p. 471)

mineral Una sustancia sólida formada en la naturaleza, de composición química definida y estructura cristalina.

mixture
A combination of two or more substances that do not combine chemically but remain the same individual substances. Mixtures can be separated by physical means.

mezcla Una combinación de dos o más sustancias que no se combinan químicamente sino que permanecen siendo las mismas sustancias individuales. Las mezclas se pueden separar por medios físicos.

molecule
A group of atoms that are held together by covalent bonds so that they move as a unit. (p. 371)

molécula Un grupo de átomos que se mantienen unidos por medio de enlaces covalentes de tal manera que se mueven como una sola unidad.

momentum (moh-MEHN-tuhm)
A measure of mass in motion. The momentum of an object is the product of its mass and velocity. (p. 64)

momento Una medida de la masa en movimiento. El momento de un objeto es el producto de su masa y su velocidad.

moraine (muh-RAYN)
A deposit of till left behind by a retreating glacier. Moraines can form along a glacier's sides and at its end. (p. 596)

morrena Un depósito de sedimentos glaciares dejado por un glaciar que retrocede. Las morrenas pueden formarse en los costados de un glaciar o en su extremo.

motion
A change of position over time. (p. 11)

movimiento Un cambio de posición a través del tiempo.

multicellular organism
An organism that is made up of many cells. (p. 793)

organismo multicelular Un organismo compuesto de muchas células.

N

nanotechnology
The science and technology of building electronic circuits and devices from single atoms and molecules. (p. 167)

nanotecnología La ciencia y tecnología de fabricar circuitos y aparatos electrónicos a partir de átomos y moléculas individuales.

natural resource
Any type of matter or energy from Earth's environment that humans use to meet their needs. (p. 751)

recurso natural Cualquier tipo de materia o energía del medio ambiente de la Tierra que usan los humanos para satisfacer sus necesidades.

natural selection
The process through which members of a species that are best suited to their environment survive and reproduce at a higher rate than other members of the species. (p. 801)

selección natural El proceso mediante el cual los miembros de una especie que están mejor adecuados a su medio ambiente sobreviven y se reproducen a una tasa más alta que otros miembros de la especie.

net force
The overall force acting on an object when all of the forces acting on it are combined. (p. 43)

fuerza neta La fuerza resultante que actúa sobre un objeto cuando todas las fuerzas que actúan sobre él son combinadas.

neutron
A particle that has no electric charge and is located in an atom's nucleus. (p. 331)

neutrón Una partícula que no tiene carga eléctrica y que se encuentra en el núcleo de un átomo.

Newton's first law
A scientific law stating that objects at rest remain at rest, and objects in motion remain in motion with the same velocity, unless acted on by an unbalanced force. (p. 45)

primera ley de Newton Una ley científica que establece que los objetos en reposo permanecen en reposo, y que los objetos en movimiento permanecen en movimiento con la misma velocidad, a menos que actúe sobre ellos una fuerza no balanceada.

Newton's second law
A scientific law stating that the acceleration of an object increases with increased force and decreases with increased mass. (p. 50)

segunda ley de Newton Una ley científica que establece que la aceleración de un objeto aumenta al incrementar la fuerza que actúa sobre él y disminuye al incrementar su masa.

Newton's third law
A scientific law stating that every time one object exerts a force on another object, the second object exerts a force that is equal in size and opposite in direction back on the first object. (p. 57)

tercera ley de Newton Una ley científica que establece que cada vez que un objeto ejerce una fuerza sobre otro objeto, el segundo objeto ejerce una fuerza de la misma magnitud y en dirección opuesta sobre el primer objeto.

nonmetal
An element that is not a metal and has properties generally opposite to those of a metal. (p. 493)

no metal Un elemento que no es un metal y que tiene propiedades generalmente opuestas a las de los metales.

nonrenewable resource
A resource that exists in a fixed amount or is used up more quickly than it can be replaced in nature. (p. 752)

recurso no renovable Un recurso que existe en una cantidad fija o se consume más rápidamente de lo que puede reemplazarse en la naturaleza.

nuclear fission (FIHSH-uhn)
The process of splitting the nuclei of radioactive atoms, which releases huge amounts of energy mainly in the form of radiation and heat energy. (p. 765)

fisión nuclear El proceso de rotura de los núcleos de átomos radioactivos, el cual libera inmensas cantidades de energía, principalmente en forma de radiación y energía calorífica.

nucleus
The central region of an atom where most of the atom's mass is found in protons and neutrons. (p. 331)

núcleo La región central de un átomo donde se encuentra la mayor parte de la masa del átomo en la forma de protones y neutrones.

oceanic-continental subduction
A boundary along which a plate carrying oceanic crust sinks beneath a plate with continental crust. (p. 637)

subducción océano-continente Un límite a lo largo del cual una placa de corteza oceánica se hunde bajo una placa de corteza continental.

oceanic-oceanic subduction
A boundary along which a plate carrying oceanic crust sinks beneath another plate with oceanic crust. (p. 636)

subducción océano-océano Un límite a lo largo del cual una placa de corteza oceánica se hunde bajo otra placa de corteza oceánica.

opportunist
A species characterized by a relatively short life span, with relatively large quantities of offspring, as compared with a competitor species. (p. 875)

oportunista Una especie caracterizada por una vida relativamente corta, que produce relativamente grandes cantidades de crías, en comparación con una especie competidora.

optics (AHP-tihks)
The study of light, vision, and related technology. (p. 289)

óptica El estudio de la luz, la visión y la tecnología relacionada a ellas.

orbit
The elliptical path one celestial body follows around another celestial body. An object in orbit has a centripetal force acting on it that keeps the object moving in a circle or other ellipse. (p. 80)

órbita El camino elíptico que un cuerpo celeste sigue alrededor de otro cuerpo celeste. La fuerza centrípeta actúa sobre un objeto en órbita y lo mantiene en un movimiento circular o elíptico.

ore
A rock that contains enough of a valuable mineral to be mined for a profit. (p. 492)

mena Una roca que contiene suficiente mineral valioso para ser extraído con fines lucrativos.

organism
An individual living thing, made up of one or many cells, that is capable of growing and reproducing. (p. xxxiii)
organismo Un individuo vivo, compuesto de una o muchas células, que es capaz de crecer y reproducirse.

original remains
A fossil that is the actual body or body parts of an organism. (p. 716)
restos originales Un fósil que es en realidad el cuerpo o partes del cuerpo de un organismo.

outer core
A layer of molten metal, mainly nickel and iron, that surrounds Earth's inner core. (p. 614)
núcleo externo Una capa de metal fundido, principalmente níquel y hierro, que rodea al núcleo interno de la Tierra.

Pangaea (pan-JEE-uh)
A hypothetical supercontinent that included all of the landmasses on Earth. It began breaking apart about 200 million years ago. (p. 620)
Pangea Un supercontinente hipotético que incluía todas las masas continentales de la Tierra. Empezó a fracturarse aproximadamente hace 200 millones de años.

pascal Pa
The unit used to measure pressure. One pascal is the pressure exerted by one newton of force on an area of one square meter, or one N/m^2. (p. 92)
pascal La unidad utilizada para medir presión. Un pascal es la presión ejercida por un newton de fuerza sobre un área de un metro cuadrado, o un N/m2.

Pascal's principle
A statement that says when an outside pressure is applied at any point to a fluid in a container, that pressure is transmitted throughout the fluid with equal strength. (p. 102)
principio de Pascal Un enunciado que dice que cuando una presión externa es aplicada a cualquier punto de un líquido en un contenedor, esta presión es transmitida a través del fluido con igual fuerza.

period
A horizontal row in the periodic table of the elements. Elements in a period have varying properties. (p. 342)
período Un renglón horizontal en la tabla periódica de los elementos. Los elementos en un período tienen distintas propiedades.

periodic table
A table of the elements, arranged by atomic number, that shows the patterns in their properties. (p. 338)
tabla periódica Una tabla de los elementos, organizada en base a número atómico, que muestra los patrones en sus propiedades.

photosynthesis
In green plants, the endothermic process in which light is absorbed and used to change carbon dioxide and water into glucose and oxygen. (p. 414)
fotosíntesis En plantas verdes, el proceso endotérmico en el cual se absorbe luz y se usa para cambiar dióxido de carbono y agua a glucosa y oxígeno.

pitch
The quality of highness or lowness of a sound. Pitch is associated with the frequency of a sound wave—the higher the frequency, the higher the pitch. (p. 221)
tono La cualidad de un sonido de ser alto o bajo. El tono está asociado con la frecuencia de una onda sonora: entre más alta sea la frecuencia, más alto es el tono.

planet
A spherical body, larger than a comet or asteroid, that orbits the Sun, or a similar body that orbits a different star.
planeta Un cuerpo esférico, más grande que un cometa o un asteroide, que orbita alrededor del Sol, o un cuerpo similar que orbita alrededor de una estrella distinta.

Plantae (PLAN-tee)
Part of a classification system that divides all living things into six kingdoms. Kingdom Plantae includes multicellular organisms, such as trees, grass, and moss, that are capable of photosynthesis, capturing energy from the Sun. (p. 843)
Plantae Parte de un sistema de clasificación que divide a todos los organismos vivos en seis reinos. El reino Plantae incluye a organismos multicelulares, como árboles, pasto y musgo, que son capaces de fotosintetizar, capturando la energía del Sol.

polar covalent bond
The unequal sharing of electrons between two atoms that gives rise to negative and positive regions of electric charge. (p. 371)
enlace polar covalente El compartir electrones desigualmente entre dos átomos y que lleva a la formación de regiones de carga eléctrica positiva y regiones de carga eléctrica negativa.

polarization (POH-luhr-ih-ZAY-shuhn)
A way of filtering light so that all of the waves vibrate in the same direction. (p. 272)

polarización Una manera de filtrar la luz para que todas las ondas vibren en la misma dirección.

pollution
The release of harmful substances into the air, water, or land. (p. 884)

contaminación La descarga de sustancias nocivas al aire, alagua o a la tierra.

population density
A measure of the number of organisms that live in a given area; the population density of a city may be given as the number of people living in a square kilometer. (p. 865)

densidad de población Una medida de la cantidad de organismos que viven un área dada; la densidad de población de una ciudad puede expresarse como el número de personas que viven en un kilómetro cuadrado.

population dynamics
The study of the changes in the number of individuals in a population and the factors that affect those changes. (p. 861)

dinámica de población El estudio de los cambios en el número de individuos en una población y los factores que afectan a estos cambios.

population size
The number of individuals of the same species that live in a given area. (p. 864)

tamaño de la población El número de individuos de la misma especie que vive en un área determinada.

position
An object's location. (p. 9)

posición La ubicación de un objeto.

potential energy
Stored energy; the energy an object has due to its position, molecular arrangement, or chemical composition. (p. 122)

energía potencial Energía almacenada; o la energía que tiene un objeto debido a su posición, arreglo molecular o composición química.

power
The rate at which work is done. (p. 130)

potencia La razón a la cual se hace el trabajo.

precipitate
n. A solid substance that forms as a result of a reaction between chemicals in two liquids. (p. 396)
v. To come out of solution.

precipitado *s.* Una sustancia sólida que se forma como resultado de la reacción entre sustancias químicas en dos líquidos.
precipitar *v.* Salir de solución.

pressure
A measure of how much force is acting on a certain area; how concentrated a force is. Pressure is equal to the force divided by area. (p. 91)

presión Una medida de cuánta fuerza actúa sobre cierta área; el nivel de concentración de la fuerza. La presión es igual a la fuerza dividida entre el área.

primary colors
Three colors of light—red, green, and blue—that can be mixed to produce all possible colors. (p. 274)

colores primarios Tres colores de luz, rojo, verde y azul, que se pueden mezclar para producir todos los colores posibles.

primary pigments
Three colors of substances—cyan, yellow, and magenta—that can be mixed to produce all possible colors. (p. 275)

pigmentos primarios Tres colores de sustancias, cian, amarillo y magenta, que se pueden mezclar para producir todos los colores posibles.

prime meridian
An imaginary north-south line that divides the planet into the Eastern Hemisphere and the Western Hemisphere. The prime meridian passes through Greenwich, England. (p. 447)

primer meridiano Una línea imaginaria de norte a sur que divide al planeta en hemisferio oriental y hemisferio occidental. El primer meridiano pasa a través de Greenwich, Inglaterra.

prism
An optical tool that uses refraction to separate the different wavelengths that make up white light. (p. 273)

prisma Una herramienta óptica que usa la refracción para separar las diferentes longitudes de onda que componen la luz blanca.

product
A substance formed by a chemical reaction. A product is made by the rearrangement of atoms and bonds in reactants. (p. 395)

producto Una sustancia formada por una reacción química. Un producto se hace mediante la reorganización de los átomos y los enlaces en los reactivos.

projection
A representation of Earth's curved surface on a flat map. (p. 448)

proyección Una representación de la superficie curva de la Tierra en un mapa plano.

Protista (proh-TIHS-tuh)
Part of a classification system that divides all living things into six kingdoms. Kingdom Protista includes mostly single-celled organisms with cells similar to those of the Plantae, Animalia, and Fungi kingdoms. (p. 843)

Protista Parte de un sistema de clasificación que divide a todos los organismos vivos en seis reinos. El reino Protista incluye principalmente a organismos unicelulares con células parecidas a las de los reinos Plantae, Animalia y Fungi.

proton
A positively charged particle located in an atom's nucleus. (p. 331)

protón Una partícula con cargada positivamente localizada en el núcleo de un átomo.

pulley
A wheel with a grooved rim that turns on an axle; one of the six simple machines. (p. 156)

polea Una rueda con un canto acanalado que gira sobre un eje; una de las seis máquinas simples.

pupil
The circular opening in the iris of the eye that controls how much light enters the eye. (p. 303)

pupila La apertura circular en el iris del ojo que controla cuánta luz entra al ojo.

pyroclastic flow (PY-roh-KLAS-tihk)
A dense cloud of superheated gases and rock fragments that moves quickly downhill from an erupting volcano. (p. 692)

corriente piroclástica Una nube densa de gases sobrecalentados y fragmentos de rocas que desciende rápidamente de un volcán en erupción.

R

radiation (RAY-dee-AY-shuhn)
Energy that travels across distances in the form of electromagnetic waves. (p. 251)

radiación Energía que viaja a través de la distancia en forma de ondas electromagnéticas.

radio waves
The part of the electromagnetic spectrum that consists of waves with the lowest frequencies. (p. 258)

ondas de radio La parte del espectro electromagnético que consiste de las ondas con las frecuencias más bajas.

radioactivity
The process by which the nucleus of an atom of an element releases energy and particles. (p. 350)

radioactividad El proceso mediante el cual el núcleo de un átomo de un elemento libera energía y partículas.

reactant
A substance that is present at the beginning of a chemical reaction and is changed into a new substance. (p. 395)

reactivo Una sustancia que está presente en el comienzo de una reacción química y que se convierte en una nueva sustancia.

reactive
Likely to undergo a chemical change. (p. 346)

reactivo Que es probable que sufra un cambio químico.

recrystallization
The process by which bonds between atoms in minerals break and re-form in new ways during metamorphism. (p. 525)

recristalización El proceso mediante el cual los enlaces entre los átomos de los minerales se rompen y se vuelven a formar de diferentes maneras durante el metamorfismo.

recycling
The reusing of materials that people would otherwise throw away, such as paper, glass, plastics, and certain metals. (p. 762)

reciclaje El reutilizar los materiales que la gente de otra forma desecharía, como el papel, el vidrio, los plásticos y ciertos metales.

reference point
A location to which another location is compared. (p. 10)

punto de referencia Una ubicación con la cual se compara otra ubicación.

reflection
The bouncing back of a wave after it strikes a barrier. (p. 201)

reflexión El rebote de una onda después de que incide sobre una barrera.

refraction
The bending of a wave as it crosses the boundary between two mediums at an angle other than 90 degrees. (p. 201)

refracción El doblamiento de una onda a medida que cruza el límite entre dos medios a un ángulo distinto a 90 grados.

regular reflection
The reflection of parallel light rays in the same direction. (p. 290)

reflexión especular La reflexión de rayos de luz paralelos en la misma dirección.

relative age
The age of an event or object in relation to other events or objects. (p. 723)

edad relativa La edad de un evento u objeto en relación a otros eventos u objetos.

relative motion
The idea that the observation of motion depends on the observer. (p. 13)

movimiento relativo La idea de que la observación del movimiento depende del observador.

relief
In geology, the difference in elevation between an area's high and low points. (p. 453)

relieve En geología, la diferencia en elevación entre los puntos altos y bajos de un área.

relief map
A map that shows the differences in elevation in an area. Relief maps can show elevations through the use of contour lines, shading, colors, and, in some cases, three-dimensional materials. (p. 444)

mapa de relieve Un mapa que muestra las diferencias en elevación de un área. Los mapas de relieve pueden mostrar elevaciones mediante del uso de curvas de nivel, sombreado, colores y, en algunos casos, materiales tridimensionales.

remote sensing
A method of using scientific equipment to gather information about something from a distance. Most remote-sensing methods make use of different types of electromagnetic radiation. (p. 458)

sensoramiento remoto Un método de reunir información sobre algo a distancia usando equipo científico. La mayoría de los métodos de sensoramiento remoto hacen uso de diferentes tipos de radiación electromagnética.

renewable resource
A natural resource that can be replaced in nature at about the same rate as it is used. (p. 752)

recurso renovable Un recurso natural que puede reemplazarse en la naturaleza casi al mismo ritmo al que es utilizado.

resonance
The strengthening of a sound wave when it combines with an object's natural vibration. (p. 224)

resonancia El fortalecimiento de una onda sonora cuando se combina con la vibración natural de un objeto.

respiration
The exothermic process by which living things release energy from glucose and oxygen and produce carbon dioxide and water. (p. 418)

respiración El proceso exotérmico mediante el cual los organismos vivos liberan energía de la glucosa y del oxígeno y producen dióxido de carbono y agua.

retina (REHT-uhn-uh)
A light-sensitive membrane at the back of the inside of the eye. (p. 303)

retina Una membrana sensible a la luz en la parte trasera del interior del ojo.

rift valley
A deep valley formed as tectonic plates move apart, such as along a mid-ocean ridge. (p. 627)

valle de rift Un valle profundo formado cuando las placas tectónicas se separan, como a lo largo de una dorsal oceánica.

robot
A machine that works automatically or by remote control. (p. 169)

robot Una máquina que funciona automáticamente o por control remoto.

rock
A naturally formed solid that is usually made up of one or more types of minerals. (p. 503)

roca Un sólido formado de manera natural y generalmente compuesto de uno o más tipos de minerales.

rock cycle
The set of natural, repeating processes that form, change, break down, and re-form rocks. (p. 506)

ciclo de las rocas La serie de procesos naturales y repetitivos que forman, cambian, descomponen y vuelven a formar rocas.

S

sandbar
A ridge of sand built up by the action of waves and currents. (p. 588)
barra de arena Una colina de arena que se forma por la acción de las olas y las corrientes.

satellite
A body that orbits a more massive body. A natural satellite is also called a moon.
satélite Un cuerpo que orbita otro de mayor masa. Un satélite natural también se denomina luna.

scattering
The spreading out of light rays in all directions as particles reflect and absorb the light. (p. 271)
dispersión La disipación de los rayos de luz en todas las direcciones a medida que las partículas reflejan y absorben la luz.

screw
A simple machine that is an inclined plane wrapped around a cylinder. A screw can be used to raise and lower weights as well as to fasten objects. (p. 159)
tornillo Una máquina simple que es un plano inclinado enrollado alrededor de un cilindro. Un tornillo se puede usar para levantar o bajar pesos y también para sujetar objetos.

second s
A unit of time equal to one-sixtieth of a minute.
segundo Una unidad de tiempo igual a una sesentava parte de un minuto.

sediment
Solid materials such as rock fragments, plant and animal remains, or minerals that are carried by water or by air and that settle on the bottom of a body of water or on the ground. (p. 517)
sedimento Materiales sólidos como fragmentos de rocas, restos de plantas y animales o minerales que son transportados por el agua o el aire y que se depositan en el fondo de un cuerpo de agua o en el suelo.

sedimentary rock (SEHD-uh-MEHN-tuh-ree)
Rock formed as pieces of older rocks and other loose materials get pressed or cemented together or as dissolved minerals re-form and build up in layers. (p. 506)
roca sedimentaria Roca que se forma cuando los pedazos de rocas más viejas y otros materiales sueltos son presionados o cementados o cuando los minerales disueltos vuelven a formarse y se acumulan en capas.

seismic wave (SYZ-mihk)
The vibrations caused by an earthquake. (p. 655)
onda sísmica Las vibraciones ocasionadas por un terremoto.

seismograph (SYZ-muh-GRAF)
An instrument that constantly records ground movements. (p. 660)
sismógrafo Un instrumento que registra constantemente los movimientos del suelo.

sensor
A mechanical or electronic device that receives and responds to a signal, such as light. (p. 459)
sensor Un dispositivo mecánico o electrónico que recibe y responde a una señal, como la luz.

simple machine
One of the basic machines on which all other mechanical machines are based. The six simple machines are the lever, inclined plane, wheel and axle, pulley, wedge, and screw. (p. 154)
máquina simple Una de las máquinas básicas sobre las cuales están basadas todas las demás máquinas mecánicas. Las seis máquinas simples son la palanca, el plano inclinado, la rueda y eje, la polea, la cuña y el tornillo.

sinkhole
An open basin that forms when the roof of a cavern becomes so thin that it falls in. (p. 583)
sumidero Una cuenca abierta que se forma cuando el techo de una caverna se vuelve tan delgado que se desploma.

slope
A measure of how steep a landform is. Slope is calculated as the change in elevation divided by the distance covered. (p. 453)
pendiente Una medida de lo inclinada de una formación terrestre. La pendiente se calcula dividiendo el cambio en la elevación por la distancia recorrida.

soil horizon
A soil layer with physical and chemical properties that differ from those of soil layers above or below it. (p. 552)
horizonte del suelo Una capa del suelo con propiedades físicas y químicas que difieren de las de las capas del suelo superior e inferior a la misma.

soil profile
The soil horizons in a specific location; a cross section of soil layers that displays all soil horizons. (p. 552)
perfil del suelo Los horizontes del suelo en un lugar específico; una sección transversal de las capas del suelo que muestra todos los horizontes del suelo.

solar cell
A device that converts the energy of sunlight into electrical energy. (p. 769)

celda solar Un aparato que convierte la energía de la luz del Sol en energía eléctrica.

sonar
Instruments that use echolocation to locate objects underwater; acronym for "sound navigation and ranging." (p. 235)

sonar Instrumentos que usan la ecolocación para localizar objetos bajo agua; acrónimo en inglés para "navegación y determinación de distancias por sonido."

sound
A type of wave that is produced by a vibrating object and that travels through matter. (p. 213)

sonido Un tipo de onda que es producida por un objeto que vibra y que viaja a través de la materia.

speciation
The evolution of a new species from an existing species. (p. 804)

especiación La evolución de una nueva especie a partir de una especie existente.

species
A group of living things that are so closely related that they can breed with one another and produce offspring that can breed as well. (p. xxxiii)

especie Un grupo de organismos que están tan estrechamente relacionados que pueden aparearse entre sí y producir crías que también pueden aparearse.

speed
A measure of how fast something moves through a particular distance over a definite time period. Speed is distance divided by time. (p. 16)

rapidez Una medida del desplazamiento de un objeto a lo largo de una distancia específica en un período de tiempo definido. La rapidez es la distancia dividida entre el tiempo.

streak
The color of a mineral powder left behind when a mineral is scraped across a surface; a method for classifying minerals. (p. 479)

raya El color del polvo que queda de un mineral cuando éste se raspa a lo largo de una superficie; un método para clasificar minerales.

stress
The force applied by an object pressing on, pulling on, or pushing against another object. (p. 649)

tensión La fuerza aplicada por un objeto que presiona, jala o empuja contra otro objeto.

subduction
The process by which an oceanic tectonic plate sinks under another plate into Earth's mantle. (p. 634)

subducción El proceso mediante el cual una placa tectónica oceánica se hunde bajo otra placa y entra al manto de la Tierra.

subscript
A number written slightly below and to the right of a chemical symbol that shows how many atoms of an element are in a compound. (p. 363)

subíndice Un número que se escribe en la parte inferior a la derecha de un símbolo químico y que muestra cuantos átomos de un elemento están en un compuesto.

system
A group of objects or phenomena that interact. A system can be as simple as a rope, a pulley, and a mass. It also can be as complex as the interaction of energy and matter in the four parts of the Earth system.

sistema Un grupo de objetos o fenómenos que interactúan. Un sistema puede ser algo tan sencillo como una cuerda, una polea y una masa. También puede ser algo tan complejo como la interacción de la energía y la materia en las cuatro partes del sistema de la Tierra.

T

taxonomy
The science of classifying and naming organisms. (p. 824)

taxonomía La ciencia de clasificar y ponerle nombre a los organismos.

technology
The use of scientific knowledge to solve problems or engineer new products, tools, or processes.

tecnología El uso de conocimientos científicos para resolver problemas o para diseñar nuevos productos, herramientas o procesos.

tectonic plate (tehk-TAHN-ihk)
One of the large, moving pieces into which Earth's lithosphere is broken and which commonly carries both oceanic and continental crust. (p. 616)

placa tectónica Una de las grandes piezas en movimiento en las que la litosfera de la Tierra se rompe y que comúnmente lleva corteza oceánica y continental.

terminal velocity
The final, maximum velocity of a falling object. (p. 89)

velocidad terminal La velocidad máxima final de un objeto en caída libre.

theory
In science, a set of widely accepted explanations of observations and phenomena. A theory is a well-tested explanation that is consistent with all available evidence.

teoría En las ciencias, un conjunto de explicaciones de observaciones y fenómenos que es ampliamente aceptado. Una teoría es una explicación bien probada que es consecuente con la evidencia disponible.

theory of plate tectonics
A theory stating that Earth's lithosphere is broken into huge plates that move and change in size over time.

Teoría de la tectónica de placas Una teoría que establece que la litosfera de la Tierra está formada por enormes placas que se mueven y cambian de tamaño con el tiempo.

till
Sediment of different sizes left directly on the ground by a melting, or retreating, glacier. (p. 596)

sedimentos glaciares Sedimentos de diferentes tamaños depositados directamente en el suelo por un glaciar que se derrite o retrocede.

topography
All natural and human-made surface features of a particular area. (p. 452)

topografía Todas las características de superficie de origen natural y humano en un área particular.

trait
Any type of feature that can be used to tell two species apart, such as size or bone structure.

rasgo Cualquier característica que puede usarse para diferenciar a dos especies, como el tamaño o la estructura ósea.

transform boundary
A boundary along which two tectonic plates scrape past each other, and crust is neither formed nor destroyed. (p. 626)

límite transcurrente Un límite a lo largo del cual dos placas tectónicas se rozan y no se forma corteza ni se destruye.

transmission (trans-MIHSH-uhn)
The passage of a wave through a medium. (p. 269)

transmisión El paso de una onda a través de un medio.

transverse wave
A type of wave in which the disturbance moves at right angles, or perpendicular, to the direction in which the wave travels. (p. 189)

onda transversal Un tipo de onda en el cual la perturbación se mueve en ángulo recto, o perpendicularmente, a la dirección en la cual viaja la onda.

trough (trawf)
The lowest point, or valley, of a wave. (p. 193)

valle El punto más bajo de una onda.

tsunami (tsu-NAH-mee)
A water wave caused by an earthquake, volcanic eruption, or landslide. (p. 666)

tsunami Una ola de agua ocasionada por un terremoto, erupción volcánica o derrumbe.

U

ultrasound
Sound waves with frequencies above 20,000 hertz, the upper limit of typical hearing levels in humans, used for medical purposes, among other things. (p. 222)

ultrasonido Ondas sonoras con frecuencias superiores a 20,000 hertzios, el límite superior de los niveles auditivos típicos de los humanos. Estas ondas tienen usos médicos, entre otros.

ultraviolet light
The part of the electromagnetic spectrum that consists of waves with frequencies higher than those of visible light and lower than those of x-rays. (p. 261)

luz ultravioleta La parte del espectro electromagnético que consiste de ondas con frecuencias superiores a las de luz visible y menores a las de los rayos X.

unicellular organism
An organism that is made up of a single cell. (p. 792)

organismo unicelular Un organismo compuesto de una sola célula.

uniformitarianism
(YOO-nuh-fawr-mih-TAIR-ee-uh-nihz-uhm)
A theory stating that processes shaping Earth today, such as erosion and deposition, also shaped Earth in the past, and that these processes cause large changes over geologic time. (p. 732)

uniformismo Una teoría que afirma que los procesos que le dan forma a la Tierra hoy en día, como la erosión y la sedimentación, también le dieron forma a la Tierra en el pasado; además, afirma que estos procesos ocasionan grandes cambios en tiempo geológico.

vacuum
A space containing few or no particles of matter. (p. 217)

vacío Un espacio que no contiene partículas de materia o bien contiene muy pocas.

variable
Any factor that can change in a controlled experiment, observation, or model. (p. R30)

variable Cualquier factor que puede cambiar en un experimento controlado, en una observación o en un modelo.

vector
A quantity that has both size and direction. (p. 22)

vector Una cantidad que tiene magnitud y dirección.

velocity
A speed in a specific direction. (p. 22)

velocidad Una rapidez en una dirección específica.

vertical
Going straight up or down from a level surface.

vertical Que está dispuesto hacia arriba o hacia abajo de una superficie nivelada.

vestigial organ (veh-STIHJ-ee-uhl)
A physical structure that was fully developed and functional in an earlier group of organisms but is reduced and unused in later species. (p. 810)

órgano vestigial Una estructura física que fue completamente desarrollada y funcional en un grupo anterior de organismos pero que está reducido y en desuso en especies posteriores.

vibration
A rapid, back-and-forth motion. (p. 213)

vibración Un movimiento rápido hacia delante y hacia atrás.

visible light
The part of the electromagnetic spectrum that consists of waves detectable by the human eye. (p. 260)

luz visible La parte del espectro electromagnético que consiste de ondas detectables por el ojo humano.

volcano
An opening in the crust through which molten rock, rock fragments, and hot gases erupt; a mountain built up from erupted materials. (p. 690)

volcán Una abertura en la corteza a través de la cual la roca fundida, fragmentos de roca y gases calientes hacen erupción; una montaña formada a partir de los materiales que surgen de una erupción.

volume
An amount of three-dimensional space, often used to describe the space that an object takes up.

volumen Una cantidad de espacio tridimensional; a menudo se usa este término para describir el espacio que ocupa un objeto.

watt W
The unit of measurement for power, which is equal to one joule of work done or energy transferred in one second. For example, a 75 W light bulb converts electrical energy into heat and light at a rate of 75 joules per second. (p. 131)

vatio La unidad de medición de la potencia, el cual es igual a un julio de trabajo realizado o energía transferida en un segundo. Por ejemplo, una bombilla de 75 W convierte energía eléctrica a calor y luz a un ritmo de 75 julios por segundo.

wave
A disturbance that transfers energy from one place to another without requiring matter to move the entire distance. (p. 185)

onda Una perturbación que transfiere energía de un lugar a otro sin que sea necesario que la materia se mueva toda la distancia.

wavelength
The distance from one wave crest to the next crest; the distance from any part of one wave to the identical part of the next wave. (p. 193)

longitud de onda La distancia de una cresta de onda a la siguiente cresta; la distancia de cualquier parte de una onda a la parte idéntica de la siguiente onda.

weathering
The process by which natural forces break down rocks. (p. 543)

meteorización El proceso por el cual las fuerzas naturales fragmentan las rocas.

wedge
A simple machine that has a thick end and a thin end. A wedge is used to cut, split, or pierce objects, or to hold objects together. (p. 158)

cuña Una máquina simple que tiene un extremo grueso y otro extremo delgado. Una cuña se usa para cortar, partir o penetrar objetos, o para mantener objetos juntos.

weight
The force of gravity on an object. (p. 79)

peso La fuerza de gravedad sobre un objeto.

wheel and axle
A simple machine that is a wheel attached to a shaft, or axle. (p. 156)

rueda y eje Una máquina simple que es una rueda unida a una flecha, o a un eje.

work
The use of force to move an object over a distance. (p. 115)

trabajo El uso de fuerza para mover un objeto una distancia.

x-rays
The part of the electromagnetic spectrum that consists of waves with high frequencies and high energies; electromagnetic waves with frequencies ranging from more than 10^{16} hertz to more than 10^{21} hertz. (p. 262)

rayos X La parte del espectro electromagnético que consiste de las ondas con altas frecuencias y altas energías; las ondas electromagnéticas con frecuencias de más de 10^{16} hertzios hasta más de 10^{21} hertzios.

Index

Page numbers for definitions are printed in **boldface** type.
Page numbers for illustrations, maps, and charts are printed in *italics*.

A

abrasion, **544**, *545*
absolute age, **727**, 729, 740
absorption, **269**, 273
abyssal anglerfish, 815
acceleration, **25**, 25–31, *26, 34,* 49–55, *53,* 60
    average, 28
    force, mass, and, 50–53, *50, 51, 52, 53,* 56, *56,* 67, *70, 86*
    gravitational, 78–79, *79, 80, 81,* 123, 148, *149*
    negative, *26, 29, 30,* 31
    velocity, time, and, 25, *26,* 27–31, *28, 30, 34*
accuracy, **R22**
acid rain, 546–547, 582–583, **704**
acid test, 484–485, *485*
acoustics, *231,* **231**
actinides, 341
action and reaction, 57–60, *59, 60, 66, 70,* 85, 158
adaptation, **802**, *803.* See also natural selection.
aeolipile, 109, *109,* 111
aftershocks, **666**
Age of Mammals, 737
ages of rocks, 621, 628–629, 723–729, 740
    absolute age, **727**, 729, 740
    half-life, **727**, *728*
    index fossils, 725–726, 729
    layers, 724–725, 729, *736*
    radioactive dating, 727–729, *728*
    relative age, **723**, 723–724, 729, 740
age structure, 867, *867*
AIDS, 882
air, 372, *372.* See also atmosphere.
    density of, 94
    weight of, *94*
air bags, 47, 408, *408*
air pollution, 547
air pressure, 94, 100–101
air resistance, **89**, *89,* 152
Aleutian Islands, 636
alkali metals, 347
alkaline earth metals, 347
alloys, 348
alluvial fans, **581**
alpine glaciers, 594, *595*
the Alps, *635*
alternative energy sources, 752–753, 767–773
altitude, air pressure and, 94
aluminum, 347, *347*
amber, 716
ammonia, 363, *364*
    molecular structure, 374, *374*
ammonites, 743
amplification, *231,* **231**
amplitude, 192, *193,* **193**, *194, 195,* 205, 231

AM waves, 258, *258*
analysis, critical, R8
ancestor, **809**
    and taxonomy, 826
angle of incidence, 290, *290,* 294
angle of reflection, 290, *290,* 294
anglerfish, 815
angles, measuring, 294
Animalia, *842,* **843**, 844, *844*
animals
    biomass energy, 772
    fossil fuels, 754
    humans, 733, 737
    mammals, 737
    one-celled organisms, 720
    and soil formation, 554, *555*
Antarctica
    fossils, 720
    ice cores, 721
    meteorites, 509
anvil (ear), 215, *215*
apatite, *483,* 490
aperture, 310, *311*
Appalachian Mountains, 640, *640,* 682
Archaea, *842,* **843**, 846, *846,* R64
    domain, 841, *841*
Archean eon, 734–735
Archimedes, 109, *109*
area, **R43**
    force, pressure, and, 91–95, *92, 93,* 104
Aristotle, 108, *108*
armadillo, 809
artificial lenses, 305–306
artificial light, 266–268
ash, 692, *692,* 701, *701*
astatine, 342
asteroids, 716, 737
asthenosphere, **615**, *615,* 621–622, 642, 651
    causes of plate movement, 621–622
    convection currents, **621**, 621–622, *622,* 624–625
    ridge push, 622, *622*
    slab pull, 622, *622*
astronomy, 84
atmosphere, xxxii, **438**, *438,* 441–442, 751
    air pollution, 756–758
    study of, 721
atmosphere (unit of pressure), 94
atomic mass, **337**, 344–345
atomic mass number, **332**
atomic model, *331*
atomic number, **332**
atomic particles, *331,* 331–332
atomic size, 343, *343*

atoms, **xxxvii**, 329–335, 354, *354*, 386–389, 473, *473*, 727
  atomic number, **332**
  change in identity, 350, 352
  in chemical reactions, 393, 395, 397, 403–405, 407
  compounds and, 361–362, 364, *364*, 382
  electrons, **331**, *331*, 331–332, 388
  ion formation, 334–335, 368, 377
  mass, **337**, 344–345
  mass number, 332
  model, *331*
  nanotechnology and, 167
  neutral, 332
  neutrons, *331*, **331**, 332–333, *333*, 350, 354, *354*
  nuclear fission, **765**, *766*
  nuclear power, 765–767, *766*, *767*, 776
  nucleus, *331*, **331**, 354, *354*, 388
  particles, *331*, 331–332
  protons, **331**, *331*, 354, *354*
  radioactive, 350–352
  ratios of, in compounds, 362, 364, *364*
  size, 332, 343, *343*
  structure, 331–332
  types, in Earth's crust, 330, *330*
  types, in humans, 330, *330*
audion, 388
audio tape, 239
automobile. *See* car.
averages, calculating, 120, **R36**
axle. *See* wheel and axle.

B

Bacteria, *842*, **843**, 847, *847*, R64
  domain, 841, *841*
bacteria and soil formation, 554
balanced forces, **43**, 43–47, **45**, 59, **86**
barrier islands, **588**, 588–589, 600
basalt, *511*, *512*
base isolators, 671, *671*
batteries, 387
Beagle, H.M.S., *798*
bears, 828–829, *829*
beetle, bombardier, 413, *413*
Bernoulli's principle, **100**, 100–101, 104
  in nature, *101*
Bernoulli, Daniel, 100
bias, **R6**
  scientific, R6
  sources of, R6
bicycles
  efficiency of, *152*
  forces acting on, *44*
binomial nomenclature, **832**, 832–833, *833*. *See also* taxonomy.
biological evidence, for evolution, 810–812
biological relationships, 826–827, *827*. *See also* taxonomy.
bioluminescence, *264*, **265**, 265–266
biomass energy, 772, **772**, 776
bioremediation, 759
biosphere, **xxxv**, 439, *439*, 441–442, 751
birth, 871. *See also* growth, population.
block-and-tackle system. *See* pulley.

blue jays, 828, *828*
Bohr, Niels, 388
boiling point, of compounds, 377–378
bombs, 692, *692*
bond energy, 410–412
  in endothermic reactions, 411, 413, *413*, 424
  in exothermic reactions, 411, *412*, 424
bonds. *See* chemical bonds.
boundaries of tectonic plates, 626–642
  convergent boundaries, **626**, 634–637, *635*, *636*, *639*, *642*, 684
  divergent boundaries, **626**, 626–632, *627*, *639*, 642
  transform boundaries, **626**, 638, *639*, 642
  volcano formation, 693
Boyle, Robert, 386
braces, 671, *671*
brachiopods, 743
breeding, 801, *801*
bristlecone pine, 844
bromine, 342
Buckland, William, 745
buildings in earthquakes, 670–674, *670–671*
buoyancy, **98**, 98–99, 104, 109
  density and, *99*
Burgess Shale, 855

C

calcite, 476, *480*
calcium, 336, 347, 362, *362*
calcium chloride, 362, *362*, 382
calderas, 696, *696*
Cambrian period, 734
cameras, 310, *311*, 315
  digital, 310, *311*
car, 755, 773, *773*
  catalytic converter, 420, *421*
  design of, xlii–xliii
  fuel-cell powered, xliii, *xliii*
  gas consumption, xliii
  pollution and, xliii, 420, 421
caracals, 825, *825*
carbon, 336, 718, 729
  forms of, 378–379, *379*
  hydrocarbon, 420, *421*
  in living things, 330, 336
carbonates, 476
carbon dioxide, 363, 371, *371*, 414, 418–421, *421*, 439, 692, 703, 772
  formation, 404
  mapping flow of, 462
carbon films, 718, *719*
Carboniferous period, *734–735*
carrying capacity, **862**
  for humans, 878
Cascade Mountains, 637
cast fossils, 718, *719*, 740
catalyst, *400*, **400**, 420
catalytic converter, 420, *421*
catapult, 108, *108*
cats, 825, *825*, 834, *834*
cause-and-effect relationship, **R5**
caverns, 582–583
caves, 521, 582–583

CD (compact disc), 239, *239*
cell phones, 259, *259*, 263
cells
 cone, **304**
 hair (ear), 215, *215*, 232, *232*
 rod, **304**
Cenozoic era, 735, 737
change over time, 731–732, *733*
changes, population, 867–868, *868*. See also growth, population.
Chapter Investigations
 atomic masses, 344–345
 chemical bonds, 380–381
 chemical reactions, 416–417
 creating stream features, 584–585
 earthquakes, 672–673
 field guides, 848–849
 geologic time scale, 738–739
 lenses, 300–301
 mineral identification, 486–487
 natural selection, 806–807
 plate tectonics, 624–625
 rock classification, 530–531
 stringed instrument, 240–241
 sustainable resource management, 886–887
 testing soil, 558–559
 topographic maps, 456–457
 volcanoes, 698–699
 wavelength, 198–199
 wavelength and color, 276–277
 wind power, 774–775
chemical bonds, 361, 367–382
 Chapter Investigation, 380–381
 in chemical reactions, 410–413, *412, 413*
 comparison of, 372, *372*
 covalent, **370,** *370,* 370–372, *371, 372,* 378–379, 382
 electrons and, 367–368, 382
 Internet activity, 359
 ionic, *368,* 368–369, *372,* 377–378, 382
 metallic, **376,** 376–377, *377,* 382
 models, *370*
 polar covalent, **370,** *371, 372*
 properties of substances and, 376–379
 structure of materials and, 373–374
chemical compounds, 358–382
 atoms and, 361–362, 364, *364,* 382
 covalent, 374, *374,* 378
 formulas, 363–364, *364*
 ionic, 369, *372,* 373, 377–378
 names of ionic compounds, 369
 new, 397
 properties, 361–362, 376–379, 382
 with same elements, 364–365, *365*
 structure, 373–374, *374*
 substances and, 361
 synthesis, 397
chemical energy, 128
chemical equations, 404–408
 balancing, 405–408
 coefficients, 406–407
 conservation of mass, 404, 405, 408, 424
chemical formulas, **363,** 363–364, *364*
 how to write, 363

chemical reactions, 390–424, **393,** 424
 atoms and, 393, 395, 397, 403–405, 407
 catalyst in, *400,* **400,** 420
 in catalytic converters, 420, *421*
 Chapter Investigation, 416–417
 chemical changes, 395, *395*
 classification of, 397
 conservation of mass, 402–403, **403,** 404, 405, 408, 424
 electronics and, 422–423, *423*
 endothermic, **411,** *413,* 413–414, 424
 energy changes in, 410–415, 424
 equations of, 404–408
 evidence of, 396, *396,* 424
 exothermic, **411,** *411,* 411–413, *412,* 424
 in firefighting, 409
 in industry, 420–423, 424
 Internet activity, 391
 iodine clock, 401
 in living things, 412–413, 414, 415, 418–419, 424
 photosynthesis, **414,** 414–415, 418, 419
 products, **395**
 rates and factors, 398–400, *399,* 401
 reactants, **395**
 respiration, **418,** 418–419
 thermite reaction, 411, *411*
chemical weathering, **546,** 546–547, 562, 566
Chicxulub crater, 794, *795*
chips, 422–423, *423*
chloride ion, 335, *335,* 368
chlorine, 336, 342, 362, *362*
 atom, 332, 333, *333,* 335, *335*
cichlids, *804,* 804–805
cinder cone volcanoes, 694–695, *695,* 708
cinders, *692,* **692**
cinnabar, 489
class, 834, *834, 835*
classification, 820–825, **824,** 831–838, *R64–R67. See also* taxonomy.
 and binomial nomenclature, **832,** 832–833, *833*
 compared to taxonomy, 824
 and dichotomous keys, **836,** *837*
 and field guides, 838, *838*
 of fossils, 857
 and hierarchy, *834,* 834–836, *835*
 Internet activity, 821
 and Linnaeus, 831
cleavage, **480–481**
climate, 548, 552–553. *See also* environment; weather.
 change over time, 732
 and diversity, 782–785
 effects of volcanoes on, 704
 evidence of continental drift, 619
 ice core studies, 721
 and mass extinctions, 784–785
 and population growth, *879*
clock gene, 813
cloning fossils, 857
closed system, 437
clumped spacing, *866,* 866–867
coal, 519, *519,* 704, 752–753, 755, *755,* 776
coastal mountains, *636,* 637, 642
coastlines, 587–589
cochlea, 215, *215*
cockroaches, 870

coefficients, 406–407
collisions, **66**, *67, 68, 70*. See also momentum.
    of molecules and pressure, 93
colors, 272–275
    mixing, 274, 275, *275*
    primary, *274*, **274**
    reflection and absorption, 273, *273*
    wavelength and, 272–275, 276–277
color spectrum, 273
combustion, *397*, **397**
    gasoline, 420
    methane, 405, *405*, 406, *406*, 412, *412*
    respiration, **418**, 418–419
combustion reaction, 397
compact disc (CD), 239, *239*
compass rose, 445
competition, as limiting factor, 872, *872*, 873
competitors (reproductive), **876**, *876*
composite volcanoes, 695, *695*, 708
compounds. See chemical compounds.
compressional waves, 190
compressions, 216, *216*
computer chips, 758
computer modeling, of fossils, 857
computers
    modeling forces, 111
    scientific use of, xli
concave lens, *297*, **297**
    images formed by, 299
    nearsightedness and, 305, *305*
concave mirror, *292*, **292**, *293*
    in telescopes, 308, *309*
concentration, 398, *399*
cone cells, **304**
conic projections, 449–450
conservation, 563–564, **761**, 776
    natural resources, 760–762
    nonrenewable resources, 752–759
    renewable resources, 767–773
conservation of mass. See law of conservation of mass.
conservation tillage, 563
constants, **R30**
constructive interference, 203, *203*
contact force, *42*
contact lens, 306, *306*
continental-continental collisions, **635**, *635*, 642, 684, **684**, *684, 685*
continental crust, 615, 616, 621
    folded mountains, 684, **684**, *684*, 685
    hot spots, **631**, 631–632, *632*, 693
    rift valleys, 630–631, *630, 631*, 642, 693
    subduction, **634**, 642
continental glaciers, 594, *595*
continents, 615
    coastal mountains, *636*, 637, 642
    continental drift, **618**, 618–623, *620*, 642
    convergent boundaries, **626**, 634–637, *635, 636, 639*, 642, 684
    divergent boundaries, **626**, 626–632, *627, 639*, 642
    formation of, 537, 538
    oceanic-continental subduction, *636*, **637**, 642, 681
    Pangaea, 620, **620**, *620*
    spreading centers, 621, 627
    subduction, **634**, 634–637, 642
    tectonic plates, **616**

theory of plate tectonics, 620–623
transform boundaries, **626**, *638, 639*, 642
contour lines, **453**, *453*, 454–455
contour plowing, 564
control group, 129, R30
convection, **621**, 621–622
convection currents, **621**, 621–622, *622*, 624–625
convergent boundaries, **626**, 634–637, *635, 636, 639*, 642, 684
convex lens, *297*, **297**, *298, 299*, 300–301
    in cameras, 310, *311*
    farsightedness and, 305, *305*
    images formed by, 299, *299*
    in microscopes (objective lens), 308, *309*
    in telescopes (objective lens), 308, *309*
convex mirror, *292*, **292**, *293*
copper, 347, *347*, 382, 471, *473*
    properties of bonds in, 377, *377*
coral reefs, *520*
core, 614, *614*
core of the Earth, 504
cornea, *303*, **303**, 304, 306
    surgery on, 306
covalent bond, *370*, **370**, 370–372, *371, 372*, 378, *379*, 382
covalent compounds
    properties of, 378
    structure of, 374, *374*
Crater Lake, 696, *696*
craters, 694, 702
creep, 576–577
crest, **193**, 206
Cretaceous extinction, 785, 794–795
Cretaceous period, 735
critical analysis, R8
    of statements, R8–R9
crop rotation, 563
cross braces, 671, *671*
crust, **440**, 475–476, 508, *508*, 614, **615**, 622, 623, *623*, 642. See also continental crust; minerals; oceanic crust; rocks.
crystals, 373, **474**, 474–475, *475*
    in igneous rock, 512–513
    of ionic compounds, 369, *369*
    recrystallization, **525**, 527
    size, 512–513
Curie, Marie, 350, 388
Curie, Pierre, 388
current (electrical), 135
cycle, 222
cylindrical projections, 448–449

D

daddy longlegs, 824, *824*
Dalton, John, 331
damage from earthquakes, 664–671, 674
    buildings and structures, *670*, 670–671
    fires, 664, 666
    landslides, *654*, 666
    liquefaction, **666**, 670
    tsunamis, 654, **666**, 666–667, *667*, 701–702

damage from volcanoes, 704
    air pollution, 703–704
    landslides, 701
    lava flows, 700–701
    mudflows, 701–702
    pyroclastic flows, 701
    steam explosions, 702
    volcanic ash, 701, 704
dams, 768, *768*
Darwin, Charles, 798–804
    and natural selection, 801–804
    and population growth, 863
    voyage of, *798–799*, 799–800
data
    analyzing, xli, 463
    describing, R36–R37
data tables, making, R23
dating fossils, 790–791, 856
da Vinci, Leonardo, 110
Davy, Humphrey, 387
dawn redwoods, 855
death, 871. *See also* growth, population.
decibel, **228**, 230, *230*
decimals, 764, **R39**, R40
    adding, R39
    dividing, R40
    multiplying, R40
    in scientific notation, 353
    subtracting, R40
decline, population, 861–863, *862*. *See also* growth, population.
decomposition, *397*, **397**
    of sodium azide, 408
    of water, 395, *395*, 413, *413*
deep-ocean trenches, **636**, *636*, 637, 642
deep-sea vents, 706, *706*
Deep Space 1 (spacecraft), *29*
DeForest, Lee, 388
deltas, **581**, *581*
density, **99**, **482–483**
    air, *94*
    buoyancy and, 99
    mass, volume, and, 99
    of materials, 613
    water, *95*
density, population, **865**, *865*, 865–866. *See also* growth, population.
    as limiting factor, *872*, 873
deposition of soil, 570–604, **573**, 600
    alluvial fans, **581**
    Chapter Investigation, 584–585
    deltas, **581**
    dunes, **589**, 589–590
    floodplains, **580**
    glaciers, 596–598, 600
    loess, **590**, 590–591
    longshore drift and currents, 587–589
    moraines, **596**
    oceans, 574, 586–589
    oxbow lakes, **580**
    till, **596**
desertification, **561**
desert pavement, 591
design, technological, xlii–xliii
destructive interference, 204, *204*

development. *See* evolution.
developmental evidence, for evolution, 812, *812*
Devonian period, 734
diamond, 378, *379*, *382*, 433, 483, 489
dichotomous keys, **836**, *837*
diffraction, **202**, *202*, 202–203, *203*, 206
diffuse reflection, **290**
diffusion, 315, *315*
digital cameras, 310, *311*
dinosaur fossils, 856
dinosaurs
    disappearance, 716
    eggs, 746
    fossil formation, *717*
    hearts, 747
    Mesozoic period, *735*, 736–737
    South Pole, 720
    speed, 722
    theropods, *717*
    trace fossils, 718, *719*, 722
diorite, *512*
direction. *See also* vectors.
    of force, 42, 43, 147, *149*
directions, 445
disease, as limiting factor, *872*, 873
displacement, 99, 104
dissolving, 546–547
distance
    distance-time graph, 20, *21*, 30, *31*, 34
    force, work, and, 115–119
    gravity and, 78, 104
    measuring, 11, 24
    speed and, 16–19, 23, 24, 34
distribution, population, 868, *868*. *See also* growth, population.
    and Darwin, *799*
divergent boundaries, **626**, 626–632, *627*, *639*, 642
diversity, 782. *See also* evolution.
divides, **579**, *581*, 600
DNA, 813–814, *814*. *See also* genetic material.
    and fossils, 857
    and taxonomy, 814, 828
Dobson spectrophotometer, 537
domains, **841**, *841*
    and kingdoms, *841*, *842*, 843–847
Doppler effect, **226**, *227*
Doppler ultrasound, 236
drag, 89. *See also* air resistance.
drainage basins, **579**, 600
drought, 874
dunes, **589**, 589–590, 592

E

ear, 215, *215*
ear canal, 215
eardrum, 215, *215*
Earth. *See also* Earth's history; tectonic plates.
    change over time, xxxv, 536–539
    curvature of, 80, *81*
    gravity, xxxvii, 78, 79
    heat, xxxv, 767
    interior, xxxv
    mass and weight on, *80*

orbit around Sun, 80
processes, xxxv
surface, xxxv
system, xxxv, **437**, 536–539
Earth's history, 613, 712–743. *See also* plate tectonics.
  ages of rocks, 723–729, 740
  change over time, 731–732, 733
  Chapter Investigation, 738–739
  early life, 733, *734*, 736
  first humans, 733
  fossils, 715–721, 740
  geologic time scale, **733**, 733–737, *734–735*, 740
  ice cores, **721**
  Internet activity, 713
  original remains, **716**
  radioactive dating, 727–729, *728*
  tree rings, 720
  uniformitarianism, **732**
  Unit Project, 722
earthquakes, 186, *186*, 187, *187*, 441, 575, 641, 646–676, 732
  aftershocks, **666**
  buildings and structures, 670–674, *670–671*
  Chapter Investigation, 672–673
  damage from, 664–671, 674
  energy release, 655–662
  epicenters, 656, **656**, *656*, 661, *661*, 674
  fault-block mountains, 687–688
  faults, 649–653, 656, 669, 674
  focus, 656, **656**, *656*, 662, *662*, 674
  folded mountains, **684**, *685*
  Internet activity, 647
  landslides, 654, 666, 701
  liquefaction, **666**
  locating, 661, *661*
  magnitudes, 662–663, *665*, 665–666
  moment magnitude scale, 663, *665*, 665–666
  prediction, *668*, 668–669
  primary waves, 658, *659*
  Richter scale, 665–666
  risks of, in the U.S., *668*
  secondary waves, 658, *659*
  seismic gaps, 669, *669*
  seismic waves, **655**, 655–658, *656*, *659*, 674
  seismograms, 660–662, *661*
  seismographs, **660**, 660–662, *660*, *661*
  study of Earth's layers, 614
  subduction zones, 656
  surface waves, 658, *659*
  tectonic plate boundaries, 650, *650*
  tsunamis, 654, **666**, 666–667, *667*, 701–702
  Unit Project, 654
  volcanoes, 697, 701
Earth science, xxxiv. *See also* science.
echolocation, *235*, **235**
Edison, Thomas, 238, 239
efficiency, **150**, *150*, 150–152, *153*
  calculating, 150, *153*
  friction and, *150*, 151, 156
  ideal mechanical advantage and, 160
Einstein, Albert, 84, 111, 330
einsteinium, 330
electric current, 387
electric field, 249–250, *250*

electricity, 128, 135, 146, 151, **754**, 755, 765–767, 776
  acid rain, **704**
  renewable sources, 767–773
electrolysis, 395, *395*
electromagnetic (EM) waves, 246–277, **249**. *See also* laser; light.
  artificial light, 266–268
  as a disturbance, 249–250
  formation of, 250, *250*
  frequencies, 254, 255, 257
  gamma rays, 257, *257*, **262**
  infrared light, 256, *256*, **260**, 260–261, *261*
  Internet activity, 247
  laser light and, 314
  light waves and materials, 269–275, 278
  measuring, 257
  microwaves, 253, *253*, 256, *256*, 259, **259**
  radio waves, 255, 256, *256*, *258*, **258**
  sources of, 250
  spectrum, 256–257
  sunlight, 264–265, 278
  traits, 249–253, 278
  travel of, 251
  ultraviolet light, 257, *257*, *261*, **261**
  uses of, 255–262, 278
  visible light, 257, *257*, **260**
  x-rays, 257, *257*, *262*, **262**
electromagnetic energy, 128
electromagnetic spectrum, *256–257*, **256–257**
electron cloud, *331*, 332, 354, *354*
electrons, **331**, *331*, 331–332, 388
  chemical bonds and, 367–368, 382
  discovery of, 387
  ion formation and, *334*, 334–335, *335*
elements, xxxvii, 329–333, **473**, **727**, *728*
  atoms and, 331
  atoms of, in Earth's crust, 330, *330*
  atoms of, in human body, 330, *330*, 336
  carbon. *See* carbon.
  compounds and, 361–365, 382
  density, trends of, 343
  half-lives, 352, *352*
  halogens, 342, *342*, 349, *349*
  ion formation and periodic table, 368
  metalloids, 350, *350*, 354
  metals, **347**, 347–348
  names and symbols, 330
  noble gases, 349, *349*
  nonmetals, **349**, *349*, 354
  organization of, 337, 354, *354*
  periodic table of, 337–343, **338**, *340–341*, 346–352
  properties of, and compound properties, 361–362
  rare earth (lanthanides), 341, 348, *348*
  reactive, **346**, 347, *347*
elevation, *453*, **453**
  contour lines to show, 455
ellipse, 80
emigration, **871**. *See also* growth, population.
emu, *799*
endothermic reaction, **411**, *413*, 413–414, 424
  Chapter Investigation, 416–417
  photosynthesis, **414**, 414–415, 418, 419

energy, **xxxv**, xxxvii, 121–128, 138
   bond energy, 411, *412, 413*, 424
   chemical, 128
   and chemical reactions, 410–415
   conservation of, **126**, *126, 127*, 128, *138*
   efficiency and, 151, 152
   elastic potential, 122
   electrical, 128, 135, 146, 151
   electromagnetic, 128
   in endothermic reactions, *413,* 413–414, 414–415, 424
   in exothermic reactions, 411–412, *412,* 414–415, 424
   forms of, 128
   kinetic, **122,** *122,* 124, 125–128, *127, 138,* 187
   law of conservation of, **xxxvii**
   mechanical, **125,** 125–128, *127,* 146, 151
   nuclear, 128
   potential, **122,** *122,* 123, 125–128, *127, 138,* 148, *149*
   power, time, and, 133–136
   radiant, 128
   storage and release, 414–415
   thermal, 128, 151
   transfer of, 121–128, *122,* 133–135, *134, 135, 149*
   transformation of, 121, 122, 125–128, *127*
energy sources, 776
   alternative, 752–753
   biomass, **772**
   coal, 752, 755, *755*
   earthquakes, 655–663, 674
   ethanol, 772
   fossil fuels, **754,** 754–759
   geothermal, 705, **770,** 770–771
   heat, xxxv, 767
   hydrogen fuel cells, **772,** 772–773
   natural gas, *756,* 756–757, 767
   non-renewable, 752–759
   nuclear power, 765–767, *766, 767*
   oil, *756,* 756–757, 759
   renewable, 767–773
   solar, 769
   water, 768
   waves, 657
   wind, 771
energy transfer, 185–188
   EM waves, 252, 253
   laser, 314
   sound, 213, 217
engine. *See also* motor.
   efficiency of car, 151, 152
   power of different types, 132
   steam, 109–110, *109, 110,* 132
environment. *See also* habitat.
   human impact on, *883,* 883–885, *884, 885*
   as limiting factor, 872, 873, *873,* 874
   and population growth, 867–868
environmental concerns
   conservation, 760–762
   dams, 768, *768*
   electricity production, 755
   erosion, 752
   fossil fuels, 754–759
   nonrenewable resources, 752–753
   pollution, 755–759

radioactive waste, 767
recycling, 762–763
renewable resources, 767–773
enzymes, 400, *400*
eons, 734, 740
epicenters, of earthquakes, 656, **656,** *656,* 661, *661,* 674
epochs, 734, 740
equations, chemical, 404–408
equator, *10,* **446**
eras, 734, 740
erosion of soil, 570–603, **573,** 600, 752
   Chapter Investigation, 584–585
   creep, 576–577
   desert pavement, 591
   glaciers, 593–598, 600
   longshore drift and currents, 587–589
   mass wasting, 575–577
   mudflows, 576
   oceans, 574, 586–589
   slumps, 576–577
eruptions, volcanic
   effects on air, 703–704
   effects on land, 700–703
   effects on water, 704–706
   monitoring of, 696–697
ethanol, 772
Eukarya, 841, *841,* R64–R67
eukaryotic cells, 841, *841*
European Alps, *635*
Europium, 348
evaluating, R8
   media claims, R8
evidence collection, xl
evidence for evolution, 808–814
   developmental, 812, *812*
   fossil, 809
   genetic, 813–814
   and scientific theory, 808–809
   structural, 810, *811*
evolution, **797,** 797–819
   Darwin's theory of, 799–803
   and early organisms, 792–793
   evidence for, 808–814
   Lamarck's theory of, 798
   and mass extinctions, 795
   and natural selection, 801–805, *803*
   and species evolution, 847
   and taxonomy, 826
exfoliation, **544,** *545*
exothermic reaction, *411,* **411,** 411–413, *412,* 424
   Chapter Investigation, 416–417
   in living things, 412–413, *413,* 419
experiment, **xl.** *See also* lab.
   conclusions, R35
   constants, determining, R30
   controlled, **R28,** R30
   designing, R28–R35
   hypothesis, writing, R29
   materials, determining, R29
   observations, recording, R33
   procedure, writing, R32
   purpose, determining, R28
   results, summarizing, R34
   variables, R30–R31, R32

experimental group, R30
exponents, 254, 353, **R44**
extinction of species, 720, 736
extinctions
    human impact on, 883
    mass, 784–785, 794–795
extrusive igneous rock, **511**, 512, 515
eye. See human eye.
eyepiece lens, 308, *309*
eyesight. See vision.

F

fact, **R9**
    different from opinion, R9
false color images, **460**, *460*
family, 834, *834*, 835
famine, 874
farming
    conservation, 563–564
    soil loss, 561
farming pollution, 884, *884*
farsightedness, 305, *305*, 306
fault-block mountains, **686**, 686–688, *687*
faults, **649**, 649–653, *656*, 669, 674
faulty reasoning, **R7**
Fermi, Enrico, 330
fermium, 330
fiber optics, **313**, *313*
field, 249–250
field guides, 838, *838*
filament, 267, *267*
finches, 800, *800*
    Internet activity, 787
fires, 664, 666, 700, 873
fires and chemical reactions, 419
first law of motion. See Newton's laws of motion.
fishing, excessive, 885
fish, sargassum, 827, *827*
floating. See buoyancy.
floods, 732
fluids, **88**, 88–89, *93*, 93–95, 98–103
    friction in, 88–89, *89*
    pressure in, *93*, 93–95
    transmission of force through, 102–103, 104
fluorescence, **267**, 484–485, *485*
fluorescent light bulbs, **267**, 267–268
fluorine, 342
fluorite, 478, *478*
FM waves, 258, *258*
focal length, *298*, **299**
focal point, *292*, **293**, *297*, *298*
focus of an earthquake, *656*, **656**, *656*, 662, *662*, 674
folded mountains, 684, **684**, *684*, 685
foliated rocks, 528–529
foliation, **528**
force, xxxv, xxxvii, 38–70, **41**, *42*
    acceleration, mass, and, *50*, *51*, *52*, *53*, *56*, *67*, *70*, *86*
    action and reaction, 57–60, *59*, *60*, *66*, *70*, *85*, *158*
    applied, *116*
    area and, 91–95, 104
    balanced, *43*, 43–47, *45*, *59*, *86*
    buoyancy, **98**

centripetal, **54**, *55*, 80, *81*
changing direction of, 42, 43, 147, *149*
contact, *42*
direction of motion changed by, 53–55
distance, work, and, 115–119, *116*, *118*, 138
friction, **xxxvii**, **85**, *85–89*
gravitational, **xxxvii**, 42, *42*, 77–84
input, 146–147, *146*, 149–153, *155*, 160–162
Internet activity, 39
machines, work, and, 145–152, *146*, *147*, 155–162, *155*, *172*
mass, distance, and, 77–85, *78*, 104
multiplication of, 146, 147
needed to overcome friction, *86*, *87*, *104*
net, *43*, 44, *93*, 98, *99*, 149
output, 146–147, *146*, 150–153, *155*, 160–162
physical, xxxv
strong, 111
transmission through fluids, 102–103
types of, 42
unbalanced, *43*, 43–47, *45*, *47*, *70*
waves and, 186
formulas, **R42**. See also chemical formulas.
    wave speed, 196–197
fossil fuels, **754**, 754–759
    coal, 755
    natural gas, *756*, 756–757, 767
    oil, *756*, 756–757, *759*
    plastic, 757
    pollution, 755, 757–759
fossil record, 791, *791*
fossils, 519, *519*, 619, *619*, **715**, 715–720, 740, 744–747, **789**, 789–791, *790*
    carbon films, 718, *719*
    classification of, 857
    and climate changes, 782
    dating, 790–791, 856
    dinosaur, 856
    discovering, 854–857
    as evidence for evolution, 809
    extinction of species, 720
    formation, 717
    history of, 854–857
    hominid, 856
    index fossils, **725**, 725–726
    and Lamarck, 798
    microfossils, 746
    molds and casts, 718, *719*
    one-celled organisms, 720
    original remains, **716**
    petrified wood, 718, *719*
    Phanerozoic eon, 735
    Precambrian time, 735
    protecting, 854
    South Pole, 720
    and taxonomy, 828
    trace fossils, 718, *719*
    types of, 790
    Unit Project, 722
fractions, **R41**
fractures, **481**
frame of reference, *13*. See also motion, observations.
free fall, 83, 90

frequency, 192, *193,* **193,** 194, 206, 242
    Doppler effect and, 227
    electromagnetic, 254, 255
    fundamental tone, 225
    natural, 224
    of sound waves, 221–227, *222*
    wavelength and, 194, *194,* 222
friction, **xxxvii,** 42, 44, **85,** 85–89, *86, 87,* 110
    air resistance, **89,** *89,* 152
    compound machines and, 165
    efficiency and, *150,* 151, 152, 156
    fluids and, 88–89, *89*
    force needed to overcome, *86, 87, 104*
    heat and, *87*
    reducing, 152
    surfaces and, 86–88
    weight and, *87*
Frontiers in Science
    Climate and Life, 782–785
fulcrum, 109, **155,** *155, 162,* 163, *172*
fullerene, 379, *379*
fumaroles, 705
Fungi, *842,* **843,** 846, *846*
fungi and soil formation, 554

G

gabbro, *504,* 511
Galápagos islands
    current research at, 810
    Darwin's voyage to, *798–799,* 799–800
Galilei, Galileo, 44, 110
    theory of motion, 44–45
gallium, 339
gamma rays, 256, *257,* **262**
garnet, 480, *480*
gases, 692
    inert, 349, *349*
    studying, 386
gasohol, 772
gears, *165*
    mechanical advantage of, 165
    used in nanotechnology, *167*
Geiger counter, 350
gemstones, 489, 495
gene, **813**
genetic evidence
    for evolution, 813–814
    for taxonomy, 828–829, *829*
genetic material. See also DNA.
    and natural selection, 802
genus, **832,** *835*
    and binomial nomenclature, 832–833
    and classification, 834
Geographic information systems, **461,** 461–462, *461–462*
geologic time scale, **733,** 733–737, *734–735,* 740
    Chapter Investigation, 738–739
    eons, 734
    epochs, 734
    eras, 734
    periods, 734
geology, 732–740
geometry of gems, 495

geosphere, **xxxv,** *439,* **440,** 441–442, 751
geothermal energy, **770,** 770–771, 776
geysers, **705,** *705*
glaciers, **593,** 593–598, *595,* 600
    alpine, 594, *595*
    continental, 594, *595*
    lake formation, 597–598
    movement, *595*
Global Positioning Systems (GPS), 447
globes, 443–450, 464
Glomar Challenger boat, 621
glow sticks, 412, 418
glucose
    formula, 366
    in respiration, 418–419
glue, 375
glyptodon, *798,* 809
gneiss, *525*
Goddard, Robert H., 111
gold, 330, 332, *332,* 491
Grand Canyon, *736*
granite, 510, *510, 511,* 548
graphite, 379, *379, 382, 481,* 491
graphs, 730
    bar, *711, R7,* R26, R31, R34
    circle, *476, 508, 754, 756, 761, 778,* R25
    distance-time, 20, *21,* 30, 31, *34*
    double bar, R27
    line, *401,* 730, R24, R34
    using, 233
    velocity-time, *30,* 31, *90*
    wave properties, 194, *195*
gravity, **xxxvii,** 42, *42,* 60, **77,** 77–84, *78, 79, 104*
    acceleration, mass, and, 78–79, *79,* 148, *149*
    distance, mass, and, 77–85, *78, 104*
    Earth's, 78–81, *80, 81,* 123
    effect on light, *84,* 111
    energy and, 123, 126, *127*
    erosion, 573
    glacier movement, *595*
    internet activity, 75
    mass wasting, 575–577
    orbit and, 80–83, *81*
    weight and, 79–80, *80*
    work and, 118–119, *119, 158*
Great Lakes formation, 598
Great Rift Valley, 631, *631,* 652, 693
Greek philosophy, theory of motion in, 44, 108
groundwater, 582–583
group, in periodic table, *340, 342,* **342,** 346–350, 354, *354*
growth, population, 861–863, *862, 863,* 870–874
    Darwin's theory of, 863
    factors for, 881–882
    human, 879–883, *881*
    human limitations on, 881–882
    increase and decrease of, 871
    limiting factors of, 872–874
    predicting, 867–868, 881–882
gypsum, *481,* 491

H

habitat
    for human populations, 879, *879*
    and population growth, 867–868
Hadeon eon, 734–735
hair cells, ear, 215, *215*, 232, *232*
hair dryer, energy use of, *135*
Hales, Stephen, 386
half-life, **352, 727,** *728*
halite, 472, *473*. See also salt.
halogen light bulbs, 267, *267*
halogens, 342, *342*, 349, *349*
hammer, 215, *215*
hardness, **483**, 484
Hawaiian Islands, 631, *631*, *632*, 693, 694, 700
health, 755
hearing loss, 232, 233
heat, xxxv, 767. See also energy; energy sources.
    friction and, *87*, 151
heat rays (infrared light), **260,** 260–261, *261*
hematite, *479*
hemoglobin, 336
hertz, **222,** 223, 257
hierarchy, *834*, 834–836, *835*. See also taxonomy.
Himalayas, 635, 653, 684, *685*
history of Earth *See* Earth's history.
HIV, 882
Hoba meteorite, 509
hog farming, 884, *884*
holograms, 312
hominid fossils, 856
horsepower, 132. See also power; Watt.
hot spots, **631,** 631–632, *632*, 693, 707
hot springs, 704–705, *705*
human body, elements in, 330, *330*, 336
human ear, 215, *215*
human eye, 302–304, *303*, 316
    compared with camera, *310*, *311*
    formation of image, *303*, 304
human populations, 878–885
    carrying capacity for, 878
    compared to mice, 814, *814*
    environmental impact of, *883*, 883–885, *884*, *885*
    growth of, 879–883, *881*
    habitat for, 879, *879*
    impact of technology on, 880, *880*
humans, 733, 737, 755
    classification of, 836
humus, **551,** 554, *555*
Hutton, James, 731–732, 745
hydraulics, *103*, 166
hydrocarbon, 420, *421*
hydrochloric acid, 364
hydrogen, 330, 336, 767, 772–773
    compounds of, 364–365
hydrogen fuel cells, **772,** 772–773, *773*, 776
hydropower, **768,** 776
hydrosphere, **xxxv,** *438*, **438**–**439**, 441–442, 751
hypothesis, **xl, R3,** R29

I

ice, 716
    erosion, 574, 600
    glaciers, 593–598
    soil formation, 544, 545
ice ages, 721, 732, 737
icebergs, 594
ice cores, **721**
Iceland, 705
ideal mechanical advantage, 160–162
igneous rock, **506,** *508,* 510–515, 532, 691
    composition, 513
    crystal size, 512–513
    fossil formation, 717
    landforms, 514–515
    origins, 511
    parent rocks, 524
    radioactive dating, 729
    in sedimentary layers, 725
    textures, 512–513
image, **291,** 291–292, *292,* 292–293, *293*, 299, 309
immigration, **871.** See also growth, population.
impact winter, 785
incandescence, **265,** 266–268
incandescent light bulb, 267, *267*
incidence, angle of, 290, *290*, 294
inclined plane, *147*, 148, *149*, 154, **158,** *158*, 159, *160*. See also wedge.
    ideal mechanical advantage of, *160,* 160–161
index contour lines, 455
index fossils, **725,** 725–726, *725, 726*
inert gases, 349, *349*
inertia, **46,** 47. See also momentum.
inference, **R4,** R35
infrared light, 256, *256,* **260,** 260–261, *261*
infrared spectroscopy, 324
infrared waves, 128
infrasound, 222
inner core, **440, 614,** *614,* 642
inner ear, *215*
insects
    abundance of, 844
    new discoveries of, 839
intensity, sound, **228,** 228–232, *230,* 242
interference, **203,** *203,* 203–204, *204*
interior of Earth, *614,* 614–616. See also plate tectonics.
International System of Units, R20–R21
Internet activity
    chemical bonding, 359
    chemical reactions, 391
    earthquakes, 647
    history of Earth, 713
    interior of Earth, 611
    mapping technology, 435
    minerals, 469
    natural resources, 749
    periodic table, 327
    rocks, 501
    soil formation, 541
    volcanoes, 679
    wind erosion, 571
intrusive igneous rock, **511,** 512, 514, *514*

Investigations. *See* Chapter Investigations.
iodine, 342, 370, *370*
    molecular structure, 374, *374*
iodine clock reaction, 401
ionic bond, **368,** *368,* 368–369, *372,* 382
ionic compounds
    names of, 369
    properties of, 377–378
    structures of, 373
ions, **334**
    formation, *334,* 334–335, *335,* 368
    negative, 335, *335, 368,* 368–369
    periodic table and, 342–343, 368, *368*
    positive, 334, *334, 368,* 368–369
iris, 303, *303*
iris, camera, 310, *311*
island arcs, *636,* **636,** 642
isolation of populations, 805
isotopes, **332,** 332–333, *333*
    atomic mass number and, 337
    half-life, 352, *352*
    radioactive, 350, 351–352

J

jaguars, *825*
Japan, 636
jays, 828, *828*
jellyfish, movement of, *57,* 58
joule, **117,** *123, 124,* 131
Jurassic period, 735

K

kangaroos, movement of, *60*
kelp, 845, *845*
kettle lakes, **597**
kilowatt, 131
kinetic energy, **122,** *122, 124,* 125–128, *127, 138,* 187
    of sound waves, 216
kingdoms, 834, *834, 835, 842,* 843–847
    and taxonomy, *841, 842*
    table of, R64–R67
kudzu plant, 883, *883*

L

lab, R10–R35. *See also* experiment.
    equipment, R12–R19
    safety, R10–R11
laboratory equipment
    beaker, R12, *R12*
    double-pan balance, R19, *R19*
    force meter, R16, *R16*
    forceps, R13, *R13*
    graduated cylinder, R16, *R16*
    hot plate, R13, *R13*
    meniscus, R16, *R16*
    microscope, 308, *309,* R14, R14–R15
    ruler, metric, R17, *R17*
    spring scale, R16, *R16*
    test tube, R12, *R12*
    test-tube holder, R12, *R12*
    test-tube rack, R13, *R13*
    triple-beam balance, R18, *R18*
lakes
    formation, 597–598
    kettle, **597**
    oxbow, 580
Lamarck, Jean-Baptiste de, 798
land-dwelling organisms, 793–794
landforms and soil formation, 552
landscape architecture, 565
landslides, 575, 654, 666, 701
Langmuir, Irving, 388
lanthanides (rare earth elements), 341, 348, *348*
laser, *311,* **311,** 311–314, *312*
    fiber optics, *313,* **313**
    future uses, 314, *314*
    making, 312
    visual uses, 312, 313
laser beams, 312, *312*
latitude, 10, *10,* 446, **446–447**
lava, **490,** 510–512, 515, **691,** 700–702
Lavoisier, Antoine, 402–403, *403*
law of conservation of mass, 402–403, **403,** 424
    in chemical equations, 404, 405, 408
law of reflection, **290,** 291, 292, 294
laws of motion. *See* Newton's laws of motion.
layers of Earth, *614,* 614–616, 642
    asthenosphere, **615,** *615,* 642
    continents, 616
    core, 614, *614*
    crust, *614,* **615**
    inner core, **614,** *614,* 642
    lithosphere, **615,** *615,* 615–616, 642
    mantle, *614,* **615,** 642
    outer core, **614,** *614,* 642
leafy sea dragon, 827, *827*
leaves, identifying, *837*
LEDs (light emitting diodes), 268, *268*
legends, **445**
lenses, *297,* **297,** 297–301, 316
    camera, 310, *311,* 315, *315*
    concave, *297,* **297,** 299, 305, *305*
    contact, 306, *306*
    convex. *See* convex lens.
    corrective, 305–306
    eyepiece, 308, *309*
    gravitational, *84*
    human eye, 303, *303*
    long, 315, *315*
    microscope, 308, *309*
    mirrors and, 307
    objective, 308, *309*
    telescope, 308, *309*
    wide-angle, 315, *315*
Leonardo da Vinci, 110
lever, 109, *146, 153,* 154, **155,** *162, 172*
    compound machines using, 164, 165, *166, 172*
    first-class, *155*
    force and, *155*
    ideal mechanical advantage of, *162*
    in human body, 163
    real-world examples, *163,* 164
    second-class, *155*
    third-class, *155*

Lewis, G.N., 388
lift, 101
light
    artificial, 266–268
    bending by gravity, *84*, 111
    color, 272–277
    diffused, 315, *315*
    infrared, **260**, 260–261, *261*
    laser. *See* laser.
    materials and, 269–275, 278
    neon, 268
    optics and 286–315. *See also* optics.
    refraction and, *201*, **201**, 206, 295–296, *296*, *298*
    speed of, 251
    sunlight, 264–265, 278
    ultraviolet, *261*, **261**
    visible, 128, **260**, *311*
    white, 272
light bulbs, 267, *267*
light emitting diodes (LEDs), 268, *268*
light filters, 271, 272
lightning, 196, 220
limestone, 520–521, 548, 582–583
limiting factors, **872**. *See also* growth, population.
    density dependent, *872*, 873–874
    environmental, 872, 873, *873*, 874
Linnaeus, Carolus
    and binomial nomenclature, 832
    classification by, 831–833, 843, 845
    Internet activity, 821
liquefaction, **666**, 670
liquids. *See* fluids; hydraulics; water.
lithium, 330
lithosphere, **615**, *615*, 615–616, 640, 642, 651
    theory of plate tectonics, **622**, 622–623
    volcanoes, 693
living matter, 767
lizard fossils, 854
lobster fishing, 885, *885*
locating earthquakes, 661, *661*
location, ways of describing, 9, *10*
longitude, 10, *10*, *446*, **447**
longitudinal waves, **190**, 194, *194*, 206
long lens, 315, *315*
longshore currents, **587**
longshore drift, **587**
loudness, 228–232, *230*, 242
Lucy (fossil), 856
luminescence, **265**
luster, **480**
lynx, *825*

M

machines, 108–110, **145**, 145–169, *146*, *172*
    compound, **164**, 164–169, *172*
    efficiency of, **150**, *150*, 150–152, **153**
    electronic, 146
    force, work, and, 145–152, *146*, *147*, 155–162, *155*, *172*
    Internet activity, 143
    mechanical advantage of, **147**, 160–162
    perpetual motion, 109, 110
    robotic, 2–5, *2*, *4*, 168, **169**
    simple, 146, **154**, 154–162, 163, *172*. *See also* inclined plane; lever; pulley; screw; wedge; wheel and axle.
magma, **490**, 507, 510–512, *514*, *527*, 691, *691*, 694
magma chambers, *691*
magnesium, 330, 347
magnetic field, 250, *250*
magnetic reversals, **628**, *628*, 628–629, 642
magnets, 485
magnitudes of earthquakes, 662–663, *665*, 665–666
mammals, 737, 753
mammoth, discovery of, 745
mantle, **440**, *614*, **615**, 642
manufacturing
    methods, 167
    robots used in, 169
map legends, **445**
mapping technology, 443, 458–462, 464
    conic projections, 449–450
    cylindrical projections, 448–449
    false color images, **460**, *460*
    Geographic information systems, **461**, 461–462, *461–462*
    Internet activity, 435
    interpreting data, 463
    Mercator projection, 448–449
    planar projections, 450
    remote sensing, 430–433, **458–459**
    satellite imaging, *459*, *460*
maps, 443–450, 464
    Chapter Investigation, 456–457
    contour lines, **453**, *453*, 454–455
    land features, 444
    latitude and longitude, *446*, **446–447**
    legends, **445**
    Mercator maps, 449
    projections, **448**, 448–450
    relief, 444, **453**
    scale, **445**
    slope, **453**
    topographic symbols, 455
    topography, 452–457, *453*, *454*, 464
map scale, **445**
marble, *528*
Mariana Trench, 636
Mars, exploration of, 2–5
Mars Exploration Rover (robot), 3–5, *3*
mass, 46, 49–53
    acceleration, gravitation, and, 78–79, *79*, 148, 149
    force, acceleration, and, 50, 51, 52, 53, 56, 67, 70, 86
    gravitation, distance, and, 77–85, *78*, *104*
    inertia and, 46
    momentum, velocity, and, 64–65, *65*, 70
    volume, density, and, 99
    weight and, compared, 79–80, *80*
mass extinctions, **794**, 794–795
    and climate, 784–785
mass wasting, **575**, 575–577
math skills. *See also* units of measurement.
    area, 516, 549, **R43**
    averages, 120, **R36**, **R37**
    creating a line graph, 599
    decimal, 764, **R39**, R40
    describing a set of data, R36–R37

eliminating outlying values, 120
equivalent rates, 633
exponents, 254, **R44**
finding averages, 869
formulas, 18, 23, 51, 52, 53, 65, 92, 117, 123, 124, 125, 131, 133, **R42**
fractions, 477, **R41**
graphs, using, 233, 730
line graphs, 90, 401
mean, 120, 191, 689, **R36**
measuring angles, 294
median, 191, **R36**
mode, 191, **R37**
multiplication, 663
percents, 153, 477, **R41**
proportions, 451, **R39**
range, **R37**
rates, 633, **R38**
ratios, 153, 366, **R38**
scientific notation, 254, 353, **R44**
significant figures, 56, **R44**
surface area, 549
units, 24
using proportions, 796
volume, **R43**
writing percents, 830
matter, **xxxv,** xxxvii
conservation of, xxxvii
particles and, xxxvii
physical forces and, xxxvii
Mauna Loa volcano, 694, 696, 700
mean, 120, 191, 689, **R36**
measurement. See also geologic time scale; metric system.
acceleration, 28, 51
amplitude, **193**
area, 92, **R43**
density, 99
distance, 11, 24
Earth's gravity, 78
energy, 121
force, 51, 80
frequency, **193,** 206
International System of Units (SI), R20–R21
mass, 51
power, 131, 132
pressure, 92, 94
speed, 18
temperature, R21
using map scales, 445, 451
volume, **R43**
wavelength, **193,** 206
weight, 80
work, 117
mechanical advantage, **147,** 157, 160. See also efficiency; machines.
calculating, 147
compound machines, 165
ideal, 160–162
mechanical waves, **187,** 213, 217
mechanical weathering, 543–545, **544,** *545,* 566
median, 191, **R36**
medicine
from nature, 322–325
radioactivity in, 351

medium, **187,** 188, 217, 218–219, 251, 252, 295, 296, *296*
EM waves, 251, 252
light, 269–275, 278
refraction in, 295, 296, *296*
sound, 217, 218–219
total internal reflection and, 313, *313*
Mendeleev, Dmitri, 338, *338,* 339
Mercator projection, 448–449
mercury, 347
Mesosaurus fossils, 619, *619*
Mesozoic era, 735–737
metallic bond, **376,** 376–377, *37,* 382
metalloids, 350, *350,* 354
metals, 342, **347,** 347–348
alkali, 347
alkaline earth, 347
alloys, 348
properties and bonds, 376–377
reactive, 347, *347*
transition, *347,* 347–348
metamorphic rock, **506,** *508,* 524–529, 532
foliated rocks, 528–529
foliation, **528**
formation, 524–527
metamorphism, **524**
nonfoliated rocks, 529
recrystallization, **525,** 527
metamorphism, **524**
meteorites, 509, 536, 785, 794, *795*
methane, *364*
bonding of, *370,* 370–371
combustion, 405, *405,* 406, *406,* 412, *412*
molecular structure, 374, *374*
metric system, R20–R21
changing metric units, R20, *R20*
converting U.S. customary units, R21, *R21*
temperature conversion, R21, *R21*
microchips, 422–423, *423*
microfossils, 746
microgears, *167*
microgravity, *83*
microorganism fossils, 857
microorganisms and soil formation, 554, *555*
microscope, 308, *309,* R14, R14–R15. See also laboratory equipment.
making a slide or wet mount, R15, *R15*
viewing an object, R15
microtechnology, 166–167
microwave oven, 253, *253*
microwaves, 253, *253,* 256, *256,* 259, **259**
Mid-Atlantic Ridge, 627
middle ear, 215, *215*
mid-ocean ridges, **620,** 620–621, 627, *627,* 642
minerals, 468–499, **471–472,** 503–504, 752–753, 757, 776
acid test, 484–485, *485*
appearance, 478–480
carbonates, 484
Chapter Investigation, 486–487
characteristics, 471–474, 496
chemical makeup, 473
cleavage, **480–481**
color, 479
crystal makeup, 474–475

density, **482–483**
dissolving, 546–547
fluorescence, 484–485, *485*
formation, 472–473, 490, *491*, 496
fracture, **481**
gemstones, 489, 495
grouping, 475 476
hardness, **483**, 484
Internet activity, 469
luster, **480**
magneticism, 485
metamorphic rocks, 528–529
mining, 492–494
note-taking strategies, 470
ores, **492**
properties, 478–485, 496
radioactivity, 485
recrystallization, **525**
remote sensing to find, 432, 433
rust, 547
streak, **479**
uses, 488–489, 496
vocabulary strategies, 470
mining, 492–494, 562, 755
mirrors, 289–293, 316
   concave, *292*, **292**, *293*
   convex, *292*, **292**, *293*
   flat, 291–292, *292*
   lenses and, 307
Mississippi River, 578–579
   deltas, **581**
   floodplains, **580**
moats, 671, *671*
mode, 191, **R37**
Mohs scale, 483, *483*
molds, 846
molds and casts, 718, *719*, 740
molecular structure, 374, *374*
   studying, 324
molecule, **371**
   air, 94
   carbon-based. *See* carbon.
   collision of, 93–95
   fluid, *93*, 93–95
   nanotechnology and, 166–167
   water, *93*, 94, *95*
moment magnitude scale, 663, *665*, 665–666
momentum, **64**, 64–69, *65*, *67*, *70*. *See also* inertia.
   conservation of, **67**, *68*, *69*
   transfer of, 66, *67*
   velocity, mass, and, 64–65, *65*, *70*
money, *758*
Moon
   exploration of, 111, *111*
   mass and weight on, *80*
   orbit around Earth, 80
moraines, **596**, 598
motion, 6–34, **11**, *34*. *See also* inertia; Newton's laws of motion.
   Aristotle and, 108
   Bhaskara and, 109
   circular, 54, *55*
   direction of, force, and, 53–55, *55*, *116*
   direction of, work, and, *116*
   fluids, and, 88–89, *89*, 100–101, 104

force, work, and, 115–119, *116*, *118*, 138, 148–149, *149*
friction and, 42, *42*, 44, 85, 86–87, *86*, *87*
Galileo and, 110
Internet activity, 7
Leonardo da Vinci and, 110
observations, 13–14, 34
perpetual, 109, 110, 126
relative, 13–14, *14*, 34
motors, 151. *See also* engine.
mountains, 441, **444**, *444*, 678–689, 708
   change over time, 732
   continental-continental collisions, *635*, 642, 684
   continental crust, 615
   elevation, *453*, **453**
   erosion, 683, *683*
   fault-block mountains, **686**, 686–688, *687*, 708
   folded mountains, 684, **684**, *684*, *685*, 708
   formation of, 684–686, *685*, 708
   Himalayas, 635, 653, 684, *685*
   mid-ocean ridges, **620**, 620–621, 627, *627*, 642
   oceanic-continental subduction, 681
   plate boundaries and formation of, *635*, 642, 681, 684
   ranges and belts, 682, *682*
   rift valleys, *627*, **627**, 642
   sediment, 683, *683*
   volcanoes, 441, 576
Mount Everest, 681
Mount Pinatubo, 696–697, 702, 704
Mount Rainier, 697
Mount Shasta, 700
Mount St. Helens, 576, 637, 694–695, *695*, 704
Mount Vesuvius, 697
mouse DNA, 814, *814*
mudflows, 576, 701–702
multicellular organisms, **793**
mushrooms, 846, *846*
music, 236–237
musical instruments, 237, *237*, 240
mutation, 802

N

naming species, 832–833, *835*. *See also* taxonomy.
nanotechnology, 166–167, **167**, *167*, 314
natural frequencies, 224
natural gas, 752–753, *756*, 756–757, 767, 776
natural medicines, 322–325
natural resources, 748–779, **751**
   biomass energy, **772**
   Chapter Investigation, 774–775
   conservation, 760–762, **761**
   fossil fuels, **754**, 754–758
   geothermal energy, **770**, 770–771
   hydroelectric energy, **768**, 776
   hydrogen fuel cells, **772**, 772–773
   Internet activity, 749
   nonrenewable resources, **752**, 752–759, 776
   nuclear energy, 765–767
   plastic, 757
   pollution, 755–759
   recycling, **762**, 762–763
   renewable resources, **752**, 752–753, 767–773

solar energy, 769
Unit Project, 759
uses, 751–758, 776
wind, 771
natural selection, **801**, 801–805, *803*. See also evolution.
elements of, 802–803
and speciation, 804–805
nearsightedness, 305, *305*, 306
negative ions, 335, *335, 368,* 368–369
neon lights, 268
Neptunium, 330
neutral atoms, 332
neutron, **331,** *331,* 354, *354*
number of, 332–333, *333*
Newton's laws of motion, 44, 45, *60,* 61, *70,* 109, 110, 111
first, 44–47, **45,** *45, 60*
second, 49–55, **50,** *50, 55, 60,* 78
third, **57,** 57–59, *59, 60, 67,* 68–69
Newton, Sir Isaac, 44, 45, 80, 109, 110
newton (unit of force), 51, *92, 117, 123*
New Zealand, 705
nitrogen, 336, 371, *371,* 554
compounds, 364
noble gases, 349, *349*
nonfoliated rocks, 529
nonmetals, **349,** *349,* 354
nonrenewable resources, **752,** 752–759, 776
normal faults, 652, *652,* 674
normal line, 296, *296*
North American Plate, 650
note-taking strategies, **R45–R49**
combination notes, 40, 144, 184, *184,* 288, *288,* 392, *392,* 542, 572, R45, *R45*
concept map, R49, *R49*
content frame, 680, R45, *R45*
main idea and detail notes, 360, *360,* 436, 572, 648, 750, R46, *R46*
main idea web, 114, 144, 328, *328,* 502, 572, 750, R46, *R46*
mind map, R47, *R47*
outline, 8, 144, 212, *212,* 714, R48, *R48*
supporting main ideas, 76, 144, 248, *248,* 470, 572, 612, 750, R47, *R47*
Venn diagram, R49, *R49*
nuclear energy, 128
nuclear fission, **765,** *766*
nuclear magnetic resonance spectoscopy, 324
nuclear power, 765–767, *766, 767,* 776
nucleus, *331,* **331,** 354, *354,* 388
numbers. See also math skills.
meaningful, 56
outlying, 120

O

objective lens, 308, *309*
observations, **xl, R2,** R5, R33
qualitative, R2
quantitative, R2
obsidian, *504*
ocean floor, 538

oceanic-continental subduction, *636,* **637,** 642, 681, 684, *684,* 685
oceanic crust, 615–616
age, 621
deep-ocean trenches, **636,** *636,* 637, 642
evidence of continental drift, 620–621
folded mountains, 684, **684,** *684,* 685
island arcs, **636,** *636,* 642
magnetic reversals, **628,** *628,* 628–629, 642
mid-ocean ridges, **620,** 620–621, 627, *627,* 642
oceanic-continental subduction, *636,* **637,** 642, 681, 684, *684,* 685
oceanic-oceanic subduction, **636,** *636,* 642, 693
rift valleys, **627,** *627,* 642, 693
subduction, *636,* 636–637, 642
transform boundaries, 638, *639,* 642
trenches, 621
oceanic-oceanic subduction, **636,** *636,* 642, 693
oceans, 537, 538, 539
currents, 439
erosion and deposition, 574, 586–589
ocean waves. See waves, ocean.
ocelots, 825
oil, 752–753, *756,* 756–757, 759, 776
Old Faithful geyser, 705, *705*
On the Origin of Species, 804, 863
opaque materials, 270, *270*
open system, 437
operational definition, **R31**
opinion, **R9**
different from fact, R9
opportunists (reproductive), **875,** *875*
optical fibers, 313, *313*
optical tools, 307–315
optic nerve, 303, *303*
optics, 286–315, **289.** See also visible light.
fiber, *313,* **313**
human eye. See human eye.
Internet activity, 287
lenses and refraction, 295–301
mirrors and reflection, 289–294
photography, 315
technology, 307–314, 316
orbit, **80,** 80–83, *81*. See also force, centripetal.
humans in, 83
velocity needed to achieve, 82
order, 834, *834,* 835
Ordovician period, 734
ores, **492**
organic matter, 551, 554, *555,* 566
organism development, 792–793, *792–793.* See also evolution.
original remains, **716**
oscilloscope, 225, *225*
osmium, 343
outer core, **440, 614,** *614,* 642
outer ear, 215, *215*
outliers, 120
overfishing, 885
overproduction, 802, *803.* See also natural selection.
overtone, 225
oxygen, 439, 537
in combustion, 397, *397,* 405, *405*
compounds, 364–365
in photosynthesis, 365, 414
in respiration, 418–419
ozone, 537

P

Pacific Plate, 650
Pacific Tsunami Warning Center, 667
Paleozoic era, 734–736
pandas, 828–829, *829*
Pangaea, 620, **620**, *620*
paper, 757
parent rocks, 524
particle
    atomic, *331*, 331–332
particle accelerators, 389
Pascal's principle, **102**, 102–103, *102*, 104
Pascal, Blaise, 102
pascal (unit of pressure), **92**, 94
Patterson, Clair C., 536
pendulum, *126*
percents, 153, **R41**
period, *340*, *342*, **342**, 354, *354*
periodic table, 337–350, **338**, *340–341*, 354, *354*
    atomic size and, 343, *343*
    density of elements and, 343
    group, *340*, *342*, **342**, 354, *354*
    halogens, *342*, *342*, 349, *349*
    how to read, 339, *339*
    Internet activity, 327
    Mendeleev's, 338, *338*
    metalloids, 350, *350*, 354
    metals, 347–348
    modern table, 339, *340–341*
    noble gases, 349, *349*
    nonmetals, 349, **349**, 354
    organization of, *339*, 342–343
    period, *340*, *342*, **342**, 354, *354*
    regions, 346, *346*
    trends and patterns, 342–343
periods, geologic, 734, 740
Permian extinction, 784–785, 794
Permian period, 734–735
petrified wood, 718, *719*
Phanerozoic eon, 735–737
Philippine Islands, 636
phonograph, 239
phosphorus, 336
photography, 315
photoresist, 422–423
photosynthesis, **414**, 414–415, 418
    equation, 419
phyllite, *525*, *528*
phylum, 834, *834*, 835
physical evidence, for taxonomy, 828, *828*
physical science, xxxvi. *See also* science.
phytoplankton, 782
Piltdown man, 856
pine trees, 844, *875*
pitch, **221**, *222*, 223, 225, *225*
    Doppler effect and, 226–227
plains, **444**, *444*
planar projections, 450
plane, inclined, *147*, 148, *149*, 154, **158**, *158*, 159, *160*
Plantae, 842, **843**, 844, *844*
plants, 752–754, 757, 772, 776, 877
    and soil formation, 544, *545*, 554, *555*
plastic, 757
plateaus, **444**, *444*

plate tectonics, 610–645, *641*
    asthenosphere, **615**, *615*, 642
    boundaries, 626–641, 650, *650*, 656, 693
    causes of movement, 621–622
    Chapter Investigation, 624–625
    coastal mountains, *636*, 637, 642
    continental-continental collision, **635**, *635*, 642, 684
    continental drift, **618**, 618–623, *620*, 642
    convection, **621**
    convection currents, **621**, 621–622, *622*, 624–625
    convergent boundaries, **626**, 634–637, **635**, *636*, *639*, 642, 684
    core, 614, *614*
    crust, *614*, **615**, 642
    deep-ocean trenches, **636**, *636*, 637, 642
    density of materials, 613
    disturbed layers of rock, 724, *724*
    divergent boundaries, **626**, 626–632, *627*, *639*, 642
    hot spots, **631**, 631–632, *632*, 693
    inner core, **614**, *614*, 642
    Internet activity, 611
    island arcs, **636**, *636*, 642
    layers of Earth, *614*, 614–616, 642
    lithosphere, **615**, *615*, 615–616, 642
    magnetic reversals, **628**, *628*, 628–629, 642
    mantle, *614*, **615**, 642
    mountain formation, 681
    oceanic-continental subduction, *636*, **637**, 642, 684, *684*, 685
    oceanic-oceanic subduction, **636**, *636*, 642, 684, *684*, 685, 693
    outer core, **614**, *614*, 642
    Pangaea, 620, *620*, **620**
    ridge push, 622, *622*
    rift valleys, 630–631, *630*, *631*, 642, 693
    slab pull, 622, *622*
    spreading centers, 621, 627
    subduction, **634**, 634–637, 642
    tectonic plates, **616**, 621–623, *623*
    theory of, 620–623, *622*, 640
    transform boundaries, **626**, 638, *638*, *639*, 642
    Unit Project, 641
platypus, *799*
pneumatic trough, 386
point of view. *See* frame of reference.
polar covalent bond, *371*, **371**, *372*
polarization, *272*, **272**
pollution, 167, 752, 757–758, 884, *884*
    biomass energy, **772**
    cars, 755, 773
    electricity production, 755
    fossil fuels, 756–757, 759
population density, *865*, **865–866**. *See also* growth, population.
population dynamics, **861**. *See also* growth, population.
population growth. *See* growth, population.
population mapping, 461
populations, 858–891. *See also* human populations.
    age structure of, 867, *867*
    changes in, 867–868, *868*
    density of, **865**, *865*, 865–866
    distribution of, 868, *868*
    growth limitations on, 870–874
    human. *See* human populations.
    Internet activity, 859

reproductive strategies of, 875–876
size of, *864*, 864–865
spacing of, *866*, 866–867
stages of, 861–863, *862*
position, **9**, 9–14, *34*. *See also* reference point; motion.
    energy transfer, speed, and, 121
    potential energy and, 122
    ways of describing, *10*
positive ions, 334, *334*, 368, 368–369
postreproductive organisms and age structure, 867
potassium, 336, 347
potential energy, **122**, *122*, 123, 125–128, *127*, *138*, *148*, *149*
power, **130**, 130–135, *132*, *138*
    energy, time, and, 133–135, *134*, *135*, *138*
    everyday usage, *135*
    work, time, and, 130–132, *132*, *138*
power plants, *754*, 755. *See also* electricity.
praseodymium, 348
Precambrian time, *734*, 735
precipitate, *396*, **396**
precision, **R22**
prediction, **xli**, **R3**
    earthquakes, 668–669
    volcanoes, 696–697
predictions, population
    factors for, 867–868
    human, 881–882
prereproductive organisms and age structure, 867
pressure, **91**, 91–96, 524–527
    air, *94*
    area, force, and, 91–95, *92*, *93*, *104*
    atmospheric, *94*
    in fluids, *93*, 93–95, 100–103, *101*, *102*, *104*
    water, *93*, *95*
primary colors, *274*, **274**, 278
primary pigments, *275*, **275**, 278
primary waves, 658, *659*
prime meridian, *10*, *446*, **447**
principal axis, *297*, **297**
prism, *273*, **273**, 296, *296*
products, **395**
projections, **448**, 448–450
projections, population
    factors for, 867–868
    human, 881–882
prokaryotic cells, 841, *841*
propane, *364*
proportions, **R39**
protecting fossils, 855
Proterozoic eon, 735
Protista, *842*, **843**, 845, *845*
protons, *331*, **331**, 354, *354*
    relation to element, and, 332
pulley, *147*, *154*, **156**, *156*, *157*, *172*
    block-and-tackle system, using, 157
    fixed, *156*, 157
    mechanical advantage of, 157
    movable, 157
pumice, *511*
pupil, *303*, **303**
P waves, 658, *659*
pyrite, 480, *480*, 482
pyroclastic flows, **692**, 701

Q

qualitative observations, R2
quantitative observations, R2
quarks, 389
quartz, 422, *422*, 481, *481*, 482, 489, 491
Quaternary period, 735, 737

R

raccoons, 829, *829*
radar, 259
radiation, **xxxv**, **251**
radioactive dating, 727–729, *728*
radioactive waste, 767
radioactivity, **350**, 388, 485
    detection, 350
    medical uses, 351, *351*
radiometric dating, 856
radio waves, 255, *256*, *258*, **258**
radius, 161
rainbows, 296, *296*
rainfall, 720
ramp. *See* inclined plane.
random spacing, *866*, 866–867
range, **R37**
range, population, 866
rare earth elements (lanthanides), 341, 348, *348*
rates, 17, 633, **R38**
ratios, 153, 366, **R38**
reactants, **395**
    changes in, 398–399, *399*
reaction, 57–60, *59*, *60*, 66, 77, 85, 158
reactions. *See* chemical reactions.
reactive, **346**
reactive metals, 347, *347*
reasoning, faulty, **R7**
reconstruction, evolutionary, 792–793
recrystallization, **525**, 527
recycling, **762**, 762–763, 776
Red Sea, 630
reference point, **10**, *10*, 34
reflecting telescope, 308, *309*
reflection, *201*, **201**, 206, 273, 289, 290, 315
    angle of, 290, *290*, 294
    diffuse, **290**
    law of, **290**, 291, *292*, 294
    in photography, 315, *315*
    regular, *290*, **290**
    total internal, 313, *313*
refracting telescope, 308, *309*
refraction, *201*, **201**, 206, 315
    of light, 295–296, *296*, 298
    in photography, 315, *315*
    rainbows and, 296, *296*
regular reflection, *290*, **290**
relative age, **723**, 723–724, 729, 740
relief, **453**, *453*
relief maps, *444*, **444**
remote sensing, 430–433, **458–459**
renewable resources, **752**, 752–753, 767–773, 776
    biomass energy, **772**
    geothermal energy, **770**, 770–771

hydroelectric energy, **768**, *768*
hydrogen fuel cells, **772**, *772–773*
solar energy, 769
wind energy, 771
reproductive organisms and age structure, 867
reproductive strategies, 875–876
resonance, **224**
respiration, **418**, 418–419
    equation, 419
retina, *303*, **303**, 304, 305–306
reverse faults, *652*, 652–653, 674
rhyolite, 510, *510*, *511*
Richter scale, 665–666
ridge push, 622, *622*
rift valleys, **627**, *627*, **630**, 630–631, *631*, 693
Ring of Fire volcano belt, 693, *693*
robins, 824
robots, 2–5, *2*, *4*, *168*, **169**, *169*
    Mars exploration and, 2–5
rock cycle, 503–508, **506**, *507*, 532
rocket, 111
rock folds, 684, *684*, *685*
rocks, 472, 500–525, **503**, 740, 752–753, 776
    absolute age, 727, 729
    ages, 621, 628–629, 723–729, 740
    asthenosphere, 651
    Chapter Investigation, 510–511
    classification, 505–506
    continental drift, 619, 621, 642
    cycle, 503–508, **506**, *507*
    erosion, 683, *683*
    fossils, **715**, 715–721
    from space, 509
    half-life, **727**, *728*
    igneous, **506**, 508, 510–515, 532, 691, 717, 725, 729
    Internet activity, 501
    lava, 510–512, 515
    layers, *724*, *725*, *736*, 744
    lithosphere, 651
    magma, **490**, *507*, 510–512, 691, *691*, 694
    magnetic reversals, **628**, *628*, 628–629, 642
    mechanical weathering, 543–545
    metamorphic, **506**, 508, 524–529, 532
    movement along faults, 649–651
    note-taking strategies, 502
    on the sea floor, 628–629
    porous/nonporous, 756
    radioactive dating, 727–729, *728*
    sedimentary, **506**, 508, 517–523, 532, 683, *683*, 717–718, 723–724, *724*, 729, *736*
    soil formation, 543–548
    till, **596**
    uses, 504–505
    vocabulary strategies, 502
    volcanic ash, cinders, and bombs, **692**, *692*, 701, *701*
rockslides, 575
Rocky Mountains, 682
rod cells, **304**
roses, 824
rounding numbers, 56
ruby crystal, 312, *312*
rust, 546–547, *547*

S

safety, R10–R11
    animal, R11
    chemical, R11
    clean up, R11
    directions, R10
    dress code, R10
    electrical, R11
    fire, R10
    glassware, R11
    heating, R10
    icons, R10–R11
    lab, R10–R11
    sharp object, R11
salmon, 802, *803*
salt, 490, 495, 521, 546. *See also* sodium chloride.
Salton Sea, 884, *884*
San Andreas Fault, 638, **638**, 650, 653
sand, *476*, 556
    dunes, **589**, 589–590, 592
    longshore drift and currents, 587–589
    plants and animals in, 592
    in sedimentary rock, 517–518, 523
sandbars, **588**, 600
sargassum fish, 827, *827*
sargassum seaweed, 827, *827*
satellite mapping, 458–460, *459*, *460*
scale, **445**
scanning tunneling microscope (STM), 375, 389
scattering, *271*, **271**
schist, 524, *524*, *525*
Schmitt, Harrison "Jack", 539
science, nature of, xxxviii–xli
Scientific American Frontiers, 2, 4
scientific notation, 254, 353, **R44**
scientific process, xxxviii–xli
    asking questions, xxxix
    determining what is known, xxxix
    interpreting results, xli
    investigating, xl
    sharing results, xli
scientific theory, 808–809
screw, 154, *158*, **159**, *159*
sea dragon, leafy, 827, *827*
sea floors. *See* oceanic crust.
seahorse, 827, *827*
seat belts, *47*
seaweed
    kelp, 845, *845*
    sargassum, 827, *827*
secondary waves, 658, *659*
second law of motion. *See* Newton's laws of motion.
sediment, **517**, 683, *683*
sedimentary rock, **506**, *508*, 517–523, 532, 682, *682*
    caves, 521
    coal, 519
    disturbed layers, *724*
    formation, 518–519, 522
    fossil formation, 717–718, 729
    igneous rock in, 725
    layers, 522–523, *736*
    limestone, 520–521
    parent rock, 524

radioactive dating, 729
re-formed from dissolved minerals, 521
relative age, **723**, 723–724, 729, 740
undisturbed layers, *724*
seeds, survival of, 877
seismic gaps, 669, *669*
seismic waves, **655**, 655–659, *656*, *659*, 674
seismograms, 660–662, *661*
seismographs, **660**, 660–661, 660–662, 674
selection, *803*. *See also* natural selection.
semiconductors, 350, 353, *353*, 422
sensors, **459**
shale, 524, *524*, 525
shaping the land, 600
    water, 578–589
    wind, 589–592
sharp objects, R11
shear walls, 671, *671*
shield volcanoes, 694, *694*, 708
Sierra Nevada, 688
significant figures, 56, **R44**
silica, 691
silicates, 475, 513
silicon, 422–423, *423*, 769
   in Earth's crust, 330
Silurian period, 734
sinkholes, **583**
sinking. *See* buoyancy.
SI units, R20–R21
size of Earth, 621
size, population, *864*, 864–865
skydiving, *89*
slab pull, 622, *622*
slate, *525*
slides, making, R15, *R15*
slope, *453*, **453**
slope (steepness), 148, *149*, 160
slumps, 576–577
Smith, William, 745
smog, 756
sodium, 336, 347, *347*
   ion, 334, *334*
sodium azide, 408
sodium chloride, 369, *369*, 372
soil, 573
   erosion, 752
   formation, 700, 702
soil conservation, 563–564
soil deposition. *See* deposition of soil.
soil erosion. *See* erosion of soil.
soil formation, 540–548, 550–553. *See also* deposition of soil.
   chemical weathering, 546–547, 566
   climate, 548, 552–553
   composition, 551
   fertilizer use, 561
   Internet activity, 541
   living organisms, 554, *555*
   mechanical weathering, 543–545, **544**, *545*, 566
   nutrients, 554, 557, 560
   organic processes, 551, 554, *555*, 566
   rates of weathering, 548
soil horizons, *552*, **552**
soil profile, **552**

soil properties
   chemistry, 557
   color, 557
   pore space, 557
   texture, 556
soil use, 560–565, 566. *See also* erosion of soil.
   Chapter Investigation, 558–559
   conservation, 563–564
   construction and development, 562
   farming, 561, 563–564
   land-use practices, 561–563
   mining, 562
   water purification, 560
solar cells, **769**, 776
solar energy, 769, *769*, 776
solar system, 539
solids, 473, 474–475
sonar, *235*, **235**
sonic booms, 220, *220*
sound, 190, 210–241, **213**, 242
   acoustics, *231*, **231**
   in air, 216, *216*, 217, 218–219
   amplification, *231*, **231**
   changes in, 221
   different materials and, 218
   Doppler effect, **226**, 227
   frequency and pitch, 221–227, *222*, 242
   intensity, **228**, 228–232, *230*, 242
   Internet activity, 211
   loudness, 228–232, *230*, 242
   mediums, 217, 218–219
   music, 236–237
   pitch, **221**, *222*, 223, 225, *225*, 226–227, 242
   quality, 225
   recorded, 238, 239, *239*
   sonic booms, 220, *220*
   speed of, 218–220
   temperature and, 219
   ultrasound, 178–181, **222**, 223, 234–236
   uses of, 178–181, 234–239, 242
   vibration, **213**, 214, 216
   as a wave, 213–220, *216*, 242
sound frequencies, 221–227, *222*
   heard by animals, 223
   high and low, 222
   natural, 224
   sound quality, 225
sound waves, 190, 214, 657
   detection of, 215, *215*
   mechanical wave, 213
   production of, 214, *214*
   vibration of particles, *216*, 216–217
South Pole, 720–721
spacecraft, *29*, *53*, 81–83, *83*, 169
   velocity needed to achieve orbit, 82
space elevator, 314, *314*
space rocks, 509
space station, 539
space travel, 769, 772
spacing, population, *866*, 866–867
speciation, **804**, *804*, 804–805
species, 834, *834*. *See also* taxonomy.
   and binomial nomenclature, 832–833
   and classification, 834
   development of, *804*, 804–805

evolution of, 847
and genus, 832–834
introduced, 868, *868*, 883, *883*
naming, 832, 833, *835*
spectroscopy, 324
speed, 12, **16,** 16–23, *17, 18, 23, 34.* See also velocity.
average, 19, 23
instantaneous, 19
of light, 218, 251
relation to velocity, 22–23
time, distance, and, 16–23, *17, 18, 20, 21, 24, 34*
using distance-time graph to show, 20, *21*
stability, population, 861–863, *862*
stages of population growth, 861–863, *862, 863.* See also growth, population.
Standardized Test Practice, 37, 73, 107, 141, 175
analyzing data, 73
analyzing descriptions, 427
analyzing experiments, 245
analyzing graphics, 175
classification, 853
common ancestors, 819
earthquakes, 677
history of Earth, 743
interpreting diagrams, 107, 209, 281, 319
interpreting graphs, 37
interpreting tables, 357, 385
minerals, 498
natural resources, 779
plate tectonics, 645
population growth, 891
rocks, 535
shaping the land, 603
soil formation, 569
understanding experiments, 141
views of Earth, 467
volcanoes, 711
starlings, 868, *868*
steam engine, 109–110, *109, 110,* 132
steam explosions, 702
steering wheel, example of wheel and axle, 156
Steller's jays, 828, *828*
Steno, Nicolaus, 744
stirrup, 215, *215*
streak, **479,** 488
streams, 579, *581*
alluvial fans, **581**
channels, 580
deltas, **581**
stress, **649**
strike-slip faults, 653, *653,* 674
strip cropping, 564
structural evidence, for evolution, 810, *811*
subduction, **634,** 634–637, 642, 693
subscripts, **363**
in chemical equations, 407
in chemical formulas, 363–364
sulfur dioxide, 703–704
sunlight, 264–265, 278, 752–753, 756, 767, 769, 776
effects of volcanoes on, 704
formation of fossil fuels, 754
supersonic speed, 220
surface area, 548. See also pressure.
air resistance and, *89*
in chemical reactions, 398–399, *399*

surface waves, 658, *659*
survival, of seeds, 877
synthesis reaction, *397,* **397**
synthetic compounds, 324–325
system, Earth, **437**
systems. See energy, conservation of; momentum, conservation of.

T

tables, R23
taking notes. See note-taking strategies.
tar, 716
taxon, **826**
taxonomy, **824,** 826–829, 840–847. See also classification.
compared to classification, 824
development of, 840
and DNA, 814
and domains, **841,** *841*
genetic evidence for, 828–829, *829*
physical evidence for, 828, *828*
and species evolution, 847
technology. See also DNA; genetic evidence.
acoustical engineering, 231, *231*
age of solar system, measuring, 536
alloys, 348
applications of Bernoulli's Principle, 101
audiogram, 233, *233*
battery, 387
cameras, 310, *311,* 315
catalytic converter, 420, *421*
catapult, 108
cell phone, 259, 263
chemical technology, 420
cochlear implants, 180–181
compound machines, **164,** 164–166, *166*
computer modeling, 111
core sample collection, 538, *538,* 621, *621*
corrective lenses, 305–306
earthquake-resistant buildings, *670,* 670–671, *671*
electrical energy and appliances, 135, *135*
electrolysis, *395,* 395
electronic products, 422–423, *423*
elements in industry, 347–350
exploration of Earth, 437–442
false-color images, 430–431, 435, **460,** 460
fiber optics, **313**
and fossils, 854, *854,* 856, *856,* 857
gamma rays, *257,* **262**
Geographic information systems (GIS), **461,** *461,* 461–462, 462
Global Positioning System (GPS), 447
holograms, 284, 312
and human population growth, 880, *880*
hydraulics, 103
hydrogen fuel cells, xliii, **772,** 772–773, *773,* 776
infrared light, *256,* **260,** 260–261
International Space Station, 538
lasers, 285, **311,** 311–312, 314
lighting, 266–268
machines, 142–171, **145**
mapping, 458–462
microchips, 422–423

microscopes, 308, *309*
microwaves, 253, *256*, **259**
minerals, uses of, 488–489
miniaturization, 166
musical instruments, 236–237, *237*
nanotechnology, **167**
nature of, xlii–xliii
objects used to do work, 119, *119*
optics, 286, 315, **289**
oscilloscope, 225, *225*
ozone levels, measuring, 537
particle accelerator, 389, *389*
particle detector, *xxxviii*
PCR, 857
photography, 315
radar, 259
radio waves, *256*, **258**
radioactive dating, 727–729, *728*
radioactivity in medicine, 351
radiometric dating, 790, 856, *856*
recorded sound devices, 239
remote sensing, 430–433, **458**, 458–459, *459*
robot, 2–5, *2*, *4*, *168*, **169**
scanning electron micrograph, *239*
scanning tunneling microscope, xl, *xl*, 375, 389
seismographs, **660**, *660*, *661*
semiconductor, 350, 422
sonar, **235**, *235*
sonic boom, 220, *220*
spacecraft, 29, *81*, *82*, 111
spectroscopy, 324
steam engine, 109–110
telephone, 238, *238*
telephones as example of changes in, 797, *797*
telescope, reflecting and refracting, 283, *283*, 308, *309*
tracking plate movement with lasers, 633
ultrasound, *179*, 179–181, **222**, 234–236
ultraviolet light, *257*, **261**
volcanoes, monitoring of, 606–609, 697
x-rays, *257*, **262**
tectonic plates, **616**, 621–623, *623*. See also plate tectonics.
telephone, 238, *238*, 259
telescope, *256*, 283, *283*, 308, *309*
television, 256, 258
temperature, 399, *399*, R21, *R21*
 inside the Earth, 510
 metamorphic rock, 524–527
 reaction rate and, 399, *399*
 speed of sound and, 219
 unit conversion, R21, *R21*
terminal velocity, 89, 90
terraces, 564
Terra satellite, 608–609, *609*
Tertiary period, 735, 737
theory of plate tectonics, 620–623, **622**, 622–623, 640. See also plate tectonics.
theory, scientific, 808–809
thermal energy, 128
thermite reaction, 411, *411*
theropods, *717*, 746
third law of motion. See Newton's laws of motion.
till, **596**

timbre, 225
time. See geologic time scale.
 distance, speed, and, 16–23, *17*, *18*, *20*, *21*, 24, 34
 distance-time graph, 20, *21*, *30*, 31, *34*
 energy, power, and, 133–135, *134*, *135*, 138
 velocity, acceleration, and, 25, *26*, 27–31, *28*, *30*, 34
 velocity-time graph, *30*, 31, *90*
 work, power, and, 130–132, *132*, 138
Timelines in Science
 fossils, 854–857
timeline, understanding forces, 108–111
topography, **452**, 452–457, *453*, *454*, 464
topsoil, 552
tortoises, Galápagos, 800
total internal reflection, 313, *313*
trace fossils, 718, *719*
traits, 826
 and DNA, 813–814
transform boundaries, **626**, *638*, *639*, 642
transition metals, *347*, 347–348
translucent materials, 270, *270*
transmission, **269**, 270–271
transparent materials, 270, *270*
transverse waves, **189**, 206
 graph of, *194*, *195*
trash, 761
trees, 720, 752–753, 776
trees and soil formation, 554
T. rex, 722
Triassic period, 734–735
trilobites, 743
trough, **193**, 206
tsunamis, 205, *205*, 654, **666**, 666–667, *667*, 701–702
tungsten, 267, *267*
turtles, 834–836, *835*
Tyrannosaurus, rex, 747

U

ultrasound, 178–181, **222**, 223, 234–236
ultrasound scanner, 178–181, 236, *236*
ultraviolet light, 257, *257*, *261*, **261**
unicellular organisms, **792**
uniformitarianism, **732**
uniform spacing, *866*, 866–867
United States Geological Survey (USGS), 455
Unit Projects
 earthquakes, 654
 fossils, 722
 gem cutting, 495
 landscape architecture, 565
 life on the dunes, 592
 mapping for an Olympic Stadium, 463
 oil spills, 759
 plate tectonics, 641
 rocks from space, 509
 volcanoes, 707
units of measurement, 24. See also metric system.
 decibel, **228**
 hertz, **222**, 223, 257
 horsepower, 132
 joule, 117
 kilogram, 51
 kilogram-meter per second (kg·m/s), 65

kilometers per hour (km/h), 23
meters per second (m/s), 18, 24
meters per second squared (m/s^2), 28, 51
newton, 51–53
pascal, 92
watt, 131
wavelength, **193**, 206
uranium, *766*, 766–767, 776
uranium 235, 727–729, 752–753

V

vacuum, **217**, 251
    EM waves and, 251
vacuum, acceleration in, 79
valleys, 580
variables, **R30**, R31, R32
    controlling, R17
    dependent, **R30**, R31
    independent, **R30**
    isolating, 129
variation, 802, *803*. See also natural selection.
vector, **22**, *22*
    acceleration, 26
    of force, 42
    momentum, 65
    velocity, *22*
velocity, **22**, *22*, 25–31, *26*, *34*. See also speed.
    acceleration, time, and, 25, *26*, 27–31, *28*, *30*, *34*
    average, 23
    escape, 82
    kinetic energy, mass, and, 124, 126
    momentum, mass, and, 64–65, *65*, *70*
    needed to achieve orbit, 82
    relation to speed, 22–23
    terminal, *89*, *90*
    velocity-time graph, *30*, 31, *89*, *90*
vestigial organs, **810**, *811*
vibration, **213**, 214–215, *216*
views of Earth, 434–467
    Internet activity, 435
    mapping, 458–462
    maps and globes, 443–450, 464
    note-taking strategies, 436
    topography, 452–457
    using technology, 437–442, 458–462, 464
    vocabulary strategies, 436
visible light, 257, *257*, **260**, *311*. See also optics.
vision, 302–306
    correction of, 305–306
    farsightedness, 305, *305*, 306
    formation of images, *303*, 304
    nearsightedness, 305, *305*, 306
vocabulary strategies, 714, R50–R51
    description wheel, 8, 114, 212, *212*, 288, *288*, 360, *360*, 470, 542, 612, R50, *R50*
    four square, 76, 114, 184, *184*, 288, *288*, 392, *392*, 572, 714, 750, R50, *R50*
    frame game, 248, *248*, 288, *288*, 328, *328*, R51, *R51*
    magnet word, 40, 114, 502, 542, 648, 714, R51, *R51*
    word triangle, 144, 436, 542, 680, 714, R51, *R51*
vocal cords, 214, *214*
volcanic ash, 692, *692*, 701, *701*, 704
volcanic bombs, 692, *692*

volcanic cinders, 692, *692*
volcanic gases, 692, 703–704
volcanoes, 440, 576, 606–609, 630, 641, **690**, 690–711, 721, 732, *733*. See also lava; specific volcanoes, e.g. Mount St. Helens.
    benefits from, 700, 702
    calderas, 696, *696*
    Chapter Investigation, 698–699
    cinder cones, 694–695, *695*, 708
    coastal mountains, *636*, 637, 642
    composites, 695, *695*, 708
    craters, 694, 696, *696*, 702
    damage from, 700–704
    dangers of, 701–702
    deep-sea vents, 706, *706*
    eruptions, signs of, 697
    formation, 637, 642, 693, 708
    fumaroles, 705
    geysers, **705**, *705*
    hot spots, **631**, 631–632, 693, 704–705, 707
    hot springs, 704–705, *705*
    Internet activity, 679
    landslides, 701
    lava, **691**, 700–702
    magma, 691, *691*, 694
    magma chambers, *691*
    monitoring, 606–609, 696–697, 707
    mudflows, 701, 702
    oceanic-oceanic subduction, 693
    pyroclastic flow, **692**, 701
    Ring of Fire belt, 693, *693*
    rock fragments, 692, *692*
    shapes and sizes, *694*, 694–696, *695*
    shield volcanoes, 694, *694*, 708
    steam explosions, 702
    structure, *691*
    subduction zones, 693, *693*
    Unit Project, 707
Volta, Alessandro, 387
volume, **R43**
    buoyancy and, 109
    displacement and, 99, 104
    mass, density, and, 99

W

water, xxxiii, xxxv, *93*, 94, 95, *364*, 365, *365*, 371, *371*, *372*, 579, 692, 752–753, 767–768, 776. See also buoyancy; hydraulics.
    alluvial fans, **581**
    caverns, 582–583
    chemical weathering, 546–547
    deltas, **581**
    divides, **579**
    drainage basins, **579**
    and early organisms, 793–794
    electrolysis, 395, *395*, 413, *413*
    erosion, 573–574, 600
    floodplains, **580**
    groundwater, 582–583
    hot springs, 704–705
    and human technology, 880, *880*
    hydroelectric energy, **768**, 776
    hydrosphere, **xxxv**

landscape architecture, 565
  as limiting factor, 874
  longshore drift and currents, 587–589
  meanders, 580
  molecular structure, 374, *374*
  physical states, 394, *394*
  pollution, 561, 562, 757–758
  pressure in, *93*, *95*
  purification of, 560
  sedimentary rock, 522–523
  shaping the land, 578–589, 600
  soil formation, 544, *545*, 546–547
  streams, 579–580, *581*
  used to power machines, *119*
  waves, 586–589
water waves. *See* waves, ocean.
water wheels, *119*
Watt, James, 110, 132
watt (unit of power), **131**
wavelength, 192, *193*, **193**, 206
  color and, 272–275, 276–277
  frequency and, 194, *194*, 222
waves, 182–205, **185**, 586–589, 600, 657–658, *659*
  AM (amplitude modulation), 258, *258*
  amplitude, 192, *193*, **193**
  behavior, 200–204
  classification, 188–190
  compressional, 190
  diffraction, **202**, *202*, 202–203, *203*, 206
  electromagnetic, 246–277. *See also* electromagnetic waves.
  energy and, 185–190
  FM (frequency modulation), 258, *258*
  frequency, 192, *193*, **193**, 194, 206. *See also* frequency.
  height, 191, 192
  Internet activity, 183
  light. *See* light.
  longitudinal, **190**, 194, *194*, 206
  mechanical, **187**, 213, 217
  medium. *See* medium.
  model, *188*
  ocean, 186, 188, 189, 191, 196–197
  properties, 192–197
  reflection, *201*, **201**, 206, 290–293, *290*, *292*, *293*
  refraction, *201*, **201**, 206, 296, *296*, *298*
  rope, 185, 186, *186*, 189, *189*
  sound, 190, 210–241. *See also* sound; sound waves.
  speed of, 192, 196–197, 220
  transverse, **189**, 194, *195*, 206
  wavelength, 192, *193*, **193**, 194. *See also* wavelength.
weather, 438–439, 441–442, 704, 720, 873. *See also* climate.
  acid rain, 546–547
  soil formation, 548, 552–553
weathering, **543**
  chemical, 546–548, 566
  mechanical, 543–545, 548, 566
  rates, 548
  soil formation, 543–548, 550–553
wedge, 154, **158**, *158*, 159
  compound machines using, 165, *172*
  real-world examples, *158*, 159
  used to hold objects together, 159
  used to separate objects, 159
Wegener, Alfred, 618–620
weight, **79**
  friction and, 87
  gravitation and, 79–80, *80*
  mass and, compared, 79–80, *80*
weightlessness, *83*
wet mount, making a, R15, *R15*
whales, 95
wheel and axle, 154, **156**, *156*, *161*, *172*
  compound machines using, 164–165, *165*, 166, *172*
  mechanical advantage of, *161*, 165
  real-world examples, 156, *159*, *161*
white light, 272
wide-angle lens, 315, *315*
wildfire, 873
wind, 752–753, 767, 771, 774–776
  deposition, 589–591, 600
  erosion, 571, 574, 600
  Internet Activity, 571
  sedimentary rock, 522–523
  used to power machines, 119
windbreaks, 564
windmills, 119, 771, *771*
wings, 101
wood, 757, 772
work, **115**, 115–135, *118*, *138*
  distance, force, and, 115–119, *116*, *118*, *138*, 148–149, *149*
  energy transfer and, 121, 126, *127*
  gravitation and, 118–119, *119*
  input, 150–152, *150*, 153
  Internet activity, 113
  machines, force, and, 145–152, *146*, *147*, 155–162, *155*, *172*
  output, 150–152, *150*, 153
  time, power, and, 130–132, *132*, *138*

x-rays, 257, *257*, 262, **262**, 324

yeasts, 846, *846*
Yellowstone National Park, 632, 704–705, *705*, 707

zebra mussels, 883
zincite, *482*

Acknowledgments

Photography

Cover © Grafton Marshall Smith/Corbis; **i** © Grafton Marshall Smith/Corbis; **iii** *left (top to bottom)* Photograph of James Trefil by Evan Cantwell; Photograph of Rita Ann Calvo by Joseph Calvo; Photograph of Linda Carnine by Amilcar Cifuentes; Photograph of Sam Miller by Samuel Miller; *right (top to bottom)* Photograph of Kenneth Cutler by Kenneth A. Cutler; Photograph of Donald Steely by Marni Stamm; Photograph of Vicky Vachon by Redfern Photographics; **vi** © Arthur Tilley/Getty Images; **vii** © Mike Chew/Corbis; **viii** © Chip Simons/Getty Images; **ix** © Alan Kearney/Getty Images; **x** © Digital Vision/PictureQuest; **xi** From General Chemistry by P. W. Atkins, © 1989 by Peter Atkins. Used with permission of W.H. Freeman and Company; **xii** © Steve Starr, Boston Inc./PictureQuest; **xiv** © Robert Patrick/Corbis Sygma; **xv** © Douglas Peebles; **xvi** *bottom* © Richard T. Nowitz/Corbis; **xvii** © Burke/Triolo/Artville: Bugs and Insects; **xxii–xxiii** Photographs by Sharon Hoogstraten; **xxxii–xxxiii** © Nick Vedros & Assoc./Stone/Getty Images; **xxxiv–xxxv** Doug Scott/age fotostock; **xxxvi–xxxvii** © Galen Rowell/Corbis; **xxxviii** AP/Wide World Photos; **xxxix** © David Parker/IMI/University of Birmingham High, TC Consortium/Photo Researchers; **xl** *left* AP/Wide World Photos; *right* Washington University Record; **xli** *top* © Kim Steele/Getty Images; *bottom* Reprinted with permission from S. Zhou et al., SCIENCE 291:1944–47. © 2001 AAAS; **xlii–xliii** © Mike Fiala/Getty Images; **xliii** *left* © Derek Trask/Corbis; *right* AP/Wide World Photos. **xlviii** © The Chedd-Angier Production Company.

Motion and Forces

1 © Brett Froomer/Getty Images, **2–3** Courtesy of NASA/JPL/Caltech; **3** © Stocktrek/Corbis; **4** *top* Courtesy of NASA/JPL/Caltech; *bottom* © The Chedd-Angier Production Company; **6–7** © Lester Lefkowitz/Corbis; **7** Photographs by Sharon Hoogstraten; **9** © Royalty-Free/Corbis; **11** © Globus, Holway & Lobel/Corbis; **12** *top* Photograph by Sharon Hoogstraten; *bottom* © The Image Group/Getty Images; **14** *top* © Georgina Bowater/Corbis; *bottom* © SuperStock; **15** © Graham Wheatley/The Military Picture Library/Corbis, **16, 17** Photographs by Sharon Hoogstraten; **18** © Gunter Marx Photography/Corbis; **19** Photograph by Sharon Hoogstraten; **21** © Tom Brakefield/Corbis; **22** © David M. Dennis/Animals Animals; **23** © Kelly-Mooney Photography/Corbis; **24** © Gallo Images/Corbis; **25** © 1986 Richard Megna/Fundamental Photographs, NYC; **27** Photograph by Sharon Hoogstraten; **28** © Royalty-Free/Corbis; **29** Courtesy of NASA/JPL/Caltech; **30** © Robert Essel NYC/Corbis; **32** *top* © Mark Jenkinson/Corbis; *bottom* Photographs by Sharon Hoogstraten; **34** *top* © Globus, Holway & Lobel/Corbis; *center* Photograph by Sharon Hoogstraten; **36** © David M. Dennis/Animals Animals; **38–39** © Arthur Tilley/Getty Images, **39, 41** Photographs by Sharon Hoogstraten; **42** © John Kelly/Getty Images; **43** *left* © AFP/Corbis; *right* © Reuters NewMedia Inc./Corbis; **44** © Michael Kevin Daly/Corbis; **45** *left* © Jim Cummins/Getty Images; *right* © Piecework Productions/Getty Images; **46** Photograph by Sharon Hoogstraten; **47** © Jeffrey Lynch/Mendola Ltd.; **48** *left, inset* © Bill Ross/Corbis; *right* Dr. Paula Messina, San Jose State University; **49, 50** Photographs by Sharon Hoogstraten; **52** AP/Wide World Photos; **53** NASA; **54** Photograph by Sharon Hoogstraten; **55** AP/Wide World Photos; **56** *top* Clare Hirn, Jewish Hospital, University of Louisville and ABIOMED; *bottom* John Lair, Jewish Hospital, University of Louisville and ABIOMED; **57** © Danny Lehman/Corbis, **58, 59** Photographs by Sharon Hoogstraten; **60** © Photodisc/Getty Images; *background* © David C. Fritts/Animals Animals; **62** *top* Digital image © 1996 Corbis/Original image courtesy of NASA/Corbis; *bottom* Photographs by Sharon Hoogstraten; **64, 66** Photographs by Sharon Hoogstraten; **68** © TRL Ltd./Photo Researchers; **69** © Charles O'Rear/Corbis; **70** *top* © Photodisc/Getty Images; *bottom* Photographs by Sharon Hoogstraten; **71** © Siede Preis/Getty Images; **72** Photographs by Sharon Hoogstraten; **74–75** © Mike Chew/Corbis; **75, 77** Photographs by Sharon Hoogstraten; **80, 81** Photographs of models by Sharon Hoogstraten; **80** *left* NASA; *right* © Photodisc/Getty Images; **81** *top, bottom, background* NASA; **82** Photograph by Sharon Hoogstraten; **83** NASA; **84** *left* © Royalty-Free/Corbis; *right* NASA/ESA; **85** © John Beatty/Getty Images; **86, 87** Photographs by Sharon Hoogstraten; **88** *top* © Al Francekevich/Corbis; *bottom* Photograph by Sharon Hoogstraten; **89** © Joe McBride/Getty Images; **90** © NatPhotos/Tony Sweet/Digital Vision; *inset* © Michael S. Yamashita/Corbis; **91** Photograph by Sharon Hoogstraten; **92** © Wilson Goodrich/Index Stock; **93** © Royalty-Free/Corbis; **94** © Philip & Karen Smith/Getty Images; **95** © Ralph A. Clevenger/Corbis; **96** *top* © Stephen Frink/Corbis; *bottom* Photographs by Sharon Hoogstraten; **98, 99, 100** Photographs by Sharon Hoogstraten; **101** Photograph of prairie dogs © W. Perry Conway/Corbis; **103** © Omni Photo Communications Inc./Index Stock; **104** *top, bottom* Photographs by Sharon Hoogstraten; *center* © Royalty-Free/Corbis; **105** Photograph by Sharon Hoogstraten; **106** *left* © Joe McBride/Getty Images; *right* Photograph by Sharon Hoogstraten; **108** *top* © Erich Lessing/Art Resource, New York; *bottom* © Dagli Orti/The Art Archive; **109** *top left* © SPL/Photo Researchers; *top right* Sam Fogg Rare Books & Manuscripts; *bottom* © Dorling Kindersley; **110** *left* © Victoria & Albert Museum, London/Art Resource, New York; *top right* Photo Franca Principe, Institute and Museum of the History of Science; *center right* © Scala/Art Resource, New York; *bottom right* © Dorling Kindersley;

111 top © Gerald L. Schad/Photo Researchers; bottom NASA; 112–113 © Digital Vision; 113 top Image Club Graphics; center Photograph by Sharon Hoogstraten; 115, 116 Photographs by Sharon Hoogstraten; 117 © Rob Lewine/Corbis; 118 Photograph by Sharon Hoogstraten; 119 © Reinhard Eisele/Corbis; 120 © Roger Allyn Lee/SuperStock; 121 Chris Wipperman/KCPDSA; 123 © Patrik Giardino/Corbis; 124 © Tony Anderson/Getty Images; 125 Photograph by Sharon Hoogstraten; 126 © 1988 Paul Silverman/Fundamental Photographs, NYC; 127 © Tony Donaldson/Icon Sports Media; 129 © AFP/Corbis; 130 Photograph by Sharon Hoogstraten; 131 © Pete Saloutos/Corbis; 132 © Digital Vision; 133 Photograph by Sharon Hoogstraten; 134 © Walter Hodges/Corbis; 135 © Grantpix/Index Stock; 136 top © David Young-Wolff/PhotoEdit; bottom Photographs by Sharon Hoogstraten; 138 © Pete Saloutos/Corbis; 140 Photographs by Sharon Hoogstraten; 142–143 © Balthazar Korab; 145 Photograph by Sharon Hoogstraten; 146 © David Young-Wolff/PhotoEdit; 147 © Joseph Sohm/ChromoSohm Inc./Corbis; 149 © Brad Wrobleski/Masterfile; 150 © Michael Macor/San Francisco Chronicle/Corbis SABA; 151 Photograph by Sharon Hoogstraten; 152 © Jean-Yves Ruszniewski/Corbis; 153 © Royalty-Free/Corbis; inset © Felicia Martinez/PhotoEdit; 154, 155 Photographs by Sharon Hoogstraten; 156 © Tom Stewart/Corbis; 157 Photograph by Sharon Hoogstraten; 158 top © David Butow/Corbis SABA; bottom © Peter Beck/Corbis; 159 © Henryk T. Kaiser/Index Stock; 160 © Tony Freeman/PhotoEdit; 161 © Todd A. Gipstein/Corbis; 163 AP/Wide World Photos; 164 © Tony Freeman/PhotoEdit; 165 © Lester Lefkowitz/Corbis; 166 Hurst Jaws of Life; 167 © David Parker/Photo Researchers; 168 top AP/Wide World Photos; bottom © Robert Caputo/Stock Boston; background © Royalty-Free/Corbis; 170 top © Photodisc/Getty Images; bottom Photograph by Sharon Hoogstraten; 172 © ThinkStock/SuperStock; 173 top left Photograph by Sharon Hoogstraten; 174 © Tony Freeman/PhotoEdit.

Waves, Sound, and Light
177 © David Pu'u/Corbis; 178–179 © Paul Kuroda/SuperStock; 179 left © B. Benoit/Photo Researchers; right © Powerstock/SuperStock; 180 top © Stephen Frink/Corbis; bottom © The Chedd-Angier Production Company; 181 © George Stetten, M.D., Ph.D; 182–183 © Peter Sterling/Getty Images; 183, 185 Photographs by Sharon Hoogstraten; 187 Photograph courtesy of Earthquake Engineering Research Institute Reconnaissance Team; 188 © Michael Krasowitz/Getty Images; 189 Photograph by Sharon Hoogstraten; 191 © John Lund/Getty Images; 192 © Greg Huglin/Superstock; 193 © Arnulf Husmo/Getty Images; 195 Richard Olsenius/National Geographic Image Collection; 196 Photograph by Sharon Hoogstraten; 198 top © 1990 Robert Mathena/Fundamental Photographs, NYC; bottom Photographs by Sharon Hoogstraten; 199, 200 Photographs by Sharon Hoogstraten; 201 © 2001 Richard Megna/Fundamental Photographs, NYC; 202 top © 1972 FP/Fundamental Photographs, NYC; bottom Photograph by Sharon Hoogstraten; 203 © 1998 Richard Megna/Fundamental Photographs, NYC; 204 © Hiroshi Hara/Photonica; 205 Takaaki Uda, Public Works Research Institute, Japan/NOAA; 206 bottom center © 2001 Richard Megna/Fundamental Photographs, NYC; bottom right © 1972 FP/Fundamental Photographs, NYC; 210–211 © Chip Simons/Getty Images; 211, 213 Photographs by Sharon Hoogstraten; 215 © Susumu Nishinaga/Photo Researchers; 217 Photographs by Sharon Hoogstraten; 218 © Jeff Rotman/Getty Images; 219 © John Terence Turner/Getty Images; 220 left © Reuters NewMedia Inc./Corbis; background © Jason Hindley/Getty Images; 221 Photograph by Sharon Hoogstraten; 223 left (top to bottom) © Will Crocker/Getty Images; © Dorling Kindersley; © Photodisc/Getty Images; © Dorling Kindersley; © Photodisc/Getty Images; © Stephen Dalton/Animals Animals; © Steve Bloom/Getty Images; top right © Don Smetzer/Getty Images; bottom right Brian Gordon Green/National Geographic Image Collection; 224 Photograph by Sharon Hoogstraten; 225 © Dorling Kindersley; 226 © Michael Melford/Getty Images; 228 © Tom Main/Getty Images; 229 Photograph by Sharon Hoogstraten; 231 left © Roger Ressmeyer/Corbis; right Symphony Center, Home of the Chicago Symphony Orchestra; 232 © Yehoash Raphael, Kresge Hearing Research Institute, The University of Michigan; 233 © Chris Shinn/Getty Images; 234 Photograph by Sharon Hoogstraten; 235 top left © Stephen Dalton/OSF/Animals Animals; top right © Paulo de Oliveira/Getty Images; bottom left © AFP/Corbis; bottom right U.S. Navy photo by Photographer's Mate 3rd Class Lawrence Braxton/Department of Defense; 236 © Fetal Fotos; 239 © Andrew Syred/Photo Researchers; 240 top left © Reuters NewMedia Inc./Corbis; bottom Photographs by Sharon Hoogstraten; 241 Photograph by Sharon Hoogstraten; 242 bottom left © Stephen Dalton/OSF/Animals Animals; bottom right © Paulo de Oliveira/Getty Images; 244 © Photodisc/Getty Images; 246–247 © Alan Kearney/Getty Images; 247 top, center Photographs by Sharon Hoogstraten; bottom The EIT Consortium/NASA; 249 Photograph by Sharon Hoogstraten; 251 NASA, The Hubble Heritage Team, STScI, AURA; 252 Photograph by Sharon Hoogstraten; 254 top Palomar Observatory/Caltech; center NASA/MSFC/SAO; bottom NASA/CXC/ASU/J. Hester et al; background NASA/JHU/AUI/R. Giacconi et al.; 255 Photograph by Sharon Hoogstraten; 256 left © China Tourism Press/Getty Images; center © David Nunuk/Photo Researchers; right © Dr. Arthur Tucker/Photo Researchers; 257 left to right © Jeremy Woodhouse/Getty Images; © Sinclair Stammers/Photo Researchers; © Hugh Turvey/Photo Researchers; © Alfred Pasieka/Photo Researchers; 260 Photograph by Sharon Hoogstraten; 261 top © Dr. Arthur Tucker/Photo Researchers; bottom © Thomas Eisner, Cornell University; 262 © Martin Spinks; 263 © Photodisc/Getty Images; inset © David Young-Wolff/Getty Images; 264 Robert F. Sisson/National Geographic Image Collection; 265 © George D. Lepp/Corbis; 266 top © Raymond Blythe/OSF/Animals Animals; bottom Photograph by Sharon Hoogstraten; 268 © Traffic Technologies; 269 Photograph by Sharon Hoogstraten; 270 © Jeff Greenberg/Visuals Unlimited; 271 © Raymond Gehman/Corbis; 272 © Charles Swedlund; 273 top © Ace Photo Agency/Phototake;

bottom © Dorling Kindersley; **274** Photograph by Sharon Hoogstraten; **276** *top* © Michael Newman/PhotoEdit; *bottom* Photographs by Sharon Hoogstraten; **277** Photographs by Sharon Hoogstraten; **278** *center right* Robert F. Sisson/National Geographic Image Collection; *bottom* © Ace Photo Agency/Phototake; **282** *top* The Granger Collection, New York; *bottom* © Jack and Beverly Wilgus; **283** *top* The Granger Collection, New York; *center left* Diagram of the eye from the *Opticae thesaurus. Alhazeni Arabis libri septem, nunc primum editi* by Ibn al-Haytham (Alhazen). Edited by Federico Risnero (Basleae, 1572), p. 6. Private collection, London; *center right* Courtesy of NASA/JPL/Caltech; *bottom* © Royal Greenwich Observatory/Photo Researchers; **284** *top* © Stock Connection/Alamy; *center* © Florian Marquardt; *bottom* © Museum of Holography, Chicago; **285** *top* © Bettmann/Corbis; *bottom* © Bob Masini/Phototake; **286–287** © Tom Raymond/Getty Images; **287** *top, center* Photographs by Sharon Hoogstraten; *bottom* © Philippe Plaily/Photo Researchers; **288** Photograph by Sharon Hoogstraten; **290** © Laura Dwight/Corbis; **291** Photograph by Sharon Hoogstraten; **292** © Michael Newman/PhotoEdit; **293** Photographs by Sharon Hoogstraten; **294** Peter McBride/Aurora; **295** Photograph by Sharon Hoogstraten; **296** © Richard H. Johnston/Getty Images; **298** © Kim Heacox/Getty Images; *background* © Photodisc/Getty Images; **299** © T. R. Tharp/Corbis; **300** *top* © Ruddy Gold/age photostock america, inc.; *bottom* Photograph by Sharon Hoogstraten; **301** Photographs by Sharon Hoogstraten; **302** © CMCD, 1994; **304** Photograph by Sharon Hoogstraten; **306** © Argentum/Photo Researchers; **307** Photograph by Sharon Hoogstraten; **309** *top* © Andrew Syred/Photo Researchers; *center* Luna and Planetary Institute, CIRS/Library; *bottom* NASA; **310** Photograph by Sharon Hoogstraten; **311** Use of Canon Powershot S45 courtesy of Canon USA; **312** © Philippe Psaila/Photo Researchers; **313** *top* © Photodisc/Getty Images; *bottom* © Tom Stewart/corbisstockmarket.com; **314** Bradley C. Edwards, Ph.D.; **315** *top* © Photodisc/Getty Images; *center* © PhotoFlex.com; *bottom* © Michael Goldman/Photis/PictureQuest; **316** © Michael Newman/PhotoEdit.

Chemical Interactions
321 © Photodisc/Getty Images; **322–323** © David Cavagnaro/Peter Arnold, Inc.; **323** Joel Sartore/National Geographic Image Collection; **324** © The Chedd-Angier Production Company; **325** © Colin Cuthbert/Photo Researchers; **326–327** IBM Research, Almaden Research Center; **327, 329** Photographs by Sharon Hoogstraten; **330** NASA; **332** © Pascal Goetgheluck/Photo Researchers; **333** Photograph by Sharon Hoogstraten; **336** © Cnri/Photo Researchers; **337** Photograph by Sharon Hoogstraten; **338** *left, right* The Granger Collection, New York; **344** *top* © A. Hart-Davis/Photo Researchers; *bottom* Photograph by Sharon Hoogstraten; **346** Photograph by Sharon Hoogstraten; **347** *left* © Charles D. Winters/Photo Researchers; *center* © Rich Treptow/Visuals Unlimited; *right* © Corbis Images/PictureQuest; **348** © Peter Christopher/Masterfile; **349** © M. Gibbon/Robertstock.com; **350** © Superstock; **351** *top* © Simon Fraser/Photo Researchers; *bottom* Photograph by Sharon Hoogstraten; **353** © Alfred Pasieka/Photo Researchers; *inset* © John Walsh/Photo Researchers; **358–359** © Digital Vision/PictureQuest; **359, 361** Photographs by Sharon Hoogstraten; **362** *left* © Rich Treptow/Visuals Unlimited; *center, right* © E. R. Degginger/Color-Pic, Inc.; **363, 365** Photograph by Sharon Hoogstraten; **366** © Lawrence M. Sawyer/Photodisc/PictureQuest; **367** © IFA/eStock Photography (PQ price control)/PictureQuest; **369** © Runk and Schoenberger/Grant Heilman Photography, Inc.; **372** © The Image Bank/Getty Images; **373** Photograph by Sharon Hoogstraten; **375** © Astrid & Hanns-Frieder Michler/Photo Researchers; *inset* © Volker Steger/Photo Researchers; **376** Photograph by Sharon Hoogstraten; **377** © David Wrobel/Visuals Unlimited; **378** © Rob Blakers/photolibrary/PictureQuest; **379** *left* © E. R. Degginger/Robertstock.com; *right* © C. Swartzell/Visuals Unlimited; **380** *top* © David Young-Wolff/Getty Images; *bottom* Photograph by Sharon Hoogstraten; **381** Photograph by Sharon Hoogstraten; **382** *left* © Rich Treptow/Visuals Unlimited; *center, right* © E. R. Degginger/Color-Pic, Inc.; **386** From Hales, *Vegetable Statiks* [1727]; **387** *top* The Granger Collection, New York; *bottom* Mary Evans Picture Library; **388** *top* AP/Wide World Photos; *bottom* © Dorling Kindersley; **389** *top, bottom* © David Parker/Photo Researchers; **390–391** From *General Chemistry* by P. W. Atkins, © 1989 by Peter Atkins. Used with permission of W.H. Freeman and Company; **391, 393** Photographs by Sharon Hoogstraten; **394** © Daryl Benson/Masterfile; **396** *top left* © Science VU/Visuals Unlimited; *top right* © 1992 Richard Megna/Fundamental Photographs, NYC; *bottom left* © E. R. Degginger/Color-Pic, Inc.; *bottom right* © Larry Stepanowicz/Visuals Unlimited; **398** Photograph by Sharon Hoogstraten; **401** © Corbis Images/PictureQuest; *inset* © Andrew Lambert Photography/Photo Researchers; **402** © Wally Eberhart/Visuals Unlimited; **403** *top* The Granger Collection, New York; *bottom* Photograph by Sharon Hoogstraten; **404** © William Ervin/Photo Researchers; **406** © Maximilian Stock Ltd./Photo Researchers; **408** © Index Stock; **409** *left, inset* Courtesy of Chicago Fire Department; *center* Uline; *bottom right* Photograph by Sharon Hoogstraten; **410** Photograph by Sharon Hoogstraten; **411** *top* NASA; *bottom* © 1992 Richard Megna/Fundamental Photographs, NYC; **412** © Jeffrey L. Rotman/Corbis; **413** Thomas Eisner and Daniel Aneshansley, Cornell University; **415** © Harald Sund/Brand X Pictures/PictureQuest; **416** *top* AP/Wide World Photos; *bottom* Photographs by Sharon Hoogstraten; **417** Photograph by Sharon Hoogstraten; **418** © Runk and Schoenberger/Grant Heilman Photography, Inc.; **419** Photograph by Sharon Hoogstraten; **420** © Tom Yhlman/Visuals Unlimited; **421** *background* © Conor Caffrey/Photo Researchers; **422** © Arnold Fisher/Photo Researchers; **423** *left to right* © Bruce Forster/Getty Images; © Colin Cuthbert/Photo Researchers; © Fontarnau-Gutiérrez/age fotostock america, inc.; © D. Roberts/Photo Researchers; **424** © 1992 Richard Megna/Fundamental Photographs, NYC.

Earth's Surface

429 © Per Breiehagen/Getty Images; **430–431** Courtesy of NASA/JPL/Caltech; **431** *top* Carla Thomas/NASA; *bottom* Diamonds North Resources, Ltd.; **432** *top* Carla Thomas/NASA; *bottom* © The Chedd-Angier Production Company; **433** © William Whitehurst/Corbis; **434–435** NASA; **435** *top left* © NASA; *center left* SeaWiFS Project/NASA Goddard Space Flight Center; *bottom left* National Air & Space Museum/Smithsonian Institution; *top right* Courtesy of L. Sue Baugh; *center right* Bike Map courtesy of Chicagoland Bicycle Federation. Photograph by Sharon Hoogstraten; *bottom right* NASA Goddard Space Flight Center; **437** Photograph by Sharon Hoogstraten; **438–439** NASA; **438** *bottom left* © David Parker/Photo Researchers; *bottom center* © R. Wickllund/OAR/National Undersea Research Program; **439** *bottom center* University of Victoria, Victoria, British Columbia, Canada; *bottom right* © Peter and Georgina Bowater/Stock Connection/PictureQuest; **440** © Photodisc/Getty Images; **441** Photograph by Sharon Hoogstraten; **442** © A. Ramey/PhotoEdit/PictureQuest; **443** Photograph by Sharon Hoogstraten; **444** U.S. Geological Survey; **447** © David Parker/Photo Researchers; **448** Photograph by Sharon Hoogstraten; **451** © Jerry Driendl/Getty Images; **452** Photograph by Sharon Hoogstraten; **453** *top* © Stan Osolinski/Getty Images; *bottom* U.S. Geological Survey; **454, 456** *top left* U.S. Geological Survey; *bottom left, center right, bottom right* Photographs by Sharon Hoogstraten; **458, 459** *top right* © Space Imaging; *bottom background* © Paul Morrell/Getty Images; *bottom left* National Oceanic and Atmospheric Administration/Department of Commerce; **460** *top left, top center* Eros Data Center/U.S. Geological Survey; *bottom right* Photograph by Sharon Hoogstraten; **462** Photo courtesy of John D. Rogie, 1997; **463** © Lynn Radeka/SuperStock Images; **464** *top* NASA; *lower center* U.S. Geological Survey; *bottom left, background,* © Paul Morrell/Getty Images; *bottom left* National Oceanic and Atmospheric Administration/Department of Commerce; **466** U.S. Geological Survey; **468–469** © Steve Starr, Boston Inc./PictureQuest; **469** *top right, center right* Photographs by Sharon Hoogstraten; *bottom right* © Dan Suzio/Photo Researchers; **471** Photograph by Sharon Hoogstraten; **472** © Andrew J. Martinez/Photo Researchers; **473** *left* © Astrid & Hanns-Freider/Photo Researchers; *center* © Charles D. Winters/Photo Researchers; **474** Photograph by Sharon Hoogstraten; **475** *top left, center* © Charles D. Winters/Photo Researchers; *top right* Photograph by Malcolm Hjerstedt. Courtesy of F. John Barlow/SANCO Publishing; *bottom left* © Biophoto Associates/Photo Researchers; *bottom center* © Dorling Kindersley; *bottom right* © Phil Degginger/Color Pic, Inc.; *top* © David Young Wolff/PhotoEdit; *bottom* © Doug Martin/Photo Researchers; **477** *background* © Joyce Photographics/Photo Researchers; *top* © Dorling Kindersley; **478, 479** Photographs by Sharon Hoogstraten; **480** *top left* © Charles D. Winters/Photo Researchers; *top right* © Mark A. Schneider/Photo Researchers; *bottom* Photograph by Sharon Hoogstraten; **481, 482** Photographs by Sharon Hoogstraten; **483** *top, center right* Photographs by Sharon Hoogstraten; *bottom right* © Thomas Hunn/Visuals Unlimited; **484** Photograph by Sharon Hoogstraten; **485** *top left, center* © Mark A. Schneider/Visuals Unlimited; *top right* Photograph by Sharon Hoogstraten; **486** *top left* © Martin Miller/Visuals Unlimited; *bottom left, right* Photographs by Sharon Hoogstraten; **487, 488** Photographs by Sharon Hoogstraten; **489** *top left* © Geoff Tompkinson/PhotoResearchers; *center left* © A.J. Copely/Visuals Unlimited; *bottom left* © Charles D. Winters/Photo Researchers; *top right* © Charles Falco/Photo Researchers; *center right, bottom right* © Dorling Kindersley; **491** *top right, center left* © Mark A. Schneider/Photo Researchers; *center right* © Andrew J. Martinez/Photo Researchers; *bottom right* © M. Claye/Photo Researchers; **493** *top* © Mervyn P. Lawes/Corbis; *bottom* Photograph by Sharon Hoogstraten; **494** Newmont Mining Corp.; **495** *top left* © Dorling Kindersley; *top right* © Louis Goldman/Photo Researchers; *center left, bottom left* © Dorling Kindersley; **496** *center* © Charles D. Winters/Photo Researchers; *bottom left* © Astrid & Hanns-Freider/Photo Researchers; *bottom right top* © Photodisc/Getty Images; *bottom right middle* © Dorling Kindersley; *bottom right* © Photodisc/Getty Images; **498** *left* NASA/Science Photo Library; *right* NASA; **500–501** Stephen Alvarez/NGS Image Collection; **501** *top, center* Photographs by Sharon Hoogstraten; *bottom* Courtesy of L. Sue Baugh; **503** Photograph by Sharon Hoogstraten; **504** *top left* © Dorling Kindersley; *top right* © Doug Martin/Photo Researchers; *bottom* © The Image Bank/Getty Images; **505** *top* © James Lyon/Lonely Planet Images; *bottom* Photograph by Sharon Hoogstraten; **507** *center left, bottom* © Andrew J. Martinez/Photo Researchers; *center right* © Arthur R. Hill/Visuals Unlimited; **509** *background* Arne Danielsen, Norway; *left* © Charles O'Rear/Corbis; *right* © Detlev Van Ravenswaay/Photo Researchers; **510** Photograph by Sharon Hoogstraten; **511** *top left* © Arthur R. Hill/Visuals Unlimited; *top center, top right* © Joyce Photographics/Photo Researchers; *bottom center* © Mark Schneider/Visuals Unlimited; *bottom right* © Dorling Kindersley; **512** *top* © Andrew J. Martinez/Photo Researchers; *bottom* © Breck P. Kent; **513** Photograph by Sharon Hoogstraten; **514, 515** © Francois Gohier/Photo Researchers; **516** *background* © Dr. Juero Aleon/Photo Researchers; **517** Photograph by Sharon Hoogstraten; **519** *left* © Carolyn Iverson/Photo Researchers; *right* © Ted Clutter/Pennsylvania State Museum Collection/Photo Researchers; **520** *top left* Photograph by Sharon Hoogstraten; *center* Courtesy of L. Sue Baugh; *bottom right* © Norbert Wu/Norbert Wu Productions/PictureQuest; *bottom left;* National Oceanic and Atmospheric Administration **521** *top* © Look GMBH/eStockPhotography/PictureQuest; *bottom* © Corbis; **522** Photograph by Sharon Hoogstraten; **523** *left* © 1991 Ned Haines/Photo Researchers; *center* © Wayne Lawler/Photo Researchers; *right* © Jim Steinberg/Photo Researchers; **524** Photograph by Sharon Hoogstraten; **525** *right (top to bottom)* © Andrew J. Martinez 1995/Photo Researchers; © Andrew J. Martinez 1995/Photo Researchers; Boltin Picture Library; © Breck P. Kent; © 1996 Andrew J. Martinez/Photo Researchers; **526** Photograph by Sharon Hoogstraten; **528** *top left* The Boltin Picture Library; *top right* Photograph courtesy of John Longshore; *bottom left* © E.R. Degginger/Color-Pic, Inc.; *bottom right* © Patricia Tye/Photo Researchers; **530** *top* Will Hart/PhotoEdit; *center, bottom* Photographs by Sharon Hoogstraten;

531 © Corbis; 532 *top left, top center* © Andrew J. Martinez/Photo Researchers; *upper center section left* Arthur R. Hill/Visuals Unlimited; *lower center section, left* © Andrew J. Martinez/Photo Researchers; *right* Photograph by Sharon Hoogstraten; *bottom left, center* © Andrew J. Martinez/Photo Researchers; *bottom right* © Breck P. Kent; 534 © G.R. Roberts Photo Library; 536 *top* © Chris Butler/Photo Researchers; *bottom* © Detlev van Ravenswaay/Photo Researchers; 537 *top* © Jim Brandenburg/Minden Pictures; *center* J.W. Schopf/University of California, Los Angeles; *bottom* Japan Meteorological Agency; 538 *top left* © Simon Fraser/Photo Researchers; *top right* © Chase Studios/Photo Researchers; *bottom* Courtesy of the Ocean Drilling Program; 539 *top* NASA Goddard Space Flight Center; *bottom* STS-113 Shuttle Crew/NASA; 540–541 © Wendy Conway/Alamy Images; 541 *top right, center* Photographs by Sharon Hoogstraten; 543 Photograph by Sharon Hoogstraten; 545 *background* © Photodisc/Getty Images; *inset top* © Susan Rayfield/Photo Researchers; *inset center, bottom left* Photographs courtesy of Sara Christopherson; *inset bottom right* © Kirkendall-Spring Photographer; 546 Photograph by Sharon Hoogstraten; 547 *top left* © Bettmann/Corbis; *top right* © Runk/Schoenberger/Grant Heilman Photography; *bottom* © Cheyenne Rouse/Visuals Unlimited; 549 *background* © Ecoscene/Corbis; *inset* © Michael Nicholson/Corbis; 550 Photograph by Sharon Hoogstraten; 551 *left* © Joel W. Rogers/Corbis; *right* © Barry Runk/Grant Heilman Photography; 552 © Barry Runk/Grant Heilman Photography; 553 *top left* © Sally A. Morgan/Corbis; *top right* © Peter Falkner/Photo Researchers; *bottom left* © Tony Craddock/Photo Researchers; *bottom left* © Tui de Roy/Bruce Coleman, Inc.; 556 © Barry Runk/Grant Heilman Photography; 557 © Jim Strawser/Grant Heilman Photography; 558 *top left* © Larry Lefever/Grant Heilman Photography; *center right, bottom left* Photograph by Sharon Hoogstraten; 560 © Cameron Davidson/Stock Connection, Inc./Alamy Images; 561 AP/Wide World Photos; 562 *top* © Steve Strickland/Visuals Unlimited; *bottom* Betty Wald/Aurora; 563 Photograph by Sharon Hoogstraten; 564 *left* © Charles O'Rear/Corbis; *right* © Larry Lefever/Grant Heilman Photography; 565 *center inset* Courtesy of Teska Associates, Evanston, Illinois; 566 *top right* © Runk/Schoenberger/Grant Heilman Photography; *bottom* © Larry Lefever/Grant Heilman Photography; 568 © Barry Runk/Grant Heilman Photography; 570–571 © A.C. Waltham/Robert Harding Picture Library/Alamy Images; 571 *center right* Photograph by Sharon Hoogstraten; 573 © Bernhard Edmaier/Photo Researchers; 574 Photograph by Sharon Hoogstraten; 575 AP/Wide World Photos; 576 *top* Photograph by L.M. Smith, Waterways Experiment Station, U.S. Army Corps of Engineers. Courtesy, USGS; *bottom* © Thomas Rampton/Grant Heilman Photography; 577 © Troy and Mary Parlee/Alamy Images; 578 Photograph by Sharon Hoogstraten; 579 © Bill Ross/Corbis; 580 *top* © Kevin Horan/Stock Boston/PictureQuest; *bottom* © Yann Arthus-Bertrand/Corbis; 581 © 1992 Tom Bean; 582 © Charles Kennard/Stock Boston/PictureQuest; 583 © Reuters NewMedia, Inc./Corbis; 584 © Peter Bowater/Alamy Images; 586 © John and Lisa Merrill/Getty Images; 587 © Robert Perron; 588 Photograph by Sharon Hoogstraten; 589 © Tim Barnwell/Picturesque/PictureQuest; 590 © John Shaw/Bruce Coleman, Inc.; 591 *top* © 1994 Tom Bean; *right* © Goodshoot/Alamy Images; 592 *background* © Gustav Verderber/Visuals Unlimited; *inset left* © Gary Meszaros/Bruce Coleman, Inc.; *inset right* © Lee Rentz/Bruce Coleman, Inc.; 593 Photograph by Sharon Hoogstraten; 595 *left* © Bernard Edmaier/Photo Researchers; *right* © ImageState-Pictor/PictureQuest; 596 *top* © Norman Barett/Bruce Coleman, Inc.; *bottom* © Jim Wark/Airphoto; 597 *top* © 1990 Tom Bean; *bottom* Photograph by Sharon Hoogstraten; 599 © Charles W. Campbell/Corbis; 600 *top* © Bernhard Edmaier/Photo Researchers; *center* © John and Lisa Merrill/Getty Images; 602 © Tom Bean.

The Changing Earth
605 © Roger Ressmeyer/Corbis; 606–607 © Stephen and Donna O'Meara/Photo Researchers; 607 *top* NASA/GSFC/METI/ERSDAC/JAROS, and U.S./Japan ASTER Science Team; 608 *top left* U.S. Geological Survey; *inset* Photograph by T. Miller/U.S. Geological Survey; *bottom* The Chedd-Angier Production Company; 609 NASA/GSFC/METI/ERSDAJAROS, and U.S./Japan ASTER Science Team; 610–611 Tony Waltham/Geophotos; 611, 613, 616, 618 Photographs by Sharon Hoogstraten; 619 © 1995–2002 Geoclassics. All rights reserved.; 624 Worldsat International/Photo Researchers; 626, 629 Photographs by Sharon Hoogstraten; 631 *top* © Christophe Ratier/NHPA/Photo Researchers; *bottom* © NASA/Photo Researchers; 633 *left* © Dr. John Brackenbury/Photo Researchers; *right* NASA; 634 Photograph by Sharon Hoogstraten; 635 © John Coletti/Stock Boston/PictureQuest; 637 Photograph by Sharon Hoogstraten; 638 © Lloyd Cluff/Corbis; 639 © Paul Chesley/Getty Images; 641 *left* © Albrecht G. Schaefer/Corbis; *right* © Mitch Diamond/Index Stock/PictureQuest; 646–647 © Robert Patrick/Corbis Sygma; 647, 649, 651 Photographs by Sharon Hoogstraten; 652 © Martin Miller/University of Oregon, Eugene, Oregon; 653 NOAA/National Geophysical Data Center; 654 *left* U.S. Geological Survey; *inset* © Bettmann/Corbis; 655, 657 Photograph by Sharon Hoogstraten; 663 AP/Wide World Photos; 664 Photograph by Sharon Hoogstraten; 665 © Mark Downey; 666 U.S. Geological Survey; 667 Commander Dennis J. Sigrist acting Director of the International Tsunami Information Center/NOAA; 670 © Roger Ressmeyer/Corbis; 672 *top* © Michael S. Yamashita/Corbis; *bottom left, bottom right* Photograph by Sharon Hoogstraten; 673 Photograph by Sharon Hoogstraten; 678–679 © Douglas Peebles; 679, 681 Photographs by Sharon Hoogstraten; 682 U.S. Department of the Interior; 683, 684 © Martin Miller/University of Oregon, Eugene, Oregon; 685 © Tim Hauf Photography/Visuals Unlimited; 686 Photograph by Sharon Hoogstraten; 687 © Martin Miller/University of Oregon, Eugene, Oregon; 688 © Phil Schermeister/Corbis; 689 © William Ervin/Photo Researchers; 690, 692 Photograph by Sharon Hoogstraten; 694 © G.R. Roberts Photo Library; 695 *left* © Tom Bean/Corbis; *right* © Krafft-Explorer/Photo

Researchers; **696** © F. Gohier/Photo Researchers; **697** NASA/Carnegie Mellon University; **698** *top* © Krafft-Explorer/Photo Researchers; *bottom left, right* Photographs by Sharon Hoogstraten; **700** *top* © James A. Sugar/Corbis; *bottom* © Mark E. Gibson/Corbis; **701** *top* © Stephen and Donna O'Meara/Volcano Watch International/Photo Researchers; *bottom* © Sid Balatan/Black Star Publishing/PictureQuest; **702** U.S. Department of the Interior, U.S. Geological Survey, Reston, Virginia; **703** Photograph by Sharon Hoogstraten; **704** © The Image Bank/Getty Images; **705** © Simon Fraser/Photo Researchers; **706** © Peter Ryan/Photo Researchers; **707** *top right* © James Leynse/Corbis; *top left* © Raymond Gehman/Corbis; *center* Courtesy of the General Libraries, The University of Texas at Austin; *bottom* © Jeff Foott/Panoramic Images/National Geographic Image Collection; **708** *bottom left* © Sid Balatan/Black Star Publishing/PictureQuest; *bottom center* © The Image Bank/Getty Images; *bottom right* © Simon Fraser/Photo Researchers; **710** © Roger Ressmeyer/Corbis; **712–713** © Louis Psihoyos/psihoyos.com; **713** *top right* © Digital Vision; *center right* Photograph by Sharon Hoogstraten; *bottom right* © Chris Butler/Photo Researchers; **715** Photograph by Sharon Hoogstraten; **716** *top left* Latreille-Cerpolex; *center left* © Alfred Pasteka/Photo Researchers; *bottom left* © Dominique Braud/Animals Animals; **717** *bottom left, bottom right* Courtesy, American Museum of Natural History; **718** © 2001 Tom Bean; **719** *background* © Images Ideas, Inc./PictureQuest; *top left* © Dorling Kindersley; *top right* © John Elk III; *center right* © Kaj R. Svensson/Photo Researchers; *bottom right* © Francesc Muntada/Corbis; **720** © Doug Wilson/Corbis; **721** *top left* © B & C Alexander; *top right* © Maria Stenzel/National Geographic Image Collection; **722** © Chris Butler/Photo Researchers; *inset* © Robert Dowling/Corbis; **723** *left* Courtesy of The Bicycle Museum of America; *center* © Softride, Inc.; *right* © Photodisc/Getty Images; **724** *bottom left* © Tom Bean 1993; *bottom right* © Dr. Morley Read/Photo Researchers; **725** *top right* © Asa C. Thoresen/Photo Researchers; *bottom right* © Sinclair Stammers/Photo Researchers; **726** *bottom* Photograph by Sharon Hoogstraten; **728** *background* © G. Brad Lewis/Getty Images; **730** *left* © Jonathan Blair/Corbis; *inset* AP Wide World Photos; **731** Photograph by Sharon Hoogstraten; **732** © Sime s.a.s./eStock Photography/PictureQuest; **733** *left, right* © John Marshall Photography; **734** *bottom left* Mural by Peter Sawyer © National Museum of Natural History, Smithsonian Institution, Washington, D.C.; *bottom right* Exhibit Museum of Natural History, The University of Michigan, Ann Arbor, Michigan; **735** *bottom left* © Ludek Pesek/Photo Researchers; *bottom right* © Steve Vidler/SuperStock; **736** © Tom Bean; **737** © Sisse Brimberg/National Geographic Image Collection; **738** *top* © Jonathan Blair/Corbis; *left, right* Photographs by Sharon Hoogstraten; **740** *center left* © Asa C. Thoresen/Photo Researchers; **744** *top* The Granger Collection; *bottom* © Tom Bean/Corbis; **745** *top* © Gianni Dagli Orti/Corbis; *center* The Natural History Museum, London; *bottom* Courtesy British Geological Survey; **746** *top left* © Sally A. Morgan/Ecoscene/Corbis; *top right* © Bettmann/Corbis; *bottom* © James King-Holmes/Photo Researchers; **747** *top* © Mark A. Klinger/Carnegie Museum of Natural History; *bottom* © The Field Museum; **748–749** © Richard Folwell/Photo Researchers; **749** *top right, center right* Photographs by Sharon Hoogstraten; **751** © Corbis; **753** *top* © SuperStock; *bottom* © Gunter Marx Photography/Corbis; **757** Photograph by Sharon Hoogstraten; **758** *left* Diane Moore/Icon SMI; *top right* © Corbis; *bottom right* © Photodisc/Getty Images; **759** *left* © Photolink/Photodisc/PictureQuest; *inset* © Dr. Tony Braun/Photo Researchers; **760, 761** Photograph by Sharon Hoogstraten; **762** *top* Photograph by Sharon Hoogstraten; *bottom* © David Young-Wolff/PhotoEdit; **763** José Azel/Aurora; **764** *top* © Dick Luria/Index Stock/PictureQuest; *bottom* © Johnston Images/Picturesque/PictureQuest; **765** Photograph by Sharon Hoogstraten; **767** © Steve Allen/Brand X Pictures/PictureQuest; **768** © Beth Davidow/Visuals Unlimited; **769** © Martin Bond/Photo Researchers; **770** © James Stilling/Getty Images; **771** © Lynne Ledbetter/Visuals Unlimited; **772** Andrew Carlin/Tracy Operators; **773** © California Fuel Cell Partnership; **774** *top* © M.L. Sinibald/Corbis; *bottom left, right* Photograph by Sharon Hoogstraten; **775** Photograph by Sharon Hoogstraten; **776** *top left* (1) © SuperStock; *top left* (2) © Gunter Marx Photography/Corbis; *bottom* José Azel/Aurora.

Life Over Time

781 © Martin Siepman/Age Fotostock America Inc.; **782, 783** *background* © Alfredo Maiquez/Lonely Planet Images; **783** *top left* © Donald Windsor; *bottom right* Reprinted with permission from "Timing the Radiations of Leaf Beetles: Hispines on Gingers from Latest Cretaceous to Recent" Peter Wilf and Conrad C. Labandeira, SCIENCE V. 289:291-294 (2000). © 2000 AAAS.; **784** *bottom* © The Chedd-Angier Production Company; *top* Courtesy, Earth Sciences and Image Analysis, NASA-Johnson Space Center; **785** © The Natural History Museum, London; **786, 787** © Richard T. Nowitz/Corbis; **790** *top* © Mark A. Schneider/Photo Researchers, Inc.; *center* © Sinclair Stammers/Photo Researchers, Inc.; *bottom* © Novosti/Science Photo Library/Photo Researchers, Inc.; **791** *bottom* © Field Museum/Photo Researchers, Inc.; **793** *top* © Ken M. Johns/Photo Researchers, Inc.; **794** *bottom* © Lynette Cook/Photo Researchers, Inc.; **795** *top right* © D. Van Ravenswaay/Photo Researchers, Inc.; *bottom right* © David Parker/Photo Researchers, Inc.; *top left* © D. Van Ravenswaay/Photo Researchers, Inc.; **796** *top* © Paddy Ryan/Animals Animals; *bottom* © Layne Kennedy/Corbis; **797** *left* © Corbis-Royalty Free; **798, 799** *background* © Ralph Lee Hopkins/Lonely Planet Images; *bottom* © The Natural History Museum, London; *top* © The Granger Collection, New York; **799** *top right* © Volker Steger/Photo Researchers, Inc.; *right* © Zig Leszczynski/Animals Animals; *left* © Theo Allots/Visuals Unlimited; **800** *bottom right, top left, top right* © Tui De Roy/Minden Pictures; *bottom left* © Richard I'Anson/Lonely Planet Images; *background* © Ralph Lee Hopkins/Lonely Planet Images; **801** *right* © Hans Reinhard/Bruce Coleman, Inc.; *center, left* © Larry Allan/Bruce Coleman, Inc.; **803** *top left* © Bruce

Coleman, Inc.; *background* © Paul Souders/Accent Alaska; **804** *top* © Hans Reinhard/Bruce Coleman, Inc.; *bottom, center* © Jane Burton/Bruce Coleman, Inc.; **805** © John Winnie, Jr./DRK Photo; **806** *top* © Marian Bacon/Animals Animals; **808** © Ed Degginger/Color-Pic, Inc.; **809** © Mark A. Schneider/Photo Researchers, Inc.; **811** *background* © Corbis-Royalty Free; **812** *center, left* © Photodisc/Getty Images; *right* © Mark Smith/Photo Researchers, Inc.; **814** © Photodisc/Getty Images; **815** © Norbert Wu; **816** *bottom* © Mark A. Schneider/Photo Researchers, Inc.; *top* © Tui de Roy/Bruce Coleman, Inc.; **818** © Hans Reinhard/Bruce Coleman, Inc.; **820, 821** © Burke/Triolo/Artville: Bugs and Insects; **821** *top right* © Ed Block/Corbis; **823** *top* © Robert Pickett/Corbis; *bottom* © U.S. Fish & Wildlife Service; **824** *right* © David I. Roberts/Photo Researchers, Inc.; *left* © S.J. Krasemann/Photo Researchers, Inc.; **825** *center* © Renee Lynn/Photo Researchers, Inc.; *bottom left* © Tom McHugh/Photo Researchers. Inc.; *top right* © Len Rue, Jr./Bruce Coleman, Inc.; *bottom right* © Frans Lanting/Minden Pictures; **827** *right* © Bill Kamin/Visuals Unlimited; *bottom left* © Norbert Wu; *center, top left* © Dave Fleetham/Tom Stack & Associates; *background* © E.R. Degginger/Photo Researchers, Inc.; **828** *top* © D. Ditchburn/Visuals Unlimited; *bottom* © M.H. Sharp/Photo Researchers, Inc.; **829** *top right* © Tom Brakefield/Bruce Coleman, Inc.; *top left* © Fritz Polking/POLKI/Bruce Coleman, Inc.; *bottom left* © G.C. Kelley/Photo Researchers, Inc.; *bottom right* © Tom McHugh/Photo Researchers, Inc.; *background* © Corbis-Royalty Free; **830** © Mary Evans Picture Library; **831** *top* © Photodisc/Getty Images; **833** *left, right* © Judy White/GardenPhotos.com; *center* © Tom J. Ulrich; **834** *left* © Joe McDonald/Visuals Unlimited; *right* © Photodisc/Getty Images; **835** *right* © John Mitchell/Photo Researchers, Inc.; *background* © Visuals Unlimited; **837** *top right* © Robert Della-Piana/photolibrary/PictureQuest; *background* © Photodisc/Getty Images; **838** From *A Field Guide To The Birds Of Eastern And Central North America,* Fifth Edition by Roger Tory Peterson. Text copyright © 2002 by Marital Trust B u/a Roger Tory Peterson and the Estate of Virginia Peterson. Reprinted by permission of Houghton Mifflin Company. All rights reserved.; **839** *background* © Link/Visuals Unlimited; *bottom* © George Bryce/Animals Animals; **840** © Ken Lucas/Visuals Unlimited; **841** *left* © CNRI/Photo Researchers, Inc.; *center* © Wolfgang Baumeister/Photo Researchers, Inc.; *right* © Biophoto Associates/Photo Researchers, Inc.; **842** *top to bottom* © Corbis-Royalty Free; © Sharna Balfour/Gallo Images/Corbis; © Eric Grave/Photo Researchers, Inc.; © Rico & Ruiz/Nature Picture Library; © Dr. Jeremy Burgess/Photo Researchers, Inc.; © Eye of Science/Photo Researchers, Inc.; *background* © Courtesy of NASA/Corbis; **844** *center* © Jim Zuckerman/Corbis, *right* © Masa Ushioda/Bruce Coleman, Inc.; *left* © M. & C. Photography/Peter Arnold, Inc.; *top* © Ed Degginger/Earthscenes; **845** © Jeff Foott/Bruce Coleman, Inc.; **846** *right* © Mark Taylor, Warren Photographic/Bruce Coleman, Inc.; *bottom* © Dr. M. Rohde, GBF/Photo Researchers, Inc.; *left* © Cordelia Molloy/Photo Researchers, Inc.; **847** © Gary Gaugler/Visuals Unlimited; **848** © Corbis-Royalty Free; **850** © John Mitchell/Photo Researchers, Inc.; **854** *bottom right* © Visuals Unlimited; *bottom left, top right* The Natural History Museum Picture Library, London; **855** *top left* American Museum of Natural History Library; *bottom right* © O. Louis Mazzatenta/National Geographic Image Collection; *center* © Peter Scoones/Photo Researchers, Inc.; *top right* © Geoff Bryant/Photo Researchers, Inc.; **856** *top left* © Science/Visuals Unlimited; *top right* © Kevin O. Mooney/Odyssey/Chicago; *center right* © Ira Block/National Geographic Image Collection; *bottom left* © James King-Holmes/Photo Researchers, Inc.; **857** *top left* © John Reader/Science Photo Library; *bottom left* © David Parker/Photo Researchers, Inc.; **858, 859** *background* NASA; **861** © David M. Phillips/Photo Researchers, Inc.; **863** *left* © Photo Researchers, Inc.; *right* © Wayne Lynch/DRK Photo; **864** *right* © Darrell Gulin/DRK Photo; *left* © Thomas Wiewandt/Corbis; **865** *left* © Stephen J. Krasemann/DRK Photo; *right* © D. Cavagnaro/DRK Photo; **866** *center* © Visuals Unlimited; *right* © Judy White/GardenPhotos.com; *left* © Betty Press/Animals Animals; **867** © Jim Sulley/The Image Works; **868** © Anthony Merciecca/Photo Researchers, Inc.; **869** *left* © Rod Planck/Photo Researchers, Inc.; *right* © Michael Abbey/Photo Researchers, Inc.; **871** © OSF/N. Rosing/Animals Animals; **872** © Tom Brakefield/Corbis; **873** © Najlah Feanny/Corbis; **875** *right* © Martha Cooper/Peter Arnold, Inc.; *bottom* © Dennis Flaherty/Photo Researchers, Inc.; **876** © Stephen J. Krasemann/DRK Photo; **877** *left* © Raymond Gehman/Corbis; *top right* © David Sieren/Visuals Unlimited, Inc.; *bottom right* © George Bernard/Science Photo Library; **879** *bottom right* © Rob Crandall/The Image Works; *bottom left* © Grant Heilman/Grant Heilman Photography; *top right* © Ed Degginger/Color-Pic, Inc.; **880** *left* © Bob Daemmrich/The Image Works; *right* © Geri Engberg/The Image Works; **881** NASA; **883** *top* © Ray Coleman/Photo Researchers, Inc.; *bottom* © John Serrao/Photo Researchers, Inc.; **884** *top* © Donald Speckler/Animals Animals; *bottom* © Janis Burger/Bruce Coleman, Inc.; **885** © Jeff Greenberg/The Image Works; **886** © Gaetano/Corbis; **888** *center* © Najlah Feanny/Corbis; *bottom* © Bob Daemmrich/The Image Works; **890** © Photo Researchers, Inc.; **891** © Wayne Lynch/DRK Photo.

Backmatter
R28 © Photodisc/Getty Images.

Illustrations and Maps

Accurate Art Inc. 107, 175, 209, 467, 535, 603, 743; Ampersand Design Group 15, 315,409, 421; Argosy 186, 189, 190, 194, 195, 201, 206, 231, 237, 769, 771, 773; Richard Bonson/Wildlife Art Ltd. 511, 614–615, 642, 644, 676, 683, 685, 687, 691, 705, 708, 792, 793, 816 *(top);* Peter Bull/Wildlife Art Ltd. 588, 590, 595, 597, 621, 644, 656, 662, 674, 726; Eric Chadwick 274, 275; Steve Cowden 122, 188, 227, 230, 258; Stephen Durke 331, 332, 333, 334, 335, 354, 368, 369, 370, 371, 372, 374, 379, 382, 384, 394, 395, 397, 412, 413, 421, 426,473, 481,628, 669, 671,

674; Chris Forsey **527, 659**; Luigi Galante **555, 566**; Patrick Gnan/Deborah Wolfe Ltd. **835**; David A. Hardy **440, 512, 514, 532**; Gary Hincks **491, 507, 508, 577, 581, 627, 628, 630, 632, 635, 638, 639, 642, 694–695, 708, 736**; Ian Jackson/Wildlife Art Ltd. **811**; Mapquest.com, Inc. **10, 60, 129, 168, 445, 446, 451, 460, 461, 462, 464, 492, 516, 538, 553, 594, 598, 617, 620, 623, 627, 631, 632, 635, 636, 638, 639, 640, 642, 650, 661, 667, 668, 669, 674, 682, 685, 693, 717, 732, 733, 736, 798–799, 868, 879, R58–R59, R62–R63**; Janos Marffy **719, 728, 740, 755**; Morgan, Cain & Assoc. **556**; NOAA/NGDC (National Geophysical Data Center) **R60–R61**; Laurie O'Keefe **809, 812, 816** *(bottom);* Mick Posen/Wildlife Art Ltd. **803, 837, 852**; Precision Graphics **652, 653, 674, 696, 756**; Tony Randazzo/American Artists Rep. Inc. **13**; Mike Saunders **545, 548, 566**; Peter Scott/Wildlife Art Ltd. **800, 804, 816** *(center);* SlimFilms **671, 674, 754, 766, 768, 770**; Dan Stuckenschneider **102, 135, 156, 157, 158, 159, 161, 162, 165, 172, 173, 238, 253, 267, 278, 309, 311, 312, 316, R11–R19, R22, R32**; Dan Stuckenschneider based on an illustration by Matt Cioffi **168**; Raymond Turvey **587**; Bart Vallecoccia **214, 215, 302, 303, 305, 311, 316**; Rob Wood **545, 582**; Ron Wood/Wood Ronsaville Harlin **725, 742.**

Formulas

Word Form	Symbolic Form	Purpose
Volume = length • width • height	$V = lwh$	to calculate the volume of a rectangular object
Density = $\dfrac{\text{mass}}{\text{Volume}}$	$D = \dfrac{m}{V}$	to calculate the density of an object
Speed = $\dfrac{\text{distance}}{\text{time}}$	$S = \dfrac{d}{t}$	to calculate the speed of an object
acceleration = $\dfrac{\text{final velocity} - \text{initial velocity}}{\text{time}}$	$a = \dfrac{v_{final} - v_{initial}}{t}$	to calculate the acceleration of an object
Force = mass • acceleration	$F = ma$	to calculate the force, mass, or acceleration of an object; called Newton's second law
momentum = mass • velocity	$p = mv$	to calculate the momentum of an object
Pressure = $\dfrac{\text{Force}}{\text{Area}}$	$P = \dfrac{F}{A}$	to calculate the pressure on an object
Work = Force • distance	$W = Fd$	to calculate work
Gravitational Potential Energy = mass • gravitational acceleration • height	$GPE = mgh$	to calculate the gravitational potential energy of an object
Kinetic Energy = $\dfrac{\text{mass} \cdot \text{velocity}^2}{2}$	$KE = \dfrac{1}{2} mv^2$	to calculate the kinetic energy of an object
Mechanical Energy = Potential Energy + Kinetic Energy	$ME = PE + KE$	to calculate the mechanical energy of an object
Power = $\dfrac{\text{Work}}{\text{time}}$	$P = \dfrac{W}{t}$	to calculate power based on work
Power = $\dfrac{\text{Energy}}{\text{time}}$	$P = \dfrac{E}{t}$	to calculate power based on energy
Efficiency (%) = $\dfrac{\text{Output work}}{\text{Input work}} \cdot 100$	$E(\%) = \dfrac{W_{out}}{W_{in}} \cdot 100$	to calculate the efficiency of a machine
Mechanical Advantage = $\dfrac{\text{Output force}}{\text{Input force}}$	$MA = \dfrac{F_{out}}{F_{in}}$	to calculate a machine's mechanical advantage
Speed = wavelength • frequency	$S = \lambda f$	to calculate the speed of a wave
Current = $\dfrac{\text{Voltage}}{\text{Resistance}}$	$I = \dfrac{V}{R}$	to calculate the relationships among current, voltage, and resistance; called Ohm's law
Electrical Power = Voltage • Current	$P = VI$	to calculate power
Energy used = Power • time	$E = Pt$	to calculate the total energy used

The Periodic Table of the Elements

1									
1 **H** Hydrogen 1.008	2								
3 **Li** Lithium 6.941	4 **Be** Beryllium 9.012								
11 **Na** Sodium 22.990	12 **Mg** Magnesium 24.305	3	4	5	6	7	8	9	
19 **K** Potassium 39.098	20 **Ca** Calcium 40.078	21 **Sc** Scandium 44.956	22 **Ti** Titanium 47.87	23 **V** Vanadium 50.942	24 **Cr** Chromium 51.996	25 **Mn** Manganese 54.938	26 **Fe** Iron 55.845	27 **Co** Cobalt 58.933	
37 **Rb** Rubidium 85.468	38 **Sr** Strontium 87.62	39 **Y** Yttrium 88.906	40 **Zr** Zirconium 91.224	41 **Nb** Niobium 92.906	42 **Mo** Molybdenum 95.94	43 **Tc** Technetium (98)	44 **Ru** Ruthenium 101.07	45 **Rh** Rhodium 102.906	
55 **Cs** Cesium 132.905	56 **Ba** Barium 137.327	57 **La** Lanthanum 138.906	72 **Hf** Hafnium 178.49	73 **Ta** Tantalum 180.95	74 **W** Tungsten 183.84	75 **Re** Rhenium 186.207	76 **Os** Osmium 190.23	77 **Ir** Iridium 192.217	
87 **Fr** Francium (223)	88 **Ra** Radium (226)	89 **Ac** Actinium (227)	104 **Rf** Rutherfordium (261)	105 **Db** Dubnium (262)	106 **Sg** Seaborgium (266)	107 **Bh** Bohrium (264)	108 **Hs** Hassium (269)	109 **Mt** Meitnerium (268)	

Period
Each row of the periodic table is called a **period**. As read from left to right, one proton and one electron are added from one element to the next.

Group
Each column of the table is called a **group**. Elements in a group share similar properties. Groups are read from top to bottom.

58 **Ce** Cerium 140.116	59 **Pr** Praseodymium 140.908	60 **Nd** Neodymium 144.24	61 **Pm** Promethium (145)	62 **Sm** Samarium 150.36
90 **Th** Thorium 232.038	91 **Pa** Protactinium 231.036	92 **U** Uranium 238.029	93 **Np** Neptunium (237)	94 **Pu** Plutonium (244)

 Metal   Metalloid   Nonmetal    Solid    Liquid   Gas